Worldwide Tax Summaries

Corporate Taxes 2010/11

All information in this book, unless otherwise stated, is up to date as of 28 May 2010.

Design Services 24501 (08/10).

Foreword

Welcome to *Worldwide Tax Summaries – Corporate Taxes 2010/11*, which provides quick and easy access to information on corporate tax rates and rules in 139 countries worldwide. The country summaries – written by our local PwC tax specialists – include information about changes in legislation, residency, gross income, deductions, tax credits, tax administration, other taxes and tax rates. *All information in this book, unless otherwise stated, is up to date as of 28 May 2010*. Please also visit our online version of these summaries at www.pwc.com/taxsummaries. Each country summary is reviewed and updated as necessary on a periodic basis and each web page shows the date of the latest update to that information.

If you have any queries, or need more detailed advice on any aspect of tax, please get in touch with us. The PwC tax network has member firms throughout the world who can offer you high quality advice and support, whenever and wherever you need it, and our specialist networks can provide both a domestic and cross-border perspective to the tax challenges you are facing. We've also included for reference a list of some of our key specialists at the back of this book, to help you locate the right person, in both our major territories and networks.

We hope this book will be a useful reference tool, to help you manage taxes around the world.

Yours sincerely

Richard Collier-Keywood
Vice Chairman, Tax
+44 20 7213 3997
richard.collier-keywood@uk.pwc.com

Contents

Country chapters

Country chapters

Corporate taxes in Albania

For more information, contact:

Peter Burnie
PricewaterhouseCoopers Consulting d.o.o.
Airport City Belgrade
88a Omladinskih brigada st.
11000 Belgrade
Serbia
Tel: +381 11 3302 138
Email: peter.burnie@rs.pwc.com

Significant developments

All taxpayers must submit tax returns electronically. Depending on the category of taxpayers, the electronic filing comes into force on the following dates:

- Taxpayers registered with the Regional Directorate of Large Taxpayers – starting from 1 January 2010;
- Taxpayers registered for VAT and corporate income tax with the regional tax offices – starting from 1 March 2010;
- Taxpayers registered for VAT and subject to personal income tax for small business – starting from 1 July 2010; and
- State institutions submitting tax returns for personal income tax and social and health contribution – starting from 1 March 2010.

Taxes on corporate income

The corporate income tax rate in the country is 10%.

The following entities are exempt from tax on profit: foundations or non-banking financial institutions established to support development policies of the government through credit activities. In addition, film studios and cinematographic productions (among other types of entity/activity) that are licensed and funded by the National Cinematographic Centre are exempt from the corporate income tax.

Corporate residence

Based on Albanian legislation, a legal entity is deemed to be resident in Albania if either of the following is true:

- The legal entity has its head office in Albania; or
- The legal entity has its place of effective management in Albania.

Other taxes

Value-added tax (VAT)

Taxable persons are all individuals and legal entities registered, or required to be registered for VAT purposes. The VAT registration threshold in Albania is ALL 5 million. However, for specific services defined in the VAT law, the VAT registration threshold is ALL 2 million. Any person providing taxable supplies and whose annual turnover does

Albania

not exceed ALL 5 million is not required to register, although voluntary registration is possible.

The standard VAT rate is 20% and the standard VAT period is the calendar month.

Foreign entities that carry out business activities in Albania are subject to 20% VAT in Albania when one of the following conditions exists:

- Services rendered are related to immovable property located in Albania; or
- Services are rendered in Albania.

In both cases, total turnover must exceed ALL 5 million per annum. If these conditions are met, the foreign entity is obliged to register and pay the VAT in Albania by nominating a tax representative.

In case of a foreign entity's noncompliance, the tax liabilities and respective penalties derived from such noncompliance will be paid by the local beneficiary of these services.

The following activities are subject to 0% VAT:

- Export of goods;
- The provision of services relevant to the processing of semi-finished goods intended for export;
- The supply of goods and services related with the international transport of goods or passengers; and
- The supply of goods and services in relation to trading and industrial activities at sea.

The VAT on machinery and equipment imported by Albanian registered entities for use in their own business activity (i.e., not for resale) is subject to the VAT deferral scheme under which the payment of the VAT is postponed for up to 12 months, with a possibility of extension for an additional 12-month period.

Taxable transactions include the import of goods into Albania by a taxable person. The following transactions are also taxable:

- Transactions performed for no consideration or for a consideration less than the market value;
- Barter transactions; and
- The private use of taxable goods by a taxable person (self-supply).

The following services are exempt from VAT in Albania:

- The lease of land (unless the rental period does not exceed two months);
- The lease of buildings is exempt from VAT, except cases where there is a contract between parties in which the supply is deemed as taxable;
- Financial services;
- Postal service (only if there are no imports or other postal service and the annual turnover doesn't exceed ALL 8 million);
- Gambling, casino and totalisator services;
- Written media and books;

- Advertising in electronic media (TV);
- Interest payments on leasing transactions; and
- Export of services.

The sale of land and buildings is not subject to VAT, although the construction process itself is subject to VAT.

A supply made by a non-profit organisation against a reduced payment is an exempt supply in the following case:

- The supply of services by religious or philosophical organisations for the purpose of spiritual welfare; and
- If the organisation makes the above supplies against a full payment and the annual turnover is above ALL 5 million, then this entity is required to be registered for VAT.

Non-profit organisations that do not supply the goods mentioned above are subject to VAT if the annual turnover is above ALL 5 million.

When commodities are transferred through a lease contract or through a sale contract, the VAT is applied to the whole value of the commodities and is calculated on each instalment, regardless of when the ownership is transferred.

Taxable entities have the right to claim for VAT reimbursement if the following two conditions are met:

- The period in which VAT credits are carried forward exceeds three months; and
- The total amount of VAT credits is equal to or greater than ALL 400,000.

VAT registered taxpayers who are in a VAT credit position have the right to request (if all legal conditions are met) the reimbursement of the VAT credit within 30 days after the request is submitted to the relevant tax authority. In case the tax authorities do not proceed with the reimbursement, the taxpayer is entitled to reduce payment of other tax obligations up to an amount equal to the VAT reclaimed.

In relation to the VAT evaluation by tax authorities and the right of the taxpayer on appealing this evaluation with the Tax Appeal Directorate, the taxpayer is entitled to reimbursement in case the VAT evaluation after appealing is decreased or waived.

All taxpayers are required to submit their tax returns and sales and purchase books electronically.

Depending on the category of taxpayers, the electronic filing, after it comes into force, is due on the following dates:

- The deadline for the electronic filing of the VAT books is the fifth day of the consecutive month.
- The deadline for the electronic filing of tax returns and the payment of the related tax liability is the fourteenth day of the consecutive month.

Excise duties

Albania levies excise tax on the following products: fruit juice and refreshments; beer, wine, tobacco and other alcoholic drinks; petroleum; cosmetic articles, perfumes and

Albania

candescent lamps. The excise tax on candescent lamps, cosmetic articles and perfumes is defined as a percentage of the sales turnover, whereas the excise tax for other products is based on quantity.

The excise tax paid on fuel used in greenhouses as well as in production of industrial and agricultural products is reimbursable.

Importers of "malt" and "cigarette paper in tubular form together with the filter" that are not authorised as excise taxpayers and are engaged in the production of beer and cigarettes, must provide a request to the General Directory of Tax in order to receive the authorisation to import "malt" and "cigarette paper in tubular form together with the filter" for trading purposes. The authorisation is issued by the General Director of Taxation and is valid for one year with the right of renewal.

Branch income

Branch offices in Albania are subject to the same taxes as all other forms of legal entities.

Income determination

Inventory valuation
Inventory is valued at the end of each tax period using the methods stipulated in the Accounting Law, which should be applied systematically.

Capital gains/losses
Capital gains/losses derived from the sale of a company's fixed assets are taxed at the same rate as the company's ordinary business income.

Fiscal losses may be carried forward up to three years. Losses may not be carried forward if more than 25% of direct or indirect ownership of the share capital or voting rights of the company are transferred during the tax year.

Transfer pricing
Transfer pricing adjustments may be made if the conditions set in a transaction between related parties differ from those that would have been set if the parties were independent. In particular, the following are regarded as related parties: (1) a legal entity and any person who owns, directly or indirectly, at least 50% of the shares or voting rights in that entity; and (2) two or more legal entities if a third person owns, directly or indirectly, at least 50% of the shares or voting rights in each entity.

Controlled foreign company legislation
There is no controlled foreign company legislation.

Deductions

Depreciation and depletion
The declining balance basis method of depreciation is used for buildings and machinery and other fixed structures installed in the building. They are depreciated at an annual rate of 5%. The depreciation of intangible assets is calculated separately for each asset using the straight-line method at the rate of 15%. For other assets, depreciation is calculated on a declining balance basis. The maximum depreciation

rates are 25% for computers, software products and information systems, and 20% for all other assets. Land, fine art, antiques and jewellery are non-depreciable assets.

Other deductions

Representation and reception expenses exceeding 0.3% of the annual turnover are not deductible.

Sponsorship expenses exceeding 3% of profit before tax and sponsorships of press and publications exceeding 5% of profit before tax are also not deductible.

The costs of in-kind benefits not taxed via payroll, dividends, fines and other tax-related sanctions, expenses for gifts as well as any expense which the taxpayer does not support with a fiscal invoice, are not deductible for corporate income tax purposes.

The interest paid on outstanding loans and prepayments exceeding four times the amount of net assets should be added to the corporate tax base. This rule does not apply to banks and insurance companies.

The corporate income tax base should be increased by the amount of interest paid in excess of the average 12-month credit interest rate applied in the banking system, as determined by the Bank of Albania.

Bad debts are only deductible if all of the following conditions are met:

* An amount corresponding with the bad debt was included earlier in income;
* The bad debt is removed from the taxpayer's accounting books; and
* All possible legal action to recover the debt has been taken.

The amounts allocated to special reserve accounts in banks and insurance companies are deductible.

Group taxation

There is no group taxation in Albania.

Tax incentives

There are no tax incentives applicable in Albania.

Withholding taxes (WHT)

The gross amount of interest, royalties, dividends and shares of partnerships' profits paid to non-resident companies are subject to 10% withholding tax, unless a double tax treaty provides for a lower rate.

Withholding tax of 10% is levied on the gross amount of payments for technical, management, installation, assembly or supervisory work, as well as payments to management and board members.

If a non-resident company does not create a permanent establishment in Albania, and a double tax treaty exists between Albania and the home country of the foreign company, the payment of withholding tax can be avoided.

Albania

Double tax treaties
Albania has signed 30 double tax treaties, of which 28 are already in force.

Tax administration

The tax year is the calendar year. The final tax return for corporate income tax is due by 31 March of the year immediately following that tax year. Predetermined advance payments of corporate income tax are due by the fifteenth of each month.

Advance payments of profit tax payable by the small business category are payable on a quarterly basis.

For advance payments, companies can decide to use their prior fiscal year after tax profit within six months of the subsequent year and submit the decision to the tax authorities no later than 31 July. The decision should state the amount allocated as statutory reserves, the amount to be used for investments and/or for increase in share capital as well as the amount to be distributed as dividends.

Companies have the obligation to pay the tax on dividends to the tax authorities no later than 30 July of the year the financial results are approved, regardless of whether the dividend has been distributed to the shareholders.

Companies have the obligation to submit to the National Registration Center every decision taken by their board of directors within 30 days from the decision's date.

Corporate taxes in Angola

For more information, contact:

Pedro Calixto
PricewaterhouseCoopers
16th floor, BPC Building
Largo Saydi Mingas
Luanda, Angola
Tel: +244 222 395 004
Email: pedro.calixto@ao.pwc.com

Significant developments

The most significant corporate tax change in 2009 was the approval of the new minimum taxable income for corporate income tax purposes, which is structured by sector of activity and province in Angola where the company is located.

Taxes on corporate income

The standard tax rate of 35% is levied on the taxable income of the following corporate income taxpayer groups:

- Group A – Tax is levied on actual profits as shown in taxpayers' accounting records (e.g., public and private companies, permanent establishments of foreign entities);
- Group B – Tax is levied on taxpayers' presumable profit (taxpayers not included in groups A or C); and
- Group C – Taxation is based on profits that taxpayers could normally earn/obtain (e.g., small family companies).

Special regimes, rules and tax rates are provided for the oil and gas industry and the mining industry.

Exemptions from corporate income tax are provided for:

- Agricultural companies (for up to 10 years);
- "Corporative organisms";
- Culture associations;
- Companies that manage their own property; and
- Non-resident shipping operators (as long as reciprocity exists).

Corporate residence

Tax is assessed on the worldwide income of business entities with a head office or effective management in Angola, or on income attributable to a non-resident company deemed to have a permanent establishment in Angola.

Other taxes

Stamp tax
Stamp tax is payable on a wide variety of transactions and documents, at rates that are of value set in specific amounts or on a percentage basis of value.

Angola

Important examples include:

- Receipts – 1%;
- Companies' incorporation – 0.20%; and
- Share capital increase – 0.50%.

Consumption tax

There is no value-added tax (VAT) or sales tax in Angola.

A consumption tax exists, which is similar to that of an excise duty. Local production, importation of goods, and a few services (e.g., hotels, restaurants, electricity, water supply and telecommunications) are subject to this tax.

The rates vary from 2% to 30%, depending on the service or goods imported or produced locally.

Real estate income tax

Real estate income tax (IPU) is due on actual or deemed income from real estate located in Angola.

Buildings used for activities subject to corporate income tax are exempt from IPU.

Other exemptions are provided for:

- "Corporative organisms" and economic associations;
- Recognised religious associations;
- Buildings owned by public services, humanitarian organisations, charity organisations, schools, museums and other public and social services;
- Consular representations of foreign countries (reciprocity applies); and
- New habitation buildings.

The IPU tax rate is 30%. Hotel buildings considered to be of public interest may benefit from a 50% tax reduction over a period of 15 years.

Taxable income is 80% of the annual rent received. Maintenance and conservation expenses are deductible if exceeding 20% of rental income.

Investment income tax

Investment income tax (IAC) is due on interests, dividends and royalties and other income of a similar nature. In Angola, the IAC code divides such income into two taxable sections as follows:

- Section A
  - Interest on loans and credit facilities;
  - Income derived from credit contracts; and
  - Income derived from deferred payments.

Tax is due at the moment that the interest or income is earned or at the moment when it is presumed to have been earned.

A minimum annual interest rate of 6% is deemed on loan agreements.

- Section B
  - Dividends;
  - Capital remunerations of members of "corporative organisms";
  - Bonds interest;
  - Interest on shareholders' loans;
  - Income derived from dividends not collected until the end of the year; and
  - Royalties.

For the purposes of this group of income, note that:

a. The concept of royalties includes the remuneration of any kind attributed to the use of or consent to use copyrighted literature; arts or science works, including movies and films or recordings for radio or television transmissions; patents; brands; drawings or models of a plan; formulas or secret processes. The concept of royalties also applies to the use of or the consent to use industrial, commercial or scientific equipment and information related to an experience acquired on the industrial, commercial or scientific sector.
b. A minimum annual interest rate equal to the rate used by commercial banks on credit operations is deemed interest for shareholders' loans, except if proven that these loans do not earn any interest.

Tax is due at the moment the effective attribution of income (dividends) is earned (interest) or paid (other income).

The IAC rate is 15%, except for the following income for which the rate is 10%:

- Dividends;
- Capital remuneration of members of "corporative organisms";
- Bonds interest; and
- Royalties.

Tax is withheld by the payer on dividends, royalties and bonds and shareholders' loans. In any other situation, tax is assessed by the competent local tax office (i.e., on interest from ordinary loans – other than domestic bank loans – and credit facilities, current accounts, sales on credit and late payment on these loans). When the payment of interest is made to a non-resident company that is not a shareholder, Angolan law establishes that the tax obligation shifts to the Angolan resident entity paying the interest. This investment income tax payable is a cost for corporate income tax purposes and, in addition, 65% of its value is credited against corporate income tax.

Branch income

Branch taxable income is taxed on the same basis as separate legal entities. Income remitted by a branch to the head office is not subject to (dividends) taxation.

Income determination

The taxable income results of the profits computed in accordance with Angolan accounting regulations, and adjusted in accordance with the provisions of the corporate income tax code, most commonly relate to:

Angola

- Costs, if not contributing to generate profits;
- Excessive depreciation;
- Provisions other than for bad debts (limited), stocks (limited) and pending court decisions;
- Penalties;
- Non-documented costs; and
- Adjustment to intergroup charges (although transfer pricing regulations are vague and the tax authorities have not been enforcing them systematically).

Depreciation

Depreciation should be computed using the straight-line method; any other method must be approved by the tax authorities.

Furthermore:

a. The tax depreciation rates should respect the limits imposed by Government Ruling 755/72.
b. Depreciation not accounted for at cost are not permitted as a deduction in the following years.
c. 30% of the increase on depreciation resulting from a legal revaluation of fixed assets is not accepted for tax purposes, as well as the total increase in depreciation resulting from free revaluation of the fixed assets.

Bad debts

Write-off of debts is considered as a tax cost only if the write-off resulted from a bankruptcy court process.

Provisions

The only provisions accepted as costs for tax purposes are:

- Doubtful debts – within an annual limit of 2% of the client's current total account value and provided that a 6% accumulated provision limit is not exceeded;
- Inventory depreciation – within limits that vary from 1% and 8% (annual and accumulated) depending on the nature of the company's activity;
- Those respecting the limits and rules imposed by the Insurance Supervision Institute for insurance companies, as well as the Central Bank for Financial Institutions; and
- Provisions for possible losses resulting from a court process.

Donations

Donations are accepted as a tax cost up to a limit of 2% of the taxable income if the donations are granted to Angolan education, science, charity and cultural institutes. If granted to Angolan government, central and local administration bodies, the donations are totally accepted as tax costs.

Deductions

The following values can be deducted from the net profit on the calculation of the taxable income:

- Dividends received, provided that the share participation is owned for two consecutive years (or since the incorporation of the entity where the participation is held) and the share participation is not less than 25%;
- Dividends and interest of public bonds owned by insurance companies to fund their technical reserves; and
- Profits retained and that, in the three following financial years, have been reinvested by the company in new installations or, equipment may be deductible from the taxable profit the following three years after the investment is finalised (benefit not yet regulated).

Transfer pricing

Despite the existence of the arm's-length principle in Angolan corporate tax law, there are no detailed regulations on transfer pricing. Taxpayers should be aware that, in light of existing generic rules included in the corporate tax code, the tax authorities do have means to adjust inter-company charges.

Losses carried forward

Tax losses are deductible from the taxable income of the following three years. Carryback of losses is not allowed.

Group taxation

There are no special rules for group taxation in Angola.

Tax incentives

Special regulations, such as the law of private investment and following regulations such as Decree Law No. 17/03, provide tax and customs incentives for investment projects in strategic economic development areas and sectors (that can go up to 15 years of corporate tax exemption). The oil and gas, financial and mining economic sectors are, however, regulated by specific laws.

Withholding taxes (WHT)

Withholding tax is applicable to payments for services provided to Angolan entities. For Angolan taxpayers this is regarded as an advance payment of the corporate income tax due at the year-end, and for non-resident companies it is a final tax.

The payments subject to this withholding tax are those related to:

a. Construction, improvement, repair or conservation of immovable property withheld at a rate of 3.5% on the gross payments (corporate income tax rate of 35% applicable on a 10% deemed margin); and
b. Other services, namely technical assistance and management fees, withheld at a rate of 5.25% on the gross payments (corporate income tax rate of 35% applicable on a 15% deemed margin).

Angola

Tax administration

Tax returns
The tax year follows the calendar year, and the annual corporate tax return must be submitted by the last business day of May of the year following the year to which the income relates.

Tax payment
Tax is paid in four instalments. The first three correspond to advance payments based on the expected tax to be paid or, if unknown at that date, 75% of the taxable income computed on the previous year multiplied by the tax rate (35%). The instalments are paid in January, February and March, and the final instalment is paid with the submission of the annual tax return on the last business day of May.

A

For more information, contact:

Charles Walwyn
PricewaterhouseCoopers
11 Old Parham Road
St. John's, Antigua
Tel: +1 268 462 3000 ext. 121
Email: charles.walwyn@ag.pwc.com

Significant developments

There have been no significant tax or regulatory developments in the past year.

Taxes on corporate income

Corporation tax currently is imposed at a rate of 25% on all companies except financial institutions registered under the Banking Act. If a financial institution maintains its residential mortgage rates at or below 7% throughout the taxation year, then it shall pay income tax at a rate of 22.5%. The corporate tax rate was 30% prior to 1 January 2008.

Corporate residence

A corporation is deemed to be a resident if it is incorporated in Antigua, if it is registered as an external company doing business in Antigua, or if the central management and control of its business are exercised in Antigua.

Other taxes

Life insurance premium tax
A premium tax of 3% is levied on the premium income (net of agent's commission) of all life insurance companies, whether resident or non-resident.

General insurance premium tax
A premium tax of 3% is levied on the premium income, excluding motor business (net of agent's commission), of all general insurance companies, whether resident or non-resident.

Stamp tax on transfer of property
Stamp tax is levied on the consideration for the sale or the value of property as assessed by the Chief Valuation Officer, whichever is higher.

	%
Vendor (parent or grandparent) (husband or wife)	1%
Purchaser (child or grandchild) (husband or wife)	1%

Antigua and Barbuda

	%
Vendors who are citizens of Antigua	7.5%
Vendors who are non-citizens of Antigua	7.5%

In addition, non-citizens will be required to pay a land value appreciation tax at the rate of 5%, which is assessed on the difference between the value of property when purchased, plus improvements, and the value of property at the time of sale.

	%
Purchasers who are citizens of Antigua	2.5%
Purchasers who are non-citizens of Antigua	2.5%

In addition, non-citizens will be required to pay 5% of the value of property with reference to a non-citizens license required to hold property in Antigua and Barbuda.

Stamp tax on transfer of shares
Stamp tax is levied on the market value of the shares or book value of the shares, whichever is higher.

	%
Vendors	5.0%
Purchasers	2.5%

Non-citizens must obtain a license (at a cost of XCD 400) to hold shares or be a director in a company that owns land or has a lease on land in excess of five acres for a period greater than five years.

Property tax
Property tax is levied at graduated rates on the basis of the market value of the real property (as assessed by the Property Valuation Department) and its use (residential or commercial).

Rates of tax are as follows:

- Agricultural land 0.10%;
- Residential land 0.20%;
- Residential building 0.30%;
- Buildings classified as other property 0.50%; and
- Land classified as other property 0.40%.

Allowances and tax rebates available as follows:

- Dwelling house allowance of XCD 150,000 from the taxable value;
- Rebates to pensioners of between 10% and 50% depending on the annual income of the pensioner;
- 5% rebate for payment of tax on or before the due date;
- New dwelling house will be exempt from tax for the first two years of being habitable; and
- Tax rebate available to special development property and property for public use of between 25% and 100%.

Sales tax

Antigua and Barbuda Sales Tax (ABST) was introduced on 29 January 2007. The ABST is applicable to a wide range of goods and services. The standard rate is 15%; hotel accommodation carries a rate of 10.5%.

A period in the ABST Act represent one month. The XCD 300,000 registration threshold covers a period of 12 months. The threshold for registration is XCD 300,000 in taxable activity per 12 month period.

A number of services including financial services, international and local transportation, sale of residential land, education, long-term accommodation (greater than 45 days), medical and veterinary services, are exempt. Certain supplies are zero-rated, including exports, basic food items, water, electricity for residential use, sale of residential property, construction of new residential premises and fuel. Intergroup transactions are taxable.

Hotel tax

Hotel taxes were repealed on 29 January 2007 with the introduction of the Antigua and Barbuda Sales Tax.

Branch income

Branch income is taxed on the same basis and at the same rate as that of corporations.

Recharges of expenses from head office to the branch will be subject to withholding tax at a rate of 25%. The recharges have to be justifiable, consistent and cannot just be based on a percentage allocation.

A resident branch of a foreign company shall be regarded as a separate company and shall be taxed on the same basis as that of a locally registered corporation.

Income determination

Inventory valuation

Inventories are generally stated at the lower of cost or net realisable value. First-in, first-out (FIFO) and average cost methods of valuation are generally used for book and tax purposes. However, the Commissioner of Inland Revenue will normally accept a method of valuation that conforms to standard accounting practice in the trade concerned. Last-in, first-out (LIFO) is not permitted for tax or book purposes.

Capital gains

Capital gains are not subject to tax.

Inter-company dividends

Dividends received by a company resident in Antigua from another company resident in Antigua are taxed at the rate of 25%. Credit is given to the recipient for the tax on the dividend in computing the tax liability.

Foreign income

An Antiguan corporation is taxed on foreign branch income as earned and on foreign dividends as received. Double taxation is avoided by means of foreign tax credits where active tax treaties exist and through deduction of foreign income taxes in

Antigua and Barbuda

other cases (UK and The Caribbean Community, CARICOM). There is also relief from Commonwealth taxes.

Stock dividends
An Antiguan corporation may distribute a tax-free stock dividend proportionately to all shareholders.

Deductions

Depreciation and depletion
Depreciation allowed for tax purposes is computed by the diminishing-balance method at prescribed rates. Initial allowances are granted on industrial buildings and on capital expenditures incurred on plant and machinery by a person carrying on a trade or undertaking, as defined. In addition, an annual allowance of 2% is granted on all buildings. Conformity between book and tax depreciation is not required. Any gain on the sale of depreciated assets is taxable as ordinary income up to the amount of tax depreciation recaptured.

Net operating losses
Income tax losses may be carried forward for six years following the year in which the loss was incurred. However, the chargeable income of a company in any one income year may not be reduced by more than one half by losses brought forward. No carryback of losses is permitted.

Payments to foreign affiliates
An Antiguan corporation may claim a deduction for royalties, management fees and interest charges paid to foreign affiliates, provided the payments are equal to or less than what the corporation would pay to an unrelated entity. The deductibility of any payments to a foreign affiliate will be subject to an arm's-length test.

Cultural and social contribution
A deduction of 50% of all substantial contributions made by any person with respect to sport, education or culture in Antigua and Barbuda is allowed against a person's assessable income from trade, business or profession. Contributions must be in excess of XCD 10,000 in any assessment year and deductions during any assessment year will be limited to XCD 250,000.

Interest
No deduction is allowed for interest on loans owing to shareholders, directors, their spouses, children or relatives, or to any related parties. Only interest paid to banks and financial institutions licensed under the Financial Institutions (Non-Banking) Act on loans borrowed at commercial rates and terms is deductible.

Restriction on rents paid
Rents paid by a company to shareholders, directors, their spouses, children or relatives, or to any related parties in excess of 5% of the otherwise chargeable profits of the company may not be deducted.

Restriction on compensation
Salaries, wages, directors' fees and other payments made for services rendered by the shareholders, directors, their spouses, children or relatives in excess of 25% of otherwise chargeable profits may not be deducted.

A

Group taxation

Group taxation is not permitted.

Tax incentives

Inward investment and capital investment
Tax incentives are currently available under the following legislation:

1. Fiscal Incentives Ordinance 1975: This ordinance provides to manufacturers of an "approved product" exemption from taxes for varying periods, up to a maximum of 15 years. After the period of exemption, relief by way of tax credits of up to 50% of income tax paid on profits derived from certain export sales may be obtained. The net losses arising during the tax holiday period (i.e., the excess of accumulated tax losses over total profits) may be carried forward and relieved against profits following the expiration of the tax holiday in accordance with the normal rules for set-off of losses.
2. International Business Corporations Act 1982: An international business company is exempt from the payment of corporate income tax and withholding tax.
3. The Investment Authority Act 2006: The Act provides the framework for the promotion of investment opportunities in Antigua and Barbuda by introducing a system of registration of businesses, an investment code and a range of incentives that are available to both local and foreign investors. The available incentives and concessions to which an investor would be entitled for consideration are as follows:

    a. Exemption from the payment of customs duty;
    b. Reduction of property tax;
    c. Exemption from income tax;
    d. Reduction of stamp duty; and
    e. Exemption from withholding tax.

The amount of the incentive and concessions will depend on the amount of the investment and the number of employees in the proposed business.

The investment categories are as follows:

1. Capital investment of up to XCD 1 million or employs up to 26 persons: This investor could qualify for exemption from the payment of customs duty on certain imports, reduction in property tax by up to 10%, exemption from the payment of corporate income tax and withholding tax for up to three years and a reduction of stamp duty by up to 10% on the sale of land and buildings used in the business operation;
2. Capital investment of over XCD 1 million, employs over 26 persons and has at least one director or owner who is a resident of Antigua and Barbuda: This investor could qualify for exemption from the payment of customs duty on certain imports, reduction in property tax by up to 20%, exemption from the payment of corporate income tax and withholding tax for up to five years and a reduction of stamp duty by up to 20% on the sale of land and buildings used in the business operation;
3. Capital investment of over XCD 10 million, employs over 51 persons and has at least one director or owner who is a resident of Antigua and Barbuda: This investor could qualify for exemption from the payment of customs duty on certain imports, reduction in property tax by up to 30%, exemption from the payment of corporate

income tax and withholding tax for up to 10 years and a reduction of stamp duty by up to 30% on the sale of land and buildings used in the business operation;

4. Capital investment of over XCD 25 million, employs over 75 persons and has at least one director or owner who is a resident of Antigua and Barbuda: This investor could qualify for exemption from the payment of customs duty on certain imports, reduction in property tax by up to 40%, exemption from the payment of corporate income tax and withholding tax for up to 12 years and a reduction of stamp duty by up to 40% on the sale of land and buildings used in the business operation;

5. Capital investment of over XCD 75 million, employs over 100 persons and has at least one director or owner who is a resident of Antigua and Barbuda: This investor could qualify for exemption from the payment of customs duty on certain imports, reduction in property tax by up to 50%, exemption from the payment of corporate income tax and withholding tax for up to 15 years and a reduction of stamp duty by up to 50% on the sale of land and buildings used in the business operation; and

6. Capital investment of over XCD 100 million, employs over 150 persons and has at least one director or owner who is a resident of Antigua and Barbuda: This investor could qualify for exemption from the payment of customs duty on certain imports, reduction in property tax by up to 75%, exemption from the payment of corporate income tax and withholding tax for up to 20 years and a reduction of stamp duty by up to 75% on the sale of land and buildings used in the business operation.

Withholding taxes (WHT)

Tax is currently withheld from income as follows:

Recipient	Dividend	Dividend preferred shares	Interest and rentals	Management fees, royalties and other payments to a non-resident	Interest on bank deposits
	%	%	%	%	%
Resident corporations and individuals	Nil	Nil	Nil	Nil	Nil
Non-resident corporations	25	25	25	25	25
Non-resident individuals	25	25	20	25	Nil
Residents of a CARICOM member state:					
Corporations	Nil	15	15	15	15
Individuals	Nil	15	15	15	Nil

Interest payments on bank deposits made to non-resident individuals are not subject to withholding tax. Interest payments on bank deposits made to non-resident corporations are taxed at the rate of 25%.

Where a non-resident lends money at arm's length for the purpose of promoting industrial, commercial, scientific, housing, or other development, the rate of withholding tax is 10%. Prior approval must be sought from the Commissioner of Inland Revenue and it is recommended that Cabinet approval also be obtained.

Withholding taxes become due at the time of payment or accrual and must be paid within seven days thereof.

Tax treaties

There is a tax treaty with the United Kingdom and a double taxation agreement between member states of CARICOM.

Tax administration

Returns

Taxes are assessed on a fiscal-year basis. The taxpayer must file a corporate income tax return within three months of the fiscal-year end, which includes audited financial statements, and the authorities would subsequently raise an assessment.

If a return is not filed on a timely basis the authorities have the power to issue estimated assessments. There is a 5% penalty for late filing (minimum of XCD 500). The taxpayer can object to assessments raised within 30 days and ask the Commissioner of Inland Revenue to review and revise. In the event that the objection is unsuccessful, the taxpayer may appeal to the Tax Appeal Board. The Commissioner of Inland Revenue has the power to enforce the collection of tax prior to the determination of any objection or appeal. The Commissioner also has the discretion to order a stay on the collection and payment of the whole or part of any assessed tax until such time as the objection or appeal is finalised if it would be unjust not to do so. Assessments for the past six years may be reviewed and revised.

Payment of tax

Advance tax is payable in monthly instalments and is ordinarily based on the tax chargeable and assessed in the previous fiscal-year. The standard amount of each instalment is determined as one-twelfth of the tax chargeable in the previous fiscal-year. If the assessment for the prior year has not been finalised, the Commissioner of Inland Revenue can raise an assessment based on his best judgment.

The balance of tax due after deduction of advance tax, as notified in the assessment, is payable at the time of submitting the annual corporate tax return, which must not be later than three months after the financial year-end or one-month of service of the final assessment.

Tax is deemed to be in default if not paid within 30 days of the date on which it becomes due and payable. A penalty of 20% and interest of 1% per month is charged on unpaid taxes in default.

Corporate taxes in Argentina

For more information, contact:

Jorge San Martín
PricewaterhouseCoopers
Edificio Bouchard Plaza
Bouchard 557
C1106ABG Ciudad de Buenos Aires
Argentina
Tel: +54 11 4850 6706
Email: jorge.a.san.martin@ar.pwc.com

Significant developments

From a Tax Treaty network perspective, Argentina has revoked the double tax treaty with Austria. The termination of the tax treaty became effective on 1 January 2009. On the other hand, five tax information exchange agreements (TIEAs) were signed with Andorra, Bahamas, Monaco, San Marino and Costa Rica.

The Argentine Executive Power, on 21 October 2009, introduced new rules that provide tax benefits for investments in new capital assets earmarked for industrial activities and infrastructure works (Law No. 26,360). The tax benefits consist of either accelerated depreciation (three, four, or five years) or a reimbursement of VAT for the relevant investment, but the taxpayer will be able to request both benefits in some cases *(please refer to Tax incentives section)*.

An amnesty programme (Law No. 26,476) was approved in December 2008, allowing delinquent taxpayers to satisfy tax liabilities with substantial discounts on interest charges. The amnesty applied to tax and social security liabilities accruing prior to 31 December 2007. Delinquent taxpayers could pay down the balances in up to 120 instalments. The amnesty programme closed on 31 August 2009 and also permitted employers to formally declare disguised labour relationships free of any obligation for unpaid payroll taxes and social security contributions. The amnesty also provided for forgiveness of tax penalties (fines). The amounts collected by the Argentine Revenue Service, however, fell short of expectations.

The tax cost of doing business in the city of Buenos Aires has been increased. On 1 January 2009, all contracts executed in or with effects in the city of Buenos Aires, as well as financial transactions related to this jurisdiction that involve a financial entity established in Buenos Aires, become subject to stamp tax. Stamp tax had been abolished in the city of Buenos Aires as from January 2003 and re-established as from 12 January 2009. *(Please refer to section Stamp tax.)*

The Province of Buenos Aires passed a regional measure (Law No. 14,044) that raised local tax rates and imposed a new tax called "tax on charitable donations and transfers of wealth".

Taxes on corporate income

Profits tax

The rate of profits tax on net taxable business profits is 35%. Legal entities resident in Argentina are subject to tax on Argentine and foreign-source income. Legal entities resident are able to claim any similar taxes actually paid abroad on foreign-source income as a tax credit. The tax rate applies on net income determined on a worldwide basis.

Corporations, limited liability partnerships and branches, as well as other entities, are required to make a flat and final income tax withholding of 35% from dividend payments to resident or non-residents beneficiaries, to the extent that the amount of such dividends exceeds the net taxable income determined at a corporate level in accordance with the general tax rules.

Argentine-source income (royalties, interests, etc.) received by foreign entities is subject to withholding tax in full and final settlement *at sour*ce. *(Please refer to section Withholding Taxes.)*

Tax on minimum notional income
In addition to the profits tax, there is a tax on minimum notional income. The rate is 1% on the value of fixed and current assets. The presumed tax, imposed annually is applied only in excess of the profits tax of the same fiscal year. In addition, payment of this presumed tax, not offset by the profits tax, will be treated as payment on account of profits tax chargeable during a maximum period of 10 years.

Banking and insurance entities are only subject to this tax on the 20% of the corresponding taxable assets.

Corporate residence

Corporate residence is determined on the basis of centres of activity, which may be the location of a company's economic activity or management activity. Centres of activity in Argentina of non-Argentine corporations are treated as permanent establishments.

Argentina taxes its corporate residents on a worldwide basis, and a tax credit for taxes paid abroad is available.

Other taxes

Value-added tax (VAT)
It is assessable on the sales value of products (e.g., raw materials, produce, finished or partly finished merchandise) with few exemptions, and on most services (such as construction, utilities, professional and personal services not derived from employment, rental, etc.) and on import of goods and services. The general tax rate is 21%, although certain specific items are subject to a 10.5% and 27% rate. It is payable by filing monthly tax returns.

The increased rate of 27% applies on "utilities services" not rendered to final consumer in family (e.g., telecommunications, household gas, running water, sewerage and energy).

A reduced rate of 10.5% will apply on certain transactions, such as (but not limited to):

• Construction of housing;
• Interest and other costs on personal loans granted to final consumers by financial institutions;

Argentina

- Sales and imports of living bovine animals, supply of publicity and advertising in some specific cases;
- Any passenger transportation operating inside the country when the distance does not exceed 100km;
- Medical assistance in some specific cases; and
- Certain capital goods depending on the Custom Duty Code.

Exemptions

Among others, the following transactions are exempt from VAT:

- Sales of books, ordinary natural water, common bread, milk, medicine, postage stamps; aircraft used in commercial activities and for defence or internal safety, and ships or boats acquired by the National Government; and
- Supply of services such as: services rendered by the Government (National, Provincial or Local) or by public institutions, school or university education provided by private institutions subject to public educational programmes; cultural services supplied by religious institutions; hospital and medical care and related activities, transportation services for sick or injured persons in vehicles specially designed for the purpose; tickets for theatre, cinema, musical shows and sport events, the production and distribution of motion picture films; local transport of passengers (taxis, buses, etc.) up to 100km., international transportation; rental of real estate for housing purposes.

Exemption on importation

The following transactions shall be exempted from taxation:

- Final importation of goods qualifying for exemption from customs duties under special regimes for tourists, scientists and technicians, diplomatic agents, etc.; final importation of samples and parcels exempted from customs duties.

Exports of goods and services are treated as a zero rated transaction. Nevertheless, input VAT related to these transactions can either be used as a credit against output VAT or refunded pursuant to a special procedure. *(Please refer to Other issues.)*

Services rendered within the country shall be deemed to be exports if they are effectively applied or economically utilised outside the country.

VAT law also establishes that services rendered abroad but utilised in Argentina ("importation of services") are subject to tax through a self-assessment mechanism.

There is also a system of standard VAT collections and withholdings under which liable parties (who are registered as such), Custom and other entities are required to act as a VAT collection or withholding agent with regard to sale, purchase or import transactions.

VAT paid on purchases, final imports, and rental of automobiles not considered as inventory, cannot be computed by the purchaser as a VAT credit. The same tax treatment applies to other services, such as those provided by restaurants, hotels and garages.

Turnover tax (gross income tax)

Each of the 24 jurisdictions into which Argentina is divided imposes a tax on gross revenues from the sale of goods and services. Exports of goods are exempt, and certain industries are subject to a reduced tax rate. Rates, rules and assessment procedures are determined locally.

Information on tax rates of the economically largest jurisdictions is as follows:

Jurisdiction	General Rate	Commerce	Services	Industry
Province of Buenos Aires	3.5%	3% – 4.5%	3.5% – 4.5%	1% – 3%
City of Buenos Aires	3%	3%	3%	1% – 3%
Córdoba	4%	2% al 7%	4%	0.5% – 1%
Mendoza	3%	3%	3%	1.5%
Santa Cruz	2.5%	2.5%	2.5%	1.5%
Santa Fe	3.5%	1% al 15%	1% al 15%	0%

Excise taxes

This tax is assessable on a wide variety of items sold in Argentina (not on exports), principally on tobacco, wines, soft drinks, spirits, gasoline, lubricants, insurance premiums, automobile tires, mobiles services, perfumes, jewellery and precious stones. The bases of the assessment and tax rate of some items are:

Products	Rates	
	Nominal	Effective
Tobacco	16% – 20% – 60%	19.05 – 25%
Alcoholic drinks	20%	25%
Beers	8%	8.70%
Soft drinks	4% – 8%	4.17% – 8.70%
Jewellery and precious stones	20%	25%

Tax on financial transactions – on credits and debits on bank accounts

Bank account movements (deposits and withdrawals) are subject to this national tax at the following rates:

- 0.6% of deposits and withdrawals in bank accounts opened in local financial entities; and
- 1.2% of any transactions made in a bank without using a bank account.

The 34% or 17%, respectively, of tax paid on bank account deposit transactions and movement of funds, respectively, is creditable against income tax and minimum notional income tax and/or respective tax advances.

Wealth tax

This annual tax is levied on the shares or holding in the capital of local companies owned by individuals or undivided estates domiciled in Argentina or abroad, and/or companies and/or any other type of legal person domiciled abroad. It shall be assessed and paid directly by the local company, as a full and final payment on behalf of the shareholders (the issuing company has the right to recover from the shareholder the tax paid).

Argentina

The applicable tax rate is 0.5% on the value of the participation, which is generally calculated on the difference between assets and liabilities arising from the financial statements closed at 31 December or during the respective fiscal year.

Stamp tax

Levied by each of the 24 jurisdictions, and applies principally to contracts and agreements, deeds, mortgages, and other obligations, agreements and discharges of a civil, financial or commercial nature of which there is written evidence or, in certain instances, that are the subject of entries in books of account. The average tax rate is 1% applicable on the economic value of the contract.

In the city of Buenos Aires, the standard tax rate is 0.8% of the aggregate amount of the transactions, contracts, and deeds that are subject to the stamp tax. It also establishes special rates of 0.5%, 1%, and 2.5%; and in the case of transactions involving uncertain consideration, a fixed tax of ARS 1,000 (on the fulfilment of certain conditions).

Payroll taxes

Foreign and local nationals working for a local company must be included on the local payroll and will be considered as a local employee for local labour, tax and social security purposes and so both the local company and the employees will be subject to the corresponding regulations.

All the compensation paid in Argentina or abroad for work performed for the local company will be considered as local compensation and should be reported to the tax and social security authorities, as the case may be, and included in the salary slips and recorded in the local labour books.

The local employer must withhold income tax on an actual and monthly basis and make the corresponding payments to the tax authorities through monthly withholding tax returns. Individual tax rates range from 9% to 35% and personal deductions are available.

The local entity must issue salary slips every month for each employee included on its payroll, considering the total compensation mentioned above.

Employer social security contributions add up to 23% to 27% to payroll cost. There is a compulsory thirteenth-month salary. There is no restriction regarding the employment of foreigners, provided they hold working visas.

Workers' (Employees') Compensation: Argentine labour regulations determine different forms of compensation for employees. These include, but are not limited to, the following:

- Vacation compensations; and
- Compensation in a case of termination of employment contract with employee (prior notice of dismissal and to a severance payment, both based on seniority), etc.

Main social taxes and contributions assessable on salaries are as follows:

	Percentage of gross monthly earnings (including 13th month salary)	
	Employer (2,3)	Employee (1)
Pension fund	17/21	11%
National unemployment fund	–	–
Family allowances fund	–	–
Social services institute for pensioner	–	3%
Social health care plan	6%	3%
Total	23/27	17

1. Social security charges borne by employees are applicable up to a monthly salary cap which currently amounts to ARS 10,119.08 (updated as of May 2010).
2. Contributions made by employers are applicable to total compensation without application of any cap.
3. Employer's contribution to the national unemployment fund, family allowances fund, and social services institute for pensioners is paid at a unified rate of 17%. The rate is increased to 21% for companies the main activity of which consists of service rendering or commerce, provided the amount of their total annual sales average for the last three years exceeds USD 13.67 million (at the current exchange rate of USD 1.00 = ARS 3.90 equivalent to ARS 48 million).

Import and export duties

The levels of import duty currently range between 0% and 35%, except in cases where specific minimum duty is applied or which involve merchandise with a specific treatment. These percentages were established considering the individual competitive conditions prevailing in different production sectors and the relative advantages of contributing to the introduction of equipment and technology for local industry. In general, merchandise originating from LAIA (Latin America Integration Association – ALADI) countries is entitled to preferential duty.

In the case of export transactions, goods are valued based on the FOB clause and the approach is based on their theoretical value, rather than a positive basis as in the case of imports.

Since March 2002, definitive exports of all goods are subject to export duties. The rates vary from 5% to 45%, depending on the tariff code of the merchandise (while 5% is the current typical applied higher rates are considered for exports of agricultural products or hydrocarbons).

Branch income

The rate of profits tax on net taxable profits from Argentine sources and from activities performed abroad by the branch is 35%. Branches are also subject to Minimum Notional Income Tax.

Income determination

Inventory valuation

Inventory valuation is based on the latest purchase. Thus, LIFO may not be elected for tax purposes. Conformity between book and tax reporting is not required.

Argentina

Capital gains
Capital gains and losses attract normal profits tax treatment, except that losses from the sale of shares and other equity interests may be offset only against the same type of income.

Inter-company dividends
These dividends are not included in the tax base by the recipient if distributed by an Argentine company. However, see "Withholding taxes"; tax is levied if the dividends are distributed by a foreign company.

Foreign income
Foreign income received or held undistributed abroad (in case of investments in non-stock companies) by resident corporations is subject to tax. Argentina does not have a CFC regimen. Tax losses from foreign source can only be offset against income of foreign source.

Stock dividends
These dividends are tax exempt if distributed by an Argentine company. However, see "Withholding taxes" section; tax is levied if the dividends are paid by a foreign company.

Transfer pricing rules
The transfer pricing regulations governing inter-company transactions, adopt principles similar to those of the Organisation for Economic Co-operation and Development (OECD) pursuant to which companies must comply with the arm's-length principle in order to determine the value of goods and services in their transactions with foreign related companies.

The following taxpayers, among others, must generally file, together with their annual income tax return, a supplementary return (transactions encompassed by regulations governing transfer prices) and the transfer pricing study:

a. Taxpayers carrying out transactions with related individuals or legal entities. Related parties - "Two or more persons are considered to be related parties when one of them takes part, either directly or indirectly, in the administration, control or capital of the other, or when a person or group of persons takes part either directly or indirectly in the administration, control or capital of those persons" set up, domiciled or located abroad;
b. Taxpayers carrying out transactions with related individuals or legal entities set up, domiciled or located in countries with low or no taxation, whether related or not;
c. Argentine residents carrying out transactions with permanent establishments located abroad and owned by them; and
d. Argentine residents, owners of permanent establishments located abroad, for transactions carried out by the latter with persons or other type of related entities domiciled, set up or located abroad.

The Regulatory Decree provides the specific applicable rules to determine the fairness of the transfer pricing methodology. These rules are similar to those set by the OECD and contemplate six methods, including the following:

1. Comparable Uncontrolled Price – CUP;
2. Resale Price Method – RPM;
3. Cost Plus;

4. Profit Split Method – PSM;
5. Transactional Net Margin Method – TNMM; and
6. Special Method for Export of goods with prices quoting in transparent markets.

There is no specific hierarchy, as each particular transaction must be analysed based on the assets, functions and risks involved and on information available. Regulations establish that the most appropriate method is that which reflects the economic reality of the transactions.

Deductions

General rule
Expenses necessary to generate, maintain and preserve taxable income, and related to the company activity, are usually tax deductible, with a few exceptions, to the extent they are fair and reasonable.

Net operating losses
Net operating losses (NOLs) may be carried forward five years. Loss carrybacks are not permitted. Furthermore, foreign source losses must be offset by income from similar sources.

Losses on derivatives and hedging transactions can be only offset against income from the same transaction.

Payments to foreign affiliates
Transactions between related parties should be at arm's length. This principle is extended to transactions with companies located in low or no tax jurisdictions. (Please refer to *Transfer pricing rules* section above). Payments to foreign affiliates or related parties and companies located in low or no tax jurisdictions that represent income of Argentine source are tax deductible, provided they are paid before the due date for filing the tax return and the corresponding withholding is paid to the tax authorities. Otherwise they would be deducted in the fiscal year in which they are paid.

Technical assistance and services that involve transfer of technology should be covered by agreements duly registered with the National Institute of Intellectual Property for information purposes. These transactions are governed by the Transfer of Technology Law (Law No. 22,426).

Taxes
Except for profits tax and the tax on minimum notional income, all taxes are deductible.

Depreciation and depletion
Depreciation is generally computed on a straight-line basis over the technically estimated useful life of the assets or, alternatively, over their standard useful lives (e.g., machinery and equipment – 10 years; furniture – 10 years). Depreciation of buildings and other constructions on real estate is 2% per annum on cost (on a straight-line basis), unless it can be proved that useful life is less than 50 years.

Depreciation of automobiles whose original cost exceeds ARS 20,000 is not deductible. Related expenses (gasoline vouchers, insurance, rentals, repairs and maintenance, etc.) are deductible up to an amount of ARS 7,200 per car per year.

Argentina

Conformity between book and tax depreciation is not required.

Profit or loss on the sale of depreciated property is determined with reference to cost less depreciation, restated for inflation as at March 1992, and is included in ordinary taxable income.

Percentage depletion is available for natural resources (mines, quarries, woods).

Foreign exchange
The general rule is that the foreign exchange results (gain or losses) have to be recognised on an accrual basis. However, in some cases cash basis is applicable.

Foreign exchange losses can only be offset against foreign source taxable income.

Other significant items
Donations
When made to societies and associations expressly exempt from assessment to profits tax, donations are admissible deductions up to a maximum of 5% of the donor's net taxable profits, provided certain requirements are fulfilled.

Representation expenses
If adequately documented, representation expenses are permissible deductions up to 1.5% of the amount of salaries accrued during the fiscal year. According to Regulatory Decree, the representation expenses are payment made in order to represent the company in the market, improve and maintain its relationship with suppliers, client, etc.

Directors' fees
Amounts up to the greater of 25% of after-tax profit or ARS 12,500 per individual are deductible in the financial year to which they refer, provided they are approved and available for the director before the due date of the tax return, or in a later year of payment.

Convertibility Law
Although the Convertibility Law is no longer in place, the adjustment of inflation for tax purposes is not yet in force. There is a strong debate regarding the reinforcement of this procedure for fiscal years ended up to December 2002. However, no final decision is in view. The wholesale price index for 2004 was 8%, for 2005 was 11% and for 2006 was 7.8%.

Thin capitalisation
Thin capitalisation rules apply as a restriction on the deductibility of interest arising from debts of a financial nature, contracted by taxpayers with controlling non-resident entities and can be summarised as follows:

- Interest subject to a 15.05% withholding (i.e., paid on loans granted by certain banking institutions), the portion of interest stemming from financial liabilities exceeding two times the shareholders' equity are not deductible for tax purposes and treated as dividends.
- Interest subject to a 35% withholding tax is fully deductible.

- According to the Regulatory Decree of the Income Tax Law, the thin capitalization rules would also be applicable to any case where a lower withholding rate of 35% is applicable (for instance, interest payments to a controlling company resident of certain tax treaty countries).

Group taxation

Group taxation is not permitted.

Tax incentives

Province of Tierra del Fuego Regime
Companies set up in province of Tierra del Fuego enjoy a general tax exemption and important benefits in customs matters, based on a system established by Law No. 19,640 and supplementary regulations. Tax exemption includes income tax, tax on minimum notional income, tax on personal wealth and excise tax. The VAT benefit consists on the release from payment of the technical balance of the tax (VAT debits less VAT credits). Also a reduction of the prevailing rate for tax on financial transactions and the exemption from taxation on the transfer of fuels is contemplated.

Mining activity
Law No. 24,196/93 created an investment regime for mining activity and is applicable to natural and legal persons. Mining ventures included within this regime enjoy fiscal stability (i.e., tax rates will remain basically the same) for a term of 30 years, except for VAT, which will adjust to the general regime. Furthermore, the regime grants incentives for profits tax, tax on assets, import duties, and any other tax for introduction of certain assets. Additionally, the possibility to obtain a VAT reimbursement during the exploration stage set forth by Law No. 24,196/93 has been regulated by General Resolution 1641 (Official Gazette 27 February 2004).

Forestry
Law No. 25,080 established an investment regime for plantation, protection and maintenance of forests. It contains rules similar to those for mining activity tax incentives:

- Fiscal stability for a period of thirty (30) years. The period may be extended to 50 years.
- Refund of value-added tax (VAT) resulted in the purchase or final importation of goods, leases, or services effectively for forestry investment project in a period of less than 365 days.

Export incentives
Exports of goods and services are exempt from value-added and excise taxes. The temporary importation of raw materials and intermediate and packaging goods for the manufacture of products for export is free from duties with the obligation of offering sufficient guarantees for the import. A reimbursement regime is in place for VAT credits paid to suppliers in relation to the export activity.

Oil and gas industry
Argentine government has enacted Law No. 26,154 through which grants attractive benefits to the oil and gas sector to encourage the exploration of the nation's hydrocarbons reserves.

Argentina

This new legislation grants special incentives to investments in underdeveloped regions, speeding reimbursement of VAT (after a three-month period, inputs will be credited against other federal taxes or returned to the taxpayer), exempting from import duties, and offering an accelerated depreciation – three years – for income tax purposes.

In addition, a three-year relief from minimum notional income tax, which is levied at 1% rate on the company assets, is provided by the law.

The incentive package will be in effect for 15, 12 or 10 years, depending on whether the activities are performed in areas identified as i) continental platform, ii) within the country other than continental platform and iii) currently in production, respectively.

The above benefits will apply to the exploration permits granted as from the enactment of the Law (1 November 2006) and up to five years, for the cases mentioned in i), four years, for those described in ii) and three years in the latter cases.

There also exists a Promotion Regime established by the Law No. 26,190, which grants similar benefits for the exploration of alternative source of energy (e.g., wind energy).

Biotechnology industry

A promotional tax regime for development and production of modern biotechnology was introduced by Law No. 26,270. Pursuant to this law, the beneficiaries of the projects that qualify for this regime will be entitled to the following benefits:

- Income tax: accelerated depreciation of capital goods, special equipment, parts or components of newly acquired goods destined for the promoted project;
- VAT: Early refund of the tax applicable to the assets acquired for the project; and
- Social security contributions: the amount representing 50% of social security contributions actually paid on the payroll salaries involved in the project shall be converted into a tax credit bond that may be applied to payment of national taxes.

Software industry

A Software Promotion Regime was established through the enactment of Law No. 25,922. Taxpayers carrying out software related activities as their main purpose may qualify for the benefits granted by the new legislation. The main tax incentives contemplated by the Regime are as follows:

- Fiscal stability for a ten-year period covering national taxes;
- Reduction of social security charges (70% of these charges may be credited against certain national taxes); and
- Income tax relief (up to 60% of the applicable tax).

While most of the software related activities qualify for the fiscal stability benefit, the remaining incentives only apply to software research and development, quality control procedures and software exports.

Capital investment and infrastructure works

Law No. 26,360 introduced a transitory regime aimed at promoting investments in new capital goods other than automobiles addressed to industrial activities as well as infrastructure works – excluding civil works – from October 2007 until September 2010. According to this regime, taxpayers will be able to obtain (i) early recovery of value-added tax paid for the purchase of assets or infrastructure works by means of a refund or a credit against certain other national taxes; or, alternatively, (ii) an accelerated depreciation system for income tax purposes applicable to investments on new projects made during the above period.

Province incentives on local taxes

Most of the provinces have legislation establishing incentives for the development of industries within their boundaries, especially industries that utilise or develop their natural resources and provide work for their residents. The incentives, in general, consist of exemptions from provincial and municipal taxes.

Various provinces have investment promotion regimes. Even when there are certain differences among these regimes, generally they include the following incentives:

* Exemption from provincial taxes such as turnover tax, stamp duty, real estate tax, etc;
* Reduced public utility rates;
* Support for infrastructure and equipment projects; and
* Facilities for the purchase, rental, or lease without charge of public property.

These regimes are not automatically applied and a special procedure should be followed to be entitled to the respective benefits.

Free trade zones

The free trade zones offer exporters the possibility to import free from customs duties, statistics rate and VAT, all the necessary equipment for construction of a "turnkey plant" within the zones. Furthermore, exporters manufacturing within the zones enjoy the benefit of buying supplies and raw materials from third countries, without having to pay duties or taxes that lead to increased prices.

Customs authority regulating these goods considers them as stored in a third country; therefore, incoming products are subject to inspection with the sole purpose of classifying quantity and type. In other words, goods enjoy a duty-free status until they enter the Argentine customs territory. Goods may remain in the free zone for a maximum period of five years.

Withholding taxes (WHT)

Equalisation corporate tax

Corporations, limited liability partnerships, and certain other entities are required to make a flat and final income tax withholding of 35% from dividend payments or profit distributions to resident or non-resident payees, to the extent that the amount of such dividends or profit distributions exceeds the taxable income of the distributing company, determined by applying the general tax rules (i.e., without considering any exemptions, abatements and other adjustments arising from special promotional laws) included in their retained earnings at the end of the fiscal year, immediately preceding the date of payment or distribution.

Other payments

Other payments to residents and to non-residents are subject to withholding tax rates as following:

Argentina

Recipient	Interest	Royalties (1), (2)
	%	%
Resident corporations	6 or 28 (3)	6 (4)
Resident individuals	6 or 28 (3)	6 (4)
Non-resident corporations and individuals:		
Non-treaty:	15.05 or 35	21 or 28
Treaty:		
Australia	12	10 or 15
Belgium	0 or 12 (5)	3,5,10 or 15
Bolivia	15.05 or 35	21 or 28
Brazil	15.05 or 35	21 or 28
Canada	12.5	3,5,10 or 15
Chile	15.05 or 35	21 or 28
Denmark	12 (5)	3,5,10 or 15
Finland	15	3,5,10 or 15
France	15.05 or 20 (6)	18
Germany	10 or 15 (7)	15
Italy	15.05 or 20 (5)	10 or 18
Netherlands	12	3,5,10 or 15
Norway	12.5 (8)	3,5,10 or 15
Spain	12.5	3,5,10 or 15
Sweden	12.5	3,5,10 or 15
Switzerland	12	3,5,10 or 15
United Kingdom	12 (5)	3,5,10 or 15

Notes

The numbers in parentheses refer to the following notes:

1. Withholding from payments of interest and royalties to non-residents is based on a flat rate of 35% applied to an assumed percentage gross profit margin. This margin is not contestable, but the resultant rate may be limited by bilateral treaty. Under the 1998 tax reform, the general margin for interest paid for credits obtained abroad is 100%. However, a margin of 43% is applicable (1) if the debtor is a local bank, (2) if the creditor is a foreign financial institution located in a country not considered as a low or no tax jurisdiction or in countries that have signed an agreement with Argentina for exchange of information and have no bank secret, which are under the supervision of the respective central bank, (3) if the interest is paid on a loan dedicated to the purchase of tangible assets other than cars, (4) if the interest is paid on debt certificates (private bonds) issued by local companies and registered in certain countries that have signed an agreement with Argentina for the protection of investments, and (5) on interest paid on time deposits with local banks. "Royalties" covers a variety of concepts. The rates given in this column relate specifically to services derived from agreements ruled by the Foreign Technology Law, as follows:

    a. Technical assistance, technology and engineering not obtainable in Argentina – 21% (35% on assumed profit of 60%);
    b. Cessation of rights or licenses for invention patents exploitation and technical assistance obtainable in Argentina – 28% (35% on assumed profit of 80%). (On non-registered agreements the rate is 31.5% (profit of 90% is assumed) or 35% (profit of 100% is assumed), depending on the case.)

Several other concepts of "royalties" are subject to rates that, in turn, may be limited by treaty. A broad sample of these concepts and the non-treaty effective rates is set forth in Note 2.

2. Payments to non-residents (only) for "royalties," rentals, fees, commissions, and so on, in respect of the following are subject to withholding at the rates given below on the basis of assumed gross profit margins (Note 1) unless limited by treaty. The treaty concerned should be consulted to determine any limitation in each case.

	%
Freight and passenger bookings (other than those covered by special treaties), news and feature services, insurance underwriting	3.5
Containers	7.0
Copyright	12.25
Rental of movable assets	14.0
Motion picture, video and sound tape rentals and royalties; radio, television, telex and telefax transmissions; any other means for projection, reproduction, transmission, or diffusion of image or sound; sale of assets located in Argentina (9,10)	17.5
Rental of real estate (9)	21.0
Any other Argentine-source income (unless the non-resident is or was temporarily resident)	31.5

3. The higher tax rate is applicable on non-registered taxpayers. On interest paid to corporations by financial entities or stock exchange/open market brokers, income tax must be withheld at 3% (10% if not registered); individuals are tax exempt.
4. Resident corporations and individuals who are registered for tax purposes are subject to 6% withholding (28% if not registered).
5. Interest is exempt if paid on credit sales of machinery or other equipment, specific bank loans at preferential rate or loans by public entities.
6. The treaty limits taxation of interest to 20% (registered).
7. The 10% rate is applicable to interest on credit sales of capital equipment, any bank loan or any financing of public works; otherwise 15%.
8. Interest paid on loans with guarantee of the Norwegian Institute for Credit Guarantees, or paid in relation to imports of industrial equipment is tax exempt.
9. Deduction of actual costs and expenses may be optionally exercised.
10. Gains on the sale of shares are exempt, except for companies, permanent establishments, or other entities residing abroad whose main activity based on their statutes consists of investments to be made outside of their country of formation. These entities are subject to income tax withholding at the definite flat rate of 17.5%.

Tax administration

Returns
Tax is assessed on a fiscal-year, self-assessment basis. The due date for filing the profits and the notional income tax return is during the second week of the fifth month after the fiscal year end. Tax returns are filed electronically.

Payment of tax
Instalment payments on account of both profits tax and minimum notional income tax must be made in the course of the tax year. The instalment payments must be made at a monthly basis beginning in the first month after the due date of filing of the tax returns.

Argentina

Penalties

Penalties derived from tax infractions may be applied by tax authorities, as follows:

*   Failing to file the tax return: fines range between ARS 200 and ARS 400 (approximately USD 50 – and USD 100).
*   Tax omission or incorrect tax determination: The fines that range from 50% to 100% of unpaid taxes or incorrect tax calculation.
*   Tax avoidance: fines range between two and 10 times the avoided tax.
*   Certain tax infractions may be penalised by closing the business premises for three to 10 days. In addition, fines ranging between ARS 300 – ARS 30,000 (approximately USD 76 to USD 7,600) may be imposed.
*   Simple evasion: Entities or individuals evading payment of social security contributions or withholdings, or both, payable to the Tax Authorities under the social security regime, through deceitful declarations, malicious concealment or any fraudulent or deceitful procedure, either through action or omission, in excess of twenty thousand pesos (ARS 20,000) per fiscal period, shall be punished with two to six years' imprisonment. Such amount will be ARS 100,000 in the case of taxes, it being applied by tax and by fiscal year.
*   If the infringement qualifies as aggravated evasion: Imprisonment could be extended from three years and six months to nine years in certain situations.

Interest on late payments

Late payment of taxes is subject to a monthly 2% interest rate. Interest will start accruing on the day after the filing due date.

Exchange control regime

As a result of the devaluation of the Argentine peso at the beginning of 2002, several regulations were issued to limit the transfer of money abroad. They have been made more flexible up to date.

Regulations referring to the entrance of funds to the country, the obligation of liquidation of foreign currency in the Exchange Market of payments of exports of goods and services, remain in force. The terms to comply with the liquidation obligation vary between 60 and 360 days.

There are no restrictions for the payment abroad of interest, dividends or profits, royalties and other commercial payments duly supported by the corresponding documentation. Payment abroad for other concepts may be subject to further filing requirements.

In addition, it should be particularly highlighted that a rule issued by the central bank in mid-2005 requires a compulsory one-year temporary deposit equivalent to 30% of funds brought by non-residents to Argentina, which must be kept in a reserve (encaje) for the term of one year. This deposit is made in foreign currency and does not earn interest.

There are some exceptions, as for instance, direct investments such as interest in Argentine companies (minimum 10%) or real estate which are not subject to this rule, or if the funds were borrowed for the acquisition of fixed assets and the re-payment term is longer than two years.

Other issues

VAT – export reimbursement regime

Exporters are able to file an export return with the tax authorities, reporting the VAT receivables related to their exports to be reimbursement on VAT paid in relation to the export operations. This return has to be filed within the following tax period in which the export took place. A report certified by a public accountant with respect to the value, registrations and other characteristics related to the refund must be attached to the export return.

The tax credit related to exports and other taxable activities can only be refunded in proportion to the exports, and can be fully refunded to a cap of 21% of the FOB value of the exported products.

There is no specific method stated in the legislation for allocating the tax credit related to exports, but taxpayers are able to use any methods of calculation that would be suitable to their business model. This calculation has to be approved by the tax authorities.

Finally, it is important to highlight that the tax authorities have to approve the tax credit to be refunded.

Legal entities

Foreign Companies in Argentina, carrying out their business or activity in Argentina, must have a local legal vehicle, being the most common legal entity types the following.

*   Branch;
*   Corporation (Sociedad Anónima, so-called "S.A."); and
*   Local Limited Liability Company (Sociedad de Responsabilidad Limitada, so-called "S.R.L.").

Argentine Corporations and Limited Liability Partnerships, as Argentine residents, are subject to the Argentine tax system. Branches of foreign companies, whatever the nature of their activities, are taxed under the same rules as those applicable to Corporations and Limited Liability Partnerships.

Several documents are required to register an entity with the relevant authorities. Some of said documentation must be filed in the original language, duly translated and certified with the Apostille issued pursuant to The Hague Convention or legalised by the Argentine Consulate of the company's place of origin.

At present, the minimum capital requirement to incorporate a local Corporation ("Sociedad Anonima") is ARS 12,000 (approximately USD 3,000). There are not special requirements regarding the minimum amount of capital for Limited Liability Partnerships.

A Branch does not require capital contributions unless it is engaged in certain specific activities (e.g., banking and financing). The Branch must carry its financial statements separately from those of the foreign company.

The three legal types are subject to the same legal, tax and accounting regulations.

Corporate taxes in Armenia

For more information, contact:

Nerses Nersisyan
PricewaterhouseCoopers
1 Northern Avenue
Business Center NORD, 5th floor
Yerevan 0001, Armenia
Tel: +374 10 592150
Email: nerses.nersisyan@am.pwc.com

Significant developments

The simplified tax rules were repealed, effective 1 January 2009. As a transitional measure, the profit tax liability of taxpayers moving from simplified tax to the profits tax may not be less than 2% of revenues or more than 10% of revenues for the 2009 calendar year.

In conjunction with the repeal of the simplified tax, the annual revenue threshold requiring monthly value-added tax (VAT) reporting increased from AMD 60 million to AMD 100 million per year.

Businesses with sales exceeding AMD 58.35 million in the preceding calendar year (other than businesses that require a license that costs more than AMD 100,000 to operate and businesses producing excisable goods) are not required to account for VAT on their sales in the subsequent calendar year, until their sales in that subsequent year exceed AMD 58.35 million. However, there are no clear rules to explain how businesses should deal with input taxes once they are required to report VAT on the sales exceeding the threshold.

Businesses may register voluntarily for VAT.

Until 2008, qualifying small legal entities could opt to use the simplified taxation system if their gross turnover for the previous year did not exceed AMD 50 million.

Taxes on corporate income

Armenian entities and foreign entities doing business in Armenia through a permanent establishment are liable for corporate income tax. The standard rate is 20%.

Taxpayers engaged in agricultural production are exempt from tax on that income.

Taxpayers engaged in certain activities (e.g., car repair service, casinos, public baths and showers, gas refilling stations for motor vehicles, billiard games, organisation of computer games) must use the presumptive tax system. Under that system, the taxpayer pays a fixed tax based on the location and area occupied by the business, and will not be required to pay profit tax or VAT. The rate of tax depends on the activity undertaken.

Corporate residence

A

Resident entities are legal and business entities whose existence is established under Armenian law. Non-resident entities are those whose existence is established under foreign law.

Other taxes

Value-added tax (VAT)
Armenia's current VAT law was enacted in 1997 and is based loosely on the principles of the EU Sixth Directive. Armenia operates the input-output model of VAT. VAT-registered persons may deduct the VAT paid on their inputs from the VAT charged on their sales and account for the difference to the tax authorities.

The standard rate of VAT on domestic sales of goods and services and the importation of goods is 20%. Exported goods and related services are zero-rated. Advertising, consulting, engineering, legal, accounting, translation, data processing, banking, financial and insurance services provided to non-residents are zero-rated if the non-resident's place of business is outside Armenia. Various supplies, including most financial and education services, are VAT-exempt.

Services supplied in Armenia by non-residents that are not registered in Armenia are subject to application of a VAT reverse charge.

Except for cash purchases up to AMD 300,000 per transaction up to a maximum of AMD 3 million per month, an input tax credit will only be available if payment is remitted through a bank and the goods or services are obtained for commercial purposes.

Excise tax
Excise tax is payable on alcoholic beverages, tobacco products, petrol and diesel fuel, whether imported or produced domestically.

Property tax
Property tax is assessed on buildings, motor vehicles and means of water transport. The tax base for buildings is determined based on their cadastral value. The tax rate on public and industrial buildings is 0.3% annually of the property value. Property tax is assessed and collected at the municipal level.

Land tax
Land tax is paid by landowners and the permanent users of state-owned land. Tax on rented land is levied on the lessor. The land "cadastre" (valuation system) is used to determine the value of the land. Land tax for agricultural lands is calculated at 15% of the net income determined by the "cadastral" evaluation. For non-agricultural land the rate is 0.5% to 1.0% of the "cadastral" value of the land. Land tax is assessed and collected at the municipal level.

Branch income

When a foreign company conducts business in Armenia through a permanent establishment and maintains separate accounting records for that permanent establishment, taxable income generally should be determined on the same basis as

Armenia

for domestic entities. The law on profit tax indicates that a permanent establishment is taxable on dividends received from Armenian companies and may not carryforward losses, which differs from the treatment of domestic entities. However, the permanent establishment may be able to overcome this restriction under a relevant tax treaty.

If it is not possible to determine taxable profit based on the "direct" method (taxable income less deductible expenses), income is determined based on a method agreed upon between the taxpayer and the tax authorities. The law explicitly recognises the allocation method (the taxpayer allocates a portion of its worldwide income and expenses to Armenia) as a possible approach.

Armenia has no special tax rules for non-commercial representative offices established to engage in liaison-type activities. Such offices are subject to the normal corporate income tax, but an exemption from income tax may be available under a relevant tax treaty if the activities of the representative office are not sufficient to constitute a permanent establishment for the foreign entity.

Income determination

Taxable profits are defined as the difference between a taxpayer's gross income and deductible expenses. Gross income encompasses all revenues received by a taxpayer from all economic activities, unless the revenues are expressly exempt from inclusion under the law. Deductible expenses encompass all necessary and documented expenses that are directly related to conducting business or earning profit, unless a specific provision in the law restricts the deduction.

Deductions

Expenses incurred in the furtherance of a taxpayer's business activities generally are deductible, unless a specific provision in the law provides otherwise (refer below).

As a general rule, interest is deductible if the related debt is used to fund business activities of the taxpayer and the interest rate is not more than double the Central Bank of Armenia rate (currently, the deductible interest rate is capped at 26%). Armenia does not have thin capitalisation rules.

Lease payments on operating leases are deductible. The lessor claims a deduction for depreciation of the leased assets. Financial leasing is treated for tax purposes as if a sale had been made. The lessee includes the value of the property in the relevant group of fixed assets and claims depreciation charges. The lessee also deducts the interest and commission elements of the lease payments in the period in which they are payable. Similarly, the lessor recognises taxable income for the total principal amount of the lease at the time when the asset is transferred, and recognises the interest and commission element of the payments over the term of the lease.

The following are key items that are not deductible for corporate income tax purposes:

- Expenses that are not supported by relevant documentation;
- Expenses incurred for advertising outside Armenia are limited to the greater of 3% of gross income or 20% of the value of services or goods exported from Armenia;
- Training of staff outside Armenia is limited to the lesser of 4% of the gross income of the reporting year or AMD 3 million per employee;

A

- Expenses for foreign trips are limited to 5% of the gross income of the reporting year;
- Representative expenses are limited to the lesser of 0.5% of the gross income of the reporting year or AMD 5 million; and
- Payments with respect to goodwill and amortisation of goodwill.

Companies are entitled to carryforward losses to the five subsequent income years.

Group taxation

There is no group taxation in Armenia.

Tax incentives

Taxpayers engaged in agricultural production are exempt from tax on that income.

Withholding taxes (WHT)

Payments to non-residents are subject to the following withholding tax rates:

- Payments for insurance, reinsurance, and transportation are taxed at 5%.
- Other income received from Armenian sources is taxed at 10%.

Withholding tax rates for non-residents may be reduced under a relevant tax treaty.

Tax administration

Returns
The annual profits tax return for resident entities must be filed by 15 April. The corresponding tax is payable by 25 April.

Payment of taxes
Taxpayers are required to make advance profits tax payments by the twenty-fifth day of each month. Each advance payment is equal to 1/16 of the profits tax paid for the previous year. For payments before the previous year's tax is calculated (e.g., January to March), tax is paid based on the last filed tax return, and an adjustment is made in the first advance tax payment made after the previous year's tax is calculated to correct the amount paid. If advance payments exceed the profits tax liability for the year, the excess may be refunded.

Advance payments are not required if a taxpayer's profit for the proceeding year was less than AMD 500,000. Thus, newly established companies do not need to make advance payments until 25 April of the year following the start of operations.

Armenia also has a monthly minimum profits tax. If the advance profits tax payable is less than 1% of revenues for the previous month less depreciation charges (up to a maximum of 50% of revenues), the excess is paid as a minimum profits tax. The minimum profits tax is applied against profits tax payable for the year. Any excess is applied against the profits tax liability for the subsequent year.

Armenia

Branches of foreign companies pay advance profits tax biannually, but only if their profit tax for the proceeding year exceeded AMD 2 million. Each advance payment is equal to 1/4 of the profits tax paid for the previous year. Branches are not subject to the minimum profits tax. The annual tax return for branches is filed by 15 April. However, the corresponding tax only needs to be paid within one month of receiving a payment notification from the tax authorities about the final amount of the calculated profit tax.

Corporate taxes in Aruba

For more information, contact:

Hans Ruiter
PricewaterhouseCoopers
L.G. Smith Boulevard 62
Oranjestad, Aruba
Tel: +1 297 522 1647
Email: hans.ruiter@an.pwc.com

Significant developments

Corporate income tax
As of 1 January 2007, the corporate income tax rate was reduced from 35% to 28%
(except for special regime companies).

As of 1 January 2007 two fiscal facilities were abolished. Specifically, it is no longer
possible to claim a deduction for investments or recover capital costs by using the
accelerated depreciation method.

Turnover tax
As of 1 January 2007, Aruba introduced a turnover tax on revenues realised on the sale
of goods or provision of services. At introduction, the turnover tax rate was 3%. On the
export of goods, a 1% tariff may apply. As of 1 January 2010, the 3% rate was reduced
to 1.5%.

Offshore regime
Officially, the Aruba offshore regime was abolished as of 1 January 2003. As a result of
transitional legislation, existing offshore companies could follow the previous regime
up until 31 December 2007.

Taxes on corporate income

Resident companies are taxed on worldwide income. Non-resident companies are
taxed on the following Aruba sourced income:

- Income allocated to a permanent establishment or permanent representative
  in Aruba;
- Income from real estate located in Aruba; and
- Interests on loans secured by a mortgage on real estate located in Aruba.

The corporate income tax rate on Aruba as of 1 January 2007 amounts to 28%. Aruba
does have some special tax regimes (imputation payment company, free zone company,
Aruba Exempt Company), which are ultimately taxed at a lower tax rate.

Corporate income tax is levied on the income as reflected in the profit and loss
statement less any allowable deductions based on local Aruba tax and case law.

Aruba

Corporate residence

A corporation that is organised under Aruba laws is a resident. Furthermore, corporations that are managed and controlled in Aruba will often be deemed residents, depending on each corporation's specific circumstances.

Other taxes

Ground tax
If a person or company owns real estate property in Aruba as of 1 January of the respective tax year, a 0.4% ground tax is due on the amount that exceeds the value of the real estate minus a general exemption of AFL 60,000.

Real estate transfer tax
If real estate situated in Aruba is transferred, the buyer of the real estate must pay transfer tax on the *sales price* of the real estate (unless the value registered at the tax department is higher, in which case the registered value is the basis for the levy). The rate for the transfer of the legal ownership of real estate with a value not exceeding AFL 250,000 is 3%. The rate for the transfer of the legal ownership of real estate with a value exceeding AFL 250,000 is 6% (due on the total amount).

If shares in a real estate company are sold, no transfer tax is due.

Import duties
Import duties are imposed by a tariff, which is set as a percentage of the Cost, Insurance and Freight value of the product. A classification rule has been published that categorises various imported products into groups. A tariff ranging from 0% to 50% is levied on the various groups of products.

Foreign exchange commission
A foreign exchange commission (FEC) is due when residents make a payment abroad. The FEC is calculated as 1.3% of payments abroad. In the text of the law, a payment abroad is defined as:

- A payment with local currency or a payment against a florin account, whether or not by electronic transfer;
- A payment with foreign currency or a payment against a foreign currency account, whether or not by electronic transfer; or
- A payment against a foreign currency account abroad or against an inter-company account with a person or entity abroad, whether or not by electronic transfer.

Insofar as the payment is a result of one of the following legal transactions:

- The purchase of foreign currency or foreign exchangeables;
- Obtaining control over receivables in one or more foreign currencies; or
- An addition to an account of a non-resident of Aruba at a bank or an institution abroad.

An exemption from the FEC exists for inter-island bank transactions, as follows:

- Purchase of Antillean banknotes by Aruba residents and the purchase by Aruba residents of bank cheques in Antillean guilders and drawn from exchange banks situated in the Dutch Antilles;
- Transfers in Antillean guilders to residents of the Dutch Antilles by Aruba residents; or
- Transactions in Aruba and Antillean banknotes between exchange banks on Aruba and on the Dutch Antilles.

Furthermore, FEC will be levied on the purchase of foreign currencies (except Antillean guilders) with Aruba florins.

According to the policy of the Central Bank of Aruba, another exemption for the foreign exchange tax applies when cash is transferred to a foreign bank account of an Aruba resident. In order to apply for this exemption, certain formalities must be met. First, the foreign bank account of the Aruba resident must be registered at the Central Bank of Aruba. Secondly, the Central Bank of Aruba must grant a so-called exemption for requirements. Also, certain overviews of transactions regarding the foreign bank account must be filed with the Central Bank of Aruba on a quarterly basis.

Turnover tax

Every company that sells goods or provides services in Aruba is subject to a business turnover tax ("Belasting op Bedrijfsomzetten" or BBO) on the company's entire turnover or operating revenues, excluding interest. The general turnover tax rate is 1.5% as of 1 January 2010. The rate levied on the revenues realised by the export of goods is 1%.

Goods are defined as all physical objects except water, gas and electricity. Services are defined as all services rendered for payment. A payment is defined as all income received relating to the sale of goods or services. If a payment is non-monetary, the fair market value should be taken into account.

In the case of goods, the taxable event occurs either where the transportation starts (if sold abroad) or the physical location of the goods. In case of services, case law stipulates (contrary to the text of the law) that the taxable event occurs where the services are rendered.

Some exceptions apply. For example, no BBO is levied on the supply of immovable property if transfer tax is paid on the supply. Furthermore, exemptions apply to interest received, payments for hotel rooms or leasing of apartments (insofar as room tax has been paid on the proceeds) and casino revenues (insofar as gambling duties are due on these revenues).

Branch income

Tax rates on branch profits are the same as on other corporate profits. In principle, the transfer of profits to the head office is not subject to taxation.

Aruba

Income determination

Inventory valuation
Inventories may generally be stated on a LIFO (last-in, first-out) or FIFO (first-in, first-out) basis, provided the method chosen conforms to the sound business practice. Conformity of book and tax reporting is not required.

Capital gains
Capital gains are taxed as ordinary income. However, capital gains realised on the disposal of a shareholding qualifying for the participation exemption, are tax exempt. The capital gain realised on the disposal of assets may be carried over to a special tax deferral reinvestment reserve, but must be deducted from the acquisition costs of the new asset. In principle, this reinvestment reserve cannot be maintained for more than four consecutive years. If the reserve has not been used after four years, the remainder will be subject to taxation. Capital losses are tax-deductible, unless these losses are incurred on shares to which the participation exemption is applicable.

Inter-company dividends
Provided the conditions of the participation exemption are met, an Aruba company is exempt from taxation on all benefits from the participation, including inter-company (cash) dividends. In general, the participation exemption applies if an Aruba company holds shares in another company. If shares are held in a foreign entity, the participation exemption only applies if the shares are not held as an investment and the foreign entity is subject to tax on its profit. Please note that costs that are made for participation (this includes administration costs, interest, management expenses and such) are not deductible from the taxable result of the Aruba parent company.

Foreign income
An Aruba resident company is subject to corporate income tax on its worldwide income. Double taxation of certain foreign source income is avoided by means of the exemption method. If there is no legal possibility to exempt income and prevent double taxation, the foreign tax paid can be claimed as a deduction.

Stock dividends
Stock dividends are allowed and treated as regular dividend income. The stocks will be valued at market value for tax purposes.

Deductions

Depreciation and depletion
Depreciation of tangible fixed assets, excluding land, is taken over the estimated useful life of the asset. The basis for the depreciation includes all costs incurred with the purchase of this asset less the residual value. The straight-line method is customary; however, the declining balance method is also acceptable.

Net operating losses
A net operating loss (NOL) may be carried forward to the five years following the tax year that the loss was incurred. If the NOL has not been offset against profits within this period, the remaining NOLs expire. Losses incurred by an imputation payment company may be carried forward indefinitely. Carrybacks are not permitted.

Payments to foreign affiliates

If interest or other payments (all compensation paid for the use of material and/or immaterial goods or rendered services) are made, these payments should be made at arm's length. If the transaction is not at arm's length, only the arm's-length payment may be deducted from the taxable income.

Even if the transaction is at arm's length, the interest or other payments are still not deductible from the taxable result of the Aruba company, unless the Aruba company provides evidence that one of the following is true:

- The receiving company is not (in)directly related to the Aruba company;
- The receiving company pays an effective tax rate of at least 15%; or
- The shares in the receiving company are (for at least 50% of the shares and the voting rights) directly or indirectly listed at a qualified stock exchange.

A relation with the taxpayer is deemed to exist if one of the following is true:

- The taxpayer has an interest of at least one-third in another entity;
- An individual or entity has an interest of at least one-third in the taxpayer; or
- A third party has an interest of at least one-third in another entity, while this third party also has an interest of at least one-third in the taxpayer.

If an at arm's-length payment is made to an affiliated company that is subject to taxation, but pays an effective tax rate of less than 15%, 75% of the payment made is allowed as a deduction.

Taxes

Taxes paid by the company, with the exception of the corporate income tax, are tax-deductible. Taxes paid by the company with respect to the purchase of an asset (for instance paid real estate transfer tax in case of obtaining real estate) should be included in the cost of the asset.

Other significant items

As of 1 January 2007, it is no longer possible to claim the investment allowance or recover capital costs by using the accelerated depreciation method.

Group taxation

Aruba tax authorities allow Aruba resident companies with wholly owned companies to file a consolidated tax return (fiscal unity). In order to apply for this facility, a request must be filed with the Aruba tax authorities. The Aruba tax authorities provide conditions for the application of this regime. Advantages of this regime are that recognition of inter-company profits may be deferred and that losses may offset profits within the group.

Tax incentives

Aruba corporate income tax legislation no longer provides tax incentives. The legislation does provide incentives for certain special purpose vehicles, such as the Imputation Payment Company, the Aruba Exempt Company and the transparent company that can be used to reduce the overall tax liability.

Aruba

Withholding taxes (WHT)

Dividend withholding tax

A dividend withholding tax is levied on all (formal and non-formal) dividend distributions of Aruba-based companies. The tax rate is:

- 10% of the dividend distribution;
- 5% of the dividend distribution if the shares of the distributing company or the receiving company are (for at least 50% of the shares and the voting rights) directly or indirectly listed at a qualified stock exchange; and
- 0% if the participation exemption *(see Taxes on corporate income section)* is applicable.

Dividends between countries of the Dutch kingdom are subject to the Regulation for the Dutch kingdom (hereinafter: the Regulation).

In certain situations the Regulation reduces the rate of the dividend withholding tax from 10% to 7.5% or even 5%. The dividend withholding tax can be reduced to:

- 7.5% if the parent company owns at least 25% of the paid in capital of the distributing company; or
- 5% if the parent company owns at least 25% of the paid in capital of the distributing company and the dividend is at the parent company level, subject to a profit tax of at least 5.5%.

If a company is incorporated under Aruba law and transfers its factual place of management to another country, all dividend distributions by this relocated company will remain subject to the Aruba dividend withholding tax.

Dividend distributions include, among others:

- Formal dividend distributions;
- Liquidation payment;
- Bonus shares;
- Paying back of share capital, unless strict conditions are met; and
- Imputation payment.

Formal requirements

Within 15 days after a dividend becomes payable, a dividend withholding tax return must be filed, together with payment of the amount due. A dividend is payable if it is at the disposal of the shareholder, i.e., the board of directors of the distributing company does not have to take any more action in order for the shareholder to claim the dividend. A dividend is also payable if the debt becomes interest bearing, because of the distribution.

A statement of approval of the Central Bank of Aruba is required if dividends are distributed to a foreign shareholder. If the dividend exceeds AFL 750,000 a license from the Central Bank of Aruba is required.

Tax administration

Returns

Once a corporate income tax return is issued by the authorities, taxpayers are obliged to file annual returns within two months. If within six months after the tax year has ended no return has been issued, the taxpayer is obliged to request a return within two weeks after the six months have passed. It may be argued that this obligation does not exist if a taxpayer is not subject to taxation.

If the final corporate income tax return cannot be filed within the required two-month period, a request for an extension may be filed. The tax inspector may grant an extension for a maximum period of 12 months.

Payment of tax

The corporate income tax, individual income tax and ground tax are due upon receipt of an assessment. The amount of tax due must be paid within two months after the date of the assessment.

Corporate taxes in Australia

For more information, contact:

Ian Farmer
PricewaterhouseCoopers
Darling Park Tower 2
201 Sussex Street
Sydney, New South Wales 2000
Australia
Tel: +61 2 8266 2802
Email: ian.farmer@au.pwc.com

Significant developments

New measures for the "taxation of financial arrangements" (TOFA) were enacted in March 2009 with effect for income years commencing on or after 1 July 2010 (although a taxpayer may have been able to elect to apply the new measures to income years commencing on or after 1 July 2009). These measures provide tax timing rules – accruals, realisation, fair value, retranslation, financial reports and hedging – for gains or losses in respect of financial arrangements, along with revenue account treatment of the resulting gains or losses. "Financial arrangement" is widely defined to cover arrangements that involve a cash settlable legal or equitable right to receive, or obligation to provide, something of economic value in the future. Exemptions from the new regime may be available having regard to the duration of the arrangement or the nature of the relevant taxpayer and the annual turnover or value of assets of that taxpayer. *See "Income determination"*.

For thin capitalisation purposes, following the cessation of a four-year transitional period after the introduction of International Financial Reporting Standards (IFRS) in Australia, which applied from tax years commencing on or after 1 January 2005, when calculating safe harbour debt amounts for thin capitalisation purposes, the provisions were amended to allow departure from the Australian equivalents to IFRS in relation to certain intangible assets and to exclude deferred tax assets and liabilities and surpluses and deficits in defined benefit superannuation funds. *See "Interest" under "Deductions"*.

Legislation was enacted in May 2009 to provide a one-off tax benefit for certain capital expenditure in respect of 'depreciating assets', where the taxpayer commences to hold the asset under a contract entered into between 13 December 2008 and 31 December 2009 (or where the taxpayer commences to construct the asset between those dates) and the asset is used or installed ready for use by 31 December 2010. The "investment allowance" provides an additional deduction of up to 50% for "small business entities" and up to 30% for other business taxpayers for the cost of purchasing new depreciating assets, and on expenditure that enhances existing depreciating assets where the cost of the asset or the expenditure is at least AUD 10,000 (or AUD 1,000 in the case of small business entities). *For further details, see "Investment allowance" under "Tax incentives"*.

On 5 January 2010, the Assistant Treasurer released a consultation paper setting out the proposed high-level design of the taxation laws to modernise the controlled foreign company (CFC) rules. The Government announced the modernisation of the CFC rules in May 2009 as part of wider reforms to Australia's foreign source income anti-tax-deferral (attribution) rules. Details of the changes have yet to be finalised. It is expected that the earliest commencement date for the new rules will be for income

A

years commencing on or after 1 July 2010. *For further details, see "Foreign income" under "Income determination".*

Legislation was introduced into Parliament in May 2010 to change the tax treatment of expenditure on research and development (R&D) from 1 July 2010. The current concessional deductions will be replaced with an R&D tax credit. For companies with an annual turnover of less than AUD 20 million, there will be a 45% refundable tax credit, equivalent to a 150% tax concession, and for companies with a turnover of greater than AUD 20 million, they will have access to a non-refundable 40% tax credit, equivalent to a 133% tax concession. *See "Tax incentives".*

In May 2010, the government released its interim response to the recommendations made following the comprehensive review of Australia's tax system ("Henry Review") which commenced in May 2008. One of the key changes proposed by the government is that it will reduce the company tax rate from its current rate of 30% to 29% in the 2013-14 income year and to 28% from the 2014-15 income year (with a 28% rate to apply to small business companies from 2012-13), in conjunction with the introduction of a proposed new Resource Super Profits Tax (RSPT) on natural resource projects from 1 July 2012. No legislation has been developed for these proposals which will be subject to extensive consultation.

Taxes on corporate income

Companies are subject to federal tax on their income at a flat rate of 30%. There are no state or municipal taxes on income.

Corporate residence

A company is a resident of Australia for income tax purposes if it is incorporated in Australia or, if not incorporated in Australia, it carries on business in Australia and either (1) its central management and control are in Australia or (2) its voting power is controlled by shareholders who are residents of Australia.

Other taxes

Goods and services tax (GST)
The federal government levies GST at a rate of 10%, and distributes the revenue to state governments. The GST is a value-added tax (VAT) applied at each level in the manufacturing and marketing chain and applies to most goods and services, with registered suppliers getting credits for GST on inputs acquired to make taxable supplies.

Food with some significant exceptions, exports, most health, medical and educational supplies, and some other supplies are "GST-free" (the equivalent of "zero-rated" in other VAT jurisdictions) and so not subject to GST. A registered supplier of a GST-free supply can recover relevant input tax credits, although the supply is not taxable.

Residential rents, the second or later supply of residential premises, most financial supplies, and some other supplies are "input-taxed" ("exempt" in other VAT jurisdictions) and are not subject to GST. However, the supplier cannot recover relevant input tax credits, except that financial suppliers may obtain a reduced input tax credit of 75% of the GST on the acquisition of certain services.

Australia

Health insurance is GST-free. Life insurance is input taxed. General insurance is taxed. "Reverse charges" may apply to services or rights supplied from offshore, where the recipient is registered or required to be registered, and uses the supply solely or partly for a non-creditable supply.

Luxury car tax

The luxury car tax is levied by the federal government at the rate of 33% of the value of the car that exceeds the luxury car tax threshold (AUD 57,180 for the 2009-10 financial year) and is payable on the GST-exclusive value above the threshold. No input tax credit is available for luxury car tax, regardless of whether the car is used for business or private purposes.

Wine equalisation tax (WET)

The federal government levies WET at the wholesale level at a rate of 29%, in addition to 10% GST, which is calculated on the price including the WET, and it applies to wine from grapes, fruit and certain vegetables, mead and sake. Retailers do not receive an input tax credit for WET. Up to a maximum of AUD 500,000, a rebate is available to a wine producer of 29% of the wholesale price (excluding WET or GST) for wholesale sales, and of 29% of the notional wholesale selling price for retail sales and applications for own use.

Import and excise duties

Imports into Australia are subject to duties under the Australian Customs Tariff. The top duty rate is 5%, other than for clothing and finished textiles which are currently taxed at 10% (to be reduced to 5% in 2015). A TCF Strategic Investment Program will operate until 2015.

Australia now has comprehensive free trade agreements with the United States, Thailand, Singapore, New Zealand and Chile. In addition, a regional free trade agreement between Australia, New Zealand and Southeast Asian nations commenced on 1 January 2010, which progressively eliminates all barriers to trade in goods, services and investments.

Excise duties are imposed at high levels on beer, spirits, liqueurs, tobacco, cigarettes and petroleum products. A fuel tax credit system provides a credit for fuel tax (excise or customs duty) that is included in the price of taxable fuel. Broadly, credits are available to entities using fuel in their business and to households using fuel for domestic electricity generation and heating.

Fringe benefits tax (FBT)

The federal government levies FBT on employers at the rate of 46.5% on the "grossed-up value" of non-salary and wages fringe benefits provided to employees (and/or the employee's associates) by the employer or associates. The grossing-up of the value ensures tax neutrality between providing benefits and cash remuneration. FBT generally is deductible for income tax purposes. There are some exemptions from FBT, including some minor benefits, remote area housing in certain circumstances, and specified relocation costs. In addition, there are some concessional valuation rules, in particular for living-away-from-home benefits.

Stamp duty

All states and territories impose a stamp duty on a wide variety of transactions at different rates. All jurisdictions impose a stamp duty on real estate conveyances, but most exempt conveyances of goods (not associated with other property) from stamp duty. The imposition of duty on share transfers involving unlisted entities differs from state to state. Corporate reconstruction exemptions are available. Advice from a stamp duty specialist should usually be obtained where substantial stamp duty may be imposed because the amount of duty may depend on the form of the transaction.

Payroll tax

States and territories impose a tax on employers' "payroll" (broadly defined). The various jurisdictions have harmonised their payroll tax legislation, but some differences remain, particularly tax rates and the thresholds for exempting employers whose annual payroll is below a certain level, after taking into account grouping rules. For example, in New South Wales the rate is 5.75% from 1 January 2009, 5.65% from 1 January 2010 and the annual exemption threshold is AUD 638,000. In Victoria the rate is 4.95% from 1 July 2008 and the annual exemption threshold is AUD 550,000. A variety of rates and thresholds apply in other state and territory jurisdictions.

Insurance tax

States impose taxes on insurance premiums, which may be substantial.

Land tax

All states and territories (except the Northern Territory) impose a tax based on the unimproved capital value of land. In general, the principal place of residence and land used for primary production is exempt from land tax.

Local municipal taxes

Local taxes, including water, sewerage and drainage charges, are levied based on the unimproved capital value of land and include a charge for usage (for example water usage).

Superannuation guarantee levy

The federal government effectively requires employers to contribute 9% of an employee's earnings base, subject to limited exceptions, to a registered superannuation fund or retirement savings account on behalf of the employee. Failure to make these contributions will result in the employer being liable for a non-deductible superannuation guarantee charge.

No level of Australian government imposes a social security levy.

Branch income

Branch profits are subject to ordinary corporate rates of taxation, and there is no withholding on repatriated profits.

Income determination

Inventory valuation

Inventory generally may be valued at cost (full absorption cost), market selling value or replacement price. Where, because of obsolescence or other special circumstances, inventory should be valued at a lower amount, the lower valuation generally may be chosen, provided it is a reasonable valuation. Special rules apply, however, regarding the valuation of trading stock for certain companies joining a consolidated group.

Australia

Last-in, first-out (LIFO) is not an acceptable basis of determining cost, nor is direct costing in respect of manufactured goods and work-in-progress.

Conformity is not required between book and tax reporting. For tax purposes inventory may be valued at cost, market selling value or replacement price, regardless of how inventory is valued for book purposes. Those who choose to come within the small-business entity measures (broadly defined as taxpayers who carry on business and who, together with certain "connected" entities, have an "aggregated turnover" of less than AUD 2 million for the year) may ignore the difference between the opening and closing value of inventory, if on a reasonable estimate this is not more than AUD 5,000.

Capital gains

A capital gains tax (CGT) applies to assets acquired on or after 20 September 1985. Capital gains realised on the disposal of such assets are included in assessable income and are subject to tax at the company's corporate tax rate, if the disposal is by a company. In order to determine the quantum of any gain for any assets acquired before 21 September 1999, the cost base is indexed according to price movements since acquisition, as measured by the official Consumer Price Index until 30 September 1999 (provided the asset has been held for at least 12 months). There is no indexation of the cost base for price movements after 1 October 1999. Disposals of plant and equipment are subject to general rules rather than the CGT rules. Capital losses are allowable as deductions only against capital gains and cannot be offset against other income. In calculating capital losses there is no indexation of the cost base.

Residents of Australia generally are liable for the tax on gains on the disposal of assets wherever situated, subject to relief from double taxation if the gain is derived and taxed in another country. However, the capital gain or capital loss incurred by a company from a CGT event in relation to shares in a foreign company is reduced by a percentage reflecting the degree to which the foreign company's assets are used in an active business, if the company holds a direct voting percentage of 10% or more in the foreign company for a certain period before the CGT event. Attributable income from CGT events happening to shares owned by a controlled foreign company (CFC) are reduced in the same way. Capital gains and capital losses made by a resident company in respect of CGT events happening in respect of "non-tainted" assets used to produce foreign income in carrying on business through a permanent establishment in a foreign country are disregarded in certain circumstances.

For CGT events occurring on or after 12 December 2006, non-residents are subject to Australian CGT only where the assets are "taxable Australian property" – that is, Australian real property, or the business assets of Australian branches of a non-resident. Australian CGT also applies to "indirect Australian real property interests", being non-portfolio interests in interposed entities (including foreign interposed entities), where the value of such an interest is wholly or principally attributable to Australian real property. "Real property" for all these purposes is consistent with Australian treaty practice, extending to other Australian assets with a physical connection with Australia, such as mining rights and other interests related to Australian real property. A "non-portfolio interest" is an interest held alone or with associates of 10% or more in the interposed entity.

CGT rollover relief is available for scrip-for-scrip (stock for stock) takeovers between companies (and also trusts) provided at least 80% of the target entity is acquired. This

A

rollover is not limited to listed or Australian entities. Special rules apply to determine the cost base of interests acquired by the acquiring entity in the target where the scrip-for-scrip arrangement consists of a "restructure" (broadly where just after completion of the arrangement the market value of the replacement interests issued under the arrangement by the replacement entity is more than 80% of the market value of all the shares (including options, rights and similar interests to acquire shares) issued by the replacement entity).

"Demerger" rollover relief is available where the head entity of a group transfers ownership of one or more of its subsidiaries to its shareholders provided at least 80% of the interests in the demerged entity are acquired by the owners of the head entity of the group and they receive interests in the demerged entity in the same proportion as their original interests. There are other requirements which must be satisfied in respect of each of these rollovers.

Rollover relief from CGT is available on the transfer of unrealised gains on assets, which are taxable Australian property between companies sharing 100% common ownership where the transfer is between non-resident companies, or between a non-resident company, on the one hand, and, on the other hand, a member of a consolidated group or multiple entry consolidated (MEC) group, or a resident company that is not a member of a consolidated group. *See "Group taxation."*

Inter-company dividends

A "gross-up and credit" mechanism applies to franked dividends (dividends paid out of profits which have been subject to Australian tax) received by Australian companies. The corporate shareholder grosses up the dividend received for tax paid by the paying company (i.e., franking credits attaching to the dividend) and is then entitled to a tax offset (i.e., a reduction of tax) equal to the gross-up amount. A company with an excess tax offset entitlement converts the excess into a carryforward tax loss using a special formula. Dividends paid to another resident company that are unfranked (because they are paid out of profits not subject to Australian tax) are taxable, unless they are paid within a group that has chosen to be consolidated for tax purposes. Dividends paid between companies within a tax consolidated group are ignored for the purposes of determining the taxable income of the group.

An exemption from withholding tax is available for dividends that are "unfranked" under the dividend imputation rules *(see below)* and are declared to be conduit foreign income (CFI) received by non-resident shareholders (or unitholders) in an Australian corporate tax entity (CTE). These rules may also treat the CFI component of an unfranked dividend received by an Australian CTE from another Australian CTE as not taxable to the recipient, provided it is on-paid within a specified timeframe. Broadly, income will qualify as CFI if it is foreign income, including certain dividends, or foreign gains, which are not assessable for Australian income tax purposes or for which a foreign income tax offset has been claimed in Australia. Alternatively (and subject to certain conditions), if a foreign owned company resident in Australia receives a taxable unfranked dividend with no CFI component from a resident company in which they hold at least 10% of the voting power, a deduction may be allowed to the extent that the dividend is on-paid to a non-resident 100% parent company. In that case, the unfranked dividend on-paid to the non-resident parent generally will attract dividend withholding tax (subject to treaty relief – *see "Withholding taxes"*).

Australia

Foreign dividends are not assessable and are not eligible for a tax offset if received by an Australian resident company from a foreign affiliate where the recipient company has a voting power of at least 10% in the foreign affiliate. Income of a non-resident entity in which Australian residents hold interests is not assessable when repatriated to Australia where the income has been previously attributed to those residents and taxed in Australia *(see below)*.

Dividends paid out of share capital accounts are unfrankable.

Where a company transfers an amount (e.g., profits) to a share capital account from another account, the capital account will become a tainted share capital account. Until it becomes "untainted," any distribution debited to such an account is treated as an unfrankable dividend, and not as a return of capital.

A dividend imputation system allows Australian corporations (and New Zealand companies that have chosen to be a "New Zealand franking choice company") to pass tax credits to individual resident shareholders, certain superannuation entities, life insurance companies in respect of their superannuation (Australian retirement plan) business and certain registered organisations, such as registered trade unions and friendly societies, in respect of Australian tax imposed on profits from which dividends (including stock dividends treated as dividends) are paid.

A resident corporation (or New Zealand company that has chosen to be a "New Zealand franking choice company") receiving a franked dividend, that is, a dividend paid out of Australian taxed profits, may further distribute the imputed tax credits to its own resident shareholders.

Franked dividends paid to non-residents are exempt from dividend withholding tax.

Companies that are effectively wholly owned by non-residents (known as "exempting companies") may provide franking benefits only in limited circumstances. However, non-resident shareholders in receipt of franked dividends from exempting companies are exempt from dividend withholding tax.

There is legislation designed to prevent the selective streaming of franking credits to different shareholders. Selection plans under which shareholders are given a choice of a tax-free bonus share (stock dividend), unfranked dividend or franked dividend in lieu of another dividend are no longer effective.

Under debt and equity classification rules there may be situations where interest income is treated as if it were a dividend. Similarly, dividends paid on shares that are debt interests will not be frankable.

The dividend imputation system operates in the following way. The company's franking account is credited with tax paid. The corporate entity paying a dividend may determine the extent to which a dividend is franked, subject to anti-streaming rules and benchmarking rules that limit the ability to change the franking percentage in later periods. As indicated above, fully franked inter-company dividends effectively are untaxed under a "gross-up and credit" method. A shareholder is entitled to franking credits on dividends only in respect of ordinary shares held "at risk" for at least 45 days (90 days for preference shares). There is an exemption from these franking credit trading rules for individuals, provided the imputation rebates received in the year of income do not exceed AUD 5,000 and the individual is not obliged to make a payment related to the dividend.

Foreign income

On 5 January 2010 the Assistant Treasurer released a consultation paper setting out the proposed high-level design of the taxation laws to modernise the controlled foreign company (CFC) rules. The government announced the modernisation of the CFC rules in May 2009 as part of wider reforms to Australia's foreign source income anti-tax-deferral (attribution) rules. Details of the changes have yet to be announced by the government, although consultation on the new rules has commenced. The current basis upon which the foreign income of corporations resident in Australia is taxed is set out below, together with some of the key features of the proposals as released for consultation. The commencement date for the new rules has not been announced but is expected to be no earlier than for income years commencing on or after 1 July 2010.

1. Non-active income of foreign companies controlled by Australian residents (determined by reference to voting rights and dividend and capital entitlements) may be attributed to those residents under rules which distinguish between companies resident in "listed countries" (e.g., Canada, France, Germany, Japan, New Zealand, the UK and the US) and in other "unlisted" countries. In general, if the CFC is resident in an unlisted country and it fails the "active income test" (typically because it earns 5% or more of its income from passive or "tainted" sources), the CFC's "tainted income" (very broadly, passive income and gains, and sales and services income which has a connection with Australia) is attributable. If a CFC is resident in a listed country, a narrower range of tainted income is attributed even if the CFC fails the active income test. It is currently proposed under the new rules that the term "control" will take its ordinary meaning, rather than the current bright-line test of voting interest and entitlements to capital and dividends. With regard to the type of income to be attributed, it is proposed that sales and services income, which has a connection with Australia derived by a CFC will no longer be attributable. It is proposed that passive income, defined in broadly similar terms to the existing rules, will continue to be attributable, however, a carve out is proposed where the income arises in the ordinary course of the active conduct of a trade or business, or which are profits from assets or financial arrangements that were held for the predominant purpose of producing "active income". It is also proposed that passive income received from a company which is a member of the same "CFC group" will not be attributable provided that payment of the amount does not provide a "benefit", such as a deduction, to the payer for Australian tax purposes (either as a resident or as a CFC).
2. When income previously taxed on attribution is repatriated, it is not assessable for tax.
3. Dividends received directly by a resident company from a foreign company are not assessable for tax where the resident company has a (non-portfolio) voting interest of at least 10% in the foreign affiliate and does not receive the dividend in its capacity as a trustee. The basis upon which distributions may qualify for such relief (i.e., where the payee has a voting interest of at least 10% in the payer) is currently under consideration as part of the redesign of the CFC rules. The proposal is currently that the relief should only be available where the distribution is in respect of an "equity interest" (as defined for tax law purposes) and the Australian resident recipient company holds a "total participation interest" of at least 10% or the Australian resident is an attributable taxpayer. It is proposed that the relief will also

Australia

be available where the distribution is received by an Australian resident company indirectly through a trust or partnership.

4. Active foreign branch profits of a resident company from carrying on business through a permanent establishment in a foreign country and capital gains made by a resident company from the disposal of "non-tainted assets" used in deriving foreign branch income are not assessable for tax, except income and capital gains from the operation of ships or aircraft in international traffic. It is not known at this stage whether the changes mentioned above to the rules governing the CFCs will necessitate changes to the taxation treatment of foreign branch profits to align the treatment of offshore investment through a permanent establishment with investment made via a subsidiary.

5. Foreign income of Australian resident corporations and income of such taxpayers which is subject to foreign income taxes that is not effectively exempt (as broadly described above) is subject to tax, but, in most cases an offset for foreign income tax paid is allowed to the extent of Australian tax payable on such income. For income years commencing prior to 1 July 2008, such offsets generally were confined to foreign tax paid in respect of foreign sourced income and computed in three separate classes: passive income, offshore banking income and other income. In addition, it was possible to carryforward excess credits for a period of up to five years. The ability to carryforward excess credits was removed for income years commencing on or after 1 July 2008, subject to transitional rules permitting conversion of some existing carried forward balances to foreign income tax offsets. For income years commencing on or after 1 July 2008, there is no longer a quarantining of deductions or losses associated with the derivation of foreign source income.

6. There are also measures to deal with passive foreign investment funds (FIFs) (including interests in foreign companies, foreign trusts and foreign life insurance policies). Essentially, and subject to important qualifications, the FIF rules tax (attribute) increases or deemed increases in the value of interests held by Australian residents in offshore entities (wherever located), except for some categories that are specifically exempted. Investments in foreign companies listed on approved stock exchanges that are principally engaged in certain active businesses are exempt. There are several other exemptions. Legislation is currently proposed to repeal the FIF rules (with effect from the 2010-11 income year) and replace them with a narrow anti-avoidance rule (proposed Foreign Accumulation Fund (FAF) regime) which, in broad terms, is directed at schemes entered into for holding or acquiring an interest in a FAF with the sole or dominant purpose of obtaining a "tax deferral benefit".

7. In certain circumstances, foreign limited partnerships, foreign limited liability partnerships, US limited liability companies and UK limited liability partnerships will be treated as partnerships (i.e., as a flow-through entity) rather than as a company for the purposes of Australia's income tax laws.

Stock dividends

Stock dividends, or the issue of bonus shares, as they are known under Australian law, are in general not taxed as a dividend, and the tax treatment is the spreading of the cost base of the original shares across the original shares and the bonus shares. However, if a company credits its share capital account with profits when issuing bonus shares, this will "taint" the share capital account (if it is not already a tainted share capital account), causing the bonus share issue to be a dividend. Certain other rules may apply to bonus share issues, depending on the facts.

A

Financial arrangements

New measures for the "taxation of financial arrangements" (TOFA) apply for arrangements entered into from income years commencing on or after 1 July 2010, although a taxpayer may elect to apply the new measures to arrangements entered into from income years commencing on or after 1 July 2009. A taxpayer may also elect to have the new rules apply to all pre-existing financial arrangements that the taxpayer has at the start of the first income year to which new rules apply.

"Financial arrangement" is widely defined to cover arrangements that involve a cash settlable legal or equitable right to receive, or obligation to provide, something of economic value in the future.

The new measures provide for six tax timing methods for determining gains or losses in respect of financial arrangements, along with revenue account treatment of the resulting gains or losses to the extent that the gain or loss is made in earning assessable income or carrying on a business for that purpose. The default methods are the accruals method and the realisation method, one or other of which will apply depending on the relevant facts and circumstances of a particular financial arrangement. The accruals method will apply to spread an overall gain or loss over the life of the financial arrangement where there is sufficient certainty that the expected gain or loss will actually occur. A gain or loss that is not sufficiently certain is dealt with under the realisation method. Alternatively, a taxpayer may irrevocably choose one of four elective methods – fair value, retranslation, financial reports and hedging – to determine the tax treatment of financial arrangements covered by the legislation. Qualification criteria must be met before the elective methods may be used. Generally, these criteria require that the taxpayer prepare a financial report in accordance with Australian (or comparable) accounting standards and be audited in accordance with Australian (or comparable) auditing standards.

Exemptions from the new regime may be available having regard to the duration of the arrangement or the nature of the relevant taxpayer and the annual turnover or value of assets of that taxpayer. Certain types of financial arrangements are excluded from the new rules, including leasing and hire purchase arrangements. Foreign residents are taxable on gains from financial arrangements under the new measures to the extent that the gains have an Australian source.

Foreign exchange gains and losses

Foreign currency gains and losses are recognised when realised regardless of whether there is a conversion into Australian dollars, and are included in or deducted from ordinary income, subject to limited exceptions. There are exceptions to the timing and characterisation aspects of the realisation approach where the foreign currency gain or loss is closely linked to a capital asset. Rollover relief is available for the issuer of a succession of short-term foreign currency bill or securities, to the extent that money remains outstanding under the facility. To reduce compliance costs with foreign currency denominated bank accounts caused by the first-in, first-out (FIFO) approach mandated in the rules, taxpayers may elect to disregard gains or losses on low balance transaction accounts that satisfy a *de minimis* exemption, or may elect for retranslation by annually restating the balance of the account by reference to deposits, withdrawals, and the exchange rates at the beginning and end of each year. Entities or parts of entities, satisfying certain requirements, are able to choose to account for their activities in a currency other than Australian dollars for income tax purposes as an intermediate step to translating the result into Australian dollars. For foreign exchange

Australia

gains and losses associated with "financial arrangements" as defined, the practical impact of these foreign exchange rules will be reduced for those taxpayers eligible to elect certain tax timing methods under the taxation of financial arrangement measures (as previously discussed).

Deductions

Depreciation and depletion
A capital allowances regime allows a deduction for the decline in value of depreciating assets held by a taxpayer. The "holder" of the asset is entitled to the deduction and may be the economic, rather than the legal owner. A "depreciating asset" is an asset that has a limited effective life and can reasonably be expected to decline in value over the time it is used, but does not include land, trading stock or, subject to certain exceptions, intangible assets. Deductions are available for certain other capital expenditure.

Intangible assets that are "depreciating assets" (if they are not trading stock) are:

* Certain mining, quarrying or prospecting rights and information;
* Items of intellectual property;
* "In-house" software;
* Indefeasible rights to use an international telecommunications submarine cable system;
* Spectrum licenses under radio communications legislation;
* Datacasting transmitter licenses; and
* Telecommunications site access rights.

Goodwill and trademarks are not depreciating assets, and tax amortisation is not available.

Taxpayers that do not qualify as a small-business must depreciate the asset over its useful life (known as "effective life"), using either straight-line (known as the "prime cost" method) or diminishing-value method (straight-line rate multiplied by 200% for depreciating assets acquired on or after 10 May 2006).

Taxpayers may self-determine the effective life of a unit or plant or may choose the effective life contained in a published determination of the Commissioner of Taxation.

Non-small-business taxpayers are able to choose to write-off all items costing less than AUD 1,000 through a low-value pool at a diminishing-value rate of 37.5%.

For those who satisfy the "small business entity" threshold (broadly defined as taxpayers who are carrying on business and who, together with certain "connected" entities, have an "aggregated turnover" of less than AUD 2 million for the year), a simplified depreciation system applies with more attractive depreciation rates.

"Project pool" rules allow expenditure that does not itself form part of a depreciating asset to be deductible over the life of a project that is carried on for a taxable purpose. Amongst other things, items that fall within the rules include the following:

* Amounts paid to create or upgrade community infrastructure for a community associated with the project.

A

- Site preparation costs for depreciating assets (except horticultural plants in certain circumstances).
- Amounts incurred for feasibility studies for a project.
- Environmental assessment costs applicable to the project.
- Amounts incurred to obtain information associated with the project.
- Amounts incurred in seeking to obtain a right to intellectual property.
- Costs of ornamental trees or shrubs.

The so-called "blackhole" expenditure provisions allow a five-year straight-line write-off for capital expenditure incurred on or after 1 July 2005 in relation to a past, present or prospective business, to the extent that the business is, was or is proposed to be carried on for a taxable purpose. The expenditure is deductible to the extent that it is not elsewhere taken into account (for example by inclusion in the cost base of an asset for capital gains tax purposes) and that it is not denied deductibility for the purposes of the income tax law (for example, by the rules against deducting entertainment expenditure).

Special rules apply for primary producer assets, such as horticultural plants, water and land care assets, and the treatment of expenditure on research and development (R&D) *(see "Tax incentives")* and expenditure on certain Australian films.

A "luxury car" cost limit applies for depreciating the cost of certain passenger motor vehicles (AUD 57,180, cost limit for the 2009-10 income year).

Expenditure on the development of "in-house" software may be allocated to a "software development pool" and written off over three years, starting in the year after the expenditure was incurred (40% in year two, 40% in year three, and 20% in year four). Amounts spent on acquiring computer software or the right to use it (except where the acquisition is for developing in-house software) generally is treated as incurred on acquiring a depreciating asset, deductible over its "effective life" commencing in the first year it is first used or installed ready for use. Such effective life recently was amended from two and one-half to four years. "Shrink-wrapped" software acquired or manufactured for sale generally will be treated as trading stock.

A loss arising on the sale of a "depreciating asset" (depreciated value of the asset less sale consideration) is generally an allowable deduction. A gain on the sale of a "depreciating asset", to the extent of depreciation recaptured, generally is taxed as ordinary income. Gains exceeding the amount of depreciation recaptured are also taxed as ordinary income.

A one-off tax benefit is available for certain capital expenditure in respect of "depreciating assets" *(see above)* where the taxpayer commences to hold the asset under a contract entered into between 13 December 2008 and 31 December 2009 (or where the taxpayer commences to construct the asset between those dates). This "investment allowance" provides an additional tax deduction of between 10% and 50% for the cost of purchasing new depreciating assets, and on new expenditure that enhances existing depreciating assets, where the cost of the asset or the new expenditure meets certain investment thresholds. *See "Investment allowance" under "Tax incentives"*.

Australia

The cost of income-producing structural improvements, the construction of which started after 26 February 1992 is eligible for write-off for tax purposes on the same basis as that of income-producing buildings, that is, at a rate of 2.5% per annum.

Subject to exceptions referred to below, capital expenditure incurred after 15 September 1987 in the construction or improvement of non-residential buildings used for producing assessable income is amortised over 40 years at an annual 2.5% rate. Capital expenditure on the construction of buildings used for short-term traveller accommodation (e.g., hotels, motels) and industrial buildings (typically, factories) is amortised over 25 years at an annual 4% rate where construction commenced after 26 February 1992. The cost of eligible building construction that commenced after 21 August 1984 and before 16 September 1987 (or construction contracted before 16 September 1987) is amortised over 25 years at an annual 4% rate. There is no recapture of the amortised amount upon disposal of the building, except where the expenditure is incurred after 13 May 1997, in which case recapture will apply, subject to certain transitional rules.

Similar provisions apply in relation to income-producing residential buildings on which construction commenced after 17 July 1985.

The cost of consumables may be either written off immediately, or as used. The following expenditure attracts an immediate 100% deduction: environmental protection activities, dealing with pollution and waste; "landcare" operations; exploring or prospecting for minerals; mine site rehabilitation; and certain expenditure in respect of the establishment of carbon sink forests.

Tax depreciation is not required to conform to book depreciation.

Percentage depletion based on gross income or other non-cost criteria is not available.

Net operating losses

Losses may be carried forward indefinitely, subject to compliance with tests of continuity of more than 50% of ultimate stock ownership or compliance with a "same business" test. For consolidated group companies, the ability to utilise these losses is determined by a modified version of these tests. *See "Group taxation"*. More liberal rules apply when determining continuity of majority underlying ownership of certain "widely held" companies and companies which are majority-owned by "widely held" companies or certain other entities. These more liberal rules have two main effects: (1) the continuity of majority underlying ownership test may be satisfied by testing at certain points of time, without testing throughout the intervening periods, and (2) in certain cases, special concessional tracing rules deem entities to hold voting, dividend or capital stakes in the company so that tracing through to the ultimate beneficial owners of those stakes is not needed. In particular, registered shareholdings of less than 10% are taken to be held by a single notional shareholder, in general avoiding the need to identify small ownership interests and the risk of failing the continuity of ownership test because of small shareholder "churn". Companies (including tax consolidated groups) can choose the proportion of their carryforward losses to be deducted in a year. Making this choice deals with the situation where untaxed franked dividends and the imputation credit on such dividends would otherwise absorb carryforward and current year losses.

Payments to foreign affiliates

A corporation can deduct royalties, management service fees and interest charges paid to non-residents, provided the amounts are commercially realistic and referrable to activities aimed at producing assessable income.

Interest

Special rules classify financial arrangements as either debt or equity interests. These rules focus on economic substance rather than legal form and take into account related schemes, and extend beyond shares. In this situation, interest expense on non-share equity would be treated as a dividend, which is potentially frankable, and would be non-deductible for the paying company/group.

Thin capitalisation measures apply to the total debt of the Australian operations of multinational groups (including branches of those groups). The measures cover investment into Australia of foreign multinationals and outward investment of Australian-based multinationals, and include a safe-harbour debt-to-equity ratio of 3:1. Interest deductions are denied to the extent that borrowing exceeds the safe-harbour ratio. Where borrowing exceeds the safe-harbour ratio, multinationals are not affected by the rules if they can satisfy the arm's-length test (that the borrowing could have been borne by an independent entity). A further alternative test is available for outward investing entities based on 120% of their worldwide gearing.

The thin capitalisation rules apply to inward investment into Australia, where a foreign entity carries on business through an Australian permanent establishment or has direct investments in Australia or in broad terms five or fewer non-residents have at least 50%, or a single non-resident has at least 40% of an Australian entity that has incurred interest expenses that might otherwise be deductible against its Australian taxable income. Separate rules apply to financial institutions. To facilitate their inclusion in the rules, branches are required to prepare financial accounts.

International Financial Reporting Standards (IFRS), equivalents of which apply in Australia from 1 January 2005, make it more difficult for some entities to satisfy thin capitalisation rules because of the removal of internally generated intangible assets from the balance sheets. A four year transitional measure, applying from tax years commencing on or after 1 January 2005, allowed taxpayers to calculate safe harbour debt amounts using the pre-1 January 2005 standards. Legislation now allows departure from the Australian equivalents to IFRS in relation to certain intangible assets and to exclude deferred tax assets and liabilities and surpluses and deficits in defined benefit superannuation funds from applicable calculations.

Financial arrangements

New measures for the "taxation of financial arrangements" (TOFA) apply with effect for arrangements entered into from income years commencing on or after 1 July 2010, although a taxpayer may elect to apply the new measures to arrangements entered into from income years commencing on or after 1 July 2009. The new measures provide for two default methods and four elective methods for determining gains or losses in respect of financial arrangements, along with revenue account treatment of the resulting gains or losses to the extent that the gain or loss is made in earning assessable income or carrying on a business for that purpose. *See "Financial arrangements" under "Income Determination".*

Australia

Foreign exchange gains and losses

Foreign currency gains and losses are recognised when realised, regardless of whether there is a conversion into Australian dollars, and are included in or deducted from ordinary income, subject to limited exceptions. *See "Foreign exchange gains and losses" under "Income Determination".*

Taxes

In general, goods and services tax (GST) input tax credits, GST and adjustments under the GST law are disregarded for income tax purposes. Other taxes, including property, payroll, fringe benefits tax and other business taxes, excluding income tax, are deductible to the extent they are incurred in producing assessable income or necessarily incurred in carrying on a business for this purpose, and are not of a capital or private nature.

Other significant items

Where expenditure for services is incurred in advance, deductibility of that expenditure generally will be prorated over the period during which the services will be provided, up to a maximum of 10 years.

Subject to limited exceptions, deductions are denied for expenditure on "entertainment", which broadly is defined as entertainment by way of food, drink or recreation, and accommodation or travel to do with providing such entertainment.

The amount of a commercial debt "forgiven" (other than an intra-group debt within a tax consolidated group) that is not otherwise assessable or does not otherwise reduce an allowable deduction is applied to reduce the debtor's carryforward tax deductions for revenue tax losses, non-deducted capital losses, non-deducted capital expenditure, and other capital cost bases in a certain order. Any amount not so applied is not assessable to the debtor. "Forgiveness" includes the release, waiver or extinguishment of a debt (other than by full payment in cash) and the lapsing of the creditor's recovery right by reason of a statute of limitations. Under current law, the net forgiven amount may in certain circumstances be apportioned among a non-consolidated group of companies related to the debtor (legislation to effectively repeal this rule, with effect for debts forgiven in the 2010-11 and later income years, has been introduced into Parliament, but is not yet law).

General value shifting rules apply to shifts of value, direct or indirect, in respect of loan and equity interests in companies or trusts. Circumstances in which these rules may apply include where there is a direct value shift under a scheme involving equity or loan interests, or where value is shifted out of an asset by the creation of rights in respect of the asset, or where there is a transfer of assets or the provision of services for a consideration other than at market value. The value shifting rules may apply to the head company of a tax consolidated group or MEC group for value shifts also involving entities outside the group, but not to value shifting between group members, which the tax consolidation rules address. *See "Group taxation".*

Group taxation

A tax consolidation regime applies for income tax and capital gains tax purposes for companies, partnerships and trusts ultimately 100% owned by a single head company (or certain entities taxed like a company) resident in Australia. Australian resident companies that are 100% owned (either directly or indirectly) by the same foreign company and that have no common Australian head company between them and the non-resident parent are also allowed to consolidate as a multiple entry consolidated group (MEC group). The group that is consolidated for income tax purposes may differ from the group that is consolidated for accounts or for GST purposes. Groups that choose to consolidate must include all 100%-owned entities under an "all-in" rule and the choice to consolidate is irrevocable. However "eligible tier-1 companies" (being Australian resident companies that have a non-resident shareholder) that are members of a potential MEC group, are not all required to join a MEC group, when it forms, but may form two or more separate MEC groups, if they so choose, of which the same foreign "top company" is the 100% owner. If an eligible tier-1 company joins a particular MEC group, all 100% subsidiaries of the company must also join the group. While the rules for forming and joining MEC groups allow more flexibility than with consolidated groups, the ongoing rules for MEC groups are more complex, particularly for tax losses and on the disposal of interests in eligible tier-1 companies, which are subject to cost pooling rules, although for practical purposes these rules are relevant only if the non-resident is holding or disposing of an "indirect Australian real property interest". *See "Capital gains" under "Income determination".*

A single entity rule applies to members of a consolidated or MEC group so that for income tax purposes the subsidiary members are taken to be part of the head company, while they continue to be members of the group and intra-group transactions are not recognised. In general, no group relief is available where related companies are not members of the same consolidated or MEC group. However, *see previously under "Capital gains" in "Income determination"* for exceptions with regard to certain capital gains tax rollovers.

Consolidated groups file a single tax return, and calculate their taxable income or loss ignoring all intra-group transactions.

When a consolidated group acquires 100% of an Australian resident entity, so that it becomes a subsidiary member, the cost base of certain assets (in general, those that are non-monetary) of the joining member are reset for all tax purposes, based on the purchase price plus the entity's liabilities, subject to certain adjustments. In this way, an acquisition of 100% of an Australian resident entity by a consolidated group is broadly the tax equivalent of acquiring its assets. Subject to certain tests being passed, tax losses of the joining member may be transferred to the head company, and may be utilised subject to a loss factor, which is broadly the market value of the joining member divided by the market value of the group (including the joining member). The value of the loss factor (referred to as "the available fraction") that applies for transferred losses may be reduced by capital injections (or the equivalent) into the member before it joined, or into the group after the loss is transferred.

Franking credits, foreign tax credits carried forward under the former foreign tax credit regime and tax losses remain with the group when a member exits, and the cost base of shares in the exiting member is calculated based on the tax value of its assets at the time of exit, less liabilities subject to certain adjustments.

Generally members of the group are jointly and severally liable for group income tax debts on the default of the head company, unless the group liability is covered by a tax sharing agreement (TSA) that satisfies certain legislative requirements. A member who enters into a TSA generally can achieve a clean exit from the group where a payment is made to the head company in accordance with the TSA.

Australia

Tax incentives

Inward investment

Depending on the nature and size of the investment project, state governments may give rebates from payroll, stamp and land taxes on an ad hoc basis and for limited periods.

Capital investment

Incentives for capital investment are as follows.

1. Accelerated deductions are available for capital expenditures on the exploration for and extraction of petroleum and other minerals, the rehabilitation of former mineral extraction sites, certain environmental protection activities, the establishment of certain "carbon sink" forests and for certain expenditure of primary producers.
2. A temporary "investment allowance" provides an additional deduction of between 10% and 50% for the cost of purchasing new tangible "depreciating assets" *(see "Depreciation and depletion" under "Deductions")*, and for new expenditure on enhancing existing depreciating assets where the cost of the asset or the new expenditure is at least AUD 10,000 (or AUD 1,000 in the case of small business entities, such that generally where the annual "aggregated turnover" of the taxpayer and certain associated taxpayers is under AUD 2 million).

In summary, the investment allowance deduction that can be claimed is as follows:

	First use time (Note 2) is on or before 30 June 2010	First use time (Note 2) is after 30 June 2010 but on or before 31 December 2010
Small business entity		
Investment commitment time (Note 1) between 13 December 2008 and 31 December 2009 (inclusive)	50%	50%
Other taxpayers		
Investment commitment time (Note 1) between 13 December 2008 and 30 June 2009 (inclusive)	30%	10%
Investment commitment time (Note 1) between 1 July 2009 and 31 December 2009 (inclusive)	10%	10%

Note 1: The investment commitment time is generally the time at which the taxpayer enters into a contract under which the taxpayer starts to hold the depreciating asset (or incurs expenditure to enhance an existing depreciating asset), or starts to construct the asset.

Note 2: The first use time is generally the time at which the taxpayer starts to use the asset or have it installed ready for use.

There is no entitlement to the investment allowance outside the parameters specified above.

In each case, to be entitled to make the claim, it must be reasonable to conclude that at the time the asset is first used or installed ready for use, or the new expenditure is incurred on improving the asset, the asset will be principally used in Australia for the principal purpose of carrying on a business. This investment allowance deduction is available to the "holder" of the depreciating asset and is in addition to the normal capital allowance deductions able to be claimed in relation to such assets. This means that except in the case of the lease of a "luxury car", it will generally be the lessor who is entitled to the investment allowance (assuming the other criteria are satisfied). In the case of hire purchase contracts and arrangements treated as such under the tax law, the holder of the asset is generally the entity that hires the asset from the hirer.

The investment allowance is not available for the purchase of trading stock or land, or to improvements to land which are not treated under the tax law as depreciating assets but the cost of which may be deducted under the structural improvement capital allowance provisions (see "Depreciation and depletion" under "Deductions"). Intangible assets, which may qualify for a capital allowance as a depreciating asset – such as "in-house software", patents, copyright, registered designs (and licences in respect thereof) and mining, prospecting and quarrying rights/information – do not qualify for investment allowance.

3. Subject to changes proposed with effect from 1 July 2010 (see below), deductions of up to 125% of amounts expended apply to eligible R&D expenditure incurred by a company incorporated in Australia on projects whose details are set out in an R&D plan that has previously been approved by the company's board of directors or an authorised person. To qualify the company must lodge a registration application with Innovation Australia not later than 10 months after the end of the relevant income year. The concessional deduction may be cancelled retrospectively if subsequent exploitation of the results is not on normal commercial terms and is not "of the kind to be expected of hypothetical persons dealing with each other at arm's length and from positions of similar or like or roughly equivalent bargaining power." Expenditure in acquiring or gaining access to certain pre-existing technology, known as "core technology expenditure," is deductible at a rate of 100% of the amount expended if the purpose of acquiring the technology is to carry on eligible R&D. The deduction in any year cannot exceed one-third of the amount of expenditure incurred in that year on R&D related to that core technology. Undeducted "core technology expenditure" may be carried forward for deduction in future years, subject to the same requirements. There is an R&D tax offset for certain small companies and a 175% premium rate deduction for certain expenditure years where companies increase their R&D expenditure over the average expenditure for the preceding three-year period. In certain circumstances, an Australian company undertaking R&D activities in Australia wholly or principally on behalf of a foreign related entity, may be able to claim the 175% rate.

Special grant programmes may be available to assist corporations in the conduct of certain research and development in Australia. These grants are awarded on a discretionary basis.

Within a consolidated regime, R&D concessions are claimed by the head company on behalf of the group.

As mentioned above, the government proposes to change the tax treatment of expenditure on R&D. For income years commencing on or after 1 July 2010, the

Australia

current concessional deductions will be replaced with an R&D tax credit. For companies with an annual turnover of less than AUD 20 million, there will be a 45% refundable tax credit, equivalent to a 150% tax concession. This equates to a cash saving of 15% every dollar of R&D spend, and will be refundable where the company is in a tax loss position. For companies with a turnover of greater than AUD 20 million, they will have access to a non-refundable 40% tax credit, equivalent to a 133% tax concession. This equates to a cash saving of 10 cents for every dollar of R&D spend. Generally, only R&D activities undertaken in Australia qualify for the new R&D tax incentive. However, R&D activities conducted overseas also qualify in limited circumstances where the activities cannot be undertaken in Australia. The 175% premium concession and international premium concession will be abolished. Eligibility criteria will be tightened to support "only genuine R&D". Legislation to give effect to the proposals was introduced into Parliament on 13 May 2010.

4. There are a number of tax concessions aimed at encouraging investments in the venture capital sector. Non-resident pension funds that are tax-exempt in their home jurisdiction, are residents of Canada, France, Germany, Japan, UK, US, or another country prescribed by regulation, and satisfy certain Australian registration requirements are exempt from income tax on the disposal of investments in certain Australian venture capital equity held at risk for at least 12 months. A similar exemption is extended to other tax-exempt non-resident investors, including managed funds and venture capital fund-of-funds vehicles and taxable non-residents holding less than 10% of a venture capital limited partnership. These investors are able to invest in "eligible venture capital investments" through an Australian resident venture capital limited partnership or through a non-resident venture capital limited partnership. For periods from 1 July 2002 until the end of the 2006-07 income year, the exemption applies only to investors from the United States, United Kingdom, Japan, Germany, France and Canada, Finland, France, Italy, the Netherlands, New Zealand, Norway, Sweden, and Taiwan. Thereafter, the restriction on the country of residence of non-resident investors no longer applies (although general partners of specified classes of limited partnership are excluded). "Eligible venture capital investments" is limited to specified interests in companies and trusts. Detailed rules in the legislation prescribe the nature of such investments and the characteristics, which such companies and trusts and their investments must possess.

5. There is a venture capital tax concession for "pooled development funds" (PDFs). PDFs are investment companies established to provide equity capital to small and medium-size enterprises. PDFs are taxed on their net income at 25%, except for income from small and medium-size enterprises, which is taxed at 15%. PDFs are entitled to imputation credits on the receipt of franked dividend income. Dividends from PDFs are tax exempt. Gains on the sale of shares in a PDF are exempt from tax, and losses are not deductible. The existing PDF arrangements have been progressively replaced by a newer investment vehicle called an early stage venture capital limited partnership (ESVCLP). The existing PDF arrangements closed to new registrations from 21 June 2007. For income years commencing on or after 1 July 2007 a new investment vehicle called an early stage venture capital limited partnership (ESVCLP) has been introduced. The thresholds for qualification include requirements that, amongst other things, the committed capital of ESVCLP must be at least AUD 10 million but not exceed AUD 100 million, the investments made must fall within prescribed parameters as to size and proportion of total capital and the ESVCLP must have an investment plan approved by Innovation Australia. Where the thresholds for their application are met, the ESVCLP provisions provide

flow-through tax treatment to domestic and foreign partners with the income and capital received by the partners being exempt from taxation. As the income will be tax exempt, the investor will not be able to deduct investment losses.

6. The taxable income derived from pure offshore banking transactions by an authorised offshore banking unit in Australia is taxed at the rate of 10%.

7. Taxation incentives currently are provided to both investors in, and producers of, films in Australia. However, the provisions which, subject to a number of conditions, provided an accelerated deduction for certain capital expenditures on films made wholly or substantially in Australia are being phased-out, with no deductions being available after the 2009-10 income year. These provisions regarding film incentives have been replaced with refundable tax offsets which are available to companies for certain expenditure incurred in Australia in producing specified classes of film or undertaking specified post, digital or special effects production activities in respect of specified classes of films. The concessions are only available to a company that is either an Australian resident or a non-resident carrying on business through an Australian permanent establishment and which has been issued with an Australian Business Number. The availability of the offsets is subject to a number of conditions, including meeting registration and "minimum spend" requirements. The rate of the offset varies from 15% to 40% depending upon the nature of the relevant film and activities undertaken.

8. There is an Entrepreneurs' Tax Offset (ETO) of up to 25% for businesses run by small business entities, which can include companies with an annual turnover of up to AUD 75,000.

Other incentives

Cash grants for export-market development expenditure are available to eligible businesses seeking to export Australian-source goods and services.

Withholding taxes (WHT)

Recipient	Dividends (1)	Interest (2)	Royalties (3)
	%	%	%
Resident corporations or individuals	Nil	Nil	Nil
Non-resident corporations or individuals:			
Non-treaty	30	10	30
Treaty:			
Argentina	10/15 (4)	12	10/15 (5)
Austria (46)	15	10	10 (6)
Belgium	15	10	10 (6)
Canada	5/15 (7)	10 (7)	10 (6)(7)
Chile (47)	5/15	5/10/15	5/10 (6)
China, P.R. (8)	15	10	10 (6)
Czech Republic	5/15 (9)	10	10 (6)
Denmark	15	10	10 (6)
East Timor (Timor Sea Treaty) (10)	15 (11)	10 (11)	10 (11)
Fiji	20	10	15 (6)
Finland (12)	0/5/15 (37)	0/10 (38)	5 (6) (39)

Australia

Recipient	Dividends (1)	Interest (2)	Royalties (3)
	%	%	%
France (13)	0/5/15 (13)	0/10 (13)	5/10 (6) (13)
Germany	15	10	10 (6)
Hungary	15	10	10 (6)
India	15	15	10/15 (14)
Indonesia	15	10	10/15 (15)
Ireland, Rep. of	15	10	10 (6)
Italy	15	10	10 (6)
Japan (40)	0/5/10/15 (40)	0/10 (40)	5 (6)(40)
Kiribati	20	10	15 (6)
Korea, Rep. of	15	15	15 (6)
Malaysia	0/15 (16)	15	15 (6)
Malta	15 (17)	15	10 (6)
Mexico	0/15 (18)	10/15 (19)	10 (6)
Netherlands	15	10	10 (6)
New Zealand (45)	0/5/10/15 (45)	0/10 (45)	5/10 (6) (45)
Norway	0/5/15 (35)	0/10 (41)	5 (6) (42)
Papua New Guinea	15/20 (20)	10	10 (6)
Philippines	15/25 (21)	15	15/25 (22)
Poland	15	10	10 (6)
Romania	5/15 (23)	10	10 (6)
Russian Federation	5/15 (24)	10	10 (25)
Singapore	15	10	10 (6)
Slovak Republic	15	10	10 (6)
South Africa (43)	5/15 (43)(36)	0/10(43)	5 (6)(43)
Spain	15	10	10 (6)
Sri Lanka	15	10	10 (6)
Sweden	15	10	10 (6)
Switzerland	15	10	10 (6)
Taipei/Taiwan	10/15 (26)	10	12.5 (6)
Thailand	15/20 (27)	10/25 (28)	15 (6)
United Kingdom (44)	0/5/15 (29)	0/10 (30)	5 (6)
United States	0/5/15/30 (31)	0/10/15 (32)	5 (6) (33)
Vietnam	10/15 (34)	10	10 (6)

Notes

Numbers in parentheses refer to the following notes:

1. Dividends paid to non-residents are exempt from dividend withholding tax except when paid out of a company that has not borne Australian tax (i.e., unfranked dividends). Dividends include those stock dividends that are taxable. The rates shown apply to dividends on both portfolio investments and substantial holdings other than dividends paid on or after 26 June 2005 in connection with an Australian permanent establishment (PE) of the non-resident. Unfranked dividends paid to non-residents are exempt from dividend withholding tax to the extent that the dividends are declared by the company to be "conduit foreign income". There is also a deduction from 1 July 2000 in certain cases to compensate for the company tax on inter-entity distributions where these are on-paid

by holding companies to a 100% parent that is a non-resident *(see "Inter-company dividends" under "Income determination")*. Dividends paid to a non-resident in connection with an Australian PE on or after 26 June 2005 are taxable to the non-resident on a net assessment basis (i.e., the dividend and associated deductions will need to be included in the determination of the non-resident's taxable income – the dividend is not subject to dividend withholding tax), and a franking tax offset is allowable to the non-resident company for franked dividends received.

2. Australia's interest withholding tax rate is limited to 10% of gross interest although the treaty may allow for a higher maximum limit. An exemption from withholding tax can be obtained for interest on certain public issues or widely held issues of debentures. Provisions exist to ensure that discounts and other pecuniary benefits derived by non-residents on various forms of financings are subject to interest withholding tax. Interest paid to non-residents by offshore banking units is exempt from interest withholding tax where offshore borrowings are used in offshore banking activities (including lending to non-residents). An offshore borrowing is defined as a borrowing from (1) an unrelated non-resident in any currency or (2) a resident or a related person in a currency other than Australian currency.

3. Royalties paid to non-residents (except in respect of a PE in Australia of a resident of a treaty country) are subject to 30% withholding tax (on the gross amount of the royalty), unless a double taxation agreement provides for a lesser rate.

4. For Australian-sourced dividends which are "franked" under Australia's dividend imputation provisions and paid to a person who directly holds at least 10% of the voting power of the company, the limit is 10% (although note that Australia does not impose withholding tax on franked dividends). For Argentinean-sourced dividends paid to a person who holds at least 25% of the capital in the company, the limit is 10%. A 15% limit applies to other dividends.

5. Source-country tax is limited to 10% of the gross amount of royalties in relation to copyright of literary, dramatic, musical, or other artistic work; the use of industrial or scientific equipment; the supply of scientific, technical or industrial knowledge; assistance ancillary to the above; or certain forbearances in respect of the above. Source-country tax is limited to 10% of the net amount of royalties for certain technical assistance. In all other cases it is limited to 15% of the gross amount of royalties.

6. Tax is limited to the indicated percentage of gross royalty.

7. Under a protocol signed on 23 January 2002 the maximum withholding tax rate on interest is 10%. The Protocol adopts a 5% dividend withholding tax rate to franked dividends paid by an Australian resident company and in the case of dividends paid by a Canadian resident company (other than a non-resident owned investment corporation) to a company that holds directly at least 10% of the voting power in the dividend company (although note that Australia does not impose withholding tax on franked dividends). Otherwise the maximum withholding tax rate on dividends will continue to be 15%. The protocol has effect in Australia in relation to dividends, interest and royalties derived on or after 1 January 2003.

8. Except Hong Kong and Macau.

9. The treaty between Australia and the Czech Republic allows Australia to impose a 5% withholding tax on the franked part of a dividend in certain circumstances (although note that Australia does not impose withholding tax on franked dividends). In the Czech Republic a rate of 15% applies to the gross amount of dividends if the dividends are paid to a company, which holds directly at least 20% of the capital of the company paying the dividend.

10. East Timor does not have a comprehensive double tax agreement with Australia. However, the Timor Sea Treaty governs the taxation rights between the two countries for petroleum-related activities conducted in the Joint Petroleum Development Area of the Timor Sea by any person or entity, irrespective of the residency status of that person or entity.

11. Where the Timor Sea Treaty applies to third-country resident payees, only 10% of the total gross interest, dividend or royalty payment is subject to Australian withholding tax, as follows: interest – 10% of total gross interest paid is subject to withholding tax at a rate of 10%; dividends – 10% of total gross unfranked dividends paid is subject to withholding

Australia

tax at a rate of 15%, or at the relevant double tax agreement rate of the recipient; royalties – 10% of total gross royalties paid is subject to withholding tax at a rate of 10%, or at the relevant double tax agreement rate of the recipient. However the other 90% of each such amount is subject to East Timorese withholding tax at the same rates.

12. The current agreement came into force on 10 November 2007 and has effect in Australia in respect of withholding taxes for income derived on or after 1 January 2008 and in respect of other income, profit or gains derived on or after 1 July 2008.

13. On 20 June 2006 Australia and France signed a new agreement. The new agreement has effect in Australia in respect of withholding tax on income derived on or after 1 January 2010, being the calendar year next following 1 June 2009, which was the date on which the new agreement entered into force. The source country will exempt inter-corporate non-portfolio (i.e., minimum 10% shareholding) dividends paid out of profits that have borne the normal rate of company tax. There is a 5% rate limit for all other non-portfolio dividends. A rate limit of 15% will continue otherwise to apply for dividends. A rate limit of 10% applies to interest except no tax will be chargeable in the source country on interest derived by a financial institution resident in the other country or a government or political or administrative subdivision or local authority or central bank of the other country. The rate limit for royalties reduced to 5% from 1 January 2010. Amounts derived from equipment leasing (including certain container leasing) are excluded from the royalty definition and treated either as international transport operations or business profits.

14. The source-country limit under the Indian agreement is 10% for royalties paid in respect of the use of or rights to use industrial, commercial or scientific equipment or for the provision of consulting services related to such equipment. In other cases the limit is 15%.

15. The source-country limit under the Indonesian agreement is 10% for royalties paid in respect of the use of or the right to use any industrial, commercial or scientific equipment or for the supply of scientific, technical, industrial, or commercial knowledge or information, and it is 15% in other cases.

16. A nil dividend withholding tax rate applies to franked dividends paid by an Australian resident company to an entity that holds directly at least 10% of the voting power in the dividend paying company, otherwise a 15% withholding tax rate applies. In relation to dividends paid by a company resident of Malaysia, no withholding tax applies.

17. Source-country tax in Malta is limited to the tax chargeable on the profits out of which the dividends are paid.

18. A nil dividend withholding tax rate applies to franked dividends paid (in Mexico, those dividends that have been paid from the net profit account) to a company that holds directly at least 10% of the voting power in the dividend paying company. In all other cases, a 15% withholding tax rate will apply to dividends.

19. Source-country tax is limited to 10% when interest is paid to a bank or an insurance company, derived from bonds and securities that are regularly and substantially traded on a recognised securities market, paid by banks (except where the prior two criteria apply) or paid by the purchaser to the seller of machinery and equipment in connection with a sale on credit. It is 15% in all other cases.

20. For Australian-source dividends, the limit is 15%. Where dividends are sourced in Papua New Guinea, the limit is 20%.

21. Source-country tax is limited to 15% where relief by way of rebate or credit is given to the beneficial owner of the dividend. In any other case, source-country tax is limited to 25%.

22. Source-country tax generally is limited to 15% of gross royalties if paid by an approved Philippines enterprise. In all other cases, the rate is limited to 25% of the gross royalties.

23. Source-country tax (Australia) is limited to 5% where a dividend is paid to a Romanian resident company that holds directly at least 10% of the capital of the Australian company paying the dividend to the extent that the dividend is fully franked. Source-country tax (Romania) is limited to 5% where a dividend is paid to an Australian resident company that holds directly at least 10% of the capital of the Romanian company paying the dividend if the dividend is paid out of profits that have been subject to Romanian profits tax. In other cases it is limited to 15%.

24. Source country tax generally is limited to 15%. However, a rate of 5% applies where the dividends have been fully taxed at the corporate level, the recipient is a company which has a minimum direct holding in the paying company and has invested a minimum of

AUD 700,000 or the Russian ruble equivalent in the paying company; and where the dividends are paid by a company that is a resident in Russia, the dividends are exempt from Australian tax.

25. The agreement with the Russian Federation is the first of Australia's new treaties to include spectrum licenses in the definition of royalties.

26. Source-country tax (Taiwan) is limited to 10% of the gross amount of the dividends paid to a company which holds at least 25% of the capital of the company paying the dividends. A rate of 15% applies in all other cases. To the extent that dividends are franked because they are paid out of profits that have borne Australian tax, they are exempt from dividend withholding tax. *See Note (1) above.* The treaty allows Australia to impose a 10% withholding tax on the franked part of a dividend.

27. The source-country limit where the recipient has a minimum 25% direct holding in the paying company is 15% if the paying company engages in an "industrial undertaking"; 20% in other cases.

28. The source-country limit is 10% when interest is paid to a financial institution. It is 25% in all other cases.

29. Source country tax is generally limited to 15%. However, an exemption applies for dividends paid to a listed company which satisfies certain public listing requirements and which controls 80% or more of the voting power in the company paying the dividend, and a 5% limit applies to dividends paid to other companies with voting power of 10% or greater in the dividend paying company.

30. Source country tax is generally limited to 10%. However, generally nil interest withholding tax is payable where interest is paid to a financial institution or a government body exercising governmental functions.

31. Source country tax is generally limited to 15%. Exceptions are: no source country tax is chargeable on dividends to a beneficially entitled company, which satisfies certain public listing requirements, and holds 80% or more of the voting power in the company paying the dividend. A 5% limit applies to dividends paid to other companies with voting power of 10% or greater in the dividend paying company. No limit applies to US tax on dividends paid on certain substantial holdings of Australian residents in US real estate investment trusts (REITs). In practical terms US tax on these dividends is increased from 15% to the current US domestic law rate of 30%. The 15% rate applies to REIT investments made by certain listed Australian property trusts subject to the underlying ownership requirements not exceeding certain levels. Investments in REITs by listed Australian property trusts acquired before 26 March 2001 are protected from the increased rate.

32. Source country tax generally is limited to 10%. However, generally nil interest withholding tax is payable where interest is paid to a financial institution or a government body exercising governmental functions. Rules consistent with US tax treaty policy and practice will allow interest to be taxed at a higher 15% rate (the rate that generally applies to dividends) and for tax to be charged on intra-entity interest payments between a branch and its head office.

33. Amounts derived from equipment leasing (including container leasing) are excluded from the royalty definition.

34. Source-country tax is limited to 15% (Australia) and 10% (Vietnam).

35. A nil withholding rate will apply in certain cases to inter-corporate dividends where the recipient holds directly at least 80% of the voting power in the dividend paying company for the 12-month period prior to payment. A rate of 5% applies to all other inter-corporate dividends where the recipient holds directly 10% or more of the voting power of the company paying the dividend. A general limit of 15% applies to all other dividends.

36. Prior to 1 January 2009, a nil withholding tax rate applied to dividends paid out of profits that have borne the normal rate of company tax and are paid to a company which holds directly at least 10% of the capital of the dividend paying company. A 15% rate applied in all other cases.

37. For dividend income derived on or after 1 January 2008, a nil withholding rate applies to inter-corporate dividends where the recipient holds directly 80% or more of the voting power of the company paying the dividend. A 5% rate limit applies on all other inter-corporate dividends where the recipient holds directly 10% or more of the voting power of the company paying the dividend. A 15% rate applies in all other cases.

Australia

38. A rate limit of 10% will apply to interest except no tax will be chargeable in the source country on interest derived by a financial institution resident in the other country or a government or political or administrative subdivision or local authority or central bank of the other country.
39. Amounts derived from equipment leasing (including certain container leasing) are excluded from the royalty definition and treated either as international transport operations or business profits. The rate of 5% applies to royalties derived on or after 1 January 2008. Before that date, a 10% rate applied.
40. On 31 January 2008 Australia and Japan signed a new agreement. The new agreement has effect in Australia in respect of withholding taxes on income derived on or after 1 January 2009. The source country will exempt inter-corporate dividends where the recipient holds directly 80% or more of the voting power of the company paying the dividend and certain "limitation of benefit" thresholds are met. A 5% rate limit will apply on all other inter-corporate dividends where the recipient beneficially holds directly 10% or more of the voting power of the company paying the dividend. A rate limit of 10% will otherwise apply for dividends. However where the dividends are paid by a company that is a resident of Japan, which is entitled to a deduction for the dividends in Japan, the rate limit is 15% where more than 50% of the assets of the paying company consist, directly or indirectly of real property situated in Japan and 10% in all other cases. Special rules apply to distributions to Japanese residents by real estate investment trusts (REITs). A rate limit of 10% applies to interest except no tax will be chargeable in the source country on interest derived by a financial institution resident in the other country or a government or political subdivision or local authority or central bank or other specified entity of the other country. From 1 January 2009, a 5% withholding tax rate on royalties applies. Before 1 January 2009, a general limit of 10% withholding tax on royalties applied. Under the new agreement, amounts derived from equipment leasing (including certain container leasing) will be excluded from the royalty definition and treated either as international transport operations or business profits.
41. A general rate limit of 10% applies to interest. However, in respect of interest derived on or after 1 January 2008 no tax will be chargeable in the source country on interest derived by a government of the other country (including its money institutions or a bank performing central banking functions) from the investment of official reserve assets and on interest derived by a financial institution resident in the other country (excluding interest paid as part of a back-to-back loan arrangement).
42. The rate limit for royalties of 5% applies to royalties derived on or after 1 January 2008. Before that date, a 10% rate applied.
43. On 31 March 2008 Australia and South Africa signed a protocol amending the agreement. The provisions of the new Protocol relating to Australian withholding taxes have effect in respect of income derived by a non-resident on or after 1 January 2009. A 5% rate limit will apply on all inter-corporate dividends where the recipient beneficially holds directly 10% or more of the voting power of the company paying the dividend. A rate limit of 15% will otherwise apply for dividends. From 1 January 2009, a general rate limit of 10% applies to interest. However no tax will be chargeable in the source country on interest derived by a government of the other country (including a bank performing central banking functions) and on interest derived by a financial institution resident in the other country (excluding interest paid as part of a back-to-back loan arrangement). From 1 January 2009, a 5% rate on royalties applies. Before 1 January 2009, a general limit of 10% withholding tax on royalties applied.
44. On 28 October 2008, it was announced that the Australian and the United Kingdom governments would commence negotiations on a revised tax treaty. Submissions were due to be lodged with Australian Treasury by 14 November 2008.
45. On 26 June 2009, a new double tax agreement was signed between Australia and New Zealand. The new treaty will replace the existing agreement signed in 1995 and the 2005 amending protocol. The new treaty takes effect for withholding tax purposes on 1 May 2010. From 1 May 2010, a nil withholding tax rate will apply in certain cases to inter-corporate dividends where the recipient holds directly at least 80% of the voting power in the dividend paying company. A rate of 5% will apply on all other inter-corporate dividends where the recipient holds directly 10% or more of the voting power of the

company paying the dividend. A general limit of 15% will apply for all other dividends, including those paid prior to 1 May 2010. From 1 May 2010, source country tax on interest will continue to be limited to 10%. However, no tax will be chargeable in the source country on interest derived by a government or a political subdivision or local authority of the other country (including a government investment fund or a bank performing central banking functions) or on interest derived by a financial institution which is unrelated to and dealing wholly independently of the payer (excluding interest paid as part of a back-to-back loan arrangement and, for New Zealand payers, where that person has not paid approved issuer levy). From 1 May 2010, the royalty withholding tax rate reduced from 10% to 5%.

46. The government announced on 4 February 2010 that negotiations to update Australia's tax treaty with Austria would take place in March 2010.

47. Australia and Chile signed a new DTA on 10 March 2010. The new agreement has not yet entered into force.

Other payments

A Pay-As-You-Go (PAYG) withholding regime applies to require the deduction and remittance of taxes on behalf of foreign resident individuals and entities that are in receipt of the following types of payments:

Type of payment	Rate of withholding
Payments for promoting or organising casino gaming junket arrangements	3%
Payments for performing artists, sportspersons, including payments to support staff such as art directors, bodyguards, coaches, hairdressers and personal trainers	– if recipient is a company, 30%
	– if recipient is an individual, the applicable non-resident marginal tax rate, (this effectively codifies existing ATO practice in relation to these types of payments)
Payments under contracts entered into after 30 June 2004 for the construction, installation and upgrading of buildings, plant and fixtures and for associated activities	5%

Managed investment trust distributions

For income years commencing on or after 1 July 2007, a "non-final" withholding tax at the rate of 30% applied to distributions ("fund payments") to non-residents, directly or through an intermediary, of income (other than dividends, interest, royalties, foreign source income and capital gains on assets that are not taxable Australian property) by a "managed investment trust" with defined connections to Australia. For fund payments made in income years commencing on or after 1 July 2008, a new regime applies, with divergent outcomes, depending upon whether or not the recipient of such fund payments is resident of a country identified as being one with which Australia has an effective exchange of information (EEOI) arrangement. For EEOI countries, the tax changes to a non-final withholding tax at a 22.5% rate in the first year of income commencing on or after 1 July 2008, a final withholding tax at a 15% rate in the second year (i.e., 2009-10 income year) and a final withholding tax at a 7.5% rate thereafter. For residents of non-EEOI countries, a final withholding tax at a 30% rate applies. EEOI countries have been identified by regulation to be the Netherlands Antilles and Bermuda and the countries with which Australia has concluded DTAs

Australia

other than Austria, Belgium, Greece, Korea, Malaysia, the Philippines, Singapore, and Switzerland. Australia has entered into EEOI agreements with Antigua & Barbuda, Aruba, Belgium, Jersey, Isle of Man, the British Virgin Islands, Gibraltar, Malaysia, Samoa Singapore, Guernsey and the Cook Islands, however, these countries have not yet been identified in regulations to be EEOI countries.

Tax administration

Returns

A corporation (including the head company of a tax consolidated group) generally lodges/files a tax return on the basis of a 1 July to 30 June year of income. However, a corporation may apply to adopt a substitute year of income, for example, 1 January to 31 December. A return is lodged/filed under a self-assessment system that allows the Australian Taxation Office (ATO) to rely on the information stated on the return. Where a corporation is in doubt as to its tax liability regarding a specific item, it can ask the ATO to consider the matter and obtain a binding private ruling.

Payment of tax

A PAYG instalment system applies to companies other than those whose annual tax is less than AUD 8,000 that are not registered for GST. Most companies are obliged to pay instalments of tax for their current income year by the twenty-first days of the fourth, seventh and tenth months of that year and by the twenty-first day of the month immediately following that year. Instalments are calculated on a quarterly basis by applying an "instalment rate" to the amount of the company's actual "ordinary income" (ignoring deduction) for the previous quarter. The instalment rate is notified to the taxpayer by the ATO and determined by reference to the tax payable for the most recent assessment. The ATO may notify a new rate during the year on which subsequent instalments must be based. Taxpayers can determine their own instalment rate, but there may be penalty tax if the taxpayer's rate is less than 85% of the rate that should have been selected.

Final assessed tax is payable on the first day of the sixth month following the end of that income year or such later date as the Commissioner of Taxation allows by a published notice.

Corporate taxes in Austria

For more information, contact:

Herbert Greinecker
PwC PricewaterhouseCoopers GmbH
Erdbergstraße 200
1030 Vienna
Austria
Tel: +43 1 501 88 3300
Email: herbert.greinecker@at.pwc.com

Significant developments

As a result of two Austrian Tax Reforms made in 2009 ("Budgetbegleitgesetz 2009" and "Konjunkturbelebungsgesetz 2009"), inter alia, the international participation exemption was extended to also cover portfolio dividends (investments less than 10% and no minimum holding period) from European Union (EU) based companies which therefore are exempted from corporate income taxation on shareholder level. Furthermore, for economic recovery reasons, an accelerated depreciation for fixed assets in the year of purchase was introduced. The accelerated depreciation (30%) covers acquisitions of assets made in 2009 and 2010. Moreover, a new recapture taxation mechanism was established being relevant for the Austrian tax group scheme.

In April 2010, a draft for a reform of the Austrian Corporate Income Tax Act ("Abgabenänderungsgesetz 2010") was forwarded to the Austrian Parliament, which contains the introduction of an advanced ruling opportunity. If this new regulation is implemented, legally binding information in the fields of transfer pricing, group taxation and mergers & acquisitions can be requested from the Austrian tax authorities for the payment of an administrative fee.

Furthermore, a first draft for Austrian transfer pricing guidelines was recently issued by Austrian tax authorities, which is expected to enter into force within the year 2010. The guidelines represent the Austrian authority's understanding of the OECD transfer pricing guidelines and will be of relevance for the interpretation of Austrian income tax law by the tax administration.

Taxes on corporate income

Basis of corporate income tax (Körperschaftsteuer)
Corporations (i.e., GmbH, AG) are subject to unlimited taxation in Austria with their entire (domestic and foreign) income if they have their legal seat or place of effective management in Austria. A non Austrian corporate tax resident (neither legal seat nor place of effective management in Austria) is subject to limited taxation with certain sources of income in Austria.

Due to the qualification of corporations as independent tax subjects, a distinction must always be made between tax ramifications at the level of the company and those at shareholder level. At the level of the company, profits are taxed at the standard rate of 25% while at shareholder level the profit distributions are usually subject to a withholding tax of 25%.

Austria

Profits of corporations are subject to (federal) corporate income tax only. There is no additional local income tax levied at company level.

Rates of corporate income tax (Körperschaftsteuer)
The corporate income is taxed at a flat rate of 25% regardless of whether profits are retained or distributed.

There is also a minimum corporate income tax, payable by companies in a tax-loss position. The minimum corporate income tax amounts to EUR 437.50 for limited liability companies (GmbH) and EUR 875 for stock corporations (AG) for each full quarter of a year. To promote the formation of new companies the minimum corporate income tax is reduced to EUR 273 for the first four quarters. The minimum corporate income tax can be carried forward without time limitation and be credited against future corporate income tax burdens of the company.

Corporate residence

A corporation is resident in Austria for tax purposes if either it is registered in Austria (legal seat) or its place of effective management is located in Austria. The "place of effective management" is located where the day-to-day management of the company is actually carried out and not where singular board decisions are formally made. However, the definition of place of effective management under Austrian tax law does not significantly deviate from its definition under the OECD guidelines (see commentary to the OECD Sample Double Tax Convention).

Other taxes

Value-added tax (Mehrwertsteuer)
Generally, the Austrian valued-added tax (VAT) law is based on the 6th EU VAT Directive. Under the Austrian VAT law, companies and individuals carrying out an active business on a permanent basis are qualified as entrepreneurs for VAT purposes. As entrepreneur they have to charge their supplies of goods or services provided to their customers with Austrian VAT at a rate of 20%. A certain limited range of goods and services (such as food, books, passenger transportation, cultural events) is taxed at the reduced rate of 10%. Certain transactions are exempted from Austrian VAT (e.g., export transactions).

Entrepreneurs are entitled to deduct Austrian input VAT insofar the input VAT does not result from goods/services purchased which are directly linked to certain VAT exempt sales (interest income, insurance premium, etc.). However, certain transactions are exempt from Austrian VAT (e.g., export transactions) without limiting the ability of the entrepreneur to deduct the related input VAT. To be entitled to deduct input VAT, the entrepreneur must obtain an invoice from his supplier which fulfils certain formal requirements.

Entrepreneurs have to file monthly or quarterly VAT returns by the fifteenth of the second month following the month concerned or by the fifteenth of the second month following the quarter concerned. The balance of the VAT due and the input VAT deducted has to be paid to the tax office (if VAT burden) or is refunded by the tax office (if input VAT position) to the electronic tax account of the entrepreneur. A separate report has to be filed by the entrepreneur at the tax office showing the cross-border intra EU-transactions made (EC sales listings report).

Excise taxes

Excise taxes are imposed on certain products including petroleum, tobacco products and alcoholic beverages.

Stamp duty

Stamp duty is imposed in connection with certain legally predefined transactions for which a written contract has been established (e.g., lease contracts, loan or credit agreements, bills of exchange, assignments of receivables). The Austrian administration's understanding of a "written contract" is very broad and covers not only paper-contracts but also contracts concluded by electronic means (e.g., electronically signed e-mails).

The stamp duty is triggered upon the establishment of a legal relationship if at least one Austrian party is contractually involved or – even if a contract is concluded between non-Austrian parties only – if the subject of the contract relates to Austria (e.g., lease contract on Austrian real estate).

However, various possibilities are available for most legal transactions subject to stamp duty to structure them in a way without triggering stamp duties (e.g., setting up of contracts abroad, offer-acceptance procedure, usage of audio-tapes).

The stamp duty rates for the most common legal transactions follow:

Legal transactions	Duty
Lease agreements	1.00%
Certificates of bonds	1.00%
Loan agreements	0.80%
Cash credit agreements non-recurring or revolving during a period of five years	0.80%
Cash credit agreements with a maturity exceeding five years	1.50%
Bill of exchange	0.13%
Assignment of receivables	0.80%

Capital transfer tax (Gesellschaftsteuer)

Capital transfer tax is imposed at a rate of 1% on the initial contribution of capital, other contractual or voluntary contributions in cash or in kind and certain hybrid financing instruments to Austrian corporations. However, in many cases a taxable event for capital transfer tax purposes can be eliminated by careful structuring (e.g., contributions made by the indirect shareholder of an Austrian company – so called "grandparent contributions" – do not trigger capital transfer tax).

Real estate tax

Local authorities annually levy real estate tax on all Austrian real estate property whether developed or not. The tax is levied on the assessed standard ratable value ("Einheitswert") of immovable property. The assessed value is usually substantially lower than the market value. The effective tax rate depends on the intended use of the real estate and is calculated using a special multiplier.

Austria

Tax rates:

- Agricultural area and forestry
  - 1.6% for the first EUR 3,650 of the assessed standard ratable value; and
  - 2% for the amount of the assessed standard ratable value exceeding EUR 3,650.

- Buildings and property is taxed at 2% of the assessed standard ratable value. This multiplier is reduced for:

  - Single family houses
    - To 0.5% for the first EUR 3,650 of the assessed standard ratable value; and
    - To 1% for the next EUR 7,300.

  - Leasehold und shared property
    - To 1% for the first EUR 3,650 of the assessed standard ratable value; and
    - To 1.5% for the next EUR 3,650.

  - All other property
    - To 1% for the first EUR 3,650 of the assessed standard ratable value.

After the assessed standard ratable value is multiplied by the relevant multiplier the real estate tax is calculated by using a special municipal rate fixed by each municipality (maximum 500%). Finally the tax amount is reduced by a general reduction of 25% as stated by law and increased by a 35% inflation adjustment.

Real estate transfer tax
Tax is levied on any transaction which causes a change in the ownership of Austrian real estate or in the person empowered to dispose of such property. Tax liability arises when a sales contract or other legal transaction is concluded transferring the right of title to another party. Generally speaking, tax on the sale of real estate is calculated on the payment received for the transfer of the property. Real estate transfer tax is generally calculated on the basis of the acquisition price. However, in the case of corporate restructuring under the Reorganisation Tax Act and in case of real estate transfers free of consideration, the two-fold (in the case of the former) and the threefold (in the case of the latter) assessed standard ratable value for tax purposes is taken as the tax base.

Tax exemptions:

- Real estate transactions with a tax base of EUR 1,100 or below.
- Real estate transactions in connection with business transfers free of charge with a tax base of up to EUR 365,000 if the donee is an individual and the donor is older than 55 years of age or is (due to physical or mental illness) permanently unable to work.
- Donation of real estate to a husband or wife for the acquisition or construction of a dwelling of up to 150 square metres in order to fulfil immediate living space requirements.
- Under certain circumstances the splitting of real estate within the scope of a partnership.

Tax rates:

Facts of the case	Percentage
Transfer to the husband, wife, parent, child, grandchild, stepchild, adopted child, son in law or daughter in law of the transferor	2%
Acquisition by the husband or the wife in the case of a divorce or an annulment of a marriage	2%
Acquisition by other individuals	3.5%

An additional 1% registration fee (same tax base as Real Estate Transfer Tax) becomes due upon incorporation to the land register.

Branch income

Austrian branches of foreign corporations are taxed in the same way as Austrian corporations, except that inter-company dividends received by Austrian branches of non-EU corporations are not tax exempt (*see Income determination*), and Austrian tax losses can be carried forward only if they exceed non-Austrian profits. Books and records generally can be kept abroad but must be brought to Austria in case of a tax audit (upon official request).

Income determination

Taxable income is determined based on statutory accounts under Austrian GAAP adjusted for certain deductions and additions prescribed by the tax law.

Inventory valuation
In general, inventories are valued at the lower of cost or market. If specific identification during stock movements is not possible, other methods, such as last-in, first-out (LIFO) and first-in, first-out (FIFO) are permitted when shown to be appropriate. Conformity between financial book keeping and tax reporting is required.

Capital gains/exit taxation
Generally, capital gains (short-and long-term) are part of the normal annual result of a corporation and therefore are taxed at the ordinary corporate income tax rate (25%).

A special tax treatment applies to capital gains with respect to the exit of taxable assets. In the case of a transfer of assets which formed part of a business from Austria to a foreign country (e.g., allocation of assets to foreign branch), latent capital gains generally are taxed at the time of the transfer. However, if these assets are transferred to an EU member state, capital gains taxation can be postponed upon request until the assets are sold or transferred outside the EU.

Inter-company dividends (inbound)
Domestic dividends/EC portfolio dividends
Dividends received from an Austrian company at corporate shareholder level are generally excluded from the tax base (no minimum stake, no minimum holding period). However, this tax exemption does refer to domestic dividends only but not to capital gains or losses.

Austria

Additionally, dividends received from companies located within the EU or from countries within the European Economy Area (EEA) with which an agreement on comprehensive administrative assistance was established (currently only Norway), are also tax exempt if the foreign company is subject to a tax similar to the Austrian corporate income tax and if the foreign corporate income tax rate is not below 15%.

International participation exemption
Dividends received from a foreign company are also tax exempt at corporate shareholder level, if the Austrian company holds at least 10% of the issued share capital for a minimum holding period of one year (international participation exemption). Furthermore, both capital gains and capital losses derived from shares qualifying for the international participation exemption are tax neutral. This means a deduction of capital losses is no longer available. However, the parent company can exercise an (irrevocable) option for each single participation acquired to treat both capital gains and capital losses taxable (spread of losses and depreciations over a period of seven years). The option refers to capital gains (losses) only and does not affect the tax treatment of ongoing dividend distributions. In the case of presumed tax abuse, the participation exemption for dividends and capital gains is replaced by a tax credit (switch-over-clause). The credit system will be applied if the foreign subsidiary does not meet an active-trade-or-business test (i.e., passive income from royalties, interest, etc. is greater than 50% of total income of subsidiary) and is not subject to an effective foreign minimum corporate income tax rate of more than 15%. The domestic and foreign participation exemptions are available to Austrian resident corporations and to Austrian branches of EU corporations only, but not to Austrian branches of non-EU corporations.

Austrian withholding tax (WHT) on inter-company dividends (outbound)
Under Austrian domestic law, there is generally a 25% WHT on dividends (profit distributions) paid to a foreign parent company. The WHT has to be deducted and forwarded by the Austrian subsidiary to the tax office.

Reduction of WHT according to double taxation treaties (DTT)
To end up with the reduced WHT rate as defined under the DTT applicable, Austrian tax law provides for the following alternative methods of WHT relief refund method or exemption at source method.

Refund method
The Austrian subsidiary generally has to withhold 25% WHT on profit distributions to the foreign parent company and the parent company has to apply for a refund (of the difference between 25% WHT and the lower DTT rate). In the course of the refund process, the Austrian tax administration analyses whether the foreign shareholder can be qualified as beneficial owner of the dividends paid. If the refund is approved by the Austrian tax authority, dividend distributions within the following three years can be done without deduction of WHT (for distributions of a comparable size and provided the foreign holding structure did not change in the meantime).

Exemption at source method
Relief at the source is available only if the direct parent company issues a written declaration confirming that it is an "active" company carrying out an active business that goes beyond the level of pure asset management and has own employees and office space at its disposal (substance requirements).

WHT on dividends paid to EU-companies
With regard to dividends paid to EU-resident corporate shareholders Austria has implemented the EU Parent/Subsidiary Directive according to which domestic WHT is reduced to zero. The requirements for the reduction are that the EU-resident parent company – which also has to meet the substance requirements mentioned above (Exemption at source method) – must directly own at least 10% of the share capital of the Austrian subsidiary for a period of at least one year. In case of foreign EU shareholders being qualified as pure holding companies, the Austrian tax administration does not allow an exemption at source but claims the application of the refund method (as discussed above).

Provided the requirements according to the EU Parent/Subsidiary Directive are not met, Austrian WHT has to be deducted. If an EU parent company cannot credit the Austrian WHT deducted against the CIT of its resident state (e.g., because the foreign dividend income is exempted from the CIT or due to a loss position of the shareholder), it is entitled to apply for a refund of the Austrian WHT. This application has to include a confirmation/documentation that the Austrian WHT could (fully or partly) not be credited at the level of the parent company.

Foreign income
Austrian resident corporations are taxed on their worldwide income. If a double taxation treaty is in force, double taxation is mitigated either through an exemption or by granting a tax credit equal to the foreign withholding tax at the maximum. If foreign withholding tax cannot be credited at the level of the Austrian corporation (e.g., due to a loss position), Austrian tax law does not allow to carry forward the foreign withholding tax to future assessment periods. However, if the source of the income is a non-treaty country, exemption or a tax credit shall be available based on unilateral relief (representing a discretionary decision of the Austrian Ministry of Finance only but no legal entitlement for the applicant). Special rules for taxing undistributed income of foreign subsidiaries are applicable only to foreign investment funds.

Please note that Austrian Tax Law does not define special CFC rules. However, under certain circumstances, Austrian tax administration – under a substance over form approach – taxes passive income of foreign subsidiaries of Austrian companies located in low tax jurisdictions *(see switch-over rule under section Inter-company dividends-inbound)*.

Stock dividends
A conversion from revenue reserves (retained earnings) to capital by a company does not lead to taxable income for the shareholder (but triggers capital transfer tax). However, capital reductions are treated as taxable income if within 10 years prior to the capital reduction the above-mentioned increase in capital was repaid to the shareholder. Otherwise, they are tax exempt.

Interest income
Interest income is taxed at the general rate of 25%. Interest payments to non-resident companies are – under Austrian tax law – not subject to WHT (provided no Austrian real estate property is used as security).

Rents and Royalties
Rental income is treated as normal business income.

Austria

On royalties paid to a non-resident company, Austrian WHT at a rate of 25% has to be deducted. This tax rate can be reduced under an applicable DTT *(see topic Withholding taxes)* or under the application of the EU Interest Royalty Directive which was implemented in Austrian Tax Law.

Partnership income
Partnerships are not classified as tax subjects separate from their owner (partners). The partnership income is calculated at the level of the partnership but taxed at the level of its owners as income from trade or business *(see Individual taxes)*.

Deductions

Expenditures in connection with the conduct of one's personal life are basically not deductible.

There is no carryback period for deductions. However, losses can be carried forward to a certain limit *(see section Tax losses)*.

Depreciation and depletion
Only the straight-line method is accepted for tax purposes, whereby the cost is evenly spread over the useful life of an asset. For certain assets, depreciation rates relevant for tax purposes are prescribed by the tax law and shown in the chart below:

	Allowed amount
Buildings (industrial use)	3.0%
Buildings (banking, insurance)	2.5%
Other buildings	2.0%
Automobiles	12.5%

Goodwill arising in the course of an asset deal for tax purposes must be amortised over 15 years. Goodwill arising in the course of a share deal can be amortised only if the acquired company is included in a tax group *(see Group taxation)*. Goodwill arising as a result of a corporate merger cannot be amortised.

Trademarks are usually amortised over 15 years. Other intangibles have to be depreciated over their useful lives.

For tangible fixed assets subject to depreciation and acquired within the fiscal years 2009 and 2010, an accelerated depreciation of 30% is allowed in the first year. Items excluded from this regulation include buildings, automobiles and low value items.

Tax depreciation is not required to conform to financial depreciation under Austrian GAAP. If depreciated property is sold, the difference between tax value and sale proceeds is taxed as a profit or loss in the year of sale.

Taxes losses
Tax losses can be carried forward without any time limit. However, tax loss carryforwards generally can be offset against taxable income only up to a maximum of 75% of the taxable income for any given year. Again, some exceptions to that rule apply, such as, in connection with tax groups *(see section Group taxation rules)* or in

case of liquidations allowing to charge tax loss carryforwards available against 100% of annual taxable income.

Payments to foreign affiliates

Generally, there are no restrictions on the deductibility of royalties, interest and service fees paid to foreign affiliates, provided they are at arm's length (which should be appropriately documented by agreements, contracts, calculation sheets, etc.). Payments to affiliated companies not meeting arm's-length standards are treated as a hidden distribution of earnings, i.e., they are not tax deductible and withholding tax is usually triggered at source. *For further information see section Transfer pricing.*

However, the domestic implementation of the EU Interest Royalty Directive which abolishes withholding taxes on cross-border payments of interest and license fees (regardless of whether taken out by deduction or by assessment) between affiliated companies in the Member States, has to be considered.

Taxes

Austrian and foreign taxes on income and other personal taxes, as well as the VAT insofar as it relates to non-deductible expenditures, are non-deductible. Other taxes, such as payroll or capital transfer taxes, are deductible.

Interest payments

Interest payments (also inter-company) are generally tax deductible, if they meet the general arm's-length requirements. *For further information see section Thin capitalisation rules.*

Fines and penalties

Fines and penalties are generally not tax deductible.

Meals and entertainment

The deductibility of entertainment expenses is restricted to advertising expenses. The deductibility of costs for business lunches generally is limited to 50% of actual expenses incurred (provided the business lunch had the purpose of acquiring new business).

Accrued expenses

Certain accruals (such as provisions for liabilities and impending losses) running for more than 12 months as of the closing date of the accounts are accepted for tax purposes at 80% of their value only. Exempted from this reduction are provisions for personnel benefits (severance payments, pensions, vacations and anniversary awards) for which specific reduction and computation methods have been provided and provisions which were already calculated by discounting a future obligation.

In general, lump-sum accruals and accruals for deferred repairs and maintenance are not allowed for tax purposes.

Financing costs

A deduction of interest incurred in connection with loans/credits used for the acquisition of participating interests is allowed from 2005 onwards even if the respective dividend income is tax exempt under the international participation exemption *(see Inter-company dividends)*. Other financing cost (fees, legal advice, etc.) being directly related to tax exempt dividend income are not deductible. However, foreign exchange expenses or profits accumulated in connection with the financing

Austria

of tax exempted international participations are treated as deductible respectively taxable item.

Charitable contributions
Charitable contributions are tax deductible up to a limit of 10% of the prior year profit.

Organisational and start-up expenses
Generally, organisational and start-up expenses are tax deductible.

Payment to directors
Payments to a member of the supervisory board ("Aufsichtsrat") are tax deductible up to a limit of 50%. Payments to members of the executive (managing) board are tax deductible without special limitation.

Group taxation

Group taxation rules
In 2005, a new group taxation system replaced the "Organschaft" concept under which Austrian resident companies as well as foreign companies (with restrictions) may be taxed as a unit. Under the 2005 system, two or more companies can form a tax group provided the parent company directly or indirectly owns more than 50% of the shares in the subsidiaries. The tax group also can include foreign group members. If a group member withdraws from the group within a minimum commitment-period of three years, all tax effects derived from its group membership must be reversed.

Within a tax group, all of the taxable results (profit and loss) of the domestic group members are attributed to their respective group parent. From foreign tax group members, tax losses in the proportion of the shareholding quota are attributed to the tax group parent. Foreign tax losses utilised by the Austrian tax group parent are subject to recapture taxation at the time they are utilised by the tax group member in the source state, or in the moment the group member withdraws from the Austrian tax group. Under the recapture taxation scheme, the Austrian tax group has to increase its Austrian tax base by the amount of foreign tax losses used in prior periods (limited to the amount of tax losses actually utilised by the foreign tax group member).

For the purpose of the application of the recapture taxation scheme, a withdrawal from the tax group is also assumed if the foreign group member significantly reduces the size of its business (compared to the size of the business at the time the losses arose). Reduction of size is measured on the basis of business parameters such as turnover, assets, balance sheet totals and employees, while the importance of the respective criteria depends on the nature of the particular business.

Goodwill / badwill arising in the course of a share deal (acquisition of an active business company from a third party contractor) must be amortised/appreciated over 15 years provided that the acquired company is included in a tax group.

Write-downs of participations in tax group members are not tax deductible.

Transfer pricing
Under Austrian Tax Law there are no explicit transfer pricing regulations available defining in detail the local requirements with regards to arm's length, the documentation standards required, penalties, etc. However, Austria applies the OECD

transfer pricing guidelines referring to the OECD model tax convention. According to these guidelines, all business transactions between affiliated companies must be carried out under consideration of the arm's-length principle. Where a legal transaction is deemed not to correspond to arm's-length principles, the transaction price is adjusted for corporate income tax purposes. Such an adjustment constitutes either a constructive dividend or a capital contribution. Currently, there is the option of applying for a non-binding ruling at the tax authorities only.

In March 2010, a draft for a reform of the Austrian Corporate Income Tax Act was published, which covers the introduction of an advanced ruling mechanism. If this new regulation is implemented, binding information in the fields of transfer pricing, group taxation and mergers & acquisitions can be requested from the Austrian tax authorities against payment of an administrative fee (the fee rate depends on the size of the applicant's business).

Furthermore, a first draft of Austrian transfer pricing guidelines was recently issued by Austrian tax authorities, which is expected to enter into force within 2010 (the guidelines are still under review and were not disclosed to the public). The guidelines represent the Austrian authority's understanding of inter-company business relationships with regards to their arm's-length classification and will be based on the OECD transfer pricing guidelines.

Thin capitalisation rules

There are no explicit tax regulations available under Austrian tax law stipulating the minimum equity required by a company (thin capitalisation rules). Basically, group financing has to comply with general arm's-length requirements. Therefore, an Austrian group entity being financed by an affiliated entity must be able to document, that it would have been able to obtain funds from third party creditors under the same conditions as from an affiliated financing entity. Therefore, the appropriate ratio between an Austrian company's equity and debt will mainly depend on the individual situation of the company (profit expectations, market conditions, etc.) and its industry. Nonetheless, the fiscal authorities in administrative practice (no "safe-harbour" rule) tend to accept a debt-equity ratio of approximately 3:1-4:1. However, the debt-equity ratio accepted by tax authorities also strongly depends on the average ratio relevant for the respective industry sector. If an inter-company loan for tax purposes is not accepted as debt, it is reclassified into hidden equity and related interest payments into (non deductible) dividend distributions.

Furthermore, under Austrian commercial law (for companies subject to statutory audits) a minimum equity ratio of 8% is claimed. If the equity ratio of the company falls below 8% and its earning power (virtual period for debt redemption) at the same time does not meet certain requirements, a formal and public reorganisation process would have to be initiated.

Tax incentives

Research and development (R&D)

R&D costs are fully deductible at the time they accrue. An R&D tax bonus payment at 8% (R&D expenses x 8% = tax refund) or alternatively an allowance of 25% to 35% of qualifying R&D expenses (R&D expenses x 25% / 35% = tax allowance) can be claimed. Since 2005, the R&D tax bonus payment and allowance is also available in case of contract R&D, however, R&D incentives cannot be claimed by both principal

Austria

and agent. Also R&D expenses incurred at foreign EU/EEA-permanent establishments of Austrian companies qualify for the allowance or the tax bonus payment (however, it qualifies for the tax bonus payment only if the permanent establishment suffers a tax loss).

Employment
A tax bonus payment of 6% or alternatively an allowance of 20% can be claimed for expenditures in connection with the training of employees. These incentives can be claimed for external training expenditures and for in-house training expenditures, provided that there is a dedicated in-house training department (for in-house training expenditures the allowance only can be applied for).

A new premium scheme for apprenticeships started in June 2008. This premium is based on the amount of actual wage as set out in the applicable collective contract, and provides tax free subsidies, depending on the duration of the apprentice's employment.

Inward investment
For investment in certain regions, government grants and subsidies are available and are generally individually negotiated.

Withholding taxes (WHT)

The following table lists the countries with which Austria has signed a double taxation treaty (DTT) and provides details of the amount of Austrian withholding taxes.

Numbers of letters in parenthesis in the chart refer to footnotes with more explanation below the chart.

Recipient:	Dividends (1, 2) in %	Interest (3) in %	Royalties, licenses (4) in %
Resident corporations	0 / 25 (5)	0 / 25	0
Resident individuals	25 (6)	0 / 25	0
Non-resident individuals			
Non-treaty:			
Corporations and business enterprises	25	0	20
Individuals	25	0	20
Treaty:			
Albania (7)	15 / 5*	0	5
Algeria	15 / 5+	0	10
Argentina (8) (DTC was recalled by Argentina in 2008)			
Armenia	15 / 5+	0	5
Azerbaijan	5 / 10 / 15 (9)	0	5 / 10 (10)
Australia	15	0	10
Bahrain (11)			
Barbados (12)	15 / 5+	0	0
Belarus (White Russia)	15 / 5*	0	5
Belgium	15	0	0 / 10**

Recipient:	Dividends (1, 2) in %	Interest (3) in %	Royalties, licenses (4) in %
Belize	15 / 5*	0	0
Brazil	15	0	10 / 15 / 25 (13)
Bulgaria (14)	0	0	0
Canada	15 / 5+	0	10
China	10 / 7*	0	10 / 6 (15)
Croatia	15 / 0+	0	0
Cyprus	10	0	0
Czech Republic (16)	10 / 0+	0	5 (17)
Cuba	15 / 5*	0	5 / 0 (18)
Denmark (19)	15 / 0+	0	0
Egypt	10	0	0 / 20 films
Estonia	15 / 5*	0	10 / 5 (20)
Finland	10 / 0+	0	5
France	15 / 0+	0	0
Georgia	10 / 5+ / 0** (21)	0	0
Germany	15 / 5+	0	0
Greece (22)	15 / 5*	0	7
Hungary	10	0	0
India	10	0	10
Indonesia	15 / 10*	0	10
Iran	10 / 5*	0	5
Ireland	10	0	0 / 10**
Israel	25	0	10
Italy	15	0	0 / 10**
Japan	20 / 10**	0	10
Kazakhstan	15 / 5+	0	10
Kyrgyzstan	15 / 5*	0	10
Korea	15 / 5*	0	10 / 2 (23)
Kuwait	0	0	10
Latvia (24)	10 / 5*	0	10 / 5 (25)
Liechtenstein	15	0	10 / 5 (26)
Lithuania	15 / 5*	0	10 / 5 (27)
Luxembourg	15 / 5*	0	0 / 10**
Malaysia	10 / 5*	0	10 / 15 films
Malta	15	0	0 / 10 (28)
Macedonia (29)	15 / 0+	0	0
Mexico	10 / 5+	0	10
Moldova	15 / 5*	0	5
Mongolia	10 / 5+	0	5 / 10 (30)
Morocco (31)	10 / 5*	0	10
Netherlands	15 / 5*	0	0 / 10**
Nepal	15 / 10+ / 5*	0	15
New Zealand (32)	15	0	0

Austria

Recipient:	Dividends (1, 2) in %	Interest (3) in %	Royalties, licenses (4) in %
Norway	15 / 5*	0	0
Pakistan (33)	15 / 10+++	0	10
Philippines	25 / 10+	0	15
Poland	15 / 5+	0	5
Portugal	15	0	5 / 10 (34)
Romania	5 / 0*	0	3
Russia	15 / 5* (35)	0	
Russian Federation (36)	0	0	0
San Marino	15 / 0+	0	0
Saudi Arabia (37)	5	0	10
Singapore	10 / 0+	0	5
Slovakia (38)	10	0	5
Slovenia	15 / 5*	0	5
South Africa	15 / 5*	0	0
Spain	15 / 10**	0	5
Sweden	10 / 5*	0	0 / 10**
Switzerland	15 / 0+++ (39)	0	0
Thailand	25 / 10*	0	15
Tunisia	20 / 10*	0	10 / 15 films
Turkey (40)	15 / 5*	0	10
Ukraine	10 / 5+	0	5
United Kingdom	15 / 5*	0	0 / 10**
United Arab Emirates	0	0	0
USA	15 / 5+	0	0 / 10 films
Uzbekistan	15 / 5+	0	5
Venezuela (41)	15 / 5++	0	5
Vietnam (42)	15 / 10* / 5***	0	10 / 7.5 (43)

Notes

1. Dividends – Dividend distributions attributable to a prior release of paid-in surplus or other shareholder contributions (classified as capital reserves) are deemed to be a repayment of capital, i.e., no withholding tax is incurred. At the shareholder's level, dividends received and those classified as contribution refund will reduce the tax basis assessment for investments. To the extent to which the tax basis would become negative, such dividends are treated as taxable income (unless taxation is eliminated by a tax treaty). Regarding tax free dividend distributions *refer to chapter "Holding companies"* and *chapter "Exemption for domestic investments"*.
2. Under certain treaties the amount of the withholding tax is dependent on the extent of the proportion of issued share capital held by the recipient. Where this is the case, all rates are given. Those marked with + refer to an investment of 10%, ++ to 15%, those marked with +++ refer to an investment of 20%, those marked with * refer to an investment of 25%, those marked with ** refer to an investment of 50% and those marked with *** refer to an investment of 70 %.
3. Interest – Interest on cash deposits in EUR or foreign currency in bank accounts and fixed interest bearing securities in foreign currency (issued after 31 December 1988) and on fixed interest bearing securities denominated in Austrian Schillings or EUR (issued after 31 December 1983) are subject to a 25% withholding tax. If the recipient is an individual, this

withholding tax is final (no further income taxation and inheritance taxation). Companies receiving interest payments may obtain an exemption from withholding tax if they provide the bank or other custodial agent with a written confirmation from the recipient that such interest payments constitute a part of the recipient's operating revenues (exemption statement). Interest payments to non-residents without a permanent establishment in Austria are generally not subject to withholding taxation. At interest payments between affiliated companies the regulations stipulated by the EU interest directive have to be taken into consideration.

4. Royalties, etc. – In case of payments to countries marked with "***" the rate is nil unless more than 50% of the issued share capital of the company paying the royalties is held by the recipient, in which case the rate given applies. At royalty payments between affiliated companies the regulations stipulated by the EU interest directive have to be taken into consideration

5. If the recipient holds a participation of less than 25% in the distributing company, the dividends are subject to a 25% withholding tax. Since dividends distributed by an Austrian corporation to another Austrian corporation are generally not subject to taxation (see "Determination of income"), the withholding tax is credited against corporation income tax upon assessment of the recipient corporation for the respective tax year.

6. Withholding tax on dividends from Austrian companies is final, i.e., no further income tax is collected from the recipient (provided an individual).

7. The treaty was signed on 14 December 2007 and entered into force on 1 September 2008. It is applicable by the beginning of the fiscal year 2009.

8. The treaty was recalled by Argentina in 2009. Austrian tax citizens are protected by § 48 BAO against double taxation. Austria will try to enter into new negotiations with Argentina.

9. 5% for shares of at least 25% and worth at a minimum of USD 250,000, 10% for shares of at least 25% and worth at least USD 100,000, 15% in all other cases.

10. 5% for industrial licenses and know-how not more than three years old; 10% in all other cases.

11. The new treaty was signed on 2 July 2009 but has not entered into force yet. It will not be applicable before 2011.

12. The treaty entered into force on 1 April 2007 and will be applicable by the beginning of the fiscal year 2008.

13. 10% for copyright license fees in connection with literature, science and art; 25% for trademarks license fees; 15% in all other cases

14. The new treaty was signed on 12 February 2009 but has not entered into force yet. It will not be applicable before 2011.

15. Industrial, commercial or scientific equipment – 6%, 10% in all other cases.

16. The treaty was entered into force on 22 March 2007 and will be applicable by the beginning of the fiscal year 2008.

17. 5% for license income from copyrights, brands, plans, secret formulas or procedures, computer software, industrial, commercial or scientific use of equipment and information.

18. 0% for copyright royalties in connection with the production of literary, dramatic, musical or artistic work – 5% in all other cases.

19. The new treaty was signed on 25 May 2007 and entered into force on 27 March 2008. It is applicable by the beginning of the fiscal year 2009.

20. 5% for leasing of mobile goods and 10% for other licenses.

21. 0% for shares of at least 50% and worth at a minimum of EUR 2,000,000, 5% for shares of at least 10% and worth at least EUR 100,000, 10% for shares in all other cases.

22. The treaty entered into force on 1 April 2009 and is applicable by the beginning of the fiscal year 2010.

23. 2% for license income from industrial, commercial or scientific use and 10% for other licenses.

24. The treaty entered into force on 16 May 2007 and will be applicable by the beginning of the fiscal year of 2008.

25. For the use of commercial or scientific equipment – 10% in all other cases.

26. 5% in case of direct (or indirect over a patent-realisation-company) payments of royalties by companies of the other member state (with an industrial establishment in the other member state) and 10% for other licenses.

Austria

27. 5% in case of license income from industrial, commercial or scientific use and 10% for other licenses.
28. 0% for copyright license fees in connection with literature, art and scientific use and 10% for other licenses.
29. The treaty was signed on 7 September 2007 and entered into force on 20 January 2008. It is applicable by the beginning of the fiscal year 2008.
30. 10% for the right of use of copyrights to artistic, scientific or literary as well as cinematographic works and 5% for other licenses.
31. The new treaty was signed on 13 September 2006 and entered into force on 13 November 2006. It was applicable by the beginning of the fiscal year 2007.
32. The treaty was signed on 21 September 2006 and entered into force on 1 December 2007. It is applicable by the beginning of the fiscal year 2008.
33. The treaty entered into force on 1 June 2007 and will be applicable by the beginning of the fiscal year 2008.
34. For Portugal, the rate of withholding tax is 5%, but 10% if more than 50% of the issued share capital is owned by the recipient.
35. 5% if capital share amounts to at least 10% and worth at least USD 100,000. 15% in all other cases.
36. The treaty applies to Tajikistan and Turkmenistan. With Russia a new treaty has been ratified.
37. The treaty entered into force on 1 June 2007 and will be applicable by the beginning of the fiscal year 2008.
38. Until a new treaty will be established, the treaty with Czechoslovakia remains applicable.
39. For dividend distributions retroactive as of 1 January 2000.
40. The new treaty was signed on 28 March 2008 and entered into force on 1 October 2009. It is applicable by the beginning of the fiscal year 2010.
41. The treaty entered into force on 17 March 2007 and will be applicable by the beginning of the fiscal year of 2008.
42. The new treaty was signed on 2 June 2008 and entered into force on 1 January 2010. It is applicable by the beginning of the fiscal year 2011.
43. 7.5% on fees for technical services, 10% on royalties.

Tax administration

Tax returns
The standard tax assessment period in Austria is the calendar year. However, a company's financial year may deviate. When the tax and financial years deviate, the tax assessments for a year are based on the profits derived in the financial year(s) ending in the respective calendar year (e.g., if tax year 1 June 2009 – 31 May 2010: assessment FY 2010).

Tax return due dates
Generally, the CIT return has to be submitted electronically by June 30 of the calendar year following the year in which the fiscal year of the company ends. However, if the company submits the tax return via a certified tax advisor the tax return can be submitted by 31 March of the second following year at the latest, if the company will not be formally requested by the tax office to file it earlier.

Statute of limitation
The right to assess CIT is subject to a limitation period of five years after the end of the calendar year in which the fiscal year ends. Additionally, the limitation period can be extended for another year in case of certain interruptive events (e.g., tax audit, tax assessment) take place within the general limitation period. According to the Austrian tax law the maximum limitation period is 10 years.

Payment of tax

Corporate income tax is prepaid in quarterly instalments during the calendar year, with a final settlement subsequent to the annual assessment. Prepayments of corporate income tax generally are based on the most recently assessed tax year's tax burden (unless the taxpayer can show that its tax charge for the current year will be lower).

The difference between income tax or corporate income tax as per the final assessment and the prepayments made is interest bearing, from 1 October of the year subsequent to the year when the tax claim arose up to the date when the assessment is released (late payment interest). Interest at a rate of currently 2.38% is applied to underpayments (as well as overpayments) of tax.

Electronic filing of annual corporate income tax returns

The annual corporate income tax return (as well as the annual VAT return) has to be filed by electronic means. In the case of a company that reasonably be expected to file tax returns electronically due to the lack of technical prerequisites, filing of the tax return is allowed to be done via pre-printed forms.

Audit cycle

In general, companies are audited every three to four years. The audit period usually covers three to four fiscal years, so generally each fiscal year is audited.

Other issues

Choice of business entity

The most important types of companies in Austria are the limited liability corporation (GmbH), and the joint stock corporation (AG). Foreign investors generally choose the GmbH since it provides a higher degree of corporate law control and allows for lower equity provision.

As a legal entity the GmbH exists upon registration with the Companies' Register. The application for registration must contain the notarised signatures of all managing directors. The articles of association must be drawn up in the form of a notarial deed (written document executed by a public notary) and must as minimum requirements include the name of the company as well as its seat, the business purpose, the amount of registered capital and the capital contribution of each of the various owners.

A GmbH's minimum registered capital amount is EUR 35,000. Generally, one half of the registered capital must be raised in cash while the remainder may be contributed in the form of assets (contributions in kind). Of the original capital contributions to be paid in cash one fourth, however at least EUR 17,500 must actually be paid upon incorporation. Under certain conditions, the capital can be provided exclusively in the form of assets (incorporation in kind). The articles of association may provide for additional capital contributions payable by the owners on the basis of a resolution adopted by the shareholder meeting.

The minimum share capital of an AG is EUR 70,000. For an AG, the same payment regulations apply as for a GmbH. But the owners can agree upon a further capital contribution going beyond the nominal value of the shares (premium). The premium is shown on the company's balance sheet as a capital reserve.

Austria

Since 2004 the company type Societas Europaea (SE) can be chosen in Austria. The SE is a stock corporation based on community law. The advantages of this legal form are the simplification of organisational structures (in particular for international groups) and the possibility of cross-border transfers of corporation seats without loss of the legal identity. The SE allows the choice of a business location under an economic point of view as well as the choice of the most favourable legislation. The minimum share capital required for the incorporation of a SE is EUR 120,000 while the statutory seat of the corporation must be located in the same country where the place of management is located in.

Restructuring measures (M&A from a business perspective)

Transfers of assets and undertakings can be realised with retroactive effect and be tax neutral within the framework of the Austrian Reorganisation Tax Act.

The legislation administers the following areas (Article I-VI):

- Mergers (within EU also cross border) of corporations;
- Special conversion (from corporations to partnerships);
- Contribution of businesses and exchange of shares;
- Merger of partnerships;
- Demerger of partnerships; and
- Demerger of corporations.

If the reorganisation qualifies for the application of the Austrian Reorganisation Tax Act, the reorganisation steps are realised tax neutral. Existing tax loss carryforwards can be transferred under certain conditions as well. Furthermore, several other tax privileges are granted under the Reorganisation Tax Act for stamp duties, capital transfer tax, etc.

Corporate taxes in Azerbaijan

For more information, contact:

Movlan Pashayev
PricewaterhouseCoopers
The Landmark Office Plaza III
12th floor, 90A Nizami Street
Baku AZ1010, Azerbaijan
Tel: +994 12 497 25 15
Email: movlan.pashayev@az.pwc.com

Significant developments

Electronic value-added tax (VAT) invoices

Electronic VAT invoices (e-VAT) have been implemented, replacing hardcopy VAT invoices, effective as of 1 January 2010. E-VAT invoices are generated in the Ministry of Taxes' electronic tax filing system, which provides an automatic record of the issuance date. Unused hardcopies of VAT invoices should be destroyed after 1 January 2010.

The Law on the Special Economic Regime for Export-Oriented Oil and Gas Activities

The Law on the Special Economic Regime for Export-Oriented Oil and Gas Activities was implemented on April 2009 and will remain effective for 15 years. This law avails the following tax incentives to contractors and subcontractors (excluding foreign subcontractors without permanent establishment in Azerbaijan):

- Local companies are permitted to choose between the application of i) profit tax at a rate of 20%, or ii) 5% withholding tax on gross revenues.
- Foreign subcontractors are taxable only by a 5% withholding tax.
- A 0% VAT rate.
- Exemption from dividend tax and taxation on branch's net profits.
- Exemption from customs duties and taxes.
- Exemptions from property tax and land tax.

In order to enjoy these benefits, the relevant taxpayer should obtain a special confirmation certificate from the Ministry of Industry and Energy.

The Law on Special Economic Zones

The Law on Special Economic Zones (SEZ) became effective on 6 June 2009 and introduces the concept of SEZ. The companies operating in these zones will derive the following tax benefits:

- A 0.5% tax levied on profits from supplied goods, performed services or works;
- A 0% VAT rate; and
- Customs exemptions.

In order to operate from a SEZ, a special residency certificate is necessary. However, the following companies may not apply for this certificate:

- Parties producing or processing oil and gas;
- Parties producing alcoholic beverages and tobacco; or
- Television or radio broadcasting companies.

Azerbaijan

Exemptions for banks

From 1 January 2009 until 2012, Azerbaijani banks, insurance and re-insurance companies are exempt from corporate income tax (CIT) on the portion of their income directed to increase their charter capital.

Taxes on corporate income

According to the changes into the Tax Code (Code) in June 2009, effective as of 1 January 2010, the profit tax rate is reduced from 22% to 20%. Profit tax is imposed on domestic enterprises, as well as permanent establishments (PE) of non-residents.

The Code also stipulates payment of taxes based on a simplified system for enterprises not registered as VAT payers and whose annual gross revenue is less than AZN 150,000 starting from 1 January 2010, except for enterprises producing excisable goods, credit and insurance organisations and investment funds and professional participants in the securities market. The simplified tax is imposed on gross revenue at a rate of 4% in Baku and at a rate of 2% in other regions of Azerbaijan. A special rate of simplified tax is set for enterprises involved in residential construction at a fixed amount of AZN 10 per square metre plus an applied co-efficient, which is determined by regional executive authorities.

There are other tax regimes applicable under special agreements concluded between the Azerbaijan government and foreign oil companies: Production Sharing Agreements (PSA) and Host Government Agreements (HGA). The PSA and HGA regimes apply to all enterprises involved in these agreements, including foreign oil companies functioning as contractors and foreign service companies providing services to the contractor or the operating company.

As of 1 January 2010, there are 31 signed and ratified PSAs and two HGAs, each with its own separate tax regime. Each PSA and HGA contains a tax article that outlines the tax regime for that particular agreement. While there are several similarities with respect to tax terms in the various PSAs, there are some differences, other than merely differing tax rates (e.g., taxation of foreign subcontractors) or reporting requirements. Additionally, Tax protocols for each PSA and HGA, which provide specific guidance regarding the procedures for payment of taxes and filing of reports, are negotiated with the Ministry of Taxes and other executive authorities.

Corporate residence

A resident enterprise is any legal entity established in accordance with the legislation of the Azerbaijan Republic and performing entrepreneurial activity or any entity that is managed in Azerbaijan.

A PE of a foreign legal entity is also subject to taxation with respect to the income attributable to such PE. A PE is an establishment of a foreign legal entity, through which it fully or partially performs commercial activities (for these purposes, a PE may be considered a management unit, office bureau, agency, construction site, etc.) for more than 90 consecutive days within any 12-month period. Activities of auxiliary or preparatory nature (e.g., exclusively storing or exhibiting goods or products belonging to a non-resident, purchasing goods, or collecting data by a non-resident enterprise for its own purposes, etc.) do not create a PE.

Other taxes

Value-added tax (VAT)
VAT is levied on the supply of goods and services and on the import of goods.

Taxable persons
Any person who is, or is to be, registered as a VAT payer is regarded a taxable person.

Companies are required to register for VAT if their taxable income exceeds AZN 150,000 for the previous 12 months beginning from 1 January 2010 (previously, it was AZN 22,500 and three months respectively).

Taxable transactions
Supply of goods and services in Azerbaijan and imports into Azerbaijan are subject to VAT.

Taxable amount
The taxable base is established by starting with the value of the goods and services without adding the VAT amount, but including any customs duty and excise duty if applicable.

The value of taxable imports consists of the value of the goods determined in accordance with the customs legislation and taxes and duties (other than VAT) to be paid upon importation to Azerbaijan.

The amount of VAT to be paid is the difference between the amount of VAT received on taxable supplies of goods and services and VAT paid on the purchase of goods and services necessary to generate taxable supplies of goods and services.

The Cabinet of Ministers can grant exemptions for the import of goods and equipment used for production purposes or to provide advanced technology know-how. Such exemptions are granted for a specific period and in a specific area, and can only be granted if it is impossible to satisfy the respective needs from local resources.

Rates
The standard rate of VAT is 18%.

The zero rating applies to:

- Exportation of goods and services;
- Importation under the PSA and HGA regimes;
- Importation of goods, the supply of goods, and the implementation of works and provision of services to grant recipients on the expense of financial aid (grants) received from abroad;
- International and transit cargo and passenger transportation, as well as the supply of works and services directly connected with international and transit flights; and
- The supply of gold and other valuables to the National Bank of Azerbaijan.

Excise duty
Excise duties are paid by companies and organisations, including companies with foreign investment, as well as branches, divisions and other independent subdivisions of companies in Azerbaijan that render services and sell self-produced goods.

Azerbaijan

The following operations are subject to excise duties:

- Release of excise goods produced in Azerbaijan outside the premises of the building in which they were produced; and
- Import of excise goods pursuant to the customs legislation of Azerbaijan.

Excise duties are imposed on tobacco products and alcoholic beverages, light vehicles, leisure and sports yachts, petroleum and lubricants.

Property tax
Property tax is levied on both movable and immovable tangible assets owned by individuals and companies.

Taxable persons
Taxable persons comprise:

- Resident companies, including companies with foreign investment that are treated as residents under Azerbaijani law, international organisations engaged in economic activities, and other enterprises;
- Branches and affiliated companies of such taxpayers;
- Agencies and representative offices of foreign legal entities located in Azerbaijan; and
- Non-resident companies performing activities through a PE on the territory of Azerbaijan.

Enterprises can combine their assets and cooperate as joint owners. Joint owners are liable to pay tax according to their interest in the property concerned.

Tax base
The tax base varies according to the residency status of the taxpayer. Resident companies are subject to tax on their tangible assets recorded on their balance sheet. Non-resident companies carrying out a business activity through a PE in Azerbaijan are only subject to tax on their tangible assets connected with the PE.

The following assets are exempt:

- Facilities used for the purposes of the environment, fire protection and civil defence;
- Product lines, railways and motorways, communication and power lines, melioration and watering facilities;
- Automobile transport taxed for the road tax; and
- Facilities of companies involved in education, health, culture and sports that are used only for the purposes of such areas of activity.

Tax rates
The tax is imposed on the average annual book value of the taxable property at the rate of 1%.

Administration
Companies are required to report the average annual value of taxable property and pay tax on a quarterly basis, subject to any necessary recalculations at the end of the

year. Tax payments are due within 15 days of the second month of each quarter. The payment should be 20% of the previous year property tax amount.

The tax on water and air transport means is estimated on 1 January each year by the tax offices based on data provided by the organisations responsible for registration of means of transport. The tax is assessed on the person named in the registration document.

Where an asset changes ownership during the tax year, the tax liability is defined as the liability of the new owner.

Land tax

Land tax is levied on the land resources on the territory of Azerbaijan that are in the possession of or used by individuals or companies.

Taxable persons
Companies and individuals who own, hold or use land must pay land tax.

Taxable base
Land plants that are in ownership or used are subject to land tax. Exemptions apply to various types of land owned or used for public purposes by the state or other public authorities. The government may grant further tax exemptions and reliefs.

Tax rates
The rate of land tax for agricultural land is AZN 0.06 per unit. The units are determined by the relevant authority on the basis of the purpose, geographical location and the quality of agricultural land in the administrative regions.

The rate of land tax for industrial, construction, transport, telecommunications, trade and housing servicing and other dedicated land varies from AZN 2 to 10 per 100 m2, depending on the city or region.

Assessment and procedure of payment
Companies must compute the exact amount of the land tax each year on the basis of documents evidencing the title of ownership, possession and use. The computation must be submitted to the tax authorities by 15 May of each year. The tax must be paid by 15 August and 15 November in equal amounts.

Individuals receive each year before 1 July a calculation from the authorities for the tax amount due by them. The tax must be paid by 1 August.

Branch income

In addition to profit tax paid by a PE of a non-resident, the amounts transferred from the net profit of such PE to the non-resident is taxed at a rate of 10%.

Income determination

Profit tax is levied on an enterprise's taxable profits. Profits are defined as the difference between the gross income and deductions.

Azerbaijan

Inventory valuation
Inventory valuation is determined according to national accounting standards.

An inventory valuation method is not stipulated for tax purposes.

Capital gains
There is no separate capital gains taxation in Azerbaijan. Proceeds from the disposal of capital assets are included in the ordinary taxable income.

Inter-company dividends
Inter-company dividends distributed to residents and non-residents are taxable at payment of source. Therefore, the received dividend amounts of legal entities and physical persons are not taxable for profit (income) tax purposes.

Foreign income
Resident taxpayers must pay tax on worldwide income. A non-resident enterprise operating in Azerbaijan through a PE must pay tax on the gross income generated from Azerbaijan sources less any related deductions attributable to the PE.

According to the Tax Code, if a resident of Azerbaijan Republic directly or indirectly holds more than 20% of charter capital or possesses more than 20% of the voting shares of a foreign legal entity that, in turn, received income from a state with a favourable taxation, then such income of the resident shall be included in its taxable income.

A state with a favourable taxation is considered a country in which the tax rate is two or more times lower than that determined under the Tax Code of Azerbaijan Republic, or a country in which the laws on confidentiality of information about companies exist, which allow secrecy to be maintained concerning financial information, as well as the actual owner of property or income receiver.

Gross income of a non-resident enterprise generated from Azerbaijan sources and not connected with a PE will be taxed at the source of payment without any deductions allowed for expenses.

A non-resident enterprise generating income through the assignment of property not connected with a PE shall pay tax on the gross income received during a calendar year from Azerbaijan sources, after deducting expenses for the period that relates to such income.

Dividends
Dividends received from Azeri sources and previously taxed at the source of payment are not included in the taxable profits of the recipient.

Deductions

All expenses connected with generating income, except for non-deductible expenses and expenses with limited deductibility, are deductible from income.

Road, property, land and mining taxes are also deductible.

Non-deductible expenses
Non-deductible expenses are as follows:

- Capital expenses
- Expenses connected with noncommercial activity
- Entertainment and meal expenses, accommodation and other expenses of a social nature incurred for employees

Expenses deductible within certain limits
- Interest on loans received from overseas and/or from related parties may be deducted, limited to the interest rate on loans with similar currency and maturity at the interbank credit auction. In absence of such an auction, deductions for interest may not exceed rates of 125% of the interbank auction credit rates published by the National Bank of Azerbaijan Republic.
- The amount of repair expenses deductible each year is limited to the amount of the tax written down value of each category of fixed assets as of end of the previous year. For building and premises, the limit is 2%, for machinery and equipment the limit is 5%, and for other fixed assets the limit is 3%. An amount exceeding these limits shall be taken as an increase of the residual balance value of the fixed assets in the appropriate category.
- Actual business trip expenses are deductible from income within the standards established by the Cabinet of Ministers.
- A legal entity engaged in insurance activities is entitled to deduct allocations to reserve insurance funds within the standards established by the legislation of the Azerbaijan Republic.
- A taxpayer shall be entitled to a deduction for doubtful debts connected with goods, work and services that have been realised where income from them was previously included in the gross income received from entrepreneurial activity. Doubtful debt deduction shall be allowed only if the debt is written off as worthless in taxpayer's books. Banks and credit entities engaged in certain types of banking activities shall be entitled, dependent from classification of assets in order established under legislation, to deduct from income amounts assigned for establishment of special reserve funds in accordance with procedures established by the relevant executive authority.

Depreciation
Depreciation may be calculated at the following rates:

- Buildings and premises – up to 7%;
- Machines, equipment and calculation appliances – up to 25%;
- Means of transportation – up to 25%;
- Working cattle – up to 20%;
- Expenses incurred for geological and exploration works, as well as for preparatory works for the production of natural resources – 25%;
- Intangible assets with an undetermined period of use – up to 10%; for those with a determined period of use – pro-rata amount as per the useful life, in years; and
- Other fixed assets – up to 20%.

Net operating losses
Taxable losses incurred by legal entities may be carried forward for five years to offset future taxable profit, without limitations.

Azerbaijan

Foreign tax credit for residents

Azeri legal entities are taxed on worldwide profit; however, any tax paid overseas up to the tax amount that would be calculated under Azeri law will be allowed to offset the Azeri profits tax. The tax credit may not exceed the tax that would be imposed on such income in Azerbaijan. This credit applies only to residents of Azerbaijan.

Group taxation

Each taxpayer is liable to fulfil his own tax liabilities. Azeri Tax Legislation does not have the concept of "group taxation".

Tax incentives

The rate of profit tax levied on production enterprises, in which the number of employees belonging to public organisations of invalids includes a minimum of 50% of invalids, shall be reduced by 50%. In determining the right to such privileges, invalids substituting permanent employees or subcontractors (i.e., those without an employment contract) are not included into the average number of employees.

The Law on the Special Economic Regime for Export-Oriented Oil and Gas Activities

The Law on the Special Economic Regime for Export-Oriented Oil and Gas Activities was adopted in April 2009 and will remain effective for 15 years. This law avails the following tax incentives to contractors and subcontractors (excluding foreign subcontractors without permanent establishment in Azerbaijan):

*   Local companies are permitted to choose between i) profit tax at a rate of 20%, or ii) 5% withholding tax on gross revenues.
*   Foreign subcontractors are taxable only by a 5% withholding tax.
*   A 0% VAT rate.
*   Exemption from dividend tax and taxation on branch's net profits.
*   Exemption from customs duties and taxes.
*   Exemptions from property tax and land tax.

In order to derive these benefits, the relevant taxpayer should obtain a special confirmation certificate from the Ministry of Industry and Energy.

The Law on Special Economic Zones

The Law on Special Economic Zones (SEZ) became effective in June 2009. The companies operating in these zones shall have the following tax benefits:

*   A 0.5% tax levied on profits from supplied goods, performed services or works;
*   A 0% VAT rate; and
*   Customs exemptions.

In order to operate in a SEZ, a special residency certificate is necessary. However, the following companies may not apply for this certificate:

*   Parties producing or processing oil and gas;
*   Parties producing alcoholic beverages and tobacco; or
*   Television or radio broadcasting companies.

As of April 2010, no SEZ were established in Azerbaijan.

Withholding taxes (WHT)

Income received from Azerbaijan sources not attributable to a PE (base) of a non-resident in Azerbaijan is subject to withholding tax at the following rates:

- Dividends paid by resident enterprises – 10%;
- Interest paid by residents, PEs of non-residents, or on behalf of such PEs (except for interest paid to resident banks or to PEs of non-resident banks) – 10%;
- Rental fees for movable and immovable property and royalties –14%;
- Leasing, risk insurance or reinsurance payments – 4%;
- Telecommunications or international transport services – 6%; and
- Other Azeri source income – 10%.

If a resident enterprise or a PE of a non-resident receives interest, royalties or rental fees taxable at the source of payment in Azerbaijan, it is entitled to consider the tax deducted from the source of payment, providing the documents supporting the tax deduction are in place.

Tax administration

Returns
Resident enterprises and PEs of non-residents must file profit tax returns for a calendar year by 31 March of the following year. During liquidation of a legal entity or a PE of a non-resident, the tax return should be submitted within 30 days after the adoption of a decree on liquidation.

A non-resident that has no PE in Azerbaijan and receives income subject to withholding tax at the source of payment (except for dividends and interest) may file a tax return with respect to such income and expenses, connected with the generation of the income, for purposes of reassessment of profit tax at the rate of 20%.

If a taxpayer applies for an extension of time to file the profit tax return prior to the expiration of the filing deadline and at the same time settle the full tax amount due, the filing deadline may be prolonged for up to three months. The prolongation of the terms for filing the return will not modify the terms of tax payment.

Legal entities and entrepreneurs that withhold tax at the source of payment are obliged to file the withholding tax report with the tax authority within 20 days following the end of the quarter.

Tax payments
Taxpayers must make advance quarterly tax payments of profit tax by the fifteenth day of the month following the end of the calendar quarter. Payments are determined either (1) as 25% of tax for the past fiscal year or (2) by multiplying the amount of actual income through the quarter by a ratio of tax to gross income for the previous year.

Corporate taxes in Bahrain

For more information, contact:

Ebrahim Karolia
PricewaterhouseCoopers
9th Floor BMB Centre, PO Box 21144
Diplomatic Area
Manama, Kingdom of Bahrain
Tel: +973 17540 554 ext. 250
Email: ebrahim.karolia@bh.pwc.com

Significant developments

There have been no significant legislative or regulatory developments in Bahrain.

Taxes on corporate income

There are no taxes in Bahrain on income, sales, capital gains or estates, with the exception in limited circumstances to businesses (local and foreign) that operate in the oil and gas sector or derive profits from the extraction or refinement of fossil fuels (defined as hydrocarbons) in Bahrain. For such companies, a tax rate of 46% is levied on net profits for each tax accounting period. A company's accounting period should normally follow the (Gregorian) calendar year.

Corporate residence

The income tax law No. 22 of 1979 does not define residence. In the case of businesses operating in the oil and gas sector, profits from taxable activities in Bahrain are taxed in Bahrain irrespective of the residence of the taxpayer.

Other taxes

There are no other taxes on corporate income levied in Bahrain. However, companies are subject to stamp duties, customs duties, as well as a series of corporate registration fees, licence fees and certain municipal taxes (for example, on leases of property and registration of land title).

Branch income

Profit from branch income is taxable in Bahrain if it is derived from activities in the oil and gas sector.

Income determination

There are no specific rules with respect to the calculation of specific items of income, such as inventory valuation, capital gains, inter-company dividends, foreign income or stock dividends. However, the income tax law requires the taxable profits to be calculated using generally accepted accounting principles.

Deductions

The law generally allows deductions for all costs associated with taxable activities in Bahrain, such as the cost of production, refinement and other operational losses.

Depreciation and depletion
Tax deductions may be claimed with respect to reasonable amounts for depreciation, obsolescence, exhaustion and depletion incurred during the taxable year for properties used by the taxpayer in a trade or businesses from which income, taxable under the income tax law, is derived. Generally, such amounts may be claimed on a straight-line basis over the estimated remaining useful life of the properties, unless otherwise approved by the Minister of Finance.

Net operating losses
Unutilised losses may be carried forward and deducted up to an amount equivalent to the net income in future years as defined by the Bahrain income tax law. Carryback of losses is not permitted.

Payments to foreign affiliates
There are no specific restrictions in the income tax law pertaining to payments made to foreign affiliates.

Taxes
All taxes and duties not imposed by the Bahrain income tax law, including customs duties, may be deducted from the taxable income as stipulated in Bahrain's income tax law.

Other significant items
All reasonable and justifiable costs of production and exploration of products sold during the current taxable year are deductible for tax purposes, provided that these expenses have not been deducted elsewhere in calculating net taxable income.

Group taxation

There is no legislation or mechanism for group relief or the taxation of group activities in Bahrain.

Tax incentives

There are no tax incentives in Bahrain.

Withholding taxes (WHT)

There are no withholding taxes on the payment of dividends, interest or royalties.

Tax administration

Returns
An estimated income tax statement must be submitted on or before the fifteenth day of the third month of the taxable year. Where applicable, a taxpayer may also be required to file an amended estimated income tax statement quarterly, unless a final income tax statement has been provided.

Bahrain

Approved accountants must prepare a certified tax return for the return to be acceptable to the authorities.

Payment of tax

Taxes are payable in 12 equal monthly instalments. Payments are due starting the fifteenth day of the fourth month of the taxable year. Income tax as per the final/ amended income tax statement will form the basis of tax payments for the next 12 months, and any excess income tax paid will be credited and used in the first invoice following the establishment of the credit by the Minister.

Corporate taxes in Belarus

For more information, contact:

Kristina Krisciunaite
UAB PricewaterhouseCoopers
J. Jasinskio 16B
LT-01112 Vilnius
Lithuania
Tel: +370 5 239 2365
Email: kristina.krisciunaite@lt.pwc.com

Significant developments

As a result of major tax reform in 2009, the Tax Code of Belarus (Tax Code) has replaced all other tax laws, effective 1 January 2010. From the effective date forward, in order to establish a new tax or to change an existing tax, the Parliament will have to amend the Tax Code, except in cases when a new state tax is established by order or decree of the President of Belarus.

A new rule has been established for cases where there is uncertainty or ambiguity surrounding tax legislation for a taxpayer. In these situations, the tax authorities must resolve the issue in favour of the taxpayer.

Another significant development entitles a taxpayer to appeal any decision of the tax authorities related to the taxpayer's request concerning application or enforcement of the tax legislation, with regards to a certain tax issue, in court.

Several new amendments resulted from the tax reform effective 1 January 2010, which abolished the following taxes:

- 1% turnover tax (state);
- 3% vehicle acquisition tax (state);
- 5% retail sales tax (local); and
- Parking tax (local).

Certain modifications in tax rates and administering and filing procedures with regard to value-added tax (VAT) and corporate income tax (CIT) have been set by the Tax Code.

The standard VAT rate increased from 18% to 20% and is levied on supplies of goods, works and services in 2010. The requirement to maintain records of purchases in support of input VAT deductions was abolished. Taxpayers are no longer required to issue and maintain VAT invoices of mandatory form for work and services supplied. Certain taxpayers, whose total sales revenue does not exceed BYR 3,815 billion calculated on an accrual basis from the beginning of the year, may qualify for VAT filing and payment on a quarterly basis.

The timeframe for tax refund decisions, notifications and distributions from the tax authorities was adjusted. Tax authorities now have two days to make a determination of a refund (reduced from 10 days). Once the determination is made, a taxpayer must be notified of the offset of tax within five business days (reduced from 10 days). The

Belarus

tax refund from the budget after the offset is made should be received from the tax authorities within five business days (reduced from one month).

Contrary to VAT, a company may file and pay CIT on a quarterly basis, irrespective of the amount of sales revenue. A reduced 12% CIT is levied on dividends derived from local or foreign sources, and capital gains from disposal of shares or stocks in Belarusian entity.

A company is entitled to deduct for CIT any business related costs if supported by proper documents, except for certain costs specifically restricted by the Tax Code.

Restrictions on the deductibility of marketing and advertising expenses, and management and consultancy fees for CIT purposes were annulled as of 1 January 2010.

Significant changes in land tax were also introduced. In 2010, a company will have to calculate land tax in percentage to cadastral value of a land plot, rather than at a flat rate in BYR per hectares as it was calculated in 2009. Provided that average rate of 1% is levied on cadastral value of the land plots (related to production/manufacturing areas located in Minsk, the capital of Belarus), the amount of land tax charged may significantly increase in 2010.

Local authorities (Councils of Deputies) are entitled to change (increase or reduce, but not more than twice) the established rates of land tax and immovable property tax for certain taxpayers.

Pursuant to the e-filing initiative of the ministry of taxes all Belarusian taxpayers will benefit from electronic tax filing starting from 2011, which is not currently mandatory.

Taxes on corporate income

The standard corporate income tax (CIT), also known as profits tax, rate is 24%.

Exemptions
The following types of income are exempt from CIT:

1. "Target financing" received from the budget. The taxpayer is required to hold separate accounting records of income and expenses derived and incurred within "target financing".
2. Amounts payable to a shareholder, whether in cash or in kind, not in excess of its contribution to the statutory capital of a legal entity in case of:
   • Its liquidation;
   • A shareholder's withdrawal from a legal entity; or
   • If the shares are purchased by a legal entity from its shareholder.
3. Payments to a shareholder in the value of its shares or as a result of an increase in their nominal value made by the legal entity's sources, as long as such payments do not change the percentage of participation of either shareholder.
4. Goods (works, services), material rights and monetary means granted:
   • To the successors by a legal entity in case of its restructuring; and
   • As an inter-company transfer pursuant to corporate decision;

- To taxpayers engaged in crop production, animal husbandry, fish farming and beekeeping, provided that this income is spent for the appropriate activities; and
- As a foreign gratuitous help on conditions stipulated by the president.
5. Monetary means or assets received by a taxpayer from its shareholders as their contributions to the statutory capital, not in excess of amounts provided by the statutory documents.
6. Penalties paid by a taxpayer as a result of a violation of contract terms.
7. Fees associated with court cases (court related fees).

Local taxes
Area development tax
There is a local area development tax due on net profits.

The tax is paid by any legal entity, including foreign companies acting via a permanent establishment in Belarus, conducting business in the prescribed territory (city, region, and area).

The tax base for area development tax is the taxpayer's taxable profits minus the amount of CIT paid. The permitted rate for area development tax should not exceed 3%.

The tax is reported and paid on a quarterly basis, and is not deductible expenses for the purposes of CIT.

Corporate residence

A company is resident in Belarus if it is incorporated in Belarus. According to local legislation, a foreign company is deemed to have a permanent establishment (PE) in Belarus in cases where:

- It permanently carries out commercial activities in Belarus in whole or in part;
- It carries out its activities through a dependent agent;
- It uses a building site or construction, assembly or equipment objects; or
- It provides services or performs works within a period of 90 days continuously or in the aggregate during a calendar year.

Double taxation treaties (DTT) may establish different rules of PE recognition. According to domestic law, where there is a DTT, the provisions of the treaty shall prevail.

Notwithstanding the activities which create a PE in Belarus, a foreign company must be registered with the local tax authorities controlling the territory where activities are carried out, before starting a business in Belarus.

Any profits derived by a foreign company via a PE in Belarus are subject to 24% CIT and 3% area development tax. Expenses incurred by a foreign company either in Belarus or abroad that relate to a PE can be deducted subject to local deductibility restrictions.

Belarus

Other taxes

Value-added tax (VAT)

The standard VAT rate is 20%, whereas the preferential rate is 10%.

In general, local supplies of goods, works and services made by a taxpayer performing its economic activities in Belarus, as well as the importation of goods are subject to VAT.

Place of supply rules established by the Tax Code of Belarus should be followed to determine whether goods, works and services are supplied locally, and therefore, subject to tax in Belarus.

When a foreign company, which does not have a PE registered in Belarus, sells goods or provides works and services that are considered local supplies according to the place of supply rules, the VAT due on such supplies is paid by the purchaser registered with the local tax authorities from its own funds. This VAT could be deducted against output VAT, if any, or refunded from the budget in the established order.

Some exceptions apply to provision of construction and other similar works.

Exemptions with credit (zero-rated) include, but are not limited to:

- Supply of goods exported outside of Belarus;
- Provision of works and services involving maintenance, loading, reloading and any other similar works and services related to supply of exported goods;
- Transportation and any directly linked ancillary services related to the export or import of goods, including transit forwarding, as well as exported works for goods processing;
- Works and services related to the manufacturing of goods (excluding processing of imported goods) exported from Belarus to Russia; and
- Works and services related to repair (modernisation, conversion) of vehicles (including parts of vehicles) imported from Russia to Belarus for the mentioned purposes, with subsequent export of renovated vehicles.

In order to apply zero-rated VAT on goods carried out from Belarus, VAT payers must hold supporting documents as evidence that these goods were actually exported from Belarus to other state. Application of zero-rated VAT on respective works and services must be supported by the appropriate documents, which have to be provided to the local tax authorities where the taxpayer is registered for tax purposes.

Exemptions without credit include, but are not limited to:

- Disposal of shares in resident legal entities;
- Supply of material rights for industrial property objects (e.g., inventions, utility models, industrial designs, breeding achievements, integrated circuits, know-how, trade names, trademarks and service marks);
- Supply of securities, derivatives and other similar financial instruments, certain limitations apply;
- Fiduciary management services related to funds and assets owned by an individual or an entity, securities, derivatives and other similar financial instruments;

- Provision of all types of insurance and re-insurance (co-insurance) services rendered by insurance and re-insurance agents;
- Supply of medicines, medical equipment, instruments, medical products, as well as drugs, devices, equipment, veterinary products, under certain conditions;
- Personal or public health care services, under certain conditions;
- Social services supplied by institutions for children and young people care, nursing homes for the elderly and/or by care/guardianship institutions for disabled or by other non-profit entities;
- Supply of services in the field of culture and art, under certain conditions;
- Public services (services of barbers, baths and showers; laundry and dry cleaning services; watch repairing; manufacturing and repair of clothing and footwear; repair and maintenance of household appliances; repair of personal and household goods);
- Services provided by religious organisations, if these services correspond to the purposes set out in their canons, statutes and other documents;
- Funeral services, maintenance of the graves, tombstones, fences and other objects associated with burial, as well as works on their production, under certain conditions;
- Supply of postage stamps, postcards and envelopes marked, excise and control (identification) stamps for marking of goods at their nominal value, stamps which can be used as a confirmation of fees and charges payable in accordance with the legislation;
- Supplies of jewels as well as related services, under certain conditions;
- Retail trade of goods in duty-free shops, under certain conditions;
- Communication services rendered to individuals;
- Legal services supplied by certified lawyers;
- Research and development, design and technological works and services, under certain conditions;
- Education and training services;
- Lotteries and gambling, under certain conditions;
- Financial services supplied by the banks, under certain conditions; and
- Goods and equipment imported into Belarus, under certain conditions.

In order to apply exemptions, taxpayers should ensure that their services and goods supplied meet the appropriate VAT exemption requirements.

State dues

State dues are payable by legal entities that apply to the state institutions for the issuance of documents having legal force or other deeds, bring the cases before the courts for consideration, use bills of exchange in their activities, etc.

State dues include the following payments and duties:

- State fees (payable on suits, applications, appeals and other documents that are submitted to or claimed from the courts or prosecution authorities, payable on applications for state registration of a legal entity, notary public services, real estate registration services, etc.);
- Patent fees (payable for registration and use of intellectual property);
- Stamp fees (payable on activities with bills of exchange); and
- Consular fees (payable on the activities of state consular and diplomatic departments performed under the request of any applicant).

Belarus

Offshore charge

An offshore charge is levied upon the following activities of domestic entities:

- Any transfer of funds to an entity registered in an offshore jurisdiction (blacklisted territory) or to a third party who is a creditor of that entity, or to the bank account of a blacklisted territory;
- In kind performance of obligation to an offshore entity, with some exceptions; and
- Any transfer of material rights and obligations as a result of changes in commitment (cession or transfer of debt) between a domestic entity and an offshore entity.

Tax relief is granted to: (1) repayment of loans including interests on them, borrowed from entities located in blacklisted territories, (2) payments due under international marine cargoes and forwarding services and (3) payments for bank operations under certain conditions.

An offshore charge is paid at 15% rate and is deductible for CIT purposes.

Land tax

Belarusian and foreign entities are subject to land tax collected by the local tax authorities with respect to land that they own or use in Belarus.

Tax base depends on a plot location and purpose and is normally determined pursuant to cadastral value of a land plot.

Land for public roads and railways, as well as forest land, is exempt.

The tax is payable on an annual basis at the rates established by the Appendixes to the Tax Code of Belarus. Tax rates for agricultural plots vary from BYR 90 to BYR 24,402 per hectare. Tax rates on the land plots located in towns and rural areas range from 0.36% – 12% payable on the cadastral value.

Land tax is deductible, with some exceptions, for CIT purposes.

Real estate tax

Real estate tax is levied at the annual rate of 1% on the residual value of the following objects:

- Buildings, including separated premises, and constructions, late construction in progress (if construction works take longer than the deadline established in technical documentation), owned by legal entities; and
- Buildings and constructions, including houses, garden houses, villas, other kind of accommodation (e.g., apartments, rooms), farm buildings as well as construction in progress, located in the territory of Belarus, owned by individuals.

The tax base of buildings and constructions, located in the territory of Belarus and leased by individuals to legal entities, will be the contract value of the leased real estate not less than its value established by the evaluation. Evaluation is conducted in the manner approved by the President of Belarus.

When the real estate subject to taxation is located in Belarus and leased by a resident company to a lessee, the lessee is considered a real estate taxpayer provided that the leased real estate is accounted for in its balance sheet. The lessee is also obliged to pay the tax due on real estate leased from foreign companies that are not considered as having a PE in Belarus.

For objects located in Belarus such as trunk pipelines, oil pipelines, gas pipelines, stations, warehouses, plants and other objects related to the trunk pipelines, which are owned by a foreign company and leased to any legal entity, the tax is paid by the owner (i.e., by the foreign company).

Amount of tax, except the tax due on late construction in progress (if construction works take longer than the deadline established in technical documentation), is deductible for CIT purposes.

Excise taxes
Excise taxes are imposed on the following goods produced and sold in or imported to Belarus:

- Rectified ethyl alcohol and alcoholic drinks, including beer and wine;
- Alcohol-containing food products in the form of solutions, emulsions, suspensions, produced with the use of ethanol from all types of raw materials, other alcohol-containing products;
- Tobacco (excluding raw tobacco), including cigarettes, cigars, cigarillos and smoking tobacco;
- Energetic products, including petrol, kerosene, diesel and bio diesel, gasoline, fuel, marine fuel, oils for diesel engines and engines with a carburetor and an injector;
- Liquefied hydro carbonated gas and compressed natural gas used as motor fuel; and
- Vans and passenger cars, including those converted to cargo (HS codes 8702, 8703 and 8704).

The tax rate depends on the type and quantity of goods. Rates of excise taxes are stipulated by the Appendixes to the Tax Code of Belarus.

The Tax Code of Belarus provides a detailed procedure for calculation and inclusion of the excise tax into deductible expenses as well as into the accounting records of a taxpayer.

Excise taxes paid on the purchasing/importation of excisable goods to be used in manufacturing of goods or provision of works and services in Belarus are considered as deductible for CIT purposes, with certain exceptions.

Customs payments
The following charges are considered customs payments:

- Import duties;
- Export duties;
- Special anti-dumping and countervailing duties;
- VAT and excise taxes due upon importation of goods; and
- Fees for customs processing/services.

Rates of import duties as well as description of goods subject to them are established by the Belarus Customs Tariff.

Belarus

Export duties are not levied on exported goods, with the following exceptions: certain soft oil, light distillates; fuels and gasoline, wasted petroleum products, propane, butane, ethylene, propylene and other liquefied gases, petroleum coke, petroleum bitumen, benzol, toluene, xylenes, etc.

Import duties are temporarily not levied on importation of certain goods such as some food products, some textile fabrics, latex, certain chemical substances, coke and semi-coke of peat, whether or not agglomerated, retort carbon, soluble classes of wood pulp, high tenacity fibres made of nylon or other polyamides with certain exceptions, and some others.

Import and export duties are calculated on the customs value of the goods, which is defined pursuant to methods and procedures established by the Customs Code of Belarus. Generally, the following components are considered when calculating the customs value of imported goods:

- Contract price of the goods;
- Rebates and discounts provided by a supplier, under certain conditions;
- Transportation related expenses;
- Insurance premiums;
- Cost of containers and other package;
- Royalties or other similar fees; and
- Part of direct or indirect income to be derived by the seller from future resale, transfer or other use of imported goods.

Special, anti-dumping, and countervailing duties could be imposed as a measure to protect economic interests of Belarus.

Tax base for VAT calculation due on imported goods (further – import VAT) includes the total amount of customs value, import duty and excise tax paid, if any.

Generally, the taxpayer is required to pay customs duties before the customs clearance of the appropriate goods; however, under certain conditions, a taxpayer may be provided with an extension of payment deadlines or allowed to pay only part of customs duties. It is also possible to pay customs duties in advance.

Ecological (environmental) tax

The tax is imposed on pollutants discharged into the environment, storage and disposal of industrial wastes; production and (or) importation of plastic, glass containers, container-based paper and paperboard, other products that could generate waste or do harm to the environment after the loss of their consumer characteristics, importation of goods packed in plastic, glass bottles and containers from paper and paperboard with certain exceptions, oil refining, oil transportation via trunk pipelines, oil products in transit, etc.

The following are excluded from taxation, including but not limited to:

- Pollutants discharged into the air by mobile sources (cars, vehicles, etc.);
- Importation of plastic, glass containers, container-based paper and cardboard used for packing goods for export, if they are accounted separately; and
- Seizure of minerals from the subsoil during the construction of underground parts of buildings and other construction projects not related to mining.

The tax base of environmental tax is the actual quantity of respective pollutants used/discharged. Tax rates of environmental tax are stipulated by the Tax Code of Belarus.

Environmental tax paid, with certain exceptions, is treated as deductible for CIT purposes.

Tax on natural resources

This tax is payable on the actual value of extracted natural resources. It depends on the kind and quantity of extracted resources.

Tax rates are established by the Tax Code of Belarus and are applied on natural resources that have been extracted by a taxpayer within established limits. Natural resources extracted over established limits are taxed by a standard tax rate multiplied by 10.

Tax paid on resources extracted within established limits or if the limits are not established (for certain type of resources), is treated as deductible for CIT purposes.

Local taxes

Service tax

Taxpayers of service tax are all legal entities. Tax base is the taxpayer's income derived from the provision of respective services, excluding the amount of service tax.

Provision of the following services is subject to service tax:

- Markets, fairs, exhibitions;
- Hotels (campgrounds, motels);
- Restaurants (bars, cafes);
- Disco, billiards, bowling clubs, hairdressers (beauty salons), solarium, cosmetic services;
- Real estate, cellular mobile telecommunication, cable TV, maintenance and repair of vehicles for individuals; and
- Tourism.

The service tax rate should not exceed 5%. The tax is added to the price of services including VAT.

Tax on providers (suppliers)

The tax is levied on legal entities engaged in gathering/purchasing of wild plants (or parts thereof), mushrooms, and technical and medical raw materials of floral origin for their further industrial processing or resale.

Tax base is the cost of gathered items defined on the basis of procurement (purchasing) prices.

Tax rates do not exceed 5%. Tax on providers is treated as CIT deductible expenses.

Branch income

Foreign legal entities pay tax on profits attributable to a PE. A PE is broadly defined as "a branch, division, office, bureau, agency, or any other place through which a foreign legal entity regularly carries out its business activities in Belarus". Belarus' various DTT

Belarus

may define a PE differently, which could in some cases result in tax relief. Conducting business through an agent may also create a taxable PE in Belarus.

A PE's profits are computed on substantially the same basis as Belarusian legal entities, including the composition of tax deductible expenses. The Tax Code provides for the deductibility of expenses incurred abroad by a head office with respect to its PE in Belarus (including a reasonable allocation of administration costs).

To calculate a PE's taxable income, a foreign company is required to provide a tax authority with financial documents (i.e., accounting records, income statement, general ledger accounts, invoices, statements of services/works fulfilment, etc.) supporting the amount of revenue earned and expenses incurred. Generally, PE's taxable income is defined on revenue less costs basis. Documentary support of each revenue and/or costs item is required.

When it is not possible to calculate a profit attributable to a PE, this profit can be calculated by the Tax Authority using one of the following methods:

- A profit sharing method (i.e., gross foreign profit is allocated to PE by using one of the following coefficients related to a PE – working time costs, expenses incurred, services/works performed); or
- Benchmarking method (tax authority performs benchmarking study by collecting the respective ratios/indexes of other entities engaged in similar activities).

Head office expenses related to a PE are considered for calculation of taxable income in Belarus and require confirmation of an independent foreign auditor. Splitting of expenses is highly recommended in the audited financial statements of the parent company (head office).

If a foreign company is deemed to have a PE in Belarus, it will have to register with a local tax authority and declare related profit. Profit related to a PE will be taxed by CIT at a rate of 24% and 3% area development tax.

Foreign legal entities operating in Belarus through a PE are required to follow the filing and payment schedules established for Belarusian legal entities, although they shall submit CIT returns on a quarterly basis within established reporting deadlines and annual tax report by 15 April of the following year.

Foreign legal entity is allowed to operate in Belarus via its representative office or to set up a resident legal entity.

A representative office of a foreign company is defined as the structural subunit registered with the ministry of foreign affairs, which is entitled either to engage in commercial activities in Belarus or not, conclude contracts and undertake obligations according to the power of attorney issued to the management official of the branch by its head company (founder).

The representative office is not considered a legal person.

A representative office conducting commercial activities is taxed in the same manner as a PE or as a local resident company, with some exceptions.

A non-commercial representative office pays taxes due on its primary and auxiliary activities, such as real estate tax (with some exceptions), customs duties, input VAT, personal income tax, social security contributions due on employment of individuals, etc.

Income determination

Inventory valuation

Under domestic accounting legislation, stock used in the production and included in the cost of produced goods could be generally valued by the following methods:

- Cost of each unit;
- Average cost;
- Weighted-average cost;
- Last-in, first-out (LIFO); and
- First-in, first-out (FIFO).

The inventory valuation method must be established by the taxpayer's accounting policy and the same method is to be used for CIT purposes.

Capital gains

Capital gains from disposal of shares/stocks in a Belarusian entity are taxed as part of the taxpayer's profits and are subject to 12% CIT. No tax exemptions are provided by the Tax Code for the capital gains taxation.

Inter-company dividends

Dividends distributed by a resident company to another resident company are subject to 12% CIT, which is withheld by a paying company.

The Tax Code provides no exemptions for taxation of inter-company dividends.

Dividends distributed by a foreign entity represent non-operating income of a receiving Belarus entity and are subject to 12% CIT payable by the receiving entity in Belarus, irrespective of the fact that the foreign entity has paid the withholding tax (WHT) on dividends distributed.

Foreign income

If a Belarusian legal entity derives income subject to taxation abroad, the tax paid abroad may be deducted from the calculated CIT according to domestic legislation.

In accordance with the Tax Code, the amount deducted from CIT may not exceed that part of the tax calculated in Belarus that is attributed to the income received in a foreign jurisdiction. If there is a valid DTT with the country in question, the provisions of the treaty regarding avoidance of double taxation shall apply.

Deductions

Depreciation

Intangible and tangible assets may be depreciated using the directly proportional (straight-line) depreciation method, indirect disproportionate depreciation method, production depreciation method, or a declining-balance depreciation method. Depreciation may not exceed maximum rates established by the law.

Belarus

Net operating losses
Pursuant to local tax rules, net operating losses shall not be carried forward nor carried back. They must be fully recognised in the year incurred.

Taxes
Generally, the following taxes, dues and other compulsory charges to the budget are deductible for CIT purposes (including but not limited to):

- Excise taxes paid at purchasing/importation of excisable goods to be used in manufacturing of goods or provision of works and services in Belarus, with some exceptions;
- Environmental tax, with certain exceptions;
- Real estate tax, except the tax due on late construction in progress;
- Land tax, with some exceptions;
- Tax on natural resources, with some exceptions;
- State dues;
- Offshore charge;
- Tax on providers; and
- Payments for social and other mandatory security.

The following taxes shall not be deducted for CIT purposes:

- VAT paid, with certain exceptions;
- Corporate income tax; and
- Area development tax.

VAT can be treated as deductible for CIT purposes only if acquired goods, works or services are used for production or sale of goods, works or services that are VAT exempt.

Other significant items
Deductible expenses include all the usual costs that an entity actually incurs for the purpose of earning income or receiving economic benefit unless the Tax Code of Belarus or presidential regulations provide otherwise.

Limited deductible expenses are:

1. Depreciation or amortisation of fixed assets (for tax purposes assets cannot be depreciated faster than indicated in the relevant tax and accounting legislation);
2. Modernisation and reconstruction of fixed assets (the value of modernisation or reconstruction is included in the acquisition costs);
3. Business trips;
4. Representation;
5. Management fees payable to outsourcing companies, deductible with restrictions
6. Natural losses, with certain exceptions;
7. Cost of fuel and energy resources, deductible with restrictions established for certain entities;
8. Environmental tax and tax on natural resources, deductible with restrictions;
9. Bad debts, deductible only if proved and specific criteria are met;
10. Social insurance contributions and expenses for the benefit of employees, deductible with restrictions;
11. Membership fees, contributions and premiums, deductible with restrictions; and

12. Premiums on certain types of voluntary insurance, deductible with restrictions.

Non-deductible expenses:

1. Expenses on provision or acquisition of works and services not related to the taxpayer's business activities;
2. Construction, maintenance and other works, including all types of repair of assets that are not used for the purpose of earning income or receiving economic benefit;
3. Default interest (forfeit), fines and other sanctions paid to the state budget;
4. Certification related expenses (testing (analysis) of samples, if the results are negative);
5. Dividends paid and similar type of payments;
6. Contributions made to the authorised share capital;
7. Expenses incurred on purchase and/or creation of depreciable assets;
8. Depreciation for tangible and intangible assets not used in business, as well as for tangible assets that are not in operation;
9. Cost of assets or material rights transferred as advance or a pledge to a third party;
10. Expenses covered by reserves for future expenses created by a taxpayer in the prescribed manner;
11. Interest on overdue loans, as well as on loans related to the acquisition of tangible and intangible assets, other long-term assets; and
12. Other expenses, not related to the deriving of income and not attributed to operating activities of the entity as well as expenses that are not considered as allowable deductions under the Tax Code of Belarus.

Group taxation

Currently, group taxation legislation and regimes are not available in Belarus. Each Belarusian entity is regarded as a separate taxpayer and may not deduct tax losses of any other group entity. Belarus Tax Code does not allow the deduction of foreign losses from domestic taxable income, or domestic losses from foreign taxable income.

Tax incentives

Amounts not exceeding 5% of entity's gross profit granted to the health, education, social welfare, culture, sports state institutions, or spent for acquisition of goods, works or services for the benefit of the named institutions, are not taxed with CIT.

Entities employing disabled persons, if their number exceeds 50% of the average number of employees for the reporting period, are exempt from CIT due on taxable profit derived from production activity.

Profit of entities engaged in baby food production is exempt from CIT.

Profit derived by insurance companies from investments of insurance reserves under the contracts of voluntary life insurance is not taxable with CIT.

Entities engaged in manufacturing of prosthetic and orthopedic devices (including dental prostheses), provision of rehabilitation and disability services are exempt from CIT due on profit derived from sales of these items.

Belarus

Entities deriving profit from sales of plants (except for flowers, ornamental plants), livestock (except for farming), fish farming and beekeeping, provided the entities raise them, are not considered as taxpayers of CIT.

Profit from the services provided by hotels located at tourist sites established by the President of Belarus is exempt from CIT for three years starting from the commencement of its activities, with certain exceptions.

Profit derived by motels, hotels, campgrounds, maintenance stations, objects of trade and catering, cleaning, located on the roadsides of national highways is not taxable with CIT for five years starting from the day when the permission for such activities was received.

The profit is excluded from CIT if it is spent for financing of capital investments for production purposes (capital investments tax incentive) as well as for the repayment of bank loans received and used for this purpose. Capital investments are defined as any purchase of fixed assets or construction in progress, any capital construction in the form of new construction and (or) creation of fixed assets, reconstruction and modernisation of fixed assets or construction in progress. This tax relief is provided if a taxpayer meets certain established requirements.

Entities engaged in production of laser-optical equipment, accounting for at least 50% of the entity's total production, can benefit from a reduced CIT rate of 10% (whereas standard CIT rate is 24%), under certain conditions.

Entities that are members of the Scientific and Technological Association established by Belarusian State University, in accordance with legislation are entitled to apply 5% CIT rate on their profit derived from sales of IT and provision of IT development services.

High-technology producers included in the special list approved by the President of Belarus are taxed at 12% CIT with regard to the profit derived from sales of their own high-tech goods, works and services, under certain conditions.

Entities, which are registered in Belarusian Free Economic Zones, are exempt from CIT in relation to goods, works and services of their own production for five years starting from the date when the profits were declared. After expiration of this term, the CIT rate is 12%.

Moreover, residents of Free Economic Zones are granted, under certain conditions, a partial VAT relief, and a relief for a real estate tax on buildings and constructions located in Free Economic Zone.

Withholding taxes (WHT)

Domestic legislation
The following income of a foreign entity in Belarus not derived through a PE is deemed to be Belarusian-source income:

- Freight charges, (including demurrage) and freight-forwarding services (excluding freight charges for the marine transportation and forwarding services) – 6%;
- Interest on any type of debt obligations including securities – 10%;
- Royalties – 15%;

- Dividends and other similar income – 12%;
- Penalties, fines and other sanctions received for breach of contractual liabilities – 15%;
- Income derived from sports, entertainment activities or performers' activities – 15%;
- Income derived from innovative, design, research and development activities, design of technological documentation engineering design and other similar works and services – 15%;
- Income from provision of guarantees – 15%;
- Income from provision of disk space and/or communication channel for placing information on the server and services for its maintenance – 15%;
- Proceeds from the sale, transfer (with title) or lease of immovable property located in Belarus – 15%;
- Income derived by a foreign entity from the sale of an enterprise as a complex of assets located in Belarus – 15%;
- Capital gains (income from the sale of shares/stocks) in local companies – 12%;
- Income from the sale of securities (except shares) – 15%; and
- Income derived from provision of works and services – 15%.

In calculation of WHT due on certain types of income a taxpayer is permitted to deduct related expenses following the rules specified by the Tax Code.

Generally, the tax is withheld and paid to the budget by a local entity, an individual entrepreneur, a branch or a PE of a foreign company. When certain types of Belarusian-source income is received (capital gains, sale, transfer of title of ownership or lease of immovable property, provision of licenses for software and other copyright objects, etc.), a WHT shall be paid directly by a foreign entity.

Currently Belarus has approximately 60 DTT with foreign countries. Where a treaty for the avoidance of double taxation with the country in question contradicts the local tax regulations, the treaty provisions prevail.

Reduction of or an exemption from withholding taxes under a DTT may be obtained if a special residence certificate is completed and provided to the tax authorities before the payment is made.

If the payment that is covered by the DTT has already been made and WHT at the local rate was withheld, it is possible to obtain an appropriate refund (reduction) by completing a special claim for a refund. The claim for a refund must be filed with additional documents, such as a residence certificate, copies of the contract and other documents related to the payment.

Dividends, interest, royalties
Currently, foreign entities are subject to WHT on loan interest paid by Belarusian companies and PEs of foreign companies at a rate of 10%. WHT is not applied on:

- Interests on loans to domestic entities when these loans are made from accumulated profits on securities/shares issued by a foreign entity; and
- Interest on loans under syndicated loan agreements.

Belarusian WHT rate on royalties paid to a foreign entity is 15%. Dividends paid are subject to WHT at the rate of 12%.

Belarus

DTT include provisions for reduction of withholding taxes on dividends, interest and royalties.

Offshore companies

A blacklisted territory is a territory which is included in the list of offshore territories established by the president, has a preferential tax treatment and/or does not disclose of the information related to financial transactions made by resident entities.

A list of 52 offshore territories has been published. With certain exceptions specified in the law, all payments to offshore companies or their branches for any kind of work or services, commodities, interest on loans, insurance premiums, guarantees, etc. are subject to offshore charge, which is deductible for CIT purposes.

Special tax treatments

Belarus Tax Code provides special tax treatments, which are applicable to a certain taxpayer depending on its location, amount of revenue and individuals employed, types of business, etc. Special tax treatments include but not limited to:

- Simplified taxation;
- Tax on farmers and other producers of agricultural products;
- Tax on gambling business;
- Tax on lotteries;
- Tax on electronic interactive games; and
- Free economic zones.

In case where activities fulfil the criteria of a special tax treatment, the taxpayer is not permitted to use the general taxation regime with regard to income deriving from those activities, with certain exceptions. Concerning simplified taxation and tax on farmers, the taxpayer is entitled to determine whether to apply such treatment or not.

Tax administration

Returns

Corporate income tax

Whether a company has taxable income or not, the CIT return shall be submitted on a monthly or quarterly basis, depending on the reporting period applied by the taxpayer, by the twentieth day of the month following the reporting period.

PEs of foreign companies shall submit tax returns on a quarterly basis within established reporting deadlines and an annual tax report by the fifteenth of April of the following year. Annual CIT return must be audited by a local certified auditor.

CIT withheld on inter-company dividends must be reported by a tax withholding entity no later than the twentieth day of the month following the month in which the dividends were accrued.

WHT on payments other than inter-company dividends

A tax-withholding entity must submit a WHT return to the tax authorities no later than the twentieth day of a month following the month when the payment was made.

VAT
VAT return shall be submitted on a monthly basis, by the twentieth day of the month following the reporting period.

Offshore charge
The tax is reported on a monthly basis, no later than the twentieth day of the month following the reporting period.

Land tax
The tax is reported annually, no later than 20 February of the next reporting year.

Immovable property tax
Tax reporting obligation must be fulfilled by a taxpayer before 20 January of the reporting year.

Excise taxes
The tax is reported on a monthly basis, no later than the twentieth day of the month following the reporting period.

Customs payments
Customs payments are calculated in customs declarations (i.e., no special customs return).

Ecological (environmental) tax
The tax is reported and paid on a quarterly basis. Certain exemptions are provided to legal entities effecting tax payments on the basis of established annual limits. These taxpayers will have to fill an annual tax return and provide it to a tax authority no later than 20 April of the calendar year.

Tax on natural resources
The tax is reported and paid on a quarterly basis. Those taxpayers, who calculate the tax on the basis of annual limits for extraction, fulfil tax reporting and payment liability on an annual basis.

Service tax
The tax is reported and paid on a quarterly basis.

Tax on providers (suppliers)
The tax is reported and paid on a quarterly basis.

Payment of tax
Corporate income tax
CIT must be paid before the twenty-second day of a month following the reporting period.

PEs of foreign entities are subject to quarterly tax payments due no later than the twenty-second day of the month following the reporting period (quarter). Furthermore, the remaining CIT, if any, shall be paid within 10 days after the date established for filing the annual tax return (i.e., no later than 25 April).

CIT on inter-company dividends shall be paid no later than the twenty-second day of a month following the month when dividends were paid.

Belarus

WHT on payments other than inter-company dividends
WHT is to be calculated, withheld and paid by a Belarusian company or a PE of a foreign company no later than the twenty-second day of a month following the month when the payment was made.

VAT
VAT shall be paid on a monthly basis, no later than the twenty-second day of the following month.

Offshore charge
The tax is paid on a monthly basis, no later than the twentieth day of the month following the reporting period.

Land tax
Generally, the tax is paid quarterly by equal parts, before the twenty-second of the second month of each quarter. Concerning payment terms for land tax due on agricultural plots, some exceptions can be applied.

Immovable property tax
The tax is paid on a quarterly basis by equal parts, no later than the twenty-second day of a first month of each quarter.

Excise taxes
The tax is paid on a monthly basis, no later than the twentieth day of the month following the reporting period.

Customs payments
Generally, customs payments are made before customs clearance. Payments in advance are also possible. A taxpayer may be provided with a payment extension or qualify for payment in instalments, if certain conditions are met.

Corporate taxes in Belgium

For more information, contact:

Frank Dierckx
PricewaterhouseCoopers
Woluwe Garden
Woluwedal 18
B-1932 Sint-Stevens-Woluwe
Belgium
Tel: +32 2 710 43 24
Email: frank.dierckx@be.pwc.com

Significant developments

Dividends-received deduction (DRD)

Belgian tax-resident companies (or Belgian branches) can deduct 95% of dividends received from qualifying holdings from their net taxable income. The previous conditions were that the company (or branch) had to have held or committed to maintaining a shareholding of at least 10% or having a minimum acquisition value of EUR 1,200,000 in the subsidiary for at least one year. Credit institutions, insurance companies and broker-dealer companies did not have to meet this condition. As of 1 January 2010, the minimum acquisition value has been raised from EUR 1,200,000 to EUR 2,500,000.

In addition, the exemption provided for credit institutions, insurance companies and broker-dealers companies has been abolished. As from tax year 2010, the minimum threshold requirement also applies to these companies.

Under Belgian tax law, any "excess" DRD in a given tax year (i.e., that could not be used in the year in which it arose due to a lack of net taxable income) could in principle not be carried forward, and thus was forfeited. Pursuant to judgments against Belgium by the European Court of Justice (ECJ) for breach of the EU Parent-Subsidiary directive, the Belgian tax administration issued two practice notes in June and October 2009 in which it acknowledged that excess DRD for European Economic Area (EEA) dividends and certain non-EEA dividends (subject to conditions) can be carried forward to future tax years.

Any unused portion of the DRD from dividends received from an EEA subsidiary or a subsidiary from a country with which Belgium has concluded a double tax treaty with a non-discrimination clause on dividends can be carried forward to future tax years. The possibility of carrying forward the unused portion of DRD from qualifying non-EEA dividends has not been codified, but should continue to apply based on the October 2009 practice note. The same is also true for dividends from Belgian subsidiaries.

Payments made to tax havens

Starting 1 January 2010, companies subject to Belgian corporate income tax or Belgian non-resident corporate income tax that make direct or indirect payments to recipients established in tax havens are obliged to declare them, if they exceed EUR 100,000 during the tax year. The reporting has to be made on a special form to be attached to the (non-resident) corporate tax return.

Belgium

A tax haven is defined as: (i) a jurisdiction regarded by the OECD as not being cooperative concerning transparency and international exchange of information or (ii) a jurisdiction where the nominal corporate tax rate is less than 10%. A royal decree containing the list of countries where the nominal corporate tax rate is lower than 10% is published. The countries which are mentioned in the royal decree are the following:

Abu Dhabi / Ajman / Andorra / Anguilla / the Bahamas / Bahrain / Bermuda / British Virgin Islands / Cayman Islands / Dubai / Fujairah / Guernsey / Jersey / Jethou / Maldives Islands / Isle of Man / Micronesia (Federation of) / Moldavia / Monaco / Montenegro / Nauru / Palau / Ras el Khaimah / Saint-Barthelemy / Sark / Sharjah / Turks and Caicos Islands / Umm al Qaiwain / Vanuatu / Wallis-and-Futuna

In the event of non-reporting, the payments will be disallowed for corporate income tax purposes. Where the payments have been reported duly and timely, their tax deductibility will be subject to the ability of the taxpayer to prove that (i) said payments were made as part of genuine, proper transactions and (ii) they were not made to an entity under an artificial construction.

Notional interest deduction (NID)
Belgian companies (and Belgian branches) can claim tax relief for their cost of capital by deducting notional (deemed) interest, which is calculated on their adjusted accounting net equity. The NID rate for a given tax year is based on the 10-year government bond interest rate of the calendar year, two years prior to the tax year (e.g., for tax year 2011 reference is made to 2009 government bonds).

For budgetary reasons, the NID rate for tax years 2011 and 2012 (i.e., financial years ending between 31 December 2010 (included) and 30 December 2011 (included)) has been capped at 3.8% (4.3% for SMEs).

A provision has been included in Belgium's non-resident (corporate) tax rules for the tax credit for research and development and NID to be transferable to an acquiring company in the case of a tax-exempt reorganisation, as if a reorganisation had not taken place. A similar provision already has been included in the resident (corporate) tax rules. It applies on and after 12 January 2009.

Automobile costs
Rules related to the tax deductibility of automobile costs in the hands of Belgian companies (and Belgian branches) recently have been changed to introduce a system where the deductibility rate varies in a range between 50% and 120% of the automobile costs, depending on the CO_2 emission of the automobile. Prior to 1 January 2010, the deductibility ranged from 60% to 90%.

Moreover, after 1 January 2010, the deduction for fuel costs has been limited to 75%.

Finally, the rules for determining the benefit in-kind arising from the private use of company automobiles are also amended. Prior to 1 January 2010, the benefit in-kind was calculated on the basis of a fixed number of privately-driven kilometres (in principle 5,000 or 7,500), multiplied by a coefficient related to the fiscal horsepower of the automobile. From 1 January 2010, this is determined on the basis of a coefficient related to the CO_2 emission of the automobile.

Research and development (R&D) incentives

As of 1 July 2009, 75% of the payroll tax withheld from wages of qualifying researchers by a Belgian company or establishment does not need to be remitted to the Belgian Tax Revenue provided that the researchers are employed in research and development programmes and have a qualifying degree (such as a degree in (applied) sciences, veterinary medicines, bio-technology, etc.). For the employee's personal tax liability, the Belgian Tax Revenue considers that the payroll withholding tax amount entirely was withheld.

Taxes on corporate income

The corporate tax is levied at a rate of 33% plus a crisis tax, which is a 3% surtax, for an effective rate of 33.99%.

Reduced rates

A progressive scale of reduced rates applies to taxpayers with lower amounts of taxable income. If the taxable income is lower than EUR 322,500, the following scales apply (including the 3% crisis tax):

	%
EUR 0 up to EUR 25,000	24.98
EUR 25,001 up to EUR 90,000	31.93
EUR 90,0501 up to EUR 322,500	35.53

Even if their taxable income does not exceed the aforesaid ceilings, certain companies are excluded from the reduced rate, and thus, always subject to the basic corporate income tax rate. These companies include:

1. Finance companies which are defined as companies that own participations whose investment value exceeds, at the closure date of the annual accounts, 50% of the paid-up capital, possibly revalued, or 50% of the paid-up capital plus taxable reserves and recorded (taxable or tax free) capital gains of the companies that want to benefit from the reduced rates. Participations that exceed 75% of the paid-up capital of the companies held are not taken into account for the purpose of this computation;
2. 50% or more subsidiaries;
3. Companies that distribute dividends exceeding 13% of their paid-up capital at the beginning of the taxable period;
4. Companies that, per taxable period, do not attribute a tax deductible remuneration of at least EUR 36,000 to at least one key individual (known as dirigeant d'entreprise/bedrijfsleider);
5. Companies belonging to a group that also holds a coordination centre. (Note that the status of coordination centre (whereby companies and permanent establishments could benefit from a special (low) tax regime) expires on 31 December 2010 at the latest); and
6. Collective investment companies (e.g., BEVEK (Beleggingsvennootschap met veranderlijk kapitaal)/SICAV (Société d'investissment à capital variable), BEVAK (Beleggingsvennootschap met vast kapitaal)/SICAF (Société d'investissmenet à capital fixe), VBS (Vennootschap voor belegging in schuldvorderingen/SIC (Société

Belgium

d'investissment en créances)), organisations for financing pensions and recognised coordination centres).

Surcharge

A surcharge is due on the final corporate tax amount upon assessment. For tax year 2011 (financial year as per 31 December 2010), this surcharge equals to 2.25%. However, such surcharge can be avoided if sufficient advance tax payments are timely made. The advance tax payments can be made in quarterly instalments. In the situation where the company's financial year ends on 31 December 2010, the due dates for the advance tax payments are 12 April 2010, 12 July 2010, 11 October 2010 and 20 December 2010. Advance tax payments give rise to a tax credit. The tax credit amounts to 3%, 2.25%, 2%, or 1.5% of the advance tax payment made, depending on whether such payment has been made respectively in the first, second, third or fourth quarter (percentages applicable for tax year 2011). If the total amount of credits exceeds the surcharge, no surcharge is due, but the excess is not further taken into account for the final tax computation. The taxpayer can choose to either have the excess reimbursed by the tax authorities as the excess can be used as an advance tax payment for the next year.

Secret commissions tax

A special assessment of 309% (300% plus 3% crisis tax) is applicable to the so-called "secret commissions," that is, any expense of which the beneficiary is not identified properly by means of proper forms timely filed with the Belgian tax authorities. These expenses consist of:

- Commission, brokerage, trade or other rebates, occasional or non-occasional fees, bonuses or benefits in kind forming professional income for the beneficiaries;
- Remuneration or similar indemnities paid to personnel members or former personnel members of the paying company; and/or
- Lump-sum allowances granted to personnel members in order to cover costs proper to the paying company.

The secret commissions tax is not applicable if the payor demonstrates that the payments have been reported in the beneficiary's Belgian tax return. The 309% rate also is applicable to hidden profits that are not part of the property of the company, with the exception for certain specific hidden reserves. The special assessment of 309% and the expenses themselves are, however, fully deductible for corporate income tax purposes.

Belgian ruling practice

Belgium has a long tradition of providing formal and informal rulings. Currently, a taxpayer may request an advance tax ruling on a wide range of subjects including but not limited to: corporate tax, individual tax, non-resident income tax, legal entity income tax, VAT, customs, and registration duties. The request should cover a "specific and concrete" operation, which effectively is envisaged to be realised in a foreseeable future. The ruling should be filed before the transaction takes place. In practice the ruling decision should be granted prior to the filing of the corporate tax return of the year of the transaction. A ruling is binding upon the Belgian tax authorities for five years. Delivery of a requested ruling takes, on average, three months.

The Ruling Office is autonomous from the Belgian tax authorities and has the legal authority to issue decisions, which are binding upon the Belgian tax authorities. The

Ruling Office increasingly has adopted a constructive approach towards the taxpayer and is seen in the Belgian tax practice as a powerful insurance instrument ascertaining the Belgian tax treatment of contemplated operations.

Corporate residence

A company that is not excluded from the scope of Belgian corporate income tax is, in principle, considered to be a resident of Belgium for tax purposes if it has its registered office, its principal place of business, or its seat of management in Belgium. The seat of management has been defined by Belgian case law as the place from where directing impulsions emanate or the place where the company's effective management and central administration abide, meaning the place where the corporate decision-making process actually takes place.

Other taxes

Value-added tax (VAT)
Scope of VAT
The following transactions are subject to VAT in Belgium:

a. The supply of goods effected for consideration by a taxable person acting as such;
b. The supply of services effected for consideration by a taxable person acting as such;
c. The importation of goods; and
d. Intra-Community supply of goods for consideration by a taxable person acting as such or by a non-taxable legal person.

Standard and other rates and their application to goods and services
The standard rate is 21%. It applies to all goods and services not qualifying for one of the reduced VAT rates.

12% for supplies of goods and services including, but not limited to:

a. Restaurant and catering services, excluding beverages;
b. Phytopharmaceutical products;
c. Pay television;
d. (Inner) tubes; and
e. Certain combustible material.

6% for supplies of goods and services including, but not limited to:

a. Works on immovable property (limited in time and with strict conditions);
b. Basic necessities such as food and pharmaceuticals;
c. Some printed materials;
d. Transport services of persons;
e. Hotels and camping; and
f. Admission to cultural, sporting and entertainment venues.

Exempt with credit ('zero-rated') for supplies of goods and services including, but not limited to:

a. Exports and certain related services;
b. Intra-Community supplies of goods;

Belgium

c.   Certain transactions on goods placed in a Customs or VAT warehouse cross-border passenger transportation by ship or aircraft;
d.   Supplies to diplomats and international organisations; and
e.   Certain supplies of goods and services to certain vessels and aircraft mainly involved in international passenger transport.

Exempt without credit for supplies of goods and services such as:

a.   Healthcare services;
b.   Social services;
c.   Education services;
d.   Sport services;
e.   Cultural services;
f.   Services of lawyers and notaries;
g.   Banking services;
h.   Interest charges;
i.   Financial services;
j.   Insurance services;
k.   Land and real estate sales; and
l.   Property leasing and letting.

It should be noted that specific conditions may apply to the above two categories.

VAT grouping
VAT grouping came into effect in Belgium on 1 April 2007. Under a VAT group, independent legal persons are treated as one single taxable person for VAT purposes if they are closely linked financially, economically, and organisationally. Hence, for VAT purposes, all supplies of goods and services to or by the group members are deemed to be made to or by the group itself.

The application of a VAT group has, amongst other, the following consequences:

*   No issuance of "inter-company" invoices between companies in the VAT group;
*   No charging of VAT between companies in the VAT group;
*   Filing of one VAT return for all companies in the VAT group;
*   No risks of incorrect VAT treatment of transactions between companies in the VAT group; and
*   No cascade of the limitation of the right to deduct VAT when charging costs to companies in the VAT group.

The biggest advantages for entering into a VAT group are in our view the cost saving further to administrative simplification, the elimination of the risk of an incorrect VAT treatment for intra-group transactions and potential cash flow benefits.

Registration duties
Purchases and transfers of real estate located in Belgium, including buildings (except new buildings, which are subject to VAT as described above), are subject to registration duties at the rate of 12.5% on the higher of transfer price or fair market value (except in the Flemish Region, where the applicable rate is 10%). Note that the registration duties on the sale of real estate can be lowered to 1%-2% in a so called split sale of the real estate, whereby, the long-lease right is transferred to a special purpose vehicle (SPV) and the bare ownership is transferred to another SPV. However, a ruling is recommended (specific conditions apply).

No registration duty is due upon a capital contribution; only a fixed fee of EUR 25 is due. However, the contribution (in property or usufruct, which is the right to use or benefit from property) to a Belgian or foreign company by a natural person of real estate located in Belgium that wholly or partially is used as a dwelling is subject to a registration duty of 12.5% (10% in the Flemish Region).

Stamp duties

Stamp duties are due on transactions relating to public funds that are concluded or executed in Belgium, irrespective of their (Belgian or foreign) origin, to the extent that a professional intermediary intervenes in these transactions. Exemptions for non-residents and others are available.

Branch income

Branch profits are subject to the basic tax rate for Belgian corporations of 33.99% (including the 3% crisis tax) plus the possible surcharge for absence/insufficiency of advance payments *(see "Taxes on corporate income")*. Transfers of branch profits to the head office abroad do not give rise to further taxation in Belgium. Branches can benefit from the reduced corporate income tax rates under specific conditions *(see "Taxes on corporate income")*. The specifications for the applicable conditions include:

1. To determine whether the EUR 322,500 ceiling of taxable income is exceeded and whether the "EUR 36,000 remuneration" requirement is satisfied, reference needs to be made to the branch's results only.
2. All other conditions must be satisfied at the level of the foreign company, taken as a whole.

Capital gains realised on real estate located in Belgium by non-resident companies are subject to a professional withholding tax at the basic tax rate of 33.99%. The professional withholding tax is in fact an advance payment of the final Belgian non-resident corporate income tax. Indeed, the professional withholding tax can be offset against the final Belgian non-resident corporate income tax. Any balance is refundable.

In general, the taxable basis will be determined on the basis of the separate set of accounts of the Belgian branch. The taxable basis would then be determined as the difference between the profits actually realised and the tax deductible costs actually incurred in the hands of the Belgian branch. Please note, however, that no legal requirement exists to keep a separate set of accounts in the hands of the permanent establishment (PE), in case no legal branch is deemed to exist in Belgium.

Should no separate set of accounts be kept, the taxable basis in the hands of the Belgian branch, in principle, will be determined on the basis of article 182, §1, 3°, a) of the Royal Decree implementing the Belgian Income Tax Code. As a result, the yearly taxable basis would be determined on 10% of the gross turnover realised in Belgium with a minimum of EUR 7,000 per employee and an absolute minimum of EUR 19,000. Note that the European Court of Justice ruled that this "minimum taxable basis" is in violation with the freedom of establishment. It is still applied in practice, though. Note that such determination of the taxable basis is often formalised in a written agreement with the local Belgian tax inspector without, however, deviating from the tax law criteria as mentioned before.

Belgium

Income determination

Inventory valuation

Belgian accounting law provides for the following four methods of inventory valuation: the method based on the individualisation of the price of each item; the method of the weighted average prices; the last-in, first-out (LIFO) method; and the first-in, first-out (FIFO) method. All of these methods are accepted for tax purposes.

Capital gains

Capital gains are subject to the standard corporate income tax rate. For tax purposes, a capital gain is defined as the positive difference between the sale price less the costs related to the disposal of the asset (which are tax-deductible) and the original cost of the acquisition or investment less the depreciations and write-offs, which have been deducted for tax purposes. However, capital gains realised on tangible fixed assets and on intangible assets on which depreciation has been claimed for tax purposes and which have been held for more than five years can be subject to a deferred and spread taxation regime, provided the proceeds of the transfer are reinvested fully in tangible or intangible assets (subject to depreciation) in Belgium within three years (or five years in case of reinvestments in buildings, vessels, or aircrafts). If all the above conditions are met, the taxation of the net capital gain is spread over the depreciation period (allowed for tax purposes) of the asset that is acquired to fulfil the reinvestment obligation. Deferred and spread taxation occurs at the basic corporate income tax rate.

Net capital gains realised on shares are exempt if dividends from such shares would – in case of distribution – meet the so-called "taxation conditions" under the participation exemption regime (see below). The "minimum participation condition" provided under that regime needs not be satisfied for capital gain exemption.

Inter-company dividends

Dividends received by a Belgian company are first included in its taxable basis on a gross basis when the dividends are received from a Belgian company or on a net basis, that is, after deduction of the foreign withholding tax, when they are received from a foreign company.

Then, a dividend-received deduction (DRD) of 95% of the above amount can be applied under certain conditions. Any unused portion of the DRD from dividends received from an EEA subsidiary or a subsidiary from a country with which Belgium has concluded a double tax treaty with a non-discrimination clause on dividends can be carried forward to future tax years. The possibility of carrying forward the unused portion of DRD from qualifying non-EEA dividends has not been codified, but should continue to apply based on the October 2009 practice note. The same also applies for dividends from Belgian subsidiaries.

The DRD is subject to a minimum participation condition and a taxation condition.

According to the minimum participation condition, the recipient company must have, at the moment of attribution, a participation of at least 10% or an acquisition value of at least EUR 2,500,000 in the distributing company. However, that condition, does not apply to dividends received or attributed by investment companies, nor to dividends attributed by inter-municipal organisations. The beneficiary of the dividend must have been holding the full legal ownership of the underlying shares for at least one year prior to the dividend distribution or commit to hold it for a minimum of one year (share-per-share test). Furthermore, the shares should be booked as "financial fixed assets". This condition was contested by the European Commission.

The taxation condition, in summary, means that the dividend income received must have been subject to tax at the level of the distributing company or its subsidiaries.

The taxation condition is based on five so-called "exclusion" rules and certain exceptions to these rules. Basically, the exclusion rules apply to:

1. Tax haven companies, that is, companies that are not subject to Belgian corporate income tax or to a similar foreign tax, or that are established in a country where the common taxation system is notably more advantageous than in Belgium. Countries, in which the minimum level of (nominal or effective) taxation is below 15% qualify as tax havens for the application of the regime (a list of tainted countries has been published). The common tax regimes applicable to companies residing in the EU are, however, deemed not to be notably more advantageous than in Belgium.
2. Finance, treasury or investment companies that, although are subject in their country of tax residency to a taxation system similar to that of Belgium, as mentioned in item 1 above, nevertheless benefit from a taxation system that deviates from the one commonly applicable.
3. Offshore companies, which are companies receiving income (other than dividend income) that originates outside their country of tax residency and in these countries such income is subject to a separate taxation system that deviates substantially from the common taxation system.
4. Companies having branches that benefit globally from a taxation system notably more advantageous than the Belgian non-resident corporate taxation system. This exclusion is deemed not applicable to EU companies with an EU branch.
5. Intermediary holding companies, that is, companies (with the exception of investment companies) that redistribute dividend-received income, which, on the basis of regulations mentioned under items 1 through 4 above, would not qualify for the dividend-received deduction for at least 90% of its amount in case of direct holding.

While this is a summary of the major exceptions, numerous exceptions to these exclusion rules exist and need to be analysed on a case-by-case basis.

Thin capitalisation rules
There is no general thin capitalisation rule in Belgium, but only two specific rules.

The deduction of interest paid by a Belgian company or branch can be denied partially when the beneficial owner of such interest is not subject to tax or is subject, with respect to the interest received, to a tax regime that is significantly more advantageous than the ordinary Belgian income tax system. In that case, the interest charge is considered a disallowed expense to the extent that the outstanding total amount of loans (on which the interest is calculated) – other than fixed interest securities – from such beneficiary exceeds seven times the sum of taxable reserves (at the start of the financial year) and paid-up capital (at the end of the financial year) of the interest paying company (7/1 debt equity ratio).

Payments that are subject to the special thin capitalisation rule, interest due on advances or loans (other than bonds) granted to a Belgian company by shareholders (private individuals only) of that company or by any person (not being a Belgian tax

Belgium

resident company) acting as a director, manager (known as gérant/zaakvoerder), payments to liquidators or those exercising a similar function in the company, or by the spouse or minor children of such persons, may be recharacterised as dividend income to the extent that the interest rate exceeds the applicable market rate, or the amount of such advances or loans exceeds the sum of the paid-up capital (at year-end) and taxable reserves (at the start of the financial year) of the Belgian company.

Foreign income
A Belgian resident company is subject to corporate tax on its worldwide income. However, the following exceptions apply.

* Foreign source profits not exempt from taxation by virtue of a double tax treaty are taxable at the basic corporate tax rate in Belgium (i.e., 33.99%). Income realised by foreign branches located in countries with which Belgium has concluded a double tax treaty is exempt from Belgian corporate income tax.
* Unless a more advantageous provision (e.g., a so-called tax sparing provision) would apply based on a double tax treaty concluded by Belgium *(see list in the Withholding tax section),* a foreign tax credit is granted under Belgian tax law with respect to foreign royalty income, provided that this income has effectively been subject to taxation in its source country. This foreign tax credit is equal to 15/85 of the net frontier amount (i.e., after deduction of foreign withholding tax) of the royalty. The foreign tax credit is included in the taxable basis of the recipient company (grossing-up). It is only creditable against Belgian income tax to the extent that said foreign income is included in the taxable basis of the Belgian company. Excess foreign tax credit, if any, is not refundable.
* Unless a more advantageous provision (e.g., a so-called tax sparing provision) would apply based on a double tax treaty concluded by Belgium *(see list in the Withholding tax section),* the Belgian beneficiary of foreign interest income is entitled to a foreign tax credit under Belgian tax law, provided that this income effectively has been subject to taxation in its source country. The computation of the foreign tax credit is based on the net frontier interest income (i.e., after deduction of foreign withholding tax). The tax credit as described above is included in the taxable base of the Belgian lender (grossing-up). It is creditable against the corporate income tax due but is not refundable in case of excess.
* Undistributed income of subsidiaries, whether or not they are foreign, is not subject to any Belgian income tax.

Bonus shares – stock dividends
Distribution of bonus shares to the shareholders in compensation for an increase of the share capital by incorporation of existing reserves is, in principle, tax-free. The situation may be different if the shareholder has the choice between a cash or stock dividend.

Depreciation
Depreciation of an asset is tax deductible to the extent that it results from a devaluation of the asset and the devaluation effectively occurred during the taxable period concerned. The depreciation methods that are accepted by Belgian tax law are the straight-line method (linear method) and the double-declining balance method. In the latter case, the annual depreciation may not exceed 40% of the acquisition value. The double-declining method may not be used for intangible fixed assets, automobiles, minibuses and automobiles used for mixed purposes and for assets, the use of which has been transferred to a third party (e.g., in the case of operational leasing).

Depreciation rates are based on the estimated lifetime of the assets concerned. However, intangible fixed assets have to be depreciated over a period of at least five years for tax purposes (except R&D expenses, for which the minimum depreciation period is three years).

Belgian accounting and tax laws allow depreciation of goodwill arising at the occasion of an asset deal. For Belgian tax purposes, the depreciation period, which depends on the elements included in the goodwill, is a minimum of five years (according to the Minister of Finance, "clientele" (client lists) should be depreciated over a period of 10 to 12 years), and the straight-line method must be applied. The aforesaid accounting and tax depreciation is not available in the case of mergers or de-mergers that occur tax-free (i.e., that, among other things, follow the continuity principle from an accounting perspective).

For the year of acquisition of an asset, only the proportionate share of an annual depreciation calculation can be accepted as depreciation for income tax purposes (in principle to be computed on a daily basis). This provision, however, does apply only to companies that cannot be considered as small- or medium-sized companies (SMC) as defined by article 15 of the Belgian Companies Code. An SMC is a company that does not exceed more than one of the following criteria: 50 employees, a turnover of EUR 7.3 million, or total asset value of EUR 3.65 million. These thresholds are to be evaluated on a consolidated level. According to the position of the central tax administration, no depreciation can be accepted for the year in which the asset is disposed of. On the other hand, ancillary expenses incurred at the time of acquisition will have to be depreciated in the same way as the asset to which they relate (thus, no full deduction in the year of acquisition, except for SMCs). Alternatively ancillary expenses relating to the acquisition of land can be written down and such write-downs, if they are justified, may constitute a deductible expense.

Incorporation costs, at the election of the taxpayer, may be deducted fully in the year of incorporation or spread in fixed amounts over a number of years as determined by the taxpayer.

Net operating losses

Tax losses can be carried forward without any limitation in time. However, in case of change in control of a Belgian company (e.g., if the shares of this company are transferred and along with them the majority of the voting rights), the amount of tax loss carryforward available in that company (before the change of control) can no longer be offset against future profits, unless the change can be justified by legitimate needs of a financial or economic nature in the hands of the loss realising company (i.e., evidence must be brought that the change is not purely tax driven). A ruling can be obtained from the Belgian tax authorities to obtain upfront certainty on the Belgian tax treatment of the contemplated operation, so as to ensure the losses are not forfeited as a result of a change of control. The condition of legitimate needs of a financial or economic nature is considered to be fulfilled when the employees and activities of the company are maintained by the new shareholder or when the company's control is acquired by a company belonging to the same consolidated group of companies as the former controlling company.

In the case of a tax-free merger or (partial) de-merger, Belgian tax law provides for a partial transfer/maintenance of the rollover tax losses of the absorbed/absorbing company. The carried forward tax losses of the companies involved are then reduced

Belgium

based on the proportionate net fiscal value of the company (before the restructuring) compared to the sum of the net fiscal values of both the merging entities (before the restructuring).

There is no tax loss carryback provision under Belgian tax law.

Payments to foreign affiliates
A Belgian corporation can claim a deduction for royalties, management service fees, and interest charges paid to foreign affiliates, provided such amounts are at arm's length. However, when such payments are made, either directly or indirectly, to a foreign person or entity or to a foreign branch, which is not subject to tax or is subject with respect to the payments received to a tax regime that is notably more advantageous than the Belgian tax regime on such income, there is a reversal of the burden of proof. Such charges will be disallowed unless the Belgian enterprise can prove that the payments are reasonable and that they correspond to genuine and real transactions.

Effective 1 January 2010, companies subject to Belgian corporate income tax or Belgian non-resident corporate income tax that make direct or indirect payments to recipients established in tax havens are obliged to declare them if they exceed EUR 100,000 during the tax year. The reporting has to be made on a special form to be attached to the (non-resident) corporate tax return. In the event of non-reporting, the payments will be disallowed expenses for corporate income tax purposes.

Fees, commissions, etc., paid to beneficiaries located in foreign countries, which are not properly reported on Form 281.50 and Summary Form 325.50, will, in principle, be subject to the secret commissions tax (of 309%), unless the taxpayer can prove that the beneficiaries have declared this income in their Belgian tax return.

Disallowed expenses
As a general rule, expenses are tax deductible in Belgium provided that they are incurred in order to maintain or to increase taxable income, they relate to the taxpayer's business activity, they are incurred or have accrued during the taxable period concerned, and that evidence of the reality and the amount of such expenses is provided by the taxpayer. Notwithstanding the aforesaid rule, the following expenses are not tax deductible in Belgium (this list is not exhaustive):

- Belgian resident and non-resident corporate income tax including advance tax payments, any surcharge imposed in case of insufficient advance tax payments and any interest for late payment of the corporate income tax, Belgian movable withholding tax as well as any foreign tax credit granted in relation with foreign movable withholding tax. Immovable withholding tax (i.e., real estate tax), secret commissions tax and foreign taxes, however, are considered as tax deductible.
- Regional taxes and contributions, including penalties, increases, ancillary expenses and interest for late payment (certain exceptions apply).
- Any administrative and judicial fines or penalties (except for VAT proportionate fines).
- Depending on the CO_2 emission of the automobile, a rate from 0% to 50% must be disallowed (except for financial costs incurred in relation to automobiles and automobile telephone expenses that remain fully tax deductible). Costs relating to automobiles that have a zero CO_2 emission (electric vehicles) are 120% tax deductible.

- 25% of fuel expenses for automobiles.
- 31% of restaurant expenses.
- 50% of representation expenses and business gifts (there are exceptions).
- Advantages granted to employees for social reasons with certain exceptions (e.g., hospitalisation insurance premiums, gifts of a small value).
- Capital losses on shares (except in the case of liquidation, up to the amount of paid-up capital of the liquidated company).
- Brokerage, commissions, commercial discounts, or others allocated directly or indirectly to a person in the form of a Belgian public bribery.
- Interest, royalties, or fees paid or attributed, either directly or indirectly, to non-resident taxpayers or foreign branches that are not subject to tax or are subject with respect to the income received at a notably more favourable tax regime than the Belgian tax regime on such income, unless the Belgian taxpayer can prove that those payments are made with respect to real and genuine transactions and provided that the payments do not exceed normal limits for such transactions (arm's-length principle).
- Interest paid, to the extent that it exceeds an amount corresponding to the market rate, taking into account factual circumstances proper to the appraisal of the risk linked to the operation, and particularly the financial situation of the debtor and the duration of the loan. The latter test, however, is not applied with respect to interest paid to a Belgian-based financial institution.
- Direct or indirect payments to recipients established in tax havens, which are not properly reported (if they exceed EUR 100,000 per tax year).

Provisions – bad debt reserve
Provisions and bad debt reserve are tax deductible provided that:

- They are set up to cover clearly identified losses and charges, and thus, not to cover "general" risks that have been rendered probable by events, which took place during the taxable period concerned;
- They are booked at the end of the financial year in one or more separate accounts on the balance sheet;
- They are reported on a specific form enclosed with the tax return; and
- They relate to losses and charges that are deductible for Belgian tax purposes.

Group taxation

Belgium does not apply any tax consolidation mechanism with respect to corporate tax.

Transfer pricing
The arm's-length principle is formally codified in the Belgian Income Tax Code. Indeed, Belgian tax law contains standard anti-abuse provisions dealing with artificial profit shifting (deductibility of costs, excessive expenses, granting and receiving of so-called abnormal or benevolent benefits, deductibility of interest paid to a tax haven, deductibility of excessive interest).

If a Belgian resident company grants an "abnormal" or "benevolent" advantage (this is, generally speaking, an advantage which has no arm's-length character) this abnormal or benevolent advantage should be added back to its taxable income as a disallowed expense (= permanent difference), unless the advantage is taken into account to determine the taxable basis of the beneficiary. Notwithstanding the above exception, the abnormal or benevolent advantage should be added back to the taxable income

Belgium

when the advantage is being granted to a non-resident affiliated company. Such granted abnormal or benevolent advantages can be offset against any tax deductible items (i.e., tax losses carried forward, notional interest deduction, etc.).

If a Belgian tax resident company receives an "abnormal" or "benevolent" advantage, and to the extent that such benefit is received from a related company, the advantage received cannot be offset by the Belgian company against its (current year or carryforward) tax losses or other tax deductions (e.g., dividends-received deduction, notional interest deduction, investment deduction). According to the tax authorities (Parliamentary Question of 2004), the taxable basis of a Belgian company must be at least equal to the amount of the advantage received.

No specific transfer pricing documentation requirements or rules on the selection of transfer pricing methods are foreseen in the Belgian tax legislation. Nevertheless, transfer pricing requirements have been developed, mainly by the tax authorities, which are in line with the OECD transfer pricing requirements and the EU Code of Conduct. Based on these requirements, it is advisable to proactively compile a coherent and consistent documentation set, although there is no legal obligation to do so.

Tax incentives

Notional interest deduction (NID)

Belgian corporate income taxpayers are allowed to claim a NID for tax purposes reflecting the economic cost of the use of capital, equal to the cost of long-term, risk-free financing. The NID-rate is, in principle, based on the average rate on 10-year Belgian government bonds. The NID rate will be adjusted annually (with a maximum upwards or downwards variation of, in principle, 1%) again by making reference to the average interest rate on 10-year Belgian government bonds of the prior year, but capped at maximum 6.5% (7% for SMEs). For tax years 2011 and 2012 (financial years as per 31 December 2010 and 31 December 2011), the NID rate is capped at 3.8% (4.3% for SMEs).

As for determining the basis on which this deduction is calculated, the company's share capital plus its retained earnings, as determined for Belgian GAAP purposes and as per the last year-end date, will have to be taken into account.

Certain adjustments to the equity should be made in order to avoid double use. The accounting equity as per the last year-end date has to be reduced by, among other things, the following items (all valued at the same year-end date): (1) the fiscal net value of financial fixed assets qualifying as "participations and other shares" and (2) in the case of a company that has foreign PE, located in a jurisdiction with which Belgium has concluded a tax treaty, the positive difference between the net book value of assets attributable to the foreign PE and the liabilities (other than equity).

In addition, adjustments should be made in order to avoid abuse. The accounting equity as per the last year-end date has to be reduced by, among other things, the following items:

1. The net book value of tangible fixed assets whose corresponding costs unreasonably exceed the needs of the company;
2. The book value of any other passive investment that are not acquired in order to produce a regular income;

3. The book value of real estate (rights) used/occupied by either individuals having a director or liquidator mandate in the company or by their spouse or dependent children;
4. Revaluation gains in respect of assets, other than the aforementioned assets, and capital subsidies.

Components of the accounting equity and adjustment items (e.g., qualifying participations) are adjusted upwards or downwards on a proportionate basis in cases where these change occur in the course of the financial year.

The unused part of the NID can be carried forward for a maximum of seven years if there is insufficient tax capacity in the year that the deduction is claimed. No advance ruling from the Belgian Ruling Office is required for claiming the deduction. Furthermore, a FIFO approach (first in, first out) applies regarding the combined application of carryforward NID and NID of the current financial year. This means that the carryforward NID can be utilised to offset taxable profits before the current year NID.

The Belgian ruling commission already has issued several positive ruling decisions, whereby, it has confirmed that a company may opt to waive partially or fully the notional interest deduction. Notional interest deductions that have been waived, however, may not be carried forward to later tax years.

Investment deduction

Belgian tax residents can claim an investment deduction, which corresponds to a part of the acquisition or investment value of investments in new fixed assets, irrespective of whether these assets have been purchased or produced. These assets, however, should be used exclusively for professional purposes and cannot be placed at the disposal of a third party. Furthermore, the assets should be amortisable.

The deduction equals a percentage of the investment made, which depends on the nature of the investment and on the person claiming the deduction. For assessment year 2011, the percentages are:

	Individuals	Legal persons
Patents	13.5%	13.5%
Environmentally friendly R&D investments	13.5%	13.5%
Energy-saving investments	13.5%	13.5%
Air filter systems in bars, restaurants, etc.	13.5%	13.5%
Charge station for electric cars	13.5%	13.5%
Security investments	20.5%	20.5% (*)
Other investments	3.5%	0%

* This is only applicable for companies held for more than 50% by private individuals and for SMCs as defined by article 15 of the Belgian Companies Code (see the "Depreciation" section).

Companies can spread the investment deduction with respect to environmentally friendly R&D investments over the amortisation period of the asset. In such a case, the applicable percentage is increased up to 20.5%.

Belgium

In case of insufficiency or absence of taxable profits, the investment deduction can be carried forward without any limitation in time or in amount. Certain restrictions apply as to the maximum amount of investment deduction carried forward that is tax deductible in a given year.

Under certain conditions the investment deduction carried forward can be lost after a change of ownership *(see "Net operating losses" section)*. Note that the investment deduction for patents and R&D cannot be combined with the tax credit for patents and R&D.

R&D tax credit
As an alternative to the above investment deduction for patents and R&D, a company can opt for a tax credit for which the advantage corresponds to the advantage of the investment deduction. The investment deduction implies a deduction of the taxable basis, while the tax credit is a reduction of the tax due. A key advantage of the tax credit for patents and R&D patents is that it is refundable if it has not been deducted for five subsequent tax years. The amount of the tax credit should be deducted from the basis of the notional interest deduction.

Reduced payroll tax for qualifying researchers
As from 1 July 2009, 75% of the payroll tax withheld from wages of qualifying researchers by a Belgian company or establishment does not need to be remitted to the Belgian Tax Revenue provided that the researchers are employed in research and development programmes and have a qualifying degree (such as a degree in (applied) sciences, veterinary medicines, bio-technology, etc.). For the employee's personal tax liability, the Belgian Tax Revenue considers that the payroll withholding tax amount entirely was withheld.

Patent income deduction (PID)
The PID allows a taxpayer to deduct – as an extra tax deduction in the tax return – 80% of qualifying gross patent income. Therefore, only 20% of gross patent income will be taxable at the normal corporate tax rate, resulting in an effective tax rate of maximum 6.8%.

Qualifying taxpayers are corporate taxpayers in Belgium that are involved in the development or further improvement of patents through an in-house R&D centre. They include both Belgian companies and Belgian PEs of foreign companies. The company must be the owner, licensee, or usufruct holder of the patents for which they claim the benefits of the PID. To benefit from the PID, the R&D centre should qualify as a "branch of activity" or "line of business", which means that it should be a division of an entity that is capable of operating autonomously. The Belgian company or PE should have relevant substance to perform and supervise research and development activities, but may use subcontractors, related or unrelated, in its development of the patents or extended patent certificates. The law specifically provides that the R&D centre can be located outside Belgium but must belong to a Belgian legal entity.

Belgian companies or PEs, acting as "contract R&D" service providers on behalf of another company cannot qualify for PID because they are not the owners, holder of beneficial rights to or licensee of the patent.

Qualifying patents
The PID applies where patents or supplementary protection certificates are owned by a Belgian company or establishment as a result of its own patent-development activities

(partly or fully) in an R&D centre in Belgium or abroad. The PID also applies where patents or supplementary protection certificates are acquired by a Belgian company or establishment from a related or unrelated party, in full ownership, joint ownership, usufruct, or via license agreement, provided it has further improved the patented products or processes in the company's R&D centre in Belgium or abroad.

Other intellectual property (IP), such as copyrights, know-how, designs, trade or marketing intangibles, are not eligible for the Belgian PID.

The Belgian company or establishment can license the patents to other parties. Alternatively, it can use the patents, which are owned by it or licensed to it, to manufacture and supply patented products or services.

For patents licensed by the Belgian company or establishment to any party, whether related or unrelated, the tax deduction amounts to 80% of the relevant patent income to the extent the income does not exceed an arm's-length price, is permitted.

For patents used by the Belgian company or establishment for the manufacture of patented products, manufactured by itself or by a contract manufacturer on its behalf, the tax deduction is 80% of the license fee (known as embedded royalties) that the Belgian company would have received had it licensed the patents used in the manufacturing process to an unrelated party.

The tax deduction for patent income is available to all corporate taxpayers in Belgium. This includes essentially all Belgian resident companies and Belgian permanent establishments of non-resident companies.

No advance ruling is required to benefit from this deduction since it is applicable generally and automatically. Only minor compliance formalities apply. The taxpayer should submit a special application form together with the corporate income tax return.

"Excess profit" rulings

Belgium introduced the arm's-length principle in the Belgian Income Tax Code. While it already had instruments to adjust upward a taxpayer's Belgian taxable basis in case of non-arm's-length dealings, the new measure now also allows multinational companies to achieve a unilateral downward tax adjustment. Belgium will refrain from taxing profits that a Belgian tax-resident company would not have realised if it had not been a party to related-party dealings.

As the cost structure (or the profit potential) of a member of a multinational group of companies will normally differ from that of a stand-alone entity, its profit will normally also be higher. Applying the arm's-length principle, this profit differential, which does not result from the functions performed and risks assumed by the respective entities, should not be allotted to the Belgian group member. As such, Belgian tax law allows for unilateral adjustments of the Belgian tax base similar to the corresponding adjustments in article 9 of the OECD Model Convention. The underlying assumption is that the "excess profit" forms part of the profits of the foreign related party.

The part of profit that is deemed to derive from related-party dealings and that is exempted from taxation in Belgium and how the "part-of-the-profits-of-the-foreign-related-party" condition should be interpreted will need to be submitted to the Belgian

Belgium

Ruling Office to obtain a ruling in advance. Such rulings are granted for renewable periods of five years and are based on a detailed functional, economic analysis of the relevant Belgian activities with a view to determining a profit level commensurate with the company's functional and risk profile.

Withholding taxes (WHT)

Domestic corporations and branches of foreign corporations paying dividends, interest, royalties, and/or certain rentals are required to withhold tax. The standard rates applicable under Belgian tax law are fixed at 25% for dividends and 15% for interest, royalties, and certain rentals. However, some withholding tax reductions/exemptions are foreseen under Belgian domestic tax law.

1. A reduced Belgian withholding tax of 15% applies to dividend distributions relating to non-preference shares subscribed in cash, issued as from 1 January 1994 and which, upon issuance, are nominative or have been deposited with a financial institution in Belgium, on condition that the distributing company does not irrevocably renounce its right to benefit from the reduced rate of withholding tax.
2. A reduced Belgian withholding tax of 15% is possible for dividend distributions relating to non-preference shares issued as from 1 January 1994 in the context of a public offering (i.e., shares quoted on the stock exchange) on condition that the distributing company does not irrevocably renounce its right to benefit from the reduced rate of withholding tax.
3. Under certain conditions, a reduced withholding tax of 15% applies to dividend distributions made by companies quoted on a stock market or by companies whose capital has been (partly) contributed by a PRIVAK/PRICAF, which must also be quoted on a stock market. A PRIVAK/PRICAF is a company with the sole objective of collective investment in non-quoted companies and in growth companies.
4. A withholding tax exemption on dividends is foreseen if both the receiving and distributing companies are subject to Belgian corporate income tax, if the receiving company holds a minimum shareholding of at least 10% for at least one year in the capital of the subsidiary and if certain formalities are complied with. If the one-year holding requirement is not fulfilled at the time of distribution, the distributing company provisionally should withhold the amount of withholding tax due (but it does not have to pay the tax authorities). Once the one-year holding requirement is met, the provisionally withheld tax amount can be paid out to the parent company. If the one-year holding requirement eventually is not complied with (e.g., because the Belgian participation is disposed of by the parent company before the one-year holding requirement is met) then the Belgian company has to pay the amount provisionally withheld increased by interest for late payment (at an annual rate of 7%) to the competent services of the Belgian tax authorities.
5. A withholding tax exemption is foreseen also for the distribution of profits made by a Belgian subsidiary to an EU parent company, if both the parent and subsidiary have a legal form that is mentioned in the Annex to the EU Parent-Subsidiary directive, if both are subject to corporate income tax, and if the parent company holds during an uninterrupted period of at least one year a shareholding of at least 10% in the capital of the distributing company. The same procedure as that described under point 4 above applies in case the one-year holding requirement is not met at the moment of the dividend distribution.
6. A 10% tax is applicable to profits that are attributed or made payable as a result of the full or partial liquidation of a company or the acquisition by a company of its own shares. However, the exemption of Belgian withholding tax is maintained for liquidation proceeds distributed by a BEVEK (Beleggingsvennootschap

met veranderlijk kapitaal)/SICAV (Société d'investissment à capital variable), for dividends resulting from tax-free mergers and for liquidation proceeds resulting from the redemption of own shares by a company listed on a regulated stock exchange. If the conditions of items 4 and 5 above apply, an exemption is also available.

7. The application of the Parent-Subsidiary directive to dividend payments has been extended towards non-EU-resident companies. Dividends distributed towards a country that has concluded a tax treaty with Belgium containing a qualifying exchange of information clause, can be exempt from withholding, tax subject to the same conditions as laid down in the Parent-Subsidiary directive.

8. There is a withholding tax exemption on interest on loans granted by professional investors to banks established in the EEA or in a country which has concluded a double tax treaty with Belgium. For example, banks situated in France, the UK or the US, thus, should be able to benefit from this exemption.

9. No Belgium interest withholding tax arises where two related companies with tax residence outside Belgium are involved in a financial transaction with the intervention of a Belgium based intra-group financial enterprise. Under these circumstances, the Belgium intra-group financial enterprise is not required to retain Belgium interest withholding tax if the entity merely intervenes as "paying agent intermediary."

10. Belgian domestic tax law also provides for a withholding tax exemption on the following movable income sourced in Belgium (this list is not exhaustive):

    a. Income from deposits allocated or attributed to non-resident savers by Belgian banks.

    b. Income from bonds, treasury bonds, or other similar instruments of which the beneficiaries are identified as financial institutions.

    c. Income from receivables (this includes income from commercial receivables) or loans of which the beneficiaries are identified as financial institutions or professional investors. Professional investors are defined as any Belgian resident company or branch not being a financial institution or any equivalent. As a result, interest payments between two Belgian companies are exempt from withholding tax. This exemption has been extended by virtue of the Royal Decree of 3 July 2005. As a result, on transactions with banks situated in a country with which Belgium has concluded a double tax treaty, no withholding will be due. In practice this means that on transactions with inter alia French, UK and US banks no withholding will be due.

    d. Income from bonds paid by a Belgian resident financial institution or by a Belgian resident company to non-resident savers, provided that such bonds are registered on a nominal basis with the debtor of the income during the entire period to which the interest relates and that the foreign beneficiaries of the interest are not located in a tax haven country or held by more than 50% by Belgian residents.

    e. Income from bonds and loans granted by "eligible quoted companies" and "eligible intra muros financial companies" to non-residents (under certain conditions).

    f. Interest payments between a Belgian company and an EU tax resident company in case of direct or indirect shareholding of at least 25% for an uninterrupted period of at least one year (i.e., transposition of EU Interest & Royalty directive in Belgian tax law).

Belgium

With respect to payments made to non-resident corporations or individuals, withholding tax exemptions and/or reductions can also be found in the double taxation treaties concluded by Belgium.

Recipient	Dividends	Interest (c)	Royalties, certain rentals (c)
	%	%	%
Non-resident corporations and individuals			
Non-treaty:	25	15	15
Treaty:			
Albania	5, 15 (a)	5	5
Algeria	15 (a)	15	5, 15
Argentina	10, 15 (a)	12	3, 5, 10, 15
Armenia	5, 15 (a)	10	8
Australia	15 (a)	10	10
Austria	15 (a)	15	10
Azerbaijan	5, 10, 15 (a)	10	5, 10
Bangladesh	15 (a)	15	10
Belarus	5, 15 (a)	10	5
Brazil	10,15 (a)	10, 15	10, 15, 20 (d)
Bosnia-Herzegovina (1)	10,15 (a)	15	10
Bulgaria	10 (a)	10	5
Canada	5, 15 (a)	10	0, 10
Chile	0, 15 (a)	5, 15	5, 10
China, P.R. (2)	10 (a)	10	10
Croatia	5, 15 (a)	10	0
Cyprus	10, 15 (a)	10	0
Czech Republic	5, 15 (a)	10	5, 10
Denmark	15 (a)	10	0
Ecuador	15 (a)	10	10
Egypt	15, 20 (a)	15	15, 25 (d)
Estonia	5, 15 (a)	10	5, 10
Finland	5, 15 (a)	10	5
France	10, 15 (a)	15	0
Gabon	15 (a)	15	10
Georgia	5, 15 (a)	10	5, 10
Germany	15, 25 (a)	0, 15	0
Ghana	5, 15 (a)	10	10
Greece	5, 15 (a)	5, 10	5
Hong Kong	0, 5, 15 (a)	10	5
Hungary	10 (a)	15	0
Iceland	5, 15 (a)	10	0
India	15 (a)	10, 15	20 (d)
Indonesia	10, 15 (a)	10	10
Ireland, Rep. of	5 (a)	15	0
Israel	15 (a)	15	10
Italy	15 (a)	15	5

Recipient	Dividends	Interest (c)	Royalties, certain rentals (c)
	%	%	%
Ivory Coast	15 (a)	16 (a) (d)	10
Japan	5, 15 (a)	10	10
Kazakhstan	5, 15 (a)	10	10
Korea, Rep. of	15 (a)	10	10
Kuwait	0, 10 (a) (d)	0	10
Kyrgyzstan (3)	15	15	0
Latvia	5, 15 (a)	10	5, 10
Lithuania	5, 15 (a)	10	5, 10
Luxembourg	10, 15 (a)	0, 15	0
Macedonia (1)	10, 15 (a)	15	10
Malaysia	0, 15 (a)	10	10
Malta	15 (a)	10	0, 10
Mauritius	5, 10 (a)	10	0
Mexico	5, 15 (a)	10, 15	10
Moldova (3)	15	15	0
Mongolia	5, 15 (a)	10	5
Montenegro (1)	10, 15 (a)	15	10
Morocco	6.5, 10 (a)	10	10
Netherlands	5, 15 (a)	0, 10	0
New Zealand	15 (a)	10	10
Nigeria	12.5, 15 (a)	12.5	12.5
Norway	5, 15 (a)	15	0
Pakistan	10, 15 (a)	15	15, 20 (d)
Philippines	10, 15 (a)	10	15
Poland	5, 15 (a)	5	5
Portugal	15 (a)	15	10
Romania	5, 15 (a)	10	5
Russia	10 (a)	10	0
San Marino	0, 5, 15 (a)	10	5
Senegal	15, 16 (a)	15, 16	10
Serbia (1)	10, 15 (a)	15	10
Singapore	0, 5, 15 (a)	5	5
Slovakia	5, 15 (a)	10	5
Slovenia	5, 15 (a)	10	5
South Africa	5, 15 (a)	10	0
Spain	15 (a)	10	5
Sri Lanka	15 (a)	10	10
Sweden	5, 15 (a)	10	0
Switzerland	10, 15 (b)	10 (b)	0
Taiwan	10 (a)	10	10
Tajikistan (3)	15	15	10
Thailand	15, 20 (a)	10, 25	5, 15
Tunisia	5, 15 (a)	5, 10	11
Turkey	15, 20 (a)	15	10

Belgium

Recipient	Dividends	Interest (c)	Royalties, certain rentals (c)
	%	%	%
Turkmenistan (3)	15	15	0
Ukraine	5, 15 (a)	2, 10	0, 10
United Arab Emirates	5, 10 (a)	5	0,5
United Kingdom	5, 10 (a)	15	0
United States	0, 5, 15 (a)	0, 15	0
Uzbekistan	5, 15 (a)	10	5
Venezuela	5, 15 (a)	0, 10	5
Vietnam	5, 10, 15 (a)	10	5, 10, 15

Notes

1. The treaty concluded with ex-Yugoslavia is still applicable to Bosnia-Herzegovina, Macedonia, Serbia and Montenegro.
2. Not applicable to Hong Kong. Note that a new treaty with China has been signed (but not yet into force). The rates under the new treaty are 5% and 10% for dividends, 10% for interest, and 7% for royalties.
3. The treaty concluded with the (ex-) USSR is still applicable to Kyrgyzstan, Moldova, Tajikistan, and Turkmenistan.
a. The treaty contains a qualifying exchange of information clause. Hence, the rate of 0% is applicable subject to the same conditions as invoked by the Parent-Subsidiary directive (see above).
b. Under the Bilateral II agreement concluded between Belgium and Switzerland, a rate of 0% is applicable under certain conditions.
c. With respect to EU countries, a withholding tax exemption is applicable provided that the conditions laid down in the Interest & Royalty directive are met (see above).
d. Since the Belgian domestic rate for interest and royalties is maximum 15%, the higher treaty rate will in principle not be applicable on interest and royalties arising from Belgium

The treaties which are currently in force are listed above. The following tax treaties are signed, modified, or under renegotiation but have not yet entered into force (including some for the exchange of information clause): Armenia, Azerbaijan, Australia, Bahrain, China, Congo, Croatia, Denmark, Isle of Man, Finland, France, Germany, Iceland, Italy, Japan, Luxembourg, Macao, Malaysia, Malta, Moldova, the Netherlands, New Zealand, Norway, Qatar, Rwanda, San Marino, Seychelles, Singapore, Spain, Tajikistan, Uganda, and the United Kingdom.

Tax administration

Tax returns
As a general rule, the annual resident or non-resident corporate tax return cannot be filed less than one month from the date when the annual accounts have been approved and not later than six months after the end of the period to which the tax return refers. For instance, assuming that the accounting year has been closed on 31 December 2009, the corporate tax return needs to be filed, in principle, by 30 June 2010 at the latest (this deadline is often postponed).

Payment of tax
Corporate income tax is payable within two months following the issue of the tax assessment. Interest for late payment is charted at the rate of 7% per year.

Corporate taxes in Bermuda

For more information, contact:

Richard (Rick) Irvine
PricewaterhouseCoopers
Dorchester House
7 Church Street West
Hamilton HM 11, Bermuda
Tel: +1 441 299 7136
Email: richard.e.irvine@bm.pwc.com

Significant developments

There have been no recent significant developments.

Taxes on corporate income

Income tax and taxes on capital gains are not imposed on corporations in Bermuda.

Corporate residence

Entities that are incorporated in Bermuda are considered to be resident in the country.

Other taxes

Bermuda does not impose withholding taxes on payments made from Bermuda.
Bermuda does impose an Annual Company Fee based upon the capital of the company.

Bermuda does impose a stamp duty; however, exempt companies are not subject to the
stamp duty. All companies that employ persons in Bermuda must pay a payroll tax and
a social insurance tax.

Social insurance tax

If an employer has employees in Bermuda for 26 or more weeks in a calendar year, the
employer will have to register and obtain an account number from the Department
of Social Insurance (DSI) (unless previously registered) and pay social insurance tax
for its employees. At the same time, the employer must also apply for and obtain from
the DSI a social insurance number for each employee, which is required to pay social
insurance. Once the employer has registered for a social insurance account number
and the employees have obtained social insurance numbers, the DSI will automatically
send an electronic print-out to the employer with an itemised list of employees as
well as the amount of social insurance tax due for the month. Under certain facts and
circumstances, the employer may also file an Employee Amendment Form, which
shows any change in status (i.e., termination or unpaid leave) of employees that could
affect the amount of social insurance tax due.

The amount of social insurance tax due is calculated as BMD 60.80 per employee
per week (effective 1 April 2010), with the employer and employee each paying half
of the liability (or BMD 30.40). The employer must pay and remit monthly (for all
employees) to the DSI the total social insurance tax due per employee. The amount of
social insurance tax due per month is based on the number of Mondays in the month
and must be paid by the end of the following month.

Bermuda

Payroll tax

Under Section 3 of the Payroll Taxes Act of 1995, an employer (viewed as the entity that has control over an individual's remuneration) is required to remit payroll taxes (currently 16% on all remuneration paid or given up to a maximum compensation of BMD 750,000) for each of its employees whose employment in Bermuda exceeds four consecutive weeks in a calendar year (whether or not with one or more employers). If an employee's stay in Bermuda is for a period of less than four consecutive weeks, the employer is not obligated to remit the payroll taxes.

Once an employee's service period in Bermuda has exceeded four consecutive weeks, the employer must register the employee with the Office of the Tax Commissioner (OTC). The employer must obtain a payroll tax account number by filing an application with the OTC, if no previous account exists for such employee. The application must be filed within seven days after the end of the quarterly tax period (the four quarters end on 1 January, 1 April, 1 July and 1 October) in which the employee's stay exceeded four consecutive weeks. A payroll tax return and remittance of tax must be filed with the OTC 15 days after the end of each quarterly period (i.e., 15 January, 15 April, 15 July and 15 October). A return is due only when an employee's stay exceeds four consecutive weeks in a tax period. The employer may recover from the employee a maximum of 5.75% of the 16% payroll tax, and the employer is allowed an exemption of BMD 600 (of remuneration paid) per employee for each quarterly tax period. Penalties for tax returns filed late are 5% of the payroll tax due for each month (or part thereof) that the tax return is late (with a maximum of 30%).

Compensation subject to the payroll tax under the Payroll Taxes Act includes all remuneration paid or given to the employee. Remuneration includes:

* Wages, salary, leave pay, commission, gratuity, fee, bonus, perquisite, or allowance;
* Money paid under a profit-sharing scheme;
* Money or anything of value paid or given to an employee or ex-employee in connection with the permanent termination of his employment;
* Any amount paid with respect to a retirement or provident fund, scheme or society, or under a hospital or health insurance scheme;
* The value of meals, boarding, lodging, or other benefit of any kind, whether provided in cash or otherwise;
* The rental value of any place of residence provided rent-free or the difference between the rent paid and the rental value if the rent paid is lower than the rental value; and
* Any gain on the exercise or right to acquire company stock based on services rendered.

All employers or self-employed persons are required to report remunerations up to a maximum of BMD 350,000 per annum per employee, deemed employee or self-employed person. There is no payroll tax on remunerations above BMD 750,000.

The Payroll Taxes Act is extremely broad in its definition of remuneration. Therefore, a Bermuda employer should take caution when calculating the amount of remuneration paid to an employee.

Annual company fee

Every exempted company shall in the month of January forward to the Registrar of Companies a declaration signed on behalf of the company as to the company's principal business and its assessable capital, together with the appropriate fee payable.

Where the assessable capital of the exempted company is:

BMD 0 – 12,000	BMD 1,870
BMD 12,001 –120,000	BMD 3,820
BMD 120,001 – 1,200,000	BMD 5,890
BMD 1,200,001 – 12,000,000	BMD 7,850
BMD 12,000,001 – 100,000,000	BMD 9,815
BMD 100,000,001 – 500,000,000	BMD 17,530
BMD 500,000,001 or more	BMD 29,220

Branch income

Branch income is not applicable in Bermuda.

Income determination

Income determination is not applicable in Bermuda.

Deductions

Deductions are not applicable in Bermuda.

Group taxation

There are no group taxation rules in Bermuda.

Tax incentives

Bermuda offers no specific tax incentives.

Withholding taxes (WHT)

There are no withholding taxes in Bermuda.

Tax administration

Tax administration is not applicable.

Corporate taxes in Bolivia

For more information, contact:

César O Lora Moretto
PricewaterhouseCoopers
Avenida Mariscal Santa Cruz y Yanacocha
Edificio Hansa, 19th floor
La Paz, Bolivia
Tel: +591 2 240 8181
Email: cesar.lora@bo.pwc.com

Significant developments

Bolivian citizens approved the project of the State Political Constitution (CPE) through the referendum dated 25 January 2009, which was entered into force in February 2009. The CPE introduced three main changes with respect to tax policies, which are as follows:

- Debts caused by economical damage to the state have no statute of limitations. Note, that to date, there are no regulations that provide what should be interpreted as economical damage, and it is not yet clear whether taxes should be included within this definition. If the definition does apply to taxes, this would apply from the moment the new CPE was effective (i.e., as of February 2009);
- Municipal governments now have legal authority to create, modify and eliminate taxes (including council taxes and special contributions) previously approved by the Bolivian congress, that are not analogous to national taxes. However, regulations related to this matter have not yet been passed; and
- Coming into force is the "worldwide income" concept, through which the municipal governments have legal authority to tax income generated by their residents and companies abroad. Legislation has not yet regulated how this change will be implemented, such as providing clear definitions of residence and domicile, etc.

Taxes on corporate income

Pursuant to Law 1606, all companies in Bolivia are subject to corporate income tax at a rate of 25%. The taxable base is the profit arising from financial statements prepared in accordance with Bolivian generally accepted accounting principles, adjusted for tax purposes (i.e., by nondeductible and non-taxable items), as per the requirements established in the tax law and regulations.

Surcharge
Law 1731 introduced an additional corporate income tax at a rate of 25%, which affects only extractive activities of nonrenewable natural resources (mining and oil/gas). This additional tax is calculated on the same basis as the normal corporate income tax, except that two additional deductions are allowed: (i) up to 33% of the accumulated investment as from 1991; and (ii) 45% of the gross revenue of each extractive operation (e.g., a field or a mining site) with a threshold of BOB 250 million for each extractive operation.

Special industries

In addition to the general corporate income tax rate of 25%, all mining companies are also subject to an additional tax, calculated on the taxable net profits of: (i) 12.5%, if the mining company carries out exploitation activities; and (ii) 7.5%, if the mining company carries out manufacturing activities with raw minerals that add value.

Mining companies are also subject to mining royalties at a rate of between 1% and 7% (depending on the kind of mineral), calculated on the total sales price. Note that there is a 60% discount on the rates of mining royalties if minerals are sold within the Bolivian market. Mining royalties can be offset with corporate income tax if official mineral prices are lower than the prices established by the tax law; however, in this case, mining royalties paid will not be deductible for corporate income tax purposes.

Taxes on professionals working as independents

Professionals (e.g., lawyers, accountants, economic or engineering advisors, etc.) are subject to corporate income tax at a rate of 12.5% on their revenue net of value-added tax (VAT). Professionals can offset 50% of this tax with input VAT paid on purchases for their personal consumption.

Corporate residence

A corporation is considered resident in Bolivia if it has been incorporated in Bolivia.

Note that Bolivian commercial laws allow foreign corporations to carry out isolated commercial acts in Bolivia without the obligation to constitute a permanent representation in Bolivia, however such corporations cannot carry out habitual commercial acts without fulfilling the requirements established to constitute a company in Bolivia. Unfortunately, Bolivian legislation does not include provisions to regulate situations that could trigger "permanent establishment" issues, nor does it define what should be understood by "carrying out habitual commercial acts".

Other taxes

Value-added tax (VAT)

VAT is levied on the sale of movable goods and provision of services carried out within Bolivian territory at a rate of 13%, including definitive imports. Since this tax is included in the final price, the effective tax rate amounts to 14.94% (13% / 87%).

Tax on gross income

The tax on gross income (also known as "transaction tax") generally taxes gross income arising from the performance of any economic or commercial activity (including non-profitable activities) at a rate of 3% on a monthly basis. However, exceptions exist for the sale of investments (as defined by the Stock Exchange Law) and the sale of minerals, oil and gas within the local market, as long as such sales will ultimately be exported.

Corporations pay either corporate income tax or transaction tax, whichever is higher, on an annual basis. From an administrative perspective, corporate income tax is due and paid at the end of each tax year and is considered an advanced payment of transaction tax, while transaction tax is due monthly. If during the year the cumulative monthly transaction tax due exceeds the corporate income tax prepayment, the taxpayer will be subject to transaction tax on a monthly basis until the end of the tax

Bolivia

year. For example, a corporation pays corporate income tax for the 2009 fiscal year in April 2010. This payment is considered a prepayment for the transaction tax due between May 2010 and April 2011.

Property tax on real estate and vehicles
Real estate and vehicles are subject to a property tax calculated at different rates based on a scale value determined by the municipal government. Corporations pay this tax based on book values. However, for accounting purposes, book value can never be less than BOB 1. Please note that, in the case of vehicles, when accounting residual values are equal to BOB 1, the property tax should continue to be paid based on tax residual values determined by the tax law (10.7% on the gross value of the asset) until the vehicle is written-off.

Taxes on specific goods for consumption (excise tax)
Specific goods are taxed at the following rates:

Product	Tax rate (%)
Cigarettes and tobacco for pipes	50
Vehicles (except those of high capacity and weight, which will pay a 10% rate of excise tax)	18

Other specific products taxed by specific measure:

Product	Bs
Soft drinks (except natural water and fruit juices)	0.28/Litre
Maize liquor	0.58/Litre
Alcohol	1.11/Litre
Beers with 0.5% or more volumetric degrees	2.26/Litre
Wines	2.26/Litre
Ciders and sparkling wines (except maize liquor)	2.26/Litre
Liquors and creams in general	2.26/Litre
Rum and vodka	2.26/Litre
Other brandies/liquors	2.26/Litre
Whiskey	9.40/Litre

Special tax on hydrocarbons and derived products
This tax is charged on the commercialisation of these products within the local market, regardless of whether they are produced in Bolivia or imported.

Product	Bs
Gasoline	1.23/Litre
Premium gasoline	2.18/Litre
Aviation gasoline	1.85/Litre
Kerosene	0.29/Litre
National jet fuel	0.32/Litre
International jet fuel	4.27/Litre
National diesel oil	1.25/Litre
Agro fuel	0.62/Litre

Product	Bs
Fuel oil	0.39/Litre

Direct tax on hydrocarbons

Direct tax on hydrocarbons (IDH) is applied on the production of hydrocarbons, measured at the wellhead point, at a rate of 32%. To determine the taxable base for this tax, production of hydrocarbons must be valued taking into account the average sales price and considering the market (internal/external) where such hydrocarbons were sold.

Financial transaction tax

The financial transaction tax is levied on bank transactions (deposit or transfer of funds), carried out within the domestic financial system, at a rate of 0.15%.

Branch income

Branch income is subject to the same tax applicable to other types of Bolivian corporations (i.e., corporate income tax of 25%). However, note that net profits of Bolivian branches are deemed to be distributed to the head office at the annual filing due date for corporate income tax (i.e., 120 days after the fiscal year end); hence, a Bolivian branch must withhold 12.5% on such deemed distributed profits – note this can be avoided as long as the head office decides to reinvest Bolivian branch's net profits.

Income determination

Bolivia taxes the income generated by corporations following the "income source" principle. Therefore, income arising from goods and assets located or utilised economically within Bolivian territory and from any activity carried out within the country is considered Bolivian income source. Hence, such income is subject to corporate income tax, regardless of the nationality/residence of the parties involved in generating such income or the place where the contracts were subscribed.

Taxable income is determined based on the financial statements prepared under Bolivian generally accepted accounting principles; then the income is adjusted for tax purposes in accordance with guidelines provided by Law 843 and Supreme Decree 24051 with respect to nondeductible and non-taxable items. In general terms, expenses may be deducted as long as they are necessary to generate Bolivian-sourced income and are properly documented.

Foreign income

Bolivian corporations are taxed only on income generated within Bolivian territory.

Deductions

As a general principle, all expenses required to generate or preserve taxable income may be deducted for corporate income tax purposes.

In broad terms, the following items are nondeductible for tax purposes, according to current legislation:

1. Owners' or shareholders' personal withdrawals and living expenses;

Bolivia

2. Salaries, as well as associated compensations, paid to employees without the application of withholding taxes (i.e., RC-IVA);
3. Fees paid to individuals (i.e., acquisition of goods and services) for which no withholding taxes have been withheld;
4. Amortisation of trademarks and other intangible assets, unless a price has been paid to acquire them;
5. Interest paid to owners or shareholders, to the extent the interest rate exceeds the rate of LIBOR (London Interbank Offered Rate) plus 3% in the case of foreign owners/shareholders, and to the extent the interest rate exceeds the official interest rate on loans published by the Central Bank of Bolivia for national owners/shareholders. Interest deductible on shareholder loans may not exceed 30% of the total interest paid to third parties;
6. Corporate income tax;
7. Taxes paid in the acquisition of fixed assets. These taxes must be included in the cost of the asset and depreciated accordingly;
8. Provisions that are not specifically authorised by the tax law and regulations;
9. Depreciation of fixed assets that include a revaluation reserve; and
10. Losses arising from illegal acts.

Net operating losses
Tax losses can be carried forward with no time limit.

Payments to foreign affiliates
Payments to foreign affiliates are subject to a 12.5% withholding tax with no restriction, if the Bolivian company is remitting Bolivian-sourced income (e.g., interest on loans, provision of any kind of services, royalties, etc.).

Taxes
Taxes effectively paid by the corporation as a direct taxpayer are deductible for tax purposes. Any transaction tax (tax on gross income) that has been offset against corporate income tax paid is not deductible for corporate income tax purposes.

Other significant items
Donations are not deductible unless made to nonprofit organisations that are not subject to corporate income tax. These donations are deductible up to a maximum of 10% of the donor's net taxable profit.

Provisions for employees' severance payments are also deductible. Provisions of other bonuses (e.g., Christmas, productivity bonuses, etc.) accrued on behalf of employees are tax deductible, as long as they are paid prior to the annual income tax filing due date and the company demonstrates it has withheld taxes (if applicable).

Group taxation

Bolivia does not include group taxation rules within its legislation.

Tax incentives

Inward and capital investments
No incentives are granted for domestic or foreign investment.

Other incentives
Foreign exchange transactions are legal, and a system of free-floating exchange rates exists.

Export activities benefit from reimbursement of VAT and customs duties paid in the process of producing goods to be exported (with some limitations for oil/gas companies). Note that tourist and lodging services by hotels to foreign tourists without a residence or address in the country are exempt from VAT.

Regional tax incentives
New investments in manufacturing in the states of Oruro and Potosi are entitled to tax exemptions granted by Laws 876, 877, 967 and 2809.

Exemption	Conditions of exemption
Import tariffs and VAT on imported machinery	Machinery imported exclusively for the new industry until start-up of operations.
Import tariffs on imported inputs	They do not replace domestic inputs of the same kind and are destined to a transformation process. The exemption is granted for the first 10 years of operation.
Transaction tax	For 10 years as from the start-up of operations.
Corporate income tax	For 10 years from the start-up of operations if the amount exempt is reinvested in fixed assets in the following fiscal year.

Withholding taxes (WHT)

Payments made to Bolivian residents
Dividends paid to Bolivian residents, either individuals or corporations, are not taxable.

Payments made by corporations to individuals with respect to the acquisition of goods or provision of services that are not supported with an invoice or fiscal receipt are subject to a withholding tax of 8% on goods and 15.5% on services.

Payments to non-residents
Dividend payments, distributions of profits to the head office by Bolivian branches, interest payments, royalty payments and fees paid for any type of services made to non-residents are subject to a withholding tax of 12.5%.

Tax treaties
Bolivia currently has in force double tax treaties with the Andean Community, Argentina, France, Germany, Spain, Sweden and the United Kingdom.

Beneficial withholding tax rates on dividend distributions are provided by double tax treaties with Spain and Sweden at 10% and 0%, respectively, provided the Spanish or Swedish holding company demonstrates it is the ultimate beneficial owner and holds more than a 25% interest in the Bolivian company.

Bolivia

Tax administration

Returns
Corporate income tax is assessed on a self-assessment basis every fiscal year. Tax returns must be accompanied by audited financial statements (if applicable) and ancillary tax information as requested by the tax authorities.

The fiscal year varies according to the activity of the corporation. Banks and commercial and other service activities have a fiscal year end as of 31 December; industrial, oil and gas companies as of 31 March; agribusiness and forestry companies as of 30 June; and mining companies as of 30 September.

Payment of tax
Corporate income tax is payable in one annual payment except for mining companies, which are obliged to make advance payments on a monthly basis with respect to the additional tax (i.e., 12.5% and 7.5% for exploitation and manufacturing mining companies, respectively).

Corporate taxes in Bosnia and Herzegovina

For more information, contact:

Peter Burnie
PricewaterhouseCoopers Consulting d.o.o.
Airport City Belgrade
88a Omladinskih brigada st.
11000 Belgrade
Serbia
Tel: +381 11 3302 138
Email: peter.burnie@rs.pwc.com

Significant developments

Stabilisation and association agreement

The agreement is taking Bosnia and Herzegovina (BiH) a step closer to European Union (EU) accession. The custom tariff for products from the EU is being lowered to zero. The agreement is applicable as from 1 January 2009.

Excise duty

The law on excise duties prescribes that cigarettes will be subject to proportional duty (42% of retail price) and specific duty (BAM 0.15 for a pack of cigarettes – 20 cigarettes per pack).

The BiH Indirect Tax Authorities (ITA) have also introduced a minimal excise duty that will be paid, which is being calculated on the basis of the most popular cigarette brand in the last period. The excise duty paid may not be lower than the excise duty paid for the most popular brand.

In accordance with law and according to reports on issued excise duty stamps by the ITA, the retail price of the most popular brands in the period 1 July 2008, through 30 June 2009, was BAM 1.20 for a pack of cigarettes.

By using the adequate methodology, the ITA announced the minimal excise duty in the amount of BAM 40 for 1,000 pieces (BAM 0.80 for one package of 20).

The minimal excise duty is applicable as from 1 January 2010.

Taxpayers and other persons who sell cigarettes were required to count their inventory of cigarettes on 1 January 2010, and submit the count to the relevant regional centre by 10 January 2010.

Taxes on corporate income

Corporate income tax (CIT)

Bosnia and Herzegovina consists of two entities: Federation of Bosnia and Herzegovina (FBiH) and Republika Srpska (RS), and a separate administrative-territorial body: Brčko District. Direct taxes are imposed on entity and district level, while indirect tax regulations are on the state level. Corporate income tax systems in BiH have been partially harmonised in the past few years, but significant differences remain.

Bosnia and Herzegovina

Federation BiH (FBiH)

A taxpayer is a business association or other legal entity performing independent and permanent business activity through the sales of products and providing services on the market for the purpose of generating profit.

A taxpayer is also a non-resident who generates profits through business activity from a business unit in the territory of FBiH.

A non-resident, whose registered seat or management is not in FBiH, and does not have a business unit in FBiH, is subject to withholding tax for income generated in FBiH.

The CIT rate in FBiH is 10%.

Republika Srpska

A CIT payer in Republika Srpska is:

*   A legal entity from Republika Srpska that generates income from any source in Republika Srpska or abroad;
*   A business unit of a legal entity that generates income in the territory of Republika Srpska;
*   A foreign legal entity that conducts business activity and has a permanent establishment (PE) in Republika Srpska, for income that is related to that PE;
*   A foreign legal entity that generates income from immovable property in Republika Srpska, for the income generated in Republika Srpska; and/or
*   A foreign legal entity that generates income in Republika Srpska, not mentioned above, and is subject to withholding tax (WHT) in accordance with the CIT law of Republika Srpska.

The CIT rate in Republika Srpska is 10%.

Brčko District

CIT payers per Brčko District income tax law are business persons that generate income from their business entities:

*   Unlimited taxpayers are resident persons no matter where the income was generated; and
*   Limited taxpayers are foreign persons whose non-resident entity generated income in the territory of Brčko District.

Business persons are physical and legal entities, as well as associations and organisations.

If a legal entity or the management is seated in Brčko District, then that business entity is a resident of Brčko District.

The CIT rate in Brčko District is 10%.

Corporate residence

Federation BiH

Under Federation BiH (FBiH) CIT law, a resident is a legal entity whose headquarters (registration) is entered into a court registry or whose management and supervision over the business activities is located in the FBiH.

A PE of a non-resident is a permanent place of business through which the non-resident performs activity in whole or partially throughout the territory of the FBiH.

A PE as per FBiH CIT law is considered as follows:

- Management headquarters;
- Branch office;
- Business office;
- Factory;
- Workshop;
- Location of natural resources extraction;
- Construction site (construction or mounting project) when the work is performed during the period exceeding six months;
- Providing consulting or business services lasting for the period exceeding three months consecutively over a 12-month period; and
- A representative acting independently on behalf of a non-resident related to the activities of signing a contract or keeping supplies of products delivered on behalf of a non-resident.

Republika Srpska

In CIT law of Republika Srpska, a resident is a legal entity registered in Republika Srpska.

A PE shall be considered a place of business of a non-resident in Republika Srpska (i.e., construction works, installation and assembly works, infrastructure used for research or exploitation of natural resources or supervisory of the same). A PE shall also be a place of business where an individual or legal person has the authorisation to conclude contracts for a foreign legal entity.

Brčko District

A business entity is considered to be a resident of Brčko District if it is a legal person seated in the Brčko District or the management of a legal entity is seated in the Brčko District.

Other taxes

Value-added tax (VAT)

The standard rate is 17%. The VAT regime applies equally throughout the state of BiH. There is no reduced VAT rate in BiH.

Taxable persons are all individuals and legal entities registered, or required to be registered, for VAT. Any person making taxable supplies of goods and services that exceeds or is likely to exceed a threshold of BAM 50,000 (EUR 25,000) is required to register as a VAT payer.

Bosnia and Herzegovina

The export of goods is zero-rated.

Taxable transactions include the supply of goods and services in BiH by a taxable person, as well as the importation of goods to BiH by any person. The following transactions are also taxable:

- Transactions for no consideration or for a consideration less than the market value; and
- The private use of taxable goods by a taxable person (self-supply).

The following services are exempt from VAT in BiH:

- The leasing and subletting of residential houses, apartments and residential premises for a period of longer than 60 days;
- The supply of immovable property, except for the first transfer of the ownership rights or the rights to dispose of newly constructed immovable property;
- Financial services;
- Insurance and reinsurance services;
- Educational services provided by private or public educational institutions; and
- Postal services.

The VAT period is one calendar month.

Any tax credit that has not been used after a period of six months shall be refunded. Registered exporters are to be refunded within 30 days.

Excise duties
BiH levies excise tax on the following products: petroleum products; tobacco products; non-alcoholic drinks; alcohol and alcoholic drinks; beer and wine; coffee (unroasted, roasted and ground coffee and coffee extracts). The duties on petroleum products and drinks are set at a specific amount per litre, and the coffee excise is a specific amount per kilo.

There is a single excise regime throughout BiH.

Customs duties
The customs policy law and the rates of customs tariffs to be applied exist and are largely based on EU standards. BiH has signed the Stabilisation and Association Agreement (SAA) and the Central European Free Trade Agreement (CEFTA).

Branch income

Representative offices of foreign companies are permitted, although the concept of an international branch has not been recognised.

Income determination

Taxable profit is profit determined by adjusting the accounting profit as stated in the profit and loss statement and determined in accordance with International Financial Reporting Standards (IFRS) and accounting legislation, in accordance with the provisions of the CIT law.

Federation BiH

Income for assessment of taxable profit shall be income from the sales of products, services, goods, materials and financial, extraordinary and other income calculated in the profit and loss balance in accordance with accounting regulations and International Accounting Standards (IAS).

Dividends realised based on participation in the capital of other taxpayers shall not be included in the tax base. Shares in the profit of a business association will be considered dividends.

Income on the basis of collected written-off debt, in the event when these were included in the income in a previous period and were not subject to tax allowable or recognised expenditure, shall not be included in the tax base.

Expenses of production in accordance with accounting regulations and IAS shall be recognised in the value of stocks of unfinished production, semi products and finished products for the calculation of taxable profit.

Taxable base shall include profit from liquidation, and capital gain from the balance sheet.

Republika Srpska

The tax base for a fiscal year is the difference between taxable revenue and deductible expenditures for such fiscal year.

Taxable revenue for the purpose of computing the tax base includes all revenue from whatever source derived whether in cash or in kind or whether related or unrelated to the legal person's economic activity.

In the event of revenue received in the form of property (other than cash) or services, the amount of revenue is equal to the market price of the property or services received.

Expenditures are deductible from revenue in computing the tax base if the expenditures directly relate to the realised revenue.

Capital gain is realised through the sale or other type of transfer of capital or investment assets and represents a difference between the sales price and adjusted base of an asset. The sales price is the contracted price (i.e., the market price established by the competent tax authority in case it finds the contracted price to be lower than the market price).

Deductions

Depreciation – Federation BiH

Depreciation cost shall be allowed only if it relates to the property subject to depreciation and being used.

Depreciation of fixed assets shall be recognised as an expenditure in tax balance up to the amount established by proportionate application of the highest annual depreciation rates, prescribed by the BiH government.

Bosnia and Herzegovina

The property being depreciated with a value of less than BAM 1,000 may be fully deducted in the purchase year, on condition that the property was put in function.

Purchase value of computer hardware and software may be deducted fully in the year the purchase was made.

Depreciated assets, once depreciated, shall not be re-included in depreciation calculation for the purposes of tax balance.

Depreciation expenditure is tax allowed for increase of fixed assets value due to revalorisation in accordance with IAS/IFRS, up to the amount of calculated depreciation on the revalorisation base, and by using the proportion method prescribed by law.

Other tax allowable expenses
Expenditures are deductible from revenue in computing the tax base if the expenditures directly relate to the realised revenue.

Representation costs pertaining to business activity shall be recognised as expenditures in the amount of 30% of representation costs.

Costs of humanitarian, cultural, educational, scientific and sports purposes (except professional sports) shall be recognised as an expenditure in the amount of up to 3% of total income in the tax period.

Expenses of membership fees to the chambers shall be recognised as an expenditure in the amount not exceeding 0.1% of total income in the tax period, with the exception of membership fees regulated by the law.

Expenses based on sponsorship shall be recognised in the amount of 2% of total income in a tax period.

Tax allowable expenditures include expenditures of reservation for risks and expenditures in accordance with the laws and other regulations and reservations based on the contract for the following:

- Reservations for severance pay paid up to the prescribed amount;
- Reservations for expenditures of natural resources renewal;
- Reservations for expenditures in guaranteed time frames;
- Reservations for initiated court procedures; and
- Reservations for potential credit losses of banks and microcredit organisations.

The expenses occurring based on the write-off of disputable bills received are considered as tax allowable.

Tax treatment of losses
Tax losses shown in tax balance may be transferred against the profit in a future tax period but not exceeding five years. Tax losses are utilised on a first-in, first-out (FIFO) basis.

Tax credit for tax paid outside BiH

When a taxpayer generates income or profit through business activities outside of FBiH (directly or through a business unit) and pays the profit tax on such activities, the tax paid abroad shall be credited up to the amount of the profit tax that would have been paid for the income or profit generated by the same activities in FBiH.

Depreciation – Republika Srpska

Depreciation deductions are allowed only with respect to depreciable assets that are being used.

A depreciable asset is any tangible or intangible asset that is held for use in the production or supply of goods and services, for rental to others, or for administrative purposes. Land or any other asset that does not decrease in value through wear and tear or obsolescence is not considered a depreciable asset.

Other tax allowable expenses

Expenditures that are recognised and deductible from revenue also include the following:

* 30% of the cost of entertainment, meals and amusements related to the legal person's economic activity;
* Contributions to public institutions, humanitarian, cultural and educational organisations in the amount not exceeding 3% of the fiscal year's total revenue, and any excess contribution may be carried forward three years to apply against future contributions;
* Sponsorship expenses in an amount not exceeding 2% of the fiscal year's total revenue; and
* Scholarships to students in an amount up to 75% of average monthly net salary per employee in Republika Srpska in accordance with the latest published data from the body in charge of statistics.

A legal person using the accrual form of accounting is allowed a deduction with respect to bad debts and reserves.

Legal persons – other than banks, authorised credit institutions or insurance companies – shall be entitled to a bad debt deduction that arose in connection with a sale of goods or services but only if the revenue from the sale was previously included in the tax base of the legal person. For this purpose, a credit or trade receivable is considered a bad debt only if one of the following is true:

* It is more than 12 months past the due date for payment of the invoiced receivable;
* The creditor has sued for the receivables or an enforced collection procedure is initiated due to receivables;
* They are registered in the bankruptcy procedure of the debtor; or
* An agreement has been reached with the debtor who is not a physical or related person in the bankruptcy or liquidation procedure.

In the case of a bank or other authorised credit institution, a deduction is allowed for increases in the reserve account for customary losses due to unpaid loans, and the amount may not exceed 20% of the tax base.

Bosnia and Herzegovina

In the case of an insurance or reinsurance company, a deduction is allowed for increases in reserves as registered in accounting documents and as authorised according to applicable law. For insurance contracts pertaining to reinsurance, reserves are to be reduced so that they cover only part of the risk remaining with the insurer, and the amount may not exceed 20% of the tax base.

The tax savings resulting from a reduction or cancellation of any reserve that is collected later on comprises the taxable revenue at the moment of collection in accordance with this law.

Tax treatment of losses
Losses are carried forward and compensated for through reduction of the tax base in the following five years.

Tax losses are utilised on a FIFO basis.

Payment of foreign profit tax
If a legal entity from Republika Srpska obtains revenue from a foreign state and the revenue is taxed both in Republika Srpska and in the foreign state, then the tax paid to the foreign state, whether paid directly or withheld and remitted by another person, is to be credited from the Republika Srpska's profit tax, unless such legal entity from Republika Srpska elects to treat the foreign tax as a deductible expenditure in determining the fiscal year tax base.

Group taxation

Federation BiH
A headquarters company and its branches shall form a business association when there is direct or indirect control between them with no less than 90% share.

A business association shall hold the right to request tax consolidation on the condition that all businesses in the group are residents of FBiH.

A request for tax consolidation shall be filed to the authorised branch office of the tax authorities by a headquarters company.

Each group member is required to file its tax balance, and the headquarters of the business association shall file a consolidated tax balance for the group.

The consolidated tax balance shall offset losses of one or more businesses against the profit of other businesses in the association.

Individual group members shall be liable for the tax calculated per consolidated balance proportionately to the profit from the individual tax balance, and the payer of calculated tax per consolidated balance shall be the headquarters.

Once approved, tax consolidation shall be applied for the consecutive period of no less than five years.

When one, several or all the businesses in the association later opt for individual taxation, all group members shall be obliged to pay the difference proportionately on behalf of the tax privilege they used.

Republika Srpska

An affiliated group of legal persons located within Republika Srpska may elect to file a consolidated annual tax declaration.

An affiliated group of legal persons is a group of one or more legal entities from Republika Srpska that are connected through the ownership of stock with a common parent provided that the common parent owns at least 80% of the stock in a legal person that is included in the affiliated group. If the common parent does not own at least 80% of the stock in a legal person that is included in the affiliated group, then the parent may file a consolidated tax declaration if one or more other legal persons in the affiliated group own at least 80% of the stock in such legal person.

Tax incentives

Federation BiH

For a taxpayer who established in the year for which the CIT is calculated, more than 30% of totally generated income by exportation is being relieved from CIT for that year.

A taxpayer who invested in production within the territory of FBiH for five consecutive years for a minimum fee of BAM 20 million will be relieved from taxation for a period of five years, starting with the first year in which it has invested at least BAM 4 million.

A taxpayer who employs more than 50% of handicap or special needs individuals within its company for a period of time longer than one year is relieved from CIT for the year in which more than 50% of handicap or special needs individuals are employed within the company.

Republika Srpska

There are no CIT incentives available in Republika Srpska.

Withholding taxes (WHT)

Federation BiH (FBiH)

WHT in FBiH shall be the tax calculated on non-resident income generated throughout the territory of FBiH.

The base for calculation of WHT is the gross amount paid by a resident of FBiH to a non-resident based on the dividends, interest, royalties and other intellectual property rights, compensations for market research, tax consulting services, auditors' services, fun and sports events, premium insurance for insurance or reinsurance of risk in FBiH, telecommunication services between FBiH and other countries, as well as all other services performed on the territory of FBiH.

Withholding tax shall be paid at the rate of 5% on dividend payments and 10% for interest, royalties and other, if not reduced under a tax treaty.

Republika Srpska

Any legal or physical person from Republika Srpska, as well as any foreign legal or physical person with PE in Republika Srpska who pays revenue to a foreign legal person is to withhold tax from the total payment of revenue and is to remit the withheld tax to the Public Revenues Account of Republika Srpska.

Bosnia and Herzegovina

The WHT applies to the following revenue payments, regardless of whether the revenue is received in Republika Srpska or abroad:

- Payment of interest or its functional equivalent under financial instruments and arrangements from a resident;
- Payment for entertainment or sporting activities carried out in Republika Srpska regardless of whether the revenue is received by the entertainer or sportsman or by another person;
- Payment for the performance of management, consulting, financial, technical or administrative services, if the revenue is from a resident or if the revenue is paid by or included in the books and records of a PE in Republika Srpska or if such payment is deducted for the purpose of determining the tax base;
- Payment in the form of insurance premiums for the insuring or reinsuring of risks in Republika Srpska;
- Payment for telecommunication services between Republika Srpska and a foreign state;
- Payment of royalties;
- Payment of lease for movable property; and
- Payment for the performance of other services in Republika Srpska.

Withholding tax is not due on dividend payments.

The WHT rate in Republika Srpska is 10%.

Tax administration

Federation BiH
A taxpayer is obliged to file correctly and accurately a completed tax return (declaration) with the tax balance to the authorised branch office of the tax administration within 30 days after the deadline for submitting financial statements.

The deadline for submission of annual calculation of business results is 28 February of the following year.

Republika Srpska
Tax declaration for a tax year shall be filed no later than 90 days upon the end of the tax year, and in case of a calendar year, no later than 31 March of the current year for the previous year.

A taxpayer shall pay the profit tax pursuant to the final tax declaration.

Corporate taxes in Botswana

For more information, contact:

Butler Phirie
PricewaterhouseCoopers
Plot 50371, Fairground Office Park
Gaborone
Botswana
Tel: +267 395 2011
Email: butler.phirie@bw.pwc.com

Significant developments

The following changes to taxation were confirmed by the Ministry of Finance and Development Planning and will take effect on 1 July 2011 (i.e., in the tax year 2011/12):

- The current two-tier system of company tax and additional company tax (ACT) is to be abolished and to be replaced with a flat corporate tax rate of 25% with no ACT component; and
- Withholding tax (WHT) on dividends to resident and non-resident shareholders is to be reduced from 15% to 7.5%.

Taxes on corporate income

Company tax is imposed at a rate of 15% for non-manufacturing companies and 5% for manufacturing companies. ACT is imposed at a rate of 10% and the ACT amount could be carried forward up to 5 years to be set off against WHT payable on dividends paid.

International Financial Services Centre (IFSC) companies are taxed at a flat rate of 15%. Companies must apply for a certificate to be classified as IFSC companies, which deal only in specified services and only with non-residents.

Corporate tax calculation/non-manufacturing company fiscal year ending 30 June 2011:

Corporate tax calculation		
Net income before taxation		BWP 1,000,000
Add		
Depreciation	50,000	
Accounting loss on disposal of machinery and equipment	5,000	
Donations	1,000	
Balancing charge (Tax profit on disposal of machinery and equipment)	35,000	91,000
		1,091,000
Less		
Accounting profit on disposal of industrial buildings	33,000	

Botswana

Corporate tax calculation

Net income before taxation		**BWP 1,000,000**
Initial allowance:		
Industrial buildings at 25% on cost	100,000	
Annual allowances:		
Commercial buildings at 2.5% on cost	5,000	
Industrial buildings at 2.5% on cost	10,000	
Plant and machinery at 15% on cost	40,000	
Office equipment at 10% on cost	2,000	
Computer equipment at 25% on cost	10,000	
Motor vehicles at 25% on cost (Subject to BWP 175,000 limit for motor cars)	20,000	
Approved training expenditure (Additional 100% of cost of 20,000)	20,000	240,000
		851,000
Add – Taxable capital gain on disposal of property		49,000
Taxable income		BWP 900,000
Tax thereon 25% of 900,000		BWP 225,000

Notes

1. Exchange rate of the pula at 31 December 2009: USD 1 = BWP 6.76.
2. CIT at a rate of 15% plus ACT at a rate of 10%/proposed rate of 25%.

Corporate residence

Corporate residence is determined on the basis that a company's registered office or place of incorporation is in Botswana or it is managed and controlled in Botswana.

Other taxes

There are no other taxes on income.

Branch income

Company tax at the rate of 25% is payable on branch profits.

Income determination

Inventory valuation
Inventories are valued at cost less such amounts, if any, that the Commissioner General believes are reasonable as representing the amount by which the value of such stock has been diminished because of damage, deterioration, obsolescence or other cause. Although not expressly excluded by legislation, last-in, first-out (LIFO) has not been accepted in practice by the tax authorities.

Capital gains
Gains from disposal of specified capital assets (immovable property and marketable securities, including shares in private companies) are included in taxable income in the hands of the corporate taxpayer. Acquisition costs of immovable property are subject to a 10% compound annual addition for inflation for the period from acquisition to

30 June 1982, and thereafter to an inflation addition based on the increase in the consumer price index to the date of sale. For other gains, no inflation allowances are granted, but the taxable gain is set at 75% of the total gain.

The aggregate amount of capital losses is set-off against the aggregate amount of capital gains in the same tax year. Any excess of loss is deducted from aggregate gains over losses accruing in the succeeding tax year only. Capital losses cannot, in any circumstances, be deducted against other income.

Inter-company dividends

Dividend income is not subject to tax. A withholding tax of 15% (proposed rate – 7.5%) is deducted from dividend payments.

Foreign income

Resident corporations are not generally taxed on a worldwide income basis. However, interest and dividend income from a foreign source is taxed in the hands of the resident company on an accrual basis. Relief is given for any withholding tax imposed on such income.

Deductions

Depreciation and depletion

Annual and capital allowances available are as follows.

Companies other than mining companies:
Annual taxation allowances for expenditures incurred on machinery and equipment before 30 June 1982 can be claimed up to 100%. This allowance may be for any proportion of previously unclaimed expenditure. For expenditure incurred on machinery and equipment after 30 June 1982, annual allowances are granted, calculated on cost by the straight-line method on the basis of the expected useful lives of the individual assets. Guidelines are provided for expected useful lives of different categories of assets, which vary from four to 10 years. Book depreciation is not required to conform to tax depreciation. The capital allowance claimable on a company motorcar is restricted to a maximum of BWP 175,000.

An initial allowance of 25% of cost is granted on certain industrial buildings. All industrial and commercial buildings (excluding residential properties) are granted a 2.5% annual allowance based on cost or, in the case of an industrial building on which an initial allowance has been claimed, the original cost less the initial allowance.

Balancing allowances and charges are brought to account on the disposal of assets on which allowances have been claimed. Where disposal value of an item of machinery or equipment exceeds the difference between expenditure incurred on the asset and allowances granted, the whole amount is taxable as corporate income or the balancing charge can be offset against further additions of new equipment, thus providing rollover relief.

However, there is no rollover relief on motorcars except where the cars are used in a car rental or taxi service business.

Botswana

Mining companies:
Mining companies are taxed in accordance with the provisions of the Twelfth Schedule to the Botswana Income Tax Act. A summary of the information contained in this schedule is set out below:

1. Mining profits, other than profits from diamond mining, shall be taxed according to the following formula:

$$\text{Annual tax rate} = 70 \text{ minus } \frac{1{,}500}{x}$$

   where x is the profitability ratio, given by taxable income as a percentage of gross income provided that the tax rate shall not be less than the company tax rate (currently 25%).
2. Head office expenses allowed as a deduction in ascertaining gross revenue from mineral licence shall be limited to 1.5% of gross income for the year of assessment, and any excess of such expense above the limit shall be treated and taxed as a dividend.
3. Where a foreign controlled resident company has a foreign debt-to-equity ratio in excess of 3:1 at any time during the year of assessment, the amount of interest paid by the resident company during that year on that part of the debt that exceeds the ratio shall be disallowed as a deduction and the amount so disallowed shall be treated and taxed as a dividend.
4. Where the interest rate on a loan made by a foreign-based company to an affiliate company resident in Botswana is considered by the commissioner to be in excess of the market rate, such excess will be disallowed as a deduction and taxed as a dividend.
5. In ascertaining the business chargeable income of any person for any tax year from a business of mining, there shall be deducted from his business income an allowance, to be known as a mining capital allowance, computed in accordance with 100% of the mining capital expenditure made in the year in which such expenditure was incurred, with unlimited carryforward of losses.
6. Diamond mining is usually taxed in terms of an agreement with the Government of Botswana.

Net operating losses
Losses may be carried forward for five years, with the exception of farming, mining and prospecting operations, for which there is no time limit. There is no allowance for carrybacks.

Payments to foreign affiliates
Royalties, interest and service fees paid to foreign affiliates are generally deductible, provided such amounts are at arm's length and withholding tax is paid.

Taxes
Any taxes paid are specifically disallowed in computing a company's taxable income.

Other significant items
An allowance is granted for dwelling houses erected for employees by a business other than a mining business. The amount of the allowance is the lower of cost or BWP 25,000 for each dwelling house constructed.

A deduction of 200% of the cost of an approved training expenditure is allowed.

As of 13 February 1984, companies with shareholders having 5% or more of the equity, either directly or indirectly, are classified as close companies, and there are additional tax regulations in respect of these shareholders.

Small companies, that is, resident private companies whose gross income does not exceed BWP 300,000, may elect that the company be taxed as a partnership.

Expenses incurred by the company for having its shares listed on the Botswana Stock Exchange are deductible in determining the chargeable income of the company.

Group taxation

There are no concessions for group taxation, other than for wholly-owned subsidiary companies of the Botswana Development Corporation.

Tax incentives

Inward investment
To encourage investment in Botswana, extra tax reliefs on revenue or capital account will be granted for specific business development projects if the government is satisfied that such projects are beneficial to Botswana.

Withholding taxes (WHT)

WHT at the following rates must be deducted from payments to residents and non-residents unless a double taxation agreement exists.

Residents	%
Interest	10
Dividends (Proposed rate 7.5%)	15
Payments due under certain construction contracts	3
Non-residents	**%**
Interest	15
Dividends (Proposed rate 7.5%)	15
Payments due under certain construction contracts	3
Payments for royalties, management or consultancy fees	15
Payments for entertainment fees	10

Botswana has tax agreements with the following countries, which provide for withholding at the rates shown.

Treaty	Dividends	Interest	Royalties	Management and consultancy fees
	%	%	%	%
Mauritius	*5 or 10	12	12.5	15
South Africa	**10 or 15	10	10	10
Sweden	15	15	15	15
United Kingdom	*5 or 12	10	10	7.5
France	*5 or 12	10	10	7.5

Botswana

Treaty	Dividends	Interest	Royalties	Management and consultancy fees
	%	%	%	%
Russia	*5 or 10	10	10	10
Barbados	*5 or 12	10	10	10
Seychelles	*5 or 10	7.5	10	10
Namibia	10	10	10	15
Zimbabwe	*5 or 10	10	10	10
India	*7.5 or 10	10	10	10

Notes

*   5% or 7.5% rate of withholding tax is applicable if the beneficial shareholder is a company resident in the double taxation agreement country and holds at least 25% of the share capital in the company paying dividends. Otherwise, the other rate applies (10% or 12% as the case may be).

** 10% rate of WHT is applicable if the beneficial shareholder is a company resident in the double taxation agreement country and holds at least 25% of the share capital in the company paying dividends.

Tax administration

Returns
Botswana has a fiscal year ending on 30 June. However, a business may select its own accounting year, which may end on a date other than 30 June. This accounting year is accepted for the computation of the company's taxable income, which will be the last accounting period prior to 30 June.

The system is one that requires all taxpayers to file tax returns in standard format (providing information relating to taxable income earned). Self-assessment, which means that the return submitted constitutes the assessment, was introduced effective 1 July 2001.

Payment of tax
Under the self-assessment tax procedures, if the tax payable for a tax year exceeds BWP 50,000, then the tax is required to be paid in equal quarterly instalments over the period of the 12 months ending on the company's financial year-end date. Where the tax is less than BWP 50,000, then the tax is payable within four months from the company's financial year-end date.

Corporate taxes in Brazil

B

Significant developments

On 16 December 2009, Brazil's Executive Branch published Provisional Measure (PM) 472 which, among other provisions, includes new thin capitalisation rules that can be summarised as follows:

- Interest paid or credited by a Brazilian entity to a related party (individual or legal entity), not resident or domiciled in a tax haven jurisdiction, may only be deducted for income tax purposes if the interest expense is viewed as necessary for the activities of the local entity and the amount of debt granted by the related party does not exceed twice the amount of its participation in the net equity of the Brazilian entity. A second test also needs to be performed including the total amount of debts with any foreign related party. If under either "debt/equity" test a 2:1 ratio is exceeded, the portion of interest related to the excess debt amount will not be deductible for Brazilian income tax purposes.
- Similar provisions are also applicable to interest paid or credited by a Brazilian entity to an individual or legal entity (whether or not a related party) resident or domiciled in a tax haven or favourable tax regime jurisdiction. In these cases, the interest expense would only be deductible for Brazilian income tax purposes if the expense is viewed as ordinary and necessary as referenced above, and the total amount of the Brazilian entity's debt with any foreign party resident or domiciled in a tax haven jurisdiction does not exceed 30% of the entity's net equity.

The two above-mentioned rules also apply to cases where a guarantor, representative or any other intervening party is a related party or resident of a tax haven jurisdiction (respectively).

It should be noted that the above-mentioned rules are still pending final approval by the authorities and as such might be subject to further changes.

Taxes on corporate income

Corporate income tax (IRPJ)
Federal income tax is assessed at the fixed rate of 15% on taxable income.

Corporate income tax is generally computed on the basis of annual taxable income. For tax purposes a company's year-end is 31 December. A different year-end for corporate purposes is irrelevant.

Brazil

Surcharge
Corporate taxpayers are also subject to a surcharge of 10% on the annual taxable income in excess of BRL 240,000.

Social contribution on net income (CSLL)
All legal entities are subject to a social contribution to the federal government at the rate of 9% (except for financial and insurance institutions, which are taxed at the rate of 15%), which is not deductible for income tax purposes. The tax basis is the profit before income tax, after some adjustments.

Brazilian taxpayers have the option (subject to some restrictions) to calculate IRPJ and CSLL on net income using an "actual profits" method ("Lucro Real"), which is based on total taxable income (book results before taxes), adjusted by certain additions and deductions as determined in the legislation. Brazilian taxpayers have also the option to calculate IRPJ and CSLL using a "presumed profits" method ("Lucro Presumido"). Under the "presumed profits" method, the income is calculated on a quarterly basis on an amount equal to different percentages of gross revenue (based on the entity's activities) and adjusted as determined by the prevailing legislation.

Whenever the tax basis is negative (tax loss), it may be carried forward without any time limitation. However, the use of tax losses is limited to 30% of each year's taxable income. There is no carryback.

Corporate residence

A corporation is considered resident in Brazil if it has been incorporated in Brazil, and its tax domicile is where its head office is located.

Other taxes

Import tax
Import tax ("Imposto de Importação", or II) is levied on the CIF (Cost, Insurance and Freight) price of the imported good. The rates depend on the degree of necessity and are defined in accordance with the product's tariff code contained in the Mercosur Harmonised System (NCM/SH). The rates tend to be in the range of 10% to 20%, although there are many exceptions which are subject to higher or lower rates.

Value-added tax (VAT)
VAT is payable on imports, sales and transfers of goods and products in the form of a federal excise tax ("Imposto sobre Produtos Industrializados", or IPI) at various rates in accordance with the nature of the product (normally around 10% to 15%, but in certain cases ranging to over 300%); and a state sales and service tax ("Imposto sobre as operações relativas à Circulação de Mercadorias, e sobre a prestação de Serviços de transporte interestadual e intermunicipal e de comunicação", or ICMS) with rates ranging from 7% to 25%.

Except for services related to freight and transportation, communications, and electric energy, which are subject to ICMS, income from services rendered is normally subject to a municipal service tax ("Imposto Sobre Serviços de qualquer natureza", or ISS) – which is not a value added tax – with rates ranging from 2% to 5%.

COFINS

COFINS ("Contribuição para o Financiamento da Seguridade social"), levied at the rate of 7.6% is a monthly federal social assistance contribution calculated as a percentage of revenue. A COFINS credit system is meant to ensure the tax is applied only once on the final value of each transaction. However, some taxpayers (such as financial institutions, telecommunication companies, cooperatives and companies, which opt to calculate Brazilian corporate income tax and social contribution on net income using a "Presumed Profit" method) are still subject to the previous COFINS system, that is, COFINS is applied at the rate of 3% and no credit system is allowed.

PIS

PIS ("Programa de Integração Social") levied at the rate of 1.65% is also a federal social contribution calculated as a percentage of revenue. A PIS credit system is meant to ensure the tax is applied only once on the final value of each transaction. However, some taxpayers (such as financial institutions, telecommunication companies, cooperatives and companies which opt to calculate Brazilian corporate income tax and social contribution on net income using a "Presumed Profit" method) are still subject to the previous PIS system, that is, PIS is applied at the rate of 0.65% and no credit system is allowed.

PIS and COFINS on imports

Importation of goods and services are also subject to PIS and COFINS (in addition to all other taxes imposed on import transactions). PIS and COFINS are imposed on the Brazilian entity or individual (the importer of goods or services) and applied at the rates of 1.65% and 7.6%, respectively. The contributions paid upon import transactions may, in some instances, be creditable.

IOF

IOF ("Imposto sobre operações de crédito, câmbio, seguro e sobre operações relativas a títulos e valores mobiliários", or Tax on Financial Transactions) is a tax levied primarily on certain financial transactions, such as loans, foreign exchange operations, insurance and securities and transactions with gold (as a financial asset) and foreign exchange instruments. The applicable rate will vary depending on the transaction. The IOF rate may be reduced to 0% in some cases, such as: (i) exchange transactions relating to the inflow of revenues in Brazil deriving from the export of goods and services; (ii) exchange transactions relating to the inflow and outflow of resources in and from Brazil, stemming from foreign loans and financing obtained as from 23 October 2008; (iii) liquidation of exchange operations for the purposes of repatriation of funds invested in the stock market; and (iv) remittances of interest on net equity and dividends relating to investment in the stock market.

CIDE

CIDE ("Contribuição de Intervenção no Domínio Econômico", or Contribution for the Intervention in the Economic Domain) is a contribution levied at the rate of 10% on remittances made by corporate taxpayers for royalties and for administrative and technical services provided by non-residents. CIDE is payable by the local entity, and therefore, not creditable to the non-resident. CIDE does not represent a liability to the foreign recipient. CIDE is not applied on the payments relating to the license to use, market or sublicense software, provided that it does not involve transfer of technology.

Brazil

Property taxes

A property tax named IPTU ("Imposto Predial e Territorial Urbano") is levied annually based on the fair market value of property in urban areas at rates that generally vary according to the municipality and location of the property. In the municipality of São Paulo, the basic IPTU rate is 1% for residential properties or 1.5% for commercial properties (both rates may be increased or decreased according to the market value of the property). Another property tax – ITBI ("Imposto de Transmissão de Bens Imóveis Inter Vivos") is levied at the transfer of immovable property, with rates also varying based on the municipality were the property is located. The ITBI rate in the municipality of São Paulo is currently 2%, applied over the market value of the property.

A state property transfer tax – ITCMD ("Imposto sobre Transmissão Causa Mortis e Doações") is normally payable at rates varying from state to state on inheritances and donations of goods and rights. In the State of São Paulo, ITCMD is charged at the rate of 4%.

Branch income

Profits of branches of foreign corporations are taxable at the normal rates applicable to local corporations.

Income determination

Inventory valuation

Brazilian income tax regulations require that inventory may be valued at the actual average cost or by the cost of the most recently acquired or produced goods. Rulings to the effect that last-in, first-out (LIFO) is not acceptable have been given.

Capital gains

Capital gains deriving from the sale of assets and rights, including shares/quotas, are taxed as ordinary income. However, profits on certain long-term sales of permanent assets may be computed for tax purposes on a cash basis. Profits on long-term contracts may be computed on a percentage-of-completion basis. When these contracts are entered into with the government or government-owned companies, the profit may be recognised on a cash basis for tax purposes.

Except during the year when incurred, capital losses may be offset only against capital gains. Unused capital losses are treated similarly to income tax losses with regard to limits on use and carryforward period.

Capital gains derived by non-residents (including transactions carried out abroad between two non-resident investors, involving assets or rights located in Brazil), are taxed in Brazil. The Brazilian source performing the remittance of capital gains to the non-resident (whether a Brazilian acquirer or the local solicitor of a foreign acquiring entity) would withhold the applicable income tax on such amounts on behalf of the latter at the rate of 15% (or 25% if the beneficiary is located in a tax haven jurisdiction).

Foreign income

Brazilian resident companies are taxed on worldwide income. Profits of foreign subsidiaries, affiliates and controlled companies are taxed at the date of the financial statements in which the profits are calculated, regardless of remittance. Double taxation could be avoided by means of foreign tax credits.

Foreign exchange gain
With respect to foreign exchange gain, which may arise from receivables or liabilities denominated in foreign currency, Brazilian tax legislation allows the local company to elect to consider the related effect, for tax computation purposes, either upon accrual or cash basis (i.e., actual receipt/payment of funds).

Stock dividends
Stock dividend distributions are not subject to withholding tax.

Financial income
Fixed-rate interest income from short-, medium-, or long-term financial market transactions, including swap transactions, is subject to withholding income tax at rates ranging from 15% to 22.5%. Non-fixed financial gains related to stock/commodities exchange and/or futures market transactions are taxed at the rates of 20% (day-trade) and 15% (all other cases). The total income or gain is considered taxable income, and the tax withheld may be offset against the total tax due by the corporate taxpayer.

Interest on net equity
Companies can pay interest (calculated on a pro rata basis and up to a given rate known as the "long-term interest rate" (TJLP) – which is currently set at 6.00% in 2010) to partners and/or share/quotaholders, based on the company's net equity. Such interest, which may not exceed the highest of 50% of the annual profits or 50% of the accumulated earnings and profits, is deductible for both income tax and social contribution purposes and is subject to 15% tax at the source. Whenever the beneficiary is a legal entity subject to normal income tax in Brazil, the tax withheld at the source may be taken by the recipient as a tax credit against the normal corporate income tax due or the tax due at the source on distributions of interest. If the beneficiary is a Brazilian resident individual, such interest will not become subject to any further taxation.

Deductions

Depreciation and depletion
Depreciation is allowable on a straight-line basis over the useful life of the asset. The annual rates normally allowable are 10% for machinery, equipment, furniture and installations; 20% for vehicles; and 4% for buildings. Accelerated depreciation is allowed for companies with a two or three working shift operation by increasing normal rates by 50% and 100%, respectively.

Depletion allowances are allowed for natural resources on a useful-life basis. Special incentive depletion allowances are granted for mining operations.

Net operating losses
Tax losses may be carried forward without any time limitation. However, the tax loss compensation may not reduce taxable income by more than 30% of its amount prior to the compensation itself. Tax loss is defined as the accounting loss adjusted for tax purposes. There is no carryback.

Brazil

Payments to foreign affiliates and related companies
Royalties and technical service fees payable to foreign companies with a direct or indirect controlling interest in the Brazilian company are deductible for tax purposes (observing applicable deduction limits), provided the contract has been duly registered with the National Institute of Industrial Property (INPI) and approved by the Brazilian Central Bank. Brazilian legislation recently introduced thin capitalisation rules, which restrict the deductibility of interest expenses in Brazil. Deductibility of interest is also conditioned to approval of the respective contract by the Brazilian Central Bank. However, on unregistered related-party loans the deductible interest may not exceed interest calculated using the six-month US dollar deposit LIBOR (London Interbank Offered Rate) rate plus 3%. Amounts paid, credited, delivered or remitted at any title, direct or indirectly, to individuals or legal entities residing in tax haven jurisdictions (as provided by Brazilian legislation) should not be considered tax deductible provided that operational substance can be allocated abroad.

Foreign exchange loss
With respect to foreign exchange loss, which may arise from receivables or liabilities denominated in foreign currency, Brazilian tax legislation allows the local company to elect to consider the related effect, for tax computation purposes, either upon accrual or cash basis (i.e., actual receipt/payment of funds).

Losses on bad debts
Losses are tax deductible, depending on the amounts, time overdue and administrative and/or legal actions taken to recover losses. Losses arising from inter-company transactions are not tax deductible.

Taxes/contributions
Taxes, contributions and related costs, such as late-payment interest, are deductible for tax purposes on the accrual basis. This rule does not apply to taxes/contributions being or to be challenged by the taxpayer at any level of litigation, which are deductible for tax purposes only on a cash basis.

Other deductions
Among others, travel expenses may only be considered deductible if they are duly documented and substantiated. Donations are deductible up to certain limits if recipients are registered as charitable institutions. At the option of the company, research and development expenditures may be deducted when incurred or deferred until termination of the project and then amortised over a period of not less than five years. Expenses of group medical care and health insurance programmes for employees and contributions to private supplementary pension schemes are considered deductible if supplied to all employees indistinctly.

Group taxation

Consolidated tax returns are not permitted in Brazil.

Tax incentives

Inward investment
Total or partial exemption from duty, excise tax and social contributions on imported equipment is granted on certain approved investment projects.

Regional incentives

Income tax exemptions or reductions are also available for companies set up in specified regions within Brazil, primarily the north and northeast regions. These incentives are designed to accelerate the development of certain less-developed regions and industries considered to be of importance to the economy.

Capital investment

Approved investment projects are granted accelerated depreciation on nationally produced equipment and access to low-cost financing. Sales of some capital equipment are exempt from state sales tax.

Other incentives

Brazilian corporate taxpayers can apply a percentage of their income tax liability on deposit for reinvestment and investment in their own approved investment projects. These approved investment projects are normally granted total or partial income tax exemption. Excise and sales tax exemptions are granted to exporters of manufactured goods.

As from 2005, Brazilian legislation has introduced tax incentives for projects focusing on technological innovation.

Withholding taxes (WHT)

Profits/dividends distributed to resident or non-resident beneficiaries (individuals and/or legal entities) relating to periods beginning on or after 1 January, 1996 are not subject to withholding income tax. This provision is also applicable to dividends paid to non-resident companies located in a tax haven jurisdiction.

The withholding tax rate applicable to payments for services rendered by non-resident companies or individuals is generally 15% but can be increased to 25% in certain cases.

Payments for services, royalties and interest to non-resident companies located in a tax haven jurisdiction are subject to withholding income tax at the rate of 25%.

Certain types of income paid by Brazilian companies to non-resident recipients are subject to withholding tax as follows:

Recipient	Dividends (1)	Interest	Royalties
	%	%	%
Non-resident companies and individuals:			
Non-treaty:	0	15	15
Tax Haven	0	25	25
*Treaty (2):			
Argentina	0	15	15
Austria	15	15	25, 15, 10
Belgium	15, 10	15, 10	20, 15, 10
Canada	15	15, 10	25, 15
Chile	15, 10	15	15
China, P.R.	15	15	25, 15

Brazil

Recipient	Dividends (1)	Interest	Royalties
	%	%	%
Czech Republic	15	15, 10	25, 15
Denmark	25	15	25, 15
Ecuador	15	15	25, 15
Finland	10	15	25, 15, 10
France	15	15, 10	25, 15, 10
Hungary	15	15, 10	25, 15
India	15	15	25, 15
Israel	15, 10	15	15, 10
Italy	15	15	25, 15
Japan	12.5	12.5	25, 15, 12.5
Korea, Rep. of	15, 10	15, 10	25, 15, 10
Luxembourg	25, 15	15, 10	25, 15
Mexico	15, 10	15	15, 10
Netherlands	15	15, 10	25, 15
Norway	15	15	25, 15
Peru	15, 10	15	15
Philippines	25, 15	15, 10	25, 15
Portugal	15, 10	15	15
Slovak Republic	15	15, 10	25, 15
South Africa	15, 10	15	15, 10
Spain	15, 10	15, 10	15, 10
Sweden	25	25	25
Ukraine	15, 10	15	15

Notes

1. Note that the remittance of dividends is not subject to taxation in Brazil, since 1 January 1996.
2. Treaty rates in excess of those in force for non-treaty countries are automatically reduced. *The treaty concerned should be consulted to confirm that the tax reduction is applicable in each case.

Tax administration

Returns
With few exceptions, corporate entities, including those that are foreign-controlled, must file an annual adjusting tax return consolidating the monthly results of the previous calendar year. This tax return must normally be filed by the end of June following the tax year ending on 31 December.

Supporting documentation must be retained for at least five years.

Payment of tax
In the case of income tax, it is calculated monthly and prepayments must be paid by the last working day of the subsequent month. Any amounts of income tax due for the year (exceeding the prepayments performed) must be paid by the last working day of March of the subsequent year.

When income tax is calculated quarterly, the taxpayer must perform the applicable payment by the last working day of the month subsequent to the end of the quarter. There is an option to pay the tax due at the end of each quarter in three instalments, the first one starting from the subsequent month to the end of the quarter.

Public digital bookkeeping system – SPED

Brazil is currently implementing a new public system of digital bookkeeping known as SPED, which aims at gradually replacing paper copies of invoices and tax records for electronic files. SPED can be defined as an instrument that unifies the activities of reception, validation, storage and legalisation of records and documents that are part of the commercial and tax bookkeeping of companies, through a single, computerised flow of data.

Comprised by three pillars (electronic invoice, digital fiscal bookkeeping and digital accounting bookkeeping), the implementation of the SPED requires adjustments on the relationship with tax authorities, clients, suppliers and, mainly, on the internal operational processes, which will demand an integrated action from different areas (tax, accounting, IT, supplies, production, commercial, and others). On the other hand, occasional inconsistencies from databases, as well as operational errors related to tax and accounting information to be generated, usually unknown to the companies' administration, will be subject to an increased visibility and monitoring by the Brazilian tax authorities.

Other issues

Transfer pricing

The Brazilian transfer pricing rules apply to import and export transactions of goods, services and rights between related parties (the legislation provides a broad list of the parties considered as "related" for transfer pricing purposes). Under such rules, the transfer price determined between related parties will be acceptable, for Brazilian tax purposes, if it is determined that such price is at arm's length according to one of the traditional methods established by the legislation (no profit methods available). Moreover, all operations with jurisdictions considered as tax havens will also be subject to transfer pricing rules whether involving related parties or not.

Furthermore, interest arising from loans contracted with foreign related parties, which are not registered with the Brazilian Central Bank (BACEN), will also be subject to compliance with such rules. Operations involving royalty agreements will not be subject to the rules below if the related contract is registered with the BACEN and the Brazilian Institute of Industrial Property (INPI).

Therefore, the adequacy of the price practiced between the related parties in any operations involving goods, services and rights, may be supported through the application of one of the following methods, as determined under the Brazilian transfer pricing regulations (the company may choose the most convenient method):

- Methods used on import transactions:
    1. Comparable Independent Price Method (PIC);
    2. Resale Price Less Profit Method (PRL); and
    3. Production Cost Plus Profit Method (CPL).
- Methods used in export transactions:
    1. Export Sales Price Method (PVEx);

Brazil

2. Resale Price Method; and
3. Acquisition or Production Cost Plus Taxes and Profit Method (CAP).

Relief of proof rules for inter-company export transactions is available.

For more information, contact:

Irina Tsvetkova
PricewaterhouseCoopers
9-11 Maria Louisa Blvd., 8th Floor
1000 Sofia, Bulgaria
Tel: +359 2 9355 126
Email: irina.tsvetkova@bg.pwc.com

B

Significant developments

Corporate income tax rate
The rate of corporate income tax is 10%.

Withholding taxes
The withholding tax rate on interest, royalties, capital gains, rentals and technical services is 10%. The withholding tax rate on dividends and liquidation quotas is 5%.

One-off taxes
All one-off taxes (applicable to certain types of expenses) are levied at a rate of 10%.

Tax exemption for dividends payable between European Union (EU)/ European Economic Area (EEA) companies
As from 1 January 2009, dividends and liquidation quotas payable to or by an EU/EEA-based company are tax exempt without special conditions, similar to dividends and liquidation quotas payable between Bulgarian companies.

Thin capitalisation
The Bulgarian debt-to-equity ratio for thin capitalisation purposes is 3:1. In addition, the period for carryforward of restricted interest costs is five years.

Corporate reorganisations
Deferral of taxation is provided in the tax law for certain types of corporate reorganisations in accordance with the EU Merger Directive.

Taxes on corporate income

Corporate income tax
In general, corporate income is subject to tax at a flat rate of 10%.

Alternative tax
Income earned by organisers of games of chance is subject to 12% or 15% alternative tax, applied on a specific tax basis (e.g., the total value of the stakes made). In addition, a special tax regime applies to the operation of commercial maritime vessels as per their net tonnage at a rate of 10%.

Bulgaria

Corporate residence

A corporation is resident in Bulgaria for tax purposes if it is incorporated in Bulgaria. Permanent establishments (PE) of foreign tax residents (e.g., branches) are treated as separate entities similar to Bulgarian residents for tax and accounting purposes.

Other taxes

Value-added tax (VAT)

VAT was initially introduced on 1 April 1994. As of the date of Bulgaria's accession to the European Union (EU) on 1 January 2007 new VAT legislation entered into force, which is based on the provisions of Council Directive 2006/112/EC. Respectively, new concepts (e.g., intracommunity supplies and acquisitions, triangulation, distance sales) and a number of changes (e.g., VAT treatment of real estate, place of supply rules for certain services) were introduced. As of 1 January 2010 the so called VAT Package amendments were implemented in the Bulgarian VAT legislation.

The tax base includes the agreed price, customs and excise duties, if any, and certain other expenses (e.g., commission, packing, transport, insurance costs charged by the supplier to the purchaser, statutory taxes and fees), but does not include damages and interest for late payment.

The standard VAT rate is 20%. A reduced VAT rate of 7% applies to certain tourist services. Some activities are zero-rated, including intracommunity supplies, exports of goods to countries outside the EU, as well as international transport of goods (i.e., transport to or from countries outside of the EU).

Some supplies are VAT exempt without the right to a VAT credit, including (but not limited to) certain land transactions; leasing of residential property to individuals, financial, insurance, gambling, educational and health services. Options to charge VAT exist for certain land transactions, leasing of residential property to individuals and finance lease contracts.

The following statutory periods for VAT refunds apply:

- 30 days – For persons that have performed supplies subject to zero-rate within the last 12 months, exceeding 30% of the total value of all taxable supplies performed by them in the same period as well as by large investors meeting certain specific conditions; and
- Two months and 30 days – In all other cases.

The following mechanism for VAT recovery applies to VAT-registered companies: the positive or negative difference between the output VAT charged by the company and the input VAT for the respective month for which recovery is claimed results, respectively, in VAT payable or refundable. The VAT payable should be remitted to the state budget not later than the fourteenth day of the month following the respective month. VAT refundable is offset against any VAT payable in the following two months, and any remainder is effectively recovered within 30 days thereafter.

It is possible to claim a refund for VAT paid with respect to assets acquired not earlier than five years prior to the VAT registration, under certain conditions. If the assets are real estate, the term is 20 years.

Excise duties

Excise duties are charged as a percentage of the sales price or customs value or as a flat amount in BGN per unit unless a suspension regime applies. For 2010, excisable products include petrol and diesel fuel, heavy oil, beer and spirits, tobacco products and electricity.

The Excise Duties and Tax Warehouse Act introduced the tax warehousing regime and regulates the production, storage and movement of excisable products.

Property tax

The property tax rate is determined by each municipality and currently ranges from 0.01% to 0.25% of the tax value of property. Individuals and legal entities that are owners of immovable property, that is land and buildings, are liable for property tax. For individuals and residential properties of the enterprises, the tax value is determined by the municipal authorities based on certain statutory criteria. The tax value of non-residential properties of the enterprises is the gross book value. As of 1 January 2011 the taxable based for such properties would become the higher between the property's gross book value and its tax value determined by the respective municipal authorities.

A garbage collection fee is payable for immovable property at a rate determined by the local municipal council annually.

Transfer tax

A transfer tax is due on the value of transferred real estate or motor vehicles, subject to certain exemptions (e.g., contributions in kind and acquisitions under the Law on Privatisation and Post-privatisation Control). The rate of the transfer tax ranges from 0.1% to 3% and is determined by each municipality.

Company expenses

The following corporate expenses are subject to one-off tax:

* Representative expenses related to a company's business;
* Social expenses provided to employees in kind (monetary social expenses are subject to personal income tax); and
* Expenses related to the exploitation and maintenance of cars where they are used for management activities (as distinguished from administrative activities).

The rate of the one-off tax with respect to the above expenses is 10%. Both the expenses and the related one-off taxes are deductible for corporate income tax purposes.

Branch income

Corporate income tax

Although branches are not deemed to be separate legal persons, branches of non-resident companies have separate balance sheets and profit and loss accounts and are subject to corporate income tax at the standard rate of 10% as well as other general taxes (e.g., VAT, property tax).

Representative offices of foreign entities are not allowed to carry out business activities and are not subject to corporate income taxation. A representative office registered

Bulgaria

under the Encouragement of Investments Act may perform only those activities that are not regarded as "economic activities" (e.g., marketing activities normally carried out by a representative office and auxiliary to the activities of its head office). Representative offices do not constitute PEs of the non-resident entities, unless they engage in business activities in breach of the law.

Withholding tax (WHT)

Profits repatriated by a branch to its head office abroad are not subject to WHT. However, certain income payable by a Bulgarian branch or a PE to other parts of the enterprise abroad may trigger WHT (e.g., income from technical services, interest, royalties), unless the respective expenses are not tax allowed at the branch or the PE or are recharged at cost.

Income determination

Taxable result

The taxable result is based on the statutory accounting principles relating to profit/loss and adjusted for tax purposes. Statutory accounting is maintained on an accrual basis in line with the applicable accounting standards.

Small and medium-sized companies may apply specific national standards for the financial statements of small and medium-sized companies, or optionally, International Financial Reporting Standards (IFRS). The principles provided by the Standards for the Financial Statements of Small and Medium-sized Companies are similar to those provided by IFRS. Certain types of companies, including banks and insurance companies, are obliged to apply IFRS.

Inventory valuation

Inventory valuation and revaluation methods applicable under accounting standards may be used for tax purposes. Companies may choose the method of inventory valuation, but must apply the chosen method consistently throughout the accounting period. An inventory of assets and liabilities is carried out in each accounting period. Accounting gains and losses realised upon revaluation of inventory would not be recognised for tax purposes and would form a temporary tax difference. These gains and losses would be recognised for tax purposes in the period when the inventory is disposed.

Capital gains

Realised capital gains are included in corporate income and are taxed at the full corporate tax rate. Exchange rate gains and losses are reported in the profit and loss account and reflected in the assessment of taxable profit. Capital gains from securities will not be subject to taxation if resulting from shares in listed companies and tradable rights in such shares on a regulated securities market in the EU/EEA.

Inter-company dividends

Inter-company dividend payments between Bulgarian companies and dividends distributed by EU/EEA residents *to Bulgarian companies (except for dividends from special purpose investment companies or in case of "hidden distribution of profits") are not included in the tax* base of the recipient company. Dividends distributed by Bulgarian companies to foreign shareholders and resident individuals are subject to 5% withholding tax under the domestic legislation *(see Withholding taxes section for exceptions for payments to EU/EEA tax residents and under double tax treaties (DTTs))*.

Foreign income

Income derived outside Bulgaria by resident legal entities and income derived in Bulgaria by Bulgarian branches of non-residents is included in the taxable base for the purpose of corporate income tax, regardless of whether such income is subject to taxation abroad.

In instances where the provisions of a DTT are applicable, a tax credit or exemption for the foreign tax paid may be allowed. There is also a unilateral tax credit which may not exceed the amount of the tax that would be payable in Bulgaria for the same type of income. Undistributed income of foreign subsidiaries of a Bulgarian resident company is not taxed.

Stock dividends

No explicit regulation with respect to stock dividends exists in the Bulgarian corporate income tax act. Rather, the tax treatment of stock dividends would follow accounting treatment.

Deductions

Depreciation and depletion

For accounting purposes, depreciation is calculated in accordance with the straight-line, progressive, or declining methods of depreciation. Accounting regulations permit Bulgarian companies to establish a depreciation schedule for each tangible and intangible fixed asset on the basis of the method chosen by the company.

For tax purposes, only the straight-line method is permitted. For machines and equipment that are part of the initial investment, accelerated depreciation may also apply, subject to certain conditions.

Net operating losses

The taxpayer has the right to carryforward tax losses incurred in a given year over the following five years. The loss subject to carryforward is the negative amount of the financial result adjusted for tax purposes with certain add-backs and deductions specified in the tax legislation.

Tax losses may be reversed up to the amount of the positive financial result after tax adjustments (without the effect of the loss subject to be carried forward itself).

Carryforwards of foreign-source losses may only offset income from the same source. However, EU/EEA-source losses may offset income from other sources, including Bulgarian sources. Loss carryback is permitted in very specific cases.

Payments to foreign affiliates

Payments to foreign affiliates may be subject to recalculation by the tax authorities if such payments are not made at arm's length.

Thin capitalisation rules

Interest payable by local companies to local or foreign persons may be restricted by the thin-capitalisation rules (which also apply to interest due to non-affiliated companies).

The tax deductibility for interest expenses that exceed interest income is restricted to 75% of the accounting result of the company, exclusive of interest income and expense.

Bulgaria

If the accounting result of the company before including the effect of the interest income and expenses is a loss, none of the net interest expense will be deductible for tax purposes. Interest on bank loans and interest under financial lease agreements are subject to thin capitalisation regulations only when the agreements are between related parties or guaranteed by or extended at the order of a related party.

The thin capitalisation rules do not apply if the debt-to-equity ratio does not exceed 3:1 for the respective tax period.

Interest expenses restricted in a given year under the thin capitalisation rules may be deducted from the financial result for tax purposes during the following five consecutive years. This reversal may be made up to the tax allowed interest expenses, as per the above formula.

Other significant items

Companies may deduct for tax purposes the tax-allowable depreciation costs (booked depreciation costs are added back to the taxable income).

Capital gains from shares in listed public companies, tradable rights in such shares as well as from units of collective investment schemes realised on a regulated stock exchange in the EU/EEA are not recognised for tax purposes.

Group taxation

No group consolidation is permitted for tax purposes in Bulgaria. All companies must pay tax on the basis of individually assessable profits and losses.

Tax incentives

Tax incentives may apply in certain circumstances, including:

* Performance of agricultural activities (the incentive is awaiting the approval of the European Commission);
* Hiring of long-term unemployed, handicapped or elderly persons; and
* Investment in regions with high unemployment.

Withholding taxes (WHT)

Income subject to withholding tax

Bulgarian companies are required to withhold tax on payments of dividends and liquidation proceeds; interest (including that incurred under finance lease agreements and on bank deposits); royalties; fees for technical services; payments for the use of properties; payments made under operating leasing, franchising and factoring agreements; and management fees payable to non-residents.

Capital gains from the transfer of shares in a Bulgarian company or immovable property located in Bulgaria realised by a non-resident are also subject to domestic withholding tax, however, the tax is payable by the non-resident. Capital gains from securities are not subject to withholding tax, if result from shares in listed companies and tradable rights in such shares on a regulated securities market in the EU/EEA.

Dividends and liquidation proceeds are taxed also where payments are made to resident individuals and non-profit organisations. *(For details on dividend payments between domestic companies see Inter-company dividends under the Income determination section.)* Dividends capitalised into shares (stock dividends) are not subject to withholding tax.

In addition, Bulgaria has negotiated a transitional period for implementing the Directive 2003/49/EC on a common system of taxation applicable to interest and royalty payments made between associated companies of different EU member states, which abolishes withholding tax on income from interest and royalty payable between EU resident companies. During the transitional period, the tax rate on such income in Bulgaria should not exceed 10% until 31 December 2010 and 5% between 1 January 2011 and 31 December 2014.

Certain types of income (other than dividends) accrued by a PE of a foreign person to other parts of its enterprise located outside the country is subject to withholding tax (except for that mentioned under the "Branch income" category).

Dividends
When a dividend is accrued to a non-resident company or a resident individual, it is subject to withholding tax at a rate of 5% unless the rate is reduced by an applicable DTT. No differentiation is made between portfolio and substantial holdings for purposes of this withholding tax on dividends.

Dividends distributed by a Bulgarian resident company to an entity that is a tax resident in an EU/EEA member state are not subject to Bulgarian withholding tax.

Interest
A 10% rate applies to interest (including interest from bank deposits) payable to a non-resident, unless the rate is reduced by an applicable DTT.

Interest on borrowings by the government or the Bulgarian National Bank from international financial institutions is not taxable if the respective loan agreements contain relevant exemption arrangements (international treaties override domestic legislation).

Royalties
Royalties payable to foreign persons are taxed at a rate of 10% at source unless the rate is reduced by an applicable DTT.

Capital gains and technical services
Capital gains and technical service fees payable to foreign residents are subject to 10% withholding tax, unless the rate is reduced by an applicable DTT. As per the domestic legislation, technical services include installation and assembly of tangible assets as well as consultancy services and marketing research.

The following is a summary of the main parameters of the Bulgarian DTTs as of 11 May 2009:

Recipient	Dividends*	Interest	Royalties	Capital gains
	%	%	%	%
Albania (3, 6, 9, 29)	5/15	10/0	10	0/10

Bulgaria

Recipient	Dividends*	Interest	Royalties	Capital gains
	%	%	%	%
Algeria (25)	10	10/0	10	0
Armenia (1, 6)	5/10	10/0	10	0
Austria (12, 28)	0	0	0	0
Azerbaijan (6, 29, 35)	8	7	5/10	0
Belarus (6)	10	10/0	10	0
Belgium (6, 10, 28)	10	10/0	5	0
Canada (16, 9, 29)	10/15	10	10	0/10
China (2, 6, 9, 18, 29)	10	10/0	7/10	0/10
Croatia	5	5	0	0
Cyprus (3, 27, 28)	5/10	7	10	10/0
Czech Republic (11, 28)	10	10/0	10	0
Denmark (3, 28)	5/15	0	0	0
Egypt (6)	10	12.5/0	12.5	10
Estonia (9, 16)	0/5	5	5	0/10
Finland (4, 9, 12, 28)	10	0	0/5	0/10
France (5, 28)	5/15	0	5	0
Georgia (6)	10	10/0	10	0
Germany (28)	15	0	5	10
Greece (28)	10	10	10	0
Hungary (6, 28)	10	10/0	10	0
India (6)	15	15/0	15/20	10
Indonesia (6)	15	10/0	10	0
Iran (6, 9, 29)	7.5	5/0	5	10/0
Ireland (3, 6, 9, 28, 29)	5/10	5/0	10	0/10
Israel (19, 20, 21, 22)	10/7.5-12.5	0/5/10	7.5-12.5	7.5-12.5
Italy (28)	10	0	5	0
Japan (3, 6)	10/15	10/0	10	10
Jordan (6, 29)	10	10/0	10	0
Kazakhstan (8, 9, 29)	10	10/0	10	0/10
Kuwait (3, 23)	0/5	0/5	10	0
Latvia (3, 9, 25, 26, 28, 29)	5/10	5/0	7/5	0/10
Lebanon (6)	5	7/0	5	0
Lithuania (16, 30, 29)	0/10	10/0	10	0/10
Luxembourg (3, 10, 28)	5/15	10	5	0
Macedonia (3, 6)	5/15	10/0	10	0
Malta (12, 17, 28)	0/30	0	10	0
Mongolia (6)	10	0/10	10	0
Morocco (5, 9, 29)	7/10	10	10	0/10
Moldova (3, 6, 9, 29)	5/15	10/0	10	0/10
The Netherlands (3, 7, 9, 28)	5/15	0	0/5	0/10
Norway	15	0	0	0
North Korea (6)	10	10/0	10	0
Poland (6, 28)	10	10/0	5	0
Portugal (3, 6, 28)	10/15	10/0	10	0

Recipient	Dividends*	Interest	Royalties	Capital gains
	%	%	%	%
Romania (3, 6)	10/15	15/0	15	0
Russian Federation (6)	15	15/0	15	0
Serbia (3)	5/15	10	10	0
Singapore (6)	5	5/0	5	0
Slovak Republic (28)	10	10	10	0
Slovenia (3, 24, 28, 29)	5/10	5/0	5/10	0/10
South Africa (3, 6, 24, 29)	5/15	5/0	5/10	0/10
South Korea (5, 6)	5/10	10/0	5	0
Spain (3, 28)	5/15	0	0	0
Sweden (9, 28, 29)	10	0	5	0/10
Switzerland (3, 10, 13)	5/15	10/0	0/5	0
Syria	10	10/0	18	0
Thailand (14, 15)	10	10/15	5/15	10
Turkey (3, 6, 9)	10/15	10/0	10	0/10
Ukraine (3, 6, 9, 29)	5/15	10/0	10	0/10
United Arab Emirates (6, 23, 35)	5/0	2/0	5/0	0
United Kingdom (28)	10	0	0	0
USA (16, 25, 29, 31, 32, 33, 34)	5/10	5/10	5	0
Uzbekistan (6, 29)	10	10/0	10	0/10
Vietnam (6, 9)	15	10/0	15	0/15
Zimbabwe (3, 6, 9, 29)	10/20	10/0	10	0/10

Notes

*Under Bulgarian domestic legislation, dividends distributed to non-residents are subject to 5% withholding tax, unless the recipient is a resident of an EU/EEA member state.

1. The lower rate applies to dividends paid out to a non-resident that is the direct owner of at least USD 40,000 forming part of the capital of the company making the payment.
2. The withholding tax on royalties for use of (or right to use) industrial, commercial or scientific equipment is reduced to 7%.
3. The lower rate applies to dividends paid out to a foreign company that controls directly at least 25% of the share capital of the payer of the dividends. In the specific cases of the different countries, more requirements may be in place.
4. There is no withholding tax on royalties for the use of (or the right to use) scientific or cultural works.
5. The lower rate applies to dividends paid out to a foreign company that controls directly at least 15% of the share capital of the payer of the dividends.
6. There is no withholding tax on interest when paid to public bodies (government, the central bank, and, in several cases, certain governmental bodies).
7. 5% royalties are applicable if the Netherlands applies withholding tax under its domestic law.
8. Up to 10% branch tax may be imposed on PE profits.
9. The 10% rate on capital gains from securities applies in specific cases that are described in the respective treaty.
10. The zero rate on interest applies if the loan is extended by a bank and also for industrial, trade and scientific equipment on credit.
11. The zero rate on interest applies if the interest is paid to public bodies (government, municipality, the central bank or any financial institution owned entirely by the

Bulgaria

government), to residents of the other country when the loan or the credit is guaranteed by its government, or if the loan is extended by a company for any equipment or goods.

12. The Council of Ministers has stated its intention to renegotiate the DTTs with Austria, Malta and Finland.

13. A 5% rate on royalties applies if the Swiss Confederation introduces in its domestic law withholding tax on royalties paid to non-residents.

14. The 10% rate on interest applies if the interest is received from a financial institution, including an insurance company.

15. The 5% rate on royalties applies if the royalties are paid for the use of copyright for literary, art or scientific work.

16. The lower rate applies to dividends paid out to a foreign company that controls directly at least 10% of the share capital of the payer of the dividends.

17. The zero rate applies to dividends payable by a Bulgarian resident entity to an entity resident in Malta. The 30% rate applies to dividends payable by a Maltese entity to a Bulgarian entity.

18. There are indications that there may be some amendments to the treaty, which are not yet officially promulgated in Bulgaria.

19. The 10% rate applies to dividends distributed by companies that enjoy a reduced or zero corporate income tax by virtue of a tax incentive for investments. In all other cases the rate is equal to one half of the applicable rate as per the national legislations of Bulgaria and Israel. Nevertheless, the withholding tax rate may not be less than 7.5% or more than 12.5%.

20. The 5% rate applies to interest payable to banks or other financial institutions. The zero rate applies to interest payable to certain public bodies (governments, municipalities, central banks) or to residents of the other country when the loan or credit is guaranteed, insured or financed by a public body of that country or by the Israeli International Trade Insurance Company.

21. The rate on royalties is equal to one half of the applicable rate as per the national legislations of Bulgaria and Israel. Nevertheless, the withholding tax rate may not be less than 7.5% or more than 12.5%.

22. The rate on capital gains from securities is equal to one half of the applicable rate as per the national legislations of Bulgaria and Israel. Nevertheless, the withholding tax rate may not be less than 7.5% or more than 12.5%. However, capital gains from transfers of shares in entities whose real estate properties exceed 50% of their assets are taxed in the country in which the real estate is located.

23. The zero rate applies to dividends and interest paid to certain public governmental and local bodies as well as entities fully owned by the state.

24. The 5% rate on royalties applies if the royalties are paid for the use of copyright for literary, art or scientific work; as well as for the use of industrial, commercial or scientific equipment.

25. There is no withholding tax on interest when paid to and beneficially owned by public bodies (government, local public authorities, the central bank or any financial institution wholly owned by the government), as well as on interest derived on loans guaranteed by the foreign government or based on an agreement between the governments of the states.

26. The 7% rate on royalties applies if the royalties are paid for the use of, or the right to use, cinematograph films and films or tapes for radio or television broadcasting, any patent, trademark, design or model, plan, secret formula or process.

27. The zero rate applies for capital gains from shares in a Bulgarian resident company that are traded on the Bulgarian Stock Exchange.

28. In accordance with the EU Parent-Subsidiary Directive implemented in the Bulgarian legislation, dividends distributed by a Bulgarian resident company to an entity that is a tax resident in an EU member state may not be subject to Bulgarian withholding tax.

29. Full withholding tax at source may be levied on capital gains from the sale of shares in companies, the main assets of which are directly or indirectly holdings in real estate situated in Bulgaria, and in some other cases (subject to the specifics stipulated in the respective treaty).

30. There is no withholding tax on interest when paid to public bodies (government, the central bank, governmental institutions) or any financial institution wholly owned by the government.
31. Pension funds and charities are considered resident persons.
32. The zero rate does not apply to dividends distributed to real estate investment trusts (REITs).
33. The zero rate does not apply to interest paid under a back-to-back loan.
34. The benefits of the treaty are limited to entities that satisfy certain criteria (Limitation of Benefits clause).
35. The 5% rate on royalties applies if the royalties are paid for the use of, or the right to use, any patent, design, model, plan, secret formula, process, or know-how.

Under some DTTs, technical service payments fall within the definition of royalty payments and are taxed accordingly. The Bulgarian government has signed a new DTT with Austria which has not entered into force yet.

Tax administration

Returns
Annual profit must be declared no later than 31 March of the year following the financial (tax) year. The financial and tax years coincide with the calendar year. Along with their annual corporate income tax returns companies are required to file financial information for their business activities during the year in a standard statistical form not subject to a financial audit. Up until 2008, companies were required to file audited annual financial statements along with their returns but this practice was abolished in 2009. The self-assessment principle is applied.

Payment of tax
If a company ended the preceding financial year with a taxable profit, it is liable for advance corporate income tax payments each month in the current year at the rate of 10%. The monthly taxable base for the second, third and fourth quarters is one-twelfth of the annual taxable profit for the preceding year multiplied by a coefficient determined in the State Budget Act for the current year. However, the taxable base for the advance payments during the first quarter is one-twelfth of the taxable profit of the company for the year before the preceding year multiplied by a coefficient defined in the State Budget Act for the current year.

Corporate taxpayers having a tax loss or zero taxable result in the previous year and companies established during the current year make quarterly advance payments during the current fiscal year. The base of the quarterly advance payments is the profit for the corresponding period accumulated from the beginning of the current year.

Companies with a net sales revenue below BGN 200,000 for the preceding year and newly incorporated companies (if not established as a result of a transformation of another entity) are not required to make advance payments of corporate income tax.

Overpayment of corporate tax may be offset against advance and annual payments of the respective taxes due for the next period. The difference between the annual tax declared in the corporate income tax return and the advance tax paid for the corresponding year must be paid by the deadline for submitting the tax return on 31 March of the following year.

Corporate taxes in Cambodia

For more information, contact:

Jean Loi
PricewaterhouseCoopers (Vietnam) Ltd.
Saigon Tower, Fourth Floor
29 Le Duan, District 1
Ho Chi Minh City, Vietnam
Tel: +84 8 3823 1502
Email: jean.loi@kh.pwc.com

Significant developments

Accommodation tax
The accommodation tax is effective from 1 January 2007. The accommodation tax
rate is 2% and is imposed on the room charges including all taxes and all other charges
except accommodation tax and VAT. Hotel owners or their representatives are required
to submit the return on a monthly basis and make lodgement and payment of taxes
to the tax department by the fifteenth day of the following month for real regime
taxpayers and by the tenth day of the following month for estimated regime taxpayers.

Statutory audit requirement
The Ministry of Economy and Finance (MoEF) issued a Prakas dated 26 July 2007
requiring all enterprises (physical or legal persons) that meet the following criteria to
have their financial statements audited by an independent external auditor registered
with the Kampuchea Institute of Certified Public Accountants and Auditors (KICPAA):

- Annual turnover above KHR 3,000,000,000;
- Total assets above KHR 2,000,000,000; and
- More than 100 employees.

Qualified Investment Projects (QIP) registered with the Council for the Development
of Cambodia (CDC) are required to have their financial statements audited by
independent external auditors registered with the KICPAA.

The enterprises and QIP are required to prepare their financial statements in
accordance with Cambodian Accounting Standards.

The Prakas does not state the deadline for enterprises and QIP to submit their audited
financial statements. However, the deadline for financial statements to be audited is
six months after year-end, i.e., for the financial year ending 31 December 2009, the
deadline is 30 June 2010.

Taxes on corporate income

Corporate tax
Cambodia's taxation rules vary according to the taxpayer's regime. Real regime
taxpayers include large or incorporated taxpayers. The majority of foreign investors
will fall into the real regime. Unless otherwise stated, our comments are therefore
restricted to real regime taxpayers.

Resident taxpayers are subject to tax on worldwide income/profits while non-residents are taxed on Cambodian sourced income/profits only. Residents earning foreign sourced income can receive credits for foreign taxes paid. A permanent establishment (PE) is taxable on its Cambodian sourced income only.

Resident taxpayers include companies organised, managed or having their principal place of business in Cambodia.

The standard rate of corporate income tax (Tax on profit or ToP) for companies and PEs is 20%. Oil and gas and certain mineral exploitation activities are subject to tax at the rate of 30%. Insurance activities are taxable at a rate of 5% on the gross premium income. QIP are entitled to tax holidays.

Additional tax on profit on dividend distribution
The dividend-paying company is required to pay an additional ToP at the time of dividend distribution if the profit was previously subject to a 9% or 0% ToP.

A shareholder is entitled to establish a special dividend account from which the relevant dividend may be paid without further additional ToP obligations.

A dividend will be exempt from tax in the hands of the shareholder if additional ToP and withholding Tax (for non-resident shareholders) has been paid by the company.

Corporate residence

Any legal person or pass-through organised or managed in Cambodia, or having its principal place of business in Cambodia is a resident. A PE shall be considered a resident legal person with respect to its Cambodian source income only.

The term legal person means any enterprise or organisation carrying on a business whether or not officially recognised by the competent institutions of the Royal Government. The term legal person includes any government institution, religious, charitable, or non-profit organisation. For a non-resident person, the term legal person means any permanent establishment in Cambodia. The term legal person does not include a pass-through or a sole proprietorship.

Other taxes

In addition to the ToP, the following taxes may affect certain investors:

Minimum tax
Real-regime taxpayers are subject to a separate minimum tax, unless the taxpayer has been granted the status of a QIP by the CDC. The minimum tax is an annual tax with a liability equal to 1% of the annual turnover of the taxpayer for the year in question. The tax is due irrespective of the taxpayer's profit or loss position.

If a taxpayer's ToP liability exceeds the minimum tax, the taxpayer will only pay the ToP, otherwise minimum tax will apply.

Cambodia

Value-added tax (VAT)
VAT is applicable to real-regime entities and is charged at 10% on the value of the supply of most goods and services. Exported goods and services rendered outside Cambodia are zero-rated. In addition, 0% VAT applies to the supporting industries or contractors who directly supply goods or services to the export-oriented garment manufacturers, textile and footwear industries. Some supplies are VAT exempt, the main categories being public postal services, medical and dental services, electricity, transportation of passengers by wholly state-owned public transport systems, insurance services and primary financial services. Strict record-keeping requirements exist.

Specific tax on certain merchandise and services
The Specific tax is a form of excise tax that applies to the importation or domestic production and supply of certain goods and services. Specific Tax on domestically produced goods is generally applied to the "ex-factory selling price". The "ex-factory selling price" is defined as 65% of the selling price before VAT and any discount. For imported goods, the tax is due on the CIF (cost, insurance and freight) value inclusive of customs duty. For hotel and telecommunication services, the tax is payable based on the invoice prices. For local and international air transportation of passengers the tax is payable based on the air ticket value issued in Cambodia for travel within and outside Cambodia.

Import and export duties
Import duties are levied on a wide range of products at varying rates, although exemptions may be available as an investment incentive. As a requirement of Cambodia's membership of Association of South East Asia Nations (ASEAN), various import duties have been reduced as part of the Common Effective Preferential Tariffs scheme. Export duties are levied on a limited number of items, such as timber and certain animal products (including most seafood).

Tax on house and land rent
Businesses (other than real-regime entities) that rent land, buildings, certain equipment, storage facilities and so forth, are liable for the Tax on house and land rent. The tax is levied at 10% of the rental fee. This tax may not apply where the ToP has been withheld from the rental payment.

Patent tax
Registered businesses must pay a (relatively nominal) patent tax on initial business registration and annually thereafter. Patent tax is levied with reference to turnover or estimated turnover.

Fiscal stamp tax
Fiscal stamp tax is paid on certain official documents and, perhaps more importantly for foreign investors, certain advertising costs.

Tax for public lighting (TPL)
The TPL applies to the distribution of tobacco and alcohol products. TPL is imposed on all chains of supply at the rate of 3% on the value of the taxable products inclusive of other taxes (but not VAT for real-regime taxpayers). The tax is payable on a monthly basis.

Tax on unused land

Land in towns and other specified areas that have no buildings, construction sites not in use and even certain built-upon land, is subject to the Tax on Unused Land. The tax is calculated at 2% of the market value of the land per square metre, as determined by the Commission for Evaluation of Unused Land as at 30 June each year. The owner of the land is required to pay the tax by 30 September each year.

Registration tax (property transfer tax)

The transfer of title of certain assets (such as land and vehicles) is subject to registration tax, which is generally levied at 4% of the transfer value.

Tax on means of transportation

This tax imposes a number of statutory fees on the registration of certain vehicles used to transport goods including trucks, buses, motor vehicles and ships.

Branch income

Tax rates for branch income are the same as those for corporate profits.

Income determination

Inventory valuation

Inventory can be valued at weighted-average cost, first-in, first-out (FIFO) or current value at the close of the period, where this value is lower than the purchase price or production cost. Work-in-progress should be valued at production costs.

Capital gains

Capital gains form part of taxable profit.

Inter-company dividend

Inter-company dividends may be exempted *(see Withholding tax section)*.

Foreign income

Residents are taxed on their worldwide income/profits. Tax credits are available for foreign taxes suffered.

Deductions

Depreciation

Property should be depreciated at rates according to four classes of assets as specified in the tax legislation. Land is not considered a depreciable asset. The straight-line or the declining-balance method is specifically required to be used for each class of assets. Special depreciation is available to assets purchased by a QIP and used in manufacturing and processing. The special depreciation regime allows the use of 40% depreciation in the year of purchase or first year of use of assets.

Net operating losses

Tax losses may be carried forward for up to five years subject to certain criteria. The criteria include:

- The loss must be recorded in the ToP return and submitted to the tax department on time;

Cambodia

- The business objective of the company has not changed; and
- The ownership of the company has not changed. The tax regulations contain various provisions indicating that losses will be forfeited if there is a change of ownership of a company. However, the tax regulations do not provide clear guidance on what constitutes "a change in ownership".

In addition, a tax loss carried forward cannot be used if a company is subject to a unilateral tax reassessment during a tax audit. The tax department can issue a unilateral reassessment if there is evidence of obstruction of the tax laws. Losses cannot be carried back.

Payments to foreign affiliates
Certain losses incurred on sales to (51%) related parties are non-deductible. Other transfer pricing provisions are present where there is 20% common ownership.

Taxes
Non-deductible taxes include taxes that are not a charge to the enterprise (e.g., withholding taxes and ToP).

Other significant items
Interest deductibility in any year is limited to the amount of interest income plus 50% of the net profits excluding interest income and interest expense. The excess non-deductible interest expense can be carried forward to the following tax years indefinitely.

Group taxation

There is no provision for group taxation.

Tax incentives

Inward investment
Most investments will require registration with the Ministry of Commerce (MoC) and other relevant ministries. The Council for the Development of Cambodia (CDC) may also be approached for purposes of seeking investment incentives. CDC licensing is however, not mandatory (except for certain large or politically sensitive projects) and may in fact not be possible for projects that fall within the Negative List, i.e., trading activities, import and export, any transportation services (except for the railway sector), currency and financial services, production of tobacco products, provision of value-added services of all kinds, telecommunication services and real estate development. The investment incentives available have been significantly changed following the implementation of the New Law on Investment. The current investment incentives include ToP holiday of up to six years, import duty exemptions and exemption from minimum tax.

Under the New Law on Investment, all QIP registered with the CDC are required to obtain a certificate of compliance from the CDC on an annual basis in order to continue enjoying the investment incentives.

Capital investment
There are no tax incentives for capital investment in Cambodia.

Withholding taxes (WHT)

WHT only needs to be withheld on payments made by resident taxpayers. The WHT constitutes a final tax when withheld for payments to non-residents/residents.

Payment/recipient	%
Interest paid by a resident taxpayer:	
Resident, other than a Cambodian bank	15
Non-resident	14
Interest paid by a resident taxpayer bank:	
Resident individual on non-fixed-term savings accounts	4
Resident individual on fixed-term savings	6
Rent:	
Resident	10
Non-resident	14
Payments for services:	
Non-real regime resident taxpayer	15
Non-resident for 'management or technical services' (not defined)	14
Royalties:	
Resident	15
Non-resident	14
Dividend:	
Non-resident	14

WHT must be remitted by the payer on a monthly basis, by the fifteenth day of the succeeding month.

At the time of writing Cambodia had not negotiated any double taxation agreements.

Tax administration

Returns and payment of tax
Returns for the Tax on Profit are to be filed annually within three months of year-end. The standard tax year is the calendar year, although different accounting year-ends may be granted upon application. 1% Prepayments of Tax on Profit are due on a monthly basis, by the fifteenth day of the succeeding month.

Cambodian incorporated companies are technically required to adopt the Cambodian Accounting Standard, which is similar to International Accounting Standards, as their accounting system.

Corporate taxes in Cameroon, Republic of

For more information, contact:

Nadine Tinen
Fidafrica SARL
Rue du Maréchal Joffre
Immeuble Bel-Air
Douala Akwa
Republic of Cameroon
Tel: +237 33 43 24 43/44/45
Email: nadine.tinen@cm.pwc.com

Significant developments

No significant tax or regulatory developments have taken place regarding corporate taxation in the past year.

Taxes on corporate income

Taxable profits

Cameroon corporate tax rate is 38.5%. The 38.5% corporate tax rate is 35% + 10% surcharge.

The basic corporate tax rate of 35% is reduced to 30% for companies during their first three years of listing on the national stock exchange of Cameroon.

The minimum tax is 1.1% based on the turnover.

The profits subject to the company tax are determined with sole regard to profits earned by businesses carried on or transactions effected in Cameroon.

The net taxable profits are established after deduction of all charges directly entailed by the exercise of activities subject to assessment in Cameroon.

Corporate residence

Resident corporations in Cameroon are taxed on their worldwide income; non-resident corporations are taxed only on Cameroon source income.

An entity is deemed resident if its registered office, centre of activity or management is located in Cameroon or if it has resident employees in Cameroon that provide services to customers.

Other taxes

Value-added tax (VAT)

VAT shall be levied on natural persons or corporate bodies which automatically, habitually or occasionally carry out taxable transactions consisting of provisions of services or sales of goods.

The standard VAT in Cameroon is 19.25%. This is a 17.5% basic tax rate plus 10% surcharge. Exports are zero VAT rated. An excise duty to the rate of 25% is applicable to the cigarettes, drinks, cosmetics or products known as of luxury: jewels, precious stones. A reduced rate of excise duty (12.5%) shall apply to soft drinks and private vehicles with engine capacities of 2 000 cm³.

The VAT paid upstream is recoverable, except where otherwise stated.

Business licence tax

Any natural person or corporate body carrying on trade, industry or profession in Cameroon shall be liable to a business licence tax. The business licence is paid annually according to a graduated scale. The tax is assessed on turnover.

New enterprises shall be exempt from the payment of the business licence during the first two years of operation.

Registration duty

The registration duty applies to certain deeds listed by the general tax code. The assessment basis depends on the nature of transactions and the rate varies from 1% to 15%.

Social security contributions

Employer and employee must contribute on a monthly basis to Cameroon's National Social Insurance Fund 11.2% and 2.8%, respectively. The basis of contribution is capped at XAF 300, 000 per month. Employers in Cameroon must also contribute 1.75%, 2.5% or 5% of total salaries, depending on the risk category of activities performed by employees. The calculation basis in this category is the gross salary including the benefits in kind assessed for their actual amount.

Capital duty

The formation of a company and subsequent capital increases in Cameroon are not subject to registration duties. This exemption has been provided by the Finance Law for 2010.

Payroll tax

Employers in Cameroon are required to make monthly contributions of 2.5% of the total amount of salaries and fringe benefits of their employees to the Housing Loan and Employment Fund of Cameroon.

Real property tax

Cameroon property tax is payable annually on real estate with or without an ownership certificate or an administrative or judicial order issued. Tax is charged at 0.1% of the assessed property value, with the usual 10% local tax.

Transfer tax

The sale of a business in Cameroon is subject to a transfer tax rate of 15%.

Branch income

The local branch of any foreign company is taxed at the same rate as a company. The net profits (after corporate income tax) of entities having their residence or head office outside Cameroon (such as the branch of a foreign company) are assumed to be distributed each fiscal year to companies not located in Cameroon.

Cameroon, Republic of

Income determination

Inventory valuation
Stocks shall be valued at cost price; however, if the market price is lower than the cost price, the undertaking shall make provisions for depreciation of inventory.

Capital gains
Capital gains are normally taxed at full corporate rates.

Inter-company dividends
Subject to international conventions, inter-company dividends are subject to a 16.5% withholding tax.

Foreign income
As matter of both fact and law, except in a few cases, revenue from entities located outside Cameroon but earned by corporate bodies situated in Cameroon shall be subject to the corporate income tax in Cameroon.

Stock dividends
Subject to international conventions, stock dividends shall be subject to a 16.5% withholding tax.

Deductions

Depreciation and depletion
Depreciation is generally computed on a straight-line basis over the useful life according to the rates provided for by the Tax Code, including those which might have already been deferred in times of deficit.

The following depreciation rates are generally accepted for tax purposes:

- Construction – the rates vary from 5% to 20%.
- Stationary equipment and tools – the rates vary from 5% to 20%.
- Portable equipment – the rates vary from 10% to 100%.
- Transport equipment – the rates vary from 10% to 33.33%.
- Railway lines – the rates vary from 1% to 10%.
- Engines – the rate is 5%.
- Rehabilitation – the rates vary from 5% to 25%.
- Furniture fittings and other equipment – the rates vary from 10% to 33.33%.
- Fishing equipment and fishing vessels – 15%.

The deduction of depreciation can be carried forward indefinitely.

Net operating losses
Any loss sustained in a given year can be carried forward up to the fourth year following the recording of the loss.

Payments to foreign entities
Head office overhead expenses for operations carried out in Cameroon and the remuneration of certain effective services (studies, technical, financial or accounting assistance) provided to Cameroonian firms by foreign natural persons or corporate

bodies are not totally deductible. Fees paid are deductible up to a maximum of 10% of the taxable profit before deducting the expenses concerned.

Group taxation

There is specific taxation of groups within the Economic and Monetary Community of Central Africa (CEMAC) area.

Where a joint stock company and a private limited company own either registered stock in a joint stock company or shares in a private limited company, the net proceeds of the share in the second company paid to the first during the financial year shall be deducted from the total net profit of the latter, less a percentage for costs and charges. This percentage is fixed at 10% of the total amount of the proceeds. This system shall apply in the following circumstances:

- When the stocks or shares owned by the parent establishment represents at least 25% of the capital of the subsidiary firm;
- When the parent and subsidiary firms have their registered office in a CEMAC state (Cameroon, Central African Republic, Chad, Gabon, Equatorial Guinea and Republic of Congo); and
- When the stocks or shares allotted at the time of issue are still registered in the name of the participating company which undertakes to retain them for at least two consecutive years in registered form.

Tax incentives

Three major tax incentives are granted in Cameroon under the tax systems.

The system of reinvestment relief
Any natural person or corporate body reinvesting in Cameroon may be granted, under certain conditions, a reduction in company tax or personal income tax.

The reinvestment must take a form described by the general tax code as construction or extension of permanent buildings for industrial, agricultural, forestry, tourism or mining purposes, including technical offices, housing salaried workers free of charges, etc.

Note that, total investment less than XAF 25,000,000 are not eligible for reinvestment relief.

The reinvestment relief consists of deduction from the taxable basis an amount equal to 50% of the investment effected by the undertaking and approved by the tax authorities.

The special fiscal regime for structuring projects
This regime applies to major enterprises with annual turnover not less than XAF 1 billion and small- and medium-sized enterprises with annual turnover of less than XAF 1 billion.

Cameroon, Republic of

The tax incentives consist of:

- Exemption from payment of the business license tax for the first two years of operation;
- Fixed registration fee of XAF 50,000 for transfers of real estate which directly concern the establishment of the project;
- Exemption from payment of VAT on local purchases of building materials and on imports related to the establishment of the project; and
- Extension of the carryover period for deficits from four to five years.

A taxpayer must apply, required conditions must be met and authorisation must be issued for this tax incentive to be granted.

The system applicable to the exchange sector
Companies whose ordinary shares are listed on the Cameroon Stock Exchange shall be entitled to the following company tax reductions:

- 20% for a period of three years for capital increases which represent at least 20% of the share capital;
- 25% for a period of the three years for capital increases or transfers of shares which represent at least 20% of the share capital; and
- 28% for a period of three years from the date of listing for capital increases or transfers of shares which represent less than 20% of the share capital.

Companies whose ordinary shares are listed on the bond market in Cameroon shall be entitled to pay company tax at a reduced rate of 30% for three years, effective from the date of listing.

Withholding taxes (WHT)

A special tax is levied at an overall discharging rate of 15% on income paid to natural persons and corporate bodies domiciled outside of Cameroon by enterprises or establishments based in Cameroon for various services provided or used in Cameroon. The tax is withheld at source by the Cameroonian entity which pays the remuneration.

Dividends
A withholding tax of 16.5% (15% withholding tax plus 10% surcharge) applies to dividends paid to both Cameroon residents and non-residents. The tax rate may be reduced under an applicable tax treaty.

Interest
The payment of 16.5% withholding tax on interests from foreign loans has been suspended by decree N° 76-64 dated February 1976.

Royalties
Royalties paid to non-residents are subject to a 15% withholding tax (the 10% local tax is not applicable). The tax rate may be reduced under an applicable tax treaty.

Tax treaties
Cameroon has tax treaties with France, Canada, Tunisia and States members of CEMAC (Cameroon, Gabon, Equatorial Guinea, Congo, Chad and Central African Republic).

Tax administration

Payment of taxes and tax return (corporate tax)

An instalment representing 1.1% of turnover realised during each month shall be paid to the tax authorities not later than the fifteenth of the following month.

Advance payment of 1% on imports or purchases of goods for resale is withheld at source by the supplier.

The balance is paid at the latest on 15 March following the fiscal year-end when submitting the tax return.

On or before 15 March, taxpayers are expected to submit to the tax administration the annual return of revenue derived from their business venture during the period serving as tax base.

This return must be presented in conformity with the Organisation for the Harmonisation of Business Law in Africa (OHADA) accounting system.

The tax year in Cameroon is the calendar year.

Tax credit

A surplus tax payment can be offset against future taxes of the same nature to be paid. For the specific case of VAT, a reimbursement process is provided for by the General Tax Code under certain conditions.

Taxes paid abroad are not considered as tax credits unless provided as such by international tax treaties.

Corporate taxes in Canada

For more information, contact:

Saul Plener
PricewaterhouseCoopers LLP
Suite 3000, Box 82
77 King Street West
Royal Trust Tower, TD Centre
Toronto, Ontario, M5K 1G8, Canada
Tel: +1 416 941 8299
Email: saul.plener@ca.pwc.com

Significant developments

Canada's corporate summary includes all 2010 federal, provincial and territorial budgets. The numerous tax changes this year, many of a highly technical nature, may affect taxpayers engaged in international transactions. Other measures enhance targeted programmes, such as film and media tax credits and incentives for scientific research and experimental development. The summary is based on enacted and proposed legislation and assumes that the proposed legislation will become law.

Corporate income tax rates
Federal corporate income tax rates decreased commencing 2008, and will continue to decline gradually until 2012. Provincial corporate rates tend to be on the decline.

Capital tax
All provincial general capital taxes are scheduled to be eliminated by 1 July 2012.

Taxable Canadian property
Commencing 5 March 2010, taxable Canadian property will exclude shares of corporations, and certain other interests, that do not derive their value (over a 60-month look-back period) principally from real or immovable property situated in Canada, Canadian resource property, or timber resource property. Therefore, with some exceptions, non-residents will no longer be required to report dispositions of these properties and obtain a clearance certificate.

Stock options
Significant changes to the rules for stock options permit only the employer or employee (not both) to claim a tax deduction for cashed-out stock options and eliminate employee elections to defer the payment of tax on stock option benefits until the shares are sold (relief may be available). The changes also eliminate the undue hardship exemption for withholdings on stock option benefits and require withholdings in connection with these benefits after 2010. Grandfathering rules may apply.

Tax avoidance
A proposed regime will make an "avoidance transaction" that meets certain conditions a "reportable transaction" that must be reported to the Canada Revenue Agency. The proposals (as modified to reflect public consultations) will apply to transactions entered into after 2010, and those that are part of a series of transactions completed after 2010.

Non-resident trusts (NRTs) and foreign investment entities (FIEs)

The 2010 federal budget announced that the draft rules for NRTs and FIEs will be somewhat simplified and better targeted. The revised proposals will be subject to further public consultation. The NRT rules generally will apply commencing 2007; trusts subject to the draft rules will be considered resident for Canadian income tax purposes. An election will allow a trust to elect to be deemed resident for the 2001 and subsequent years.

C

The FIE rules have been essentially eliminated. The enacted version of the rules for offshore investment funds property will continue to apply, with some modifications, for taxation years ending after 4 March 2010. A taxpayer that filed under the FIE proposals for previous years can either have those years reassessed or be entitled to a deduction in the current year for the income previously included.

Specified investment flow-throughs (SIFTs)

Certain earnings of SIFTs (i.e., publicly traded income trusts and partnerships) are subject to a SIFT tax and are deemed to be a dividend when distributed. These rules apply starting the 2007 taxation year, for SIFTs first publicly traded after 31 October 2006, and starting the 2011 taxation year, for other SIFTs. New rules facilitate the conversion of SIFT trusts into corporations, generally for transactions that occur after 13 July 2008 and before 2013.

Group taxation

The federal government will consider whether the tax system could be improved by new rules for the taxation of corporate groups, such as the introduction of a formal system of loss transfers or consolidated reporting.

International Financial Reporting Standards (IFRS)

Canada will move to IFRS from Canadian generally accepted accounting principles (GAAP), which could affect the measurement and reporting of income taxes for financial statement purposes and the calculation of Canadian taxes payable. Canada's adoption of IFRS is effective for fiscal years beginning after 31 December 2010, with earlier adoption permitted in certain circumstances. IFRS will be mandatory for "publicly accountable enterprises" and elective for other enterprises.

Provincial sales tax harmonisation

On 1 July 2010, provincial sales tax in British Columbia and Ontario will be harmonised with the federal goods and services tax (GST).

Taxes on corporate income

Federal income tax

The following rates apply for 31 December 2010 year-ends. For non-resident corporations, the rates apply to business income attributable to a permanent establishment in Canada. Different rates may apply to non-resident corporations in other circumstances. Non-resident corporations may also be subject to branch tax (*see below*).

	Federal rate
	%
Basic rate	38.0
Less – Provincial abatement (1)	10.0

Canada

	Federal rate
Federal rate	28.0
Less – General rate reduction (2), (3) or manufacturing and processing (M&P) deduction	10.0
Net federal tax rate (4), (5)	18.0

Notes

1. The basic rate of federal tax is reduced by a 10% abatement to give the provinces and territories room to impose corporate income taxes. The abatement is available in respect of taxable income allocated to Canadian provinces and territories. Taxable income allocable to a foreign jurisdiction is not eligible for the abatement and normally is not subject to provincial or territorial taxes.
2. The general rate reduction does not apply to the first CAD 500,000 of active business income earned in Canada by Canadian-controlled private corporations (CCPCs), investment income of CCPCs, manufacturing and processing (M&P) income, income of credit unions, most deposit insurance corporations, mutual fund corporations, mortgage investment corporations and investment corporations, which may benefit from preferential tax treatment.
3. The general rate reduction and M&P deduction increased from 9% to 10% on 1 January 2010, and will increase to 11.5% on 1 January 2011 and to 13% on 1 January 2012.
4. Provincial taxes apply in addition to federal taxes. Provincial tax rates are noted below.
5. For small CCPCs, a federal rate of 11% applies to the first CAD 500,000 of active business income. A federal rate of 18% (19% before 2010) is levied on active business income above CAD 500,000. Investment income (other than most dividends) of CCPCs is subject to tax at the federal rate of 28%, in addition to a refundable federal tax of 6-2/3%, for a total federal rate of 34.7%.

Provincial/territorial income tax

All provinces and territories impose income tax on income allocable to a permanent establishment in the province or territory. Generally, income is allocated to a province or territory by using a two-factor formula based on gross revenue and on salaries and wages. Provincial and territorial income taxes are not deductible for federal income tax purposes. The rates given apply to 31 December 2010 year-ends. The rates do not take into account provincial tax holidays, which reduce or eliminate tax in limited cases.

	Provincial/territorial (1), (2)
	%
Alberta	10.0
British Columbia (3)	10.5
Manitoba (4)	12.0
New Brunswick (5)	11.5
Newfoundland and Labrador	14.0 or 5.0
Northwest Territories	11.5
Nova Scotia	16.0
Nunavut	12.0
Ontario (6)	13.0 or 11.0
Prince Edward Island	16.0
Quebec	11.9
Saskatchewan (7)	12.0 or 10.0
Yukon Territory	15.0 or 2.5

C

Notes

1. When two rates are indicated, the lower rate applies to M&P income.
2. In all provinces and territories, the first CAD 500,000 (CAD 400,000 in some jurisdictions) of active business income of a small CCPC is subject to reduced rates that range from 0.9% to 8.0%, depending on the jurisdiction. British Columbia, Manitoba, Newfoundland and Labrador, Nova Scotia, Ontario and Prince Edward Island intend to decrease their rates for small CCPCs.
3. British Columbia's rate decreased from 11% to 10.5% on 1 January 2010 and will decrease to 10% on 1 January 2011.
4. Manitoba's rate decreased from 13% to 12% on 1 July 2009, and subject to balanced budget requirements, will decrease to 11% at a date to be determined.
5. New Brunswick's rate decreased from 13% to 12% on 1 July 2009, and will decrease to 11% on 1 July 2010, to 10% on 1 July 2011 and to 8% on 1 July 2012.
6. The lower Ontario rate applies to profits from manufacturing and processing, and from farming, mining, logging and fishing operations carried on in Canada and allocated to Ontario. This rate will decrease from 12% to 10% on 1 July 2010.
   Ontario's non-M&P rate will decrease from 14% to 12% on 1 July 2010, to 11.5% on 1 July 2011, to 11% on 1 July 2012 and to 10% on 1 July 2013.
   Corporations subject to Ontario income tax may also be liable for corporate minimum tax (CMT) based on adjusted book income. The CMT is payable only to the extent that it exceeds the regular Ontario income tax liability. The CMT rate will decrease from 4% to 2.7% on 1 July 2010 and the CMT thresholds will increase as shown in the following table:

		Taxation years ending	
		before 1 July 2010	after 30 June 2010
Thresholds for CMT to apply*	Total Assets	> CAD 5 million	≥ CAD 50 million
		or	and
	Annual gross revenues	> CAD 10 million	≥ CAD 100 million

* Thresholds apply on an associated basis.

7. Saskatchewan's M&P rate is as low as 10% (reduced from the 12% non-M&P rate), depending on the extent to which the corporation's income is allocated to the province.

Corporate residence

As a general rule, corporations resident in Canada are subject to Canadian income tax on worldwide income. As a result of special provisions in the Income Tax Act, almost all corporations incorporated in Canada are resident in Canada. A corporation not incorporated in Canada may be considered resident in Canada if its central management and control are exercised in Canada.

A corporation incorporated in Canada will cease to be a Canadian resident if it is granted articles of continuance in a foreign jurisdiction or if it is a predecessor corporation in a cross-border amalgamation. Similarly, a foreign corporation will become resident in Canada if it is continued in Canada or is a predecessor corporation of an amalgamated corporation that is resident in Canada.

Non-resident corporations are subject to income tax on income derived from carrying on a business in Canada and on capital gains arising upon the disposition of taxable Canadian property. The purchaser of the taxable Canadian property is generally required to withhold tax from the amount paid unless the non-resident vendor has obtained a clearance certificate.

Canada

Taxable Canadian property includes, among other things, real or immovable property situated in Canada, both capital and non-capital property used in carrying on a business in Canada and shares in Canadian-resident corporations that are not listed on a stock exchange. In certain circumstances, shares in Canadian-resident corporations that are listed on a stock exchange, shares in non-resident corporations and interests in non-resident trusts will be considered taxable Canadian property. However, commencing 5 March 2010, taxable Canadian property will exclude shares of corporations, and certain other interests, that do not derive their value (over a 60-month look-back period) principally from real or immovable property situated in Canada, Canadian resource property, or timber resource property. Therefore, with some exceptions, non-residents will no longer be required to report dispositions of these properties and obtain a clearance certificate.

Withholding tax at a rate of 25% is imposed on interest (other than most interest paid to arm's-length non-residents, commencing 2008), dividends, rents, royalties, certain management and technical service fees, and similar payments, made by a Canadian resident to a non-resident of Canada.

Canadian income tax and withholding tax can be reduced or eliminated if Canada has a treaty with the non-resident's country of residence. A list of treaties that Canada has negotiated and applicable withholding tax rates is provided under *"Withholding taxes arising in Canada", below.*

Other taxes

Goods and services tax
The federal goods and services tax (GST) is levied at a rate of 5%. It is a value-added tax applied at each level in the manufacturing and marketing chain and applies to most goods and services. However, the tax does not apply to sales of zero-rated goods, such as exports and groceries, or to tax-exempt supplies, such as certain services provided by financial institutions.

Generally, businesses pay GST on their purchases and charge GST on their sales, and remit the net amount (i.e., the difference between the GST collected and the input tax credit for the tax paid on purchases). Suppliers are entitled to claim input tax credits on zero-rated goods and services, but not on tax-exempt supplies.

Harmonised sales tax
Newfoundland and Labrador, New Brunswick and Nova Scotia harmonised their sales tax systems with the GST and impose a single sales tax rate of 13% (15% in Nova Scotia starting 1 July 2010). The 13% rate includes an 8% provincial sales tax component (10% in Nova Scotia starting 1 July 2010) and the 5% GST. It is imposed on essentially the same base as the GST. On 1 July 2010:

* In British Columbia, the 7% Social Services Tax and the 5% federal GST will be replaced with a 12% harmonised sales tax; and
* In Ontario, the 8% Retail Sales Tax and the 5% federal GST will be replaced with a 13% harmonised sales tax.

Transitional rules will apply in British Columbia and Ontario.

Retail sales tax

British Columbia, Manitoba, Ontario, Prince Edward Island and Saskatchewan levy retail sales tax at rates ranging from 5% to 10% on most purchases of tangible personal property for consumption or use in the province and on the purchase of specific services. As mentioned, on 1 July 2010, retail sales tax in British Columbia and Ontario will be replaced with the harmonised sales tax.

Quebec's sales tax is structured essentially in the same way as the GST. Quebec has widened its sales tax base to include most of the goods and services subject to the GST. The general Quebec sales tax rate is 7.5% (8.5% in 2011 and 9.5% after 2011). Quebec administers the GST in that province.

Only Prince Edward Island and Quebec levy their sales tax on prices that include the GST.

Alberta and the three territories (the Northwest Territories, Nunavut and the Yukon) do not impose a retail sales tax.

Property tax

Property taxes are levied by municipalities in Canada on the estimated market value of real property within their boundaries and by provinces on land not in a municipality. In most provinces, a general property tax is levied on the owner of the property. Some municipalities levy a separate business tax, which is payable by the occupant if the premises are used for business purposes. These taxes are based on the assessed value of the property at tax rates that are set each year by the various municipalities. School taxes, also generally based on the value of real property, are levied by local and regional school boards or the province.

Land transfer tax

All the provinces and territories levy a land transfer tax or registration fee on the purchaser of real property within their boundaries. These levies are expressed as a percentage, primarily on a sliding scale, of the sale price or the assessed value of the property sold, and are generally payable at the time title to the property is registered. Rates generally range from 0.02% to 2%, depending on the province or territory, but may be higher if the purchaser is a non-resident. Some exemptions (or refunds) are available. Additional land transfer taxes apply for properties purchased in the municipalities of Montreal or Toronto. Other municipalities may also impose these taxes and fees.

Federal capital taxes

The federal Large Corporations Tax (Part I.3 Tax) was eliminated on 1 January 2006. The Financial Institutions Capital Tax (Part VI Tax) is imposed on banks, trust and loan corporations and life insurance companies at a rate of 1.25% when taxable capital employed in Canada exceeds CAD 1 billion. The tax is not deductible in computing income for tax purposes. It is reduced by the corporation's federal income tax liability. Any unused federal income tax liability can be applied to reduce Part VI Tax for the previous three and the next seven years. Unused income taxes that can be carried back from taxation years ending after 30 June 2006 are calculated using capital tax rates and thresholds that applied before 1 July 2006 (i.e., 1.25% rate for capital over CAD 300 million; 1% between CAD 200 million and CAD 300 million; nil below CAD 200 million). The thresholds are shared among related financial institutions. In effect, the tax constitutes a minimum tax on financial institutions.

Canada

Provincial capital taxes

Every province, except Alberta, imposes a tax on capital employed within the province. The tax is deductible for federal income tax purposes. The federal government has proposed to limit the deductibility of capital taxes, but has delayed implementing this proposal indefinitely. As an interim measure, any increase in these taxes, with certain exceptions, is not deductible. Furthermore, the federal government has proposed to provide financial incentives to provinces that eliminate their capital taxes before 1 January 2011.

Provincial capital taxes are imposed at the following rates for 31 December 2010 year-ends. Certain exemptions and reduced rates apply.

	General (%)	Banks, trust and loan corporations (%)
Alberta	—	—
British Columbia (1)	—	0.082 or 0.247
Manitoba (2)	0.3	3
New Brunswick	—	3
Newfoundland and Labrador	—	4
Nova Scotia (3)	0.125	4
Ontario (4)	0.074	0.223 or 0.179
Prince Edward Island	—	5
Quebec (5)	0.12	0.49
Saskatchewan (6)	—	3.25

Notes

1. British Columbia's financial institutions capital tax was eliminated on 1 April 2010. On 1 April 2009, for financial institutions with either a head office in British Columbia or net paid-up capital of CAD 1 billion or less, the rate decreased from 0.67% to 0.33% and for other financial institutions, the rate decreased from 2% to 1%. A financial institutions minimum tax that was to apply starting 1 April 2010, will not come into effect.
2. Manitoba's general rate decreased from 0.3% to 0.2% for taxation years commencing after 1 January 2010, and will be eliminated on 1 January 2011. These changes do not apply to Crown corporations, for which the rates will remain 0.3%, nor to certain manufacturing and processing companies for which capital tax was eliminated on 1 July 2008. Other rates apply to the first CAD 21 million of taxable capital employed in Manitoba.
3. Nova Scotia's general rate decreased from 0.2% to 0.15% on 1 July 2009, and will decrease to 0.1% on 1 July 2010 and to 0.05% on 1 July 2011. These rates are doubled for corporations with taxable capital under CAD 10 million. The general capital tax will be eliminated on 1 July 2012.
4. Ontario's general capital tax was reduced or eliminated for certain manufacturing and resource corporations on 1 January 2007. On 1 January 2010, Ontario's general rate decreased from 0.225% to 0.15%, and its financial institutions rate decreased from 0.675% (deposit-taking institutions) and 0.54% (other) to 0.45% and 0.36%, respectively. Lower rates apply to financial institutions with taxable capital of CAD 400 million or less. Capital tax will be eliminated for all corporations on 1 July 2010.
5. Quebec's general rate decreased from 0.24% to 0.12% on 1 January 2010, and will be eliminated on 1 January 2011. In addition, capital tax was reduced or eliminated for certain manufacturing corporations, commencing with taxation years ending after 13 March 2008.
   Quebec's financial institution rate of 0.49% includes a 0.24% base rate and a 0.25% compensatory tax on paid-up capital. A compensatory tax of 3.9% (2% for taxation years ending before 31 March 2010 or beginning after 31 March 2014) on payroll also applies.

Quebec's base rate decreased from 0.48% to 0.24% on 1 January 2010, and will be eliminated on 1 January 2011.

6. Saskatchewan's rate for financial institutions that have taxable paid-up capital of CAD 1.5 billion or less is 0.7%.

Additional taxes on insurers

All provinces and territories impose a premium tax ranging from 2% to 4.4% on insurance companies (both life and non-life). In addition, Manitoba and Nova Scotia impose a capital tax on all insurance companies, while Ontario and Quebec impose a capital tax on life insurance companies only. Quebec also levies a compensatory tax on insurance premiums at a rate of 0.55% (0.35% for taxation years ending before 31 March 2010 or beginning after 31 March 2014).

Part III.1 tax on excess designations

Federal Part III.1 tax applies at a 20% or 30% rate if, during the year, a CCPC designated as eligible dividends an amount that exceeds its general rate income pool (GRIP), or a non-CCPC pays an eligible dividend when it has a positive balance in its low rate income pool (LRIP). A corporation subject to Part III.1 tax at the 20% rate (i.e., the excess designation was inadvertent) can elect, with shareholder concurrence, to treat all or part of the excess designation as a separate non-eligible dividend, in which case Part III.1 tax will not apply to the amount that is the subject of the election.

Eligible dividends are designated as such by the payor and include dividends paid by:

- Public corporations or other corporations that are not CCPCs, that are resident in Canada and are subject to the federal general corporate income tax rate (i.e., 18% in 2010); or
- CCPCs, to the extent that the CCPC's income is:
  - Not investment income (other than eligible dividends from public corporations); and
  - Subject to the general federal corporate income tax rate (i.e., the income is active business income not subject to the federal small business rate).

Non-eligible dividends include dividends paid out of either income eligible for the federal small business rate or a CCPC's investment income (other than eligible dividends received from public companies).

Provincial payroll taxes

Employers in Manitoba, Newfoundland and Labrador, Ontario and Quebec are subject to payroll tax. Maximum rates range from 1.95% to 4.3%. In addition, Quebec employers with payroll of at least CAD 1 million must allot 1% of payroll to training or to a provincial fund. Employers in the Northwest Territories and Nunavut must deduct from employees' salaries a payroll tax equal to 2% of employment earnings.

Social security taxes

For 2010, employers are required to pay, for each employee, government pension plan contributions up to CAD 2,163.15 and employment insurance premiums up to CAD 1,046.30. However, Quebec employers contribute, per employee, a maximum of CAD 822.53 in employment insurance premiums and up to CAD 442.50 to a Quebec parental insurance plan.

Canada

Excise taxes and duties
Excise duties are levied at various rates on alcohol, alcoholic beverages (other than wines) and tobacco products manufactured in Canada, while imports are subject to customs duties *(see below)*.

Excise tax is imposed on petroleum products and automobiles. In addition, a 10% federal excise tax applies to insurance premiums paid or payable by a Canadian resident to an insurer that is not authorised under Canadian or provincial law to transact the business of insurance. Certain premiums are exempt, including those for life, personal accident, marine and sickness insurance.

Custom duties
Custom duties are generally intended to protect Canadian industry from foreign competition and not as a source of revenue. The majority of most-favoured-nation (MFN) duty rates are below 10%; notable exceptions are textiles and apparel and certain food products (the latter is subject to "tariff rate quotas"). Many products are duty-free regardless of their country of origin. Goods imported from developed countries with which Canada does not have trade agreements will attract the MFN duty rate.

Qualifying goods that originate in the North American Free Trade Agreement (NAFTA) territory (Canada, the United States and Mexico) can enter Canada duty-free. Canada has implemented free trade agreements (FTAs) with several other countries (i.e., Chile, Costa Rica, the European Free Trade Association countries, Israel, Peru) and has signed or is negotiating agreements with several other countries. Like the NAFTA, these agreements set out rules of origin for determining whether the goods are eligible for preferential duty rates under the particular FTA.

Canada extends preferential duty rates to most (but not all) products imported from developing countries (the General Preferential Tariff) and has granted further concessions to goods originating in Least-Developed Developing Countries. In either case, goods must satisfy rules of origin and be shipped directly to Canada from the beneficiary countries to qualify for these rates. Canada applies the general duty rate of 35% to only two countries (North Korea and Libya).

Branch income

A non-resident corporation will be subject to income tax at normal corporate rates on profits derived from carrying on a business in Canada. However, Canada's tax treaties generally restrict taxation of a non-resident's business income to the portion allocable to a permanent establishment located in Canada.

In addition, a special 25% "branch tax" applies to a non-resident's after-tax profits that are not invested in qualifying property in Canada. The branch tax essentially is equivalent to a non-resident withholding tax on funds repatriated to the foreign head office. In the case of a company resident in a treaty country, the rate at which the branch tax is levied may be reduced to the withholding tax rate on dividends prescribed in the relevant tax treaty (generally 5%, 10% or 15%). Some of Canada's treaties prohibit the imposition of branch tax or provide that branch tax is payable only on earnings in excess of a threshold amount. The branch tax does not apply to transportation, communications and iron-ore mining companies. Nor does it apply to non-resident insurers, except in special circumstances.

Whether or not a treaty applies, a non-resident corporation that has a permanent establishment in Canada may be subject to federal capital taxes (i.e., financial institutions capital tax) and provincial capital taxes *(see Provincial capital taxes under Other taxes above)*.

Income determination

Inventory valuation

In most cases, all property included in an inventory can be valued at fair market value, or each item can be valued at its cost or fair market value, whichever is lower. Most well-established and reasonable approaches to inventory costing can be used for tax purposes, except for the last-in, first-out (LIFO) method. Conformity between methods used for book and tax reporting is not mandatory, but the method chosen should be used consistently for tax purposes. Inventory must be valued at the commencement of the year at the same amount as at the end of the immediately preceding year.

Capital gains

Half of a capital gain constitutes a taxable capital gain, which is included in the corporation's income and taxed at ordinary rates. Capital losses are deductible, but generally only against capital gains. Any excess of allowable capital losses over taxable capital gains in the current year can be carried back three years and forward indefinitely, to be applied against net taxable capital gains from those years, except in the case of an acquisition of control. No particular holding period is required. Intent is a major factor in determining whether the gain or loss is income or capital in nature. Complex transitional rules ensure that gains and losses accrued to the end of 1971 have no tax effect. Capital gains were not taxable before 1972.

Interest, rents and royalties

Interest that accrued, became receivable by or was received by a corporation, and rents and royalties received by a corporation are taxable as income from a business or property, as the case may be.

Inter-company dividends

Dividends received by one Canadian corporation from another Canadian corporation generally can be deducted in full in determining taxable income. However, dividends on certain preferred shares are an important exception and are taxed at full corporate rates. The intent is to allow preferred share investors to transfer benefits of accumulated deductions or losses from the entity that incurred the expense.

Dividends on most preferred shares are subject to a 10% tax in the hands of the recipient, unless the payer elects to pay a 40% tax (instead of a 25% tax) on the dividends paid. The payer can offset the tax against its income tax liability. The tax is not imposed on the first CAD 500,000 of taxable preferred-share dividends paid in a taxation year. Nor does it apply to dividends paid to a shareholder with a "substantial interest" in the payer (i.e., at least 25% of the votes and value).

Dividends received by private corporations (or public corporations controlled by one or more individuals) from Canadian corporations are subject to a special refundable tax of 33$\frac{1}{3}$%. The tax is not imposed if the recipient is connected to the payer (i.e., the recipient owns more than a 10% interest in the payer) unless the payer was entitled to a refund of tax in respect of the dividend. When the recipient pays dividends to its shareholders, the tax is refundable at CAD 1 for every CAD 3 of dividends paid.

Canada

Foreign income

Corporations resident in Canada are subject to Canadian federal income taxes on worldwide income, including income derived directly from carrying on business in a foreign country, as earned. In addition, resident corporations may be taxable currently on certain passive and active income earned by foreign subsidiaries and other foreign entities. Relief from double taxation is provided through Canada's international tax treaties, as well as foreign tax credits and deductions for foreign taxes paid on income derived from non-Canadian sources.

Canada intends to sign Tax Information Exchange Agreements (TIEAs) with non-treaty countries. To encourage non-treaty countries to enter into TIEAs:

- An exemption will be available for dividends received out of active business income earned by foreign affiliates resident in non-treaty countries that have agreed to a TIEA with Canada; and
- Active business income earned by foreign affiliates in non-TIEA, non-treaty countries will be treated as foreign accrual property income (FAPI), which is taxable on an accrual basis, if a TIEA with Canada is not concluded within a specified time period.

Foreign investment income earned directly, other than dividends, is taxed as earned, with foreign tax credits available in respect of foreign withholding taxes. Dividends received by private corporations from non-connected foreign corporations are subject to the special refundable tax of 33^1/$_3$% referred to above, to the extent that the dividends are deductible in determining taxable income.

The tax treatment of foreign dividends depends on whether the payer corporation is a foreign affiliate of the recipient. A foreign corporation is considered a foreign affiliate of a Canadian corporation if the Canadian corporation owns, directly or indirectly, at least 1% of any class of the outstanding shares of the foreign corporation and the Canadian corporation and related persons (together) own, directly or indirectly, at least 10% of any class of the outstanding shares of the foreign corporation.

Dividends received from foreign corporations that are not foreign affiliates are taxed when received, with foreign tax credits available in respect of foreign withholding taxes. Dividends received from foreign affiliates are permitted to flow tax-free between corporations, subject to certain limitations. These limitations pertain to the nature of the earnings from which the dividends were paid, the underlying foreign taxes paid and withholding tax paid.

Canadian corporations are taxed on certain investment income (foreign accrual property income) of controlled foreign affiliates (e.g., more than 50% voting shares owned by the Canadian corporation, related parties or a limited number of Canadian residents, among other things) as it is earned, whether or not distributed. A grossed-up deduction is available for foreign income and withholding taxes paid in respect of the income.

In light of recommendations made by the Advisory Panel on Canada's System of International Taxation and others, the federal government has reconsidered the draft rules that change the tax treatment of certain investments in foreign investment entities (FIEs) and in non-resident trusts (NRTs) that generally were to apply for taxation years beginning after 2006. The 2010 federal budget announced that the draft rules for FIEs and NRTs will be somewhat simplified and better targeted. The revised proposals will be subject to further public consultation.

The FIE rules have been essentially eliminated. The enacted version of these rules for offshore investment funds property will continue to apply, with some modifications, for taxation years ending after 4 March 2010, and the normal reassessment period will be extended by three years for these properties. A taxpayer that filed under the FIE proposals can either have those years reassessed or be entitled to a deduction in the current year for the income previously included.

The NRT rules treat non-resident trusts as being resident for Canadian income tax purposes. The NRT rules will generally apply commencing 2007. An election will allow a trust to elect to be deemed resident for the 2001 and subsequent years.

Stock dividends

If the payer is resident in Canada, stock dividends are treated for tax purposes in the same manner as cash dividends. The taxable amount of a stock dividend is the increase in the paid-up capital of the payer corporation because of the payment of the dividend. Stock dividends received from a non-resident are exempt from this treatment. Instead, the shares received have a cost base of zero.

Foreign exchange gains and losses

The foreign exchange gains and losses of a Canadian taxpayer that arise from business transactions (i.e., on income account), including the activities of a branch operation, are generally fully includable in income or fully deductible, as the case may be. Any method that is in accordance with generally accepted accounting principles may be used to determine foreign exchange gains or losses on income transactions, providing the treatment is consistent with previous years and conforms to the accrual method of accounting.

A foreign exchange gain or loss that is on capital account is treated the same as any other capital gain or loss. The accrual method of accounting cannot be used for purposes of reporting gains or losses on capital account. This follows from the Canada Revenue Agency's view that a taxpayer has not made a capital gain or sustained a capital loss in a foreign currency until a transaction has taken place. Therefore, paper gains and losses are disregarded.

Partnership income

For Canadian tax purposes, a partnership is treated as a conduit, and the partners are taxed on their share of the partnership income, whether or not distributed. A corporation is not restricted from being a member of a partnership. Income is determined at the partnership level and is then allocated among the partners according to the terms of the partnership agreement. However, certain deductions, such as depletion allowances, exploration and development expenses and donations, will flow through to be deducted by the various partners directly, as will any foreign tax credits, dividend tax credits or donation credits. Partners may deduct expenses incurred directly, such as interest on borrowings to acquire partnership interests, in computing income from the partnership.

Earnings of specified investment flow-throughs (SIFTs)

Certain earnings of SIFTs (i.e., publicly traded income trusts and partnerships) are subject to a SIFT tax and are deemed to be a dividend when distributed, starting

Canada

the 2007 taxation year for SIFTs first publicly traded after 31 October 2006, and starting the 2011 taxation year for other SIFTs. These rules are intended to discourage corporations from converting to income trusts and effectively force existing trusts to consider either restructuring or abandoning the income trust model. The rules do not apply to Real Estate Investment Trusts that meet certain conditions.

Deductions

Business expenses
Business expenses that are reasonable and paid out to earn income are deductible for income tax purposes unless disallowed by a specific provision in the Income Tax Act. Some expenses are deductible subject to limitation, e.g., charitable donations, entertainment expenses and the cost of providing an automobile to employees. Deduction of capital expenditures is specifically prohibited, but special provisions may allow depreciation or amortisation of these expenditures. Because Canadian corporations are taxable on worldwide income, there are basically no territorial limits on the deductibility of related expenses. Payments to affiliates are deductible if they reflect arm's-length charges.

Depreciation
Generally, depreciation for tax purposes (capital cost allowance) is computed on a pool basis, with only a few separate classes (pools) of property. Annual allowances are generally determined by applying a prescribed rate to each class on the declining-balance basis. For example, the prescribed annual rate on most furniture and fixtures is 20%, on automotive equipment 30% and on most buildings 4% to 10%. In the year of acquisition, only half of the amount otherwise allowable may be claimed on most classes of property. Generally, capital cost allowance may not be claimed until the taxation year the property is available for use. The taxpayer can claim any amount of capital cost allowance up to the maximum. Capital cost allowance previously claimed may be recaptured if assets are sold for proceeds that exceed the undepreciated cost of the class.

Temporary incentives to accelerate depreciation:

- For eligible manufacturing and processing machinery and equipment acquired after 18 March 2007, and before 2012, revise the rate and method from 30% declining balance to 50% straight-line; and
- For eligible computers and systems software acquired after 27 January 2009, and before 1 February 2011, increase the rate from 55% declining balance (half-year rule) to 100% (no half-year rule).

Mining and oil and gas activity
Generally, mining and oil and gas companies are allowed a 100% deduction for exploration costs and certain preproduction development costs. Other development costs are deductible at the rate of 30% on a declining-balance basis. Capital property costs are subject to the depreciation rules noted above under *Depreciation section*. In addition, in certain cases, significant asset acquisitions and assets acquired for a new mine or major expansion benefit from accelerated depreciation up to 100% of the income from the mine. For certain oil sands assets acquired after 18 March 2007, accelerated depreciation will be reduced gradually starting 2011 and will be eliminated by 2015.

Provinces levy mining taxes and royalties on mineral extraction and on oil and gas production. These provincial levies are mostly deductible.

Investment tax credits (ITCs) are available federally (and in some provinces) to individuals who invest in shares to fund prescribed mineral exploration expenditures. The federal credit in 2010 for qualified "flow-through" share investments is 15% of qualifying mining grassroots exploration expenditures. Certain mining exploration and preproduction expenditures that are incurred by a Canadian corporation and not used for flow-through are eligible for a 10% ITC. These credits can be used to offset current taxes payable or carried over to certain previous or subsequent taxation years.

Net operating losses
Net operating losses generally may be carried back three tax years and forward 20 (10 years if the loss was incurred in taxation years ending before 2006 and after 22 March 2004, seven years if before 23 March 2004). Special rules may prohibit the use of losses from other years when there has been an acquisition of control of the corporation.

Losses from a business or property
In 2003, the federal government released draft legislation that would have allowed a loss from a business or property to be claimed only if there is a "reasonable expectation of profit" from that business or property. Subsequently, the federal government announced that a revised proposal would be developed and released, although one is still forthcoming. When released, the measures likely will apply only prospectively. Furthermore, Quebec has rules that limit the deductibility of investment expenses for Quebec tax purposes.

Payments to foreign affiliates
Royalties, management fees and similar payments to affiliated non-residents are deductible expenses to the extent that they are incurred to earn income of the Canadian company and do not exceed a reasonable amount (fair market value in most cases).

Interest
Interest on borrowed money used for earning business or property income or interest in respect of an amount payable for property acquired to earn income is deductible, provided the interest is paid pursuant to a legal obligation and is reasonable in the circumstances.

Thin capitalisation rules can limit interest deductions when debt owing to certain non-resident shareholders (or persons not dealing at arm's length with a non-resident shareholder) exceeds two times the corporation's equity.

The Anti-Tax-Haven Initiative, which would have restricted the deductibility of certain interest payable after 2011 on investments in debt or equity of foreign affiliates, was repealed. The rule would have prevented multinational corporations from using tax havens and other tax avoidance structures to generate two expense deductions (one in Canada and another in a foreign subsidiary) for only one borrowing (so-called double-dipping).

Canada

Taxes

Neither federal nor provincial income taxes are deductible in determining income subject to tax. The tax treatment of federal capital taxes and provincial payroll and capital taxes is discussed above.

Scientific research and experimental development (SR&ED)

Canada provides a generous combination of deductions and tax credits. Current and capital expenditures on research and development can be deducted in the year incurred or carried forward indefinitely to be used at the taxpayer's discretion to minimise tax payable.

In addition, a taxpayer can benefit from the ITC, which is generally a 20% non-refundable credit on SR&ED expenditures that can be applied against taxes payable. Alternatively, this tax credit can be carried back three years or forward 20 to be applied against taxes owing.

A qualifying CCPC can qualify for a 35% refundable tax credit annually on its first CAD 3 million in expenditures. This enhanced credit is subject to certain income and capital limitations.

SR&ED ITCs have been extended to certain salary and wages (limited to 10% of salary and wages directly attributable to SR&ED carried on in Canada) incurred in respect of SR&ED carried on outside Canada.

In addition to the federal research and development incentives, all provinces (except Prince Edward Island) and the Yukon provide tax incentives to taxpayers that carry on research and development activities.

Business meals and entertainment

Deductions by a corporation for business meals and entertainment expenses are limited to 50% of their cost. This includes meals while travelling or attending a seminar, conference or convention, overtime meal allowances and room rentals and service charges, etc., incurred for entertainment purposes. If the business meal and entertainment costs are billed to a client or customer and itemised as such, the disallowance (i.e., the 50% not deductible) is shifted to the client or customer.

Doubtful accounts and bad debts

A reasonable reserve for doubtful accounts may be deducted for tax purposes. The reserve calculation should be based on the taxpayer's past history of bad debts, industry experience, general and local economic conditions, etc. Special rules apply for determining reserves for financial institutions. A taxpayer may deduct the amount of debts owing that are established to have become bad debts in the year, provided the amount has previously been included in the taxpayer's income or relates to loans made in the ordinary course of business. Recoveries of bad debts previously written off must be included in income in the year of recovery.

Fines and penalties

Most government-imposed fines and penalties are not deductible. Fines and penalties that are not government-imposed are generally deductible, if they were made or incurred by the taxpayer for the purpose of gaining or producing income from the business or property.

Other significant items

Transfers of losses and other deductions between unrelated corporate taxpayers are severely limited after an acquisition of control.

Three-quarters of capital expenditures for goodwill and certain other intangible properties can be amortised at a maximum annual rate of 7%, on a declining-balance basis. A portion of proceeds may be taxable as recapture or as a gain on disposition.

Charitable donations made to registered Canadian charitable organisations are deductible in computing taxable income, generally to the extent of 75% of net income. A five-year carryforward is provided.

Insurance premiums relating to property of a business are generally deductible, but life insurance premiums are generally not deductible if the company is the named beneficiary. However, if a financial institution lender requires collateral security in the form of life insurance, a deduction is allowed for the associated net cost of any pure insurance for the period.

Group taxation

Group taxation is not permitted. However, the federal government will explore whether the tax system could be improved by new rules for the taxation of corporate groups, e.g., the introduction of a formal system of loss transfers or consolidated reporting.

Transfer pricing

Canadian transfer pricing legislation and administrative guidelines are generally consistent with the Organisation for Economic Co-operation and Development (OECD) Guidelines. Statutory rules require that transactions between related parties be carried out under arm's-length terms and conditions.

Penalties may be imposed when contemporaneous documentation requirements are not met. A taxpayer will be deemed not to have made reasonable efforts if the taxpayer does not maintain complete and accurate documentation to evidence that it has determined and used arm's-length prices for its related party transactions. The documentation must be prepared on or before the taxpayer's documentation due date, which is six months after the end of the taxation year.

The transfer pricing penalty is 10% of the transfer pricing adjustment, if the adjustment exceeds the lesser of CAD 5,000,000 and 10% of the taxpayer's gross revenue for the year. The penalty is not deductible in computing income, applies regardless of whether the taxpayer is taxable in the year and is in addition to any additional tax and related interest penalties.

Canada has an Advance Pricing Agreement (APA) programme that is intended to help taxpayers determine transfer prices acceptable to the local tax authorities and, when negotiated as bilateral or multilateral APAs, with tax authorities in other jurisdictions. Under this programme, 210 APAs have been completed or are in progress.

Many of Canada's international tax agreements contain provisions concerning income allocation in accordance with the arm's-length principle. These include a Mutual Agreement Procedure, which is a treaty-based mechanism through which taxpayers

Canada

can petition competent authorities for relief from double taxation resulting from transfer pricing adjustments

Tax incentives

Regional incentives
In specified regions of Canada (i.e., Atlantic provinces, the Gaspé region and Atlantic offshore region) a 10% federal ITC is available for various forms of capital investment (generally, new buildings and/or machinery and equipment to be used primarily in manufacturing or processing, mining, oil and gas, logging, farming or fishing). The ITC is fully claimed against a taxpayer's federal tax liability in a given year. Unused ITCs reduce federal taxes payable for the previous three years and the next 20.

The provinces and territories may also offer incentives to encourage corporations to locate in a specific region. Income tax holidays are available in Newfoundland and Labrador, Nova Scotia, Ontario, Prince Edward Island and Quebec for certain corporations operating in specific industries (e.g., in Ontario and Quebec, commercialisation of intellectual property; in Prince Edward Island, bioscience or aviation) or meeting certain conditions (e.g., major investment projects for Quebec; job creation for Newfoundland and Labrador).

Industry incentives
Canada offers many tax incentives at the federal, provincial and territorial level, for various industries and activities, including those related to:

- Research and development *(see Scientific research and experimental development under Deductions above)*;
- Film, media, computer animation and special effects and multi-media productions;
- Manufacturing and processing; and
- Environmental sustainability.

Withholding taxes (WHT)

Withholding taxes arising in Canada
Canada is continually renegotiating and extending its network of treaties, some with retroactive effect. This table summarises withholding tax rates on payments arising in Canada. The applicable treaty should be consulted to determine the withholding tax rate that applies in a particular circumstance.

Recipient	Dividends (1)	Related-Party Interest (2)	Royalties (3)
	%	%	%
Resident corporations and individuals	Nil	Nil	Nil
Non-resident corporations and individuals:			
Non-treaty	25	25	25
Treaty:			
Algeria	15	15	0 or 15
Argentina	10 or 15 (5)	12.5	3, 5, 10 or 15
Armenia	5 or 15 (5)	10	10

Recipient	Dividends (1)	Related-Party Interest (2)	Royalties (3)
	%	%	%
Australia	5 or 15 (5)	10	10
Austria	5 or 15 (5)	10	0 or 10
Azerbaijan (8)	10 or 15 (5)	10	5 or 10
Bangladesh	15	15	10
Barbados	15	15	0 or 10
Belgium	5 or 15 (5)	10	0 or 10
Brazil	15 or 25 (5)	15	15 or 25
Bulgaria	10 or 15 (5), (6)	10	0 or 10 (6)
Cameroon	15	15	15
Chile (6)	10 or 15 (5)	15	15
China, P.R. (7)	10 or 15 (5)	10	10
Columbia (4)	5 or 15 (5)	10	10 (6)
Croatia	5 or 15 (5)	10	10
Cyprus	15	15	0 or 10
Czech Republic	5 or 15 (5)	10	10
Denmark	5 or 15 (5)	10	0 or 10
Dominican Republic	18	18	0 or 18
Ecuador	5 or 15 (5)	15	10 or 15 (6)
Egypt	15	15	15
Estonia (8)	5 or 15 (5)	10	10 (6)
Finland	5 or 15 (5)	10	0 or 10
France	5 or 15 (5)	10	0 or 10
Gabon	15	10	10
Germany	5 or 15 (5)	10	0 or 10
Greece (4)	5 or 15 (5)	10	0 or 10
Guyana	15	15	10
Hungary	5 or 15 (5)	10	0 or 10
Iceland	5 or 15 (5)	10	0 or 10
India	15 or 25 (5)	15	10, 15 or 20
Indonesia	10 or 15 (5)	10	10
Ireland, Republic of	5 or 15 (5)	10	0 or 10
Israel	15	15	0 or 15
Italy (9)	5 or 15 (5)	10	0, 5 or 10
Ivory Coast	15	15	10
Jamaica	15	15	10
Japan	5 or 15 (5)	10	10
Jordan	10 or 15 (5)	10	10
Kazakhstan (8)	5 or 15 (5)	10	10 (6)
Kenya	15 or 25 (5), (6)	15	15
Korea, Republic of	5 or 15 (5)	10	10
Kuwait	5 or 15 (5)	10	10
Kyrgyzstan (8)	15 (6)	15 (6)	0 or 10
Latvia (8)	5 or 15 (5)	10	10 (6)

Canada

Recipient	Dividends (1) %	Related-Party Interest (2) %	Royalties (3) %
Lebanon (4)	5 or 15 (5)	10	5 or 10
Lithuania (8)	5 or 15 (5)	10	10 (6)
Luxembourg	5 or 15 (5)	10	0 or 10
Malaysia	15	15	15
Malta	15	15	0 or 10
Mexico	5 or 15 (5)	10	0 or 10
Moldova	5 or 15 (5)	10	10
Mongolia	5 or 15 (5)	10	5 or 10
Morocco	15	15	5 or 10
Namibia (4)	5 or 15	10	0 or 10
Netherlands	5 or 15 (5)	10	0 or 10
New Zealand	15	15	15
Nigeria	12.5 or 15 (5)	12.5	12.5
Norway	5 or 15 (5)	10	0 or 10
Oman	5 or 15 (5)	10 (6)	0 or 10
Pakistan	15	15	0 or 15
Papua New Guinea	15	10	10
Peru (6)	10 or 15 (5)	15	15
Philippines	15	15	10
Poland	15	15	0 or 10
Portugal	10 or 15 (5)	10	10
Romania	5 or 15 (5)	10	5 or 10
Russia (8)	10 or 15 (5)	10	0 or 10
Senegal	15	15	15
Singapore	15	15	15
Slovak Republic	5 or 15 (5)	10	0 or 10
Slovenia	5 or 15 (5)	10	10
South Africa	5 or 15 (5)	10	6 or 10
Spain	15	15	0 or 10
Sri Lanka	15	15	0 or 10
Sweden	5 or 15 (5)	10	0 or 10
Switzerland	5 or 15 (5)	10	0 or 10
Tanzania	20 or 25 (5)	15	20
Thailand	15	15	5 or 15
Trinidad and Tobago	5 or 15 (5)	10	0 or 10
Tunisia	15	15	0, 15 or 20
Turkey (4)	15 or 20 (5)	15	10
Ukraine (8)	5 or 15 (5)	10	0 or 10
United Arab Emirates	5 or 15 (5)	10	0 or 10
United Kingdom	5 or 15 (5)	10	0 or 10
United States (10)	5 or 15 (5)	0	0 or 10
Uzbekistan (8)	5 or 15 (5)	10	5 or 10
Venezuela	10 or 15 (5), (6)	10	5 or 10

Recipient	Dividends (1)	Related-Party Interest (2)	Royalties (3)
	%	%	%
Vietnam	5, 10 or 15 (5)	10	7.5 or 10
Zambia	15	15	15
Zimbabwe	10 or 15 (5)	15	10

Notes

1. Dividends – In its treaty negotiations, Canada is prepared to accept a withholding tax rate of 5% on "direct dividends", i.e., dividends paid by a Canadian affiliate to a foreign parent or other corporation with a substantial interest in the affiliate.
2. Interest – Commencing 2008, Canadian withholding tax is eliminated on interest (except for "participating debt interest") paid to arm's-length non-residents, regardless of their country of residence.
   Most treaties have an explicit provision for higher withholding tax on interest in excess of fair market values in non-arm's-length circumstances.
3. Royalties – In its treaty negotiations, Canada is prepared to eliminate the withholding tax on arm's-length payments in respect of rights to use patented information or information concerning scientific experience. It is also willing to negotiate exemptions from withholding tax for payments for the use of computer software.
   Canada does not levy withholding tax on "cultural royalties", other than payments in respect of motion picture and television films, etc. Different rates may apply in the case of immovable property (e.g., payments that relate to Canadian natural resources). Most treaties explicitly provide for higher withholding tax on royalties in excess of fair market value in non-arm's-length circumstances. A nil rate of tax may apply in certain circumstances.
4. The treaty has been signed, but is not yet in force. Absent a treaty, Canada imposes a maximum 25% rate of withholding on dividends, interest and royalties.
5. The lower (lowest two for Vietnam) rate applies if or when the beneficial owner of the dividend is a company that owns/controls a specified interest in the paying company. The nature of the ownership requirement, the necessary percentage (10%, 20%, 25% or higher) and the relevant interest (e.g., capital, shares, voting power, equity percentage) vary by treaty.
6. If the other state (Canada for the treaty with Oman) concludes a treaty with another country providing for a lower withholding tax rate (higher rate for Kenya), the lower rate (higher rate for Kenya) will apply in respect of specific payments within limits, in some cases.
7. Canada's treaty with China does not apply to Hong Kong.
8. The treaty status of the republics that comprise the former USSR is as follows:
   • Azerbaijan, Estonia, Kazakhstan, Kyrgyzstan, Latvia, Lithuania, Russia, Ukraine and Uzbekistan—new treaties entered into force (see table for rates); and
   • Other republics – no negotiations are underway.
   Belarus, Tajikistan and Turkmenistan will not honour the treaty with the former USSR As a result, Canada will impose a maximum 25% rate of withholding on dividends, interest and royalties until a new treaty enters into force. For other republics that comprise the former USSR, the status of the former treaty with the USSR is uncertain. Because the situation is subject to change, Canadian taxpayers are advised to consult with the Canada Revenue Agency as transactions are carried out.
9. A new treaty with Italy was signed on 3 June 2002. Upon ratification, its provisions will apply:
   • For purposes of non-resident withholding tax, to amounts paid or credited after 31 December of the calendar year the treaty is ratified; and
   • For other taxes, for taxation years beginning after that date.
   The rates in the table are from the new treaty. Under the new treaty, the withholding tax rate will:

Canada

- Be reduced from 15% to 5% on dividends paid to a company that owns at least 10% of the payor's voting stock (the rate will remain 15% on other dividends);
- Be reduced from 15% to 10% on interest, but certain interest payments will be exempt; and
- Remain 10% on royalties, but certain royalties for the use of computer software, patents and know-how will be subject to a rate of 5% and certain copyright royalties will be exempt.

10. The fifth Protocol to the Canada-US treaty entered into force on 15 December 2008. The provisions of the Protocol generally apply:
    - For purposes of non-resident withholding tax, to amounts paid or credited on or after 1 February 2009; and
    - For other taxes, to taxable years beginning after 2008.

    The rates in the table are from the Protocol. Under the Protocol, the withholding tax rate will:
    - Remain 5% on dividends paid to a company that owns 10% or more of the payor's voting shares and 15% on other dividends;
    - Be eliminated on cross-border interest payments between:
        - Arm's-length persons – retroactive to 1 January 2008 (however, Canada has already eliminated withholding tax on most interest paid to arm's-length non-residents, *see footnote 2*); and
        - Related persons – subject to the Limitation of Benefits article, over three years from 10% to 7%, retroactively on amounts paid or credited after 31 December 2007, to 4% on 1 January 2009 and to nil on 1 January 2010; and
    - Remain 10% or zero on royalties.

Tax administration

Returns

Both the federal and the provincial corporation tax systems operate on an essentially self-assessing basis. The tax year of a corporation, which is normally the fiscal period it has adopted for accounting purposes, cannot exceed 53 weeks. The tax year need not be the calendar year. Once selected, the tax year cannot be changed without approval from the tax authorities.

All corporations must file federal income tax returns. Alberta and Quebec tax returns must also be filed by corporations that have permanent establishments in those provinces, regardless of whether any tax is payable. Corporations with permanent establishments in other provinces that levy capital tax must also file capital tax returns. Tax returns must be filed within six months of the corporation's tax year-end. No extensions are available.

Effective for taxation years ending after 2009, certain corporations with annual gross revenues exceeding CAD 1 million are required to electronically file (E-file) their federal corporate income tax returns via the Internet. Also, starting 2010, information return filers that submit more than 50 information returns annually must E-file via the Internet. There will be a one-year transitional period before penalties are assessed for failure to E-file.

Functional currency

The amount of income, taxable income, and taxes payable by a taxpayer is determined in Canadian dollars. However, certain corporations resident in Canada can elect to determine their Canadian tax amounts in the corporation's "functional currency" commencing taxation years beginning after 13 December 2007.

C

Payment of tax

Corporate tax instalments are generally due on the last day of each month (although some CCPCs can remit quarterly instalments, if certain conditions are met). Any balance payable is generally due on the last day of the second month following the end of the tax year.

Assessments, audit cycle and statute of limitations

The tax authorities are required to issue an assessment notice within a reasonable time following the filing of a tax return. These original assessments usually are based on an initial high level review of the corporation's income tax return and either indicate agreement with the return (which is the result in the majority of cases) or outline in detail any differences that arise from this limited initial review.

A reassessment of the tax payable by a corporation that is not a Canadian-controlled private corporation may be made within four years from the date of mailing of the original notice of assessment, usually following a detailed field audit of the return and supporting information. The limitation period is three years for Canadian-controlled private corporations. The three- and four-year limits are extended a further three years to permit reassessment of transactions with non-arm's-length non-residents. Reassessments generally are not permitted beyond these limits unless there has been misrepresentation or fraud. Many larger corporations have their returns audited annually. Smaller corporations generally are subject to less frequent audits, covering more than one year's return. Occasionally, a specific industry or a particular type of transaction may be selected for more intensive examination. Different time limits may apply for provincial reassessments.

Appeals

A taxpayer that disagrees with a tax assessment or reassessment may appeal. The first step is to file a formal notice of objection within 90 days from the date of mailing of the notice of assessment or reassessment, setting out the reasons for the objection and other relevant information. Different time limits may apply for provincial reassessments. Corporations that qualify as "large corporations" must file more detailed notices of objection. The Canada Revenue Agency will review the notice of objection and vacate (cancel), amend or confirm it. A taxpayer that still disagrees has 90 days to appeal the Canada Revenue Agency's decision to the Tax Court of Canada, and if necessary, to the Federal Court of Appeal and the Supreme Court of Canada. However, the Supreme Court accepts few income tax appeals.

Topics of focus for tax authorities

Topics of interest to Canadian tax authorities include:

- The deductibility of:
  - Royalty payments made by Canadian corporations to non-arm's-length non-residents;
  - Business restructuring expenses incurred by a group of corporations located in more than one country;
  - Interest paid on loans if the funds derived from the loans are used offshore; and
  - Guarantee fees paid by Canadian corporations to related non-resident corporations;
- The offshoring of Canadian-source income by factoring the accounts receivable of Canadian corporations;
- Treaty shopping to reduce Canadian withholding taxes and capital gains tax; and

Canada

- Surplus stripping to reduce Canadian withholding taxes by artificially increasing a Canadian corporation's paid-up capital and subsequently distributing the surplus as a return of capital.

Foreign reporting
Reporting requirements apply to taxpayers with offshore investments. The rules impose a significant compliance burden for taxpayers with foreign affiliates. Failure to comply could result in substantial penalties.

Other issues

Forms of business enterprise
Canadian law is based on the British common-law system, except in Quebec where a civil-law system prevails. The principal forms of business enterprise available in Canada are the following:

- Corporation – Whether public or private, incorporated federally or provincially, a Canadian corporation is a legal entity distinct from its shareholders.
- Partnership – A business relationship between two or more "persons" (i.e., individuals, corporations, trusts or other partnerships) formed for the purpose of carrying on business in common. A partnership is not treated as a legal entity distinct from its partners.
- Sole proprietorship – An unincorporated business operated by an individual that is carried on under the individual's own name or a trade name.
- Trust – A relationship whereby property (including real, tangible and intangible) is managed by one person (or persons, or organisations) for the benefit of another. Trusts may hold commercial enterprises.
- Joint Venture – Generally, refers to the pursuit of a specific business objective by two or more parties whose association will end once the objective is achieved or abandoned. A joint venture is not treated as a legal entity distinct from the participants.

Foreign investors usually conduct business in Canada through one or more separate Canadian corporations, although during the start-up period, operation as a branch of a profitable foreign corporation may be preferable. In addition, foreign investors may participate as partners in partnerships carrying on business in Canada or as joint venturers.

Corporate taxes in Cayman Islands

For more information, contact:

Frazer Lindsay
PricewaterhouseCoopers
P.O. Box 258, Strathvale House
90 North Church Street
George Town, Grand Cayman
Cayman Islands, KY1-1104
Tel: +1 345 914 8606
Email: frazer.lindsay@ky.pwc.com

Significant developments

There are no recent significant developments.

Taxes on corporate income

Corporate, capital gains, value-added tax (VAT), profits, payroll or other direct taxes are not imposed on Cayman companies.

Corporate residence

Since no corporate, capital gains, VAT, profits, payroll or other direct taxes are currently imposed on Cayman companies, corporate residency is not relevant in the context of Cayman Islands taxation.

Entities engaged in "scheduled" trade and business in the Cayman Islands (as defined in the Trade & Business Licensing Law) are required to have a trade and business license. Effecting and concluding contracts in the Cayman Islands and exercising, in the Cayman Islands, powers necessary for the carrying on of a business outside the Cayman Islands is generally not considered to be engaging in trade and business in the Cayman Islands.

Other taxes

Stamp duty and/or import duty is paid, at various rates, on importation of most goods, transfers of land/property and execution of certain documents.

Branch income

Branches are treated the same as other corporations doing business in the Cayman Islands.

Income determination

Since no corporate, capital gains, VAT, profits or other taxes are imposed on Cayman companies, income determination is not relevant in the context of Cayman Islands taxation.

Cayman Islands

Deductions

Not applicable as corporate, capital gains, VAT, profits or other taxes are not imposed on Cayman companies.

Group taxation

Not applicable as corporate, capital gains, VAT, profits or other taxes are not imposed on Cayman companies.

Tax incentives

Not applicable as corporate, capital gains, VAT, profits or other taxes are not imposed on Cayman companies. However, Cayman entities carrying on business outside the Cayman Islands can register as exempted companies (i.e., a company formed primarily to do business outside of the Cayman Islands and subject to certain requirements) and can apply under the Tax Concessions Law for an undertaking to be issued by the Governor-in-Council (i.e., the Cayman Islands government) exempting such company from any tax on profits, income, gains or appreciation which might be introduced in the period of 20 years following the grant of such concessions. The concession is extendable for a further 10 years after expiry. "Exempted limited liability partnerships" – certain partnerships formed primarily to do business outside of the Cayman Islands – can apply under the Exempted Limited Partnership Law for a similar concession which is for 50 years (rather than 20 years).

Withholding taxes (WHT)

Currently, no withholding taxes are imposed on dividends or payments of principal or interest.

Tax administration

There are no tax treaties; however, there are tax information exchange agreements between the Cayman Islands and a number of countries. *Please refer to the Cayman Islands Tax Information Authority's website for the latest list* (http://www.tia.gov.ky/html/assistance.htm).

The Cayman Islands agreed with the United Kingdom government to implement the Savings Directive and so the Reporting of Savings Income Information (European Union) Law (2007 Revision) came into force, setting out a reporting regime whereby Cayman paying agents making interest payments to individuals who are tax resident in a EU member state may have to report interest paid. The Cayman Tax Information Authority receives or facilitates submission of such information reporting.

No tax returns, forms or procedures are required to be completed for tax compliance purposes.

Corporate taxes in Chile

For more information, contact:

Francisco Selame
PricewaterhouseCoopers
Avenida Andrés Bello 2711
Torre de la Costanera, Cuarto Piso
Santiago, Chile
Tel: +56 2 940 0460
Email: francisco.selame@cl.pwc.com

Significant developments

Law No. 20,326, dated 29 January 2009, introduced amendments to the stamp tax. For operations performed during 2009, the stamp tax duty rate is reduced to 0%. For operations performed during the first half of 2010 (i.e., until 30 June), the normal rate, which varies, is reduced by half.

Law No. 20,316, dated 9 January 2009, introduced amendments to the tax benefits of charitable donations.

Law No. 20,343, dated 28 April 2009, introduced a beneficial tax regime applicable to capital gains in the transfer of certain publicly offered debt instruments, the purpose of which is to promote non-banking financing and to increase the liquidity on companies' cash flows to generate more activity in the stock market.

Taxes on corporate income

First category tax

The basic tax on income of a Chilean legal entity domiciled or resident in Chile and engaged in commerce, mining, fishing or industry is the First Category income tax, which is assessed at a rate of 17% on the entity's worldwide income. Non-domiciled and non-resident shareholders and partners are subject to an "additional" withholding tax of 35% on their Chilean-source distributions or remittances, with a credit granted for the First Category tax paid on the underlying profits. This results in an effective tax rate of 35%.

Corporate residence

Companies incorporated in Chile are considered to be domiciled in the country.

Other taxes

Value-added tax (VAT)

VAT is payable on transfers and services at a rate of 19%. The same tax is applicable to imports.

Chile

Stamp tax

Stamp tax is payable on the execution of certain legal documents, and its rate varies depending on the document being executed. However, pursuant to Law No. 20,326 of 29 January 2009, the stamp tax duty rate for operations performed during 2009 was 0%. For the first half of 2010 (i.e., until June 30), the normal stamp tax duty rate has been reduced by half.

Special taxes

Alcoholic and non-alcoholic beverages and certain luxury items, such as jewels, are subject to additional sales taxes ranging from 13% to 50%.

Branch income

Branches of foreign corporations that are operating in Chile are taxed on their Chilean-source income. Branches are subject to the First Category income tax, which is assessed at a rate of 17%. Branches are also subject to a 35% "additional" tax on amounts remitted or withdrawn during a given calendar year, less a credit for the First Category income tax paid, which is payable in April of the year following the distribution. Thus, the tax burden for a branch is 35%.

Income determination

For purposes of the First Category tax, as a general rule, corporate revenue must be determined on an accrual basis.

Inventory valuation

Last-in, first-out (LIFO) is not allowed. Inventories must be valued in accordance with monetary correction provisions, basically by adjusting raw material content and direct labour to replacement cost (which is generally the most recent cost), but excluding indirect costs. No conformity is required between book and tax reporting for income determination.

Capital gains

Capital gains are subject to normal taxation unless special provisions, such as those pertaining to gains on the sale of shares or monetary correction on capital repayments, establish exemptions.

Inter-company dividends

Dividends received from Chilean corporations are exempt from the First Category tax.

Foreign income

Resident corporations are subject to taxes on their worldwide income. In general, foreign income and dividends received by a domestic corporation are subject to Chilean taxation in the financial year when received (i.e., on a cash basis). A tax credit for taxes paid abroad is granted, subject to the regulations of the income tax law.

Branches of foreign corporations are taxed on their income without regard to the results of the head office.

Stock dividends

Stock dividends are not taxed.

Deductions

Net taxable income of a taxpayer is arrived at by deducting from gross income the expenses incurred to generate the income that have not been already deducted from gross revenue as costs.

Depreciation and depletion

Depreciation rates are calculated based on the estimated useful life of the assets. The normal periods of depreciation for new assets under normal conditions are as follows: heavy machinery, 15 years; trucks, seven years; factory buildings, in general, 20 years to 40 years. At the request of the Foreign Investment Committee or the taxpayer, the Internal Revenue Service (IRS) may reduce the normal useful life.

Taxpayers may recover capitalised costs by using the accelerated depreciation method for up to one-third of the normal useful life with respect to new or imported fixed assets, provided that the normal period of depreciation is at least three years.

Accelerated depreciation may be used only to reduce the taxable basis of the First Category tax. For the purpose of the tax applicable to distributions, accelerated depreciation is not considered.

No conformity is required between book and tax depreciation.

Annual depreciation is taken by the straight-line method. Gains or losses on the sale of fixed assets are considered ordinary profits or losses.

Normally, the sale of fixed assets is not subject to VAT, unless the assets are sold before the end of their useful lives or within four years from the date of acquisition. The sale of immovable property as fixed assets is subject to VAT only when the sale takes place within 12 months from the date of acquisition. For tax purposes, depletion for natural mineral resources is allowed on a unit-of-production basis.

Net operating losses

An indefinite carryforward of losses is allowed. Consistent with monetary correction, losses are carried forward, adjusted by the cost-of-living increase. No carrybacks are allowed, except in a case where a taxpayer has retained tax profits and has a subsequent tax loss.

Payments to foreign affiliates

The deductibility of payments made abroad for the use of trademarks, patents, formulas, and consulting and similar services is limited to a maximum of 4% of the income derived from sales and services in the corresponding year, unless the royalty is subject to income tax of greater than 30% in the country of the beneficiary.

Transfer pricing regulations are in line with general Organization for Economic Co-operation and Development (OECD) principles.

Taxes

Taxes imposed by Chilean laws are deductible, provided they are related to the normal activities of the company. However, income taxes and special contributions for promotion or improvement are not deductible.

Chile

Other significant items

As a general rule, expenses are not deductible for income tax purpose if they are not incurred to generate taxable income.

Group taxation

Consolidated returns are not allowed.

Tax incentives

Inward investment
The principal incentives are the following:

- Tax benefits and other incentives for companies operating in the northernmost and southernmost parts of the country; and
- Tax benefits to forestry companies, contracts for oil operation and nuclear material operations.

Capital investment
The principal incentives to encourage foreign capital contributions are statutory guarantees covering the repatriation of capital, remittance of profits, non-discrimination toward foreign investment, and access to the foreign exchange market for remittance purposes. In general, foreign investors are subject to the same legislation as national investors. A guaranteed income tax rate of 42% may be granted for 10 years or, provided the capital investment project exceeds USD 50 million, 20 years for the development of industrial or extractive projects.

The overall rate comprises the corporate tax on profits and withholding tax on dividend or branch profit distributions. The tax rate on dividend or profit distributions is the difference between 42% and the underlying tax paid at a corporate level. The option to be subject to an overall effective tax rate of 42% without change for 10 or 20 years is usually not exercised by foreign investors, because the current combined effective tax rate on profits and dividend distribution is 35% under the general tax regime.

Under the Foreign Investment Contract, a foreign investor may petition for tax stability with respect to VAT and customs duty regimes. With respect to customs duties, however, stability is granted only for the importation of certain machinery and equipment not available in Chile.

The Andean Pact is not in force in Chile.

Other incentives
The principal incentives for exports can be summarised as follows:

- Taxes paid in the importation or acquisition of goods required in the export activity are reimbursed;
- VAT on exports is zero-rated; and
- Chile has signed free-trade agreements with Australia, Bolivia, Canada, Central America (i.e., Costa Rica, El Salvador, Guatemala, Honduras, Nicaragua), China, Colombia, the European Union, Mexico, Panama, Peru, Republic of South Korea, Turkey, and United States. All these agreements provide for reduced customs duties.

Withholding taxes (WHT)

Dividends paid to a non-resident recipient are subject to a 35% withholding of "additional" tax, with a credit available that is equivalent to the income tax effectively paid at the corporate level, corresponding with the First Category tax paid by the corporation. This credit is added to the amount that is distributed to form the taxable base for the "additional" tax. Consequently, the tax burden for a non-resident recipient of dividends, including taxes at the company level, is 35%.

Branches are subject to a 35% "additional" tax on amounts remitted or withdrawn, less the First Category tax credit. *See Branch income section.*

In the case of a foreign investor that has applied for the 42% tax invariability, the effective tax burden is also 42%.

Interest paid to non-residents is subject to additional withholding tax at a general 35% rate. Interest on loans granted by foreign banking or financial institutions is subject to a sole 4% Additional withholding tax. Thin capitalisation rules requesting a 3:1 debt: equity ratio become applicable when the debt generating interest subject to the 4% rate is secured by related entities.

Royalties paid to non-residents are subject to additional withholding tax at a 30% rate. Royalty payments in connection to software are subject to additional withholding tax at a 15% rate. Such rate is increased in case the beneficiary of the payment is resident in a tax haven or in case the payment is made to a related entity.

Tax treaties
Chile has in force double taxation treaties with the following countries: Argentina, Brazil, Canada, Colombia, Croatia, Denmark, Ecuador, France, Ireland, Malaysia, Mexico, New Zealand, Norway, Paraguay, Peru, Poland, Portugal, Republic of South Korea, Spain, Sweden and the United Kingdom.

Please note that Chile has signed double taxation treaties with Belgium, Russia, Switzerland, Thailand, Australia and the United States of America, which are not yet in force.

Tax administration

Returns
The tax year coincides with the calendar year. The tax system is one of self-assessment by the taxpayer, with occasional auditing by the tax authorities. Tax returns must be filed with the IRS before 30 April of each year with respect to the income of the previous calendar year.

Payment of tax
Taxes are payable when the annual tax return is submitted in April of each year. Taxpayers, in general, are subject to monthly advance payments on account of their yearly income taxes. The difference between the advance payments and the final tax bill is payable in cash at the time the tax return is filed. If prepayments exceed the final tax bill, the excess is reimbursed by the Treasury.

Corporate taxes in China, People's Republic of

For more information, contact:

Cassie Wong
PricewaterhouseCoopers Consultants Shenzhen Limited, Beijing Branch
26/F Office Tower A, Beijing Fortune Plaza
7 Dongsanhuan Zhong Road
Chaoyang District
Beijing 100020
People's Republic of China
Tel: +86 10 6533 2222
Email: cassie.wong@cn.pwc.com

Significant developments

The Ministry of Finance and the State Administration of Taxation (SAT) jointly released a tax circular Caishui [2009] No.59 on 30 April 2009 to outline the corporate income tax (CIT) treatment for corporate restructuring transactions. Circular 59 addresses the CIT treatments for six forms of restructuring transactions, namely, change in legal form, debt restructuring, equity acquisition, assets acquisition, merger, and spin-off. The general principle is that enterprises undergoing corporate restructuring should recognise the gain/loss from the transfer of relevant assets/equity at fair value when the transaction takes place. However, if certain prescribed conditions are satisfied, the parties involved could opt for special tax treatments, which are essentially tax deferral treatment. In other words, recognition of gain/loss of the transferor from transfer of assets/equity can be deferred with respect to the equity-payment portion and the transferee may take over the transferor's tax basis of the acquired assets/equity. Such special tax treatments are only available to a very few specific types of cross-border transactions. Circular 59 is retroactively effective from 1 January 2008.

Also since year 2009, the Chinese tax authorities have strengthened their tax administration on transfer pricing and income derived by non-tax resident enterprise (TREs). The SAT has released a number of tax circulars addressing the tax administration of transfer pricing, foreign contractors and service providers, withholding tax on passive income, direct and indirect transfer of an equity interest in a Chinese company by non-TREs, etc. In addition, the SAT has also released circulars relating to the claiming of treaty benefits by non-TREs and interpretation of certain articles and terms in the tax treaties, such as dividends, royalties, beneficial ownership, etc. Aggressive tax planning (including but not limited to tax-avoidance and treaty-abusive arrangements) not supported by reasonable commercial purposes and substance will be subject to scrutiny of the Chinese tax authorities.

Taxes on corporate income

Under the CIT law effective 1 January 2008, the standard tax rate is 25%. There is no local or provincial income tax in China.

A lower CIT rate is available for the following sectors/industries:

- Qualified new/high tech enterprises are eligible for a reduced CIT rate of 15%. An enterprise has to fulfil a set of prescribed criteria and be subject to an assessment in order to qualify as a new/high tech enterprise.

- Integrated circuit (IC) production enterprises with a total investment exceeding RMB 8 billion, or which produce integrated circuits with a line-width of less than 0.25um are eligible for the reduced CIT rate of 15%.
- From 1 January 2009 to 31 December 2013, qualified technology-advanced service enterprises in 20 cities (such as Beijing, Shanghai, Tianjian, Guangzhou, Shenzhen, etc.) are eligible for the reduced CIT rate of 15%. This incentive is only available to certain technology-advanced service sector members and an enterprise has to fulfil a set of prescribed criteria and be subject to an assessment in order to qualify as a technology-advanced service enterprise.
- Qualified small and thin-profit enterprises are eligible for the CIT rate of 20%. An enterprise has to fulfil certain conditions in order to qualify as a small and thin-profit enterprise.

Corporate residence

The TRE concept is introduced in the CIT law whereby TREs are subject to CIT on their worldwide income. Enterprises established in China are always TREs. A foreign enterprise with a place of effective management in China is also regarded as a TRE.

A non-TRE that has no establishment or place in China is taxed only on its China-source income. A non-TRE with an establishment or place in China shall pay CIT on income derived by such establishment or place from sources in China as well as income derived from outside China which effectively is connected with such establishment or place. "An establishment or a place" is defined in the CIT regulations as establishments and places in China engaging in production and business operations, including:

1. Management organisations, business organisations, representative offices;
2. Factories, farms, places where natural resources are exploited;
3. Places where labour services are provided;
4. Places where contractor projects, such as construction, installation, assembly, repair and exploration, etc., are undertaken;
5. Other establishments or places where production and business activities are undertaken; and/or
6. Business agents who regularly sign contracts, store and deliver goods, etc., on behalf of the non-TRE.

If the non-TRE is from a tax jurisdiction which has entered into a tax treaty with China, the definition of "permanent establishment" in the treaty should prevail over the above definition of "establishment or place" in the CIT regulations.

Other taxes

Turnover taxes
China has a turnover tax system consisting of three taxes – value-added tax (VAT), business tax, and consumption tax. The regulations for the turnover taxes were amended in late 2008 and the amended regulations became effective from 1 January 2009.

Value-added tax (VAT)
The sales or importation of goods and the provision of repairs, replacement, and processing services are subject to VAT. VAT is charged at a standard rate of 17% and the

China, People's Republic of

rate for small-scale taxpayer is 3%. The sales of certain necessity goods may be subject to VAT at a reduced rate of 13%, as specified in the VAT regulations.

Starting on 1 January 2009, the VAT system was changed from a production-based VAT system to a consumption-based VAT system which means that input VAT on fixed assets is fully recoverable except for situations specified in the VAT regulations.

Export of goods from China may be entitled to a refund of VAT incurred on materials purchased domestically. The refund rates range from 0% to 17%. There is a prescribed formula for determining the amount of refund, under which many products do not obtain the full refund of input VAT credit and suffer different degree of export VAT costs.

Business tax
A business tax is imposed on services, transfer of intangible assets and immovable property taking place within China. Starting from 2009, services taking place within China are referring to services where either the service provider or the service recipient, or both are in China. This may make services even being rendered outside China subject to business tax in China. Business tax rates are 3% or 5%, except for the leisure and entertainment industry which may be subject to a rate of up to 20%. Business tax is not recoverable but is deductible for income tax purpose.

Consumption tax
A consumption tax is imposed on 14 categories of goods, including cigarettes, alcoholic beverages, certain luxury and environmental unfriendly items. The tax liability is computed based on the sales amount and/or the sales volume depending on the goods concerned. It is not recoverable but is deductible as an expense for income tax purposes.

Real estate tax
A real estate tax, which is based on the value of the property or rental received, is assessed on land and buildings used for business purpose or leased. The tax rate is 1.2% of the original value of buildings. A tax reduction of 10% to 30% is commonly offered by local governments. Alternatively, tax may be assessed at 12% of the rental value. Real estate tax is deductible for income tax purpose.

Land appreciation tax
A land appreciation tax is levied on the gain from the disposal of properties at progressive rates from 30% to 60%. Land appreciation tax is deductible for income tax purpose.

Customs duties
In general, a customs duty is charged in either specific or ad valorem terms. For specific duty, a lump sum amount is charged based on a quantitative amount of the goods (e.g., RMB 100 per unit or per kg). For ad valorem duty, the customs value of the goods is multiplied by an ad valorem duty rate to arrive at the amount of duty payable. The applicable duty rate generally is determined based on the origin of the goods.

An exemption from customs duty applies to machinery and equipment imported by a foreign investment enterprise within the amount of its total investment, for its own use if the project falls within the encouraged category of the "Catalogue for the Guidance of Foreign Investment Industries", and the imported machinery or equipment is not within the list of commodities that are not exempted from customs duty.

A customs duty and VAT exemption may be allowed on importation of raw materials for contract processing or import manufacturing. Goods may be imported into, and exported out of, designated Free Trade Zones and Bonded Logistics Zones without liability to customs duty or VAT.

Stamp tax
All enterprises and individuals who execute or receive "specified documentation" including 11 types of contracts and a few specified documents are subject to stamp tax. The stamp duty rates vary between 0.005% on loan contracts to 0.1% for property leasing and property insurance contracts. A flat amount of RMB 5 applies to certification evidencing business licences and patents, trademarks or similar rights.

Motor vehicle acquisition tax
A motor vehicle acquisition tax at a rate of 10% of the taxable consideration will be levied on any purchase and importation of cars, motorcycles, trams, trailers, cart and certain types of trucks.

Deed tax
A deed tax, generally at rates from 3% to 5%, may be levied on the purchase or sale, gift or exchange of ownership of land use rights or real properties. The transferee/assignee is the taxpayer.

Vehicle and vessel tax
A vehicle and vessel tax is a tax that is levied on all vehicles and vessels registered within China. A fixed amount is levied on either a yearly or quarterly basis. Transport vehicles generally are taxed on a fixed amount according to their own weight, with passenger cars, buses and motorcycles being taxed on a fixed unit amount. Vessels are taxed on a fixed amount, according to the deadweight tonnage.

Urban and township land-use tax
An urban and township land-use tax is levied on taxpayers who utilise land within the area of city, country, township and mining districts. It is computed annually based on the space of area actually occupied by a taxpayer multiplied by a fixed amount per square metre that is determined by the local governments.

Resource tax
A resource tax may be levied, generally on a tonnage or volume basis, at rates specified by the Ministry of Finance in consultation with relevant ministries of the State Council on natural resources including crude oil, natural gas, coal, other raw nonmetallic metals, raw ferrous metals, nonferrous metallic minerals and salt (including solid and liquid salt). In lieu of a resource tax, mine area usage fees are collected from joint ventures exploiting crude oil or natural gas.

Branch income

Under the CIT law, a branch of a non-TRE in China is taxed at the branch level. If there is more than one branch, they may elect to file their tax at the main office in China on a consolidated basis. There is no further tax upon remittance of branch profits.

China, People's Republic of

Income determination

Taxable income is defined as "gross income in a tax year after deduction of non-taxable income, tax exempt income, various deductions and allowable losses brought forward from previous years". The accrual method of accounting should be used.

Gross income refers to monetary and non-monetary income derived by an enterprise from various sources including but not limited to the sales of goods, provision of services, transfer of property, dividend, interest, rental, royalty, and donation.

Non-taxable income refers to fiscal appropriation, governmental administration charges, governmental funds and other income specified by the central government.

An unrealised gain or loss due to changes in the fair value of financial assets, financial liabilities and investment properties held by an enterprise is not taxable/deductible for CIT purpose. The gain/loss is taxable/deductible only when the asset/liability actually is disposed or realised.

Capital gains are treated in the same way as ordinary income of a revenue-nature for a TRE.

An exemption exists for CIT on dividend derived by a TRE from the direct investment into another TRE except for where the dividend is from stocks publicly traded on the stock exchanges and the holding period is less than 12 months.

The worldwide income of a TRE and its branches both within and outside China is taxable. A foreign tax credit is allowed for foreign income taxes paid on foreign-source income. The CIT law contains a controlled foreign enterprise rule under which the unremitted earning of a foreign company controlled by Chinese enterprises may be taxable in China.

Interest, rental and royalty income and income from stock transactions are treated as ordinary income.

Inventory must be valued according to costs. In computing the cost of inventories, the enterprise may choose one of the following methods: first-in first-out (FIFO), weighted average or specific identification.

Unrealised exchange gain (loss) from the year-end translation of assets (liabilities) denominated in foreign currency generally is taxable (deductible).

Partnerships registered in China are not subject to CIT. The income of a partnership is taxable at the partners' level.

Deductions

Generally, an enterprise is allowed to deduct reasonable expenditures which actually have been incurred and are related to the generation of income.

Depreciation of fixed assets
Fixed assets with useful lives of more than 12 months must be capitalised and depreciated in accordance with the CIT regulations. Generally, depreciation is

calculated by the straight-line method. Shorter tax depreciation life or accelerated depreciation may be allowed due to advancement of technology or suffering from constant vibration or severe corrosion. Production-nature biological assets, such as livestock held for breeding and commercial timber, also have to be capitalised and depreciated using the straight-line method.

Under the straight-line method, the cost of an item less residual its value is depreciated over the useful life of the asset. Residual value should be reasonably determined based on the nature and usage. The CIT law provides minimum useful lives for the following assets.

	Years
Buildings and structures	20
Aircrafts, trains, vessels, machinery, mechanisms and other production equipment	10
Appliances, tools and furniture, etc., related to production and business operations	5
Means of transport other than aircraft, trains and vessels:	4
Electronic equipment	3
Production-nature biological assets in the nature of forestry	10
Production-nature biological asset in the nature of livestock	3

Amortisation of intangibles and goodwill
A deduction is allowed for amortisation of intangible assets, such as, but not limited to, patents, trademarks, copyrights, land use rights. Generally, intangible assets have to be amortised over a period of not less than 10 years. For an intangible asset obtained through capital contribution or assignment, it can be amortised according to the useful life prescribed in the laws or agreed in the contracts, if any. However, acquired goodwill is not deductible until the invested enterprise entirely is transferred or liquidated.

Wages and staff welfare
Reasonable wages and salaries of employees incurred by an enterprise are tax-deductible. Directors' fees are also tax-deductible.

Basic social security contributions including basic pension insurance, basic medical insurance, unemployment insurance, injury insurance, maternity insurance and housing funds, that are made by an enterprise in accordance with the scope and criteria as prescribed by the State or provincial governments are deductible.

Commercial insurance premiums paid for investors or employees shall not be tax-deductible unless it is paid for safety insurance for workers conducting special types of work.

Staff welfare expense, labour union fees and staff education expenses are tax-deductible up to 14%, 2% and 2.5% of the total salary expenses respectively.

Reserves and provisions
Provisions for asset impairment reserves (e.g., bad debt provisions) and risk reserves generally are not tax-deductible unless otherwise prescribed in the tax rules. Financial institutions and insurance companies may deduct certain provisions and reserves subject to the caps specified in the relevant tax circulars.

China, People's Republic of

Contingent liability
The CIT law does not specifically address the deductibility of contingent liability. According to the general principle of the CIT law, contingent liability is a liability that an enterprise has not actually incurred and thus shall not be tax-deductible.

Assets loss
The tax deduction of most types of assets loss (including bad debt loss) is subject to approval by the tax authorities.

Research and development (R&D) expense
For R&D expenses incurred for new technology, new products or new craftsmanship, an extra 50% of the actual expenses incurred are also tax-deductible as an incentive.

Interest expense
Interest on loans generally is tax-deductible. For interest expenses on borrowings from non-financial institutions by a non-financial institution, the portion that does not exceed the commercial rate is deductible. The tax deduction of interest paid to related parties is subject to the thin capitalisation rule under the CIT law.

Payment to affiliates
Management fees for stewardship nature are not deductible but services fees paid for genuine services provided by affiliates in China or overseas and charged at arm's length should be deductible. Other payment to affiliates, such as royalty, is also tax-deductible provided that the charge is at arm's length.

Entertainment expense
Entertainment expenses are tax-deductible to the less of 60% of the costs actually incurred and 0.5% of the sales or business income of that year. The excess amount must not be carried forward to and deducted in the following tax years.

Advertising expense and business promotion expense
Advertising expenses and business promotion expenses are deductible up to 15% (30% for certain specified industries) of the sales (business) income of that year unless otherwise prescribed in the tax regulations. Any excess amount is allowed to be carried forward and deductible in the following tax years. Advertising expenses and business promotion expenses incurred by the tobacco industry are entirely not tax-deductible.

Charitable donation
A charitable donation is tax-deductible up to 12% of the annual accounting profit.

Organisational and start-up expense
Organisational and start-up expense is tax deductible fully in the first year of operation.

Other non-deductible expenses
In addition, the following expenditures are non- tax deductible expenditures: CIT payments; tax surcharges; penalty, fine and loss arising from confiscation of property; non-charitable donation; and sponsorship expenditures which are non-advertising and non-charitable in nature.

Tax loss
Tax losses can be carried forward for no longer than five years starting from the year subsequent to the year in which the loss was incurred.

Group taxation

Group taxation is not permitted under the CIT law unless otherwise prescribed by the State Council.

Transfer pricing regime

All enterprises are required to conduct transactions with related parties on an arm's-length basis. The Chinese tax authorities are empowered to make adjustments to transactions between related parties which are not conducted at arm's length and resulting in the reduction of taxable income of the enterprise or its related parties using the following appropriate methods: comparable uncontrolled price method, resale price method, cost plus method, transactional net margin method, profit split method, and other methods which are consistent with the arm's-length principle. China also adopts stringent requirements on the disclosure of related party transactions in the filing of the annual tax return. In addition, there is also a requirement to prepare contemporaneous transfer pricing documentation if the amount of related parties' transactions with an enterprise exceed a certain prescribed threshold.

The CIT law also contains transfer pricing provisions relating to cost sharing arrangements and advance pricing arrangements. In addition, it also contains a few tax avoidance rules such as controlled foreign corporation rules (CFC rules), thin capitalisation rule and general anti-avoidance rules.

Controlled foreign company (CFC) rule

Under the CFC rule, the undistributed profits of CFCs located in low-tax jurisdictions with an effective income tax rate of less than 12.5% may be taxed as a deemed distribution to the TRE shareholders. The Chinese tax authorities have published a list of countries ("White List") that they do not regard to be low-tax jurisdictions.

Thin capitalisation rule

The CIT law has a thin capitalisation rule disallowing interest expense arising from excessive related party loans. The safe harbour debt/equity ratio for enterprises in the financial industry is 5:1 and for enterprises in other industries is 2:1. However, if there is sufficient evidence to show that the financing arrangement is at arm's length, these interests may still be deductible fully even if the ratios are exceeded.

Dividend

CIT is exempted on dividend derived by a TRE from the direct investment into another TRE except where the dividend is from stocks publicly traded on the stock exchanges and the holding period is less than 12 months.

Tax incentives

The CIT law adopts the "Predominantly Industry-oriented, Limited Geography-based" tax incentive policy. Key emphasis is placed on "industry-oriented" incentives aiming at directing investments into those industry sectors and projects encouraged and supported by the state. The tax incentive policies mainly include the following and are applicable to both domestic and foreign investments:

Tax reduction and exemption

CIT may be reduced or exempted on income derived from the following projects:

China, People's Republic of

Projects/industries	CIT incentive	Valid period
Agriculture, forestry, animal-husbandry and fishery projects	Exemption or 50% reduction	All years as long as it is engaged in these projects
Specified basic infrastructure projects	3 + 3 years tax holiday	Starting from the first income-generating year
Environment protection projects and energy/water conservative projects	3 + 3 years tax holiday	Starting from the first income-generating year
Qualified new/high tech enterprises established in Shenzhen, Zhuhai, Shantou, Xiamen, Hainan and Pudong New Area of Shanghai after 1 January 2008	2 + 3 years tax holiday	Starting from the first income-generating year
Newly established software production enterprises	2 + 3 years tax holiday	Starting from the first profit-making year
Integrated Circuits production enterprises with a total investment exceeding RMB 8 billion, or which produce integrated circuits with a line-width of less than 0.25um provided that its operation period exceeds 15 years	5 + 5 years tax holiday	Starting from the first profit-making year
Integrated Circuits production enterprises which produce integrated circuits with a line-width of less than 0.8um	2 + 3 years tax holiday	Starting from the first profit-making year

Notes

In the above table, "2 + 3 years tax holiday" refers to two years of exemption from CIT followed by three years of 50% reduction of CIT. Likewise, "3 + 3 years tax holiday" refers to three years of exemption plus three years of 50% reduction of CIT.

For income derived from the transfer of technology in a tax year, the portion that does not exceed RMB 5 million shall be exempted from CIT; and the portion that exceeds RMB 5 million shall be allowed a 50% reduction of CIT.

A CIT exemption applies to the dividend derived by a TRE from the direct investment into another TRE except where the dividend is from stocks publicly traded on the stock exchanges and the holding period is less than 12 months.

A CIT exemption applies to the income derived by recognised non-profit-making organisations engaging in non-profit-making activities.

Reduced tax rate
The CIT rate may be reduced under certain conditions. For details, please refer to the *Taxes on corporate income section*.

Reduction of revenue
Where an enterprise uses resources specified by the state as its major raw materials to produce non-restricted and non-prohibited products, only 90% of the income derived is taxable.

Offset of certain venture capital investment
For a venture capital enterprise that makes an equity investment in a non-listed small- to medium-sized new/high tech enterprise for more than two years, 70% of its investment amount may be used to offset against the taxable income of the venture capital enterprise in the year after the holding period has reached two years. Any portion that is not utilised in that year can be carried forward and deducted in the following years.

Investment tax credit

Enterprises purchasing and using equipment specified by the state for environmental protection, energy and water conservation, or production safety purposes are eligible for a tax credit of 10% of the investment in such equipment. Any unutilised amount can be carried forward and creditable in the following five years.

Other incentives

There are also tax incentives in relation to the deduction of expenses and cost. For details, please refer to the *Deductions section*.

Foreign tax credit

A TRE is allowed to claim foreign tax credit in relation to foreign income tax already paid overseas in respect of income derived from sources outside China based on a country-basket principle. The creditable foreign tax also includes foreign income tax paid by qualified CFCs. However, the creditable amount may not exceed the amount of income tax otherwise payable in China in respect of the foreign sourced income. In addition, there is a five-year carryforward period for any unutilised foreign tax.

Withholding taxes (WHT)

Foreign enterprises without establishments or places in China shall be subject to a unilaterally concessionary rate of withholding tax at 10% on gross income from dividend, interest, lease of property, royalties, and other China-source passive income unless reduced under a tax treaty. Nevertheless, dividends distributed by a foreign investment enterprise out of its pre-2008 profit are still exempted from withholding tax.

Withholding tax rates under China's tax treaties with other countries/nations are as follows (as at 30 April 2010).

	Dividends	Interest (1)	Royalties (2)
	%	%	%
Albania	10	10	10
Algeria	10, 5 (3a)	7	10
Armenia	10, 5 (3a)	10	10
Australia	15	10	10
Austria	10, 7 (3b)	10, 7 (4a)	10, 6
Azerbaijan	10	10	10
Bahrain	5	10	10
Bangladesh	10	10	10
Barbados	5	10	10
Belarus	10	10	10
Belgium	10	10	10, 6
Brazil	15	15	25, 15 (5a)
Brunei	5	10	10
Bulgaria	10	10	10, 7
Canada	15, 10 (3f)	10	10
Croatia	5	10	10
Cuba	10, 5 (3a)	7.5	5

China, People's Republic of

	Dividends	Interest (1)	Royalties (2)
	%	%	%
Cyprus	10	10	10
Czech Republic	10	10	10
Denmark	10	10	10, 7
Egypt	8	10	8
Estonia	10, 5 (3a)	10	10
Ethiopia (6)	5	7	5
Finland	10	10	10, 7
France	10	10	10, 6
Georgia	10, 5, 0 (3c)	10	5
Germany	10	10	10, 7
Greece	10, 5 (3a)	10	10
Hong Kong Special Administrative Region	10, 5 (3d)	7	7
Hungary	10	10	10
Iceland	10, 5 (3a)	10	10, 7
India	10	10	10
Indonesia	10	10	10
Iran	10	10	10
Ireland, Rep. of	10, 5 (3b)	10	10, 6
Israel	10	10, 7 (4a)	10, 7
Italy	10	10	10, 7
Jamaica	5	7.5	10
Japan	10	10	10
Kazakhstan	10	10	10
Korea, Rep. of	10, 5 (3a)	10	10
Kuwait	5	5	10
Kyrgyzstan	10	10	10
Laos	5	5 (in Laos) 10 (in Mainland China)	5 (in Laos) 10 (in Mainland China)
Latvia	10, 5 (3a)	10	10
Lithuania	10, 5 (3a)	10	10
Luxembourg	10, 5 (3a)	10	10, 6
Macao Special Administrative Region	10	10, 7 (4a)	10
Macedonia	5	10	10
Malaysia	10	10	15 (5b), 10
Malta	10	10	10
Mauritius	5	10	10
Mexico	5	10	10
Moldova	10, 5 (3a)	10	10
Mongolia	5	10	10
Morocco	10	10	10
Nepal (6)	10	10	15
Netherlands	10	10	10, 6
New Zealand	15	10	10

	Dividends	Interest (1)	Royalties (2)
	%	%	%
Nigeria	7.5	7.5	7.5
Norway	15	10	10
Oman	5	10	10
Pakistan	10	10	12.5
Papua New Guinea	15	10	10
Philippines	15, 10 (3g)	10	15 (5b), 10
Poland	10	10	10, 7
Portugal	10	10	10
Qatar	10	10	10
Romania	10	10	7
Russia	10	10	10
Saudi Arabia	5	10	10
Seychelles	5	10	10
Singapore	10, 5 (3a)	10, 7 (4a)	10, 6
Slovak Republic	10	10	10
Slovenia	5	10	10
South Africa	5	10	10, 7
Spain	10	10	10, 6
Sri Lanka	10	10	10
Sudan	5	10	10
Sweden	10	10	10, 7
Switzerland	10	10	10, 6
Tajikistan	10, 5 (3a)	8	8
Thailand	20, 15 (3a)	10	15
Trinidad and Tobago	10, 5 (3e)	10	10
Tunisia	8	10	10, 5 (5c)
Turkey	10	10	10
Turkmenistan (6)	5, 10 (3a)	10	10
Ukraine	10, 5 (3a)	10	10
United Arab Emirates	7	7	10
United Kingdom	10	10	10, 7
United States	10	10	10, 7
Uzbekistan	10	10	10
Venezuela	10, 5 (3h)	10, 5 (4a)	10
Vietnam	10	10	10
Yugoslavia	5	10	10

Notes

Source: State Administration of Taxation, China

* This table is a summary only, and does not reproduce all the provisions relevant in determining the application of withholding taxes in each tax treaty/arrangement.
* The former Czechoslovak Socialist Republic is divided into Czech Republic and Slovak Republic.

China, People's Republic of

- The former Yugoslavia is divided into Bosnia, Croatia, Macedonia, Serbia, Slovenia, and Yugoslavia.
- There is no tax treaty signed between China and Bosnia and Serbia.
- The numbers in parentheses refer to the following numbered Notes.

1. Nil on interest paid to government bodies except for Australia, Brunei, Cyprus, Israel, Slovenia and Spain. Reference should be made to the individual tax treaties.
2. The lower rate on royalties applies for the use of or right to use any industrial, commercial or scientific equipment.
3a. The lower rate applies where the beneficial owner of the dividend is a company (not a partnership) that directly owns at least 25% of the capital of the paying company.
3b. The lower rate applies where the beneficial owner of the dividend is a company that directly owns at least 25% of the voting shares of the paying company.
3c. The lowest rate (i.e., 0%) applies where the beneficial owner is a company that owns directly or indirectly at least 50% of the capital of the paying company and the investment exceeding EUR 2 million. The lower rate (i.e., 5%) applies where the beneficial owner is a company that directly or indirectly owns at least 10% of the capital of the paying company and the investment exceeding EUR 100,000.
3d. The lower rate applies where the beneficial owner of the dividend is a company that directly owns at least 25% of the capital of the paying company.
3e. The lower rate applies where the beneficial owner of the dividend is a company that directly or indirectly owns at least 25% of the capital of the paying company.
3f. The lower rate applies where the beneficial owner of the dividend is a company that owns at least 10% of the voting stock of the paying company.
3g. The lower rate applies where the beneficial owner of the dividend is a company that directly owns at least 10% of the capital of the paying company.
3h. The lower rate applies where the beneficial owner is a company (other than a partnership) which directly owns at least 10% of the capital of the paying company.
4a. The lower rate applies to interest payable to banks or financial institutions.
5a. The higher rate applies to trademarks.
5b. The higher rate applies to copyright of literary, artistic or scientific work including cinematograph films or tapes for television or broadcasting.
5c. The lower rate applies to royalties paid for technical or economic studies or for technical assistance.
6. These tax treaties have not yet entered into force as of 30 April 2010.

In addition to the above tax treaties, a number of these countries have entered into investment protection treaties with China.

Tax administration

Tax return due dates and payment of tax

The tax year commences on 1 January and ends on 31 December. Enterprises are required to file their annual income tax return and settle the tax payment within five months after the end of the tax year, together with an audit certificate of a registered public accountant in China. Information on related party transactions must be filed with the annual income tax return. In addition, enterprises are required to file and pay provisional income taxes on a quarterly or monthly basis within 15 days following the end of each month/quarter. Three options are available to the taxpayer in computing the provisional tax: (1) actual profits of the month/quarter, (2) average monthly or quarterly taxable income of the preceding year, or (3) other formulas approved by the local tax authorities.

Statute of limitations

For unintentional errors, such as, calculation errors, etc., committed by the taxpayer in its tax filing, the statute of limitation is three years and extended to five years if the amount of tax underpaid is RMB 100,000 or more. For transfer pricing adjustments, the statute of limitation is 10 years. There is no statute of limitation for tax evasion, refusal to pay tax or defrauding of tax payment.

Audit cycle

There is no fixed audit cycle in China. Tax audit targets are selected pursuant to certain criteria.

Recent focus of Chinese tax authorities

Since year 2009, the Chinese tax authorities have strengthened their tax administration on transfer pricing and income derived by non-TREs. The SAT has released a number of tax circulars addressing the tax administration of transfer pricing, foreign contractors and service providers, withholding tax on passive income, direct and indirect transfer of equity interest of a Chinese company by non-TREs, etc. In addition, the SAT has also released circulars relating to the claiming of treaty benefits by non-TREs and interpretation of certain articles and terms in the tax treaties, such as dividends, royalties, beneficial ownership, etc. Aggressive tax planning (including but not limited to tax-avoidance and treaty-abusive arrangements) not supported by reasonable commercial purposes and substance will be subject to scrutiny of the Chinese tax authorities.

Other issues

Foreign investment incentives and restrictions

The tax incentives under the corporate income tax law are applicable to both Chinese domestic enterprises and foreign investment enterprises. Foreign investment is categorised as encouraged, permitted, restricted or prohibited. The details of each category are provided in the "Catalogue for the Guidance of Foreign Investment Industries" promulgated by the Ministry of Commerce on a needed basis from time to time.

Choice of business entity

Foreign companies, enterprises or individuals may, subject to approval from the Ministry of Commerce or other relevant ministries, establish equity joint ventures, contractual joint ventures, wholly foreign-owned enterprises or representative offices in China. Certain foreign financial institutions including banks and insurance companies may, subject to approval, set up branches in China. Starting from 1 March 2010, foreign investors are allowed to establish foreign invested partnership in China.

Exchange controls

Foreign exchange transactions are administered by the State Administration of Foreign Exchange (SAFE) and its branches. The regulatory administration on foreign exchange transactions of an enterprise depends on whether the transaction is a current account item or a capital account item. Current account items refer to ordinary transactions within the context of international receipts and payments, including, but not limited to, balance of payments from trade, labour services, and unilateral transfers. Capital account items refer to items of increase or decrease in debt and equity due to inflow or outflow of capital within the context of international receipts and payments, including, but not limited to, direct investment, all forms of loans, and investment in securities.

China, People's Republic of

If a transaction falls under the category of capital account items, generally prior approval from the SAFE should be obtained. Generally, a payment that falls under the category of a current account may be remitted to overseas if supported with proper contracts, invoices and tax payment/exemption certificates.

Intellectual properties
Patents, trademarks and copyrights are governed by separate laws and administered by separate governmental bodies. The government encourages the development and transfer of intellectual properties. The transfer of technology and technical services are currently exempted from business tax.

Mergers and acquisitions (M&A) activities
Both Chinese domestic and foreign investors increasingly are using M&A transactions to establish or expand their Chinese operations.

The Ministry of Finance and the SAT jointly released a tax circular Caishui [2009] No.59 on 30 April 2009 to outline the "CIT treatment for corporate restructuring transactions. Circular 59 addresses the CIT treatments for six forms of restructuring transactions, namely, change in legal form, debt restructuring, equity acquisition, assets acquisition, merger, and spin-off. The general principle is that enterprises undergoing corporate restructuring should recognise the gain/loss from the transfer of relevant assets/equity at fair value when the transaction takes place. However, if certain prescribed conditions are satisfied, the parties involved could opt for special tax treatments, which are essentially tax deferral tax treatment. In other words, recognition of gain/loss of the transferor from transfer of assets/equity can be deferred with respect to the equity-payment portion; and the transferee may take over the transferor's tax basis of the acquired assets/equity. Such special tax treatments are only available to a very few specific types of cross-border transactions. Circular 59 is retroactively effective from 1 January 2008.

General anti-avoidance rules (GAAR)
There is a GAAR provision in the CIT law allowing the Chinese tax authorities to make adjustments to taxable revenue or taxable income where business arrangements, structures, or transactions are entered into without reasonable commercial purpose. The Chinese tax authorities may initiate GAAR investigation if they suspect that an enterprise undertakes any of the following arrangements: abuse of preferential tax treatments, abuse of tax treaties, abuse of corporate structure, use of tax havens for tax avoidance purposes or other arrangements that do not have a reasonable commercial purpose.

Corporate taxes in Colombia

For more information, contact:

Carlos Chaparro
PricewaterhouseCoopers Servicios Legales y Tributarios
Calle 100 #11A-35 Piso 3
Bogotá, Cudinamarca
Colombia
Tel: +57 1 634 0555
Email: carlos.chaparro@co.pwc.com

Significant developments

Colombia has signed double taxation treaties with Spain, Chile, Switzerland, Canada and Mexico, the first two of which are in force as of 30 April 2010 while the others are still being finalised or awaiting ratification process. In addition, negotiations for double taxation treaties with China, Korea, and Germany have recently commenced.

The last tax reform of Colombia was enacted in late December 2009 as Law 1370 (promulgated 30 December). The scope of this reform is quite limited and refers to three tax matters basically, as follows. The equity tax originally due to expire in 2010 has been rolled over into to 2011 (accruing only once), at rates substantially higher than those that applied from 2007 through 2010. The so-called 40% fixed asset super-deduction, which was enacted as an investment incentive, has been reduced to 30% without any other changes. Lastly, beginning 2010, Free Trade Zone users subject to the corporate income tax (CIT) of 15% can no longer claim the 30% fixed asset super deduction as noted below.

A tax reform is likely to take place in Colombia in 2010 or in 2011 amid a fall in tax collections and slow recovery of the economy.

Taxes on corporate income

National companies (i.e., incorporated in Colombia under Colombian law) are taxed on worldwide income. Foreign non-resident companies and local branches of foreign companies are taxed on their Colombian source income only. The current general income tax rate is 33% which is applied on taxable income, with taxable income being generally defined as the excess of all operating and non-operating revenue over deductible costs and expenses. The current general capital gains tax rate is also 33%. However, qualifying businesses located at Free Trade Zones enjoy a reduced rate of 15% (while subject to capital gain tax at 33%).

The customary costs and expenses of a business are generally acceptable as deductible expenditure for income tax purposes provided they are necessary, reasonable and provided they have been realised during the relevant tax year under the accrual or cash method of accounting, as the case may be.

Corporate income taxpayers are required to pay a minimum amount of income tax which is determined based on the so-called presumptive income method, an alternate and rather simple income tax computation method. Under it, presumptive income is measured as 3% of net assets (or tax equity) as of 31 December of the prior tax year

Colombia

as reported by the tax payer on the corresponding income tax return. Income tax rate is then applied to the greater of regular taxable income (revenue less allowable costs and expenses) or presumptive taxable income (certain business activities are exempted from presumptive taxable income).

Shares and equity interests held in national companies, the net value of assets affected by force majeure events or the net value of assets that are being used in start-up, unproductive enterprises are excluded from the minimum presumptive tax computation.

There are no graduated tax rates for corporate income tax purposes in Colombia; the general rate is a flat rate. Also, the income tax is a national tax that applies to every qualifying taxpayer operating anywhere in the country, under the general rule noted above and the specific rules noted below.

In an effort to continue to attract local and foreign investments, a 2005 law created a Stability Agreement Regime whereby taxpayers can, upon satisfaction of several requirements, including the payment of a fee on the investment commitment, agree with the government on a contract that any future adverse changes to direct taxes are not to apply. However, to the extent changes are for the benefit of the taxpayer (i.e., income tax rate reduction), these are to be applied. An investor has to satisfy certain requirements to obtain a legal stability contract, which include the payment of a premium of 0.5% or 1% on the investment commitment, the definition of which is a new investment or enhancement of one existing which is worth over COP 3,862,500,000 or more.

In Colombia, as a general rule there are no industry-specific income tax rates, there are no dual income tax rates or hybrid tax systems relating to corporate income or tax consolidation. The only material deviation from the statutory income tax rate that is worth mentioning is the special income tax rate that applies for certain free trade zone users, which is 15% (as opposed to the statutory 33% income tax rate).

Corporate residence

Corporate residence is determined by the place of incorporation of any given company. For income tax purposes, companies incorporated under foreign laws and which have their main domicile abroad are considered "foreign companies", whereas any company incorporated in Colombia under Colombian law qualifies as a national company even if fully owned by foreign shareholders.

The concept of permanent establishment has not been defined by Colombian income tax laws. This concept is only relevant in the context of double taxation treaties.

Other taxes

Equity tax
For taxable years 2007 through 2010, individual (required to make income tax filings) and corporate income taxpayers are subject to an equity tax based on net equity held as of 1 January 2007 provided it amounted to COP 3,000,000,000 or more, at the annual rate of 1.2%. Net equity is generally defined as gross assets less allowable liabilities as reported on the income tax return.

The life of the equity tax has been extended to 2011 for those taxpayers who hold an amount of tax net equity that is also equal to or greater than COP 3,000,000,000 but less than COP 5,000,000,000 as of 1 January 2011 (the tax rate being 2.4%). Where the tax net equity is equal to or greater than COP 5,000,000,000, a 4.8% rate will apply.

The 2011 equity tax is payable in eight equal instalments starting in 2011 through 2014. The 2011 equity tax is not deductible for income tax purposes and cannot be offset against any tax receivables.

Beginning 2010, cross-border related party liabilities (other than for short termed imports) are not to be treated as such to arrive to a net equity basis for purposes of equity tax and presumptive taxable income.

Value-added tax (VAT)

The Colombian sales tax or value-added tax (VAT) taxes the sale in the country of any items of tangible personal property that are not fixed assets and are not covered by an exemption, the provision of services within the national territory (certain services supplied outside Colombia but imported also attract VAT) and the importation of tangible personal property that is not covered by an exemption.

The Colombian sales tax is a value-added tax based on a credit-debit system throughout the entire chain of a business. However, certain products are only taxed at the manufacturer level (one-phase VAT). For purposes of VAT calculation, the VAT taxpayer may credit against any output VAT collected to customers that (input) paid to vendors (certain limitations apply).

The general VAT rate is 16%. However, certain services and goods are taxed at 10% (i.e., coffee, rice) and 20% (i.e., mobile phone services). Luxury goods attract higher rates.

Under current law there are VAT exemptions available for the following items, among others:

- Equipment and materials for the construction, installation, assembly and operation of environmental monitoring and control systems;
- Imports of raw materials and supplies made under the so-called Plan Vallejo (*see below for description*) for further processing and incorporation into products that are to be exported subsequently;
- Temporary importation of heavy machinery and equipment for basic industries (mining, hydrocarbons, heavy chemistry, the iron and steel industry, metallurgy, power generation and transmission, and the water industry);
- Importation of machinery and equipment that is not produced in the country for recycling and processing of waste and refuse;
- Regular imports by major exporters of industrial equipment not produced in the country for the transformation of raw material;
- Freight transportation;
- Public transportation of passengers in the national territory by water or land;
- Transportation of gas and hydrocarbons,
- Interest and other financial income from credit operations;
- Financial leasing;
- Medical care services; and

Colombia

- Public utilities.

A non-resident supplier of VAT-subject services does not require a VAT registration. Rather, it is the locally-based recipient that must apply a reverse-charge rule. No VAT fiscal representation is allowed.

Vallejo plan for raw materials
This type allows the receipt, within the national customs territory, under Decree Law 444 of 1967 and Order 1860 of 1999, with total or partial suspension of customs duties, of specific goods destined to be totally or partially exported within a certain period of time, after having undergone transformation, manufacture or repair, including the materials needed for these operations. Under this type, machinery, equipment and spare parts may also be imported, to be used partially or entirely in the production and sale, of goods and services destined for export. The goods so imported remain under restrictions of sale.

Starting on 1 January 2007, customs duty exemptions for the importation of capital goods, spare parts and intermediate goods were eliminated, except for products for the agricultural sector not related with subsidies (Order 11 of 2003, Ministry of Commerce). Plan Vallejo benefits are granted by direct operation to the importer of goods, raw materials or supplies, who produces and exports the finished goods, or by indirect operation to the importer or producer of intermediate goods sold to the exporter, or to whoever provides the associated services with the production of the goods to the exporter.

Stamp tax
The stamp tax rate has been reduced to 0% for documents executed beginning 2010.

As a rule, a 0.5% to 1.5% stamp tax applied until 2009 on written agreements and contracts where the related contract value exceeded a certain threshold (COP 142,578,000 approx. in 2009). Under certain circumstances, the deductibility for income tax purposes of the expenditures associated with a written contract can depend upon full payment of the related stamp tax.

Financial transactions tax
The financial transactions tax, which is formally known as the Gravamen a los Movimientos Financieros (GMF), is a permanent tax on financial transactions the collection of which is the responsibility of regulated financial institutions and the Central Bank (Banco de la República).

The taxable event is the carrying out of financial transactions that involve the withdrawal of resources deposited in checking or savings accounts as well as in deposit accounts with Banco de la Republica, and the issuance of cashier's cheques.

The tax rate is 0.4%. After 2007, 25% of the total tax paid is deductible for income tax purposes, regardless of whether or not the transactions have a causal nexus with the income producing activity of the taxpayer.

The law establishes a series of operations and transactions that are exempted from this tax.

Industry and trade tax

This is a municipal tax that is imposed on revenue obtained from the exercise of industrial, commercial or service activities in any Colombian municipal jurisdiction. It can be viewed as a special form of a turnover tax.

The industry and trade tax rates are determined by each municipality, and as a rule they range between 0.2% and 1%. All of this tax can be deducted for income tax purposes when effectively paid.

Property tax

The property tax is another municipal tax which is imposed on real property located in urban, suburban or rural areas. It is levied on both improved and unimproved real estate. Therefore, the property taxpayers are the owners or holders of real property.

The taxable base of this tax is the current cadastral value of the property, as adjusted for inflation. In some cities, such as Bogotá, the taxable base is the value of the property as appraised by the taxpayer directly.

Property tax rates depend upon the nature and usage of the property, and generally range between 0.4% and 1.2%.

This tax is fully deductible for income tax purposes provided the same has a causal nexus with the income producing activity of the taxpayer (for example, where the tax is paid on rental property).

Branch income

Branch income is taxed at the same rate as corporate income, which is 33%. Beginning 2007 the 7% remittance tax on branch profits was eliminated. However, the 7% remittance tax will still apply to retained profits incurred prior to 2007.

Income determination

Income taxes on dividend income

The so called double income taxation on corporate earnings was eliminated from the Colombian tax system many years ago. This means that shareholders of Colombian companies are, as a rule, not required to pay any income taxes on dividend distributions, but only to the extent that dividends are paid out from earnings that were taxed at corporate level prior to distribution. When the dividends are paid out from earnings that went untaxed at corporate level, a foreign shareholder is required to pay income taxes on the dividends at 33% (in which case the tax is paid as a withholding tax collected by the distributing company). Certain double taxation treaties offer limited or full relief for the 33% dividend income tax.

Deductions

In Colombia, the customary costs and expenses of a business are generally acceptable as deductible expenditure for income tax purposes provided they are necessary, reasonable and have been realised during the relevant tax year under the accrual method of accounting. Examples of common (and not so common) deductions include the items below.

Colombia

Depreciation
As a general rule, the acquisition cost of tangible fixed assets is fully depreciable for income tax purposes. The normal estimated useful lives are as follows:

Asset	Years
Buildings and pipelines	20
Machinery and equipment, office furniture and fixtures	10
Vehicles and computer equipment	5

Depreciation rates can be increased by 25% for each additional eight-hour shift of asset use (and pro rata for fractions thereof). When tax depreciation exceeds book depreciation, the taxpayer is required to establish a reserve equivalent to 70% of the difference. Recapture of depreciation on the sale of depreciated property is taxed at 33%.

Depletion
It is available under certain specific circumstances, since generally recovery of costs takes place via amortization.

Amortisation of intangible assets
Taxpayers can amortise, for income tax purposes, the cost of any acquired intangible asset over a period of five years at a minimum, unless the taxpayer is able to prove that the amortization period should be less because of the specific nature or conditions of the business.

Interest
Taxpayers are generally entitled to deduct any interest paid to financial institutions or to third parties.

Tax loss carry-forwards
Net tax losses (adjusted for inflation) incurred in 2007 or thereafter may be carried forward without limitation. There is no loss carryback. Certain limitations apply to the offset of losses transferred on merger reorganisations.

Payments to foreign related parties
Royalties and similar charges
Royalties and the costs of exploitation or acquisition of all kinds of intangible property that are charged by foreign related parties are admissible as income tax deductions, provided that the corresponding withholding taxes are collected at generally 33% (10% in most double taxation treaties). Other types of payments are subject to the general rules for expenses incurred abroad.

Management overhead expenses
Management overhead expenses paid to a foreign related party (e.g., the parent company) are deductible provided they are subject to transfer pricing regulations and meet the arm's-length test, and provided the management services are real and are specifically related to the income producing activity of the local subsidiary which pays them. These expenses must also be carefully documented such that the local subsidiary can provide evidence to the authority of the fact that they are specifically related to its Colombian operations: to the planning and direction of the operations, the setting and implementation of management controls, the measurement of progress

made toward specific business goals, the related financial results, etc. Where these services are supplied inside Colombia, a 33% withholding tax is also required to ensure deductibility.

Interest
Interest and related financial costs (including foreign exchange losses) paid to foreign related parties are deductible provided they are subject to transfer pricing regulations and meet the arm's-length test. Furthermore, interest and the related financial costs paid on short-term financing relating to imports of merchandise and raw materials directly supplied by foreign related parties are also deductible for income tax purposes. In most cases, interest paid to non-resident lenders is not subject to withholding tax while at the same time being fully deductible (arm's-length principle must be satisfied for related party loans). However, only financial institutions registered with the Colombian Central Bank are permitted to extend loans into Colombia.

Net operating losses
Expenses incurred abroad
As a general rule, expenses incurred abroad which are not subject to withholding taxes are limited to 15% of the taxpayer's net income as computed before deducting such expenses. However, these expenses are fully deductible when they have to be capitalised under Colombian Generally Agreed Accounting Principles (GAAP).

Special deductible items
Colombian income tax laws have established certain special deductible items which include the following:

- All of the industry and trade tax and real property tax actual payments and 25% of the financial transactions tax actual payments are deductible;
- The so-called productive fixed asset super-deduction, which is equal to 30% of the acquisition cost of any productive, tangible fixed assets is deductible for the taxpayer in the year in which the qualifying assets are acquired (or built, as the case may be). In addition, all of the acquisition cost's are available as a tax amortisation or depreciation base;
- 125% of the investments made in certain scientific and/or technological projects or in professional training projects of governmental, public or private institutions of higher education are deductible. This deduction cannot exceed 20% of the taxpayer's net income as determined before subtracting the amount of the investment;
- All of the investments made for the control and improvement of the environment. This deduction cannot exceed 20% of the taxpayer's net income as determined before subtracting the amount of the investment; and
- Starting in 2007, tax losses may be carried forward and set-off against the regular taxable income obtained by the taxpayer in any subsequent taxable year.

Group taxation

Group taxation or group consolidation is not allowed for income tax purposes in Colombia.

Colombia

Tax incentives

Special corporate income tax relief items or incentives include the ones noted below.

As items of exempt income, the law has established the following:

1. Income obtained by publishing companies from the publication of scientific and cultural books, until year 2013;
2. The principal and interest (as well as related commissions and fees) paid pursuant to public foreign debt operations;
3. Income from the sale of electric power generated from wind, biomass, or agricultural waste, for a period of 15 years, provided the seller issues and negotiates Greenhouse Gas Reduction Certificates;
4. Income obtained from slow yield crops and plantations, including cocoa, rubber, palm oil, citrus and other fruits;
5. Income obtained from river transportation services with shallow draft vessels and barges, for a period of 15 years, starting in 2003;
6. Income obtained from hotel services offered in new hotels that are built within 15 years counted from 2003, for a term of 30 years, until 2032;
7. Income obtained from hotel services offered in refurbished or enlarged hotel facilities, where the related work is started within 15 years counted from 2003, for a term of 30 years;
8. Income obtained from ecotourism services, for 20 years starting in 2003;
9. Income obtained from investment in new forestry plantations, sawmills and plantations of timber-yielding trees; and
10. Income obtained from new medicinal and software products developed in Colombia and protected under new patents registered with the authorities, with a high content of national research and technology, until 2013.

Special income tax rate for free trade zones

Free trade zone (FTZ) industrial users enjoy a special income tax rate. The so-called FTZ industrial goods users and industrial service users pay corporate income taxes at a rate of 15% only, on income earned from their FTZ operations. Effective 1 January 2010, the 30% fixed asset super-deduction is not available for 15% income tax rate-subject taxpayers.

Withholding taxes (WHT)

The Colombian tax system provides for withholding taxes as a general mechanism of advance tax collection. Under the law, as a general rule all corporate entities (and big individual merchants) are required to collect or withhold taxes from payments made to third parties. The withholding tax collection agents must collect the applicable withholding tax amounts, deposit the withheld amounts with the authority, file monthly withholding tax returns and issue withholding tax certificates to the payees. The payees who are also income tax return filers credit the withheld taxes against the annual income tax liability computed on their returns.

As noted above, foreign non-resident persons are taxed on their Colombian source income only. Generally, the full tax liability accruing on payments made to foreign non-resident persons is satisfied via the collection of the applicable withholding taxes. The withholding tax rate on payments made to foreign non-resident persons for taxable dividends, royalties, and taxable interest is 33%. On payments made for consulting, technical assistance and technical services the withholding tax rate is 10% (whether supplied inside or outside Colombia). On payments made for software licences the withholding tax rate is 26.4%.

On other types of payments which give rise to Colombian source income the general withholding tax rate is 14%, with the foreign non-resident payee being required to file an income tax return in Colombia to report the final income tax liability, at 33% of net income (and being entitled to a refund where the final liability is less than the amount withheld at the 14% rate or being required to pay the deficit should the case be the opposite).

Exempt interest

Interest paid under foreign loans is not treated as Colombian-source income and thus is not subject to withholding taxes where the operations carried out by the local debtor qualify as activities that are considered of interest for the economical and social development of the country.

The scope of the activities that are considered of interest for the economic and social development of the country is relatively wide. The applicable regulations mention as qualifying activities for these purposes those related to the primary, manufacturing, and services sectors; as examples of qualifying service activities the regulations mention transportation, engineering, hotel services, tourism, health care services and the construction and sale of housing units.

Summary chart

Type of payment	Withholding tax rate
Dividends	33%
Royalties	33%
Taxable interest	33%
Royalties on software licences	26.4%
Technical assistance, consulting and technical services	10%
Other types of payments	14%

Tax administration

Tax returns

For income tax purposes, the taxable period is the calendar year, with no exceptions being admissible. The statute of limitations is generally two years following the actual filing of the return (a longer or shorter statute of limitations applies in certain cases).

Payment of tax

For income tax purposes, corporate taxpayers are divided into "large taxpayers" and "other taxpayers." Large taxpayers pay their estimated outstanding income tax liability (outstanding after deducting applicable withholding taxes from the estimated final liability) in five instalments over the year in which they file their annual income tax return.

Income tax return filing due dates are set by the government every year. Usually they fall in the months of April and May.

Colombia

Foreign tax credit

Foreign income taxes are creditable subject to certain limitations. Generally, the amount of the credit cannot exceed the Colombian income tax rate (33% or 15%, as the case may be). Double taxation treaties provide for more comprehensive credit systems as well.

Other issues

Choice of business entity

The most common type of company used in Colombia since the beginning of 2009 has been the so-called simplified stock company or simplified corporation, known as a SAS (sociedad por acciones simplificada). Besides SAS, foreign investors also use branch offices of an offshore entity as their investment vehicles in Colombia.

As a general rule, from a high-level perspective, there are no differences between a branch office and a subsidiary (such as a SAS) as far as Colombian taxation is concerned. All the taxes discussed above would apply equally to a branch operation or a subsidiary operation. Now, from a commercial perspective, and specifically from the perspective of corporate liability, operating through a branch office means that the head office is exposed to direct liability for all the obligations of the branch, tax obligations included. Operating through a subsidiary means that only the subsidiary is liable for its obligations as a general rule, that is to say that the shareholders are not liable for company obligations. Of corporations, the advisable choice would be a SAS which is very flexible in nature, easy to incorporate and can be held by one single shareholder (regular corporations require a minimum of five shareholders).

Corporate taxes in Congo, Democratic Republic of

For more information, contact:

David Guarnieri
PricewaterhouseCoopers Tax & Legal DRC
13 Avenue Mongala
Midema Building
Kinshasa 1
Democratic Republic of Congo
Tel: +243 810 536 849
Email: guarnieri.david@cd.pwc.com

Significant developments

No significant developments in corporate taxation have occurred in the Democratic Republic of Congo (DRC) in the past year.

Taxes on corporate income

Corporate tax in the DRC is paid on profits realised by a company, which carries out any operational activity in the country.

Foreign-sourced profits (e.g., dividends received from a foreign subsidiary, for instance) are exempt from corporate tax.

The corporate tax rate is currently 40% (30% for mining companies), with a minimum of 0.1% of the yearly turnover, which cannot be less than USD 2,500.

Please note that turnover includes all exceptional profits and interest received, in essence any credits on the income statement, which have the nature of income or gain.

Corporate residence

The set of rules related to tax residence are determined by:

- Ordinance-Law No. 69/009 dated 10 February 1969.
- Tax doctrine:
  - Circular No. 02372/CAB/FIN/73 dated 8 May 1973;
  - Circular No. 3749 dated 27 November 1989; and
  - Note of Service No. 01/036/DGI/GE/MMJ/2006 dated 28 March 2006.

The set of rules can be summarised as follows:

- Article 68 of Ordinance-Law No. 69/009 dated 10 February 1969 states that:
  - Foreign companies that carry out an activity in the DRC are taxable on profits they realised through permanent establishments or fixed establishments located in the DRC.
- According to Article 69, a foreign company is deemed as having a permanent establishment (PE) in the DRC in the following cases:
  - It has a material place of business (head office, branch, etc.) or any other fixed or permanent installations producing revenues in the DRC; or

Congo, Democratic Republic of

- Without having a material place of business, it carries out a professional activity under its own name during a period of at least six months, insofar as such an activity cannot be considered as a technical assistance to a local company.

Other taxes

Tax on rental income

Rental income related to buildings, houses, offices, premises, warehouses, etc. is taxed in the DRC at the rate of 22%.

In order to secure the payment of this tax, the tax code has put into practice a withholding tax system.

The tenant is liable to withhold 20% of the rentals paid and to refund this tax to the authorities.

Branch income

Tax rates on branch profits are the same as on corporate profits.

However:

- The costs involved abroad by the head office of the branch are not deductible in the DRC.
- The branch is submitted to the taxation of deemed distributed profits on top of corporate tax, i.e., on profits realised branch will pay:
  - Corporate tax on profits (40%); and
  - A 20% tax based on 50% of the net profits after deduction of corporate tax.

Income determination

Taxable income consists of profits from any industrial, commercial, agricultural or real estate operations entered into by the taxpayer in the DRC, as well as any increases of assets invested as a result of such activities and any increases derived from capital gains either realised or not, of any nature and origin.

To arrive at taxable income, the taxpayer may deduct all costs actually incurred in the production of income of the company, during the year, such as:

- Rents actually paid and rental expenses linked to buildings or parts of buildings used in the exercise of the activity and any overheads derived from their maintenance, lighting, etc.;
- Overheads costs, from maintenance of furniture and equipment used in connection with the company's activities;
- Wages, salaries, bonuses and allowances of employees and workers used in the operation, benefits in kind if these have been added to remunerations paid;
- Depreciation of fixed assets used in the company's operations; and
- Interest costs on funds borrowed from third parties and invested in the company's operations and similar type expenses, such as annuities or fees related to the operation.

Please note if the borrower is a private limited company ("Société Privée à Responsabilité Limitée" or SPRL) and if the lender is one of its shareholders, the interests on loan paid are not deductible from the corporate tax basis.

Deductions

Professional expenses directly related to the acquisition of income are tax-deductible.

The following are examples of expenses which may not be deducted to arrive at taxable income:

- Expenses of a personal nature, such as accommodation, school fees, leave indemnities and any other expenses not necessarily incurred in the business;
- Income tax;
- Legal or administrative fines of any nature;
- Expenses linked to rental properties as a landlord as well as related depreciation expenses; and
- Provisions.

Estimated tax losses can be carried forward for the next five years following the tax loss year; however, the losses must be deducted from the first profits of the company. A company may get audited up to five years after submission of tax return, in practice there is a tax audit every year.

In respect of payments made by a local company to a foreign one, for services (management services, technical assistance services), Ordinance No. 69/009 of 10 February 1969 and its subsequent modifications, provides that such expenses are deductible, provided:

- The services rendered can be clearly identified;
- The services cannot be rendered by a local company; and
- The amount paid for the service is not overstated and is commensurate to the nature of the service itself.

Technical assistance/management services must be clearly formalised in an agreement, including the modalities of calculation of the corresponding fees payable.

Group taxation

There is no group taxation regime per the DRC tax legislation.

Tax incentives

An Investments Code was issued by Law No. 004/2002 dated 21 February 2002.

This code allows for a certain number of tax, customs and general order measures designed to favour direct investments.

The preferential tax treatment measures of the Investments Code apply to direct investments and/or to entities that carry them out.

Congo, Democratic Republic of

The regime of the Investments Code does not apply to numerous sectors, notably:

- Mining and hydrocarbons;
- Banking and insurance; and
- Trade.

Particularly, the Investments Code grants appointed investors an exemption of corporate tax during the investment period.

Moreover, such advantages are granted for a determined period depending on the location of the investments – three years (Kinshasa), four years (Lubumbashi, Kolwezi) and five years (Katanga).

Withholding taxes (WHT)

According to Article 13 of the Tax Code, the following payments are subject to a WHT:

- Dividends paid by a local company to its shareholders;
- Royalties: the tax law defines royalties as any kind of remuneration paid for the use, or for the concession of a copyright on art works, scientific works, film works, brands, charts, any design, or formula or any secret process or recipe, as well as for the use of industrial, commercial or scientific equipment and for intellectual property in any industrial, commercial or scientific field;
- Interest on funds borrowed for business purposes.

Please note, if the interest is paid to a local company, the WHT does not apply as the interest is included in the taxable income of the company charging such interest.

The DRC has not entered into a double tax treaty (DTT) with any other nation.

As such, in order for a beneficiary to benefit from WHT paid, it will have to take advantage of its own country's tax legislation, in order to identify double tax credits. Therefore, it is impossible to get any WHT reimbursed.

WHT rate and payments
The rate of WHT is 20% which is based on the gross amount of sums paid.

If the payee does not withhold the tax from the amount invoiced and pays on his own the tax of 20%, then the tax authorities consider that the basis of the 20% tax is composed of the amount invoiced plus the amount of the tax. Consequently, in the case that the DRC company takes in charge the corresponding WHT, the WHT rate will be 20/80 and the amount of tax will not be tax-deductible.

However, for royalties, the WHT is charged on the net amount of the royalties paid.

The tax authorities consider that the net amount of royalties is calculated by deducting 30% from the royalties invoiced (i.e., the taxable basis will be 70% of the royalties invoiced).

Mining companies are, under certain conditions exempt from withholding tax on interest paid and are subject to a 10% withholding tax on dividends paid to their shareholders.

Tax administration

Payment of corporate tax is required when submitting the yearly tax return (by 31 March of the following year).

Like other taxes, the corporate tax is payable in local currency through a DRC bank account by a wire transfer to the bank account of the Public Treasury. Consequently, in order to operate in the DRC, the opening of a bank account in a DRC bank is mandatory. Moreover, the Tax Authorities require the bank account number of the applicant in order to grant a taxpayer number.

However, the collection of corporate tax is on an instalment basis or by way of prepayments (depending on taxpayer type).

Instalments of corporate tax
Instalments, in respect of corporate tax only, apply to taxpayers who come under the supervision of two specific kinds of tax departments – the Directorate General (DGE), the department of the tax authorities in charge of the most important taxpayers, and the Centre des Impôts (CDI), tax centres.

These taxpayers have to pay two instalments each representing 40% of the corporate tax paid during the previous fiscal year (including the amounts assessed by the Tax Authorities). This, therefore, totals 80% of the tax actually paid in the previous year. The first instalment must be paid before 1 August, and the second instalment before 1 December. Both payments are offset against the final corporate tax due for the fiscal year. The balance is paid when the tax return is submitted.

Prepayments of corporate tax (Précompte BIC)
Prepayments of corporate tax are to be paid by taxpayers (excluding those under the supervision of DGE and the CDI), in respect of import and export activities by wholesalers, and on the settlement of invoices relating to provisions of services or for building works.

Prepayments of corporate tax are withheld at source and collected by the Customs Authorities (OFIDA) for imported and exported goods, local manufacturers, wholesalers or semi-wholesalers, beneficiaries of services rendered and employers or contracting authority, for building works on the settlement of the invoices.

Amounts withheld at source must be refunded monthly to the Tax Authorities and they are creditable against the final corporate tax to be paid at the end of the fiscal year by the importer, exporter, service provider, etc.

The prepayment rate is 1% based on invoice value.

Corporate taxes in Congo, Republic of

For more information, contact:

Prosper Bizitou
PricewaterhouseCoopers Tax & Legal
88 Avenue du Général de Gaulle
Pointe Noire
Republic of Congo
Tel: +242 534 09 07
Email: prosper.bizitou@cg.pwc.com

Significant developments

The Republic of the Congo had no major tax developments in 2010.

Taxes on corporate income

The majority of corporate income tax (CIT) provisions in the Congolese General Tax Code arise from the implementation, under Congolese law, of CEMAC regulation No. 02/01/UEAC-050-CM-06, which revised the Act No. 3/72-153-UDEAC dated 22 December 1972.

Tax rates

The standard corporate income tax (CIT) rate in the Republic of Congo is 36%, with certain exceptions.

The minimum tax payable is 1% of the annual turnover and cannot be less than EUR 1,524.49 (EUR 762.25 if annual turnover is less than EUR 15,244.90).

A 2% minimum tax is payable by companies showing losses during two consecutive fiscal years. The 2% rate is applied to the sum of gross turnovers and products and benefits realised by the company in the most recent year in which it earned a profit. The 2% tax is not deductible for CIT purposes. However, in a company's first profit-making year after incurring the losses, half of the 2% tax is deductible.

The CIT rate for agricultural companies is 25%.

A tax rate of 30% applies for:

- Property companies;
- Revenues resulting from leasing or occupation of built or empty lands received by public establishments and non-profit making organisations; and
- Revenues resulting from capital assets that are not subject to tax on securities received by public establishments, non-profit-making organisation or communities.

A tax rate of 35% is applied on a deemed profit equal to 22% of the total gross remuneration (i.e., an effective tax rate of 7.70% of the taxable turnover made in Congo) derived from services rendered by:

- Foreign companies that qualified for the simplified tax regime; and

- Local companies and branches realising more than 70% of their annual turnover with oil companies and oil services companies (in this case, the deemed profit tax is regarded as an advance payment of CIT levied at the rate of 36% on net profits).

A 20% withholding tax (WHT) is imposed on income sourced in Congo that is derived by foreign companies not necessarily engaged in activities in Congo.

Corporate residence

Resident companies
Congolese registered companies are taxed on the territoriality principle. As a result, Congolese companies carrying out business out of Congo are not taxed in Congo on the related profits.

Non-resident companies
In the absence of a tax treaty providing otherwise, a non-resident company is liable for CIT on income realised in the Congo or deriving from or resulting from work or services of any nature supplied or used in the Congo.

Other taxes

Value-added tax (VAT)
Under the provisions of the VAT Law No. 12-97, dated 12 May 1997, all economic activities conducted in the Republic of Congo are subject to VAT, regardless of their purpose, their profitability or the legal status of the business performing them, and irrespective of whether these activities are habitual or occasional or originate in Congo or from a foreign country. Therefore, any person, natural or legal, engaged in an industrial, commercial or professional activity is subject to VAT unless specifically exempt by law.

Section 8 of the VAT law states a service is considered as provided in the Republic of Congo, when this service is used or exploited in the Republic of Congo.

The Congolese VAT rate is 18%. In addition to VAT, there is a sales tax (surtax), calculated at the rate of 5% applied to the amount of VAT, which must be invoiced and paid at the same time as the VAT. Therefore, the VAT rate is globally 18.9%. The surtax is not deductible (final cost).

A VAT return must be filed on a monthly basis before the fifteenth of every month.

Business tax and accessory taxes
The business tax is a tax paid by traders and professionals. The business tax is imposed on most commercial, industrial and professional enterprises (including branches of foreign enterprises), although some traders are exempt.

Tax is charged on the actual or deemed annual rental value of the tangible assets of the enterprise, on the power of the machines and on the average number of employees.

Any new taxpayer undertaking an activity requiring a trading licence must declare it in writing to the tax administration, within 15 days following the start of the business.

Congo, Republic of

For the first tax year, the business tax is paid on the basis of the date on which the business started. The tax is due from the first day of the quarter during which the business started.

The contribution called business tax ("patente," in French) is a tax collected by local communities. This tax, paid during the first three months of every year, includes both a fixed and variable fee depending on the specifications of the profession. The principal amount of the tax is increased with "additional centimes", "communal centimes", and "contributions to the National Investment Fund" (accessory taxes).

Computer royalty
The 2003 Finances Act instituted a computer royalty, applicable without exception or exemption to all importation and exportation of goods. The royalty applies on the customs taxable value of any imported or exported goods in the Republic of Congo. The rate is fixed at 2%, as per the 2004 Finances Act.

Oil and gas
Specific rules and caps apply for the upstream (production) oil and gas industry.

Customs duties
When applicable, import duties are payable at rates ranging from 5% to 30% on the customs value of imported goods. Customs value is calculated on the cost, insurance and freight level (CIF).

Customs duties rates

Group	Rates (%)
Basic necessities	5%
Raw materials and capital goods	10%
Intermediate and miscellaneous goods	20%
Consumer goods	30%

Additional entry taxes
Additional entry taxes apply on the importation of goods:

- CEMAC integration tax: 1% on CIF value;
- Statistic tax: 0.20% on CIF value;
- Organisation for the Harmonisation of Business Law in Africa (OHADA) contribution: 0.05% on CIF value; and
- Economic Community of Central African States (CEEAC) contribution: 0.04% on CIF value.

Rent tax
Rent tax is payable annually on the rental of built property. The tax is equal to one-twelfth of the rents due within the year. The tax also applies on non-built property for business purposes. The tax is imposed on the occupant of the premises (whether the occupant is the owner, a tenant or a subtenant).

The tax is due annually on 28 February at the latest. For new lease agreements, the tax is due within three months of the effective date of the lease agreement and is calculated as a proportion of the rents due until the end of the year.

The tax is paid by the tenant on behalf of the owner, or by the subtenant on behalf of the tenant.

Tenant and subtenants make a once-a-year deduction between 1 January and 30 April of the same year from all the rents due to the owner.

A 50% fine, assessed on the amount of the tax, is due for any late payment of the real estate tax.

Registration fees and stamp duties
Registration fees amount to 5% of the value of the annual rent paid during the tax year, including premises charges if any (Article 18 of the Congolese General Tax Code, Part II, Book I). "Additional centimes" also apply at a 5% rate of the registration fees. Stamp duties and registration fees should be paid for the total duration of the lease agreement. In the case where the lease agreement is renewed, stamp duties and registration fees should be paid for the renewable period.

Stamp duty ranges from XAF 200 to XAF 20,000 on certain documents.

Examples of documents that are subject to stamp duty include:

- Letters of agreement and other letters, which are prepared for use as evidence of act, fact or condition of civil nature;
- Notarial deeds and their copies; and
- Visas and flight tickets.

Transfer of company shares are subject to a 5% registration fee.

Tax on company-owned cars
This tax, which applies to company-owned cars from the previous fiscal year, is due 1 March at the latest.

With the exception of estate cars, private company cars, which fall into the category of own-used cars for the issuance of vehicle registration documents, are subject to tax. The tax rates vary from XAF 200,000 for engine ratings nine horsepower and below, to XAF 500,000 for the rest. Any late payment of the tax is subject to a 100% penalty.

Cars registered more than 10 years ago are exempt from tax.

Land tax on built properties
Land tax is payable annually on built properties. However, properties built for the purpose of accommodation are exempt for 10 years and properties built for business purposes are exempt for five years. The effective rate is determined every year by the local council.

The tax is levied on the rental value after a deduction of 25% (decline, maintenance and repair expenses) for properties built for business purposes. The tax is levied on the cadastral value after a deduction of 25% (decline, maintenance and repair expenses) for properties built for accommodation purposes. The tax is due from the owner.

Congo, Republic of

Land tax on non-built properties

Land tax is payable annually on non-built properties. However, properties intended for plantations and breeding are temporarily exempt for a three to 10 year range. The effective rate is determined every year by the local council.

The tax is levied on 50% of the cadastral value, determined every year by the Ministry of Finances. The tax is arbitrarily assessed by hectares in rural areas according to the nature of the plantations. The tax is due from the owner.

Branch income

Tax rates on branch profits are the same as for domestic corporations. No tax is withheld on transfers of profits to the head office.

Income determination

Determination of income

Taxable income is based on financial statements prepared according to generally accepted principles and the standard statements of the Organisation for Harmonisation of Business Law in Africa (OHADA) treaty.

Business expenses are generally deductible, unless specifically excluded by law.

Capital gains

Capital gains are treated as ordinary business income and are taxed at the standard corporate income tax rate of 36%.

However, a capital gain realised on the disposal of a fixed asset in the course of trading is excluded from income for a period of three years, if the taxpayer reinvests the gain in new fixed assets for the business.

If the business is totally or partially transferred or discontinued, only half of the net capital gain is taxed if the event occurs less than five years after the start-up or purchase of the business and only one-third of the gain is taxed if the event occurs five years or more after the business is begun or purchased. However, if the business is not carried-on in any form, the total gain is taxed.

Dividends

Dividends paid by a Congolese company are subject to a 20% withholding tax on securities income (Impôt sur les Revenus des Valeurs Mobilières or IRVM) unless a different rate applies under an international tax treaty (France, CEMAC, OCAM). This IRVM is regarded as an advance payment for the final calculation of CIT.

Dividends are treated as ordinary business income and are taxed at the standard income tax rate of 36% for resident corporations.

After three years, profits credited to the non-compulsory reserve are considered to be dividends and are accordingly subject to the 20% WHT on dividends.

Inter-company dividends

Dividends received from a Congolese company (DivCo) by a commercial company incorporated in Congo (HoldCo) are exempt from CIT and subject to a final 20% WHT if the following conditions are met:

- HoldCo and DivCo are incorporated in the CEMAC;
- HoldCo holds 25% of the capital of DivCo; and
- HoldCo holds the shares for at least two years from the date of purchase.

However, 10% of dividends that are deemed to represent the share of cost and expenses are included in the taxable profits of HoldCo and liable for the CIT.

If the above conditions are not met, dividends received from a Congolese company by another Congolese company are subject to a 20% WHT, which is an advance payment of the recipient's CIT.

Deductions

Generally, a deduction is allowed for all expenditures incurred to obtain, collect and maintain business profits.

To be deductible, expenses should be incurred necessarily for the normal purposes of the business, and be supported by suitable evidence.

Depreciation and depletion

In general, all types of fixed assets, except land, are depreciable for tax purposes, as long as they can be shown to have been acquired for business purposes of the corporation. Goods costing less than EUR 152.44 per item may be written-off on purchase as expenses. Depreciation must be calculated on the original purchase price. The straight-line method is used. The General Tax Code sets forth maximum rates of depreciation.

Depreciation recorded when the company is in a loss position may be carried forward without limitation and deducted from the first available taxable profits, provided it was appropriately disclosed in the annual corporate income tax return.

Recoverable and identifiable packaging is regarded as fixed assets. They are recorded in a fixed asset account at the time of purchase. This packaging is regarded as returnable packaging when the supplier intends to act as the sole owner of the packaging.

Unrecoverable packaging is recorded as an expense and deductible for tax purposes.

Exceptional accelerated depreciation may be authorised in certain circumstances for heavy equipment with a value of more than EUR 60,979.60. This special accelerated depreciation does not apply to private vehicles owned by the enterprises.

Exceptional depreciation method

The exceptional depreciation method is an accelerated depreciation method.

Companies may elect the accelerated depreciation method for heavy materials and equipments that:

Congo, Republic of

- Are purchased new for a value higher than EUR 60,979.60;
- Have a useful life of at least three years;
- Are used for manufacturing, processing, transport and handling; and
- Are bound to an intensive use.

The application for the accelerated depreciation must be submitted to the head office of taxes within three months of the purchase of the assets to be depreciated. The option is granted upon approval of the ministry in charge of finances. According to the implementation instructions adopted by the head office of taxes on 24 January 2003, if the administration fails to respond to the application for accelerated depreciation within three months, the application is tacitly granted.

The accelerated depreciation rate is 40%.

The normal annual depreciation is calculated on the residual value of the assets.

According to the implementation instructions adopted by the head office of taxes on 24 January 2003, a 40% deduction may be taken in the year of acquisition of the previously mentioned assets, increased with the normal rate calculated on the residual value after application of the accelerated depreciation. These assets are depreciated on a straight-line basis thereafter.

Net operating losses
For tax purposes, losses may be carried forward to offset profits earned in the three succeeding fiscal years. Carryback losses are not permissible. Tax consolidation is not available.

Payments to foreign affiliates
Allowable deductions include sums paid abroad to foreign companies for:

- Actual services, notably overheads for the operations made for the benefit of a company based in Congo, including: costs of studies, technical, financial and accounting assistance, commissions and fees, and interests; and
- Use of patents, licenses, trademarks, drawings, manufacturing processes, patterns and similar rights to the extent the payer proves they correspond to actual operations, and they are neither abnormal, nor excessive.

Subject to the provisions of tax treaties (France, CEMAC and OCAM), the deduction is allowed within a limit of 20% of taxable profits before deduction of the expenses in question.

In the event of losses, the rate is applied on the results of the last profit exercise, which is not prescribed. In the absence of profits during the period out of prescription, the sums paid are not allowed as tax deductions.

When the sums are not allowed, as a whole or in part, in the deductible expenses, they are deemed to be paid benefits, and are subject to tax on the dividends at the rate of 20%.

Royalties for the transfer or concession of patents, trademarks, drawings and other similar titles, are deductible to the extent the payer proves they are still valid. When these royalties benefit an enterprise contributing in the management or share capital of an enterprise in the Republic of Congo, they are deemed to be paid benefits, and are subject to tax on the dividends at the rate of 20%.

Commission or brokerages, relating to goods purchased on behalf of enterprises based in Congo, are allowable tax deductions up to 5% of the purchase amount made by the central purchasing office, the head office or the intermediaries. The reductions shall benefit enterprises based in Congo. An original supplier's invoice must be attached to the intermediary's invoice.

The payer shall prove that:

- The purchases necessitated the interventions of a broker or intermediary;
- The commissions provided better supply conditions compared with the actual situations on the market; and
- The commissions are not excessive compared with the nature of the services.

Taxes
Taxes, other than income taxes, are usually deductible. Examples of deductible taxes include: customs duties, excise duties, payroll taxes, business license tax, registration taxes and unrecoverable value-added tax.

Corporate income tax itself is not deductible, nor is the special tax on company-owned cars.

Taxes withheld on remuneration paid to third parties (third parties taxes) and remitted to the tax office by a Congolese enterprise are not deductible.

Interest paid to shareholders
Interests are deductible subject to the following two conditions:

1. General limit – regardless of the form under which a legal entity is registered, the deduction is allowed in the limit of the interest calculated at the rate of the advances in current accounts on states funds of the Bank of the States of Central Africa (BEAC) raised by two points. Currently, the ceiling for the deduction of interests is 7.25%.
2. For private limited companies and public limited companies – the deduction is allowed according to the status of control over the management of the enterprise.
   a. Shareholders who have control over the company *de facto* or *de jure*: The deduction is allowed only to the extent that the sums paid do not exceed, for the shareholders as a whole, half of the paid-up capital and are within the limit sets forth in condition 1 (General limitation).
   b. Other shareholders:
      The limit indicated in condition 1, General limitation applies.

Group taxation

There is no tax provision in Congo for group taxation.

Tax incentives

Law No. 008-92 of 10 April 1992 giving rise to the Investment Code, modified by Law No. 07/96 of 6 March 1996, was repealed by Law No. 6-2003 of 18 January 2003.

Congo, Republic of

The new investment regime in Congo was set out by Law No. 6-2003 of 18 January 2003, which established the investment charter. The charter's application, Decree No. 2004-30 of 18 February 2004 established modes of business registration.

1. Scope – the following may be registered under the investment charter:
   - Businesses wishing to pursue an activity in the Republic of Congo, except for activities such as brokerage, trade, import and production of arms, import or processing of toxic waste and by products;
   - Under certain conditions, commercial activities linked to collection, storage, distribution and export of locally produced products, except alcoholic beverages and tobacco;
   - New activities (as opposed to pre-existing activities);
   - Forestry businesses benefiting from a forestry permit called the forestry development unit; and
   - New companies coming from the redemption of a registered company.
2. Conditions of eligibility for the investment charter – which are required to be eligible for the investment charter, the company must satisfy the conditions below:
   - Be registered with the Trade and Personal Credit Registry in Congo;
   - Create permanent employment, to be carried out over a minimum of 280 days per year;
   - Maintain company share capital equal to or greater than 20% of investments;
   - Primarily use local principal materials necessary for the production of the finished or semi-finished product, with equal conditions concerning price, quality and time of delivery to outside, in the case of industry;
   - Primarily use local business services, with equal conditions concerning quality, price, time of realisation regarding payments to external businesses, for the case of service businesses;
   - Be registered at the Congolese National Welfare Fund;
   - Open an account at a local bank or any other financial, savings or credit establishment duly established; and
   - Primarily use a local workforce, with the same expertise as the foreign workforce.
3. Registration procedure – entitlement to the benefits prescribed by the charter is subject to obtaining a registration agreement, provided by the National Investment Commission.
4. Fiscal and customs benefits set out by the Investment Charter – these benefits vary according to privileged regimes, motivation measures and in a general manner.

Privileged regimes
The charter sets out three privileged regimes:

- General regime (G);
- Special regime (S); and
- Preferential development zone regime.

General regime (G)
The general regime applies to businesses that fulfil the aforementioned general requirements, and carry out investments greater than or equal to EUR 152,450.

Special advantages are conferred according to the period of activity of the registered business.

- During the set-up period and the first three exploitation tax years, the company receives several benefits.

  In customs matters, the company benefits from the provisions of the CEMAC customs code relative to asset improvement mechanisms for export activity and from the suspension of customs duty in the form of temporary admission or franchise for natural resource research activities.

  In fiscal matters, the company benefits from the 50% reduction of registration fees for business foundation, increases in capital, company mergers, transfer of company stocks and shares.

- For the three first exploitation tax years and until the first year of sale or first service, the following fiscal benefits are added with the aforementioned reduction of registration duties:

  - Total exemption from the tax on company earnings:
    - Companies that are subject to CIT because of their size of activity will be exempt from CIT; and
    - Businesses that are subject to personal income tax because of their size or activity will be exempt from personal income tax.
  - The authorisation to proceed to accelerated depreciation;
  - The authorisation to carryforward losses for the first three tax years; and
  - The application of zero-rate VAT on exported products.

Special regime (S)
The special regime applies to businesses that fulfils the aforementioned general requirements, and carry out investments between EUR 45,734 million and EUR 152,450 million.

As well as the advantages of the aforementioned (G) regime, businesses registered under the (S) regime benefit during the set-up period and the first three exploitation tax years, from the moderation of registration duties for the foundation of the business, increases in capital, company mergers, transfer of company stocks and shares.

This moderation of registration duties is granted exclusively by decree of the Minister in charge of the Economy and Finances, upon a decision of the National Investment Commission.

Preferential development zone regime
All exporting businesses registered under the investment charter are eligible for the preferential development zone system, including free-trade zones.

The institution, organisation and function of the preferential development zone are fixed by a specific text.

Incentive measures
Respect for the aforementioned general requirements set out by the charter is a prerequisite for benefiting from these motivation measures.

Export incentives
This measure is reserved for businesses that export at least 20% of their production.

Congo, Republic of

The benefits are:

- The provisions of the CEMAC customs code, relating to asset improvement mechanisms;
- Customs exemption, export duties and taxes on manufactured products, except computing fees and statistic tax; and
- Application of a zero-rate VAT on exported products.

Non-manufactured goods remain subject to the common law export system.

Incentive to reinvest earnings
This measure is reserved for businesses that carry out new investments of at least one-third of existing assets.

The benefit conferred consists in a 50% reduction of the tax on company earnings, for the three years following the realisation of the investment.

Notwithstanding, this benefit is granted upon the following conditions:

- The business declares to the permanent secretary of the National Investment Commission its investments, planned investment and the state of existing capital assets;
- The National Investment Commission, on the report of checking teams, verifies if the new investments correspond to one-third of the preceding capital assets;
- All investments are realised within one year;
- Investments generate new employment;
- Investments increase capacity of production by at least 10%; and
- The business has sound ethical concerns.

Incentives to set up in remote areas
All new businesses registered under (G) or (S) regimes, which are located in a remote area, benefit from a reduction of 50% on the tax on company earnings in the fourth and fifth year following the first three tax years for which the business benefited from total exemption from the tax on earnings or the tax on businesses subject to personal income tax.

The business is considered as belonging to a remote area from the moment its production units are set-up and 90% of the production unit workforce is working in the remote location.

The appraisal of a zone's location results from the exclusive competency of the National Investment Commission.

Incentives for social and cultural investment
All new businesses registered under (G) or (S) regimes, carrying out investments of a social and cultural character, may benefit from a fiscal reduction by ministerial decree of the Minister in charge of Finance and the Economy, upon the decision of the National Investment Commission.

These benefits may not, however, be added to those mentioned above and allocated to remote areas, even if the business concerned is set-up in such a location.

General measures
For the duration of the privileged regime, and subject to current texts, the company shall enjoy fiscal stability in terms of local and state taxes.

Privilege regimes (G) and (S) are allocated only once and are not renewable. The business may receive fiscal and customs advantages pertaining to the set-up period.

Fiscal advantages concerning the exploitation period are applicable only after the set-up period.

The end of the set-up period is certified by decision of the Minister in charge of Economy and Finance, after the adoption of the verification report by the National Investment Commission.

General guarantees
During the privileged regime period, and subject to respect for the currently applicable texts, the company benefits from local and state fiscal stability.

Withholding taxes (WHT)

The Republic of Congo is a member of the Economic and Monetary Community of Central Africa (CEMAC), established by the treaty signed on 16 March 1994 in N'Djamena (Chad) that became effective in June 1999. The organisation replaced what was then the Customs and Economic Union of Central Africa (UDEAC) and adopted its commitments. The CEMAC unites the following six states: Cameroon, Central African Republic, Republic of Congo, Gabon, Equatorial Guinea, and Chad.

The Republic of Congo has signed the following tax treaties:

The tax treaty of the Common Organisation for Africa and Madagascar (OCAM):
The member states of this organisation adopted a tax cooperation agreement 29 January 1971, which was ratified by the Republic of Congo on 3 September 1971. The OCAM, which initially had 14 members, had 17 members when it was dissolved by the Conference of Heads of State in 1985. Those members were Cameroon, Central African Republic, Chad, Congo, Ivory Coast, Dahomey, Gabon, High Volta, Madagascar, Mauritius, Niger, Rwanda, Senegal, Togo, and the Democratic Republic of Congo. The Republic of Congo has not denounced the application of this tax treaty.

The tax treaty of the CEMAC Convention:
The Republic of Congo signed the UDEAC Convention of 13 December 1966, which was designed to avoid or to limit double taxation among the member states: Cameroon, Central African Republic, Congo, Gabon, Equatorial Guinea and Chad. This tax treaty remains significant to companies interested in affiliate creation in Central Africa countries.

The tax treaty between the Republic of Congo and the French Republic:
This tax treaty, which concluded on 27 November 1987, was designed to avoid double taxation and to prevent tax evasion related to income tax, inheritance tax, registration law and stamp duty.

Congo, Republic of

Services, dividends, attendance fees

Services

The tax regime set forth for foreign suppliers is defined in Section 185 Ter of the Congolese General Tax Code, Part 1. According to the provisions of Section 185, as well as the wide interpretation made by the Congolese Tax Authorities, the services rendered by the foreign suppliers should be subject to a 20% WHT.

In addition, Section 185 Ter provides that companies, which have no tax residence in the Congo, are subject to a 20% WHT if they earn revenues realised in the Congo or coming from the Congo, and which come from works or services of any nature performed or used in the Congo.

The provisions of the Section 185 Ter do not apply to resident suppliers of a country, which has signed an international tax treaty with the Congo, provided certain conditions are met.

Dividends

Dividends distributed by a Congolese company are subject to a 20% WHT unless a different rate applies under an international tax treaty (France, CEMAC, OCAM). The same rate applies for dividends distributed to a resident shareholder.

Under the tax treaty between France and Congo, the applicable WHT rate is 15%. There is no specific rate defined in the CEMAC and OCAM tax treaties.

Attendance fees

Attendance fees are subject to a 22% WHT unless a different rate applies under an international tax treaty (France, CEMAC, OCAM).

Payments to local independent contractors

Payments to local independent contractors (self-employed contractors – i.e., those not registered with the Congolese Trade Registry) are subject to a WHT at the rate of 5% from such payments to be remitted to the Public Treasury.

Late remittance of the tax is subject to a penalty of 100% if the late payment exceeds two months, and a penalty of 50% if the late payment does not exceed two months.

WHT rates summary

Recipient	Dividends	Interest	Royalties
	%	%	%
Resident corporations	20	Nil	Nil
Resident individuals	20	Nil	Nil
Non-resident corporations and individuals: (Non-treaty)	20	20	20
Treaty (3):			
France	15	Nil	15
OCAM	Nil	Nil	Nil
CEMAC	Nil	Nil	Nil

Tax administration

Tax returns

Taxable business profits are computed on the basis of normal accounting principles as modified by certain tax adjustments.

The final corporate tax return (annual tax return) is a specific form (Document Statistique et Fiscal "DSF", in French) which should be prepared in accordance with OHADA accounting principles. The form cannot be completed electronically.

The books must be maintained in French and in XAF. This accounting system must follow the OHADA chart of account. All entries have to be booked under OHADA standard, throughout the year.

The annual tax return must be filed within four months following the end of the fiscal year of the company (i.e., before 1 May).

Payment of tax

Resident companies are required to pay quarterly instalments of tax (15 February, 15 May, 15 August and 15 November).

These quarterly instalments are generally calculated with reference to the most recent corporate tax return.

Special calculations of instalments apply to new taxpayers.

Based on the self-assessment system, when submitting annual tax returns due by 1 May every year, taxpayers must pay the amount of tax calculated in the annual tax return to the extent this amount exceeds tax instalments paid during the year.

Corporate taxes in Costa Rica

For more information, contact:

Ramon Ortega
PricewaterhouseCoopers
Edificio Bank of Nova Scotia
3rd floor
Avenida John F Kennedy, Esquina con Avenida Lope de Vega
Santo Domingo
Dominican Republic
Tel: +1 809 567 7741
Email: ramon.ortega@do.pwc.com

Significant developments

There have been no significant tax or regulatory developments regarding corporate taxation in the past year.

Taxes on corporate income

Taxable income is taxed at a 30% rate.

However, the law establishes special regulations for small companies whose gross income does not exceed CRC 78,231,000. For this category, the following tariffs will be applied: 10% will apply for companies with gross income up to CRC 41,112,000; 20% for companies with gross income of more than CRC 41,112,000, but not more than CRC 82,698,000. Companies with gross over CRC 82,698,000 will pay the regular 30% income tax rate.

Please note that these income tax brackets are adjusted yearly, effective 1 October to 30 September. The tax brackets listed are for the 2010 fiscal year.

Corporate residence

In most cases, the place where a company is incorporated is regarded by Costa Rican authorities as the corporate residence. However, any business that carries on industrial, agricultural or commercial activity in Costa Rica is subject to income taxation on local income in the same way as a registered business, irrespective of the place of incorporation. Such corporations doing business in Costa Rica are subject to the permanent establishment (PE) rules.

On the other hand, under the Costa Rican income tax law, income from transactions carried out abroad may be regarded as non-Costa Rican-source income and, therefore, are not subject to income taxes.

Other taxes

Franchise tax
The payments realised abroad for the use of a franchise will be subject to remittances abroad, with a 25% withholding tax (WHT).

Capital gains tax

At present, there is no capital gains tax on the sale of real estate or securities when such sales are not a habitual activity. There is capital gain tax, at the regular rate, on the sale of depreciable assets when their sale price is higher than their adjusted basis (book value).

Sales tax

A fixed sales tax rate of 13% is applied at all stages of the sale of merchandise or the invoicing of certain limited services. The tax is levied on (i) sales of merchandise within the national territory (except sales of land, buildings, exports, and certain basic necessity items, such as basic foodstuffs, certain medicines and veterinary products); (ii) the value of services performed by restaurants, bars, motels, printing companies, social and recreational clubs, and painting and repair shops, and others; and (iii) imports consisting of merchandise for personal use or consumption or to satisfy commercial needs.

Selective consumption tax

The selective consumption tax may be applied at a rate of up to 100% and is levied on goods that are considered non-essential. The tax base is either the cost, insurance and freight (CIF) price plus import duties for imported items or the sales value for item produced in Costa Rica. The tax is levied at only one stage in the sale of merchandise. Payment of the tax is required at the time of importation or, for articles produced in Costa Rica, within 15 days of the month of the sale.

Property tax

Each local municipal government is in charge of real estate appraisal. The property tax to be applied throughout Costa Rican territory is 0.25% of the appraised value, registered in the respective municipality when the tax liability originates. The first CRC 13,203,000 is exempt from property tax if the taxpayer is an individual who owns only one piece of property within the country. Tax will be levied on the amount in excess of CRC 13,203,000 for the year 2010.

Real estate transfer tax

Real estate transfer is calculated as 1.5% of the selling price of the real estate or its tax value, whichever is greater.

Branch income

Branch income is subject to income tax at the rates applicable for corporate income taxes. There is a WHT of 15% on dividends distributed within the country and a 15% tax, in lieu of a dividend WHT, on profits transferred abroad.

Income determination

Inventory valuation

Inventories are generally stated at cost and may be valued at the compound average cost, first-in, first-out (FIFO), last-in, last-out (LIFO), retailer, or specific identification methods. Because all entities are required to keep legal records, any adjustments necessary as a result of the use of different inventory valuation methods for tax and financial purposes should be recorded.

Costa Rica

Capital gains
Capital gains and losses on the disposition of non-depreciable fixed assets or shares of other companies are excluded for income tax purposes if such dispositions are not a habitual activity.

Inter-company dividends
Dividends between domestic subsidiaries and other domestic corporations are not subject to taxes. There are no ownership requirements to qualify for this exclusion.

Foreign income
Foreign-source income is not taxable.

Stock dividends
Stock dividends are subject to income tax at 15% or 5% if the stock is registered at an approved Costa Rican stock market.

Dividends paid in the form of stock of the distributing company are allowed and exempt from taxes.

Deductions

Depreciation and depletion
The straight-line and sum-of-the-years-digits methods of depreciation are allowed.

	Years
Buildings	2 to 6
Machinery and equipment	7 to 15
Furniture and fixtures	10
Vehicles	10
Agricultural plantations	10 to 50

The tax administration, at the request of the taxpayer, could adopt technically acceptable special depreciation methods in cases duly justified by the taxpayer. In addition, the tax administration could authorise, through general resolution, accelerated depreciation methods on new assets, acquired by corporations with monetary activities requiring constant technological update, higher installed production capacity and productive reconversion processes, in order to maintain and strengthen their competitive advantage.

Net operating losses
Losses incurred by industrial and agricultural enterprises may be carried forward and deducted from the taxable profits for the following three and five years, respectively. Loss carrybacks are not allowed.

Payments to foreign affiliates
Corporations may claim deductions for royalties, technical and management service fees, and interest charges paid to foreign affiliates, provided that a tax of 25% for royalties, franchises and other services, and a tax of 15% for interest is withheld. However, the deductions for technical and management service fees may not exceed 10% of gross sales in the aggregate if paid to the parent company.

Taxes

With the exception of sales tax, selective consumption tax, specific taxes over consumption and special duties over them established by law, penalties and interest paid over any tax obligation, and the income tax itself, all other taxes are deductible expenses when determining taxable income.

Group taxation

There is no group taxation in Costa Rica.

Tax incentives

Free zones

Entities established in free zones may enjoy exemption from import duties on goods, income tax, sales tax, export tax, selective consumption tax, real estate transfer tax, and WHT on payments abroad, as well as the discretionary use of foreign currency generated abroad. However, these incentives will be affected by the rules established by the World Trade Organisation, in force in the year 2015.

Drawback industries

Special benefits exist for industries that import semi-manufactured materials for assembly in Costa Rica and export finished products. Benefits consist of duty-free imports of raw materials for subsequent export as manufactured products. Machinery for these industries may also be imported duty-free.

Tourism development

The Incentive Law for Tourism Development grants several tax benefits, such as exemption from import duties on certain tourism service-related goods and from property tax for companies dedicated to tourism, but only for those with a signed tourism agreement.

Withholding taxes (WHT)

Payments to non-domiciled foreign corporations or individuals

Regarding payments to non-domiciled foreign corporations or individuals, taxes are withheld as follows:

1. Dividends – 15%
   Withholding depends on the origin or source of the retained earnings. Total or partial exemption will be authorised by the tax authorities to the extent that a foreign tax credit is totally or partially disallowed to the taxpayer in the taxpayer's country of residence. This exemption will not be allowed, however, if this type of income is not taxable to the taxpayer in the country of residence.
2. Interest and other financial expenses – 15%
   No tax is withheld if the recipient is a bank or a financial institution recognised as a first-class bank by the Central Bank of Costa Rica or a supplier of merchandise. Interest or financial expenses paid to parties other than those aforementioned are subject to a 15% WHT.

   An 8% WHT applies to interest on bearer documents issued by financial entities registered at the Central Bank's General Auditor's Office or stock exchange. No WHT applies to interest paid on securities issued by the Workmen's Bank or the

Costa Rica

Mortgage Housing Bank and its authorised institutions or on foreign currency securities issued by the state banks.

3. Special tax on banks and non-resident financial entities
   Banks or non-resident financial entities that are part of a local financial group are payers of taxes established in this article. The taxpayers mentioned in the "interest and other financial expenses" section should pay, in lieu of tax on remittances abroad, a local currency tax equivalent to USD 125,000 per annum. The tax period will run from 1 January to 31 December of each year.
4. Royalties, patents, trademarks, franchises, and formulas are subject to a 25% WHT.
5. For technical service and management fees, a 25% tax is withheld.
6. Personal services from a Costa Rican source are subject to the following withholdings: employees, 10%; directors, 15%; others, depending on the nature of the services rendered, 30%.
7. Transportation and communication services are subject to an 8.5% WHT.

Tax treaties

Costa Rica is a full member of the Central American Common Market, which guarantees free trade among the countries of the area. It also has a free-trade bilateral treaty in force with Mexico (1994), the Dominican Republic (1998), Chile (1998), Canada and Panama, and the CAFTA-DR entered into force on 1 January 2009. These agreements aim to provide favourable conditions for the exchange of merchandise between contracting parties.

The only tax treaty in force between Costa Rica and the United States, effective since 12 February 1991, is a Tax Information Exchange Agreement, whereby both countries agree to exchange information, from and/or in relation to public and private entities and individuals, at the request of the party's corresponding authority, in relation to any tax relevant issue.

Tax administration

Returns

With certain exceptions, all corporations must file by 15 December a tax return on the basis of a fiscal year ended 30 September. Entities with an operating period of less than four months may present a return together with the following year's tax return. Current legislation contemplates that other fiscal year-ends may be adopted with the prior approval of the tax authorities.

The tax system is one of self-assessment with occasional auditing by the tax authorities.

Payment of tax

In March, June and September all corporations and taxpayers must prepay instalments that total 75% of the average income taxes paid in the past three fiscal years, or the amount paid in the prior year, whichever is greater. Failure to pay on these dates results in the accrual of interest unless the taxpayer has requested, on a timely basis, that the tax authorities eliminate the corresponding payments. Any amount owed in excess of the instalments should be paid by 15 December.

Corporate taxes in Croatia

For more information, contact:

Ivo Bijelic
PricewaterhouseCoopers d.o.o.
Alexandera von Humboldta 4
10000 Zagreb
Croatia
Tel: +385 1 6328 802
Email: ivo.bijelic@hr.pwc.com

Significant developments

The Corporate Income Tax Act was introduced on 1 January 2007.

The amendments of the Corporate Income Tax Ordinance were introduced on 1 January 2010.

The Tax Incentives Act was introduced on 1 January 2007.

The Act on Special State Care Areas was introduced on 1 July 2009.

Taxes on corporate income

Profit tax

Profit tax is paid by: enterprises engaged in independent activities on a long-term basis for the purpose of deriving profit; branches of foreign enterprises; enterprises that control shares in capital (unless the object of investment itself pays profit tax); and natural persons who choose to pay profit tax instead of personal income tax.

The tax base is the difference between revenue and expenditures, adjusted for increasing and decreasing items. Croatian residents pay profit tax on profit derived in Croatia and abroad, and non-residents, for example, branches, pay profit tax only on profits derived in Croatia. The tax base also includes gains arising from liquidation, sale, change of legal form and division of the taxpayer where it is determined at the market rates.

The profit tax base is reduced by the following items:

- Revenues from dividend and profit sharing;
- Unrealised profits from value adjustments of shares (increase of financial asset value), if these were included as profit in the P&L account;
- Revenues from collected written-off claims that were included in the tax base in the previous tax periods, but not excluded from the tax base as recognised expenditure;
- The amount of depreciation not recognised in previous tax periods, up to the amount prescribed by the Corporate Income Tax Act; and
- The amount of tax relief or tax exemption in line with special regulations (i.e., costs of education, costs of research and development (R&D) and costs of a new employee's salary).

Croatia

The profit tax base is increased by the following items:

- Unrealised losses from value adjustments of shares (decrease of financial asset value), if these were included as expenses in the P&L account;
- The amount of depreciation in excess of the amounts prescribed by the Corporate Income Tax Act;
- 70% of entertainment costs (food and drink, gifts with or without the printed firm logo or product brand and expenses for vacation, sport, recreation and leisure-time, renting cars, vessels, airplanes and holiday cottages);
- Entertainment costs will not include the costs of goods and merchandise adapted by a taxpayer for business entertainment purposes, labelled "not for sale", and other promotional objects with the name of the firm or merchandise or other advertising objects (glasses, ashtrays, table cloths, mats, pencils, business diaries, cigarette-lighters, tags, etc.) put to use in the selling area of the purchaser and given to consumers provided that their value does not exceed HRK 80 per item;
- 30% of the costs, except insurance and interest costs, incurred in connection with owned or rented motor vehicles or other means of personal transportation (personal car, vessel, helicopter, airplane, etc.) used by managerial, supervisory and other employees, provided that the use of means of personal transportation is not defined as salary;
- Non-business costs, incurred in connection with the private life of shareholders and company members (withdrawals) as well as employees (entertainment, relaxation, sport and recreation costs), including value-added tax;
- Hidden profit distribution;
- The costs of forced collection of tax and other levies;
- Fines imposed by competent bodies;
- Penalty interest accumulated between associated persons;
- Privileges and other economic benefits granted to natural or legal persons for the purpose of causing or preventing a certain event in favour of the company (generally related to commissions paid to parties acting on behalf of the taxpayer);
- Gifts in excess of the amounts prescribed by the Corporate Income Tax Act;
- Interest not recognised as expenditure pursuant to the provisions of the Corporate Income Tax Act; and
- Any other expenditure not directly related to profit earning, as well as other increases in the tax base, which were not included in the tax base.

Thin capitalisation

Interest on loans from a shareholder or a member of a company holding at least 25% of shares or voting power of the taxpayer will not be recognised for tax purposes, if the amount of the loan exceeds four times the amount of the shareholder's share in the capital or their voting power. Interest on loans obtained from financial institutions is exempt from this provision. A third-party loan will be considered to be given by a shareholder if it is guaranteed by the shareholder.

Related party transaction

Prices between a Croatian entity and its foreign related parties must be set at fair market value (the arm's-length principle).

If the prices between related entities are different than those between non-related resident and non-resident entities, the tax base must be calculated with prices that would be charged between unrelated companies. In order to determine the market value of the related party's transaction, the following methods can be used:

- Comparable uncontrolled price;
- Resale price;
- Cost plus;
- Profit split; and
- Net-profit.

Tax incentives and exemptions
Investment incentives are usually organised as corporate tax credits. Tax rates can be reduced for up to 10 years upon completion of various conditions. *See Tax incentives section below.*

Tax losses
Tax losses may be carried forward and utilised within five years following the year in which the losses were incurred and must be utilised in the order in which they occurred. The losses may not be transferred to any third entity except in the case of merger, demerger or acquisition.

Local taxes
A trade name may be subject to taxation at the amount up to HRK 2,000, depending on the decision of the municipal or city.

Corporate residence

Profit tax is payable by enterprises engaged in independent activities in Croatia on a long-term basis for the purpose of deriving a profit, including Croatian domestic entities, branches of foreign enterprises and domestic business units of foreign entities.

Permanent establishment
Definition of a business unit of a non-resident is based on the Organisation for Economic Co-operation and Development (OECD) guidelines, which provides that a non-resident's business unit is a place of management, a branch, an office, a factory, a workshop, a mine, an oil or gas well, a quarry or any other place of extraction of natural resources or construction site or project for a period longer than six months, including agents acting in its name, having the right to conclude contracts or hold stock of products which it distributes on the Croatian market in the name of a foreign entrepreneur. The business unit of a non-resident also includes the performance of services (i.e., advisory and business consulting services) for the same or a related project, which lasts for more than three months in a 12-month period.

Other taxes

Value-added tax (VAT)
VAT was introduced on 1 January 1998 at a rate of 22%. As of 1 August 2009, the general VAT rate was increased to 23%. VAT is a consumption tax and has a neutral effect on enterprises by operation of the input and output mechanism. Accordingly, the tax burden is borne by the final consumer. A VAT-registered entity must calculate its VAT liability or refund and submit a monthly (by the end of the following month) VAT return to the relevant Tax Authority Office or a quarterly VAT return if the taxpayer is classified as small. An annual VAT return must be submitted by 30 April of the following year.

Croatia

Where the amount of input tax credits exceeds the entity's VAT liability, a taxpayer is entitled to a refund of the difference or may choose to use the difference as a VAT prepayment.

VAT taxpayers are defined as entrepreneurs that deliver goods or perform services in Croatia. An "entrepreneur" is a legal entity or a natural person that continuously and independently performs an activity for the purpose of deriving profit. In addition to those that may be regarded as "normal" taxpayers, domestic enterprises receiving imported services from foreign enterprises and legal entities and individuals that issue invoices or receipts including VAT without authorisation are also liable to pay VAT.

A taxpayer is required to register for VAT where turnover in the previous year exceeded HRK 85,000. Voluntary registration is also possible.

Foreign entrepreneurs may also become VAT registered in Croatia through a tax representative. This will entitle them to reclaim input VAT incurred in Croatia.

In addition to foreign individuals, foreign legal entities are now also entitled to claim a VAT refund under reciprocity agreement terms.

VAT is also payable on the sale of new buildings.

The VAT base for goods and services supplied domestically is the consideration received. Where no consideration is provided, for instance where goods are exchanged, the VAT base is the market value of the good or service. The VAT base of imports is the customs value as prescribed by customs regulations, increased by customs duties, import duties, special taxes and other fees paid during customs clearing.

VAT paid to the customs office at the time of import can be credited to the taxpayer's VAT account and offset against any domestic VAT liability. If goods are exempt from import duty, they are also VAT exempt. A VAT entity must self-assess VAT on imported services provided by a foreign entity. This VAT can be reclaimed through the VAT return as described above.

Exempt supplies are similar to those contained in the EU's Sixth Directive and include rental of residential property (with some exceptions); granting of credits and credit guarantees; transactions related to bank accounts, interest, winnings from special games of chance in casinos, slot machine clubs and other forms of gambling; supplies of domestic and foreign legal tender, securities and shares and supplies of gold by the central bank.

The most significant change is that banks, insurance companies, medical and educational institutions are no longer institutionally exempt from VAT. Other exemptions include:

- Services and deliveries of goods by public institutions in the field of culture, such as museums, galleries, archives, libraries, theatres including religious communities and institutions, primary and secondary schools, universities and student catering and boarding institutions;
- Medical services, including services conducted by doctors, dentists, nurses, physiotherapists, and biochemistry laboratories engaged in private practices including services of medical care performed in healthcare institutions,

and services performed by social care institutions and child and adolescent care institutions;
- Supplies (transfers) of real estate (land, buildings, parts of buildings, housing premises, and other structures) with the exception of newly built buildings; and
- Temporary imports of goods which are exempt from customs duty.

The following supplies are zero-rated or 'VAT free' under the Croatian VAT legislation:

- Bread and milk including baby food used as a substitute for mother's milk;
- Books of a scholarly, scientific, artistic, cultural and educational character as well as school textbooks (primary, secondary and tertiary education, including materials printed on paper and other media, such as CD-ROMs, video cassettes and audio tapes);
- Certain medicines and surgical implants;
- Scientific journals; and
- Services rendered by cinemas.

There is also a reduced rate of 10% for services related to:

- Organised stays (accommodation or accommodation with breakfast, full or half board, in all kinds of commercial hospitality facilities) and agency fees with respect to the above mentioned services.
- Daily and periodic newspapers and magazines (with the exception of those that consist entirely of advertisements or are used mainly for advertising purposes).

VAT-registered entities are required to issue an invoice (R-1 or R-2) which clearly illustrates the VAT base amount and the rate of VAT charged (0%, 10% or 23%) as well as the tax amount as a separate figure.

On 26 March 2008, the new Regulation on Modifications and Amendments to the VAT Ordinance came into force, introducing new customs duty and tax relief on financial aid from the European Union (EU). The VAT regulations set tax relief rates for the provision of goods and services abroad when this is stated in an international agreement which is binding on the Republic of Croatia. There is a wider range of customs duty and tax relief, and special tax and VAT relief for project beneficiaries who have received financial aid from EU for the purchase of goods and services from abroad or inland.

Real estate tax
The acquisition of real estate is subject to taxation. Real estate includes agricultural, construction and other land as well as residential, commercial and other buildings. Transactions include the sale, exchange and any other means of acquiring real estate for consideration.

Tax is charged at 5% of the market value of the real estate on the contract date.

Excise duties
There are a number of excise duties levied on specific products. They are levied at a fixed amount and are payable by the producer or importer. VAT is applied first, after which the fixed amounts are added.

- Oil derivatives: Tax ranging from HRK 300 to HRK 3,600 per 1,000 litres.

Croatia

- Tobacco products: Tax on cigarettes may reach up to HRK 180 per 1,000 pieces plus 30% proportional special (excise) tax from retail price; for cigars HRK 1,100 per 1,000 pieces; for cigarillos HRK 220 per 1,000 pieces and HRK 136 per kilogram for tobacco.
- Beer: HRK 40 per 1% volume fraction of the actual alcohol contained in one hectolitre o finished product.
- Soft drinks: HRK 40 per hectolitre for domestically produced brands and imported soft drinks. Some soft drinks, including mineral water and natural fruit juices are exempt.
- Alcohol:
  - Excise duty on products with the volume of actual alcohol content between 15% and higher, wages in the amount of HRK 800 per hectolitre of finished product.
  - Excise duty on products with the volume of actual alcohol content of less than 15%, is paid in the amount of HRK 500 per hectolitre of finished product.
  - Excise duty on ethyl alcohol is to be paid in the amount HRK 5,300 per hectolitre of pure alcohol.
- Imported coffee: HRK 5 to HRK 20 per kilogram.
- Passenger cars and motor cycles: from 13% to HRK 177,500 plus 63% of the amount exceeding HRK 500,000.
- Imported boats and aircrafts: from 5% to HRK 445,000 plus 16% of the amount exceeding HRK 4,000,000.
- Luxury products: 30% of the sales value of the product without VAT.
- Liability and comprehensive road vehicle insurance premiums: for obligatory motor vehicle insurance premium, 15% of the contractual amount; and for comprehensive motor vehicle insurance premium, 10% of the contractual amount.

Chamber of Commerce contribution

Employers pay a mandatory contribution to the Croatian Chamber of Commerce. The amount varies between HRK 55 to HRK 5,500 depending on company size and 0.0075% of total income.

Branch income

Foreign corporations carrying on business in Croatia are taxed on their Croatian source income at a 20% rate.

Income determination

Inventory valuation

Inventories are generally valued at the lower of their acquisition cost or net realisable value. Taking into consideration the accounting principles set out in the Accounting Act and the International Accounting Standards (IAS), a company can choose to adopt the most favourable method.

Capital gains

Capital gains or losses are covered by the profit tax regime. They are either an increasing or decreasing item to the profit tax base.

Inter-company dividends

Inter-company dividends are treated as income under the profit tax regime but are not included in the tax base.

Deductions

Depreciation

Most companies depreciate assets on a straight-line basis. This is because depreciation calculated this way at the prescribed rates is recognised for tax purposes. Companies are, however, free to use any depreciation method defined in the IAS and to estimate the useful lives of all fixed assets in accordance with their accounting policies.

However, depreciation expenses in excess of the amount allowed for tax purposes are taxable. The value adjustment of tangible fixed assets rarely occurs in practice, except in the case of financial assets and claims.

The Corporate Income Tax Act no longer allows taxpayers to wholly write-off plant and equipment acquired or built during the tax period.

Plant and equipment depreciation begins in the period in which it is installed or ready for use. Plant and equipment includes: tools of trade, information technology infrastructure including software, furniture and fittings and motor vehicles (excluding vehicles for personal use).

If the taxpayer writes off a portion of a depreciable asset, the remaining undepreciated portion will be depreciated at the rate prescribed by law. According to the Corporate Income Tax Act, the taxpayer can double depreciation rates.

Land and forests are not depreciated.

Goodwill paid on the acquisition of a business must be amortised over five years. It is usually the difference between the estimated statistical value of assets and liabilities and their book value.

However, goodwill arising from mergers and acquisitions is not recognised for taxation purposes.

Tax losses

Tax losses can be carried forward for up to five years. If a taxpayer does not utilise a tax loss within five years, the tax loss will expire.

Payments to foreign affiliates

The treatment of payments made to foreign affiliates is dealt with through the mechanism of the profit tax base. The profit tax base is increased for any concealed profit payments made. The Tax Administration may audit the expenditure of non-resident taxpayers, examining expenditure on goods and services abroad as well as management, intellectual property and other fees and payments that may have the character of a profit transfer. If the Tax Administration discovers that transactions have been used to conceal profit transfers, the difference between the declared price/fee and the average market price/fee will be added back into the taxpayer's tax base.

Group taxation

There are no group taxation provisions in Croatia.

Croatia

Tax incentives

The Corporate Profit Tax Act provides the following relief and incentives for taxpayers.

Investment incentives
Investment incentives are usually organised as corporate tax credits. It means that tax rates can be reduced for up to 10 years upon completion of various conditions.

General incentives apply for investors profit earned as a result of an investment under the following conditions:

Investment amount	Tax benefit rate (%)	Period	Necessary to employ
From EUR 300,000 to EUR 1.5 million	10	10 years	10 employees
More than EUR 1.5 million	7	10 years	30 employees
More than EUR 4 million	3	10 years	50 employees
More than EUR 8 million	0	10 years	75 employees

Tax benefits cannot exceed investment amount.

Other concessions and exemptions
Other concessions and exemptions are generally available to companies including the following:

*   Companies established in mountain regions that employ more than five persons on a permanent basis, will enjoy up to a 75% corporate income tax reduction in the period starting from 2008 until the end of 2010.
*   Taxpayers in custom free zones can take advantage of incentives prescribed in the Investment Incentives Act. Taxpayers that were engaged in or participating in the building of infrastructure within a zone, in projects with a value exceeding HRK 1 million before July 2008, and that did not fully utilise the incentive prescribed by the Investment Incentive Act, are exempt from paying profit tax until the full amount has been used but no later than 31 December 2016.
*   Taxpayers whose business activities are based on agriculture or fishing in areas under special state care and employing more than five persons on a permanent bases (certain limitations apply), will be exempted from the payment of any corporate income tax until EU accession up to 100%.
*   Taxpayers with business activities other than agriculture or fishing in areas under special state care and who employ more than five persons on a permanent basis (subject to certain limitations and depending on the area) will be exempt from tax, up to a certain amount of the CIT rate, as prescribed by local legislation. Exemptions will be gradually decreased until year 2014 or 2017, when it will no longer be applicable.
*   Companies established in the territory of the City of Vukovar and employing more than five persons on a permanent basis will be exempted from the payment of any corporate income tax until EU accession.

Major investment incentives:

- Non-refundable money subsidy in an amount of up to 5% of justified costs related to investment in significant projects (max amount of up to EUR 1 million) may be granted to a company providing that certain conditions are met).
- A significant project investment consists of high economic activity, such as the construction of a new plant or industrial facility, initiation of a new economic activity or new technology development, with investment in assets greater than EUR 15 million. At least 100 workplaces must be opened upon expiration of one year of investment.

Research and development incentives

Registered scientific organisations, centres of scientific excellence, individual scientists and groups of scientists are entitled to apply for the state subsidies and tax incentives for scientific research, basic research, applied research and development research.

Depending on the type of research (e.g., scientific, basic, applied research or technical feasibility) and size of entrepreneur (i.e., small, medium or large entrepreneur, according to the Accounting Act), the percentage of the costs covered by state subsidy can vary between 25% and 100%. Additionally, the corporate income tax base can be decreased (depending on the same criteria) by up to 150% of the amount of the costs covered by the state subsidy, where the corporate income tax liability decrease is granted up to the amount of the percentage of the costs covered by state subsidy.

Withholding taxes (WHT)

Taxpayers who pay fees for the use of intellectual property rights (the right to reproduction, patents, licenses, copyrights, designs or models, manufacturing procedures, production formulas, blueprints, plans, industrial or scientific experience and such other rights), or fees for market research services, tax consulting services, legal, auditing or such other services, or interest to foreign legal entities, natural persons excluded, shall, when making the payment, calculate and withhold tax at a rate of 15%. In addition to the current withholding tax rate of 15%, an increased rate of 20% is introduced. It applies to all services paid to foreign entities whose place of seat or management is in a country with the profit tax rate below 12.5%. This provision does not apply to the European Union member countries.

Tax is not withheld from interest payments on the following:

- Commodity loans for the purchase of good used for carrying out a taxpayer's business activity;
- Loans granted by a non-resident bank or other financial institution; and
- To holders of government or corporate bonds, who are non-resident legal persons.

The withholding tax rate on dividends is 0% regardless of the period in which the dividends were received.

Croatia

Tax administration

All profit tax taxpayers are obliged to submit an annual profit tax return to the tax authorities no later than four months after the end of the tax period for which profit tax is assessed. Every taxpayer is required to make monthly profit tax instalments (on the last day of each month) on the basis of the previous year's tax return.

In the first year of operation, taxpayers are not obliged to pay any corporate income tax advances.

Profit tax is assessed at the end of the calendar year, and the assessed amount, less any instalments made, is payable by the day of submission of the tax return (i.e., at the latest by the end of the fourth month following the end of the tax and accounting year). If a domestic taxpayer has paid tax abroad on profit derived abroad, the tax paid will be included in its profit tax, up to the amount of tax paid abroad where no double-tax treaty exists with the country in question.

The Ministry of Finance administers taxation matters through the Tax Administration and the Financial Police. These organisations have responsibilities and powers defined by law.

Corporate taxes in Cyprus

For more information, contact:

Panikos Tsiailis
PricewaterhouseCoopers
Julia House
3 Themistocles Dervis Street
CY-1066 Nicosia
Cyprus
Tel: +357 22 555 255
Email: panikos.n.tsiailis@cy.pwc.com

Significant developments

No significant developments in corporate taxation have occurred in Cyprus in the past year.

Taxes on corporate income

Corporation tax
The corporate tax rate in Cyprus is 10% on taxable income.

Life insurance companies
When the tax payable on profits arising from the life insurance business does not exceed 1.5% of the gross amount of premiums, the difference is paid in addition to the corporate tax.

International Collective Investment Schemes
The International Collective Investment Schemes (ICIS) law, enacted in 1999, provides the required legal framework for the registration, regulation of operations, and supervision of ICIS.

ICIS can take the following legal forms:

1. International fixed capital company;
2. International variable capital company;
3. International unit trust scheme; and
4. International investment limited partnership.

The sole objective of ICIS is the collective investment of funds of the unitholders. ICIS are exempt from tax on profits arising on disposal of titles. Dividend income is also exempt (with minor limitations) whereas interest income is taxed at the rate of 10%.

ICIS set-up in Cyprus can utilise the double taxation treaty (DTT) network of Cyprus.

Corporate residence

All companies managed and controlled in Cyprus are treated as tax resident in Cyprus.

Cyprus

Other taxes

Defence contribution
A contribution for the defence of the Republic is imposed on certain types of income. Dividends are generally exempt from defence contribution subject to certain rarely applicable limitations *(see section titled Tax incentives)*.

Interest received by closed-ended or open-ended (collective investment schemes (CIS) is taxed under income tax law after deducting expenses at the standard corporate tax rate of 10%.

Interest received by other companies in the ordinary course of business including interest closely connected to the ordinary course of business is taxed under income tax law after deducting expenses at the standard corporate tax rate of 10%. When companies receive interest that does not satisfy the conditions prescribed immediately above, the interest is subject to special defence contribution (SDC) without expense deduction at the rate of 10%.

Rental income (reduced by 25%) is subject to defence contribution at the rate of 3%.

Value-added tax (VAT)
The standard rate of VAT is 15%. There are also two reduced rates of VAT, 5% and 8%. Exports, most foodstuffs (except those taxed at 5% or 15%) and most medicines (except those taxed at 5%), are zero-rated. Some supplies are exempt, the main categories being rents, insurance, financial services, certain education, health and welfare, and supplies of real estate (except supply of new buildings before the first use) including supplies of land and second-hand buildings.

Social security
Employed persons are compulsorily insured under a state-administered social insurance fund. Contributions to the fund are borne by both employer and employee.

The employer's contributions are made as a percentage of earnings to the following funds:

	%
Social insurance fund	6.8
Redundancy fund	1.2
Training development fund	0.5
Social cohesion fund	2.0
	10.5

With the exception of the social cohesion fund, the maximum amount of monthly earnings on which the contributions are made is EUR 4,216.

The referenced contributions are an allowable deduction for corporate tax purposes.

Immovable property tax
Immovable property is subject to property tax, which is levied on the market value of the property as of 1 January 1980, and is payable by the end of September each year.

The tax rates vary from 0 per thousand to 3.5 per thousand on values of up to EUR 854,300 and 4 per thousand on any excess.

Branch income

The rate of tax on branch profits is the same as on corporate profits. No further tax is withheld on transfers of profits to a foreign head office.

Income determination

Inventory valuation
Inventories are generally stated at the lower of cost and net realisable value. Last-in, first-out (LIFO) is not permitted for taxation purposes. First-in, first-out (FIFO) is permitted. Conformity between book and tax reporting is not required.

Capital gains
Capital gains tax is imposed at the rate of 20% on gains arising from the disposal of immovable property situated in Cyprus, and of shares in companies (other than companies whose shares are listed in any recognised stock exchange) that own immovable property situated in Cyprus. Liability is confined to gains accruing since 1 January 1980. The costs deducted from gross proceeds on the disposal of immovable property are its market value at 1 January 1980, or the costs of acquisition and improvements of the property, if made after 1 January 1980, as adjusted for inflation up to the date of disposal on the basis of the consumer price index in Cyprus.

Inter-company dividends
All dividends are excluded from the taxable income of the recipient company.

Foreign income
Resident corporations are subject to tax on their worldwide income. However, foreign-branch income, as well as dividend income from abroad, is exempt from taxation in Cyprus (with some minor limitations). Where foreign income is taxed in Cyprus, double taxation is avoided, either through unilateral relief by giving credit for foreign taxation or by treaty relief. This credit may not exceed the Cyprus taxes imposed on the same income.

Stock dividends
A Cyprus corporation can distribute tax-free dividends of common stock (bonus shares) proportionately to all common stock shareholders.

Deductions

Depreciation and depletion
Depreciation is computed on a straight-line basis at rates that vary, depending on the life and type of asset. Tax depreciation is not required to conform to book depreciation. Gains on the sale of depreciated property are taxable as ordinary income to the extent of depreciation allowed.

Net operating losses
Tax losses can be carried forward indefinitely and set-off against taxable profits of future years. Carrybacks are not permitted.

Cyprus

Payments to foreign affiliates

A Cyprus corporation can claim a deduction for royalties and interest charges paid to foreign affiliates, and a reasonable amount of head office expenses of an overseas company, provided such expenditures can be justified as having been incurred in the production of the income. In the case of insurance companies, the amount of head office expenses should not exceed 3% of the net premiums in Cyprus for the general insurance business and 2% for the life insurance business.

Taxes

Taxes that are deducted in computing profits for corporate tax purposes include VAT not recovered and the employer's share of contributions to the social insurance and other funds.

Other significant items

Charitable donations or contributions made for educational, cultural, or other charitable purposes to the Republic, or to approved charitable institutions, are wholly deductible, provided that these expenses are supported with relevant vouchers.

Any expenditure on scientific research of a capital nature for which no capital allowance is granted is deductible from taxable income and spread equally over the year in which it has been incurred and the five subsequent years. Scientific expenditure of a revenue nature is deducted in the year incurred.

Any expenditure incurred on the acquisition of patents, patent rights and intellectual property is deductible from taxable income, and spread equally over the life of the patents or patent rights.

Group taxation

Group relief provisions allow, subject to certain conditions, companies of the same group to transfer losses from the loss-making companies to profitable companies. A group includes only Cypriot resident companies with a 75% direct or indirect holding relationship.

Tax incentives

The following tax incentives exist:

1. Profits from disposals of corporate titles are unconditionally exempt from income tax. Titles is defined as shares, bonds, debentures, founders' shares, and other titles of companies or other legal persons incorporated in Cyprus or abroad and options thereon as well as futures/forwards on titles, short positions on titles, swaps on titles, depositary receipts, repos, units in open or close CIS, ICIS, undertakings for collective investments of transferable securities, investment trusts and funds, mutual funds, real estate investment trusts and units in stock exchange indices.
2. Dividends earned from foreign investments are exempt from income tax in Cyprus. Dividend income is also exempt from defence contribution unless:
   a. More than 50% of the paying company's activities result directly or indirectly in investment income; and
   b. The foreign tax is significantly lower than the tax burden in Cyprus, i.e., less than 5%.

3. Profits from a permanent establishment (PE) abroad are exempt from income tax. This exemption is always applicable unless:
   a. More than 50% of the foreign PE's activities result directly or indirectly in investment income; and
   b. The foreign tax on the income of the foreign PE is significantly lower than the tax burden in Cyprus, i.e., less than 5%.
4. For ship-owning companies, the profits derived by the owner or bare boat charterer of an European Union (EU) or European Economic Area (EEA) (as well as foreign subject to conditions) ship from its operation, as well as the salaries and benefits of the captain, the officers and the crew, are fully exempt from corporate and income tax. A similar exemption applies to charterers and ship managers. Instead of corporate tax, ship owners, charterers and managers pay tonnage tax (TT) on the net tonnage of the ships they own, charter or manage. In addition, there is no tax on dividends paid at all levels of distribution by the above persons out of profits subject to TT and related capital gains and no capital gains tax on the sale or transfer of a ship, share in a ship or shares in a ship owning company. This treatment applies until 2020.

Reorganisations

Transfers of assets and liabilities between companies can occur without tax consequences within the framework of a tax-exempt qualified reorganisation.

Reorganisations include mergers, demergers, partial divisions, transfers of divisions of activities and exchanges of shares.

Withholding taxes (WHT)

The following tables give a summary of the WHT provided by the DTT entered into by Cyprus.

Paid from Cyprus

Recipient	Dividends (1)	Interest (1)	Royalties (1)
	%	%	%
Non-treaty countries	Nil	Nil	Nil (2)
Treaty countries:			
Austria	10	Nil	Nil
Belarus	5 (18)	5	5
Belgium	10 (8)	10 (6,19)	Nil
Bulgaria	5 (23)	7 (6)	10
Canada	15	15 (4)	10 (5)
China, P.R.	10	10	10
Czech Republic (29)	Nil (30)	Nil	Nil (31)
Denmark	10 (8)	10 (6)	Nil
Egypt	15	15	10
France	10 (9)	10 (10)	Nil (3)
Germany	10 (8)	10 (6)	Nil (3)
Greece	25	10	Nil (12)
Hungary	Nil	10 (6)	Nil
India	10 (9)	10 (10)	10 (16)

Cyprus

Recipient	Dividends (1)	Interest (1)	Royalties (1)
	%	%	%
Ireland, Rep. of	Nil	Nil	Nil (12)
Italy	Nil	10	Nil
Kuwait	10	10 (6)	5 (7)
Lebanon	5	5	Nil
Malta	15	10	10
Mauritius	Nil	Nil	Nil
Moldova (27)	5 (28)	5	5
Norway	Nil	Nil	Nil
Poland	10	10 (6)	5
Qatar (29)	Nil	Nil	5
Romania	10	10 (6)	5 (7)
Russia	5 (17)	Nil	Nil
San Marino	Nil	Nil	Nil
Singapore	Nil	10 (6,25)	10
Slovak Republic	10	10 (6)	5 (7)
South Africa	Nil	Nil	Nil
Seychelles	Nil	Nil	5
Sweden	5 (8)	10 (6)	Nil
Syria	Nil (8)	10	10
Thailand	10	15 (21)	5 (22)
USSR (former) (20)	Nil	Nil	Nil
United Kingdom	Nil	10	Nil (3)
United States	Nil	10 (10)	Nil
Yugoslavia (former) (26)	10	10	10

Received in Cyprus

Recipient	Dividends	Interest	Royalties
	%	%	%
Treaty countries:			
Austria	10	Nil	Nil
Belarus	5 (18)	5	5
Belgium	10 (8)	10 (6,19)	Nil
Bulgaria	5 (23)	7 (6,24)	10 (24)
Canada	15	15 (4)	10 (5)
China, P.R.	10	10	10
Czech Republic (29)	Nil (30)	Nil	Nil (31)
Denmark	10 (8)	10 (6)	Nil
Egypt	15	15	10
France	10 (9)	10 (10)	Nil (3)
Germany	10 (8)	10 (6)	Nil (3)
Greece	25 (11)	10	Nil (12)
Hungary	5 (8)	10 (6)	Nil

Recipient	Dividends	Interest	Royalties
	%	%	%
India	10 (9)	10 (10)	15 (15)
Ireland, Rep. of	Nil	Nil	Nil (12)
Italy	15	10	Nil
Kuwait	10	10 (6)	5 (7)
Lebanon	5	5	Nil
Malta	Nil	10	10
Mauritius	Nil	Nil	Nil
Moldova (27)	5 (28)	5	5
Norway	Nil (13)	Nil	Nil
Poland	10	10 (6)	5
Qatar (29)	Nil	Nil	5
Romania	10	10 (6)	5 (7)
Russia	5 (17)	Nil	Nil
San Marino	Nil	Nil	Nil
Singapore	Nil	10 (6,25)	10
Slovak Republic	10	10 (6)	5 (7)
South Africa	Nil	Nil	Nil
Seychelles	Nil	Nil	5
Sweden	5 (8)	10 (6)	Nil
Syria	Nil (8)	10 (4)	10
Thailand	10	15 (21)	5 (22)
USSR (former) (20)	Nil	Nil	Nil
United Kingdom	15 (14)	10	Nil (3)
United States	5 (9)	10 (10)	Nil
Yugoslavia (former) (26)	10	10	10

Notes

The numbers in parentheses refer to the following numbered notes:

1. Under Cyprus legislation there is no WHT on dividends, interests and royalties paid to non-residents of Cyprus.
2. Royalties earned on rights used within Cyprus are subject to WHT of 10%.
3. A rate of 5% on film and TV royalties.
4. Nil if paid to a government or for export guarantee.
5. Nil on literary, dramatic, musical or artistic work.
6. Nil if paid to the government of the other state.
7. This rate applies for patents, trademarks, designs or models, plans, secret formulas or processes, or any industrial, commercial or scientific equipment, or for information concerning industrial, commercial or scientific experience.
8. A rate of 15% if received by a company controlling less than 25% of the voting power.
9. A rate of 15% if received by a person controlling less than 10% of the voting power.
10. Nil if paid to a government, bank or financial institution.
11. The treaty provides for WHT on dividends but Greece does not impose any withholding tax in accordance with its own legislation.
12. A rate of 5% on film royalties.
13. A rate of 5% if received by a person controlling less than 50% of the voting power.
14. This rate applies to individual shareholders regardless of their percentage of shareholding. Companies controlling less than 10% of the voting shares are also entitled to this rate.

Cyprus

15. A rate of 10% for payments of a technical, managerial or consulting nature.
16. Treaty rate is 15%, therefore restricted to Cyprus legislation rate.
17. A rate of 10% if a dividend is paid by a company in which the beneficial owner has invested less than USD 100,000.
18. If investment is less than EUR 200,000, dividends are subject to 15% WHT which is reduced to 10% if the recipient company controls 25% or more of the paying company.
19. No WHT for interest on deposits with banking institutions.
20. Armenia, Kyrgyzstan, Tajikistan and Ukraine apply the USSR/Cyprus treaty.
21. A rate of 10% on interest received by a financial institution or when it relates to sale on credit of any industrial, commercial or scientific equipment or of merchandise.
22. This rate applies for any copyright of literary, dramatic, musical, artistic or scientific work. A 10% rate applies for industrial, commercial or scientific equipment. A 15% rate applies for patents, trade marks, designs or models, plans, secret formulas or processes.
23. This rate applies to companies holding directly at least 25% of the share capital of the company paying the dividend. In all other cases the WHT is 10%.
24. This rate does not apply if the payment is made to a Cyprus international business entity by a resident of Bulgaria owning directly or indirectly at least 25% of the share capital of the Cyprus entity.
25. A rate of 7% if paid to a bank or financial institution.
26. Slovenia, Serbia and Montenegro apply the Yugoslavia/Cyprus treaty.
27. The treaty is effective from 1 January 2009.
28. This rate applies if received by a company (excluding partnerships) that holds directly 25% of the shares. A rate of 10% applies in all other cases.
29. The treaty is effective as from 1 January 2010.
30. This rate applies if received by a company (excluding partnership) that holds directly at least 10% of the shares for an uninterrupted period of no less than one year. A rate of 5% applies in all other cases.
31. A rate of 10% for patent, trademark, design or model, plan, secret formula or process, computer software or industrial, commercial or scientific equipment, or for information concerning industrial, commercial or scientific experience.

Tax administration

Returns
Business organisations are required to prepare audited accounts based on International Financial Reporting Standards (IFRS). Tax returns are completed based on these accounts on a calendar-year basis. The tax return needs to be submitted to the tax authorities by 31 December of the year following the relevant tax year.

Payment of tax
Corporate entities must pay provisional tax on the current year's income in three equal instalments on 1 August, 30 September, and 31 December. A final payment must be made on or before 1 August of the following year on a self-assessment basis to bring the total payments of tax to the total actually due according to the tax return.

Corporate taxes in Czech Republic

For more information, contact:

Paul Stewart
PricewaterhouseCoopers Česká republika, s.r.o.
Business Community Centre
Katerinská 40/466
120 00 Praha 2, Czech Republic
Tel: +420 251 151 111
Email: paul.stewart@cz.pwc.com

Significant developments

The amendment to the Income Taxes Act broadens the scope of non-residents' income from sources in the Czech Republic to include income in connection with the transfer of shares in Czech-seated companies, even in the case of a transfer between two non-residents (only income from a Czech tax resident buyer was included until 2008). The capital gain participation exemption now applies to gains from the sale of Czech subsidiaries' realised European Union (EU) incorporated companies (previously, the exemption applied only to Czech permanent establishment of these companies). The amendment cancels participation exemption for EU companies when the Czech subsidiary is in the liquidation process (taxation of dividends is contrary to Parent Subsidiary Directive). Thin capitalisation rules have been softened retroactively from January 2008 when the inclusion of non-related party loans into debt/equity ratio was cancelled as well as the cap for interest rate. Dividend and interest exemption paid to Norway or Iceland is now available and exemption of licences from Czech withholding taxes based on the EU I/R Directive will be available from 1 January 2011.

The elections in May 2010 may result in tax changes implemented by the Parliament and new government. There are discussions that tax rates should be slightly increased after the elections. If any changes are approved, they will likely be effective from 1 January 2011, at the earliest.

Taxes on corporate income

Corporate income tax applies to the profits generated by all companies, including branches of foreign companies. Corporate partners in general partnerships (i.e., unlimited) and corporate general partners (i.e., unlimited) in a limited partnership are subject to corporate income tax on their share of the profits in the partnership.

The corporate income tax rate is 19% for 2010, going forward. The corporate income tax rate was 20% in 2009. The 19% rate applies to all business profits, including capital gains from the sale of shares (if not exempt under the participation exemption regime).

There is a special tax rate of 15% levied on dividend income of Czech tax resident entities from non-resident entities.

Corporate residence

A company is resident in the Czech Republic for tax purposes if it is registered in, or has a place of management located in the Czech Republic.

Czech Republic

Other taxes

The taxes discussed below may apply in addition to the corporate income tax.

Value-added tax (VAT)
VAT is charged at 20% on the supply of goods and services within the Czech Republic, but certain supplies (such as groceries) are taxed at a rate of 10%. Exports are generally exempt from VAT with a credit. Some supplies are exempt without a credit, including the lease of real estate (with certain exceptions), financial and insurance services, radio and TV broadcasting, education, health, and welfare.

Road tax
Road tax is payable with respect to vehicles (including private vehicles) used for commercial purposes. Foreign vehicles are also liable to road tax while in the Czech Republic. Rates vary depending on engine capacity and vehicle size.

Real estate tax
Real estate tax is payable by the owner of land or buildings. The amount of the tax is dependent on area, location and usage of the land or buildings.

Transfer taxes
Real estate transfer tax is levied on the transferor of real estate at a rate of 3% on the greater of the transaction price or the officially appraised value. Inheritance and gift taxes are levied on the recipient of other property transferred by inheritance or gift. The inheritance tax rates range from 0.5% to 20%, and the gift tax rates range from 1% to 40% on the value of the transferred property.

Excise taxes
Excise tax is charged on the production or import of tobacco products, wines, spirits, beer, fuel, and lubricants.

Environmental taxes
Environmental taxes are imposed on electricity and natural gas, and on certain solid fuels. The environmental taxes have a character similar to excise taxes.

Branch income

A foreign company can trade in the Czech Republic through a Czech branch. A branch usually creates a Czech permanent establishment (PE) of the foreign entity for corporate income tax purposes (depending on the character of the activities carried out through the branch). The basis of taxation is the same as for corporations (i.e., tax base is calculated as taxable revenues less tax-deductible costs). In some cases, it may be possible for taxpayers to negotiate with the tax authorities regarding the basis on which profits are attributed to the branch.

A branch is liable for tax on its attributable profits at the standard corporate income tax rate.

Income determination

Capital gains

No separate capital gains tax is levied in the Czech Republic. Capital gains are included in the corporate income tax base and taxed as ordinary income in the year in which they arise.

Capital gains from the sale of shares may be exempt from Czech taxation if the following conditions are met:

1. The Czech or EU parent holds at least 10% of the shares of the subsidiary for at least 12 months;
2. The subsidiary is a tax resident of the Czech Republic;
3. Both the parent and the subsidiary have one of the legal forms listed in the Annex to the EU P/S directive; and
4. If the subsidiary is not a tax resident of the Czech Republic or another EU member state, the exemption can be applied, provided that the subsidiary is a tax resident of a country where there is a double-tax treaty in place with the Czech Republic, it has a legal form similar to a limited liability company or a joint stock company, and it is subject to corporate income tax at the nominal rate of at least 12% in a year when dividends are paid.

Inter-company dividends

Dividends received by Czech tax resident corporations from non-resident entities are subject to a special tax rate of 15% (unless exempt under the participation exemption regime – *see discussion below*).

Dividends paid by Czech tax resident corporations to Czech resident entities are subject to 15% final withholding tax, unless exempt under the participation exemption regime.

Dividends paid by Czech tax resident corporations to Czech non-resident entities are subject to 15% final withholding tax, unless exempt under the participation exemption regime or decreased under the relevant double-tax treaty.

Participation exemption regime

Dividend income may be exempt from Czech taxation (i.e., withholding tax, when a Czech company is paying dividends and corporate income tax or a Czech company is receiving dividends) if the following conditions are met:

- The Czech or EU parent holds at least 10% of the shares of the subsidiary for at least 12 months;
- The subsidiary is a tax resident of the Czech Republic or another EU member state.
- Both the parent and the subsidiary have one of the legal forms listed in the Annex to the EU P/S directive;
- Regarding dividends paid, provided that conditions above are met, the exemption also applies when dividends are paid by a Czech subsidiary to Switzerland, Norway or Iceland; and
- Regarding dividends received, if the subsidiary is not a tax resident of the Czech Republic or another EU member state, exemption on dividends received by a Czech resident may be applied, provided that the subsidiary is a tax resident of a country where a double-tax treaty with the Czech Republic is in place, it has a legal form similar to a limited liability company or a joint stock company, and it is subject to

Czech Republic

corporate income tax at the nominal rate of at least 12% in a year when dividends are paid.

Foreign income

Companies resident in the Czech Republic are taxed on their worldwide income. A Czech corporation is taxed on its foreign branch income when earned (accrual basis) and on foreign dividends when approved by general meeting.

Participation exemption regime is available *(see above)*.

There is no controlled foreign companies (CFC) legislation in the Czech Republic.

Exchange gains and losses

Realised as well as unrealised foreign exchange gains and losses are accounted for in profit and loss accounts and represent taxable revenues or tax-deductible costs, respectively.

The default functional currency is Czech crown (CZK). A Czech company cannot opt for any foreign currency to be the functional currency for tax purposes.

Inventory valuation

Stock (i.e., inventory) is valued at cost. Czech legislation specifically provides for the use of the arithmetical average cost and first-in, first-out (FIFO) methods to value stock. Last-in, first-out (LIFO) and the replacement-cost methods (except for livestock) may not be used.

Deductions

Depreciation and depletion

Methods of tax depreciation are prescribed by tax legislation and are independent from depreciation methods for accounting purposes. Tax depreciation is calculated on an asset-by-asset basis, applying the straight-line or accelerated basis methods of depreciation at statutory rates. Under both methods, depreciation expense in the first year is lower than for subsequent years. The company may choose which method to apply to a new asset, but once the choice is made, it cannot be altered. All assets are classified into six groups, which determine the number of years over which the asset will be written off, as follows:

Depreciation group	Minimum depreciation period (years)	Examples
1	3	Office machines and computers, tools
2	5	Engines, motor vehicles, machines, audio-visual equipment
3	10	Elevators, escalators, turbines, air conditioning equipment, electric motors and generators
4	20	Buildings made of wood and plastic, long-distance lines and pipes
5	30	Buildings (except for those listed in groups 4 and 6), roads, bridges, tunnels
6	50	Administrative buildings, department stores, historical buildings and hotels

"Tangible assets" (i.e., assets which are subject to tax depreciation) are defined by tax legislation generally as assets with economic useful lives of greater than one year and acquisition prices higher than CZK 40,000. Certain assets, such as buildings, are always considered tangible assets.

Taxpayers are not obliged to depreciate a tangible asset for tax purposes every year. Depreciation may be interrupted in any year and continued in a later year without a loss of depreciation potential.

Tangible assets are generally depreciated by the taxpayer with ownership title. Certain exceptions apply, for instance, technical appreciation of a rented asset carried out by a tenant may be depreciated by that tenant, subject to certain conditions.

Depreciation can start only once the assets are put into use and comply with the requirements of specific laws.

Certain assets have special depreciation methods (e.g., moulds are depreciated based on expected life or number of products).

The value to be used as the basis for tax depreciation depends on how the asset is acquired, for example:

- Acquisition cost (construction and equipment costs, architect fees, legal fees, notary's fees, etc.), if the asset is acquired for consideration; or
- Internal costs incurred, if the asset is acquired or produced internally.

"Intangible assets" are also defined by tax legislation as software, valuable rights, intangible results of research and development (R&D) and other assets regarded as assets for accounting purposes, provided that they:

- Were acquired from a third party or developed internally for the purpose of trading with them;
- Have an acquisition price of more than CZK 60,000; and
- Have a useful life of greater than one year.

Intangible assets are depreciated for tax purposes based on the number of years that the taxpayer has a license for the assets, if the license is for a limited number of years. Otherwise, depreciation for tax purposes will vary depending on the asset (e.g., software is depreciated over for 18 months, results of R&D is depreciated over 36 months, etc.).

Travel expenses and meal allowances
Payments for travel expenses and meal allowances that are made to employees are tax-deductible, but only within the statutory limits.

Net operating losses
Losses incurred in a tax year may be carried forward to offset taxable profits generated in the following five tax years. Losses may not be carried back.

Payments to foreign affiliates
Generally, deductions may be claimed for royalties, management service fees and interest charges paid to foreign affiliates, provided such amounts are at arm's length.

Czech Republic

Thin capitalisation

Thin capitalisation rules apply in the Czech Republic and may limit the tax deductibility of interest payments on debt financing from related parties as well as from third parties.

Below is a brief summary of the thin capitalisation rules:

- The tax-deductibility test applies not only to interest but also to all so-called "financial costs" on loans (e.g., interest plus other related costs, such as bank fees).
- Thin capitalisation applies only to related-party loans.
- The debt-to-equity ratio for related-party loans is 4:1.
- Unrelated-party loans (e.g., bank loans) guaranteed by a related party are not considered related-party loans for thin capitalisation purposes. If, however, a bank provides a back-to-back loan to a Czech entity where the loan is provided to the bank by a related party, such a bank loan to the Czech entity is considered a related party loan.
- Interest on profit-participating loans is not deductible for tax purposes.

Taxes

Road tax, real estate tax and most other taxes, with the exception of gift and inheritance taxes, are deductible, as are social security contributions paid by an employer with respect to employees.

Income tax is not tax-deductible.

Other deductions

Fees paid to members of other statutory bodies of companies for their services are not deductible for tax purposes.

Certain charitable donations are deductible. The minimum deductible donation is CZK 2,000 and the maximum deductible donation is 5% of the tax base (a maximum of up to 10% of the tax base is possible if gifts are granted to universities or R&D centres).

Research and development (R&D) credits

Costs (e.g., salaries, depreciation of assets) incurred by a taxpayer on R&D projects may be deducted twice for tax purposes: once as normal tax-deductible costs and then again as a special tax allowance. However, not all R&D costs may be deducted, including fees for services purchased.

Group taxation

Currently, the Czech Republic does not permit group taxation. Each company in a group is taxed individually.

Tax incentives

Investment incentives

Investment incentives are available only to Czech entities (including Czech subsidiaries of foreign companies) engaged in the manufacturing industry. Incentives include income tax relief, financial support for the creation of new jobs, financial support for training or retraining of employees and a transfer of land at a specially reduced price.

The former programmes for the support of business support service centres and for the development of technology centres, which were focused primarily on investments in human capital as well as the training or retraining of skilled staff, were abolished based on the decision of the Ministry of Industry and Trade in July 2008. However, these activities currently are supported by the EU structural funds, especially under the operational programmes Enterprise and Innovation.

Film industry support programme

Film production or co-production companies may apply for cash subsidy to cover a part of costs incurred in the Czech Republic in respect of production of audiovisual work. Eligible costs are represented by payments for goods and services related directly to the project if they were provided by the Czech tax residents in the territory of the Czech Republic. In this case, the subsidy amounts to 20%. Remuneration paid to actors and members of film unit can be also considered as eligible provided that they are subject to Czech withholding tax. The amount of subsidy for these costs is 10%. The amount of the subsidy is paid after the project finalization. In order to qualify for subsidy, the project has to fulfil certain financial and objective conditions. One of the conditions is a cultural test, which may ensure that only quality projects connected to the European culture are supported.

R&D allowance

Up to 100% of specific R&D expenses (or costs) incurred in a given tax year may be deducted from the tax base as a special tax allowance. These costs are deducted twice for tax purposes: once as a normal tax-deductible cost and then again as a special tax allowance.

The following costs can be included in the R&D tax allowance:

- Direct costs (e.g., personnel costs of research and development engineers, consumed materials);
- Tax depreciation of fixed assets used for R&D activities; and
- Other operational expenses directly related to the realisation of R&D activities (e.g., telecommunications fees, electricity, water, gas).

Only qualifying expenses are deductible for tax purposes and must be separately identified from other expenses (or costs). This allowance does not apply to costs of purchased services or intangible results of R&D acquired from other entities, except for expenses (or costs) incurred in connection with the certification of the results of R&D projects. In addition, expenses that were supported from public sources are also excluded.

Any non-utilised R&D allowance may be carried forward for three subsequent years.

A taxpayer may request a binding ruling with respect to R&D costs from the respective tax office in the event that the taxpayer is unsure of whether certain R&D costs are eligible for the allowance.

Czech Republic

Withholding taxes (WHT)

Czech corporations are required to withhold tax on payments of dividends, interest and royalties as follows:

Recipient	Dividend (1)	Interest (2)	Royalties (3)
	%	%	%
Resident corporations	15	0	0
Resident individuals	15	0	0
Non-resident corporations, individuals:			
Non-treaty:			
Corporations	15	15	15
Individuals	15	15	15
Treaty:			
Albania	5/15	0/5	10
Australia	5/15	10	10
Austria	0/10	0	0/5
Belarus	10	0/5	10
Belgium	5/15	10	0/10
Brazil	15	10/15	15/25
Bulgaria	10	0/10	10
Canada	5/15	0/10	0/10
China, P.R.	10	0/10	10
Croatia	5	0	10
Cyprus	0/5	0	0/10
Denmark	15	0	0/5
Egypt	5/15	0/15	15
Estonia	5/15	0/10	10
Ethiopia	10	0/10	10
Finland	5/15	0	0/1/5/10
France	10	0	0/5
Georgia	5/10	0/8	5/10
Germany	5/15	0	5
Greece	Local rates	0/10	0/10
Hungary	5/15	0	10
Iceland	5/15	0	10
India	10	0/10	10
Indonesia	10/15	0/12.5	12.5
Ireland, Rep. of	5/15	0	10
Israel	5/15	0/10	5
Italy	15	0	0/5
Japan	10/15	0/10	0/10
Jordan	10	0/10	10
Kazakhstan	10	0/10	10
Korea, Rep. of	5/10	0/10	0/10
Latvia	5/15	0/10	10

Recipient	Dividend (1)	Interest (2)	Royalties (3)
	%	%	%
Lebanon	5	0	5/10
Lithuania	5/15	0/10	10
Luxembourg	5/15	0	0/10
Malaysia	0/10	0/12	12
Malta	5	0	5
Mexico	10	0/10	10
Moldova	5/15	5	10
Mongolia	10	0/10	10
Netherlands	0/10	0	5
New Zealand	15	0/10	10
Nigeria	12.5/15	0/15	15
Norway	5/15	0	0/5
Philippines	10/15	0/10	10/15
Poland	5/10	0/10	5
Portugal	10/15	0/10	10
Romania	10	0/7	10
Russia	10	0	10
Singapore	5	0	10
Slovak Republic	5/15	0	0/10
Slovenia	5/15	0/5	10
South Africa	5/15	0	10
Spain	5/15	0	0/5
Sri Lanka	15	0/10	0/10
Sweden	0/10	0	0/5
Switzerland	5/15	0	10/5
Tajikistan	5	0/7	10
Thailand	10	0/10	5/10/15
Tunisia	10/15	0/12	5/15
Ukraine	5/15	5	10
United Arab Emirates	0/5	0	10
United Kingdom	5/15	0	0/10
United States	5/15	0	0/10
Uzbekistan	10	0/5	10
Venezuela	5/10	0/10	12
Vietnam	10	0/10	10
Yugoslavia (former)	5/15	0	10

Notes

1. The lower rate applies if the recipient is a company that owns at least a certain amount of the capital or a certain amount of the voting shares of the company paying the dividend directly.
2. The lower rate applies mostly in situations when the interest is received by the government or a state-owned institution or is paid by the government.
3. The lower rate applies mostly to cultural royalties.

Czech Republic

Tax administration

Returns
A corporation may choose between the calendar year or an accounting year as its tax year.

Returns must be filed within three months of the end of the tax period.

A three-month extension of the filing deadline is available if a taxpayer is represented by a registered tax advisor or if the taxpayer is subject to a statutory accounting audit.

In some special cases, a filing deadline of less than three months may apply (e.g., upon merger or liquidation). This shorter deadline may, however, be extended if approved by the tax office.

Payment of tax
Tax payments are due on the same day as the filing deadline.

A company is obliged to make corporate income tax advances based on its last known tax liability. The tax advances are paid semi-annually or quarterly, depending on the amount of the last known tax liability.

Upon filing a tax return, tax advances paid during the year for which the tax return is filed will offset the tax liability declared in the tax return. Any outstanding amount must be paid on the date the tax return is due. Any overpayment will be refunded upon request or may be credited against future tax liabilities.

Corporate taxes in Denmark

For more information, contact:

Henrik Faust Pedersen
PricewaterhouseCoopers
Strandvejen 44
DK 2900 Hellerup, Denmark
Tel: +45 39 45 94 14
Email: henrik.faust.pedersen@dk.pwc.com

D

Significant developments

Participation exemption improved with effect from 2010

Previously, a company was required to pay tax on any capital gain on the sale of shares in a subsidiary, unless the company owned the shares for at least three years. Effective 2010, the three-year holding period requirement has been removed. As a consequence, shares can now be disposed of free of capital gains tax, regardless of the length of the ownership period, provided that the shares qualify as either "subsidiary shares" or "group shares". *See Income determination*.

The change in law also removes the requirement that shares in a subsidiary must be held for at least 12 months for a dividend to be distributed in a tax-free manner. This requirement has been removed with effect for dividends declared in the calendar year 2010 and later. Consequently, dividends on "subsidiary shares" and "group shares" are tax-free.

On the other hand, the new law introduces harsh rules for taxation of shareholdings that do not qualify as "subsidiary shares" or "group shares". Dividends received and capital gains realised or accrued on such shareholdings are fully taxable to the corporate shareholder.

Taxes on corporate income

Since 2007, the corporate income tax rate has been 25%. There is no local corporate income tax or similar surcharge.

Corporate residence

A corporation is resident in Denmark for tax purposes if it is incorporated in Denmark and registered in the Companies Register as having a Danish place of business. Further, foreign companies having their actual place of management in Denmark are also tax resident in Denmark. The actual place of management is typically the place where the management decisions concerning the company's day-to-day operations are made.

Other taxes

Value-added tax (VAT)
The general VAT rate is 25% of the price charged (exclusive of VAT).

Denmark

Stamp tax
Stamp tax is payable on a few documents, such as a deed of transfer of real estate (0.6% of the transfer sum). There is no stamp duty on transfer of shares.

Hydrocarbon income tax
A special corporate income tax is levied on profits from the exploration and extraction of oil and gas on the Danish continental shelf at a rate of 52% under the new system (70% in the old system). Corporation income tax (25%) is deductible in computing the hydrocarbon tax.

Employer's tax (social security charges)
The employer's contribution to ATP (old-age pension) charges is DKK 2,160 per annum for a full-time employee.

Companies that provide VAT-exempt services are liable to pay the employer's tax, which is calculated on the total annual salary cost. The rate can be up to 9.13%, which is the rate for banks and other financial institutions, the most significant sector paying the employer's tax. This tax is deductible for income tax purposes. Other than these taxes, an employer's obligation for social security taxes is minimal. The main social security charge is an additional income tax of 8% on salaries and wages, which is borne by employees.

Environmental taxes
Danish companies must pay environmental taxes, which were introduced to reduce companies' energy consumption, discharges of fluids with an environmental impact and emission. The tax is paid to the company that provides the energy, who pays the tax to the Danish tax authorities.

In general, almost all VAT registered companies in Denmark can receive a reimbursement of some of the taxes. From 2010 the environmental taxes have increased, the possibilities to get a reimbursement have been decreased and the majority of companies will likely suffer a significant increase in tax costs from 2010.

Branch income

Danish branches and permanent establishments (PE) of foreign companies are taxed under the same rules and rates as Danish resident companies. There is no branch remittance tax or other similar tax on branch profits.

Income determination

Taxable income generally is calculated as income determined for accounting purposes that is adjusted and modified for several items, as prescribed by the tax laws. Typical timing differences include reserves, work in progress and depreciation.

A Danish company is not taxed on its worldwide income. Instead, income from a PE outside Denmark or from real estate located abroad is excluded from taxable income. This main rule is subject to modifications, particularly where the PE would constitute a taxable controlled foreign corporation (CFC) *(more details follow)*.

Capital gains

Gains and losses realised on the sale of tangible and intangible assets, including goodwill, are generally included in taxable income. However, gains realised on the sale of shares are tax-exempt if the shares qualify as either "subsidiary shares" or "group shares".

"Subsidiary shares" are shares held by a corporate shareholder that holds a minimum of 10% of the share capital in a subsidiary that is located in the European Union (EU), European Economic Area (EEA) or a country with which Denmark has a double taxation treaty. A special anti-avoidance rule applies, which is targeted at Danish shareholders joining their shareholdings in order to reach the 10% threshold.

"Group shares" are defined as shares in companies with which the shareholder is jointly taxed or might be jointly taxed. The definition of a group is therefore the same as in the joint taxation rules and generally corresponds to the definition of a group for accounting purposes. The location where the companies are registered is irrelevant, as long as the companies are affiliated.

If the shares do not constitute group shares, subsidiary shares or treasury shares, they constitute portfolio shares. Gains on portfolio shares are fully taxable regardless of holding period. Losses on the sale of portfolio shares generally are tax-deductible. However, special rules may apply for losses on unlisted shares.

Gains realised on the sale of real estate property are taxable whereas losses are not tax-deductible unless the property is a building qualifying for tax depreciation. A loss realised on the sale of land and other buildings may be utilised only against taxable profits on the sale of real estate properties in the same year or may be carried forward infinitely.

Gains and losses on financial instruments generally are included in taxable income, according to the mark-to-market principal, which is required. There are special rules for losses on certain share-based contracts.

Inter-company dividends

Dividends received on "subsidiary shares" or "group shares" are tax exempt regardless of the length of the ownership period, whereas dividends received on portfolio shares are fully included in taxable income.

Despite whether the shares qualify as "subsidiary shares" or "group shares", dividends are fully taxable if received from a foreign company that can deduct the dividends paid, unless a tax exemption is provided for in the EU parent/subsidiary directive.

Foreign income

As a general rule, foreign source income, such as interest, is included in taxable income. However, income from a PE or real estate outside Denmark is excluded from taxable income.

The income of a foreign subsidiary may be taxed in the hands of its Danish parent company if the subsidiary constitutes a CFC.

Denmark

Stock dividends

Stock dividends may be distributed to shareholders free of tax provided that the dividends are in proportion to the existing shareholdings (bonus shares).

Deductions

Depreciation and depletion

Tax depreciation need not be in conformity with book depreciation.

Annual depreciation allowances on machinery and equipment may be claimed under the diminishing-balance method at up to 25%. The depreciation base is the cost of fixed assets less (1) sales proceeds from disposals and (2) depreciation allowances previously claimed.

For ships, the depreciation rate is 20% in the year of construction and a 12% declining balance basis in subsequent years.

Depreciation allowances on buildings (other than residential buildings and office buildings not adjoining an industrial building) may be claimed at up to 4% on the straight-line basis.

Acquired goodwill and other intangible property rights can be amortised at up to one-seventh per year on a straight-line basis. Costs related to the purchase of patents or know-how (including rights/licenses to utilise patents or know-how) can either be fully expensed in the year of acquisition or amortised over a seven-year period on a straight-line basis.

Certain restrictions regarding the depreciable value of goodwill apply in the case of group transactions. Goodwill on the purchase of shares cannot be amortised for tax purposes.

Amortisation of the cost of acquisition or exploitation of natural resources is subject to special rules.

Airplanes, trains and utility plants can be depreciated only at a 15% declining balance (presently subject to phasing-in rates).

Rails, telecommunications facilities and certain other long-life plant and equipment can be depreciated only at a 7% declining balance.

Depreciation allowances that are recaptured as part of a capital gain on the sale of an asset generally are fully taxable.

Net operating losses

Tax losses may be carried forward indefinitely.

Certain restrictions on the right to carry tax losses forward apply when more than 50% of the share capital or 50% of the voting rights at the end of the financial year are owned by shareholders different from those that held control at the beginning of the income year in which the tax loss was incurred.

Similarly, under certain circumstances, tax losses are cancelled if a Danish company receives a debt forgiveness or comparable transaction. However, there are numerous exceptions (e.g., inter-company transactions).

Payments to foreign affiliates

A Danish corporation can claim a deduction for royalties, management fees and similar payments made to foreign affiliates, provided that such amounts are made on an arm's-length basis and reflect services received. Interest at normal commercial rates paid to foreign affiliates generally will be allowed as a deduction but is subject to very complex thin capitalisation and interest relief limitation rules.

Taxes

Taxes are non-deductible for income tax purposes, except for employer's tax and nonrecoverable VAT.

Group taxation

Mandatory Danish tax consolidation

A mandatory tax consolidation regime obliges all Danish resident companies and Danish branches that are members of the same domestic or international group to file a joint group tax return. The definition of a group generally corresponds with the definition of a group for accounting purposes. The tax consolidated income is equal to the sum of the taxable income of each individual Danish company and branch that are a member of the consolidated group.

The top parent company participating in the Danish tax consolidation group will be appointed the role of a so-called management company; this company is responsible for settling advance and final corporate tax payments of all group members.

Elective cross border tax consolidation

A non-Danish subsidiary may be included as a member to a Danish tax grouping provided that the group includes all of its foreign companies and branches in the Danish tax grouping. In effect, this all-or-nothing provision rules out the possibility for major international groups to have their Danish subgroup file a Danish group tax return that includes only certain hand-picked (typically loss-making) foreign group members.

If a general cross-border tax consolidation is established, it will be binding for 10 years – however, with certain possibilities of "breaking" the 10-year period (e.g., in connection with takeovers).

The comments under *Mandatory Danish tax consolidation* with respect to the calculation of the tax consolidation income, "management" company, etc., generally also apply to international tax consolidation.

Thin capitalisation and interest relief limitations

Danish resident companies and Danish branches of foreign companies are subject to three sets of restrictions, each of which may seriously limit or disallow Danish tax relief for financing costs. There is no recharacterisation of interest as dividends.

Firstly, there is the thin capitalisation rule under Section 11 of the Corporate Income Tax Act. This rule works to disallow gross interest costs on related party debt to the

Denmark

extent the overall debt to equity ratio exceeds 4 to 1. Related party debt is defined so as to include external bank debt if group member companies or shareholders have provided guarantees to the bank. Section 11 does not apply if the controlled debt is less than DKK 10 million.

Secondly, there is an asset-based rule under Section 11B. To the extent a Danish tax group as a whole has net financing costs in excess of DKK 21.3 million (full-year amount for 2009 and 2010), tax relief may be obtained only within an amount equal to 6.5% (rate applicable for 2009) of the tax basis of certain assets of the group (rate applicable for 2010 is 5%).

Thirdly, there is an Earnings before Interest & Tax (EBIT) based rule under Section 11C. This rule works to limit interest relief to an amount equal to 80% of the Danish tax group's taxable EBIT income. The rule applies the same definition of net financing costs as Section 11B, and it also allows for a minimum deduction of DKK 21.3 million in cases where EBIT is too low or negative.

Controlled foreign company rules
According to the Danish CFC rules, a Danish company has to include in its taxable income the total income of a subsidiary, foreign or Danish, if such subsidiary qualifies as a CFC. A subsidiary qualifies as a CFC if all of the following criteria are met:

1. The Danish company, together with other group member companies, directly or indirectly owns more than 50% of the capital or controls more than 50% of the voting rights in the subsidiary
2. More than half of the subsidiary's taxable profits, as hypothetically assessed under Danish tax laws, are predefined CFC- income types (mainly interest, royalty, capital gains, etc.)
3. During the income year, the subsidiary's CFC assets (assets, where the return is characterised as CFC income type) make up more than 10% of the subsidiary's total assets.

There is no black-or-white list that exempts subsidiaries resident in certain countries.

Transfer pricing
Danish transfer pricing rules apply to transactions between related parties (e.g., intergroup transactions), whether the transactions are made between residents or non-residents. The rules apply when a company or person directly or indirectly owns at least 50% of the share capital or 50% of the voting rights in another company.

Companies are obliged to disclose in the annual tax return certain information regarding type and volume of intragroup transactions. Companies also are obliged to maintain detailed and extensive transfer pricing documentation to substantiate that intragroup transactions are conducted in accordance with arm's-length principles. A company is subjected to fines for failure to comply with the documentation rules.

Tax-free restructuring
Restructuring such as mergers, demergers, share exchanges, drop-down of assets, etc., can in many cases be carried out tax-free under the provisions of the EU Mergers Directive as implemented into Danish law. These types of restructuring can be carried out in a tax-exempt manner without prior approval from the tax authorities. However,

several objective conditions must be fulfilled. Formation, merger, reorganisation and liquidation expenses are mostly non-deductible.

Tax incentives

Capital expenditures
A small variety of tax incentives are available in the form of deductions for capital expenditures.

Danish tax law allows for an immediate write-off of capital expenditures for research and development (R&D). Alternatively, the taxpayer may choose to take tax depreciation in the same year and the following four years on a straight-line basis. Costs incurred in connection with the exploration for raw materials may also be fully deducted in the same year.

Costs related to purchase of patents, know-how (including rights/licenses to utilise patents or know-how) may either be fully expensed in the year of acquisition or amortised over a seven-year period on a straight-line basis.

Tonnage Tax Scheme
Danish tax law provides for a special tax scheme for shipping entities.

The main principle of the Tonnage Tax Scheme is that qualifying shipping entities are not taxed on the basis of their actual income derived from their business, but on a fictitious income based on the net tons carrying capability of their fleet used for purposes covered by the Tonnage Tax Act.

The Tonnage Tax Scheme is available to Danish shipping entities organised as limited liability companies (A/S or ApS), foreign shipping companies with the place of management and control in Denmark, and EU shipping companies with a PE in Denmark.

The Scheme is available upon application to the Danish tax authorities. A decision to enter into the scheme is binding for a period of 10 years.

As a general rule, group related shipping companies based in Denmark must make the same choice regarding the Tonnage Tax Scheme. However, shipping companies that do not have the same management or operating organisation and do not conduct business in related fields may be exempt from the joint decision provision.

The Tonnage Tax Scheme is restricted to certain types of business activities. The entity must carry out commercial transportation of passengers or cargo between different destinations. The ships must be owned, or chartered on a "bareboat" or "time-charter with a call/buy option by the company" basis, and have a minimum gross tonnage of 20 tons. Certain restrictions apply for ships chartered on a time charter basis without a call/buy option. The ships must be strategically and commercially run from Denmark.

Income from activities that are carried out in close connection with this business, such as the usage of containers and loading facilities, etc. may also be included in the Tonnage Tax Scheme. Ships used for exploration, diving, fishing, towing, sand dredging, etc., are specifically exempt from the Scheme. The same applies for certain types of ships, such as barges, floating docks, etc. However, EU or European Economic

Denmark

Community registered ships used for towage activities at sea (i.e., not in and around ports) during at least 50% of its operating time during the income year may be included in the tonnage tax system.

Ship operating companies may also use the Danish Tonnage Tax Scheme. A ship operator is defined as a company doing business with crew management and technical management of ships qualified for use in the tonnage tax system. It is a requirement that the ship operator has taken over the full operating responsibility and all obligations and responsibilities according to the International Safety Management codex.

Taxable income
The taxable income for the part of the business that qualifies for the Tonnage Tax Scheme is determined for each ship as a fixed amount per 100 net tons (NT) per day according to the following:

Ship net ton	Fixed amount per day
0 to 1,000 NT	DKK 7.8 per day per 100 NT
1,001 to 10,000 NT	DKK 5.6 per day per 100 NT
10,001 to 25,000 NT	DKK 3.35 per day per 100 NT
Over 25,000 NT	DKK 2.2 per day per 100 NT

The income is taxed at the ordinary corporate tax rate (25%). No deductions relating to shipping income will be allowed. Special rules apply for financial income and financial expenses, and in relation to so called "thin capitalisation". Income that does not qualify for the tonnage tax scheme is taxed according to the general tax provisions in Denmark.

Depreciation
Shipping entities that apply the Tonnage Tax Scheme from the time of their establishment may not deduct depreciation for tax purposes. Special rules apply for shipping entities that were already in existence when they elected to become subject to the Scheme and for entities that elect to include certain other assets at a later point in time that were not previously subject to the Scheme.

Gains on the sale of ships
Gains on the sale of ships that have not been used in the Scheme prior to 1 January 2007 are tax exempt. The same applies to gains on the sale of contracts on the delivery of ships, provided that the ship was destined to be delivered after 1 January 2007. Gains on the sale of ships used in the scheme in prior years are taxable. The taxable gain is calculated as the sale price minus the purchase price plus improvements. Any losses on ships acquired and sold within the same income year as the income year in which a gain is realised may be offset against the gain.

Withholding taxes (WHT)

On payments to foreign corporations and non-resident aliens
Dividends
Dividends paid to a parent company in another EU member state or a state with which Denmark has a double tax treaty are exempt from withholding tax provided that the shares qualify as subsidiary shares. The same applies for dividends paid on group

shares (that are not also subsidiary shares, i.e., holding below 10%) provided that the recipient company is resident within the EU/EEA.

Dividends paid on portfolio shares to a foreign shareholder are levied withholding tax of 28%. A change in law has reduced the rate to 27% with effect from 2012. If the portfolio shareholder is situated in a country with which Denmark has a Tax Information Exchange Agreement (TIEA), the tax rate on the dividend is reduced to 15% and the difference between the higher withholding rate and the lower tax rate may be reclaimed. However, the reduced rate does not apply if the shareholder is resident outside the EU and together with related entities own more than 10% of the capital in the Danish distributing company.

Interest
Interest generally is not subject to withholding tax unless paid to a foreign group member company that is tax resident outside the EU and outside any of the states with which Denmark has concluded a tax treaty. In this situation, interest withholding tax is levied at 25%. Certain other exemptions apply, mainly relating to CFC taxation.

Royalties
Royalties are subject to a 25% withholding tax. In most cases, the payer may reduce its withholding in accordance with the tax treaty applicable to the payee. Also, the EU Interest/Royalty Directive may provide an exemption from withholding tax if the payee is an immediate parent, sister or subsidiary company resident in the EU.

Recipient	Dividend		Interest (2)	Royalty
	Qualifying companies(1a+b)	Others		
	%	%	%	%
Resident corporations	Nil	28	Nil	25 (5)
Resident individuals		28	Nil	25
Non-treaty(4):				
Non-resident corporations	28	28	25 (3+5)	25 (5)
Non-resident individuals		28	Nil	25
Treaty:				
Argentina	Nil (1a)	15	Nil	3/5/10/15
Australia	Nil (1a)	15	Nil	10
Austria	Nil (1a+b)	15	Nil	Nil
Bangladesh	Nil (1a)	15	Nil	10
Belgium	Nil (1a+b)	15	Nil	Nil
Brazil	Nil (1a)	25	Nil	25/15
Bulgaria	Nil (1a+b)	15	Nil	Nil
Canada	Nil (1a)	15	Nil	Nil/15
Chile	Nil (1a)	15	Nil	5/15
China, P.R.	Nil (1a)	10	Nil	10
Cyprus	Nil (1a+b)	15	Nil	Nil
Czech Republic	Nil (1a+b)	15	Nil	5
Egypt	Nil (1a)	20	Nil	20

Denmark

Recipient	Dividend		Interest (2)	Royalty
	Qualifying companies(1a+b)	**Others**		
	%	%	%	%
Estonia	Nil (1a+b)	15	Nil	5/10
Faroe Islands	Nil (1a)	15	Nil	Nil
Finland	Nil (1a+b)	15	Nil	Nil
Georgia	Nil (1a)	10	Nil	Nil
Germany	Nil (1a+b)	15	Nil	Nil
Greece	Nil (1a+b)	18	Nil	5
Greenland	Nil (1a)	15	Nil	10
Hungary	Nil (1a+b)	15	Nil	Nil
Iceland	Nil (1a+b)	15	Nil	Nil
India	Nil (1a)	25	Nil	20
Indonesia	Nil (1a)	25	Nil	15
Ireland, Rep. of	Nil (1a+b)	15	Nil	Nil
Israel	Nil (1a)	15	Nil	10
Italy	Nil (1a+b)	15	Nil	5
Jamaica	Nil (1a)	15	Nil	10
Japan	Nil (1a)	15	Nil	10
Kenya	Nil (25%)	28	Nil	20
Korea, Rep. of	Nil (1a)	15	Nil	10/15
Croatia	Nil (1a)	10	Nil	10
Latvia	Nil (1a+b)	15	Nil	5/10
Lithuania	Nil (1a+b)	15	Nil	5/10
Luxembourg	Nil (1a+b)	15	Nil	Nil
Macedonia	Nil (1a)	15	Nil	10
Malaysia	Nil (1a)	Nil	Nil	Nil
Malta	Nil (1a+b)	15	Nil	Nil
Mexico	Nil (1a)	15	Nil	10
Morocco	Nil (1a)	25	Nil	10
Netherlands	Nil (1a+b)	15	Nil	Nil
New Zealand	Nil (1a)	15	Nil	10
Norway	Nil (1a+b)	15	Nil	Nil
Pakistan	Nil (1a)	15	Nil	12
Philippines	Nil (1a)	15	Nil	15
Poland	Nil (1a+b)	15	Nil	5
Portugal	Nil (1a+b)	10	Nil	10
Romania	Nil (1a+b)	15	Nil	4
Russia	Nil (1a)	10	Nil	Nil
Serbia (6)	Nil (1a)	15	Nil	10
Singapore	Nil (1a)	10	Nil	10
Slovak Republic	Nil (1a+b)	15	Nil	5
Slovenia	Nil (1a+b)	15	Nil	5
South Africa	Nil (1a)	15	Nil	Nil
Sri Lanka	Nil (1a)	15	Nil	10

Recipient	Dividend		Interest (2)	Royalty
	Qualifying companies(1a+b)	Others		
	%	%	%	%
Sweden	Nil (1a+b)	15	Nil	Nil
Switzerland	Nil (1+a)	Nil (7)	Nil	Nil
Taiwan	Nil (1a)	10	Nil	10
Tanzania	Nil (1a)	15	Nil	20
Thailand	Nil (1a)	10	Nil	5/15
Trinidad and Tobago	Nil (1a)	20	Nil	15
Tunisia	Nil (1a)	15	Nil	15
Turkey	Nil (1a)	20	Nil	10
Uganda	Nil (1a)	15	Nil	10
Ukraine	Nil (1a)	15	Nil	10
United Kingdom	Nil (1a+b)	25	Nil	Nil
United States	Nil (1a)	15	Nil	Nil
Venezuela	Nil (1a)	15	Nil	5/10
Vietnam	Nil (1a)	15	Nil	15
Zambia	Nil (1a)	15	Nil	15

Notes

1. Denmark does not operate a system of withholding tax on dividends when the parent company holds:
   a. At least 10% of the share capital of the distributing Danish company, provided the receiving company is resident in a EU/EEA member state or a state with which Denmark has entered a double tax treaty (subsidiary shares).
   b. Less than 10% of the share capital in the distributing company provided that the receiving company is an EU/EEA-resident and the distributing and the receiving company are affiliated companies (group shares).
2. Interest generally is not subject to withholding tax unless paid to a foreign group member company that is tax resident outside of the EU and outside of any of the states with which Denmark has concluded a tax treaty. In this situation, interest withholding tax is levied at 25%.
3. Exemptions apply if the receiving company is directly or indirectly controlled by a Danish parent company or if the receiving company is controlled by a company resident in a state with which Denmark has a double tax convention and that company may be subject to CFC taxation. Finally, an exemption applies if the receiving company establishes that the foreign taxation of interest is not less than three-quarters of the Danish corporate taxation and that the interest is not paid to another foreign company subject to taxation less than three-quarters of the Danish corporate taxation.
4. Denmark has terminated its treaty with Spain and France with effect from 1 January 2009. The termination means that each country will tax the relevant income according to its domestic tax rules. New treaties are not expected to be agreed in the near future. Companies in Spain and France receiving dividends from a Danish company may, however, qualify for tax exempt dividend since they are EU member states.
5. The EU Interest/Royalty Directive may provide an exemption from withholding tax if the payee is an immediate parent, sister or subsidiary company resident in the EU.
6. Serbia has succeeded in the treaty between Denmark and Yugoslavia.
7. A new protocol to the treaty between Denmark and Switzerland has been signed, allocating taxing rights of 15% on dividends to the source state. The amendment has, however, not yet entered into force.

Denmark

Tax administration

Returns
Tax returns are completed on the basis of audited financial accounts with adjustments for tax. Tax returns should be filed no later than six months following the end of the accounting year. Corporations with an accounting year-end that falls in the period from January 1 to March 31 must file a tax return no later than 1 August in the same calendar year.

The tax system, in practice, is based on self-assessment. Tax assessments are made automatically by the tax authorities on the basis of the tax return. However, the tax authorities may subsequently audit the tax return. The general statute of limitations is 1 May in the fourth calendar year after that of the end of the relevant accounting period. This limitation is extended for another two years with respect to inter-company (transfer pricing) issues.

Payment of tax
Corporate income tax must be paid on a current year basis in two equal instalments due on 20 March and 20 November. The authorities request payments of 50% of the average of the last three years' final income tax. In addition, voluntary additional payments may be made at the same dates; such voluntary payments are adjusted by 0.7% when set against the final tax bill.

The final tax bill is settled by 20 November in the following year. Underpaid tax is then payable by 20 November with a surtax of 5.1% of the tax amount (rate for 2010 tax year). Overpaid tax is refunded by November of the following year with interest of 1.6% (rate for 2010 tax year).

Corporate taxes in the Dominican Republic

For more information, contact:

Ramon Ortega
PricewaterhouseCoopers
Edificio Bank of Nova Scotia
3rd floor
Avenida John F Kennedy, Esquina con Avenida Lope de Vega
Santo Domingo
The Dominican Republic
Tel: +1 809 567 7741
Email: ramon.ortega@do.pwc.com

Significant developments

No significant developments from January through to April 2010.

Taxes on corporate income

The current corporate income tax rate is 25%.

Corporate residence

A company is resident when it is registered and/or incorporated under the Law of the Dominican Republic (DR). However, a foreign entity registered in the DR as a branch or permanent establishment is subject to local tax in the same manner.

Dividends remitted abroad or paid locally are subject to a withholding tax of 25%. This withholding tax may be used as a credit against the company's corporate income tax of the same period, as long as the dividends were paid out of profits which had already been subject to the corporate income tax.

Other taxes

Internal and consumption taxes collected at customs upon import

These taxes are assessed at various rates depending on the nature of the goods and its origin since free trade agreements exist (such as the United States-DR-Central American Free Trade Agreement (CAFTA)), which decrease the custom duties rates for goods imported from the member countries.

Excise tax

There are two kinds of selective consumption tax:

- Specific tax for alcoholic goods and cigarettes (adjusted by inflation annually):
  - Alcohol: range from DOP 335.88 to DOP 411.86 for every litre of absolute alcohol; and
  - Cigarettes: DOP 31.29 for a 20 pack and DOP 15.64 for a 10 pack.

- *Ad valorem* which ranges from 19.50% to 130% and is applied on the consumption of certain imported goods (listed in the law) that are considered to be nonessential, rendering of telecommunications services (10%), insurance services (10%) and

0.0015% over the value of cheques or wire transfers made through financial entities (this tax does not apply to cash withdrawals or credit card use).

Value-added tax (VAT)

VAT is applied to industrialised goods (movable) and services. The rate is 16%. Zero rates apply to exports.

Real estate transfer tax

This tax is assessed at a basic rate of 3%.

Stamp taxes

Stamp taxes have been abolished.

Asset tax

Asset tax/Law No. 557-05 imposes a 1% tax on total assets. Share investments in other companies, land in rural areas, immovable property pertaining to livestock and agriculture, and tax advance payments are excluded from this tax base.

Depreciation, amortisation and reserves for bad debts are allowable deductions for application of the 1% tax on total assets.

This tax shall be filed and liquidated through the Annual Corporate Income Tax Return (Form IR-2) and paid, applying the following rule:

- The asset tax is an alternative/minimum tax.
- The income tax is allowed as a credit against the asset tax.
- If the income tax is greater than the asset tax, the obligation to pay the asset tax is considered to be cancelled and instead the income tax is paid.

If the income tax is less than the asset tax, the difference (in order to complete the asset tax value) shall be paid in two equal instalments as follows:

- First instalment: shall be paid during 120 days subsequent to closing date; and
- Second instalment: shall be paid within six months after first quote's due date.

The entities may request a temporary exemption from the asset tax, such as entities that require large capital (among other requirements established by General Ruling 3-06) may make such request, which shall be submitted at least 90 days before the filing due date. The local internal revenue service (IRS) shall evaluate the merits of the request and approve or deny as appropriate.

If the entity has an income tax credit arising from excess advance payments, it may request the refund of such balance be applied against the asset tax.

In the case of financial institutions, power generation and distribution, pension funds entities and stock brokerage companies, the tax is calculated based on the book value of fixed assets.

According to rule 07-2007, construction companies may seek exemption from the asset tax, provided that such entities meet the requirements established in this rule.

Dominican Republic

Branch income

Branch profits are taxed at the same rate as corporate profits (25%). There is no withholding tax on branch profit remittances to the company's headquarters, provided corresponding annual corporate tax has been paid.

Income determination

Inventory valuation
The last-in, first-out (LIFO) method of inventory valuation is accepted for fiscal purposes. Other methods may be authorised upon request.

Conformity between book and tax reporting is not required.

Capital gains
Capital gains are added to the ordinary taxable income and subject to the same tax rate of 25%. Capital gain is determined by deducting the acquisition cost adjusted by the inflation rate from the sale amount.

Inter-company dividends
Dividends distribution is subject to a 25% withholding tax that should constitute a tax credit against the annual corporate income tax corresponding to the same fiscal period of the distribution.

Foreign income
Dominican-resident companies, branches and permanent establishments are subject to taxation on income from Dominican sources and on income from foreign sources arising from investments and financial gains. Tax determined on income from foreign source is subject to a credit mechanism. Taxes paid in the country where the income is originated can be credited up to the amount of the tax payable in DR on the same income.

Stock dividends
Stock dividends are not subject to taxation.

Deductions

Depreciation and depletion
Depreciation allowances on fixed assets are determined by the declining balance method at the following rates:

Class	%
Buildings	5
Furniture, fixtures, computers, vehicles, etc.	25
Other assets not specified	15

The fiscal book value is adjusted by the annual inflation rate.

Net operating losses
The carryforward of losses of legal entities can be used to offset profits up to the fifth period following the period in which the losses were generated, with a maximum

Dominican Republic

amortisation of 20% in each period. For the fourth period the deduction allowed should not exceed 80% of the net taxable income. In the fifth period, the percentage is 70%.

Payments to foreign affiliates
Payments to foreign affiliates for royalties, interest, or service fees are deductible, provided 25% withholding tax was paid.

Payments on interest (loans) abroad to foreign financial institutions are subject to a withholding tax of 10%.

Taxes
In principle taxes are not deductible neither interest and surcharges imposed on it, inheritances, donations, fringe benefit tax and penalties related to all taxes.

Other significant items
For tax purposes, the following significant items should be considered:

- Bad debts are deductible only in the year the loss is suffered. Authorisation may be obtained to use an alternative method which consists in creating a provision, allowing the deduction only in the year the bad debts qualify as doubtful, up to 4% of the balance of the accounts receivable at year-end;
- Amortisation of intangible assets, such as patents, author's rights, drawings, franchises, and contracts without set expiration date, is not deductible;
- Changes in method are not allowed without advance approval; and
- Bonuses to employees are deductible within the year if paid before 120 days after year-end.

Group taxation

Group taxation is not permitted.

Tax incentives

In the DR the following incentive laws exist:

- Tourism;
- Alternative energy;
- Industrial renovation and modernisation;
- Industrial Free Trade Zone operations; and
- Border development.

Withholding taxes (WHT)

Dividends in cash to resident and non-resident individuals and corporations are subject to a WHT of 25%.

The WHT on payments to foreign corporations, which are not permanently established in the Dominican Republic, are as follows:

Dominican Republic

	Interest/ Dividends	Royalties	Technical assistance	Other services
	%	%	%	%
Non-treaty, basic	25*	25	25	25
Treaty (Canada)	18	18	25	25

Note

* Payments on interest (loans) to foreign financial institutions are subject to a withholding tax of 10%.

Tax administration

Returns
The Corporate Annual Tax Return must be filed and taxes paid within 120 days after year-end. Tax authorities may allow extensions of up to 60 days, upon request.

Tax returns are based on self-assessment and must be filed on electronic forms supplied by the Internal Tax Department.

Payment of tax
The balance of any tax due must be paid no later than the due date for filing the return. Corporations domiciled in the country and permanent establishments of foreign enterprises shall be obliged to make monthly advance payments of tax related to the period in progress.

Year-end dates established by the DR tax code
Corporate bylaws should establish as year-end, one of the following: 31 December, 31 March, 30 June, or 30 September. Once the year-end is selected, any change should be authorised by the tax authorities.

Year ending 31 December 2009

Pretax income	DOP 1,000,000
Add – Non-deductible expenses:	
Charitable contribution in excess of limitation	25,000
Tax on compensation-in-kind (120,000 at 25%)	30,000
Total of nondeductible expenses	55,000
Deduct:	
Dividends from domestic operation	50,000
Carryover loss	100,000
Total deductions	150,000
Taxable income	DOP 905,000
Tax at 25%	DOP 226,250

Corporate taxes in Ecuador

For more information, contact:

Pablo Aguirre
PricewaterhouseCoopers
Diego de Almagro N 32-48 with Whimper
Edificio IBM
Quito, Pichincha
Ecuador
Tel: +593 2 256 2288
Email: pablo.aguirre@ec.pwc-ag.com

Significant developments

A new tax reform was introduced at the end of 2007, 2008, 2009 and 2010 modifying many subjects on local tax legislation.

The reforms include a remittance tax ("Impuesto a la Salida de Divisas" – ISD) and changes to the Income Tax Law, including income tax (creating additional limitations on deducting expenses) and value-added tax (VAT) (imposing a 12% VAT on the importation of services).

The International Financial Reporting Standards' (IFRS) final implementation deadline for companies (except for financial institutions) was suspended until 2012 (for companies with assets lower than USD 4 million).

Taxes on corporate income

Taxes on corporate income are levied at the following rates:

	Rate %
Distributed or undistributed profits of local corporations and branches	25.0
Reinvested profits of local corporations and branches	15.0
Oil companies with production sharing contracts	25.0
For oil companies with risk service contracts:	
Distributed profits	44.4
Undistributed profits (under certain investment conditions)	25.0

Resident entities are taxed their on worldwide income. Non-resident entities are subject to tax on Ecuadorian-source income only.

Corporate residence

Corporate residence is determined by the place of incorporation. For foreign branches, it is the place stated in the domiciliary deed.

Other taxes

Value-added tax (VAT)

VAT is levied at the rates of either 12% or 0% on the ownership transfer of goods, import of goods and services, as well as services rendered within the country. Royalties and intangible property imported or locally paid are also levied with a 12% VAT.

The following are transactions exempt from VAT:

- In-kind contributions to capital of companies;
- Inheritance and assets obtained from liquidation of companies;
- Transfer of business as a whole, amalgamations, mergers, takeovers and spin-offs;
- Donations to public entities and non-profit organisations; and
- Transfers of shares and securities.

Goods and services, which are subject to 0% rate, are explicitly listed in the law. Among others, the following goods are taxed at a 0% rate upon either importation or local transfer of ownership:

- Most agricultural goods and foodstuff when these remain in their natural state; this includes refrigerated or packaged goods that have not undergone further processing. Also included in this category are milk, meats, sugar, salt, bread, butter and margarine, flour and cooking oil;
- Drugs, medicines and other pharmaceutical products, including raw materials for their production;
- Fertilisers, insecticides, animal foods and similar products, including the raw materials required for processing such goods;
- Agricultural machinery and equipment;
- Goods that are exported; and
- Paper, books, magazines and newspapers.

Among others, the following services are taxed at a 0% rate:

- Transportation of persons and cargo, except air transportation of persons and local air transportation of cargo;
- Book printing services;
- Housing rental;
- Water, electric, sewage and other public services, including garbage collection;
- Financial services; and
- Exported services.

12% VAT paid on imports and local purchases can be deducted from 12% VAT charged on sales or services rendered. The VAT paid on raw materials, fixed assets or components required for the production of goods or rendering of services is also creditable when the final product is considered taxable at 12%. Similarly, VAT paid on raw materials, services, components or fixed assets necessary for production of export goods is also recoverable.

VAT may not be recovered (by either tax credit or other means) on the local acquisition or import of goods and services that are used for the production of goods or services taxed at a rate of 0%. In these cases, nonrecoverable VAT is part of the cost of

Ecuador

the purchased goods and services or an expense, both deductible for income tax computation purposes.

Companies designated by the government as special taxpayers are required to withhold 30% of VAT applicable on their purchases of goods taxed at 12% and 70% of VAT applicable on their purchase of services taxed at 12%, except with respect to services rendered by professionals, in which case 100% of VAT charged must be withheld.

Municipal assets tax
The municipal asset tax is levied on all individuals and companies required to keep accounting records in accordance with Ecuadorian tax legislation. This tax is levied at a rate of 1.5 per thousand (or 0.15%) of total assets less current and contingent liabilities as shown on the balance sheet.

Municipal real estate tax
The city government assesses the municipal property tax, which ranges from between 0.25 per thousand and 5 per thousand (0.025% to 0.5%) of the commercial value of the property, as determined by valuation carried out every five years by the city government, for both urban and rural properties (rural property is taxed at a maximum of 3 per thousand or 0.3%).

Municipal tax on capital gain in the transfer of real estate (Plusvalía)
The real estate transfer tax applies to the transfer of real estate. It is taxed at 10% of profits, except in the case of first transfer after September 2004. In that case the rate is half of the property's value.

Special consumption tax (Impuesto a los Consumos Especiales – ICE)
This tax is imposed on domestic and imported goods which are explicitly listed in the law. This tax is levied at a progressive rate from 5% to 35% on certain automobiles and 15% on airplanes, helicopters and boats. The tax on cigarettes, alcoholic beverages and soft drinks ranges from 10% to 150%. It must be paid monthly and is collected upon sales. The ICE tax base for imported goods is the "*ad valorem*" value.

Foreign assets tax (Impuesto a los Activos en el Exterior)
The tax base is the average monthly balance of cash deposits held in foreign entities by private entities registered in the stock market and regulated by the Superintendent of Banks and Companies. Monthly tax rate is 0.084%.

Remittance tax (Impuesto a la Salida de Divisas)
Remittance tax is imposed on the transfer of money abroad in cash or through cheques, transfers or courier of any nature carried out with or without the mediation of the Ecuadorian financial system. Beginning January 2010, the rate is 2%.

Branch income

Distributed or retained branch profits (as well as reinvested profits of oil companies operating under risk-service contracts) are taxed at a 25% rate. No further taxes are payable when profits are remitted to headquarters. Re-invested profits are levied at a 15% income tax rate. Companies must increase their share capital within the following fiscal year to be beneficiaries of the income tax rate reduction. There is not a branch remittance tax in Ecuador.

Income determination

Inventory valuation

The valuation of inventories is not specifically treated in the tax law. Ecuadorian accounting standards must be applied; inventories are carried at acquisition cost. Last-in, first-out (LIFO); first-in, first-out (FIFO) and average cost methods are used, with average cost being the preferred method.

Capital gains

Occasional gains from stock sales are tax exempt, and gains from investment funds and investment trusts are income tax exempt, as long as the income has been taxed at source. Gains on the sale of fixed assets are added to the taxable base and levied at regular income tax rates, except gains derived from occasional sales of real estate, which is tax exempt.

Dividends

Dividends received by a resident company from another resident company's profits that have been subject to tax are exempt. However, dividends paid to tax havens are taxable subject to withholding at source.

Inter-company dividends

Dividends received by an Ecuadorian company from another domestic company are exempt from income taxes. The same treatment applies to dividends received by a branch of a foreign company from a domestic company. Dividends remitted abroad to non-tax haven countries are not subject to additional income tax withholding.

Foreign income

Foreign-source income is considered exempt for tax purposes; companies must demonstrate the income tax payment abroad. Tax haven countries are not considered to be part of this exemption.

Stock dividends

The distribution of stock dividends is not subject to tax.

Deductions

Depreciation and amortisation

Straight-line depreciation at rates specified by law applies. The director of the Internal Revenue Service of Ecuador authorises higher rates of depreciation in cases such as obsolescence, excessive use and faster than expected wear-out of assets.

Depreciation rates are as follows:

	%
Real estate (except land), aircraft, naval crafts, and similar property	5
Facilities, machinery, equipment and furniture	10
Vehicles, trucks and tractors used for construction	20
Computer equipment and software	33

Depreciation rates apply to the cost of assets.

Ecuador

Net operating losses

The carryforward of losses is allowed to a maximum of five years, with an amortisation limit of 25% per year over the taxable base. There is no loss carryback.

Payments to foreign affiliates

In most cases, payments made abroad are deductible, as long as income taxes have been withheld (at the rate of 25% over the taxable base). Professional fees, royalties, commissions or any payment made abroad is subject to withholding at a rate of 25% over the taxable base. Payments on imports are deductible and are not subject to withholding of income taxes.

Taxes

Taxes, rates, levies and contributions to the social security system related to the generation of taxable income are deductible. Interest and fines paid as penalties imposed on late payments of tax obligations and on income tax payments are not deductible for income tax calculation purposes.

Other significant items

The tax law refers to other deductions, the most important of which are as follows:

- Organisation, experimentation and preoperational expenses. These expenses are to be amortised over five years at the rate of 20% per year.
- Interest on debts incurred for business purposes.
- Foreign loan interests are deductible to the extent that they are registered with the Ecuadorian Central Bank (ECB) and do not exceed the maximum rates established by ECB. Interest on foreign loans that are not registered with the ECB are non-deductible.
- Intangible assets are amortised either within the terms specified in the contract or over a 20-year period.

Statutory profit sharing

According to the Ecuadorian Labour Code, companies must distribute 15% of their pre-tax earnings amongst their employees. This profit sharing is a deductible expense for corporate income tax purposes.

Financial system

As a general rule, operations that exceed USD 5,000 should be performed through any institution of the Ecuadorian financial system, otherwise such operations will become non-deductible.

Thin capitalisation rule

A thin capitalisation rule on foreign loans granted by related parties at a 3:1 ratio over equity must be considered. For branches of a foreign corporation, only capital must be considered.

Group taxation

Group taxation is not permitted.

Tax incentives

Social security system
Taxes, rates, levies and contributions to the social security system that are related to the generation of taxable income are deductible.

Net employee increase and handicapped employees
An amount equivalent to one and a half and one times remunerations of handicapped and new employees, respectively, can be considered an additional deduction for income tax calculation purposes. New employees must be working with the company for at least six months.

Withholding taxes (WHT)

Dividends paid to a non-resident generally are not subject to WHT. However, dividends paid to a non-resident in a tax haven are subject to WHT at source.

Interest paid on loans obtained from non-residents is subject to a 25% WHT unless reduced by tax treaty. Royalties paid to a non-resident are subject to 25% WHT unless reduced by tax treaty.

Revenues from occasional services provided by non-resident individuals are levied at 25% of the total revenue. Payments made abroad to non-resident individuals and companies are subject to a 25% withholding tax. Other payments made abroad, other than dividends or profits, are subject to a 25% income tax withholding. For 2009, a 5% income tax withholding applied on interest remitted abroad. The rates at which the loan has been contracted should not exceed the rates set by the ECB.

Periodically, the Internal Revenue Service of Ecuador establishes withholding percentages on local payments, which are not greater than 10%. Local payments (including interest paid by financial institutions) are subject to 1%, 2% or 8% withholding.

Tax treaties
As a member of the Andean Community, Ecuador has adopted Decision 578, which provides relief from double taxation for individual or company members. Furthermore, Ecuador has similar tax treaties with Belgium, Brazil, Canada, Chile, France, Germany, Italy, Mexico, Romania, Spain and Switzerland.

Tax administration

Returns
The fiscal year is the calendar year from 1 January to 31 December. The tax system operates on the basis of self-assessment, with subsequent inspection by the tax authorities.

Payment of tax
Tax filing deadlines begin on April 10 and continue up to April 28. The tax due dates are determined by the ninth digit of the company's Tax Identification Number (TIN).

Corporations are required to keep accounting records and must make advance income tax payments based on the following calculation:

Ecuador

The sum of 0.4% of the taxable income plus 0.4% of total assets plus 0.2% of total equity, and 0.2% of deductible expenses less withholdings taxes held on the fiscal year.

Advance payments are made in two equal payments in July and September. Differences between advance payments and the income tax returns must be paid. If the difference is in favour of the taxpayer, the taxpayer must request a reimbursement from the Internal Revenue Service.

Other Issues

Transfer pricing
The transfer pricing regime is based on the Organisation for Economic Co-operation and Development (OECD) guidelines. Related party transactions must be carried out at arm's length. Documentation requirements exist.

Corporate taxes in Egypt

For more information, contact:

Sherif Mansour
PricewaterhouseCoopers\Mansour & Co
Plot No 211
Second Sector
City Centre
New Cairo 11835, Egypt
Tel: +20 2 2759 7700 ext. 7888
Email: sherif.mansour@eg.pwc.com

E

Significant developments

On 10 June 2005, the Egyptian Cabinet passed a new income tax law that replaced Law 157 of 1981. The following information summarises some of the developments in the tax system under the new law.

Corporate definitions
The term "corporate" covers the following definitions under the new tax law:

1. Juridical Persons – The following shall be considered juridical persons:
   - Associations of capital and partnerships under whatever the law they are subject to, as well as de facto corporations;
   - Cooperative societies and their unions subject to the exemptions prescribed for them by the law;
   - Public authorities and other public juridical persons, with regard to the taxable activity they exercise, subject to the exemptions prescribed in the laws establishing them; and
   - Foreign banks, companies and establishments even if their head offices are abroad and their branches are in Egypt.
2. Corporation de facto – A de facto corporation is a partnership established between natural persons without fulfilling the procedures of establishment or registration, with the exception of cases resulting from inheriting an individual firm.

Taxes on corporate income

The corporate tax rate is 20% for the income generated for all types of business activities except for oil exploration companies, the profits of which are taxed at 40.55%. In addition, the profits of the Suez Canal Authority, the Egyptian Petroleum Authority and the Central Bank of Egypt are taxable at a rate of 40%.

The foreign tax paid by a resident company on its profits earned abroad is deductible from the tax payable in Egypt; however, losses incurred abroad are not deductible.

Non-resident corporations and partnerships pay taxes on income derived from their permanent establishments (PE) in Egypt.

Egypt

Corporate residence

A foreign business can incorporate under the Egyptian law, choosing one of several legal forms including Joint Stock Company, Limited Liability Company, Branch or a Representative Office.

Corporations and partnerships are classified as residents of Egypt if they meet one of the following conditions:

- The entity is established according to the Egyptian law;
- The government or a public authority owns more than 50% of the capital of the entity; and/or
- The effective place of management is in Egypt.

The executive regulations of the law indicate that Egypt is considered as the effective place of management if the entity meets two of the following conditions:

- Managerial decisions take place in Egypt;
- Members of the board of directors hold their meetings in Egypt;
- Members of the board of directors reside in Egypt; and/or
- The major shareholders (owners of more than 50% of the shares or voting rights) reside in Egypt.

Other taxes

Sales tax
The standard sales tax rate is 10% of the value of commodities (except for those referred to in special schedules of the law) and 5% to 10% for specific services.

The Sales Tax Department is responsible for assessing the tax on the sales of locally produced goods and imported goods, except for those exempted by a special decree.

Consequently, all natural persons and legal entities are required to collect general sales tax and remit it to the Sales Tax Department. This includes manufacturers and providers of taxable services and every importer of commodities or taxable services. In addition, there are plans to introduce a newly developed sales tax law.

Stamp tax
There are two distinct types of stamp tax, which is imposed on legal documents, deeds, banking transactions, company formation, insurance premiums and other transactions, as follows:

- The nominal stamp tax is imposed on documents, regardless of their value. The tax rate for items such as contracts is EGP 1 for each paper; and
- Percentage or proportionate stamp tax is levied based on the value of transactions.

A proportional tax at the rate of 0.4% is imposed on the balances of credit facilities and loans and advances provided by Egyptian banks or branches of foreign banks during the financial year, with the bank paying 0.1% on the balance at the end of each quarter of the year. The bank and the customer each bear half of the tax.

Loans from other establishments are not subject to this tax.

Real estate taxes

The new real estate tax law was effective from January 2010. The new law takes into consideration the different variables that can affect the value of a property, such as location, value of similar buildings and the economic situation of the district in which the property is located. This is to be updated every five years.

Branch income

The Egyptian tax treatment of a branch is similar to that of a Joint Stock Company/ Limited Liability Company.

In addition, the Egyptian tax law treats every company in a group of companies as a separate legal entity. Thus, affiliated companies or subsidiaries can not shift the profits/ losses within the group.

Branches of foreign corporations operating in Egypt receive tax treatment identical to that of corporate entities for the results of their activities in Egypt.

Treaties allow Egypt to tax only those business profits attributable to PE of foreign enterprises in Egypt.

A branch, but not a subsidiary, may deduct a 'head office charge' of an amount up to 7% of its taxable income.

Income determination

Capital gains

A foreign company is taxed on all capital gains realised in Egypt. However, capital gains on the sale of Egyptian securities listed on the Egyptian Stock Exchange are not taxable.

Dividends

Dividends distributed by a company residing in Egypt are not subject to corporate taxes. Conversely, dividends that non-resident companies distribute are subject to the Egyptian corporate tax, after deducting foreign taxes paid abroad.

Foreign income

Income from any source, domestic or foreign, received by a corporation within Egypt is subject to corporate tax. The scope of tax covers the activities carried out inside and outside Egypt, which are administered or managed within Egypt.

The foreign tax paid by a resident company on its profits incurred abroad is deductible from the tax payable in Egypt; however, losses incurred abroad are not deductible.

Stock dividends

Stock dividends receive the same treatment as ordinary dividends.

Transfer pricing

Transfer pricing rules were introduced in Egypt for the first time by Law No. 91 for the year 2005. The law introduced the arm's-length principal, specifying that any transaction between related parties should be at arm's length (i.e., market value).

Egypt

The law does not specify penalties with regard to transfer pricing. However, the law states that the Egyptian tax authorities may adjust the pricing of transactions between related parties if the transaction involves elements that would not be included in transactions between non-related parties, and whose purpose is to shift the tax burden to tax exempt or non-taxable entities. Where this is the case, the tax authorities may determine the taxable profit on the basis of the neutral price. The acceptable methods for determining such neutral price, according to the rule of the law, are as follows:

- Comparative free price same as Comparable Uncontrolled Price method (CUP);
- Total cost with an added margin of profit (same as Cost Plus method); and
- Resale price.

The law does not provide any documentation specifications and no guidelines have been issued.

For the time being it is advisable for all multinational enterprises established in Egypt to locate their group/company's transfer pricing policy, review it, and assess what documentation is available to prove this policy.

Deductions

Depreciation
The new tax law changed the depreciation rates for tax purposes to the following:

- 5% of the cost of purchasing, establishing, developing, and renovating buildings and establishments is deductible based on the straight-line method;
- 10% of the cost of purchasing, developing, and improving intangible assets is deductible based on the straight-line method;
- Computers, information systems, software, and data storage sets are depreciated at a 50% rate on a declining balance method; and
- All others assets are depreciated at a rate of 25% of the depreciation basis for each fiscal year, on a declining balance method.

Accelerated depreciation
A company may deduct 30% accelerated depreciation from the cost of new or used machines and equipment used in industries during the first fiscal year of their employment.

Net operating losses
A company may carry losses forward for a period not to exceed five years. Nevertheless, if a change occurs in the ownership of its capital exceeding 50% of the shares, stocks, or the voting rights, and if the company changes its activity, the company cannot carry the losses forward.

In general, companies cannot carry losses back, except for contracting companies, which are allowed a loss carryback period of five years.

Other significant items
Donations to the government are tax deductible, and donations to Egyptian charities are deductible up to 10% of taxable income.

Payments to head office

A branch may deduct head-office charges up to 7% of its taxable income. Refer to Article No. 74 of the Egyptian executive regulations of the Law 91/2005 (ER). Moreover, the branch or subsidiary should withhold taxes before the payment of interest, royalties, and service fees to non-resident foreign corporations or affiliates.

Non tax-deductible costs

The following items are not tax-deductible costs:

- Reserves and appropriations of all different types;
- Financial fines and penalties paid by the taxpayer because he or one of his subordinates has committed a deliberate felony or misdemeanour;
- Income tax payable according to the income tax law;
- Interest settled on loans that exceeds twofold the credit and discount rates announced by the Central Bank;
- Interest on loans and debts of all different kinds, as paid to non-taxable or tax-exempt individuals;
- Profit shares, distributed dividends, and the attendance fees paid to shareholders for attending the general assembly's meetings;
- Compensation and allowances obtained by the chairmen and board members; and
- Workers profit share to be distributed according to the law.

Group taxation

There are no group taxation rules in Egypt.

Tax incentives

Egypt offers no specific tax incentives. Under the new income tax law, the tax incentives granted to investment companies were abolished.

Withholding taxes (WHT)

A corporation paying invoices must withhold 0.5% to 5% of payments, depending on the services and commodities, to local taxpayers and remit them quarterly to the Tax Department.

Payments of interest, royalties, and services by a domestic corporation to foreign or non-resident bodies are subject to WHT as follows:

Interest

Interest expenses are deductible for tax purposes after offsetting any tax-exempt interest income.

Interest expense deductions are limited to an interest rate that does not exceed twice the discount rate as determined by the Central Bank of Egypt at the beginning of the calendar year in which the tax year ends.

Interest on loans with a three-year term or more entered into by private sector companies are exempt from WHT, while loans of less than three years are subject to 20% tax on interest. However, an applicable tax treaty between Egypt and the foreign country may result in the reduction of such tax rate.

Egypt

New ministerial decree
A new ministerial decree was issued on 29 December 2009, declaring that the reduced rate of WHT on interest or royalties provided by an applicable double tax treaty (DTT) should be ignored when withholding the tax. However, under certain conditions, the foreign recipient of payments would be able to get a refund for the amount resulting from the variance between the normal rate of 20% and the reduced treaty rate.

Tax treaties
Egypt has concluded DTTs with about 50 countries, which could change the tax treatment of transactions carried out between Egyptian entities and residents of a treaty country.

Royalties
Royalty payments are subject to the WHT. However, an applicable DTT signed between Egypt and the foreign country might result in a reduction in this rate. *(Please refer to the new ministerial decree affecting the treatment of interest and royalty payments.)*

Service payments
Service payments may be exempt from the WHT if there is an applicable DTT signed between Egypt and the foreign country.

Tax administration

Tax returns
The tax year is the financial year of the taxpayer. The taxpayer is required to assess taxes due for every financial year and settle them with the tax return.

Payment of tax
A taxpayer is subject to a WHT system for all money received from other taxpayers. These advance payments are deducted from taxes assessed per the tax return, and the balance is payable in a lump sum at the date of submitting the tax return.

Other issues

In Egypt, there are several laws regulating projects, such as: the Investment Law, Companies' Law, Tax Law, Capital Market Law, etc. These laws cover all investment activities in Egypt; whether in the industrial or commercial field.

Changes to the Egyptian law
Since May 2008, Egypt witnessed many changes in its economy as a result of the Law no. 114. This law has been issued with the intention of decreasing the gap between those who are financially secure and those who are not.

The Law was designed to increase the tax rates imposed on several commodities and services, as well as decreasing the subsidies of some (e.g., petroleum) from one side, and increasing the basic salaries of employees (especially government employees) from the other.

The main points of the Law are as follows:

- All government employees are granted a special monthly increase at a rate of 30% of April 2008's basic salary. This is optional for private companies, and is exempt from tax for both government and private company employees;
- An amendment to law 147 for the year 1984 with the imposition of a state development duty on vehicles and driving licenses;
- An increase in general sales tax rates imposed on cigarettes and petroleum products;
- An abolishment of law no. 17 for the year 1991 which previously provided an exemption of treasury bills from income tax;
- An addition of a final paragraph to article 29 of the law of investment guarantees and incentives (Law 8 of 1997) which indicates that in all cases, projects in the fields of: fertiliser industries, iron and steel, oil processing, and natural gas processing, transport, and liquidification, will not be authorised for establishment under the free zone system; and
- All licenses of investment projects established under free zone systems existing on the enactment date of this law (5 May 2008) will terminate in the fields of: fertiliser industries, iron and steel, oil processing, and natural gas processing, transport, and liquidification.

E

Corporate taxes in El Salvador

For more information, contact:

Edgar Mendoza
PricewaterhouseCoopers
Centro Profesional Presidente
Avenida La Revolución y Calle
Circunvalación, Colonia San Benito
San Salvador
El Salvador
Tel: +503 2 243 5844
Email: edgar.mendoza@gt.pwc.com

Significant developments

In mid-2007, the tax authorities improved the system for filing and paying the monthly tax returns electronically (i.e., value-added tax (VAT) and income tax advance payment returns). Since 2008 this benefit was also extended to the annual corporate income tax (CIT) returns.

These improvements include:

- Reduction of steps needed to complete registration;
- Reduction of steps needed to complete the process of filing tax returns;
- Speed-up of payment process by providing more effective links to the banks accepting payment in the local financial system;
- The system issues a certified copy of the tax return filed and payment; and
- Previously, a formal contract had to be downloaded and installed but now the taxpayer only has to check a box to accept or not check the box to reject the stated terms and conditions.

Recent changes in legislation approved on December 2009 include:

- Tax Code: transfer pricing regulations, new obligations on representations, billing and reports;
- VAT: new reform on VAT and restrictions on deduction of tax credits; and
- ISR: new income taxed in El Salvador, and new conditions/deductions for costs and expenses.

Taxes on corporate income

The corporate income tax rate applicable is 25%.

Taxable income is net of costs and expenses considered necessary for generating and maintaining the related source of income, and other deductions allowed by law. Gross income, on the other hand, comprises income or profits collected or accrued, either in cash or in kind, from any sources such as business, capital and all types of products, gains, benefits or profits, whatever their origin might be, as well as condoned debts.

Juridical entities are required to follow the accrual method of accounting, which means that income is reported although not collected, and costs and expenses are reported when incurred and not when paid for.

For tax purposes, income is computed for 12-month periods, also known as taxable periods, and the tax period for juridical entities begins on 1 January and ends on 31 December of each year.

Corporate residence

A company incorporated in El Salvador is a domiciled entity in the country for tax purposes and subject to 25% CIT. Also, branches from foreign companies authorised in El Salvador and/or entities operating as a permanent establishment are considered domiciled for tax purposes and subject to the mentioned income tax rate.

Other taxes

VAT ("Impuesto al Valor Agregado" or IVA)

VAT is levied at a rate of 13% over the taxable amount. As a general rule, the taxable amount is the price or remuneration agreed upon by the parties. For imports, the taxable amount is the customs value.

The following transactions are subject to VAT when performed within the Salvadoran territory:

1. Transfer/sale of tangible movable goods;
2. Withdrawal of tangible movable goods from the inventory made by the company for self-consumption by its partners, directors or personnel;
3. Import of goods and services; and
4. The supply of services of any type whether permanent, regular, continuous or periodic; technical advice and project designs; lease and sublease agreements over tangible goods; lease and sublease agreements over real estate for commercial purposes; lease of services in general; construction of real estate properties or building contracts; auctions; freight, whether inland, air or maritime; lease, sublease and any form of use regarding trademarks.

The following imports are exempt from VAT:

- Imports made by diplomats and consulate representatives of foreign nations with presence in the country according to international agreements adopted by El Salvador;
- Imports made by international organisations to which El Salvador is a party;
- Traveller's luggage according to customs regulations;
- Donations to non-profit organisations;
- Imports made by municipalities, if the goods imported are for the public benefit of the community;
- Imports of machinery by taxpayers duly registered for this purpose which will be part of the taxpayer's fixed assets; and
- Vehicles for public transportation, which can only be transferred after five years.

The following services shall be exempt from VAT:

- Health services rendered by public institutions;
- Lease and sublease of real estate properties for housing;
- Services rendered under a labour relationship, and those rendered by public and municipal employees;

El Salvador

- Cultural public performances authorised by competent authorities;
- Educational services rendered by authorised entities, i.e., "Ministerio de Educación" (the Ministry of Education);
- Interest on deposits and loans, provided by local financial institutions or entities registered at the Salvadoran Central Bank (BCR);
- Interest on securities issued by the government and/or private entities traded through a stock exchange;
- Water supply by public institutions;
- Public transportation; and
- Insurance premiums covering individuals, and reinsurance in general.

Exports are levied at 0% VAT. Foreign source income is not subject to VAT.

VAT taxes paid by a registered taxpayer company on its purchases (tax credits) are credited against VAT taxes charged to its customers (tax debits), on a monthly basis.

Income tax advance payment

A 1.5% tax rate is applied to gross revenues obtained, and paid monthly as advance payments which are applied against the CIT at the end of the year.

Tax on transfer of real estate properties

Transfers of real estate property are taxed according to the value of the real estate, at a tax rate of 3% applicable over amounts exceeding USD 28,571.43.

Tax on simple or sweetened soft drinks

This is an *ad valorem* tax levied at 10% over the selling price to the public as suggested by the manufacturer, importer or distributor, excluding VAT and returnable bottle taxes.

Tax on the production and importation of alcohol and spirits

This tax is levied on domestic or imported alcohol and spirits at rates ranging from 0.0825 and 0.15 over each 1% of alcohol volume per litre or in proportion thereof. At the beginning of 2010 spirits and alcohol also have an *ad valorem* tax levied at 5% over the selling prices to the public as suggested.

Tax on tobacco products

This tax is levied at USD 0.005 per cigarette, cigar, little cigarette or any other tobacco product. Also, an *ad valorem* tax is levied at 39% over the suggested consumer selling price reported, excluding items such as VAT taxes, the specific tax established by the law.

Annual business tax

Companies are required to register themselves with the Registry of Commerce, and pay an annual business licence fee assessed on the company's assets, as follows:

From USD 2,000 to USD 57,150	USD 91.43
From USD 57,151 to USD 114,286	USD 137.14
From USD 114,287 to USD 228,572	USD 228.57
An additional charge for each office, branch or agency property of a company	USD 34.29

If the assets exceed the amount of USD 228,572, there is an additional duty of USD 11.43 for each USD 100,000 or fraction thereof. In any case, the relevant duties are limited to USD 11,428.57.

Social security contributions

Monthly employee's salary USD	Employer's rate
0 – 685.71	7.50%
Over 685.71	0%

Pension fund (AFP Confía)

Monthly employee's salary USD	Employer's rate (%)
0 – 5,354.52	6.75%
Over 5,354.52	0%

Payroll tax

Monthly employee's salary USD	Employer's rate
0 – 685.71	1%
Over 685.71	0%

Municipal taxes

Municipal taxes are assessed according to a progressive tariff list issued by each municipality applicable to the company's assets located in each municipality. Taxes are paid on a monthly basis. The tariff lists are applied separately to commercial, industrial and financial sectors.

Stamp taxes

No stamp taxes are assessed as the pertinent law was abrogated in 1992.

Branch income

In El Salvador tax rates on branch profits are the same as for domestic corporations. No tax is withheld on transfers of profits to the head office provided the entity distributing them reports them and pays the corresponding income tax thereon.

Administrative offices: the law does not provide a separate treatment to administrative offices located in El Salvador. The general regulations in this respect indicate that branches, agencies and/or establishments permanently operating in the country, with owned or leased installed infrastructure, employing domestic staff, and performing their economic activities in a material and perceptible manner in the country are subject to the same taxes as companies duly incorporated.

Income determination

Inventory valuation

For tax purposes, taxpayers are authorised to use any one of the following inventory methods, provided they are technically appropriate for the particular business and are consistently applied and their audit is easy:

- Purchase or manufacturing costs;
- Last purchase costs;
- Direct average allocation costs;
- Average costs;

El Salvador

- Last-in, first-out;
- First-in, first-out;
- Specific methods for fruits and farm products; or
- Specific method for cattle.

Other than the methods enumerated above, taxpayers are not permitted to use other methods for valuing their inventories except with prior authorisation of the tax office, provided that in the latter's judgement, the method in question contains clear determination and bona fide elements available to the office. Once an inventory valuation method is adopted, the taxpayer may not change it without the tax office's prior authorisation.

Capital gains
Capital gains are taxed at a flat rate of 10% of net profits, except when gains are realised within 12 months following the purchase date, as capital gains in this case are taxed as ordinary income. Capital losses can be offset against capital gains only. Whenever capital losses exceed capital gains, the remaining balance may be carried forward to future capital gains within a five-year period.

Inter-company dividends
Profits or dividends remitted or credited to shareholders are non-taxable provided the entity distributing them reported and paid the correspondent income taxes.

Foreign income
Under the territoriality source of income principle, extraterritorial income is not taxable in the country, with the exception of income/other benefits from securities and other financing operations.

Stock dividends
Stock dividends are not taxable provided the entity distributing them reported and paid the correspondent income taxes.

Deductions

All business expenses considered necessary to produce taxable income and/or maintain income sources (freight, marketing, power, telecommunications, water, salaries, lease contracts, merchandise and transport insurance, fuel and interest paid on loans used by income generating sources, and similar ones, among other items) are deductible for income tax purposes.

Depreciation
Depreciation is normally calculated by a straight line method.

	Rate %
Buildings	5
Machinery	20
Vehicles	25
Other movable assets	50

Depletion
Amortisation of new software is admitted at a constant and maximum 25% over purchase or production costs.

Interest expense

If a loan is made by a foreign company or bank that is not registered by the Central Bank, income tax will be withheld at 20%. If the foreign bank is registered by the Central Bank in 2010 then 10% income tax will be withheld.

Net operating losses

Operating losses cannot be carried forward to future years. Salvadorian legislation does not allow for the carryback of losses except for capital losses.

Payments to foreign affiliates

Remittance of royalties, interest income and service fees to foreign affiliates are deductible provided proper contracts are in place and withholding tax of 20% is applied and if these services have actually been received. Payments to entities located in tax haven regimes, are subject to a withholding tax rate of 25%.

Taxes

Other than penalties and interest charges on unpaid taxes, income, VAT and conveyance of real estate property taxes, and state and municipal taxes and duties on imports of goods and services rendered by the company are not deductible.

Other significant items

The deductibility of charitable donations is limited to 20% of the amount resulting from deducting the donation amount from the donor's net income of the respective tax period.

Amortisation of goodwill, trademarks and other similar intangible assets are not deductible for income tax purposes.

Group taxation

Tax grouping

There are no grouping rules in El Salvador between independent entities.

Tax incentives

El Salvador offers a wide range of incentives to attract foreign investment and drive new commercial and industrial developments. There are no restrictions on foreign ownership or on mergers, acquisitions or joint ventures. There are three specific laws in El Salvador that seek to encourage foreign investment by improving the country's competitiveness in all areas involving the granting of tax incentives. These laws are the Industrial and Commercial Free Zone Law, Law of International Services and the Export Reactivation Law.

The Industrial and Commercial Free Zone Law No. 405 dated 3 September 1998, grants companies the following incentives:

* Income tax exemption;
* VAT exemption;
* Municipal tax exemption;
* Exemption from real estate transfer taxes when land is intended to be used for productive activities;

El Salvador

- Exemption from duties for imports on machinery, raw materials, equipment and intermediate goods used for production; and
- Option to sell merchandise or services linked to international trade produced in the free zone in the Salvadoran market is permitted as long as companies pay the corresponding import taxes, income tax, VAT, and municipal taxes on the final goods admitted.

Any foreign company may establish and function in a free zone or bonded warehouse if they are engaged in: production, assembly, manufacturing, processing, transformation, or commercialisation of goods and services; and/or rendering of services linked to international or regional trade, such as gathering, packaging and repackaging, cargo consolidation, distribution of merchandise and other activities connected or complementary to them.

The most recently approved Law of International Services No. 431, dated 11 October 2007, grants the same benefits as the Free Zone Law, but the beneficiaries are companies operating in Service Centres specially created according to this law and dedicated to international services as defined therein.

The Export Reactivation Law No. 460 ("Ley de Reactivación de las Exportaciones") dated 15 March 1990, grants reimbursement of 6% free on board (FOB) value of exports destined outside the region.

Withholding taxes (WHT)

Payments or amounts credited to non-residents arising from income obtained in El Salvador are subject to a 20% withholding tax. Income earned in El Salvador covers income from assets located in the country, and from any activities performed or capital invested in the land, and from services rendered or used in the national territory, regardless of whether they are provided or paid outside the country. Income from services used in the country is income earned in El Salvador by the service provider, irrespective of whether the relevant income generating activities are performed abroad. Payments to foreign entities located in tax haven regimes are subject to a withholding tax rate of 25%.

Payments to domiciled individuals with respect to services rendered other than under a labour relationship, are subject to a 10% withholding tax.

The acquisition of intangible goods among domiciled entities in the country is subject to a 10% withholding tax.

Tax administration

Taxing authorities: national taxes, fees and other contributions on all types of goods, services and income in El Salvador are levied by the National Congress, while local governments (municipalities) may suggest contribution rates and propose their approval to the National Congress by way of a specific law.

Ministry of Finance ("Hacienda"): The Ministry controls the State's finances and defines and guides the government's financial policy, and also harmonises, directs and implements its policies on taxation, through the following agencies:

- Internal Revenue Service ("Dirección General de Impuestos Internos" or DGII): was created by Law No. 451, dated 22 February 1990, replacing the former Direct Revenues Services, and is charged with managing and collecting the country's main internal revenues.
- Customs Authority ("Dirección General de Aduanas" or DGA): DGA was created by Law No. 903, dated 14 December 2005, replacing the former Customs Revenues Service, and its main function is the exercise of its customs powers, to facilitate and control international trade within its domain, and monitor and collect duties and taxes imposed upon merchandise entering and exiting the territory.

Returns
VAT returns are filed on a monthly basis within the first 10 working days of each month following the period under taxation.

In addition, public and private legal entities, domiciled in the country for tax purposes, other than farm and cattle concerns, are required to make income tax advance payments at 1.5% of gross revenues. These advance payments are due, together with the corresponding return, within 10 working days following the corresponding calendar month.

CIT annual returns must be filed each year no later than 30 April, following the end of the year under taxation. In El Salvador the fiscal year is from 1 January to 31 December.

These requirements are mandatory irrespective of the fact that no income taxes are ultimately payable.

Payment of tax
Taxes are due on the date established for filing the tax returns. In El Salvador tax payments are made together with the filing of tax returns, and payments shall be made at the banks of the local financial system.

Corporate taxes in Equatorial Guinea

For more information, contact:

Dominique Taty
Fidafrica SA
Immeuble Alpha 2000
20th Floor
Rue Gourgas – Plateau
Abidjan 01
Côte d'Ivoire
Tel: +225 20 31 54 67
Email: d.taty@ci.pwc.com

Significant developments

There have been no significant tax regulatory developments regarding corporate taxation in the past year.

Taxes on corporate income

The corporate income tax rate is 35%.

Corporate residence

If a legal entity exceeds a total of three months within a calendar year or a total of six months within two calendar years performing activities in Equatorial Guinea, the legal entity is considered as resident. On the contrary, a non-resident company is, according to the regulations in force, a company, which spends less than three months in Equatorial Guinea performing its activities.

Other taxes

Social security
Employers contribute 1% of gross salary to the worker protection fund (Fondo de Proteccion del Trabajador) and 21.5% to the National Social Security Fund (INSESO). This is done monthly.

Minimum income tax
Minimum income tax is 1% of the turnover of the company for the previous year.

Transfer tax
For the transfer of goods between residents and non-residents, there is a 3% tax on the value of the consideration.

Real estate transfers between residents are taxed at the rate of 5%. The rate increases to 25% on real estate transfers between residents and non-residents.

Value-added tax (VAT)
VAT is 15% in Equatorial Guinea.

Real property tax

Urban property tax equals 1% of 40% of the value of the land and building on such land. Rural property tax is XAF 100 for each hectare or fraction thereof.

Stamp taxes

Stamp duties are payable on a variety of instruments and transactions and vary depending on the contract.

Branch income

Branch income is treated the same as corporate income. *See Taxes on corporate income.* There is no branch remittance tax.

Income determination

Inventory valuation

Inventory is generally stated at market value.

Capital gains

Capital gains are usually subject to corporate income tax. Some exemptions are possible.

Dividends

All dividends received by a resident company are subject to corporate tax. However, the recipient company may offset any domestic tax withheld from dividends against its company tax liability.

A participation exemption applies so that only 10% of the net dividends received by a corporate shareholder is subject to tax if the:

* Shareholder holds at least 25% of shares; and
* Shareholder holds these shares for at least two consecutive years.

Dividends received by foreign shareholders are subject to a 25% tax.

Inter-company dividends

Whenever an incorporated company or a limited company has, either registered shares in an incorporated company or interest in a limited company, the net proceeds of the shares of stock or the interest in the second company earned through the first during the fiscal year will be deducted from the total net profit of the parent company, minus a quarter of expenses and liens. This proportional part is established at 10% of the amount of these proceeds, and represents the management expenses already deducted from overhead.Nevertheless, this provision is only applicable in the following conditions:

1. That shares of stock or interest owned by the parent company represent at least 25% of the capital of the subsidiary; and
2. That the shares of stock or interest conferred in the share issue have always remained registered in the name of the participating company and the latter is committed to keeping them as registered for at least two consecutive years.

Equatorial Guinea

Foreign income

Resident corporations are taxed on their worldwide income. Controlled foreign company legislation applies if at least 35% of share capital is held by a resident.

Non-resident entities are subject to a 10% withholding tax on gross income derived from sources in Equatorial Guinea.

Deductions

Depreciations

	%
Structures:	
Commercial, industrial buildings, garages, workshops and hangars	5
Processing booth	5
Dams and dykes	5
Factories	5
Residential houses	5
Removable or temporary buildings	20
Electric ovens	10
Material and permanent tools:	
Steam boiler	10
Cement vat	5
Electric transmission cables – in final material	15
Electric transmission cables – in temporary material	20
Oil refinery machines	20
Hydraulic dams	10
Compression dams	10
Motors or heavy oils	10
Oil deposits	10
High output heavy-duty transformers	10
Steam turbines and machines	10
Mobile material:	
Mechanical kneaders	15
Excavators	15
Hogsheads, brewery, distillation or experimentation vats	10
Wood-carving machines or devices	20
Purification machines or devices	10
Lamination machines	10
Light machinery, lathes and similar items	20
Manufacturing material, including its tools	20
Drills	20
Small tools	100
Transportation material:	
Roads	25
Naval and air material	20
Containers	20
Automobile material: Light, used in city	25

	%
Automobile material: Light rental or school vehicle	33.33
Automobile material: Heavy (trucks)	33.33
Tractors	20
Tractors used by foresters	33.33
Material for port manipulation: Lift vehicles	20
Material for port manipulation: Cranes	10
Furnishings and facilities:	
Facilities, layouts and development	20
Office furnishings	10
Office material	15
Computer material	25
Reprographic material	33.33
Ships or fishing boats	15
Hotels, coffee shops and restaurants:	
Pots, glassware, kitchen utensils	50
Laundry	33.33
Silverware	20
Decorative material	20
Carpeting, curtains, painting	25
Refrigerators, air conditioning	25
Kitchen ovens	20
Material subjected to the action of chemical products:	
Buckets, containers, receptacles or diffusers of chemical products	20
Product recycling devices	20
Bleaching devices	20
Baking devices	20
Fixed asset expenses	20

E

Interest
No thin capitalisation rules exist in Equatorial Guinea.

Net operating losses
Net operating losses can be carried forward for three years (five years if in the oil and gas industry). Losses cannot be carried back. Losses of one entity cannot be transferred to another entity in a reorganisation. Except for new companies, companies with losses for three consecutive years will be de-registered from the tax registry.

Payment to foreign affiliates
There is a deduction limit of 50% of the intermediary tax result for technical assistance.

Group taxation

Equatorial Guinea law does not provide for taxation of groups.

Equatorial Guinea

Tax incentives

Some exemptions are approved for some specific economic sectors (oil and gas exploration, public work, etc.). Investment law also provides tax exemptions.

There is no foreign tax credit.

Withholding taxes (WHT)

WHT is 6.25% on payments to residents.

There is a 10% tax on interest, royalties, and incomes earned in Equatorial Guinea by non-residents. This is not a withholding tax in principle but tax authorities consider it as a WHT. Dividends paid to non-residents are subject to 25% WHT.

Withholding tax on the oil and gas sector
The tax regime of the 6.25% or the 10% WHT linked to the oil and gas sector is defined by Sections 466 to 477 of the Tax Code.

In Equatorial Guinea, according to Section 461-2 of the Tax Code:

* A 6.25% withholding tax is imposed in the oil and gas sector on payments made to a resident registered entity;
* A 10% withholding tax is imposed in the oil and gas sector on payments made to a non-registered entity.

The tax basis is composed of the total amount paid to the provider.

Withholding tax on movable incomes
There is a withholding tax on movable incomes paid to non-residents.

Tax administration

A company's tax year must correspond with its financial year.

Returns
Corporate income tax returns must be filed within the first four months of the year following the taxable fiscal year.

The minimum company tax of 1% of the previous year's turnover is payable by 31 March with final instalment paid on 30 April.

Payment of tax
Payment of the corporate income tax must be made within fifteen days of the date of receipt of the tax liquidation from the Tax Authorities.

Penalties
Penalties apply for late payment, failure to pay and understatement of tax liability.

Corporate taxes in Estonia

For more information, contact:

Villi Tõntson
PricewaterhouseCoopers AS
Pärnu mnt 15
EE10141 Tallinn
Estonia
Tel: +372 614 1970
Email: villi.tontson@ee.pwc.com

E

Significant developments

Estonia is regarded as offering a relatively favourable income tax regime as all undistributed corporate profits are tax exempt. However, the provision in the tax legislation that would have further reduced the income tax rate was abolished in 2009 and thus the 21% income tax rate continues to be levied in 2010. The previous version of the legislation gradually reduced the income tax rate by 1% per annum until reaching an 18% income tax rate in 2012.

On 1 January 2010, the tax treaties with Isle of Man, Israel and Macedonia became effective.

Taxes on corporate income

All undistributed corporate profits are tax exempt. This exemption covers both active (e.g., trading) and passive (e.g., dividends, interest, royalties) types of income, as well as capital gains from the sale of all types of assets, including shares, securities and immovable property. This tax regime is available to Estonian companies and permanent establishments (PE) of foreign companies that are registered in Estonia.

The taxation of corporate profits is postponed until the profits are distributed as dividends or deemed to be distributed, such as in the case of transfer pricing adjustments, expenses and payments that do not have a business purpose, fringe benefits, gifts, donations and representation expenses.

Distributed profits are generally subject to the 21% corporate income tax (21/79 on the net amount of profit distribution). For example, a company that has profits of 100 available for distribution can distribute dividends of 79, on which it must pay corporate income tax of 21.

From the Estonian perspective, this tax is considered a corporate income tax and not a withholding tax, so the tax rate is not affected by an applicable tax treaty. Certain distributions are exempt from such tax *(see Inter-company dividends section)*.

Corporate residence

A legal entity is considered resident in Estonia for tax purposes if it is established under Estonian law. There is no management and control test for the purpose of determining corporate residency. All tax treaty tie-breakers for legal entities are based on competent

Estonia

authority procedures. Estonian general partnerships and limited partnerships have legal identity and therefore are considered residents in Estonia for tax purposes.

A PE (including a branch registered in the Commercial Register) of a foreign entity is deemed to be a non-resident taxpayer.

Other taxes

Value-added tax (VAT)
The following transactions are subject to Estonian VAT:

* Taxable supplies of goods and services (the place of supply of which is Estonia);
* Taxable imports of goods; and
* Taxable intra-community acquisitions of goods.

The standard VAT rate is 20%. A reduced rate of 9% is applied to books, periodicals with few exceptions, hotel accommodation services and listed pharmaceuticals.

The VAT rate on the export of goods and certain services is 0% (i.e., exemption with credit). Some services, such as health care, insurance, certain financial and transactions with securities, are exempt (i.e., exempt without credit).

Transactions in real estate are generally exempt from VAT but there are certain significant exceptions (e.g., transactions in new and significantly renovated buildings). Taxpayers can elect to add VAT to real estate transactions if certain conditions are met.

If the taxable supplies of Estonian businesses or a PE of a foreign business in Estonia exceed EEK 250,000 in a calendar year, VAT registration is required. Voluntary registration is also possible. Certain transactions of foreign businesses require Estonian VAT registration without any threshold.

The VAT accounting period is generally a calendar month, and the VAT should be declared and paid on or before the twentieth day of the following month.

Under certain conditions, a European Union (EU) taxable person that is not registered for VAT in Estonia will be entitled to a refund of input VAT paid in Estonia. Non-EU taxable persons are entitled to claim VAT refunds based on reciprocity.

On 1 January 2008, Estonia implemented a system which allows, under certain conditions, a company to account for VAT on imports on the VAT return without paying VAT to the customs authority (Article 211 Recast of 6th Directive).

Excise duties
Excise taxes are levied on tobacco, alcohol, electricity, some packaging materials and motor fuel.

Customs duties
After becoming a member of the EU, Estonia also became a member of the Customs Union. The Community Customs Code and related implementation regulations will apply, meaning that:

* Trade between Estonia and other EU countries is customs-free;

- Imports from non-EU countries are subject to EU customs tariffs; and
- Numerous free trade agreements concluded between EU and non-EU countries apply to Estonia.

Social security and unemployment insurance

Employers operating in Estonia (including non-residents with a PE or employees in Estonia) must pay social tax on certain payments to individuals at the rate of 33% (where 20% is used for financing public pension insurance and 13% is used for financing public health insurance). Social tax paid by employers is not capped and mainly applies to salaries, directors' fees and service fees paid and fringe benefits granted to individuals.

In addition to social tax, employers are also required to pay and withhold unemployment insurance contributions. From 1 August 2009, employers must pay 1.4% and employees must pay 2.8% (collected by employers through payroll withholding). The contributions mainly apply to salaries and service fees paid to individuals.

Compulsory accumulative pension scheme

Resident employees born after 31 December 1982 are obliged to join the compulsory accumulative pension scheme and make 2% contributions to the scheme (mostly collected by employers through payroll withholding). The contributions mainly apply to salaries, directors' fees and service fees. For resident employees born before 1983, joining the pension scheme is voluntary, but after joining, it becomes compulsory and the employees may not subsequently exit the scheme. In addition to the 2% contribution made by the employee, 4% of the social security contribution payable by the employer (33%) will be transferred to the employee's pension account.

Due to the recession and weak economic situation, state contributions (4%) have been temporarily suspended for the period from 1 June 2009 through to 31 December 2010. However, upon voluntary request, an employee may continue (2%) contributions from 1 January 2010 and the state will continue its contributions at a 2% rate from 1 January 2011.

Land and property taxes

Land is subject to an annual land tax, which is calculated on the assessed value of land at rates between 0.1% and 2.5%, depending on municipality. The tax is paid by the owners of land, or sometimes by the users of land, generally in two instalments by 31 March and 1 October. There is no property tax (i.e., tax on the value of buildings).

Property transfers are generally subject to state and notary fees.

Heavy goods vehicle tax

The heavy goods vehicle tax is paid for the following classes of vehicles that are registered with the Estonian National Motor Vehicle Register and are intended for the carriage of goods: (1) lorries with a maximum authorised weight or gross laden weight of not less than 12 tons; (2) road trains composed of trucks and trailers with a maximum authorised weight or gross laden weight of not less than 12 tons. The tax is paid by the owners or users of the vehicles.

Estonia

Gambling tax
Gambling tax is imposed on amounts received from operating games of skill, totalisator, betting, lotteries and promotional lotteries. Tax is also charged on gambling tables and machines used for games of chance located in licensed premises. The tax is paid by authorised operators.

Local taxes
Local taxes can be imposed by rural municipalities or city councils. The list of local taxes which the local authorities may impose include sales tax, boat tax, advertisement tax, road and street closure tax, motor vehicle tax, tax on keeping animals, entertainment tax and parking charges . Most commonly, the Estonian local authorities have imposed parking charges, advertisement tax, sales tax and road and street closure tax, but the fiscal significance of these taxes is almost non-existent. The 1% sales tax has been introduced in Tallinn, the capital of Estonia, from 1 June 2010.

Branch income

Registered PEs of non-residents, much as with resident companies, are subject to corporate income tax only in respect of profit distributions, both actual and deemed, as defined in domestic law.

Transactions and dealings between a head office and its PE(s) should be conducted on arm's-length terms. Thus, such profits should be attributed to a PE of a non-resident taxpayer that the PE would be expected to make if it were a distinct and separate taxpayer engaged in the same or similar activities, and under the same or similar conditions, and dealing in a wholly independent manner with its head office.

Income determination

Distributable profits are determined based on financial statements drawn up in accordance with Estonian GAAP or IAS/IFRS and there are no adjustments to accounting profits for tax purposes (e.g., tax depreciation, tax loss carryforward or carryback, etc.).

The corporate income tax liability associated with the distribution of dividends is accounted for as an expense at the time the dividends are declared, regardless of when the profits were generated or distributed.

Inter-company dividends
Dividends paid by Estonian companies are generally subject to 21/79 corporate income tax at the level of the distributing company. However, dividends distributed by Estonian companies are exempt from corporate income tax if the distributions are paid out of:

- Dividends received from Estonian, EU, European Economic Area (EEA) and Swiss tax resident companies (except tax haven companies) in which the Estonian company has at least a 10% shareholding;
- Profits attributable to a PE in EU, EEA or Switzerland;
- Dividends received from all other foreign companies in which the Estonian company (except tax haven companies) has at least a 10% shareholding, provided that either the underlying profits have been subject to foreign tax or if foreign income tax was withheld from dividends received; or

- Profits attributable to a foreign PE in all other countries provided that such profits have been subject to tax in the country of the PE.

Certain domestic and foreign taxes can also be credited against the 21/79 corporate income tax charge under domestic law or tax treaties.

Deductions

Depreciation and depletion
There is no adjustment of accounting profits for depreciation or depletion for tax purposes. Distributable profits are determined based on financial statements drawn up in accordance with Estonian GAAP or IAS/IFRS.

Net operating losses
There is no adjustment of accounting profits for net operating losses for tax purposes. Distributable profits are determined based on financial statements drawn up in accordance with Estonian GAAP or IAS/IFRS.

Payments to foreign affiliates
Payments to foreign affiliates are deductible for tax purposes (i.e., not subject to 21/79 corporate income tax as deemed profit distributions) if the payment serves a business purpose, provides a benefit to the payer, is at arm's length and is substantiated by sufficient documentation.

Payments to foreign affiliates may also be subject to various withholding taxes. Certain payments to affiliates located in tax haven countries are always subject to 21/79 corporate income tax or a 21% withholding tax rate.

Taxes
All taxes paid are deductible for income tax purposes. In certain circumstances domestic or foreign taxes may be creditable against the 21/79 corporate income tax charge under domestic law or an applicable tax treaty.

Fringe benefits
Employers operating in Estonia (including foreign companies that have a PE or employees in Estonia) are liable to Estonian taxation on any fringe benefits granted to their employees (including directors).

Fringe benefits are subject to an exceptional tax treatment in Estonia, as only the employer is obliged to pay taxes on the fringe benefits furnished to the employee. Taxable fringe benefits received by a resident employee are generally not included in the taxable income of the employee for Estonian tax purposes. Fringe benefits are subject to 21/79 corporate income tax and 33% social tax. For example, where the amount of the benefit is 100, the income tax due by the employer would be 27 (21/79 x 100) and the social tax due 42 (0.33 x 127), for a total fringe benefit tax charge of approximately 69.

Gifts, donations and representation expenses
The 21/79 corporate income tax is generally due on gifts and donations. Gifts and donations made to certain qualifying recipients are only subject to 21/79 corporate income tax if such expenses exceed one of two limitations:

Estonia

- 3% of the calculated social tax base for the existing calendar year; or
- 10% of the profit of the last financial year according to statutory financial statements.

Representation expenses, those expenditures whose character and primary purpose is for representational or entertainment related activities, are generally subject to 21/79 corporate income tax only if they exceed the threshold of EEK 500 per month plus 2% of the calculated social tax base of the calendar month in which the expenses are paid.

Other significant items

The 21/79 corporate income tax is generally due on expenses and payments that do not have a business purpose and that are regarded as deemed profit distributions. These may include, for example, late payment interest on tax arrears, penalties imposed by law, bribes, purchase of services or settlement of obligations not related to taxpayer's business and acquisition of assets not related to taxpayer's business.

Furthermore, there are specific anti-tax haven rules treating certain transactions and dealings with tax haven companies as deemed profit distributions, which are therefore subject to 21/79 corporate income tax. These include:

- Acquisition of securities issued by a tax haven entity (exception for certain listed securities);
- Acquisition of an ownership interest in a tax haven entity;
- Payment of fines or penalties to a tax haven entity, unless settled by court or arbitrage; and
- Granting loans or making prepayments to a tax haven entity or otherwise acquiring a claim against a tax haven entity.

Group taxation

There is no form of consolidation or group taxation for corporate income tax purposes.

Tax incentives

There are no special tax incentives in Estonia. However, the entire Estonian corporate tax system, which provides for an indefinite deferral for taxing corporate profits, may be viewed as a tax incentive that promotes reinvestment of profits and thus stimulates economic growth.

Withholding taxes (WHT)

Withholding agents must withhold income tax from certain payments. Withholding agents include resident legal entities, resident individuals registered as sole proprietorships or acting as employers, and non-residents having a PE or acting as employers in Estonia. The tax must be reported and paid by the tenth day of the month following the payment. Income tax is not withheld from payments to resident companies, registered sole proprietorships and registered PEs of foreign companies. The following rules are in place with respect to payments that are subject to WHT:

1. There is no WHT on dividends.

2. There is no WHT on interest payments to non-residents on the condition that the interest charged does not significantly exceed the arm's-length rate at the time the debt is incurred and the interest payments are made. A 21% Estonian WHT rate will thus apply only to the part of interest that significantly exceeds the arm's-length amount.

3. Royalties (including payments for the use of industrial, commercial or scientific equipment) paid to non-residents are generally subject to a 10% WHT rate under domestic law, but reduced rates may be available under double tax treaties. Certain royalty payments to associated EU and Swiss companies that meet certain conditions are exempt from withholding tax.

4. Rental payments to non-residents for the use of immovable property located in Estonia and movable property subject to registration in Estonia (excluding payments for the use of industrial, commercial or scientific equipment) are subject to a 21% withholding tax rate under domestic law, but double tax treaties may exempt payments for the use of movable property from WHT.

5. Royalties and rental payments to resident individuals are subject to a 21% WHT rate.

6. Payments to non-resident companies for services provided in Estonia, including management and consultancy fees, are subject to a 10% withholding tax rate under domestic law, but may be exempt under double tax treaties. Service fee payments to tax haven entities are always subject to a 21% WHT rate.

7. Salaries, directors' fees and service fees paid to individuals are subject to a 21% withholding tax rate under domestic law, but double tax treaties may exempt service fee payments to non-resident individuals from WHT.

8. Payments for the activities of non-resident artistes or sportsmen carried out in Estonia are subject to a 10% WHT rate.

9. Certain pensions, insurance benefits, scholarships, prizes, lottery winnings, alimony, etc., paid to non-residents and resident individuals are subject to a 21% WHT rate under domestic law.

For non-residents without a PE in Estonia, the tax withheld from these payments at domestic or treaty rates constitutes final tax in terms of their Estonian source income and they do not have any tax reporting requirements in Estonia.

For certain types of Estonian source income, non-residents are liable under Estonian domestic law to self assess their Estonian tax and submit a tax return to the Estonian tax authorities. These types of income include:

- Taxable capital gains;
- Profits derived from business conducted in Estonia without a registered PE; and
- Other items of income from which tax was not withheld but should have been withheld.

Estonia has effective tax treaties with: Armenia, Austria, Azerbaijan, Belarus, Belgium, Bulgaria, Canada, the People's Republic of China, Croatia, the Czech Republic, Denmark, Finland, France, Germany, Georgia, Greece, Hungary, Iceland, Ireland, Isle of Man, Israel, Italy, Kazakhstan, Latvia, Lithuania, Luxembourg, Macedonia, Malta, Moldova, the Netherlands, Norway, Poland, Portugal, Romania, Singapore, Slovakia, Slovenia, Spain, Sweden, Switzerland, Turkey, Ukraine, the United Kingdom, and the United States. Treaties have also been concluded with Albania, Republic of Korea, Russia and Serbia, but these are not yet effective.

Estonia

The following withholding tax rates apply to dividends, interest and royalties paid to a recipient beneficial owner resident in a tax treaty country. The lower of the domestic or the treaty rate is given.

Recipient	Dividends	Interest	Royalties
	%	%	%
Non-treaty	0	0/21 (2)	0/10 (3)
Treaty:			
Armenia	0	0/21	10
Austria	0	0/21	0/5/10 (4)
Azerbaijan	0	0/21	10
Belarus	0	0/21	10
Belgium	0	0/21	0/5/10 (4)
Bulgaria	0	0/21	0/5
Canada	0	0/21	10
China, People's Rep. of	0	0/21	10
Croatia	0	0/21	10
Czech Republic	0	0/21	0/10
Denmark	0	0/21	0/5/10 (4)
Finland	0	0/21	0/5/10 (4)
France	0	0/21	0/5/10 (4)
Germany	0	0/21	0/5/10 (4)
Georgia	0	0/21	10
Greece	0	0/21	0/5/10 (4)
Hungary	0	0/21	0/5/10 (4)
Iceland	0	0/21	5/10 (4)
Ireland, Rep. of	0	0/21	0/5/10 (4)
Isle of Man	0	0/21	0
Israel	0	0/21	0
Italy	0	0/21	0/5/10 (4)
Kazakhstan	0	0/21	15
Latvia	0	0/21	0/5/10 (4)
Lithuania	0	0/21	0/10
Luxembourg	0	0/21	0/5/10
Macedonia	0	0/21	5
Malta	0	0/21	0/10
Moldova	0	0/21	10
Netherlands	0	0/21	0/5/10 (4)
Norway	0	0/21	5/10 (4)
Poland	0	0/21	0/10
Portugal	0	0/21	0/10
Romania	0	0/21	0/10
Singapore	0	0/21	7.5
Slovakia	0	0/21	0/10
Slovenia	0	0/21	0/10
Spain	0	0/21	0/5/10 (4)

Recipient	Dividends	Interest	Royalties
	%	%	%
Sweden	0	0/21	0/5/10 (4)
Switzerland	0	0/21	0/5/10 (4)
Turkey	0	0/21	5/10 (4)
Ukraine	0	0/21	10
United Kingdom	0	0/21	0/5/10 (4)
United States	0	0/21	5/10 (4)

Notes

1. Under the domestic law, the rate is nil for all non-resident individual and corporate shareholders.
2. The rate is nil on the condition that the interest paid to a non-resident does not significantly exceed the arm's-length rate at the time the debt is incurred and the interest payments are made. Estonian withholding tax at the domestic rate of 21% will thus apply only to the part of interest that significantly exceeds the arm's-length amount. This withholding tax could be reduced under tax treaties.
3. The rate is nil for arm's-length royalties paid to an associated EU or Swiss company if certain conditions are met.
4. The lower 5% rate applies to royalties paid for the use of industrial, commercial or scientific equipment.

Tax administration

Tax return
The tax period is a calendar month. The combined corporate income tax and payroll tax return (form TSD with appendices) must be submitted to the local tax authorities by the tenth day of the month following a taxable distribution or payment. Tax returns may be filed electronically via the Internet.

Payment of tax
Corporate income tax and payroll taxes must be remitted to the local tax authorities by the tenth day of the month following a taxable distribution or payment. No advance corporate income tax payments are required.

Advance rulings
An advance ruling system became available in Estonia on 1 January 2008. The aim of the procedure is to provide certainty on the tax consequences of specific transactions or combination of transactions taking place in the future. The ruling is binding on the authorities (and not on the taxpayer) if the transaction was made within the deadline and the description provided in the ruling and the underlying legislation has not been substantially changed in the meantime. Estonian legislation specifically excludes obtaining rulings when the interpretation of the legislation is objectively clear, the situation is hypothetical or the main purpose of the planned transaction is tax avoidance. In addition, transfer pricing valuation issues are excluded from the scope of the binding ruling system.

Corporate taxes in Fiji Islands

For more information, contact:

Jerome Kado
PricewaterhouseCoopers
Level 8
Civic Tower
262 Victoria Parade
Suva, Fiji Islands
Tel: +679 331 3955
Email: jerome.kado@fj.pwc.com

Significant developments

The following changes became effective 1 January 2010:

- The Tax Administration Decree was promulgated with the stated intention of harmonising the administration of various tax laws including income tax and value-added tax (VAT);
- Companies listed on the South Pacific Stock Exchange will be subject to a reduced corporate tax rate of 20% in 2010, provided the companies have been listed on the stock exchange for at least three years and have at least a 40% resident shareholding;
- The Branch Profit Remittance Additional Normal Tax of 15% has been repealed.
- The 150% deduction on capital expenditure by a non-resident company for reinvestment of profits in Fiji has also been repealed;
- The cap on deductible head office expenses is reduced from 5% to 3%.
- In the case of the sale of shares in a company, the total value of retained earnings is now to be deemed as dividends distributed to shareholders;
- The provisions in relation to withholding tax have been amended to include the imposition of 15% withholding tax on payments for professional services and other services of a similar nature;
- The threshold for VAT registration has been increased to FJD 50,000; and
- The VAT provisions were amended to include forfeited deposits as taxable supplies, which is subject to VAT.

Taxes on corporate income

Normal tax is payable on taxable income at the following rates:

	Rate (%)
Non-resident shipping companies in respect of outgoing business from Fiji	2
Companies listed on the South Pacific Stock Exchange provided the companies have been listed in the stock exchange for at least three years and have at least 40% resident shareholding	31 (in 2008) 29 (in 2009) 20 (in 2010 and subsequent years)
Mutual insurance companies in respect of life insurance income and non-mutual insurance companies to the extent their life insurance business is deemed to be mutual	30 (in 2008) 29 (in 2009) 28 (in 2010 and subsequent years)

	Rate (%)
Other companies including non-resident	31 (in 2008)
companies carrying on business in Fiji	29 (in 2009)
(e.g., branch profits)	28 (in 2010 and subsequent years)

Corporate residence

A company incorporated in Fiji is resident in Fiji. A company not incorporated in Fiji is resident in Fiji if it carries on business in Fiji and either its practical management and control are in Fiji, or its voting powers are controlled by shareholders who are residents of Fiji.

Other taxes

Resident interest withholding tax
A withholding tax of 31% is deductible from payments to, or on the accrual of, interest for resident depositors by banks and other financial institutions. However, this tax is not payable where the depositor obtains a valid certificate of exemption or where interest received does not exceed FJD 200 per annum.

Land sales tax
The profits arising from the sale of undeveloped land in Fiji, if not included in taxable income for income tax purposes, may be subject to land sales tax at rates ranging from 6.5% to 30%.

Excise tax
Excise tax is payable on tobacco and alcohol products manufactured in Fiji. The government has also removed excise duty on carbonated drinks but imposes a 3% fiscal duty on the raw materials.

The government has introduced a new import excise tax (in addition to existing tariffs imposed) that will be levied on selected goods. These include:

- Alcohol and tobacco;
- Used or second hand LPG powered motor vehicles plus 15% import excise;
- New or used licensed mini buses;
- Some goods which are also locally manufactured; and
- Certain white goods and luxury items.

Value-added tax (VAT)
The threshold amount for VAT registration has been increased from FJD 30,000 to FJD 50,000 for the supply of goods and from FJD 15,000 to FJD 50,000 for the supply of services effective 1 January 2010.

The supply of financial services, residential accommodation and education by an approved institution is exempt. The supply of exports and international transportation is zero-rated. However, as of 1 January 2009, the export of services is zero-rated only under certain conditions.

The sale of edible oil, tin fish, rice, flour, tea, powdered milk and kerosene are zero-rated.

Fiji Islands

Beginning 1 January 2009, VAT refunds can no longer be transferred or assigned to another registered person.

Directors of companies with insufficient funds may be held liable for any outstanding VAT or income tax liability of the company and may be sued in their personal capacity under certain conditions.

Hotel turnover tax

Under the Hotel Turnover Tax Act of 2006, hotel turnover tax (HTT) at the rate of 5% is imposed on hotel charges.

For ease of administration to both hoteliers and the Fiji Islands Revenue and Customs Authority (FIRCA), the due date for payment is aligned with the VAT Decree requirements (i.e., end of the following month).

Directors have been included in the definition of accountable persons in the HTT Act. An accountable person is a person who is operating a licensed hotel which has levied the HTT on hotel charges and must account for it.

Record keeping

The HTT Act includes a seven year record keeping requirement.

The HTT liability may be offset against other tax refunds consistent with the Income Tax Act, VAT Decree and the Gambling Turnover Tax Act.

Branch income

The tax rate on branch profits is the same as the rate on profits of a resident corporation (29% in 2009 and 28% in 2010 and subsequent years).

Income determination

Inventory valuation

Inventories are normally valued at the lower of cost and net realisable value. While the first-in, first-out (FIFO) method is acceptable, the last-in, first-out (LIFO) method is not, for either book or tax purposes. Conformity between book and tax reporting is not required. There are no special provisions for valuing inventories or determining inventory flows.

Capital gains

Currently, capital gains are not subject to tax, although gains realised from the sale or other disposition of property acquired for the purpose of resale or as part of a profit-making undertaking or scheme are taxable as ordinary income.

Inter-company dividends

Resident corporations may exclude from taxable income dividends received from a company incorporated in Fiji. There are no ownership requirements for this exclusion.

Fiji Islands

Foreign income

Resident corporations are taxed on their worldwide income. Foreign income sourced from a non-treaty country are subject to income tax in Fiji with credits available for tax paid on such income. Income derived from a treaty country is taxed according to the treaty. A credit is allowed in Fiji for foreign tax paid on the foreign income, limited to the lesser of the Fiji tax payable or the overseas tax paid on such income. There are no special provisions for taxing undistributed income of foreign subsidiaries.

Stock dividends

Bonus shares are tax-free, except where paid out of the revenue or profits of investment or service-type companies. Tax-free stock dividends issued by private companies may be taxable upon sale of the shares.

Other significant items

Where a foreign-controlled business in Fiji produces less income than might be expected, the revenue authorities may determine the income for tax purposes.

A person normally residing outside Fiji, which disposes of an interest in land in Fiji held directly or through a shareholding in a company, may be assessed to income tax on the profit on that disposal.

Liability of directors/shareholders

Directors/shareholders of companies in liquidation may be held liable for any outstanding tax liability of the company. Directors/shareholders of private companies or companies with insufficient assets may also be held liable for any outstanding tax liability of the company under certain conditions.

Deductions

Depreciation and depletion

Depreciation is calculated on the cost of an asset on the straight-line basis. The rates of depreciation are based on the estimated life of the asset. Upon disposal of an asset, recoupment of depreciation claimed is taxable or the excess of tax written-down value over sale proceeds is deductible. The taxpayer has an option to set-off recoupment of depreciation against the cost of replacement assets. Conformity between book and tax depreciation is not required.

There are seven broad bands of depreciation rates for assets acquired after 1 January 1998, and the prescribed effective life of the asset is used to determine the relevant depreciation rate.

An optional 20% loading, which applies on the broadband rate, may be claimed. Buildings have been subject to new depreciation rates from 1 January 2001. Accelerated depreciation will apply for certain buildings built up to 31 December 2010 (i.e., if the buildings are completed on or before 31 December 2010, the accelerated depreciation will apply to the building even after 2010).

Renewable energy plant and water storage facilities also qualify for accelerated depreciation.

Assets acquired before 1 January 1998 will continue to be depreciated at the former rates.

Fiji Islands

Accelerated depreciation is available on capital expenditure on buildings constructed between certain specified dates that are to be used for agricultural, commercial or industrial purposes or on multi-storey, multi-unit residential buildings, as well as on other capital expenditure considered of benefit for the economic development of Fiji. Up to one-fifth of the expenditure may be claimed in each of any five years of an eight-year period.

Capital expenditure aimed at economising on the consumption of fuel, electricity or its derivatives or on an asset using energy sources indigenous to Fiji may be eligible for accelerated depreciation at varying rates or for an investment allowance (in addition to normal depreciation) of up to 40% of expenditure.

The cost of the acquisition of a mining lease or tenement and the cost of development of mines may be written off in equal instalments in any five of the first or last eight years of a nine-year period, commencing with the year in which the expenditure was incurred.

A deduction for depletion of other natural resources is not available.

Thin capitalisation
There are no thin capitalisation rules in Fiji.

Net operating losses
Losses may be carried forward for eight years (previously six years), provided the company can demonstrate a minimum 51% continuity of shareholding between the year of loss and the year of claim. Notwithstanding the change in ownership, losses may also be carried forward where a company carries on the same business in the carried forward year as it did in the loss year. Loss carrybacks are not permitted.

Losses incurred in agricultural or pastoral pursuits may be carried forward indefinitely.

Donations
The deduction threshold for contributions to approved charitable organisations is FJD 100,000.

There are certain other specific donations which qualify for varying levels of deductions including donations to the Fiji Heritage Foundation, which qualify for a deduction of 150%, and cash donations exceeding FJD 50,000 to the Poverty Relief Fund for Education, which qualify for a deduction of 200%.

Sports fund
A 150% deduction is available to a taxpayer in respect of any cash donation made exceeding FJD 100,000 to a Sports Fund (as approved by the Commissioner of Inland Revenue) for purposes of sports development in the Fiji Islands.

Payments to foreign affiliates
Subject to the normal rules of deductibility, a deduction can be claimed for royalties, management service fees and interest charges. However, as of 1 January 2008, any deductions claimed by any company (whether incorporated in Fiji or not, carrying on business in Fiji) in respect of head office charges or any other like payments shall not exceed 5% of total gross Fiji income. Effective 1 January 2010, the limit was reduced to 3%.

Fiji Islands

Taxes

Taxes levied on income are not deductible.

Other significant items

Provisions for expenses not yet incurred (e.g., provisions for bad debts or future maintenance) are not tax-deductible. A deduction is permitted in respect of amounts subsequently paid or written off.

Group taxation

Group taxation is not permitted.

Tax incentives

The tax incentives are designed primarily to promote export sales and to encourage the development of industries that are considered of benefit to the economic development of Fiji.

Export income deduction

A deduction for export income is allowed in accordance with the following:

Year of assessment	Percentage of export income to be deducted
2008 to 2010	50%
	100% (on the island of Vanua Levu)

"Export income" means profit derived by a taxpayer from the business of exporting goods and services, and the Commissioner of Inland Revenue may, where separate records for export income are not maintained, determine such income on the basis of a formula as set out in the legislation.

The definition of "export income" has been clarified to mean "net profit".

The 5th Schedule of the Income Tax Act – "Export Incentives" – has been repealed. However, the existing beneficiaries are expected to continue to enjoy the incentives under this schedule until the expiry of the incentives granted.

Investment allowance

From 2001, an investment allowance equal to 40% of the qualifying expenditure is available as a deduction for agricultural, forestry or marine resources business; an information technology business; or a rural manufacturing business. This allowance may be claimed in addition to normal depreciation.

A qualifying expenditure means expenditure of FJD 50,000 or more incurred in any of the years from the 2001 year of assessment to 2010 year of assessment, for the purpose of acquiring a capital asset(s).

Information communication technology (ICT) tax incentives

The income of an information communication technology operator may be exempt from income tax as follows:

1. Operating on or before 1 January 2009 in the declared Kalabu Tax Free Zone, from 1 January 2007 to 31 December 2016; or

Fiji Islands

2. Granted a licence after 1 January 2009, for a period of 13 years from the date of issue of the licence.

Provided that the business employs 50 employees or more for six months within the income year and 60% or more of the total value of its services in that income year is exported.

"Information communication technology business" means an entity engaged in software development, call centres or internet service provision, but does not include an internet café or any retail or wholesale of information technology products or the repair, sale or service of any such products.

Employment taxation scheme
Salary and wages paid to first-time employees for the first 12 months of employment qualify for a 150% deduction. This deduction is available until 31 December 2010.

Capital investment
The following incentives are available for capital investment:

Hotel industry – The Hotels Aid Act was repealed and the Income Tax Act was amended effective 1 July 2007. Approved capital expenditure incurred in building, renovating or expanding a hotel is subject to an investment allowance of 55% of the approved expenditure, in addition to normal depreciation.

Under the Short Life Investment Package (SLIP) the following concessions are available:

- Exemption from income tax for a period of 10 years provided that the capital investment in the hotel is more than FJD 7,000,000;
- Duty-free entry of all capital equipment, plant and machinery upon receiving provisional approval from the Minister; and
- Permission to generate own electricity, the excess to be sold to the Fiji Electricity Authority.

Mining industry – An approved mining company may for a specified period be exempt from income tax or taxed at a lower rate. The holder of a valid prospecting license may write off approved expenditure on prospecting for minerals against income from all sources.

From 1 January 2005, a 150% deduction is available for direct capital expenditure incurred by commercial banks in rural banking programmes.

From 1 July 2005, a 300% deduction is available for capital expenditure of at least FJD 40,000 spent for ICT business, agriculture, forestry, mining, manufacturing, textile, clothing and footwear, timber manufacturing, fishery manufacturing or shipbuilding business set up between 1 July 2005 and 31 December 2010 on the island of Vanua Levu.

From 1 January 2006, a 200% deduction is available for capital expenditure incurred by entities in the agriculture and fisheries sector not enjoying other concessions under the Income Tax Act. The incentive will be available until 31 December 2010.

From 1 January 2006, investors engaged in value adding processes in the food processing, agricultural processing, fisheries or forestry business may be able to claim a 100% deduction with respect to amounts invested or re-invested (for expansion), provided that the businesses meet the 50% local content rule.

Tax incentives are available to taxpayers engaged in new ICT business and for existing taxpayers so engaged who are able to show a significant increase in capacity and the number of employees as follows:

- 80% tax exemption for businesses employing more than 101 employees;
- 60% tax exemption for those that employ between 60 to 100 employees; or
- 40% tax exemption for those employing 10 to 59 employees.

A 150% deduction is available for costs incurred for the development of ICT business by any taxpayer employing 500 or more employees. This deduction is available till 31 December 2012.

From 1 January 2009, the following income tax exemption may be available to a taxpayer engaged in commercial agricultural farming and agro-processing subject to certain conditions:

- Any new activity approved and established between 1 January to 31 December 2009, for a period of four to 10 consecutive fiscal years depending on the level of capital investment; or
- Any new activity approved and established from 1 January 2010 to 31 December 2014 with a capital investment of at least FJD 2,000,000, for a period of 10 consecutive fiscal years.

Effective 1 January 2009, income derived by a taxpayer from a new activity in processing agricultural commodities into bio-fuels may be exempt from income tax for a period of 10 years under certain conditions.

From 1 January 2009, exemption from income tax for a period of five years may be available to a taxpayer engaging in renewable energy projects and power cogeneration.

From 1 January 2009, an investment allowance equal to 60% of the qualifying expenditure is available as a deduction for investment in Fixed Line Next Generation Networks. A qualifying expenditure means expenditure of FJD 50,000 or more incurred in any of the years between the years of assessment 2009 and 2012, for the purpose of acquiring a capital asset(s).

Other incentives
Other incentives include the following:

Filmmaking and audiovisual incentives
Incentives are available for filmmaking and for the development of the audio-visual industry in Fiji. These incentives include:

- Availability of an exemption from tax or tax at a reduced rate on the income of non-resident employees of an approved non-resident company engaged or intending to be engaged in making a film in Fiji;

Fiji Islands

- Availability to a resident entity (excluding an entity holding a broadcast license in television or radio in Fiji or with substantial shareholdings in the same) of a deduction of up to 150% of monies expended on audio-visual production in respect of income in the year the monies are expended. "Audio-visual productions" include production for exhibition or sale of theatrical films, broadcast television, direct-to-video and video disk programme, audio recording, computer software and interactive websites;
- Exemption from tax on the income derived by a taxpayer from the commercial exploitation of a copyright until the taxpayer has received from the commercial exploitation a return of up to 60% of the monies expended. The monies expended must be of a capital nature and in relation to the audio-visual production costs in respect of a qualifying audio-visual production; and
- Tax concessions are also available for residents of areas declared as studio city zones by the appropriate government Minister.

Dividends
Any dividend from a company incorporated in Fiji, received or accrued to a resident company other than a unit trust, is exempt from tax.

As of 1 January 2005, transfer of property by private companies to shareholders and associates shall be deemed to be a dividend paid by that company.

A 150% deduction is available on expenses incurred in reorganising a company for the purpose of listing on the South Pacific Stock Exchange.

Entities in the following sectors with maximum turnover threshold of FJD 300,000 may be exempt from income tax:

- Agriculture;
- Fisheries; and
- Tourism.

Tax on land sales
Non-residents of Fiji would no longer be subject to income tax on profit from the sale of land acquired purely for investment purposes. However, land sales tax may be applicable. Profit from the business of buying and selling land is subject to income tax.

Withholding taxes (WHT)

Recipient	Dividends %	Interest %	Royalties %	Know-how, management fees %	Professional fees %
Resident corporations	Nil	31 (1)	Nil	Nil	Nil
Resident individuals	Nil (2)	31 (1)	Nil	Nil	Nil
Non-resident corporations and individuals:					
Non-treaty	15	10	15	15	15
Treaty:					
Australia	20	10	15	15	Nil to 15 (5)
Japan	15	10	15	15	Nil to 15 (5)

Recipient	Dividends %	Interest %	Royalties %	Know-how, management fees %	Professional fees %
Korea, Rep of	10 or 15 (3)	10	10	10	Nil to 15 (5)
Malaysia	15	15	15	15	Nil to 15 (5)
New Zealand	15	10	15	15	Nil to 15 (5)
Papua New Guinea	17	10	15	15	Nil to 15 (5)
Singapore	5 or 15 (4)	10	10	10	Nil to 15 (5)
United Kingdom	15	10	15	15	Nil to 15 (5)

Notes

1. Applies to interest (over FJD 200) on savings and deposits with commercial banks and other financial institutions, unless the taxpayer has provided a tax identification number to the financial institution.
2. Any dividend that has been paid or credited in favour of a resident individual in respect of shares of a company listed on the South Pacific Stock Exchange is not subject to tax.
3. 10% of gross amount of dividends if beneficial owner is a company (other than a partnership) that holds directly at least 25% of the capital of the company paying the dividends; 15% in all other cases.
4. 5% of gross amount of dividends if beneficial owner is a company (other than a partnership) that holds directly at least 10% of the capital of the company paying the dividends; 15% in all other cases.
5. Depending on the provisions of the applicable double taxation agreement.

Tax administration

The Tax Administration Decree (TAD) was promulgated effective 1 January 2010 with the stated intention of harmonising the administration of the various tax laws including income tax and VAT.

Returns

Tax is assessed on income derived during the calendar year preceding the year of assessment. Returns are therefore generally accepted on a calendar-year basis, although approval is also given to use a fiscal-year basis. For purposes of assessment of returns completed on a fiscal-year basis, the calendar year in which more than one-half of the fiscal year falls is deemed to be the calendar year in which the income is derived. The Fiji tax system is not based on self-assessment. Returns of income contain information on the basis of which assessments are raised by the tax authorities.

A Tax Agent Lodgement Programme was introduced in 2003 to spread the lodgement of tax returns. In conjunction with this program, the advance tax payments will be increased to 100% in three instalments by the seventh month after the end of the taxpayer's fiscal year-end as follows:

- First advance – due on the last day of the financial year;
- Second advance – due three months after the end of the taxpayer's fiscal year-end; and
- Third advance – due seven months after the end of the taxpayer's fiscal year-end.

Fiji Islands

Penalties
Administrative penalty provisions have been amended and increased by the TAD.

Provisions have been introduced to allow for distress of business assets once a company goes into liquidation.

The TAD provides for various ways to ensure the collection of taxes including, but not limited to:

1. Departure Prohibition Order – A departure prohibition order may be used by the tax office to prevent taxpayers from leaving the country without settling outstanding taxes;
2. Garnishee orders – The tax office may garnish bank accounts for outstanding taxes;
3. Registration of charges on personal and real properties of the taxpayer;
4. Distress and sale of personal property; and
5. Temporary closure of business.

Binding rulings
The TAD has introduced a binding ruling system. However, the provisions will only apply after the Minister of Finance has appointed a date by notice in the Gazette.

Anti-avoidance provisions
The anti-avoidance provisions of the Fiji Income Tax Act have been amended to strengthen the same.

Corporate taxes in Finland

For more information, contact:

Klaus Keravuori
PricewaterhouseCoopers Oy
PL 1015, Itämerentori 2
00101 Helsinki
Finland
Tel: +358 9 2280 1928
Email: klaus.keravuori@fi.pwc.com

F

Significant developments

The Finnish income tax system is expected to undergo some changes in the coming years. The working group on the reform should complete its work in May 2010. According to the public conversation around the working group, most significant changes will concern taxation of dividends and a decrease in the corporate income tax rate.

Taxes on corporate income

The corporate tax rate is 26%.

Corporate residence

A company is deemed to be resident on the basis of incorporation. Consequently, a company is deemed to be resident in Finland, if it is incorporated (registered) in Finland.

Finnish resident companies are subject to Finnish tax on their worldwide income (unlimited tax liability). Also Finnish permanent establishments (PE) of non-resident companies are subject to Finnish tax on their worldwide income attributable to the PE. A PE is, in general, formed in line with the OECD Model Convention.

Other taxes

Value-added tax (VAT)
The general VAT rate increased from 22% to 23% as of 1 July 2010. The reduced rate of 12% previously applied to food and animal feed, increased to 13% effective as of the same date. The VAT rate of 13% also applies to restaurant and catering services, which were taxed at the standard rate of 22% until 1 July 2010. The reduced VAT rate of 8% applied to books, accommodation and passenger transport increased to 9% as of 1 July 2010.

A zero rate applies to, e.g., subscriptions to newspapers and periodicals, intra-Community supplies of goods and exports of goods. Additionally, certain services, including financial services, insurance services and certain educational services, are exempted from tax.

Finland

The introduction of the so-called Tax Account system as of January 2010 has changed VAT reporting and payment including the due dates. Please see more in section *"Tax administration"*.

Real estate tax

Municipalities impose a real estate tax. The tax is levied on the taxable value of buildings and land. The municipal council determines the applicable tax rates, although the minimum and maximum tax rates are set by tax legislation, such as from 0.32% to 0.75% for permanent dwellings and from 0.6% to 1.35% for other real estate. The tax is deductible from taxable business income if the real estate is used for business purposes. The tax is deductible from taxable income of the so-called other source of income if the real estate is used to acquire other taxable income than business income.

Transfer tax

A transfer tax of 4% of the sales price is payable on the transfer of real estate situated in Finland. The transfer of shares in Finnish companies and other domestic securities is subject to a transfer tax of 1.6%. Generally, the transfer tax is payable by the transferee.

No transfer tax is payable on the transfer of securities made through the stock exchange. Similarly, no transfer tax is payable if both the seller and the transferee are non-residents. Transfer tax is, however, always payable on transfers between non-residents if the transferred shares are shares in a Finnish housing or real estate company.

Social security contributions

According to the Finnish social security legislation both Finnish and foreign employers have a liability to pay several social security payments in Finland in case the employee performs his tasks partly or wholly in Finland. The liability concerns all employers, regardless of the form of the company and whether the foreign company has a permanent establishment (PE) in Finland. The percentage rates for the employer's (and employee's) social security contributions are revised on an annual basis.

Compulsory social security contributions payable by the employer in 2010 according to the paid salaries are as follows:

- Employer's social security charge: 2.23% (no cap);
- Employer's pension insurance contribution: 16.9% (on average, no cap);
- Employer's unemployment insurance contribution: 0.75% for the first EUR 1,846,500 of gross salaries and 2.95% for the portion of the gross salaries exceeding EUR 1,846,500 (no cap);
- Group life insurance premium: 0.072% (on average, no cap); and
- Accident insurance premium: 1.0% (on average, no cap).

The new rates for employer's social security charge are applicable to salaries paid as of 1 January 2010.

If the employee is regarded as a foreign-posted employee and has an E-101 certificate or a certificate of coverage from his home country, neither the aforementioned employer's social security contributions nor the employee's social security charges are payable in Finland.

Branch income

As a general rule, a branch is taxed like a corporation (tax rate 26%) on the profits attributable to it, provided the branch constitutes a PE in Finland. No tax is withheld on transfers of (taxed) profits to the head office.

Income determination

Companies and other legal entities can have as many as three sources of income (i.e., the Source of Income from Business Activities, the Source of Agricultural Income and the Source of Other Income). The net taxable income is calculated separately for each source. The expenses of one source of income cannot be deducted from the taxable income of another source, and a loss from one source of income cannot offset taxable income from another source. All taxable income received by a company is taxed at the rate of 26% irrespective the source to which it is attributable. Typically Finnish companies are taxed mainly in accordance with Business Income Tax Act (BITA, Business Source), but it is not rare that a company would also have income taxed in accordance with Income Tax Act (ITA Other Income). Common income taxable in the "Other Income" basket is certain kinds of rental income.

In general, Finland has a very broad income concept and taxable income includes all income derived from a company's activities, though there are some significant exceptions, including (among others):

- Capital contributions by shareholders;
- In most cases, dividends from unlisted companies *(See more in Dividends section below)*;
- Liquidation gains and capital gains qualifying for the participation exemption *(see more below in section Capital gains)*;
- Proceeds from disposal of company's own shares; and
- Merger gain.

There is no general distinction between capital gains and other income; capital gains of a company are taxed as part of its general income either in the "business income" basket or the "other income" basket. No rates other than the general 26% are applied to any part of taxable income of a company.

Taxable income of a company generally is computed on accrual basis: income is taxable in the year it is earned. Exemptions to this main rule exist, including unrealised exchange gains and losses, which are taxable/deductible on the year of the rate change.

Inventory valuation
Inventories may be written down to the lower of direct first-in, or first-out (FIFO) cost, or replacement cost or net realisable value. Conformity between book and tax reporting is required.

Capital gains
Capital gains and losses are generally included in the taxable business income (i.e., sales proceeds are included in the taxable income and the undepreciated balance of the asset sold is deducted in the sales year) and treated as ordinary income. However, the entire stock of machinery and equipment is treated as a single item, and the capital

Finland

gain on machinery and equipment is entered as income indirectly by deducting the selling price from the remaining value of the stock of machinery and equipment.

Capital gains arising from the sale of shares are tax exempt under certain circumstances (participation exemption). Specifically, capital gains arising from the sale of shares are tax exempt if:

- The seller is not engaged in venture capital business;
- The seller has owned continuously for a period of at least one year at least 10% of the share capital of the target company; and
- The shares must be part of the seller's fixed assets and the shareholding must be included in the seller's business income source for tax purposes:
  - The target company cannot be a real estate company, a housing company or a company the activities of which mainly include owning of real estates; and
  - The target company must be a Finnish company, a company referred to in the European Commission (EC) Parent-Subsidiary Directive or a company resident in a country with which Finland has concluded a tax treaty which applies to the target company's dividend distribution.

However, a capital gain is taxable to the extent that the gain corresponds with a previous tax-deductible write-down or provision made in connection with the acquisition cost of shares, subsidies received for acquiring shares, or previous capital losses deducted for Finnish tax purposes from intragroup transfer of the shares.

Capital losses in the corresponding situations are non-deductible.

Dividends
Dividends received by a Finnish company are tax exempt in most cases. However, dividends received are partly taxable (75%) if:

- The dividend is received on shares belonging to the financial assets and the receiving company does not own at least 10% of the equity of the distributing company that is resident in another European Union (EU) member state and covered by the EC Parent-Subsidiary Directive (note that only financial, pension and insurance institutions may have assets which are considered as financial assets);
- The dividend is received from a company other than Finnish or EU resident; and
- The dividend is received from a publicly quoted company and the receiving company is not a publicly quoted company, and the shareholding is less than 10% of the equity of the distributing company.

Dividends that a Finnish company receives from other than a company resident in Finland or another EU member state are, however, fully taxable (100%), if there is no applicable tax treaty. Note, that most of the Finnish tax treaties include provision enabling tax exempt dividend from the tax treaty country in case of at least 10% shareholding.

Income from controlled foreign corporations (CFC)
The Finnish CFC regime was amended in 2009 for the purpose of bringing the regime into compliance with European Community law.

Finland

The CFC rules are applicable with respect to foreign entities in low tax jurisdictions controlled by Finnish residents. The undistributed profits of such foreign entities may be taxed as profit of the Finnish resident direct or indirect shareholders. The entity is deemed to be controlled by Finnish residents if at least 50% of the capital or total voting rights are directly or indirectly held by Finnish residents, or if Finnish residents have the right to at least 50% of the profits of the entity. The taxable person in such a case is the Finnish resident shareholder who owns directly or indirectly at least 25% of the capital of the corporate body or have right to at least 25% of the profits of the entity. A foreign entity is considered to be low taxed if the actual income tax burden of the foreign corporation in its state of residence is lower than three-fifths of the tax burden of a comparable Finnish corporation, i.e., currently effective rate is less than 15.6% (three-fifths of the Finnish tax rate of 26%).

Foreign PEs of non-resident companies can be regarded as equal to foreign companies provided that the PE's profits are not taxed in the head office state. Due to the transitional period, the PE provision would be applicable to PEs of foreign entities only as of 1 January 2015.

Certain types of businesses are excluded from the scope of the CFC Rules (e.g., income principally from industrial, manufacturing or shipping activities, as well as sales or marketing activities related to such activities if they are directed principally to the country of residence of the sales or marketing company). Also companies resident in a country with which Finland has a double tax treaty generally are outside the scope of the CFC Rules if the company does not benefit from any special tax incentives in that treaty country. Tax treaty countries that are not covered by this rule are exhaustively mentioned in a specific "black list" provided by the Ministry of Finance. As of January 2010, these countries are Barbados, Bosnia-Herzegovina, Georgia, Macedonia, Malaysia, Moldova, Montenegro, Serbia, Singapore, Switzerland, United Arab Emirates and Uzbekistan.

In addition to these two mentioned exclusions, the Finnish CFC rules are not applicable in cases of genuine economical establishment in a foreign country, which is either an EU/European Economic Area (EEA) member state or a tax treaty state not on the "black list". The genuine economical establishment is evaluated in light of the requirements of the business in question and paying special attention to capable personnel and office space, etc., located in the low tax jurisdiction.

Foreign income
A Finnish corporation is taxed on foreign dividends when the decision to distribute dividend is made and on foreign branch income and other foreign income (e.g., interest and royalties) as earned. The principal method of avoiding double taxation is the credit method, although the exemption method is still applied in few older treaties. Foreign tax can be credited at maximum in the same proportion of Finnish tax payable on the same income as the combined amount of income from foreign are in proportion to the same income source. Unused credit of foreign tax paid may be carried forward for five years.

Stock dividends
Stock dividends (bonus shares) may be distributed to stockholders, which are corporations and other legal entities with some exceptions, free of tax on the shareholder *(see Dividends section above)*.

Finland

Deductions

Deductions

As with taxable income, the concept of deductible costs is wide and covers, in general, all costs incurred in the pursuance of taxable income. Significant exceptions to this rule include (among others):

- Income taxes (see below), tax late payment interests and punitive tax increases;
- 50% of entertainment costs;
- Fines and other punitive payments;
- Capital losses, and liquidation losses if capital gains from the sale of shares of a target company would qualify for participation exemption *(see the Income Determination: Capital gains section)*;
- Losses from the disposal of a company's own shares; and
- Merger losses.

As the accrual method is applied to calculation of taxable income, expenses are usually deductible on the year they are realised (obligation to pay has arisen).

Depreciation and depletion

Maximum annual rates of depreciation calculated on net book value (declining-balance method) are 25% for machinery and equipment and from 4% to 20% for buildings and other constructions, depending on the type and estimated life of the asset. Net book value is defined as cost less accumulated depreciation and, in the case of machinery and equipment, proceeds on disposal of the assets. The straight-line method is applied to certain intangible assets and capitalised expenditures and to assets with long economic use, such as dams. Tax depreciation is limited to the cumulative charges made in the books.

The maximum amount of depreciation from the acquisition cost of new buildings, machinery and equipment, taken into use in 2009 and 2010 in production activities, are temporarily doubled *(see more detail in the Tax incentives section)*.

The capital cost of mines, sandpits, quarries and peat bogs is written off in proportion to the quantities extracted. Short-lived items (the economic life of which is three years or less) may be written off immediately. Land is not a depreciable asset.

Costs related to qualifying intangible property are usually amortisable over a period of 10 years or a shorter period if the economic life is proven to be less than 10 years.

Net operating losses

Losses may be carried forward for 10 subsequent years. The right to carryforward may be forfeited, such as in cases where there is a direct or indirect change in the ownership of the company operating at a loss. Loss carrybacks are not allowed.

Goodwill

Acquired goodwill is amortisable for tax purposes over its economic life, up to a maximum of 10 years.

Payments to foreign affiliates
A Finnish corporation may claim a deduction for royalties, service fees and interest charges paid to foreign affiliates, provided the underlying transaction is beneficial to it and the amounts paid are at arm's length.

Taxes
No income taxes are deductible when determining taxable income. However, the real estate tax is deductible.

Group taxation

Companies within a group are not consolidated for income tax purposes. However, via group contributions (lump sum payments of cash based on annual taxable profits), group companies may even out their taxable profits and losses, which leads effectively to the same result as would consolidation. A group contribution is a deductible cost for the granting company and taxable income for the receiving company, provided that all of the following are true:

- Both companies belong to a structure where there is a direct or indirect common ownership of at least 90% and the structure has existed for the entire tax year;
- Both companies are Finnish resident for tax purposes;
- Both companies are limited liability companies or co-operatives with business activities (have a source of income from business activities, *see Income determination section*);
- The contribution is recorded in the accounts for both of the companies so that it has a P/L effect;
- The accounting period for both companies ends at the same date; and
- The amount of contribution does not exceed the taxable income of the granting company.

Based on case law, the ownership chain may also be traced via foreign entities, provided there is a tax treaty between Finland and the country wherein the ultimate parent for the group is resident.

Thin capitalisation
There is no special legislation governing thin capitalisation. A Finnish company may deduct interest payments to affiliates provided that the amount of debt and rate of interest are at arm's length: if not, a possibility for application of general anti-avoidance provision may exist.

Transfer pricing
All transactions between related parties must happen at arm's length. The requirement is imperative even in relation to purely domestic transactions. If the arm's-length requirement is not followed, income or deductions of a company may be adjusted for tax purposes, in addition to which a risk for substantial penalties exists.

A Finnish company is obliged to prepare transfer pricing documentation to support transactions between its non-Finnish related parties. Documentation is subject to statutory requirements regarding content, which vary depending on the volume of related party transactions. The documentation requirement does not concern small- and medium-sized companies that have less than 250 employees and feature a turnover of no larger than EUR 50 million or a balance sheet of no more than EUR 43 million.

Finland

Thresholds are calculated at group level. Failure to present appropriate documentation may lead to a punitive tax increase.

Tax incentives

Small- and medium-sized companies
It is possible for small- and medium-sized companies carrying on certain production activities or tourism in developing areas to make use of increased depreciation.

The maximum amount of depreciation allowed for the acquisition costs of new machinery and buildings, put into use in 2009 and 2010 for production activities, may be doubled for tax purposes. Accelerated depreciation rates also apply to new factories and workshops as well as new machinery and equipment acquired for use in old factories and workshops, as follows:

- 25% – 50% (new machinery and equipment used in production); and
- 7% – 14% (new buildings used in production).

Double depreciation may be deducted from taxable income for the 2009 and 2010 tax years. Depreciation is calculated as a percentage of the depreciable acquisition costs, for example:

If the capitalised acquisition cost of a piece of machinery put into use in 2009 is EUR 100,000, the depreciation would be as follows:

- Depreciation in 2009 EUR 50,000 (50% of 100,000); and
- Depreciation in 2010 EUR 25,000 (50% of 50,000).

The remaining EUR 25,000 is depreciated according to normal rules (25%, declining-balance method). Conformity with accounting is required.

Research and development (R&D) activities
Qualifying R&D related costs may be, under certain circumstances, deducted annually, despite the fact that under general rules they should be capitalised.

Withholding taxes (WHT)

Finnish corporations paying certain types of income are required to apply the following withholding tax rates on payments to foreign corporations and non-resident aliens (see Note 1).

Tax rates on dividends and other payments from Finland to non-residents in 2010 are presented in the table below.

According to domestic legislation, interest paid to a non-resident is usually tax exempt in Finland. Dividends paid to a company referred in the EC Parent-Subsidiary Directive owning at least 10% of the capital of the dividend distributing company are tax exempt.

No withholding tax is levied on dividend payments received by companies resident in the EU/EEA area (other than in Liechtenstein), which would have been tax-free if paid to a Finnish corporate body, if the withholding taxes cannot be credited in the company's state of residence.

See below for tax to be withheld at source, by countries of residence (of recipient). For countries not included in table, the rate is 28%.

Each tax treaty should be studied carefully because there are often exceptions to general rules.

	Dividend (portfolio)/ interest on cooperative capital	Dividend * (direct investment)	Investment fund profit share **	Royalty ***
	%	%	%	%
Argentina	15	10 (25%)	28	15 18)
Armenia	15	5 (25%)	0	10 6)
Australia	15	5 (10%)6,14	28	5 8)
Austria	10	0 (10%)14	0	5
Azerbaijan	10	5 (25%) 8)	28	5 4)
Belarus	15	5 (25%)	0	5
Barbados	15 5)	5 (10%)14	28	5 1,5)
Belgium	15	0 (10%)	0	5 1)
Bosnia-Herzegovina	15	5 (25%)	0	10
Brazil (see protocol)	28	28	28	28
Bulgaria	10	0 (10%)	0	5 1)
Canada	15	5 (10%) 14	28	10 1)
China, P.R. of	10	10	28	10 9)
Croatia	15	5 (25%)	0	10
Cyprus	28 23)	0 (10%)	28	28
Czech Republic	15	0 (10%)	0	10 16,1)
Denmark (Including the Faroe Islands)	15	0 (10%)	0	0
Egypt	10	10	28	25
Estonia	15	0 (10%)	28	10 12)
France	0	0	0	0
Germany	15	0 (10%)	See dividend	5 1)
Georgia	10	5 (10%)8) or 0 (50%)8)	0	0
Great Britain	0 5)	0	0 5)	0 5)
Greece	13	0 (10%)	0	10 1)
Hungary	15	0 (10%)	0	5 1)
Iceland	15	0 (10%)	0	0
India	15	15	28	20 6)
Indonesia	15	10 (25%)	28	15 4)
Ireland, Rep. of	0 5)	0 (10%)14	0 5)	0 5)
Israel	15	5 (10%)	0	10
Italy	15	0 (10%)	0	5 1)
Japan	15	10 (25%)8)	0	10
Korea, Rep. of	15	10 (25%)	0	10
Kyrgyzstan	15	5 (25%)	0	5

Finland

	Dividend (portfolio)/ interest on cooperative capital	Dividend * (direct investment)	Investment fund profit share **	Royalty ***
	%	%	%	%
Latvia	15	0 (10%)	28	10 12)
Lithuania	15	0 (10%)	28	10 12)
Luxembourg	15 10)	0 (10%)10)	0	5 1,10)
Macedonia	15	0 (10%)14)	0	0
Malaysia	15	5 (10%)	28	5
Malta	15	0 (10%)	0	0
Mexico	0	0	28	10
Moldova	15	5 (25%)	0	7 6)
Morocco	15	15	0	10
Netherlands	15	0 (15%)	0	0
New Zealand	15	15	28	10
Norway	15	0 (10%)	0	0
Pakistan	20 20)	12 (25%)	28	10
Philippines	28	15 (10%)14)	28	25 3)
Poland	15	0 (10%)	0	10 1)
Portugal	15	0 (10%)	0	10
Romania	5	0 (10%)	0	5 19)
Russia	12	5 (30%)7)	0	0
Serbia and Montenegro	15	5 (25%)	0	10
Singapore	10 15)	5 (10%)14,15)	28	5 15)
Slovak Republic	15	0 (10%)	0	10 1,16)
Slovenia	15	0 (10%)	0	5
South Africa	15	5 (10%)	0	0
Spain	15	0 (10%)	0	5
Sri Lanka	15	15	0	10
Sweden	15	0 (10%)	0	0
Switzerland	10	0 (20%)	0	0
Tanzania	20	20	0	20
Thailand	28	20 (25%)13)	28	15
Turkey	20	15 (25%)	28	10
Ukraine	15	5 (20%)	0	10 17)
United Arab Emirates	28 22)	28 22)	28 22)	28 22)
United States	15 21)	5 (10%)14,21)	0	0
Uzbekistan	15	5 (10%)14)	0	10 6)
Vietnam	15	10 (25%) or 5 (70%)	28	10
Zambia	15	5 (25%)	28	15 1,11)

Notes

* The recipient is a company whose share in the company making the payment is at least the percentage indicated in parentheses.

** No tax on profit shares meant in EC Directive 2003/48/EC (§ 3.7, Act on Tax at source).

*** No tax on royalties between associated companies meant in EC Directive 2003/49/EC (§ 3 b-f, Act on Tax at source).

1. Tax is not levied on literary, scientific or artistic royalties *(for film royalties see text of treaty)*.
2. The tax rate is 10% on use of films, literary, scientific or artistic works and 25% on use of trademark or royalties paid for usufruct.
3. The tax rate is 15% on films, tapes used in television or radio broadcasts, use of copyright of literary, artistic or scientific works or royalty paid for usufruct.
4. The tax rate is 10% on literary, scientific, artistic and film royalties.
5. The tax rate for an individual is 28% if income is tax exempt in the country of residence.
6. A lower tax in certain cases, as for India *see article V in protocol 1997*.
7. Foreign capital > USD 100,000 when dividend becomes due and payable.
8. For additional requirements, see the treaty.
9. The tax rate is 7% on industrial, scientific and commercial royalties.
10. The tax rate is 28% if the recipient is a special holding company.
11. The tax rate is 5% on royalties from films and tapes.
12. The tax rate is 5% on royalties paid for the use of industrial, commercial or scientific equipment.
13. The tax rate is 15% if the payer is also an industrial enterprise.
14. The 10% is calculated on the total voting stock.
15. The tax rate is 28% on an unremitted amount, if free from tax in Singapore.
16. The tax rate is 1% for a finance lease of equipment and 5% for an operating lease of equipment and computer software.
17. The tax rate is 5% for the use of secret process or for know-how, no tax for computer software or patent.
18. The tax rate is 10% on industrial royalty, 3% on royalties to news agency and 5% on artistic royalty to the author or his *mortis causa* successor.
19. The tax rate is 2.5% on royalties paid for the use of industrial, commercial or scientific equipment or computer software.
20. The tax rate is 15% if the recipient is a company.
21. No tax on dividends to qualified parents-subsidiaries and pension funds (Article 10 paragraph 3).
22. No tax if the recipient proves that he has domicile (individual) or is incorporated in the United Arab Emirates.
23. The tax rate is 19.5% if paragraph 3 of Act on Tax at source (RP 113/2008) is applicable.

Non-treaty areas include: Andorra, Antigua and Barbuda, Bahama Islands, Bahrain, Belize, Bermuda, Cayman Islands, Cyprus, Grenada, Greenland, Guernsey, Hong Kong, the Spitzbergen, Jan Mayen, Jersey, Liberia, Macao, Mauritius, Monaco, Netherlands Antilles, Panama, Vanuatu, Virgin Islands.

Tax administration

Issues in focus

Current issues in special focus of tax audits are transfer pricing and permanent establishments.

Tax returns

The tax year is generally the calendar year. A company having an accounting period other than the calendar year is taxed for the accounting period or the accounting periods ending during the calendar year. A company must file a corporate income tax return within four months from the end of the accounting period.

Finland

Payment of tax

Income taxes are levied as prepayments during the tax year. After the assessment of the taxes, any excess prepayments are refunded without application. If the total prepayments are less than the actual income tax to be paid, the remaining amount is levied by the local tax office.

The tax account system

As of the beginning of 2010, a new system for reporting and paying unprompted taxes – such as VAT and employer's social charges – was introduced. Tax Account is a taxpayer-specific information system under which unprompted taxes are declared on a monthly basis. There are changes in the existing system of monthly returns, due dates, payments and refunds. Payments are made through regular payment channels.

Tax types not covered by Tax Account are income tax, real estate tax, inheritance tax, gift tax, forestry fees and transfer tax. It is important to note that withholding taxes are henceforth declared through the Tax Account.

Other issues

Company restructurings

In accordance with the EC directive 2009/133/EC on mergers, divisions, partial divisions, transfers of assets and exchanges of shares concerning companies of different Member States, it is possible to carry out the said restructurings tax neutral, if statutory conditions are met. In cross-border situations, both parties should be resident in the EU. Principal of going concern is applied in taxation, i.e., the receiving company receives the assets with the values the transferring company had for those assets in its taxation.

Corporate taxes in France

For more information, contact:

Michel Combe
Landwell & Associés
Crystal Park
61 rue de Villiers
92208 Neuilly-sur-Seine Cedex
France
Tel: +33 1 56 57 45 86
Email: michel.combe@fr.landwellglobal.com

Significant developments

Attractive research and development (R&D) tax credit regime

The 2010 Finance Act extended for one additional year (2010) the ability for companies, which are subject to corporate income tax, to elect to receive an immediate refund of the R&D tax credit.

Tax consolidation group

Beginning in January 2009, a French subsidiary can be included in a tax consolidated group even if its parent company is not located in France. However, at least 95% of the share capital of the foreign company must be held, directly or indirectly, by the French company that is head of the tax consolidated group. In addition, the foreign company must be subject to corporate income tax, be located in the European Union or in a member state of the European Economic Area whose tax treaty with France includes a mutual administrative assistance clause to fight tax fraud and tax evasion and hold 95% of the lower-tier subsidiary's shares.

A permanent establishment of a foreign company and subject to French corporate income tax can be a member of a French tax consolidated group if the shares of the foreign company are held by other French companies, which are members of the consolidated group.

Provisions on the tax neutrality of intra-group transaction flows (e.g., dividends, provisions, waivers of debts, interest, and capital gains on the sales of shares) have been modified to treat tax consolidated groups with an intermediate foreign company the same as other tax consolidated groups.

Business tax

The business tax has been replaced by the territorial and economic contribution, known in French as "Contribution Economique Territoriale" (CET) beginning 1 January 2010. CET comprises two different taxes: the companies' land contribution, known in French as "Cotisation Foncière des Entreprises" (CFE) and the companies' added value contribution (CVAE). Although they have a similar scope, the taxes are subject to very different rules. The CFE tax is based on the rental value of assets that are subject to the land tax, excluding movable goods and equipment. For industrial plants, the taxable base is reduced by 30%. There is a specific rental value for each town and an upgrading ratio is set forth at national level each year.

The CVAE is based on a company's added value. Only taxpayers, which are not exempt from the CFE and whose turnover is greater than EUR 152,500, are subject to CVAE.

France

However, tax relief equal to the amount of the tax is provided for companies whose turnover is under EUR 500,000. The tax rate for companies whose turnover ranges from EUR 500,000 to EUR 50 million is assessed according to a progressive scale, which ranges from 0 to 1.5%. There is an upper ceiling on the added value that applies to the CET. As a consequence, a tax relief applies and is equal to the excess of the sum of CFE and CVAE over 3% of the added value of the company.

VAT package
Beginning on 1 January 2010, for VAT business-to-business (B2B) suppliers of services are taxable at the location of the customer and no longer at the location of the supplier. For business-to-consumer (B2C) suppliers of services, the place of taxation remains where the supplier is established.

With the new VAT package, taxation in the state of the customer applies only to taxable persons, partly taxable persons, and non-taxable legal persons that are registered for VAT.

Specific new VAT rules apply to transportation leases, cultural, arts and sports services, electronic and telecommunication services, and transportations of goods.

Transfer pricing documentation
Beginning on 1 January 2010, the Amended Finance Act of 2009 introduces new French transfer pricing documentation requirements concerning large corporations located in France (i.e., with annual turnover or amount of gross assets in excess of EUR 400 million).

According to this new provision, the documentation must contain general information regarding the relevant group of companies, including notably activities, operational and legal structures of the related companies, functions performed and risks borne, main intangible assets, group transfer pricing policy, amongst others.

Anti-avoidance rules applicable to non-cooperative states or territories (NCST)
Under NCST for French tax purposes, a state or territory is considered non-cooperative if it meets at least one of the following criteria:

1. It is not a member of the European Community;
2. It has been reviewed and monitored by the OECD Global Forum on Transparency and Exchange of Information;
3. It has not concluded at least twelve administrative assistance agreements/treaties that allow a complete exchange of information for tax purposes; or
4. It has not concluded an administrative assistance agreement/treaty with France.

Under the new tax regime, the French parent-subsidiary regime will no longer be applicable to dividends paid from entities located in an NCST with respect to tax years beginning on or after 1 January 2011.

Beginning on 1 January 2010, withholding tax on passive income is increased to 50% for transactions with an NCST person or entity.

Payments (e.g., interests, royalties, payments for services) made to an NCST person or entity are as a general rule not tax deductible. In addition it is no longer possible to offset withholding tax in France with any foreign withholding tax borne by the entity located in a NCST.

Moreover, concerning shareholders (individuals and companies) located in a NCST, a tax amounting to 50% is levied on capital gains derived from the disposal of shares in French companies whatever the level of shareholding.

Taxes on corporate income

France levies a corporate income tax at a rate of 33.33%.

Concerning large size companies, a social contribution tax amounting to 3.3% is assessed on the corporate tax amount from which a EUR 763,000 allowance is withdrawn.

A patent box regime allows income derived from the sale or license of patents or patentable inventions to be taxed at the reduced rate of 15%, under certain conditions.

Reduced tax rates of 15% or 8% apply to certain capital gains. *See "Capital gains" under the "Income determination" section.*

No tax is levied on income at the regional or local level.

A withholding tax is levied on French branches of foreign non-EU corporations at the rate of 25%, or a reduced tax treaty rate (e.g., for the United States, 5%) on net profits. Refund (limited or full) of tax may be claimed to the extent that the taxable amount exceeds the dividend(s) actually distributed by the foreign corporation during the twelve months following the close of the fiscal year concerned, or the dividends are distributed to residents of France.

Corporate residence

France is defined as metropolitan France (excluding Monaco, but including the continental shelf), Corsica and the overseas departments (French Guyana, Guadeloupe, Martinique, Reunion).

A French company, which as a general rule is a company incorporated under French commercial laws, is subject to corporate tax in France on its worldwide income, with the exception of income attributable to foreign business activity (if there is no treaty in force between France and the relevant foreign country) or to a foreign permanent establishment (if a tax treaty does apply).

A foreign company is subject to corporate tax in France on income attributable to a French business activity or to a French permanent establishment, as well as on income from real estate located in France.

Other taxes

Value-added tax (VAT) known as turnover taxes in France
Turnover taxes are assessed on goods sold and services rendered in France. The normal rate is 19.6%. Other rates of 5.5% and 2.1% apply to specific sales and services (for example, restaurant, transports of travellers and sales of books are taxable at the 5.5%

France

reduced rate). Exports and certain specific services invoiced to non-French residents are zero-rated.

Registration duties
Registration duties mentioned hereafter are imposed on the purchaser. However, the seller may be liable for these duties in case of non settlement by the purchaser.

Transfer of goodwill
The transfer of goodwill is subject to a registration duty at a rate of 3% on the part of the transfer price amounting from EUR 23,000 to EUR 200,000 and at a rate of 5% on the part exceeding EUR 200,000.

Transfer of shares
The transfer of shares of Société anonyme (SAs, which are corporations) and Société par Actions Simplifiées (SASs, which are simplified corporations) is subject to registration duty at a rate of 3% with a maximum of EUR 5,000 per transfer.

The transfer of interests or quotas in legal entities whose capital is not divided into shares (e.g., Société à responsabilité limitée – SARLs), which are a form of private limited liability corporate entity is subject to a registration duty of 3%.

The transfer of shares in non-quoted companies whose assets consist principally of immovable property is subject to a registration duty of 5%.

Transfer of real estate
The sale of land and buildings is subject to registration duty at a rate of 5.09% on the transfer price, including expenses.

Real estate tax
All properties located in France are subject to a 3% real estate tax. The tax is assessed on the fair market value of the real estate, in proportion to the direct or indirect interest held. All entities in the chain of ownership are jointly liable for the payment of the tax.

Automatic exemptions apply in three situations. First, to entities whose French real estate assets represent less than 50% of their total French assets. Second, to entities listed on a regulated market whose shares, units or rights are significantly traded on a regular basis. Third, to entities having their registered office in France, in an EU Member State or in a country that has concluded a double tax treaty with France providing for an administrative assistance or a non-discrimination clause, where:

1. Their direct or indirect interest in the French real estate is less than either EUR 100,000 or 5% of the fair market value of the French real estate;
2. They are pension funds or public charities recognised as fulfilling a national interest whose activities justify the need to own French real estate; or
3. They are non-listed French real estate funds ("société de placement à prépondérance immobilière à capital variable" (SPPICAV) or "fonds de placement immobilier" (FPI)) or foreign funds subject to equivalent regulations.

Where an automatic exemption does not apply, a claim may be submitted for conditional exemption.

Branch income

Tax rates on branch profits are the same as on corporate profits. However, as a principle, branch profits are deemed to be distributed to the head office.

Profits realised in France by foreign corporations whose head offices are located in a European country are not subject to branch withholding tax, provided that certain conditions are met (e.g., effective head office in a European country or foreign corporation subject to corporate taxation).

Income determination

Inventory valuation
Inventories must be valued at the lower of cost or market. Cost must be determined in accordance with the first-in, first-out (FIFO) or the average-cost method. The last-in, first-out (LIFO) method is prohibited.

Capital gains
Capital gains generally are taxable as ordinary income and subject to French corporation tax at the standard rate of 33.33%, regardless of the duration of ownership of the assets sold.

However, a reduced rate of 15% increased by the social contribution on benefits is applied to capital gains on the disposal of patents or patentable inventions, as well as on income from the licensing of patents or patentable inventions.

Gains on the sale of shares in subsidiaries held for at least two years benefit, since 1 January 2007, from a large size relief (95% of such capital gains are excluded from corporate income tax, the remaining 5% portion being taxed at the standard 33.33% rate).

Capital gains realised by non-resident investors on the sale of participations in French companies that are subject to corporate income tax continue to be taxed at the rate of 18% (if the non-resident investor has held at least 25% of the share capital of the French company at any time over the past five years) or 33.33% (for French real property companies, depending on the specific wording of the applicable tax treaties).

See also the developments concerning "Anti-avoidance rules applicable to NCST" in the *"Significant developments"* section.

Inter-company dividends
French parent companies (i.e., companies incorporated in France and holding qualifying shares that represent at least 5% of the issued capital of subsidiaries, French or foreign) have the option of excluding 95% of the subsidiaries net dividends from corporate income tax (a 5% of charges and expenses must be added back to the parent company's taxable results). The French parent-subsidiary regime extends to certain shares without voting rights. There is no formal commitment to hold the shares for at least two years and companies can benefit from this regime from the acquisition date of the shares. However, the obligation remains to hold the shares over this period of time. Certain shares of listed real estate companies are not eligible to the French parent-subsidiary regime.

F

France

Foreign income and new Controlled Foreign Company (CFC) rules

Resident corporations are not taxed on foreign source income derived from activities carried out abroad through foreign branches. Foreign income is not taxable until actually repatriated to French resident corporations. As a result, undistributed income of foreign subsidiaries is not taxable. The only exception to the territoriality principle is provided by Article 209 B of the tax code, known as the Controlled Foreign Company rules. The controlled foreign company rules provide that:

- The percentage of shares, which have to be owned by the French company in the foreign legal entity or permanent establishment: French corporations are required to include in their taxable income profits made by their more than 50% owned foreign subsidiaries and branches. The 50% holding is determined by direct and indirect control of shares and voting rights.
- Introduction of an anti-avoidance rule: The minimum holding threshold has to be reduced to 5%, if over 50% of the share capital of the foreign entity is indirectly held through French or foreign companies controlled by the French parent company. However, if the shares in the foreign entity are listed on a regulated market, the French tax authorities will have to demonstrate that the French parent company, together with other entities holding shares in such foreign entity, is acting in concert.
- Notion of privileged tax regime: The CFC rules are applicable if the foreign legal entity or permanent establishment in which the French company owns the requisite percentage of shares is in a country with a privileged tax regime. A privileged tax regime is defined by the French tax code as a tax regime in which a foreign jurisdiction subjects taxable income of a foreign entity to at least 50% or lower of the income tax liability which would have been incurred in France, had the activity of the foreign entity been performed in France.
- Profits of the foreign entity which fall under the CFC rules are no longer taxed separately. They are now aggregated with the other taxable profits of the French parent company. Consequently, any tax losses incurred by the French parent company may be offset against the foreign entity's profits.
- Safety clauses: The French parent company can avoid the application of the CFC rules if it demonstrates that the foreign entity carries an effective trading or manufacturing activity, conducted from its country of establishment or registered office. Furthermore, the CFC rules in principle are not applicable with respect of foreign branches or subsidiaries located in another EU country. However, this exception is not applicable if the French tax authorities can demonstrate that the foreign entity located in another EU country constitutes an artificial arrangement, set up to circumvent French tax legislation. This concept is similar to the "abuse of law" concept, although it does not have all the same characteristics.

Deductions

Carryforward of losses

France imposes no time limit on the carryforward of losses by companies.

Bad debts

Bad debts which are definitively non recoverable are treated, from a tax point of view, as losses.

Under certain conditions, a tax deductible reserve can be established for debts whose recovery is uncertain.

Charitable donations

Charitable donations made by companies to certain foundations or societies are deductible up to 60% of their amount (limited to EUR 5,000 of the turnover before taxes).

Depreciation and depletion

Tax consequences of the IAS/IFRS accounting rules
As a result of the entry into force of IAS/IFRS accounting rules, which took effect on 1 January 2005, the definition as well as methods of valuation and depreciation of fixed assets have been modified.

The depreciation of fixed assets has to be carried out component by component. The components of a fixed asset have to be depreciated separately according to their own lifetime.

In order to mitigate the tax consequences of the change in the accounting rules, the amendments provide that the increase or decrease in the taxable profits of companies arising from the changes of adopting IAS/IFRS accounting rules will be spread over a period of five years, unless the increase or decrease does not exceed EUR 150,000.

Declining-balance depreciation
Declining-balance depreciation is allowed for certain new and renovated assets whose useful life is more than three years.

For assets bought or manufactured between 4 December 2008 and 31 December 2009, the rate is computed by multiplying the rate of straight-line depreciation by:

- 1.75 if the useful life of the asset is three or four years;
- 2.25 if the useful life of the asset is five or six years; and
- 2.75 if the useful life of the asset is more than six years.

For assets bought or manufactured after 31 December 2009, the rate is computed by multiplying the rate of straight-line depreciation by:

- 1.25 if the useful life of the asset is three or four years;
- 1.75 if the useful life of the asset is five or six years; and
- 2.25 if the useful life of the asset is more than six years.

Goodwill

Under French tax rules, goodwill (e.g., clientele, trade-marks) cannot be depreciated.

R&D and software expenses

Concerning R&D and software expenses, a business may elect to immediately deduct costs incurred in research and development of software or to amortise their cost straight-line over a maximum period of five years. The cost of acquiring software may be written off straight-line over 12 months.

The cost of patents acquired can be depreciated over a five year period.

France

Net operating losses

For tax purposes, the distinction between ordinary losses and losses corresponding to deferred depreciation, has been eliminated. Companies subject to corporate tax can carryforward their losses for an unlimited period of time.

Corporations may also elect to carryback net operating losses (NOLs). Losses of a given fiscal year may be offset against undistributed taxable profits of the three preceding years. The lower of the tax paid on these profits or the potential tax savings represented by the tax loss of the fiscal year is a tax credit. Such credit may be offset against corporate income tax of the following five fiscal years, and thereafter, any excess credit may be refunded.

Thin capitalisation rules

Under current rules, the tax deduction of interest paid by a French company to its foreign controlling shareholders is subject to the following three restrictions:

Interest rate limitation

Under the amended article 212 of the French Tax Code, tax deduction of interest paid to related parties is limited to the higher of (i) the average annual interest rate applied by credit institutions to companies for medium-term variable rate loans or (ii) the interest that the borrowing company could have obtained from independent banks under similar circumstances. This rate is 4.81% for financial years ending on 31 December 2009. Having passed this interest rate test, French indebted companies have to pass a second test: the debt ratio.

Debt ratio

That part of interest paid to related parties, which is deductible under the rate limitation test is disqualified, if it exceeds all of the three following limitations during the same financial year:

i.   Interest relating to financing of any kind granted by related parties within the limit of 1.5 times the net equity of the borrower;
ii. 25% of an adjusted net income before tax ("résultat courant avant impôt" defined as the operating income, increased by certain items); and
iii. Interest income received from related parties (i.e., no limitation on thin capitalisation grounds when the borrowing company is in a net lending position vis-a-vis related entities).

The portion of the interest which exceeds the three above limits is not deductible, except if it is lower than EUR 150,000.

Carryforward of excess interest

That part of the interest which is not deductible immediately by the borrowing company can be carried forward, without time limit, for relief in subsequent years, provided there is an excess capacity during such years. The amount in excess is, however, reduced by 5% each year, from the second financial year following the financial year in which the interest expense has been incurred.

Exceptions

(i) The thin capitalisation rules do not apply to interest payable by banks and credit institutions, and also to certain specific situations such as interest in connection with intra-group cash pools or with certain leasing operations; and

(i) The thin capitalisation rules do not apply if the French indebted company can demonstrate that the debt-to-equity ratio of the worldwide group to whom it belongs exceeds its own debt-to-equity ratio.

Deductibility is also facilitated within a French tax consolidated group. The thin capitalisation rules apply to each company member of the group taken on a stand-alone basis. Any excess interest incurred by such company is, however, not carried forward by it. Instead, it is appropriated at group level.

Payments to foreign affiliates
Payments to foreign affiliates are allowed, as long as they meet the arm's-length test. If they do not, article 57 of the French Tax Code provides that income directly or indirectly transferred to the foreign affiliate, through either the increase or the reduction of the purchase or sales price of goods and services, or through any other means, must be added back to taxable income. For the purpose of this provision, foreign affiliates are defined as parent or sister companies.

Where the payments are made to companies located in a country with a privilege tax regime *(see above in the "Significant developments" section, Foreign income and CFC rules)*, the French taxpayer must prove that the transaction is bona fide and that the amount due is not exaggerated.

Taxes
Most taxes, including unrecoverable VAT, registration taxes and business tax, are deductible. The major exceptions are corporate income tax and tax penalties.

Group taxation

French corporations and their 95% owned domestic subsidiaries may elect to file one single tax return, thus, allowing offset of losses of one group corporation against the profits of a related corporation. The tax is levied on the aggregate income after certain adjustments for intra-group provisions such as debt waivers, dividend distributions, have been made.

Other group consolidation systems are available with the prior authorisation of the Ministry of Finance, as follows:

1. "Bénéfice consolidé" – The 50% owned subsidiary consolidation system allows the combined reporting of profits and losses of all controlled branches, subsidiaries, and partnerships, whether French or foreign.
2. "Bénéfice mondial" – Worldwide tax consolidation allows French corporations to include in their French tax return the results of their foreign activities carried out by branches.

When shares in a company that will be integrated into the group are acquired by a group company from individuals or legal entities that control this group, either directly or indirectly, a portion of the group's overall financial expense incurred by the members of the group is progressively added back to the group's taxable income on a straight-line basis over a nine year period.

France

Tax incentives

R&D tax credit

The tax code classifies eligible technical and scientific research operations in three areas: fundamental research, applied research, and experimental development.

The eligible expenditures include:

- Tax deductible depreciation expenses relating to fixed assets, created or acquired newly, and assigned to eligible research and development works/projects, including patents acquired;
- Costs relating to staff qualifying as scientists and/or engineers (staff costs relating to "young graduate doctor" are retained up to 200% of their amounts during the 24 months following their hiring by the company);
- Expenses resulting from outsourced research and development works/projects;
- Expenses incurred for patent registration and/or in connection with the defense of patents;
- Expenses relating to the monitoring of technical developments; and
- Premiums paid in connection with insurance contracts relating to the legal defense of patents.

The R&D tax credit is determined on the basis of the eligible R&D expenses incurred during the calendar year.

Currently, the R&D credit equals 30% of the R&D eligible expenses incurred during the year up to EUR 100 million in eligible R&D expenses and 5% beyond this amount. In addition, eligible R&D expenses incurred by the company can be included in the basis for computation on the tax credit up to 100% of that amount.

Moreover, the 30% "standard" rate is increased to 50% and 40% for the first and the second year, respectively, during which the company incurs eligible R&D expenses, or after the expiration of a period of five consecutive years during which the company did not benefit from the tax credit, provided in both cases, that the concerned company is not affiliated with another company which benefited from the R&D tax credit within the same time period.

Inward investment

No particular incentives are available to foreign investors in France. However, the government offers a comprehensive programme of tax incentives and development subsidies to encourage investment in underdeveloped areas.

Capital investment is encouraged through the declining-balance method of depreciation as well as through exceptional depreciation for certain capital expenditure.

Withholding taxes (WHT)

Payments to resident corporations and individuals are not subject to withholding taxes.

Payments to non-resident corporations and individuals are subject to withholding taxes, as follows.

	Dividends		
Column 1	**Column 2**	**Column 3**	**Column 4**
Country of residence	**Individuals and non-parent companies**	**Parent companies**	**Shareholding required to be a parent**
	%	%	%
Non-treaty:	25	25	–
Treaty:			
Algeria	15	5	10
Argentina	15	15	–
Armenia	15	5	10
Australia	15	0	10
Austria	15	0	10
Bahrain	0	0	–
Bangladesh	15	10	10
Belgium	15	0 (1)	10
Benin	25	25	–
Bolivia	15	15	–
Botswana	12	5	25
Brazil	15	15 (2)	–
Bulgaria	15	5/0 (1)	15/10
Burkina Faso	15 (25)	25 (2)	–
Cameroon	15	15	–
Canada	15	5	10
Central African Republic	15	5	10
China	25	25	0
Comoro Islands	15/25	15/25	–
Congo, Rep. of	25	15	10
Croatia	15	0	10
Cyprus	15	10/0 (1)	10
Czech Republic	10	0 (1)	10
Denmark	25/18 (48)	0 (1)	–
Ecuador	15	15	–
Egypt	0	0	–
Estonia	15	5/0 (1)	10
Finland	15/0	5/0 (1)	10
Gabon	15	15	–
Germany	15	0 (3)	10
Ghana	15	5	10
Greece	25/18 (48)	25/0 (1)	10
Hungary	15	5/0 (1)	10
Iceland	15	5	10
India	10	10	–
Indonesia	15	10	25
Iran	20	15	25
Ireland, Rep. of	15	10/0 (1)	50/10

France

	Dividends		
Column 1	Column 2	Column 3	Column 4
Country of residence	Individuals and non-parent companies	Parent companies	Shareholding required to be a parent
	%	%	%
Israel	15	5	10
Italy	15	5/15 or 0 (1)	10
Ivory Coast	15	15	–
Jamaica	15	15	10
Japan	10	5	10
Jordan	15	5	10
Kazakhstan	15	5	10
Korea, Rep. of	15	10	10
Kuwait	0	0	–
Latvia	15	5/0 (1)	10
Lebanon	0	0	–
Lithuania	15	5/0 (1)	10
Luxembourg	15	5/0 (1)	25/10
Holding company (5)	25	25	–
Macedonia	15	0	10
Madagascar	25	15	25
Malawi	25	25	–
Malaysia	15	5	10
Mali	15/25	25 (2)	–
Malta	15	5/0 (1)	10
Mauritania	25	25	–
Mauritius	15	5	10
Mayotte	15/25	25 (6,2)	–
Mexico	15	5/0	10/5
Monaco	25	25	10
Mongolia	15	5	10
Morocco	15/0	15/0 (10)	–
Namibia	15	5	10
Netherlands	15	5/0 (1)	25/10
New Caledonia	15	5 (46)	–
New Zealand	15	15	–
Niger	25	–	–
Nigeria	15	12,5 (46)	10
Norway	15	0	10
Oman	0	0	–
Pakistan	15	10	10
Philippines	15	10 (46)	10 (47)
Poland	15	5	10
Polynesia, French	25	25	25
Portugal	15	5/0 (1)	10

	Dividends		
Column 1	**Column 2**	**Column 3**	**Column 4**
Country of residence	Individuals and non-parent companies	Parent companies	Shareholding required to be a parent
	%	%	%
Qatar	0	0	–
Romania	10	0 (1)	10
Russia (10)	15	15/10/5 (11)	–
Russian Federation	15	5	10
St. Pierre & Miquelon	15	5	–
Saudi Arabia	0	0	–
Senegal	15	15 (5)	–
Singapore	15	10	10
Slovakia	10	10/0 (1)	20
South Africa	15	5	10
Spain	15	0	10
Sri Lanka	25	25	–
Sweden	15	15/0 (1)	10
Switzerland (12)			
A (13)	15	0 (12)	10 (12)
B (14)	15 (12)	15/0 (12)	10 (12)
C (15)	25	25	–
Thailand	25	15	25
Togo	15/25	25 (2)	–
Trinidad and Tobago	15	10	10
Tunisia	25	25	–
Turkey	20	15	–
Ukraine (17)	15	5/0	10/50
United Arab Emirates	0	0	–
United Kingdom	15	5/0 (1)	10
United States	15	5/0	10/80
Uzbekistan	10	5	10
Venezuela	15	5/0	10
Vietnam	15	5	10
Zambia	25	25	50
Zimbabwe	15	10	25

France

Column 1	Interest Column 5	Royalties Column 6	Distributions Column 7
Country of residence	For instruments other than borrowings		Automatically levied on after-tax profits of permanent establishments
	%	%	%
Non-treaty: (18, 19, 20)	18 (21)	33.33	25
Treaty:			
Algeria	10	10/5 (44)	0
Argentina	16/0	18	5
Armenia	10/0	10/5 (44)	5
Australia	10	5	15
Austria	0	0	0
Bahrain	0	0	25
Bangladesh	10 (8)	10	15
Belgium	15/0 (49)	0	10/0 (28)
Benin	16	0	25 (22)
Bolivia	15	15	0
Botswana	10	10	5
Brazil	15/10	10/15/25 (23)	15
Bulgaria	0	5/0 (49)	5/0 (28)
Burkina Faso	16	0	25 (22)
Cameroon	15/0	15 (25)	15
Canada	10 (8, 24)	10 (25)	5
Quebec	10	10	5
Central African Republic	16	0	25 (22)
China	10/0	10/6 (26)	0
Comoro Islands	10 to 15	33.33	25 (22)
Congo, Rep. of	0	15	15
Croatia	0	0	0
Cyprus	10/0 (8, 49)	0 (27, 49)	10/0 (28)
Czech Republic	0	0/5/10 (29, 45, 49)	0 (28)
Denmark	18/0 (49)	33.33/0 (49)	25/0 (28)
Ecuador	15/10/0 (30)	15	15
Egypt	15	15/10 (31)	0
Estonia	10/0 (49)	5/10/0 (45, 49)	0
Finland	10/0 (8, 49)	0	15/0 (28)
Gabon	10	10	0
Germany	0	0	0
Ghana	10	10	0
Greece	0	5/0 (49)	25/0 (28)
Hungary	0	0	5/0 (28)
Iceland	0	0	5
India	10	0	0

Column 1	Interest Column 5	Royalties Column 6	Distributions Column 7
Country of residence	For instruments other than borrowings		Automatically levied on after-tax profits of permanent establishments
	%	%	%
Indonesia	15/10/0 (8)	10	10
Iran	15/0 (8)	10	15
Ireland, Rep. of	0	0	25/0 (28)
Israel	10/0 (8)	10/0 (27, 25)	5/10
Italy	10/0 (8, 49)	5/0 (29, 49)	0
Ivory Coast	15	10/0 (32)	0
Jamaica	10/0	10	10
Japan	10	0	0
Jordan	10/0 (8)	5/15/25 (23)	5
Kazakhstan	10/0	10	5
Korea, Rep. of	10 (8)	10	5
Kuwait	0	0	25
Latvia	10/0 (49)	5/10/0 (45, 49)	0
Lebanon	0	33.33	25
Lithuania	10/0 (49)	5/10/0 (45, 49)	0
Luxembourg	10/12/0 (49)	0	5/0 (28)
Holding company (5)	10 to 15	33.33	25
Macedonia	0	0	0
Madagascar	15/0 (8)	10/15 (34, 35)	25
Malawi	15	0/33.33 (25)	10
Malaysia	15 (8)	10 (35)	15
Mali	16	0	25 (22)
Malta	10/0 (49)	10/0 (29, 49)	10/0 (28)
Mauritania	16	0	25 (22)
Mauritius	16/0	15/0 (29)	15
Mayotte	0	0	25 (22)
Mexico	5/10/0	10 (26, 29)	0
Monaco	15	33.33	25
Mongolia	10/0	5 (29)	0
Morocco	15/10	10/5 (36)	0
Namibia	10/0	10 (29)	0
Netherlands	10/0 (8, 49)	0	0
New Caledonia	0	10 (29)	10
New Zealand	10/0 (8)	10	15
Niger	16	0	25 (22)
Nigeria	12.5 (8)	12.5	25
Norway (5)	0 (8)	0	0
Oman	0	0	25

France

Column 1	Interest Column 5	Royalties Column 6	Distributions Column 7
Country of residence	For instruments other than borrowings		Automatically levied on after-tax profits of permanent establishments
	%	%	%
Pakistan	10/0	10	0
Philippines	15/0 (8)	15	10
Poland	0	10/0 (29)	25
Polynesia, French	0	33.33	25 (22)
Portugal	12/0 (8, 49)	5/0 (49)	15/0 (28)
Qatar	0	0	25
Romania	10/0 (49)	10/0 (49)	10/0 (28)
Russia	0 (8)	0	0
Russian Federation	10/0	0	25
St. Pierre & Miquelon	0	10 (29)	10
Saudi Arabia	0	0	25
Senegal	15/0	0	0
Singapore	10/0 (8)	0/33.33 (37)	15
Slovakia	0	5/0 (29)	10
South Africa	0	0	0
Spain	10/0 (49)	5/0 (38, 49)	0
Sri Lanka	10/0 (8)	10/0 (39)	25
Sweden	0	0	0 (28,29)
Switzerland (12)			
A (13)	0 (12)	5/0 (12, 40)	0 (12)
B (14)	0 (12)	5/0 (12, 40)	0 (12)
C (15)	0 to 15	33.33	0 (12)
Thailand	10/3/0	5/15 (36)	25
Togo	16	0	25 (22)
Trinidad and Tobago	10/0 (8)	0/10 (26)	10
Tunisia	12/0 (8)	5/15/20 (41)	25 (22)
Turkey	15/0	10	7.5
Ukraine	10/0	0/10	25
United Arab Emirates	0	0	0
United Kingdom	0	0	0 (28)
United States	0 (42)	0	5
Uzbekistan	5/0	0	0
Venezuela	5/0 (8)	5	0
Vietnam	0	10	0
Zambia	15	0/33.33 (25)	10
Zimbabwe	10/0	10	0

Explanation of columns

Column 2: Companies not qualifying as parents and individuals are subject to the withholding tax rates as indicated in this column.

Columns 3 and 4: Column 3 indicates the withholding tax rate for dividends paid to a foreign "parent" company. To be considered as a parent company, the foreign company must hold a specified percentage of the French company's share capital or voting rights. These minimum percentages range from 0% to 50%, as indicated in Column 4, and certain other conditions must be met (see each treaty). If no percentage is indicated, either no minimum shareholding is required, or the tax treaty does not reduce the withholding tax rate of 25%.

From 1992, no withholding tax is levied on dividends paid to an EU parent company by a French company that actually are subject to corporate tax, provided the following is the case:

- The EU parent company has held a minimum percentage of the share capital of the distributing company, directly and continuously for at least two years. From 1 January 2009, with a view to benefiting from the withholding tax exemption, the participation required is 10%;
- The EU parent company is the effective beneficiary of the dividends;
- The EU parent company has its effective seat of management in an EU State and is not deemed to be domiciled outside the EU under an applicable tax treaty;
- The EU parent company is one of the legal forms enumerated by the relevant Directive.
- The EU parent company is subject to corporate income tax in the member State where it has its effective seat of management; and
- There is an anti-avoidance rule.

Column 5: French domestic law exempts interest on most types of debt from withholding tax. Minor exceptions to this general rule include interest on current accounts, claims and certain coupon bonds. French tax treaties often reduce the withholding rate to nil in these situations.

Moreover, as of 1 January 2004, there is no requirement to withhold income tax on interest and royalties paid to EU companies if all the following conditions are met:

- The taxpayer is a French resident company or a French permanent establishment of a company resident in another EU member State;
- The recipient of the income is an EU resident company; and
- The taxpayer and the recipient are at least 25% associates, which means that either one holds directly 25% or more of the share capital or voting rights in the other, or a third party holds directly 25% or more of the capital or voting rights in them both.

Column 7: Withholding tax automatically is imposed on after-tax profits of a permanent establishment unless certain conditions are met. The rate is 25% or the reduced tax treaty rate.

Notes

1. See 1 in *"Explanation of Columns 3 and 4"*.
2. Exceptions where the dividends are excluded from the taxable income of the company which has received the dividends.
3. A rate of 15% is applicable for dividends distributed by certain companies.
4. The dividend withholding tax rate is eliminated if the recipient owns 15% or more in votes or value of the distributing corporation and is (a) a company regularly traded on either the Japanese or the French stock market, (b) a company more than 50% owned by the government of either country, (c) an individual or a quoted company resident in either country, or (d) any combination of (a), (b), and (c): anti-avoidance rule.
5. The 1929-type Luxembourg holding companies are not entitled to any of the benefits of the France-Luxembourg tax treaty.

France

6. A 25% rate applies if dividends are not included in the income taxed to either corporate or income tax.
7. No withholding tax applies if dividends are taxable in Morocco.
8. Full or partial exemption is applicable when specific conditions provided by the treaty are met.
9. These are taxed when attached to a permanent establishment in France.
10. The 26 November 1996 tax treaty came into force on 9 February 1999.
11. The 5% rate applies to dividends when three conditions are fulfilled, as follows. (1) The effective recipient of the dividends must have invested at least EUR 76,224.51 in the company that pays these dividends. (2) The recipient must be a company liable for corporate tax. (3) The latter company must be exempt from corporate tax. The rate is 10% when only condition (1) or conditions (2 and 3) are fulfilled. In all other cases the rate is 15%.
12. An addendum signed on 22 July 1997 modifies the provisions of the French-Swiss tax treaty relating to dividends, interest and royalties, and provides for the removal of the 5% withholding tax on profits realised by French permanent establishments of Swiss resident companies.
13. The rate indicated applies to Swiss resident companies controlled by Swiss residents.
14. The rate indicated applies to Swiss resident companies that are controlled by non-Swiss residents (non-UE) (Article 11.2.b ii) and meet the conditions of Article 14 of the tax treaty. In the case of column 3, the 15% rate applies to these companies, provided both the recipient and the distributing company are not quoted on a stock exchange. If these conditions are not met, the tax exemption applies.
15. The rate indicated applies to Swiss resident companies controlled by non-Swiss residents but not complying with Article 14 of the tax treaty.
16. The 15% rate applies to dividends paid to an industrial company.
17. The 5% rate applies to gross dividends if the effective recipient is a Ukrainian company that holds directly or indirectly at least 10% of the French company's capital. The rate is 0% if the participation exceeds 50% and EUR 762,245. It is 15% in all other cases.
18. Non-treaty recipients of royalties and management fees are subject to a 33.33% withholding rate. Where a treaty exists, management fees are exempt from withholding tax unless they are included in the definition of royalties subject to withholding tax.
19. In France, the withholding tax is levied on a provisional basis at 25% of the net profit. This amount is reduced to the extent it exceeds the dividends actually paid by the company during the previous 12 months, and the amount of dividends paid to residents of France. Consequently, if the foreign head office undertakes not to distribute dividends in a given year, the after-tax profits of its French branch are not subject to withholding tax, even when they are transferred abroad.
20. Withholding tax on interest on loans with a contract is 0%, while withholding on other interest is in a range from 15% to 50%. For treaty rates, consult the individual entry in the table.
21. The withholding tax rate can be 60% for certain securities if the investor's identity is not disclosed.
22. The withholding tax is levied on the following amount-French net profit divided by the total foreign company net profit, multiplied by the amount of the distribution.
23. The rate of 10% is applicable on royalties for the use of literary, artistic, or scientific works, including films, 25% on royalties for the use of trademarks, and 15% otherwise.
24. Exemption is granted only to recipients actually subject to income tax on the payment in their own country.
25. No withholding tax is applicable on a royalty arising from the use of or the right to use literary, artistic, or scientific works (excluding film).
26. Withholding tax is reduced to 6% for royalties paid for the lease of industrial, commercial, or scientific equipment.
27. A rate of 5% (Cyprus) and 10% (Israel) is applicable on royalties paid for the use or the right of the use of films.
28. Profits realised in France by foreign corporations whose head offices are located in a European country are not subject to withholding taxes if certain conditions concerning

the foreign corporation are met (effective head office in a European country; foreign corporation subject to corporate taxation).

29. No withholding tax is applicable on a royalty arising from the use or the right to use literary, artistic or scientific works.
30. The rate is reduced to 10% in certain circumstances (for equipment or bank loans) mentioned in the treaty, or nil in other circumstances.
31. The rate of 25% is applicable on royalties paid for the use of trademarks.
32. No withholding tax is levied on certain royalties paid in the field of audiovisual techniques.
33. The 5% rate is levied on royalties paid for the use of literary, artistic, and scientific works. The 25% rate is levied on royalties paid for the use of trademarks.
34. The rate of 15% is applicable on royalties paid for the use of industrial property and trademarks.
35. A rate of 33.33% is applicable on royalties paid for the use of or the right to use films.
36. The rate of 5% is applicable on royalties paid for the use of literary, artistic, or scientific works, excluding films.
37. The rate of 33.33% is applicable on royalties paid for the use of literary and artistic works, including films, and for information concerning commercial experience.
38. No withholding tax is levied on royalties paid for the use of or the right to use literary or artistic works, excluding films and recordings.
39. No withholding tax is levied on royalties paid for the use of or the right to use copyrights or films.
40. No withholding tax is levied on royalties paid for the use of or the right to use industrial, commercial, or scientific equipment.
41. The rate of 20% is applicable on royalties paid for the use of trademarks, 15% for the use of industrial property, and 5% for the use of literary, artistic, or scientific works.
42. Taxed in certain circumstances provided by the treaty.
43. No withholding tax is applicable on a royalty arising from the use of or the right to use literary, artistic, or scientific works, films, recordings, or computer software.
44. The rate of 5% is applicable on royalties for the use of literary, artistic, or scientific works, not including films.
45. The rate of 5% is applicable on royalties for the use or the right to use industrial, commercial, or scientific equipment.
46. The reduced rate is applicable if the beneficial owner is a company (other than a partnership).
47. Voting shares solely.
48. French domestic law decreases the withholding tax rate from 25% to 18% concerning individuals who are resident in another EU member state, in Iceland and in Norway.
49. See 49 in Explanation of column 5 above.

Tax administration

Payment of tax
Payment of tax is made during the fiscal year by way of four instalments totalling 33.33% of the taxable income of the preceding year.

Currently, for companies which have a gross income in excess of EUR 500 million, the last down-payment is now assessed on the basis of the estimated taxable income of the present year (in case of significant increase of the taxable profits in comparison with the previous fiscal year). This modification leads to an anticipated payment of corporate income tax.

Late payment interest
For a reassessment after a tax audit, late-payment interest is currently 4.8% per year or 0.4% per month.

France

The ruling system

To secure the tax status of a situation, foreign companies and individuals can request a private ruling from the French tax authorities as to whether their activities constitute a permanent establishment or fixed base.

The French tax authorities have to provide an answer within three months after the receipt of the request. In the absence of response from the French tax authorities within this period of time, the foreign company or individual will be deemed not to have a permanent establishment in France.

Individual advanced pricing agreements

Advanced Pricing Agreements (APAs) are available for taxpayers only on the basis of international agreements entered into in accordance with Article 25 of the OECD Model Tax Convention. Currently, taxpayers are allowed to enter into APAs with the French tax authorities on a unilateral basis. In practice, taxpayers are entitled to submit their transfer pricing policy to the French tax authorities. Agreement of the tax authorities to the APA precludes a later challenge.

For more information, contact:

Christophe Relongue
PricewaterhouseCoopers Tax and Legal Gabon
366 Rue Alfred-Marche
Libreville
Republic of Gabon
Tel: +241 74 59 11
Email: christophe.relongoue@ga.pwc.com

Significant developments

There have been some significant tax and regulatory developments regarding corporate and personal taxation in Gabon.

Law No. 27/2008 dated 22 January 2009 instituted a new tax code in Gabon. The Code became applicable as of May 2009 (except for the provisions relating to payroll taxes which became applicable from 1 January 2010).

The new tax code introduced two sets of rules relating to the form and the substance of the law. Notable changes that the new tax code has introduced include:

- Tax provisions per the former Gabonese tax code;
- Provisions relating to registration duties and stamp duties;
- The last finance bills; and
- The Economic and Monetary Community of Central Africa (CEMAC) provisions as well as the Organisation for the Harmonisation of Business Law in Africa (OHADA) provisions on accountancy.

In substance, the new tax code contains a number of changes concerning the deductibility of expenses and the introduction of more consistent provisions relating to transfer pricing.

Deductibility of expenses
The former Gabonese tax code listed expenses that were permissible deductions (as well as related conditions). Per the new tax code, this list has been replaced by rules to be applied in order to determine the deductibility of an expense. It has also defined the notion of mismanagement ("acte anormal de gestion"), which had not been defined in previous tax laws.

Transfer pricing
New rules concerning transfer pricing have been introduced. All payments considered to be a result of mismanagement will be subject to the corporate income tax rate at 35% plus penalties.

Other changes
The new Gabonese tax code has introduced rules related to tax procedure ("procedures fiscales"), notably when the tax administration performs tax audits and also in the case of misuse by the tax authority (and the collection of tax). Rules relating to tax procedure were not consistent under the former Gabonese tax code. Under the new code, new rules have been introduced relating to:

Gabon, Republic of

- The basis of tax: The new tax code introduces a number of obligations which taxpayers must comply with relating to the preservation of accounting documents;
- The audit of tax: The new tax code introduces a modification to the number of years within which a tax audit may be performed, the framework in which such an audit may take place and rules regarding protection of the taxpayer; and
- The collection of tax: The new tax code introduces rules relating to the administration and recovery of taxes, which includes various sanctions which may be applicable, (e.g., notice to third party, external constraints, blocking of the taxpayer's bank accounts); and rules relating to litigation and appeal (including identifying various parties).

Taxes on corporate income

Corporate tax is assessed on the profits minus deductible expenses and charges. Profits are composed of all operations carried out by enterprises during the period of taxation, including notably fixed assets capital gains.

The rate of the corporate income tax is fixed at 35%.

There is, however, a lower limit, known as the "Impôt Minimum Forfaitaire" (IMF) which is calculated as 1% of the global turnover carried out during the fiscal-year of the taxation, with a minimum of XAF 1,000,000. The tax cannot be less than this amount even in the case of a negative turnover.

New companies are exempt from this minimum tax during the first two fiscal years of their existence.

Companies liable to the corporate income tax must pay the General Tax Office two instalments on 30 November and 30 January. The balance of the due tax must be paid on 30 April. The first instalment must equal one-quarter of the tax assessed the previous year and the second instalment must equal one-third of this tax.

Corporate residence

Subject to the provisions of international tax treaties, companies carrying out operations in Gabon are subject to taxation in Gabon.

Other taxes

Value-added tax (VAT)
VAT is a cumulative tax levied on the sale of goods and the provision of services rendered or used in Gabon.

There are three rates of VAT:

- Standard rate: 18% (applies to all transactions unless otherwise provided for by the law);
- Reduced rate: 10% (applies to manufacturing operations and sales of products mentioned in a limitative list provided by article 221 of the new Gabonese tax code, including mineral water, chicken, sugar, cement, etc.); and
- Zero-rate: 0% (applies to exports and international transports).

Gabon, Republic of

Franchise tax (Patente)
Each person who carries on a trade, business or activity that is not expressly exempted is liable to franchise tax. It is a fixed duty established according to a general tariff varying from XAF 10,000 to XAF 500,000, according to the size, nature and location of the company.

Tax on property
Tax on buildings (CFPB) is 15% of the rental value of the building after deduction of 25% for deterioration and maintenance. Tax on non-built property is 25% of the taxable revenue corresponding to 4 to 5% of the rental value or 10% of the purchase value.

Registration duties
Since the publication of the Law No. 27/2008, provisions relating to registration duties are provided by the Gabonese tax code.

Registration duties are fixed, proportional or progressive, depending on the nature of the acts and transfers in question.

Stamp duty
The stamp contribution is levied on all paperwork relating to civil and judicial actions and to documents which could be produced in court as evidence.

All signatories for mutually binding contracts, lenders and borrowers for loans and ministerial officials who receive or modify deeds announcing unstamped deeds or books are jointly responsible for the payment of stamp duties and fines.

Tax on insurance premiums
Insurance or annuity agreements made with insurance companies or any other Gabonese or foreign insurer are subject to an annual obligatory tax.

The tax is levied on the sums charged by the insurer and on any accessory payments made to this party by the insured party according to the following rates:

Nature of the policies	Rates
Marine policies	5%
Life policies	Exempt
Fire policies	30%
Other (e.g., personal liability, transportation)	8%
Reinsurance	Exempt

Social security contributions
Employers must contribute to the social security system (National Social Security Fund or CNSS).

The taxable basis is made up of gross salaries including indemnities having the function of a salary and any benefits in kind.

However, there is an annual ceiling of XAF 18,000,000 or XAF 1,500,000 per month.

Gabon, Republic of

The social contributions are determined according to the following rates:

	Rates
Family allowances	8%
Industrial accidents (work injuries)	3%
Retirement pensions	5%
Health evacuation funds	0.6%
Medication distribution	2%
Hospitalisations	1.5%
TOTAL	20.1%

Branch income

Taxation of branch income is the same as for corporate income. However, a 10% tax on profit is due at the time the profit is taken by the head office of the branch located abroad.

Simplified tax regime for oil subcontractors
There is a simplified tax regime specific to the oil sector which is a lump-sum tax regime granted for a triennial period. The rates for the 2009, 2010 and 2011 fiscal years is 8.68% corresponding to corporate income tax (5.6%) and personal income tax for expatriate employees (3.08%).

Features of this specific regime are as follows:

- The option for this regime is irrevocable;
- The option is granted by the Director of the General Tax Office to foreign companies;
- The subcontractor must have signed, with an oil company, a temporary agreement for the provisions of services to this company;
- The option is no longer granted to companies that have been in Gabon for more than nine years. The duration of nine years is calculated from the year during which the company started its activities in Gabon; and
- The subcontractor must constitute a Gabonese branch office.

Specific regime for regional offices ("quartiers généraux")
A regional office is a company or a branch that renders various administrative services such as management or accounting exclusively to other companies of the same group based in a given geographical area (usually a group of countries).

Taxation is based on the expenses of the regional office. A lump rate ranging between 5% and 12% of the operating expenditures is applied to determine the basis taxable to corporate income tax.

Income determination

Capital gains
Capital gains arising from the transfer of assets must be used for the calculation of taxable profits. However, the tax on capital gains can be deferred if a company reinvests an amount equal to the capital gain and the sale price of the transferred asset back into its fixed assets within three years.

Inter-company dividends
Inter-company dividends are taxed at a reduced rate in full discharge of 10% if paid and received by or from companies with their registered office in a Central African Economic and Monetary Community (CEMAC) country, shares were allotted at the time of issue or kept for two years and the Gabonese company owns more than 25% of the share capital of the subsidiary.

Foreign income
Foreign interest, royalties and dividends are included in the taxable income, subject to international tax treaties (some treaties state that certain/all types of income listed are not includable in Gabon taxable income).

Deductions

Depreciation and depletion
The straight-line method and accelerated depreciation are permitted. Tax and book conformity is obligatory. Annual depreciation must be booked to preserve tax deductibility.

The main depreciation rates provided by the Gabonese tax code are the following:

Nature of the assets	Rates
Buildings	8%
Machinery, equipment	From 8% to 20%
Office furniture	15%
Office equipment	20%
Vehicles	From 20% to 33.3%
Computing equipment	From 25% to 33.3%

Net operating losses
There is a three-year carryforward for net operating losses (NOL). Depreciation deferred in the accounts can be carried forward indefinitely.

Payments to foreign affiliates
Management fees paid to a foreign parent company are deductible under the following conditions: (1) they reflect real transactions, (2) they do not present an abnormal characteristic, and (3) they are not exaggerated. Management fees determined in a lump sum basis are not deductible.

Interests paid to shareholders are deductible only within the limit of the Central Bank's (BEAC) normal rate for advances plus two percentage points, on the condition that the registered capital is entirely paid. The portion exceeding the ceiling is not deductible and is thus subject to taxation.

Other significant items
1. Legal reserve: 5% of net profit must be transferred to a special reserve until it equals 10% of the share capital.
2. To be tax deductible, provisions must relate to existing liability or loss. General provisions are not deductible.
3. Fines and third-party taxes borne by companies are not tax deductible.

Gabon, Republic of

Group taxation

Group taxation is not permitted.

Tax incentives

Tax credits for job creation
There is a mechanism in place for granting corporate tax credits for any salaried appointments of Gabonese personnel.

This tax credit is equal to 20% of the gross salary paid to new employees, and is subject to the creation of a minimum number of jobs, according to the size of the company:

- Two jobs, for companies with less than 20 employees;
- Three jobs, for companies with 20 to 50 employees; or
- Five jobs, for companies with more than 50 employees.

Note: The tax credit is granted only on newly created jobs since the preceding fiscal year subject that the contracts concluded with the employees are for an undetermined duration and that the new jobs do not result from the diminution of existing jobs.

Inward investment
The Investments Law in force in Gabon is a result of Law No. 15/98 of 23 July, 1998.

It comprises an Investments Charter by which the Republic of Gabon reaffirms its commitment to a strategy of economic and social development based on the expansion of the private sector.

Due to the provisions of the Investments Law, any private investment in Gabon can benefit from:

- A common law framework;
- Privileged frameworks; and
- Specifically agreed frameworks.

Depending on the frameworks it is eligible for, a company can benefit from customs privileges and tax breaks.

Capital investment
New companies are exempt from the minimum taxation of corporate income tax during the first two years of operations.

Withholding taxes (WHT)

10% WHT
This tax is due on the amounts listed in article 206 of the new Gabonese tax code when they are paid by a debtor established in Gabon to individuals or companies subject to corporate income tax or personal income tax that do not have a permanent professional base in Gabon.

This tax notably concerns sums paid as a remuneration of all types of services which have been substantially provided or used in Gabon, as well as payments such as industrial property royalties and interests to non-resident foreign individuals or companies.

Net profits carried out by branches of foreign companies having their head offices abroad are also subject to a 10% withholding tax in Gabon before they are taken into account by the foreign companies.

Transferable securities income tax (IRCM) at rate 15%

This tax is due on revenues from stocks and shares paid to legal entities. It is due by beneficiaries of these revenues and must be withheld by the distributing company.

Tax treaties

Tax treaties provide that certain/all types of income are not includable in Gabon taxable income. Gabon has tax treaties with France, Belgium, the other countries of CEMAC (former UDEAC) and the African and Malagasy Common Organisation (OCAM).

Tax administration

Returns

Returns (statistical and fiscal declaration or DSF) for the previous calendar year are to be filed before 30 April of each year. Companies are required by law to have a 31 December closing of any fiscal year.

Payment of tax

Tax is payable in two instalments on 30 November and 30 January, the balance of the tax being paid on 30 April.

Corporate income tax has to be paid by Gabonese public limited companies (SA), limited liability companies (SARL), Gabonese branches of foreign companies and all permanent establishments in Gabon.

Corporate taxes in Georgia

For more information, contact:

Sergi Kobakhidze
PricewaterhouseCoopers
#7 Bambis Rigi St.
Business Center Mantashevi
Tbilisi 0o105, Georgia
Tel: +995 32 50 80 50
Email: sergi.kobakhidze@ge.pwc.com

Significant developments

To attract foreign investment, the Georgian government has reduced tax rates on passive income:

- The tax rate on dividends paid to non-residents is 5%. The rate will reduce to 3% from 1 January 2011 and to 0% from 1 January 2012; and
- The tax rate on interest paid to non-residents is 5%. The rate will reduce to 0% from 1 January 2011.

The government introduced the concept of a free industrial zone (FIZ) in 2008. Various tax and duty exemptions are available to businesses located in a FIZ.

Taxes on corporate income

The corporate income tax (CIT) rate is 15%. Taxable profit is defined as gross income minus deductible expenses.

Corporate residence

A resident enterprise is any legal entity that is established under the laws of Georgia or has its place of effective management in Georgia. Resident enterprises are subject to tax on worldwide income.

Other taxes

Value-added tax (VAT)

The standard rate of VAT is 18% and applies to the sale of all goods and services supplied in Georgia. Goods are considered to be supplied in Georgia if they are transferred in or their shipment originates in Georgia. Services generally are considered to be supplied in Georgia if they are performed in Georgia. However, special rules apply for services relating to immovable property and certain services provided to non-residents.

Zero rating applies to exported goods and international transportation. VAT-exempt supplies include financial services, goods and services required for oil and gas operations, and medical services.

Reverse-charge VAT applies to services provided to Georgian taxpayers by a non-resident entity.

A taxpayer is a person who is registered or required to be registered as a taxpayer. Any person whose annual taxable turnover exceeds GEL 100,000 in any continuous period up to 12 months or who produces or imports excisable goods must register as a taxpayer. In addition, an enterprise that expects to perform one-off taxable transaction of more than GEL 100,000 must also register as a VAT payer before effecting the transaction.

Property tax

Property tax is payable at the rate of 1% on the annual average residual value of fixed assets (except for land) on the balance sheet of Georgian entities or foreign entities with taxable property in Georgia. For property acquired before 2005, the average residual value must be multiplied by a coefficient of between one and a half and three, depending on the acquisition date.

Land tax

Land tax rates per square metre depend on the use of the land plot (urban and non-urban) and its location. The base tax rate is GEL 0.24 per square metre.

Excise tax

Excise tax is levied on specified goods that are produced in Georgia or imported. Excise tax generally is calculated with reference to the quantity of goods (e.g., volume, weight), or in the case of automobiles, on the basis of the engine's displacement and vehicle age.

Excise tax applies to the following goods:

- Alcoholic drinks;
- Condensed natural gas, except for pipeline;
- Oil distillates;
- Goods produced from crude oil;
- Tobacco products;
- Automobiles; and
- Ferrous and nonferrous metal scrap.

The export of excisable goods is taxed at 0%, with the exception of the export of ferrous and nonferrous metal scrap.

Branch income

Branch income is taxed at the general rate of 15%. There is no tax on branch profit remittances.

Income determination

Taxable profit is determined as the difference between the gross income of a taxpayer and the relevant deductions granted under the Georgian tax code. A foreign enterprise carrying out economic activities in Georgia through its permanent establishment (PE) is considered a taxpayer with respect to its gross income earned from Georgian sources, which can be reduced by deductions attributable to such income.

Georgia

Deductions

Expenses

Expenses connected with the receipt of income generally are deductible from income, provided sufficient primary documentation is available.

The following expenses are not deductible:

- Expenses not related to the generation of income (such as tax fines and penalties); and
- Expenses related to the receipt of income exempted from corporate tax.

The deduction of certain expenses is subject to limitations, including:

- Representation expenses are deductible up to 1% of gross income;
- Charitable donations are deductible up to 8% of taxable profit; and
- Repair expenses are directly deductible up to 5% of the book value of the relevant asset at the end of the year. Any excess must be capitalised and deducted through depreciation.

Interest paid on loans

Interest paid on loans is deductible up to a 30% annual interest rate (this will reduce to 24% in 2011).

Georgia currently has no thin capitalisation rules in force. However, new rules will apply from 1 January 2011. Interest expense may be disallowed if a company's debt-to-equity ratio exceeds 3:1. The thin capitalisation rules will not apply to financial institutions, entities that have gross income of less than GEL 200,000, and entities with interest expense that is less than 20% of their taxable income before deducting such interest expense.

Bad debts

A taxpayer is entitled to deduct bad debts only if the following conditions are all met:

- The bad debt is related to the taxpayer's goods or services sold;
- Income received from the sale of goods or services was previously included in taxable gross income; and
- The bad debt has been written off and recorded as such in the taxpayer's accounting records.

Depreciation

The declining balance method of depreciation applies to fixed assets for tax purposes. The maximum rate of depreciation is 20% for most fixed assets; though buildings and construction are subject to depreciation at the rate of 5% (there are other groups and rates – please contact us for additional information).

The taxpayer is entitled to fully deduct costs of purchased, produced or leased fixed assets in the year when the fixed assets are put into operation (a form of capital allowance). In case the taxpayer employs the right of full deduction in this manner, this method should not be changed for five years.

Losses
Losses may be carried forward for five years but may not be carried back.

A taxpayer may elect to extend the period to 10 years. However, this also results in the statute of limitations period being extended from six to 11 years.

International financial companies, free warehouse enterprises and international enterprises are not entitled to carryforward losses.

Leasing
If assets are transferred under a financial lease, the lessee is treated as the owner of the assets for tax purposes (i.e., if assets are on the lessee's balance sheet, the lessee pays property tax on the assets and may deduct depreciation). A lease is characterised as a financial lease if any of the following requirements are met:

- Title of ownership to the leased assets is transferred to the lessee at the end of the lease period;
- The lease term exceeds 75% of the economic life of the assets;
- The expected residual value of the leased assets at the end of the lease period is less than 20% of the market value of the leased assets; and
- The current discounted value of payments for the lease period equals or exceeds 90% of the value of the leased assets.

New rules apply for assets leased from 1 January 2010. Financial leasing will be treated in the same manner as operational leasing, provided the following conditions are met:

- The discounted value of income generated from leasing applying a 15% discount rate should not be less than the difference between the present value of the asset and its expected residual value;
- At the end of the lease term, the lessee may acquire the leased asset at its residual value, which may not be higher than 15% of the asset's fair market value at the beginning of the lease term; and
- At the end of the financial lease of the leased fixed asset may not be disposed for a price lower than the asset's residual value.

Offsetting taxes paid abroad
Income tax or profit tax paid on income earned from outside Georgia may be credited against tax payable in Georgia. The amount of credited taxes may not exceed the Georgian tax payable on the foreign income.

Group taxation

There is no group taxation in Georgia.

Tax incentives

The following are exempt from profit tax (the list is not exhaustive):

- Income of budgetary, international and charitable organisations (including grants, membership fees and donations), except for the profit from commercial activity;
- Profit received from financial services conducted by international financial companies;

Georgia

- Gains on sales of securities issued by international financial companies; and
- Income received from reexporting goods from an independent warehouse via a free warehouse enterprise.

Free industrial zone (FIZ)
The following rules apply for enterprises located in a FIZ:

- Income received by an international enterprise from its permitted activities conducted in a FIZ is exempt from income tax;
- The importation of foreign goods into a FIZ is free of customs duties and VAT-exempt;
- Operations carried out in FIZ are VAT-exempt;
- Property located in FIZ is exempt from property tax; and
- The personal income tax of employees is paid by those individuals through self-reporting.

Withholding taxes (WHT)

Foreign legal entities earning income from Georgian sources, other than through a PE, are subject to WHT at the following rates:

	%
Dividends (reducing to 3% from 1 January 2011)	5
Royalties	10
Interest (reducing to 0% from 1 January 2011)	5
Insurance and re-insurance	0
International transportation/communication, oil & gas subcontractor income	4
Income from services rendered in Georgia	10
Other Georgian source income	10

Tax administration

A corporate tax return should be submitted and any taxes paid before 1 April of the year following the reporting period.

CIT is paid in advance in equal instalments on a quarterly basis before the fifteenth day of the month following the end of the previous quarter. The advance instalments are estimated according to the previous year's annual tax. A taxpayer with no prior-year corporate tax obligation is not required to make advance payments. Excess corporate tax payments may be offset against other tax liabilities.

The tax treatment of foreign legal entities is of the same as for local companies.

The tax departments under the Ministry of Finance are responsible for administrative matters.

Corporate taxes in Germany

For more information, contact:

Dieter Endres
PricewaterhouseCoopers AG
Friedrich-Ebert-Anlage 35-37
60327 Frankfurt am Main
Germany
Tel: +49 69 9585 6459
Email: dieter.endres@de.pwc.com

Significant developments

A new coalition government took office in the last quarter of 2009. It caused parliament to enact a number of specific measures for 2010 – mainly in reaction to the worldwide financial crisis – but otherwise has announced that for the next four years priority is to be given to a return to financial and budgetary stability, rather than to any major reform of the tax system. In particular, there will be no tax cuts before 2013. The main corporate tax measures enacted were:

- The suspension of the curtailment of loss relief provisions to enable corporate recovery of a troubled business in 2008 and 2009 has now been extended indefinitely. The same curtailment provisions have been repealed for reorganisations solely within groups and otherwise to the extent the loss carryforward is covered by hidden reserves in German assets other than shareholdings;
- The interest limitation threshold of EUR 3 million for 2008 and 2009 has now been prolonged indefinitely. Unutilised taxable EBITDA (earnings before interest, tax, depreciation and amortisation) above this threshold may now be carried forward; and
- The deemed implicit interest charge in property rentals has been reduced from 65% to 50% of the rent paid. The amount of rental disallowed for trade tax, thus, falls from 16.25% of the total to 12.5%.

The Accounting Modernisation Act, an accounting reform, was enacted in 2009, intended as a simpler alternative for – in particular – unquoted companies to full International Financial Reporting Standards (IFRS) statements. From the tax point of view, the most radical change is the abolishment of the strict requirement for conformity between book and tax reporting. This has been replaced by a provision allowing a company to exercise all options permitted under the tax acts in its own tax interest without regard to the accounting treatment for the item in question. As a consequence, full deferred tax accounting is now mandatory. The Accounting Modernisation Act must be applied to accounting years ending in 2010. Application of this act is permitted but not required for 2009. IFRS statements remain mandatory for the published group accounts of quoted companies, whilst the Accounting Modernisation Act statements are the basis for the tax returns of all companies.

Germany

Taxes on corporate income

Corporation tax (Körperschaftsteuer)
German business profits are subject to two taxes, corporation tax and trade tax. Corporation tax is levied at a uniform rate of 15% and is then subject to a surcharge of 5.5% (solidarity levy).

Trade tax (Gewerbesteuer)
The effective rate of trade tax varies by location from a minimum of 7%, which is the legal minimum and applies in a few small villages in depressed areas, to the Munich rate of 17.1%. The local rates in most cities range between 14% and 16%, whilst those in small towns can be as low as 12%. The basis for this tax is the adjusted accounting profit: in particular 25% of all financing costs over EUR 100,000, including the implicit financing costs in leasing, rental and royalty payments, is added back to taxable income.

If the basis for the two taxes is identical (unlikely in practice), the overall burden on corporate profits earned in Munich would be 33%. In Frankfurt the burden would be 31.9% and in Berlin 30.2%.

Corporate residence

A corporation is resident in Germany for tax purposes if either its place of incorporation or its main place of management is in Germany.

Germany taxes its corporate residents on their worldwide income.

Value-added tax (VAT)
Proceeds of sales and services effected in Germany are subject to value-added tax under the common system of the EU at the standard rate of 19% (7% on certain items, such as food and books). The taxpayer generally is entitled to deduct the VAT charged on his inputs from that payable on his outputs.

Excise taxes
Excise taxes on fuel, electric power, insurance, and some other products are not a compliance issue for businesses other than dealers in bonded goods and insurance companies, although they can be a significant additional cost factor for business users. These excise taxes also have an environmental element in as much as the rates are set to discourage excessive use of pollutants. There is, however, no tax on pollution as such. Energy producers (such as power stations) can claim a refund of the excise tax borne in the cost of the energy products used in the production process.

Social security contributions
All employers are required to account for social security contributions on wages and salaries paid up to set monthly limits. There are four separate insurances for old-age pensions, unemployment benefits, health and invalidity care. Employees regularly earning more than EUR 4,162.50 per month can opt out of the health and invalidity insurances provided they take out appropriate cover with a private insurance company. The pension and unemployment insurances are compulsory for all employees. The upper monthly salary limits are EUR 5,500 (EUR 4,650 in the eastern part of Germany) for the pension and unemployment insurances and EUR 3,750 for the health and invalidity risks. The rates are:

- Pension insurance 19.9% – of which one-half is borne by the employee by salary deduction;
- Unemployment insurance 2.8% (employee's share is 1.4%);
- Health insurance 14.9% (7.9% employee's share); and
- Invalidity insurance 1.95% (employee's share is one-half).

There is also an additional charge of 0.41% (up to a monthly salary limit of EUR 5,500) on the employer alone to protect the insurance institutions from the risk of lost contributions on employer insolvency.

Real estate transfer tax

Real estate transfer tax is levied at 3.5% of the consideration on all conveyances of German property.

It is also levied on indirect transfers from the acquisition of at least 95% of the shares in property owning companies. This applies to shares in the shareholder throughout the corporate chain. If the transfer is indirect, and therefore without its own specific consideration, the basis for the tax is 12.5 times the annual rentable value. This value is derived from rents actually achieved over the past three years or estimated from statistics maintained by the local authority.

The tax is not levied on direct or indirect transfers without consideration in the course of a corporate reorganisation under the laws of a member state of the EEA (European Economic Area), provided at least 95% of the ultimate interest in the property remains unchanged for five years before and after the transaction.

Real estate transfer tax is currently under attack before the Constitutional Court.

Customs duties

Customs duties are levied under a common system on imports into the EU. The rate is set at zero on most imports from EU candidate countries and on many from countries with which the EU has an association agreement. For manufactured produce from other countries the rates generally lie within the range of 0-10%. The basis is the import value of the goods and thus includes uplifts for royalty or other payments associated with their use but not apparent from the transit documents. The European Commission also sets "countervailing" duties from time to time on specific imports from specific countries in order to counter dumping attempts. The countervailing duty rate is set to fully absorb the dumping margin and is therefore usually much higher than 10%.

Branch income

Both corporation tax and trade tax are imposed on the taxable income of a foreign company's German branch. The rates are the same for branches as for resident German companies, although the withholding tax on dividend distributions by German companies is not deducted from profits transferred by a German branch to its foreign head office.

Germany

Income determination

General
Strict conformity between book and tax reporting is no longer required, once the Accounting Modernisation Act takes effect (generally for 2010). Rather, a company must draw up its financial statements according to the dictates of fair presentation, but may exercise all valuation and other options in the tax acts in its own best tax interest without regard to the accounting treatment for the item concerned. IFRS financial statements are not accepted as a basis for computing taxable income.

Inventory valuation
Inventories normally are valued at the lowest of actual cost, replacement cost and net realisable value. However, any write-downs below actual cost must be for specific reasons. If specific identification of the inventories is not possible, valuation at either standard or average cost is acceptable. The last-in, first-out (LIFO) method is accepted as an option. First-in, first-out (FIFO) is not accepted unless its assumption accords with the facts, although in practice the condition is often fulfilled.

Long-term liabilities and accruals
Non-interest bearing long-term liabilities, other than advance payments received, must be discounted at 5.5% per year. A similar provision applies to refurbishment (to restore an asset to its original condition) and other accruals which accumulate over time.

Capital gains
Generally, capital gains realised by a corporate entity from a disposal of business assets are treated as ordinary income. It is possible to postpone the taxation of part or all of the gain on real estate by offsetting the gain against the cost of a replacement property.

Capital gains from the sale of investments in other companies are exempt from corporation and trade taxes. Corresponding losses are not deductible. However, 5% of the capital gains are added back to taxable income as non-deductible directly related expenses.

Dividends
Dividends received are exempt from corporation and trade taxes, regardless of the level of shareholding and the length of time it has been held. However, portfolio dividends are subject to trade tax. 5% of the tax-free gross dividend is added back to taxable income as non-deductible business expenses. Banks do not enjoy this exemption on dividends from securities held for trading.

Foreign income
Foreign income, except dividends, received by a German corporation from foreign sources, is included in taxable income for corporation tax unless a tax treaty provides for exemption. Foreign permanent establishment income, in most cases, is exempt from corporation and trade taxes, whilst double taxation on most items of passive income (e.g., interest and royalties) is avoided by foreign tax credit or, at the taxpayer's option, by a deduction of the foreign taxes as an expense.

Irrespective of any tax treaty, income from a foreign branch or partnership is not charged to trade tax.

Germany

A Foreign Tax Act sets anti-avoidance (including CFC) rules with respect to subsidiaries in certain lines of business subject to a low-tax regime. A low tax regime is one in which the rate applicable to the income in question is less than 25%. Most forms of passive income fall under the CFC rules, which essentially attribute it to the German shareholder as though he had earnt it direct. Active business income is not generally caught where the business operates from properly established facilities. Investment income held in an EU/EEA subsidiary (except Liechtenstein) is also exempt from attribution, provided the subsidiary is commercially active in its country of operation and maintains at least a minimum establishment.

Other provisions give the tax office the right to insist on full disclosure of all the facts and circumstances surrounding a transaction as a condition for the deduction of a business expense incurred within an essentially tax-free environment for the supplier. This rule operates independently of ownership or shareholding considerations.

Stock dividends
In principle, a declaration of stock dividends (by converting reserves to capital stock) by a company will not lead to taxable income for the shareholder or to other tax effects. Subsequent capital reductions, however, will be treated as cash dividends in most circumstances. There is no German tax reason for distributing a stock dividend as opposed merely to leaving accumulated profits on the books to be carried forward. The decision, therefore, depends upon the situation in the investor's home country.

Deductions

Depreciation, amortisation and depletion
Depreciation on movable fixed assets is calculated on the straight-line method over the asset's anticipated useful life. The declining balance method is not available for assets acquired in 2008, although it may be continued for additions up to 31 December 2007. The option was reintroduced for movable fixed assets capitalised in 2009 and 2010 at a maximum of two and a half times the straight-line rate, but in no case to exceed 25%. Depreciation takes the residual value of the asset into account, only if it is material, with any gains on a sale being treated as normal business income.

Buildings are amortised on a variety of straight-line or reducing rate systems designed to reach a full write-down between 25 and 50 years, depending on the age of the building and on whether the taxpayer was its first owner.

Intangibles are amortised straight-line over their estimated useful lives with goodwill over 15 years.

In addition to normal depreciation, special depreciation is deductible for tax purposes in certain limited circumstances (small businesses, ancient monuments, buildings in designated renovated city zones).

Interest limitation
Annual net interest expense (the excess of interest paid over that received) is only deductible up to 30% of EBITDA for corporation and trade tax purposes. The 30% limitation applies to all interest, whether the debt is granted by a shareholder, related party or a third party.

Germany

This limitation does not apply where the total net interest expense for the year is less than EUR 3 million or where the net amount paid to any one shareholder of more than 25% (or his related party) is no more than 10% of the total. If the company is part of a group, this latter concession is dependent on the demonstration that the equity to gross assets ratio of the company is no more than two percentage points below that of the group as a whole. Unused EBITDA potential may be carried forward for up to five years to cover future excess interest cost. This carryforward is otherwise subject to the same principles as the loss carryforward, including the curtailment of the carryforward on change of shareholder(s).

It is emphasised that the interest limitation is additional to, and not a substitute for, the transfer pricing requirement that related party finance be at arm's length.

Net operating losses (NOLs)
NOLs are carried forward without time limit. For corporation tax (but not trade tax), there is an optional carryback to the previous year of up to EUR 511,500. The loss relief brought forward claimable in any one year is limited to EUR 1 million plus 60% of current income exceeding that amount. The remaining 40% of income over EUR 1 million is charged to trade and corporation taxes at current rates. This is referred to as "minimum taxation". The loss carryforward ceases, if a single (immediate or ultimate) shareholder acquires more than 50% of the issued capital (voting rights) within a five year period.

An acquisition of between 25% and 50% leads to a corresponding reduction in the loss carryforward. These forfeiture rules do not apply to share acquisitions in connection with the recovery of a troubled business, where the change is part of a group internal reorganisation without effect on the single ultimate shareholder, or inasmuch as the loss carryforward is covered by hidden reserves in the company's assets that, on realisation will lead to German taxation. This excludes the appreciation in value of shareholdings in other companies as well as business assets held in foreign permanent establishments.

Payments to foreign affiliates
A German corporation can claim a deduction for royalties, management service fees and, subject to the interest limitation, interest charges paid to foreign affiliates, provided the amounts are at arm's length. Detailed provisions covering both form and substance define this. In particular, all services must be covered by prior written agreement, and it is also necessary to conclude agreements for the purchase and sale of goods in writing where this would be usual between third parties (e.g., for quantity rebates on sales). The substance tests must be satisfied, both as to value for money and as to business relevance. Thus the manager of a German subsidiary must be able to show both an adequate business benefit from a related party transaction and that the company could not have got a better deal on the open market. These and all other aspects of inter-company (related-party) trading fall under strict and extensive documentation requirements, breach of which can lead to serious penalties.

Taxes
All taxes borne are deductible except for corporation tax, trade tax, and VAT on non-deductible expenses. Late payment interest and similar charges are also not deductible.

Special features for trade tax

There are a number of differences between the income subject to trade tax and to corporation tax.

The most significant are the trade tax disallowance of one-quarter of the interest costs, including interest included implicitly in leasing, rental and royalty charges. Banks have an exemption from this interest disallowance.

Group taxation

If a German parent holds more than 50% of the voting rights in a domestic subsidiary, the two may conclude a formal, five-year, court registered profit pooling agreement. The ensuing relationship is then referred to as an *Organschaft*. Effectively, the annual results of an *Organschaft* are pooled in the accounts and tax returns of the parent. Profits and losses within a group, can therefore, be offset, but there is no provision for the elimination of intra-group profits from the total tax base.

Tax incentives

Germany does not offer tax incentives except in very limited circumstances, not usually of direct business relevance (e.g., special depreciation for buildings under a conservation order). Partly, this is a question of the state budget, partly it reflects the constitutional requirement for equal treatment for all taxpayers.

Other incentives

Investment grants of 10% or 20% are available on capital investment in new manufacturing facilities or hotels in the eastern part of Germany. The system is to be phased out by 2013.

Local authorities may offer facilities on favourable terms, such as the provision of cheap land on industrial estates.

Withholding taxes (WHT)

Domestic corporations paying certain types of income are required to withhold tax as shown in the following tables. There is also a solidarity levy of 5.5% on the tax due.

General

Recipient of German-source income	Dividends[1]	Interest[1,2,3]	Royalties	Movable asset rentals[4]
	%	%	%	%
Resident corporations and individuals	25	25	–	–
Non-resident corporations and individuals[1]				
EU corporations[5,6]	–	–	–	–
Non-treaty corporations	25	25	15	15
Non-treaty individuals	25	25	15	varies

Germany

Notes

1. Corporate recipients of dividend and interest income (interest on convertible and profit-sharing bonds) can apply for refund of the tax withheld over the corporation tax rate of 15% regardless of any further relief available under a treaty.
2. Generally, only interest paid by banks to a resident is subject to a withholding tax. 25% tax is also withheld from income on convertible or profit-sharing bonds.
3. Interest paid to non-residents other than on convertible or profit-sharing bonds is generally free of withholding tax. Tax on loans secured on German property is not imposed by withholding, but by assessment to corporation tax at 15% (plus solidarity levy) of the interest income net of attributable expenses. The tax authorities can order a withholding tax of 15.825% (including solidarity levy) if ultimate collection of the tax due is in doubt. Both forms of tax are reduced by treaty relief.
4. Movable asset rentals are taxed by assessment rather than by withholding. For corporations, the rate is the standard 15% corporation tax rate (plus solidarity levy) unless reduced by treaty.
5. Where the EC Parent/Subsidiary Directive applies, dividends paid by a German company to a qualifying parent company resident in another EU member state are exempted from German withholding tax. The minimum shareholding is 10%, to be held continuously for at least one year.
6. The EC Interest and Royalties Directive exempts payments from withholding tax, if made to an associated company in another EU member state. The association must be through a common shareholding of at least 10%, to be held continuously for at least one year.

Treaty rates

Recipient of German-source income	Dividends[1]	Interest[1,2,3]	Royalties	Movable asset rentals[4]
	%	%	%	%
Algeria	5 / 15	10	10	–
Argentina[5]	15	10 / 15	15	15
Armenia[5,6]	15	5	–	–
Australia[5]	15	25	10	10
Austria[5]	5 / 15	–	–	–
Azerbaijan[7]	5 / 15	– / 10	5 / 10	–
Bangladesh[5]	15	25	10	10
Belarus[7]	5 / 15	– / 5	3 / 5	5
Belgium[5,8]	15	– / 25	–	–
Bolivia[5]	10	25	15	15
Bosnia-Herzegovina[5,9]	15	25	10	10
Bulgaria[5]	15	25	5	5
Canada[10]	5 / 15	– / 10	– / 10	10
China, P.R.[5]	10	25	10	7
Croatia[5]	5 / 15	25	–	–
Cyprus[11]	10 / 15	10	– / 5	–
Czech Republic[12]	5 / 15	–	5	5
Denmark[5]	5 / 15	25	–	–
Ecuador	15	10 / 15	15	15
Egypt[5,13]	15	25	15	15
Estonia[5]	5 / 15	25	10	5
Finland[14]	10 / 15	–	– / 5	5

Recipient of German-source income	Dividends[1]	Interest[1,2,3]	Royalties	Movable asset rentals[4]
	%	%	%	%
France	5 / 15	–	–	–
Georgia[5]	– / 5 / 10	25	–	–
Ghana[5]	5 / 15	25	8	–
Greece	25	10	–	–
Hungary	5 / 15	–	–	–
Iceland	5 / 15	–	–	–
India[5]	10	25	10	10
Indonesia[5,29]	10 / 15	25	10 / 15	10
Iran	15 / 20	15	10	10
Ireland, Rep. of	10	–	–	–
Israel[28]	25	15	– / 5	5
Italy[5,18]	15	25	– / 5	5
Ivory Coast[5]	15	25	10	10
Jamaica[24]	10 / 15	10 / 12.5	10	10
Japan	15	10	10	10
Kazakhstan[5]	5 / 15	25	10	10
Kenya	15	15	15	15
Korea, Rep. of[5]	5 / 15	25	10	2
Kuwait[5]	5 / 15	25	10	10
Kyrgyzstan[5]	5 / 15	25	10	–
Latvia[5]	5 / 15	25	10	5
Liberia[15]	10 / 15	10 / 20	10 / 15	10
Lithuania[5]	5 / 15	25	10	5
Luxembourg	10 / 15	–	5	5
Macedonia[5,9]	15	25	10	10
Malaysia[16]	5 / 15	15	10 / 15	10
Malta[5]	5 / 15	25	–	–
Mauritius[5,17]	5 / 15	– / 25	15	15
Mexico[5]	5 / 15	25	10	10
Moldova[5,6]	15	25	–	–
Mongolia[5]	5 / 10	25	10	10
Montenegro[5,9]	5 / 15	25	10	10
Morocco	5	10	10	10
Namibia[5]	10 / 15	25	10	10
Netherlands[19]	10 / 15	–	–	–
New Zealand[5]	15	25	10	10
Norway[5]	– / 15	25	–	–
Pakistan[5]	10 / 15	5	10	10
Philippines[5,20]	10 / 15	25	10 / 15	10
Poland[5]	5 / 15	25	5	5
Portugal[5]	15	25	10	10
Romania[5]	5 / 15	25	3	–

Germany

Recipient of German-source income	Dividends[1]	Interest[1,2,3]	Royalties	Movable asset rentals[4]
	%	%	%	%
Russia[5]	5 / 15	25	–	–
Serbia[5,9]	15	25	10	10
Singapore[5]	5 / 15	25	8	8
Slovakia[12]	5 / 15	–	5	5
Slovenia[5]	5 / 15	25	5	–
South Africa[21]	7.5 / 15	10	–	–
Spain	10 / 15	10	5	5
Sri Lanka[5]	15	25	10	10
Sweden[5]	– / 15	25	–	–
Switzerland[5]	– / 15	25	–	–
Tajikistan[5]	5 / 15	25	5	–
Thailand[22,24]	15 / 20	– / 10 / 25	5 / 15	–
Trinidad and Tobago[23,24]	10 / 20	10 / 15	– / 10	10
Tunisia[25]	10 / 15	10	10 / 15	–
Turkey[5] (treaty has been terminated as of December 31, 2010)	15 / 20	25	10	10
Turkmenistan[5,6]	15	25	–	–
Ukraine[5,22]	5 / 10	25	– / 5	–
USSR[5,6]	15	–	–	–
United Arab Emirates[26]	26	26	26	26
United Kingdom[21]	15	–	–	–
United States[5,27]	– / 5 / 15	25	–	–
Uruguay[5]	15	25	15	15
Uzbekistan[5,22]	5 / 15	25	3 / 5	–
Venezuela[5]	5 / 15	25	5	5
Vietnam[5]	5 / 10 / 15	25	10	10
Yugoslavia[5,9]	15	25	10	10
Zambia	5 / 15	10	10	10
Zimbabwe[5]	10 / 20	25	7.5	7.5

Notes

1. Corporate recipients of dividend and interest income (interest on convertible and profit-sharing bonds) can apply for refund of the tax withheld over the corporation tax rate of 15% regardless of any further relief available under a treaty.
2. Generally, only interest paid by banks to a resident is subject to a withholding tax. 25% tax is also withheld from income on convertible or profit-sharing bonds.
3. Interest paid to non-residents other than on convertible or profit-sharing bonds is generally free of withholding tax. Tax on loans secured on German property is not imposed by withholding, but by assessment to corporation tax at 15% (plus solidarity levy) of the interest income net of attributable expenses. The tax authorities can order a withholding tax of 15.825% (including solidarity levy) if ultimate collection of the tax due is in doubt. Both forms of tax are reduced by treaty relief.
4. Movable asset rentals are taxed by assessment rather than by withholding. For corporations, the rate is the standard 15% corporation tax rate (plus solidarity levy) unless reduced by treaty.

5. The treaty does not (effectively) limit the taxation of profit-based interest income; thus the domestic rate (plus solidarity levy) applies.
6. The USSR treaty continues in force with Armenia, Moldova and Turkmenistan.
7. The lower royalty rate applies to commercial and industrial, as opposed to cultural, royalties.
8. Mortgage interest to a Belgian business is exempt unless the recipient holds at least 25% of the voting rights in the payer.
9. The Yugoslav treaty continues in force with Bosnia-Herzegovina, Macedonia and Serbia. Its applicability to Montenegro is still awaiting clarification.
10. The higher royalty rate applies to film and TV royalties, licenses to use trademarks and names, and to franchises.
11. The 5% royalty rate applies to films and TV.
12. The Czechoslovak treaty continues to apply to the Czech Republic and to Slovakia. Interest on profit-sharing bonds is taxed as a dividend.
13. The tax on trademark royalties is also subject to solidarity levy.
14. The higher royalty rate of 5% applies to commercial, industrial and scientific royalties.
15. There is no treaty relief for copyright or trademark royalties, except for those on films and TV.
16. There is no treaty relief for copyright royalties, except for those on films and TV.
17. Interest to banks is exempt. Otherwise, tax is levied at the domestic rate (including solidarity levy) without treaty relief.
18. Cultural royalties are exempt.
19. Interest on convertible and profit-sharing bonds taxed as a dividend; mortgage interest is exempt.
20. The 15% royalty rate applies to copyrights.
21. Treaty relief on interest, royalties and rentals is conditional on taxation in country of receipt.
22. The 5% royalty rate applies to copyrights.
23. Royalties for copyrights, except for films and TV are exempt.
24. The 10% interest rate applies in certain circumstances where the recipient is a bank.
25. The 15% royalty rate applies to patents, trademarks, films and TV.
26. The former UEA treaty expired on December 31, 2008. A new treaty has been initialled, but not yet signed or published. On ratification, it is to have retroactive effect to January 1, 2009.
27. The dividend exemption applies to corporate shareholders with at least 80% throughout the previous 12 months.
28. The 5% royalty rate applies to industrial, commercial, film and TV royalties.
29. The 10% royalty rate applies to access to industrial, commercial or scientific experience.

Tax administration

Returns
Returns are filed for each calendar year and reflect the financial statements for the business year ending in that calendar year. Assessments are issued once the tax office has reviewed the return.

Electronic returns
Monthly or quarterly returns for withholding taxes from employee salaries, dividends, interest, royalties and other payments and for VAT must be submitted electronically. Electronic filing of the annual returns for trade tax, income tax and VAT is encouraged, but is not yet required. For corporation tax, it is not yet available, though it will be required for 2011.

Germany

Payment of tax

Taxes are payable in quarterly instalments during the year, with a final settlement when the assessment is issued. The quarterly instalments are based on the estimated ultimate liability. Usually, this is the total tax due shown by the last assessment issued as adjusted by any rate changes in the meantime. The corporation tax instalments are due on the tenth of March, June, September and December. For trade tax, the due dates are the fifteenth of February, May, August and November. Failure to pay by the due date followed by three days of grace leads to a penalty of 1% per month.

Corporation and trade tax assessments bear interest on the net amount payable after deduction of all credits and previous payments. The rate is 0.5% per month simple interest and the period runs from 1 April of the second year following the year of assessment. Interest on a corporation tax assessment for 2008, for example, runs from 1 April 2010, though only on amounts unpaid by that date. The interest period is independent of the actual date of assessment. It thus runs in retrospect on assessments issued later, for example following a tax audit.

Value-added tax (VAT)

VAT is administered by the tax office responsible for the corporation tax assessment of a company. It is based on returns filed monthly or quarterly by the tenth of the following month (monthly where the output tax in the previous year was more than EUR 7,500) drawn up on the basis of the actual transactions during the filing period as shown in the books of account. A permanent filing extension of one month is available against an advance payment of one-eleventh of the total net tax due during the previous year. Otherwise, payment is due when the return is filed.

Legally, VAT is an annual tax. Each taxpayer must file an annual return for each calendar year, regardless of the actual accounting date for the business. Filing is together with the corporation and trade tax returns. If the annual return does not agree with the total of the monthly or quarterly returns, the tax office can be expected to ask for a detailed explanation and to penalise any irregularity.

Rulings

Tax offices are able to issue binding rulings in respect of planned transactions provided the taxpayer can show a particular interest in the tax consequences of the intended action. The fee varies between EUR 121 and EUR 91,456, depending upon the amount of tax involved.

Advance pricing agreements (APA)

A taxpayer can request the Central Tax Office to negotiate an APA on related-party transactions with a foreign tax authority on his behalf. The vehicle is the mutual agreement procedure under the treaty and the fee is a lump sum EUR 20,000 for each new agreement.

Corporate taxes in Ghana

For more information, contact:

Darcy White
PricewaterhouseCoopers
No. 12 Airport City
Una Home, 3rd Floor
Accra
Ghana
Tel: +233 302 761 576
Email: darcy.white@gh.pwc.com

Significant developments

The principal legislation governing income taxes in Ghana is the Internal Revenue Act, 2000 (Act 592), with amendments in 2002, 2003, 2004, 2005, 2006, 2007 and 2008.

Other tax enactments are also contained in the Internal Revenue Regulations, 2001 (legislative instrument or L.I. 1675), 2002 (L.I. 1698), 2003 (L.I. 1727), 2004 (L.I. 1803), 2005 (L.I. 1811), 2006 (L.I. 1820), and 2007 (L.I 1831).

The recent budget for 2008 contained minor changes which have been enacted by Parliament. These changes related mainly to penalty amounts and branch profit tax, which is now classified as a final tax.

Taxes on corporate income

National income tax is payable on the following:

1. Income accruing in, derived from, brought into or received in Ghana in respect of gains or profits from a trade, business, profession or vocation;
2. Dividends, interest or discounts;
3. Any charge or annuity;
4. Royalties, premiums and any other profits arising from property, including rents; and
5. Receipts, including royalties and deferred payments of any kind.

The corporate tax rate is 22% (this rate is applicable for three years for companies listed after 1 January 2004) for companies listed on the Ghana Stock Exchange (GSE), and 25% for companies that are not listed. The rate for companies engaged in non-traditional export and rural banking is 8% after 10 years (due to a special exemption); bank lenders to the agricultural and leasing sectors pay 20% corporate tax; and companies in the hotel industry pay 25%.

Corporate residence

Corporate residence is determined by the place where the trade, business, profession or vocation is carried on. Hence, where a non-resident corporate body carries on any trade, business, profession or vocation in Ghana (part of the operations of which may be carried on outside Ghana), the full gains or profits of the trade, business, profession or vocation are deemed to be derived from Ghana.

G

Ghana

If the corporate body's activities are carried on entirely outside Ghana, the mere supply of goods or services to Ghana does not constitute carrying on trade or business in Ghana.

Other taxes

Gift tax
The gift tax rate is nil up to GHC (Ghana Cedi) 50 and 5% thereafter, where the value of the gift exceeds GHC 50.

Value-added tax (VAT)
Service tax/entertainment; betting; hotel accommodation and food; food served in restaurants and snack bars; and advertisements, which formerly attracted a 15% service tax, are now subject to VAT at a rate of 12.5% and a national health insurance levy (NHIL) of 2.5%. Most professional services are also subject to the same VAT and NHIL rates, including the following:

- Management services;
- Insurance brokerage and other services;
- Financial, tax and economic consulting;
- Engineering and technical services;
- Accounting services;
- Courier services;
- Legal services;
- Provision of satellite television;
- Architectural services;
- Mobile cellular phone services; and
- Services rendered by surveyors.

Exports of goods and services are zero-rated. Unless specifically exempt, supplies of all goods and services are subject to VAT.

Other taxes
Other taxes include customs and excise duties which are imposed on the importation of goods at the port of entry and certain manufactured goods produced or imported into Ghana. There are also property taxes and business rates which are nominal amounts.

Branch income

The rates on branch profits are the same as on corporate profits. However, the profits for the period deemed to arise in connection with the operations of the branch may, at the discretion of the tax authorities, be computed by reference to the total consolidated profits of the entire group, taking into account the proportion that the turnover of that branch bears to the total consolidated turnover of the group. When repatriating branch profits, the amount to be repatriated is subject to an additional tax of 10%.

Income determination

Inventory valuation
There is no statutory guidance on the principles of stock valuation for income tax purposes. Any method of valuation of stock (inventory) and work-in-progress based on sound accounting principles is acceptable, provided it is adopted and consistently

applied from one period to another. In practice, inventory is normally valued for tax purposes at the lower of cost and net realisable value.

Capital gains

A capital gains tax is payable by every person, including a corporate body, on any capital gain accruing or derived from the realisation of any chargeable asset, including buildings of a permanent or temporary nature; business and business assets, including goodwill; land other than agricultural land; and any assets declared as chargeable by legislative instrument made under the law.

Capital gains in excess of GHC 50 are subject to tax at 5% thereafter. However, gains resulting from a merger, amalgamation, reorganisation, reconstruction and gains accruing to or derived from a venture capital financing company are exempt from capital gains tax. Details of further exemptions can be found in the income tax laws of Ghana.

Inter-company dividends

The gross dividends received by one Ghanaian company from another, regardless of whether it is a subsidiary of the company, are normally exempt from corporate income tax if the dividends were taxed in the first instance.

Foreign income

Resident corporations are taxed on their foreign income as and when it is brought into or received in Ghana. Foreign income is taxed together with other income derived in Ghana, and double taxation is avoided through treaties or foreign tax credits. No special rules exist for taxing undistributed income of foreign subsidiaries.

Stock dividends

The issue of stock dividends is permitted under Section 74 (1) of the Ghana Companies Code 1963, Act 179. It is, however, subject to income tax at the dividend tax rate of 8%.

Other significant items

Specific exemptions from tax include the following:

- Income of a local authority;
- Income of a statutory or registered building society;
- Income of an ecclesiastical, charitable or educational institution;
- Income of organisations formed for the purpose of promoting social or sporting amenities not for profit;
- Income accruing from a farming enterprise for a limited period;
- Income of a registered trade union;
- Income of rural banks for the first 10 years of operations;
- Gain or profit from the business of operating ships or aircraft by non-resident corporate bodies;
- Investment income of a pension or provident society;
- Income or profit of any registered cooperative society; and
- Income of a company engaged in the construction and sale or leasing of residential premises during the first five years following commencement of operations of the company.

Ghana

Deductions

Depreciation and depletion
Depreciation of capital assets in the accounts of a business is not an allowable deduction in computing taxable profits. It is replaced by capital allowances at statutorily prescribed rates. These allowances are available on capital expenditure for the following types of depreciating assets used in a trade:

- Plant and machinery;
- Trawlers and dredges;
- Furniture, fixtures and fittings;
- Airplanes and helicopters;
- Industrial buildings;
- Mines and oil wells;
- Ships; and
- Timber concessions.

Allowances are granted only on the following conditions:

1. The taxpayer must own the asset.
2. Capital expenditure must be incurred.
3. The asset must be used in the trade.
4. The asset must be in use up to the end of the basis period.

Capital allowances are granted for every year in which the asset is in use. In some cases, balancing allowances and charges are made where use continued until immediately before disposal of the asset.

For intangibles, such as patents, trademarks and copyrights, the law allows deduction of fees and expenditure incurred in obtaining the grant and the cost of registration and renewals.

For capital expenditure for acquisition of Ghanaian mineral concessions and related interest in land, an annual write-down allowance is allowed of 80% of the cost base added to the pool during the basis period and 50% of the balance of the pool, if any. There is also an additional 5% allowance calculated on the previous year's additions.

Net operating losses
Losses can be carried forward and deducted from assessable income of the five years immediately succeeding the year in which the loss was incurred. This provision covers the following industries: farming and agro-processing, mining, manufacturing (for export only), tourism and ICT (software development).

Carryback of losses is permitted for persons deriving income relating to a long term contract. Long term contract of a business refers to a contract for manufacture, installation or construction.

Payments to foreign affiliates
No special restrictions are imposed on the deductibility of royalties, interest and service fees paid to foreign affiliates, provided they are expenses incurred wholly, exclusively and necessarily in the production of the income. However, the Commissioner may

disallow certain transactions if the Commissioner is of the opinion that they are artificial or fictitious.

Taxes

No taxes are deductible in determining taxable income.

Other significant items

No special deductions are allowed. Principal non-deductible items include the following:

- Domestic or private expenses, including cost of travel between residence and place of business or employment;
- Any disbursement or expense not being wholly and exclusively paid or expended for the purpose of acquiring income;
- Capital withdrawn or any sum employed or intended to be employed as capital;
- Capital employed in improvement;
- Any sum recoverable under an insurance contract of indemnity;
- Rent of or any expense in connection with premises or a part of premises not occupied or used for the purpose of producing business income;
- Any amount paid or payable in respect of any income tax, profits tax or similar tax, whether due within or outside Ghana;
- Any payment to a provident, savings or other society or fund unless specifically allowed by the tax commissioner;
- Any sum payable by way of mortgage or debenture interest by any person to a non-resident person, except where tax has been deducted and accounted for; and
- Depreciation of any fixed assets of a permanent nature.

Group taxation

No form of combined reporting of results of operations by a group or affiliates is permitted.

Tax incentives

Inward investment

Under the Ghana Investments Promotion Centre Act 1994, various incentives are available to encourage investments in the country, particularly in the areas of agriculture, manufacturing industries engaged in export trade or using predominantly local raw materials or producing agricultural equipment, etc., construction and building industries, mining, and tourism. Incentives generally include exemption from customs import duties on plant and machinery; reduced corporate income tax rates; more favourable investment and capital allowances on plant and machinery; reduction in the actual corporate income tax payable where appropriate; retention of foreign exchange earnings where necessary; guaranteed free transfer of dividends or net profits, foreign capital, loan servicing, and fees and charges in respect of technology transfer; and guarantees against expropriation by the government.

Capital investments

Venture capital tax incentives:

- Relief from stamp duty in each year on subscriptions for new equity shares in venture capital funds;

Ghana

- Full tax exemption from corporate income tax, dividend tax and capital gains tax for five years;
- Carryforward of losses from disposal of shares during the tax-exempt period to the post-exempt period up to five years; and
- Chargeable income tax deduction equal to 100% of their investment for financial institutions which invest in venture capital subsidiaries.

Withholding taxes (WHT)

Income	Rate (%)
From employees' monthly salaries	*
Resident persons	
Interest (excluding individual & resident financial institutions)	8
Dividend	8
Rent (for individuals and as investment income)	8
Fees to part-time teachers, lecturers, examiners and endorsement fees	10
Commissions to insurance agents, sales persons, and fees to directors, board members, etc.	10
On commissions of lotto agents	5
Supply of goods and services exceeding GHC 50	5
Non-resident persons	
Dividend	8
Royalties, natural, resources payments and rents	10
Management, consulting and technical service fees and endorsement fees	15
Interest income	8
Short-term insurance premium	5

*Graduated tax rates as per regulations made under the decree.

Tax administration

Returns
The tax year runs from 1 January to 31 December. Corporations with financial periods other than the calendar year are taxed on their financial period ending during the calendar year. Separate provisions exist for commencement and cessation of business.

The tax administration system is an information return system, with subsequent assessment being issued by the tax authorities. Upon request to the Internal Revenue Service (IRS), a taxpayer is given Income Tax Form 22A for completion and submission to the IRS. This form provides the relevant information for determining taxable income and is filed by the taxpayer or an appropriate agent.

Companies are expected to submit a return four months after the end of the financial year. They may file an application for extension of filing time not to exceed two months.

The following are to be furnished together with a return:

1. Certified statement of turnover for the period covered by the return;
2. Copy of certified accounts of the business for the period; and
3. An estimate of the tax due on the income declared and remittance of the tax so computed.

Assessments

An assessment may be made on the company after the beginning of each year of assessment. If the return is considered incorrect and inadequate, additional assessments may be made as often as necessary. The tax authorities may make a provisional assessment before a return is filed, which can serve as a tax credit against the final assessment based on the return.

Payment of tax

Where the assessment has been finalised, the tax is payable within 30 days after service of the notice. At the discretion of the Tax Commissioner, the time for payment may be extended. Without notice or demand from the Commissioner, a taxpayer is required to pay not less than the total of the tax paid or payable in respect of the preceding year of assessment. This may be paid by equal quarterly instalments at the end of March, June, September and December in each year of assessment, but such payments are not deemed to be the actual tax payable.

Where tax is not paid by the due date, a penalty is assessed at 10% of the tax payable in addition to the tax unpaid up to three months after the due date; thereafter, the penalty is 20%.

Corporate taxes in Gibraltar

For more information, contact:

Edgar Lavarello
PricewaterhouseCoopers
International Commercial Centre
Casemates Square
Gibraltar
Tel: +350 200 73520
Email: edgar.c.lavarello@gi.pwc.com

Significant developments

Following the 2009 budget, the following changes have taken place:

* From 1 July 2009, a 5% reduction in the corporate income tax rate from 27% to 22%;
* Confirmation that the "low rate" announced in the 2007 budget will be 10%. The effective date for this rate will be 1 January 2011. Energy and utility providers will pay a 10% surcharge and will thus suffer an effective rate of 20%;
* The preceding year basis of assessment will be abolished in favour of an actual basis as of 1 January 2011 (commencement provisions will be abolished and transitional rules will be introduced);
* Effective 1 July 2009, a "start-up" rate of 10% will be introduced, which will apply to any business established in Gibraltar after 1 July 2009, and will be assessed on an actual year basis; and
* Start-up rate will also be available, on certain conditions, to businesses that have recently been established.

Taxes on corporate income

Generally, companies are subject to Gibraltar taxation on income accrued in, derived from, or received in Gibraltar, and are assessed on the prior-year basis. The main exemption to this is dividends which are taxed on a worldwide basis, although tax can be mitigated provided certain criteria are met (see *Income determination section*). Audited accounting profits are subject to certain adjustments, as set out below, to arrive at taxable profits.

Commencement provisions operate, whereby a company's profits for the first accounting period form the basis of more than one year of assessment. An imputation system is used, whereby tax paid by a company is imputed to the shareholder recipients of dividends paid from the company's profits.

The prior-year basis of assessment will be abolished in favour of an actual basis as of 1 January 2011. Commencement provisions will be abolished and transitional rules will be introduced.

Corporation tax rates
The standard rate of corporation tax is 22%, but there is a "small company" rate of 20% that applies where the profits of an accounting period are less than GBP 35,000

per annum and a marginal rate is charged on profits of between GBP 35,000 and GBP 43,333.

A "small company" is one whose trading activities in any year has a minimum of 80% of its total trading receipts derived from sources other than the following: dividends, interest or discounts, rents, royalties, premiums and any other profits arising from property.

The Gibraltar Government has confirmed that a "low rate" of corporation tax of 10% will be put into effect on 1 January 2011, with utility and energy providers paying an extra 10% surcharge.

Start-up relief

With effect from 1 July 2009, a "start-up" rate of 10% will be introduced, which will apply to any business established in Gibraltar after 1 July 2009. The start-up tax will be assessed on a current actual year basis, i.e., the tax will be assessed on the actual profits from 1 July to 30 June of the following year.

This scheme will also be available, on certain conditions, to businesses that have been recently established. Those conditions are as follows:

- The business must have commenced after 1 July 2007;
- For companies that commenced trading after 1 July 2007 but before 1 July 2008, the first tax year for which the company will be liable is 2008/2009, and tax will be payable in respect of this period at the rate of 27%, the rate for the subsequent two tax years will be 10%;
- For companies that commenced trading after 1 July 2008 but before 1 July 2009, the first tax year will be the 2009/2010 tax year and the profits assessed will be for the period from commencement of trade to 30 June 2009, taxed at the rate of 10%. The second tax year will be the 2010/2011 tax year and the company will be assessed on an actual preceding year basis at the rate of 10%; and
- For companies that have commenced trading after 1 July 2009 the first tax year will be the 2009/2010 tax year and will be based on the profits from the commencement of trade to 30 June 2010 at the rate of 10%. The second tax year will be the 2010/2011 tax year and the company will be assessed on an actual current basis.

As an anti-avoidance provision, the start-up relief will not apply in respect of any commercial activity carried out before 25 June 2009 and which is reorganised by the taxpayer in the name of a different entity for the purpose of benefiting from this scheme.

Exempt company

An exempt company is not subject to taxes in Gibraltar. In order to qualify for such status, the exempt company must demonstrate that it is not beneficially owned by Gibraltarians (or residents of Gibraltar) and does not trade with such persons.

The legality of this status was challenged by the European Union (EU) under the EU State Aid Rules in July 2001. In January 2005 the Government of Gibraltar reached an agreement with the EU Commission to permit existing tax-exempt companies to continue enjoying such status until 31 December 2010, provided that neither the

G

Gibraltar

beneficial ownership nor the activities of the company change, in which case by default they become ordinarily resident entities taxable at the standard rate above.

No new exemptions have been granted since 30 June 2006.

On 31 December 2010 the tax exempt company legislation will be repealed and all tax exempt companies will as from 1 January 2011 be subject to taxation at the rate of 10%.

Corporate residence

A company will be considered resident in Gibraltar if the management and control of its business is exercised from Gibraltar.

The location of central management and control will be established under legal principles laid down in the United Kingdom and is the place of the highest form of control and direction over a company's affairs, as opposed to decisions on the day-to-day running of the business.

Other taxes

Value-added tax (VAT)
There is no VAT in Gibraltar.

Customs and excise duties
Goods imported into Gibraltar from outside are, with some exceptions, generally subject to import duty at the applicable rate, which is usually 12%. Different rates apply to food, alcohol and tobacco (among others).

Estate duty
There is no estate duty in Gibraltar.

Property tax
A general business property rate is levied on all businesses in Gibraltar.

Stamp duty
Stamp duty is payable on the transfer or sale of any Gibraltar real estate or shares in a company owning Gibraltar real estate (on an amount based on the market value of said real estate) at the following rates:

- Less than GBP 160,000 – 0%;
- Between GBP 160,000 and GBP 250,000 – 1.26%;
- Between GBP 250,000 and GBP 350,000 – 1.60%; and
- Over GBP 350,000 – 2.50%.

Gaming tax
Gaming tax is levied at 1% of the gaming income. The tax paid is subject to a minimum of GBP 85,000 and maximum of GBP 425,000.

Capital duty
Capital duty of GBP 10 is payable on the initial authorisation of capital or any subsequent increase thereto.

Social insurance

Employers are obliged to pay a proportion of social insurance on behalf of their employees.

Employers' social insurance contribution for employees paid weekly is calculated as 20% of gross earnings, subject to a minimum of GBP 15.00 and a maximum of GBP 29.97 per week.

Employers' social insurance contribution for employees paid monthly is calculated as 20% of gross earnings, subject to a minimum of GBP 65.00 and a maximum of GBP 129.87 per month.

Branch income

The basis for taxation of branches of foreign enterprises is the same as for companies.

Income determination

Generally, companies are subject to Gibraltar taxation on income accrued in, derived from, or received in Gibraltar, the main exception to this are dividends which are taxed on a worldwide basis, although tax on this can be mitigated (see below).

Where a taxpayer seeks to reduce their liability to tax by creating an artificial split between activities in Gibraltar and outside the Commissioner shall use the anti-avoidance provisions of Section 13 of the Income Tax Act and any other means to defeat such an attempt.

Inventory valuation

Inventory is valued at the lower of historical cost or net realisable value. The last-in, first-out (LIFO) method is not permitted. Generally there are no material differences between accounts prepared on a normal accounting basis and those prepared on a tax basis.

Capital gains

Capital gains are not subject to tax in Gibraltar.

Dividends

Except in the case where the income forms part of the company's trading receipts, dividend income from companies listed on a recognised stock exchange is not taxable in Gibraltar. There is no tax on dividends paid by a Gibraltar company to a non-resident individual or to a corporate entity wherever resident.

Dividends received from participating interests or from any subsidiaries in the participating interest group are not liable to taxation in Gibraltar. A participating interest exists where there is a direct or indirect shareholding of at least 10%, as from 1 January 2009, in a company registered in the EU (or a company which is registered in a country which has a bilateral agreement with the EU).

Interest

Except in the case where the income forms part of the company's trading receipts, interest received from financial institutions is not taxable in Gibraltar.

Gibraltar

With respect to non bank loans, where the situs of a loan is outside Gibraltar there is no source of income which would give rise to a liability to tax in Gibraltar in respect of the interest received on that loan.

The situs of a loan will depend upon:

- The place of residence of the debtor;
- The source from which the interest is paid;
- The place where the interest is paid; and
- The nature and location of the security for the debt.

Unless there are compelling reasons to the contrary, where loans are primarily secured on assets situated in Gibraltar they are likely to have their situs in Gibraltar.

Deductions

For the purpose of ascertaining the assessable income there shall be deducted all outgoings and expenses wholly and exclusively incurred in the production of the income. No deduction shall be allowed in respect of:

- Domestic or private expenses;
- Expenses not incurred wholly and exclusively in the generation of income;
- Any expenses of a capital nature;
- Any sum recoverable under an insurance contract or contract of indemnity;
- Property expenses not incurred for the purposes of producing income;
- Any tax charges under the Income Tax Act;
- Depreciation of assets (although capital allowances are available, *see below*); and
- Employee remuneration not accompanied by a certified statement of name, addresses and amount of remuneration.

Capital allowances
Plant and machinery
The first GBP 30,000 of capital expenditure on plant and machinery is fully deductible. After the first year, assets are written down at a rate of 25% on a straight-line basis.

Information technology
The first GBP 50,000 of capital expenditure on information technology investment is fully allowable against taxable profits and as for plant and machinery, any balance over the specified amount is written down at a rate of 25% per annum on a straight-line basis.

Motor vehicles
Capital expenditure on motor vehicles is written down at a rate of 25% on a straight-line basis (N.B. vehicles which are primarily suited for the conveyance of any goods or burden other than passengers are considered as plant and machinery).

Operating losses
A trading loss incurred in an accounting period may be offset against trading income arising in the same period or subsequent period, provided that within a period of three years there has not been both a change in the ownership of the company and a major change in the nature or conduct of the trade.

There is no provision for the carrying back of losses.

Group taxation

Companies are assessed on an individual basis and trading losses of group members may not be offset against profits of other members of the group.

Thin capitalisation
There are no debt-to-equity ratio rules.

Transfer pricing
Where a non-resident individual transacts business with a resident individual and the transaction reduces the profits of the resident individual by more than the ordinary profits which might be expected to arise from that business, then in the case where the non-resident individual has a "close connection" and can exercise "substantial control" over the resident individual, the non-resident shall be assessable and chargeable to tax in the name of the resident individual as if such individual was an agent for the non-resident.

Also, by using the anti-avoidance provisions of Section 13 of the Income Tax Act the Commissioner is able to disregard a transaction if he is of the opinion that the transaction is either artificial or fictitious.

Tax incentives

Exempt company
See Taxes on Corporate income section.

Development aid
In order to encourage private development in Gibraltar, promoters and developers of approved projects are offered certain incentives such as tax relief, import duty relief and rates relief.

In order to qualify for the above relief the project needs to be a new project the aim of which is:

*   To create a tangible immovable asset in Gibraltar that will remain in existence after the applicant has ceased to derive the benefits under the license; and
*   To provide more than two additional units of housing accommodation in Gibraltar; or
*   To contribute materially to the development of the tourist industry in Gibraltar; or
*   To afford any new employment opportunities or career prospects in Gibraltar; or
*   Otherwise to improve materially the economic or financial infrastructure of Gibraltar; and the project shall be one which is for the economic benefit of Gibraltar.

The project needs to be completed within a specified time (dependent on the type of project) following the issue of the licence and the applicant must not expend less than the prescribed amount for the project.

Application for development aid must be made to the Minister for Trade.

Gibraltar

Deduction of approved expenditure on premises

For taxpayers with an interest in a building situated in Gibraltar an allowance is available for approved expenditure on the painting, decorating, repair or enhancement of the frontage of that building.

The approved amount will be available as a deduction against the taxpayer's income. This deduction is in addition to any deduction, relief or allowance given in accordance with any other provision of the Income Tax Act in respect of the same expenditure.

The claim for the deduction must be made within two years after the end of the year of assessment with respect of which the deduction is claimed.

Withholding taxes (WHT)

There is no WHT in Gibraltar except in the following cases:

* Interest payments on Gibraltar situs loans payable to non-financial institutions at the corporate tax rate;
* Payments to subcontractors in the construction industry. Unless the subcontractor is in possession of an exemption certificate, tax is withheld at the rate of 25% of the amount which relates to the labour and profit element of the contract;
* Payments to employees (under the "Pay As You Earn" system).

Tax administration

Returns

Tax returns are due by 30 September following the year in which the income is assessed.

Payment of tax

Tax for any year of assessment is due on the later of 28 February in the year of assessment or 60 days after the issue of the assessment. Tax paid after the due date incurs a 10% charge.

Appeals

If a taxpayer disputes an assessment, he may appeal against that assessment by notice in writing addressed to the Commissioner within 21 days of the date of service of the notice of the assessment.

Corporate taxes in Greece

For more information, contact:

Mary Psylla
PricewaterhouseCoopers
268 Kifissias Avenue
GR-152 32 Athens
Greece
Tel: +30 210 6874 543
Email: mary.psylla@gr.pwc.com

Significant developments

The new tax law 3842/2010 adopted by the Greek Parliament amended significantly the Greek tax regime, by introducing new provisions affecting all fields of taxation. The most important amendments in the field of corporate taxation are the following:

- Introduction of a system of dual corporate income tax (CIT) rates for non-distributed and distributed profits of legal entities. Non-distributed profits are taxed at a rate of 24% (which will gradually decrease to 20% by 2014), while distributed profits are taxed at a rate of 40%. The new rates apply to profits arising from balance sheets drafted as of 31 December 2010 onwards. As of that period, the withholding tax (WHT) rate of 10% on dividends distributed by Greek Societes Anonymes to resident or non-resident beneficiaries is abolished. Until then, the existing system of a 25% corporate tax rate plus 10% dividend WHT applies.
- Introduction of significant restrictions on the deduction of expenses from the gross income of enterprises paid to companies established in countries included in the catalogue of non-cooperating states or states with preferential tax treatment.
- Companies incurring a gain from the sale of listed shares are subject to a capital gains tax of 10% or 20% depending on whether the shares are sold within three or 12 months from their original acquisition, respectively (application for shares acquired from 1 January 2011).
- Introduction of certain important changes on real estate taxes.
- Moreover, by virtue of law 3833/2010 a one-off special lump sum contribution aimed to address the current fiscal deficits is imposed on the total net income of legal entities by fiscal year 2009. It is likely that such a contribution will also apply for 2010 and 2011, depending on the progress of the Greek economy, as monitored by the European Union (EU) and the International Monetary Fund (IMF).
- Finally, as of 15 March 2010, the value-added tax (VAT) standard rate is increased from 19% to 21% and the reduced rate from 9% to 10%. Such taxes are further expected to increase to 23% and 11%, respectively, as of 1 July 2010. Various exemptions from VAT are abolished (e.g., services of lawyers, notaries, freelance land registrars and judicial clerks, authors, artists, medical and hospital care, diagnosis services, etc.).

Taxes on corporate income

For companies closing balance sheets as of 31 December 2010 onwards, two CIT rates apply for non-distributed and distributed profits of legal entities respectively.

Greece

Non-distributed profits are taxed at a rate of 24%. Corporate income tax rates will gradually decrease to 20%, from 24% currently in force, by 2014 as follows:

- 24%: for accounting periods starting from 1 January 2010 to 31 December 2010;
- 23%: for accounting periods starting from 1 January 2011 to 31 December 2011;
- 22%: for accounting periods starting from 1 January 2012 to 31 December 2012;
- 21%: for accounting periods starting from 1 January 2013 to 31 December 2013; and
- 20%: for accounting periods starting from 1 January 2014 onwards.

Moreover, distributed profits will be subject to a 40% company tax paid at the level of the company. A credit is provided for corporate tax paid on such profits. The way the law is drafted, the 40% tax does not appear to apply as a dividend WHT but as an increased corporate tax payable on distributed profits. As of the drafting of this text, no further details have been provided by the Greek tax authorities on the application of this new regime.

Local/state/provincial tax rates
No local taxes on income are paid at a local level. However, it should be noted that the aforementioned rates are reduced by 40% for profits of companies derived from activities carried out on islands with less than 3,100 inhabitants (Article (Art.) 118 par.2 Income Tax Code (ITC)).

Special one-off contribution on profits
A one-off special lump sum contribution aimed to address the current fiscal deficits is imposed on the total net income of legal entities by fiscal year 2009. It is likely that such contribution will also apply for 2010 and 2011, depending on progress of the Greek economy.

The special one-off contribution is imposed on the total net income declared by legal entities or on the total net income of legal entities publishing financial statements under IFRS, whichever is higher, provided that it exceeds EUR 100,000. The abovementioned lump sum is calculated based on a progressive scale of rates and more specifically, at 4%, 6%, 8% and 10% for income from EUR 1 up to 300,000, from EUR 300,001 up to 1,000,000, from EUR 1,000,001 up to 5,000,000 and exceeding EUR 5,000,001, respectively. The amount of the lump sum is reduced so that the remaining total net income does not fall under EUR 100,000. A similar lump sum was imposed on the net income of legal entities by fiscal year 2008, provided that it exceeded EUR 5,000,000, within a progressive range of scales, from 5% for income up to EUR 10,000,000 to 10% for income exceeding EUR 25,000,000.

Corporate residence

Corporate residence is determined primarily by place of incorporation. However, the corporate law rules based on the effective management criterion the place of legal seat could be relevant.

Permanent establishment (PE)
Subject to related tax treaty provisions, foreign corporations are subject to Greek taxation if they maintain a PE in the country. Such PE may arise in cases of foreign companies maintaining inventories from which orders are filled; maintaining offices, warehouses, factories, etc.; carrying out any other operations for the purposes of

exploiting natural resources; processing raw materials or agricultural products in their own factories or through third parties; or providing services of a technical or scientific nature (surveys, designs or research) (Art. 100 ITC).

Other taxes

Value-added tax (VAT)
As of 1 July 2010, the standard VAT rate will be 23%. There is a reduced rate of 11% on basic necessities (5.5% on books, newspapers and periodicals as of 1 July 2010). Supplies of goods and services to individuals and legal entities subject to VAT and established in EU countries (intra-Union supplies) are exempt from VAT. Exports of goods and certain services to non-EU countries are also exempt. As of 1 January 2007, shopping centres lease contracts may be subject to VAT, on condition that the taxable person opts for the submission to taxation of the leasing right. The term "shopping centres" is defined by means of a Ministerial Decision. With the noted exception, real estate leases are generally exempt from VAT.

Stamp taxes
Rentals of non-residential properties are subject to 3.6% stamp duty (with the exception of shopping centres subject to VAT).

In general, loans and interest may be subject to a 2.4% stamp duty. However, there are a number of exemptions, the main one covering bank loans and bond issues.

Other stamp duties may apply, in certain limited cases.

Excise taxes
Excise taxes are imposed on energy and electricity products (e.g., petrol, natural gas, electricity etc.), tobacco and alcoholic products. The imposed tax rates vary according to the category of products and detailed provisions including:

- Industrialised tobacco products are taxed generally at a standard tax rate of 65% on the weighted average retail price, with minimum amount of collection of EUR 78 per 1,000 cigarettes. Also a proportional excise tax is calculated at the rate of 58.823%.
- Alcoholic products/beverages are taxed at EUR 1.884 per 100 litres, subject to further deductions of certain alcoholic products.
- Taxation of energy products vary significantly in respect to the classification of the product and further detailed provisions. Indicatively, petrol with lead is taxed a EUR 621 per 1,000 litres, airplane gasoline at EUR 637 per 1,000 litres, diesel fuel at EUR 382 per 1,000 litres, diesel used for heating at EUR 382 per 1,000 litres, kerosene at EUR 410 per 1,000 litres, etc.
- Electricity is subject to excise tax at the rate of EUR 5 for non-business and EUR 2.5 for industrial/commercial use.

Real estate tax
An annual real estate tax is imposed effective from 2010 onwards on real estate located in Greece, which is owned on 1 January of the tax year by individuals or legal entities, regardless of nationality or residence. Real estate tax on individuals is imposed at a progressive tax rate from 0.1% to 1% with a tax free amount of EUR 400,000 per owner. Specifically for years 2010, 2011 and 2012, taxable real estate of individuals

Greece

exceeding EUR 5,000,000 in value, is taxed at a 2% rate on the value exceeding EUR 5,000,000.

The applicable tax rate for legal entities amounts to 0.6%, 0.3% or 0.1% depending on their profit or non-profit making character and the use of the properties. The tax rate remains reduced at 0.33% for real estate owned by hotel enterprises and used for their business activities.

An exemption from real estate tax is provided for buildings built within three years from the issuance of the initial building permit, unless these have been leased or in any other way used, from the year 2011 onwards.

Special real estate tax
The special real estate tax of 3% effective as of 1 January 2003, on legal entities owning real estate property in Greece on the objective value of such property, is increased to 15% as of 1 January 2010. This tax is mainly directed against property held, directly or indirectly, by offshore companies for the purpose of tax avoidance of transfer and inheritance taxes by the real owners. In this context exemptions apply to listed companies, companies with registered shares up to the individual shareholder (provided such shareholder holds a tax registration number in Greece), companies for which the income derived from the real estate property does not exceed the income from other activities, EU banks, insurance companies, investment funds, etc.

Real estate transfer tax
Each transfer of real estate, which is not subject to VAT, is subject to real estate transfer tax. The tax rates of the real estate transfer tax amount to 8% for the value up to EUR 20,000 and at 10% for the exceeding value of the real estate.

Exemptions from real estate transfer tax for the acquisition of primary residences are determined according to the value of the property.

Contribution tax on capital accumulation
A 1% tax contribution is imposed on capital accumulation by (1) business companies and joint ventures; (2) associations of all degrees and any other form of company, legal entity, or union of persons or society aiming to make profits; and (3) branches of foreign companies (unless of EU origin). For Societe Anonyme (SA) companies an additional 0.1% duty is payable on capital to the competition committee.

Branch income

For profits arising with respect to balance sheets drafted as of 31 December 2010 onwards, profits of branches of foreign companies are subject to CIT at the standard rate of 24% currently in force, to be reduced to 20% by 2014 (Art. 99 ITC). Post-tax profits remitted to the foreign head office are taxed at a rate of 40% (i.e., equalised to a distribution from a Greek company).

Income determination

Capital gains
In general, capital gains are included in the taxable profits of Greek companies. Certain special rules apply in the case of sales of shares in listed or non-listed entities.

Capital gains tax on sale of listed shares

Companies incurring a gain from the sale of listed shares are subject to a capital gains tax of 10% or 20% depending on whether the shares are sold within three or 12 months from their original acquisition, respectively (application for shares acquired from 1 January 2011). Thereafter, the capital gains derived from the sale of the relevant shares is booked in a special reserve account after the deduction of losses derived from similar transactions. In case of distribution or capitalisation, capital gains are taxed at the rate of distributed profits by deducting the tax withheld. No further tax is imposed on foreign resident investors. In the case of application of taxation of capital gain, according to the aforementioned, transaction duty of 0.15%, currently in force, shall not apply.

Transfer tax on sale of non-listed shares

The sale of Greek shares non-listed on the Stock Exchange triggers a 5% tax calculated on the transfer value as either agreed by the parties or determined on the basis of a "minimum-value" formula set forth by law, whichever is the higher. The aforementioned 5% tax is also due in the case of transfer of foreign non-listed shares by a Greek tax resident, calculated on the consideration agreed. In the case where the seller is a Greek corporation, the payment of the 5% tax does not exhaust the transferor's tax liability. Any capital gains arising thereof, are further subject to tax at the standard CIT rate (i.e., they are included in the taxable profits of the company). It should be noted that the 5% tax paid at the time of the transfer may, under certain conditions, be provided as a credit against the company's annual corporate liability.

Moreover, gains arising from the sale of parts of limited liability companies (LLC) are subject to a 20% tax rate. In the case the seller is an individual, the taxation exhausts any further income tax obligation regarding such income. In the case the seller is a Greek entity, the tax liability is not exhausted and the respective capital gain is taxed according to the general tax provisions with the 20% tax being credited against the final income tax liability.

Dividend income

Distributed profits are taxed at a rate of 40% (application for profits arising from balance sheets drafted as of 31 December 2010) at the level of the distributor company. No further WHT is imposed on dividends.

Taxation of 40% on distributed profits of the legal entities does not exhaust the tax liability of beneficiary individuals. The dividend amount is further taxed based on the progressive tax scale applicable to individuals with a credit being provided for the corporate tax paid by the distributing legal entities, based on a certificate issued by the latter in the name of the individual.

On the contrary, taxation of 40% on distributed profits of the legal entities is designed to exhaust the tax liability in case the beneficiaries are legal entities.

Foreign income (anti-deferral regime, unremitted earnings)

Resident corporations are taxed on their worldwide income. Foreign income received by a domestic corporation is taxed together with other income. If related income tax is paid or withheld abroad, a tax credit is generally available up to the amount of the applicable Greek income tax. Losses incurred abroad can only be offset against foreign profits.

Greece

There are no special anti-deferral regimes or CFC rules in Greece.

Interest income

Interest income is generally taxable. There are certain special rules that govern the receipt of interest income from bonds by banks and insurance companies.

Inventory valuation

Inventories are stated at the lower of cost or market (replacement value). The Greek tax system recognises various valuation methods such as first-in, first-out (FIFO), last-in, first-out (LIFO), weighted average, etc.

Partnership income

Both general partnerships ("Omorrythmi Etairia", or OE) and limited partnerships ("Eterrorythmi Etairia", or EE) are not tax transparent. They are generally taxed at a rate of 25%, but there are special rules on income determination or cases where partners are individuals.

Rents/royalties income

Income derived from rents and royalties is taxed as ordinary income.

Stock transactions

Stock dividends are treated as cash dividends for income tax purposes.

Deductions

In general, expenses are deductible subject to certain conditions. The following is a list of certain key conditions or restrictions on expense deductibility:

- In general, accrued interest from loans or credits of a company, with the exception of interest on arrears due to the debt of taxes, duties, contributions and fees to the state and other legal entities governed by public law, interest on loans for the purchase of shares in any type of company, to the extent that this participation is transferred within a two-year period, interest on loans used for the purchase of shares in a legal entity established in non-cooperating states or states with preferential tax regime, interest paid to companies established in such states, which cannot be deducted from gross profits of companies.
- Hotel expenses, expenses for corporate gifts, education of personnel, special clothing of personnel, mobile telephone expenses, etc., subject to specific conditions set out in Art. 31 of the ITC.
- Payroll expenses are not deducted when they are not paid through professional bank accounts or cheques paid through the same accounts.
- The value of raw and ancillary materials and other goods (plus processing thereon), which is paid to a legal entity whose role consists exclusively of the invoicing of the transactions, while the delivery of goods or provision of services is conducted by a third party, is not deducted from the gross profits of companies.
- Car expenses are generally deductible up to 70% for motor vehicles up to 1.600cc and 35% for motor vehicles exceeding 1.600cc.
- Expenses concerning transactions realised between Greek companies and entities established in preferential tax regimes may be deductible for Greek companies, on the condition that satisfactory evidence is provided that the transactions are real, usual and do not result in the transfer of profits, income or capital for the purpose of tax evasion or tax avoidance.

- Expenses concerning transactions realised between Greek companies and entities established in a non-cooperating state are non-tax-deductible.

Accrued expenses

Accrued expenses are, in principle, non-deductible until they become final and settled, supported by respective invoices.

Bad debt

Tax-deductible bad debt provisions are calculated at 0.5% on the stated value of invoices for sale of goods or provision of services, after a reduction for discounts, sales to the State or other entities governed by public law and the special consumption tax imposed in certain cases. Special restrictions and rules apply to certain transactions, while there is a recapture system for provisions which are not realised.

Charitable contributions

Donations and sponsorships paid to charitable institutions, non-profit making foundations, churches and monasteries and various other welfare institutions may be deductible up to 10% of the total net profits or income arising from the balance sheet of the legal entity.

Depreciation of fixed assets/amortisation of intangibles

Depreciation of tangible assets is compulsory for financial years ending after 30 December 1997 (not compulsory for financial years ended within the period from 1 January 1992 through 30 December 1997). Fixed assets with acquisition value of up to EUR 1,200 each may be written off to profit and loss in the year acquired or when used in operations. Depreciation is computed on the basis of the straight-line method or, in some cases, the declining-balance method on the acquisition value, increased by any additions and improvements. The straight-line method or the declining-balance method must be used consistently. However, new companies, for the three consecutive financial years that follow the financial year in which their productive operation commenced, are permitted to depreciate all their fixed assets either at 0% or at a rate equal to 50% of the applicable rate, provided that the selected rate will not change from year to year. If the declining-balance method is used, the straight-line method rates increase three times.

For each category of assets maximum and minimum annual depreciation rates are determined by a presidential decree. Companies may select any rate within this range, provided that this is consistently applied.

Taxes

Taxes, other than income tax and real estate tax, are recognised as deductible expenses only if supported by related tax returns and payment receipts, and are borne by the company.

Fines and penalties

Fees received from activities constituting a criminal offence, from penal clauses, fines and penalties are not recognised as deductible expenses.

Goodwill

There are some court cases which support the deductibility of goodwill as a start-up expense but the specifics of each case must be carefully considered.

Greece

Special restrictions on transactions with non-cooperative states and states with preferential tax treatment

Greek tax law has established rules in relation to non-cooperating states and states with preferential tax treatment in Art. 51A and B of the ITC.

Non-cooperating states are defined as states that on the 1 January 2010 are not EU member states and which, up to the aforementioned date, have not concluded agreements of administrative assistance in the tax sector with Greece or with, at least, 12 other states. Such states will be enumerated in an annual Ministerial Decision, and will normally follow the relevant list of the Organization for Economic Co-operation and Development (OECD).

An individual or legal entity, irrespective of its legal form, is considered located in a preferential tax regime, even if its residence of registered office is located in an EU member state, in case it is not subject to taxation in this state or is *de facto* not subject to taxation, or is subject to tax on income or capital at an amount which is lower than 50% of the tax that would have been due, in accordance with Greek tax legislation, if such entity were resident or were maintaining a PE in Greece.

Greek tax law enumerates a number of serious restrictions on transactions with the aforementioned entities, which could lead to a material increase of the tax burden of a Greek counterparty company.

Net operating and capital losses

Losses can be carried forward five years. Carrybacks are not permitted.

Organisational and start-up expenses

The amount of start-up expenses (including costs for acquisition of real estate) is amortised, either as a lump sum during the year of its realisation, or in equivalent instalments within a five year period. Specifically, expenses realised by financial leasing companies in relation to the acquisition of real estate, which will constitute the object of an agreement of the same law, may be depreciated in equivalent amounts, in analogy to the years of duration of the agreement.

Payments to foreign affiliates

Royalties, interest and service fees paid to foreign affiliates are deductible expenses under certain requirements and conditions.

Pension expenses

Group life insurance premiums, which include pension plans, may be deducted up to EUR 1,500 per employee.

Payment for directors

Fees of board members are taxed at source at a rate of 35%. Such amounts are tax-deductible.

Bonuses (benefits in cash, on top of regular remunerations and overtime payments) paid to executives of credit institutions up to financial year 2013 are subject to special increased taxation. Taxation is based on the general progressive tax scale applicable to individuals provided the total annual income of the executive does not exceed EUR 60,000 and the amount of the bonus does not exceed 10% of the total annual regular remuneration. For amounts exceeding the outlined limitations, taxation at source based on a progressive tax scale is provided as follows:

- Up to EUR 20,000: 50%;
- EUR 20,001 – 40,000: 60%;
- EUR 40,001 – 60,000: 70%;
- EUR 60,001 – 80,000: 80%; and
- EUR 80,001 and above: 90%.

Group taxation

Consolidation/group taxation rules
Group taxation is not permitted.

Transfer pricing regime
Article 26 of L.3728/2008 on "Monitoring the Markets and other provisions" of the Ministry of Development *(see also Ministerial Decision A2-8092/2008, 31 December 2008 and Informative Circular of 7 May 2009)* introduced, for the first time in Greece, rules on the documentation of prices of intergroup transactions with the intention of "detecting possible overpricing of intergroup transactions, expanding artificially the cost of sold products and services, having as a consequence the reduction of the gross profit of enterprises in Greece, picturing the increase of sale prices to the final consumers as necessary and justified".

In accordance with the relevant transfer pricing rules, companies operating in any form in Greece are obliged to apply to their transactions with companies that are connected to them, terms in accordance with the arm's-length principle.

For this purpose, the companies document the prices for all their inter-group transactions with a complete and standardised study of documentation of prices. The study consists of the "basic documentation file", concerning groups in which the parent company is Greek and the "Greek documentation file", with regard to Greek subsidiaries of foreign groups and foreign companies operating in any form in Greece.

These files must be made available when requested by the competent authorities of the Ministry of Development within 30 days from the notification of the relevant request. Moreover, companies that have inter-company transactions submit annually, within four months and 15 days from the end of the accounting period, to the Ministry of Development a catalogue in which the data of their intergroup transactions, and specifically the number and their value, are documented. In case of non-compliance with these obligations, an independent fine is imposed, equal to 10% of the value of the transactions for which the relative documentation was not submitted or the foreseen catalogue was not submitted timely.

If an infringement of the arm's-length principle is established, the competent tax authorities are immediately informed in order for the provisions of tax legislation and the imposition of the relevant tax penalties to apply.

In parallel to the aforementioned regimes, transfer pricing is also regulated by the ITC.

The aforementioned provisions of Art. 39 and 39A ITC were amended by Article 11, par.13 of L.3842/2010. Specifically, the provisions expanded the frame of application

Greece

of the provision to leases of movable or immovable property, while the condition of (direct or indirect) tax avoidance taxes for the application of the provision was abolished. Moreover, the new provisions provide for a fine 20% on the surplus net profits arising on behalf of enterprises in case of infringement of the arm's-length principle, as well as a fine equal to 20% on the value of the transaction in case of non-compliance, faulty compliance or overdue filing of the required documentation. With reference to the obligation of documentation, the deadline within which enterprises are obliged to present the file is 30 days and the minimum amount of transactions for which documentation is required is EUR 100,000 annually.

Thin capitalisation rules
Article 3 of L.3775/2009 established, for the first time, rules on thin capitalisation of enterprises in Greece.

According to the relevant thin capitalisation rules, accrued interest on loans paid to affiliated companies are deductible on the condition that the debt to equity ratio is 3:1.

The aforementioned provisions of Article 3 of L.3775/2009 were amended by Article 11, par.7, of L.3842/2010. Specifically, the new provisions extended the exceptions from the application of the thin capitalisation rules to banks, factoring companies, as well as special vehicle companies of L.3156/2003 and L.3601/2007 (an exception was already in force for leasing companies). It was, moreover, provided that loans assumed by third companies and for which any kind of guarantee has been issued by the aforementioned connected companies are added to the total amount of loans undertaken by the connected companies. Finally, the relevant provisions abolished the clause of non-application of thin capitalisation rules for loans that had been concluded until the publication of L.3775/2009 (namely until 21 July 2009) (grandfathering clause), thus as of 2010 the debt equity ratio covers also older loans.

Tax incentives

New tax incentives are expected in June 2010. The following tax incentives were provided by tax L. 3842/2010.

Incentives for the maintenance of workplaces
Legal entities, which suffer a reduction of turnover for two consecutive accounting periods without reducing their workforce, can enjoy a reduction of the tax rate by three percentage units. However, a revocation of the granted benefit and imposition of further tax in case of reduction of personnel or increase of the turnover within the three-year period is provided.

Incentives for the development of young entrepreneurship
An exemption is provided from income tax for three years regarding profits derived from the exercise of a personal business or freelancers, in the case the entrepreneur in question has not exceeded 35 years of age. The same applies to partnerships that are established exclusively by individuals, who have not exceeded 35 years of age.

Some other very specific incentives, including exemption from income tax on profits derived from activities connected with certain patents, are also provided for in Greek tax legislation.

Withholding taxes (WHT)

Recipient	Dividends	Interest	Royalties
	%	%	%
Resident individuals and companies	10, Nil (1)	20, 10 (2)	Nil
Non-resident individuals and companies:			
Non-treaty	10, Nil (1)	40 (2)	25 (3)
Treaty:			
Albania	5	5	5
Armenia	10	10	5
Austria (4)	5, 15 (5)	8	7
Azerbaijan (*)	8	8	8
Belgium	5, 15 (9)	5, 10 (8)	5
Bulgaria	10	10	10
Canada (*)	5, 15 (9)	10	10, Nil (16)
China	5, 10 (6)	10	10
Croatia	5, 10 (6)	10	10
Cyprus	25	10	5, Nil (7)
Czech Republic	Domestic	10	10
Denmark	38	8	5
Egypt	10	15	15
Estonia	5, 15 (6)	10	5, 10 (14)
Finland	47	10	10, Nil (11)
France	Domestic	10	5
Georgia	8	8	5
Germany	25	10	Nil
Hungary	45	10	10
Iceland	5, 15 (6)	8	10
India	Domestic	Domestic	Domestic
Ireland	5,15 (9)	5	5
Israel	Domestic	10	10
Italy	15	10	5, Nil (11)
Korea, Rep. of	5, 15 (6)	8	10
Kuwait	5	5	15
Latvia	5, 10 (6)	10	5, 10 (14)
Lithuania	5, 15 (6)	10	5, 10 (14)
Luxembourg	38	8	5, 7 (10)
Malta	5, 10 (6)	8	8
Mexico	10	10	10
Moldova	5, 15 (6)	10	8
Morocco (*)	5, 10 (6)	10	10
Netherlands	35	10, 8 (15)	5, 7 (10)
Norway	40	10	10

G

Greece

Recipient	Dividends	Interest	Royalties
	%	%	%
Poland	Domestic	10	10
Portugal	15	15	10
Qatar (13)	5	5	5
Romania	45	10	5, 7 (10)
Russia	5, 10 (6)	7	7
Saudi Arabia (13)	5	5	10
Serbia (*)	5, 15 (6)	10	10
Slovakia	Domestic	10	10
Slovenia	10	10	10
South Africa	5, 15 (6)	8	5, 7 (10)
Spain	5, 10 (6)	8	6
Sweden	Domestic	10	5
Switzerland	35	10	5
Tunisia (*)	35	15	12
Turkey	15	12	10
Ukraine	5, 10 (6)	10	10
United Kingdom	Domestic	Nil	Nil
United States	Domestic	Nil Domestic (12)	Nil
Uzbekistan	8	10	8

Notes

1. The 10% WHT applies only to distribution of dividends by Greek SAs. Profits distributed by Greek Eteria Periorismenis Euthinis (EPEs, or limited liability companies) are not subject to any WHT. For dividends distributed from profits arising from balance sheets drafted as of 31 December 2010 onwards, the 10% WHT is abolished.
2. Interest earned on deposits with banks operating in Greece, as well as on any kind of bonds, is subject to WHT at the rate of 10% withheld at source. WHT on interest payable to non-Greek residents is 40%.
3. Payments of royalties and service fees to foreign residents are subject to a WHT at the rate of 25%.
4. The new double taxation treaty (DTT) concluded between Greece and Austria will apply to income earned as of 1 January 2010. For payments realised up to 31 December 2010 the former DTT applies, which provides for a WHT of 8% for interest payments and 7% for royalty payments.
5. The rate of 5% will apply if the beneficial owner is a company which holds directly at least 25% of the voting power of the company paying the dividends.
6. The rate of 5% applies in case the beneficiary is a company (excluding a partnership) and directly holds, at least, 25% of the capital of the paying company.
7. The rate of 5% is applicable only for the right to use cinematograph films.
8. Rate of 5% applies to loans not incorporated into negotiable instruments and granted by banks.
9. A rate of 5% is applicable to shareholders of 25% and above.
10. The rate is 5% if the royalties consist of payments of any kind received as a consideration for the use of or the right to use any copyright of literary, artistic or scientific work, including cinematograph films.
11. Exemption (nil rate) applies to payments of any kind received as a consideration for the use of, or the right to use, any copyright of literary, artistic or scientific work including cinematograph films and films or tapes for television or radio broadcasting.
12. Interest (on bonds, securities, notes, debentures, or on any other form of indebtedness) received from sources within Greece by a resident or corporation of the United States

(US) not engaged in trade or business in Greece through a PE therein, shall be exempt from Greek tax but only to the extent that such interest does not exceed 9% per annum; but such exemption shall not apply to such interest paid by a Greek corporation to a US corporation controlling, directly or indirectly, more than 50% of the entire voting power in the paying corporation.

13. The DTT will apply to income earned as of 1 January 2011.
14. The 5% rate is applicable if the royalties consist of payments of any kind received as a consideration for the use of industrial, commercial or scientific equipment, and the 10% rate is applicable for all the other cases.
15. The 8% rate is applicable when the beneficiary of the interests is a bank or a financial institution, 10% rate is applicable for all the other cases.
16. Exemption (nil rate) applies to copyright royalties and other like payments in respect of the production or reproduction of any cultural or artistic work (but not including royalties in respect of motion picture films nor royalties in respect of works on films or videotapes or other means of reproduction for use in connection with television broadcasting.
(*) Although the DTT has been ratified it is not in force, since the instruments of ratification have not been exchanged yet, as of May 2010.

In general, it should be noted that certain DDTs may include specific clauses on specific cases that are not all captured in the table; hence, a careful review of each DDT is highly advisable.

Tax administration

Audit cycle
Tax audit procedures
The tax audit commences with the issuance of an audit order for tax open years, usually not more than five. The order concerns the audit of all tax issues (income tax, VAT, WHT, capital gain tax, etc.). The duration of the audit may vary from a few weeks to a few months, in certain cases.

Following the audit and the notification of tax audit findings, the company may:

- Negotiate with the tax authorities in an effort to reduce the tax burden and achieve an out of court settlement. An out-of court settlement offers the possibility to reduce additional taxes (not the principal amount of tax) at the rates provided now under the provisions of L.2238/94 (reduction of the additional tax to 3/5). The conclusion of such a settlement presupposes that the company accepts the findings of the audit (e.g., of expenses) for the audited years and is likely to face the same issues in the following years as well.
- Take the case to court (filing of a recourse), which necessitates an advance payment (25% of the taxes and penalties assessed). The first decision normally takes two to three years and another six to eight years until a decision by the Court of Appeal and Supreme Court is issued.
- Incorporate both of the aforementioned options in one document.
- Request a court settlement (after the filing of the recourse).

Criminal sanctions are also imposed on the company's representative under certain conditions, which are waived in the case of settlement on the amount of taxes assessed.

Tax auditors' practice
The complexity of the Greek tax legislation and the vagueness of its requirements enable the tax auditors to dispute either the company's results reflected in its accounting records or to disallow expenses. This is true in all tax audits and in spite of

companies' endeavours to comply with the tax requirements, tax audits always result in assessment of additional taxes and penalties.

The amount of additional taxes depends mainly on the following:

- Company's vulnerability because of nature of business and transactions;
- Taxes already paid on the basis of the company's income tax returns;
- Profits declared by competitors; and
- Weaknesses and shortcomings which the tax auditors might reveal, if a full audit is carried out.

In respect of deductible expenses, the legislation prescribes, among other requirements, that such expenses must be of a "business" nature, without defining what a business expense is. Consequently, the tax auditors dispute the deductibility of various items arguing that, in their opinion, they are not contributing to the company's business.

In a worst-case scenario, if serious violations are detected that make the audit verifications impossible, then the validity of the accounting books may be contested, resulting in the deemed (out-of-books) profit calculation and the imposition of heavy penalties and additional taxes.

Specifically, the validity of the books may be contested on the basis of the kind and gravity of infringements, which are divided in two categories:

- Infringements determining the books as "inadequate"; and
- Infringements determining the books as "inaccurate".

In the extreme cases, where the accounting books are treated as 'inadequate' or 'inaccurate', the taxable income and the tax due by the company will not be calculated according to book figures; but instead, the out of books determination method is applied, according to which the company's gross income of each financial year will be multiplied by the net profit rates defined by the Greek Ministry of Finance. These rates have been defined on the basis of the business activities of each company. In cases where the books are deemed to be 'inaccurate', these rates would be surcharged by 40% to 80%, depending on the kind of infringement from which the inaccuracy of the books has resulted.

Statute of limitations
The right of the Greek State to seek to collect unpaid taxes is normally five years starting from the end of the year in which the relevant tax return should be filed. For example for taxes due in 2009, the clearance VAT return should be filed in 2010 and the statute of limitation expires on 31 December 2015. However, in the case where a return is not filed then the statute of limitation is extended to 10 years. Furthermore, it should be noted that the statutes of limitation may be extended by law. This has happened many times in the past. Thus, the statutes of limitation for tax audit cases regarding accounting years 2000, 2001, 2002 and 2003 and fictitious or forged invoices' cases has been extended until 31 December 2010.

Tax return due dates
Income tax returns of Greek SAs, EPEs and branches of foreign companies are filed on a special form within four months and 10 days from the end of their financial year, which

can be on either 30 June or 31 December. By a decision of the Minister of Finance, the filing date for SAs may be extended a few days, depending on the last digit (figure) of their tax registration number (known in Greece as the arithmos phorologikou metroou or AFM). Branches and subsidiaries (at least 50% participation) of foreign companies may follow the financial year of the parent company. A Greek company that is at least 50% held by another Greek company that is in turn a subsidiary of a foreign company that has participation with the same or higher percentage may also follow the financial year of the foreign parent company. The income tax return constitutes the basis for assessment.

Tax returns are required to be submitted electronically from 2011 onwards.

Payment of tax

Income tax and tax prepayment (80% [100% for banks operating in Greece] of the current year's income tax less tax withheld at source) based on the tax return are paid in eight equal monthly instalments, the first of which should be paid upon filing. For newly established companies the pre-payment is reduced to 50% for the first three years of their operating. A deduction of 1.5% in case of a lump sum payment of income tax liability applies to tax returns filed from 2010 onwards.

Other issues

Exchange controls

In general, exchange controls have been long abolished in Greece.

Choice of business entity

The main differences between a subsidiary (i.e., SA, EPE or LLC) and a branch of a company from the law/establishment perspective are as follows:

1. A subsidiary is a separate legal entity from its parent company, whereas a branch does not form a separate legal entity, does not have its own shareholders and consequently the funds needed for its operation are transferred from the overseas parent company;
2. The parent company of a branch must be either the equivalent of a Greek SA or a LLC, whereas there is no such restriction for subsidiaries;
3. The day-to-day management of a branch is exercised by the legal representative, a person appointed by the parent company, whereas an SA is represented by its board of directors (BoD) and a LLC is administered and directed by the administrator(s);
4. No minimum capital is required for the establishment of a branch, nevertheless the share capital of the parent company should be at least EUR 60,000 if it is an SA and EUR 4,500 if it is a LLC;
5. An SA appears to be a more prestigious type of company than a branch and a LLC. This has a mainly psychological effect. Certain investors still tend to opt for the establishment of an SA company, particularly if they would like to participate in public tenders, etc.

The main legal differences between a SA and a LLC in Greece from a company law/ establishment perspective are as follows:

1. An SA is managed by a BoD consisting of at least three members, whereas a LLC can be managed by only one individual, the administrator (legal entities are permitted to be appointed as BoD members or administrators). Both BoD members

Greece

and administrators have to acquire a Greek tax registration number and a Greek residence permit before the establishment of the companies. Obtaining a residence permit for non-EU citizens is a time consuming procedure.

2. The shareholders of an SA are not required to be registered with the Greek tax authorities, whereas the partners of an LLC have to be registered with the Greek tax authorities and this may prove to be a time consuming procedure;

3. An SA is established by virtue of registration or approval (in case the company's share capital is higher than EUR 3,000,000 as well as in special cases) of the notarial deed which embodies the company's Articles of Association (AoA). The announcement of the Ministry of Development, containing a summary of the AoA, must be published in the "Bulletin of Societes Anonymes and Limited Liability Companies" of the Government Gazette. Generally, the registration of a SA requires approximately one to two working days after submission of relevant documentation. However, the time period may be extended to 10 working days, in the case that a special approval by the Ministry of Development is required. Whereas a LLC is established by a notarial deed, which incorporates the company's AoA, filed with the relevant authority (Registry with the Court of First Instance). A summary of the AoA must be published in the "Bulletin of Societes Anonymes and Limited Liability Companies" of the Government Gazette. Such registration usually takes three to five working days after the signature of the notarial deed;

4. An SA company is supervised by the Greek Ministry of Development (Prefecture), which necessitates certain filings to be performed (e.g., minutes of BoD, general announcements, financial statements, etc.). Whereas, at least at this stage, no supervising authority exists for an LLC and thus its filing requirements are less restrictive.

As of May 2010, there is a draft law in place that is expected to materially enhance and simplify the formation process for all Greek companies.

Corporate taxes in Guatemala

For more information, contact:

Edgar Mendoza
PricewaterhouseCoopers
Edificio Tívoli Plaza, 6a Calle 6-38 Zona 9
Cuarto Nivel
Guatemala City, Guatemala
Tel: +502 2420 7800
Email: edgar.mendoza@gt.pwc.com

Significant developments

No significant corporate tax developments noted for Guatemala in the past year.

Taxes on corporate income

The tax system of Guatemala is a unitary system, whereby income of all kinds, other than capital gains, is lumped together and subject to a single tax. The components of gross income subject to tax are usually business income, interest, dividends, rent, salaries and services. Dividends and other income payable abroad are taxed separately by way of withholding taxes.

There are two income tax regimes: general and optional.

General income tax regime
A rate of 5% is applicable to a company's gross income from Guatemalan sources (less exempt incomes).

A rate of 5% on gross revenue is applicable to juridical entities and individuals performing mercantile and non-mercantile activities, domiciled in Guatemala.

The tax is payable under flat tax withholdings (the tax is to be retained by either the customer or the recipient of services) or by direct remittances to the tax office made monthly within the first 10 working days of the month following the invoice date.

Optional income tax regime
A rate of 31% is applicable to a company's taxable income from Guatemalan sources.

A rate of 31% is applicable on net income of individuals or juridical entities domiciled in Guatemala. Under this system, the tax is determined and paid at the end of each quarter, without prejudicing the end-of-period final tax liquidation.

The annual final tax liquidation period begins on 1 January and ends on 31 December of each year.

Under this system, income taxes are payable as advance quarterly payments, and the balance is due upon filing the returns, which are due after the end of the fiscal period (31 December) but no later than 31 March of each year. Quarterly advance tax payments are applied to the final income tax liability computed as of the end of year.

Guatemala

The income tax return shall be accompanied by the documents required by the regulations, which might include:

- A balance sheet;
- A statement of results of operations;
- A statement of cash flows; and
- A statement of cost of production.

Documents must be duly certified by a professional or an independent accounting firm. The financial statements that accompany the return shall agree with both those recorded in the financial statements ledger and those destined for publication.

Both the income tax return and exhibits thereto shall be signed by the taxpayers, their agent or their legal representative or by any other responsible persons so determined by this law and the tax code.

Salaries and wages, dividends, or profits and fees are subject to withholding taxes. Remittances abroad for services, commissions, interest, rents, royalties and technical service fees are subject to flat income tax withholdings.

Although both business enterprises and individuals are required to file tax returns, individuals are not required to file tax returns if their annual income from personal services does not exceed GTQ 36,000 or if their income from personal services has been subject to withholding taxes in amounts no less than the tax due.

Corporate residence

The place of incorporation determines corporate residence. Any entity incorporated according to Guatemalan law is required to have its fiscal and corporate domicile in Guatemalan territory.

Other taxes

Value-added tax
A 12% value-added tax (VAT) is levied on the sale or transfer of merchandise and on non-personal services rendered or effected in Guatemala. The tax is payable to the government by way of the invoice method, whereby the tax charged to the customers is offset by the VAT paid over purchases, and the government collects the net resulting amount. The issuance and circulation of credit titles is VAT-exempt.

Sale of goods
The taxable amount on the sale of goods includes the sales price less any discounts provided under sound commercial practices plus other charges shown on the invoice.

Services
The taxable amount of services includes the price of the service, less any discounts provided under sound commercial practices, plus financial charges and products used to render the services.

Other issues
1. Imports: The tax base is the value declared for import duties' computation purposes.
2. Leases of movable or immovable property: The tax base is the value of the lease.

Exempted sales and services
- Importations made by:
  - Cooperatives legally constituted as registered on imported machinery, equipment, and other goods relating to the activity or service of the cooperative;
  - Individuals and juridical entities under temporary importation regulations; and
  - Diplomatic and consular missions accredited before the Guatemalan government.
- Banking institution services and their agents.
- The issuance, circulation and transfer of credit bonds, value bonds and stocks of any kind.
- Interest accrued by credit bonds and other obligations issued by mercantile partnerships, negotiated through an authorised stock exchange.
- Exports of goods and services.
- Contributions and donations to educational, cultural, assistance or security service partnerships, constituted as not-for-profit entities.

G

Stamp taxes
Other than sales invoices, contracts and documents subject to VAT and other minor exemptions, a stamp tax must be paid on all documents covering commercial and legal transactions (e.g., collection of dividends), either by preparing the document on papel sellado, which is special stamped paper, or by affixing stamps on the documents. This tax is also assessed on documents issued abroad, other than drafts or promissory notes and commercial invoices from foreign suppliers. Letters of credit and acceptances involving international transfers of funds are generally exempt from stamp taxes. The normal tax rate is 3% and is calculated on the face value of the documents or on the gross value of the related transaction.

Real estate tax
Real estate taxes are assessed annually at GTQ 2 per thousand on declared property values of from GTQ 2,000 to GTQ 20,000, at GTQ 6 per thousand on values from GTQ 20,000 to GTQ 70,000, and at GTQ 9 per thousand on values in excess of GTQ 70,000 (e.g., property valued at GTQ 1,000,000 will pay real estate taxes of GTQ 9,000).

Inheritance and gift taxes
Recipients of inheritances, legacies, and gifts of personal property, real property or other rights in Guatemala are subject to inheritance taxes. Inheritance, legacies, or gifts of personal property located abroad but publicly deeded in Guatemala and debt waivers executed in Guatemala are also subject to tax. The tax is levied at progressively higher rates on amounts up to GTQ 50,000 at 1% to 9% when the recipients are related to the donor (at least 12% if not) and at 6% to 14% on amounts in excess of GTQ 500,000 (at least 25% for nonrelated recipients).

Incentive stock option (ISO) tax
The ISO tax rate of 1% is assessed on the net assets of a corporation, or on the gross income of a corporation, whichever is higher, and there is no limit on the amount to be paid. Tax paid may be credited against the corporation's income tax. If the annual business tax exceeds the income tax, no reimbursement is possible.

The tax is to be paid quarterly on the basis of the corporation's opening balance sheet for each fiscal period.

Guatemala

Social security contribution
Corporations contribute 12.67% of their monthly payroll and employees contribute 4.83% of their monthly salary to social security.

Tax on interest income
Interest income earned by domiciled persons other than banks is subject to a flat withholding tax rate of 10%. The interest taxed must be included by taxpayers in their income tax returns as non-taxable income.

Branch income

Foreign-source income received by a domestic corporation is generally not considered to be from Guatemalan sources for income tax purposes. In Guatemala, individuals and business enterprises are taxed on their income derived primarily from national sources. Expenses incurred abroad by non-residents in connection with income earned from Guatemalan sources cannot be deducted for income tax purposes by merely having the supporting receipts, as the regulations to the law do not permit such a deduction for these purposes.

Income determination

Capital gains
Capital gains taxes are equivalent to 10% in the general income tax regime, and to 31% in the optional income tax regime of such gains as a flat tax. Capital losses can be netted only against capital gains.

Inter-company dividends
Dividends from domestic subsidiaries and other domestic corporations are not subject to income tax withholdings if Guatemalan income tax has been paid. However, a 3% stamp tax must be paid upon dividend payment.

Foreign income
Foreign-source income received by a domestic corporation is generally exempt from Guatemalan income tax.

Stock dividends
Stock dividends are permitted by the Commercial Code and are subject to a 3% stamp tax upon dividend payment.

Individuals and business enterprises, national and foreign, resident or domiciled in Guatemala are taxed on their income from sources within the country. In addition, personal, professional and technical services are also subject to tax when rendered abroad and charged to persons or entities resident or domiciled in Guatemala or when rendered in Guatemala and charged abroad. The law allows for two systems for income tax payment purposes, at the taxpayer's option.

Deductions

Deductions apply only under the optional income tax regime.

Depreciation and depletion

Depreciation is generally computed on a straight-line basis. Upon request by the taxpayer, the tax authorities may authorise other depreciation methods. The maximum annual rates allowed as deductible expenses are the following:

	%
Building and improvements	5
Machinery and equipment	20
Furniture and fixtures	20
Vehicles	20
Tools	25
Tree and vegetable species	15
Computer equipment and software	33.33
Any other depreciable asset	10

Tax depreciation must conform to book depreciation.

Payments to foreign affiliates

Deduction for royalties will be allowed up to 5% of gross income. Charges for technical service fees are deductible up to 1% of gross income or 15% of total salaries paid to Guatemalans, whichever is larger.

Taxes

All taxes other than income tax and VAT are deductible.

Net operating losses

Operating losses may not be carried forward for deduction from otherwise taxable profits.

Employee pension/retirement funds

The deduction of provisions to establish or increase employee pension and retirement funds or reserves is allowed, provided the government approves the related plans.

Severance compensation payments

Severance compensation payments are allowed as deductible expenses as well as limited allocations (not to exceed 8.33% of total annual salaries and wages) to a reserve for severance compensation. Provisions pertaining to actual liability for severance compensation per year are also allowed, provided the related plans, based on collective bargaining agreements, are approved by the government.

Interest expense

The deduction of interest expense is limited to a maximum of 15% annually in excess of the authorised rate for commercial banks.

Donations

Duly proven donations made to the government, the municipalities and their agencies, as well as to duly authorised not-for-profit welfare, social service and scientific associations and foundations, and universities, political parties, and guild entities are deductible. The maximum deductible amount for income tax purposes of each period shall not exceed 5% of the donor's net income up to a maximum of GTQ 500,000 per year.

Guatemala

Group taxation

No consolidation for tax purposes is permitted as each group entity is treated as an independent taxpayer, which shall file its own tax return.

Tax incentives

Exemption from payment of import duties on machinery, equipment and raw and packaging materials and from income tax is available for those corporations classified as exporting companies. These exemptions also apply to free trade zones. (Decrees 29-89, 65-89, and others).

The Law of Promotion and Development of Exports Activities and Drawback Industries is known in Guatemala as maquila. Decree No. 29-89. This law seeks to promote, encourage and develop the manufacture of products within areas controlled by the Customs Authority for export to countries outside the Central American region, as well as to regulate exporting and drawback activities.

The exporter may apply for authorisation to operate under any of the three systems provided by the law:

- Export under a temporary admission system;
- Export under the reimbursement of duties system; or
- Export under the total added national component system.

Tax incentives and benefits:

- Exemption of taxes, import duties and other charges on imports of machinery and equipment, including VAT;
- Discontinuance of VAT payments on temporary raw material imports, etc; and
- Exemption of income tax for 10 years on profits obtained under this law.

Free Trade Zones Law. Decree No. 65-89
The law seeks to encourage and regulate the establishment of free trade zones that promote domestic development by activities carried out within certain zones, particularly those that tend to strengthen export activities, generate employment and transfer technology.

Tax incentives and benefits:

- Import duties exemption; and
- Income tax exemption.
  - Ten-year period for the administrative agency;
  - Ten-year period for industrial & service permit holders;
  - Five-year period for commercial permit holders;
  - Exemption of real estate taxes for a five-year period;
  - Exemption of tax stamps on the conveyance of title over properties;
  - Dividends or profits distributed by the administrative agency and permit holders shall also be considered tax-exempted income;
  - Exemption of custom duties and any other charges on import and consumption of fuel oil, bunker, butane and propane gas used exclusively in the Free Trade Zone; and

- Foreigners working in the Free Trade Zone are subject to the provisions of the immigration law and the Labour Code.

Free Trade Zone "Santo Tomas de Castilla"-ZOLIC- Decree No. 22-73.

The Free Trade Zones are land areas subject to a special customs regime, whereby individuals or enterprises manufacture or commercialise products for export or reexportation, or offer international trade-related services.

Tax incentives and benefits:

- Taxes exemption;
- Import duties exemption; and
- Real estate tax exemption.

Withholding taxes (WHT)

On payments to non-domiciled foreign corporations or individuals:

	%
Dividends, profit participations, earnings, and other benefits (1)	10
Commissions, salaries	10
Interest (2)	10
Professional fees, royalties, technical service fees	31

Notes

1. For taxpayers that already paid corporate income tax, there is no withholding tax.
2. Interests will not be taxed (no withholding applies) when:
   - These interests are paid to a legal bank or financial institution;
   - If the interests are in connection with a loan registered in the Guatemalan banking system; and
   - The loan was used in taxable activities.

Tax treaties

Guatemala has no tax treaties in force.

Tax administration

Returns

The fiscal year runs from 1 January to 31 December.

Payment of tax

General income tax regime

Tax rate 5% on gross income. There are two kinds of payments methods: direct payment method and withholdings method.

Taxes on income are governed by the income tax law, Ley del Impuesto sobre la Renta, and its related regulations. Administration of the law is vested with the SAT.

Optional income tax regime

All corporate taxpayers are required to prepay their estimated annual income tax liability in quarterly instalments. Taxpayers may choose one of the following procedures for computing estimated quarterly tax liability:

Guatemala

1. Tax on income shown by partial closure of accounts or computation of presumed liquidation of operations at the end of each quarter;
2. Tax on 5% of overall gross income earned during the corresponding quarter of the preceding year (5% of the 30% income tax rate = 1.5%); or
3. Tax equivalent to one-fourth of the tax paid for the immediately preceding tax year.

VAT
The amount payable to the Superintendencia de Administracion Tributaria (SAT), Guatemala's tax authority, is the difference between the debits and credits of the tax period (one month) and is paid monthly by filing a tax return in the following calendar month at the end of each tax period.

Refunds of VAT
Any tax credits at the end of the period may be carried forward the next month to offset any tax debits that month. No cash refunds are allowed other than to exporters.

Other issues

Accurate and current information regarding taxation in Guatemala is often difficult to obtain as the country lacks reporting services such as those available in the United States and other countries. It is also difficult to determine how the tax laws will be applied in practice in complex situations. The laws and regulations are limited and ordinarily cover only the most common situations. The system of legal precedent resulting from court decisions is narrowly used, and each issue is resolved by reference to the respective codes. Guatemala has shown little interest in tax planning, but it is possible to have informal consultations with the tax authorities and to obtain authoritative rulings in many cases. Discrepancies between government and management criteria are commonly brought to judgment by the Constitutional Court, whose binding sentences generally abrogate the laws in dispute.

The income tax law differs from that of the United States in several basic aspects that may be of interest to a prospective investor. The comments in the preceding sections are of a general nature only; application thereof shall often be determined by reference to other laws regulating the specific industry or taxpayer, in particular, the industrial development laws.

National income is drawn principally from agriculture, poultry and cattle-raising, which together account for two-thirds of the economically active population. Taxes collected by the central government are levied on income, property, bequests and gifts, imports, exports and sales. Local taxes at countrywide level also are levied by the municipalities.

Corporate taxes in Guernsey, Channel Islands

For more information, contact:

Mark Watson
PricewaterhouseCoopers CI LLP
National Westminster House
Le Truchot
St Peter Port, Guernsey GY1 4ND
Channel Islands
Tel: +44 1481 752029
Email: m.watson@gg.pwc.com

Significant developments

The tax regime underwent radical changes with effect from 1 January 2008 with the introduction of the zero/10 tax legislation. Under this regime, the standard rate of company income tax moved to 0%, with a 10% rate applied to income derived from banking businesses and a 20% rate applied to publicly regulated utility companies and income derived from property located in Guernsey.

The new regime also saw the abolition of the "international company" designation and two categories of exempt company status with effect from 1 January 2008. As a result, a company may no longer be able to negotiate a specific rate of tax with the Income Tax Office. The only companies that may potentially qualify for the exempt company status are certain categories of collective investment schemes and unit trusts.

Taxes on corporate income

Income tax

Companies pay income tax at the standard rate of 0% on taxable income.

Income derived from a banking business is taxable at 10%. "Banking business" is broadly defined as income that arises as a result of the provision of credit facilities by any type of company and the utilisation of customer deposits. Relief is available for eligible expenses that are allocated against different streams of income.

Any income derived from the exploitation of property located in Guernsey or received by a publicly regulated utility company is subject to tax at the higher rate of 20%.

Exempt companies

Some collective investment schemes and unit trusts may qualify for exempt status, which would place them completely outside the Guernsey tax regime. For each year for which exempt status is sought, a charge of GBP 600 is levied.

One of the following conditions, among others, must be met for the company to be considered exempt:

- The company is beneficially owned outside of Guernsey; or
- No Guernsey resident individual or company has a beneficial interest in the company (with the exception of shareholders, loan creditors or nominees/trustees).

Guernsey, Channel Islands

Loans to participators
If a company makes loans with preferential terms to an individual or entity connected with the company, this will be deemed to be income in the hands of the debtor, and the creditor company will be required to account for, withhold and pay the tax. Certain exemptions apply.

Corporate residence

All Guernsey-registered companies are regarded as residents in the island unless granted exempt company status. In addition, a company will be treated as a resident in Guernsey (regardless of where it is incorporated) if shareholder control is exercised by persons resident in the island.

Other taxes

The dwellings profit tax has been abolished with effect from 28 January 2009.

Branch income

Branch income is taxed in the same manner as companies, at the appropriate rate according to the activity being undertaken.

No further tax is withheld on the transfer of profits abroad to group companies, provided no Guernsey resident individual has an interest in the company.

Income determination

Inventory valuation
Inventory is valued at the lower of historical cost or net realisable value. Use of last-in, first-out (LIFO) is not permitted. Generally, there are no material differences between accounts prepared on a normal accounting basis and those prepared on a tax basis.

Capital gains
Capital gains are not subject to tax in Guernsey.

Inter-company dividends
All dividends paid by a standard tax-paying company (0%) are deemed to have been paid from income arising after 31 December 2007, (i.e., after the introduction of the new zero/10 tax regime) unless the company elects to have them treated otherwise.

Foreign income
Resident corporations are liable to tax on their worldwide income. Income tax is levied on foreign branch income when earned, and on investment income from foreign dividends, interest, rents and royalties. Double taxation is mitigated either through unilateral relief (by giving credit for foreign taxation of up to three-quarters of the effective Guernsey rate) or by treaty relief.

Stock dividends
Stock dividends may be treated as income.

Deductions

Capital allowances

Depending on the life of an asset, annual allowances (depreciation for tax purposes) are available on machinery and equipment, including vehicles, on diminishing-balance or on straight-line basis at varying standard rates. Obsolescence allowance is given when, on disposal, proceeds of a sale are less than the unclaimed annual allowances on machinery and equipment being replaced. Any surplus of realisation value of an asset over its tax written-down value is liable to tax, up to the total amount of allowances claimed.

Limited allowances are applicable to buildings but not to the depletion of natural resources.

Net operating losses

Losses from one class of income may be used to offset the profits from another class of income if both classes are subject to tax at the same rate. Unrelieved trading losses may be carried forward to offset future trading income.

Upon cessation of trade, operating losses arising from balancing allowances may be carried back to the previous two years of charge to be relieved against past trading profits.

Payments to foreign affiliates

Guernsey-source royalties and long-term interest are subject to taxation at source. Relief is obtained by the retention of the tax deducted. Short-term interest, unless owed to an authorised bank, is not deductible, unless the advance in respect of which it is paid is used wholly and exclusively for the purposes of the trade. Other fees must be paid on an arm's-length basis.

Taxes

Local income tax paid is not deductible in computing taxable income.

Other significant items

Normally, business deductions that are incurred wholly and exclusively for the purposes of the trade are allowed.

Group taxation

Group loss relief may be claimed when both companies are members of the same group and the companies are either carrying on business in Guernsey through a permanent establishment (PE) or incorporated in Guernsey. Loss relief is available only against income taxed at the same rate.

A claim for group loss relief must be made by the claimant company within two years after the end of the calendar year in which the relevant accounting period ended, and the claim must be accompanied by a declaration by the surrendering company that it consents to the surrender.

Tax incentives

In view of the low rate of tax, no special incentives are available to local businesses.

Guernsey, Channel Islands

Withholding taxes (WHT)

Deemed distributions
A company will be required to withhold tax on any distributions made to or in reference to any Guernsey resident individual shareholders.

Furthermore, following certain trigger events, such as the sale of shares, death of the beneficial member, etc., the company is deemed to have distributed all of the Guernsey resident shareholder's share of the company's undistributed profits accumulated since 1 January 2008. All investment income is deemed to be distributed as it arises.

Although the liability to tax is the shareholder's, the company is obligated to account for, withhold and pay tax to the Income Tax Office and may then claim this back from the shareholder.

Agency
A company also is required to withhold tax when it is acting as an agent and making payments to a non-resident liable to Guernsey tax.

Tax administration

Returns
An income tax return is required to be filed one year and 15 days after the end of the calendar year in which the accounting period ends. Should a company meet the conditions below, a simplified return may be filed without either a computation or financial statements.

In order to qualify for a simplified return, a company must have none of the following:

* Guernsey employees (other than directors);
* Guernsey resident individual beneficial owners;
* Income from utilities (e.g., Guernsey water or electricity companies, etc.);
* Income from Guernsey properties;
* Income from a banking business;
* Loans to Guernsey participators; or
* Distributions made to Guernsey resident individuals.

Should a company have Guernsey resident individual beneficial members and/or make loans to participators, it will be required to submit quarterly returns accounting for distributions and deemed distributions and loans advanced.

Payment of tax
In Guernsey, tax is payable in two instalments, on 30 June and 31 December in the year of charge (calendar year). If liabilities have not been determined, this may necessitate initially raising estimated assessments based on prior year figures and raising a final assessment when the figures are agreed.

Corporate taxes in Honduras

For more information, contact:

Ramon Ortega
Edificio Bank of Nova Scotia
3rd Floor
Avenida John F Kennedy, Esquina con Avenida Lope de Vega
Santo Domingo, Dominican Republic
Tel: +809 567 7741
Email: ramon.ortega@do.pwc.com

Significant developments

Tax reforms were initiated in Decree 17-2010 that became effective on 12 May 2010.

First, a 10% tax on the distribution of profits or dividends to non-resident companies was initiated.

Distribution or payment of dividends or any other form of distribution of retained earnings or reserves to resident or domiciled individuals will be taxed at 10%.

Next, the Temporary Solidarity Contribution tax rate was increased to 10% for 2010 and 2011, 6% for 2012, 5% for 2013, 4% for 2014 and 0% for 2015.

Taxpayers with annual income over HNL 15 million will be required to withhold 1% from the payment to its suppliers on purchase of goods and machinery, if they do not use the account regime. This withholding tax will be credited against the annual income tax.

Taxes on corporate income

The corporate tax rate for a resident company is 25% of the company's period income.

In addition, the Temporary Solidarity Contribution tax rate has been increased to 10% for 2010 and 2011, 6% for 2012, 5% for 2013, 4% for 2014 and 0% for 2015. This is levied on all companies with taxable income in excess of HNL one million. For 2009 this tax was 5%. In 2007, the law established this tax as deductible for income tax purposes, however, beginning in 2008, this tax became a surcharge and non-deductible for income tax purposes.

Honduran resident companies are taxed on their worldwide income. Non-resident companies are subject to income tax only on income derived from Honduran sources.

Corporate residence

The place of incorporation is regarded by Honduran authorities as the corporate residence. Non-resident companies are companies incorporated/registered outside of Honduras. However, income taxes on corporations are levied on local income regardless of the place of incorporation. In addition, any person, natural or legal, resident in Honduras is subject to tax on both local and foreign income.

Honduras

Other taxes

Taxes and royalties
Royalties are taxed in the same manner as general income if the recipient is a local company or branch. Non-resident recipients are subject to 25% withholding tax on royalties. Royalties from mining operations are subject to 10% withholding tax. Effective 12 May 2010 all royalties paid to non-resident recipients are subject to 10% withholding income tax.

Taxes on dividends
Honduran resident individuals and non-resident individuals or companies are subject to 10% withholding tax on cash dividends. The income from dividends is considered "other income", thus non-taxable under the general income tax rates. Stock dividends are not taxable.

Net assets tax
The net assets tax applies to the gross value of assets less reserve for accounts payable and any accumulated depreciation allowed under the income tax law and other deductions allowed by law. It is a 1% tax of the net asset value of the company. The law also allows a special deduction of HNL 3,000,000. The net assets tax is in lieu of the corporate income tax when the corporate income tax is less than the amount due for net asset tax. Resident companies during their preoperative period and companies operating in Free Zones, among others, are exempt from the net assets tax.

Non-resident companies do not apply for the Net Assets Tax.

Capital gains tax
A 10% tax is applied on capital gains, regardless of the person's residence status.

Sales tax
Sales tax is charged on all sale and purchase transactions of goods and services made in Honduran territory. The general tax rate is 12%. It applies to most goods and services, with the exception of machinery and equipment, basic grains, pharmaceutical products, raw materials for the production of non-taxable goods, petroleum products, school supplies and insecticides, among others.

The import and sale of beer, other alcoholic beverages, cigarettes and other tobacco products are subject to 15% tax.

There is a 15% tax rate applicable to some PCS, cellular, internet broad band, cable TV and energy services, depending on the amount of consumption billed by the supplier.

There is an 18% tax rate levied on first class and business class air tickets.

Municipal taxes
Companies doing business in Honduras are also subject to the rules and regulations of the respective municipality. Taxes and obligations are ruled by the "Plan de Arbitrios". Some of these tax obligations are

- Industry, commerce and service tax – Based on sales volume per year;
- Personal municipal tax – (Individual tax);
- Public services tax – Tax paid for services such as waste management;

Honduras

- Real estate – Tax on asset and asset gains; and
- Sign tax – Taxation on public advertising.

The following table summarises other significant taxes.

Types of tax	Rate (%)
Sales tax	12% in general, 15% to some telecommunication, PCS, cellular, internet broad band, cable TV and energy services and 18% to business class airline tickets
Customs duties	1 to 20
Payroll taxes or contributions, paid by employers	Social security 7.2% with a ceiling of HNL 4,800 INFOP 1% Housing fund – RAP/FOSOVI 1.5%
Municipal taxes:	
Real estate tax; imposed on companies and individuals owning real estate	Various
Industry trade and service municipal tax; imposed monthly on income derived from the operations of companies; rates vary according to the annual production volume, income or sales:	Various
Up to HNL 500,000	0.0003
From HNL 500,001 to HNL 10,000,000	0.0004
From HNL 10,000,001 to HNL 20,000,000	0.0003
From HNL 20,000,001 to HNL 30,000,000	0.0002
Over HNL 30,000,000	0.00015

Branch income

Branch income is subject to income tax at the rates applicable for corporate income. Before 12 May 2010, there was no withholding tax on dividends distributed in the country or abroad.

Currently, there is a 10% withholding tax rate on dividends.

Income determination

Income is computed in accordance with generally accepted accounting and commercial principles, subject to certain adjustments required by the tax law.

- Inventories;
- Provisions;
- Tax Depreciation;
- Net operating losses/carryforwards;
- Taxes; and
- Capital gains.

Honduras

Deductions

The net taxable income of an enterprise is determined by deducting all the ordinary and necessary expenses incurred in the creation of income, including amortisation and depreciation; municipal taxes; donations made in favour of the State, the Central District, the Municipalities, and legally recognised educational institutions, charities and sporting facilities; mandatory employer-employee contributions to the social security system; and "reasonable" charges for royalties and management services.

In general, all expenses incurred in the generation of taxable income are considered as deductible for income tax purposes. However, there are some "non-deductible" expenses, even if incurred in the generation of income for example: a) interest paid to owners or shareholders; b) capital losses.

Inventories are generally valued using the first-in, first-out (FIFO), last-in, first-out (LIFO) and weighted-average cost methods.

Provisions for contingent liabilities, such as severance pay, are not deductible for tax purposes; actual payments for those liabilities are considered to be deductible expenses.

Depreciation may be computed using the straight-line method. Companies may obtain authorisation from the tax authorities to use other depreciation methods. However, after a company selects a depreciation method, it must apply the method consistently thereafter. The following are the applicable straight-line method rates for some common assets.

Asset	Rate (%)
Buildings	2.5 to 10
Plant and machinery	10
Vehicles	10 to 33
Furniture and office equipment	10
Tools	25

Companies engaged in agriculture, manufacturing, mining and tourism may carryforward losses for three years. However, certain restrictions apply. Losses may not be carried back. Some restrictions apply.

With the exception of the solidarity tax, net asset taxes, income tax and sales tax (i.e., if sales tax paid is used as a credit to net the sales tax payable to the government), taxes and contributions paid to district or municipalities are deductible expenses when determining taxable income.

Capital losses are not deductible to determine the net taxable income. Capital losses can only be netted against capital gains. Capital gains are subject to a tax rate of 10%.

Group taxation

No provisions exist for group taxation.

Tax incentives

Companies operating under a special tax regime are exempted from income tax, sales tax, customs duties and some municipal taxes. These special tax regimes are:

- Free zone
- Industrial processing zone ("Zona Industrial de Procesamiento" (ZIP))
- Temporary import regime ("Régimen de Importación Temporal" (RIT))
- Tourism incentive law
- Law of the Tourism Free Zone of the Bay Islands ("Ley de la Zona Libre Turística de las Islas de la Bahia")
- Law promoting the generation of electric energy with renewable resources ("Ley de Promoción a la Generación de Energía Eléctrica con Recursos Renovables"). There are tax exemptions for projects generating 50MW and over.

Other incentives
Drawback industries
Special benefits exist for industries that import semi-manufactured materials for assembly in Honduras and export finished products. Benefits consist of duty-free imports of raw materials for subsequent export as manufactured products. Machinery for these industries may also be imported duty-free.

Withholding taxes (WHT)

Withholding taxes for non-residents
For non-residents in Honduras, any income derived from Honduran sources is taxable under the following schedule of the Income Tax Law:

Income source	Tax Withheld (%) *Effective 12 May 2010
Real estate and movable property rent, except dividends and interest	10
Royalties from mining operations and other natural resources	10
Salaries paid for services and other remuneration for rendering of services within national territory or abroad	10
Profit transfers from branch office to head office	10
Dividends	10
Royalties	10
Interest paid on commercial operations, bonds, securities or negotiable instruments and other types of obligations	10
Income from operation of airplanes, ships and vehicles	10
Income from operation of telecommunication companies	10
Insurance premiums	10
Income obtained from public shows	10
Films and video tapes for cinemas, TV, video clubs and cable TV	10
Any other income not mentioned previously	10

Honduras

Tax administration

The Dirección Ejecutiva de Ingresos (DEI) is the tax authority in Honduras. It is responsible for the administration of the tax and customs system. Taxpayers may request approval from the DEI regarding direct or indirect taxes (e.g., accelerated depreciation methods on new assets, acquired by corporations with monetary activities requiring constant technological update, higher installed production capacity and productive re-conversion processes, in order to maintain and strengthen their competitive advantage).

The statutory tax year runs from 1 January through to 31 December. However, taxpayers may apply to use a special tax year by requesting an authorisation from the DEI. Companies must file and pay income tax on 30 April every year. Mandatory advance tax payments are payable each quarter, based on the income tax paid for the preceding tax year.

Corporate taxes in Hong Kong

For more information, contact:

Peter Yu
PricewaterhouseCoopers Limited
21/F Edinburgh Tower, The Landmark
15 Queen's Road Central
Hong Kong, SAR
Tel: +852 2289 3122
Email: peter.sh.yu@hk.pwc.com

Significant developments

Developments in tax treaty network
The Inland Revenue Ordinance (IRO) was revised in March 2010 to enable the Hong Kong Special Administrative Region (SAR) Government to obtain and exchange tax information with other jurisdictions other than those of "domestic tax interest". The legislative change paves the way for the Hong Kong SAR Government to sign comprehensive double tax agreements (CDTA) incorporating the more liberal version of Exchange of Information (EoI) article. Subsidiary legislation was also enacted to provide safeguards against possible abuse of the EoI provisions in a CDTA and for protecting the confidentiality and privacy of the information exchanged.

Following the enactment, the Hong Kong SAR Government signed a CDTA with Brunei, the Netherlands and Indonesia in March 2010 and with Kuwait, Hungary and Austria in May 2010. The newly signed CDTAs have not yet entered into force and are pending the completion of the ratification procedures of the contracting parties. Hong Kong also initialled a CDTA with Switzerland in April 2010, the formal signing of which is pending the completion of the necessary administrative procedures. In addition, agreement in principle on a CDTA has been reached between Hong Kong and Japan according to a press release released by the Hong Kong SAR Government on 31 March 2010. The third protocol to the CDTA between China and Hong Kong was signed in May 2010 to update the EoI article to the more liberal 2004 version of the Organisation for Economic Co-operation and Development (OECD) Model Tax Convention. The protocol has not yet come into force pending the completion of the ratification procedures by both sides.

New guidance on transfer pricing
Two new Departmental Interpretation and Practice Notes (DIPNs) were issued in 2009 addressing the transfer pricing issues in Hong Kong. One focuses on the administrative/procedural issues involved in providing double tax relief in a CDTA context such as when such relief is available and what are the procedures for claiming such relief while the other outlines the Hong Kong Inland Revenue Department (HKIRD)'s view on the legislative framework for transfer pricing in Hong Kong, including the statutory provisions in the IRO and the articles in a CDTA that are relevant to transfer pricing. The latter one also provides guidance on numerous transfer pricing related issues such as the application of the arm's-length principle, the acceptable transfer pricing methodologies, which are largely in line with the OECD transfer pricing guidelines. Also, it provides for the documentation that taxpayers should consider retaining to support their transfer pricing arrangements, and the interaction between the transfer pricing and sourcing rules in Hong Kong.

H

Hong Kong

2010/11 budget proposals

In the 2010/11 Budget of the Hong Kong SAR Government, measures were introduced to extend the stamp duty concession in the trading of exchange traded funds to those consisting of not more than 40% holding in Hong Kong shares and to extend the concessionary profits tax rate applicable to qualifying debt instruments. The offshore fund exemption regime was also enhanced by revising DIPN 43 – Profits Tax Exemption for Offshore Funds and updating the list of recognised exchanges covered by the exemption. DIPN 43 was revised to clarify that for the purpose of determining the location of a company's central management and control, the mere fact that the majority of the directors of the management board of the company are resident in Hong Kong would not of itself mean that the company is centrally managed and controlled in Hong Kong, and hence would not adversely affect the application of the tax exemption.

The stamp duty rate on transactions of properties valued over HKD 20 million is increased from 3.75% to 4.25%; and such transactions will no longer be eligible for deferred payment of stamp duty on chargeable agreement for sale (this was proposed in the 2010/11 Budget and at the time of writing, the legislation giving effect to this proposal has not been enacted).

Taxes on corporate income

Hong Kong adopts a territorial basis of taxation. Profits tax is payable by every person (defined to include corporation, partnership and sole proprietorship, etc.) carrying on a trade, profession or business in Hong Kong on profits arising in or derived from Hong Kong from that trade, profession or business. However, capital gains and receipts that are capital in nature are not subject to tax. Dividends are also not subject to tax in Hong Kong. The tax residence of a person is generally irrelevant for profits tax purposes. The tax treatments of public and private companies are the same.

Certain income that would not otherwise be subject to Hong Kong profits tax is deemed to arise in or be derived from Hong Kong from a trade, profession or business carried on in Hong Kong and thus becomes taxable in Hong Kong. This includes royalties received by a non-resident for the use of or right to use in Hong Kong a patent, design, trademark, copyright material, or secret process or formula or other property of a similar nature.

In general, expenses that are revenue in nature and incurred in the production of assessable profits are allowed for deduction. Please refer to the section *Deductions* for more details.

Tax losses can be carried forward indefinitely to offset against assessable profits in subsequent years of assessment but cannot be carried backward.

The tax rates are 16.5% for corporations and 15% for unincorporated businesses for year of assessment 2010/11.

There are special rules for determining the tax liabilities of certain industries such as shipping, air services, and financial services. Incomes from certain qualifying debt instruments are subject to concessionary rate. Offshore funds having Hong Kong fund managers and investment advisors with full discretionary powers will be exempt from Hong Kong profits tax on profits derived in Hong Kong from six types of "specified transactions" which are carried out or arranged by "specified persons". However, there are also specific anti-avoidance provisions in the IRO deeming certain resident persons to be subject to profits tax on their share of the non-resident person's tax exempt profits.

Corporate residence

In general, for Hong Kong profits tax purposes, corporate residency is not important in determining taxability of an entity. The decisive factors for taxability are (1) whether a corporation is carrying on a trade, profession or business in Hong Kong and (2) whether the profits are arising in or derived from Hong Kong. However, where it is necessary to determine the corporate residence, such as for the purpose of CDTA, a company incorporated in Hong Kong or a company that is normally managed or controlled/centrally managed and controlled in Hong Kong is considered as Hong Kong tax residence.

For Hong Kong profits tax purposes, whether a foreign corporation is carrying on a trade, profession or business in Hong Kong and the source of profits rather than whether there is a permanent establishment in Hong Kong are the decisive factors in determining taxability.

Other taxes

Value-added tax/goods and services tax/sales tax
Hong Kong does not have a value-added tax (VAT), goods and services tax or sales tax.

Stamp duty
Stamp duty is charged on transfer of Hong Kong stock by way of sale and purchase at 0.2% per transaction, payable half by the vendor and half by the purchaser. Hong Kong stock is defined as stock the transfer of which must be registered in Hong Kong.

For conveyance on sale of immovable property, the stamp duty payable depends on the property consideration and ranges from a flat rate of HKD 100 (for property consideration of up to HKD 2,000,000) to the highest rate of 4.25% of the consideration of the property (for property consideration exceeding HKD 20,000,000), with marginal relief upon entry into each higher rate band. For lease of immovable property, stamp duty is calculated at a specified rate of the annual rental that varies with the term of the lease. Currently, the applicable rate ranges from 0.25% (for lease period of not more than one year) to 1% (for lease period of more than three years).

Exemption is available to certain transactions such as transfer of shares between associated corporate bodies and certain stock borrowing and lending transactions, provided that the specified conditions for exemption are satisfied.

Excise tax
See the discussion on *Customs duties*.

Property tax
Property tax is charged to the owner of any land or buildings (except government and consular properties) in Hong Kong at the standard rate of 15% on the net assessable value of such land or buildings. Net assessable value of a property is the consideration

Hong Kong

payable to the owner for the right to use the land or buildings less rates paid by the owner and a 20% notional allowance.

Rental income derived by a company from a Hong Kong property is subject to profits tax. The company that is subject to profits tax may apply for an exemption from property tax in respect of the property. If no exemption is applied, the property tax paid can be used to offset against the profits tax payable by the company.

Transfer tax
Hong Kong does not have a transfer tax.

Turnover tax
Hong Kong does not have a turnover tax.

Business registration
Every person who carries on a business in Hong Kong is required to apply for business registration with a fee within one month from the date of commencement of the business.

Special registration and licence fees are applicable to banks and deposit-taking companies.

Customs duties
There is no tariff on general imports. However, duties are levied on limited categories of dutiable commodities (i.e., tobacco, liquor, methyl alcohol and hydrocarbons) regardless of whether they are imported or locally manufactured.

Capital duty
A fee of HKD 1 for all or part of HKD 1,000 of the nominal share capital, or increase in nominal share capital, is payable as capital duty. The fee is capped at HKD 30,000 per case counted on a company (rather than group) basis.

Government rates and rent
Rates are an indirect tax levied on properties in Hong Kong. Rates are charged at 5% of the rateable value which is the estimated annual rental value of a property at the designated valuation reference date of 1 October.

Privately owned land in Hong Kong is normally held by way of a government lease under which rent is payable to the Hong Kong SAR Government in return for the right to hold and occupy the land for the term (i.e., duration) specified in the lease document. Currently, government rent is calculated at 3% of the rateable value of the property and is adjusted in step with any subsequent changes in the rateable value.

Branch income

The tax rate for branch is the same as that for corporations. The Hong Kong profit of a foreign corporation with a branch in Hong Kong is determined according to the accounts maintained for the Hong Kong operation (or business). If the Hong Kong accounts do not disclose the true profits arising in or derived from Hong Kong attributable to the Hong Kong operation, the Hong Kong profit will be computed according to the ratio of turnover in Hong Kong to total turnover (or the proportion of Hong Kong assets over total assets) on the worldwide profits. Alternatively, the HKIRD tax assessor may estimate the profits of the Hong Kong branch. In certain situations, the profits of the Hong Kong branch could be estimated based on a fair percentage of the turnover in Hong Kong.

Income determination

Capital gains
Gains from realisation of capital assets or receipts that are capital in nature are not taxed.

Dividend income
Dividends from sources either inside or outside Hong Kong are not subject to Hong Kong profits tax. Hong Kong corporations may declare bonus issues (i.e., stock dividends) which are not taxable in the hands of the recipients.

Foreign income
Hong Kong resident corporations are not taxed on their worldwide income. Foreign-sourced income, whether or not remitted to Hong Kong, is not taxed. As such, there is no specific tax provision dealing with deferral or non-remittance of foreign earnings. Nor does Hong Kong have any controlled foreign corporation legislation.

Interest income
Interest income received by or accrued to a corporation carrying on a trade or business in Hong Kong is subject to profits tax. Exemption is provided to interest income derived from any deposit placed in Hong Kong with a financial institution, unless the deposit secures a borrowing the interest expense of which is deductible. This exemption, however, does not apply to interest accruing to a financial institution.

Interest accruing to a bank or financial institution will be deemed to be sourced and taxable in Hong Kong, if the interest arises through or from the carrying on of business in Hong Kong by the bank or financial institution.

Inventory valuation
Inventory may be stated at the lower of cost or market value. Last-in, first-out (LIFO) may not be used for tax purposes. First-in, first-out (FIFO) must be consistently applied.

The prevailing accounting standards require financial assets and liabilities held for trading purpose (e.g., shares and securities held as trading stock) to be carried at market value, with fluctuations in values of such assets and liabilities taken to the profit and loss accounts, irrespective of whether the profits or losses are realised. The HKIRD requires that this accounting treatment be followed in computing the assessable profits for tax purposes.

There are special tax provisions for valuation upon cessation of a business under which inventory is valued at market value, unless it is sold to a person carrying on business in Hong Kong who may deduct a corresponding amount as the cost of the inventory in computing the assessable profits.

Partnership income
Partnership business is taxed as a single entity though an individual partner can use its share of losses incurred by a partnership to offset against the assessable profits of its other business. In general, there is no special registration requirement other than

Hong Kong

business registration for a partnership. The assessable profits of a partnership are basically determined in the same way as those of a corporation with certain special rules e.g., salaries or other remunerations paid to a partner or a partner's spouse are not deductible.

Royalties income
Royalties paid or accrued to a non-resident for the use of or right to use in Hong Kong or outside Hong Kong (if the royalties are deductible in ascertaining the assessable profits of a person for Hong Kong profits tax purposes), a trademark, patent, design, copyright material, secret process or other property of a similar nature; or for the use in Hong Kong of cinema or television tape or any sound recording, are deemed to be taxable in Hong Kong.

A total of 30% of the sum receivable is deemed to constitute profits subject to tax in normal situations. Where such royalties are received by or accrued to an associated corporation, however, 100% of the sum may be deemed to constitute profits.

Unrealised exchange gains/losses
In general, unrealised gains/losses are taxable/deductible if they are recognised in the profit and loss accounts in accordance with the generally accepted accounting principles, provided that they are revenue in nature and with a Hong Kong source. The nature and source of exchange gains/losses are determined by the nature and source of the underlying transactions. Exchange gains/losses arising from ordinary business transactions (e.g., trade receivables or payables) are taxable/deductible whereas exchange gains/losses arising from capital transactions (e.g., sale of capital assets) are non-taxable/non-deductible.

Deductions

Expenses that are incurred for producing profits chargeable to tax and that are not capital in nature are generally tax deductible. In addition, special tax relief is available for certain capital expenditure. There are special rules for deduction of certain expenses (e.g., interest expenses).

Accounting treatments are usually followed in determining the assessable profits except when there is explicit rule in the IRO. Accrued expenses recognised in the profit and loss accounts in accordance with the generally accepted accounting principles are usually deductible if they are incurred for producing profits chargeable/subject to tax and are not capital in nature.

Expense items of which a tax adjustment is necessary in determining the amount of taxable profits from the accounting profits include: tax depreciation allowance vs. accounting depreciation, expenses that are capital in nature, general provisions that are non-deductible and non-deductible interest expenses on borrowings used to finance non-income producing assets, etc.

Set out below are the Hong Kong profits tax treatments of some common expense items.

Interest expenses

There is no thin capitalisation rule in Hong Kong. However deduction of interest expense is subject to stringent and complicated rules which are designed to guard against loan arrangements with an intention to avoid Hong Kong profits tax.

Bad debts

A bad or doubtful debt incurred in any trade, business or profession, proved to the satisfaction of the HKIRD to have become bad during the basis period for a year of assessment, is deductible. The deduction is limited to debts which were included as a trading receipt in ascertaining the taxpayer's assessable profits or debts in respect of money lent in the ordinary course of a money-lending business in Hong Kong.

If any bad or doubtful debt which has previously been allowed as a deduction is ultimately recovered, it will be treated as taxable profits of the basis period in which it is recovered.

Charitable contributions

A deduction is allowed for cash donations to approved charities made in the basis period for a year of assessment if the aggregate of such donations is not less than HKD 100. The deduction is limited to 35% of the assessable profits of the year of assessment.

Fines and penalties

Fines and penalties are generally not deductible as the HKIRD does not consider them to be expenses incurred for producing profits chargeable/subject to tax.

Contingent liabilities

Generally speaking, general provisions for expenses are not deductible whereas specific provisions are deductible if the HKIRD is satisfied that the amount has been incurred (i.e., the taxpayer has a legal/contractual obligation to pay such amount in future) and that the provision represents a reasonably accurate estimate of the future liability.

Tax depreciation of fixed assets

Tax depreciation allowances/deductions are available for capital expenditure incurred on the construction of buildings or structures and in the provision of machinery and plant for trade or business purposes.

1. Industrial buildings and structures – An initial allowance of 20%, in addition to an annual allowance of 4%, of the cost of construction or cost of purchase from a developer, is granted for an industrial building or structure occupied for the purpose of a qualifying trade. Provision is made for balancing allowances or charges in the year of assessment in which the building is disposed of to adjust the written-down value of the building to the disposal price. Balancing charges are restricted to the total of initial and annual allowances previously given.
2. Commercial buildings and structures – An annual allowance of 4% of the capital expenditure incurred on the construction has applied since 1 April 1998. A balancing allowance or charge applies upon disposal. Balancing charges are restricted to the total annual allowances previously given.
3. Plant and machinery – An initial allowance of 60% of the capital expenditure on machinery and plant is given for the year of assessment during the basis period in which the expenditure is incurred. An annual allowance is also given for depreciation at three prescribed rates on the reducing value of each of the three depreciation rate "pools". The three prescribed rates are 10%, 20% and 30%, and

Hong Kong

the reducing value of each of the three depreciation rate pools is original cost less initial and annual allowances and sales proceeds. Provision is made for balancing charges when machinery and plant within one of the three depreciation rate pools are sold or disposed of and the reducing value of that pool is less than the sale price, which is capped at the original amount incurred in the pool. In addition, balancing allowances or charges may be applicable upon cessation of business. Otherwise, sales proceeds are deducted in calculating the reducing value on which the annual allowance is calculated.

Book depreciation is adjusted for tax purposes in accordance with the above depreciation allowances granted under the IRO.

Special deductions
There are special deduction rules for expenditures incurred (1) for refurbishment of a building or structure, other than a domestic building or structure, (2) on environmental protection installation and machinery, (3) on environment-friendly vehicles, (4) on machinery or plant used specifically and directly for any manufacturing process, computer hardware (other than that which is an integral part of machinery or plant), computer software, and computer systems (collectively known as prescribed fixed assets), (5) for registering trademarks, designs or patents used in the production of taxable profits, (6) on the purchase of patent rights or rights to any industrial information or techniques likely to assist in the manufacture or processing of goods or materials, for use in Hong Kong, and (7) on the purchase of registered trademarks, copyrights and registered designs.

Items (3) and (7) were proposed in the 2010/11 Budget and at the time of writing, the legislation giving effect to these proposals has not been enacted.

Goodwill
Cost of acquisition of goodwill/amortisation of goodwill is not deductible as they are capital in nature.

Net operating and capital losses
Net operating losses incurred in an accounting year can be carried forward indefinitely to set off against future profits of the business. But a corporation carrying on more than one business may have losses in one business setting off against profits of the others, with any balance being carried forward. Capital losses are not tax deductible.

Organisational and start-up expenses
In general, company formation/start-up expenses that are incurred before the commencement of a trade, profession or business and that are for the establishment of the overall income producing structure are capital in nature and not tax deductible.

Payments to foreign affiliates
Royalties and service fees paid/payable by a Hong Kong corporation to foreign affiliates are deductible provided they are incurred for the production of profits chargeable/subject to tax. There is no special restriction on the deductibility of these payments. Interest payable to a foreign affiliate is not deductible if the recipient is not chargeable/subject to Hong Kong profits tax on the interest income received.

Pension expenses

A deduction is allowed for regular/ordinary contributions to a mandatory provident fund scheme or recognised occupational retirement scheme made by an employer in respect of an employee to the extent that the contributions do not exceed 15% of the employee's total emoluments for the period to which the contributions relate.

Special payments other than the ordinary contributions to a mandatory provident fund scheme or recognised occupational retirement scheme are capital in nature but can be deducted evenly over a five-year period under a specific provision of the IRO.

There are also specific rules for deduction of provisions for contributions to a mandatory provident fund scheme or recognised occupational retirement scheme.

Payments for directors

Director fees or other remunerations paid by a corporation to its directors are generally deductible under the normal deduction rule. Nevertheless, no deduction is allowed on salaries or other remunerations paid to a sole proprietor or any partners or partners' spouses of a partnership business.

Taxes paid

Taxes paid on corporate profits are generally not deductible for the purpose of calculating the assessable profits. However, the HKIRD generally accepts that a foreign tax, which is an expense that must be borne regardless of whether or not a profit is derived (e.g., a foreign withholding tax levied on the gross amount of interest or royalties received), as opposed to a charge on the profits themselves, is deductible under the general deduction provision. Where interest income or gains from the sale of a certificate of deposit or bill of exchange are deemed to be subject to profits tax, a deduction is allowed for foreign taxes of substantially the same nature of Hong Kong profits tax paid in respect of the same income, provided that the taxpayer is not eligible for double taxation relief under a CDTA.

Group taxation

Consolidated/group taxation regime

Hong Kong does not have a consolidated or group taxation regime.

Transfer pricing regime

Strictly speaking, there is no comprehensive transfer pricing legislation in Hong Kong. While a few existing provisions in the IRO may be employed by the tax authority to tackle non-arm's-length transactions, such provisions are primarily aimed at transactions with non-residents or tax avoidance transactions rather than specific legislation on transfer pricing.

As mentioned in the section *Significant developments*, two DIPNs were recently released by the HKIRD to address their views and positions on transfer pricing issues. In general, the HKIRD adopts arm's-length principle and would seek to apply the OECD transfer pricing guidelines except where they are incompatible with the express provisions in the IRO.

Thin capitalisation rules

Hong Kong does not have thin capitalisation rules.

Hong Kong

Controlled foreign company regime

Hong Kong does not have a controlled foreign company regime.

Related party transactions

There is no special treatment for related party transactions – see the section *Transfer pricing regime* above. On the other hand, there are general anti-avoidance provisions dealing with transactions entered into with a sole or dominant purpose of obtaining a tax benefit and specific anti-avoidance provisions dealing with transactions with closely connected non-residents. Under the specific provisions, if a resident person carries on a business with a closely connected non-resident person such that no profits or less than the ordinary profits are derived by the resident person in the course of such business, the non-resident person can be assessable and chargeable to tax in respect of his profits derived from such business in the name of the resident person.

Tax incentives

Foreign tax credits

Foreign tax credits are available if foreign taxes are payable/paid on income derived from a jurisdiction which has entered into a CDTA with Hong Kong and the same income is subject to tax in Hong Kong.

Research and development (R&D)

There is a specific provision allowing the deduction of expenditure incurred on research and development (including payments made to an approved research institute and in-house expenditure), provided that certain specified conditions are met.

Tax holidays

Hong Kong does not have a tax holiday programme.

Foreign investment incentives

Hong Kong does not have any specific incentives for foreign investment except that offshore funds may be exempt from profits tax under certain circumstances.

Withholding taxes (WHT)

There is no withholding tax on dividends, interest or royalties. However, the 4.95%/16.5% (for corporations) or 4.5%/15% (for unincorporated businesses) tax on royalties received by non-residents (please refer to *Royalties income* under the section *Income determination* for more details) is in effect similar to a withholding tax.

Resident consignees are required to furnish quarterly returns to the HKIRD showing the gross proceeds from sales on behalf of their non-resident consignors and to pay to the HKIRD Commissioner a sum equal to 0.5% of such proceeds. The HKIRD normally accepts this as satisfying the Hong Kong tax obligations of the non-resident.

Hong Kong has so far entered into a comprehensive double tax agreement/arrangement with Austria, Belgium, Brunei, Hungary, Indonesia, Kuwait, Luxembourg, the Netherlands, the People's Republic of China (PRC), Thailand and Vietnam. The agreements with Austria, Brunei, Hungary, Indonesia, Kuwait and the Netherlands have not yet entered into force pending the completion of the ratification procedures of the governments concerned.

The following are the non-treaty and treaty withholding tax rates for payments made from Hong Kong payers to treaty country corporate recipients. For withholding tax rates on payments received by Hong Kong recipients from treaty country payers, please refer to the summaries of the respective treaty countries.

	Dividends (1)	Interest (1)	Royalties
	%	%	%
Non-treaty	Nil	Nil	4.95 (2)
Treaty:			
Austria	Nil	Nil	3
Brunei	Nil	Nil	4.95 (3)
Belgium	Nil	Nil	4.95 (3)
Hungary	Nil	Nil	4.95 (3)
Indonesia	Nil	Nil	4.95 (3)
Kuwait	Nil	Nil	4.95 (3)
Luxembourg	Nil	Nil	3
The Netherlands	Nil	Nil	3
The People's Republic of China	Nil	Nil	4.95 (3)
Thailand	Nil	Nil	4.95 (3)
Vietnam	Nil	Nil	4.95 (3)

Notes

1. Hong Kong IRO does not impose withholding tax on dividends and interest currently. However, the treaties provide for a maximum withholding tax rate on dividends and interest should Hong Kong IRO impose such withholding tax in future. Some of the treaties also provide for a reduced withholding tax rate on dividends and interest if the conditions specified in the treaties are met.
2. Generally, royalties paid to non-resident corporations that are not otherwise chargeable to Hong Kong profits tax are subject to withholding tax at 4.95%. The 16.5% rate applies if the royalties are received by or accrued to a non-resident from an associate, unless the Commissioner is satisfied that no person carrying on business in Hong Kong has at any time wholly or partly owned the property in respect of which the royalties are paid.
3. Since a higher rate(s) is specified in the treaties, the lower non-treaty rate of 4.95% will apply.

Tax administration

Year of assessment
A year of assessment (or tax year) begins on 1 April of a year and ends on 31 March of the following year.

Tax returns
Tax return is issued on the first working day of April each year. The filing deadline is usually within a month from the date of issue. However, corporations whose financial year ended after 30 November and represented by a tax representative are normally granted an extension for filing their returns. The exact filing due date depends on the accounting year end date of the taxpayer.

The basis of assessment is the accounting profits of the financial year ending within the year of assessment with appropriate adjustments for tax purposes. A tax return is usually filed together with a tax computation showing the tax adjustments to the

Hong Kong

accounting profits in arriving at the taxable profits or allowable tax losses for a given year of assessment.

Corporate taxpayers are also required to attach their audited accounts as supporting documents when filing a profits tax return, unless they qualify as a small corporation as defined by the HKIRD (i.e., mainly those with gross income for a basis period of not exceeding HKD 2 million plus a few other conditions). Small corporations are not required to attach supporting documents with their profits tax returns but are still required to keep those documents and submit them upon request. A branch of a foreign corporation doing business in Hong Kong is required to file a profits tax return annually, and the HKIRD may require audited accounts of the foreign corporation to support the Hong Kong branch's profits tax return.

Notice of assessment will be issued after the tax return has been examined by the HKIRD. Taxpayers may be subject to post-assessment investigation or field audit under the computerised random selection procedures of the HKIRD at a later date.

Payment of tax
The dates of payment of tax are determined by the HKIRD Commissioner and specified in the assessment notice. A system of provisional tax payments applies whereby estimated tax payments are made during the current year. The provisional profits tax payable is normally estimated based on the previous year's profits tax liability. The provisional profits tax already paid is credited against the final profits tax assessed for a year of assessment, which is determined after filing of the return.

Statue of limitation
An additional assessment may be made by a HKIRD tax assessor if a taxpayer chargeable to tax has not been assessed to tax or has been assessed at less than the proper amount. The assessment must be made within the relevant year of assessment or within six years after the end of that year of assessment. The time limit for making additional assessments is extended when a taxpayer either has not been assessed, or is under-assessed, due to fraud or wilful evasion. In that case an additional assessment may be made up to 10 years after the end of the relevant assessment year.

A statement of loss is not an assessment and hence, the above six-year time limit does not apply to issue or revision of a statement of loss. A tax loss year remains technically open until the sixth year after the first year in which the taxpayer has an assessable profit after utilising all the tax losses brought forward.

Tax audit cycle
There is no specific tax audit cycle in Hong Kong. Tax audit targets are selected with reference to certain criteria determined by the HKIRD.

Topics of focus for tax authorities
Issues that are often subject to close scrutiny of the tax authority include: offshore claim of profits, capital claims of income, transactions with related parties and closely connected non-residents and deductibility of expenses (e.g., interest expenses, share-based payments and intra-group management/service fees), etc.

PricewaterhouseCoopers Worldwide Tax Summaries

Other issues

Foreign investment restrictions

In general, Hong Kong does not impose restriction to foreign investors to make investments in Hong Kong; and wholly foreign owned companies are allowed. The only exception is the restriction on foreign ownership of Hong Kong's licensed television/sound broadcasters, of which the collective foreign ownership ceiling is 49% of the voting power. In addition, an approval from the Broadcasting Authority must be obtained for holding, acquisition, or exercise of voting control by a foreign investor of more than 2% of a licensee.

Exchange controls

Hong Kong does not have any foreign exchange control. There is no restriction on entry or repatriation of capital or remittance of profits from investments. Funds can be freely remitted to persons outside Hong Kong by various means such as dividends, interest, royalties, service fees and branch profits, etc.

Choice of business entity

The principal forms through which a business can be conducted in Hong Kong are:

1. Company incorporated in Hong Kong (either private or public via listing on the Stock Exchange of Hong Kong);
2. Branch of a foreign company;
3. Representative or liaison office of a foreign company;
4. Joint venture (can be set up either as a company or partnership);
5. Partnership; and
6. Sole proprietorship.

Of the above, privately incorporated companies and branches of foreign companies are most commonly used by foreign investors, as limited liability is usually desirable.

Intellectual property regulations

The Intellectual Property Department is responsible for monitoring the intellectual property regime and ensuring the protection and enforcement of intellectual property rights in Hong Kong. The Department is also responsible for investigating complaints against infringements and has extensive powers of search and seizure. Registration and protection of patents, copyrights, trademarks and registered designs are each governed by a separate ordinance.

Merger and acquisition (M&A) activities

There are no specific restrictions on M&A activities in Hong Kong. The following tax considerations are relevant in the M&A context:

1. Hong Kong does not impose any tax on dividends or other forms of distribution of profits (e.g., distribution of branch profits to the head office);
2. Capital gains arising from a M&A transaction is not taxable in the hands of the transferor whereas amortisation of the goodwill in the transferee's accounts is not tax deductible due to its capital nature;
3. For a share deal, stamp duty is payable on the transfer of Hong Kong shares at 2% unless an exemption applies; for an asset deal, stamp duty is payable on conveyance of immovable property at progressive rate of up to 4.25%;

Hong Kong

4. Gains derived from transfer of revenue items (e.g., trade receivables) in an asset deal would be subject to profits tax;
5. There is no special tax concession/incentive relating to M&A transactions; and
6. Tax losses in the acquired company can generally be carried forward indefinitely to set off against future assessable profits. However, there are specific anti-avoidance provisions in the IRO that prevent the transfer of shares of a company with accumulated tax losses to owners of a profitable company for the sole or dominant purpose of utilising the tax losses i.e., offsetting the tax losses against the profits generated from other trade, profession or business of the transferee.

Corporate taxes in Hungary

For more information, contact:

Russell Lambert
PricewaterhouseCoopers
Wesselényi utca 16.
H-1077 Budapest
Hungary
Tel: +36 1 461 9223
Email: russell.w.lambert@hu.pwc.com

Significant developments

From 1 January 2010 the following significant changes were introduced to the Hungarian tax system.

Corporate income tax
- The corporate income tax rate has increased from 16% to 19%, but the special profit tax of 4% has been abolished.
- Sole proprietorships, foreign organisations and non-resident shareholders of a real estate company are subject to corporate income tax.
- Generally, no withholding tax is levied on payment to companies abroad. As an anti-avoidance measure, 30% withholding tax has been introduced on interest, royalties and certain service fee payments made to companies which are resident in countries with which Hungary does not have a double tax treaty.
- New definition of CFC.

Value-added tax (VAT)
Hungary was obliged to implement the EU VAT package through the Hungarian VAT legislation with effect from 1 January 2010 (that is, Regulations (EC) No. 8/2008 and No. 9/2008). The package considerably changes certain key areas of the Hungarian VAT legislation, such as the place-of-supply rules for services. The new rule contains similar rules to the EU Directive on the common system of VAT.

Environmental production product fee
From 1 January 2010, product fee is self-assessed in all cases, even imports (until 2010 the Customs Authority levied the product fee on imports as the main rule). Before 2010, the product fee return could be submitted on paper, but from 2010 it has to be submitted electronically. In 2009 the frequency of product fee return submission was not uniform (the return had to be submitted yearly, quarterly or monthly, depending on certain criteria) but from 2010 all companies have to submit their product fee returns quarterly. Unlike last year, from 2010 transactions under customs procedures (e.g., inward processing, customs warehousing), incur a product fee payment liability.

Cultural tax
The cultural tax has been abolished. (Cultural tax had to be paid on certain services, products and buildings prior to 2010.)

Energy tax
Tax rates have increased as from 1 January 2010:

Hungary

- Electricity: increased from HUF 252 (approx. EUR 0.9) to HUF 295 (approx. EUR 1.1) per megawatt hour.
- Coal: increased from HUF 2,040 (approx. EUR 8) to HUF 2,390 (approx. EUR 9) per thousand kilograms.
- Natural gas: increased from HUF 75.60 (approx. EUR 0.29) to HUF 88.5 (approx. EUR 0.34) per gigajoule.

Excise duty

Excise duty rates increased on 1 January 2010 and also on 1 April 2010. The rates effective from 1 April 2010 are listed in the *Other taxes section*.

Taxes on corporate income

Corporate income tax

Resident taxpayers are subject to all-inclusive or unlimited tax liability. Non-residents are subject to corporate income taxation on their income from their Hungarian branch's business activities.

The corporate income tax rate has increased from 16% to 19%. If certain conditions are met, the tax rate may be 10% on the first HUF 50 million of the positive tax base (approximately EUR 200,000), with the other 9% (of the total 19% rate) to be used for purposes defined in law, such as capital expenditure investments, loan repayments, and employment-related costs. Foreign organisations (foreign persons that receive interest, royalties, and/or service fees from Hungarian companies, provided that there is no double tax treaty with the country where the foreign person is resident) are subject to 30% withholding tax.

Minimum tax base

From 1 July 2007, if a company's corporate income tax base or the pre-tax profit (whichever is higher) is less than 2% of its total revenues reduced by the cost of goods sold, the value of mediated services and the income of the foreign permanent establishments ("minimum tax base"), the company can choose to file a declaration and pay corporate income tax either according to the general provisions or on its minimum tax base.

Special profit tax

Special profit tax has been abolished with effect from 1 January 2010. However, companies that use a non-calendar business year are not affected as they remain liable to special profit tax until their 2010 tax year begins.

Local taxes/local business tax

All municipalities are entitled to levy local taxes, but from 2010 their administration is delegated to the Hungarian State Tax Authority. Local taxes are deductible for Hungarian corporate income tax purposes, and are not normally treated as "income tax" in the application of the tax treaties.

The local business tax base is the net sales revenue reduced by the cost of goods sold, subcontractors' work, the costs of materials and mediated services. General service fees, depreciation and labour costs are typically not deductible for local business tax purposes. 100% of royalty, interest or dividend income is normally exempt from local business tax. The local business tax rate may differ from municipality to municipality but is capped at 2% by law. From 1 January 2010, research and development costs are also deductible from the local business tax base.

Furthermore, as of 2010 the local business tax base of a foreign PE of a Hungarian company can be exempted from the Hungarian local business tax.

Innovation contribution
Companies defined as such in the Accounting Act are subject to this contribution, except for small- and medium-sized enterprises and branches. The tax base of the innovation contribution is the same as the local business tax base. The tax rate is 0.3%.

Corporate residence

Corporations are residents for tax purposes if they are incorporated in Hungary, although foreign corporations may also be deemed to be Hungarian residents for corporate income taxation purposes if their place of effective management is in Hungary.

Foreign entities may carry out business through resident corporations or through permanent establishments (branches). Commercial representative offices may be opened for auxiliary activities which do not create a taxable presence.

Permanent establishment (PE)
Hungary treats PEs as separate and distinct entities and profit is attributed to a PE based on the principles set out in the OECD guidelines.

A permanent establishment (PE) is defined as fixed business premises (machinery or equipment) through which the entrepreneurial activity of an enterprise is partly or wholly carried on. A permanent establishment may consist of any of the following: a place of management; offices including representative offices registered in Hungary; factories and workshops; and mines, crude oil or natural gas wells, quarries, or other places from which natural resources are extracted.

Construction sites (including assembly) and related supervisory activities constitute a permanent establishment if they last, in the aggregate, for at least three months in a calendar year. All activities carried out at the same construction site qualify together as a single permanent establishment, regardless of whether they are based on separate contracts or were ordered by different persons. Construction sites are defined as sites which represent a unit for economic, business and geographical purposes.

Permanent establishments are also created by the direct utilisation of natural resources by a foreign person. A foreign person is deemed to have a permanent establishment in Hungary if it utilises natural resources or immovable property for consideration, including the alienation of any rights related to the immovable property or natural resources.

A non-resident enterprise is considered to have a permanent establishment with respect to activities undertaken on its behalf by another person if its agent is authorised to conclude contracts in Hungary on behalf of the non-resident entity and the agent regularly exercises this right or maintains a stock of goods and products from which it regularly makes deliveries in the name of the non-resident entity.

Hungary

The insurance of risks occurring in Hungary, insured on behalf of a non-resident person by another person, constitutes a permanent establishment of the foreign insurer, except for reinsurance activities.

Furthermore, as mentioned above, a foreign taxpayer must also be treated as having a permanent establishment if it has a Hungarian branch.

The definition of a permanent establishment does not include:

- Establishments used solely for the purpose of storing and presenting the goods or products of a non-resident person;
- The stockpiling of goods and products solely for the purpose of storing, presenting or processing by another person;
- Establishments used for collecting information, purchasing goods and products exclusively for the non-resident person;
- Establishments used for other activities of a preparatory or auxiliary nature; and
- Activities of independent agents, provided they are acting in their ordinary course of business.

Other taxes

Value-added tax (VAT)
VAT is payable on sales of goods and the provision of services. VAT is also payable on the importation of intra-Community acquisitions of goods and on the purchase of certain services provided to Hungarian companies by foreign suppliers.

The relevant rates are shown below:

	%
General rate	25
Most medicines	5

Certain services are exempt, including most transactions in land (an option to be taxed under the general rule is available); the letting of residential property (an option to be taxed under the general rule is available); medical, cultural, sporting, and educational services provided as public services; financial and insurance services. Intra-Community supplies of services and exports are also treated as exempt transactions. In the case of industrial sites and office rental, VAT exemption is optional.

VAT deduction is available for the business-related element of purchases made partially for non-business purposes.

Under the new general VAT liability regulations, VAT is also chargeable if an invoice is issued but the supply is not carried out.

New place-of-supply rules
The general rule for B2B services is that the place of supply is where the customer is established, whereas for B2C services the general rule remains unchanged, i.e., the place of supply is where the supplier is established. Exceptions to these rules have also been introduced (e.g., cultural services, catering services, services connected to immovable property).

Group taxation

The VAT Act allows all companies that have established business presences in Hungary and qualify as related enterprises to form a VAT group. The essence of a VAT group is that its members act under a single VAT number in their transactions (i.e., they issue invoices under a shared VAT number and submit a single, joint tax return), and product and service supplies between the members do not qualify as business transactions from a VAT perspective.

VAT recovery

If a taxpayer has a negative VAT balance in a return period, this amount can be recovered provided that the tax balance reaches or exceeds an absolute value of HUF 1 million for monthly filers, HUF 250,000 for quarterly filers or HUF 50,000 for annual filers. The VAT Act extends the application of the reverse-charge mechanism to a variety of activities in addition to the sale of waste materials, including construction and assembly and services related to real property (repairs, maintenance). The condition that only the VAT content of financially settled invoices is reclaimable continues to apply.

Directive for refunds of foreign EU taxable persons

EU-registered non-Hungarian taxable persons can recover local VAT. In the new system, refund applications will have to be submitted electronically, and the rules governing the time available/deadlines for tax authorities in certain phases of the procedure have changed. Reclaim requests should be submitted to the Tax Authority of the country where the taxable person is established.

Reporting obligations for cross-border transactions

A new requirement is that suppliers of cross-border services must submit full statements for each VAT return period of all the services supplied to taxable and non-taxable legal persons where the latter are liable for VAT in their own country. Please note that in Hungary not only EC sales but also purchase lists are required.

Excise duties

Goods subject to excise duty are:

- Petroleum products;
- Alcohol and alcoholic beverages (Any product with an alcohol content of 1.2% or more by volume qualifies as an alcohol product.);
- Beers;
- Wines;
- Sparkling wines;
- Intermediate alcoholic products; and
- Tobacco products.

Duty rates from 1 April 2010:

- Petroleum products: HUF 97,350–124,200 (approx. EUR 340–450) per thousand litres, or HUF 4,425–116,000 (approx. EUR 15–400) per thousand kilograms, depending on the type of the product;
- Alcohol products: HUF 276,100 (approx. EUR 1,050) per hectolitre of pure alcohol;
- Beer: HUF 633 (approx. EUR 2) per hectolitre per Balling (Plato) grade;
- Wines: HUF 0 for grape wines, HUF 9,400 (approx. EUR 40) per hectolitre for wines made from other types of fruit;

- Sparkling wines: HUF 14,250 (approx. EUR 50) per hectolitre;
- Intermediate alcoholic products: HUF 22,100 (approx. EUR 80) per hectolitre;
- Tobacco products:
  - Cigarettes: HUF 9,350 (approx. EUR 30) per thousand cigarettes plus 28.3% of the retail sale price, but a minimum of HUF 17,330 (approx. EUR 70) per thousand cigarettes (the tax base per cigarette also depends on the length of the cigarette (without filter): it is double if the length of the cigarette is 9-18cm, triple if the length is 18-27cm, and so on.);
  - Cigars and cigarillos: 28.5% of the retail price;
  - Fine-cut tobacco: 52% of the retail price, but a minimum of HUF 7,280 (approx. EUR 30) per kilogram;
  - Other tobacco: 32.5% of the retail price, but a minimum of HUF 7,280 (approx. EUR 30) per kilogram.

The Customs Authority is responsible for excise duty. The European Union's excise duty rules apply in Hungary.

Registration taxes
Registration tax is charged on passenger cars, motor homes and motorcycles before they can be registered and put into service in Hungary. The duty is payable with the first domestic registration or in the case of a conversion.

The registration tax rate is:

- Passenger cars: HUF 250,000 (approx. EUR 950) – HUF 9,622,000 (approx. EUR 37,000) (depends on the technical features of vehicles (cm3, engine type) and environmental classification);
- Hybrid or electrical cars: HUF 190,000 (approx. 750 EUR); and
- Motorcycles: HUF 20,000 (approx. EUR 70) – HUF 230,000 (approx. EUR 900) (depends on technical features of motorcycles (cm3).

The registration tax is levied by the Customs Authority.

Customs duties
Hungarian customs legislation and policies have been fully harmonised with EU legislation.

Environmental protection product fee
The following products are subject to the product fee: other crude oil products, tyres, packaging, batteries, commercial printing paper, and electrical and electronic products (based on customs tariff numbers applicable on 1 January 2010).

Entities liable to pay the product fee are:

- The first domestic distributor or user for own purposes.
- In the case of domestically manufactured commercial printing paper and other crude oil products: the first buyer from the first domestic distributor.
- In the case of toll manufacturing: the party that orders the toll manufacturing.

The product fee is calculated on the basis of the weight of the product multiplied by the fee rate. For example, it is HUF 6 (approx. EUR 0.02) – HUF 44 (approx. EUR 0.18) /kg for packaging, and HUF 83 (approx. EUR 0.33) – HUF 1,000 (approx. EUR 4) /kg for electrical and electronic products.

Hungary

The Customs Authority controls the payment and reporting of the product fee and carries out product fee inspections. The Customs Authority registers taxpayers by EORI customs and GLN environmental identification numbers, thus taxpayers will need to obtain both. From 1 January 2010, the product fee is self-assessed. The product fee return must be submitted quarterly to the Customs Authority via its electronic system.

The product fee penalty is generally 100% of the product fee shortfall in cases of non-payment or underpayment.

The product fee payment liability can be reduced, e.g., by meeting the mandatory recycling rate.

Environmental load charges

Environmental pollution charges were introduced to protect the natural environment, to reduce its impairment, to encourage the users of the environment to engage in activities aimed at the preservation of the natural environment, and to provide funding from the central budget for environmental protection and nature preservation. Air and water load charges were introduced on 1 January 2004 and the soil load charge from 1 July 2004, on an incremental basis.

Emitting entities liable to pay include those who operate point-source emitters subject to registration, pursue activities subject to a water right permit, or who do not use available public drainage systems and dispose of their sewage under a water right permit or a permit from the local water management authorities.

Qualifying materials include sulphur dioxide, nitrogen oxides, mercury, phosphorous, cyanides and others.

The load charge is calculated on the basis of the quantity of emitted materials multiplied by the fee rate. Basically, the amount of the fee payable depends on the hazard level of the emitted material, e.g., HUF 50 (approx. EUR 0.2) /kg for sulphur dioxide and HUF 220,000 (approx. EUR 846) /kg for mercury.

Energy tax

Goods subject to energy tax:

* Electricity;
* Coal; and
* Natural gas.

From 1 January 2010, the list of entities that can be subject to energy tax is as follows:

* Energy traders;
* End-users; and
* Producers.

Tax rates:

* Electricity: HUF 295 (approx. EUR 1) per megawatt hour;
* Coal: HUF 2,390 (approx. EUR 9) per thousand kilograms; and
* Natural gas: HUF 88.5 (approx. EUR 0.3) per gigajoule.

Hungary

The tax is self-assessed – except in the case of imports – and the Customs Authority is responsible for the related customs administration procedures.

Stamp duties
The most common types of stamp duty are gift duty and duty on transfers of property for consideration. Stamp duty is levied on movable and immovable property and property rights if they were acquired in Hungary, unless an international agreement rules otherwise.

Gift duty
Gift duty arises on the date when a contract concerning a gift is concluded.

Transfers of movable property, immovable property and property rights without consideration are subject to gift duty. In these cases, however, gift duty is only incurred if the transaction was formally documented; except for immovable property with a market value of more than HUF 150,000 where gift duty must be paid in any event.

The base of gift duty is the net value of the gift, which is the market value minus any liabilities related to the gift. The general duty rates vary depending on the base:

- 21% – up to HUF 18 million;
- 30% – on the part exceeding HUF 18 million up to HUF 35 million; and
- 40% – on the part exceeding HUF 35 million.

Transfers of assets without consideration, and acquisitions of claims without consideration including waivers of claims and assumptions of debts are exempt from gift duty, provided that the recipient is a company.

Furthermore, if a company is 100% owned by the other company in the transaction, or both companies are 100% owned by a third party, a reduced rate should be applied.

- 11% – up to HUF 18 million;
- 15% – on the part exceeding HUF 18 million up to HUF 35 million; and
- 21% – on the part exceeding HUF 35 million.

Duty on transfer of property for consideration
The obligation to pay duty on the transfer of movable and immovable property for consideration arises on the date when the contract is concluded.

For acquisitions of real estate, the stamp duty is 4% of the market value of the property. For acquisitions of direct or indirect participations (stocks, shares, co-operative shares, investor shares, converted investor shares) in a company that owns real estate, the duty base is the part of the market value of the company's properties held that represents the percentage of the participation. The stamp duty in this latter case is 4% up to HUF 1 billion and 2% of the amount exceeding HUF 1 billion up to a maximum of HUF 200 million.

There are special rules for real estate trading companies and credit institutions. Under certain circumstances, exemptions are available more generally.

Besides the above, stamp duties are also levied on certain court procedures (e.g., Court of Registration) and on submissions to certain authorities (e.g., appeals to the Tax Authority). Stamp duty is, for instance, levied in an amount of:

- HUF 100,000 on the registration of a private stock company or a limited liability company;
- HUF 600,000 on the registration of a public stock company or a European Company;
- HUF 100,000 on the registration of any other entity with legal personality;
- HUF 50,000 on the registration of a branch office; and
- HUF 50,000 on the registration of a representative office.

Property taxes
Hungarian municipalities can levy land tax or property tax at their own discretion.

Property tax
The owner of a building is subject to this tax liability on the first day of the calendar year.

The local government can determine the tax base in either of the following ways:

- The net floor space of the building expressed in square meters, with a maximum tax rate of HUF 900/m2; or
- The adjusted market value of the building, with a maximum tax rate of 3% of the adjusted market value.

Land tax
The owner of the land as is subject to this tax liability on the first day of the calendar year. Undeveloped plots of land situated within the area of jurisdiction of a local government are subject to this tax.

The local government can determine the tax base in either of the following ways:

- The actual area of the plot expressed in square meters, with a maximum tax rate of HUF 200/m2; or
- The adjusted market value of the plot, with a maximum tax rate of 3% of the adjusted market value

Transfer taxes
There is no transfer tax as such in Hungary, but transfers of direct or indirect participations in companies that own real estate may be subject to stamp duty or corporate income tax.

Stamp duty
Stamp duty has to be paid on the acquisition of a direct or indirect participation of 75% in a company that owns real estate (even if the real estate is a minor part of its total assets). Exceptions may be available if certain criteria are met.

Corporate income tax
A company and its related parties are defined as real estate holding companies if at least 75% of the market value of their assets is domestic real estate and if they have a

Hungary

foreign shareholder that is not resident in a country that has a double tax treaty with Hungary or the treaty allows capital gains to be taxed in Hungary.

The tax base of real estate holding companies in cases of share transfers and share capital decreases is the positive amount of the consideration minus the acquisition price of the shares less the costs of acquisition and of administration,. The tax rate is the same as was mentioned in the *General Information section*.

Please note that the definition of the payer for corporate income tax purposes is very different from the definition used for stamp duty purposes.

Branch income

Foreign companies may establish branch offices in Hungary. A branch office is an organisational unit of a foreign company without legal personality, vested with financial autonomy, and registered in the Hungarian companies register as a branch office of the foreign company. The provisions of the Hungarian Accounting Act apply to branch offices, which must prepare reports using double-entry bookkeeping. Statutory audits are obligatory except for the branches of corporations whose registered office address is in the EU.

A branch office is regarded as established when it has been entered into the companies register. A branch office may start operating once the application for registering the branch office has been submitted to the Court of registration, provided that it indicates "under registration" on its corporate correspondence. Until a branch has been registered, it cannot carry out any activities that are subject to official permission. A branch office is considered dissolved upon its removal from the companies register.

Branch offices are treated as permanent establishments for taxation purposes. They must determine their tax base according to the general rules applicable to Hungarian companies. Corporate income tax at the rate of 19% (or 10% on the first HUF 50 million of the positive tax bases, if certain criteria are met) is payable on the profit for the year, calculated on the basis of the Hungarian accounting system and as adjusted by specific provisions of comprehensive double tax agreements (CDTA). The definition of "permanent establishment" is similar to that in the tax treaties, but somewhat broader. In case of treaty countries, the respective treaty definition applies.

A foreign company's corporate income tax base is determined for all its domestic permanent establishments (except for branches) collectively, and for its branches separately. A branch should account for costs and revenues as if it were independent from its foreign parent company.

For a Hungarian permanent establishment, earnings before taxes are reduced by cumulated administrative costs incurred proportionately at the headquarters and any of its permanent establishments, with the maximum proportion defined as the revenues of the permanent establishment compared to all revenues of the foreign company.

The increasing items for a Hungarian permanent establishment are the administrative costs accounted by the permanent establishment, plus 5% of the revenue earned by the permanent establishment's activities but accounted elsewhere.

However, if there is a treaty between Hungary and the other country, the provisions of the treaty have priority over domestic law. Therefore, the provisions of the treaty have to be followed in the first instance and all costs related to the activity of the branch have to be allocated to the branch – without the above restrictions in domestic law – and all profit realised with respect to the branch must also be allocated to the branch. The allocation method must be consistent from year to year, unless there is a good reason for changing it.

The foreign parent must continuously provide the assets and funds required for the operation of the branch office and the settlement of its liabilities. The employees of a branch office are in a legal relationship with the foreign company, and the foreign parent exercises employer's rights. A branch is considered to be related to its parent company/headquarters, and therefore the prices used in inter-company transactions have to be at arm's length, and transfer pricing documentation has to be prepared.

Income determination

Corporate income tax base
The corporate income tax base should be calculated by modifying the accounting pre-tax profit by adjustments and deductions as provided by the CDTA.

Most common tax adjustments
The corporate income tax base is the pre-tax profit modified by tax base adjustments such as:

* Tax losses can be carried forward indefinitely without the approval of the Tax Authority provided that the company has exercised its rights in accordance with their intended purpose;
* Provisions (except for environmental purposes) created for expected future liabilities and expenses are deductible when the provision is released;
* Expenses incurred on professional training (without reference to the aim of the training) are deductible from the corporate income tax base if certain criteria are met;
* Local business tax accounted as an expense will now be only 100% deductible from the corporate income tax base, instead of the previous 200% deduction; and
* Benefits provided in kind for entertainment purposes and business gifts will qualify as non-deductible business expenses.

Bribes, "kickbacks", other illegal payments
Bribes, "kickbacks" and illegal payments are not recognised as business costs for corporate income tax purposes, thus non-deductible for the tax base.

Capital vs. ordinary transactions
Capital gains (losses) are treated as ordinary income (losses) for tax purposes. The gain on the sale of depreciable assets equals the sales revenue reduced by the net value of the asset for corporate income tax purposes.

If a participation (of at least 30%) is registered within 30 days of acquisition and held continuously for at least one year, capital gains will be exempt from corporate income tax in general. In addition, from 2010 any additional acquisitions may also be registered provided that the 30% participation was already registered.

Hungary

Dividend income
Except in the case of controlled foreign companies, dividends received and accounted as income in the given tax year are tax-free income. From 2010, the definition of CFC has changed significantly, so that foreign persons or entities established abroad and/ or foreign resident entities qualify as controlled foreign enterprises if, among other conditions, they are owned by a resident private individual who is deemed to be the beneficial owner (i.e., has a certain ownership share or voting ratio or dominant influence in the enterprise) or the majority of their income derives from Hungarian sources and in both cases the effective tax rate of the persons/entities is lower than 12.66%. Certain exceptions may be available (for companies in EU member states, OECD member states and treaty countries if a real economic presence can be proved).

Foreign investment
No special provisions in corporate tax legislation.

Foreign income (anti-deferral regime, unremitted earnings)
Income (other than dividends) earned from a foreign source is taxable unless a tax treaty provides an exemption. Foreign tax credit is available for income taxes paid abroad up to the Hungarian tax payable on the creditable income (max. 90% of income tax paid abroad), after increasing the tax base by the tax paid abroad.

From 1 January 2010, taxpayers resident in Hungary and foreign entrepreneurs must calculate their corporate income tax base exclusive of:

- Any income that is subject to taxation abroad, if so prescribed by an international treaty; and
- interest income received from abroad (defined as 75% of interest income, less the costs and expenses directly or indirectly attributable to the acquisition of such income, adjusted by the items that increase and decrease the pre-tax profit).

The foreign income has to be classified by country of origin and revenue type. The deducted tax may not exceed the lesser of either the applicable foreign tax or the applicable tax based on the taxation treaty between Hungary and the given country.

If there is no taxation treaty, the cap is 90% of the tax payable abroad, or as an absolute maximum, the tax calculated on the given tax base at the average tax rate. The average tax rate is the corporate income tax, reduced by the applicable tax allowances, divided by the tax base. Indirect costs should be allocated in proportion to the revenue of the branch office to the total revenue of the whole company, as per Section 28 (4) of CDTA.

Interest income
No specific provision exists in Hungary. From 2010, the 50% corporate income tax base adjustment related to net interest paid/received between related parties has been abolished.

Inventory valuation
Inventories are generally valued at their historical cost unless their fair market value is significantly lower than their book value, in which case, the fair market value should be recorded. Cost may be determined on the basis of FIFO or average cost.

Partnership income

Hungarian partnerships are non-transparent legal entities for taxation purposes, i.e., they are taxed in the same way as corporations.

Rents/royalties income

50% of royalty income is deductible for corporate income tax purposes up to 50% of pre-tax profit. Royalties as revenues derive from 1) permission for the exploitation of patents, from the industrial design of assets under industrial law and from know-how; 2) permission to use trademarks, business names and business secrets; 3) permission to use copyrights and similar rights attached to protected work; 4) transfers of the property described above (except for trademarks, business names and, business secrets).

Stock transactions

From 2010 non-resident shareholders of a real estate holding company are also subject to corporate income tax on their income from the sale of the shares in the real estate holding company.

Unrealised exchange gains/losses

No special provisions in corporate tax legislation.

Deductions

Common tax deductions

In general, costs and expenses incurred in relation to the taxpayer's income-generating business activity are deductible for corporate income tax purposes.

Accrued expenses

Accrued expenses are recognised for taxation purposes in the tax year they affect.

Bad debts

Under the Accounting Act, bad debts are only deductible for corporate income tax purposes if they are supported by legally valid third-party documents that the receivable cannot be collected. Expenses claimed that cannot be enforced in court and expired claims are not deductible for corporate income tax purposes.

In addition to the above, as of 2010 20% of eligible bad debts are deductible from the corporate income tax base if the debt was not settled within 365 days from the due date.

Charitable contributions

Grants made, or assets that are transferred without consideration, or liabilities assumed or services provided free of charge, will qualify as business expenses if the taxpayer has a declaration from the recipient stating that the recipient's profit will not be negative without the income received.

Grants will always qualify as non-business expenses if they are provided to a controlled foreign company or to a foreign resident company.

Contingent liabilities

No special provisions in corporate tax legislation.

Hungary

Depreciation of fixed assets/amortisation of intangibles
Accounting depreciation that is accounted as expenditure, and thus included in the accounting profit, should be added to the corporate income tax base. Tax depreciation calculated according to the CDTA reduces the tax base, even if the tax depreciation is higher than the accounting depreciation. The tax depreciation of tangible assets should be calculated using the straight-line method, on the basis of the historical value from the time when the asset was first used for business purposes.

Please find some tax depreciation rates as follows.

	%
Computers and other high-tech machinery	33/50
Vehicles	20
Other tangible assets	14.5
Buildings (long-life structure)	2
Rented buildings	5
Intangibles	same as Accounting Act

Assets newly acquired since 2003 can be depreciated at 50% annually; these instruments include, among other items, machinery and intellectual property.

Additionally, goodwill cannot be depreciated either for accounting or tax purposes if it does not lose its value during its use. However, if extraordinary depreciation is accounted on goodwill, the extraordinary depreciation will also be recognised for corporate income tax purpose. In the case of transformations, specific depreciation rules apply.

Fines and penalties
Fines and penalties are not deductible for corporate income tax purposes.

Goodwill
Although, theoretically, the Accounting Act allows for the depreciation of goodwill provided it does not depreciate, the opportunity for such depreciation is extremely limited in practice. A taxpayer cannot continue the depreciation of goodwill for tax purposes after a merger unless the acquired company revalues its assets and liabilities in the merger balance-sheet and goodwill that ceases to exist as a result of the merger is cancelled from the books.

Net operating and capital losses (carryback and carryforward periods)
From 1 January 2010, losses can be carried forward indefinitely and the Tax Authority's approval is not required. However, the Tax Authority may later audit whether a company has exercised its rights in accordance with the intended purpose of these rights when carrying losses forward. Furthermore, from this year, financial institutions can also carry losses forward.

The following existing restrictions regarding loss carryforward remain in force:

1. The earlier tax losses must be used first (FIFO principle);
2. The losses of predecessors are also deductible from the successor company's corporate income tax base; and
3. Losses cannot be carried back (except for agricultural companies).

Organisational and start-up expenses

Companies are not obliged to capitalise the costs of formation/reorganisation. The capitalisation of these costs is at the company's discretion, but the company should comply with its accounting policy. Furthermore, only the direct costs of formation/reorganisation that are not classified as investments or renovations and are likely to be recovered ultimately can be capitalised. Furthermore, expenses invoiced by subcontractors can also be included.

Payments to foreign affiliates

There is no general restriction on the deductibility of a consideration due to a foreign entity provided the payment is a justifiable business cost. General anti-avoidance provisions (abuse of law, substance-over-form) may also result in non-deductibility. If the parties are considered to be related parties under the definition of the CDTA, the Hungarian tax office is entitled to adjust the Hungarian party's tax base to reflect the market price (arm's-length price) if the parties did not make the adjustment themselves.

Considerations due for services are only deductible if the actual performance of the services is supported and the Hungarian taxpayer can prove that it benefits from the service.

Thin capitalisation rules may apply to interest on any non-banking debt in excess of three times the equity.

The consideration paid to a controlled foreign company (CFC) is not deductible for corporate income tax purposes unless the taxpayer is able to prove that it serves the purposes of business operations.

From 2010, the definition of CFC has changed significantly, so that foreign persons or entities established abroad and/or foreign resident entities will qualify as controlled foreign enterprises if, among other conditions, they are owned by a resident private individual who is deemed to be the beneficial owner (i.e., has a certain ownership share or voting ratio or dominant influence in the enterprise) or if the majority of their income derives from Hungarian sources and in both cases the effective tax rate of the persons/entities is lower than 12.66%. Certain exceptions are available (e.g., EU member states, OECD member states and treaty countries if a real economic presence can be proved).

Pension expense

No special provision in corporate taxation.

Payment for directors

No special provision in corporate taxation.

Development reserve

From 1 January 2008, 50% of pre-tax profit may be assigned as development reserve. The maximum value is HUF 500 million. However, the period available for using the development reserve has now increased from four years to six years for development reserves included in the 2008 financial statement. For other development reserves, the period remains four years.

Hungary

Royalty payments
50% of royalty income can also be deducted from the tax base (this is not limited to royalties received from related parties but applies to all royalty income).

The total deduction of 50% of royalty income from the tax base is limited to 50% of the pre-tax profit.

Tax base allowance regarding research and development (R&D)
From 2010, a tax base allowance is only applicable for R&D activities if the taxpayer carries out basic research, applied research or experimental research activities for its own purposes. The direct cost of the basic research, the applied research and the experimental research, or the amount of depreciation on the research activity (if the cost of R&D activity is capitalised), is deductible from the tax base.

300% of the direct costs of research activity (up to a maximum of HUF 50 million) is deductible from the tax base if the research activity is carried out jointly with a higher education institution, the Hungarian Academy of Sciences or a research institute established by them.

Employee benefit expenses
Employee benefits and the fringe benefit tax payable on them are tax-deductible.

Group taxation

Consolidation/group taxation rules
N/A (only available in VAT)

Transfer pricing regime
If parties qualify as related parties (as defined in the Hungarian Corporate Tax and Dividend Tax Act (CDTA)) and the price applied differs from the arm's-length price, the corporate income tax base should be modified by a proper transfer pricing adjustment. In addition, from 2010 the foreign permanent establishment(s) of a Hungarian company and the Hungarian head office also qualify as related entities and are subject to transfer pricing regulations.

Taxpayers are obliged to prepare transfer pricing documentation on intra-group transactions. The documentation has to be prepared for every contract between related parties (including in-kind contributions made at the time of establishment).

According to a Minister of Finance's Decree effective in 2010, it is possible to prepare two types of documentation (as opposed to the previous practice): country-specific documentation or consolidated transfer pricing documentation. Taxpayers may prepare consolidated transfer pricing documentation if this does not jeopardise comparability, and the contracts:

- Have the same subject matter and all their terms and conditions are identical or only slightly different; or
- Closely relate to each other.

Taxpayers are required to make a declaration in their corporate income tax returns as to which type of documentation they choose.

In summary, the requirements of the country-specific documentation have not changed as of 2010 compared to previous documentation requirements. This type of documentation must include, for example, the following:

- A functional analysis;
- Industry and company analyses;
- An economic analysis;
- A financial analysis; and
- An account of the process of selecting the transfer pricing methodology.

Consolidated transfer pricing documentation must consist of two main parts:

- The core documentation, which includes the standard data for each company within the group which is resident in any Member State of the European Union; and
- Country-specific documentation, which describes the agreements between the taxpayer and its related parties.

The documentation has to be available no later than the filing deadline for the corporate income tax return in any given year, otherwise the Tax Authority may assess a default penalty up to HUF 2 million for each case of missing or deficient documentation. We note, however, that this documentation only has to be prepared and kept in the company's files, rather than being filed with the Tax Authority.

Treatment of inter-company items
Thin capitalisation rules
Thin capitalisation rules may apply to interest on any non-banking debt in excess of three times the equity.

Controlled foreign company regime
From 2010, the definition of a CFC has changed significantly, so that foreign persons or entities established abroad and/or foreign resident entities qualify as controlled foreign enterprises if, among other conditions, they are owned by a resident private individual who is deemed to be the beneficial owner (i.e., has a certain ownership share or voting ratio or dominant influence in the enterprise), or if the majority of their income derives from Hungarian sources, and in both cases the effective tax rate of the persons/entities is lower than 12.66%. Certain exceptions may be available (for companies in EU member states, OECD member states and treaty countries, if a real economic presence can be proved).

Related party transactions
Transactions between related parties must be accounted at arm's-length prices for taxation purposes, irrespective of whether or not the underlying contracts are concluded on arm's-length terms.

If the applied price differs from the arm's-length price, and the taxpayer does not amend its tax base by the difference, the tax authority may adjust the taxpayer's tax base and may assess penalties.

Hungary

Tax incentives

Development Tax Incentive

Each development tax incentive may be claimed for a 10-year period (beginning on the completion of the development) in the corporate income tax returns over a maximum period of 14 years from the original application for the incentive. In any given tax year, the tax incentive is available for up to 80% of the tax payable, but in total up to the state aid intensity ceiling. Applications for the tax incentive only have to be submitted to the Ministry of Finance if the aggregated eligible costs of the investment exceed EUR 100 million. If the investment is below this threshold, taxpayers only need to notify the Ministry of Finance before starting the investment. Tax incentives are available for investments if:

- The current value of the investment is at least HUF 3 billion; or
- The current value of the investment is at least HUF 1 billion in certain designated areas; and provided that:

  - The investment results in the creation of new facilities or the extension of existing facilities; or
  - Substantially changed products or production processes (excluding investments in basic research, applied research and experimental development);
  - In the four years following the year in which the tax incentive is first used against the tax base:

  1. The annual average number of employees has increased by at least 150 compared with either the year before the investment was made or the average number of employees for the three years preceding the investment (by 75 in certain designated areas); or
  2. The annual wage costs have increased by 600 times the minimum wage effective on the first day of the tax year (by a multiple of 300 in certain designated areas) compared with either the annual wage costs of the year before the investment was commenced or the average annual wage cost for the three years preceding the investment.

Provided that the investment results in the creation of new facilities or the extension of existing facilities, or substantially changed products or production processes, the government may also grant tax incentives to companies that invest:

- At least HUF 100 million in equipment for zoogenic food production;
- At least HUF 100 million in environmental protection projects;
- At least HUF 100 million in broadband Internet services;
- At least HUF 100 million in the production of films and videos;
- At least HUF 100 million in basic research, applied research and experimental development projects;
- At least HUF 100 million in projects financed by an issue of stock market-quoted shares, if (1) the project is started before the last day of the third calendar year following the date of issue and (2) the total nominal value of the shares issued by the fifth year following the start of the project continuously reaches 50% of the value of the registered shares and (3) the total issue price reaches 50% of the eligible costs and (4) at the date of the application for the incentive the company has at least 25 shareholders or at least 25% of the issued shares are owned by

shareholders where each of them does not have more than 5% of the issued shares' nominal value (from 1 January 2008); and

- At least HUF 500 million in projects initiated by small- and medium-sized enterprises if certain criteria are met.

Tax incentives may also be granted for projects that create new jobs. As of 2010, the restrictions prescribed in the CDTA regarding the headcount of staff and the percentage of new entrants to the labour market that may be claimed for such investments have been abolished. The conditions prescribed in the relevant decree remain unchanged.

Tax holidays
Ongoing tax holidays can be used until 31 December 2011.

Other tax incentives
Film production companies that receive a state subsidy for their activity may deduct the amount of the subsidy from their corporate income tax base.

A tax incentive is available for small- and medium-sized enterprises (basically, those with a maximum of 250 employees; or annual net revenue of a maximum of EUR 50 million; or a maximum annual balance sheet total of EUR 43 million). Taxpayers that take a loan from a financial institution for the acquisition or production of tangible assets may deduct 40% of the interest paid on the loan from their tax due, up to a maximum deduction of HUF 6 million. However, taxpayers engaged in certain business sectors cannot use this tax incentive (e.g., transportation, agricultural activity, etc.).

In the case of software development, a taxpayer may decrease its calculated corporate income tax by 10% (or 15% in case of small- and middle-sized companies) of wage costs which were accounted for as the costs of basic research or applied research or experimental development or which arose through employing software developers. The tax incentive may be claimed in the tax year in which these costs are incurred and in the following three years, in equal instalments. However, the tax incentive claimed may not exceed 70% of the calculated corporate income tax decreased by the tax incentives specified in the CDTA (including development tax incentives).

In addition, from 2010 the expenses and costs of the reconstruction of monuments and protected buildings are deductible from the corporate income tax base.

Withholding taxes (WHT)

Under the domestic rules there is no withholding tax on dividend, interest or royalties unless anti-avoidance rules apply. From 1 January 2010, 30% withholding tax has been introduced on interest, royalties and certain service fee payments made to companies which are resident in countries with which Hungary does not have a double tax treaty.

Hungary has an extensive treaty network with maximum withholding tax rates as follows:

(1)	Dividends	Interest	Royalties
	%	%	%
Albania	5/10 (2)	0	5
Australia	15	10	10

Hungary

(1)	Dividends	Interest	Royalties
	%	%	%
Austria	10	0	0
Azerbaijan	8	8	8
Belarus	5/15 (2)	5	5
Belgium	10	15 (3)	0
Brazil	15	10/15 (4)	15/25 (5)
Bulgaria	10	10	10
Canada	5/10/15 (6) (7)	10	10
China, P.R (8)	10	10	10
Croatia	5/10 (2)	0	0
Cyprus	15/5	10	0
Czech Republic	5/15 (2)	0	10
Denmark	5/15 (2)	0	0
Egypt	15/20	15	15
Estonia	5/15 (2)	10	5/10 (10)
Finland	5/15 (2)	0	5
France	5/15 (2)	0	0
Germany	5/15/25 (2)	0	0
Greece	10/45	10	10
Iceland	5/10 (2)	0	10
India	10 (19)	10 (12)	10 (11)
Indonesia	15	15	15
Ireland, Rep. of	5/15 (2)	0	0
Israel	5/15 (2)	0	0
Italy	10	0	0
Japan	10	10	10 (13)
Kazakhstan	5/15 (2)	10	10
Korea, Rep. of	5/10 (2)	0	0
Kuwait	0	0	10
Latvia	5/10 (2)	10	5/10 (20)
Lithuania	5/15 (2)	10	5/10 (20)
Luxembourg	5/15 (2)	0	0
Macedonia	5/15 (14)	0	0
Malaysia	10	15	15
Malta	5/15	10	10
Moldova	5/15 (2)	10	0
Mongolia	5/15 (2)	10	5
Morocco	12	10	10
Netherlands	5/15 (2)	0	0
Norway	10	0	0
Pakistan	15/20 (2)	15	15
Philippines	15/20 (2)	15	15
Poland	10	10	10
Portugal	10/15	10	10
Romania	5/15 (9)	15	10 (21)

Hungary

(1)	Dividends	Interest	Royalties
	%	%	%
Russia	10	0	0
Serbia and Montenegro	5/15	10	10
Singapore	5/10 (2)	5	5
Slovakia	5/15 (2)	0	10
Slovenia	5/15 (2)	5	5
South Africa	5/15 (2)	0	0
Spain	5/15 (2)	0	0
Sweden	5/15 (2)	0	0
Switzerland	10	10	0
Thailand	15/20 (15)	10/25 (16)	15
Tunisia	12/10 (2)	12 (19)	12
Turkey	10/15 (2)	10	10
Ukraine	5/15 (2)	10	5
United Kingdom	5/15 (2)	0	0
United States	5/15 (17)	0	0
Uruguay	15	15	10/15 (18)
Uzbekistan	10	10	10
Vietnam	10	10	10

Notes

1. List of the double tax treaties Hungary is a party to and the highest rates of withholding tax a foreign-source country may charge on (the gross) income paid to Hungarian residents.
2. The lower rate applies if the recipient has a stake of at least 25% in the distributing company.
3. Interest is exempt if paid in respect of (a) commercial claims (including claims represented by negotiable instruments) and instalment payments for the delivery or supply of goods and/or services, (b) current accounts or registered loans placed by a financial institution, and (c) funds and deposits not represented by bearers' securities placed at any of the financial institutions (including public credit institutions).
4. 10% applies to bank loans used for industrial purposes, research and development, or public works.
5. 25% applies to royalties paid for the use of or the right to use trademarks.
6. The lower rate applies if the recipient has control, directly or indirectly, of 25% of the voting rights in the distributing company.
7. 10% is applicable if a non-resident owned investment corporation pays dividends to a recipient that has control, directly or indirectly, of 25% of the voting rights in the distributing company.
8. The China-Hungary Treaty does not apply to Hong Kong.
9. The lower rate applies if the recipient has a stake of at least 40% in the distributing company.
10. The lower rate applies to royalties for the use of industrial, commercial or scientific equipment, or for transmission by satellite, cable optic fibre, or similar technology.
11. The same rate applies to technical service fees.
12. The lower rate applies if the recipient has a stake of at least 10% in the distributing company.
13. Cultural royalties are exempt.
14. The lower rate applies if the recipient (other than a partnership) has a stake of at least 25% in the distributing company.

Hungary

15. The lower rate applies if the recipient has a stake of 25% in the distributing company that carries out industrial activities.
16. 10% applies if the recipient of the interest is a financial institution, including an insurance company.
17. The lower rate applies if the recipient has voting stock of at least 10% in the distributing company.
18. 10% applies to technical service fees.
19. If a lower rate is set in a treaty or agreement or minutes between India and any OECD country (excluding Hungary), then this lower rate should also be applied for India-Hungary.
20. 5% applies for the use of industrial, commercial or scientific facilities or for transmissions by means of satellite, cable, optical fibre or any similar technology.
21. 5% for commission.

Tax administration

Audit cycle
The supreme body of the company should elect an auditor for a fixed term, but not more than five years.

Auditing of annual financial statements is not statutorily compulsory if both of the conditions below are satisfied:

a. The company's annual net sales revenue (calculated for the financial year) does not exceed HUF 100 million on the average of the two financial years preceding the financial year under review; and
b. The average number of the company's employees for the two financial years preceding the financial year under review did not exceed 50 persons.

Foreign currency book-keeping
The Hungarian Accounting Act states that a company that uses a convertible foreign currency rather than the Hungarian forint in its primary economic environment (functional currency) can prepare its annual financial statement in the convertible foreign currency specified in its founding document, provided that at least 25% of its (i) income, costs and expenditures; and (ii) financial assets and financial liabilities were earned or incurred, as applicable, in such convertible currency in both the current year and the previous year.

A company will comply with the conditions if the total amount of the items listed in both point (i) and point (ii) is at least 25%. Point (ii) does not include off-balance-sheet items.

Furthermore, from 2010 all companies can prepare their annual financial statements in Euro (without the above limitation) if this is specified in their accounting policies. However this decision cannot be changed within five years.

Statute of limitations
In general, the statute of limitation is five years from the end of the calendar year in which the tax return should be filed. Self-revision interrupts the term of limitation.

For stamp duty, the statute of limitations is five years from end of the calendar year in which the tax authority gains knowledge of the acquisition of the asset(s).

Hungary

Tax return due dates
Returns
Corporate income tax must be calculated by reference to the accounting year, which is either the calendar year or, for group companies, the group's accounting year. Returns must be lodged within 150 days following the last day of the accounting year. The tax payable is determined by self-assessment.

Electronic tax returns
Tax returns may be submitted either electronically or in paper format. However, those who are legally obliged to submit monthly tax and contribution returns (e.g., employers and payers) may only submit tax returns electronically.

Payment of tax
Corporate income tax instalments must generally be reported and paid quarterly or monthly (above HUF 5 million tax payable), and 100% of the expected final payment is due by the twentieth day of the last month of the accounting year. However, a late payment penalty is only levied if the company fails to pay at least 90% of the expected final payment by the above deadline. The late payment penalty is 20% of the difference between the tax advances paid (including the top-up payment) and 90% of the actual corporate income tax liability.

Topics of focus for tax authorities
The tax authority will take more stringent measures against "aggressive tax planning" (tax planning that takes advantage of unintended administrative or legal loopholes,) using its international experience and cooperation agreements.

The following categories of taxpayers can expect to be scheduled for tax audits in 2010:

- Taxpayers whose records show frequent changes in registered address or ownership;
- Businesses that have operated for several years with substantial loans from their shareholders;
- Taxpayers that declared significant amounts of payable and deductible VAT during their pre-company period;
- Taxpayers that have been in continuous operation despite continuing losses;
- Taxpayers that spend a significant portion of their sales revenues on services;
- Taxpayers that have significant tax base decreasing items, tax allowances and subsidies related to investments; and
- Taxpayers that deduct research and development expenses.

The tax authority will also pay more attention to the actual content of transactions conducted between related parties and to the methods companies use to determine the arm's-length price.

Other issues

Foreign investment incentives and restrictions
Hungary provides incentives not based on residence, but rather on the basis of the size of investment or activity (e.g., companies that create new jobs, companies with R&D activities, etc.), or company size (e.g., for small- and medium-sized enterprises). The incentives are available to both domestic and foreign investors.

Hungary

Principal forms of doing business
- Branch;
- Partnership;
- Limited liability company;
- Private company limited by shares; and
- Public company limited by shares.

Business and tax treatment of intellectual property (IP)
IP is defined as inventions, patents, and the industrial design of assets protected under industrial law; copyrighted software products; other intellectual property; and assets without legal protection but monopolised through secrecy (e.g., know-how, production technologies and trademarks, whether purchased or created by the undertaking itself, and irrespective of whether or not used). IP is categorised as intangible assets in the balance sheet if it serves a company's business activity for more than one year. If it is used for less than one year, it is treated as costs or current assets.

Gains that are realised on the disposal of an intangible asset are taxable.

If a gain on the disposal of an intangible asset comes within the definition of royalty, 50% of this royalty revenue is exempt from corporate income tax.

Royalties are revenues derived from:

- Permission for the exploitation of patents, from the industrial design of assets under industrial law and from know-how;
- Permission to use trademarks, business names and business secrets;
- Permission to use copyrights and similar rights attached to protected work; and
- Transfers of the property described above (except for trademarks, business names and, business secrets).

If a taxpayer incurs a loss on the disposal of an intangible asset, the loss will be deductible for tax purposes.

Additionally, the tax value of the assets transferred is a tax base decreasing item for corporate income tax purposes, while the accounting value of the IP is a tax base increasing item.

The sale of an interest in an IP-holder company, or making a contribution in kind of IP to another company, or transferring IP without consideration, should be treated as in the case of any other asset.

No withholding tax is levied on royalty payments made to companies which are resident in countries with which Hungary has concluded a double tax treaty. Otherwise, 30% withholding tax rate applies.

Tax incentives are also available for IP-related activities. (For further details, please see the *Tax incentives section*).

Mergers and acquisitions (M&A) from a business and tax perspective
Mergers in Hungary are tax-free transformations provided that they qualify under the definition of preferential transformation. Preferential transformation means that a company, without going into liquidation, transfers all its assets and liabilities

to another company in exchange for the issue to its shareholders of securities representing the capital of that other company, and a cash payment not exceeding 10% of the nominal value, or, in the absence of a nominal value, of the accounting par value of those securities.

In a preferential transformation, the predecessor company does not have to amend its tax base by the difference between the adjusted book value and the book value. The adjusted book value means the historical value of assets less any depreciation deducted from the tax base plus the readjusted amount of extraordinary depreciation. Furthermore, for shareholders, the income accounted in excess of the historical value of the shares they acquire in the preferential transformation is also not taxable for corporate income tax purposes for as long as the shareholder holds its participation.

In any other case if two companies merge, the difference between the market value and the book value of the assets and liabilities is taxable for the successor company. Furthermore, the predecessor company may decrease its tax base by the amount of the difference between the adjusted book value of its assets and their book value, if the adjusted book value is the higher of the two. The company will increase its tax base if the book value is higher than the adjusted book value.

IFRS adoption
Since 2005, companies defined in Section 4 of Decision no. 1606/2002/EC (mainly companies listed on the stock exchange) have had to prepare their consolidated annual reports according to the IFRS, although it was possible to obtain an exemption until 2007 due to the ongoing harmonisation of the Hungarian regulations. However, non-listed subsidiaries of EU-listed entities are exempt from the preparation of IFRS consolidated financial statements. If a company chooses IFRS, HAR financial statements must also be prepared and filed with the Court of Registration.

Corporate taxes in India

For more information, contact:

Shyamal Mukherjee
PricewaterhouseCoopers Pvt Ltd
Building No. 10, Tower – C
17th & 18th floor,
DLF Cyber City, Gurgaon
Haryana – 122002, India
Tel: +91 12 4330 6536
Email: shyamal.mukherjee@in.pwc.com

Ketan Dalal
PricewaterhouseCoopers Pvt Ltd
PwC House, Plot No. 18 A,
Guru Nanak Road (Station Road)
Bandra
Mumbai 400 028, India
Tel: +91 22 6689 1422
Email: ketan.dalal@in.pwc.com

Significant developments

Over the past 12 months there have been numerous developments in the Indian corporate tax regime, the most significant include:

Transfer of unlisted (not tradable and not listed on any stock exchanges) shares of a company to a firm or company without consideration or for inadequate consideration is taxable income in the hands of the recipient firm or company.

Indian companies were liable to pay surcharge at the rate of 10% on the amount of income tax if the total income exceeds INR 10 million. The rate of surcharge is now reduced from 10% to 7.5% for domestic companies. There is change in surcharge in the case of foreign companies which is now 2.5%.

Minimum alternate tax
Indian companies are liable to pay Minimum alternate tax (MAT) on their income. The rate has been increased from 16.99% to 19.93%. For foreign companies the rate has increased from 15.84% to 19%. MAT is payable only where total taxable income exceeds INR 10 million.

Withholding tax
There are certain specified payments made to residents which are liable for withholding tax. The withholding tax for a fiscal year is required to be deposited with the government treasury on or before the due date of the filing of tax returns, otherwise the expense payment is not eligible as a tax deductible expense. In relation to payment made to non-residents or foreign companies, withholding tax is required now to be deposited with the government treasury within the timeline provided on a month-to-month basis.

Research and development (R&D) expenditures
Weighted deduction available in respect of expenditure incurred on scientific research in an approved in-house R&D facility has been increased from 150% to 200% for companies engaged in specified businesses.

A payment made to approved research associations undertaking research in social science or statistical research is now eligible for a weighted deduction of 125% of the payment made.

Contributions made to approved scientific research associations, universities, other institutions, are 175% deductible (which was earlier allowable at 125%) of the actual payment made.

Audit for income tax purposes
Persons carrying on business are required to get their books of accounts audited for income tax purposes where the turnover is INR 6 million (earlier the limit was INR 4 million). For persons carrying on a profession, the limit is INR 1.5 million (earlier the limit was INR 1 million). The penalty for non-compliance with this audit requirement is INR 0.15 million (earlier 0.1 million).

Non-life insurance companies
In case of non-life insurance companies, any gain or loss on realisation of investments, as the case may be, shall be added back or deducted, if it is not credited to the profit and loss account. Any provision (unrealised loss) in the profit and loss account for diminution in the value of investments is now not to be taken into consideration while computing the taxable income.

Capital expenditures
Certain specified categories of businesses are eligible now for 100% tax deduction of capital expenditure (other than on land, goodwill and financial instruments). The benefit is available for:

- Building and operating new hospitals with at least 100 beds;
- Building and operating new hotel of two star category anywhere in India; and
- Developing and building housing projects under a notified scheme for slum redevelopment or rehabilitation framed by the central/state government.

Tax holiday
Persons engaged in the business of hotels or convention centres in the National Capital Region are eligible for a tax holiday, if the date of functioning of the hotel or completion of the construction of convention centre is started by 31 July 2010 (the earlier date was 31 March 2010).

Persons engaged in the business of developing and building housing projects are eligible for a tax holiday if the housing projects (approved by the local authority on or after 1 April 2005) are completed within five years (earlier it was four years). The condition relating to built-up area of shops and commercial establishments included in the housing project has been relaxed. The amendment is applied retrospectively from tax year 2010-11.

Conversion to LLP
Conversion of a private company or an unlisted public company into a limited liability partnership (LLP) will no longer attract capital gains tax subject, if the prescribed conditions are fulfilment as detailed below:

- Turnover or gross receipts of the company being converted does not exceed INR 6 million in any of the three preceding tax years;
- Any unabsorbed business loss or depreciation allowance of the company is eligible for carryforward and set-off in the hands of the successor LLP;
- Any unutilised MAT credit in the hands of a company is not available to the successor LLP; and

India

- Transfer of shares by the shareholders of a company will not attract capital gains tax subject to fulfilment of prescribed conditions.

Dispute resolution
To facilitate quick resolution of disputes, a dispute resolution panel (DRP) comprising three Commissioners of Income Tax has been in operation since 1 October 2009 to deal with cases of foreign companies and transfer pricing orders which are prejudicial to a taxpayer.

Transfer pricing
In order to lessen the litigation under transfer pricing regulations, the Central Board of Direct Taxes will formulate safe harbour rules. The rules will provide the circumstances in which tax authorities would accept the transfer price declared by the assessee.

Social Security agreements
India has entered into social security agreements with various countries of which Belgium and Germany were recently notified.

Taxes on corporate income

For India, the financial year for tax purposes ends on 31 March. The corporate income tax rate applicable to an Indian company for the financial year 2010-2011 is 30% (plus surcharge, education cess and secondary and higher education cess). From tax year 2011-12, the surcharge for domestic companies is reduced from 10% to 7.5%. Foreign companies operating in India are taxed at the rate of 40% (plus surcharge, education cess and secondary and higher secondary education cess). Surcharge for foreign companies is 2.5%. The education cess, and the secondary and higher education secondary cess, is 2% and 1% respectively.

MAT
Companies are liable to pay the MAT on their adjusted book profits where the tax liability for the year is less than 19.93% for the assessment year (AY) 2011-12 (16.99% for AY 2010-11) of the adjusted book profits. In such cases, the tax liability is fixed at 19.93% of the adjusted book profits of the company. Sick companies (loss companies which have made losses continuously and may or may not be revived to making profits) are not subject to MAT. From tax year 2010-11, companies are allowed to take the benefit of the credit of tax paid under MAT for 10 years.

Fringe benefit tax
The Fringe benefit tax (FBT) (in addition to corporate income tax) was chargeable on the fringe benefits provided by an employer to its employees.

The FBT has been abolished as of tax year 2009-10.

Direct tax code
A new direct tax code replacing the existing Income Tax Act, 1961 is proposed and is expected to be introduced by 1 April 2011.

Corporate residence

A company is a resident of India if it:

- Is an Indian company; or
- During the financial year, the control or management of its affairs is situated wholly in India.

A company that does not fulfil either of these conditions is treated as a non-resident.

A partnership or LLP is classed as resident in India, if any portion of its control and management is in India. A partnership firm or LLP is a non-resident, if its control and management is situated wholly outside India.

Other taxes

Securities transaction tax (STT)

STT is applicable to transactions involving the purchase or sale of equity shares, derivatives, units of equity-oriented funds through a recognised stock exchange or the sale of a unit of an equity-oriented fund to any mutual fund. STT paid is eligible to be claimed as tax deductible expenditure while working out the tax computation of the income from sale of securities.

Wealth tax

All companies are liable to pay wealth tax assessed at 1% of the value of specified net assets, if the value of net wealth exceeds INR 3 million. Valuation of assets is in terms of specific rules notified by the government are detailed below.

Customs duty

Customs duty is levied by the central government on the import of goods into, and export from, India. The rate of customs duty applicable to a product proposed to be imported or exported depends upon its classification under the customs tariff. With regard to exports from India, customs duty is levied only on a very limited list of goods.

The customs tariff is aligned with the internationally recognised harmonised system of nomenclature (HSN) provided by the World Customs Organisation.

Customs duty is levied on the transaction value of the imported or exported goods. According to section 14 of The Customs Act, 1962 (CA), the concept of transaction value is the sole basis for valuation for the purposes of import and export of goods. While the general principles adopted for valuation of the goods in India are in conformity with the World Trade Organisation (WTO) agreement on customs valuation, the central government has announced independent customs valuation rules applicable to export and import of goods.

India does not have one uniform rate of customs duty. Furthermore, the customs duty applicable to any product is composed of a number of components. The types of customs duty applicable are as follows:

- The basic customs duty (BCD) is the basic component of customs duty levied at the effective rate notified under the First Schedule to the Customs Tariff Act (CTA) and

India

applied to the landed value of the goods (i.e., the cost, insurance and freight (CIF) value of the goods plus landing charges at 1%). The peak rate of BCD is 10%.
* The additional customs duty in lieu of excise duty (CVD) is equivalent to, and is charged in lieu of, the excise duty applicable on like goods manufactured or produced in India. CVD is calculated on the landed value of the goods and the applicable BCD. However, the CVD on specific consumer goods intended for retail sale in India is calculated on the basis of the maximum retail price (MRP) printed on their packs. The general rate of excise duty is currently 10% and consequently the rate of CVD is also 10%. In addition, Education Cess (EC) at 2% and Secondary and Higher Education Cess (SHEC) at 1% are also levied on the CVD.
* EC at 2% and SHEC at 1% are also levied on the aggregate of custom duties (except in cases of safeguard duty, countervailing duty and anti-dumping duty).
* Additional duty of customs (ADC) to countervail State Taxes and value-added tax (VAT) of 4% is charged in addition to the above duties on all imports subject to a few exceptions.

ADC is calculated on the aggregate of the assessable value of the imported goods, the total customs duties (i.e., BCD and CVD) and the applicable EC and SHEC.

BCD, EC and SHEC levied on the aggregate of duties of customs are a cost of any import transaction. The duty incidence arising on account of all other components may be set off or refunded subject to prescribed conditions. Where goods are imported for purposes of manufacture, the Indian manufacturer may take a credit of the CVD and ADC paid at the time of import for set-off against the output excise duty. In the case of service providers, the credit of only the CVD is available. Similarly, the central government provides exemption from payment of ADC for certain specified goods. The central government also has prescribed a refund mechanism in relation to ADC paid on goods imported for the purpose of trading in India, subject to fulfilment of the conditions prescribed under the governing notifications and circulars issued in this regard.

CENVAT (excise duty)
Central value-added tax (CENVAT) is an excise duty levied by the central government on the manufacture or production of movable and marketable goods in India.

The rate at which excise duty is leviable on the goods depends on the classification of the goods under the excise tariff. The excise tariff primarily is based on the eight digit HSN classification adopted so as to achieve conformity with the customs tariff.

The excise duty on most consumer goods, which are intended for retail sale, is chargeable on the basis of the MRP printed on the package of the goods. However, abatements are admissible at rates ranging from 20% to 50% of the MRP. Goods, other than those covered by MRP based assessment, generally are chargeable to duty on the "transaction value" of the goods sold to an independent buyer. In addition, the central government has the power to fix tariff values for charging ad valorem duties on the goods.

Typically, the duty rate is 10%. However notifications granting partial or complete exemption for specified goods from payment of excise duties are also available. EC at 2% and SHEC at 1% are applicable on the aggregate of excise duties.

The central excise duty is a modified VAT wherein a manufacturer is allowed credit of the excise duty paid on locally sourced goods and the CVD and ADC paid on imported goods. The CENVAT credit can be utilised for payment of excise duty on the clearance of dutiable final products manufactured in India. In light of the integration of goods and services tax initiated in 2004, manufacturers of dutiable final products are also eligible to avail CENVAT credit of the service taxes paid on input services used in or in relation to the manufacture of final products and clearances of final products from the place of removal subject to fulfilment of conditions.

Service tax

Service tax is levied on specified taxable services identified under Chapter V of the Finance Act, 1994 (the Act). At present over 100 services are classified as taxable under the Act. The existing rate of service tax is 10%. In addition, an EC of 2% and SHEC of 1% of the service tax have also been levied on taxable services. Thus, the effective rate of service tax is 10.30%. There is no service tax on the export of services by the service provider in India, subject to fulfilment of prescribed conditions.

The onus of payment of service tax lies with the provider of services. However, in the case of specified services such as transport of goods by road, sponsorship services import of services, the service tax liability rests with the recipient of the services.

In light of the integration of goods and services tax, a service provider can avail CENVAT credit of excise duties paid on capital goods and inputs used for providing output services, apart from availing CENVAT credit of the service taxes paid on input services subject to fulfilment of conditions.

Taxable services provided by service providers located outside India to a recipient in India are subject to service tax in terms of the Services (Provided from Outside India and Received in India) Rules, 2006. In terms of these Rules, where the taxable services are provided from outside India and received in India, the service recipient is required to become registered and to pay the tax in accordance with the relevant provisions of law.

Advance ruling for customs, excise and service tax

In order to enable foreign investors to ascertain their indirect tax liabilities arising from proposed business ventures in India, the central government has constituted the Authority for Advance Rulings (AAR) as a high level quasi judicial body. The functions of the AAR comprise giving advance rulings on a specific set of facts relating to specified matters under customs, central excise and service tax.

Advance Rulings may be sought by any non-resident investor entering a joint venture in India in collaboration with another non-resident or a resident of India, or a resident setting up a joint venture in India in collaboration with a non-resident. Through the Finance Act 2005, this facility has also been made available to an existing Joint Venture in India. The central government is also empowered to notify any other class or category of persons as eligible for availing the benefit of an advance ruling.

VAT / Central Sales Tax (CST)

Sale of movable goods in India is chargeable to tax at central or state level. The Indian regulatory framework has granted power to State Legislatures to levy tax on goods sold within that State. Such sales are, therefore, chargeable to VAT at the rates notified under the VAT laws of the relevant State.

India

All goods sold in the course of interstate trade are subject to CST.

Where goods are bought and sold by registered dealers, for trading or for use as inputs in the manufacture of other goods or specified activities (such as mining or telecommunication networks), the rate of sales tax is 2%, provided Form C is issued by the purchasing dealer. In the absence of Form C, the applicable rate would be the rate of VAT on such goods in the originating State.

CST is sought to be phased out by the year 2011. Inter-State procurement, on which CST is charged by the originating State is not eligible for input tax credit in the destination State.

State level sales tax has been replaced by VAT in all the States. Under the VAT regime, the VAT paid on goods purchased from within the State is eligible for VAT credit. The input VAT credit can be utilised against the VAT/CST payable on the sale of goods. It is, thus, ensured that the cascading effect of taxes is avoided and only the value addition is taxed.

Currently, there is no VAT on imports into India. Exports are zero-rated. This means that while exports are not charged to VAT, VAT charged on inputs purchased and used in the manufacture of export good or goods purchased for exports is available to the purchaser as a refund.

The State VAT is charged at tax rates of 1%, 4% to 6% (range). Goods other than those notified to be covered under the above rates are charged in the range of 12.5% to 16.5%. The rate of VAT depends on nature of goods involved and varies from State to State.

Turnover thresholds have been prescribed so as to exclude small traders from the ambit of the VAT. A tax under composition scheme, at a lower rate, may be levied on such small traders in lieu of the VAT.

Goods and services tax
The central government took a major step towards the transition to a national integrated goods and services tax (GST) in 2006. In this regard, a joint working group (JWG) was constituted by the Empowered Committee to study global GST models and identify suitable models for introduction in India. In 2007, the JWG recommended a dual GST model for India which was subsequently studied and approved by the Empowered Committee and the Ministry of Finance.

The Empowered Committee of the State Finance Ministers (EC) on 10 November 2009 released the First Discussion Paper on the proposed GST in India. In the discussion paper the government indicated that GST shall have two components. One levied by centre (Central GST or CGST) and the other levied by states (State GST or SGST). The CGST and the SGST would be applicable on all transactions of goods and services made for a consideration except for exempted goods and services, goods which are outside the purview of the GST and transactions which are below the prescribed threshold limits. It is proposed that GST will be implemented from 1 April 2011. Details of taxes which would be subsumed in dual GST are as follows.

The following taxes will be subsumed in CGST:

- Excise duty;
- CVD/ADC; and
- Service tax.

The following taxes will be subsumed in SGST:

- VAT
- Entertainment tax;
- Luxury tax;
- Lottery taxes;
- State cesses and surcharges; and
- Entry tax not in lieu of octroi (a municipal levy).

CST will be phased out in GST.

The input tax credit (ITC) for the CGST and SGST would operate in parallel and would be available for utilisation only against the output payment of CGST and SGST, respectively. Both CGST and SGST will be levied on import of goods and services into the country. The incidence of tax will follow the destination principle. Full and complete set off will be available on the GST paid on import of goods and services.

Octroi duty/entry tax

"Entry Tax" is a tax on entry of goods into the state from outside the state for use, consumption or sale therein. It is levied on the purchase value, which is defined to mean the amount of the valuable consideration paid or payable by a person for the purchase of any goods. The value of the specified goods can be ascertained from the original invoice for purchase of such goods.

Octroi is a municipal levy which is levied at the time of entry of specified goods into the limits of the relevant municipal corporation. Thus, octroi can be leviable, if there is movement of goods from one city to another in the same State, in the event the cities fall under the jurisdiction of two different municipal corporations.

Branch income

Branches of foreign companies are taxed on income that is received in India, or which accrues or arises in India, at the rates applicable to foreign companies. There is no withholding tax on remittance of profits to the company's head office.

Income determination

Capital gains

Capital gains refers to gains made on transfer of a capital asset, including extinguishment of the rights to an asset.

Short-term capital assets are capital assets held for a period of less than 36 months. In the case of shares, listed securities, or units of specified mutual funds or a zero coupon bond the period of holding requirement is 12 months. Capital assets that do not qualify as short-term capital assets are considered as long-term capital assets.

India

Normally, long-term capital gains are determined after increasing the cost by prescribed inflation factors. In the case of foreign companies, capital gains on transfer of shares or debentures in Indian companies are computed in the foreign currency in which the shares or debentures were acquired, and the capital gains are reconverted into Indian currency.

Capital gains are taxed as follows:

* Long-term capital gains on transfer of shares of a company, or units of an equity-oriented fund, which are subject to STT are exempt from taxation. However, such gains are taxable under MAT provisions.
* Other long-term capital gains are subject to taxation at 20% (plus the surcharge, education cess and secondary and higher secondary education cess). However, long-term capital gains arising from transfer of listed securities, units or zero coupon bonds are taxed at 10% (without adjusting the cost for inflation) or at 20% (after adjusting the cost for inflation) whichever is more beneficial to the taxpayer. These rates exclude surcharge, education cess and secondary and higher education cess.
* Short-term capital gains on the transfer of the shares of a company or units of an equity-oriented fund subject to STT are taxed at 15% (plus the surcharge, education cess and secondary and higher secondary education cess).
* Other short-term capital gains are subject to taxation at the normal corporate rates applicable to a company.

In the case of certain overseas financial organisations (e.g., off-shore funds and foreign institutional investors), long-term capital gains arising on the transfer of units purchased in foreign currency are taxable at 10% (plus the surcharge, education cess and secondary and higher education cess) on the gross amount.

Long-term capital gains earned by non-residents on transfer of bonds relating to Indian companies (issued abroad in accordance with government guidelines or approved schemes and acquired in foreign currency) are taxable at 10% (plus surcharge, education cess and secondary and higher education cess) on the gross amount of gains.

The rules of carryforward and set-off of loss for capital gains are as follows:

* Capital losses arising from the transfer of a short-term capital asset can be set-off against capital gains arising from any other asset. However, capital losses arising from the transfer of a long-term capital asset can be set-off only against capital gains arising from the transfer of any other long-term capital asset.
* Capital losses that cannot be set-off can be carried forward and set-off against the future capital gains. Losses can be carried forward for set-off for a period of eight years after the year of loss.
* Gains and losses (computed in the manner indicated under Depreciation and Depletion separately) arising on the sale of depreciable assets are classified as short-term capital gains or losses, and the gains are taxed at the same rates as business income.

Dividend income
Dividend income received from Indian companies is not taxable in the hands of all the shareholders. This applies to resident as well as non-resident shareholders.

Indian companies distributing or declaring dividends are liable to pay dividend distribution tax (DDT) at 15% (plus surcharge, education cess and secondary and higher education cess). This tax is payable at each level of distribution and is in addition to the corporate taxes payable on business profits.

As of tax year 2009-10, a holding company does not have to pay DDT on dividends paid to its shareholders to the extent that it has received dividends from its subsidiary company on which DDT has been paid by the subsidiary. However, the benefit will not be available if the holding company is itself a subsidiary (if it has a shareholding of more than 50%) of another company. An exemption from this tax has been granted in the case of declaration or distribution of dividends by special economic zone (SEZ) developers. A SEZ is a designated area which has special economic regulations and where an assessee is eligible for tax holiday.

Income received by overseas financial organisations (offshore funds) from units of specified mutual funds, or from the Unit Trust of India, that is purchased in foreign currency as well as interest received by non-residents on bonds issued abroad by Indian companies following government guidelines and acquired in foreign currency, are taxable at 10% on the gross amount of income. Dividends (other than those received from Indian companies) and interest earned by foreign financial institutions from investments in the Indian capital market are taxable at 20% on the gross amount.

Income received from units of specified mutual funds is not taxable in the hands of the recipient. The distributing mutual fund is liable to pay a distribution tax of 20% or 25% (plus surcharge, education cess and secondary and higher education cess). The above tax is not chargeable in respect of income distributed by an equity oriented fund in respect of distribution under such scheme.

Stock dividends (bonus shares) distributed are not taxed at the time of receipt in the hands of the recipient shareholders, but capital gains provisions are applicable to the sale of these stock dividends.

Foreign income
A resident company is taxed on its worldwide income. A non-resident company is taxed only on income that is received in India, or that accrues or arises, or is deemed to accrue or arise, in India. This income is subject to any favourable tax treaty provision. Double taxation of foreign income for residents is avoided through treaties that generally provide for the deduction of the lower of foreign tax, or Indian tax, on the doubly taxed income from tax payable in India. Similar relief is allowed unilaterally where no treaties exist; the resident would be taxed at the rate which would be the lower of the Indian tax rates, or the rate of the other country in which income is already taxed.

Interest income
Interest income received by a resident company is chargeable to tax at normal rates. Interest income received by a non-resident company is charged at a concessional rate.

Inventory valuation
Inventories generally are valued at cost or net realisable value, whichever is lower. Generally, there is conformity between book and tax reporting. The first-in first-out (FIFO) and average cost methods are acceptable, provided that they are consistently applied.

India

Partnership/limited liability partnership income
The partnership and limited liability partnership (LLP) are taxed as a separate legal entity. The income of partners from the partnership or LLP is exempt from tax for the individual assessment of the partner. The partnership and LLP is taxed at the rate of 30% (plus surcharge and education cess and secondary and higher education cess). The interest payment to the partner on the capital or current account is allowed as deductible expenditure; however, the maximum interest allowable for tax purposes is 12% per annum. A working partner can be paid salary, bonus, commission, or remuneration. The maximum permissible deduction in respect of remuneration payable collectively to all working partners would be based on the book profit at specified percentage for different slab of book profit.

Unrealised exchange gains/losses
There are no specific rules under the tax law for determining the nature of unrealised foreign exchange gains or losses. However, there are various judicial precedents available which lay down certain principles for classification of foreign exchange gains or losses.

Profit/loss, is considered trading profit/loss, if foreign currency is held on revenue account or as trading assets or as a part of circulating capital invested in the business.

Profit/loss is considered capital nature if a foreign currency loan is taken for capital asset or fixed asset.

Deductions

Capital v. revenue transactions
Expenditure which is revenue-in-nature would be allowed as a deduction if:

- They are incurred wholly and exclusively for the purpose of the business;
- The expenditure is not in the nature of personal expense; and
- The expenditure is not in the nature of capital expense.

Bribes, kickbacks, illegal payments
Expenditure incurred by a taxpayer which is illegal is not deemed to have been incurred for the purpose of the business or profession and no deduction will be allowed for such expenditure.

Interest
Any interest paid by a assessee (taxpayer) on capital borrowed for the purposes of their business or profession is a tax deductible expense. If the capital is borrowed for acquiring a capital asset for the purpose of extension of an existing business or profession, then interest liability pertaining to the period, until the time the asset is put to use, cannot be allowed as a tax deduction and would have to be added to the cost of such asset.

Depreciation and depletion
Depreciable assets are grouped in blocks, and each block is eligible for depreciation at a prescribed rate (usually 15%–100% for machinery, 5%–100% for buildings, 10% for furniture and 25% for intangible assets) on the opening value (net of depreciation charged in preceding years), plus cost of acquisition, less deletions, during the year. A deletion is the reduction by way of sale, discarding, demolition, or destruction of

the assets and the amount realised is reduced. Depreciation is restricted to 50% of the prescribed rate if the asset acquired is used for less than 180 days during the year of acquisition. If money receivable on the transfer exceeds the opening written-down value plus acquisitions of the block concerned, the excess is taxed as a short-term capital gain at the same tax rates as that applicable to business income.

Power-generating or power-distributing companies have the option either to use the reducing balance method provided under the normal schedule or to charge depreciation on a straight-line basis. The straight-line rates are aligned to the power companies' book depreciation rates.

Know-how, patents, licenses, franchises, and similar intangible assets form part of the block of depreciable assets provided that they are owned and put to use in the course of their business, and would be eligible for depreciation at the prescribed rate, which is 25%.

Tax depreciation is not required to conform to book depreciation.

Bad debts
The amount of any bad debt, or part thereof, which has been written off as irrecoverable in the accounts of the assessee (taxpayer) for the year, would be allowed as a tax deductible write-off.

Payments for foreign affiliates
Indian companies can claim deduction for payment of royalties, and for interest and fees for technical or management service provided by foreign affiliates, as long as they are not capital in nature, and are incurred wholly and exclusively for the purpose of the business, and that requisite tax is withheld from such payment. However, if the requisite tax is not withheld from such payment, or after withholding, it is not paid into the government treasury, a deduction for the payments is available in the year of payment of tax into the government treasury.

Taxes
All taxes (tax, duty, cess or fees by whatever name called) relating to business (other than income tax and wealth tax) incurred during the tax year are deductible in that year, provided they are paid by the following 30 September. Otherwise, they are deductible in the year of payment.

Organisational and start-up expenses
Certain expenses are incurred by taxpayers either before the start-up of a business or after start-up of business, in connection with extension of the industrial undertaking, or in connection with setting-up a new unit. One fifth of such expenditure would be allowed over a period of five years.

Expenses allowable on actual payment basis
Certain expenses ,such as but not limited to, employees' provident fund (i.e., retirement benefit funds) dues, bonus to employees, interest payable to financial institutions and banks, are allowed as tax deductible on actual payment.

Offset of losses
Loss can be carried forward and set-off against income from subsequent year(s) for periods set out in the following table:

India

Types of losses	Time limit
Unabsorbed depreciation	Unlimited
Other business losses (other than speculation business losses)	8 years
Speculation business losses	4 years
Capital losses	8 years

Group taxation

Group taxation is not provided by Indian tax law.

Tax incentives

Tax incentive provisions normally have conditions applicable for the period within which the preferred activity should be undertaken, and the period for which the tax incentive is available. It may also be necessary to fulfil certain other conditions such as 'forming' a 'new' undertaking.

Tax incentives for undertakings other than infrastructure development undertakings

New industrial undertakings located in specified "backward" states and districts are entitled to full tax exemption of profits for the first three or five years of operation, followed by a partial tax exemption of 30% of profits for the next five years. The list of backward districts has been streamlined into category A and category B districts, depending upon the current level of infrastructure development in those areas. The initial tax holiday period is five years in the case of category A districts and three years in the case of category B districts. A similar incentive is also applicable for hotels satisfying prescribed conditions.

If certain conditions are met, a tax holiday is permitted on the profits of an undertaking engaged in any of the following:

- Integrated business of handling, storage and transportation of food grains;
- Developing and building of housing project;
- Scientific research;
- Commercial production or refining of mineral oils;
- Setting up and operating a cold chain for agricultural produce;
- Processing, preservation and packaging of fruits or vegetables; and
- Operating and maintaining a hospital in a rural area.

The tax holiday periods ranges from five to 10 years and the percentage of the rebate is either 30%, 50% or 100% in initial years and 30% in later years. The number constituting 'initial' and 'later' years varies from sector to sector.

Tax incentives for infrastructure development undertakings

Enterprises engaged in the business of power generation, transmission or distribution, developing or operating and maintaining a notified infrastructure facility or an industrial park or SEZ, making substantial renovation and modernisation of the existing network of transmission or distribution lines (between specified periods), or laying and operating a cross country natural gas distribution network are eligible to a tax exemption of 100% of profits for any 10 consecutive years falling within the first

15 years of operation (20 years in the case of infrastructure projects, except for ports, airports, inland waterways, water supply projects and navigational channels to the sea). Infrastructure facility means roads, including toll roads, bridges, rail systems, highway projects, water supply projects, water treatment systems, irrigation projects, sanitation and sewerage systems or solid waste management systems, ports, airports, inland waterways, inland ports or navigational channels to the sea.

Tax incentives for exports
The export profits from a new industrial undertaking satisfying prescribed conditions established in a Free Trade Zone (FTZ), Software Technology Park (STP), or Electronic Hardware Technology Park (EHTP), or a 100% export-oriented undertaking (EOU) or a unit in a Special Economic Zone (SEZ) are exempt from income tax for 10 years, commencing from the first year of manufacture. However, this exemption is available only until the financial year 2010-2011.

The export profits from a new industrial undertaking satisfying prescribed conditions established in an SEZ is eligible for tax exemption of 100% of profits for the first five years, from the year of commencement of manufacturing, followed by a partial tax exemption of 50% of profits for the next five years. A further tax exemption of 50% of the profits for the five years is also available after that, subject to an equal amount of profit being retained and transferred to reserves in the books.

Tax incentives for units in the North Eastern Region of India
Measures are in place to facilitate the development of the Indian North Eastern Region and of the state of Sikkim. Undertakings located in these states which (a) begin to manufacture or produce any eligible article, or (b) undertake substantial expansion, or (c) commence an eligible business between 1 April 2007 to 1 April 2017, are eligible for a 100% deduction of profits for 10 consecutive years.

A list of eligible businesses have been provided by the Indian government. The eligible businesses include hotels (not below two-star category), adventure and leisure sports including ropeways, the provision of medical and health services in nursing homes with a minimum capacity of 25 beds, operating a vocational training institute for hotel management, catering and food crafts, entrepreneurship development, nursing and para-medical training, civil aviation related training, fashion design and industrial training, running information technology related training centre, manufacturing of information technology hardware and bio-technology. Businesses other than the above listed eligible businesses are not entitled to claim the tax holiday.

Tax incentives for hotels/convention centres located in specified districts
A tax holiday of five years is provided to hotels (two, three or four star) and convention centres located in the National Capital Territory of Delhi and the districts of Faridabad, Gurgaon, Gautam Budh Nagar and Ghaziabad, provided that the construction is completed and operations are started between 1 April 2007 and 31 July 2010.

Hotels located in a specified district having a World Heritage Site, if such a hotel is constructed and has started functioning at any time during the period 1 April 2008 to 31 March 2013, it would be eligible for a tax holiday for a period of five years.

India

Tax incentives for certain income relating to offshore banking units and international financial services centre

A scheduled bank, or any bank incorporated by or under the laws of a country outside India, which has an offshore banking unit in an SEZ or an international financial services unit with a specified income which is subject to prescribed conditions, is eligible for a tax exemption of 100% of the specified income for five consecutive years beginning from the year in which the permission under the Indian Banking Regulation Act, 1949 was obtained and for 50% of the specified income for five consecutive years.

Tax incentive of capital expenditure on certain specified businesses

Capital expenditure is allowed at 100% in respect of the following specified businesses:

* Setting up and operating cold chain facilities;
* Setting up and operating warehousing facilities for storage of agriculture produce;
* Laying and operating a cross-country natural gas or crude or petroleum oil pipeline network for distribution, including storage facilities being an integral part of such a network;
* Building and operating a new hotel of two-star or above category in India;
* Building and operating a new hospital with at least 100 beds; and
* Developing and building a housing project under a scheme for slum redevelopment or rehabilitation framed by the government.

The following characteristics and conditions may be noted

* Any sum received or receivable in cash or in kind on transfer, etc., of the capital asset shall be considered as business income, if expenditure on such an asset has been allowed as a deduction under this section;
* Any loss computed in respect of the above specified businesses shall be allowed to be set-off or carried forward and set-off only against the profits and gains of specified businesses; and
* The specified business should:
  * Not be set up by splitting up or reconstruction of a business already in existence;
  * Not be set up by transfer of used machinery or plant exceeding 20% of the total value of the machinery or plant used in such business; and
  * Have been approved by the prescribed authority (i.e., the government).

Withholding taxes

There is an obligation on the payer (either resident or non-resident) of income to deduct tax at source (i.e., withhold tax) when certain specified payments are credited and/or paid. Some of the expenses which require withholding of tax are as shown below:

Resident companies

Nature of payment	Rate of withholding tax (%)
Specified type of Interest	10%
Non-specified type of interest	20%
Professional and technical service fees	10%
Commission and brokerage	10%
Rent of Plant or machinery or equipment	2%

Nature of payment	Rate of withholding tax (%)
Rent of Land or Building or Furniture	10%
Contract Payment (except for Individual / HUF)	2%
Contract Payment to Individual / HUF	1%
Royalty or Fees for technical services	10%

Notes

1. Payments mentioned as above have a different threshold limit, if the payment is above that limit only then this is the payer required to withhold the tax.

Non-resident companies

Nature of payment	Rate of withholding tax (%)
Dividend	0%
Interest on foreign currency	20%
Royalty & Technical fees	10%
Long-term capital gains other than exempt income	20%
Income by way of winning horse races	30%
Other income	40%

Notes

1. Percent to be increased by surcharge and Education assessment to compute effective rate.
2. Income from units of specified mutual funds is exempt from tax in the hands of the unit-holders.
3. Dividends received from Indian companies are tax-free in the hands of the shareholder.
4. Short-term capital gains on transfer of shares of a company or units of an equity oriented fund shall be taxable at 15%, if they have been subjected to STT.
5. Long-term capital gain on transfer of shares (through stock exchange) in listed companies or units of an equity-oriented fund, are exempt from tax if they have been subjected to STT.

Treaty rates

Some tax treaties provide for lower withholding rates from certain types of income, as follows:

Country	Dividend (a)	Interest	Royalty (l)	Fee for technical services (l)
Armenia	10%	10%	10%	10%
Australia	15%	15%	15% (b) 10% in certain cases	15% / 10%
Austria	10%	10%	10%	10%
Albania	Government press release dated 29 January 2009. Treaty yet to be notified			
Bangladesh	10% (c) 15% in other cases	10%	10%	No specific provisions (e)

India

Country	Dividend (a)	Interest	Royalty (l)	Fee for technical services (l)
Belarus	10% (i) 15% in other cases	10%	15%	15%
Belgium	15%	10% (k) 15% in other cases	10%	10%
Botswana	7.5%(i) 10% in other cases	10%	10%	10%
Brazil	15%	15%	25% if royalty payments arise from the use or right to use trademarks, 15% in other cases	No specific provision (e)
Bulgaria	15%	15%	15% (g) 20% in other cases	20%
Canada	15% (c) 25% in other cases	15%	15% / 10% (b)	15% / 10% (b)
China (People's Republic of China)	10%	10%	10%	10%
Croatia	Union cabinet approved the signing of tax treaty on 19 January 2006. Treaty yet to be notified.			
Cyprus	10% (c) 15% in other cases	10%	15% (including fee for included services)	10%
Czech Republic	10%	10%	10%	10%
Denmark	15% (i) 25% in other cases	10% (k) 15% in other cases	20%	20%
Finland	10%	10%	10%	10%
French Republic	10% (f)	10% (f)	10% (f)	10% (f)
Germany (Federal Republic of Germany)	10%	10%	10%	10%
Greece	(n)	(n)	(n)	No specific provisions (e)
Hungary	10% (f)	10% (f)	10% (f)	10% (f)
Iceland	10%	10%	10%	10%
Indonesia	10% (i) 15% in other cases	10%	15%	No specific provision (e)
Ireland	10%	10%	10%	10%
Israel	10%	10%	10%	10%

Country	Dividend (a)	Interest	Royalty (l)	Fee for technical services (l)
Italy	15% (c) 25% in other cases	15%	20%	20%
Japan	10%	10%	10%	10%
Jordan (Hashemite Kingdom of Jordan)	10%	10%	20%	20%
Kazakhstan	10%	10%	10%	10%
Kenya	15%	15%	20%	17.50%
Kuwait	10%	10%	10%	10%
Kyrgyz Republic	10%	10%	15%	15%
Latvia	Government press release dated 18 September 2008. Treaty yet to be notified.			
Libyan Arab Jamahiriya	(n)	(n)	(n)	No specific provision (e)
Luxembourg	10%	10%	10%	10%
Malaysia	10%	10%	10%	10%
Malta	10% (i) 15% in other cases	10%	15% including fee for included services	10%
Mauritius	5% (c) 15% in other cases	(n)	15%	No specific provision (e)
Mexico	Government press release dated 3 April 2008. Treaty yet to be notified.			
Mongolia	15%	15%	15%	15%
Montenegro	5% (i) 15% in other cases	10%	10%	10%
Morocco	10%	10%	10%	10%
Myanmar	5%	10%	10%	No specific provision (e)
Namibia	10%	10%	10%	10%
Nepal	10% (c) in other cases 15%	10% (n) 15% in other cases	15%	No specific provision (e)
Netherlands	10% (f)	10% (f)	10% (f)	10% (f)
New Zealand	15%	10%	10%	10%
Norway	15% (i) 25% in other cases	15%	10%	10%
Oman	10% (c) 12.5% in other cases	10%	15%	15%
Philippines	15% (c) 20% in other cases	10% (m) 15% In other cases	15% subject to approval of agreement	No specific provision (e)
Poland	15%	15%	22.50%	22.50%

India

Country	Dividend (a)	Interest	Royalty (l)	Fee for technical services (l)
Portuguese Republic	10% (i) 15% in other cases	10%	10%	10%
Qatar	5% (c) 10% in other cases	10%	10%	10%
Republic of Korea	15% (d) 20% in other cases	10% (m) 15% in other cases	15%	15%
Romania	15% (i) 20% in other cases	15%	22.50%	22.50%
Russian Federation	10%	10%	10%	10%
Saudi Arabia	5%	10%	10%	No specific provision (e)
Serbia	5% (i) 15% in other cases	10%	10%	10%
Singapore	10% (i) 15% in other cases	10% (k) 15% in other cases	10%	10%
Slovenia	5% (c) 15% in other cases	10%	10%	10%
South Africa	10%	10%	10%	10%
Spain	15%	15%	10% (f)	20% (f)
Sri Lanka	15%	10%	10%	10 % (f)
Sudan	10%	10%	10%	10%
Sweden	10% (f)	10% (f)	10% (f)	10% (f)
Swiss Confederation	10%	10%	10%	10%
Syria Arab Republic	Exempt	7.50%	10%	No specific provision (e)
Tazakstan	5% (c) 10% in other cases	10%	10%	No specific provision (e)
Tanzania	10% (c) 15 % in other cases	12.50%	20%	20% on management and professional fees
Thailand	15% (c and h) 20% (i or h)	10% (m) 25% in other cases	15%	No specific provision (e)
Trinidad & Tobago	10%	10%	10%	10%
Turkey	15%	10% (k) 15% in other cases	15%	15%
Turkmenistan	10%	10%	10%	10%

Country	Dividend (a)	Interest	Royalty (l)	Fee for technical services (l)
Uganda	10%	10%	10%	10%
Ukraine	10% (i) 15% in other cases	10%	10%	10%
United Arab Emirates	10%	5% (k) 12.5% in other cases	10%	No specific provision (e)
United Arab Republic (Egypt)	No specific provision (e)	No specific provision (e)	No specific provision (e)	No specific provision (e)
United Kingdom	15%	10% (m) 15% in other cases	10% (b) 15% In other cases	10% (b) 15% In other cases
United States of America	15% (c) 25% in other cases	10% (k) 15% in other cases	10% (b) 15% In other cases	10% (b) 15% In other cases
Uzbekistan	15%	15%	15%	15%
Vietnam	10%	10%	10%	10%
Zambia	5% (j) 15% in other cases	10%	10%	10% on managerial and consultancy fees

Notes

a. The treaty tax rates on dividends are not relevant since under the current Indian tax legislation, most dividend income from Indian companies which is subject to Dividend Distribution Tax is exempt from income tax in the hands of the recipient.
b. 10% for equipment rental and ancillary services:
    • For other cases in the first 5 years – 15% if government or specified organisation is the payer and 20% for other payers; and
    • For subsequent years – 15% in all cases (income of government/government organisations exempt from Taxation in the country of source).
c. If at least 10% of capital is owned by the beneficial owner (company) of the company paying the dividend or interest.
d. If at least 20% of capital is owned by the beneficial owner (company) of the company paying dividend or interest.
e. In absence of specific provision, it may be treated as business profits or independent personal services under respective treaties, whichever is applicable.
f. The "most favoured nation" clause is applicable. The protocol to the treaty limits the scope and rate of taxation to that specified in similar articles in treaties signed by India with an OECD or another country.
g. If royalty relates to copyrights of literary, artistic or scientific work.
h. The company paying dividend is engaged in an industrial undertaking.
i. If at least 25% of capital is owned by the beneficial owner (company) of the company paying the dividend.
j. If at least 25% of capital is owned by the company during at least six months before date of payment.
k. If paid on a loan granted by a bank / financial institution.

India

I. The tax rate for royalties and fees for technical services, under the domestic tax laws, is 10%. This rate is to be increased by a surcharge at 2.5% on the income tax and education cess at 2% and secondary and higher secondary education cess at 1% on the income tax including surcharge. As a consequence, the effective tax rate is 10.558%. This rate applies for payments made under an agreement entered into on or after 1 June 2005. Accordingly, a tax resident can either use the Treaty rate or domestic tax rate, whichever is more beneficial.
m. If interest is received by a financial institution.
n. Taxable in the country of source as per domestic tax rates.

List of limited agreements between India and other countries

A list of the countries with which India has entered into limited agreements for double taxation relief with respect to income of airlines/merchant shipping follows:

Country	Government notification reference
Afghanistan	GSR 514(E), dated 30.09.1975
Bulgaria	GSR 184(E), dated 15.04.1977
Ethiopia	GSR 8(E), dated 04.01.1978 as corrected by Notification No. GSR 159(E), dated 02.03.1978
Iran	GSR 284(E), dated 28.05.1973
Kuwait	GSR 302(E), dated 31.03.1983
Lebanon	Nos. GSR 1552 and 1553, dated 28.06.1969
Oman	GSR 313(E), dated 27.03.1985
Pakistan	GSR 792(E), dated 29.08.1989
People's Democratic Republic of Yemen	GSR 857(E), dated 12.08.1988
Romania	GSR 2203 dated 20.12.1968
Russian Federation	GSR 943(E), dated 23.12.1976 as modified by GSR 419(E), dated 31.05.1984, dated GSR 952(E), dated 30.12.1992
Saudi Arabia	GSR 950(E), dated 29.12.1992
Switzerland	GSR 761, dated 29.08.1958
UAE	GSR 969(E), dated 08.01.1989
Yemen Arab Republic	GSR 2(E), dated 01.12.1987

Tax administration

Accounts for tax purposes must be made up to 31 March. The electronic return of income is required to be filed by 30 September of the financial year.

Quarterly withholding tax returns

Quarterly statement of taxes withheld are to be filed electronically with the tax authorities on or before 15 July, 15 October and 15 January for the first three calendar quarters of the financial year and on or before 15 June following the last calendar quarter of the financial year.

Payment of tax

Tax is payable in advance (if tax for the year exceeds INR 10,000) in specified instalments during the financial year (April to March) immediately preceding the assessment year in respect of the income of the financial year ending 31 March. Any balance of tax due on the basis of the return must be paid on a self-assessment basis before the return is filed.

Other issues

Mergers and acquisitions

The term "merger" has not been defined in the act but has been covered as part of under the definition of the term "amalgamation". Amalgamation is defined as merger of one or more companies with another or the merger of two or more companies to form a new company, in such a way that all the assets and liabilities of the amalgamating company or companies become the assets and liabilities of the amalgamated company and shareholders holding not less than 75% in value of the shares in the amalgamating company or companies become shareholders of the amalgamated company.

Capital gains

No capital gains tax is levied on the transfer of capital assets by an amalgamating company to the amalgamated company, provided the amalgamated company is an Indian company. Similar is the position in case of a demerger by a demerged company to a resulting company.

In case where shares of an Indian company are transferred by a foreign company or demerged foreign company to any another foreign company or resulting foreign company, there is no tax payable provided it satisfies certain specified conditions. Furthermore, the shareholder of the amalgamating company or demerged company is not liable to pay capital gains tax on the exchange of shares with that of amalgamating company or the resulting company under the scheme of amalgamation.

Carryforward of accumulated losses of amalgamating company

The losses and unabsorbed depreciation of amalgamating company are deemed to be those of the amalgamated company in the year in which the amalgamation takes place provided it satisfy certain specified conditions.

In case of amalgamation of a company owning an industrial undertaking, the amalgamated company shall achieve the level of production of at least 50% of the installed capacity of the undertaking before the end of the four years from the date of amalgamation and continue to maintain the minimum level of production till the end of five years from the date of amalgamation. If the above conditions are violated, the benefit claimed will be taxed in the hands of the amalgamated company in the year of default.

In case of demerger of a company, the accumulated losses or unabsorbed depreciation of the demerged company directly relatable to the undertaking or the division transferred is allowed to be carried forward and set-off in the hands of the resulting company.

Amalgamation or demerger of co-operative banks

An amalgamated or resulting co-operative bank is eligible for set-off and carryforward of the unabsorbed losses or accumulated depreciation of the amalgamating or demerged co-operative bank subject to fulfilment of certain conditions.

India

The following transactions are not liable for capital gains tax and, thus, tax neutral:

1. The transfer of a capital asset in business reorganisation by a predecessor co-operative bank to a successor co-operative bank; and
2. The transfer by a shareholder, in a business reorganisation of capital assets, of a share or shares held, in the predecessor co-operative bank, if the transfer is made as part of an allotment to the predecessor of any share or shares in the successor co-operative bank.

Transfer pricing
The Indian transfer pricing code stipulates that income arising from 'international transactions' between 'associated enterprises' should be computed at arm's-length price. Furthermore, any allowance for expenses or interest arising from any international transaction is also to be determined at arm's-length price.

The expressions 'international transactions' and 'associated enterprises' have been defined. Various methods for computation of arm's-length price have been specified and a taxpayer is required to adopt the most appropriate method. The taxpayer is also required to maintain a comprehensive set of prescribed information and documents relating to international transactions which are undertaken between associated enterprises. The burden of proving the arm's-length character of the transaction is primarily on the taxpayer.

Where the transfer pricing officer is of the opinion that the arm's-length price was not applied, he or she may re-compute the taxable income after giving the taxpayer an opportunity to be heard. Stringent penal provisions apply in cases of failure to comply with the provisions of the transfer pricing code.

To facilitate quick resolution of disputes, the Finance (No. 2) Act, 2009 has provided for an alternative dispute resolution mechanism and constituted a new Dispute Resolution Panel (DRP) comprising three Commissioners of Income-Tax. In cases of foreign companies, the transfer pricing orders passed by the tax officer (TO) on or after 1 October 2009 and which are prejudicial to the taxpayer, the AO shall be required to issue a draft order to the taxpayer. The taxpayer can file objections against the draft order before the DRP. After considering all evidence or objections and further enquiries, the DRP would issue binding directions to the AO within a period of nine months. The AO is required to pass an order within one month, in conformity with the directions of the DRP. Orders passed by an AO on the basis of directions of the DRP are appealable directly before the tax tribunal.

In order to lessen the litigation under transfer pricing regulations, provisions empowering the issue of safe harbour rules are contained in the tax law which would be separately issued by the Central Board of Direct. The safe harbour rules are not yet issued. The rules would provide the circumstances in which the tax authorities would accept the transfer price as declared by the assessee.

Taxpayers enjoying a tax holiday in India are also required to comply with the transfer pricing code.

Tonnage tax scheme

The tonnage tax scheme can be elected by an Indian company which has a place of effective management in India, owns at least one qualifying ship and whose main object is to carry on the business of operating ships. The tonnage tax scheme is in place of taxation on net income generated by commercial operations.

In relation to non-resident shipping companies that have a regular shipping income, there are presumptive tax provisions applicable to non-resident shipping companies with a regular shipping income. Under the tonnage tax scheme, deemed income shall be assessed at a rate of 7.5% of the amount paid or payable (whether in or out of India) for carriage of passengers, livestock, mail or goods shipped at any port in India and the amount received or deemed to be received in India on account of carriage of passengers, livestock, mail or goods shipped at any port outside India shall be treated as profits and gains of the business or profession. Tax rates as applicable to non-resident after considering the treaty provisions will be applied.

Under a presumptive tax system a taxpayer can opt to be taxed on their income at a pre-designated tax rate.

It should be noted that non-resident shipping companies who have occasional shipping income can opt for the tonnage tax scheme as well. Presumptive tax provisions are applicable to non-resident shipping companies which have occasional shipping income. For non-resident companies with occasional shipping, deemed income shall be taxed at a rate of 7.5% of the amount paid or payable (whether in or out of India) for carriage of passengers, livestock, mail or goods shipped at any port in India shall be treated as profits and gains of business or profession. Tax rates as applicable to non-resident after considering the treaty provisions.

A government company or a public company formed and registered in India with the main object to operate ships is eligible for a deduction not exceeding 50% of the profits to the extent that it is transferred to a special reserve created for the purpose which is utilised in accordance with the provisions of the Act.

Corporate taxes in Indonesia

For more information, contact:

Ray Headifen
PricewaterhouseCoopers
Jl HR Rasuna Said Kav X-7 No. 6
Jakarta 12940, Indonesia
Tel: +62 21 521 2901
Email: ray.headifen@id.pwc.com

Significant developments

The corporate tax rate was reduced from a flat rate of 28% to 25% from 1 January 2010. Public companies, subject to a minimum share listing of 40% and other conditions, are entitled to a 5% tax discount off the normal rate. Indonesian bond interest income is subject to a final tax rate of 15%, which was reduced from the previous rate of 20%.

The recent focus of the Indonesian Tax Office (ITO) has been directed at tax treaty abuse and cross-border related party transactions. This follows the general tax review that led to the 2009 and 2010 reductions in the corporate income tax rate and the introduction of the amended value-added tax (VAT) law in 2009, with effect from 1 April 2010.

The requirement to obtain the benefit of a reduced treaty withholding tax (WHT) rate as from 1 January 2010 became more difficult for foreign taxpayers to satisfy. Firstly, the ITO introduced a new form of certificate of domicile (CoD) that must be certified by a recipient's home country tax authority in the form required by the ITO. The CoD in the form prepared by the other country's tax authority may only be used in limited circumstances. Further, the CoD form also requires a number of declarations to be made by the recipient that acknowledge the use of the treaty jurisdiction was not done merely to obtain the benefit of the treaty. These declarations place onerous obligations on both the Indonesian payer and the recipient entity.

During 2009, the ITO significantly increased its focus on related party arrangements. It is now heavily focused on transfer pricing in its ongoing audits, and has indicated that it will commence a number of transfer pricing specific audits. Taxpayers must now make detailed disclosures in their annual corporate income tax return pertaining to their level of transfer pricing documentation, the method used and the reasons why the method is appropriate. Taxpayers that have not prepared adequate documentation can likely expect a tax audit.

The amendments to the VAT law, which were announced in 2009 and took effect from 1 April 2010, generally only reflect changes of an administrative nature, rather than a fundamental change in the VAT system. However, the new requirement that a valid VAT invoice be delivered at the time of the taxable delivery (as opposed to the previous deadline of the end of the month following the taxable delivery) will force a change in the administrative practices of many taxpayers.

Taxes on corporate income

Corporate tax

A flat corporate income tax rate of 25% applies from 2010. Public companies that satisfy a minimum listing requirement of 40% and certain other conditions are entitled to a tax discount of 5% off the standard rate, providing an effective tax rate of 20% in 2010. Small enterprises (i.e., corporate taxpayers with an annual turnover of not more than IDR 50 billion) are entitled to a tax discount of 50% off the standard rate, which is imposed proportionally on taxable income of the part of gross turnover up to IDR 4.8 billion.

Certain types of income are subject to a final income tax at a specified percentage of the gross amount of income, without regard to any attributable expenses:

	Tax rate (%)
Rentals of land and building	10
Proceeds from transfers of land and building rights	5
Fees for construction work performance	2/3/4
Fees for construction work planning	4/6
Fees for construction work supervision	4/6
Interest on time or saving deposits and on Bank of Indonesia Certificates (SBIs) other than that payable to banks operating in Indonesia and to government-approved pension funds	20
Interest on bonds other than that payable to banks operating in Indonesia and government-approved pension funds	15
Sale of exchange-traded shares on the Indonesian stock exchange	0.1
Income from lottery prizes	25
Forward contract derivatives	2.5

Expenses relating to gross income subject to "final" tax are not deductible

Corporate residence

A company is treated as a resident of Indonesia for tax purposes by virtue of having its establishment or its place of management in Indonesia. A foreign company carrying out business activities through a permanent establishment (PE) in Indonesia will generally be required to assume the same tax obligations as a resident taxpayer.

Other taxes

Value-added tax (VAT) / Luxury-goods sales tax (LST)

The VAT Law has been amended and took effect from 1 April 2010. The amendments are mostly administrative and do not fundamentally change the VAT system.

With a few exceptions, VAT is applicable on deliveries (sales) of goods and services within Indonesia at a rate of 10%. VAT on export of goods is zero-rated while the import of goods is subject to VAT at a rate of 10%. From 1 April 2010 zero-rated VAT is also applicable on exported services, but subject to a Minister of Finance (MoF) limitation. Currently, only certain services, including toll manufacturing services, are subject to the 0% VAT rate. Other exported services, not specifically defined by the

Indonesia

MoF, are subject to a 10% VAT rate. Inbound use or consumption of foreign services or intangible goods, with a few exceptions, is also subject to a self-assessed VAT at a rate of 10%.

The VAT law allows the government to change the VAT rate within range of 5% to 15%. However, since the enactment of the VAT law in 1984, the government has never changed the VAT rate.

In addition to VAT, some goods are subject to LST upon import or delivery by the manufacturer to another party at rates ranging from 10% to 75%, however, from 1 April 2010, the maximum rate may be as high as 200%.

Land and buildings tax
Land and buildings tax is due annually at 5% of the government-determined sales value.

In a land and building transfer, the acquirer is liable for duty on the acquisition of land and building rights at 5% of the greater of the transaction value or the government-determined value

Stamp duty
Stamp duty is nominal and payable as a fixed amount of either IDR 6,000 or IDR 3,000 on certain documents.

Branch income

Branch profits are subject to the ordinary corporate tax rate of 25%. The after-tax profits are subject to a withholding tax (WHT) at 20%, regardless of whether the profits are remitted to the home country. However, a concessional WHT rate may be applicable where a tax treaty is in force (*see Withholding taxes*).

Income determination

Inventory valuation
Inventories must be measured at cost by using either the average or first-in first-out (FIFO) methods. Once a costing method is adopted, it must be applied consistently.

Capital gains
Capital gains are generally assessable together with ordinary income and subject to tax at the standard corporate tax rate. However, gains from the transfer of land and buildings are no longer subject to tax but rather are subject to final income tax at a rate of 5% of the transaction value or the government-determined value, whichever is higher. (Refer to *Taxes on Corporate Income.*)

The proceeds from sales of shares listed on Indonesian stock exchanges are not subject to normal income tax. Instead, the proceeds are subject only to a final WHT of 0.1% of the gross sales consideration. An additional tax of 0.5% applies to the share value of founder shares at the time an initial public offering takes place, irrespective of whether the shares are held or sold. Shareholders may elect not to pay this tax, in which case the actual gain will be subject to normal tax at the time the shares are sold.

Inter-company dividends

In principle, dividend income received by a resident taxpayer from a limited liability company (generally referred to as a PT company) is taxable as ordinary income for the taxpayer receiving the dividend. However, if the dividend recipient is a PT company with a minimum shareholding of 25% in the company paying the dividend, the income tax is exempt. In this respect, the 2008 Income Tax Law removed the previous active business condition for obtaining the income tax exemption.

Where the recipient is not resident in Indonesia, a WHT rate of 20% applies, subject to variation by tax treaties *(see Withholding taxes)*.

The rule regarding inter-company dividends also applies to stock dividends (bonus shares) including dividends paid out of share premium ("agio").

Foreign income

Foreign branch income of an Indonesian company must be accounted for as Indonesian taxable income under the controlled foreign corporations (CFCs) regulation. These rules apply to Indonesian tax residents owning at least 50% of the paid-up capital (shares) in a CFC. The rules make no reference to such terms as tax avoidance or tax evasion and therefore, apply even if the CFC is domiciled in a non-tax haven country. The only situation in which the rules do not apply is when the CFC's shares are listed on a recognised stock exchange. In very broad terms, under the CFC rules, the Indonesian shareholder of the CFC is deemed to receive a dividend with respect to the CFC profits based on a shareholding proportional calculation.

Stock dividends

The rule for inter-company dividends in general also applies to stock dividends. However, the tax exemption may not be applicable if the stock dividends represent capitalisation of agio.

Exchange gains and losses

Gains and losses arising from currency fluctuations are generally recognised on an accrual basis in accordance with the prevailing Indonesian Accounting Standards, which resemble International Accounting Standards in most respects.

Deductions

Depreciation and amortisation

Depreciable/amortisable assets include both tangible and intangible property with a useful life of more than one year, except land that is owned and used in business. Depreciation and amortisation may be calculated under the straight-line method or the declining-balance method on an individual asset basis. Once a method is chosen, it should be applied consistently. In calculating depreciation, depreciable assets are divided into the following classes:

	Depreciation rate	
Class	Straight-line method	Declining-balance method
	%	%
Property:		
Useful life of 4 years	25	50
Useful life of 8 years	12.5	25

Indonesia

	Depreciation rate	
Class	Straight-line method	Declining-balance method
	%	%
Useful life of 16 years	6.25	12.5
Useful life of 20 years	5	10
Buildings:		
Permanent	5	–
Non-permanent	10	–

Special rules apply for assets used in certain business fields and/or certain areas. Tax depreciation need not conform to book depreciation.

The cost incurred for acquiring the rights, with a beneficial life of more than one year, for mining, oil and natural gas concessions; forest concessions; and other rights to exploit natural resources should be amortised by the production-unit method. Except for the right to acquire oil and natural gas concessions, the depletion rate used should not exceed 20% per annum.

Net operating losses
Losses may be carried forward for a maximum period of five years. Carrying back of losses is not permitted. Offsetting losses within a corporate group is not permitted.

Payments to foreign affiliates
Withholding tax is applied as a final tax on the recipient for payments of royalties, interest and service fees to foreign non-resident companies. Excessive and non-arm's-length payments to related parties are disallowed as deductions. The tax law denies deductions for all payments from a branch to its head office for royalties, interest and services provided by the head office (exceptions apply for loans between bank branches and their head offices).

Taxes
Land and buildings tax and regional taxes may be deducted from taxable income. With several exceptions, input VAT is also deductible against taxable income as long as it is not claimed as a credit against output VAT.

Non-deductible items
Benefits in kind
Most benefits received in-kind by employees, such as free housing, are not tax-deductible to the entity providing the benefit. Free motor vehicle and telephone expenses, including depreciation, are tax-deductible but only for 50% of the total expenses incurred. Expenses for meals and transportation made available to all staff are tax-deductible. Apart from these, benefits in kind, such as housing provided in remote areas as designated by the Minister of Finance and Integrated Economic Development Areas as designated by Presidential Decree, can also be claimed as tax-deductible expenses.

Other significant items
The Minister of Finance is authorised to make a determination on an appropriate ratio of debt to equity. Under the law, debt between related parties may be recharacterised as equity, thus giving rise to the disallowance of a tax deduction for related costs. However, the MoF has not yet issued a ruling on these matters.

Group taxation

Consolidated returns are not allowed.

Tax incentives

Inward investment

The Director General of Tax (DGT), on behalf of the Finance Minister and based on the recommendation of the National Board of Investment (BKPM) chairman, may provide the following tax concessions to Indonesian limited liability (PT) companies following their investment in certain designated business areas or in certain designated regions:

- A reduction in net income of up to 30% of the amount invested (generally amount spent on assets), prorated at 5% for six years from commercial production date, provided that the assets invested are not transferred out within six years;
- Acceleration of fiscal depreciation deductions;
- Extension of tax loss carryforwards for up to 10 years; and
- A reduction of the WHT rate on dividends paid to non-residents to 10%.

The same tax facilities may be granted by the DGT to companies conducting business in an Integrated Economic Development Area (KAPET). Specific approval must be obtained from the DGT for these tax facilities. If the company has bonded zone (KB) status, the tax facilities will also include those typically enjoyed by a KB company, for example:

- Non-collection of VAT and sales tax on certain luxury goods transactions;
- Exemption from prepaid income tax (Article 22) on the importation of capital goods and other equipment directly relating to production activities;
- Postponement of import duty on capital goods and equipment and goods and materials for processing; and
- Exemption from import duty for four years on machinery and certain spare parts.

The designation of an area as a KAPET is set out in a specific presidential decree. Currently, there are approximately 25 areas designated as KAPETs.

Reinvestment of branch profits

PEs that reinvest their after-tax profits in Indonesia within the same year or in the following year are exempt from branch profit tax on these profits. Reinvestment requires the branch head office to invest in an Indonesian company as a founder shareholder in the following tax year. Shares may not be transferred for at least two years from the date of the company commences commercial production.

Tax-neutral merger

Transfers of assets in business mergers, consolidations, or business splits must generally be dealt with at market value. Gains resulting from this kind of restructuring are assessable, while losses are generally claimable as a deduction from income.

However, a tax-neutral merger or consolidation, under which assets are transferred at book value, can be conducted but subject to the approval of the DGT. To obtain this approval, the merger or consolidation plan in question must pass a business-purpose test. Tax-driven arrangements are prohibited and therefore tax losses from the combining companies may not be passed to the surviving company.

Indonesia

Subject to a similar, specific DGT approval, the same concession is also available for business splits that constitute part of an initial public offering (IPO) plan. In this case, within one year of the DGT's approval being given, the company concerned must have made an effective declaration regarding registration for an IPO with the Capital Market Supervisory Board (BAPEPAM). In the event of complications beyond the company's control, the period may be extended by the DGT for up to four years.

Other incentives

Income earned by venture capital companies in the form of profit-sharing from their investments in Indonesia is exempt from tax, provided that the following conditions are met:

1. Entities are small or medium-scale businesses in one of the sectors designated by the Indonesian government.
2. Investments are not listed on the Indonesian stock exchange.

Withholding taxes (WHT)

Withholding tax is levied on a variety of payments to corporations and individuals, resident and non-resident, at the following rates:

	Notes	Dividends Portfolio	Dividends Substantial holdings	Interest	Royalties	Branch profits
		%	%	%	%	%
Resident corporations	6	15	Nil	15	15	N/A
Resident individuals		10	10	15	15	N/A
Non-resident corporations and individuals						
Non-treaty:		20	20	20	20	20/0
Treaty:						
Algeria		15	15	15/0	15	10
Australia		15	15	10/0	15/10	15
Austria		15	10	10/0	10	12
Bangladesh		15	10	10/0	10	10
Belgium		15	10	10/0	10	10
Brunei		15	15	15/0	15	10
Bulgaria		15	15	10/0	10	15
Canada		15	10	10/0	10	15
China		10	10	10/0	10	10
Czech Republic		15	10	12.5/0	12.5	12.5
Denmark		20	10	10/0	15	15
Egypt		15	15	15/0	15	15
Finland		15	10	10/0	15/10	15
France		15	10	15/10/0	10	10
Germany	1	15	10	10/0	15/10	10
Hungary	3, 4	15	15	15/0	15	20
India		15	10	10/0	15	10
Italy		15	10	10/0	15/10	12

	Notes	Dividends Portfolio	Substantial holdings	Interest	Royalties	Branch profits
		%	%	%	%	%
Japan		15	10	10/0	10	10
Jordan	3	10	10	10/0	10	20
Korea (North)		10	10	10/0	10	10
Korea (South)	2	15	10	10/0	15	10
Kuwait	4	10	10	5/0	20	10/0
Luxembourg	1	15	10	10/0	12.5	10
Malaysia	5	15	15	15/0	15	12.5
Mexico		10	10	10/0	10	10
Mongolia		10	10	10/0	10	10
Netherlands		10	10	10/0	10	10
New Zealand	3	15	15	10/0	15	20
Norway		15	15	10/0	15/10	15
Pakistan	1	15	10	15/0	15	10
Philippines		20	15	15/10/0	15	20
Poland		15	10	10/0	15	10
Portugal		10	10	10/0	15	10
Qatar		10	10	10	5	10
Romania		15	12.5	12.5/0	15/12.5	12.5
Russia		15	15	15/0	15	12.5
Seychelles		10	10	10/0	10	20
Singapore		15	10	10/0	15	15
Slovakia		10	10	10/0	15/10	10
South Africa	3,4	15	10	10/0	10	20
Spain		15	10	10/0	10	10
Sri Lanka	3	15	15	15/0	15	20
Sudan		10	10	15/0	10	10
Sweden		15	10	10/0	15/10	15
Switzerland	1	15	10	10/0	10	10
Syria		10	10	10	20/15	10
Taiwan		10	10	10/0	10	5
Thailand		20	15	15	15	20
Tunisia		12	12	12/0	15	12
Turkey		15	10	10/0	10	10
Ukraine		15	10	10/0	10	10
United Arab Emirates		10	10	5/0	5	5
United Kingdom		15	10	10/0	15/10	10
United States		15	10	10/0	10/0	10
Uzbekistan		10	10	10/0	10/0	10
Venezuela		15	10	10/0	20/10	10
Vietnam		15	15	15/0	15	10

Indonesia

Notes

1. Fees for technical, management and consulting services rendered in Indonesia are subject to WHT at rates of 5%, 7.5%, 10% and 15% for Switzerland, Germany, Luxembourg and Pakistan, respectively.
2. VAT is reciprocally exempt from the income earned on the operation of ships or aircraft in international lanes.
3. The treaty is silent concerning branch profit tax rate. The ITO interprets this to mean that the tax rate under Indonesian Tax Law (20%) should apply.
4. Tax only applies if the profits are remitted.
5. Subject to protocol ratification, Labuan may be excluded from the territory of Malaysia for tax treaty purposes and the WHT on interest, dividends, and royalties may be reduced to 10%.
6. In the case of dividends received by a resident shareholder, "portfolio shareholding" refers to share ownership of less than 25% of the paid-up capital. In this respect, the dividend tax withheld by the payer constitutes a prepayment of the income tax liability of the shareholder. "Substantial shareholding" refers to the share ownership of 25% of the paid-up capital or more.

Domestic WHT is also payable at the rate of 2% for most types of services where the recipient of the payment is an Indonesian resident.

The issue of beneficial ownership has come under tax office scrutiny. For treaty WHT rates to apply to passive income such as interests, dividends, and royalties, the recipient of such income must be the beneficial owner. The recipient must also provide a CoD certified by their home country tax authority, certifying that the recipient is a tax resident of that country. Without a certified CoD, a WHT at a rate of 20% will apply. These aspects need to be considered when paying income of this nature.

In addition to the above treaties, Indonesia has signed tax treaties with Armenia, Hong Kong, Iran, Myanmar, Morocco, Papua New Guinea and Tajikistan. However, these treaties are not yet effective, pending the exchange of ratification documents. There are also agreements with Saudi Arabia, Croatia and Laos for the reciprocal exemption of taxes and customs duties on the activities of the two countries' air transport enterprises.

Other than passive income such as interests, dividends, and royalties, Indonesian income tax is also collected from certain types of transactions, such as:

- Importation of goods;
- Sale of goods to the government;
- Sale or purchase of certain products;
- Sale or purchase of very luxurious goods; and
- Payment of certain services.

Tax administration

Tax returns and payments
Tax liabilities for a particular period or year must typically be paid to the State Treasury through a designated tax-payment bank and then accounted for at the DGT office through the filing of the relevant tax returns. The tax payments and tax return filing for a particular tax must be undertaken monthly or annually, depending upon the tax obligation in question.

Corporate tax returns must be filed on an annual basis. A pre-payment system operates for corporate tax whereby monthly instalments must be paid based on previous year tax liability.

Returns for transaction taxes such as WHT must be filed on a monthly basis. Payments are generally required by the tenth or fifteenth day of the following month. Under the new VAT law, which was effective from 1 April 2010, VAT filing is done on a monthly basis, with payment and filing being due no later than the last day of the month following the taxable delivery.

I

Corporate taxes in Iraq

For more information, contact:

Kenny Hawsey
PricewaterhouseCoopers Al Juraid
King Faisal Foundation Building
10th Floor – North Tower
King Fahad Road, Olaya
Riyadh
Saudi Arabia
Tel: +966 1 456 4240
Email: kenny.b.hawsey@sa.pwc.com

Significant developments

In February 2010, the Iraqi Presidency Counsel issued a new law that imposes income tax at the rate of 35% on the income realised in Iraq from contracts concluded with foreign oil companies, its branches or offices and subcontractors working in Iraq in the oil and gas production sector and related industries.

Taxes on corporate income

All income derived from Iraq is subject to tax in Iraq regardless of the residence of the recipient. In addition, income that is realised outside Iraq by Iraqi and other residents, including interest, commissions, investment returns and profits from trading in currencies, valuable metals and securities, is taxable if such income arises from funds and deposits held in Iraq.

The effective corporate income tax system method presented in Iraq for juristic persons (except partnerships), is based on the statutory income tax rate of 15% at all income levels with no progressive tax rate scale.

The income realised in Iraq from contracts concluded with foreign oil companies, its branches or offices and subcontractors working in Iraq in the oil and gas production sector and related industries should be taxed at a rate of 35%.

Corporate residence

It is important to note that the current Iraq income tax law does not clearly define a permanent establishment (PE); therefore, it is important to monitor commercial activity being performed in the country to ensure compliance with the registration requirements and tax law. The company should consult with their internal tax department and external advisers if they have signed a contract to provide any type of services inside Iraq to determine if the company should have a legal registration and begin to file corporate income tax (CIT) returns.

One of the key issues in determining when a company becomes taxable in Iraq is whether the foreign company is considered to be doing business "in Iraq" or "with Iraq". In 2009, with Instructions No. 2/2008, the Iraqi tax administration provided a clearer distinction between business in Iraq and business with Iraq.

Other taxes

In addition to the CIT, the following taxes may apply:

Stamp duty

All direct and indirect contracts related to credit facilities and other bank's activities (e.g., letter of credit contracts), are subject to the stamp fees at a rate of 0.2 of the contract value.

Custom duty

The customs duty system and procedures in Iraq are currently evolving. In March 2010, the Iraqi Presidency Counsel issued Law 12 of 2010 (Custom Tariff Law). The new law comprises 11 articles and primarily addresses custom duties on goods imported into Iraq. The law notes that customs duties shall be levied based on percentages set in the custom tariff and agricultural agenda that is annexed to the Custom Tariff Law. For the purposes of the Custom Tariff Law, the custom tariff and agricultural agenda refers to the schedule comprising itemised codified, section and notes based on the international harmonised system adopted by the World Customs Organization (WCO).

Other taxes

A sales tax of 10% of the value of services is imposed on services rendered by deluxe and first class restaurants and hotels in Iraq.

Branch income

The tax treatment for the branch is similar to the local Iraqi corporation. Therefore, in general, income tax is imposed on corporate entities and foreign branches with respect to taxable profit from all sources arising or deemed to arise in Iraq.

Income is deemed to arise in Iraq if either of the following is located there:

- The place of performance of work; or
- The place of delivery of work.

However, certain limitations apply to head office expenses. The limitation up to 10% of taxable income is allowed.

Income determination

A corporation has to determine its profit/loss according to its income statement for a tax period as established under the General Accepted Accounting Principle (GAAP). However, to reach the taxable income, positive or negative adjustments have to be made to the profit/loss as determined according to GAAP.

In general, all expenses incurred by the taxpayer in order to produce income during the year are deducted from income, provided that such expenses are confirmed by acceptable documents, with some exceptions. The expenses not deductible in accordance with Iraqi tax law include real estate tax, corporate tax, loss on assets sold and the difference between the deprecation and amortisation expenses in accordance with GAAP and Iraqi tax law.

Bribes and illegal payments are not allowed or deductable.

Iraq

Capital vs. ordinary gains

Capital gains on sales of depreciable assets are taxed at the normal CIT rates. Gains derived from the sale of shares and bonds not in the course of a trading activity are exempt from tax. Capital gains derived from the sale of shares and bonds in the course of a trading activity are taxable at the normal corporate income tax rate.

Dividend income

Under the tax law, dividends paid out of profits that have been subject to tax, are not taxed again in the hands of the shareholder.

Deductions

Net operating loss

Under the tax law, loss of a taxpayer in some sources of income arising in Iraq, substantiated by legally accepted documents, are generally deducted from profits arising from other sources. Losses, which cannot be settled in this manner, are carried forward and deducted from the income of the taxpayer over five consecutive years, provided that losses may not offset more than half of the taxable income of each of the five years, and the loss is from the same source of income from which it has arisen.

Depreciation

The Iraqi Depreciation Committee sets the maximum depreciation rates for various types of fixed assets. If the rates used for accounting purposes are greater than the prescribed rates, the excess is disallowed.

Group taxation

Iraqi law does not contain any provisions for filing consolidated returns or for relieving losses within a group of companies.

Tax incentives

In accordance with the Iraqi Investment Law, approved industrial, hotels and tourism projects are given certain custom duty and tax incentives; however, oil and gas is not one of the sectors that is normally granted investment promotion exemptions incentives.

The Board of Investment Promotion has the authority to add any sector or specific project to the list of sectors or projects that benefit from the investment promotion law incentives.

Withholding taxes (WHT)

Under the tax law, the amount due from any residing taxpayers to a non-resident, whether the payment is made in cash or credited to the account, is subject to withholding taxes (WHT) at the rate of 15%, if such amounts are related to interest on debentures, mortgages, loans, deposits and advances, as well as annual allowances, pension salaries or other yearly payments.

Tax administration

Iraqi GAAP
The Iraqi tax law requires all taxpayers to maintain books and records in accordance with Iraq's local unified accounting system (Iraqi GAAP).

These books shall constitute tax books/accounts. This accounting treatment will determine when income is accrued and costs are incurred for computing taxable profits.

Returns
The statutory time line for filing tax returns is the first day of June of the year of assessment. If the self assessment of tax is not accepted by the tax authorities, tax is assessed on the income of the taxpayer based on the information available to the tax authorities. Failure to file a tax return may lead to an estimate of income and assessment of tax by the tax authorities; however, such an assessment does not relieve the taxpayer from responsibility for non-submission of the return within the statutory time line stipulated by law.

I

Corporate taxes in Ireland

For more information, contact:

Colm Kelly
PricewaterhouseCoopers
One Spencer Dock
North Wall Quay
Dublin 1
Ireland
Tel: +353 1 792 6866
Email: colm.kelly@ie.pwc.com

Significant developments

Transfer pricing

In April 2010, Ireland enacted broad based transfer pricing legislation. The legislation endorses the Organisation for Economic Co-operation and Development (OECD) Transfer Pricing Guidelines for Multinational Enterprises and Tax Administrations and adopts the arm's-length principle. The introduction of general transfer pricing legislation in Ireland was widely anticipated and brings the Irish tax regime into line with international norms in this area. The new regime applies to domestic as well as international related party arrangements and will come into effect for accounting periods commencing on or after 1 January 2011 in relation to certain arrangements entered into on or after 1 July 2010.

The new rules will be confined to related party dealings that are taxable at Ireland's corporate tax rate of 12.5% (that is, trading transactions). Arrangements entered into between related parties prior to 1 July 2010 are excluded from the new regime and there is also an exemption for small and medium enterprises. The new rules will help multinationals to support and defend the level of income and expenses being attributed to their Irish operations

Intellectual property (IP) regime

May 2009 saw the introduction of a new, and widely welcomed, IP regime to the Irish tax code. This regime provided for a tax deduction for capital expenditure, incurred after 7 May 2009, on the acquisition of qualifying IP assets for trade purposes. Finance Act 2010 contains a number of important and significant changes to this regime which significantly enhance the regime's attractiveness and widen its availability. The list of qualifying intangible assets has been expanded with the inclusion of applications for legal protection (for example, applications for patents, trademarks, etc) as well as expenditure on certain computer software. In addition, the definition of know-how has been amended to bring it broadly in line with that in the OECD model tax treaty.

Taxation of foreign dividends

Up to 31 December 2009, the 12.5% rate of corporation tax applied to certain foreign dividends – broadly speaking, dividends paid out of the trading profits of a company resident in a country with which Ireland has a double taxation agreement. From 1 January 2010 the 12.5% corporate tax rate applies to the same type of dividends received from companies resident in non-treaty countries, that is, where the company that paid the dividend is a listed company or is part of a 75% listed group the principal class of the shares of which are substantially and regularly traded on the Irish Stock

Exchange, a recognised Stock Exchange in a country with which Ireland has a tax treaty or on such other Stock Exchange as is approved by the Minister for Finance for the purposes of this relief from double taxation.

The rules for identifying the underlying profits out of which foreign dividends are paid have also been simplified.

Foreign dividends received by an Irish company where it holds 5% or less of the share capital and voting rights in that foreign company will be exempt from corporation tax where the Irish company would otherwise be taxed on this dividend income as trading income.

Branch income

A unilateral form of credit relief for foreign taxes paid by foreign branches operating in countries with which Ireland does not have a tax treaty is available. To the extent that there were foreign taxes on branch profits that were not utilised in the relevant period (that is, where credit for foreign tax exceeds the Irish tax payable), these unused credits were lost, unless they could be used against Irish corporation tax on other foreign branch profits arising in the same accounting period. For accounting periods ending on or after 1 January 2010 any unused credits can be carried forward indefinitely and credited against corporation tax on foreign branch profits in future accounting periods.

Asset management

Finance Act 2010 introduced changes aimed at enhancing Ireland as a leading location for the management of both UCITS and non-UCITS funds. UCITS III and IV brought about fundamental changes to both the management and structuring of UCITS. One of the reforms introduced permits UCITS management companies located in one EU jurisdiction to manage UCITS domiciled in another EU jurisdiction. One of the areas of concern is whether the activities of the management company could bring a foreign UCITS within the charge to tax in the management company's home jurisdiction, for example, by creating a branch or agency or causing the fund to be regarded as tax resident there. The Finance Act provides that in the case of an Irish management company managing a non-Irish UCITS, such management company will not be regarded as a branch or agency of the non-Irish UCITS and will not bring the profits of the foreign UCITS within the charge to Irish tax or treat the foreign UCITS as an Irish regulated fund.

Following the US and OECD review of offshore domiciles, which has resulted in increased regulation and tax obligations, fund managers are being forced to consider possible alternative onshore jurisdictions for their investment fund products. As a result of its international reputation in the investment funds industry and the favourable corporate tax regime, Ireland is seeing a significant trend in investment managers moving their investment platforms there from the traditional offshore jurisdictions. Recent company law changes also allow corporate funds to migrate to Ireland through a re-registration process, whereby the fund company would benefit from its continued existence, including the ability to retain the fund's performance track record post migration and avoid potential adverse tax consequences and costs that typically arise from a merger of an offshore fund with a new onshore fund. The Irish Financial Regulator has introduced a coordinated authorisation process to facilitate speed to market, which at present is a key advantage in comparison to delays being experienced in other EU domiciles.

Ireland

Islamic finance

Towards the end of 2009, the Irish tax authorities confirmed that the Irish tax treatment of certain Islamic finance transactions, such as funds, certain ijara (leasing), takaful (insurance) and re-takaful (reinsurance) was accommodated within existing Irish tax legislation. Specific legislation was however, required to facilitate the issuance of sukuk (that is, Islamic bonds) in Ireland and this legislation was introduced earlier this year. Overall, the intention of the legislature is to ensure that Islamic finance transactions are treated in the same favourable manner as conventional financing transactions. The legislation also introduced changes in relation to the taxation (and tax impact) of UCITS management companies. The UCITS structure is one of the commonly used structures for many different types of Islamic funds such as retail Islamic equity funds, Shariah-compliant money market funds, Shariah-compliant exchange traded funds (ETFs), etc. This demonstrates the Irish government and tax authorities desire to enhance the attractiveness of Ireland as a location for Islamic finance transactions by extending to this form of financing the relieving provisions which currently apply to conventional financing.

Islamic insurance

The Irish Revenue has recently provided guidance in respect of the Irish tax treatment of general takaful (non-Life), re-takaful (reinsurance) and family (life) takaful arrangements. Legislative changes are not currently required to facilitate Islamic insurance in Ireland.

Carbon tax

A carbon tax has been introduced on mineral oils (for example, auto fuels and kerosene) which are supplied in Ireland. Relief will apply where mineral oils are supplied to an ETS (Emissions Trading Scheme) installation or for electricity generation. Pure biofuels are exempt from carbon tax. From 1 July 2010 there will be full relief for the biofuel component of the fuel. As a result, from 1 July 2010 where biofuel has been mixed or blended with any other mineral oil, the relief from carbon taxes shall apply to the biofuel content of the mixture or blend regardless of the percentage.

A carbon tax has also been introduced on natural gas and solid fuel where supplied for combustion. Again reliefs apply where these fuels are supplied to ETS installations or used in electricity generation, chemical reduction or in the electrolytical or metallurgical processes.

Tax avoidance disclosure

Finance Act 2010 introduced provisions relating to the disclosure of tax-avoidance schemes. This requires promoters of such schemes to provide information to the tax authorities within a specified time (yet to be determined) of having made the scheme available. The rules are wide reaching and essentially cover all tax heads including corporation tax, income tax, capital gains tax, stamp duty, VAT and Customs & Excise.

Other significant developments
- Further enhancements to the Research and Development tax credit regime which caters for pre-trading expenditure and other specific circumstances.
- The categories of energy efficient equipment which may qualify for 100% first year capital allowances have been extended.
- Changes have been introduced to significantly ease the administrative burden in meeting the requirements for exemption from Dividend Withholding Tax (DWT).

Ireland

The requirement for certain non-resident companies receiving dividends from Irish resident companies to provide a tax residence and/or auditor's certificate, along with a signed non-resident declaration form, in order to obtain exemption from DWT at source has been removed. Instead, a self-certification system will apply under which a "qualifying non-resident company" will provide a declaration to the dividend paying company or qualifying intermediary to claim exemption from DWT.

Taxes on corporate income

Corporation tax

Corporation tax is chargeable as follows on income and capital gains:

Standard rate on income	Higher rate on income	Capital gains rate
"trading rate"	"passive rate"	
12.5%	25%	25%

Non-trading (passive) income includes dividends from companies resident outside Ireland (with some exceptions discussed below), interest, rents and royalties. Legislation provides that certain dividend income (income from foreign trades etc.) is taxed at 12.5% – *see Income determination section below*. The higher rate also applies to income from a business carried on wholly outside Ireland and to income from land dealing, mining and petroleum extraction operations. An additional "profit resource rent" tax applies to certain petroleum activities. Depending on the profit yield of a site the tax rate applicable can range from 25% to 40%.

A rate of 10% applies until 31 December 2010 on manufacturing activities that commenced before the sunset date (July 1998) for this incentive.

Close companies *(see below for details)* may be subject to additional corporate taxes on undistributed investment income (including Irish dividends) and on undistributed income from professional services. Examples of professional services include professions such as solicitor, accountant, doctor and engineer.

Dividend withholding tax

Dividend withholding tax applies at 20% to dividends and other distributions, unless the recipient of the dividend is either a non-Irish company eligible for the Parent-Subsidiary Directive (which in Ireland requires a 5% or greater shareholding) or is an Irish company which directly or indirectly holds more than 50% of the share capital of the paying company.

Exemptions from dividend withholding tax also are available where the recipient of the distribution falls into one of the categories listed below, and provided an appropriate declaration is made to the company paying the distribution in advance of the distribution. In a move to significantly ease the administrative burden in applying for exemption for dividend withholding tax, this declaration is now self-assessed and valid for up to six years.

- Irish tax resident companies, which hold less than a 51% shareholding of the company;

Ireland

- Non-resident companies, which are resident in a country with which Ireland has a tax treaty or in another EU member state, where the company is not controlled by Irish residents;
- Non-resident companies, which ultimately are controlled by residents of a tax treaty country or another EU member state;
- Non-resident companies whose principal class of shares is traded on a recognised stock exchange in a treaty country or another EU member state or on any other stock exchange approved by the Minster for Finance (or if recipient of the dividend is a 75% subsidiary of such a listed company);
- Non-resident companies that are wholly owned by two or more companies the principal class of shares of each of which is traded on a recognised stock exchange in a treaty country or another EU member state or on any other stock exchange approved by the Minister for Finance;
- Individuals who are resident in a tax treaty country or in another EU member state; or
- Certain pension funds, retirement funds, sports bodies, collective investment funds, and employee share ownership trusts.

Companies that make a dividend distribution are required, within 14 days of the end of the month in which the distribution is made, to make a return to the tax authorities containing details of the recipient of the dividend, the reason for any exemption from dividend withholding tax and to pay over any tax withheld.

Corporate residence

A company that is incorporated, or has its place of central management and control, in Ireland will be regarded as resident in Ireland for the purposes of corporation tax and capital gains tax. This is subject to two exceptions where the company is resident in Ireland due only to its Irish incorporation.

A treaty exception applies if the Irish incorporated company is, by virtue of an Irish double tax treaty, considered to be tax resident in the treaty partner country and not resident in Ireland.

An active trading exception applies if the Irish incorporated company or its 50% affiliate carries on a trade in Ireland and the company has qualifying ownership. A 50% affiliate is essentially a company where:

- One company is a 50% subsidiary of the other or both companies are 50% subsidiaries of a third company;
- There is an entitlement to at least 50% of the profits available for distribution; and
- There is an entitlement to at least 50% of the assets available in the case of a winding up of the other company.

Qualifying ownership requires that the Irish incorporated company or a 50% or more affiliate/parent is listed on a stock exchange in an EU Member State or a territory which has a tax treaty with Ireland or, in the absence of such a listing, that the ultimate control (more than 50%) of the Irish incorporated company rests with persons who are tax resident in EU or treaty countries.

Tax residence is important because resident companies are taxable in Ireland on their worldwide profits (including gains), while non-resident companies are subject to Irish corporation tax only on the trading profits of an Irish branch or agency, and to Irish income tax (generally by way of withholding) on certain Irish source income.

Other taxes

Value-added tax (VAT)
VAT is charged at 21% on the supply of most goods and services in the course of business.

There are two lower rates being 13.5%, which applies to most building services, labour intensive services, domestic fuel and power and other reduced rate supplies, and 4.8% which applies to livestock and greyhounds.

Most exports, food, oral medicine and children's clothing and footwear are zero-rated.

Some supplies are exempt from VAT. The main exempt categories are most banking services, insurance services, medical services, passenger transport, education and training.

Zero rating is preferable to exemption because most VAT costs incurred in making a zero-rated supply can be recovered, while those incurred in making an exempt supply generally cannot.

Customs and excise duties
Many goods imported into Ireland from outside the EU are subject to customs duties. The rates of duty are provided by the EU's Common Customs Tariff.

Excise duties are chargeable on most hydrocarbon oil products, electricity supply, alcoholic drinks and tobacco products imported into or produced in Ireland.

Professional services withholding tax (PSWT)
Income tax at the standard rate (currently 20%) is deducted from payments for professional services by government departments, state bodies and local authorities. Credit is granted for any PSWT withheld against the corporation tax (or income tax for an individual) liability of the accounting period in which tax is withheld.

Relevant contracts tax (RCT)
There are special rules relating to payments made by principal contractors to sub-contractors in respect of relevant contracts in the construction, forestry and meat processing industries. Where relevant operations under a relevant contract are carried out in Ireland the RCT system applies regardless of whether or not parties to the contract are non-resident in Ireland, parties to the contract are not liable to tax in Ireland in respect of those operations, the contract is executed outside Ireland, or payments under the contract are made outside Ireland.

The principal contractor must deduct tax at a rate of 35% from such payments and remit this to the Revenue unless the sub-contractor produces a certificate (Form C2) authorising the receipt of the amount without deduction of tax, and the principal contractor obtains a Relevant Payments Card in relation to the sub-contractor. Qualification for exemption from withholding tax is a two-part test and it is critical that both parts are satisfied before any payment is made gross. The gross amount receivable

I

Ireland

under the contract is included in the computation of the profit of the sub-contractor and he is entitled to credit for, or repayment of, the tax suffered.

Local taxes

Local taxes known as "rates" are not based on income but rather are levied on the occupiers of business property by reference to a deemed rental value of the property concerned. Rates are an allowable deduction for corporation tax purposes. Local authorities are also empowered to levy charges on all occupiers for specific services, for example, water supply. These charges are also deductible for corporation tax purposes.

Stamp duty

Stamp duty is a tax on instruments. It is payable on transfers of land and on other assets whose legal title cannot be passed by delivery. It is also chargeable on all instruments of transfer executed in Ireland, and on instruments, wherever executed, which relate to Irish property or activities. The transfer of assets between associated companies may not be liable to stamp duty, provided certain conditions are met. The key conditions include:

- The companies have a 90% relationship (that is, one company is the beneficial owner of at least 90% of the ordinary share capital of the other, and is entitled to at least 90% of the profits available for distribution and is entitled to at least 90% of the assets in the case of a winding-up of the other company);
- The companies are in a group 90% relationship as defined above that can be traced as far up the group chain as is necessary to establish the qualifying relationship; and
- This relationship must be maintained for a period of two years after the transfer of the assets to avoid the relief being clawed back.

There is an exemption for transfers of intellectual property and the categories of intellectual property qualifying for this exemption are broadly similar to those for which IP capital allowances are available *(see Intellectual property regime section below)*.

Stamp duty rates are up to 6% of the value transferring (up to 9% for residential property). Stamp duty is levied at 1% on transfers of Irish shares.

A EUR 1 stamp duty applies to a policy of insurance, other than life insurance, relating to risks located in the Republic of Ireland. The stamp duty is normally collected under the terms of a composition agreement, which provides for regular, usually quarterly, payments of duty.

Health insurance policies entered into since 1 January 2009 are subject to stamp duty.

Capital duty on share capital

Ireland does not levy capital duty on share capital of companies.

Capital taxes

Ireland does not levy tax on the net worth of companies.

Social security

Employed persons are compulsorily insured under a State-administered scheme of pay-related social insurance (PRSI). Contributions are made by both the employer and the employee. Contributions by the employer are an allowable deduction for corporation tax purposes.

Insurance premium tax (IPT)

A levy of 3% of gross premiums received applies in relation to non-life insurance policies relating to risks located in the Republic of Ireland. This levy is payable four times per annum, within 30 days of the end of each quarter (that is, within 30 days from quarters ending 31 March, 30 June, 30 September and 31 December).

A levy of 1% of gross premiums received applies in relation to certain classes of life insurance policies relating to risks located in the Republic of Ireland. This levy is payable four times per annum, within 25 days of the end of each quarter (i.e., within 25 days from quarters ending 31 March, 30 June, 30 September and 31 December). Pension business and reinsurance business are excluded from the levy.

Environmental taxes

In Ireland, a levy [currently 22c per bag] is imposed upon consumers provided with a plastic bag when purchasing goods in supermarkets and other retail outlets. Under the applicable legislation, retailers are obliged to collect 22c in respect of every plastic bag or bag containing plastic regardless of size unless specifically exempted, that is provided to customers, and remit all plastic bag levies collected to Irish Revenue. As a result of the levy, most non-supermarket retailers provide paper carrier bags and a lot of retailers provide "bags for life", which are made from non-plastic material and, therefore, not subject to the environmental levy.

Carbon tax

A carbon tax has been introduced on mineral oils (for example, auto fuels and kerosene) which are supplied in Ireland. Relief will apply where mineral oils are supplied to an ETS (Emissions Trading Scheme) installation or for electricity generation. Pure biofuels are exempt from carbon tax. From 1 July 2010 there will be full relief for the biofuel component of the fuel. As a result, from 1 July 2010 where biofuel has been mixed or blended with any other mineral oil, the relief from carbon taxes shall apply to the biofuel content of the mixture or blend regardless of the percentage.

A carbon tax has also been introduced on natural gas and solid fuel where supplied for combustion. Again reliefs apply where these fuels are supplied to ETS installations or used in electricity generation, chemical reduction or in the electrolytical or metallurgical processes.

Branch income

Irish branches of foreign companies are liable to corporation tax at the rates which apply to Irish resident companies. No tax is withheld on repatriation of branch profits to the head office.

An Irish resident company with a branch or branches outside Ireland is generally taxable in Ireland on the foreign branch profits with a credit for foreign taxes paid on those profits. A unilateral form of credit relief for foreign taxes paid by foreign branches operating in countries with which Ireland does not have a tax treaty is available also. To the extent that there were foreign taxes on branch profits that were not utilised in the relevant period (that is, where credit for foreign tax exceeds the Irish tax payable),

Ireland

these unused credits were lost, unless they could be used against Irish corporation tax on other foreign branch profits arising in the same accounting period. For accounting periods ending on or after 1 January 2010 any unused credits can be carried forward indefinitely and credited against corporation tax on foreign branch profits in future accounting periods.

Income determination

Basis of income determination

Irish trading profits are computed in accordance with Irish Generally Accepted Accounting Principles (GAAP) or International Financial Reporting Standards (IFRS) subject to any adjustment required by law. Prior-year adjustments may arise on the first-time adoption of IFRS which may result in double counting of income or expenses, or of income falling out of the charge to tax. Generally speaking, in order to avoid such an outcome, transitional adjustments exist whereby amounts of income or expenses that could be double-counted or that would fall out of the charge to tax are identified and the amounts concerned are taxed or deducted as appropriate over a five year period.

Inventory valuation

Each item of inventory is valued for tax purposes at cost or market value, whichever is lower, and this will normally accord with the accounting treatment. The method used in arriving at cost or market value of inventory generally must be consistent and must not be in conflict with tax law. The FIFO (first-in, first-out) method is an acceptable method of calculation. The base-stock method has been held to be an inappropriate method for tax purposes, as has the LIFO (last-in, first-out) method.

Capital gains

Companies are subject to capital gains tax in respect of gains arising on the disposal of capital assets. The taxable gain is arrived at by deducting from the sales proceeds the cost incurred on acquiring the asset (as indexed to reflect inflation only up to 31 December 2002). The resulting gain is taxable at 25%. In cases of disposals of interests in offshore funds and foreign life assurance policies indexation relief does not apply while a tax rate of 28% applies to funds located in the European Union (EU)/European Economic Area (EEA)/DTA countries while a rate of 25% or 40% applies to funds or policies located in all other jurisdictions. Special rules apply to gains (and losses) from the disposal of development land in Ireland.

Companies that are tax resident in Ireland (that is managed and controlled in Ireland or incorporated in Ireland and not qualifying for exclusion) are taxable on worldwide gains. Non-resident companies are subject to capital gains tax on capital gains arising on the disposal of Irish land, buildings, mineral rights and exploration rights on the Irish continental shelf, together with shares in unquoted (unlisted) companies, whose value substantially (greater than 50%) is derived from these assets. Non-resident companies also are subject to capital gains tax from the realisation of assets used for the purposes of a business carried on in Ireland.

Losses arising on the disposal of capital assets may be offset against capital gains in the accounting period or carried forward for offset against future capital gains. No carryback of capital losses is permitted. There is no facility to offset capital losses against business income or to surrender capital losses within a tax group.

Irish capital gains tax legislation facilitates corporate reorganisations on a tax-free basis in situations where there is a share for share exchange.

Withholding tax on capital gains

Where any of the following assets is disposed of, the person by whom or through whom the consideration is paid (that is, the purchaser) must deduct capital gains tax at 15% from the payment:

1. Land or minerals in Ireland or exploration rights in the Irish continental shelf;
2. Unquoted (unlisted) shares deriving their value or the greater part of their value (more than 50%) from assets described in (1);
3. Unquoted (unlisted) shares issued in exchange for shares deriving their value or the greater part of their value from assets as described in (1); and
4. Goodwill of a trade carried on in Ireland.

The requirement to withhold tax is not required where the consideration does not exceed EUR 500,000 or where the person disposing of the asset produces a certificate from the Revenue Commissioners authorising payment in full. A clearance certificate may be obtained by making application on Form CG50 to the Revenue Commissioners supported by a copy of the agreement or contract for sale. The certificate may be obtained on the grounds that the vendor is Irish resident, or that no capital gains tax is due in respect of the disposal, or that the capital gains tax has been paid. Withholding tax is creditable against the capital gains tax liability of the vendor and any excess is refundable.

To avoid the requirement to withhold, clearance must be obtained before the consideration is paid. There is no exemption from the withholding procedure where the asset is held as trading stock or where the transaction is intragroup and a capital gains tax liability does not arise. Failure to obtain the certificate will lead to the purchaser being assessed to capital gains tax for an amount of 15% of the consideration.

Participation exemption from capital gains

A participation exemption is available to Irish resident companies on the disposal of a shareholding interest if:

- A minimum of 5% of the shares (including the right to profits and assets on winding up) is held for a continuous 12-month period;
- The share sale takes place during the period for which the minimum 5% holding is held;
- (the disposal is also exempt if the sale takes place within two years after meeting the holding requirement, to take account of gradual dispositions over time;
- The company whose shares are sold is resident in an EU member state (including Ireland) or in a country with which Ireland has a double taxation treaty in force at the time of the disposal; and
- A trading condition is met at the time of the disposal whereby either: (1) the business of the company whose shares are disposed of consists wholly or mainly of the carrying on of one or more trades or, (2) taken together, the businesses of the Irish holding company and all companies in which it has a direct or indirect 5% or more ownership interest consist wholly or mainly of the carrying on of one or more trades.

Ireland

If the Irish holding company is unable to meet the minimum holding requirement, but is a member of a group (that is, a parent company and its 51% worldwide subsidiaries) the gain arising on the disposal still will be exempt if the holding requirement can be met by including holdings of other members of the group. Thus, the Irish company may be exempt from capital gains tax on a disposal of shares even if it does not directly hold a significant shareholding. The exemption also applies to a disposal of assets related to shares, such as options and convertible debt. However, it does not apply to a sale of either shares or related assets that derive the greater part of their value (more than 50%) from Irish real property, minerals and mining rights, exploration and exploitation rights in a designated area and these remain liable to capital gains tax. Shares deriving their value from non-Irish real property, minerals and mining rights qualify for exemption if the other conditions are met.

Capital losses arising on the disposal of a shareholding where a gain on disposal would be exempt under the participation exemption are not deductible.

Inter-company dividends
Dividends from Irish companies are exempt from corporation tax. Dividends paid out of the trading profits of a company resident in a country with which Ireland has a double taxation agreement may be taxed at the 12.5% rate provided a claim is made. From 1 January 2010 the 12.5% corporate tax rate applies to the same type of dividends received from companies resident in non-treaty countries, that is, where the company that paid the dividend is a listed company or is part of a 75% listed group the principal class of the shares of which are substantially and regularly traded on the Irish Stock Exchange, a recognised Stock Exchange in a country with which Ireland has a tax treaty or on such other Stock Exchange as is approved by the Minister for Finance for the purposes of this relief from double taxation.

Foreign dividends received by an Irish company where it holds 5% or less of the share capital and voting rights in that foreign company are exempt from corporation tax where the Irish company would otherwise be taxed on this dividend income as trading income.

Dividends from Irish resident companies are not liable to further tax, other than a surcharge on close companies if the dividend is not redistributed. Broadly speaking, a close company is a company which is under the control of five or fewer "participators". Participators can include individual shareholders, corporate shareholders, loan creditors, any person with a right to receive distributions from the company, etc. Where not less than 35% of the shares of a company (including the voting power) are listed a company would not be regarded as a close company.

A close company surcharge of 20% is payable on certain non-trading income (for example, rental income, certain dividend income and interest income) if it is not distributed to shareholders within 18 months of the accounting period in which the income was earned. Since 31 January 2008 a close company making a distribution and the close company receiving a distribution have the option jointly to elect to have the dividend disregarded for surcharge purposes. This can give close companies the option of moving "trading income" up to a holding company without incurring a surcharge. Generally speaking close companies avoid the surcharge through the payment of dividends within the prescribed period.

Foreign income

Resident companies are liable to Irish tax on worldwide income. Accordingly, in the case of an Irish resident company foreign income and capital gains are, broadly speaking, subject in full to corporation tax. This applies to income of a foreign branch of an Irish company as well as to dividend income arising abroad.

In general, income of foreign subsidiaries of Irish companies is not taxed until remitted to Ireland, although there are special rules that seek to tax the undistributed capital gains arising from the sale of Irish land and buildings by certain non-resident close companies *(see Inter-company dividends section above for further information in relation to close companies)*.

Foreign taxes borne by an Irish resident company (or Irish branch of an EEA resident company), whether imposed directly or by way of withholding, may be creditable in Ireland. The calculation of the credit depends on the nature of the income item, but for income sources other than dividends and some related party interest the credit is limited to the Irish tax referable to the particular item of income. A system of onshore pooling of excess foreign tax credits applies to dividends from 5% or greater corporate shareholdings and excess credits in the dividend pool can be carried forward indefinitely; a similar pooling system applies to some related party interest and also to foreign branch income *(see Branch income above)*.

Stock dividends

Stock dividends taken in lieu of cash are taxed to the shareholder on an amount equivalent to the amount which would have been received if the option to take stock dividends had not been exercised. If the recipient is an Irish resident company and it receives the stock dividend from a quoted (listed) Irish company then there will be no tax. For a quoted (listed) company paying the stock dividend, dividend withholding tax with the appropriate exemptions and exclusions applies. Other stock dividends (bonus issues) are generally non-taxable.

Controlled foreign companies (CFC)

Ireland does not have CFC rules.

Thin capitalisation

Ireland does not have thin capitalisation rules.

Leasing

Ireland operates an eight-year tax depreciation life on most assets. For short life assets (that is, those with a life of less than eight years), Ireland has allowed lessors to follow the accounting treatment of the transaction in the case of finance leases. This basically allowed finance lessors to write-off their capital for tax purposes in line with the economic recovery on the asset. Earlier this year, Ireland extended this beneficial tax treatment to operating leases of certain assets. Heretofore, operating lessors of such assets were required to write-off their capital over a period of eight years which created a mismatch with the economic recovery. The change means that operating lessors may now elect to follow the accounting treatment so that they are charged to tax on the rentals received from operating lease (that is, rentals included in P&L account) without addback for depreciation and without a deduction for tax depreciation. The new approach therefore, provides a faster write-off of the capital cost of an asset where before they were relying on tax depreciation over eight years. The new provision

Ireland

applies to incremental expenditure incurred in accounting periods commencing on or after 1 January 2010

Deductions

Depreciation and depletion

Book depreciation is not deductible for tax purposes (except in the case of IP assets). Instead, tax depreciation (known as capital allowances) is permitted in respect of expenditure incurred on assets which have been put into use by the company. The rates applying are set out below:

Asset type	Tax depreciation rate
Plant and machinery	12.5% straight-line basis
Industrial buildings used for manufacturing	4% straight-line basis
Motor vehicles	12.5% straight-line basis
IP Assets	Book depreciation OR 7% straight-line basis

The allowances are calculated on the cost after deduction of grants, except for plant and machinery used in the course of the manufacture of processed food for human consumption. In this case, the allowances are calculated on the gross cost. Allowances on cars are restricted to a capital cost of EUR 24,000 and may be restricted further (to 50% or zero) depending on the level of Carbon Emissions of the vehicle.

Intellectual property (IP) regime

Legislation provides for a tax deduction for capital expenditure on the acquisition of qualifying IP assets. The definition of IP assets is widely drafted and includes the acquisition of, or the licence to use:

- Patents and registered designs;
- Trademarks and brand names;
- Know-how (broadly in line with the OECD model tax treaty definition of know-how);
- Domain name, copyrights, service marks and publishing titles;
- Authorisation to sell medicines, a product of any design, formula, process or invention (and rights derived from research into same);
- Applications for legal protection (for example, applications for the grant or registration of brands, trademarks, patents, copyright, etc.);
- Expenditure on computer software acquired for commercial exploitation; and
- Goodwill to the extent that it relates directly to the assets outlined above.

Capital allowances will be available at the same rate as the depreciation/amortisation charge for financial accounting purposes. Alternatively the company may elect to claim allowances over a period of 15 years.

Tax deductions (for example, financing costs) are available for offset against income generated from exploiting IP assets, up to a maximum deduction of 80% of the relevant IP profits. The remaining 20% is taxable at the 12.5% corporation tax rate.

Research and development (R&D) credit

Incremental R&D expenditure (over a base year of 2003) qualifies for a tax credit of 25% in addition to a tax deduction. This means that the total tax deduction on qualifying expenditure is 37.5%. Expenditure on buildings used for R&D now also can qualify for the credit as long as at least 35% of the building is used for R&D activities. This hurdle is measured over the course of four years. This is of particular assistance where R&D is carried on in a manufacturing environment.

Further enhancements to the R&D regime cater for pre-trading expenditure and other specific circumstances. Where a company incurs R&D expenditure but has not yet commenced to trade, all R&D claims in this regard must be made within 12 months from the end of the accounting period in which the company first commences to trade.

The R&D credit can be used to generate a tax refund through a carryback against prior year profits. In addition, repayment for excess credits is available over the course of a three-year cycle. Repayments are limited to the greater of the corporation tax payable by the company in the preceding 10 years or the payroll tax liability for the period in which the relevant R&D expenditure is incurred.

In addition, under Irish GAAP, companies may account for the R&D tax credit through their profit and loss account or income statement in arriving at the pre-tax profit or loss.

Accelerated capital allowances

A 100% first year capital allowance is available in respect of certain approved energy-efficient equipment. The categories of equipment that may be eligible for inclusion are:

- Information and communications technology;
- Heating and electricity provision;
- Electric and alternative fuel vehicles;
- HVAC control systems;
- Lighting;
- Motors and drives;
- Building energy management systems;
- Refrigeration and cooling systems*;
- Electro-mechanical systems*; and
- Catering and hospitality equipment*.

*Subject to Commencement Order

Trading losses

Losses are computed for tax purposes in the same way as business profits. Trading losses can be offset against other income of any nature, either in the current or preceding accounting period (of equal length). The amount of losses required to shelter the income is dependent on the tax rate which would have been applied to the income in the absence of the loss relief. Any excess losses can be carried forward indefinitely against future trading income. Certain changes in ownership may prevent the carry-forward of losses to future periods. Terminal losses which arise within 12 months of the date a company ceases to trade may be carried back three years.

Ireland

Payments to foreign affiliates

Generally, deductions can be claimed for royalties, management service charges and most interest charges paid to foreign affiliates, provided the amounts do not exceed what would be paid to unrelated entities. Depending on the circumstances certain elections may be required. As mentioned above, Ireland does not have any thin capitalisation rules.

Taxes

Taxes that are deductible in computing profits for corporation tax include value-added tax not recovered, the employer's share of PRSI contributions, and local taxes, that is, rates levied on commercial property and local authority charges.

Other significant items

In general, expenses incurred wholly and exclusively for the purposes of the trade are tax-deductible.

A deduction for interest is allowed only to the extent that borrowings are used for the purpose of a trade or other limited purposes. Expenditure on scientific R&D and payments for the acquisition of know-how in general are allowable deductions, as are the costs of obtaining or extending patents and obtaining and renewing trademarks.

Costs incurred for third-party entertainment are not tax-deductible. Entertainment includes the provision of accommodation, food, drink and any other form of hospitality including the provision of gifts. Expenditure on bona fide staff entertainment is allowable as a deduction provided its provision is not incidental to the provision of entertainment to third parties. Certain promotional costs are tax-deductible if they are incurred wholly and exclusively for the purposes of the trade.

Companies are entitled to a deduction, as a trading expense, for qualifying donations to approved charities, educational institutions, schools, churches, research foundations, sports bodies and other approved organisations which satisfy certain conditions. To qualify for a tax deduction the donation(s) to an organisation in a 12-month accounting period must amount to at least EUR 250.

Contributions to certain employee pension schemes and the cost of setting up such schemes also are deductible. Pension contributions are allowable as a deduction in the year in which they are paid.

General accruals and provisions are not tax-deductible.

Group taxation

The concept of "fiscal unity" or consolidated group tax does not exist in Ireland. However, trading losses as computed for tax purposes may be offset on a current period basis, against taxable profits of another group company. As with loss relief in a single company, the amount of losses required to shelter the income is dependent on the tax rate which would have been applied to the income in the absence of the loss relief.

A group consists of a parent company and all of its 75% subsidiaries, with all group members being tax resident in Ireland or in another member state of the EEA. Non-Irish members may only surrender losses from activities which would, if profitable, be subject to Irish tax.

Ireland

Capital losses cannot be surrendered within a group.

Relief from capital gains tax is available on intragroup transfers of capital assets. Where a capital asset is transferred from a resident company to another resident company in a 75% group, no capital gains tax charge arises. A group, for capital gains tax purposes, consists of a principal company and its 75% subsidiary companies. A 75% subsidiary is defined by reference to the beneficial ownership of ordinary share capital, owned either directly or indirectly. A capital gains tax group can include EEA resident companies for the purpose of analysing the beneficial ownership of a company.

It also is possible for an Irish resident company and an Irish branch of an EEA company in the same group to transfer capital assets without crystallising a capital gains charge, provided the asset transferred remains within the scope of the charge to Irish capital gains tax.

Subsequent to an intragroup transfer, a charge to capital gains tax will arise when either:

- The asset is sold outside the group, in which case the tax is calculated by reference to the original cost and acquisition date of the asset when first acquired within the group; or
- A company owns an asset which was transferred by a group company and subsequently leaves the group within a 10 year period of the intragroup transfer. The gain on this intragroup transfer crystallises and becomes payable at this point.

Transfer pricing
In April 2010, Ireland enacted broad based transfer pricing legislation. The legislation endorses the OECD Transfer Pricing Guidelines for Multinational Enterprises and Tax Administrations and adopts the arm's-length principle. The introduction of general transfer pricing legislation in Ireland was widely anticipated and brings the Irish tax regime into line with international norms in this area. The new regime applies to domestic as well as international related party arrangements and will come into effect for accounting periods commencing on or after 1 January 2011 in relation to certain arrangements entered into on or after 1 July 2010.

The new transfer pricing rules apply to arrangements entered into between associated persons, involving the supply or acquisition of goods, services, money or intangible assets and relating to trading activities within the charge to Irish tax at the trading rate of 12.5%. The rules confer a power on the Irish tax authorities to re-compute the taxable profit or loss of a taxpayer where income has been understated or where expenditure has been overstated as a result of certain non-arm's-length arrangements. The adjustment will be made to the Irish taxable profits to reflect the arrangement had it been entered into by independent parties dealing at arm's length. The legislation also places an obligation on a taxpayer to provide documentation "as may reasonably be required" to support the arm's-length nature of the related party arrangements and that documentation will need to be prepared on a timely basis.

However, arrangements entered into between related parties prior to 1 July 2010 are "grandfathered" and thereby excluded from the scope of the new transfer pricing rules. There is also an exemption from the new rules for small- and medium-sized enterprises. Broadly speaking, small- and medium-sized enterprises include groups employing less than 250 people and, that have either a turnover of less than EUR 50 million or assets of less than EUR 43 million.

Ireland

Tax incentives

The main tax incentives in Ireland are:

- 12.5% corporation tax rate on active business income;
- A 25% credit on incremental R&D spending over the base year of 2003 – total effective tax deduction of 37.5%;
- Ability to exploit IP at favourable tax rates;
- Accelerated tax depreciation allowances for approved energy efficient equipment;
- A 10% tax rate until 31 December 2010 for manufacturing and grant-aided service operations that were in progress prior to the sunset date for this incentive of July 1998;
- A tax exemption on patent royalties where the patents were developed in Ireland;
- Ability to carry out investment management activities for non-Irish investment funds without creating a taxable presence in Ireland for such funds; and
- An effective legal, regulatory and tax framework to allow for the efficient redomiciliation of investment funds from traditional offshore centres to Ireland.

Grants
Cash grants may be available for capital expenditure on machinery and equipment and industrial premises, training of employees, creation of employment, rent subsidies, research and development, manufacturing and exporting products, providing services to customers overseas and so on. The level of grant aid depends on a number of factors and is specific to each project. Rates depend on the location of the new industry.

Withholding taxes (WHT)

Irish resident companies are required to withhold tax on certain types of payments as set out below.

Recipient	Dividends	Interest	Patents, Royalties
	%	%	%
Resident companies	Nil	20	20
Resident individuals	20	20	20
Non-resident companies and individuals	20	20	20

Exemptions and rate reductions apply under domestic law and under tax treaties.

Recipient	Dividends (1)	Interest (2)	Patent royalties (3)
Albania**	Nil/5(4)/10	Nil/7	Nil/7
Australia	Nil	Nil/10	10
Austria***	Nil	Nil	Nil
Bahrain**	Nil	Nil	Nil
Belarus**	Nil/5(4)/10	Nil/5	Nil/5
Belgium	Nil/20	Nil/15	Nil
Bosnia-Herzegovina**	Nil	Nil	Nil
Bulgaria	Nil/5(4)/10	Nil/5	10
Canada	Nil/5(7)/15	Nil/10	Nil

Recipient	Dividends (1)	Interest (2)	Patent royalties (3)
Chile	Nil/5(6)/15	Nil/5(8)/15	10
China	Nil/5(4)/10	Nil/10	10
Croatia	Nil/5(7)/10	Nil	10
Cyprus *	Nil	Nil	Nil
Czech Republic	Nil/5(4)/15	Nil	10
Denmark	Nil	Nil	Nil
Estonia	Nil/5(4)/15	Nil/10	10
Finland	Nil	Nil	Nil
France *	Nil/20	Nil	Nil
Germany *	Nil/20	Nil	Nil
Georgia **	5(10)/10	Nil	Nil
Greece	Nil/5(4)/15	Nil/5	5
Hungary	Nil/5(7)/15	Nil	Nil
Iceland	Nil/5(4)/15	Nil	10
India	Nil/10	Nil/10	10
Israel	Nil	Nil/5(8)/10	10
Italy *	Nil/15	10	Nil
Japan	Nil/20	10	10
Korea, Rep. of *	Nil	Nil	Nil
Latvia	Nil/5(4)/15	Nil/10	10
Lithuania	Nil/5(4)/15	Nil/10	10
Luxembourg	Nil/20	Nil	Nil
Macedonia	5(6)/10	Nil	Nil
Malaysia***	Nil/10	Nil/10	8
Malta	5(6)/15	Nil	5
Moldova**	Nil/5(4)/10	Nil/5	Nil/5
Mexico	Nil/5(4)/10	Nil/5(8)/10	10
Netherlands	Nil/15	Nil	Nil
New Zealand	Nil	10	10
Norway	Nil/5(7)/15	Nil	Nil
Pakistan *	Nil/20	(5)	Nil
Poland	Nil/15	Nil/10	10
Portugal	Nil/15	Nil/15	10
Romania	Nil/3	Nil/3	3
Russia	Nil/10	Nil	Nil
Serbia**	Nil/5(4)/10	Nil/10	Nil/5/10
Slovak Republic	Nil/10	Nil	10
Slovenia	Nil/5(4)/15	Nil/5	5
South Africa****	Nil/5(7)/10	Nil	Nil
Spain	Nil	Nil	10
Sweden	Nil	Nil	Nil
Switzerland	Nil	Nil	Nil
Turkey **	5/15	10/15	10
United Kingdom	Nil/5(6)/15	Nil	Nil

Ireland

Recipient	Dividends (1)	Interest (2)	Patent royalties (3)
United States	Nil/5(7)/15	Nil	Nil
Vietnam	5(12)/10	10	5/10/15(13)
Zambia	Nil	Nil	Nil

Ireland is currently negotiating treaties with the following countries:

Argentina	Morocco
Armenia	Saudi Arabia
Azerbaijan	Singapore
Egypt	Thailand
Hong Kong	Tunisia
Kuwait	Ukraine
Montenegro	United Arab Emirates

Legislation recently has been amended to allow for favourable treatment in situations where a double-tax treaty has been signed but not yet ratified.

* These treaties are currently under renegotiation.

** Awaiting ratification

*** Protocols to the double taxation treaties with Macedonia and Austria are awaiting ratification. These protocols do not have any impact upon the exemptions and rate reductions outlined above.

**** A protocol to the double taxation treaty with South Africa is awaiting ratification. The above exemptions and rates are as per the pending protocol. Currently the above payments to South African companies are exempt from withholding taxes.

Notes

1. Individuals (and most companies) resident in countries with which Ireland has a tax treaty should be able to qualify for exemption from withholding tax subject to filing appropriate documentation.
2. Financial institutions operating in Ireland are obliged to withhold tax (deposit interest retention tax, or DIRT) at 25% out of interest paid or credited on deposit accounts in the beneficial ownership of resident companies, unless the financial institution is authorised to pay the interest gross. There is no DIRT on interest paid to non-residents where a written declaration of non-residence is completed. Certain annual interest payments are subject to withholding tax at 20%. Interest payments by companies to companies resident in other EU Member States or in treaty countries are generally not subject to withholding tax. The EU Interest and Royalties Directive may also provide an exemption from withholding tax for payments between associated companies.
3. Royalties other than patents are not generally subject to withholding tax under domestic law. Documentation and reporting may be required to access lower treaty withholding rates in other cases. The EU Interest and Royalties Directive may also provide an exemption from withholding tax for payments between associated companies. Associated companies, for the purpose of this directive, are companies where one can directly control at least 25% of the voting power of the other, or at least 25% of the voting power of both companies is directly controlled by a third company – in all cases, all companies must be resident in a member state of the EU.
4. Where the beneficial owner of the dividends is a resident of a Contracting State and is a company which holds directly at least 25% of the capital of the company paying the dividends.
5. Refer to Ireland/Pakistan double taxation treaty.

6. Where the beneficial owner of the dividends is a resident of the Contracting State and is a company which controls directly or indirectly 10% or more of the voting power in the company paying the dividends.
7. Where the beneficial owner of the dividends is a resident of the Contracting State and is a company which controls directly 10% or more of the voting power in the company paying the dividends.
8. For loans from banks and in the case of Norway certain Government funds.
9. Where the beneficial owner of the dividends is a resident of the Contracting State and is a company which controls directly 20% or more of the voting power in the company paying the dividends.
10. Where the beneficial owner of the dividends is a resident of the Contracting State and controls directly or indirectly at least 10% of the voting power in the company paying the dividend and has invested more than EUR 100,000 in the capital of the company paying the dividend. The above details in general are subject to any special relationship that may exist between the payer and the recipient, and it is assumed that the recipient does not have a permanent establishment (taxable presence) in the other Contracting State.
11. Where the beneficial owner of the dividends is a resident of a Contracting State and is a company which holds directly at least 25% of the voting power of the company paying the dividends.
12. Where the beneficial owner of the dividends is a resident of a Contracting State and is a company which holds directly at least 70% of the voting power of the company paying the dividends.
13. Refer to Ireland/Vietnam double taxation treaty.

Tax administration

Corporation tax returns must be submitted within nine months (and no later than the twenty-first day of the ninth month) after the end of the tax accounting period in order to avoid a surcharge (maximum of EUR 63,485) or a restriction of 50% of losses claimed, to a maximum of EUR 158,715. The tax accounting period normally coincides with a company's financial accounting period, except where the latter period exceeds 12 months.

A system of self-assessment and Irish Revenue audits is in operation in Ireland. Irish Revenue may undertake a Revenue audit of a company's tax return within a period of four years from the end of the accounting period in which the return is submitted.

Corporation tax payment dates are different for "large" and "small" companies. A small company is one whose corporation tax liability in the preceding period was less than EUR 200,000. Interest on late payments or underpayments is applied at approximately 10% per year.

Large companies
The first instalment of preliminary tax totalling 45% of the expected final tax liability, or 50% of the prior period liability is due six months before the end of the tax accounting period (but no later than the twenty-first day of the month).

The second instalment of preliminary tax is due 31 days before the end of the tax accounting period (but no later than the twenty-first day of the month). This payment must bring the total paid up to 90% of the estimated liability for the period.

The balance of tax is due when the corporation tax return for the period is filed (that is, within nine months of the end of the tax accounting period, but no later than the twenty-first day of the month in which that period of nine months ends).

Ireland

Small companies

Small companies only are required to pay one instalment of preliminary tax. This is due 31 days before the end of the tax accounting period (but no later than the twenty-first day of the month).

The company can choose to pay an amount of preliminary tax equal to 100% of the corporation tax liability for its immediately preceding period or 90% of the estimated liability for the current period. As is the case for large companies the final instalment is due when the corporation tax return is filed.

New start-up companies

A corporation tax holiday applies to certain start-up companies that commence to trade during 2009 or 2010. The relief will apply for three years where the total amount of corporation tax payable does not exceed EUR 40,000 in each year. Marginal relief is available where corporation tax payable is between EUR 40,000 and EUR 60,000.

Other issues

Asset management

The Finance Act 2010 introduced changes aimed at enhancing Ireland as a leading location for the management of both UCITS and non-UCITS funds. UCITS III and IV brought about fundamental changes to both the management and structuring of UCITS. One of the reforms introduced permits UCITS management companies located in one EU jurisdiction to manage UCITS domiciled in another EU jurisdiction. One of the areas of concern is whether the activities of the management company could bring a foreign UCITS within the charge to tax in the management company's home jurisdiction, e.g., by creating a branch or agency or causing the fund to be regarded as tax resident there. The Finance Act provides that in the case of an Irish management company managing a non-Irish UCITS, such management company will not be regarded as a branch or agency of the non-Irish UCITS and will not bring the profits of the foreign UCITS within the charge to Irish tax or treat the foreign UCITS as an Irish regulated fund.

Following the US and OECD review of offshore domiciles, which has resulted in increased regulation and tax obligations, fund managers are being forced to consider possible alternative onshore jurisdictions for their investment fund products. Because of its international reputation of its investment funds industry and the favourable corporate tax regime, Ireland is seeing a significant trend in investment managers moving their investment platforms there from the traditional offshore jurisdictions. Recent company law changes also allow corporate funds to migrate to Ireland through a re-registration process, whereby the fund company would benefit from its continued existence, including the ability to retain the fund's performance track record post migration and avoid potential adverse tax consequences and costs that typically arise from a merger of an offshore fund with a new onshore fund. The Irish Financial Regulator has introduced a coordinated authorisation process to facilitate speed to market, which at present is a key advantage in comparison to delays being experienced in other EU domiciles.

Islamic finance

Towards the end of 2009, the Irish tax authorities confirmed that the Irish tax treatment of certain Islamic finance transactions, such as funds, certain ijara (leasing), takaful (insurance) and re-takaful (reinsurance) was accommodated within existing

Irish tax legislation. Specific legislation was however, required to facilitate the issuance of sukuk (that is, Islamic bonds) in Ireland and this legislation was introduced earlier this year. Overall, the intention of the legislature is to ensure that Islamic finance transactions are treated in the same favourable manner as conventional financing transactions. The legislation also introduced changes in relation to the taxation (and tax impact) of UCITS management companies. The UCITS structure is one of the commonly used structures for many different types of Islamic funds such as retail Islamic equity funds, Shariah-compliant money market funds, Shariah-compliant exchange traded funds (ETFs), etc. This demonstrates the Irish government and tax authorities desire to enhance the attractiveness of Ireland as a location for Islamic finance transactions by extending to this form of financing the relieving provisions which currently apply to conventional financing.

Islamic insurance
The Irish Revenue has recently provided guidance in respect of the Irish tax treatment of general takaful (non-life), re-takaful (reinsurance) and family (life) takaful arrangements. Legislative changes are not currently required to facilitate Islamic insurance in Ireland.

Exchange control
Ireland does not have exchange control regulations.

Choice of legal entity
Foreign investors tend to operate either through an Irish legal entity or as a branch of a foreign entity. Both are equally valid means of doing business in Ireland and the choice would normally depend on the commercial fact pattern and individual circumstances of the investor parent company.

Tax avoidance disclosure
Finance Act 2010 introduced provisions relating to the disclosure of tax-avoidance schemes. This requires promoters of such schemes to provide information to the tax authorities within a specified time (yet to be determined) of having made the scheme available. A transaction which comes within the new law and which therefore must be reported to Revenue is not necessarily a tax-avoidance transaction for the purposes of existing legislation. The rules are wide reaching and essentially cover all tax heads including corporation tax, income tax, capital gains tax, stamp duty, VAT and Customs & Excise.

Corporate taxes in Isle of Man

For more information, contact:

Kevin Cowley
PricewaterhouseCoopers
Sixty Circular Road, 3rd Floor
Douglas IM1 1SA
Isle of Man
Tel: +44 1624 689689
Email: Kevin.cowley@iom.pwc.com

Significant developments

Rates

Generally, the profits of Isle of Man resident companies are taxed at 0% with two
exceptions: (i) certain profits of licensed banks, and (ii) income derived from land and
property situated in the Isle of Man, which are taxed at 10%.

Tax treaties

The Isle of Man has, since 1955, had a Tax Treaty with the United Kingdom (UK).
During 2009, it also signed tax treaties with Belgium, Estonia and Malta, and recently
entered into Tax Information Exchange Agreements (TIEAs) with Australia and New
Zealand bringing the total number of TIEAs in force to 15.

Income attributed to shareholders

Legislation has been introduced that attributes the profits of an Isle of Man resident
company to any Manx resident shareholders as if that profit had been distributed to
them. Although any resulting tax charge will fall on the shareholder, the legislation
places reporting and filing obligations on the Isle of Man resident company in respect
of profits realised and distributions made.

Taxes on corporate income

The majority of companies pay income tax at 0%. Certain profits of licensed banks
and companies who receive income from the rental or development of land situated
in the Isle of Man will pay tax at 10%. Companies are liable for income tax; there is no
separate "corporation tax" as is the case in the UK.

Licensed banks will be taxed at 10% on income from deposit taking and interest earned
from the investment of regulatory reserves only. Income earned on capital and reserves
in excess of the regulatory capital, group funded lending, fiduciary deposits, assurance,
insurance, custody, trust and corporate services will be taxed at 0%. Expenses are
allocated against 0% and 10% income streams on a pro rata basis.

Corporate residence

A company incorporated in the Isle of Man is resident for tax purposes. A company
which is incorporated elsewhere will be considered resident in the Isle of Man if it is
managed and controlled in the Isle of Man. "Managed and controlled" is generally
interpreted as being the place where the board of directors meets although this is not
always conclusive. In cases where a company is resident in the Isle of Man and also

resident in a country with which the Isle of Man has a tax treaty then a tie-breaker may operate to confirm residence.

Other taxes

Value-added tax (VAT) and customs and excise duties are levied and are similar to those in the UK.

There are no other transaction taxes in the Isle of Man other than betting duty on gaming transactions.

Branch income

The income of branches is taxed in the same way as other corporate income.

Income determination

Inventory valuation

Inventories are generally stated at the lower of cost or market value. Any method of valuation that is in accord with sound commercial principles is acceptable for tax purposes, provided it is adopted consistently at the beginning and end of the accounting period and does not conflict with tax law. In practice, inventories are normally valued for tax purposes at the lower of cost or net realisable value. A first-in, first-out (FIFO) basis of determining cost where items cannot be identified is acceptable, but not the base stock method or the last-in, first-out (LIFO) method.

In general, the book and tax methods of inventory valuation will conform.

Capital gains

There is no capital gains tax in the Isle of Man.

Foreign income

Resident corporations are liable to tax on their worldwide income. UK tax is relieved under the treaty with the UK by way of tax credits. However, the UK treaty does not cover dividends or debenture interest. Other treaties will also operate to provide relief.

The Isle of Man grants unilateral relief from double taxation in respect of all foreign-source income arising outside the UK by way of tax credit.

Certain expenses which are deductible in the computation of profits are not allowable for tax purposes. These include depreciation, unpaid but accrued pension and bonus payments, certain lease payments and interest paid to non-Manx resident lenders.

Deductions

Depreciation and depletion

Relief for depreciation is given using "capital allowances" based on a reducing-balance method. Plant and machinery, tourist premises, industrial buildings, commercial buildings within a designated area, fish processing buildings, and agricultural buildings and works have an initial allowance of 100%. There are restrictions on allowances for expensive motorcars.

Isle of Man

Isle of Man government grants are not taken into account in determining the amount of expenditure on which allowances may be given.

Tax depreciation is not required to conform with book depreciation.

Upon disposal, allowances will be reclaimed on the resale value, restricted to cost.

Net operating losses
Losses can be carried forward indefinitely against future profits from the same trade.

Trading losses incurred may be carried back against preceding year profits. There are additional rules which apply in the opening years of trade. Terminal losses in the last year of trade can be carried back against profits for the previous three years of trading.

Taxes
No local income taxes paid are deductible when calculating net taxable profit.

Other
Relief is given in calculating the taxable profit of a company if the expense is incurred in the normal course of the business and is incurred wholly and exclusively for business purposes. There are however certain exceptions to this as detailed in the Income Determination section.

Group taxation

Trading losses and excess capital allowances may be surrendered (subject to certain restrictions) between 75% affiliates resident in the Isle of Man. Similar concessions are available to members of a consortium, but only a fraction of the loss or excess may be set-off, that fraction being equal to the members' share in the consortium in the relevant year of assessment.

Although GAAP rules exist in the Isle of Man, there is no transfer pricing regime, no specific Thin Capitalisation rules and no Controlled Foreign Company regime. If, however, the Assessor of Taxes is of the opinion that the main purpose, or one of the main purposes, of any transaction is the avoidance or reduction of tax liability, he may make assessments to counteract that avoidance or reduction of tax liability.

Tax incentives

Film industry
Through its Media Development fund, the Isle of Man government can make equity investments of up to 100% for film and television productions filmed in the Isle of Man.

Capital investment
See Depreciation and depletion for tax incentives. Capital grants of up to 40% of costs of new buildings, building improvements, and new plant and machinery may also be available from the Isle of Man government.

Tax treaties
The Isle of Man has since 1955 had a tax treaty with the UK. During 2009 it also concluded treaties with Belgium, Estonia and Malta. The Isle of Man has entered into TIEAs with the United States, Netherlands, Sweden, Norway, Finland, Denmark,

Greenland, Faroes, Iceland, Ireland, UK, Australia, Germany, France and New Zealand. The Isle of Man has arrangements with the United States and Germany regarding the international operation of ships, and Shipping and Aircraft agreements with France, Netherlands and all of the aforementioned Nordic countries.

Withholding taxes (WHT)

WHT should be deducted from certain payments made to non-residents by Isle of Man resident companies as follows:

- Rent from Manx land and property – 10% if paid to a company, 20% if paid to an individual;
- Dividends – Withholding tax is not required to be deducted;
- Loan interest and royalties – Withholding tax is generally not required to be deducted but there are certain exceptions which may apply; and
- Other – The Assessor of Income Tax in the Isle of Man has the power to require the deduction of Isle of Man withholding tax at a rate of 20% on payments of taxable income made to non-resident individual.

Tax administration

Returns
Companies are required to submit income tax returns on an accounting period basis. The tax return is due for submission one year and one day following the end of an accounting period. An accounting period for tax filing purposes can be no more than 12 months and where the financial statements cover more than 12 months, two (or more) returns may be required. Fixed rate penalties apply if returns are filed late.

Payment
Payment of tax is due within one year and one day of an accounting period end. Interest is charged on tax paid late.

Other issues

There are several different entities through which businesses may operate. These include companies, limited liability companies, partnerships, limited partnerships and protected cell companies.

Corporate taxes in Israel

For more information, contact:

Gerry Seligman
PricewaterhouseCoopers Israel – Kesselman & Kesselman
Trade Tower
25 Hamered Street
Tel-Aviv 68125
Israel
Tel: +972 3 795 4 476
Email: gerry.seligman@il.pwc.com

Significant developments

There have been no significant developments in corporation taxation in Israel in the past year.

Taxes on corporate income

Foreign companies that have a branch presence in Israel and Israel incorporated companies are both subject to Israeli company tax.

The current corporate tax rate is 25% as of 2010. Pursuant to tax legislation published 23 July 2009, the corporate tax rate is scheduled to be reduced to 24% (2011), 23% (2012), 22% (2013), 21% (2014), 20% (2015) and to 18% in 2016 and thereafter.

Approved enterprises *(see Tax incentives)* are subject to reduced rates of tax depending upon the level of foreign ownership and location.

Israel does not impose local taxes on corporate income.

Corporate residence

The following are considered to be resident in Israel.

1. A company incorporated in Israel; and
2. A company whose business is controlled and managed from Israel.

In the absence of a definition of the term "management and control" either in Israeli legislation or a direct discussion of this term by the Israeli courts, it is difficult to determine whether a company that is incorporated outside of Israel shall be viewed as managed and controlled from Israel. This is a complex subject that needs to be addressed on a case by case basis. When an entity is both an Israeli tax resident and a resident of a foreign jurisdiction which is party to an income tax treaty with Israel, most treaties provide a tiebreaker test in the determination of an entity's tax residency.

Determination of tax residency is important since under Israeli tax law, an Israeli resident entity is subject to Israeli corporate tax on worldwide income while a foreign resident entity is subject to Israeli corporate tax only on income accrued or derived in Israel. Income sourcing rules determine when income is to be considered from an Israeli source.

Foreign resident entities might be exempt from corporate tax to the extent that its activities do not constitute a permanent establishment (PE) under the tax treaty applicable between Israel and the foreign resident's country of residency.

Other taxes

Value-added tax (VAT)
The current rate of VAT is 16%.

Exports of goods and certain services and various other transactions are zero-rated, and certain transactions are exempt. Banks and other financial institutions pay VAT-equivalent taxes at the rate of 16% based on their total payroll and on profits. Not-for-profit organisations pay VAT (wage tax) at the rate of 8% of their total payroll.

Real estate – capital gains
Capital gains on real estate are subject to the Land Appreciation Tax Law. The law relates to any real estate in Israel, including houses, buildings and anything permanently fixed to land; real estate rights; and leases for 25 years or more. Tax calculations closely follow the calculation of company tax on capital gains (see Capital gains below).

The tax rate on the real gain is the applicable corporate tax rate (25% in 2010).

A special tax rate may apply with respect to real estate acquired prior to 1960.

Transfer tax
The purchaser of real estate is generally subject to acquisition tax at rates of 0.5% up to a maximum of 5%.

Municipal tax
Municipal tax is levied on commercial and residential buildings by local municipalities based on the size, location and purpose of the property.

Stamp taxes
There are no stamp taxes imposed in Israel.

Customs duties
Customs duty is imposed on certain products imported into Israel. The rates of duty depend upon their classification according to the Harmonised Customs Tariff and the country of origin. Israel has concluded free-trade agreements with the United States, Canada, Mexico, the European Union, and the European Free Trade Association (EFTA).

Employer's national insurance contributions
Employers are obliged to pay national insurance contributions based on a percentage of each employee's income on a monthly basis. Employers are responsible for withholding employees' contributions from wages and remitting these together with the employer's own contributions. The employer's contribution rates (current as of May 2010) for Israeli resident employees are 3.85% up to monthly income of Israeli New Shekel (ILS) 4,809 and 5.43% on the difference between ILS 4,809 and the maximum monthly income of ILS 79,750.

Israel

For non-resident employees working in Israel who are residents of a foreign country which has a social security totalisation agreement with Israel (presently 14 agreements are in force), the above mentioned rates that apply for Israeli residents shall similarly be imposed (excluding health insurance), unless they remain employed by the foreign employer during their work period in Israel (in which case the reduced rates below apply).

For all other non-resident employees, the rates are significantly lower and are 0.54% up to monthly income of ILS 4,809 and 0.77% on the difference between ILS 4,809 and the maximum monthly income of ILS 79,750. The minimal National Insurance payments for non-resident employees do not provide any retirement benefit for the non-resident but generally provides a certain element of work accident coverage.

When an irregular salary payment in excess of one quarter of the usual salary is made, special provisions apply to the computation of social charges by which the application of this payment is equally attributed to the current month and to the past 11 months.

Israel has social security totalisation agreements with 14 countries which may allow for an exemption from Israeli National Insurance throughout the employment period of the employee in Israel.

Branch income

A branch is liable to tax at the standard corporate rate on Israel-source income. No tax is withheld on transfers of profits to the foreign head office unless the branch is an approved enterprise (*see Tax incentives*).

Income determination

In general, the annual results (i.e., the excess of income over expenses or vice versa) of an Israeli company or branch, as detailed in the taxpayer's financial statements, form the basis for computing the taxable income of the business.

The base amount is then adjusted pursuant to the provisions of the tax law to arrive at "taxable income".

Inventory valuation
Inventories are generally valued at the lower of cost or market value (net realisable value). Conformity is required between book and tax reporting of inventory. The first-in, first-out (FIFO) or weighted-average basis of valuation is acceptable; the last-in, first-out (LIFO) method is not accepted.

Capital gains
Capital gains tax is generally payable on capital gains by residents of Israel on the sale of assets (irrespective of the location of the assets) and by non-residents on the sale of the following:

* Assets located in Israel;
* Assets located abroad that are essentially a direct or indirect right to an asset, or to inventory or that are an indirect right to a real estate right or to an asset in a real estate association located in Israel. Taxation applies only in respect of that part of the consideration that stems from the above property located in Israel;

- Assets that are a share or the right to a share in an Israeli entity; and
- Assets that are a right in a foreign resident entity, which is essentially a direct or indirect right to property located in Israel. Taxation applies only with respect to that part of the consideration that stems from the property located in Israel.

The cashless transfer of rights and assets arising from certain mergers, spin-offs and asset transfers may be exempt from tax upon meeting various requirements.

Determination of the capital gain – Computation of real gain and inflationary components
Company tax on capital gains is imposed on the disposal of fixed and intangible assets where the disposal price is in excess of the depreciated cost.

For tax purposes, the capital gain is generally calculated in local currency, and there are provisions for segregating the taxable gain into its real and inflationary components. The inflationary amount is the original cost of the asset less depreciation (where applicable), multiplied by the percentage increase in the Israeli consumer price index (CPI) from the date of acquisition of the asset to the date of its sale. The inflationary amount component is exempt to the extent it accrued after 1 January 1994 and is generally subject to tax at the rate of 10% if it accrued before that date.

The real gain component, if any, is taxed at the rates set out further below.

A non-resident that invests in capital assets with foreign currency may elect to calculate the inflationary amount in that foreign currency. Under this option, in the event of a sale of shares in an Israeli company the inflationary amount attributable to exchange differences on the investment is always exempt from Israeli tax.

Sale of assets (including publicly and non-publicly traded shares)
The real gain will generally be subject to tax at the corporate tax rate applicable in the year of the gain (25% in 2010). Special exemptions may apply for non-residents *(see further below)*.

Special rule for retained profits upon sale of shares
In the case of a disposal by corporations of: (a) non-traded shares; and (b) traded shares when the seller generally directly or indirectly holds at least 10% of the sold Israeli company during the 12-month period preceding the sale, special provisions apply to such part of the real gain which is attributed to the seller's share of retained profits. The share of retained profits is the amount of gain equal to the proportional part of the retained profits of the company that the seller of the shares would have rights to by virtue of those shares. Detailed rules apply in determining this profit component.

Generally, the seller's proportionate part of the company's retained profits is taxed as if this amount had been received as dividends immediately before the sale (i.e., at a tax rate of 0% in the case of an Israeli resident corporate shareholder or at a tax rate of 25% when the seller is a non-Israeli resident corporate shareholder that generally holds 10% or more in the rights of the Israeli company, subject to a reduced rate in accordance with the provisions of an applicable tax treaty). The part of the retained profits that is attributed to the period ending on 31 December 2002 is subject to tax at the rate of 10%.

Israel

Special exemptions for non-residents
Publicly traded Israeli shares
Non-residents corporations not having a permanent establishment in Israel are exempt from tax on capital gains from the sale of shares of an Israeli company traded on the Israeli stock exchange or on a foreign stock exchange.

Where the shares were purchased by the non-resident prior to being publicly traded, capital gains tax applies for the portion of the gain that was generated up to the day of the share's public listing but not to exceed the capital gain actually arising upon the sale of the share and provided that the value on the day of public listing was more than their value on the date of purchase and that the proceeds upon sale exceeded the value on the date of purchase.

Non-publicly traded shares
For purchases after 1 January 2009, an exemption exists under domestic law for non-residents, regardless of their percentage holding in an Israeli company, from gains derived from the sale of securities not traded on a stock exchange provided the following conditions are met:

- The investment is not in a company the majority of whose assets are real estate assets in Israel;
- The capital gains was not derived by the seller's permanent establishment in Israel; and
- The shares were not purchased from a relative (as defined in the Income Tax Ordinance (ITO)) or by means of a tax-free reorganisation.

For shares purchased between 1 July 2005 and prior to 1 January 2009 more restrictive conditions apply in order to be eligible for the exemption. Detailed rules apply.

Treaty exemption
Non-residents may qualify for a tax treaty capital gain exemption depending upon the particular circumstances and the provisions of the applicable tax treaty (e.g., in some tax treaties no capital gains exemption is allowed where the holding in the sold Israeli company exceeds a certain percentage).

When assets are attributable to an Israeli permanent establishment or are real estate rights (including rights in a real estate association), a treaty exemption will generally not be available.

The Israel Tax Authority (ITA) is very sensitive to treaty shopping and it would be necessary to demonstrate to the ITA that the foreign holding entity has business substance in its country of residence and that the structuring of the holding through that entity was not implemented for tax treaty benefit purposes.

Capital losses
Capital losses may offset all capital gains (including gains from Israeli or foreign securities) and gains from the sale of property (whether Israeli or foreign source).

Where the capital loss is from a non-Israeli asset (including when carried forward into future years), the loss must first be offset against foreign source capital gains.

Capital losses derived from the sale of securities may also be offset against interest and dividend income generated from the sold security and also against interest and dividend income received from other securities (where the income was not subject to tax of more than 25%).

Capital losses from the sale of shares are generally reduced by any dividends received by the selling corporation during the 24 months preceding the sale, where tax on the dividends of at least 15% was paid.

Capital losses can generally be carried forward indefinitely and set-off only against capital gains.

Exit tax
When an Israeli tax resident, (including a company), ceases to be an Israeli resident for tax purposes, its assets are deemed to have been sold one day before it ceased being an Israeli resident. Although exit tax is primarily applicable to individuals, this might also apply to corporations incorporated outside of Israel whose management and control is transferred from Israel to another jurisdiction at a particular time.

Any gain attributable to the deemed sale of assets may be paid on the day the residency ceased or it may be postponed until the date the assets are actually realised. When the tax event is deferred to the sale date of the assets, the amount of the Israeli capital gain portion is determined by taking the real capital gain at the time of realisation, multiplied by the period of ownership from the day on which it acquired the asset until the day it ceased being an Israeli resident, divided by the entire period from the day of the asset's acquisition until the day of realisation. The Minister of Finance is authorised to prescribe provisions for the implementation of the exit tax including provisions for the prevention of double taxation and the submission of tax reports, but no provisions have yet been issued.

Foreign income
An Israeli-resident company is liable to tax on its worldwide income. Double taxation is avoided by way of a foreign tax credit mechanism that also applies unilaterally in the absence of an applicable double taxation treaty. The foreign tax credit is limited to the Israeli corporate tax payable with respect to the same income. Foreign sourced income is divided into categories ("baskets") on the basis of the income source (e.g., dividends, business income) and a particular credit limitation applies to each basket. Excess uncredited foreign income can be carried forward for the subsequent five tax years.

Dividend income
Paid to Israeli resident company
Dividends received by an Israel-resident company from another Israeli resident company which originate from income accrued or derived in Israel are exempt from corporate tax, except for dividends paid from income of an approved enterprise *(see Tax incentives)*. This affords the opportunity to transfer after tax profits within an Israeli group of companies for further investment.

Dividends received by an Israeli company from a non-resident company as well as dividends received from an Israeli company which arise from foreign source income of the distributing company are generally taxable for the receiving company at the rate of 25%. Under certain circumstances the receiving company may elect to be taxed on such dividends at the corporate tax rate in which case it would also be entitled to a

Israel

foreign tax credit with respect to corporate taxes paid by the company distributing the dividend, i.e., an "underlying" tax credit.

Paid to non-resident shareholder
Dividends paid by an Israeli company to non-resident shareholders are generally subject to tax at the rate of 20% (25% if paid to a 10% or more shareholder), subject to a reduced rate of tax under an applicable tax treaty.

Several of Israel's tax treaties have very beneficial withholding tax rates for dividends and interest being paid from Israel. The ITA is very sensitive to treaty shopping and it would be necessary to demonstrate to the ITA that the foreign holding entity has business substance in its country of residence and that the structuring of the holding through that entity was not implemented for tax treaty benefit purposes. Furthermore, many of the treaties contain a beneficial ownership clause as a condition to enjoying the treaty withholding tax rates.

Interest income
Paid to Israeli resident company
Interest income paid to an Israeli resident company is subject to the regular corporate tax rate (25% in 2010).

Paid to non-residents
Interest income paid to a foreign company is generally subject to tax at the rate of 20% or subject to a reduced rate of tax under an applicable tax treaty. *See comments above regarding treaty eligibility.*

Interest paid to a non-resident from deposits of foreign currency with an Israel bank is exempt from tax, subject to certain conditions.

In order to promote foreign investment in the Israeli corporate bonds market, there is an exemption from tax with respect to interest income received by foreign investors on or after 1 January 2009 on their commercial investments in Israeli corporate bonds traded on the Tel Aviv stock exchange (TASE). The exemption is not granted to a foreign investor that has a permanent establishment in Israel, or is related to, or holds 10% more of the means of control in, the investee company. In addition, in order for the exemption to apply to a foreign investor that has "special relations" with the investee company, or that regularly sells products to, or provides services to, or is employed by the investee company, the investor must prove that the interest rate on the corporate bond was determined in good faith.

Controlled foreign companies (CFC)
Under the CFC regime in Israeli tax law, an Israeli company or individual may be taxed on a proportion of the undistributed profits of certain Israeli-controlled non-resident companies in which the Israeli shareholder has a controlling interest (10% or more of any of the CFC's "means of control"). A CFC is a company to which a number of cumulative conditions apply including that most of its income or profits in the tax year were derived from passive sources (e.g., capital gains, interest, rental, dividend, royalties) and such passive income has been subject to an effective tax rate that does not exceed 20%.

Israel

Rent/royalties income
Rent and royalty income less allowable deductions for tax purposes are subject to tax at the regular corporate tax rate (25% in 2010).

Partnership income
From an Israeli tax perspective, a partnership is in principle a fiscally transparent vehicle. Accordingly, Israeli tax law does not tax partnerships as such, but generally each partner is taxed in respect of its share of the partnership income, with the taxable income allocated to a corporate partner taxed at the regular company tax rate. Consequently, the actual distribution of partnership income to a partner is a non-taxable event.

Deductions

General
Costs incurred by a branch or a company are deductible as a business expense for tax purposes where they are incurred "wholly and exclusively in the production of income". The amount of the deduction may be limited or disallowed further to other ITO provisions and income tax regulations.

Depreciation
The ITO and tax regulations prescribe standard annual rates of tax depreciation for assets serving in the production of taxable income. Depreciation is generally on a straight-line basis for industrial and other enterprises based on the specific asset types as set out in the tax regulations. Accelerated rates of depreciation may be available in regard to certain activities (such as industrial) where there is unusual wear and tear due to additional shifts of equipment use. Detailed rules apply. Depreciation is not permitted on land.

Goodwill
In general, under Israeli tax regulations, goodwill purchased after 1 July 2003 may be amortisable by the purchaser over a 10-year period (10% annually).

Research and development (R&D) costs
Special tax relief is provided under the ITO for R&D costs incurred (see Tax incentives).

Net operating losses
Business losses can be set-off against income from any source in the same year. Loss carrybacks are not allowed. Losses may be carried forward (generally linked to the CPI) and set-off without time limit against income from any trade or business or capital gains arising in the business, but not against income from any other source.

Excess (disallowed) expenses
Israeli tax law disallows the partial deduction of certain employee-related expenses incurred by a company doing business in Israel. These include so-called "excess expenses". Examples of these are (a) payments for business, travel and meals which exceed allowable deductions; (b) expenses incurred in respect of a benefit granted by an employer to its employees but which cannot be attributed to a particular employee, and (c) vehicle maintenance expenses.

A company is obliged to pay a monthly advance on excess expenses in the amount of 45% of the excess expense. The amount paid as an advance in respect of excess

Israel

expenses is deemed a payment on account of the regular tax advances and payments that the company must pay for corporate income tax and is set-off against them, but is not refundable (i.e., when a taxpayer's tax liability in a given year is lower than the excess expense advances paid, the unutilised amount shall be carried forward to future tax years). Detailed rules apply.

Accrued expenses

Payments are generally deductible on an accrual basis for commercially justifiable expenses representing arm's-length consideration. However, when such payments attract withholding tax, the deduction would generally be allowed provided the payment is effected within the tax year. Alternatively, such payments may be deductible in a tax year if the applicable withholding tax is deducted within three months after the tax year-end and remitted to the tax authorities within seven days of the deduction, together with index linkage differences and interest accrued since the year-end.

However, accrued expenses for severance pay, vacation pay, recreation pay, holiday allowances and sick pay are not deductible, even if there is an obligation to make these payments. They are only deductible in the year in which they are actually paid to the beneficiary or to a recognised fund.

Charitable contributions

Charitable contributions do not constitute a regular business expense. However a tax credit is granted in respect of donations to approved state and charitable institutions aggregating at least ILS 300 (for 2010) in a tax year. The donor is allowed a tax credit equal to the amount of the contribution times the corporate tax rate applicable during the year, provided the donations do not exceed the lower of the following: (i) 30% of the corporation's taxable income in that year or (ii) ILS 7.5 million (in 2010). The above figures are adjusted each year according to the CPI. Excess unused tax credits may be carried forward for three years subject to detailed rules.

Bad debt

Provisions for bad debts are deductible in the year in which it is evident that the debt has become irrecoverable. Detailed rules apply for making this determination.

Contingent liabilities

Based on Israeli court decisions, contingent liabilities may be deductible for tax purposes upon satisfying the following criterion: (i) According to accepted accounting principles the taxpayer must include in its balance sheet a suitable provision for the potential liability; otherwise its income will be considered to have been incorrectly reported; (ii) the circumstances of the case and the technical means according to accepted accounting practice, enable an agreed determination of the amount of the liability; and (iii) there is a high probability, that the potential debt with respect to which the provision was made, will become an absolute debt.

Fines and penalties

Payment of fines and penalties are generally not deductible.

Organisational and start-up expenses

Organisational and start-up expenses are generally not immediately deductible but rather are to be capitalised for tax purposes.

Pension expense

Pension fund contributions are generally deductible for the employer provided inter alia the contributions do not exceed a prescribed level and are effected on a regular basis.

Directors' fees

Payments for commercially justifiable director fees should generally be deductible.

Payments to foreign affiliates

Payments of interest, royalties and management fees to foreign affiliates are deductible if based on normal commercial terms and practices, and evidenced by an inter-company agreement and transfer pricing documentation. Where such payments attract withholding tax, the deduction will only be allowed where such tax has been withheld and paid in accordance with certain requirements. All cross-border payments to foreign affiliates for goods and services have to comply with arm's-length pricing standards (*see Group taxation*).

Group taxation

Consolidated tax returns

As a general rule, a parent company and its subsidiaries may not submit consolidated tax returns. Only groups of industrial companies in the same line of business, as well as parent companies that control industrial companies in the same line of business and have at least 80% of their assets invested in industrial companies, are eligible to file consolidated tax returns.

Transfer pricing

The ITO and its accompanying regulations contain elaborate transfer pricing provisions and include the arm's-length principle which applies to any international transaction in which there is a special relationship between the parties to the transaction, and for which a price was settled on for property, a right, a service or credit. In general, the regulations are based upon internationally recognised transfer pricing principles (i.e., United States tax regulations or Organisation for Economic Co-operation and Development (OECD) rules). These regulations generally require the taxpayer to support the pricing of international transactions with a transfer pricing study, inter-company agreements and other documentation.

Since transfer pricing is a subject that receives considerable attention from the ITA in its examination of related inter-company transactions, transfer pricing principles and documentation requirements should be carefully adhered to.

A taxpayer is required to include in its annual corporate tax return a special form entitled "Declaration of International Transactions" providing details for every cross-border transaction conducted with related parties. The taxpayer must sign the form which includes a declaration that the transactions with related parties abroad were in accordance with the arm's-length principle, as defined in the Israeli transfer pricing regulations promulgated under the ITO. As a result of this form

Israel

and declaration, the importance of appropriate transfer pricing documentation has increased.

Thin capitalisation
Israel has no statutory or regulatory provisions or other rules concerning thin capitalisation for tax purposes as exist in certain other jurisdictions. Since there are no thin capitalisation rules and Israel has no specific debt-equity ratio requirements, a company may be financed with minimum capital and there is no limit to the amount of debt that may be used. Transfer pricing principles shall apply with regards to interest charges.

Tax incentives

Approved enterprises – General
Approved enterprise (AE) status, which provides for cash and tax benefits, may be granted under the Law for the Encouragement of Capital Investments (the Law) to enterprises that increase the productive capacity of the economy, improve the balance of payments or provide new employment opportunities.

The Law differentiates between three geographical regions (A, B and C). Area A enjoys the most incentives, while Area C (generally the central area of the country) enjoys the least amount of incentives.

New AE programmes and expansion of prior existing AE programmes are governed by the Law which underwent a major amendment on 29 March 2005 (Amended Law).

AE programmes which commenced their period of benefits generally prior to 2005 are still subject to the Law's provisions prior to its amendment.

We shall primarily address the AE regime under the Amended Law.

Approved enterprises – Cash grants
Approved enterprises located in development areas A and B are eligible for cash investment grants, which vary according to the geographic location of the enterprise. Grant amounts and conditions are subject to governmental change from time to time.

Approved enterprises – Reduced tax rates
In addition to financial incentives for the establishment or expansion of an AE, various tax incentives discussed below are available once a new AE or expansion thereof is operational.

The reduced tax rates generally apply for a seven-year benefit period (or a 10-year period in certain cases of local companies established in development area A or in the case of a foreign investor company, *see below*), commencing with the year in which the AE first generates taxable income.

Generally, this seven- or 10-year period of benefits is limited to 12 years from the year of implementation. For AE plans governed prior to the amendment, the period of benefits cannot extend beyond 12 years from the year the enterprise commenced its operations or beyond 14 years from the year in which approval of status as an AE was granted, whichever is earlier.

Locally owned companies

Income derived by a company from an AE during the maximum seven-year period of benefits is generally subject to company tax at a rate of 25%.

A withholding tax rate of 15% (subject to a possible reduction under a tax treaty) applies to dividends paid from profits of an approved enterprise earned during the benefits period, if distributed either during the benefits period or during the subsequent 12 years. Note that dividends from non-approved enterprise profits that are paid to non-residents are generally subject to a maximum 25% withholding tax rate that may be further reduced under the terms of a relevant tax treaty.

Foreign investors' companies (FIC)

A company that qualifies as a FIC is entitled to enhanced tax benefits on AE income. In general, a FIC is a company having more than 25% of its share capital (in terms of rights to shares, profits, voting and the appointment of directors), and its combined share capital and investor loan capital owned by foreign residents.

A FIC benefits from reduced company tax on the profits of an AE for a period of 10 years (instead of seven years) commencing with the first year in which taxable income is generated. The total period of benefits is restricted as discussed earlier above.

A FIC enjoys reduced company tax rates applicable to its AE income as shown below:

Percentage of foreign ownership	Company tax rate
	%
Over 25% but less than 49%	25
49% or more but less than 74%	20
74% or more but less than 90%	15
90% or more	10

The foreign ownership percentage is annually determined as the lowest level retained during the specific tax year.

The Amended Law also requires that to qualify for FIC status a foreign investor must make an investment in the company of at least ILS 5 million.

Dividends paid by a FIC out of the profits of its AE are subject to tax in the hands of the recipient at the rate of 15%, without limitation as to their distribution date, provided the dividends are distributed out of AE profits derived during the benefits period.

Alternative system of tax benefits for approved enterprises (tax holiday)

Companies with new or expanding AEs may elect to forego all government cash grants and receive instead a total exemption (i.e., tax holiday) from company tax on undistributed profits of the approved enterprise for 10 years in development area A, for six years in development area B and for two years in development area C (the area in which the company's facilities are located).

The tax holiday provides an Israeli tax exemption so long as the AE profits generated in the exemption period are retained within the company. Should a subsequent distribution of such profits occur, company tax and dividend withholding tax is imposed on the income distributed, at the rates which would have been applicable if

Israel

the tax holiday had not been elected (i.e., 25% or at a lower rate if the company is a FIC with a foreign ownership percentage of 49% or more during those years).

Under certain anti-avoidance provisions applicable to tax holidays, amounts paid or credited directly or indirectly by an approved enterprise to a relative, a major shareholder or to a related entity controlled by either a relative or a major shareholder, may be treated as a deemed taxable distribution of profits by the AE.

Ireland track and strategic investment track
For companies having an AE in development area A that seek to distribute dividends while maintaining a low company and dividend tax burden, there is an "Ireland track" under which the aggregate Israeli corporate and dividend withholding tax for a foreign resident shareholder is 15% and for an Israeli resident shareholder is 24.8%. This track is in contrast to the standard alternative benefit track discussed above which provides a tax holiday provided that profits remain undistributed.

Furthermore, a "strategic investment track" allows for an exemption during the benefit period from company tax and dividend withholding tax for a company having (depending on its location within Area A of the country) very significant investment and revenue levels. This means that during the benefits period, a company eligible for benefits from income accrued under this track will have no tax liability whatsoever for its productive activity arising from such investment and for the distribution of profits. Detailed rules apply to these tracks.

Qualifying for AE status
Minimal investment amount
For entitlement of tax benefits under the alternative benefit track of the Amended Law, there must be a certain minimal investment amount ("Minimum qualifying investment") towards purchasing productive assets (e.g., machinery and equipment – but not buildings) within three years. In the case of a new factory, the minimum required investment is ILS 300,000.

For expansion of a factory, the amount of required investment shall be ILS 300,000 or the amount based on the formula shown below, whichever is higher:

Value of productive assets in the factory in the tax year prior to the year the minimum qualifying investment commences (in ILS million)	Amount of investment required expressed as a percentage of the value of the productive assets
	%
Up to 140	12
140–500	7
Above 500	5

Detailed rules apply in determining how to value the assets for purposes of these tests (including in regards to AEs operated by affiliated companies).

For AE plans governed by the Law prior to its amendment, a general condition for approval is that a minimum of 30% of the investment in fixed assets must be equity-financed.

For investors wanting to expand their current AE, a new requirement has been added to the Law that demands at least a two year waiting period before an investor can obtain AE status for its new investments. Upon completion of these investment conditions, the taxpayer must file the election of the investments implementation year. Such election must generally be filed by the filing date of the relevant annual tax return but no later than 12 months from the end of that tax year.

Automatic approval

Where an investment project meets all of the eligibility criterion under one of the alternative tracks (Standard Alternative Track, Ireland Track or strategic investment Track) as set out in the Law and in regulations to be issued, a project will automatically qualify for the AE taxation benefits under the Law with no need for prior approval from the ITA (i.e., a "green lane"). The criteria that confer tax benefits in the alternative track of the Law are handled by the ITA. A mechanism is available which enables a company to apply for a pre-ruling from the ITA, where it desires to obtain certainty as to the taxation status of its investment under the Amended Law. The application to the ITA must be submitted no later than six months following the end of the investment's implementation year (first year of potential benefits for the AE).

For AE plans governed by the Law prior to its amendment, the certification of a new or expanding approved enterprise status required interaction with the Israeli Investment Centre (IC) which had to approve the application for approved enterprise status and was responsible for issuing a final implementation approval following its determination that all requirements relating to investments in assets and minimum capital have been met.

Interruption of entitlement to benefits

Unlike the Law prior to its amendment where an AE owner was generally required to continue to operate the AE for the entire benefit period, under the Amended Law, the examination as to whether an owner is entitled to enjoy AE benefits for a tax year is determined on a year by year basis. Consequently, under the Amended Law, if in any tax year during the benefit period a company does not meet any of the conditions required under the Law, then for that tax year it is not entitled to benefits. However, if the company again meets the conditions during the benefit period, the company is entitled to the benefits during the remainder of the benefit period.

Mixed enterprises

Special rules govern the allocation of taxable income of "mixed enterprises". These are essentially entities that derive only part of their income from an AE or entities which operate under a number of approvals relating to separate investment projects. The company tax payable in respect of income from each part of a mixed enterprise is separately computed and a composite withholding tax is applicable to dividends distributed by a mixed enterprise.

Neutralisation of assets

Assets used in the operation of an enterprise that are not part of an AE are regarded as non-approved assets. Consequently, turnover which is deemed to be generated from the non-approved assets will result in non-approved enterprise income that should be taxed at the regular Israeli corporate tax rate applicable for the relevant year.

For plans operating under the Law prior to its amendment, in some cases, upon request, the Investment Centre granted neutralisation of assets that were not part of the approved investment plan, so that they would have no negative impact on the tax benefits. Neutralised assets have a "neutral" effect, as they are not considered part of

Israel

the approved investment plan or part of a non-approved plan. For certain industrial equipment, neutralisation is not available. Assets that are of a non-productive nature may receive neutralisation.

In accordance with the Amended Law, this issue arises only in connection to assets purchased which had previous use in Israel.

Research and development (R&D)
In general, under special relief provided under the ITO which was enacted for the purpose of encouraging taxpayers to invest in R&D activities, R&D costs can generally be deductible for tax purposes even when they represent capital costs.

The ITO provision generally distinguishes between two types of investors in R&D projects:

a. The R&D project is conducted or sponsored by the owner of an enterprise in the fields of industry, agriculture, transportation and energy and it is intended to develop this enterprise; or
b. The R&D costs are borne by a taxpayer that is not the owner of an enterprise in the above mentioned fields or the taxpayer participates in R&D costs of another developer in consideration for a reasonable return, when such R&D projects also enjoy government grants.

In regard to the first group of taxpayers, the R&D expenses shall be deducted in the tax year incurred when such expense has been approved as an R&D expense by the relevant government department (the approval in regard to industrial related projects is generally granted by the Office of the Chief Scientist (OCS)). When such OCS approval is not obtained, the expense shall be deducted over three tax years.

The R&D expenses incurred by the second group of taxpayers shall generally be deducted over two tax years. The deductible expenses allowed to a participant in R&D costs of another developer generally may not exceed 40% of the taxable income of the investor in the year in which the expenses had been incurred.

Withholding taxes (WHT)

Under Israeli domestic tax law, a 25% withholding tax on payments of Israeli-source income is generally deducted by an Israeli paying bank from all income remittances abroad, unless a tax certificate is obtained from the ITA authorising withholding-exempt remittances or a reduced rate of tax pursuant to an applicable tax treaty. Set out below is a listing of withholding tax rates for dividends, interest and royalties under domestic tax law and pursuant to tax treaties in force. Detailed rules apply under certain tax treaties for eligibility to the treaty reduced rates (e.g., beneficial ownership; having no permanent establishment in Israel etc.). The applicable tax treaty should be consulted to determine the relevant withholding tax rate and to examine detailed conditions that may apply for the specific circumstance.

Recipient	Dividends	Interest *	Royalties
	%	%	%
Resident corporations	0-25	25	25
Resident individuals	20 – 25	15 – 35	30

Recipient	Dividends	Interest *	Royalties
	%	%	%
Non-resident corporations:			
Non-treaty	20-25	25	25
Treaty:			
Austria	25	15	0/10 (49)
Belarus	10	5/10 (30)	5/10 (50)
Belgium	15	15	0/10 (51)
Brazil	10/15 (1)	15	10/15 (52)
Bulgaria	10/12.5 (2)	5/10 (31)	12.5 (53)
Canada	15	15	0/15 (54)
China, P.R.	10	7/10 (32)	10 (55)
Croatia	5/10/15 (3)	5/10 (33)	5
Czech Republic	5/15 (4)	10	5
Denmark	25	25	10
Estonia	0/5 (5)	5	0
Ethiopia	5/10/15 (6)	5/10 (34)	5
Finland	5/15 (7)	10	10
France	5/10/15 (8)	5/10 (35)	0/10 (56)
Germany	25	15	0/5 (57)
Greece	20/25 (9)	10	10
Hungary	5/15 (10)	0	0
India	10	10	10
Ireland, Rep. of	10	5/10 (36)	10
Italy	10/15 (11)	10	0/10 (58)
Jamaica	15/22.5 (12)	15	10
Japan	5/15 (13)	10	10
Korea, Rep. of	5/10/15 (14)	7.5/10 (37)	2/5 (59)
Latvia	5/10/15 (15)	5/10 (38)	5
Lithuania	5/10/15 (16)	10	5/10 (60)
Luxembourg	5/10/15 (17)	5/10 (39)	5
Mexico	5/10 (18)	10	10
Moldova	5/10 (19)	5	5
Netherlands	5/10/15 (20)	10/15 (40)	5/10 (61)
Norway	25	25	10
Philippines	10/15 (21)	10	15
Poland	5/10 (22)	5	5/10 (62)
Portugal	5/10/15 (23)	10	10
Romania	15	5/10 (41)	10
Russia	10	10	10
Singapore	5/10 (24)	7	5
Slovakia	5/10 (25)	2/5/10 (42)	5
Slovenia	5/10/15	5	5
South Africa	25	25	0 (63)
Spain	10	5/10 (43)	5/7 (64)
Sweden	0	25	0 (65)

Israel

Recipient	Dividends	Interest *	Royalties
	%	%	%
Switzerland	5/10/15 (26)	5/10 (44)	5
Taiwan (R.O.C.)	10	7/10 (45)	10
Thailand	10/15 (27)	10/15 (46)	5/15 (66)
Turkey	10	10	10
Ukraine	5/10/15 (28)	5/10 (47)	10
United Kingdom	15	15	0 (67)
United States	12.5/25 (29)	10/17.5 (48)	10/15 (68)
Uzbekistan	10	10	5/10 (69)
Vietnam	10	10	5/7.5/15 (70)

Notes

* Some Israeli tax treaties provide for an exemption from withholding tax on interest involving governmental and quasi-governmental parties. Such exemptions are not separately indicated in the table above.

1. 10% where beneficial owner holds directly at least 25% of the capital of the company paying the dividends.
2. At a rate which is 50% of the rate which would have been imposed but for this provision but not to exceed 12.5% and not less than 7.5%. A 10% rate applies where paid from profits generated by an enterprise entitled to special tax rates under the Encouragement of Investment Law.
3. 5% if the beneficial owner is a company (other than a partnership) which holds directly at least 25% of the capital of the company paying the dividends; 10% rate if the beneficial owner is a company which holds directly at least 10% of the capital of the company paying the dividends where that latter company is a resident of Israel and the dividends are paid out of profits which are subject to tax in Israel at a rate which is lower than the normal rate of Israeli company tax; 15% rate applies in all other cases.
4. 5% if the beneficial owner is a company (other than a partnership) which holds directly at least 15% of the capital of the company paying the dividends; 15% rate in all other cases.
5. 0% if the beneficial owner is a company (other than a partnership) which holds directly at least 10% of the capital of the company paying the dividends; 5% rate in all other cases.
6. 5% if the beneficial owner is a company (other than a partnership) which holds directly at least 10% of the capital of the company paying the dividends; 10% rate if the beneficial owner is a company which holds directly at least 10% of the capital of the company paying the dividends where that latter company is a resident of Israel and the dividends are paid out of profits which are subject to tax in Israel at a rate which is lower than the normal rate of Israeli company tax; 15% rate in all other cases.
7. 5% if the beneficial owner is a company (other than a partnership) which controls directly at least 10% of the voting power in the company paying the dividends; 15% rate in all other cases.
8. 5% if the beneficial owner is a company which holds directly or indirectly at least 10% of the capital of the company paying the dividends; 10% rate if the beneficial owner is a company which holds directly or indirectly at least 10% of the capital of the company paying the dividends and the dividends are paid out of profits which are subject to tax in Israel at a rate which is lower than the normal rate of Israeli company tax; 15% rate in all other cases.
9. At the domestic Israeli tax rate.
10. 5% if the recipient holds directly at least 10% of the capital of the company paying the dividends.
11. 10% if the beneficial owner is a company (other than a partnership) which holds directly at least 25% of the capital of the company paying the dividends.

12. 15% if the beneficial owner is a company (other than a partnership) which holds directly or indirectly at least 10% of the voting power of the company paying the dividends.
13. 5% if the beneficial owner is a company which owns at least 25% of the voting shares of the company paying the dividends during the period of six months immediately before the end of the accounting period for which the distribution of profits takes place.
14. 5% if the beneficial owner is a company which holds directly or indirectly at least 10% of the capital of the company paying the dividends; 10% rate if the beneficial owner is a company which holds 10% of the capital of the company paying the dividends and the dividends are paid out of profits which are subject to tax at a rate which is lower than the normal rate of the corporation tax; 15% rate in all other cases.
15. 5% if the beneficial owner is a company (other than a partnership) which holds directly at least 10% of the capital of the company paying the dividends; 10% rate if the beneficial owner is a company which holds directly at least 10% of the capital of the company paying the dividends where the dividends are paid out of profits which by virtue of provisions in the Israeli Law of Encouragement of Investments in Israel are exempt from tax or subject to tax at a rate that is lower than the normal rate of Israeli company tax; 15% rate in all other cases.
16. 5% if the beneficial owner is a company (other than a partnership) which holds directly at least 10% of the capital of the company paying the dividends; 10% rate if the beneficial owner is a company which holds directly at least 10% of the capital of the company paying the dividends where the dividends are paid out of profits which by virtue of provisions in the Israeli Law of Encouragement of Investments in Israel are exempted from tax or subject to tax at a rate that is lower than the normal rate of Israeli company tax; 15% rate in all other cases.
17. 5% if the beneficial owner is a company (other than a partnership) which holds directly at least 10% of the capital of the company paying the dividends; 10% rate if the beneficial owner is a company which holds directly at least 10% of the capital of the company paying the dividends and the dividends are paid out of profits which are subject to tax in Israel at a rate which is lower than the normal rate of Israeli company tax; 15% rate in all other cases.
18. 5% if the beneficial owner is a company which holds directly or indirectly at least 10% of the capital of the company paying the dividends.
19. 5% if the beneficial owner is a company (other than a partnership) which holds directly at least 25% of the capital of the company paying the dividends.
20. With respect to dividends paid to a company which holds directly at least 25% of the capital of the company paying the dividends: (a) 10% where the dividends are paid out of profits which, by virtue of provisions in Israeli law for the encouragement of investment in Israel, are exempted from tax or subject to tax at a rate that is lower than the standard rate levied on the profits of a company resident in Israel; (b) 5% where paid out of regularly taxed profits. A 15% rate applies in all other cases.
21. 10% if the beneficial owner is a company (excluding partnership) which holds directly at least 10% of the capital of the paying company.
22. 5% if the recipient holds directly at least 15% of the capital of the company paying dividends.
23. 5% if the beneficial owner is a company (other than a partnership) which holds directly at least 25% of the capital of the company paying the dividends; 10% rate if the beneficial owner is a company which holds directly at least 25% of the capital of the company paying the dividends where that latter company is a resident of Israel and the dividends are paid out of profits which are subject to tax in Israel at a rate which is lower than the normal rate of Israeli company tax; 15% rate in all other cases.
24. 5% if the beneficial owner holds directly at least 10% of the capital of the company paying the dividends.
25. 5% if the recipient holds directly or indirectly at least 10% of the capital of the company paying the dividends.
26. 5% if the beneficial owner is a company (other than a partnership) which holds directly at least 10% of the capital of the company paying the dividends; 10% rate if the beneficial owner is a company which holds directly at least 10% of the capital of the company paying the dividends where that latter company is a resident of Israel and the dividends

Israel

are paid out of profits which are subject to tax in Israel at a rate which is lower than the normal rate of Israeli company tax; 15% rate in all other cases.

27. 10% if the recipient holds at least 25% of the capital of the company paying the dividends.

28. 5% if the beneficial owner is a company (other than a partnership) which holds directly at least 25% of the capital of the company paying the dividends; 10% rate if the beneficial owner is a company which holds directly at least 10% of the capital of the company paying the dividends where that latter company is a resident of Israel and the dividends are paid out of profits which are subject to tax in Israel at a rate which is lower than the normal rate of Israeli company tax.

29. 12.5% but only if (i) during the part of the paying corporation's taxable year which precedes the date of payment of the dividend and during the whole of its prior taxable year (if any), at least 10% of the outstanding shares of the voting stock of the paying corporation was owned by the recipient corporation, and (ii) not more than 25% of the gross income of the paying corporation for such prior taxable year (if any) consists of interest or dividends (other than interest derived from the conduct of a banking, insurance, or financing business and dividends or interest received from subsidiary corporations, 50% or more of the outstanding shares of the voting stock of which is owned by the paying corporation at the time such dividends or interest is received). A 15% rate applies for payments from income derived during any period for which the paying corporation is entitled to the reduced tax rate applicable to an approved enterprise under Israel's Encouragement of Capital Investments Law (1959). A 25% rate applies in all other cases.

30. 5% for interest in connection with the sale on credit of any industrial, commercial or scientific equipment or on any loan of whatever kind granted by a bank

31. 5% for interest in the case of a bank or other financial institution.

32. 7% for interest received by any bank or financial institution.

33. 5% for interest paid on a loan granted by a bank.

34. 5% for interest paid on any loan of whatever kind granted by a bank.

35. 5% where in connection with the sale on credit of any industrial, commercial or scientific equipment, or sale on credit of any merchandise by one enterprise to another enterprise, or on any loan of whatever kind granted by a bank; 10% in all other cases. An election can be made to be taxed on the net amount of the interest as if such interest were business profits.

36. 5% for interest paid in connection with the sale on credit of any industrial, commercial or scientific equipment, sale on credit of any merchandise by one enterprise to another enterprise, or on any loan of whatever kind granted by a bank.

37. 7.5% for interest if received by any bank or financial institution.

38. 5% where paid on any loan of whatever kind granted by a bank.

39. 5% where paid on any loan of whatever kind granted by a bank.

40. 10% where paid to a bank or a financial institution.

41. 5% where paid in connection with the sale on credit of any industrial, commercial or scientific equipment, or sale on credit of any merchandise by one enterprise to another enterprise, or on any loan of whatever kind granted by a bank.

42. 2% rate applies to government debt or government-assisted debt; 5% rate applies when paid to a financial institution; 10% rate applies in all other cases.

43. 5% rate in connection with the sale on credit of any industrial, commercial or scientific equipment, or in connection with the sale on credit of any merchandise by one enterprise to another enterprise, or on any loan granted by a financial institution.

44. 5% rate for interest paid on any loan of whatever kind granted by a bank.

45. 7% rate for interest paid on any loan of whatever kind granted by a bank.

46. 10% rate for interest received by any financial institution (including an insurance company).

47. 5% rate for interest paid on any loan of whatever kind granted by a bank.

48. 10% for interest derived from a loan of whatever kind granted by a bank, savings institution, or insurance company or the like. 17.5% rate for other interest. An election may be made to be taxed on interest income as if that income were industrial and commercial profits.

49. 0% for literary, dramatic, musical or artistic work copyright royalties (excluding in respect of motion picture films or films for use in connection with television).
50. 5% for copyright royalties for literary, artistic or scientific work (excluding cinematograph films) or for the use of, or the right to use, industrial, commercial or scientific equipment or road-transport vehicles.
51. 0% for copyright royalties for literary, dramatic, musical, artistic or scientific work (excluding in respect of films for cinema or television).
52. 15% for trademark royalties.
53. The rate is 50% of the rate which would have been imposed but for the treaty provision but not to exceed 12.5% and not to be less than 7.5%.
54. 0% for copyright royalties for the production or reproduction of any literary, dramatic, musical or artistic work (but not including royalties in respect of motion pictures).
55. For industrial, commercial, and scientific equipment royalties, the 10% rate applies to the adjusted amount of the royalties (70% of the gross amount of the royalties).
56. 0% for copyright royalties for literary, artistic or scientific work (excluding cinematograph films).
57. 0% for copyright royalties for literary, dramatic, musical or artistic works.
58. 0% for copyright royalties for literary, artistic or scientific work (excluding cinematograph films or tapes for television or broadcasting).
59. 2% for industrial, commercial, and scientific equipment royalties.
60. 5% for industrial, commercial and scientific equipment royalties.
61. 10% for royalties for cinematograph films and films or video-tapes for radio or television broadcasting.
62. 5% for industrial, commercial, or scientific equipment royalties.
63. For royalties in respect of cinematograph or television films, the withholding tax rate shall not exceed tax at the rate applicable to companies on 15% of the gross amount of the royalty.
64. 5% for royalties for copyrights of literary, dramatic, musical, artistic work or for the use of, or the right to use, industrial, commercial or scientific equipment.
65. The definition of royalties does not include any royalty or other amount paid in respect of (i) the operation of a mine or quarry or of any other extraction of natural resources or (ii) in respect of cinematograph including television films.
66. 5% for royalties for literary, artistic or scientific work, excluding cinematograph films or films or tapes used for radio or television broadcasting.
67. For royalties in respect of cinematograph or television films, tax may be imposed in Israel, but not to exceed tax at the rate applicable to companies on 15% of the gross amount of the royalty.
68. 10% for copyright or film royalties
69. 5% of the gross amount of the royalties where such royalties consist of payments of any kind received as a consideration for the use or the right to use any copyright of literary, artistic or scientific work (excluding cinematograph films).
70. 5% for royalties for any patent, design or model, plan, secret formula or for the use of, or the right to use, industrial, commercial or scientific equipment or for information concerning industrial, commercial or scientific experience; 7.5% for technical fees; 15% for all other royalties.

Tax administration

Returns

The tax year is generally the calendar year. Certain entities may apply to have their tax year-end on different dates, specifically, mutual funds, government companies, quoted companies, and subsidiaries of foreign publicly listed companies.

The Israeli system is based on a combined form of assessment and self-assessment.

Israel

The statutory filing date is five months following the end of the tax year which for a calendar year taxpayer would be 31 May. It is possible however to secure extensions of the filing date.

Payment of tax
Generally, 12 monthly advance payments are levied at a fixed ratio of the company's turnover. Alternatively, a company may be required to make 10 monthly payments beginning in the second month of its tax year, each payment being a fixed percentage of the previous year's tax assessment. Penalties are imposed on overdue advance payments and on delays in the submission of tax returns. The balance of any taxes due is payable from the beginning of the following tax year and is linked to the CPI; it bears interest of 4% until paid.

Statute of limitations
The statute of limitation period for corporate tax is three years from the end of the tax year in which the relevant tax return is filed. The Commissioner of the Tax Authorities has the authority to extend this period to four years.

Other issues

Choice of business entities
Investments and business operations in Israel may be structured in a variety of ways. The following are the common types of business entities in Israel: (i) Israeli public or private company; (ii) foreign company in Israel (i.e., a branch); (iii) Israeli general or limited partnership; (iv) foreign general or limited partnership; (v) other entities such as cooperative societies; and (v) other arrangements (e.g., contractual joint ventures).

Mergers and acquisitions
Israeli tax law allows for non-taxable reorganisations in situations in which the ownership and business enterprise of the original parties is continued after the reorganisation takes place, allowing for the deferral of the tax liability until the shares or assets transferred in such reorganisations are actually sold. Different qualifying requirements and conditions apply (e.g., obtaining a ruling from the ITA in certain cases) depending upon the tax residency of the parties and the type of transfer.

Corporate taxes in Italy

For more information, contact:

Fabrizio Acerbis
TLS Associazione Professionale di
Avvocati e Commercialisti
Via Monte Rosa 91
20149
Milano, Italy
Tel: +39 02 9160 5001
Email: fabrizio.acerbis@it.pwc.com

Domenico Coldani
TLS Associazione Professionale di
Avvocati e Commercialisti
Via Monte Rosa 91
20149
Milano, Italy
Tel: +39 02 9160 5800
Email: domenico.coldani@it.pwc.com

Significant developments

The major recent changes in the tax rules enacted in 2010 are as follows:

- Penalty protection regime with transfer pricing documentation support;
- Changes to the Controlled foreign companies (CFC) rules; and
- Changes to value-added tax (VAT).

Please consider that in Italy tax updates are generally expected from June to September in connection with the finance bill and related laws approval. In this respect we suggest to review the WWTS website in order to check whether or not relevant changes affect your business.

Penalty protection regime with transfer pricing documentation support
Transfer pricing adjustments will no longer be subject to administrative penalties if during a tax audit proper documentation is provided.

Documentation content guidelines are expected to be approved by tax authorities.

Starting in 2010 the possession of the documentation must be notified with the tax authorities filing specific forms. A notification is required for previous fiscal years.

CFC rules modification
Conditions for the applicability of CFC have been modified. In addition, CFC rules may also be applicable to certain controlled companies that are not resident in tax havens.

VAT changes
The so called "VAT package" has been enacted in Italian legislation providing a new framework for the supply of services.

In order to limit abuse, from 2010 the offset of VAT credits against other taxes brings new compliance obligations.

Starting from July 2010 transactions carried out with subjects resident in "black list" countries must be disclosed in proper communication to be electronically filed with the tax authorities. An electronic communication to the tax authorities has been introduced for VAT transactions exceeding EUR 3,000. Related deadlines and conditions will be defined by the tax authorities.

I

Italy

Taxes on corporate income

Italian corporate entities are subject to State Corporate Income Tax, known as IRES (Imposta sul REddito delle Società), which is levied at 27.5% and to Regional Production Tax, known as IRAP (Imposta Regionale sulle Attività Produttive), which is levied at 3.9%.

An increase (surtax) in the IRES rate equal to 6.5% is applied to companies operating in the areas of oil and gas refining, production or trade and in electrical energy (production or trade) which have turnover in excess of EUR 25 million in the fiscal year preceding the application period.

The taxable base for IRES is determined according to principle of worldwide taxation such that regardless of the location/jurisdiction where the income is produced, to the extent that the income is legally attributable to an Italian entity, the income is taxed in Italy. IRES is charged on the total net income reported in the financial statements of the company as adjusted for specific tax rules.

There are different methods of computation for the IRAP taxable base, depending on the nature of the business carried out by the taxpayer. Labour costs (with limited exceptions), provisions for liabilities and risks and extraordinary items cannot be taken into account in determining the IRAP taxable base.

For sales and manufacturing companies, the IRAP taxable base is broadly represented by the company's gross margin in its financial statements. In addition to the non-deductible items mentioned above, interest income and expense and provisions for bad debts are excluded for purposes of the IRAP taxable base.

For banks, the IRAP taxable base is broadly defined as follows:

i.   Intermediation margin reduced by 50% of dividends;
ii. 90% of amortisation costs relating to fixed tangible and intangible assets; and
iii. 90% of other administrative expenses.

Special rules apply to financial institutions, other than banks.

IRAP is levied on a regional basis. Regions are allowed to increase or decrease the standard rate of IRAP by up to 0.9176%. Companies with facilities in different regions must allocate their overall taxable base to the different regions on the basis of the employment costs of personnel located at the various sites. Facilities become relevant to the calculation of IRAP if they have been established for more than three months. Italian companies with permanent establishments abroad (as well as shipping companies qualifying for the tonnage tax regime, *(see Tonnage tax)* are not subject to IRAP on the income earned through these permanent establishments.

Substitutive tax on reorganisations (e.g., mergers, demergers, contributions in kind)
Corporate reorganisations such as contributions in kind, mergers and demergers are in principle tax neutral even if, for financial accounting purposes, the transaction results in the recognition of higher values for the assets in question or the recognition of goodwill. Companies may elect to obtain partial or full recognition for tax purposes

of the higher financial accounting values of an asset or the goodwill arising from the corporate reorganisation provided they pay a substitutive tax.

The substitutive tax is calculated on the step-up in tax basis and is based on graduated rates of 12% to 16%. The first EUR 5 million is taxed at 12%, the tranche above EUR 5 million but less than EUR 10 million is taxed at 14%, and the amount in excess of EUR 10 million is taxed at 16%. The substitutive tax may also be paid in three annual instalments of 30% in the year of election, 40% in year two, and 30% in year three plus interest at the rate of 2.5% per year on the deferred amounts. The substitutive tax is not deductible for the purposes of IRES or IRAP.

In addition, stepped-up values of goodwill and trademarks may be depreciated for tax purposes over nine tax years instead of the normally allowed 18 years by paying a substitutive tax of 16%. The higher tax depreciation arising from this election takes effect from the tax period subsequent to the one in which the substitutive tax is paid. For example, if a merger transaction occurred in year one and the substitutive tax was paid in year two the increased tax depreciation would begin in year three.

Tonnage tax
Italian tax resident shipping companies as well as foreign shipping companies operating in Italy through a permanent establishment can qualify for the Italian tonnage tax regime. A qualifying company can elect to be subject to the tonnage tax regime. The regime basically allows the determination of a presumptive income based on the net tonnage of the qualifying ships apportioned to the effective shipping days (tonnage income). The tonnage income is subject to IRES only.

To qualify for the tonnage tax, ships must meet the following requirements: (i) a net tonnage of more than 100 net tons (NT); (ii) ships must be used for goods transportation, passenger transportation, salvage, towing and other services and (iii) must operate in international shipping as defined by the rules disciplining Italian International Registry. Ships chartered out on a bare boat charter are excluded. Chartered in ships with crew are included in the tonnage tax regime if their global net tonnage is less than 50% of the total net tonnage.

Tonnage income is calculated on the basis of the ship's net tonnage. The daily income is determined according to the following rate system: (i) from 0 to 1,000 NT: EUR 0.0090 per NT; (ii) from 1,001 to 10,000 NT: EUR 0.0070 per NT; (iii) from 10,001 to 25,000 NT: EUR 0.0040 per NT; (iv) above 25,001 NT: EUR 0.0020 per NT.

No deductions are allowed from tonnage tax income.

Income and expenses from the following activities are all deemed to be covered by the tonnage income determined as previously discussed:

*   Transport of goods;
*   Transport of passengers;
*   Salvage and towing;
*   Other services that need to be performed on the high seas;
*   Charges related to the above mentioned activities (e.g., administrative and commercial expenses, insurances fees;

Italy

- Other operations performed in close connection with the transportation operations (e.g., loading and unloading); and
- Other minor activities.

Capital gains or losses arising from the transfer of ships that have been acquired by a company, while under the tonnage tax regime, are also deemed to be included in tonnage tax income. Conversely, for capital gains arising from the transfer of a ship acquired prior to election for the tonnage tax regime, the difference between the sale price and the net tax cost as of the last tax period prior to the election for the tonnage tax regime is subject to the ordinary tax regime. Tax losses, in this latter case, are tax deductible.

An election for the tonnage tax regime should be made for all of a company's or group's qualifying vessels. So called "cherry-picking" is not allowed. Election for the tonnage tax regime is on a voluntary basis, but once elected, it remains in effect for 10 years. The election is renewable.

Corporate residence

Corporate residence of companies
Companies having their legal or administrative headquarters or their principal business activity within the Italian territory are taxable in Italy on their worldwide income. Other companies are subject to Italian corporate income tax only on their Italian-source income. Specifically, Italian non-resident companies that have permanent establishments in Italy are subject to corporation tax with respect of the taxable income generated from the permanent establishment in Italy.

A foreign company holding one or more Italian subsidiaries is deemed to be resident of Italy for tax purposes if at least one of the following conditions exists:

- The foreign company is, either directly or indirectly, held by Italian tax resident persons; or
- The board of directors of the foreign company mainly is made up of Italian resident individuals.

Corporate residence of a trust
Trusts are considered as persons subject to corporate taxation.

Residence is defined on the basis of the location of the place of management and of the main object of the trust. In the first instance, trusts that operate through an appropriate structure are deemed to be tax resident in Italy, if the said structure is located in Italy. In the absence of any such structure, trusts managed by a trustee will be deemed as tax resident in Italy, if the trustee is tax resident in Italy. In addition, trusts that have the largest part of their assets located in Italy are deemed a tax resident in Italy.

There are anti-avoidance rules for Italian non-resident trusts, which set out the specific conditions on which these trusts can become Italian tax resident.

Other taxes

VAT – General rules

Italian VAT (Imposta sul Valore Aggiunto) shall apply to the supply of goods and services carried out in Italy by entrepreneurs, professionals or artists and on importations carried out by anyone. Intra-community acquisitions are also subject to VAT taxation under certain situations.

Transactions relevant for VAT purposes in Italy are:

* Supplies of goods or services;
* Carried out by an entrepreneur, an artist or professional, in the exercise of their activity; and
* Carried out in Italy.

In the absence of one of the above elements (e.g., the supply of goods does not take place in Italy), the transaction is not subject to VAT and remains outside the Italian VAT framework. This means that the supply is not subject to VAT and that it is subject to none of the VAT requirements set forth by the Italian VAT law. Specifically listed transactions are also out of the VAT application scope (e.g., transfer of money, transfer of business parts).

Input-VAT on purchases of goods and services related to the business activity generally is allowed for recovery. Special limitations apply in relation to specific items (e.g., cars, entertainment expenses).

The Italian standard VAT rate is 20%. Reduced rates are provided for specifically listed supplies of goods and services such as 4% for listed food, drinks and listed agricultural products and 10% for electric power supplies for listed uses, listed drugs. Intra-community supplies and exports are exempt from VAT.

Specific supplies of goods and services expressly listed in the law are exempt from VAT (e.g., public postal services, hospital and medical care, education, insurance services, specific financial services, supply, leasing of particular immovable property).

Intrastat (The European Union (EU) tax information system) lists and European Community (EC) lists (which in Italy are unified in a single form) are mandatory both for intra-community exchanges of goods and the services falling in the general rule (business to business) supplied and received to/from EU established taxable persons.

VAT package

With reference to the place of supply rule, new provisions for services have been implemented in accordance to the EU Directives no. 2008/8/CE. Also Directives no. 2008/9/CE (refund procedure for persons established in a Member State other than Italy) and no. 2008/117/CE (Intrastat obligations and taxable event) (i.e., the so called "VAT package") have been implemented in Italy modifying the Italian VAT legislation (i.e., Presidential Decree No. 633/1972 and Law Decree No. 331/1993).

The main changes are:

1. Services supplied to taxable persons.

Italy

Starting 1 January 2010, services supplied by a taxable person to another taxable person (business to business) are in the scope of the Italian VAT, if the services are supplied to Italian taxable persons or to permanent establishment of an Italian non-resident entity (general rule – recipient's country).

The general rules are as follows:

- For services related to immovable property, reference must be made to the place in which the immovable property is located;
- For the transportation of passengers, the place in which the transportation takes place must be identified including the proportion of the distance covered;
- For catering and restaurant services, the place in which the activity will be physically carried out must be identified; and
- For short term hiring, leasing and similar of means of obtaining transport services, the place in which the vehicle is used must be identified (use and enjoyment rule has been implemented on these services).

2. Services supplied to final consumers.

Starting 1 January 2010, the general rule for services supplied by a taxable person to a non-taxable person (business to consumer) identifies the place of taxation with the state of residence of the supplier.

Several rules, in addition to the business to business, exist for the following:

- Brokerage services;
- Goods transport services;
- Services related to movable goods and ancillary activities related to transports;
- Long term hiring / leasing of means of transport services;
- Electronic services supplied by extra-EU suppliers; and
- Telecommunications and television/radio broadcast services.

In addition, special rules are provided for intangible services provided to final customers established outside the EU.

Disclosure of transactions with "black list" countries
Starting from 1 July 2010 a new periodical obligation to communicate by electronic means to the tax authorities is applicable to taxable persons for all supplies of goods and services carried out with business entities resident in "black list" countries. The omitted, incomplete or untrue communication will be subject to an administrative penalty.

ICI – Imposta Comunale sugli Immobili (municipal tax on real estate)
ICI is levied either on the owner or on the financial lessee of real estate (i.e., buildings, development land and agricultural land). The tax rate ranges from 0.4% to 0.7%, depending on the rate set by the municipality (Commune) where the property is located.

The taxable basis generally is determined on the basis of the so called "cadastral value" (i.e., capitalisation of the income deriving from the real estate).

Registration tax

Specific deeds and contracts must be filed with the local registration tax office either on signature or if specific circumstances occur, and the relevant tax must be paid.

Depending on the nature of the contract and on the assets object of the contract, registration tax is levied as a fixed amount or as a percentage of the value of the goods and/or rights that are the object of the contract.

VAT and registration tax on lease of immovable properties

Leases, including financial leases, of residential and commercial buildings or portion thereof generally are VAT exempt and subject to the registration tax at 2% or 1% rate.

Please refer to the table below for an overview of the tax regime applicable to the leases, including financial leases, of both residential and commercial buildings.

Registration tax table

Type of building	Lessor (VAT status)	Lessee (VAT status)	VAT	Registration tax
Residential buildings	Individual or entities not acting in the course of business (not subject to VAT)	Any	Out of scope	2%
Commercial buildings	Individual or entities not acting in the course of business (not subject to VAT)	Any	Out of scope	2%
Residential buildings	Taxable persons acting in the course of business	Any	Exempt (with non right to deduction)*	2%
Commercial buildings	Taxable persons acting in the course of business	Individual or entities not acting in the course of business (not subject to VAT)	20%	1%
		VAT taxable persons with a VAT recoverable pro-rata not higher than 25%	20%	1%
		Other cases	Exempt (with non right to deduction) with the possibility for the lessor to opt for the VAT regime (20% rate)	1%

* In some specific cases of subsidised housing, VAT is applicable at 10% reduced rate.

Italy

Branch income

The tax regime for permanent establishments (PE) is the same as for corporate Italian entities (e.g., joint-stock companies). Accordingly, a branch is subject to IRES as well as IRAP. Both taxes are determined on the basis of the relevant financial statements related to the business activities carried out by the PE.

Transfer pricing principles apply to transactions between a head office and its Italian tax resident PE.

Income determination

Basic principles for income determination
In principle, positive and negative components of a company's income statement are, respectively, taxed or deducted on an accruals basis (accrual principle) for tax purposes. Additionally, in order to be taxed, income items have to be certain to arise under a legal definition and either objectively determined or capable of objective determination as to their amount (certain and objective determination principle). Income statement items accrued in the statutory accounts that do not meet the above criteria are not allowed as a tax deduction nor taxed as income in the tax period. Deduction or taxation of income is correspondingly deferred to future tax periods when the criteria are met (for example, treatment of provisions for liabilities and risk).

Expenses generally are deductible if they relate to activities that generate revenues which form part of the company's taxable income (inherence to business principle) and provided they are included in the relevant statutory accounts (imputation principle). An exception to this general rule is made for those income statement items accrued in the statutory accounts relating to a tax period different from that in which they become relevant for tax purposes in accordance with the principles of certainty and objective determination as described above. These items are taken into account in determining taxable income in the tax period in which the latter conditions are met.

For IRAP purposes relevant income and expense are those reported in the financial statements.

Specific rules are released for entities which have adopted IFRS for Italian statutory financial reporting purposes. These provisions bring the income determination rules into line with IFRS.

Inventory valuation
Italian tax law allows the application of all the most commonly used inventory valuation methods: last-in, first-out (LIFO), first-in, first-out (FIFO), average cost. For IRES only, the reference prices used to calculate the written down value of the inventory items cannot be lower than their market prices during the final month of the tax period.

Companies operating in the oil and gas sector are required to adopt for tax purposes either average cost or FIFO.

Capital gains
Capital gains are taxable in the tax period in which they are realised.

- Fixed assets: the gain realised on the sale of fixed assets is taxable for both IRES and IRAP purposes. Additionally, for IRES purposes, tax on capital gains can be spread over a maximum of five years. This treatment is allowed, provided that the company owns the fixed assets for not less than three years.
- Financial investments: a specific participation exemption regime (PEX) is applicable. Under this regime, capital gains realised by Italian companies on sales of shareholdings are 95% exempt from IRES.

The exemption applies if the following conditions are met:

i. The shareholding is held uninterruptedly for at least 12 months prior to the sale;
ii. The investment is classified under financial fixed assets in the financial statements relating to the first tax period of uninterrupted ownership;
iii. The subsidiary is actually carrying on a commercial activity (e.g., investments in companies mainly performing management of their own real estate are not entitled to the PEX benefits); and
iv. The majority of the subsidiary's income is not generated in a tax haven country or one with a privileged tax regime.

Conditions (iii) and (iv) must be met both at the time of the sale of the investment and in the three years preceding the sale. If these conditions are not met, the capital gain realised by the company is taxed in the normal way. Capital losses arising from the sale or write-down of shareholdings meeting PEX conditions are basically not tax deductible. Likewise, the capital losses realised on sales of "non PEX" investments are tax deductible. Specific exemptions are provided for those entities that adopted IFRS for Italian statutory accounts reporting purposes.

Specific anti-dividend washing rules provide that where capital losses arise from the disposal of shareholdings which are not eligible for PEX, such losses are deductible only for the part which exceeds the tax exempt amount of dividends *(see discussion below)* received from the shares in question in the 36 months prior to the disposal. Capital gains on financial investments generally are excluded from the IRAP taxable base.

Dividends
Dividends received by Italian resident companies from Italian companies or from companies resident in countries other than tax havens are excluded from the IRES taxable base for 95% of the amount. Conversely, no exemption applies to dividends paid by entities that are resident in tax haven jurisdictions (unless those dividends derived from profits were already taxed under the Italian *CFC rules,* see below). There are specific rules for entities adopting IFRS for Italian statutory financial reporting purposes. For such entities, dividends from investments in shares and other financial instruments held for trading purposes are fully taxable.

Dividends generally are excluded from the IRAP taxable base.

CFC rules for foreign entities
An Italian company that controls, either directly or indirectly, an entity located in a tax haven jurisdiction is required to consolidate the taxable income arising in proportion to the percentage shareholding held, irrespective of whether the profits have been distributed or not.

Italy

Income from CFCs is taxed separately from the other taxable income of the business at the standard IRES rate (i.e., other tax losses cannot be used to offset income in the CFCs). Foreign taxes paid by the CFCs are recoverable by way of a corresponding tax credit.

Dividends received by an Italian shareholder from a CFC are excluded from taxable income up to the amount of the taxable income attributed under the above CFC provisions. The excess of any dividends over income already included through the CFC regime is fully taxable in the hands of the shareholder.

Where companies are located in a tax haven the CFC rules also apply for companies holding not less than the 20% of the company's share capital or entitled to not less than 20% share of the company's profits. In such instances there are specific rules to determine the taxable income attributable to the Italian resident shareholder. The taxable income is determined by applying specific income ratios to the business assets of the CFC as they appear in the relevant accounts.

Exemption from these CFC rules can be achieved by means of an advance ruling from the Italian tax authorities. To obtain such a ruling, adequate evidence must be provided to demonstrate at least one of the following:

- The foreign company is mainly and effectively engaged in sales and/or industrial activities in the "market" of the foreign host state or territory. Banks, other financial entities and insurance companies must demonstrate that most of the financial resources and related proceeds are made in or as the result of yields, respectively, from the market of the foreign host state or territory. However, this exemption cannot be requested where more than 50% of the income of the foreign subsidiary/ies derives from "passive income" (e.g., holding or investment in securities, receivables or other financial assets, transfer or license of intangible rights, etc.) or from intra-group transactions; or
- No less than the 75% of all the proceeds of the CFC have been taxed in jurisdictions that are not tax privileged countries (e.g., a company resident in Hong Kong has all of its operations in China mainland and it is subject to ordinary taxation there).

The CFC rules also extend to controlled companies that are located in a jurisdiction with a privileged tax regime that is not a tax haven, if the following conditions exist:

- The effective tax is less than 50% of the tax that would have been charged had the company been resident in Italy; and
- More than 50% of revenue derives from so-called "passive income" or from intra-group services.

By means of an advance ruling, the Italian parent company is able to obtain an exemption from these rules if it is able to provide proper evidence that the establishment of the company in the privileged tax jurisdiction is not for tax avoidance purposes (unfair tax advantage).

Foreign income

An Italian domestic corporation is taxable on all income whether produced in Italy or abroad. Profits earned by subsidiaries that are resident or located in countries or territories other than tax havens are taxed only on distribution of the relevant profits. Double taxation is, in principle, avoided by means of foreign tax credits.

Shell companies

Companies and permanent establishments of foreign enterprises can be qualified as non-operating entities if certain tests are not passed. In such a case, these entities will be assessed as having a minimum taxable income for both IRES and IRAP purposes.

For IRES purposes the average of the revenues recorded in the current fiscal year and in the two previous years must be compared to the total amount that would result by applying determined percentages to the average balance sheet value of specific assets in the current fiscal year and the two previous years.

The main assets to be taken into consideration are shares and shareholdings, financial receivables, owned or leased real estate, owned or leased tangible and intangible assets. The value of any assets that have been acquired or sold during the fiscal year must be adjusted according to the period of ownership.

An entity is deemed to be non-operative if the expected revenues determined on the above basis is higher than the average of actual revenues. As a consequence the entity is obliged to declare minimum taxable income for IRES, calculated by multiplying fixed percentages to the value of the above-mentioned assets.

This condition must be checked every year, and therefore, it is possible for an entity to be "non-operative" in one year and operative in the following year.

Tax losses generated in a tax period when the company was deemed to be non-operating cannot be carried forward.

For IRAP purposes, labour costs and other non-deductible items have to be added back to the deemed minimum IRES income as outlined above.

These rules are not applicable in the first year of a company's incorporation. Exemptions from these rules can be achieved:

- By means of an advance ruling from the Italian tax authorities aimed at assessing the specific circumstances that caused the company not to earn the minimum amount of income; or
- By specific objective situations provided for by Italian law (e.g., company directly or indirectly held by quoted companies, etc.).

Shell companies are also subject to limitations in their ability to recover VAT credits.

Deductions

Basic principles for deductible costs

The principles outlined in the section on *Income determination* also apply for deductible costs.

Interest expense

Generally, interest expense is fully tax deductible up to the amount of interest income. Thereafter, excess interest expense is deductible up to 30% of the gross operating margin (interest deduction capacity) as reported in the financial statements. Gross operating margin is defined as the difference between operating revenues and

Italy

expenses excluding depreciation of tangible and intangible assets and charges for leased assets as stated in the profit and loss account for the year.

Net interest expense in excess of the yearly limitation is carried forward indefinitely. Hence net interest expense not deducted in previous years can be deducted in any future fiscal year as long as total interest in that year does not exceed 30% of gross operating margin. If net interest expense is lower than the annual limit (i.e., 30% of gross operating margin) this difference can be carried over to increase the company's interest deduction capacity in future years. However, this latter rule is only applicable from 2010 onwards.

Where an election is made for the domestic tax consolidation regime, (as discussed in *Group taxation*), the net interest expense limitation applies to the consolidated tax group. As a consequence, if a company participating in a tax group has an excess interest deduction capacity, this excess may be used against the interest deduction deficit in another company belonging to the same tax consolidation group. Under specific conditions, non-resident subsidiaries can also be "virtually" included in the tax consolidation for the sole purpose of transferring their excess capacity over 30% of gross operating margin in order to increase the overall interest deduction capacity of the Italian group.

The above-mentioned rules are not applicable for financial institutions, such as banks and insurance companies, where the deductibility of interest expense (for both IRES and IRAP purposes) is limited to a fixed amount of 96% of the interest expense shown in the income statement of these entities.

Depreciation

All fixed assets, except land, which are used in the business of the company, are depreciable for tax purposes (for both IRES and IRAP).

For IRES, the maximum depreciation rates for fixed tangible assets are set forth in a ministerial decree. In the event that financial accounting depreciation exceeds the amounts allowed for tax purposes, temporary differences arise. Tax depreciation of fixed tangible assets is allowed from the tax period in which the asset is first used. In the first tax depreciation period, the depreciation rate cannot exceed one-half of the normal rate.

Land is not a depreciable asset. Amortisation of goodwill derived from an acquisition and amortisation of trademarks are deductible for an amount not exceeding one-eighteenth of the cost of the goodwill in any year.

Patents, know-how and other intellectual property may be amortised over a two-year period.

Concession rights may be depreciated with reference to the utilisation period as determined either by law or in the relevant agreement.

For IRAP purposes only, depreciation and amortisation (other than as related to goodwill and trademarks, see above) are deductible in accordance with the amounts reported in the financial statements, regardless of the limits outlined above.

Net operating losses (NOLs)

For IRES purposes tax losses can be carried forward and used to offset income in future tax periods. The carryforward is limited to the five tax periods following the period in which the loss is incurred. Losses arising in the first three years of life of the enterprise can be carried forward indefinitely.

For IRAP purposes tax losses are not available for carryforward.

Specific (tax anti-avoidance) rules limit the carryforward of tax losses in the event of:

- Change of control; and
- An effective change of the main activity (performed by the company carrying forward the losses).

The aforementioned changes must occur together in order for the limitations to be applicable. The change of the main activity is relevant for these purposes if it takes place in the tax period in which the change of control occurs or in the two subsequent or preceding periods.

Specific anti-abuse provisions are also applicable to NOLs in cases of merger or demerger.

In Italy tax losses may not be carried back.

Transactions with foreign affiliates – transfer pricing rules

Transactions with foreign affiliated companies should be at "fair market value" and, generally, as defined by OECD guidelines.

Italian companies transacting business with related non-resident parties may participate in special tax ruling procedures for the transfer pricing procedures used for intra-group transactions. The agreement executed between the tax authorities and the taxpayer is binding for the fiscal year during which the agreement is executed and for the following two fiscal years, unless significant changes in the circumstances relevant for the conclusion of the agreement executed by the taxpayer take place.

Purchases from suppliers resident in tax haven jurisdictions

The costs of goods and services purchased from entities which are resident in tax haven jurisdictions are deductible on the condition that the taxpayer can, upon request of the tax authorities, provide evidence that the foreign companies carry out a real business activity or that the transactions were carried out for good and sound economic reasons (e.g., better economic conditions, the foreign supplier is the sole distributor for specific products, etc.).

An official list of tax haven jurisdictions (known as the "black list") has been issued by the Ministry of Finance. A list of countries which are not considered to have a privileged tax regime (known as the "white list") is expected and countries not on this white list will be deemed tax havens. Specific disclosure is required in a company's income tax return for the expenses arising in tax haven jurisdictions.

Italy

Taxes
When calculating the IRES base, 10% of IRAP paid is deductible.

ICI (municipal tax on real estate) is not deductible for either IRES or IRAP.

Entertainment expenses
For IRES purposes expenses for gifts and entertainment which meet the requirements (both qualitative and quantitative) contained in the specific Ministerial Decree are fully deductible in the tax period in which they are incurred. Entertainment expenses which do not meet these requirements cannot be deducted.

Expenses related to gifts with a value of EUR 50 or less are entirely deductible.

Automobile expenses
For IRES purposes, deduction of the cost of company automobiles is limited to 40% of the total amount of the costs for the automobile. If automobiles are assigned to employees, the company may deduct 90% of the costs associated with the automobile.

Automobile costs may be deducted in their entirety if (i) automobiles are necessary for the company's business or if (ii) the automobiles are an essential element in the company's activity (i.e., vehicles owned by a car rental company).

Telephone expenses
For IRES purposes, up to 80% of the total expenses related to both mobile and landline telephones are deductible.

Travel expenses
For IRES purposes, the deduction for travel expenses incurred within the Municipality is limited to 75% of the amount incurred. However, the VAT related to such costs is fully recoverable.

Foreign tax credit
Where foreign-source income definitively is taxed abroad, a tax credit can be claimed for use against a company's IRES liability. The amount of the tax credit that can be claimed is the lower of the foreign tax incurred and the proportion of the IRES liability related to the foreign-source income. For partially exempt income (e.g., dividends), the foreign tax credit is reduced in proportion to the amount of the income taxable in Italy.

If an Italian company receives foreign income from more than one country, this limitation is applied separately to each country.

Foreign taxes borne by the foreign permanent establishment of an Italian resident company are allowed to be offset against the overall consolidated tax liability (IRES). For permanent establishments only, any excess over the maximum amount of foreign tax credit can be carried back or carried forward for eight years.

Group taxation

Domestic tax consolidation
Companies belonging to the same group can elect domestic tax consolidation. This allows the determination of a single IRES taxable base comprised of the taxable income

and losses of each of the participating entities. The tax consolidation does not operate for IRAP purposes.

Where an overall tax loss position arises, this can be carried forward and used against future consolidated taxable income. Conversely, tax losses arising in fiscal years preceding the domestic tax consolidation election can be carried forward and used only by the company to which these losses belong.

The taxable basis determined by each company participating in the tax consolidation arrangement is included in its entirety. No apportionment is made in relation to the percentage of control.

In order to elect validly the Italian domestic tax consolidation regime, the following conditions must be met:

- The consolidating entity must be an Italian tax resident company and it must hold, directly or indirectly, more than the 50% of the share capital of the consolidated entities (so called "legal control");
- This control must be in place from the beginning of the tax period for which the tax consolidation is applied for; and
- All of the companies participating in the group must have the same year end.

Provided that specific requirements are met, Italian permanent establishments of foreign companies can also participate in a tax consolidation.

The consolidation arrangement operates on an elective basis. Taxpayers may select whether to be included or not and it is not necessary for all the Italian group/sub-group companies to jointly elect for the tax consolidation.

Once the election is made it cannot be revoked for three fiscal years.

Worldwide tax consolidation group
A worldwide tax consolidation group is available, allowing the consolidation of foreign subsidiaries.

In addition to the requirements set out for domestic tax group system the following conditions apply:

- The ultimate parent company must be either owned by individuals who are tax residents of Italy or listed on the Italian Stock Exchange; and
- The option must be exercised for all foreign companies ("all in, all out" principle).

Income for each company is apportioned in the tax consolidation based on the actual percentage of control exercised by the ultimate parent company that is an Italian tax resident.

A number of additional requirements need to be fulfilled in order for a worldwide tax consolidation to be operative including a mandatory audit of the financial statements of all the foreign subsidiaries.

Once the election is made, it cannot be rescinded for three fiscal years.

Italy

Tax incentives

Inward investment and capital investment
A number of incentives have been established to attract new industry to southern Italy and certain depressed mountain areas in central and northern Italy.

Tax credits are given to companies that increase the number of their employees and that invest in research and development.

The possibility of taking advantage of these rules, however, depends on the taxpayer fulfilling specific conditions and on the actual availability of financial resources by the Italian state. These financial resources generally are set in the annual state budget.

"Tremonti-ter" law
The "Tremonti-ter" law provides tax relief for investments in certain types of new machinery and equipment. To benefit from this new provision, acquisition of the asset must take place between 1 July 2009 and 30 June 2010.

The relief is a tax deduction for IRES purpose of 50% of the invested amount.

This tax relief can also be used for new equipment comprising part of a complex structure. Allowable investments are on a specific list approved by a decree (i.e., specific categories in the Italian statistical business activity codes).

Recapture rules apply if the object of the investment is disposed of within two tax periods.

Withholding taxes (WHT)

Withholding tax chart
Domestic corporations paying certain types of income are required to withhold as shown on the following chart.

Recipient	Dividends	Interest	Royalties
	%	%	%
Resident corporations	0	0, 12.5, 27 (1)	0
Resident individuals	0 (2), 12.5	12.5, 27 (1)	20 (3)
EU resident corporations	0 (4), 1.375 (5)	0 (4)	0 (4)
CH resident corporations	0 (6)	0 (6)	0 (6)
Non-resident corporations and individuals:			
Non-treaty countries:	27 (7)	0, 12.5, 27 (1)	30 (3)
Treaty countries (8):			
Albania	10	0, 5 (9)	5
Algeria	15	0, 15 (9)	5, 15 (10)
Argentina	15	0, 20 (9)	10, 18 (11)
Armenia	5, 10 (12)	0, 10 (9)	7
Australia	15	0, 10 (9)	10
Austria	15	0, 10 (9)	0, 10 (13)
Bangladesh	10, 15 (14)	0, 10, 15 (15)	10
Belgium	15	0, 15 (9)	5

Recipient	Dividends	Interest	Royalties
	%	%	%
Bosnia and Herzegovina (Yugoslavia Ex)	10	10	10
Brazil	15	0, 15 (9)	15, 25 (16)
Bulgaria	10	0	5
Byelorussia	5, 15 (17)	0, 8 (9)	6
Canada	15	0, 15 (9)	0, 10 (18)
China, People's Rep.	10	0, 10 (9)	10
Croatia (19)	15	10	5
Côte d' Ivoire	15, 18 (20)	0, 15 (9)	10
Cyprus	15	10	0
Czech Republic	15	0	0, 5 (21)
Denmark	0, 15 (22)	0, 10 (9)	0, 5 (18)
Ecuador	15	0, 10 (9)	5
Egypt	27 (23)	0, 25 (9)	15
Estonia	5, 15 (24)	0, 10 (9)	5, 10 (25)
Ethiopia	10	0, 10 (9)	20
Finland	10, 15 (26)	0, 15 (9)	0, 5 (18)
France	5, 15 (27)	0, 10 (28)	0, 5 (18)
Georgia	5, 10 (29)	0	0
Germany	10, 15 (30)	0, 10 (28)	0, 5 (21)
Ghana	5, 15 (31)	10	10
Greece	15	0, 10 (9)	0, 5 (21)
Hungary	10	0	0
Iceland	5, 15 (32)	0	5
India	15, 25 (33)	0, 15 (9)	20
Indonesia	10, 15 (30)	0, 10 (9)	10, 15 (34)
Ireland, Rep. of	15	10	0
Israel	10, 15 (30)	10	0, 10 (18)
Japan	10, 15 (35)	10	10
Jordan (19)	10	10	10
Kazakhstan	5, 15 (36)	0, 10 (9)	10
Kuwait	0, 5 (37)	0	10
Latvia	5, 15 (31)	0, 10 (9)	5, 10 (38)
Lithuania	5, 15 (31)	0, 10 (9)	5, 10 (38)
Luxembourg (39)	15	0, 10 (9)	10
Macedonia	5, 15 (17)	0, 10 (9)	0
Malaysia	10	0,15 (9)	15
Malta	15	0, 10 (9)	0, 10 (21)
Mauritius	5, 15 (17)	27 (23)	15
Mexico	15	0, 15 (9)	0, 15 (18)
Montenegro (Yugoslavia Ex)	10	10	10
Morocco	10, 15 (30)	0, 10 (9)	5, 10 (18)
Mozambique	15	0, 10 (9)	10
Netherlands	5, 10, 15 (40)	0, 10 (9)	5

Italy

Recipient	Dividends	Interest	Royalties
	%	%	%
New Zealand	15	0, 10 (9)	10
Norway	15	0, 15 (9)	5
Oman	5, 10 (41)	0, 5 (9)	10
Pakistan	15, 25 (42)	0, 30 (9)	30
Philippines	15	0, 10,15 (43)	25
Poland	10	0, 10 (9)	10
Portugal	15	0, 15 (9)	12
Romania	10	0, 10 (9)	10
Russia	5, 10 (12)	10	0
Saudi Arabia (19)	5, 10 (44)	5	10
Senegal	15	0, 15 (9)	15
Serbia (Yugoslavia Ex)	10	10	10
Singapore	10	0, 12.5 (9)	15, 20 (18)
Slovak republic	15	0	0, 5 (21)
Slovenia (19)	5, 15, (17)	10	5
South Africa	5, 15 (17)	0, 10 (9)	6
South Korea	10, 15 (30)	0, 10 (9)	10
Soviet Union Ex (45)	15	0	0
Spain	15	0, 12 (9)	4, 8 (18)
Sri Lanka	15	0, 10 (9)	10, 15 (21)
Sweden	10, 15 (46)	0, 15 (9)	5
Switzerland	15	12.5	5
Syria	5, 10 (29)	0, 10 (9) (47)	18
Tanzania	10	15	15
Thailand	15, 20 (48)	0, 10 (49)	5, 15 (18)
Trinidad and Tobago	10, 20 (50)	10	0, 5 (21)
Tunisia	15	0, 12 (9)	5, 12, 16 (51)
Turkey	15	15	10
Uganda	15	0, 15 (9)	10
Ukraine	5, 15 (52)	0, 10 (9)	7
United Arab Emirates	5, 15 (18)	0	10
United Kingdom	5, 15 (53)	0, 10 (9) (28)	8
United States	0, 5, 15 (54)	0, 10 (55)	0, 5, 8 (56)
Uzbekistan	10	0, 5 (9)	5
Venezuela	10	0, 10 (9)	7, 10 (21)
Vietnam	5, 10, 15 (57)	0, 10 (9)	7.5, 10 (58)
Zambia	5, 15 (18)	0, 10 (59)	10

Notes

The numbers in parentheses refer to the notes below:

1. Rates depend on the nature of the interest and/or of the recipient. The rates on debenture loans depend on the legal instruments adopted and the redemption period, mainly:
    a. 0% applies on loan agreements and ordinary notes;
    b. 12.5% on bonds if the term of the bond issue is longer than 18 months;

   c.   27% if the bond issue period is shorter than 18 months.
2. 0% is applicable on dividends received by shareholders holding no less than the 20% of the share capital (2% in the case of listed entities), so called "qualified investments".
3. The rate is applicable on 75% of the gross amount of the royalty paid.
4. Pursuant to the EU Directives and provided that the requirements set forth therein are met, payments of dividends, interest and royalties made by an Italian company to a EU resident group company can be withholding tax exempt. Specifically for the dividends, the minimum shareholding requirement (to benefit from this exemption) is currently equal to 10%.
5. Should the full withholding tax exemption not apply, 1.375% is applicable on dividends paid to EU tax residents.
6. Pursuant to the 2004 CH/EU tax agreement and provided that the requirements contained therein are met, payments of dividends, interest and royalties made by an Italian company to a CH tax resident group company can be withholding tax exempt.
7. Non-resident persons have the right to obtain reimbursement for up to four-ninths of the withholding effected, upon proof of the actual taxation of the dividends in the foreign country where the recipient is resident.
8. Provided that all conditions are met, domestic tax legislation is applicable if more favourable for the taxpayer.
9. The 0% rate applies to interest paid to public bodies or any agency or instrumentality (including a financial institution) in relation to loans made in application of an agreement concluded between the Governments of the Contracting States.
10. The 5% rate applies to royalties arising from the use of any copyright from literary, artistic or scientific work. The 15% rate applies in all other cases.
11. The 10% rate applies to royalties arising from the use of any copyright of literary, artistic or scientific work. The 18% rate applies in all other cases.
12. Withholding tax is 5% if the foreign company holds at least 10% of the capital of the Italian company (this share should be at least USD 100,000 or its equivalent in any other currency); otherwise, the rate is 10%.
13. The higher rate applies if the Austrian company directly owns more than 50% of the capital in the Italian company.
14. Withholding tax is 10% if the foreign company holds at least 10% of the capital in the Italian company; otherwise, it is 15%.
15. The 0% rate applies to interest on public bonds. Withholding tax is 10% if the interest is derived by a bank or any other financial institution. The 15% rate applies in all other cases.
16. Withholding tax is 25% on royalties arising from use or the right to use trademarks. The 15% rate applies in all other cases.
17. The 5% rate applies if the foreign company holds directly at least 25% of the capital of the company paying the dividends. Withholding is 15% in all other cases.
18. The lower rate applies to copyright royalties, excluding films, etc.
19. In force from 1 January 2010.
20. Withholding is 18% on dividends paid by a company which is a resident of the Republic of the Ivory Coast and which is exempt from tax on its income or which is not subject to that tax at the normal rate. The 15% rate in all other cases.
21. The lower rate applies to copyright royalties, including films, etc.
22. The 0% rate applies if the Danish company has owned directly at least 25% of the capital of the company paying the dividends for a 12-month period prior to the date the dividends are declared. Withholding is 15% in all other cases.
23. The Italian domestic rates apply as no reduction is provided under the treaty.
24. The 5% rate applies if the foreign company holds directly at least 10% of the capital of the company paying the dividends. Withholding is 15% in all other cases.
25. The 5% rate applies on royalties paid for the use of industrial, commercial or scientific equipment. Withholding is 10% in all other cases.
26. 10% of the gross amount of the dividends if the beneficial owner is a company (other than a partnership) which holds directly more than 50% of the capital of the company paying the dividends. Withholding is 15% in all other cases.
27. Non-resident shareholding companies with more (less) than 10% of the capital of the company subject to 5% (15%) withholding tax.

28. The lower rate applies to interest on public bonds and trade credits, and to interest arising from the sale of equipment.
29. Withholding tax is 5% if the company holds at least 25% of the capital of the Italian company, otherwise it is 10%.
30. Withholding tax is 10% if the company holds at least 25% of the capital of the Italian company, otherwise it is 15%.
31. Withholding tax is 5% if the company holds at least 10% of the capital of the Italian company, otherwise it is 15%.
32. The 5% rate applies to dividends if the beneficial owner is a company which owns at least 10% of the capital of the company paying the dividends for a 12-month period ending on the date the dividend is declared. The 15% rate applies in all other cases.
33. Withholding tax is 15% if the company holds at least 10% of the shares of the Italian company, otherwise it is 25%.
34. The 10% rate applies on royalties in respect of payments of any kind received as a consideration for the use of, or the right to use industrial, commercial or scientific equipment, or for information concerning industrial, commercial or scientific experience. Withholding is 15% in all other cases.
35. Withholding tax is 10% if the foreign company holds at least 25% of the entire voting shares in the Italian company, otherwise it is 15%.
36. Withholding tax is 5% if the foreign company holds directly at least 10% of the capital in the Italian company, otherwise, it is 15%.
37. The higher rate applies if the Kuwaiti resident holds 75% or more of the capital in the Italian company.
38. The 5% rate applies to royalties paid for the use of industrial, commercial or scientific equipment. Withholding is 10% in all other cases.
39. Applicable only to companies that are not considered holding companies in Luxembourg.
40. The 5% rate applies if the Netherlands company has owned more than 50% of the voting shares in the Italian company for at least 12 months. The 10% rate applies if it has so owned more than 10%; the 15% rate applies in all other cases.
41. Withholding tax is 5% if the foreign company holds directly at least 15% of the capital in the Italian company, otherwise, it is 10%.
42. Withholding tax is 15% if the company holds at least 25% of the capital of the Italian company, otherwise it is 25%.
43. The 0% rate applies to interest on public bonds. The 10% rate applies to interest on other bonds. Withholding is 15% in all other cases.
44. The 5% rate applies to dividends in the country of residence of the beneficial owner if the beneficial owner is a (joint stock) company that owned at least 25% of the capital of the distributing company for at least 12 months before the distribution. The 10% rate applies in all other cases.
45. Is applied until new double tax treaties with the following countries are ratified: Azerbaijan, Moldova, Kirghizstan, Tajikistan and Turkmenistan.
46. Withholding cannot exceed 10% if the Swedish company holds at least 51% of the entire voting rights in the Italian company.
47. The lower rate applies to interest on any loan granted by a bank.
48. Withholding tax is 15% if the company in Thailand holds at least 25% of the entire voting rights of the Italian company; otherwise it is 20%.
49. The 0% rate applies to interest on public bonds and to interest received by an administrative subdivision or a local authority. The 10% rate applies if the interest is received by a financial institution (including an insurance company) and the enterprise paying the interest engages in an industrial undertaking. In case of a special relationship between the parties the treaty is not applicable to the part which exceeds the amount which would have been agreed upon by the payer and the recipient in the absence of such relationship. The excess part of the payments shall remain taxable according to the law of each Contracting State.
50. Withholding tax is 10% if the company in Trinidad and Tobago holds at least 25% of the capital of the company paying the dividends otherwise, it is 20%.

51. The 5% rate applies to copyright royalties on literary, artistic or scientific work. The 16% rate applies to a trademark, to cinematograph and television films, to industrial, commercial or scientific equipment. The 12% rate applies in other cases.
52. Withholding tax is 5% if the foreign company holds at least 20% of the capital in the Italian company, otherwise, it is 15%.
53. Non-resident shareholding companies with more than 10% of the voting power are subject to 5% withholding tax. The 15% rate applies in all other cases.
54. The 0% rate applies if the beneficial owner of the dividends is a qualified governmental entity that holds, directly or indirectly, less than 25% of the voting stock of the company paying the dividends.
    The 5% rate applies to dividends if the beneficial owner is a company which owns at least 25% of the voting rights of the company paying the dividends for a 12-month period ending on the date the dividend is declared. The 15% rate applies in all other cases.
55. The 0% rate applies on certain categories of interest that are exempt from taxation in the source State:
    a. The beneficial owner is a qualified governmental entity that holds, directly or indirectly, less than 25% of the capital of the entity paying the interest;
    b. Interest is paid with respect to debt obligations guaranteed or insured by a qualified governmental entity of either Contracting State and the recipient is the beneficial owner of the interest;
    c. Interest is paid or accrued with respect to outstanding balances between enterprises for the sale of goods, merchandise, or services;
    d. Interest is paid or accrued in connection with the sale on credit of industrial, commercial, or scientific equipment.
    The 10% rate is applied in all other cases.
56. The 0% withholding tax applies for the use of, or right to use, a copyright of literary, artistic or scientific work (excluding royalties for computer software, motion pictures, films, tapes or other means of reproduction used for radio or television broadcasting). The 5% rate applies for the use of, or the right to use, computer software or industrial, commercial, or scientific equipment. The 8% rate applies in all other cases.
57. Withholding tax is 5% if the company holds at least 70% of the capital of the Italian company; it is 10% if the company holds at least 25% of the capital of the Italian company, otherwise it is 15%.
58. Withholding tax is 7.5% on royalties for technical services.
59. The 0% rate applies to interest paid to the Zambian government or local authority thereof or any agency or instrumentality (including a financial institution) wholly owned by that government or local authority.

The Italian Parliament is expected to ratify tax treaties with Azerbaijan, Belgium, Canada, Cuba, Gabon, Iran, Lebanon, Moldova, Mongolia, Qatar and San Marino.

The treaties with Congo and Kenya have been ratified but have not entered into force.

Negotiations and re-negotiations have been initiated with Austria, Jamaica, India, Ireland, Liberia, Mexico, United Kingdom and Trinidad and Tobago.

Tax administration

Returns
Corporate income tax returns must be filed by the end of the ninth month following the tax year-end.

The filing deadline for VAT returns is 30 September because VAT follows the calendar year. The filing deadline for withholding tax agent returns is 31 July for both the simplified withholding tax return and the ordinary withholding tax return.

Italy

Payment of taxes

For IRES and IRAP purposes the tax law provides for both advance payments and settlement payments. The advance payments are equal to the net tax payable for the previous tax period and are due during the tax period to which they refer. Advance payments are split into two instalments:

* 40% by the sixteenth of the sixth month following the tax year-end; and
* 60% by the end of the eleventh month following the tax year-end.

Settlement payments are due by the sixteenth day of the sixth month following the tax year-end to which they refer.

Missed and/or late payments of taxes of whatever kind and nature incur a penalty equal to 30% of the unpaid/late paid tax.

VAT credit offset with other taxes

From 2010 to offset a VAT credit against other taxes for an amount higher than EUR 10,000, it will be necessary to wait until the sixteenth of the month following the filing of the yearly VAT return on which the credit is shown.

Furthermore, in order to avoid abuse, taxpayers intending to offset a VAT credit for an amount greater than EUR 15,000 are required to ask their tax advisors or auditors to affix their signature to the VAT return, which is known as the "conformity mark".

Administrative penalties

Failure to file a tax return implies a penalty ranging from 120% to 240% of the taxes due. Minimum penalties (ranging from EUR 258 to EUR 1,032) are applicable if no tax liability emerged in the return.

Tax return showing either a taxable income lower than the one assessed or a tax credit higher than those owed to the taxpayer (i.e., untrue tax return) implies a penalty ranging from 100% to 200% of the higher taxes ultimately due.

Omitted and/or late payments of taxes of whichever kind and nature imply a penalty equal to 30% of the unpaid/late paid tax.

Special rules apply where similar violations are repeated over various years.

Statute of limitations

The Italian tax authorities are entitled to make an assessment in relation to direct taxes (IRES and IRAP), VAT and withholding tax returns up to the end of the fourth calendar year following the year in which the tax return was filed. Under certain circumstances (e.g., no return filed or fraud giving rise to criminal law penalties) the above deadlines may be extended.

Tax disputes can be settled by accepting all the issues raised in the tax auditor's report without any challenge and by paying the related tax and reduced penalties. A number of other options to avoid tax litigation are provided for by law.

Administrative checks on tax returns may be carried out within the year following that in which the tax return has been filed for larger companies having a yearly turnover in excess of EUR 300 million (turnover to be progressively decreased to EUR 100 million).

With limited exceptions, corporations that usually are in tax loss position will be subject to specific control.

Other issues

Transfer pricing

Income deriving from operations with non-resident corporations which directly or indirectly control the Italian entity, are controlled by the Italian entity or are controlled by the same corporation controlling the Italian entity, have to be valued on the basis of the normal value of the goods transferred, services rendered and services and good received, if an increase in taxable income derives there from. Possible reductions in taxable income as a result of the normal value rule are allowed only on the basis of mutual agreement procedures or the EU Arbitration Convention.

The normal value is the average price or consideration paid for goods and services of the same or similar type, carried on at free market conditions and at the same level of commerce, at the time and place in which the goods and services were purchased or performed. For the determination of the normal value reference should be made, to the extent possible, to the price list of the provider of goods or services, and, in their absence, to the price lists issued by the chamber of commerce and to professional tariffs, taking into account usual discounts.

Other regulations

Operating guidelines provided by Ministry of Finance were released in 1980 following the 1979 OECD Transfer Pricing Report. Also the 1995 OECD guidelines are considered as a reference and the basis for any mutual agreement or advanced pricing agreements (APA) procedures. However, they have not been incorporated as such yet into the Italian tax framework and, in some cases, local practice may vary from both the 1979 and the 1995 OECD positions.

New rules to reflect the OECD guidelines are expected to be issued.

Burden of proof

As a general principle the burden of proof lies with the Italian tax authorities. However, a taxpayer is expected to demonstrate the fairness of its inter-company transactions in the event of an assessment by the tax authorities.

Particular rules apply to cross-border transactions involving counterparties (including third parties) resident in tax havens.

Adoption of IFRS and taxation

The Italian tax law provides for two basic principles and some specific rules for taxation of a company adopting IAS/IFRS in the statutory financial statements:

- Derivation principle *("Principio della Derivazione")*: the taxable base of companies is determined starting from the net income arising from the profit and loss, increased or decreased by items directly booked to equity pursuant to the application of IAS/IFRS. To such "rectified" income the general tax adjustments set forth by the Corporate Income Tax Law apply. In this respect, as exception to the general tax criteria, the accrual principle and the qualification and classification criteria stated by the IFRS are relevant for the calculation of the taxable base; and

Italy

- Neutrality principle *("Principio della Neutralità")*: such principle aims to neutralise the effects deriving from the movement to IAS/IFRS (First Time Adoption – FTA). Conversely, such principle does not grant an equal treatment for companies adopting or not IAS/IFRS (in fact, specific rules are applicable only to IAS/IFRS adopters – for example, taxation of dividend on HFT securities, derivatives, etc.).

The following specific rules applicable to IAS adopters must be considered:

- Adjustments or recognitions of transactions made in equity are relevant for tax purposes, to the extent that such items are in compliance with general tax principles;
- For equity instruments the legal classification is prevailing over the accounting one (debt vs. equity classification);
- At certain conditions, unrealised profits and losses recognised in the profit and loss become taxable and deductible (e.g., fair value on securities other than AFS, HTM and participations, on derivatives transactions not concluded for hedging reasons, etc.);
- The tax treatment of the transactions between IFRS adopters and non-IFRS adopters, in relation to operations concluded between an IFRS adopter and a non-IFRS adopter, is based on the accounting principle adopted by each company (for example, financial leasing); and
- Depreciation and amortisation are permitted within the rates provided by the tax rules, independently by the amounts booked. In this respect, the abolition of the imperative systematic depreciation of the goodwill and its substitution by the goodwill's review for impairment, does not affect the tax deduction of the goodwill amortisation that should be made for sole tax purposes.

Corporate taxes in Ivory Coast (Côte d'Ivoire)

For more information, contact:

Dominique Taty
Fidafrica SA
Immeuble Alpha 2000
20th Floor
Rue Gourgas – Plateau
Abidjan 01
Côte d'Ivoire
Tel: +225 20 31 54 67
Email: d.taty@ci.pwc.com

Significant developments

There have been some significant tax and regulatory developments regarding corporate taxation in the past years.

Further information is provided in the following sections.

Taxes on corporate income

Tax on industrial and commercial profits in Côte d'Ivoire is levied at 25%, subject to a minimum tax. The minimum tax is based on total turnover and is calculated at the rate of 0.5% (banking activities, 0.15%; oil companies, 0.10%), with a minimum of CFAF 2 million and a maximum of CFAF 30 million.

Corporate residence

In Côte d'Ivoire, companies are considered resident in tax jurisdictions where they have a registered fixed establishment.

Other taxes

Value-added tax (VAT)

VAT is a non-cumulative tax levied on the sales of goods and services at the rate of 18%. Subject to certain restrictions, VAT is recoverable. The rate is reduced to 9% for milk and pasta products, which contain 100% durum wheat semolina.

Tax on banking operations (TOB)

A cumulative tax of 10% is levied on bank services rendered.

Special tax for equipment

A tax of 0.08% is calculated on the total turnover and is paid monthly.

Business franchise tax

The business franchise tax includes a "turnover tax" and a proportional tax. The "turnover tax" is calculated on the turnover at the rate of 0.5% with a maximum of CFAF 3 million and a minimum of CFAF 300,000. The proportional tax is based on the rental value of the professional office location (based on general office rents). The rate is 18.5%.

Ivory Coast (Côte d'Ivoire)

Real-estate tax
A real estate tax is imposed at the rate of:

*   1.5% for the undeveloped lands;
*   4% on land revenue; and
*   11% on the developed land or 15% when the built property is used by the company itself. The rate is reduced to 4% for unoccupied buildings.

In case of the transfer of property through a direct sale, taxes are assessed at the following rates: 10% for lease transfers; 10% or 7.5% for the sale of real estate; and 10% for the sale of businesses.

Advance payment of property tax
Property owners are required to withhold 15% of rentals, payable every fifteenth of the month to the tax authorities. This is an advance payment on the annual real estate tax by the owner of the estate property.

Payroll tax
Taxes are levied at the rates of 2.8% for local employees and 12% for expatriate employees on the total taxable remuneration, including salaries, benefits and benefits-in-kind.

Registration taxes
Registration of capital contributions is taxed, whether the capital or increase in capital is made in cash or in kind. The rate is 0.6% for contributions up to CFAF 5 billion and 0.2% for contributions over CFAF 5 billion, with a minimum of CFAF 18,000. Increases in capital by incorporation of reserves are taxed at 6%.

In the event of a capital increase through a merger, the increase in the share capital of the acquiring company is taxed at half the rate – 0.3% for amounts up to CFAF 5 billion and 0.1% for amounts over CFAF 5 billion.

Stamp duty
A direct tax is paid for any document subject to a registration procedure, for an acknowledgment of a cash payment and for bills of exchange.

Tax on insurance premiums
Insurance premiums are subject to tax as follows:

Policy Type	%
Marine policies	7.0
Life policies	Exempted when contract's duration is more than three years
Fire policies	25.0
Health policies	8.0
Export credit insurance	0.1
Other (e.g., personal liability, transportation)	14.5

Premiums paid under commercial shipping insurance policies for maritime risks are exempt. The tax may be paid by the insurance company, its agent or the subscriber, when the subscriber pays the premiums directly abroad.

Social security contributions

Employers must contribute to the social security system (CNPS) at the following rates:

	%	Monthly ceiling (CFAF)
Family allowance	5.75	70,000
Work injury	2.0-5.0	70,000
Retirement pension	4.8	1,647,315

Tax for national reconstruction

The tax for national reconstruction was eliminated in May 2009.

Withholding tax (WHT) on public contracts

Any payment made by government bodies or public institutions for a contract for goods or services is subject to a 10% withholding tax, except the companies registered at the Directorate of Large Companies (Direction des Grandes Entreprises), with a minimum turnover over CFAF 1 billion. The tax is recoverable and may be applied to VAT and to income taxes due and withheld by employers. Contractors who do not have a permanent establishment in Côte d'Ivoire are not subject to this tax. Surplus tax payments and tax credits are refundable.

Contributions for the end of the crisis

This is a new tax enforced by FY2010 fiscal law. It is calculated at a rate of 3% on some expenses of entities which have CFAF 1 billion or more in turnover. The annual amount of the due tax is capped to CFAF 150,000,000, as per the discussions with the Government.

Withholding tax on small size businesses

The FY2010 financial law has created a 5% WHT on the remunerations paid to individual service providers registered under the forfeit and synthetic tax regimes.

Branch income

The tax rate for branch income is the same as that for corporate income. After-tax branch earnings are subject to a 12% tax (IRVM) calculated on 50% of the taxable profit. This is analogous to the WHT on dividends.

Income determination

Inventory valuation

Inventory is generally stated at the lower of cost or market value. Last-in, first-out (LIFO) and first-in, first-out (FIFO) are permitted. Book and tax conformity is required.

Capital gains

Capital gains are normally taxed at full corporate rates. However, the tax on capital gains, exclusive of recaptured depreciation, can be deferred if the gain is reinvested within three years.

Inter-company dividends

Inter-company dividends are included in taxable income at 50% of the net amount received (after 12% withholding tax). The exemption is increased to 95% for dividends

I

Ivory Coast (Côte d'Ivoire)

received from a subsidiary if a parent company domiciled in Côte d'Ivoire owns 10% of the subsidiary.

Foreign income
Resident corporations are taxed on their worldwide income, except for profits derived from business conducted through a permanent establishment (PE) outside Côte d'Ivoire. Since income derived from business conducted outside Côte d'Ivoire is not taxable, no tax credit is allowed. Interest and dividends from foreign sources are entitled to certain deductions (see "Other significant items") to alleviate instances of double taxation. Subject to provisions of tax treaties, no deductions or tax credits are allowed for revenue from royalties and services.

Stock dividends
Stock dividends are unusual, but in the event they are declared, they are not taxable to the recipient.

Other significant items
Interest from loans and dividends is brought into taxable income at 50% of the net amount earned by the company. Dividends derived from subsidiaries are brought into taxable income at 5% of the net income earned.

Deductions

Depreciation and depletion
Depreciation is generally computed on a straight-line basis over the useful life of the asset (buildings, 20 years; automobiles, three years); accelerated depreciation is sometimes permitted for machinery. The following depreciation rates are generally accepted for tax purposes:

	%
Buildings	5
Machinery, equipment	20, 10, 8
Office furniture	10
Office equipment	20
Vehicles	33.3
Computing equipment	20 to 50

A time coefficient is applied to the rate of depreciation to obtain the declining balance. Depreciation rates may be amended, but only after agreement with the tax authorities.

New plants and equipment may be depreciated at twice the normal rate in the first year of use, provided they are depreciated over at least six years. Under certain circumstances, buildings used for staff housing may be depreciated at 40% of cost in the first year. Annual depreciation must be booked to preserve tax deductibility. The whole or any part of the annual charge can then be deferred in annual accounts for fiscal years showing a tax loss. Recaptured depreciation is taxed at full rates. Tax and book conformity is obligatory.

Depletion allowances as such do not exist, but tax incentives are available for exploration to replace depleted natural reserves.

Net operating losses
Losses may be carried forward five years. Losses derived from depreciation can be carried forward indefinitely.

Payments to foreign affiliates
Reasonable royalties, interest, and management and service fees paid to foreign parent companies are tax deductible. However, the deductions should not exceed 5% of the turnover and 20% of the overhead. Otherwise, the portion exceeding the ceiling is not tax deductible; the onus is on the taxpayer to prove that expenses are justified and reflect real transactions.

Other significant items
1. Legal reserve: 10% of net profit must be transferred to a reserve for legal fees until the reserve equals 5% of the paid-up share capital.
2. To be tax deductible, provisions must relate to existing liability or loss. General reserves are not deductible.
3. Interest paid to shareholders may be deducted. The maximum interest rate allowed is related to the Banque Central des Etats de l'Afrique de l'Ouest (BCEAO) rate plus three points. The reimbursement of the loan must take place in the five years following the loan.
4. Fines and third party taxes borne by corporations are not tax deductible.

Group taxation

Group taxation is not permitted.

Tax incentives

Inward investment
Investment Law No. 95-620 of 3 August 1995 divides the country into two investment zones, offering incentives for up to five or eight years in each area.

The Investment Code provides for 100% tax exemption during the first three or six years (depending on the nature of the activity and the zone), then 50% and 25% progressively for the last two years of exemption. Exemption periods may be extended to complete a scheduled investment programme.

Incentives are divided into two programmes: "prior declaration" for investments of less than CFAF 500 million that create new activity and "prior agreement" for investments of CFAF 500 million or more that create new activity or develop an existing activity. Both programmes are handled by the Centre de Promotion des Investissements en Côte d'Ivoire (CEPICI) and are open to all sectors except trade, public works, building construction, transportation, banking and insurance.

Prior declaration investments may be exempt from tax on corporate income and the business franchise tax. Prior agreement investments benefit from exemptions varying with the size and nature of the project, as follows.

1. Creating a new enterprise or a new activity in an existing enterprise:
   - Investments of CFAF 500 million to CFAF 2 billion may be exempt from tax on corporate income; business franchise tax; import duties and taxes (with the exception of a 5% tax on machinery, equipment and spare parts).

Ivory Coast (Côte d'Ivoire)

- Investments of more than CFAF 2 billion may be exempt from property tax, in addition to the above.
2. Developing an existing activity:
   - Investments of at least CFAF 500 million may be exempt from import duties and taxes (with the exception of a 5% tax on machinery, equipment and spare parts).

These incentives may not be combined with sector-specific investment programmes, such as those for mining and hydrocarbons.

Capital investment

With prior approval of the tax authorities and varying with geographical location, 35% to 40% of the total investment in fixed assets related to commercial, industrial or agricultural activity may be deducted from taxable income. The deduction is limited to 50% of taxable profits. The balance of deduction of the first year may be carried forward over the three following years.

Export incentives

No VAT is levied on export sales.

Sales and provisions of services made to export companies, which process certain farm products (cocoa, coffee, banana, hevea, palm tree oil), and realise at least 70% of their turnover from exports are free from VAT. The exemption is granted for the purpose of avoiding new cases of VAT credits in this line of business.

Export incentives – mining industry

During the exploration phase, investments may be exempt from payroll tax; VAT on goods and services; additional tax (on the sale of goods) on imports and purchases; all import taxes and duties including VAT on materials, machines and equipment used in research activities; and half of the registration duties applicable to in-kind or cash share-capital contributions.

During the production phase, mining activities may have a five-year exemption from corporate income tax and relief from all import duties, including VAT on recovered investments required for exploitation. In addition, they may be granted temporary admission of machines and equipment that facilitate research and exploitation. A tax on profit is levied as soon as investment funds are recovered. Mining enterprises may not combine these incentives with those of the Investment Code.

Export incentives – petroleum service contractors

A special and optional tax treatment applies to petroleum service contractors that meet established criteria. Corporate tax, distribution tax, payroll tax, income tax on salaries, and the tax on insurance premiums are calculated on the turnover of the contractor. The total taxes represent 5.636% of turnover. Standard rates apply for business franchise tax and social security contributions for local personnel. The exemption from customs duties and VAT for oil companies is extended to petroleum service contractors.

Withholding taxes

Withholding taxes (WHT) are levied as follows.

1. Impôt sur le revenu des valeurs mobilières (IRVM) – 12% or 18% on dividends and directors' fees;
2. Impôt sur le revenue des créances (IRC) – 18% on interest payments, reduced to 13.5% (individuals) and 16.5% (businesses) on bank deposit interest. Foreign banks are subject to 18% tax on loan interest or 9% on equipment loans with minimum three-year terms;
3. Impôt sur les benefices non commerciaux (BNC) – 25% of 80% of revenues on royalties, license fees, and management and service fees paid by Ivorian companies to foreign companies (effective rate– 20% of net amount paid). Treaties with Belgium, Canada, France, Germany, Italy, Norway, Switzerland, and the United Kingdom provide a maximum BNC rate of 10% on royalties and Management fees (GB). The tax treaty between the member states of West African Economic and Monetary Union (UEMOA) provides a maximum BNC rate of 15%; and
4. Interest on certificates of deposit (bons de caisse) – 25%.

Tax administration

Returns
Companies are required by law to have a 31 December fiscal year-end. The corporate income tax due is returned together with annual financial statements according local generally accepted accounting principles. The deadline for the filing is 30 April for entities with more than CFAF 1 billion turnover, 30 May for entities with less than CFAF 1 billion turnover and 30 June for the entities under the Synthetic tax regime.

Payment of tax
Tax withheld must be rendered to the tax authorities by the fifteenth of each month. Other taxes are rendered on varying dates.

Corporate taxes in Jamaica

For more information, contact:

Eric Crawford
PricewaterhouseCoopers
Scotiabank Centre
Cnr of Duke & Port Royal Street
Kingston, Jamaica
Tel: +1 876 922 8323
Email: eric.crawford@jm.pwc.com

Significant developments

Major changes were effected to the rules governing the taxation of ordinary and preference dividends. Historically, persons in receipt of dividends (whether ordinary or preference) derived from a company listed on the Jamaica Stock Exchange (JSE) suffered tax at the rate of zero percent on such dividend income. Effective 1 January 2009, ordinary dividends derived by Jamaican tax residents from resident companies are also taxed at a zero rate. This tax-free treatment does not extend to non-resident shareholders in receipt of dividends from resident companies and accordingly, all dividends paid to non-resident shareholders are now fully liable to income tax thereon (subject to any treaty protection or incentive relief available).

Subject to certain conditions being met, a company may claim an income tax deduction in respect of preference dividends paid during the year of assessment. The recipient of the dividend however, will be subject to income tax at the default rate of $33^{1}/_{3}\%$ in the case of a company and 25% in the case of an individual. To the extent that these preference dividends do not qualify for this income tax deduction, they will be treated in a similar manner to ordinary dividends (i.e., they will be tax-free in the hands of Jamaican resident shareholders).

Increase in special capital allowances
As part of a stimulus package, Jamaica increased the special capital allowances available to capital expenditure on certain machinery incurred by the owner/operator of a "qualifying business" from 50% to 100% of the capital expenditure. These new rates became effective 1 January 2010 and the operator should secure approval in order to claim allowances at these rates.

Increase in the general consumption tax rate
The rate of general consumption tax (GCT) was increased to 17.5% from 1 January 2010. This new rate applies generally to all goods and services taxable at the standard rate. Within the telecommunications industry, the standard rate of 25% applies to the provision of telephone services.

Imposition of GCT on electricity consumption
Prior to 2010, the supply of electricity to the public was exempt from GCT. The following measures now apply to the consumption of electricity both by residents and commercial users:

1. Supplies of electricity to residential customers up to 200KwH per month shall be zero-rated for GCT purposes; and

2. Supplies of electricity to residential customers (in excess of 200KwH per month) and to commercial or industrial consumers shall be subject to GCT at the rate of 10%.

Taxes on corporate income

Income tax at a basis rate of 33$^1/_3$% is payable by most corporations, including Jamaican branches of foreign corporations. Building societies (similar to savings and loans) are taxed at the rate of 30% on their profits.

The income of certain organisations is specifically exempt from income tax. These include pension and superannuation funds and charitable organisations approved by the Commissioner

There are no other local taxes on corporate income.

Corporate residence

A corporation, wherever incorporated, is resident in Jamaica if the central management and control of its business is exercised there. Normally, this is the case if meetings of directors and shareholders are held in Jamaica and major policy decisions of the corporation are made there.

Other taxes

Annual fee
A fee ranging from JAD 1,000 to JAD 35,000 is payable on or before 1 September, depending on the aggregate value of the company's assets. The minimum fee and maximum fee is payable where the aggregate value of the assets is less than JAD 50,000 and greater than JAD 100 million, respectively.

Consumption taxes, custom duties
The general consumption tax (GCT) is a value-added tax (VAT). The standard rate is 17.5%. Higher rates are applicable to some goods and services (tobacco products, liquor, motor vehicles, fuels and telephone charges). The list of items and services exempt from GCT includes a wide range of grocery and household items. Certain specified drugs, as well as other items and services, are zero-rated. GCT is also charged on imported services, hence where a taxable activity consists of imported services by a person who is not resident in Jamaica, the recipient of those services shall be deemed to be the registered taxpayer, and shall pay the tax chargeable in respect of the supply. This may be available as a credit in some cases against the tax payable by the recipient of the service.

Lower rates may be applicable to some sectors, such as hotels and other businesses in the tourism sector, which is taxed at an effective rate of approximately 10% as of 1 April 2010, rather than the standard rate of 17.5%.

In addition to normal customs duties, a user fee of 2% and an environmental levy of 0.5% are imposed on the value of imports. Also with effect from 1 January 2010, an additional 5% GCT has been levied on the commercial importation of goods subject to GCT. Certain categories of imports are however excluded from this advance GCT charge.

Jamaica

Real estate tax

All land in Jamaica is valued on the "site value" or "unimproved value." Owners of properties valued at JAD 300,000 or less pay a flat rate of JAD 1,000. Where the property exceeds this value, tax is payable at 0.75% of the excess over the threshold. These new rates became effective 1 April 2010.

Construction operations levy

A levy of 2% of the gross amount is payable on contracts relating to construction and tillage operations. The levy is in the nature of tax withheld at source and must be deducted by the taxpayer from the gross payment for the construction or tillage operations and paid to the Collector of Taxes within 14 days of the month in which the gross payments are made.

The levy paid is allowable as a credit against the income tax liability of the contractor.

Branch income

Branch income is taxed at the same rate as that of local corporations and on a similar basis. The transfer of profits to head office is subject to a withholding tax of $33^1/_3$% or at a lower treaty rate, where applicable.

A branch operation, irrespective of the nature of its business activities, is subject to Jamaican tax on income derived from the island and elsewhere to the extent remitted to the island. In computing the income for tax purposes, expenses incurred outside of Jamaica, wholly and exclusively for the purpose of the branch's trade are deductible, including a reasonable proportion of head office expenses.

Transactions between the branch, its head office and affiliates should be at arm's-length values.

Income determination

Inventory valuation

Inventories are valued at the lower of cost or market value. The Commissioner of Taxpayer Audit & Assessment Department (TAAD) has made no pronouncement, but last-in, first-out (LIFO) is not generally permitted.

Any method of valuation that accords with standard accounting practice is acceptable for tax purposes, provided it is consistently applied at the beginning and end of the accounting period and it is not in contravention of the Income Tax Act.

Capital gains

There is no tax on capital gains. There is, however, a transfer tax of 4% of the sales proceeds (limited to 37.5% of the capital gain payable) on the transfer of land, building, securities, and shares. There is also stamp duty of 1% payable on the transfer/disposal of shares, and 3% for real property sold/transferred. Transactions on the Jamaica Stock Exchange are exempt.

Inter-company dividends

Inter-company (ordinary) dividends paid out of profits of a company resident in Jamaica to a shareholder resident in Jamaica can be paid without further tax.

Income tax is withheld at source on dividends paid to a non-resident shareholder. Such dividends paid are taxed at the rate of 33¹/₃% and 25% if paid to corporations and individuals, respectively. Lower rates of withholding are possible provided that the recipient is resident in a country that has concluded a double taxation agreement with Jamaica.

The term "franked income" refers to dividends received by a corporation subject to income tax, resident in the island, from which tax has been deducted at source. Where such dividends are received by a Jamaican resident company, they may be paid to that company's shareholders and all the way up the chain of companies without further deduction of tax, since the very first deduction of tax settles the tax liabilities of all subsequent recipients of the dividends.

However, the revenue authorities do not issue refunds or recognise a credit in respect of the underlying tax attributable to franked income.

Foreign income

A resident corporation is taxable on its worldwide income. Avoidance of double taxation is achieved by credits under tax treaties or, in the case of most Commonwealth countries, under the general Income Tax Act itself. Where recourse cannot be had to either of these, partial relief is granted by a deduction against income for the foreign tax.

Stock dividends

Stock dividend is not addressed specifically by our Income Tax Act. However, dividends paid, whether in cash, shares or a combination is generally subject to income tax. Where a dividend payment is not in money, it is treated as a net distribution after the deduction of income tax. Resident shareholders in receipt of stock dividends will be subject to income tax at the rate of 0%. Non-resident shareholders in receipt of stock dividends will be subject to income tax at the rate of 33¹/₃% in the case of corporations and 25% in the case of individuals.

Deductions

Depreciation and depletion

Depreciation is generally computed on the reducing balance basis over the useful life of the asset at specified rates. An election may be made for machinery and equipment to be depreciated at higher rates on the straight-line basis. Provision also exists for increased depreciation on machinery and equipment used for more than one shift in certain qualifying industries. Capital gain on depreciable property is not taxed. However, a recharge limited to the extent of the depreciation allowed (balancing charge) is taxable. Machinery and plants acquired by a "qualifying business" may be depreciated over one year instead of the estimated useful life of the asset. A qualifying business is one so designated by the Ministry of Industry Investment & Commerce.

Tax depreciation is not required to conform to book depreciation.

Net operating losses

Losses incurred may be carried forward indefinitely until fully utilised. There are provisions designed to disallow the deduction of such losses where the company that has accumulated them is sold under certain circumstances.

Jamaica

Payments to foreign affiliates

Royalties, management fees and interest charges paid to foreign affiliates are deductible to the extent that these payments are made at arm's-length rates. Withholding tax should be paid in respect of all services, unless exempted under a treaty.

Real estate taxes

Taxes on real estate from which income is derived is deductible.

Other significant items

Approved donations (not exceeding 5% of taxable income) to certain qualified charities and educational institutions are deductible.

Group taxation

Group taxation is not permitted in Jamaica.

Tax incentives

A certain number of incentive laws grant certain approved industries relief from taxation for a specified number of years. The capital may be either derived from local or foreign sources. Tax relief is given to resident shareholders on dividends paid out of tax-free profits. Relief to non-resident shareholders is generally limited to the applicable foreign tax rate.

Specific incentives are set out under the following acts:

- The Export Industry (Encouragement) Act;
- The Industrial Incentives Act;
- The Industrial Incentives (Factory Construction) Act;
- The Jamaica Export Free Zones Act;
- The Hotel Incentives Act;
- The Resort Cottages Incentives Act;
- The International Finance Companies (Income Tax Relief) Act;
- The Income Tax Act – (Agricultural & Venture Capital Incentives);
- The Urban Renewal (Tax Relief) Act 1995;
- The Motion Picture Encouragement Act;
- The Shipping Act; and
- The Factory Construction Act.

The incentives offered under the Industrial Incentives Act, the Export Industry Incentives Act and those available for the production of goods under the Jamaica Export Free Zones Act are to be phased out, given Jamaica's commitments under the World Trade Organization (WTO) agreement. This was expected to have been phased out by 1 January 2003. An extension of time has been granted for implementation until the end of 2013 with a two year phase-out period. In the meantime, approvals are being granted.

See Depreciation section for depreciation incentives available in the Income Tax Act. In addition to the aforementioned incentives, certain qualifying industries are able to write-off, over a period of time, 120% of the cost of machinery and equipment, excluding private motor vehicles.

Non-residents who place deposits with Jamaican banks can earn interest free of Jamaican tax in certain circumstances. The deposits may be designated in hard currency or Jamaican dollars.

Certain tax benefits accrue to employees and employers in respect of contributions made to an approved Employee Share Ownership Plan (ESOP) as well as the allocation of shares from such plans.

Withholding taxes (WHT)

The Jamaican Income Tax Act refers to deduction at source and not to withholding. The following references are to deduction at source. If it is proved that this exceeds the tax actually payable, refunds are made.

"Prescribed Persons" are required to withhold tax at source at a rate of 25% on interest income earned on investment instruments (subject to any lower rate as prescribed in a double taxation treaty). The Income Tax Act has been amended to provide a wider definition of the term "interest." "Prescribed persons" are entities defined as such. They include the Accountant General; banks operating under the Banking Act or the Bank of Jamaica Act; institutions operating under the Financial Institutions Act; building societies, societies registered under the Industrial and Provident Societies Act, unless certain conditions are met; the Ministry of Finance & the Public Service; life insurance companies; companies registered under the Companies Act in which the government or an agency of the government holds more than 50% of the ordinary shares and which issues interest bearing securities; issuers of commercial paper; unit trust management companies; and any person who is connected with any of the persons mentioned above (with the exception of the Accountant General).

Generally, all withholding taxes, including taxes withheld from dividend, interest, royalties, and fees must be remitted to the Inland Revenue within 14 days of the end of the month in which the payment is made.

Recipient	Dividends (1)		Interest (2) (%)	Royalties (%)	Management fees (%)
	Portfolio (%)	Substantial holdings (%)			
Resident corporations	0	0	25.0 (4)	Nil	Nil
Resident individuals	0 (3)	0 (3)	25.0 (4)	Nil	Nil
Non-treaty:					
Non-resident corporations	33⅓	33⅓	33⅓	33⅓	33⅓
Non-resident individuals	25.0	25.0	25.0	25.0	25.0
Treaty:					
Canada	15.0	22.5	15.0	10.0	12.5
CARICOM countries	0.0 (5)	0.0 (5)	15.0 (5)	15 (5)	15.0
China, P.R	5.0 (6)	5.0 (6)	7.5 (6)	10.0	33⅓
Denmark	15.0	10.0 (7)	12.5	10.0	10.0
France	15.0	10.0 (7)	10	10.0	10.0
Germany	15.0	10.0 (7)	12.5 (8)	10.0	10.0
Israel	22.5 (9)	15.0	15.0	10.0	33⅓

Jamaica

Recipient	Dividends (1)		Interest (2) (%)	Royalties (%)	Management fees (%)
	Portfolio (%)	Substantial holdings (%)			
Norway	15.0 (6)	15.0 (6)	12.5	10.0	10.0
Spain	10.0 (6)	5.0 (6)	10.0	10.0	10.0
Sweden	22.5 (6, 9)	15.0 (6)	12.5	10.0	10.0
Switzerland	15.0 (6, 7)	10.0 (6)	10.0	10.0	10.0
United Kingdom	15.0 (6, 7)	22.5 (6)	12.5	10.0	12.5
United States	15.0 (6, 7)	10.0 (6)	12.5	10.0	33⅓ (10)

Notes

The numbers in parentheses refer to the following numbered notes:

1. No tax is deducted where the dividends are paid out of franked income.
2. No withholding tax is applicable where the interest is paid by a local bank or financial institution to an approved overseas organisation, that is, a foreign bank or financial institution to an approved overseas organisation, that is, a foreign bank or financial institution approved by the Ministry of Finance & the Public Service.
3. Tax is withheld at the rate of 0% as of 1 January 2010 where ordinary dividend is paid by a company resident in Jamaica to a resident shareholder.
4. Tax is deducted from interest paid to Jamaican residents if payment is made by a prescribed person.
5. Rates apply only to specified member states.
6. The lower treaty rates do not apply if the recipient has a permanent establishment in the other territory that is "effectively connected" with the company paying the dividend.
7. A rate of 15% applies to an individual regardless of shareholding.
8. Reduced to 10% if received by a bank recognised as a banking institution under the laws of that state.
9. A rate of 22.5% applies to an individual regardless of the shareholding.
10. Nil in the absence of a permanent establishment.

A withholding tax rate of 25% is required to be withheld in respect of interest paid or credited by prescribed persons. However, certain categories of interest income earned on long-term savings accounts (LSAs) were made exempt from tax. They are as follows:

- Interest paid or credited in respect of investments or deposits made by individuals with prescribed persons if:
  - The deposit remains a minimum of five years without any withdrawal from the principal sum invested;
  - The deposit or investment (other than interest accrued or credited) does not exceed JAD 1 million dollars in any year;
  - The account is not transferable, except on the death or bankruptcy of the depositor or investor; and
  - Not more than 75% of the interest accrued in any year is withdrawn during the year.
- Benefits derived from investments in certain life insurance policies may also be exempt from income tax if specified criteria are satisfied.

Jamaica

Tax administration

Jamaica has established five taxation departments to handle tax administration.

1. The Tax Administration Services Department (TASD), which deals with the administrative issues and provides legal support to the other departments.
2. The Tax Payer Audit and Assessment Department (TAAD), which deals with the audit and assessment functions of income tax, general consumption tax (GCT/VAT), stamp duty and transfer tax.
3. The Taxpayer Appeals Department (TAD), which processes appeals to decisions made by Tax Commissioners.
4. The Customs Department, which administers taxes at the port of entry.
5. The Inland Revenue Department, which deals with all compliance and tax collection functions.

There is also a Financial Investigations Division in the Ministry of Finance which investigates customs breaches and fraudulent acts in respect of the various tax acts.

Returns

A corporation is subject to tax on its income for a calendar year. Where, however, the Commissioner of Income Tax is satisfied that a corporation normally prepares financial statements to a date other than 31 December, the company may be permitted to use the profits of its own financial year rather than the calendar year as the basis of assessment.

Payment of tax

The balance of income tax payable for a taxation year, after deduction of the instalments of estimated tax, is due on 15 March of the following year. It is the corporation's responsibility to determine the liability and settle it with the tax authorities. Quarterly instalments are based on an estimate of the year's liability or the actual tax payable for the previous year. Income tax returns are due for filing by 15 March in the year following the year of assessment.

Other issues

Corporation tax calculation
Calendar year 2010

Net profit before taxation		JAD 10,000,000
Add:		
Depreciation charged in the financial statements	500,000	
Interest payable, 2010 – accrued (1)	20,000	
Donations not approved	15,000	
Subscriptions disallowable	5,000	
Interest for late payment of income tax	4,000	
Legal fees re increase in share capital	21,000	
Bad debts – increase in general provision (2)	150,000	
Loss on sale of fixed assets	5,000	
Balancing charge (3)	7,500	
Capital expenditure charged in the financial statements	22,500	750,000
		10,750,000

Jamaica

Less:		
Interest payable, 2009 – now paid (1)	15,000	
Interest receivable, 2010 – accrued (1)	7,000	
Losses b/fwd Y/A 2009	40,000	
Capital allowances (4)	455,000	517,000
Taxable income		JAD 10,233,000
Income tax payable at 33$\frac{1}{3}$%		JAD 3,411,000
Less:		
Estimated (advance) tax payments	2,400,000	
Foreign tax credit	11,000	
Tax deducted from local bank interest	25,000	(2,436,000)
Net tax payable by 15 March 2011		JAD 975,000

Notes

1. Interest paid/received is dealt with on the cash basis, hence the adjustments for the amount receivable/payable.
2. Reserve for specific bad debts is allowed.
3. Recapture of excess tax depreciation is allowed.
4. Tax depreciation granted in lieu of book depreciation.

Corporate taxes in Japan

For more information, contact:

Hiroyuki Suzuki
Zeirishi-Hojin PricewaterhouseCoopers
Kasumigaseki Building 15 FL
2-5, Kasumigaseki 3-chome
Chiyoda-ku, Tokyo 100-6015
Japan
Tel: +81 3 5251 2400
Email: hiroyuki.suzuki@jp.pwc.com

Significant developments

The main changes in Japanese corporate tax system for the year 2010 are as follows:

- A new group taxation regime was enacted for domestic companies ("group companies") which are wholly owned by either a domestic company, foreign company or individual. Under this new regime, for example, the recognition of capital gains or losses from the transfer of certain assets between group companies is deferred until the asset is transferred to a non-group company (this rule will apply on or after 1 October 2010). Meanwhile, a group company that would otherwise qualify as a small and medium enterprise (SME) on a stand-alone basis is not eligible for the aforementioned benefits (e.g., reduced corporate tax rate, preferable allowable ratios for deductible portion of bad debt provisions, partial deductibility of entertainment expenses, carryback of tax losses, etc.) if the parent company of the group has paid-in capital of JPY 500 million or more.
- Several rules of the consolidated tax regime were amended. An important amendment states that pre-consolidation tax losses of a subsidiary can be carried forward into a consolidated tax group but may only be offset against taxable income of the subsidiary.
- Anti-tax haven controlled foreign corporation (CFC) rules are amended as follows:
  - The minimum effective tax rate for applying this rule is lowered from 25% to 20%;
  - The threshold of stock ownership which a taxpayer is required to own in a CFC is increased from 5% to 10%;
  - The holding of equity securities is disregarded on the business purpose test for the application of active business exemption where the CFC qualifies as a regional headquarters corporation; and
  - Some types of non-operating income derived by a CFC that qualifies for the active business exemption is included in the calculation of taxable income.

Taxes on corporate income

Corporation tax

The corporate tax burden (the effective tax rate) adds up from 40.87% to 42.05%, depending on the size of company. The rates are as follows:

	%
Paid-in capital of over JPY 100 million	30.0
Paid-in capital of JPY 100 million or less*:	

	%
First JPY 8,000,000 per annum	
– Fiscal year ending on and before 31 March 2009	22.0
– Fiscal year ending from 1 April 2009 to 31 March 2011	18.0
Over JPY 8,000,000 per annum	30.0

*Except for a company wholly owned by the company which has paid-in capital of JPY 500 million or more.

Enterprise tax (and special local corporate tax)

The enterprise tax is imposed on the corporation's income allocated to each prefecture. (Allocation generally is made on the basis of the number of employees.)

Based on FY2008 tax reform, the enterprise tax has been reduced and a national tax called 'Special Local Corporate Tax' has been introduced for fiscal year starting on or after 1 October 2008.

The standard rates of the enterprise tax, including the Special Local Corporate Tax are shown below.

Taxable base	Fiscal year starting before 1 October 2008	Fiscal year starting on and after 1 October 2008	Special local corporate tax
First JPY 4,000,000 per annum	5.0%	2.7%	81% of the current enterprise tax (see the immediate left column)
Next JPY 4,000,000 per annum	7.3%	4.0%	
Over JPY 8,000,000 per annum	9.6%	5.3%	

If the paid-in capital of a corporation is JPY 10 million or more and the corporation has places of business in more than two prefectures, the graduated rates above would not be applicable.

For utilities and insurance companies, the standard tax rate is shown as follows:

Taxable base	Fiscal year starting before 1 October 2008	Fiscal year starting on and after 1 October 2008	Special local corporate tax
Net revenue (net utility charges or net insurance premiums)	1.3%	0.7%	81% of the current enterprise tax (see the immediate left column)

In addition to the above enterprise tax, a "size-based" enterprise tax (Gaikei Hyojun Kazei) is applied to the company whose paid-in capital is more than JPY 100 million as of the year end. Factors such as the size of a corporation's personnel costs and its capital will determine the additional amount of tax payable, whereas, the existing profit-based enterprise tax will also continue to apply at the below tax rates. Therefore, a loss company in Japan may be required to pay tax based on value-added activities and the corporation's paid-in capital. The applicable standard rates are shown as follows:

Taxable base	Fiscal year starting before 1 October 2008	Fiscal year starting on and after 1 October 2008	Special local corporate tax
Profit-based tax:			148% of the current
First JPY 4,000,000 per annum	3.8%	1.5%	enterprise tax (see the
Next JPY 4,000,000 per annum	5.5%	2.2%	immediate left column)
Over JPY 8,000,000 per annum	7.2%	2.9%	
Additional value-based tax	0.48%	0.48%	N/A
Capital-based tax	0.2%	0.2%	N/A

Inhabitants tax

The inhabitants tax is imposed on the corporation's income allocated to each prefecture and city (municipal borough). Allocation generally is made on the basis of the number of employees, in the same way with the enterprise tax above.

The standard tax rate is 5% as the prefecture tax and 12.3% as the municipal tax. It is allowed to increase the tax rate, up to 6% for the prefecture tax and up to 14.7% for the municipal tax, depending on the determination of each local government.

In addition to the above, the inhabitant's tax is imposed on a per capita basis, in the range from JPY 70,000 to JPY 3,800,000.

Corporate residence

A company incorporated under the laws of Japan is a domestic corporation. The nationality of its shareholders or place of central management is not pertinent.

A corporation other than a domestic corporation is regarded as a foreign corporation.

A domestic corporation is taxed on its worldwide income. Meanwhile, a foreign corporation is taxed only on its Japan sourced income.

Other taxes

Family corporation tax

If an individual shareholder together with their family members own, either directly or indirectly, more than 50% of the total issued shares or voting rights of a Japanese corporation, the corporation is a family corporation (with exception for corporations with paid in capital of JPY 100 million or less) and it is subject to the family corporation tax in addition to the corporation tax.

A family corporation is liable for an additional tax at the rates shown below on undistributed current earnings in excess of the specified limits.

Taxable undistributed current earnings	%
First JPY 30,000,000 per annum	10
Next JPY 70,000,000 per annum	15
Over JPY 100,000,000 per annum	20
Inhabitants tax	Corresponding increase at rates previously shown

Japan

Consumption tax

Consumption tax (value-added tax) is levied when a business enterprise transfers goods, provides services or goods are imported in Japan. The applicable rate is 5%. Exports and certain services to non-residents are taxed at a zero rate. Specified transactions such as sales or lease of land, sales of securities and provision of public services are not subject to taxation. Consumption tax paid by the business enterprise shall be refundable by filing the consumption tax return to the extent that such transaction is recorded in the accounting book.

Business premises tax

This tax is levied and designated by each city in Japan such as Tokyo, Osaka, Nagoya, Fukuoka and other cities with a population of more than 300,000. A company that uses business premises in excess of 1,000 square metres and/or has more than 100 employees in a designated city is responsible to pay this tax based on the usage of the business (JPY 600 per square metre) and gross payroll (0.25% of gross payroll).

Fixed assets tax

The annual fixed assets tax is levied by the local tax authorities on real property and depreciable fixed assets used for business purposes. Real property is taxed at 1.7% (standard rate including city planning tax) of the value appraised by the local tax authorities. The depreciable fixed assets tax is assessed at 1.4% of cost after statutory depreciation.

Stamp duty

A stamp duty is levied on certain documents prepared in Japan. The tax amount is basically determined depending on the amount stated in the document.

Registration and license tax

Registration and license tax is levied where certain property is registered at the rate from 0.2% to 2% of taxable basis. The taxable basis varies with the subjects, e.g., the amount of capital for a company, and the amount of the estimated value by local tax authorities for real estate.

Customs duty

A customs duty is levied on imported goods based on the custom tariff table.

Branch income

Branch profits are taxed the same way as for corporate profits. However, the family corporation tax does not apply to a branch of a foreign corporation. In addition, no withholding tax is imposed on the repatriation of branch profits to the home office.

Income determination

General

The taxable income of a corporation is the aggregate income from all sources. There is no specific requirement to differentiate between the types of income. In principle, accounting for tax purposes follows generally accepted accounting principles in Japan, and income of a corporation is determined on an accrual basis.

Inventory valuation

Inventory cost should be determined by applying one of the following methods accepted for corporate tax purposes which includes actual individual cost, first-in, first-out (FIFO), weighted average, moving average, most recent retail, selling price reduction and lower of cost or market.

Capital gains

Capital gains and losses are classified as ordinary income and losses respectively.

Under certain circumstances, such as qualified reinvestment, exchange property to mention a few, taxes generally levied on capital gains may be deferred (rollover relief) as long as certain requirements are met. A special relief is available in the case of expropriation of real property by either the national or local government.

The recognition of capital gains or losses from the transfer of certain assets between group companies will be deferred until the asset is transferred to another group company or a non-group company (this rule will apply on or after 1 October 2010).

Inter-company dividends

Dividends received from a Japanese corporation are excluded from taxable income for corporate income tax purposes, provided that the recipient corporation owns 25% or more of the shares in the dividend-paying corporation. If a corporation owns less than 25% of the shares in the dividend-paying corporation, 50% of the dividends received from the dividend-paying corporation are excluded from taxable income.

An interest expense which is allocable as an investment cost of the shares that generate the dividend income (as defined above) effectively reduces the amount of dividend income. Note that this rule is not applicable to the dividends between 100% group companies.

The withholding tax for dividends is applicable at a rate of 7% (15% on and after 1 January 2012) or 20% depending on the type of stock from which the dividends were received and a tax credit may also be available for such withholding taxes.

Exemption of foreign dividends

95% of a dividend received by a company from a foreign company in which it has held at least 25% of the outstanding shares for a continuous period of six months or more, ending on the date on which the dividend is declared, can be excluded from the company's taxable income.

If the foreign company is resident in a country with which Japan has concluded a tax treaty for the avoidance of double taxation, and such treaty provides for the allowance of an indirect foreign tax credit for taxes paid by the foreign company on the profits out of which the dividend is paid where the company holds a certain percentage of the foreign company's outstanding shares (e.g., 10% based on the tax treaty between the US and Japan), that percentage will apply for the purpose of determining the availability of the above exemption to the extent that it is lower than 25%.

Foreign income

A Japanese corporation is subject to Japanese corporate income taxes on its worldwide income. However, Japanese corporations are allowed to claim a tax credit against the corporation and inhabitants taxes for foreign income taxes paid directly.

Japan

Based on the foreign dividend exemption system, as described in the *Exemption of foreign dividends section*, the indirect foreign tax credit system was repealed in 2009; any potential double taxation should be eliminated. Certain transitional measures were provided.

Foreign tax credit is not applicable for enterprise tax purposes, while foreign branch income attributable to business executed outside Japan is exempt from the enterprise tax.

Undistributed profit of a foreign subsidiary (i.e., CFCs) as well as overseas trusts located in a tax haven is included in its Japanese parent company's taxable income under certain conditions. Please note that a dividend paid by CFCs is not deductible when calculating the undistributed income.

Tax havens are defined as certain countries or territories that do not impose corporate income tax or that tax the income of a foreign subsidiary at a rate of 20% or less. And a Japanese corporation owning a 10% or more direct or indirect interest in a CFC would be required to include in its gross income, its pro-rata share of the taxable retained earnings of the CFC.

Deductions

Net operating losses
For corporate income tax and enterprise tax purposes (indirectly for inhabitants tax purposes), tax loss can be carried forward to offset future income for seven years.

When there is a change in ownership followed by certain events, such as abolish or drastic change in the business within a five-year period since business acquisition, the use of tax loss is limited.

Carryback of tax loss generally is available for one year for national corporation tax purposes. Currently, this carryback rule generally is suspended until the fiscal year ending until 31 March 2012. But for a small- or medium-sized company, defined as a company with the stated capital of JPY 100 million or less (except for a company wholly owned by the company which has paid-in capital of JPY 500 million or more after the group taxation regime is effective), it can be applied to the tax loss recognised in the fiscal year ending on or after 1 February 2009.

No carryback of losses is allowed for enterprise tax and inhabitants tax.

Taxes
The enterprise tax and business promises tax are deductible in the calculation of the taxable income for corporate tax purposes, when it is paid. However, corporate tax and inhabitants tax are not deductible. Fixed assets tax and other taxes are deductible, when it is assessed. Foreign income taxes also may be deductible if the Japanese corporation does not elect to claim a foreign tax credit.

Other significant items
Other deductions to arrive at final taxable income are listed as follows:

1. Entertainment expenses – in principle, entertainment expenses are not deductible for tax purposes. However, a corporation with paid-in capital of JPY 100 million

or less (except for a company wholly owned by the company which has paid-in capital of JPY 500 million or more after the group taxation regime is effective) may take a tax deduction up to the smaller of 90% of the actual disbursement for the entertainment expense or JPY 3.6 million (90% of JPY 4 million) for the fiscal year beginning on or after 1 April 2003 and before 31 March 2009. For the fiscal year beginning after 1 April 2009, such a corporation may take a tax deduction up to the smaller of 90% of the actual disbursement for the entertainment expense or JPY 5.4 million (90% of JPY 6 million). With regard to the expenses for eating and drinking, it is allowed to deduct up to JPY 5,000 per person for tax purposes.

2. Charitable contributions – except for certain designated donations, the tax deduction for charitable contributions is limited to the sum of 1.25% of certain taxable income plus 0.125% of paid-in capital and capital surplus. Donations subject to this limitation include economic benefits considered to be given as a subsidy. Donations to foreign affiliates are not deductible fully. In the case that a donation occurs between group companies that are wholly owned by a corporation (domestic or foreign), there will be no tax implications for either the donor or donee, i.e., no deduction for the donor and no taxation for the donee. This rule will apply on or after 1 October 2010.

3. Reserves – reserves recorded in the books of accounts, except for reserves for doubtful receivables and return of goods not sold, are not deductible for corporate tax purposes.

   a. Reserve for doubtful receivables: The limitation consists of two components: 1) an estimate of irrecoverable amounts from a debtor, and 2) a calculation of the limit in the aggregate based on either the actual historical bad debt percentage or statutory percentage (it is reduced for large corporations), excluding the irrecoverable amount of receivable in 1 above.

   b. Reserve for return of goods not sold: This reserve is available to corporations such as publishers, wholesalers of books and others, provided that the corporation sells the merchandise under an unconditional repurchase agreement.

4. Directors' remuneration – the remuneration paid to directors is deductible only in the three cases:

   a. Fixed monthly payments;

   b. Fixed payments in accordance with an advance notice to the tax office; or

   c. Performance bonuses paid in proportion to the company's earnings to directors who engage in the operation of the company's business, to the extent that certain requirements are met.

   If the amount of remuneration is deemed unreasonable by the tax authority, only the reasonable amount is deductible for tax purposes.

5. Thin capitalisation rules – the interest paid on the debt to controlling foreign shareholders is disallowed to the extent the average balance of debt on which that interest is paid is more than three times the equity of controlling foreign shareholders.

Group taxation

Consolidated tax regime

Under the consolidated tax regime, a consolidated group can report and pay national corporate income tax on a consolidated basis. A consolidated group be formed by the Japanese parent company and its 100% owned Japanese subsidiaries (directly or indirectly). The taxpayer may file an application to elect the consolidated group filing for tax purposes, but the election must include all of the parent's eligible

Japan

subsidiaries. Once the election is made, the consolidated filing, in principle, cannot be revoked unless there is a specific event, such as an ownership change that causes the qualifying conditions of a consolidated filing to fail, or an application to discontinue the consolidated group has been approved by the Commissioner of the National Tax Agency (NTA).

The taxable income of the consolidated group is computed on a consolidated basis by aggregating the taxable income or losses of each member of the consolidated group followed by the consolidation adjustments. Profits from intra-group transactions, except for transfer of certain assets as defined, should be included in the aggregate taxable income. Gains or losses from the intra-group transfer of certain assets would be deferred.

Pre-consolidation tax losses of a certain subsidiary can be carried forward into a consolidated tax group but may only be offset against taxable income of the subsidiary for the calculation of a consolidation income on or after 1 October 2010.

The consolidated national corporate income tax liability is determined by applying the corporate income tax rate to the consolidated taxable income and adjusted for consolidated tax credits. The total tax liabilities would be allocated back to each member company. The parent company files the consolidated return and pays the national corporate income tax for the group; however, each member company remains jointly and severally liable for the consolidated group's total national corporate income tax liability.

Local corporate income taxes levied on member companies would be paid on a separate company basis, but the amounts of local tax payable may be effected because of the consolidated filing.

Group taxation regime
Based on the FY 2010 tax reform, a new taxation regime has been introduced, aside from the consolidation tax regime above. This new regime is applicable to domestic companies ("group companies") that are wholly owned by either a domestic company, foreign company or individual, and automatically applies to group companies.

The key points of this regime are summarised as below:

- The recognition of capital gains or losses from the transfer of certain assets (including the transfer of assets as a result of a non-qualified or taxable merger) between group companies is deferred until the asset is transferred to another group company or a non-group company. The scope of assets is the same as that under the tax consolidation system i.e., fixed assets, land, securities, monetary receivables and deferred expenses (excluding securities for trading purposes and assets with a book value of less than JPY 10 million).
- Where a donation occurs between group companies, there is no tax implications for either the donor or donee, i.e., no deduction for the donor and no taxation for the donee. Note that this treatment is not applied to the group company owned by individuals. This is consistent with the treatment of a donation between members of a consolidated tax group.
- A dividend received from a group company can be fully excluded from taxable income without any reduction for allocable interest expense. This is consistent with the treatment of dividends between members of a consolidated tax group.

Meanwhile, a group company that would otherwise qualify as a SME on a stand-alone basis is not eligible for the aforementioned benefits (e.g., reduced corporate tax rate, preferable allowable ratios for deductible portion of bad debt provisions, partial deductibility of entertainment expenses, carryback of tax losses, etc.) if the parent company of the group has paid-in capital of JPY 500 million or more.

The above new group taxation regime is effective on 1 October 2010.

Tax incentives

Tax credit for research and development (R&D) cost
The tax credit for R&D cost is calculated based on gross R&D cost. The limitation of credit is determined on the certain portion of the corporation tax liability, as follows:

- For the fiscal year ending on or before 31 March 2009: 20% of the corporation tax liability.
- For the fiscal year beginning for the period 1 April 2009 to 31 March 2011: 30% of the corporation tax liability.

In addition to R&D credit, for tax years beginning for the period 1 April 2008 to 31 March 2012, the taxpayer may claim additional tax credits based on incremental R&D expense or excess R&D cost over sales described as follows:

1. 5% of the excess R&D costs over the annual average of R&D costs for the last three years; or
2. Excess R&D costs over 10% of the average sales amount times tax credit ratio* (* Tax credit ratio = ((R&D costs/average sales) −10%) x 0.2).

In the case that the amount of credit exceed 20% (or 30%) of the corporation tax liabilities discussed above and cannot be used in the year, this unused amount can be carried forward for one year.

Special tax credit for staff training expenses
SMEs that applied to file "blue form" tax returns under certain conditions (*see Returns under the Tax administration section*) are allowed to claim a tax credit against the corporation's income tax liability for certain staff training expenses for fiscal years beginning during the period 1 April 2008 to 31 March 2011.

The amount of tax credit is calculated using the tax credit rate for staff training expenses. The range of the tax credit rate is between 8% and 12%, depending upon the percentage of training expenses over the total labour costs.

Special tax treatment for investment in certain equipment
SMEs filing a blue tax return may elect, under certain conditions, to claim accelerated depreciation of 30% of the base acquisition cost or a special tax credit equivalent to 7% of the base acquisition cost on designated equipment to the extent that it is acquired by 31 March 2012. The maximum tax credit is limited to 20% of the taxpayers' corporate tax liability.

Japan

Withholding taxes (WHT)

Tax treaty network
As of 31 March 2010, Japan had entered into 47 tax treaties with 58 countries. Companies making certain payments are required to withhold income taxes using the following rates:

| Recipient | Dividends | | Interest | Royalties (2) |
| | Portfolio (3) | Substantial holdings (1) | | |
	%	%	%	%
Japanese corporations	7 or 20 (3)	20	Nil or 20 (4)	Nil
Resident individuals	10 or 20 (3)	20	Nil or 20 (4)	Nil
Foreign corporations, non-resident individuals:				
Non-treaty (5):	7 or 20 (3)	20	Nil, 15 or 20	20
Treaty (6):				
Australia	10	Nil or 5	10	5
Austria	20	10	10	10
Bangladesh	15	10	10	10
Belgium	15	10	10	10
Brazil	12.5	12.5	12.5	12.5, 15 or 25 (7)
Brunei	10	5	10	10
Bulgaria	15	10	10	10
Canada	15	5	10	10
China, P.R.	10	10	10	10
Czechoslovakia (former) (8)	15	10	10	Nil or 10 (8)
Denmark	15	10	10	10
Egypt (5)	15	15	Nil, 15 or 20	15 or 20 (9)
Finland	15	10	10	10
France	10	Nil or 5	10	Nil
Germany	15	10	10	10
Hungary	10	10	10	Nil or 10 (10)
India	10	10	10	10 (11)
Indonesia	15	10	10	10
Ireland, Rep. of	15	10	10	10
Israel	15	5	10	10
Italy	15	10	10	10
Kazakhstan	15	5	10	10(12)
Korea, Rep. of	15	5	10	10
Luxembourg	15	5	10	10
Malaysia	15	5	10	10
Mexico	15	Nil or 5 (13)	10 or 15	10
Netherlands	15	5	10	10
New Zealand (5)	15	15	Nil, 15 or 20	20
Norway	15	5	10	10

	Dividends			
Recipient	**Portfolio (3)**	**Substantial holdings (1)**	**Interest**	**Royalties (2)**
	%	%	%	%
Pakistan	10	5 or 7.5 (14)	10	10
Philippines	15	10	10	10 or 15 (15)
Poland	10	10	10	Nil or 10 (16)
Romania	10	10	10	10 or 15 (17)
Singapore	15	5	10	10
South Africa	15	5	10	10
Spain	15	10	10	10
Sri Lanka (18)	20	20	Nil, 15 or 20	Nil or 10
Sweden	15	Nil or 5 (19)	10	10
Switzerland	15	10	10	10
Thailand	7 or 20	15 or 20 (20)	10 or 25 (20)	15
Turkey	15	10	10 or 15 (21)	10
USSR (former) (22)	15	15	10	Nil or 10 (22)
United Kingdom	10	Nil or 5	10	Nil
United States	10	Nil or 5	10	Nil
Vietnam	10	10	10	10
Zambia	Nil	Nil	10	10

Notes

The numbers in parentheses above refer to the following notes:

The applicable treaty rates are effective as of 31 March 2010.

1. The tax treaty rates apply only to corporate shareholders. The applicable treaty should be checked for conditions required to claim the reduced rate.
2. The applicable treaty should be reviewed, because certain tax treaties exclude, such as film royalties and/or gain from copyright transfer from taxable income.
3. For certain dividends received from 1 January 2004 through to 31 December 2011, the reduced rate of 7% (for resident individuals, additional 3% will be levied) is applied instead of 20%. Thus, the withholding rate for resident individuals is either 10% or 20%, whereas, the rate for corporations or resident individuals in non-treaty countries is 7% or 20%. For residents in treaty countries, 7% or treaty rate will be applied. From 1 January 2012, 20% will be applied without exception.
4. Interest on bank deposits and/or certain designated financial instruments is subject to a 15% national withholding tax and a 5% local inhabitants withholding tax (20% combined). Taxation of such interest is fully realised by tax withholding, so resident individuals are not required to aggregate such interest income with other income. Interest on loans made by resident individuals is not subject to withholding tax; instead, it is taxed in the aggregate with other income.
5. Dividends, interest and royalties earned by non-resident individuals and/or foreign corporations are subject to a 20% national withholding tax under Japanese domestic tax laws in principle. An exception rate of 7% is applied to dividends from certain listed companies. And an exceptional rate of 15% is applied to interest on bank deposits and certain designated financial instruments. Interest on loans, however, is taxed at a 20% rate. A special exemption from withholding tax applies to certain long-term corporate bonds issued to non-residents in foreign countries.
6. Tax treaties with many countries provide reduced tax rates, as indicated. Some treaties, however, provide higher tax rates (e.g., Brazil, Thailand) or do not provide rates (e.g.,

Japan

Egypt, New Zealand). In these instances, rates specified under Japanese domestic tax laws apply. Each treaty should be consulted to see if a reduced rate for dividends (in the case of substantial holdings) is applicable.

7. Brazil – The tax treaty with Brazil provides a 25% tax rate for certain royalties (trademark). However, the withholding tax rate cannot exceed 20% on any royalties to be received by a non-resident taxpayer of Japan under Japanese income tax law. Film royalties are taxed at 15%. Any other royalties are taxed at 12.5%.
8. Czechoslovakia (former) – The treaty with the former Czechoslovakia is applied to the Czech Republic and the Slovak Republic. It stipulates that cultural royalties are tax exempt.
9. Egypt – Film royalties are taxed at 20% and other royalties are taxed at 15%.
10. Hungary – Cultural royalties are tax exempt.
11. India – The rate of 10% for royalties includes consideration for technical services.
12. Kazakhstan – The rate for royalties is reduced to 5% by Protocol.
13. Mexico – Dividends received from their subsidiaries by parent companies that have met certain conditions are exempt from withholding taxes.
14. Pakistan – The rate of 5% are applied to the company which has over 50% shares with voting right directly and the rate of 7.5% are applied to the company which has over 25% shares with voting right directly.
15. Philippines – Film royalties are taxed at 15%. Any other royalties are taxed at 10%.
16. Poland – Cultural royalties are tax exempt.
17. Romania – Cultural royalties are taxed at 10%.
18. Sri Lanka – Interest to financial institutions is tax exempt, as well as film and copyright royalties. Patent royalties are subject to 10%.
19. Sweden – If certain conditions for beneficial owners are met, dividends are taxable only in the contracting state of which the beneficial owner is a resident.
20. Thailand – Dividends paid by a corporation that is engaged in industrial undertakings are taxed at 15%. Interest to financial institutions is taxed at 10%.
21. Turkey – Interest to financial institutions is taxed at 10%.
22. The treaty with the former USSR is applied to Armenia, Azerbaijan, Belarus, Georgia, Kyrgyzstan, Moldova, Russia, Tajikistan, Turkmenistan, Ukraine, and Uzbekistan; it stipulates that cultural royalties are tax exempt.

Tax administration

Returns
Corporate income tax returns (i.e., the national corporation tax return, enterprise tax return and local inhabitants' tax return) are self-assessment tax returns.

The tax year is the corporation's annual accounting period specified in its articles of incorporation. The Japan branch of a foreign corporation must use the same accounting period that is adopted by the corporation in its home country.

If a corporation meets certain conditions, such as keeping certain accounting books, and makes an application for it in advance, it is allowed to file a "blue form" tax return. A blue form filing corporation may benefit from loss carryforward and other benefits.

A corporation (included branch) is required to file the final tax return within two months after the end of its annual accounting period. If a corporation cannot file the final return because of specific reasons, the due date of final return may be extended for one month with the tax authority's approval.

Payment of tax

Income taxes payable on the final corporate income tax return should be paid on or before the filing due date of the final tax returns (usually two months after the end of the corporation's accounting period). If an extension of time for filing is granted, the taxes may be paid on or before the extended due date with interest accrued at a rate of 4.3% (for the year 2010) per annum for the period from the day following the original due date (i.e., two months after the end of an accounting period) to the date of the actual payment.

Provisional tax payments are required for a corporation that has a fiscal period longer than six months. Provisional taxes generally are computed as one-half of the tax liabilities for the previous year, but they may be reduced by the filing of interim tax returns that reflect semi-annual results of the operations.

Consolidated taxation

The parent company will file the consolidated tax return and pay national corporate income tax for the group. The consolidated tax return and payment due dates are the same as previously discussed; however, the due date of the final return may be extended for two months.

For local corporate income taxes, the member of consolidated group would separately file the returns and pay the taxes.

Penalties

If the tax return is filed late, the late filing penalty is imposed at 15 – 20% of the tax balance due. In the case that a corporation files tax return after due date voluntarily, this penalty may be reduced to 5%.

If the amount of tax liabilities on filed tax return is assessed, the under-payment penalty is imposed at 10 – 15% of additional tax due. In the case that a corporation amends tax return and tax liabilities after due date voluntarily, this penalty may not be levied.

In addition, interest for the late payment of tax is levied at 4.3% (for the year 2010) per annum for the first two months and increasing to 14.6% per annum thereafter.

Corporate taxes in Jersey, Channel Islands

For more information, contact:

Wendy Dorman
PricewaterhouseCoopers CI LLP
Twenty Two Colomberie
St Helier, Jersey JE1 4XA
Channel Islands
Tel: +44 1534 838233
Email: wendy.dorman@je.pwc.com

Significant developments

Although not part of the European Union's (EU) fiscal territory or bound by EU law, Jersey gave commitments to change certain of its practices highlighted by the EU Code of Conduct review. This has resulted in the introduction of a zero/ten tax regime, which saw the end of the exempt company as of 31 December 2008, and the phasing out of the international business company by 2011.

The zero/ten regime was introduced in 2008 (2009 for existing companies). The new regime reduced the standard income tax rate for companies to 0%, with certain exceptions.

Financial services companies, as defined by legislation, are subject to tax at a rate of 10%. Utility companies and Jersey property source income are taxed at 20%.

All other companies are subject to 0% tax. The new zero/ten regime also has introduced a mechanism to tax Jersey resident shareholders of 0% and 10% companies on deemed distributions or attributed profits.

The new zero/ten system is currently under review and may therefore change in the future.

A 3% goods and services tax (GST) was introduced in May 2008 to raise additional revenue.

Taxes on corporate income

Income tax
Companies pay income tax at a rate of 0%, 10% or 20% on taxable income. The tax rate applies to the company as a whole the only exception being Jersey source property income, which is taxed at 20% regardless of the classification of the property holding company.

The 20% tax rate applies to Jersey based utility companies, such as telephone, gas and electricity companies. Additionally, income from Jersey real estate, including rental and property development, is subject to tax at 20%.

The 10% rate applies to financial services companies. A company is defined as a financial services company if:

- It is registered under the 1998 financial services law to carry out investment business, trust company business, or fund services business as an administrator or custodian in relation to an unclassified or an unregulated fund;
- It is registered under the 1991 banking business law; or
- It holds a permit under the collective investment funds law of 1988 as an administrator or custodian.

The 0% rate applies to all entities that are not financial services entities or utility companies, including fund managers who do not hold any of the permits mentioned above.

As a consequence of the above, companies regulated as fund managers will be liable to tax at 0% while those regulated as fund administrators will be taxed at 10%. Because these rates apply to the whole company's profits, this would have resulted in those fund service providers that were regulated to provide both fund management and fund administration services being taxed at 10% on all of their profits, irrespective of the source. This also would apply to companies with investment business licenses.

The Jersey tax authorities have indicated that they will consider, on a case by case basis, applying a concessionary basis of taxation to existing companies that are regulated as fund functionaries under more than one category and/or to carry out investment business, only in very limited circumstances. As a result, different streams of income may be taxed based on how they are regulated. However, there is no such provision in the law.

There are provisions in Jersey tax law under which Jersey resident beneficial owners of Jersey companies are subject to tax on distributed or undistributed profits.

Corporate residence

A company is regarded as tax resident in Jersey if it is incorporated in Jersey or if it has its place of central management and control in Jersey, except that a Jersey incorporated company managed and controlled elsewhere will not be regarded as Jersey resident provided certain conditions are satisfied.

Other taxes

GST
A 3% GST was introduced in May 2008.

Companies with taxable supplies of more than GBP 300,000 per annum are required to register for GST.

International services entity (ISE) status
To address the difficulty of irrecoverable input tax in the financial services sector, and to mitigate the administrative cost of GST for exporters in general, Jersey has introduced the concept of an international services entity. Where an entity qualifies for this status:

- It will not be required to register for GST;
- Services to it will be zero-rated (i.e., treated as an export) where the supply exceeds GBP 1,000; and

Jersey, Channel Islands

- Input tax on purchases less than GBP 1,000 may be reclaimed.

ISE status will automatically be available to a wide variety of service providers and administered entities based in Jersey, on application and payment of the relevant fee, including: licensed banks, licensed trust service providers, licensed fund administrators, fund managers and managed managers.

Other entities not automatically eligible under one of the headings above, including companies, partnerships, trusts, unrecognised funds and special purpose vehicles, may still obtain ISE status if they fulfil certain criteria.

The ISE must be included on a list maintained by the comptroller of income tax. The list will refer either to the entity itself or (e.g., for administered entities) a class of entities as submitted by the administrator.

Branch income

Branch income is taxed at the rate applicable to the company. No further tax is withheld on the transfer of profits abroad.

Income determination

Inventory valuation

Inventory is valued at the lower of historical cost or net realisable value. The last-in, first-out (LIFO) method is not permitted. Generally, there are no material differences between accounts prepared on a normal accounting basis and those prepared on a tax basis.

Capital gains

Capital gains are not subject to tax.

Inter-company dividends

There is no requirement to withhold tax at source when paying dividends. If a dividend is paid out of profits that have suffered tax at either a 10% or 20% rate the net dividend will be accompanied by a tax credit at the applicable rate. Repayment of the tax credit can be claimed by Jersey investment companies and financial services companies receiving the dividends, subject to certain restrictions. However trading companies subject to tax at 0% are not entitled to claim a repayment of any of the tax credit.

Foreign income

Income tax is levied on foreign branch income when earned and on foreign dividends, interest, rents, and royalties. Double taxation is mitigated by either the granting of unilateral relief to the extent of taxing foreign income net of foreign taxes or by treaty relief, which gives credit for foreign tax, however Jersey does not have an extensive tax treaty network. Concessional credit relief might be granted in certain limited circumstances upon application.

Stock dividends

Stock dividends are taxed as income.

Deductions

Capital allowances
Capital allowances are available using the diminishing-balance method on machinery and equipment, including vehicles, at a rate of 25%. For this purpose, all such assets are pooled, and the allowance is calculated by reference to the value of the pool. On disposal of an asset, the lower of cost and sale proceeds of the asset is deducted from the pool. A balancing charge is levied if the proceeds exceed the balance of the pool. Motor vehicles costing more than GBP 21,000 and greenhouses are subject to special rules and are not pooled with other assets. By concession, an alternative is to claim the full cost of replacement in the year of replacement. Capital allowances are not applicable to buildings or the depletion of natural resources.

Net operating losses
Under zero/ten legislation, no distinction is drawn between different types of income or losses arising from different trades or sources apart from Jersey property income which is separately streamed. These should be aggregated in order to arrive at the company's net relevant profits (0% companies) or tax-adjusted profits (financial services companies). Unrelieved net relevant losses or tax-adjusted losses may be carried forward and used to offset the net relevant profits or tax-adjusted profits in future accounting periods. Alternatively net relevant losses or tax-adjusted losses can be group relieved to group companies in the same income tax rate band. There are now only very limited circumstances where a company can obtain relief for carrying back losses under the new zero/ten regime.

Payments to foreign affiliates
Patent royalties are generally subject to taxation at source, and relief is obtained by retention of the tax deducted.

Taxes
Local income tax paid is not deductible in computing taxable income. ISE fees paid are a tax-deductible expense.

Other significant items
Normally, business deductions are allowed if they are incurred wholly and exclusively for the purpose of the trade.

Group taxation

Group taxation is not permitted.

The zero/ten legislation contains provisions for group relief between group companies subject to the same rate of tax. It is not possible to relieve losses between two companies taxed at different rates.

Tax incentives

There are generally no special incentives for locally owned businesses in view of the low rate of tax.

Jersey, Channel Islands

Withholding taxes

Interest and patent royalties paid by Jersey companies to non-residents are exempt from Jersey tax.

Tax administration

Returns

The tax year is the calendar year. Companies are assessed on income earned in respect of the financial year that ends within the applicable calendar year of assessment. The system relies on the filing of a return of information with the Island tax authority, which then raises an assessment (in the case of companies taxed at 10% or 20% on all or part of their income). The corporate tax return serves to provide the tax authorities with information regarding the type of company, details of the shareholders of the company and details of the dividends paid, deemed to be paid, profits attributable and shareholder loans. Companies taxed at 0% are required to submit a tax return but are not required to submit accounts and tax computations.

Payment of tax

Tax is payable in arrears during the calendar year following the year of assessment. Tax paid after a prescribed date (usually the first Friday in the December following the year of assessment) incurs a 10% surcharge.

Other issues

The zero/ten tax regime in Jersey is currently subject to review.

Corporate taxes in Jordan

For more information, contact:

Stephan Stephan
PricewaterhouseCoopers Jordan
Rajab Building 3rd floor
Yousef Al Aseer Street
Shmeisani, Amman
Jordan
Tel: +962 6 560 6629
Email: stephan.stephan@jo.pwc.com

Significant developments

The Jordanian tax regime was previously based on the application of the Jordanian Income Tax Law No. 57 of 1985 ("Old" Tax Law). The Old Tax Law was repealed and replaced by a temporary income tax law, which is effective as of 1 January 2010. This temporary income tax law was introduced by the newly appointed Jordanian government in the absence of a Parliament (after a royal edict ordering its dissolution). When the new government was sworn in during December 2009, the introduction of a new income tax law was identified on the agenda of items to be addressed. On this basis, the temporary income tax law was introduced by the new government and will be in force until a new Parliament is elected. It is expected that a new Parliament will be elected during 2010; however, an exact date is not yet known. When the new Parliament is elected, one of its tasks will be to review temporary laws, make amendments, if appropriate, and then pass the laws as final.

Taxes on corporate income

The corporate tax rates are applied based on the industry/business activities from which the taxpayer generates income. The corporate tax rates are as follows:

- 30% for banks;
- 24% for telecommunication, insurance, financial intermediation companies (including exchange and finance leasing companies); and
- 14% for other companies.

Corporate residence

An entity will be deemed to be resident if it has been established and registered in accordance with the provisions of the Jordanian legislation in force and has an office or branch practicing management and supervision of its work in the Kingdom, or whose management head office or actual office is located in the Kingdom, or which the government or any official or public institutions own more than (50%) of its capital.

Other taxes

Public shareholding companies and operating branches of foreign companies are required to withhold 1% of their net profits to fund the public universities established in Jordan. The tax is collected by the Ministry of Finance and distributed annually at the discretion of the Higher Education Council. This tax will be abolished effective as of 1 January 2011.

Jordan

Jordan also has a scientific research tax imposed at the rate of 1%.

A general sales tax similar in operation to value-added tax is imposed at the rate of 16%

A social security tax is imposed on the employee and the employer. The rates are 5.5% and 11% respectively.

Branch income

Operating branches of foreign companies registered in Jordan are taxed based on their activities/business being carried out in Jordan at the prevailing corporate income tax rates. Non-operating branches of foreign companies registered in Jordan are generally prohibited from carrying on any commercial activity in Jordan.

Income determination

Any income incurred in or from the Kingdom for any person regardless of the place of payment even if it was from illegal sources, shall be subject to tax. This includes, but is not limited to income from:

- Professional services or activities;
- Interest, commissions, discounts, currency differences, deposit profits, and profits;
- from banks and other legal resident persons;
- Royalties;
- Selling goods produced in the Kingdom whether sold in the Kingdom or exported;
- Selling or leasing of movable properties located in the Kingdom;
- Leasing immovable properties located in the Kingdom and the income from key money;
- Selling or leasing intangible assets in the Kingdom, including goodwill;
- Insurance premiums due according to insurance and re-insurance agreements for the risk in the Kingdom;
- All forms of telecommunication services, including international telecommunications;
- Transportation between the Kingdom and any foreign country;
- Re-exporting;
- Service compensation gained by a non-resident person from the Kingdom for a service provided to any person if the activity or the work related to this compensation was carried out or the output of this service was used in the Kingdom;
- Any contract in the Kingdom such as construction contracting, commercial agencies profits, and any other similar entities whether their source is inside or outside the Kingdom; and
- Any other employment or business activity, or investment, which has not been exempted according to the provisions of this law.

The following shall be exempted from tax:

- The King's allocations;
- Income of public and official institutions and municipalities, excluding its income from rent and key money;
- Income of unions, professional commissions, cooperation societies, and other societies legally registered and licensed from non-profit activities;

- Income of any religious, charity, cultural, educational, sports, or health institutions with a public character, not aiming to achieve profit and the income of charity awqaf (public endowment), and the income from the Orphans Development Fund investment;
- Income of exempted registered companies according to the companies' law, which is incurred from activities undertaken outside the Kingdom, except income derived from income sources subject to tax according to the provision of this law;
- Profits from stocks and dividends distributed by a resident to another resident, except profits of mutual investment funds of banks and financial companies;
- Capital gains incurred inside the Kingdom, other than profits from assets subject to depreciation;
- Income derived from inside the kingdom from trading in dividends and stocks, bonds, equity loan, treasury bonds, mutual investment funds, currencies, commodities in addition to futures and options contracts related to any of them, except that incurred by banks, financial companies, financial intermediation and insurance companies and legal persons who undertake out financial lease activities;
- Income from trading in immovable properties located in the Kingdom except the following:
  - Income incurred from such trade by a legal person; and
  - Income incurred from building and selling real-estates.
- Income of non-Jordanian resident investors from sources outside the Kingdom originated in investing his foreign capital, returns, profits, and investment liquidation return or selling his project, shares or stocks after taking them out of the Kingdom according to the effective Investment Law or any law that will replace it;
- Compensation paid by insurance entities, other than what is paid as a reimbursement for the loss of income from business activity or employment;
- Income from employment paid to members of non-Jordanian diplomatic or consular bodies representing other countries in the Kingdom subject to the reciprocal treatment principle;
- Income from distribution of estates or wills for the inheritors or the devisees according to the provisions of the effective legislations;
- End of service rewards for the employees according to the effective legislations or any group arrangements concluded according to the approval of the Minister as follows
  - 100% of any amount accrued before the effective date of this law; or
  - 50% of any amount accrued after the effective date of this law.
- The first JOD 4000 of monthly pension salary paid by a resident person;
- Income generated by the blind or any person totally incapable of working;
- Any income generated by banks and financial companies not operating in the Kingdom from banks operating in the Kingdom such as deposit interest, commissions, and deposit profits from investment in interest-free banks and financial companies;
- Profits gained by re-insurance companies from insurance contracts concluded with insurance companies operating in the Kingdom;
- Income covered by preventing double-taxation agreements concluded by the government to the extent of that which is covered under these agreements
- Income from employment generated, with certain restrictions from the following are also exempted from tax:
  - Meals provided for the employees at the work site;
  - Accommodation services provided for employees for work purposes; and
  - Equipment and uniforms, necessary for carrying out work activities provided to the employee by the employer.

J

Jordan

- The income of public or private pension funds and savings funds and any other funds approved by the Minister shall not be subject to tax if this income is derived from the employees and employers contributions; and
- Certain types of local origin goods and services' exports outside the Kingdom may be totally or partially exempted from tax as set forth in regulations issued for this purpose.

Deductions

Approved expenses, including the following, are deductible:

1. Foreign income tax paid for income earned from sources outside Jordan that was subject to tax under the provisions of the tax law.
2. Interest and Murabaha (profit-sharing) paid by banks or financial institutions.
3. Interest and Murabaha payable by taxpayers other than banks and financial institutions and finance leasing companies, provided that the amounts deducted do not exceed the rates set for total debt to capital or the average of ownership rights, depending on whichever is higher:

Tax period	Relative value
2010	1:6
2011	1:5
2012	1:4
2013 and following years	1:3

4. Bad debts.
5. Insurance premiums.
6. Depreciation of capital assets and amortisation of intangible assets, including goodwill.
7. Maintenance expenses for assets that were spent within the tax period provided that such expenses do not exceed (5%) of their value.
8. Taxes and fees paid on taxable activities.
9. Amounts paid as civil compensation under contracts concluded by the taxpayer for the purpose of carrying taxable activities.
10. Amounts paid by the employer for his employees to the Social Security Corporation.
11. Hospitality and travel expenses incurred by the taxpayer.
12. Expenditures for employees' medical treatment, meals during duty, travel, transport and life insurance against work injuries or death.
13. Marketing, scientific research, development and training expenses.
14. Expenses of prior tax periods, which were neither defined nor final.

Debt-to-equity rules
Jordan has no debt to equity rules beyond those stated in the legal formation papers of a corporation.

Group taxation

Group taxation is not permitted in Jordan.

Tax incentives

Jordan has had tax reductions for selective sectors categorised by development zones. Generally, these have required pre-approval.

Withholding taxes (WHT)

With respect to services performed by a non-resident juristic or natural person, under the Income Tax Law, "Amounts received or earned by the non-resident person from the Kingdom, which are derived from services provided to any person if the work or service related has been performed in the Kingdom or if the outcome of such services has been used in the Kingdom as well, is subject to tax in Jordan."

The current withholding tax rate on services performed by a non-resident juristic or natural person is 7% of the payment.

Resident juristics or natural persons that perform any services in the Kingdom are subject to a withholding tax on the services performed. The applicable withholding tax rate is the rate prevailing at the time the service is performed. The current withholding tax rate on services performed by a local subcontractor is 5% of the payment.

Services which are excluded from the 5% withholding tax regime include the following:

- Shipping services and related brokerage services;
- Road transport services and related brokerage services;
- Air transport services;
- Financing lease services;
- Hotels and restaurants services;
- Clearance services;
- Programming service provided by the companies;
- Hospital services provided by hospitals;
- Advertising services;
- Cleaning services;
- Security services;
- Training services provided by the companies;
- Insurance activities services;
- Banking services provided by banks;
- Communication activities and services provided by primary telecom companies (defined in the tax law as being communications companies individually licensed in accordance with the provisions of communications law in effect and regulations and instructions issued pursuant thereto);
- Transportation and distribution of electric power services provided by the Electricity Company Plc;
- Contracting services implemented under contractor certified by the Jordanian Contractors Association;
- Public safety services;
- Maintenance services that include value of materials and goods and labour wages;
- Food processing services, correspondence and transport and laundry provided to hospitals;
- Loading and unloading services;

Jordan

- Services that are executed by a juristic person – excluding civil companies – and have a tax number (income and sales); and
- Any other service approved by the Minister upon the recommendation of the Director General.

Tax treaties
Jordan has entered income tax treaties with Algeria, Bahrain, Canada, Croatia, the Czech Republic, Egypt, France, India, Indonesia, Iraq, South Korea, Kuwait, Lebanon, Libya, Malaysia, the Netherlands, Pakistan, Poland, Qatar, Romania, Sudan, Syria, Tunisia, Turkey, the United Kingdom and Yemen.

It has transportation agreements with a many countries and is negotiating treaties with more countries.

Tax administration

Filing requirements
Taxpayers are obliged to file tax returns before the end of the fourth month following the end of the tax period, including details related to income, expenses, exemptions and due tax. Tax returns are submitted by any of the following means approved by the department according to terms and procedures to be determined by instructions:

- Registered mail;
- Banks;
- Any licensed company to undertake the tasks of public or private mail post approved by the Council of Ministries upon the recommendation of the Minister; or
- Electronic means.

The date of filing is considered to be the earlier of the date of receipt by the department, post seal or deposit receipt at a bank or licensed company. In the case of sending electronic mail, implementation instructions have not yet been introduced to determine the approved date of submitting the same.

Fines and penalties
Failure to pay tax on the assigned dates according to the provisions of the tax law will result in a delay fine at a rate of 0.4% of the value of the tax due or any deductible amounts for each full or partial week of delay.

If a taxpayer submits a tax return and pays the declared tax in a timely manner, but the declared tax is less than the actual amount due, a shortage fee for such differences will be imposed, as follows:

- 15% of the shortage if the difference exceeds 20% but less than 50% of the tax due by law;
- 20% of the shortage if the difference does not exceed 50% of the tax due by law; and
- 80% of the shortage if the difference exceeds 50% of the tax due by law.

Other issues

The effective corporate income tax system method presented in Jordan for juristic persons (except partnerships and limited partnerships in shares), is based on statutory income tax rates at all income levels with no progressive tax rate scale; the statutory tax rates vary according to different business sectors.

Note that the corporate income tax method in Jordan does not subject all business activity to the corporate income tax. Unincorporated businesses, such as sole proprietorships and partnerships, do not pay corporate income tax. Instead, all of their income, whether it is distributed to owners as dividends or retained for additional internal investment, is "passed through" and taxed only at the level of the individual, that is, the owner or owners.

Corporate taxes in Kazakhstan, Republic of

For more information, contact:

Richard Bregonje
PricewaterhouseCoopers
29/6 Satpaev Avenue
Hyatt Regency Office Tower, 4th Floor
Almaty 050040
Republic of Kazakhstan
Tel: +7 727 298 0448
Email: richard.bregonje@kz.pwc.com

Significant developments

During November and December, 2009, the President of Kazakhstan approved a set of amendments to the Kazakhstan tax law.

The main change was the extension of the 2009 tax rates of corporate income tax and mineral production tax until 2012. Other notable changes included clarifying provisions regarding capital gains, withholding tax, double tax treaty administration, commercial discovery bonus calculations, historical costs reimbursement and excess profit tax.

Please note that some of these amendments came into force retroactively from 1 January 2009.

Customs union
From 1 January 2010, Kazakhstan, Russia and Belarus adopted a unified customs tariffs. The three countries will continue working towards unification of administrative and other procedures, which should be completed by 1 July 2010, an official date when the integrated customs territory will start functioning.

Taxes on corporate income

The tax rate for corporations is at 20% for 2010-2012 and is based on a calendar year. The tax rate will decrease to 17.5% in 2013, and 15% in 2014. All Kazakhstan legal entities and branches of foreign legal entities are subject to corporate income tax.

Corporate residence

Legal entities formed under Kazakhstan law as well as legal entities whose effective control (management) is in Kazakhstan are recognised as residents for corporate tax purposes.

Other taxes

Value-added tax (VAT)
The current VAT rate is 12%. This tax is applicable to the sales value of products, works and services, and imports. Exports of goods are taxed at a zero rate. There is a list of goods, works and services exempt from VAT.

Goods and services are subject to VAT if they are deemed to be supplied in Kazakhstan under the place of supply rules.

VAT refunds are generally available with respect to excess input VAT. However, the excess input VAT that has been formed prior to 1 January 2009, should be treated in accordance with the 2008 Tax Code. Based on these provisions, while there is a possibility of a refund of input VAT associated with zero-rated supplies, the excess input VAT not related to zero-rated supplies could only be carried forward to offset output VAT of future periods without eligibility for refund.

The VAT reporting period is the calendar quarter.

Excise taxes
Excise taxes apply to the sale and import of crude oil, gas condensate, petrol/gasoline (excluding aviation fuel), diesel fuel, spirits and alcoholic beverages, beer, tobacco and passenger cars.

Social tax
Employers must pay social tax at 11% of gross remuneration (salaries and certain benefits provided) of all employees (local and expatriate). A deduction is available for obligatory pension contributions.

Property tax
Property tax is assessed at a general rate of 1.5% of the average net book value of immovable property.

Land tax
Entities and individuals that own land plots (or land share in cases of commonly shared ownership of land plots) must pay land tax. Land tax rates vary based on the purpose for which the land is used as well as the size and quality of the land.

Vehicle tax
The vehicle tax rate is determined based on monthly calculation indices depending on the type of vehicle, engine volume, the operation period of the vehicle (aircraft only) and other factors.

Mineral production tax
The mineral production tax applies to the extracted volume of crude oil, gas condensate, natural gas, minerals and groundwater.

The tax is calculated based on the value of the extracted content, which is computed by applying average global prices to the extracted volume (adjusted for content). The determination of average global prices is based on the list of publications that are considered official sources for computation of mineral production tax (Metal Bulletin, Metal Pages, Platts Crude Oil Marketwire and Petroleum Argus).

Tax rates for crude oil and gas condensate for 2010 range from 6% to 19%, depending on the accumulated production volume for the calendar year. For hydrocarbons, rates can be reduced by 50% if they are supplied to domestic refineries on the basis of a sale/purchase agreement or tolling agreement.

K

Kazakhstan, Republic of

The tax rate for natural gas is set at 10%. For domestic sales of natural gas, tax rates range from 0.5% to 1.5%.

Tax rates for minerals which have undergone initial processing (except for widespread minerals) and for coal vary between 0% and 23%.

Excess profit tax
The excess profit tax (EPT) rates are progressive and range from 0% to 60%. The tax base is comprised of the portion of net income exceeding 25% of deductions for EPT purposes. Taxpayers may include asset acquisition costs, capital costs and losses (with certain limitations) as deductions.

Customs duties
Customs duties apply to the import of goods and the rates are established either based on a percentage (ranging between 0% and 30%) of the customs value of goods or in absolute terms in Euros. Kazakhstan is not a World Trade Organization member.

Customs fees
A customs processing fee is assessed at EUR 50 for the main page of a customs declaration plus EUR 20 for each supplemental page.

Branch income

The net income of branches of foreign legal entities is subject to a branch profits tax at a rate of 15%, which may be reduced under the terms of a double tax treaty.

Income determination

Kazakhstan legal entities are taxable on aggregate annual income earned worldwide. Non-resident legal entities, carrying out income through a permanent establishment in Kazakhstan, are taxable on income attributed to the activities of that permanent establishment. All taxpayers must apply the accrual method for recognition of income.

Inventory valuation
Inventory is valued in accordance with the international financial reporting standards and in compliance with Kazakhstan legislation.

Capital gains
Capital gains are subject to ordinary income tax rates. There is an exemption available for capital gains realised from the sale of shares and participation interests in Kazakhstan legal entities or consortiums which are not engaged in subsurface activities. There is a still-developing test for determining exactly which entities will qualify for this exemption.

Inter-company dividends
Inter-company dividends are exempt from corporate income tax in the hands of the recipient except for dividends paid by certain types of investment funds. This exemption applies to stock dividends, as well.

Foreign income
Foreign income is subject to ordinary income tax rates.

Under the controlled foreign companies (CFC) rules, if a Kazakhstan legal entity has 10% or more of direct or indirect ownership in the share capital or voting rights in a non-resident company, registered or located in a preferential tax jurisdiction, the legal entity is subject to Kazakhstan corporate income tax on the portion of the undistributed profits from the non-resident company. The list of preferential tax jurisdictions established by the government of Kazakhstan includes 63 jurisdictions.

Transfer pricing

According to the provisions of the Transfer Pricing Law, both customs and tax authorities have the right to monitor and adjust prices used in cross-border and certain domestic transactions when prices are perceived to deviate from market prices, even if such transactions are with unrelated parties.

Deductions

Allowable deductions generally include expenses associated with activities designed to generate income, unless specifically restricted for deduction by tax legislation. All expenses require supporting documentation.

Depreciation and depletion

Tax depreciation is calculated using the declining balance method at depreciation rates ranging from 10% to 40%, applied to the balances of four basic categories of assets:

1. Buildings and facilities;
2. Machinery and equipment;
3. Computers and equipment for information processing; and
4. Fixed assets not included into other groups, including oil and gas wells, transmission equipment, oil and gas machinery and equipment.

Net operating losses

Net operating losses accumulated prior to 1 January 2009, may be carried forward for up to three years. Net operating losses generated after 1 January 2009, may be carried forward for up to 10 years.

Payments to foreign affiliates

Payments to foreign affiliates are deductible for corporate income tax purposes if the payments are intended to generate income, are supported by documentation and comply with Kazakhstan transfer pricing law.

Deduction of taxes

Taxes remitted to the state treasury of Kazakhstan are deductible except for the following:

- Taxes excluded prior to the calculation of the aggregate annual income;
- Income taxes paid in Kazakhstan and other states;
- Taxes paid in the preferential tax jurisdictions; and
- Excess profit tax.

Other items

Certain expenses related to the activities aimed at generating income are deductible within limits, including expenses related to entertainment, business trips and interest (thin capitalisation).

K

Kazakhstan, Republic of

Group taxation

Kazakhstan tax law does not permit group taxation.

Tax incentives

Corporate tax investment incentives are available for certain new capital investments, including deduction of cost and subsequent repair and modernisation expenses.

Investment tax preferences do not apply to the following:

- Organisations acting on the territory of special economic zones;
- Organisations producing and/or selling excisable goods; or
- Producers of agricultural products and village consumer's cooperatives.

Withholding taxes (WHT)

Kazakhstan source income of non-residents and the proceeds from the sale of shares in subsurface users are subject to withholding tax at the rates shown in the table below.

A non-resident legal entity is exempt from dividend withholding tax if the holding period is greater than or equal to three years and 50% or more of the issuer's capital value is not a property of subsurface user.

Types of income at a source of payment	Tax rate
Dividends, capital gains, interest, royalties	15%
Any income of an entity registered in a tax haven jurisdiction	20%
Insurance premiums under risk insurance agreements	10% through 2011 (15% in 2012)
Income from international transportation services; insurance premiums under risk reinsurance agreements	5%
Other income	20% in 2010-2012, 17.5% in 2013, 15% in 2014

Notes

Benefits paid by a company to a shareholder, founder, participant or related party, falling under the definition of constructive dividends, are taxed at 15%.

In accordance with the double tax treaties as of 1 April 2010, the rate of withholding tax may be reduced as shown in the following table.

Recipient	Dividends %	Interest %	Royalties %
No treaty	0/15	15	15
Austria	5/15 (4)	10	10
Azerbaijan	10	10	10
Belarus	15	10	15
Belgium	0/5/15 (8) (4)	10	10
Bulgaria	10	10	10

Recipient	Dividends %	Interest %	Royalties %
Canada	5/15 (1)	10	10
China	10	10	10
Czech Republic	10	10	10
Estonia	5/15 (2)	10	15
France	5/15 (4)	10	10
Georgia	15	10	10
Germany	5/15 (2)	10	10
Hungary	5/15 (2)	10	10
India	10	10	10
Iran	5/15 (5)	10	10
Italy	5/15 (4)	10	10
Japan	5/15 (1)	10	10
Korea	5/15 (4)	10	10
Kyrgyzstan	10	10	10
Latvia	5/15 (2)	10	10
Lithuania	5/15 (2)	10	10
Malaysia	10	10	10
Moldova	10/15 (2)	10	10
Mongolia	10	10	10
Netherlands	0/5/15 (9) (10)	10	10
Norway	5/15 (10)	10	10
Pakistan	12.5/15 (10)	12.5	15
Poland	10/15 (3)	10	10
Romania	10	10	10
Russia	10	10	10
Singapore	5/10 (2)	10	10
Slovakia	10/15 (7)	10	10
Sweden	5/15 (1)	10	10
Switzerland	0/5/15 (9) (10)	10	10
Tajikistan	10/15 (6)	10	10
Turkey	10	10	10
Turkmenistan	10	10	10
Ukraine	5/15 (2)	10	10
United Kingdom	5/15 (1)	10	10
United States	5/15 (1)	10	10
Uzbekistan	10	10	10

Notes

The numbers in parentheses above refer to the following notes:

1. 5% if the beneficial owner is a company owning, directly (or indirectly in case of Canada, Japan and the UK), at least 10% of the voting power of the company paying the dividends.
2. 5% (10% in case of Moldova) if the beneficial owner is a company that directly holds at least 25% of the capital of the paying company.

Kazakhstan, Republic of

3. 10% if the beneficial owner is a company, directly or indirectly, holding at least 20% of the capital of the paying company.
4. 5% if the beneficial owner is a company (other than partnership) which owns not less than 10% of the capital of the paying company.
5. 5% if the recipient is a company (other than partnership) which directly owns not less than 20% of the capital of the paying company.
6. 10% if the actual owner is a legal entity that owns not less than 30% of the authorised capital of the legal entity paying the dividends.
7. 10% if the beneficial owner is a company that holds directly at least 30% of the capital of the company paying the dividends.
8. 0%, if dividends are paid in consideration of an investment of as least USD 50 million in the paying company.
9. 0% if the company receiving the dividends holds directly or indirectly at least 50% of the capital of the paying company and has made an investment in the company paying the dividends of at least USD 1 million, which investment is guaranteed in full or insured in full by the government of the first contracting state, the central bank of that state or any agency or instrumentality (including a financial institution) owned or controlled by that government, and has been approved by the government of the other contracting state.
10. 5% (or 12.5% in case of Pakistan) if the beneficial owner is a company which directly owns (or indirectly in case of the Netherlands and Pakistan) at least 10% of the capital of the paying company.

Tax administration

Returns
The tax year in Kazakhstan is the calendar year. Annual corporate income tax declarations are due by 31 March of the year following the tax year-end. For taxpayers filing electronically, a 30 calendar-day extension is usually granted upon request.

Certain taxpayers are required to submit their estimated calculation of monthly advance payments of corporate income tax.

The deadline for other tax returns is the fifteenth calendar day of the second month following the reporting period. The 30 calendar-day extension is usually granted upon request.

Payment of tax
For corporate income tax, advance payments are due every twenty-fifth day of the current month. Taxpayers with aggregate annual income during the tax period preceding the previous tax period of less than 325,000-times amount of the monthly calculation index established for the relevant financial year (approximately, USD 3.12 million) are exempt from the obligation to calculate and pay corporate income tax advance payments. Payment of any outstanding income tax liabilities is required within 10 calendar days following submission of the annual income tax declaration.

Most other taxes are payable by the twenty-fifth day of the second month following the end of reporting period.

Fines and interest penalties
Penalties are assessed on late tax payments at 2.5 times the Kazakhstan National Bank refinancing rate. As of 1 April 2010, the National Bank refinancing rate was 7% per annum.

Substantial fines are imposed for understatement of tax liabilities. Generally, the fines amount to 50% of the understated tax.

For advance corporate income tax payments, an administrative fine of 40% applies to understated advance tax payments compared with the final declared corporate income tax, if the understated amount is greater than 20% of the final declared amount.

If a taxpayer is deemed to have concealed taxable income, a fine of 150% of the concealed amount may be assessed.

Statute of limitation

The statute of limitation for tax purposes in Kazakhstan is five years. For taxpayers operating under subsurface use contracts, the tax authorities maintain the right to assess or revise the assessed amount of excess profit tax and other taxes and obligatory payments to the budget, where a methodology of calculation uses one of the following indices: internal rate of return (IRR) or internal revenue rate or R-factor (earning yield) during the effective period of a subsurface use contract and five years after the end of the effective period of a subsurface use contract.

Accounting system

Kazakhstan legal entities should maintain accounts and produce financial statements in accordance with International Financial Reporting Standards or national accounting standards (depending on the size of the company and other factors). In most cases, tax treatment follows accounting.

K

Corporate taxes in Kenya

For more information, contact:

Steve Okello
PricewaterhouseCoopers
Rahimtulla Tower
Upper Hill Road
Nairobi, Kenya
Tel: +254 20 2855116
Email: steve.x.okello@ke.pwc.com

Significant developments

Historically, one of the biggest tax incentives for investors into Kenya was the ability to carryforward tax losses indefinitely. This is now restricted to a maximum of five years, including the year in which the loss arises. This change is applicable from the years of income commencing on or after 1 January 2010 and applies to businesses as well as individuals.

Taxpayers may submit an application to the minister of finance to request an extension of the period in which losses may be carried forward where a person has provided evidence of inability to extinguish the deficit within that period.

Since 12 June 2009, withholding tax is applicable on payments made by Kenyan residents for the use of property that is located outside of Kenya. This change impacts businesses and individuals who rent property outside of Kenya. This measure effectively increases the cost of doing business in Kenya since a resident person is required to gross up rental payments as it is unlikely that the non-resident property owner would agree to bear the Kenyan tax.

The 2010/2011 Finance Bill introduced a significant change on interest free loans advanced by a related party to a thinly capitalised company resident in Kenya. The proposal is to deem an interest rate on interest free loans on which the deemed interest rate is pegged to the average 91-day treasury bill rate.

Taxes on corporate income

Corporations are taxed at the following rates:

	%
Locally incorporated companies	30
Branches of foreign companies	37.5
Export processing zone enterprises:	
First 10 years	0
Next 10 years	25
Thereafter	30
Newly listed companies:	
20% of shares listed: for three years	27
30% of shares listed: for five years	25
40% of shares listed: for five years	20

There are special provisions for non-resident shipping companies and airlines, non-residents providing broadcast, internet and messaging services, and non-resident petroleum industry subcontractors providing exploration and production services in Kenya.

Corporate residence

A company is considered resident in Kenya if:

- It is incorporated under Kenyan laws;
- The management and control of company affairs are exercised in Kenya; or
- The company has been declared by the minister, by announcement in the gazette, to be resident in Kenya for any year of income.

Other taxes

Value-added tax (VAT)

VAT is levied on the supply of taxable goods and services in Kenya, and the importation of taxable goods and services into Kenya. Certain goods and services are designated as exempt from VAT.

Exempt supplies do not count towards the registration threshold (*discussed below*) and the related input VAT is not recoverable.

The following rates apply:

	%
Standard rate on all goods and services that are neither exempt nor zero-rated	16
Electricity, diesel oil, residual fuel oils	12
Export of goods and services, certain other goods and services	0

Zero rating applies to the export of goods or services. The supply of goods or services to certain designated persons and projects are also zero rated.

The threshold for VAT registration is taxable supplies of KES 5 million per year. Registered persons must record their turnover using an approved electronic tax register or signature device. Only registered persons may recover input tax. An input tax credit is not available for several items such as non commercial vehicles, office furniture, and hospitality and entertainment services. An excess input tax credit may be carried forward or refunded, subject to certain conditions.

Some entities such as central and local governmental entities, state corporations, banks and insurance companies are required to withhold VAT on supplies received and pay the tax directly to the revenue authority.

Excise duty

Excise duty is imposed on the manufacture or importation of certain commodities, principally bottled water, soft drinks, cigarettes, alcohol, perfumes, fuels and motor vehicles at varying rates. Excise duty is also levied on mobile cellular phone and wireless telephone services at 10% and gambling services at 5%.

Kenya

Import (customs) duty

Import duty is levied under the East African Community Common Customs Management Act. Imports of goods are generally subject to import duty of 0% for raw materials and capital goods, 10% for intermediate goods and 25% for finished goods. Enterprises established in export processing zones are exempt from customs duty on machinery and inputs for exported products. Under an import duty remission scheme, import duty may be remitted for raw materials used to manufacture goods for export. This is subject to a requirement for proof of export and execution of a bond.

Compensating tax

Where a company pays dividends out of profits that have not been subject to income tax, it will be liable to pay a compensating tax. This tax effectively ensures that all distributions are paid out of profits that have been subject to income tax, prior to distribution.

Advance tax

Advance tax is payable at varying rates per year on commercial vehicles and is creditable against corporate income tax for the year.

Fringe benefit tax

The fringe benefit tax is payable by companies at 30% of the benefit arising from a loan advanced to an employee at an interest rate lower than the rates prescribed by the Commissioner. The directors and employees are not personally taxed on the benefit.

Branch income

A business carried on in Kenya through a fixed place of business gives rise to a permanent establishment (PE) as does a building site, or a construction or assembly project that has existed for six months or more. The profit of the PE is taxed at the branch tax rate of 37.5%, but there is no further taxation on the distribution of branch profits. However, there are certain restrictions with respect to costs paid to the head office.

Income determination

Companies (including a branch of an overseas company) are subject to Kenyan tax on all income accrued in or derived from Kenya.

Inventory valuation

Inventory is stated at the lower of cost or net realisable value with the exception of biological assets whose value is prescribed by the Commissioner.

Capital gains

Taxation of capital gains was suspended in 1985.

Foreign income

Income from a business carried on partly in Kenya by a resident company is taxed on a worldwide basis, but otherwise foreign source income is not taxable in Kenya. An individual resident in Kenya is taxed in respect of any employment services rendered in Kenya or outside Kenya. A non-resident individual's employment income earned in respect to services rendered to an employer resident in Kenya or PE of a non-resident employer is also taxable in Kenya.

Stock dividends

Stock dividends issued in a ratio not proportionate to shareholding of the existing equity are considered as taxable dividends to the extent of the disproportionate increase in the value of the ownership of the company.

Deductions

The general principle in Kenya is that expenses are deductible if they are incurred wholly and exclusively to generate taxable income.

Depreciation and depletion

No deduction is allowed for accounting depreciation or impairment. However, capital allowances are permitted at varying rates for certain assets used for business purposes, including buildings and machinery used in manufacturing, industrial buildings and hotels, machinery and plant, agricultural works and mining.

Accumulated losses

Effective 1 January 2010, losses calculated under the tax rules may be carried forward against income from the same source for a maximum of five years including the year in which the losses arise.

Thin capitalisation

In Kenya, a company is thinly capitalised if:

a. The company is in control of a non-resident person alone or together with four or fewer persons;
b. The company is not a bank or financial institution; and
c. The highest amount of all loans held by the company at any time exceeds the sum of three times of the revenue reserves (including accumulated losses) and the issued and paid up share capital of all classes of shares of the company.

A company which is thinly capitalised cannot claim a deduction on the interest expense incurred by the company on loans in excess of three times the sum of revenue reserves and issued and paid up capital of all classes of shares of the company. The company also can not claim a deduction any foreign exchange loss realised by the company with respect any loans from its shareholders in the period that the company remains thinly capitalised.

Payments to foreign affiliates

Transfer pricing rules based on Organisation for Economic Co-operation and Development (OECD) principles apply to transactions with foreign affiliates (both companies and branches/PE). Additionally, there are restrictions on the deductibility of expenses incurred outside of Kenya by non-residents with a Kenyan PE. Amendments in the 2010/2011 Finance Bill stated that transfer pricing is no longer limited to anti-avoidance; marital and familial relationships are now subject to transfer pricing rules.

Taxes

Kenyan income taxes are not deductible. However, foreign income taxes incurred are generally deductible as an expense if tax credit relief is not available under a double tax agreement (DTA).

Kenya

Other significant items

Donations to charities and for certain public works are deductible, subject to certain conditions.

Group taxation

Each company in a group is taxed as a separate entity

Tax incentives

Investment deduction

Qualifying investments exceeding KES 200 million incurred outside Nairobi or the municipalities of Mombasa or Kisumu are allowed an investment deduction of 150%. All other qualifying investments are allowed a 100% investment deduction in the year the asset is put into service.

Industrial building allowance

Hostels and certified education buildings qualify for an industrial building allowance at a rate of 50% on a straight-line basis.

Qualifying rental residential or commercial buildings qualify for an industrial building allowance at a rate of 25%.

Other qualifying buildings (including hotels) qualify for an industrial building allowance at a rate of 10%.

Wear and tear allowance

Expenditures incurred on heavy earth moving equipment qualify for a wear and tear allowance at a rate of 37.5%, while other self propelling vehicles (including aircraft) qualify for a wear and tear allowance at a rate of 25%.

Computers and peripheral computer hardware qualify for a wear and tear allowance at a rate of 30%.

Capital allowances were introduced, effective 1 January 2010, at a rate of 20% for computer software and 20% for telecommunications equipment not falling within the 12.5% category referred to below, purchased and used by telecommunications operators. Both these allowances are computed on a straight line basis.

All other machinery (including ships) qualify for a wear and tear allowance at a rate of 12.5%.

Export processing zone

Companies located in an approved export processing zone, principally to export goods, are taxed at a zero rate of income tax for 10 years from its commencement and at a rate of 25% for the next 10 years.

Listed companies

Companies listed on the Nairobi Stock Exchange are entitled to reduced rates of income tax for a period, depending on the proportion of share capital listed.

Withholding taxes (WHT)

Withholding taxes are levied at varying rates (3% to 30%) on a range of payments to residents and non-residents. Resident withholding taxes are either final tax or are creditable against income tax. Non-resident withholding taxes are final tax.

	Resident	Non-Resident
	%	%
Dividend > 12.5% voting power	Exempt	10
Dividend < 12.5% voting power	5	10
Interest:		
Bearer instruments	25	25
Government bearer bonds (maturity ≥ 2 years)	15	15
Bearer bonds (maturity ≥ 10 years)	10	N/A
Other	15	15
Qualifying interest:		
Housing Bonds	10	N/A
Bearer instruments	20	N/A
Other	15	N/A
Royalty	5	20
Management or professional fees	5	20
Rent/leasing:		
Immovable property	N/A	30
Others	N/A	15
Pension/retirement annuity	N/A	5
Contractual fees	3	20

Lower rates may apply to non-residents where there is a double tax agreement in force.

Tax administration

Returns
Resident companies and permanent establishments of non resident companies must file a self assessment tax return accompanied by audited or certified accounts annually. The return is due within six months following a company's year end.

Payment of tax
Quarterly payments of tax must be made during the year based on the lower of 110% of the previous year's liability or an estimate of the current year's liability. Agricultural companies are required to pay its estimated tax in two instalments of 75% and 25% in the year. Any balance of tax at the end of the year must be paid within four months of the financial year end.

Payment of agency taxes (withholding tax and PAYE)
The tax withheld from payments must be paid by the twentieth day of the month following the month in which the deduction is made.

Penalties for noncompliance
If a self assessment tax return is not submitted by the due date, a penalty of 5% on the unpaid tax for the year may be imposed, subject to a minimum of KES 10,000. Failure

Kenya

or late submission of an export processing zone company return will be subject to a penalty of KES 2,000 per day for as long as the failure continues.

A penalty of 20% and interest at 2% per month are imposed on underestimation and late payment of instalment tax and any balance of tax. Interest is charged only on the principal tax due.

Failure to make a deduction or to remit the withholding tax deducted attracts a penalty equal to 10% of the amount of tax involved (subject to a maximum of KES 1 million) and accrues interest at 2% per month.

Corporate taxes in Korea, Republic of

For more information, contact:

Young-Sik Kim
Samil PricewaterhouseCoopers
LS Yongsan Tower, 15th Floor
191 Hangangno 2-ga
Yongsan-gu
Seoul 140-702, Korea
Tel: +82 2 709 0608
Email: yskim@samil.com

Significant developments

Stimulation of corporate restructuring

Three major changes to stimulate corporate restructuring take effect on 1 July 2010. First, the types of tax-free transactions are expanded to allow companies to defer taxation in more M&A transactions. Thus, as an example, comprehensive share exchanges and comprehensive asset transfers will be eligible for the deferral of corporate income tax and dividend income tax. Further, companies engaged in these transactions will be exempt from the securities tax.

Second, the types of assets eligible for deferral of taxation on capital gains will be extended to all assets. Currently, the tax deferrals are limited to tangible fixed assets used for business purposes in the current merger and split-off taxation regime. In order to prevent possible tax evasion through M&As, the requirements for corporation's substantial consistency after a M&A transaction, which is key in determining eligibility for tax deferral, will be enhanced. Under these enhanced requirements, shareholders of the merged company will be required to hold the shares for a certain period; and the merging company will be required to hold 50% of the assets acquired in the merger for a certain period.

Third, the existing tax deferral of capital gains arising on in-kind contributions will be available in the event of capital increases through in-kind contributions and contributions by means of all assets. The current tax law limits the tax deferral to the event of corporate establishment and in-kind contributions of shares and tangible fixed assets used for business purposes.

Extension of income tax filing period

With proper application, the income tax filing period can be extended by up to a month from the statutory filing due date for companies undergoing the statutory external audit (i.e., companies listed on the Korea Stock Exchange and KOSDAQ and those having total assets worth KRW 10 billion as at the immediately preceding fiscal year-end). A daily 0.03% rate of interest will be charged for the extended period.

Higher research and development (R&D) tax credit for core technologies and strategic growth industries

Companies presently claim a tax credit in relation to qualifying R&D expenditure to the extent of either (1) 3-6% (25% for small and medium enterprises (SMEs)) of the current R&D expenses or (2) 40% (50% for SMEs) of the incremental portion of the current R&D expenses over the average of the previous four years. The tax credit will be extended to include R&D in relation to core technologies as authorised by government ministries as well as pre-designated strategic growth industries until the end of December 2012 and for these industries, the credit rate for the current R&D expenditure would be 20% (30% for SMEs).

SMEs are defined as corporations who meet certain requirements of major business type, the number of employee, size of capital or turnover under the Special Tax Treatment Control Law (STTCL). However, in case that the parent company is a large-sized company which has more than KRW 500 billion assets at the end of the prior year and this large-sized company invests directly or indirectly more than 30% in its subsidiary company, this subsidiary company is not a SME.

Taxes on corporate income

Corporation tax
The basic Korean corporate tax rates for 2010 and 2011 is 10% on the first KRW 200 million of the tax base and 22% for the excess. In FY2012 and thereafter, the respective rates will be 10% and 20%. In 2009, the respective rates were 11% and 22%.

Capital gains from the disposal of non-business purpose land or houses may be subject to an additional capital gains tax at the rates ranging from 10% to 40% after the above corporate income taxation.

Minimum tax
Corporate taxpayers are liable for the minimum tax, which is defined as the greater of 10% (to the tax base of up to KRW 10 billion, 11% on the excess until up to KRW 100 billion, 14% on the excess) of the taxable income before various deductions and exemptions pursuant to the STTCL are applied to reach adjusted taxable income or the actual tax after various deductions and exemptions.

For SMEs, the minimum tax is the greater of 7% (8% for FY2009) of adjusted taxable income or actual tax liability.

Resident tax surcharges
A resident tax surcharge of 10% on corporate income tax liability is assessed each year.

Agriculture and fishery surtax
When a corporate taxpayer claims certain tax credits or exemptions under the STTCL, a 20% of agriculture and fishery surtax is levied on the reduced corporate income tax liability.

Corporate residence

Permanent establishment
A corporation having its head office or principal office in Korea is a domestic corporation. Effective for fiscal years commencing after 31 December 2005, a corporation with a place of effective management in Korea is also treated as a domestic corporation.

A non-resident corporation is generally deemed to have a tax presence (i.e., permanent establishment) in Korea, if one of the following applies:

1. It has any fixed place of business in Korea, where the business of the entity is wholly or partly carried on;
2. It is represented by a dependent agent in Korea, who has the authority to conclude contracts on its behalf and who has repeatedly exercised that authority;
3. Its employee(s) provides services in Korea for more than six months within 12 consecutive months; or
4. Its employee(s) continuously or repeatedly renders similar services in Korea for two or more years, even if each service visit is for less than six months within 12 consecutive months.

Exceptions to a permanent establishment in Korea for a non-resident corporation include fixed places of business used only for purchasing or storage of property at which no sales activities, advertising, publicity, collecting or furnishing of information, or other activities that are preparatory or auxiliary to the conduct of business occur.

Non-resident foreign corporations without domestic places of business in Korea are generally taxed through a withholding tax on each separate item of income.

The Law for Coordination of International Tax Affairs (LCITA) was enacted on 1 January 1996. This law provides the legal basis for taxation of international transactions, focusing especially on transfer pricing rules, advance pricing arrangements (APAs) and mutual agreement procedures. The relevant law for an APA came into effect from 1 January 1997.

Other taxes

Value-added tax (VAT)

The VAT is levied at a rate of 10% on sales and transfers of goods and services, except zero-rated goods and services and exempt goods and services.

Electronic VAT invoicing will be enforced as a compulsory requirement as of 1 January 2011. If a taxpayer fails to issue the electronic VAT invoice or report electronically to tax authorities, the relevant penalties shall be imposed.

Stamp taxes

The stamp tax is levied on a person who prepares a document certifying establishment, transfer, or change of rights to property in Korea. The stamp tax ranges from KRW 100 to KRW 350,000 based on the type of taxable document.

Excise taxes

The individual consumption tax is imposed on specific luxury goods, high-priced durable consumer goods, goods subject to consumption restraints, and certain luxury activities for the purpose of supplementing the VAT single-rate scheme. Tax rates range from two to 20%; in certain circumstances a fixed amount is levied (e.g., KRW 12,000 per person for golf course greens fees).

Property taxes

A yearly tax ranging from 0.07 to 5% is charged on the statutory value of land, buildings, houses, vessels and aircraft. Five times the property tax rate is applied to property that is newly constructed or expanded in the Seoul metropolitan area for five years from its relevant registration date.

K

Korea, Republic of

Transfer taxes

A securities tax of 0.5% is imposed on the total value of securities at the time of transfer, but the government is authorised to adjust the tax rate in certain circumstances. The flexible tax rate prescribed by the Presidential Decree is 0.15 and 0.3% on transactions in the Korea Stock Exchange and Korean Securities Dealers Automated Quotations (KOSDAQ), respectively.

Turnover taxes

Not applicable.

Registration taxes

Registration tax ranging from 0.01 to 5% is also charged upon the transfer of title and incorporation. Registration upon the transfer of title and incorporation for corporations located in large cities may be subject to three times the rates otherwise applied.

Customs duties

Customs duties are generally assessed on imported goods. "Importation" refers to the delivery of goods into Korea (in case of goods passing through a bonded area, delivery of such goods into Korea from such a bonded area) to be consumed or to be used in Korea.

Acquisition taxes

Acquisition tax is charged on the price of real estate, motor vehicles, construction equipment, golf membership, boats, etc. The minimum rate is 2%. A 6% tax is charged on acquisitions in the Seoul metropolitan area and a 10% rate is applied to luxury items, such as villas, golf courses and yachts.

Branch income

In general, a branch office of a foreign corporation is taxed in the same manner as domestic companies.

Remittance of retained earnings from a Korean branch to its head office is subject to reporting to a designated foreign exchange bank in Korea under the Foreign Exchange Transaction Act.

If the tax treaty between Korea and the country in which a foreign corporation is residing allows the imposition of a branch profits tax, the tax is imposed on the adjusted taxable income of the Korean branch.

Where applicable, the branch profit tax is levied in addition to the regular corporate income tax, which is imposed at the rate of 20% (or at a reduced rate as provided in a treaty) of the adjusted taxable income of the Korean branch.

Income determination

Capital vs. ordinary transactions

Gross income consists of gains, profits, income from trade and commerce, dealings in property, rents, royalties and income derived from any ordinary transactions carried on for gain or profit. For the purposes of taxation, gross income does not include income derived from gains from capital transactions such as capital surplus, gains on reduction of paid-in capital, gains from merger, divisions, comprehensive share transfer or comprehensive share exchange. But, gains from treasury stocks transactions are taxed and losses are deductible from taxable income.

Dividend income
All distributions to shareholders are taxed as a dividend income, whether paid in cash or in stock.

However, a qualified domestic holding company that owns more than an 80% (40% in case of listed subsidiary) share ownership in its domestic subsidiary will receive 100% deduction for dividends while an 80% deduction is allowed for shared ownership of 80% (40% in case of listed subsidiary) or less. A domestic corporation other than that is not a qualified holding company will also receive a 100% deduction for shared ownership of 100%, 50% for more than a 50% (30% in case of listed subsidiary) share ownership, and 30% for shared ownership of 50% (30% in case of listed subsidiary) or less.

Foreign investment
Income of foreign subsidiaries incorporated outside Korea is not included in the taxable income of a domestic company. Income is recognised by a domestic company only upon the declaration of dividends from a foreign subsidiary. Therefore, the Korean tax impact may be delayed through deferring the declaration of dividends unless the anti-tax haven rule under the LCITA is triggered.

Korean anti-tax haven rules state that accumulated earnings (distributable retained earnings) of a domestic company's subsidiary located in a low tax jurisdiction (i.e., a tax haven where the effective tax rate on the taxable income for the past three years averages 15% or less), are taxed as deemed dividends to the domestic company, which has direct and indirect interest of 20% or more in such subsidiary.

The foreign tax paid by a qualifying subsidiary is eligible for foreign tax credit against the dividend income of a domestic company if an existing tax treaty between Korea and the country of which the foreign subsidiary is a resident allows it. A qualifying subsidiary is one in which a domestic corporation owns 10% or more of its shares for more than six consecutive months after the date of dividend declaration. Unused foreign tax credits can be carried forward for five years.

Foreign income
Domestic companies are taxed on their worldwide income, whereas foreign companies are taxed only to the extent of their Korean sourced income. A Korean company is taxed on its foreign sourced income as earned at normal corporate tax rates. To avoid double taxation, taxes imposed by foreign governments on income recognised by a domestic company are allowed as a credit against the income taxes to be paid in Korea, or as deductible expenses in computing the taxable income. In general, foreign taxes will generally be applied as credit rather than as a deduction.

Interest income
Except for certain cases, all interest income must be included in taxable income. Generally, interest income is included in taxable income as it is received.

K

Korea, Republic of

Inventory valuation
Inventories generally are stated at the lower of cost or market (LCM). Any one of seven inventory valuation methods, including LCM, specific identification, first-in, first-out (FIFO), last-in, first-out (LIFO), weighted-average, moving average, and retail method can be elected for tax purposes. The method elected should be applied consistently each year unless an application for change has been submitted before three months from the year-end. Different valuation methods may be used for different categories ((a) products and merchandise (b) semi-finished goods and goods in process (c) raw materials (d) goods in stock) and different business places.

Partnership income
A partnership taxation system is effective from 1 January 2009. It is applied to address double taxation issue for business entities, such as Hapmyong Hoesa, Hapja Hoesa and limited corporations prescribed by the Presidential Decree. A partnership's income is not subject to corporate income tax. The partners are subject to income tax on the income allocated from their partnership.

Rents/royalties income
A company engaged in the business of the rental of real properties is also taxed on the deemed rental income calculated at the financial institutions' interest rate on the lease security money as well as on the recognised rental income. Royalties are considered to be taxable income when earned.

Stock valuation
The valuation of securities or bonds shall be made using the cost method. For cost method, the weighted average cost method or moving average cost method shall be applied for the purpose of valuation of securities and individual cost method may be used for valuation of bonds.

Unrealised exchange gains/losses
Except for qualified financial institutions, unrealised foreign exchange gains and losses recognised for financial accounting purposes are not allowed as taxable income or deductions for corporate tax purposes. Therefore, the tax base for foreign currency assets and liabilities shall be the historical amount using the exchange rate at the point of transaction date.

Deductions

Business expenses
In general, expenses incurred in the ordinary course of business are deductible, subject to the requirements for documentary support.

A corporation's disbursement of KRW 30,000 or more for goods or services provided are required to be supported by corroborating documents, such as credit card sales vouchers, cash receipts and tax invoices. The corporation is required to maintain these documents for five years. If the corporation fails to maintain proper evidences, a 2% penalty shall be levied on the amount of disbursement.

Interest expense
Interest incurred in the ordinary course of business is deductible as long as the related loan is used for business purposes. There are, however, a number of exceptions to the general rule, as follows:

1. If borrowings from a foreign shareholder or from a third party under a guaranteed payment guarantee by the foreign shareholder exceeds three times the equity of the relevant foreign shareholder, the paid interest and discount fee as to the relevant excessive portion will be treated as a dividend payment and not allowed as a deduction.
2. Debenture for which the creditor is unknown.
3. Bonds and securities on which recipient of interest is unknown.
4. Construction loans and loans for the purchase of land and fixed assets up to the date in which the assets are acquired or completed must be capitalised as a part of the cost of the asset and depreciated over the life of the asset. Interest after the date of completion or acquisition is deductible as incurred.
5. Interest on loans related to non-business purpose assets or funds loaned to related parties.

Entertainment expenses

Entertainment expenses of more than KRW 10,000 on an event basis must be supported by corporate credit card vouchers, cash receipts or tax invoices in order to be deductible. In addition, the entertainment expenses in excess of tax limit are not deductible.

The deductible limit for entertainment expenses in a business year is computed as follows:

i. An amount calculated by multiplying KRW 12 million (KRW 18 million for a SME) with the number of months in the respective business year divided by 12 plus
ii. An amount calculated by multiplying the amount of gross receipts for a business year with rates listed in the following table (in the case of receipts from transactions between related parties, 20% of the amount calculated by multiplying the receipts with following rates shall be applied)

Amount of gross receipts	Rate
KRW 10 billion or less	0.2%
KRW 10 billion – KRW 50 billion	KRW 20 million + 0.1% of the excess over KRW 10 billion
KRW 50 billion or greater	KRW 60 million + 0.03% of the excess over KRW 50 billion

Employee remuneration

There is no statutory limit for employee remuneration, which includes salaries, wages, stipends, bonuses, retirement payments, pensions, meal and housing allowances as well as all other kinds of subsidies, payments and compensation. Remuneration of foreign employees is determined according to their engagement contracts.

Insurance premiums

Insurance premiums paid to an insurance company are deductible if the business enterprise is the listed beneficiary. Insurance premiums for which the beneficiary is the employee are also deductible, however, they are treated as salaries for the employees and are subject to withholding tax on earned income (this excludes the severance insurance premium or social security taxes that are borne by the corporations).

Accrued expenses

Accrued expenses are not deductible until the expenses are fixed or paid.

Korea, Republic of

Bad debts

A doubtful accounts reserve is allowed for tax purposes of up to 1% (2% for certain financial institutions) or the previous year's ratio of actual loss from bad debts to total balance of account receivables at year-end. Actual losses on bad debts are allowed when certain legal proceedings are satisfied or the statute of limitations has lapsed. The loss should first be charged against the bad debt provision.

Charitable contribution

Donations to public interest entities such as government authorities and social welfare organisations as well as donations for academic research, technical development, etc., are classified as Bub-jung donations. Bub-jung donations are tax-deductible up to 50% of the total taxable income for the concerned fiscal year after deduction of net operating loss (NOL). Ji-jung donations to public entities prescribed by Corporate Income Tax Law (CITL) are also tax-deductible up to 5% of the total taxable income for the fiscal year after the deduction of deductible Bub-jung donations and NOL. Apart from Bub-jung and Ji-jung donations, as a temporary tax concession, the STTCL allows the deduction of donations to certain public entities up to 50% of the total taxable income for the fiscal year after deduction of deductible Bub-jung donations and NOL.

The amount in excess of such a limit may be carried over for one or three years. Donations other than the statutory donations above will not be deductible for tax purposes.

Contingent liabilities

In general, contingent liabilities are not deductible, except for reserves under the following items which are counted as losses within the tax limit:

1. Reserves for retirement allowance;
2. Reserves for bad debts;
3. Liability reserves and emergency reserves prescribed in the Insurance Business Law;
4. Reserves for non-profit organisations;
5. Reserves for the write-off of a compensation claim set aside by trust guarantee funds in each business year; and
6. The amounts enumerated below are counted as losses in calculating income for the business year:
   a. The amount of gains from insurance claims used to acquire the same kinds of fixed assets as the lost fixed assets, or to improve the damaged fixed assets within two years after the beginning day of the business year following the business year in which the gains fall;
   b. The amount of a beneficiary's share of construction costs received by a domestic corporation engaged in the electricity or gas business, etc., used for the acquisition of fixed assets; and
   c. The amount of the national treasury subsidies actually used for acquisition or improvement of fixed assets for business.

Depreciation

With the exception of land, depreciation of all property, plant and equipment (PP&E), which includes buildings, machineries and auto-vehicles, used to generate income is allowed as a deduction for corporate income tax. Generally, interests on debt acquired to purchase, manufacture or construct PP&E must be capitalised until the PP&E is operational. This does not apply to the interest associated with expansion or improvement of existing PP&E. A detailed list of fixed assets, gross values (including capitalised interest), the useful lives of the assets, and the current year's depreciation charge must be submitted to the tax authorities when filing the annual corporate income tax return.

The tax law allows the following methods for calculating depreciation:

1. Straight-line or declining-balance method for tangible fixed assets, other than plant and buildings;
2. Straight-line method for plant, buildings and intangible assets;
3. Service-output or straight-line method for mining rights; and
4. Service-output, declining-balance or straight-line method for tangible fixed assets used in mining.

In determining depreciation using a straight-line method, salvage value of the assets is regarded as zero. However, where the declining-balance method is used, 5% salvage value is required. Changes in the depreciation method must be approved by the tax authorities in advance, and such approval may only be obtained in exceptional cases (i.e., merger between two corporations having different depreciation methods). Although the tax law specifies the useful lives of assets, the useful life of a fixed asset can be increased or decreased by 25% of the specified useful life at the taxpayer's election. There are no specific rules on recapture of depreciation. The selected depreciation method should be consistently applied.

Fines and penalties
Fines, penalties and interest on underpayment of income taxes are not deductible.

Goodwill
Goodwill for tax purposes is defined as "value transferred with consideration, apart from transferred assets included in business transfer, valuated by taking into account business premium factors of the transferor such as permission/license, legal privileges, geographical advantages, business secrets, credit, reputation, transaction partners, etc." Goodwill may be amortised over five years using straight-line method for tax purposes.

Net operating losses (NOL)
In general, a NOL carryover is allowed for 10 years for fiscal years commencing after 31 December 2008 (five years for the prior years). Along with the extension of the NOL carryforward period from five years to 10 years, when a taxpayer uses the NOL incurred more than five years ago, the statute of limitation shall be one year from the filing due date of the fiscal year when the NOL is utilised.

Generally, loss carrybacks are not allowed. However, SMEs can carryback a NOL for one year.

Organisational and start-up expenses
Start-up expenses such as incorporation expenses, founders' salary and registration fees and taxes are deductible when the expenses are actually paid.

Payments to foreign affiliates
With sufficient supporting documentation, interest, royalty and management service fees paid to foreign affiliates are deductible for income tax purposes.

K

Korea, Republic of

Under the LCITA, the conditions for a management service fee to be deductible are:

- The services must be provided based on an agreement entered into by the service provider prior to the service transaction;
- The provision of the service can be verified by a schedule of services, description of services, description of the company providing services and its employees, detailed explanation of expenses incurred and other supporting documentation;
- A company must be able to anticipate the company's additional profit or reduced expense through the services provided by a foreign affiliate; and
- Payment for the provided services should be consistent with arm's-length standards.

Pension expense
For tax purposes, severance allowance may be deducted up to 5% of the annual total amount of wages paid. However, the accumulated amount of the severance allowance reserve may not exceed 30% of the actual aggregate liability to employees. If a corporation subscribes to severance insurance with an insurance company to cover future payments of retirement allowances, additional tax deductions beyond the limits described above are available.

As of 2011, employers hiring five or more employees are required to set aside retirement pensions for their employees. Defined contribution (DC) and defined benefits (DB) will be two available schemes for the new retirement pension system. Under the DC scheme, the premiums paid by the employer will be deductible upon payment while the reserve under the DB scheme would be deductible subject to the limit, similar to the existing severance insurance.

Payment for directors
Bonuses paid to directors in excess of the amount determined in the articles of incorporation or at a shareholders' meeting, etc. are not deductible. Also, severance benefits paid to directors in excess of the amount prescribed in the tax law are not deductible.

Group taxation

Consolidation/group taxation rules
The consolidated corporate tax filing system can be adopted from the fiscal year commencing on or after 1 January 2010 for a domestic corporation in case where two or more wholly-owned subsidiaries exists. It is up to the election of the taxpayer, but it cannot be revoked for at least five years after the election of the consolidated tax filing.

Transfer pricing regime
The LCITA authorises the tax authorities to adjust the transfer price based on an arm's-length price (ALP) and to determine or recalculate a resident's taxable income when the transfer price of a Korean company and its foreign counterpart is either below or above an ALP.

The LCITA lists the following methods for determining an ALP: the comparable uncontrolled price (CUP) method, the resale price method, and the cost-plus method. Furthermore, the Decree elaborates upon the profit-split method, the transactional net margin method (TNMM) and the Berry Ratio method as methods for determining an ALP based on profits arising from controlled transactions.

The method used and the reason for adopting that particular one for an ALP determination must be disclosed to the tax authorities by a taxpayer in a report submitted along with his annual tax return.

Thin capitalisation rules
In case where a Korean company borrows from its controlling shareholders overseas, an amount greater than three times its equity (six times in the case of financial institutions) interest payable on the excess portion of the borrowing is characterised as dividends to which the article on dividends in tax treaty applies and therefore are treated as non-deductible in computing taxable income.

Anti-tax haven rules
In case where a Korean company invests in a company located in a tax haven, which unreasonably has reserved profits in the controlled foreign company, the profits reserved therein shall be treated as dividends paid out to that Korean company (individual), despite the fact that the reserved profits are not actually distributed.

Anti-tax haven rules are intended to regulate a company that has made overseas investments of an abnormal nature. Thus, these anti-tax haven rules apply to those Korean companies that have invested in a company incorporated in a foreign country with an average effective tax rate of 15% or less on taxable income for the past three years.

However, if a company incorporated in such a tax haven country actively engages in business operations through an office, shop, or a factory, then anti-tax haven rules will not apply.

K

Related party transactions
Under the provision of CITL, the tax authorities may recalculate the corporation's taxable income when corporate income tax is unreasonably reduced due to transactions with related parties. Generally, if the discrepancy between the transaction price and fair market value exceeds 5% of the fair market value or KRW 300 million, the transaction will be subject to this provision.

Tax incentives

Foreign taxes paid
Taxes imposed by foreign governments on income recognised by a domestic taxpayer are allowed as a credit within the limit against the income taxes to be paid in Korea, or as deductible expenses in computing the taxable income. In general, foreign taxes will be applied as credit rather than as a deduction. The excess foreign tax credit can be carried forward five years.

Inbound investment
Tax credits are generally available for qualified investment in facilities for productivity enhancement, for safety, temporary investment, etc.

Tax credit for investment in facilities for productivity enhancement
In cases where a resident makes an investment in facilities or equipment to increase productivity by, no later than 31 December 2012, in the facilities or equipments to increase productivity, 3% (7% in the case of SMEs) of such investment amount shall be deducted from income tax. The unused tax credit can be carried forward five years.

Korea, Republic of

Tax credit for investment in facilities for safety
In cases where a resident or a domestic corporation makes an investment (no later than December 31, 2012) in a facility (excluding any investment in used assets) considered to be necessary for industrial purposes, an amount of 3% of such investment shall be deducted from its income taxes. The unused tax credit can be carried forward five years

Temporary tax credit for investment
In cases where the government deems it necessary for business adjustment, the investment amount multiplied by 7% granted by the Presidential Decree (excluding any investment in used items) shall be deducted from corporate income tax. The unused tax credit can be carried forward five years

Research and development (R&D) tax incentive
The STTCL provides various tax incentives to stimulate R&D activities. These include deduction of R&D reserve, tax credit for research and manpower development expenses.

Reserves for development of technology and manpower
In cases where a corporation has set aside development of technology and manpower reserves for expenses on development of technology and manpower, on or before 31 December 2013, for expenses on development of technology and manpower, those reserves are considered as deductible expenses up to 3% of annual sales.

Tax credit for development of technology and manpower
A corporation, excluding those that run a consumer service business, may receive tax credit for each taxable year on expenses related to the development of technology and manpower.

The tax credit for research expenses on development of technology and manpower is calculated as the greater of 40% or 50% of the excess of expense incurred over the average expense incurred in the previous four years and 3~6% of R&D expense of the current year.

Tax credit for investment in facilities for technology and human resources development
A corporation purchasing facilities prescribed in the Presidential Decree with the purpose of R&D and job training is eligible for tax credit up to 10% of such investment. The unused tax credit can be carried forward five years.

Energy/environment
Tax credit for investment in energy-economising facilities
If a resident makes an investment (excluding any investment in used goods) in energy-economising facilities, not later than by 31 December 2011, 20% of such investment shall be deducted from the corporate income tax.

Tax credit for investment in facilities for environmental protection
In cases where a resident makes an investment (excluding any investment in used goods) in any facility for the purpose of environmental conservation (no later than 31 December 2010), 10% of the investment amount shall be deducted from the income taxes. The unused tax credit can be carried forward five years

Employment

Under the STTCL, where a SME has regular employees that exceed prior year's number of regular employees for the period from 1 March 2010 to 30 June 2011, KRW 3 million multiplied by the excess number of employees is deductible from corporate income taxes of the year. The unused tax credit can be carried forward five years.

Foreign investment incentives

The Korean government provides various incentives and benefits for inducing foreign investment under the Foreign Investment Promotion Law, which include the following:

- Foreign invested companies that engage in certain qualified high-technology businesses can apply for 100% exemption from corporate income tax for five years, beginning from the first year of profitable operations (from the fifth year, if not profitable until then) and a 50% reduction for the following two years in proportion to the foreign shareholding ratio. An exemption from withholding tax on dividends is available for foreign investors in the same manner as above during the same grace period. In addition, the taxpayer can apply for 100% exemption from local taxes, such as acquisition tax, registration tax, and property tax on assets acquired for their business for five years after business commencement date and 50% reduction for the following two years. For local tax exemption, some local government grants a longer exemption period (up to 15 years) in accordance with their local ordinances. Qualified foreign investment also can be eligible for the exemption from customs duties, VAT and special excise tax on imported capital goods for the first three years.
- In addition, foreign investors satisfying specified criteria are provided with tax incentives and other benefits for investment in specially designated areas including foreign investment zones (FIZ), free economic zones (FEZ), free trade zones (FTZ) and strategic industrial complexes exclusively developed for foreign invested companies. The tax incentives for qualifying foreign investors in FIZ are similar to those of the above foreign invested high-tech companies. Qualifying investors in FEZ, FTZ and strategic industrial complexes may receive the 100% exemption from corporate or individual income tax as well as local taxes for the first three years and 50% reduction for the next two years. An exemption from withholding tax on dividends is granted to qualifying foreign investors in FEZ, FTZ and such industrial complexes in the same manner as above during the same grace period. They also receive the exemption from customs duties on imported goods for the first three years.

Withholding taxes (WHT)

Foreign corporations with income derived from sources in Korea are subject to corporate income tax on such income. If the foreign corporation has no "domestic place of business" in Korea, it will be subject to tax on its Korean-source income on a withholding basis on its Korean-source income in accordance with the tax laws and the relevant tax treaty, if applicable. Any Korean source income attributable to a domestic fixed place of business of a foreign corporation will be subject to Korean income tax.

There are various limitations on these withholding taxes for residents of countries with a tax treaty with Korea. For dividends, interest, and royalties, the withholding tax rates are limited as follows.

The numbers in parenthesis refer to footnotes below the chart.

Korea, Republic of

Recipient	Dividends	Interest	Royalties
	%	%	%
Resident corporations (1)	Nil	14 or 25	Nil
Resident individuals (1)	14	14, 25 or 30	Nil
Non-resident corporations and individuals:			
Non-treaty (2)	20	14 or 20 (36)	20 (39)
Treaty:			
Albania	5 or 10 (8)	10	10
Algeria	5 or 15 (8)	10	2 or 10 (15)
Australia	15	15	15
Austria	5 or 15 (8)	10	2 or 10 (15)
Azerbaijan	7	10 (37)	5 or 10 (22)
Bangladesh	10 or 15 (3)	10	10
Belarus	5 or 15 (8)	10	5
Belgium	15	10	10
Brazil	10	10 or 15 (5)	10 or 25 (6)
Bulgaria	5 or 10 (7)	10	5
Canada	5 or 15 (8)	10	10
Chile	5 or 10 (8)	10 or 15 (31)	5 or 15 (33)
China, P.R.	5 or 10 (8)	10	10
Croatia	5 or 15 (8)	5	0
Czech Republic	5 or 10 (8)	10	10
Denmark	15	15	10 or 15 (4)
Egypt	10 or 15 (8)	10 or 15 (9)	15
Fiji	10 or 15 (8)	10	10
Finland	10 or 15 (8)	10	10
France	10 or 15 (3)	10	10
Germany	5 or 15 (8)	10	2 or 10 (15)
Greece	5 or 15 (8)	8	10
Hungary	5 or 10 (8)	0	0
Iceland, Rep. of	5 or 15 (8)	10	10
India	15 or 20 (11)	10 or 15 (12)	15
Indonesia	10 or 15 (8)	10	15
Ireland, Rep. of	10 or 15 (3)	0	0
Israel	5, 10, 15 (13)	7.5 or 10 (14)	2 or 5 (15)
Italy	10 or 15 (8)	10	10
Japan	5 or 15 (8)	10	10
Jordan	10	10	10
Kazakhstan	5 or 15 (3)	10	2 or 10 (15)
Kuwait	10	10	15
Laos	5 or 10 (3)	10	5
Lithuania	5 or 10 (8)	10	5 or 10 (38)
Luxembourg	10 or 15 (8)	10	10 or 15 (16)
Malaysia	10 or 15 (8)	15	10 or 15 (17)
Malta	5 or 15 (8)	10	0
Mexico	0 or 15 (18)	5 or 15 (19)	10

Recipient	Dividends	Interest	Royalties
	%	%	%
Mongolia	5	5	10
Morocco	5 or 10 (8)	10	5 or 10 (20)
Nepal	5, 10, 15 (32)	10	15
Netherlands	10 or 15 (8)	10 or 15 (21)	10 or 15 (22)
New Zealand	15	10	10
Norway	15	15	10 or 15 (22)
Oman	5 or 10 (3)	5	8
Pakistan	10 or 12.5 (11)	12.5	10
Papua New Guinea	15	10	10
Philippines (2)	10 or 25 (23)	10 or 15 (24)	10 or 15 (25)
Poland	5 or 10 (3)	10	10
Portugal	10 or 15 (8)	15	10
Qatar	10	10	5
Romania	7 or 10 (8)	10	7 or 10 (22)
Russia	5 or 10 (26)	0	5
Saudi Arabia, Kingdom of	5 or 10 (8)	5	5 or 10 (33)
South Africa (2)	5 or 15 (8)	10	10
Singapore	10 or 15 (8)	10	15
Slovak Republic	5 or 10 (8)	10	0 or 10 (34)
Slovenia	5 or 15 (8)	5	5
Spain	10 or 15 (8)	10	10
Sri Lanka	10 or 15 (8)	10	10
Sweden	10 or 15 (8)	10 or 15 (10)	10 or 15 (22)
Switzerland	10 or 15 (8)	10	10
Thailand (2)	10	10 or 15 (27)	5 or 10 or 15 (35)
Tunisia	15	12	15
Turkey	15 or 20 (8)	10 or 15 (28)	10
Ukraine	5 or 15 (11)	5	5
Union of Myanmar	10	10	10 or 15 (4)
United Arab Emirates	5 or 10 (3)	10	0
United Kingdom	5 or 15 (8)	10	2 or 10 (15)
United States (2)	10 or 15 (30)	12	10 or 15 (29)
Uzbekistan	5 or 15 (8)	5	2 or 15 (15)
Venezuela	5 or 10 (3)	5 or 10 (19)	5 or 10 (33)
Vietnam	10	10	5 or 15 (22)

Notes

1. Dividends and interests paid to resident individuals by corporations generally are subject to a 14% withholding rate and in addition to this, there is resident surtax of 10% on the income tax liability.
2. In addition to the indicated tax rate, resident surtax would be charged at a rate of 10% of the respective tax rate.
3. Lower rate applies in case of equity ownership of 10% or more.
4. 10% rate applies to royalties paid for the use of or the right associated with industrial activities.

5. 10% rate applies if the loan period extends to seven years or more, the recipient is a financial institution and the loan is used for certain designated purposes.
6. 25% rate applies to royalties associated with the use of trademarks or trademark rights.
7. 5% rate applies in case of equity ownership of 15% or more.
8. Lower rate applies in case of equity ownership of 25% or more.
9. 10% rate applies if the term of loans exceeds three years.
10. 10% rate applies when a recipient of interest income is a bank and income is connected with a loan with a term in excess of seven years.
11. Lower rate applies in case of equity ownership of 20% or more.
12. 10% rate applies if a recipient is a bank.
13. 5% rate applies if a recipient holds 10% or more ownership in a paying corporation but, even in case of 10% or more ownership, 10% rate applies if the dividends are paid out of profits subject to tax at a lower rate than the normal corporate tax rate of a country where a payer resides. In other cases, 15% rate applies.
14. 7.5% rate applies when a recipient of interest income is a bank or a financial institution.
15. 2% rate applies to royalties paid for use of or the right to use industrial, commercial or scientific equipment.
16. 10% rate applies if it is for the use of or the right to use industrial, commercial and scientific equipment or information.
17. 15% rate applies if royalties are for use of or the right to use cinematography films or tapes for radio or television broadcasting or any copyright of literary or artistic work.
18. 0% rate applies in case of equity ownership of 10% or more.
19. 5% rate applies if a recipient is a bank.
20. 5% rate applies to royalties for use of copyrighted literature, music.
21. 10% rate applies if the term of the loans exceeds seven years.
22. Lower rate applies if it is for the use of or the right to use patent, trademark, design or secret formula, or industrial, commercial and scientific equipment or information.
23. 10% rate applies in cases of equity ownership of 25% or more, or dividend paid by a resident company engaged in a preferred pioneer area and registered with the Board of Investment.
24. 10% rate applies in cases where the interest is paid in respect of public offering of bonds, debentures or similar obligations or interest paid by a company that is a resident of the Philippines, registered with the Board of Investment and engaged in preferred pioneer areas of investment under the investment incentive laws.
25. 10% rate applies in case of royalties paid by a company that is a resident of the Philippines, registered with the Board of Investment and engaged in preferred pioneer areas of investment under the investment incentives laws.
26. 5% rate applies if a recipient holds 30% or more of equity interest in the amount of at least USD 100,000.
27. 10% rate applies if a beneficial owner of the income is a financial institution (including insurance company) or resident of Thailand who is paid with respect to indebtedness arising as a consequence of a sale on credit by a resident of Thailand of any equipment, merchandise or services, except where the sale was between persons not dealing with each other at arm's length.
28. 10% rate applies if the term of the loan exceeds two years.
29. 10% rate applies to royalties for use of copyrighted literature, music, films, and television or radio broadcasts. Otherwise, 15% rate applies.
30. 10% rate applies if equity ownership is 10% or more and not more than 25% of the gross income of a paying corporation for a preceding tax year consists of interest or dividends.
31. 10% rate applies when a recipient of interest income is a bank or an insurance company.
32. 5% rate applies when a recipient holds 25% or more of equity interest, and 10%, when a recipient holds 10% or more of equity interest. In other cases, 15% rate applies.
33. 5% rate applies to royalties paid for the use of or the right associated with industrial, commercial or scientific equipment.
34. 0% rate applies to royalties paid for the use of academic right.
35. 5% rate applies to royalties paid for the use of or the right associated with any copyright of literary, artistic or scientific work, including software, and motion pictures and works on film, tape or other means of reproduction for use in connection with radio or television

broadcasting. 10% rate applies to royalties paid for the use of or the right to use patent, trademark, design or model, plan, secret formula or process. 15% rate applies to royalties paid for the use of or the right to use industrial, commercial or scientific equipment, or for information concerning industrial, commercial or scientific experience.
36. 14% rate applies if interest arises from bonds issued by Korean company or government bodies.
37. 0% rate applies if a recipient of interest income is government, central bank, etc.
38. 5% rate applies to royalties paid for the use of industrial, commercial or scientific equipment.
39. Effective from 1 January 2004, fees arising from rental of industrial, commercial, scientific equipment, etc., are classified as rental income subject to 2% withholding tax.

Under the new withholding tax rules, which came into effect from 1 July 2006, if a foreign company is located in a foreign jurisdiction designated by the Minister of Strategy & Finance, any Korean-source income of such foreign company will be subject to the domestic withholding rate of 20%, beginning on 1 January 2009 (previously 25%), regardless of whether or not the foreign company is resident of a treaty country. Currently, only Labuan is designated as such jurisdiction for the purpose of the new withholding tax rules. The foreign company may claim a refund of any excess withholding tax paid within three years, if it proves to the Korean Tax Office that it is entitled to the reduced treaty rates as the substantive and beneficial owner of the income. Alternatively, a foreign company may attempt to seek a pre-approval in order to have the treaty benefits apply upfront by making an application to the Commissioner of Taxation.

Tax administration

Taxable year
In Korea, the taxable year is on a fiscal-year basis as elected by the taxpayer. However, it cannot exceed 12 months.

Audit cycle
In September 2009, the National Tax Service (NTS) announced the "Plan for Tax Audits," criteria for selection of a tax audit target company are as follows.

For large companies whose sales revenue is KRW 500 billion or more, the tax audit would be conducted every four years, and the other companies are selected by the certain standards which were announced by NTS.

Statute of limitations
The statute of limitation is generally five years from the statutory filing due date of the annual corporate income tax return. However, the statute of limitation is extended further in the following cases:

1. 10 years if a taxpayer evades taxes by fraud or unjustifiable means;
2. Seven years if a taxpayer does not file its tax base by the statutory due date; or
3. 10 years for inheritance tax and gift tax (15 years in cases of fraudulent return, noncompliance with filing of tax base, or false or incomplete returns).

Along with the extension of the NOL carryforward period from five years to 10 years, when a taxpayer uses the NOL incurred more than five years ago, the statute of limitation shall be one year from the filing due date of the fiscal year when the NOL is utilised.

Korea, Republic of

Tax return due dates

A corporation must file an interim tax return with due payment for the first six months of the fiscal year and the filing/payment must be made within two months after the end of this interim six-month period.

A corporation must file an annual tax return with due payment for the fiscal year and the filing/payment must be made within three months from the end of a fiscal year.

Payment of tax

Where the tax amount to be paid by a domestic corporation is in excess of KRW 10 million, part of the tax amount to be paid may be paid in instalments within one month of the date of the expiration of the payment period (two months for SMEs).

Where the tax amount to be paid is less than KRW 20 million, the excess of KRW 10 million shall be paid in instalments; where the tax amount to be paid exceeds KRW 20 million, 50% or less of the tax amount shall be paid in instalments.

Topics of focus for tax authorities

Recently, topics of focus for tax authorities are as follows:

- Increased scrutiny for the prevention of offshore tax evasion through aggressive tax planning;
- Denial of unfair transactions between related parties;
- Entertainment expenses;
- Deductibility of management service fee or allocated expenses incurred by foreign affiliates; and
- International inter-company transactions and transfer pricing.

Other issues

Foreign investment incentives and restrictions

The Foreign Investment Promotion Act (FIPA) has been enacted to facilitate foreign investment through support and provision of convenience for foreign investment. The FIPA is the basic law for foreign investment and its subordinate acts include the Enforcement of the FIPA. Enforcement Promotion Act and Enforcement Regulations stipulating matters delegated by the Foreign Investment Promotion Act and matters required for enforcement, and regulations on foreign investment and technology import.

Also, unless stated otherwise in the FIPA, the Foreign Exchange Trade Act will apply to matters related to foreign exchange and external dealings related to foreign investments. The Tax Exemptions and Exceptions Act and its regulations on tax reductions on foreign investments, etc., will apply to tax reductions for foreign investments.

However, since foreign-invested companies are local corporations established under domestic law, the same laws that apply to purely domestic corporations will apply even if the foreign-invested company has gone through the processes as prescribed in the FIPA. Therefore, if approval and permission under each law are required, the relevant business may be conducted only after the required processes are completed.

Exchange controls

Most transactions involving foreign exchange generally do not require approval or reporting under FETA, with a few exceptions as prescribed by the FETA. Receipt of foreign exchange from outside the ROK (Republic of Korea) is freely permitted, and payments to foreign companies are not regulated. Most restrictions on Korean companies' foreign currency transactions with foreigners have been removed. However, the government continues to monitor certain flows of foreign currency in an attempt to minimise incoming speculative currency and outgoing capital flight.

Ever since Korea's currency crisis, most restrictions on short-term as well as mid- and long-term borrowings from overseas by corporations have been removed. Most foreign currency loans are allowed, and are subject to reporting to a foreign exchange bank. There are no specific regulations, except the reporting requirements, on borrowings from overseas by foreign investment companies in Korea.

Choice of business entity

The following types of commercial entities are permitted.

1. Corporation (Hoesa) – There are five classes of corporation, outlined as follows:
   a. Limited corporation:
      i. Jusik Hoesa (JH): A corporation incorporated by one or more promoters, with each shareholder's liability limited to the amount of contributed capital. This type of entity is the most commonly used in Korea.
      ii. Yuhan Hoesa (YH): A corporation incorporated by one or more members, with each member's liability limited to the amount of that member's contribution to the corporation.
      iii. Yuhan Chegim Hoesa (a newly proposed form for legislation): A corporation incorporated by one or more members, with each member's liability limited to the amount of that member's capital contribution. With significantly fewer restrictions for establishment and operation, Yuhan Chegim Hoesa provides more flexibility and self-control than YH.
   b. Unlimited corporation:
      i. Hapmyong Hoesa: A corporation incorporated jointly by more than two members who are responsible for corporate obligations, if the assets of the corporation are insufficient to fully satisfy those obligations.
      ii. Hapja Hoesa: A corporation composed of one or more partners who have unlimited liability and one or more partners with limited liability.
2. Partnership – Hapja Johap, a newly proposed form, is a legal form of partnership allowed under the Commercial Code.
3. Joint venture – A joint venture is generally established as a domestically incorporated corporation whose shareholders have limited liability regarding the obligations of the corporation under the Commercial Code.
4. Branch – A foreign corporation can perform its business operation in Korea by setting up a taxable presence in the form of a branch office.
5. Liaison office – A foreign corporation can establish a liaison office which is not allowed to execute income-generating business activities in Korea.
6. Sole proprietorship – Sole proprietorships are not a legal form of entity in Korea.

K

Corporate taxes in Kuwait

For more information, contact:

Fouad Douglas
PricewaterhouseCoopers Al-Shatti & Co.
Arraya Tower II, 23-24th Floor
Al-Shuhada Street.
Sharq
Kuwait
Tel: +965 2227 5700
Email: fouad.douglas@kwt.pwc.com

Significant developments

Tax law No. 2 of 2008, which was issued by the Kuwaiti government on 22 January 2008, amended the Kuwait Income Tax Decree No. 3 of 1955 and other corporate and taxation related matters in Kuwait.

One of the major changes of the new tax law is the reduction of the tax rates, which previously reached a maximum rate of 55%, to a flat rate of 15%.

Taxes on corporate income

Kuwait does not impose income tax on companies wholly owned by the nationals of Kuwait or other Gulf Cooperation Council countries (GCC), including Bahrain, Oman, Qatar, Saudi Arabia and the United Arab Emirates. Income tax is imposed only on the profits and capital gains of foreign "corporate bodies" conducting business or trade in Kuwait, directly or through an agent.

Governing laws
Kuwait Income Tax Decree No. 3 of 1955 and Law No. 2 of 2008, amending the income tax decree. These laws are applicable to business activities carried out in Kuwait, exclusive of the neutral zone.

Law No. 23 of 1961, applicable to business activities carried out in the neutral zone. Foreign companies carrying on trade or business in the offshore area of the partitioned neutral zone under the control and administration of Saudi Arabia are subject to tax in Kuwait on 50% of taxable profit under the above-mentioned Law.

Income subject to tax
Article 2 of the amended tax law, provides that income earned from the following activities in Kuwait shall be considered subject to tax in Kuwait:

1. Any activities or business carried out either entirely or partially in Kuwait, whether the contract has been signed inside or outside Kuwait, as well as the any income resulting from supply or sale of goods, or from providing services.
2. The amounts collected from the sale, rent, or granting of a franchise to utilise any trademarks, design, patents, copyright, or other moral rights, or those related to intellectual property rights for use of rights to publish literary, arts or scientific works of any form.
3. Commission earned or resulting from agreements of representation or commercial mediation, whether such commissions are in cash or in kind.

4. Opening a permanent office in Kuwait where the contract of purchase and sale is signed and acts as a work site in which the activities are performed or contracts are signed, whether the site is owned by the taxpayer, rented from another party, or the activities are performed in another party location in Kuwait.
5. Profits resulting from the following:
   * Any industrial or commercial activity in Kuwait;
   * Disposal of assets, either through the sale of the asset or part of the asset, or the transfer of the asset's ownership to others or any other form of disposal, including the disposal of shares in a company whose assets mainly consist of non-movable capital existing in Kuwait;
   * Granting loans in Kuwait;
   * Purchase and sale of property, goods, or related rights in Kuwait, whether such rights are related to monetary assets or moral rights such as mortgage and franchise rights;
   * Lease of property used in Kuwait;
   * Providing services, including profits from management, technical and consultancy services; and
   * Carrying out trading activities in the Kuwait Stock Exchange whether directly or through portfolios or investment funds.

Tax imposed on Kuwaiti-source income

In cases where a contract involves the performance of work both inside and outside Kuwait, the entire revenue from the contract must be reported for tax in Kuwait, including the work carried out outside Kuwait.

Tax rate

Under law No. 2 of 2008, the tax rate has been reduced to a flat rate of 15% effective for fiscal years beginning after 3 February 2008.

Capital gains

Capital gains on the sale of assets and shares by foreign shareholders are treated as normal business profits and are subject to tax at the rate stated above. Article 1 of Law No. 2 of 2008 provides for a possible tax exemption for profits generated from dealing in securities on the Kuwait Stock Exchange (KSE), whether directly or through investment portfolios.

Dividend or distribution of profits

Treatment of dividends is not specifically addressed in the amended tax law or in its bylaws. The bylaws to the amended tax law, however, require investment companies or banks that manage portfolios or funds or act as custodians of shares for foreign entities to deduct corporate tax due from payments due to foreign investors. Tax payment should be made within 30 days from the date of the deduction of tax, together with a list showing names of the foreign entities and the amount withheld from each.

Under the original tax law, no tax was imposed on dividends paid to foreign shareholders by Kuwaiti companies.

Tax exemption

The following sources of income are exempt from tax in Kuwait, as per the amended Law No. 2 of 2008:

K

Kuwait

1. Kuwaiti merchants purchasing, transporting and selling goods imported on their own account where the foreign supplier has not been involved in Kuwait operations.
2. Profits of a corporate body generated from dealing in securities listed in the KSE, whether such activities are carried out directly or through investment portfolios or funds.

Corporate residence

A foreign corporate body is any association formed and registered under the law of any country or state other than Kuwait that is registered as having a legal existence entirely separate from that of its individual members. No Kuwait-registered company is subject to income tax. However, any foreign corporate body that is a shareholder in a Kuwait-registered company undertaking business in Kuwait is subject to tax as noted above. For the purposes of this law, GCC residents and entities wholly owned by GCC residents are treated in the same manner as Kuwaiti business entities.

Other taxes

National Labour Support Tax (NLST)
NLST Law No. 19 of 2000 was issued by the Ministry of Finance (MOF) on 21 May 2000 and came into effect a year later on 21 May 2001. The purpose of the law is to encourage the national labour force to work in the private sector by closing the gap in salaries and benefits between public and private sectors.

As per the law, Kuwaiti companies listed in the Kuwait Stock Exchange (KSE) are required to pay an employment tax of 2.5% of the company's net annual profits.

Zakat
Zakat Law No. 46 of 2006 was issued on 27 November 2006 and came into effect as of 10 December 2007.

Zakat is imposed on all publicly traded and closed Kuwaiti shareholding companies at a rate of 1% of the companies' net profits.

Contribution to the Kuwait Foundation for the Advancement of Sciences (KFAS)
Published Closed Kuwaiti Shareholding Companies are required to pay 1% of their net profits as per their financial statements after their transfer to the statutory reserve and the offset of loss carryforwards, to the KFAS, which supports scientific progress.

Social security
There are no social security obligations for expatriate workers. However, for foreign employees it is generally necessary to make terminal indemnity payment calculated at 15 days' pay per year for the first five years of service and one month's pay per year thereafter.

For Kuwaiti employees, contributions are payable monthly by both the employer and employee under the Social Security Law. The employer's contribution is 11% and the employee's is 7% of monthly salary, up to a ceiling of KWD 2,250 per month. Benefits provided, include pensions on retirement and allowances for disability, sickness and death.

Branch income

Tax rates on branch profits are the same as on corporate profits.

Income determination

Income tax is imposed on the profit of a business in Kuwait as calculated by the normal commercial criteria, using generally accepted accounting principles, including the accrual basis. Note that provisions, as opposed to accruals, are not deductible for tax purposes. In addition, for contract accounting, revenue is recognised by applying the percentage of completion method. Work-in-progress carried forward may not exceed 20% of work executed.

Deductions

All expenses, other than in the nature of capital expenses and head office expenses (refer below), incurred in the conduct of a business or trade, wherever incurred, are deductible, provided that the expenditure is supported by full documentation.

Assets and depreciation
In accordance with Article 4 of Law No. 2 of 2008, depreciation is taken on a straight-line basis at specified rates. However, within 90 days prior to submission of the tax declaration, the taxpayer may request that the tax department calculate the depreciation using a different method than the straight-line method. The tax department shall accept this request provided it is based on a reasonable basis in accordance with the tax accounting principles and rules.

The principal depreciation rates are specified in the law.

Head office expenses/payments to foreign affiliates
As noted above, the deductibility of head office expenses (e.g., allocations of head office expenses), or payments to a head office may not be deductible in full. The Bylaws to the amended tax law contain specific provisions relating to head office administrative expenses and specialist tax advice should be sought on this subject. This matter is frequently raised during tax audits in Kuwait.

Relief for losses
As per the amended tax law, losses may be carried forward for a maximum of three years, provided that the following situations do not arise in the fiscal period following the period in which the loss was recorded:

- The tax declaration does not include any revenue from the business activities of the taxpayer in Kuwait;
- Change in the legal structure of the taxpayer;
- Merger of the taxpayer with another entity; or
- Liquidation or ceasing of the activities of the taxpayer in Kuwait.

Group taxation

If a foreign company conducts more than one business activity in Kuwait, one tax declaration aggregating the income from all activities is required to be submitted in Kuwait. In addition, in the case where two affiliates are involved in similar lines of

K

Kuwait

business or work on the same project, their taxable results may be aggregated for the assessment of tax.

Tax incentives

Law No. 8 of 2001: Direct foreign capital investment law
Law No. 8 of 2001 aims to encourage foreign investment participation in Kuwait, allowing up to 100% of foreign ownership in Kuwaiti businesses.

Some of the privileges under this law include:

- Exemption from income tax or any other taxes for a period of 10 years from the commencing of the actual operations of the enterprise;
- Benefits under double taxation agreements;
- Benefits under investment encouragement and protection agreements;
- Total or partial exemption from custom duties on imports;
- Recruitment of required foreign labour; and
- Allotment of land and real estate.

Law No. 12 of 1998
Law No. 12 of 1998 provides for a five-year tax holiday to non-Kuwaiti shareholders of investment and leasing companies formed in Kuwait for five years from the date of formation, if the principal business is in Kuwait.

Withholding taxes (WHT)

Apart from the withholding tax on dividends arising from trading in the KSE, there are no other withholding taxes. However, under Executive Rule No. 12 of Law No. 2 of 2008, all government bodies and private entities are required to retain the final payment due to a contractor or subcontractor until presentation of a tax clearance certificate from the MOF, confirming that the respective company has settled all of its tax liabilities. The final payment should not be less than 5% of the total contract value.

Tax treaties
Kuwait has entered into tax treaties with several countries for the avoidance of the double taxation. Treaties with several other countries are at various stages of negotiation or ratification.

However, little experience has been gained in Kuwait regarding the application of tax treaties. As a result, disputes about the interpretation of various clauses in tax treaties between taxpayers and the Director of Income Taxation (DIT) are not uncommon. Disputes with the DIT regarding tax treaties normally arise with respect to the following issues:

- Existence of a permanent establishment;
- Income attributable to a permanent establishment; or
- Tax deductibility of costs incurred outside Kuwait.

The domestic tax law in Kuwait does not provide for withholding taxes. As a result, it is not yet known how the Kuwaiti government will apply the withholding tax procedures included in the treaties listed in the table below. The withholding rates listed in the table are for illustrative purposes only.

Country	Dividends	Interest	Royalties
	%	%	%
Austria	0	0	10
Belarus	5 (c)	5 (c)	10
Belgium	10	0	10
Bulgaria	5 (j)	5 (f)	10
Canada	5/15 (m)	10	10
China	5 (a)	5 (a)	10
Croatia	0	0	10
Cyprus	10	10 (b)	5
Czech Republic	5 (j)	0	10
Ethiopia	5 (c)	5 (b)	30
France	0	0	0
Germany	5/15 (e)	0	10
Hungary	0	0	10
India	10 (n)	10 (n)	10
Indonesia	10 (c)	5 (b)	20
Italy	5	0	10
Jordan	5 (c)	5 (b)	30
Korea	10	10	15
Lebanon	0	0	30
Malta	10/15 (d)	0	10
Mauritius	0	0 (f)	10
Mongolia	5 (h)	5 (h)	10
Netherlands	10 (i)	0	5
Pakistan	10	10 (g)	10
Poland	5 (j)	5 (j)	15
Romania	1	1	20
Russian Federation	5 (c)	0	10
Singapore	0	7 (b)	10
South Africa	0	0	0
Sri Lanka	5/10	10	20
Sudan	5 (h)	5 (h)	10
Switzerland	15	10	10
Syria	0	10 (k)	20
Tunisia	10 (c)	2.5 (b)	5
Turkey	10	10	10
Ukraine	5 (f)	0	10
United Kingdom	5/15 (e)	0	10
Yugoslavia	5/10 (l)	10	10
Non-treaty countries	0	0	0

Notes

a. The rate is 0% for amounts paid to a company of which the government owns at least 20% of the equity.
b. The rate is 0% for interest paid to the government of the other contracting state. Under the Ethiopia treaty, the rate is also 0% for the interest paid to entities in which the

Kuwait

government owns a specified percentage of the equity and for interest paid on loans guaranteed by the government.

c. The rate is 0% for dividends and interest paid to the government of the other contracting state. Under the Ethiopia treaty, the rate is also 0% for dividends paid to entities in which the government owns a specified percentage of the equity.

d. The rate is 10% for dividends paid to the government of Kuwait or any of the institutions or any intergovernmental entities. The rate is 15% for other dividends.

e. The 5% rate applies if the recipient of the dividends owns directly or indirectly at least 10% of the payer. The 15% rate applies to other dividends.

f. The rate is increased to 5% if the beneficial owner of the interest carries on business in the other contracting state through a permanent establishment and the debt on which the interest is paid is connected to such permanent establishment.

g. The rate is 0% for amounts paid to the government of the other contracting state and to entities of which the government owns at least 51% of the paid-up capital.

h. For dividends and interest, the rate is 0% if the payments are made to the government or a governmental institution of the other contracting state, or to a company that is a resident of the other contracting state and is controlled by, or at least 49% of the capital is owned directly or indirectly by, the government or a governmental institution. A 0% rate also applies to interest arising on loans guaranteed by the government of the other contracting state or by a governmental institution or other governmental entity of the other contracting state.

i. A 0% rate applies if the beneficial owner of the dividends is a company that holds directly at least 10% of the capital of the company paying the dividends.

j. The rate is 0% if the payments are made to the government or a governmental institution of the other contracting state, or to a company that is resident of the other contracting state and is controlled by, or at least 25% of the capital is owned directly or indirectly by, the government or a governmental institution of the contracting state.

k. The rate is 0% if the beneficial owner of the interest is a resident in the other contracting state and the loan is secured or financed directly or indirectly by a financial entity or other local body wholly owned by the government of the other contracting state.

l. The 5% rate applies if the recipient of the dividends owns directly or indirectly at least 25% of the payer. The 10% rate applies to other dividends.

m. The rate is 5% if the beneficial owner of the dividends is a company that owns 10% or more of the issued and outstanding voting or 25% or more of the value of all of the issued and outstanding shares. The 15% rate applies to other dividends.

n. Dividends or interest paid by a company that is resident of a contracting state is not taxable in that contracting state if the beneficial owner of the dividends or interest is one of the following:
    *   The government;
    *   A political subdivision or a local authority of the other contracting state;
    *   The Central Bank of the other contracting state; or
    *   Other governmental agencies or governmental financial institutions as may be specified and agreed to in an exchange of notes between the competent authorities of the contracting state.

In addition to the above treaties, a tax treaty for the Avoidance of Double Taxation and Income Tax Evasion has recently been signed on 17 February 2010, between Japan and the State of Kuwait. However, the tax treaty has not yet been published officially and is still subject to amendment by the Parliament during their final review.

Tax administration

Tax is imposed on profits arising in a taxable period, which is defined as the accounting period of the taxpayer and further assumed to be the calendar year. However, the Director of Income Taxes may agree to a written request from the taxpayer to change the year-end to a date other than December 31. Also, at the taxpayer's request, the Director of Income Taxes may agree to extend the accounting period, provided it does not exceed 18 months. The taxpayer must submit a tax return, based on the taxpayer's books of account, within three months and 15 days of the end of the taxable period. Upon application, the Director of Income Taxes may extend the filing period by a maximum of 60 days.

The taxpayer must keep in Kuwait certain accounting records, which are subject to inspection by the Tax Department's officials. Accounting records may be in English and may be in a computerised system used to prepare financial statements, provided that the system includes the required records and the tax department is previously informed.

The tax return should be supported by the following:

1. Audited balance sheet and profit-and-loss account for the period;
2. Detailed list of fixed assets (e.g., additions, disposals, etc.);
3. List of inventory (e.g., quantities and values);
4. List of subcontractors and the latest payments to them;
5. Copies of current contracts and a statement of income and expenditure for each;
6. Trial balance, forming the basis of the accounts;
7. Last payment certificate from the client; and
8. Insurance companies must attach to the Public Budget and the tax declaration a detailed statement with the reinsured documents and the related terms and conditions.

As a general rule, an assessment is finalised only after inspection of records by the tax department. As indicated above, proper documentation must be kept to support expenditure and to avoid disallowances at the time of tax inspection. If support is considered inadequate, the assessment is apt to be made on the basis of deemed profitability. This is computed as a percentage of turnover and is fixed arbitrarily, depending on the nature of the taxpayer's business.

Payment of tax
Tax is payable in four equal instalments on the fifteenth day of the fourth, sixth, ninth, and twelfth months following the end of the tax period. If an extension is approved by the Director of Taxes, all of the tax is payable upon the expiration date of the extension. Failure to file or pay the tax on time attracts a penalty of 1% of the tax liability for every 30 days of delay or part thereof.

Objection
If a company disagrees with an assessment issued by the DIT, the company should submit an objection within 60 days from the date of the assessment. The DIT is required to resolve the objection within 90 days of the filing of the objection, after which a revised tax assessment is issued by the DIT. Upon issuance of a revised tax assessment, any additional tax is payable within 30 days. If the DIT issues no response within 90 days of filing the objection, this implies that the taxpayer's objection has been rejected.

Appeal
In case the objection is rejected or the taxpayer is still not satisfied with the revised tax assessment, the company may contest the matter further with the Tax Appeals Committee (TAC), by submitting a letter of appeal within 30 days from the date of the

Kuwait

objection response or 30 days from the expiry of the 90 days following submission of an objection if no response is provided by the DIT.

The matter is then resolved through appeal hearings and a final revised assessment is issued based on the decision of the TAC. Tax payable per the revised assessment must then be settled within 30 days from the date of issuance of the revised assessment. Failure to do so results in a delay penalty of 1% of the amount of the tax due per the final assessment for each period of 30 days or part thereof of the delay.

Other issues

Offset program
Kuwait has designed a counter-trade offset program to meet the objectives of its economic development plan. The offset program derives from the government's concern that the long-term benefits from job creation and capital accumulation resulting from government contracts with foreign suppliers unfairly accrue to the suppliers, at the expense of Kuwaiti companies and citizens. The objective of the offset program is to remedy this problem by encouraging collaborative business ventures between foreign contractors and the Kuwaiti private sector. Accordingly the offset program has been established with the following objectives:

- Promoting sustainable economic development in Kuwait, by the assimilation of modern technology and know-how in the local economy;
- Supporting projects that generate high skilled jobs for Kuwaiti nationals; and
- Attract foreign investment capital to facilitate economic development in Kuwait.

The MOF initially issued guidelines for the program in 1995. The MOF has also issued Ministerial Order 13 of 2005 reactivating the program. The following are significant aspects of the program:

- All civil contracts with a value of KWD 10 million and more, and defence contracts with a value of KWD 3 million and more attract the offset obligations for contractors. The obligations become effective on the signing date of the contract.
- The contractors covered by the offset obligation are required to invest 35% of the value of the contract with Kuwaiti government bodies.
- Offset obligators have the following options for fulfilling their offset obligation:

  1. Implement investment projects suggested by the Offset Program management;
  2. Propose their own investment projects, and seek approval of the Offset Program management;
  3. Participate in any of the funds that the Offset Program management may establish; or
  4. Purchase of commodities and services of Kuwaiti origin. The MOF is however still finalising detailed regulations in this regard.

- Contractors covered by the offset obligation must provide unconditional, irrevocable bank guarantees issued by Kuwaiti banks to the MOF equal to 6% of the contract price. The value of the bank guarantee submitted will be reduced gradually based on the actual execution of its work by the foreign contractor/supplier. The MOF has the right to cash in the bank guarantee if offset obligor fails to respect their offset obligation.

Corporate taxes in Kyrgyzstan

For more information, contact:

Richard Bregonje
PricewaterhouseCoopers
29/6 Satpaev Avenue
Hyatt Regency Office Tower, 4th Floor
Almaty 050040
Republic of Kazakhstan
Tel: +7 727 298 0448
Email: richard.bregonje@kz.pwc.com

Significant developments

Kyrgyzstan's tax system is regulated by the Tax Code No. 230 which became effective starting 1 January 2009 (tax code). The Kyrgyzstan tax system consists of both national and local taxes. National taxes set out in the tax code include a profits tax on legal entities, personal income tax, value-added tax (VAT), sales tax, excise tax, and subsurface use taxes; local taxes include property tax and land tax.

Taxes on corporate income

Pursuant to the tax code, resident and foreign legal entities carrying out business activities through a permanent establishment that earns Kyrgyzstan source income is subject to the corporate income tax called "profit tax".

Profit tax is calculated at a rate of 10% of aggregate annual income less allowed deductions. Corporate income tax is payable via quarterly advance payments (not later than twentieth day of the second month following the reporting quarter).

Corporate residence

Permanent establishment
In Kyrgyz tax legislation, a permanent establishment is a permanent place of business, through which a non-resident carries out business operations, including activities performed through an authorised person. A permanent establishment includes the following:

- Any place of management, department, office, factory, workshop, mining, oil and gas wells, land, construction site or project; and
- Any services rendered by non-residents by hiring personnel working in the territory of Kyrgyzstan for a duration of more than 183 calendar days within any consecutive12-month period.

A permanent establishment is not created in Kyrgyzstan if a non-resident is limited to the following activities in Kyrgyzstan:

- Use of warehouses or buildings exclusively for storage, demonstration activities;
- Use of a fixed place of business exclusively for preparatory purposes; or
- Performance of activities in Kyrgyzstan through an agent in cases where such agent usually performs such activities in the ordinary course of business.

Kyrgyzstan

Creation of a permanent establishment may be connected with the establishment of a branch or subsidiary. Both branches and subsidiaries are considered appropriate business vehicles for foreign investors and the choice between them would be determined by the business the investor is engaged in, along with various other factors.

Other taxes

Value-added tax (VAT)

In Kyrgyzstan, VAT is assessed on taxable supply and taxable imports. Input VAT assessed on purchases used for business purposes is generally offset against output VAT on taxable supplies. The VAT rate is 12% except for certain zero-rated supplies (such as international transportation and exports) and certain exempt turnover.

All taxpayers registered for VAT purposes are required to charge VAT on their taxable supply, and calculate and report their VAT liabilities.

Taxpayers are required to register for Kyrgyzstan VAT purposes if their taxable supply in the preceding 12 calendar months exceeds KGS (Kyrgyzstani Som) 4,000,000. Even if an entity is not required to register for VAT purposes, it may still do so voluntarily by submitting an application to the appropriate tax committee.

Place of supply of goods
Goods and services are subject to VAT if they are deemed to be supplied in Kyrgyzstan under the place of supply rules. According to these rules, transactions are deemed to be made at the place where transport of the goods begins if the goods are transported by the supplier, and in all other cases, at the place where the goods are transferred to the customer. The rules regarding services are more complicated. Services that are not specifically mentioned are deemed to be supplied at the place where the service provider has established his place of business. Certain other services are deemed to be supplied at the place of the purchaser.

Import of goods
Generally, imports of goods are subject to import VAT.

Zero-rate VAT
There are turnovers subject to zero-rate VAT. These include exports (except for certain limited types of export), and international transportation. Supply of goods (works, services) for official use of diplomatic and consular representations is taxable, but may be refunded provided that certain conditions are met.

Exempt supplies
Certain supplies are VAT-exempt, including (among others) supplies and exports of gold alloy and refined gold, supplies of pharmaceuticals, land plots, residual buildings and construction, and financial services. When a taxpayer generates both taxable and exempt supplies, input VAT proportional to the ratio of the exempt supply to the total supply should be disallowed for offset.

VAT on supplies
Taxable supply includes any sale of goods, works and services, and taxable import in Kyrgyzstan, unless the supply is specifically exempted or if the place of supply is deemed to be outside Kyrgyzstan.

VAT offset
VAT paid on services and goods purchased by a VAT payer (i.e., input VAT) and VAT paid at customs should generally be available for offset (credit) when determining a taxpayer's VAT liability. However, offset is not available for certain VAT (e.g., VAT incurred for the purpose of supplies which are deemed to be supplied outside of Kyrgyzstan).

VAT liability calculation and VAT offset carryforward
In general, the VAT liability of a taxpayer is calculated as output VAT (i.e., VAT charged by a taxpayer) less input VAT (i.e., VAT paid by a taxpayer to its suppliers) in a reporting period.

The excess of input VAT over output VAT may generally be carried forward against future VAT liabilities.

Non-deductible input VAT
The input VAT is not allowed for offset if it is subject to payment in connection with the receipt of goods (work, services) not related to entrepreneurial activity, or if it relates to inputs for VAT exempt supplies.

VAT incentives
Certain imports are VAT exempt, including imports of technological equipment, if it is used for own production purposes. Recently, a preferential offset method of VAT settlement in respect of certain fixed assets imported to Kyrgyzstan has been introduced, whereby the import VAT does not need to be paid to customs but is reflected simultaneously as input and output VAT in the VAT accounts.

VAT compliance
The tax period for VAT is a calendar month. The submission of the VAT declaration is due by the end of the month following the reporting period. Payment of the VAT liability is due by the twenty-fifth of the month following the reporting period.

Reverse-charge VAT
The current tax code does not have any provisions on reverse-charge VAT.

Customs duties and regimes
The new Customs Code entered into force from 1 January 2005. According to the Customs Code, the customs value of goods imported to the customs territory of the Kyrgyz Republic is determined by applying the following methods:

* Transaction value of imported goods;
* Transaction value of identical goods;
* Transaction value of similar goods;
* Deductive method;
* Computed method; and
* Provisional method.

Import restrictions
Generally all entities or persons have equal rights to import and export or transfer goods into the Kyrgyzstan territory, including when carrying out foreign trade activity, except in special cases as stipulated by legislation and international treaties.

Kyrgyzstan

Import of certain goods (e.g., weapons, nuclear materials, etc.) is subject to licensing.

Temporary import relief
There is a temporary import regime under which foreign goods are used in the Kyrgyz customs territory with full or partial conditional exemption from the payment of customs duties and taxes and without application of non-tariff regulatory measures. The term of the "temporary import" customs regime may not exceed two years.

Customs duties incentives
Certain items are exempt from customs payments, including transportation vehicles used in the international conveyance of passengers and goods and items of material and technical supply in transit; goods imported in the customs territory or imported from the customs territory for official and personal use by official state representatives of foreign states.

Kyrgyzstan provides preferential rates or exemptions on the importation (and export) of certain goods, including goods originating from the states which form free trade zones or a customs union with Kyrgyzstan and goods originating from developing countries, included on a special list provided by the government.

Documentation and procedures
Kyrgyzstan pays close attention to formalities/documentation and, thus, it is necessary to furnish the customs authorities with a set of required documents. For import, such documents usually include cargo customs declaration, invoices, contracts, etc.

Warehousing and storage
There is a bonded warehouse customs regime in Kyrgyzstan – a customs regime under which imports entering into the customs territory of the Republic of Kyrgyzstan goods are stored in special facilities or special areas that have the status of a customs warehouse under the customs legislation of Kyrgyzstan.

Generally, most goods (unless otherwise specifically provided for) can be placed under the bonded warehouse customs regime. The period for storage of goods at a bonded warehouse is determined by the person placing the goods into the customs warehouse, but cannot exceed three years from the date when the goods were placed under the bonded warehouse customs regime.

Re-exports
The re-export regime is similar to that used in international practice. It is defined as a customs regime under which goods previously imported into the customs territory of Kyrgyzstan are exported from this territory without payment or with a refund of the paid amounts of import customs duties and taxes and without applying the non-tariff regulatory measures with respect to the goods in compliance with Kyrgyz legislation on state regulation of foreign trade activity.

There are certain conditions under which goods can be re-exported. Customs duties and taxes are not charged for goods declared as goods intended for re-export. However, if the goods do not meet the re-export criteria, customs duties and taxes are paid in the amount which would be payable if the goods, at their importation, were declared for release for free circulation, as well as interest on them paid at the National Bank rates, as if deferment was provided with respect to the amounts at placement of the goods under the customs regime of re-export.

Excise tax

Certain goods manufactured in Kyrgyzstan or imported to Kyrgyzstan are subject to excise tax. These include, among others, certain alcohol and alcoholic drinks; fortified drinks; tobacco goods; jewellery made of gold, silver, or platinum; and oil products.

The rates of excise tax are adopted annually by the Kyrgyzstan government.

Subsurface use taxes

Under Kyrgyz legislation, subsurface users are legal entities and individuals who perform exploration and/or extraction of mineral resources.

From 1 January 2009, the Kyrgyz tax code introduced new taxes on subsurface users, both Kyrgyzstan legal entities and branches of foreign legal entities. These taxes include bonuses and royalty.

The government, depending on the type of mineral resources, establishes the bonus rates.

The royalty rates are estimated either as a percentage of sales turnover (1%–12%) or in absolute terms in KGS depending on the type of mineral resources.

Property tax

Property tax is a local tax payable by individuals and legal entities owning transport vehicles and immovable property in Kyrgyzstan, including apartment houses, apartments, boarding houses, holiday inns, sanatoria, resorts, production, administrative, industrial, and other buildings or facilities. Certain real estate may not be subject to this tax according to special lists approved by the government.

In respect of immovable property, the tax rate is established by the city or local authorities at a rate not to exceed 0.8% of the estimated value of taxable objects, except for apartment houses and apartments designated solely for residence, for which the rate may not exceed 0.35% of the estimated value. The estimation can be performed by the state competent body and independent appraisers. For transport vehicles, the tax is computed in KGS depending on engine volume.

Land tax

Land tax is paid by legal entities and individuals on the area of owned land plot. The basic rates are provided in the tax code depending on the location and purposes of the land plot.

Branch income

Branch income is subject to the profits tax as mentioned earlier. There is no special branch profits tax in addition to profits tax.

Income determination

Kyrgyzstan legal entities are taxable on aggregate annual income earned worldwide. Non-resident legal entities carrying out business through a permanent establishment in Kyrgyzstan are taxable on income attributed to the activities of that permanent establishment.

Kyrgyzstan

Aggregate annual income is comprised of all types of income, including gross revenue from the sale of goods (work, services), non-depreciable assets and other income including, but not limited to:

- Interest income (except for income already subject to withholding tax);
- Dividends;
- Royalties;
- Assets received free of charge;
- Rental income;
- Income from the reduction of liabilities;
- Foreign exchange gain; and
- Write-off liability.

The tax code envisages some profits tax privileges aimed at developing certain areas of the business economy. Currently, these include privileges/preferences for:

- Charity organisations;
- Associations of invalids of I and II groups, (i.e., persons with disability with different levels of physical disability), associations of blind and deaf persons;
- Agricultural organisations;
- Growing of berries, fruits and vegetables;
- Credit unions; and
- Companies that have been involved in the food industry for less than three years and included in the Kyrgyzstan government's list of exempt companies.

Aggregate annual income may be reduced by the value of assets donated to charity and budget organisations (limited to 10% of taxable income).

Non-taxable revenues include, inter alia, the following:

- Property received as a charter capital contribution and income from realisation of shares of organisations; and
- Property donated to special organisations using such property for development purposes under the government's social culture plan. Despite being designated as property used for social culture purposes, such property may still be used for other purposes (i.e., citizen defence projects, mining equipment, water intakes, heat networks, roads, stations).

Capital gains
Capital gains are subject to the ordinary profits tax rate. There is an exemption available for capital gains from selling shares that occur on the date of a given sale in the official lists of the stock exchange in the highest and the next-to-highest category of listing.

Inter-company dividends and stock dividends
Dividends from participation in Kyrgyz legal entities are exempt from profits tax. All other dividends are subject to the ordinary profits tax rate.

Foreign income
Generally, Kyrgyz legal entities are taxable on income earned worldwide. Foreign income is subject to the ordinary profits tax rate.

Deductions

Generally, expenses related to the earning of aggregate annual income are considered deductible for income tax purposes, including:

- Business trip expenses that were actually incurred and supported by appropriate documentation (per diems during business trips are deductible only within the established statutory limits);
- Commissions on payroll expenses for labour;
- Material and social benefits provided to employees;
- Representational expenses connected with earning income (transportation, hotel and translator services);
- Training and retraining of employees;
- Scientific development and exploration works (deductions are relevant for fixed assets); and
- Any other costs related to earning income, which can be supported by appropriate documentation in terms of their nature and amount (invoices, payment orders, receipts, etc.).

Deductions for interest actually paid on debts, where the loan proceeds were used to fund expenses incurred for the taxpayer's business activity, are allowed within limitations provided in the tax code depending on methodology and nature of the debt. For example, interest on loans connected with the purchase of depreciable assets is not deducted, but increases their value.

The principal categories of expenses which are not deductible include:

- Capital expenses and expenses connected with the purchase, production and installation of equipment;
- Fines and interest penalties paid to the state budget;
- Taxes paid in accordance with the tax code, except for land tax, property tax, VAT that cannot be offset, subsurface use taxes;
- Any losses incurred on behalf of a spouse or other family member(s);
- Any expenses incurred on behalf of any other third persons, except in cases where documentation proves business needs for such expenses;
- Pricing losses caused by rates, understated below-market prices and price incentives;
- Any losses directly or indirectly connected with sales or exchange of property by a taxpayer with family members or business partners; and
- Expenses connected with purchases of services in entertainment, vacations and leisure.

Depreciation and depletion

The tax code establishes a deduction for depreciation based on the declining balance method. Depreciable fixed assets are divided into several groups, for which maximum depreciation rates range from 10% to 50%.

Certain expenses are deductible within specified limits, including expenses on repairs, expenses on procuring and producing capital production assets, and certain other expenses.

Kyrgyzstan

Net operating losses
Net operating losses can be carried forward for up to five years. There are no provisions in Kyrgyz legislation allowing carryback of losses.

Taxes
The following taxes are allowed for deduction:

* Land tax;
* Property tax;
* VAT not allowed for offset; and
* Subsurface use taxes.

Payments to foreign affiliates
Payments to foreign affiliates are deductible for corporate income tax purposes if they are aimed at earning income and supported by documentation.

Other significant items
Deductions are generally permitted for costs related to the activities aimed at earning income, unless specifically limited or disallowed by the tax code. Examples of expenses with deductibility limits include those related to interest, repairs, expenses on procuring and producing capital production assets, and certain other expenses.

Group taxation

Group taxation is not permitted in Kyrgyzstan

Tax incentives

The tax legislation currently provides the following tax incentives:

* Investment incentives
* Tax holidays for special economic zones

Special economic zones
There are four special economic zones in Kyrgyzstan: Naryn, Karakol, Bishkek and Maimak. The special economic zones generally provide for a tax-neutral regime, exemption from customs duties and a liberal currency control regime. However, there is a special fee for incentives which varies from 0.1% to 2% of sales (depending on the region).

Withholding taxes (WHT)

Passive income from sources in Kyrgyzstan by a non-resident that is not connected with a permanent establishment is taxable at the source of payment without deductions, at the following rates:

* Dividends and interest: 10%
* Insurance premiums received under risk insurance or re-insurance agreements: 5%
* Authorship fee: 10%

Income obtained by a non-resident from performing activities and services in Kyrgyzstan, not connected with a permanent establishment, is taxable at the source of payment without deductions (with the exception of VAT) via a withholding tax mechanism:

- Income from telecommunication or freight services in international communication and transportation between Kyrgyzstan and other states: 5%
- Income from management and consulting services: 10%
- Other services and activities: 10%

Withholding tax applies to Kyrgyzstan source income regardless of whether the payment is made within or outside of Kyrgyzstan.

The application of double-tax treaties often effectively provides a reduction of withholding tax rates or, in the case of non-passive income, an income tax exemption. Note that the application of treaty privileges is not necessarily automatic and taxpayers may need to comply with certain administrative procedures to secure relief.

Tax treaties
According to the tax code, the provisions of international tax agreements and other acts to which Kyrgyzstan is a party and ratified by the president or the parliament (as appropriate), take precedence over the provisions of the tax code.

As of 1 April 2010, Kyrgyzstan has concluded double-tax treaties with the following countries:

Austria	Iran	Poland
Belarus	Kazakhstan	Russia
Canada	Latvia	Switzerland
China	Malaysia	Tajikistan
Finland	Moldova	Turkey
Germany	Mongolia	Ukraine
India	Pakistan	Uzbekistan

The table below shows withholding tax rates:

Recipient	Dividends %	Interest %	Royalties %
No treaty	10	10	10
Austria	5/10 (1)	10	10
Belarus	15	10	15
Canada	15	15	10
China	10	10	10
Finland	5/10 (1)	10	5
Germany	5/10 (1)	5	10
India	10	10	15
Iran	5/10 (1)	10	10
Kazakhstan	10	10	10
Latvia	5/10 (1)	10	5
Malaysia	5/10 (2)	10	10
Moldova	5/10 (1)	10	10

Kyrgyzstan

Recipient	Dividends %	Interest %	Royalties %
Mongolia	10	10	10
Pakistan	10	10	10
Poland	10	10	10
Russia	10	10	10
Switzerland	5/10 (1)	5	5
Tajikistan	5/10 (3)	10	10
Turkey	10	10	10
Ukraine	5/10 (3)	10	10
Uzbekistan	5/10 (3)	10	10

Notes

The numbers in parentheses above refer to the notes below:

1. 5% if the beneficial owner is a company (other than a partnership) that directly holds at least 25% of the capital of the paying company.
2. 5% if the beneficial owner is a company (other than a partnership), which owns not less than 10% of the capital of the paying company.
3. 5% if the beneficial recipient is a company, which owns not less than 50% of the capital of the paying company.

Transfer pricing
There is no special law on transfer pricing in Kyrgyzstan and rules on transfer pricing are found in the tax code. The general transfer pricing provisions set in the tax code do not follow Organisation for Economic Co-operation and Development (OECD) guidelines (thus, no advance pricing agreement (APA) mechanism is provided). According to the Kyrgyz transfer pricing regulations, the tax authorities are empowered to determine the following transactions:

* Transfers between related parties;
* Barter transactions; and
* Cross-border transactions.

Tax administration

Tax Returns and payments
The Kyrgyzstan tax code stipulates that the following key tax reports must be filed with the tax authorities:

* Aggregate Annual Income Tax Declaration (corporate and individual) – by 1 March of the year following the reporting year;
* VAT reporting – on a monthly basis, by the twenty-fifth (or, on the last day for large taxpayers) of the month following the reporting month; and
* Other tax reports – as required according to relevant legislation.

Tax authorities may grant an extension for filing a tax return for up to one month upon application by the taxpayer. Such extension does not relieve or prolong the taxpayer's obligation to pay the tax in a timely manner.

The tax payments should be made as follows:

- Advance payments on profits tax – quarterly by the twentieth of the second month of the reporting quarter;
- Final payments on profits tax and Individual tax – by 1 March of the year following the reporting year;
- Tax withheld at the source of payment by a tax agent – by the fifteenth day of the month following the month when income was paid;
- VAT – on a monthly basis, by the twenty-fifth of the month following the reporting month; and
- Other tax payments – as required according to relevant legislation.

Tax audits

The State Tax Inspectorate of the Ministry of Finance of Kyrgyzstan and its local tax authorities are the only state authorities that have the right to perform tax audits. The Kyrgyzstan tax service consists of relevant subdivisions of the revenue committee of the Ministry of Finance of Kyrgyzstan and its local authorities.

A tax audit is performed based on a written notification from the Head of the State Tax Inspectorate, which specifies the name of the company to audit, the scope of the audit, and the terms of the audit. Tax audits may be performed not more than once a year by one of the tax authorities (district, city, region, or the state tax authorities) and should not last more than 30 days. If necessary, however, a tax audit may be extended for 10 additional days with written approval from the State Tax Inspectorate.

K

Corporate taxes in Latvia

For more information, contact:

Zlata Zascirinska-Elksnina
PricewaterhouseCoopers SIA
Kr. Valdemara iela 19
LV-1010 Riga, Latvia
Tel: +371 6709 4514
Email: zlata.elksnina@lv.pwc.com

Significant developments

Incentives for shareholders to invest profits in companies
Recent changes in corporate income tax (CIT) law encourage shareholders to invest profits in the development of their company rather than take them out as dividends. Businesses may reduce their taxable income by a notional amount of interest that a taxpayer would have to pay on a loan equal to his prior-year undistributed profit. This adjustment is calculated by multiplying the annual weighted average rate of interest on loans issued to non-financial Latvian businesses as determined by the Bank of Latvia for the tax period by undistributed profits from previous periods beginning after 31 December 2008.

Deferred tax on asset replacements
Latvia will allow a deferred payment of tax on profits arising on the sale of a replaced asset in order to encourage manufacturing companies to replace inefficient and outdated plant and machinery.

If a company acquires a functionally similar asset within 12 months before or after the old equipment is disposed of, then any income (profit) on the disposal of the old equipment is ignored in this tax period (i.e., the profit is deductible from taxable income). Tax payment is deferred until the new equipment is sold and may be further postponed if the equipment is replaced.

Value-added tax (VAT)
Because of the recent amendments to the European Union (EU) Council Directive 2006/112/EC (VAT directive) and respective amendments of the VAT Act, the new place-of-supply rules for cross-border services (i.e., transactions involving a supplier and a customer located in different countries) went into force on 1 January 2010.

Additionally, new amendments to the VAT Act have been drafted to pass some of the Sixth Directive's optional provisions into domestic VAT law (including VAT grouping, VAT recovery on bad debts, reverse charges on imports). These amendments went into force on 1 December 2009.

Thin capitalisation
Thin capitalisation rules have been amended so that interest deductibility is restricted for resident company loans the same as for non-resident company loans.

Taxes on corporate income

The standard rate of CIT is 15%. There are no other taxes on corporate income. Companies operating in Free Ports *(see Tax incentives section)* and special economic zones and applying tax relief, apply CIT of 25%.

Corporate residence

A company is resident in Latvia if it is incorporated or had to be incorporated in Latvia. Under the Latvian Taxes and Duties Act, a non-resident has a permanent establishment (PE) in Latvia if all three of the following conditions are met simultaneously:

1. The non-resident uses a fixed place for activities in Latvia;
2. The place for activities is permanently used or is established for the purpose of being used permanently; and
3. The place for activities is used for the performance of commercial activities.

In addition, it is considered that a non-resident has a PE in Latvia if the non-resident performs in Latvia at least one of the following activities:

- Uses a construction site or performs building or installation activities or supervision or consultative activities related to the construction site or aforementioned activities;
- Uses equipment or installations, drilling platforms and special ships intended for the research or extraction of natural resources or carries out supervisory or consultative work related thereto;
- Within a time period, which together exceeds 30 days in any six-month period, provides services including consulting, management and technical services, utilising his or her employees or associated personnel; or
- Uses the activity of an individual, legal or other person for the benefit of his commercial activities provided that this person is authorised to enter into contracts in the name of the foreign entity and the person regularly (more than once in a taxation period) exercises such an authority.

The PE risk for the entities located in the treaty countries should be tested in accordance with the relevant double tax treaty (DTT).

Other taxes

Value-added tax (VAT)
The following rates apply:

Description of goods	%
The standard rate on supplies of goods and services, commodity imports, certain services rendered by non-residents and treated as supplied in Latvia, intra-community acquisitions of goods and personal consumption.	21%
A reduced rate on medicines, medical devices and goods, specialised baby food, domestic public transport services, household heating charges, household electricity supplies, household natural gas supplies (except gas for vehicles), firewood and wooden heating material to households, textbooks and original literature publications.	10%

Latvia

Description of goods	%
Exemption with credit on supplies of goods within the EU to taxable persons registered for VAT in other EU member states.	0%
Exemption with credit on commodity exports and imports not released for free circulation in the EU, supplies of goods and services to diplomats, supplies of goods and services financed by foreign aid, etc.	0%

A number of services are exempt, including education, financial, medical and insurance services, nursery fees and the sale of used real estate including land (except for the first sale of unused real estate, which is taxable).

Because of the recent amendments to the EU Council Directive 2006/112/EC (VAT directive) and respective amendments of the VAT Act, the new place-of-supply rules for cross-border services (i.e., transactions involving a supplier and a customer located in different countries) went into force on 1 January 2010.

Additionally, new amendments to the VAT Act have been drafted to pass some of the EU's Sixth Directive's optional provisions into domestic VAT law (including VAT grouping, VAT recovery on bad debts, reverse charges on imports). These amendments went into force on 1 December 2009.

Excise duty
An excise duty is levied on specific categories of goods, mostly as a fixed amount per unit. Excise duties are applied to the following goods, whether made in Latvia or imported:

Product	Excise amount
Oil and oil products	Up to 300 LVL depending on the type of the product
Alcohol	40–890 LVL per 100 litres (depending on the type of alcohol)
Beer	2.18 LVL for each percent of absolute alcohol, but not less than 4 LVL per 100 litres of beer (1.09 LVL on the first 10,000 hectolitres for small breweries)
Tobacco products	11 LVL per 1,000 cigars or cigarillos 22.5 LVL per 1,000 cigarettes plus 34.5% of the maximum retail selling price 23 LVL per 1,000 grams of fine-cut smoking tobacco intended for the rolling of cigarettes 23 LVL for other smoking tobacco
Coffee	100 LVL per 100kg
Certain soft drinks	4 LVL per 100 litres

Customs duty
Customs duty is levied on goods imported into Latvia. The rate of customs duty generally is between 0% and 20% of the value of imported goods, depending on the type and origin of such goods. Exports are generally exempt from customs tax.

Real estate tax
From 2010 real estate tax is payable for engineering structures such as motorways, streets, roads, bridges, elevated highways, tunnels, pipelines, communication lines and power lines, and buildings that form part of a private dwelling house development.

The following rates apply from 1 January 2010:

- The standard rate of 1.5% on the cadastral value of land, buildings and engineering structures.
- A progressive rate for dwelling houses, their parts and any parts of a non-residential building that are functionally used for living and not used in trade or business:
  - 0.1% of cadastral values up to 40,000 LVL;
  - 0.2% of cadastral values exceeding 40,000 but not exceeding 75,000 LVL; and
  - 0.3% of cadastral values exceeding 75,000 LVL.
- A double rate of 3% for uncultivated land capable of agricultural use, unless it is up to one hectare in area or subject to statutory restrictions on agricultural activity. By law, uncultivated land capable of agricultural use is agricultural land that is not used for making or growing agricultural products (including harvesting, grazing and keeping animals for agricultural purposes) or is not kept in good agricultural and environmental condition.

Newly constructed or reconstructed buildings are exempt from real estate tax for one year after completion. Other reliefs are available under the Real Estate Tax Act or determined by municipalities.

Natural resource tax

Any natural resources acquired as a result of economic activities (e.g., surface and underground water, dolomite and quartz sand), the collection of edible park snails, pollution (waste, emissions and pollutants), products harmful to the environment (e.g., lubricating oil, electric batteries, oil filters and tyres), radioactive substances, packaging, disposable tableware, vehicles, the volume of emitted greenhouse gasses, and electrical and electronic equipment and appliances are subject to a natural resource tax in Latvia.

Packaging and electrical/electronic equipment as well as certain other goods are subject to recycling in Latvia.

Lottery and gambling tax

A lottery and gambling tax is levied on licensed organisers of games or lotteries. Licence fees range from LVL 3,000 to LVL 300,000. Game organisers, gambling places and gambling machines are subject to the gambling tax. The tax rates depend on the number and type of gambling machines.

Car and motorcycle tax

Cars and motorcycles registered for the first time or after modification are subject to a car and motorcycle tax. This is payable by any individual or entity registered as the owner of a car or motorcycle.

The applicable tax rates for cars registered after 1 January 2009 in foreign countries are calculated based on the carbon dioxide (CO_2) on each kilometre constituted by the car. The rates range from LVL 0.3 to LVL 5 where the carbon dioxide is from 120 grams to 350 grams for each kilometre. The rate for newly registered motorcycles is LVL 0.10 for each cubic-centimetre of the engine's capacity.

For other cars, rates range from LVL 75 to LVL 850, depending on age and capacity. The rate for motorcycles depends on age and is 25% of the rate for cars.

Latvia

Electricity tax
This electricity tax is levied on electricity supplied to final consumers or consumed by suppliers. The rate is LVL 0.71 per mega-watt-hour. Exemptions are available to producers of electricity and for electricity used by domestic public transport and households.

Stamp duty
Stamp duties are levied on certain legal and other kinds of services, such as court trials, company formation and registration, licences for certain types of business activity, provision of information, notary services, operation of bills of exchange, and registration of real estate at the Land Registry (2% of the higher of deal value or cadastral value capped at LVL 30,000 per property).

Stamp duty is not payable if re-registration of real estate in the Land Registry is necessary due to the reorganisation process. From 1 November 2009, the maximum amount of stamp duty payable for re-registration of the title to immovable property in case of contribution in kind to a company's capital is reduced from LVL 30,000 to LVL 1,000.

Local duties
Certain activities are subject to local duties (e.g., construction permits).

Branch income

As a general rule, branches and companies are taxed alike, with certain adjustments for payments to the head office. Branch income is subject to a 15% CIT.

Income determination

Inventory valuation
Dictated by the matching and prudence concepts, stock should be valued at the lower of cost or net realisable value. Cost must be computed on a first-in,-first-out (FIFO) basis. Cost can mean purchase price or production cost. Any unrealised losses from stock revaluation are non-deductible.

Capital gains
A capital gain on the disposal of a capital asset is calculated as the difference between the sale proceeds and cost. This gain is subject to a 15% CIT as ordinary income.

Losses on the sale of shares may be carried forward and offset against future profits. However, profits on trading in securities publicly quoted in the EU or the European Economic Area (EEA) are not taxable, and losses from these securities are not deductible.

Losses on the sale of public securities traded outside the EU/EEA or non-public securities (private shares, unlisted bonds and shares, claim securities) are not deductible but may be offset chronologically in eight subsequent tax periods against income from the sale of other securities. However, if a company makes a one-off sale of securities that it has held for more than 12 months, then such losses may be offset chronologically against total taxable income from operating activities in eight subsequent tax periods.

Inter-company dividends

Dividends from Latvian companies are exempt from tax, except for dividends from companies paying CIT at a reduced rate (e.g., companies operating in special economic zones or free ports such as Riga or Ventspils). Dividends paid to non-residents may be subject to a withholding tax *(see the section Withholding taxes)*.

Dividends from companies registered in blacklisted tax havens are taxable (a list of blacklisted tax havens is approved by the Cabinet of Ministers).

Dividends paid by a non-resident company based outside blacklisted tax havens to a Latvian person, directly holding at least 25% of shares in that company at the time the dividends are paid, are exempt.

Dividends from a company resident in another EU or EEA country are also exempt.

Foreign income

Resident companies are taxed on their worldwide income. Tax paid abroad on income included in the taxable base is allowed as a credit against the CIT charged for the year. However, the credit must not exceed the Latvian tax attributable to the income taxed abroad. Any unused tax credits may not be carried forward.

Stock dividends

The distribution of new shares to a company's shareholders in proportion to their existing shareholdings (after a share capital increase by conversion of accrued capital) is not a taxable event for the shareholders.

Transfer pricing

The Latvian Regulation governing the application of the Corporate Income Tax Act states that for transfer pricing (TP) calculation purposes, use may be made of the Transfer Pricing Guidelines for Multinational Enterprises and Tax Administrations, a document issued by the Organisation for Economic Co-operation and Development (OECD).

Latvian law requires that related-party transactions be in compliance with the arm's-length principle. Under the arm's-length principle, the conditions made or imposed between two related enterprises in their commercial or financial relations must not differ from those that would be agreed between independent enterprises engaging in similar transactions under similar circumstances.

A tax audit may examine and adjust the price of a transaction in the following circumstances:

- The transaction is between related parties;
- Barters and set offs;
- A price deviation exceeds 20% of prices that the taxpayer has applied to similar goods or services over a short period; and
- Exports and imports.

The TP requirements for the arm's-length price of a related-party transaction primarily apply to transactions between two or more related companies. Latvian legislation has broadened these requirements and section 12 of the CIT Act requires the taxpayer to

Latvia

adjust his taxable income for the difference between the price applied to a transaction and the arm's-length value if the transaction involves:

- Individuals related to the company;
- Related foreign companies;
- Companies exempt from CIT or enjoying CIT relief pursuant to other Latvian laws; and
- A related company with which it forms a single tax group.

This provision may apply to any transaction, ranging from purchases and sales of fixed assets and goods, supplies of services, to loans and borrowings, and intellectual property. It should also be pointed out that the traditional view that TP rules only apply to transactions with foreign related companies is no longer consistent with the law because TP issues are now also important to companies doing business with Latvian related companies.

There are no obligatory TP documentation requirements in Latvia yet. Nevertheless, it is highly advisable to prepare the TP documentation as it may be a valuable support during tax audits.

Deductions

Fixed assets may be depreciated for tax purposes according to the reducing-balance method by applying the following rates to tax written-down values:

Types of property	%
Buildings, structures and perennial plantations	10
Technology and energy installations, fleet, railway	20
Computer hardware and software, information systems, electronic equipment	70
Other fixed assets	40
Light passenger cars (except special purpose vehicles), motorcycles and air transport means	30
Oil rigs, oil exploration and extraction ships, sea and river transport means	15

The value of new technological equipment is multiplied by a coefficient (2009-2013: 1.5) before claiming capital allowances. The effect of applying a coefficient is reversed if the new technological equipment is disposed of within five years from acquisition.

Non-business assets are ineligible for capital allowances.

Intangible assets are eligible for capital allowances on a straight-line basis over the following recovery periods:

Types of intangible assets	Years
Concessions	10
Patents, licences and trademarks	5
Research and development expenses	1

Any intangible assets not fitting into any of these categories (such as goodwill) are ineligible for capital allowances.

The cost of intangible investments is increased by a coefficient of 1.5 if such investments result in a trademark or patent being registered.

Deferred tax on asset replacements

Latvia will allow a deferred payment of tax on profits arising on the sale of a replaced asset in order to encourage manufacturing companies to replace inefficient and outdated plant and machinery.

If a company acquires a functionally similar asset within 12 months before or after the old equipment is disposed of, then any income (profit) on the disposal of the old equipment is ignored in this tax period (i.e., the profit is deductible from taxable income). Tax payment is deferred until the new equipment is sold and may be further postponed if the equipment is replaced.

Luxury vehicles

Luxury vehicles (light passenger cars with a value greater than LVL 25,424 excluding VAT) are not eligible for capital allowances. A tax deduction is denied for expenses incurred in using and maintaining luxury vehicles and for lease or hire purchase payments associated with leasing such vehicles. These rules do not, however, apply to special purpose vehicles (such as emergency vehicles and special passenger vehicles).

Net operating losses

Starting from 2010, losses may be carried forward eight years (formerly five years). According to the transitional rules, in tax periods beginning in 2008 and 2009, taxpayers will be able to offset losses to which they were entitled but unable to offset in 2007 due to lack of taxable income. This means that losses of 2002 may be offset up to 2010 (inclusive).

A company in which more than 50% of shares (a controlling interest) have changed hands may utilise its tax losses if it continues for five years the same business that it carried on during the two years prior to the change of control. When companies are reorganised by a merger or spin-off, it may be possible to utilise losses accrued.

Payments to foreign affiliates

In general, a Latvian company may deduct the full amount of royalties, service fees and interest (subject to statutory limits) made to related parties to the extent that such payments are made at arm's length. Such payments may be subject to a withholding tax (see the section "Withholding taxes"). However, if a taxpayer fails to deduct the withholding tax due, the amounts paid cease to be deductible for tax purposes.

Taxes

Excise duties, national social insurance contributions, natural resource taxes, customs duties and real estate taxes are deductible.

Other significant items

Thin capitalisation rules apply when claiming a tax deduction for interest payments on loans and leasing services.

Latvia

Taxable income should be adjusted for either:

1. Interest paid in excess of interest calculated by applying to the liability 1.2 times the average short-term interest rate at Latvian banks as determined by the Central Statistical Office for the last month of the tax period; or
2. Interest in proportion to the excess of the average liability over an amount equal to four times shareholders' equity at the beginning of the tax year less any revaluation reserve.

The higher of these calculations should be added to taxable income.

The following interest payments are fully deductible:

*   Interest paid on borrowings from credit institutions resident in Latvia, EEA member states or countries with which Latvia has an effective double tax treaty (DTT).
*   Interest paid to the Latvian Treasury, Nordic Investment Bank, European Bank for Reconstruction and Development, European Investment Bank, European Council Development Bank or the World Bank Group.
*   Interest paid on Latvian or EEA debt securities in public trading.
*   Interest expenses incurred by credit institutions and insurance institutions, regardless of the lender.
*   Interest paid on borrowings from a financial institution that:
    *   Is resident in Latvia, the EEA or a country with which Latvia has an effective DTT;
    *   Provides lending services or finance leases and is monitored by the particular country's bodies set up to supervise credit institutions or the financial sector; and
    *   Is deductible up to the amount of interest calculated by applying to the liability 1.2 times the average short-term interest rate at Latvian banks as determined by the Central Statistical Office for the last month of the tax period.

Group taxation

Group consolidation is not permitted for tax purposes. However, the members of a group of Latvian companies, whose parent owns directly or indirectly 90% of the capital of its subsidiary or subsidiaries, may surrender their current-year tax losses to one another.

Tax incentives

Donations to public benefit organisations

Under the Latvian Corporate Income Tax Act, relief may be applied in certain cases:

*   A CIT liability may be reduced by 85% of amounts donated to qualifying state-funded institutions and Latvian-registered societies, establishments and religious organisations or to institutions qualifying as public-benefit organisations under the Public Benefit Organisations Act. Such a reduction may not exceed 20% of the total CIT liability. When making a donation, the donor is not permitted to impose an obligation on the recipient of the donation or carry out any acts that may be classified and treated as consideration.

- Starting from 2011, donation relief also will be available for donations to EU/EEA entities that have statuses similar to public-benefit organisations in the country of residence.

Incentives for shareholders to invest profits in companies

Recent changes in CIT law encourage shareholders to invest profits in the development of their company rather than take them out as dividends. Businesses may reduce their taxable income by a notional amount of interest that a taxpayer would have to pay on a loan equal to his prior-year undistributed profit. This adjustment is calculated by multiplying the annual weighted average rate of interest on loans issued to nonfinancial Latvian businesses as determined by the Bank of Latvia for the tax period by undistributed profits from previous periods beginning after 31 December 2008.

Accelerated tax depreciation

The value of new technological equipment is multiplied by a coefficient (2009-2013: 1.5) before claiming capital allowances. The effect of applying a coefficient is reversed if the new technological equipment is disposed of within five years from acquisition.

The cost of intangible investments is increased by a coefficient of 1.5 for calculating capital allowances if such investments result in a trademark or patent being registered.

Free Ports and special economic zones

Companies operating in special economic zones are entitled to CIT and real estate tax relief. These areas include the free ports of Ventspils and Riga and the special economic zones of Rezekne and Liepaja.

Withholding taxes (WHT)

The following types of payments to non-residents are subject to WHT:

1. Dividends are generally subject to a 10% WHT. Double tax treaties generally reduce the rate to 5%. However, dividends paid to a company that is a resident of and meets the criteria of parent-subsidiary directive, in any EU or EEA member state, are exempt.
2. Interest payments to related non-resident parties are generally subject to a 10% WHT. Interest payments to non-related creditors are not subject to WHT. If a bank registered in Latvia pays interest to related companies at the bank's normal interest rate level, then a 5% WHT applies.
   From 1 July 2013, WHT no longer will apply to interest paid by a Latvian company to a related EU member state company that holds at least 25% of the share capital or voting power in that Latvian company and meets certain other statutory criteria. Up to 1 July 2013, Latvian companies will have to comply with transitional rules of the Corporate Income Tax Act, which provide 5% WHT on interest payments to related EU/EEA member state company.
3. Payments for intellectual property (copyright in literary or artistic works, including movies, videos and sound recordings) are subject to a 15% WHT. However, if the recipient is an EU-related company or its PE, the applicable rate is 5% up to 30 June 2013 and exempt from 1 July 2013 onwards. A 5% WHT is applied on other intellectual rights, such as patents, royalties and trademarks (exempted from 1 July 2013 onwards if the recipient is an EU-related company). Double tax treaties may reduce the rate.

Latvia

4. Rental payments for property in Latvia are subject to a 5% WHT.
5. Management and consulting fees are subject to a 10% WHT. The term "management and consulting services" means activities carried out by a non-resident directly or by outsourced personnel to ensure the management of a Latvian company or to provide necessary advice. Double tax treaties reduce the rate to 0%.
6. A 2% WHT applies to proceeds from real estate disposals. This applies to income from disposed shares or other participation in a Latvian- or foreign-registered company or other entity, if real estate in Latvia made up (in the period of disposal or the previous period, whether directly or indirectly through shareholdings in one or more other entities established in Latvia or abroad) more than 50% of the asset value of the company being disposed of.

A Latvian company can rely on a DTT to reduce the rate of WHT on any payments previously mentioned. To this end, the Latvian company must obtain a valid residence certificate for each type of payment to each recipient prior to making the actual payment. A valid residence certificate is one approved by the foreign tax authority and the Latvian tax authority.

Please see in the table below the WHT rates applicable to the following types of payment:

Recipient	Dividends (1)	Interest (2)	Royalties (3)	Rentals of industrial, commercial or scientific equipment and real estate (4)	Management fees (5)	Disposal of real estate (6)
	%	%	%	%	%	%
Related Latvian companies using certain CIT reliefs	–	5/10	5/15	5	10	2
Companies in tax havens (7)	10	5/15	15	15	15	15
Treaty:						
Albania	10/5 (8)	-5/10	5/10	5	–	2
Armenia	10/5 (8)	-/5/10	5/10	5	–	2
Austria	10/5 (8)	-/5/10	5/10	5	–	2
Azerbaijan	10/5 (8)	-/5/10	5/10	5	–	2
Belarus	10	-/5/10	5/10	5	–	2
Belgium	10/5 (8)	-/5/10	5/10	5	–	2
Bulgaria	10/5 (8)	-/5	-/5	5/7	–	2
Canada	10/5 (8)	-/5/10	5/10	5	–	2
China	10/5 (8)	-/5/10	5/10	5	–	2
Croatia	10/5 (8)	-/5/10	5/10	5	–	2
Czech Republic	10/5 (8)	-/5/10	5/10	5	–	2
Denmark	10/5 (8)	-/5/10	5/10	5	–	2
Estonia	10/5 (8)	-/5/10	5/10	5	–	2

Recipient	Dividends (1)	Interest (2)	Royalties (3)	Rentals of industrial, commercial or scientific equipment and real estate (4)	Management fees (5)	Disposal of real estate (6)
	%	%	%	%	%	%
Finland	10/5 (8)	-/5/10	5/10	5	–	2
France	10/5 (9)	-/5/10	5/10	5	–	2
Georgia	10/5 (11)	-/5/10	5/10	5	–	2
Germany	10/5 (8)	-/5/10	5/10	5	–	2
Greece	10/5 (8)	-/5/10	5/10	5	–	2
Hungary	10/5 (8)	-/5/10	5/10	5	–	2
Iceland	10/5 (8)	-/5/10	5/10	5	–	2
Italy	10/5 (9)	-/5/10	5/10	5	–	2
Ireland	10/5 (8)	-/5/10	5/10	5	–	2
Israel	10/5 (10)	-/5/10	5/10	5	–	2
Kazakhstan	10/5 (8)	-/5/10	5/10	5	–	2
Kirghizia	10/5 (8)	-/5/10	5/10	5	–	2
Lithuania	–	–	–	-/5	–	2
Luxembourg	5/10 (8)	-/5/10	5/10	5	–	2
Macedonia	5/10 (9)	-/5/10	5/10	5	–	2
Malta	5/10 (8)	-/5/10	5/10	5	–	2
Morocco	10/6 (8)	-/5/10	5/10	5	–	2
Moldova	10	-/5/10	5/10	5	–	2
Montenegro	10/5 (8)	-/5/10	5/10	5	–	2
Netherlands	5/10 (8)	-/5/10	5/10	5	–	2
Norway	5/10 (8)	-/5/10	5/10	5	–	2
Poland	5/10 (8)	-/5/10	5/10	5	–	2
Portugal	10	-/5/10	5/10	5	–	2
Romania	10	-/5/10	5/10	5	–	2
Serbia	10/5 (8)	-/5/10	5/10	5	–	2
Singapore	10/5 (8)	-/5/10	5/7.5	5	–	2
Slovak Republic	10	-/5/10	5/10	5	–	2
Slovenia	5/10 (8)	-/5/10	5/10	5	–	2
Spain	5/10 (8)	-/5/10	5/10	5	–	2
Sweden	5/10 (8)	-/5/10	5/10	5	–	2
Switzerland	10/5 (11)	-/5/10	5/10	5	–	2
Tajikistan	0/5/10 (12)	-/7	5/10	5	–	2
Turkey	10	-/5/10	5/10	5	–	2
United Kingdom	5/10 (8)	-/5/10	5/10	5	–	2
United States	10/5 (9)	-/5/10	5/10	5	–	2
Ukraine	10/5 (8)	-/5/10	5/10	5	–	2
Uzbekistan	10	-/5/10	5/10	5	–	2

Latvia

Notes

See items (1) – (6), types of payments to non-residents subject to withholding tax, as the explanations above the table.

7. 15% applies to all payments to companies located in tax havens with the following exceptions:
    *   10% for dividends paid by Latvian residents;
    *   5% for interest on deposits and current accounts paid by Latvian banks at their general rate;
    *   Repayments of loan principal are exempt; and
    *   Goods originating in the tax haven are exempt.
8. A 25% minimum shareholding required.
9. A 10% minimum shareholding required.
10. A 25% and USD 75,000 minimum shareholding required.
11. A 20% minimum shareholding required.
12. 0% – a 75% minimum shareholding is required; 5% – 25% minimum shareholding is required.

Tax administration

Returns
The fiscal year may not exceed 12 months and is normally based on the calendar year. However, companies are permitted to choose alternative start and end dates for the tax year. The first year of trading may last up to 18 months. Tax returns are filed annually, together with annual accounts.

Corporate income tax usually is paid monthly on or before the fifteenth day of each month, with a final adjustment when the annual tax return is filed. Monthly tax instalments are based on the tax liability in the previous fiscal year and adjusted by the consumer price index. A company may choose quarterly instalments if its monthly advances in the previous period were less than LVL 500. For a new company, advance payments are voluntary.

Corporate taxes in Lebanon

For more information, contact:

Wadih AbouNasr
PricewaterhouseCoopers
SNA Building, 5th Floor
Tabaris Square
Beirut
Lebanon
Tel: +961 1 200577 ext. 1610
Email: wadih.abounasr@lb.pwc.com

Significant developments

On 29 December 2009, the Ministry of Finance issued Announcement No. 3509 to clarify the method and rates of calculating the deemed profit for public work contractors, based on the type of activity they perform.

The Ministry of Finance published Decision No. 1216 dated 21 November 2009, containing a list of updated forms and declarations to be used by taxpayers starting year 2010. A listing and copies of these forms and declarations is found in Official Gazette No. 62 1/2 dated 31 December 2009. Original copies of these forms and declarations may be obtained from the Ministry of Finance.

The Ministry of Finance has introduced new fiscal obligations for Lebanese representative offices, effective financial year 2010. The major obligation is that representative offices will be required to submit annual tax declarations using specific forms which were published under the above decision.

The Ministry of Labour issued Decision No. 10/1 dated 3 February 2010 to list the professions which are restricted to Lebanese citizens, with certain exceptions.

The Budget Law for the 2010 fiscal year was submitted by the Ministry of Finance to the Council of Ministers and the Lebanese President on 15 March 2010 for approval. The new budget law calls for raising the tax on interest savings from 5% to 7%.

Taxes on corporate income

Under the income tax law in Lebanon, tax is levied based on income type. In this connection, the income tax law divides income into the following three categories:

- Chapter I – profits from industrial, commercial and non-commercial professions;
- Chapter II – salaries and wages and pension salaries; and
- Chapter III – revenues from moveable capital (chapter III mainly covers all types of dividend income, board member appropriations from profits and interest income, including interest on bonds and treasury bills).

The income tax law does not deal with what is known as global tax on income, where a progressive tax is levied on the individual's income grouped from different sources. Accordingly, where a taxpayer has income from different sources, each type of income will be taxed according to the tax chapter it falls under.

Lebanon

Real profit tax

Joint-stock companies ("Société anonyme libanaise" or SAL)
- Minimum capital: Lebanese pound (LBP) 30 million.
- Taxation: the applicable trading tax rate is 15% in addition to a dividend distribution tax of 10%, reduced to 5% in certain cases, mainly if the shares are listed.

Limited liability companies (SARL)
- Minimum capital: LBP 5 million.
- Taxation: the applicable trading tax rate is 15% in addition to dividend distribution tax of 10%.

Branch offices
Refer to section on *Branch income*.

Deemed profit tax

The deemed profit tax is imposed on, among others, insurance and savings institutions, taxable transport companies, oil refineries and public work contractors. Taxation is based on deemed profits and business income tax is levied at a flat rate of 15%. The rate of deemed profit for public contractors as approved by the Ministry of Finance is currently set at either 10% or 15% of total amounts collected per year, based on the type of activity performed by the contractor. For insurance companies the deemed profit rate varies depending on the type of insurance activity, i.e., life, motor, accident, etc. In addition to the flat rate tax imposed on deemed profits, a distribution tax of 10% is levied on dividends.

Other tax systems

Representative offices
Representative offices do not pay income taxes as long as they do not carry out commercial activities. Based on Decision No. 1/1216 effective financial year 2010, representative offices are required to submit annual tax declarations including company information and details including employee information, balance sheet, income statement, non-resident tax schedule and schedule of payments to professionals. The declaration, with all relevant documentation, should be handed as one single set. All the information included should be based on accounting records. The deadline for submitting the declaration depends on the legal form of the parent company, i.e., before 1 June of the following year for joint-stock or limited liability companies and before 1 May of the following year for others.

Holding companies
Lebanese holding companies are exempt from corporate income tax and from withholding tax on dividends. However, they are subject to a tax on their paid-up capital and reserves. In any given tax year, total tax payments on paid-up capital and reserves are capped at LBP 5 million. Holding companies are subject to a 10% tax on interest received from loans shorter than three years extended to companies operating in Lebanon. Management fees received by the holding company from companies operating in Lebanon are subject to a 5% tax. Capital gains on financial assets in Lebanese companies held for less than two years are subject to a 10% tax. Royalties received from Lebanese companies for patents and the like are taxed at a rate of 10%. Management fees and royalties received by the holding company from foreign companies are exempt from tax.

Lebanon

Offshore companies
Offshore companies are required to be registered as SAL (joint-stock) companies and, with a few exceptions, are subject to the same regulations as a joint-stock company. The business objectives of an offshore company are limited. Offshore companies are exempt from corporate income tax and from the withholding tax on dividends, and are instead subject to a lump-sum annual tax of LBP 1 million.

Corporate residence

Tax is levied on all corporeal/natural and incorporeal/artificial persons, resident in Lebanon or outside, on all profits that they generate in Lebanon. The main premise for considering profits to have been realised in Lebanon is when such profits have occurred from an effort exerted in Lebanon, irrespective of the identity of the taxpayer or his place of residency.

Income tax is levied on profits generated by two categories of taxpayers:

Taxpayers that are considered resident (for tax purposes) are every person, establishment or company even if they are not physically resident in Lebanon when they satisfy any of the following two terms:

• Have an office or a fixed place of business in their name in Lebanon even when they are not undertaking their business in a normal and repetitive manner.
• Are practising the profession or business activity in a normal or repetitive manner even if they do not have a known registered place of business in Lebanon. This is because they are considered to have practised their profession from the place in which they contact their customers even if such place is a hotel or a café.

Non-resident taxpayers consist of persons (corporeal/natural and incorporeal/artificial) residing in Lebanon and persons residing outside Lebanon. Persons residing in Lebanon subject to the non-resident tax are corporeal persons that do not satisfy any one of the following two terms:

• Practise a certain trade in a normal and repetitive manner, irrespective of whether or not they have a registered place of business; and
• Have a registered known place of business.

Persons residing outside Lebanon subject to the non-resident tax are the persons, companies and establishments that obtain from Lebanon amounts, revenues, profits or proceeds as a result of their undertaking an activity in whole or in part on Lebanese territory or as a result of their exploiting rights in Lebanon.

Other taxes

Built property tax
The built property tax is a progressive tax ranging between 4% and 14%.

Value-added tax (VAT)
The standard VAT rate in Lebanon is 10%. Unless specifically exempt, VAT is levied on all commercial transactions undertaken by business entities. Export of goods and services and export-related services, international transport and some of the

L

Lebanon

intermediate operations are zero-rated. Banking, financial services and insurance operations are exempt from VAT.

Stamp duty
Two kinds of stamp duties are levied. A proportionate stamp duty of 3 per mil is levied on all deeds and contracts (written or implied) that mention specific payments or other sums of money. A fixed stamp duty ranging between a minimum of LBP 100 and a maximum of LBP 2 million is applicable on documents in accordance with schedules appended to the stamp duty law.

Registration taxes
The estimated cost of establishing a company is USD 7,500. This includes lawyer's fees and registration fees. The registration fees will increase if the company is established with a capital exceeding the minimum requirement. However, the registration fees should not normally exceed 1% of the value of capital.

For branch offices and representative offices, establishment costs are lower and may be estimated at USD 5,000.

When transferring ownership of real estate, registration fees of approximately 6% are applicable.

Customs duties
Lebanon's application to access the World Trade Organization (WTO) was received on 30 January 1999 and the exchange of information about Lebanon's trade regime already took place. Lebanon went through both bilateral and multilateral negotiations with several WTO members.

Modern, simple and efficient assessment means are adopted by the customs authorities, e.g., electronic declarations, declaration in advance, applying international procedures in clearing the goods, selective inspection, auditing the goods after their release and adopting the unique declaration.

Customs rates are imposed and modified according to decisions from the Lebanese customs authorities. These decisions are adopted based on the need of the Lebanese markets of some goods and the will to protect national production sectors.

Safeguard measures are provided for in relation to imported goods. The purpose behind such measures is to protect the domestic production sectors when an increase of imports is witnessed when compared to the same period during the previous year.

The rates are determined based on a specific schedule created in conformity with the Harmonised System of Nomenclature. This conformity with the unified system allows Lebanon to represent an "importer friendly" environment for importers.

The normal rates are applied where there is no preferential agreement. When the origin of the good or part of the good is from a country with which Lebanon has a preferential customs treatment, preferential rates apply.

Customs rates in Lebanon are either determined in percentage or paid as a lump sum per unit of imported products.

Transfer tax

Transfer tax applies to all assets (fixed and movable) that are transferred from one party to another, except the Government and municipalities, in the way of estate, donation or any other way that does not imply a fair compensation. Transfer tax is due on the date of death or the execution of the donation. Transfer tax rates vary from 3% to 45%.

The statute of limitation does not apply to transfer tax in case of death or donation (gift). Transfers made without fair compensation within two years of the donor's death are considered part of the donor's estate and are taxed together with other estate assets and funds.

Branch income

Net income derived from a branch's operations in Lebanon is subject to Lebanese business income tax, levied at a rate of 15%. Taxable profits of foreign branch offices are deemed to be distributed and are subject to a dividend distribution tax at the rate of 10%.

Income determination

Common tax adjustments

Below are some of the most common adjustments done to accounting profits to reach taxable profits:

- Difference between fiscal and accounting depreciation;
- Non-deductible provisions such as provisions for bonuses, contingencies and charges;
- Fines and penalties are non-deductible;
- Withholding taxes borne by the company such as salary tax, non-resident tax are non-deductible;
- Gifts given by the company in cash are non-deductible;
- Gifts given by the company in-kind given to customers when the amount of each gift exceeds LBP 1 million per person per year and when the total amount of gifts in-kind exceeds 1% of the turnover are non-deductible; and
- Donations given to other than registered charitable organisations are non-deductible.

Inventory valuation

For tax purposes, inventory is valued using the weighted average cost method.

Capital gains

Under local legislation, companies are permitted to revalue their fixed assets every five years. Capital gains recognised from such a revaluation, as well as any profits that may be realised from the disposal of fixed assets are subject to a capital gains tax of 10%.

Income from disposal of shares realised by a company is subject to 10% capital gains tax when the shares are classified as financial assets in the company's balance sheet.

Income from disposal of shares realised by a company whose main activity is the acquisition of investments are subject to 15% corporate tax.

Lebanon

Inter-company dividends
Dividends received as a result of a taxable person's activity are deemed trading income and are subject to the flat corporate income tax rate of 15%. Dividends received as passive income are subject to 10% tax in Lebanon. However, dividends received from Lebanese entities are exempt from corporate tax, as the dividend tax is withheld at source, but are not exempt from further tax upon distribution from the recipient entity.

Foreign income
Income from any source, domestic or foreign, received by a corporation within Lebanon is subject to corporate tax. The scope of tax covers the activities carried out inside and outside Lebanon, which are administered or managed from Lebanon.

Stock dividends
The Lebanese law is silent on the tax implications of stock dividends. However, when share capital is increased by reducing retained earnings, no tax is applicable.

Interest income
Interest earned by corporations is added to the taxable income. Relief is given for the withholding tax suffered on bank accounts, treasury bills and bonds issue to the extent of the corporate tax due.

Partnership income
Profits of partnerships are deemed to be distributed and are taxed at progressive rates of 4% to 21%.

Rental income
Rental income should be deducted from the accounting result to reach the taxable result. Moreover, expenses related to property that is rented out should be added back to the accounting result to reach the taxable result.

A built property tax is paid on rental income at progressive rates ranging between 4% and 14%.

Royalties income
Royalties received by a holding company from Lebanese companies for patents and the like are taxed at a rate of 10%. Royalties received by holding companies from abroad are exempt from tax.

Royalties received by other than holding companies are taxed as ordinary income at 15%.

Unrealised exchange gains/losses
Unrealised exchange gains and losses are not treated differently from any other gain or loss for tax purposes, i.e., unrealised exchange gains are subject to corporate income tax at 15% and unrealised exchange losses are deductible for corporate income tax purposes.

Deductions

Depreciation and depletion
Depreciation of property, plant and equipment (at rates fixed by ministerial decree) is deductible.

Net operating losses

Tax losses may be carried forward for up to three years after the year in which they were originally incurred. The carryback of losses is not available.

Capital losses may be used to offset taxable profits of the current year but may not be carried forward.

Payments to foreign affiliates

Payments to foreign affiliates are generally subject to withholding taxes.

Based on guidance issued by the Ministry of Finance, recharges from the head office located abroad (including advertising) are deductible up to a certain limit, calculated as follows:

(Assets of the branch in Lebanon/Consolidated assets) x Central administrative expenses

However, a ceiling of 3% of the branch's revenues is applied.

Taxes

Taxes and duties incurred in the course of business (except business income tax) are deductible.

Taxes due to foreign governments on income earned in Lebanon are non-deductible.

Exceptional taxes and fines are non-deductible.

Other significant items

Deductible expenses include:

- Cost of goods sold.
- Cost of services rendered.
- Rent of business premises or, if the premises are owned by the taxpayer, their depreciation.
- Salaries, wages and other employee benefits, including end-of-service indemnities.
- General business expenses, including insurance premiums.
- Interest on business loans, under certain conditions.
- Provisions for bad debts (if a debtor has been declared bankrupt), as well as reserves for severance payments, pensions and disability payments. Surplus provisions are added to profits.
- Charitable contributions to approved charitable, social, cultural or sporting institutions, within certain limits.
- Bad debts, after all means for collection of the debt have been exhausted.
- Advertising and publicity expenses, within certain limits.
- Travel, telephone, gifts and vehicle expenses, within certain limits.
- Entertainment expenses that are properly supported.
- Board remuneration against services performed.
- Accrued expenses as long as their occurrence is certain.
- Organisation and start-up expenses are amortised over three to five years for tax purposes.
- Employees' life insurance premiums are deductible as long as they are included in the employees' benefits subject to payroll tax.

Lebanon

Non-deductible expenses include:

- Interest paid on the taxpayer's capital.
- With the exception of normal maintenance expenses, costs that increase the value of the property, plant or equipment (such costs should be capitalised and depreciated in accordance with the fiscal depreciation rates).
- Losses or share-in-costs resulting from enterprises, offices and branches situated outside Lebanon.
- Representation allowances in excess of 10% of an employee's basic salary, as well as unjustifiable and unreasonable salaries.
- Personal expenses such as payments deducted by an employer or partner for the management of the business and for certain business expenses incurred by the employer or partner.
- Appropriations made to board members that do not comprise remuneration for work done.
- Fines and penalties.
- Provisions other than those specifically allowed by law. Examples of non-deductible provisions include provisions for bad debts and provisions for slow moving items.

Group taxation

There is no group taxation in Lebanon.

Tax incentives

Holding companies
Lebanese holding companies are exempt from corporate income tax and from withholding tax on dividends. However, they are subject to a tax on their paid-up capital and reserves. In any given tax year, total tax payments on paid-up capital and reserves are capped at LBP 5 million. Interest, management fees and royalties received by holding companies from abroad are exempt from tax.

Offshore companies
Offshore companies are exempt from corporate income tax and from the withholding tax on dividends; they are instead subject to a lump-sum annual tax of LBP 1 million. Contracts related to offshore activities outside Lebanon are exempt from Lebanese stamp duty.

Permanent exemptions
Companies and organisations that are granted an indefinite exemption from business income include the following:

- Educational institutions.
- Hospitals, orphanages, asylums and other shelters that admit patients free of charge.
- Shipping, sea and air transport associations (subject to certain restrictions).
- Farmers provided they do not display farm produce and cattle outlets or sell products and meat after conversion tax.
- Syndicates and other types of professional associations.
- Miscellaneous non-profit organisations and co-operatives.
- Holding companies and offshore companies.
- Public sector bodies that do not compete with private institutions.

Lebanon

Reinvestment incentives
Industrial companies using operating profit to finance certain capital investments are exempt from up to 50% of their income tax liabilities for a period of up to four years, provided that such exemptions do not exceed the original investments made. In areas designated "development zones", 75% of a company's tax liabilities may be exempt.

In order to take advantage of this regulation, investments should consist of capital expenditure designed to increase a company's manufacturing capacity, or of investments in housing facilities for the company's staff and other employees.

Withholding taxes (WHT)

Tax on interest
The income, revenues and interest earned from accounts opened at Lebanese banks and from treasury bonds are subject to a 5% withholding tax that is non-refundable and without the possibility of carrying forward. This tax is considered as an advance payment on the current corporate income tax due to the extent of that amount and acts as a minimum tax in situations where the tax due is lower than the tax on interest paid.

Non-resident tax
Revenues earned by non-residents in Lebanon are subject to an effective tax rate of 2.25% of the revenue in the case of revenue from sale of materials and equipment, and 7.5% of the revenue in the case of sale of services. The non-resident tax is a withholding tax.

Movable capital tax
A withholding tax at a rate of 10% is levied on income derived from movable capital generated in Lebanon. Taxable income comprises:

* Distributed dividends, interest and income from shares;
* Directors' and shareholders' fees;
* Distribution of reserves or profits; and
* Interest from loans to corporations.

Tax on dividends
Tax is withheld from dividends paid to shareholders/partners at a rate of 10%. The dividend distribution tax rate may be reduced to 5% under specific conditions.

Double taxation treaties table

Country	Dividends %	Interest %	Royalties %
Non-treaty	10	10	7.5
Treaty:			
Algeria	10/15	10	7.5/10
Armenia	5/10(1)	8	5
Bahrain	10(2)	10(2)	7.5(2)
Belarus	7.5	5	5
Bulgaria	5	7	5
Cyprus	5	5	7.5(2)
Czech Republic	5	10(2)	5/7.5/10(3)
Egypt	10	10	5

Lebanon

Country	Dividends	Interest	Royalties
	%	%	%
France	10(2)	10(2)	7.5(2)
Iran	5	5	5
Jordan	10	10	7.5/10
Kuwait	10(2)	10(2)	5
Malaysia	5	10	7.5/8
Malta	5/10(4)	10(2)	5
Morocco	5/10(5)	10	5/10(7)
Pakistan	10	10	7.5
Poland	5	5	5
Romania	5	5	5
Russia	10	5	5
Senegal	10	10	7.5/10
Sultanate of Oman	5/10(6)	10	7.5/10
Syria	5	10	7.5/18
Tunisia	5	5	5
Turkey	10/15(8)	10	7.5/10
UAE	10(2)	10(2)	5
Ukraine	5/10/15(9)	10	7.5/10
Yemen	10	5	7.5

Notes

1. Shall not exceed:
   a. 5% of the gross amount of the dividends if the beneficial owner is a company (other than a partnership) which holds directly at least 25% of the equity capital of the company paying the dividends.
   b. 10% of the gross amount of the dividends in all other cases.
2. Dividends, interest, or royalties arising in a Contracting State and paid to a resident of the other Contracting State shall be taxable only in that other State.
3. Shall not exceed:
   a. 5% of the gross amount of royalties paid for the use of, or the right to use, any industrial, commercial or scientific equipment;
   b. 10% of the gross amount of royalties paid for the use of or the right to use, any copyright of literary, artistic or scientific work, including cinematograph films and films or tapes for radio or television broadcasting any software, patent, trademark, design or model, plan, secret formula or process, or for information concerning industrial, commercial or scientific experience.
4. a. Where the dividends are paid by a company which is a resident of Lebanon to a resident of Malta who is the beneficial owner thereof, the Lebanese tax so charged shall not exceed 5% of the gross amount of the dividends;
   c. Where the dividends are paid by a company which is a resident of Malta to a resident of Lebanon who is the beneficial owner thereof, the Malta tax on the gross amount of the dividends shall not exceed that chargeable on the profits out of which the dividends are paid.
5. Shall not exceed:
   a. 5% of the gross amount of the dividends if the beneficial owner is a company (other than a partnership) which holds directly at least 10% of the equity capital of the company paying the dividends.
   b. 10% of the gross amount of the dividends in all other cases.
6. Shall not exceed:

a. 5% of the gross amount of the dividends if the beneficial owner is a company (other than a partnership) which holds directly at least 20% of the equity capital of the company paying the dividends.
b. 10% of the gross amount of the dividends in all other cases.
7. Shall not exceed:
  a. 10% of the gross amount of royalties paid for the use of or the right to use, any copyright of literary, artistic or scientific work, including cinematograph films and films or tapes for radio or television broadcasting.
  b. 5% of the gross amount of royalties paid in other cases.
8. Shall not exceed:
  a. 10% of the gross amount of the dividends if the beneficial owner is a company (other than a partnership) which holds directly at least 15% of the equity capital of the company paying the dividends.
  b. 15% of the gross amount of the dividends in all other cases.
9. Shall not exceed:
  a. 5% of the gross amount of the dividends if the beneficial owner is a company (other than a partnership) which holds directly at least 20% of the equity capital of the company paying the dividends.
  b. 15% of the gross amount of the dividends in all other cases.

Tax administration

Audit cycle
The most common ways for the tax authorities to select companies for tax audits are the size of the company, the type of business and certain risk assessment measures.

Tax audits typically cover a single type of tax.

In a typical situation, a tax audit is likely to take less than one year from first information request to substantive resolution.

Statute of limitations
The tax administration has four years to collect its rights. The period is calculated from the end of year that follows the current business year.

The taxable person may request the refund of excess tax within four years starting from the end of the year where the refund right was created.

The tax administration can exceed the statute of limitations in cases where a profit or revenue has been proven by a court order, arbitration or inheritance clearance. The extension is limited till the end of the calendar year following the end of the year in which the tax administration was notified of such event.

Under the statute of limitations a company should keep its accounting books and documentation for 10 years.

Returns
Taxes on business income in any given year are based on the profits of the previous financial year. Lebanon's fiscal year runs from January to December and is based on the Gregorian calendar. With the special permission of the local tax authorities, companies may, however, use their own accounting year.

Tax returns by artificial persons (entities) must be filed by 31 March of the year following the year of income. Tax returns by capital companies must be filed by 31

Lebanon

May of the year following the year of income. If taxpayers fail to submit a tax return, realisation penalties will be due.

Payment of tax
The same deadlines for tax returns apply for tax payments.

If taxpayers fail to make payment, late payment penalties will be due.

Topics of focus for tax authorities
Lately, several topics have been of interest to the tax authorities in Lebanon, including transfer pricing, payments of royalties and management fees to non-resident parties, provisions and employee compensation.

Other issues

Foreign investment incentives and restrictions
Law No.360 was passed in 2001 to encourage investments, while the Investment Development Authority in Lebanon (IDAL) was established to implement the law's provisions. This institution became operational in January 2002 and is responsible for attracting private capital investments to Lebanon and assisting investors in the development and implementation of their projects. Article 2 of the law provides that investors who will benefit from its provisions are those who invest in the sectors of industry, agriculture and agricultural products, tourism, information technology, communications, media besides other sectors to be defined by the council of Ministers through a law to be decreed based on a proposal of the prime minister.

Foreign ownership of real estate restrictions:

- Up to 3,000m² does not require Council of Ministers approval.
- Exploitation and normal lease right extending for a period of more than 10 years cannot be attained without obtaining approval.
- Real estate owned by foreigners, for which approval has been obtained, cannot exceed over all of the Lebanese territory 3% of the total area of Lebanon. In each province, the total area owned should not exceed 3% of its area and with respect to Beirut it should not exceed 10% of its area.
- The approval is nullified if not acted upon during a period of one year.
- When approval is granted the building on the real estate should be constructed within a period of five years (renewable once by the Council of Ministers).

Exchange controls
No exchange controls are applicable in Lebanon.

Choice of business entity
Lebanon's commercial law provides for a range of business entities available to both local and foreign investors. These are:

- Sole proprietorships;
- General partnerships;
- Limited partnerships;
- Joint-stock companies (SAL);
- Limited liability companies (SARL);
- Holding companies;

- Offshore companies; and
- Representative offices.

Legal structures commonly used by foreigners in conducting business in Lebanon are joint-stock companies, limited liability companies and branch offices.

Intellectual property

The law in Lebanon does not contain a clear definition of author's rights. It protects all products of the human intellect whether written, pictorial, sculptural, scriptural or oral regardless of its value, importance, destination or form of expression.

The law provides patent protection for inventions and plant varieties and a *sui generis* protection for layout designs of integrated circuits. Furthermore, the law provides protection for undisclosed information. According to an assessment conducted by the World Intellectual Property Organization (WIPO) in July 2002, the Patent law is in complete conformity with the WTO's Agreement on Trade-Related Aspects of Intellectual Property Rights (TRIPS). It was also pointed out that the provisions of the Plant Varieties exceed the minimum requirements of the TRIPS Agreement.

The law does not explicitly protect notorious trademarks and geographical indications. However, those are provided protection via Lebanon's membership to the Paris Convention. Moreover, Geographical indications are provided protection under the provisions of the new Law on Customs, the Law on Fraud Control and the Criminal Law.

The copyright protection originally available to literary and artistic works is now extended to computer software, video films and all kind of audio-visual works. The law provides stiffer penalties for offenders and better compensation to the persons whose rights have been infringed. The manner in which the copyright is breached has also been extended.

Mergers and acquisitions (M&A) from a business and tax perspective

No specific M&A rules are applicable in Lebanon. The general tax rules will apply in case of M&A.

L

Corporate taxes in Libya

For more information, contact:

Husam Elnaili
PricewaterhouseCoopers/Al Motahedoon LLC
Aldool Street
Ben Ashour
Tripoli, Libya
Tel: +218 21 3609830 ext. 110
Email: husam.elnaili@ly.pwc.com

Significant developments

The new Income Tax Law (Law 7 of 2010) became effective on 28 April 2010. The new
Executive Regulations, which support the law, are still to be issued and the existing
Executive Regulations will remain effective. If conflict exists between the new law and
the old Executive Regulations the new law will prevail.

Taxes on corporate income

Tax is imposed annually on the same basis for Libyan controlled corporate entities,
foreign controlled corporate entities and branches of foreign companies.

Tax is levied on taxable profits at a flat rate of 20%. In addition, there is a flat rate of
Jehad Tax assessed at 4% on taxable corporate profits.

Corporate residence

Corporate residence is not specifically dealt with in the laws of Libya. The tax
authorities will seek to assess any income derived from services provided in Libya.

Other taxes

Stamp duty
Stamp Duty Law (Law 12 of 2004, as amended by Law 8 of 2010) levies a schedule
of duties and rates on various documents and transactions. The most relevant to
corporate entities is Schedule 28, which prescribes the rate of duties on contracts
for the provision of services or supply. The duty on main contracts is 1% and on
subcontracts 0.1%. Note there is a duty of 0.5% on all payments to the Tax Department
as well.

Branch income

Tax rates on branch profits are the same as on corporate profits.

However, the Income Tax Law allows the Tax Department to assess income tax on
branches of foreign companies as a percentage of turnover - the "deemed profit" basis
of assessment. Tax is therefore payable even where tax losses are declared.

The level of deemed profit applied to turnover varies according to the branch's type of the business activity. This ranges from 10% - 15% for civil works and contracting (turnkey projects), 15% - 25% for oil service and between 25% - 40% in the case of design/consulting engineers. The deemed profit percentage applied to any year will be higher than the profit percentage declared in the annual tax return.

Income determination

For any Libyan registered entity, income arising both in Libya and abroad is assessable in Libya.

Inventory valuation
Libyan taxation laws do not contain any special provisions regarding inventory valuation.

Capital gains
Any chargeable gains on the sale of capital assets are taxed as ordinary income. For entities assessed on a deemed profit basis, capital gains should be added to the deemed taxable income.

Inter-company dividends
Libyan taxation laws do not contain any special provisions regarding inter-company dividends.

Stock dividends
Stock dividends are not specifically dealt with in the laws in Libya. The current practice is for dividend distributions not to be taxed on the recipient.

Deductions

The taxable income is determined after deducting all expenditure and costs incurred in the realisation of the gross income (*see Branch income section* for more details on the deemed profit basis of assessment on branches of foreign companies).

Depreciation
Depreciation should be calculated in accordance with the Executive Regulations of the law.

Net operating losses
Losses may be carried forward and deducted from future profits, for up to five years. The Income Tax Law has no provision for the carryback of losses.

Group taxation

There is no recognition of a group for taxation purposes.

Tax incentives

Exemptions to corporate income tax exist most notably under the Investment Law. The Tourism Investment Law allows a 10 year corporate income tax holiday from the commencement of project operations. General projects registered under

Libya

the Investment Law are permitted a five year corporate income tax holiday with a possibility to extend for a further three years.

Exemptions can also exist for strategic infrastructure projects. Such exemptions must be awarded by the General People's Committee (GPC) either by ratifying the relevant contract, which includes a tax exemption clause, or by the issuance of a separate law.

Withholding taxes (WHT)
Libyan law has no withholding taxes. For unregistered foreign entities seeking to register a contract with the tax authorities income tax will be assessed (and must be settled) on a deemed profit basis at the time of registration. It may be possibly to negotiate a withholding tax in preference to the aforementioned general procedure for more a significant contract where there is greater uncertainty as to the estimated contract value.

Tax administration

Returns
The tax year is generally a calendar year, although assessments can be made on the basis of a company's own year-end, provided permission is granted in advance from the tax department and the company then adheres consistently to the same date. All corporate entities must make an annual filing within four months of its year-end or one month within its audit report, whichever is earlier.

Statute of limitations
The statute of limitations for income tax purposes is seven years.

Payment of tax
Corporate income tax is payable on a quarterly basis (10 March, 10 June, 10 September and 10 December) normally commencing the first quarter date after an assessment has been issued.

Late payment penalties
A late payment penalty is assessed on the tax due at the rate of 1% to a maximum of 12%. In addition, the remaining quarterly payments are due immediately for failing to make an instalment on time.

The new law also increases the following penalties:

* A fine of not less than three times the amount of unpaid tax due shall be applied to any person who fails to pay tax by the due date.
* Without prejudice to any harsher penalty, a fine of not less than four times the amount of tax due and unpaid will be applied to any person who, with intent to evade all or part of the tax, commits any of the following acts or abets, agrees, or aids a person who commits such an act:

  * The making of false statements in declarations submitted under this law.
  * The preparation of false accounts, books and records, reports, or budgets.
  * The use of fraudulent means to conceal or attempt to conceal taxable amounts due under this law.

Statutory books

Business entities operating in Libya are required by Libyan law to maintain a general ledger and a general journal (the "statutory books").

Before use, these must be stamped as registered with the Revenue Authorities and the Commercial Court. It should be noted that a ledger or journal will not be registered if it already contains accounting entries, i.e., one cannot register existing books of account.

Similarly, transactions pre-dating the date the books are registered will be disallowed. In theory, transactions should be entered daily, but in practice, most companies write up their statutory records on the basis of monthly transactions summaries.

The Tax Inspector will always request production of the statutory books at the commencement of a tax audit. If these are not available, a perfunctory audit of the English language (or other language) books of account will be made and it is likely that there will be a punitive increase in taxable income as a consequence.

Note, that a new commercial code is being considered that may allow approved computer based ledgers to be used instead of the traditional manual ledgers. At this juncture uncertainty exists as to who would provide such approval and on what basis.

L

Corporate taxes in Liechtenstein

For more information, contact:

Christoph Lehmann
PricewaterhouseCoopers AG
Neumarkt 4/Kornhausstrasse 26
CH-9001 St Gallen
Switzerland
Tel: +41 58 792 7268
Email: christoph.lehmann@ch.pwc.com

Significant developments

The government of the Principality of Liechtenstein has proposed a new tax law with the objective to create a tax system which is attractive and competitive for investment, but still compatible with international standards. The new tax law is planned to take effect for the fiscal year 2011.

Below is an incomplete extract of the new tax law highlighting the most important changes:

In principle, all corporations, foundations and establishments will be subject to a profit taxation of 12.5%.

To improve the attractiveness, the following elements are proposed:

- Introduction of a standardised deduction for interest on equity, which will reduce the effective tax rate depending on the profitability of the company.
- Dividend income and capital gains from disposal of participations will be tax exempted, irrespective of the capital ownership percentage and the holding period.
- Losses can now be carried forward indefinitely.
- The capital tax will be abolished.
- A tax deduction of 80% of the intellectual property (IP) income derived from research and development (R&D) will be introduced.
- A group taxation scheme for directly held subsidiaries in the European Union (EU), European Economic Area (EEA), and Switzerland (CH).
- The current taxation scheme for holding and domicile companies will be abolished, at the latest after the fiscal year 2015. This is mainly relevant for domicile companies that are engaged in commercial activities outside of Liechtenstein.
- For corporations, foundations and establishments, finally held by individuals, that only engage in the administration of its own assets, the new private funds companies tax scheme may apply. Such companies are only subject to taxation of 6% on the legally required minimal nominal capital, at minimum Swiss Franc (CHF) 1,800 per year.
- The 4% withholding tax (coupon tax) on profit distributions will be abolished. However, old reserves remain subject to the coupon tax. Interestingly, a transitional taxation of 2% in the first two years after enactment is suggested to encourage early settlement.

The new tax law proposes major changes to the current tax scheme. It is therefore recommended that persons with investments in Liechtenstein should have the changes analysed to determine how it may apply specifically to their situation.

Taxes on corporate income

Taxable income is taxed at basic rates ranging from a minimum of 7.5% to a maximum of 15%. The applicable rate is determined by the ratio of profit to capital and reserves, based on the following formula.

(Taxable income x 100) ÷ (Taxable capital x 2) = X%

If the dividend distribution exceeds 8% of taxable capital, a surcharge of one to five percentage points is added to the basic income tax rate applicable for the year in which the dividend is declared, on the basis of the following table.

Dividend in excess of percentage of taxable capital	Increase of tax rate in percentage points
8	1.0
10	1.5
12	2.0
14	2.5
16	3.0
18	3.5
20	4.0
22	4.5
24	5.0

Consequently, the maximum rate applicable is 20%.

There are two categories of companies in Liechtenstein for income tax purposes: ordinary taxed companies and privileged companies. Ordinary taxed companies are subject to income tax and capital gains tax on equity, whereas privileged companies are not taxed on income and have reduced capital taxes. Privileged companies include trusts, establishments, captive insurance companies, foreign investment companies, investment companies, domiciliary and holding companies.

For details on the taxation of domiciliary and holding companies *see Tax incentives.*

Corporate residence

A company is considered to be resident in Liechtenstein and thus subject to unlimited tax liability if its registered seat (address) or place of effective management is within Liechtenstein.

Other taxes

Value-added tax (VAT)

Liechtenstein has adopted the VAT law of Switzerland, having its own administration in Vaduz.

Any person, who irrespective of legal form carries on a business, is liable for VAT. Any person liable for VAT that is involved in domestic entrepreneurial activity with a taxable turnover which is less than CHF 100,000 within a financial year can be exempt

Liechtenstein

from taxation. Companies which are not covered with this general rule are listed under Article 10 paragraph 2c VAT and Article 45 to 49 VAT. Note that various services are VAT exempt (e.g., health area, social security, education, bank and insurance services, etc.).

The general tax rate is 7.6%. A reduced rate of 2.4% is applicable to deliveries such as food, drugs, newspapers, magazines and books. Furthermore, lodging/accommodation is taxed at only 3.6%.

Branch income

The same principles applicable to corporations also apply for branch income, provided that transactions with the head office or other branches are at an arm's-length basis. Liechtenstein taxation is imposed on the profit attributable to the branch and on the capital invested in the branch.

There is no withholding tax on profit transfers to the head office.

Income determination

Inventory valuation
Inventories must be stated at the lower of cost or market. Cost is generally determined by the first-in, first-out (FIFO) or by the average cost method. The tax authorities permit a general reserve against stock contingencies of up to one-third of the inventory cost or market value at the balance sheet date without inquiry into its justification, provided a detailed record of inventory is available for review by the tax authorities. The need for a reserve in excess of this amount (e.g., for obsolescence, slow-moving stocks) must be substantiated to the satisfaction of the tax authorities.

Capital gains
Capital gains other than those arising on the sale of real estate are classified as normal business income and are subject to tax at the regular corporate tax rates.

Capital gains from the sale of real estate are subject to a separately assessed real estate profits tax. The taxable gain is basically the difference between proceeds of the sale and the original purchase price of the property plus any capital expenditure incurred. The basic tax rate is at present 1.08%, subject to various surcharges, depending, inter alia, on how long the vendor has owned the property concerned and the amount of taxable profit. The maximum rate of real estate profits tax is presently 34.02%.

Inter-company dividends
Dividends net of foreign taxes assessed are subject to ordinary corporate taxes unless the company has holding or domiciliary status *(see Tax incentives below)*. For qualifying foreign and domestic dividends out of participations, participation relief similar to that in Switzerland is available.

Foreign income
Resident corporations operating locally are basically taxed on their worldwide income, with the exception of income from real estate and permanent establishments situated abroad.

Liechtenstein

Profits of a domestic corporation's foreign branch are usually exempt from Liechtenstein corporate income tax. However, the progression provision (i.e., exempt foreign-branch income is nevertheless included for the determination of the applicable tax rate) is applicable, and the treatment of these profits depends on the method of allocation.

The income of a foreign subsidiary is taxable only when repatriated to the Liechtenstein parent company, e.g., in the form of dividends or interest.

The proceeds from the liquidation or sale of a foreign subsidiary in excess of the carrying value of the investment are taxable as ordinary income, unless the company is a privileged company in which case the proceeds are free of tax.

Deductions

Depreciation and depletion

Depreciation of intangible and tangible fixed assets is allowed to the extent it is "commercially justified." For tax purposes, either the straight-line (depreciation based on the acquisition value) or the declining-balance method (depreciation based on the book value) may be used. Depreciation and amortisation not recorded in the statutory accounts are not deductible for tax purposes.

A special (higher) rate of depreciation may be allowed for assets used only for short periods or for assets for which a rapid decrease in value can be proved.

Rate per annum (according to "Verordnung vom 15. September 2009"):

Property type	Straight-line (in %)	Declining balance (in %)
	%	%
Immovable assets		
Real estate (dwelling houses, offices, shops, restaurant and hotel buildings, industrial buildings, factories, warehouses and parking spaces)	2.5	5
Movable assets		
Mobile structures, technical installations (air conditioning plant, water, gas and electricity mains for industrial purposes), elevators, investments in foreign real estate, high rack warehouses, airplanes	7.5	1.5
Office furniture and machines, workshop and storeroom equipment	10	20
Furniture used for the hotel and restaurant trade	12.5	2.5
Machines and accessories for production purposes, vending machines, telephone installations, operating applications	15	30
Machinery used in more than one shift or used under heavy conditions, motor vehicles	17.5	3.5
IT (hardware and software), office furniture and machines, workshop and storeroom equipment, hotel and restaurant crockery, cutlery and linen	25	50

Liechtenstein

Property type	Straight-line (in %) %	Declining balance (in %) %
Officially approved installations and equipment against water pollution, energy-saving equipment and installations using solar energy	25	50
Intangible assets		
Goodwill, patent-licence and other rights of use	20	40

Recaptured depreciation on the sale or revaluation of depreciated assets is classified as normal business income.

Net operating losses
A loss may be carried forward and offset against the profits for future years for up to a maximum of five years. Losses may not be carried back.

Payments to foreign affiliates
Interest, royalties, and license and other fees to foreign affiliates are allowable as deductions to the extent that they meet the arm's-length test (i.e., equivalent to charges that would be made by an unrelated third party).

For interest payments between affiliated companies or between shareholders and companies, Liechtenstein tax authorities publish safe harbour rules annually.

Taxes
All taxes paid, including corporate income tax but excluding the coupon (withholding) tax, are deductible from income in the accounting period in which they are paid.

Group taxation

Each corporation is taxed as a separate entity; for example, a parent company and its local subsidiaries are taxed separately; only the dividends from the subsidiaries, and not their profits, are taxed in the hands of the parent company. For some investments (more than 20% or a market value of more than CHF 2 million / holding period minimum one year), the taxation of the dividends from a subsidiary to the parent company can be exempt from taxation in the parent company.

Tax incentives

Liechtenstein is well known for its domiciliary and holding companies. A domiciliary company is a legal entity incorporated in any of the legal forms governed by the Persons and Companies Code that has its registered seat in Liechtenstein but carries out no commercial activities within the country.

A holding company is a corporate body with its registered seat in Liechtenstein whose purpose consists entirely or mainly of the administration or management of assets or investments.

The status for qualification as a domiciliary or holding company is therefore merely a question of the company's purpose. The legal form of the company (e.g., corporation, establishment (Anstalt)) may be that most suitable to the shareholders or the activities to be performed.

Business entities having the status of a domiciliary or holding company are exempt from any income tax. The benefit of this income tax exemption must, however, be considered together with the absence of any significant double taxation treaty. For instance, the double taxation treaty with Austria expressly precludes foreign-owned domiciliary and holding companies from taking advantage of the treaty. Any foreign taxes levied on the company's income are therefore final.

A capital tax of 0.1% is, however, levied on the company's net equity, i.e., on paid-in capital, all reserves and retained earnings. The capital tax is payable annually in advance; the minimum tax is CHF 1000.

Dividend distributions of domiciliary or holding companies whose capital is divided into shares are subject to a 4% coupon (withholding) tax with the exception of captive insurance companies, trusts and investment companies.

Captive insurance companies are exempt from any income tax on that part of their income derived from the captive insurance business, whereas income from third-party insurance is subject to ordinary income tax. Captive insurance companies pay a capital tax of 0.1% on net equity. For the part of net equity exceeding CHF 50 million, there is a reduced tax rate of 0.075%; for net equity in excess of CHF 100 million, the rate is further reduced to 0.05%. Captive insurance companies can apply to be subject to ordinary income and capital taxes.

Withholding taxes (WHT)

Recipient	Dividends	Interest*	Royalties
	%	%	%
Resident corporations and individuals	4	0	Nil
Non-resident corporations and individuals:			
Non-treaty	4	0	Nil
Treaty:			
Austria	4	0	Nil

* A coupon tax of 4% is levied on interest from bonds and similar loans, on time deposits with domestic banks with a term in excess of 12 months and on loans in excess of CHF 50,000 with a minimum term in excess of two years, but not on interest of normal inter-company loans.

Tax treaties
A comprehensive double taxation treaty on income is in effect with Austria, and a limited one with Switzerland.

Recently Liechtenstein initiated double taxation treaties with Luxembourg and San Marino, Uruguay and Hong Kong. Furthermore, various tax information exchange agreements (TIEAs) have been concluded.

The Governments of Liechtenstein and UK have signed a Memorandum of Understanding (MOU) Relating to Cooperation in Tax Matters, which includes the

Liechtenstein

Liechtenstein disclosure facility (LDF). According to these regulations, financial intermediaries in Liechtenstein are required to show that their UK customers have been declaring their Liechtenstein investments to HM Revenue and Customs (HMRC). Disclosure can be made between 1 September 2009 and 31 March 2015. In certain circumstances, even accounts or assets outside of Liechtenstein may be transferred to Liechtenstein in order to take advantage of the terms of the LDF.

Tax administration

Returns
Companies other than holding and domiciliary companies must file a tax return within six weeks after the adoption of the financial statements by the shareholders' meeting but no later than 1 July of the calendar year following the fiscal year-end.

The tax assessment issued by the tax administration is based on the company's tax return, including the attachments and the financial statements filed.

Holding and domiciliary companies do not file a tax return. Rather, these companies simply furnish audited financial statements to the tax authorities or, if appropriate, a declaration of the non commercial nature of operations to the Registry of Commerce within six months after the company's fiscal year-end.

Payment of tax
Companies other than holding and domiciliary companies must pay the tax within 30 days of receipt of the assessment, which is generally in the fall of each year. Payment may be made in instalments if approved by the tax administration. The taxes for holding and domiciliary companies are regularly payable in advance.

Other issues

Tax information exchange agreements (TIEA) and Liechtenstein disclosure facility (LDF)
Recently, Liechtenstein concluded various TIEAs.

Furthermore the Governments of Liechtenstein and UK have signed a Memorandum of Understanding Relating to Cooperation in Tax Matters (MOU), which includes the LDF. According to these regulations, financial intermediaries in Liechtenstein are required to be satisfied that their UK customers have been declaring their Liechtenstein investments to HMRC. Disclosure can be made between 1 September 2009 and 31 March 2015. In certain circumstances, even accounts or assets outside of Liechtenstein may be transferred to Liechtenstein in order to take advantage of the terms of the LDF.

Corporate taxes in Lithuania

For more information, contact:

Kristina Krisciunaite
UAB PricewaterhouseCoopers
J. Jasinskio 16B
LT-01112 Vilnius
Lithuania
Tel: +370 5 239 2365
Email: kristina.krisciunaite@lt.pwc.com

Significant developments

Recent amendments to the law on corporate income tax (CIT) and the law on value-added tax (VAT) that:

- Reduced the standard CIT rate from 20% to 15%.
- Reduced the CIT rate for small and medium enterprises (SMEs) from 13% to 5%;
- Increased the VAT rate from 19% to 21%;
- Allowed entities involved in investment projects are able to reduce their taxable profits up to 50% by the acquisition costs of fixed assets meeting certain criteria;
- Repealed withholding tax (WHT) on interest as of 1 January 2010 if the interest is paid to entities registered or otherwise organised in European Economic Area (EEA) member states or in countries with which a treaty for avoidance of double taxation (DTT) is applicable and fulfils other requirements of CIT law.

Taxes on corporate income

The standard corporate income (CIT) tax rate is 15%. It was reduced from 20% to 15% as of 1 January 2010.

Exemptions

The following types of income are exempt from CIT:

1. Insurance indemnity not in excess of the value of lost property or other losses or damages; the refunded part of insurance premiums in excess of the premiums deducted from income in accordance with the procedure established; and a part of insurance indemnity in excess of the premiums deducted from income in accordance with the procedure established.
2. Proceeds of a bankrupt company received from sale of its property.
3. The balance of the formation fund of an insurance company as prescribed by the law on insurance.
4. Investment income of investment companies with variable capital and closed-end investment companies acting in accordance with the law on collective investment undertakings, except for dividends and other distributable profits.
5. Income derived by health care institutions for their services that are financed from the funds of the Compulsory Health Insurance fund.
6. Income derived from revaluation of fixed assets and liabilities as established by laws and regulations, except for income derived from the revaluation of derivative financial instruments acquired for hedging purposes.

Lithuania

7. Default interest except for that received from foreign companies registered or otherwise organised in blacklisted territories or residents of such territories.
8. All or part of the profit gained from legal entities of unlimited civil liability that are payers of the corporate income tax and with income that is subject to the corporate income tax under the law or to a similar tax under respective statutes of foreign countries with certain exceptions.
9. Fees collected by seaports and airports, charges for air traffic navigation services and funds collected from the lease of seaport-owned land.
10. Results arising from adjustments made for the previous tax periods as prescribed by the law on accounting.
11. Indemnification for damages received by the company with certain exceptions.
12. Compensation received according to the Lithuanian programmes of the EU financial support relating to taking fishing ships for scrap.
13. Capital gains derived from the transfer of shares in a company incorporated in the EEA or in a country with which Lithuania has a valid double taxation treaty and which is a payer of CIT or an equivalent tax, provided: the Lithuanian holding company holds more than 25% of voting shares for a continuous period of (1) at least two years; or (2) at least three years when the shares were transferred in one of the established forms of reorganisation. Certain restrictions apply.
14. Life insurance payments received by insurance companies, provided the term of the life insurance policy is valid for not less than 10 years or at the date of the receipt of the insurance benefit, the recipient has reached the pension age in accordance with the additional law on pensions. Additionally, insurance investment income of insurance companies except for dividends and other distributable profit are exempt, along with investment insurance income of insurance companies received according to the contracts of life insurance occupational pensions concluded in accordance with the law on accumulation of occupational pensions.
15. Direct and other compensational allowances, which are received by units performing agricultural activities to maintain their level of income, which meet the requirements established in the laws and other legal acts of Lithuania.

Local taxes
There is no local or municipal CIT.

Corporate residence

A company is resident in Lithuania if it incorporates there or its activities create a permanent establishment (PE) for tax purposes. According to local legislation, a foreign company is deemed to have a PE in Lithuania when:

1. It permanently carries out commercial activities in Lithuania in whole or in part;
2. It carries out its activities through a dependent representative (agent);
3. It uses a building site or construction, assembly or equipment objects; or
4. It uses equipment, including drilling installations and ships, for exploration or extraction of natural resources.

Double tax treaties (DTTs) may establish different rules of PE recognition. According to domestic law, where there is a DTT, the provisions of the treaty take precedence.

A PE must be registered as a taxpayer with the tax authorities in the territory where its activities are carried out. Its profits are subject to the corporate income tax at the rate of 15%.

Other taxes

Value-added tax (VAT)

The standard VAT rate is 21% (applicable from 1 September 2009). The reduced rate of 9% applies to:

- Books and non-periodicals (applicable by 31 December 2010); and
- Supply of heating of residential premises and the supply of heating water (applicable by 31 August 2010).

The reduced rate of 5% applies to:

- Compensated pharmaceuticals and medical aid devices (applicable by 31 December 2010).

The compensational rate for farmers is 6%.

In general, supplies of goods and services made by a taxable person performing its economic activity for a consideration within the territory of Lithuania and imports of goods are subject to VAT.

Exemptions with credit (0%-rated; including, but not limited to):

- Supply of goods exported outside of the EU;
- Goods acquired by non-EU resident passengers in Lithuania and carried out from the EU;
- Goods and services for vessels and aircraft;
- Transportation and any directly linked ancillary services related to export of goods and any directly linked ancillary services related to the import of goods when the value of these services shall be included in the customs value of the goods;
- Transportation of imported goods carried to a VAT exemption warehouse or temporarily stored under customs' supervision, placed in a free economic zone or free warehouse, put under customs warehousing procedure, processed under customs' supervision, temporarily imported for processing without levying customs duties, temporarily imported without implicitly levying customs duties or put under internal or external transit procedure;
- Issuance of TIR and ATA documents;
- Insurance and certain financial services directly related to export of goods from the EU;
- Supply of goods to sponsorship or charity recipients registered in Lithuania and listed in the Lithuanian law on charity and sponsorship, if the goods are exported by said recipients as sponsorship or charity to non-EU organisations which may be recipients of sponsorship or charity under the law;
- Supply of maintenance and processing services for movable property supplied to non-taxable persons established outside Lithuania that have no subdivision within the country provided that the property was temporarily imported for maintenance, repair, processing, etc. in the EU and will be carried out from the EU after supply of these services;
- Services of disclosed agents participating in certain transactions of supply of goods or services to local taxable and non-taxable persons where zero-rated VAT is applied and transactions of supply of goods or services where the supply of goods or services is considered carried out outside the EU;

Lithuania

- Supply of goods to VAT payers registered in another member state when these goods are carried out from Lithuania to another member state;
- Supply of new means of transport supplied to any person when new vehicles are carried out from Lithuania to another member state;
- Supply of goods subject to excise tax when they are supplied to a company not registered for VAT purposes and the goods are carried out from Lithuania to another member state; and
- Supply of goods in certain cases related to international trade, etc.

In order to apply zero-rated VAT on goods carried out from Lithuania, VAT payers must hold supporting documents as evidence that these goods were actually exported from the EU or carried out from Lithuania to another member state.

Exemptions without credit (including but not limited to):

- Personal or public health care services under certain conditions;
- Human organs, blood, human milk and dental prostheses supplied by dentists or dental technicians;
- Transportation of ill, wounded or other persons requiring medical care by special means of transport;
- Social services supplied by institutions for children and young people, nursing homes for the elderly and/or by care or guardianship institutions for disabled or by other non-profit entities;
- Education and training services;
- Cultural and sports services rendered by non-profit entities;
- Services provided by political parties, trade unions and other non-profit membership based legal entities to their members when these services correspond to that set out in the articles of association and are provided free-of-charge, except for membership fees;
- Services provided by religious communities, other communities and centres to their members if these services correspond to the purposes of these communities set out in their canons, statutes and other documents and are provided free-of-charge, except for donations;
- Postal services and directly related goods supplied by government-listed universal postal services providers, except for individually negotiated postal services;
- Radio and TV broadcasting services provided by non-profit legal entities;
- All types of insurance and re-insurance services and related services rendered by insurance and re-insurance agents;
- Financial services meeting certain requirements;
- Lotteries and gambling;
- Postage stamps and other government-listed special signs available for sale against their nominal value (this provision shall be applied only to the postage stamps which can be used as a confirmation of payment for postal services in Lithuania);
- The letting of residential premises (except for accommodation services provided by hotels, motels, camping and other accommodation services or letting of residential premises not indicated above when the letting period is not to exceed two months);
- The letting or sale of immovable property other than residential premises (certain exceptions apply); and
- Supply of goods where the VAT payer has not deducted any proportion of the VAT on purchases and/or importation thereof (certain conditions apply).

Intra-community acquisitions are VAT-exempt provided that:

- The supply of such goods in Lithuania would be VAT-exempt or zero-rated or the imports of such goods would be VAT-exempt;
- The purchaser who is a foreign taxable person should be able to refund this VAT; and
- Triangular transactions meeting certain criteria.

In order to apply exemptions, companies should make sure their services and goods supplied meet the appropriate VAT exemption requirements.

Option to tax (applicable to):

- Leasing of immovable property;
- Sale or other transfer of old immovable property (i.e., used for more than 24 months); and
- Financial services meeting certain requirements.

Option to tax may be exercised only if the customer is a taxable person registered for VAT purposes. If a VAT payer decides to use the option to tax, it is valid for at least 24 months.

Starting from 2010 VAT refund from other member states may be claimed via the new electronic system. Electronic requests have to be submitted via the official website of the tax authorities, while the refund procedure is carried on by the tax authorities of the member state concerned.

State dues (stamp taxes)
State dues are payable on activities of state institutions, such as the issuance of documents having legal force and other deeds.

Land tax
Lithuanian and foreign entities are subject to land tax collected by the municipalities for the land they own in Lithuania. Roads for general use and forestland are exempt. The annual tax rate is 1.5% of the taxable value, which is determined according to the rules established by the government. The assessment and payment terms are set forth by the municipalities, which are also entitled to grant land tax incentives.

Land lease tax
State-owned land that is leased for Lithuanian and foreign companies is subject to land lease tax at a rate established by the municipalities. The minimum tax rate set by the government is 0.1%, and the maximum rate is 4% of the value of the land.

Real estate tax
Real estate tax at a rate ranging from 0.3% up to 1% is levied on the value of real estate owned by individuals and used for commercial purposes or owned by legal entities (with certain exemptions). Municipal councils establish a specific tax rate for real estate situated in their territories annually.

Excise taxes
Excise duty is imposed on the following goods produced in or imported into Lithuania: ethyl alcohol and alcoholic drinks, including beer and wine; processed tobacco, including cigarettes, cigars, cigarillos and smoking tobacco; energy-related products, including petrol, kerosene, gasoline, fuel oil and their substitutes and additives; coal,

Lithuania

coke and lignite; and electric energy (as of 1 January 2010). The tax rate depends on the type and quantity of goods.

Customs duties
EU customs law is applicable in full.

Environmental tax
The tax is imposed on pollutants discharged into the environment, a few specified products (e.g., tyres, batteries, etc.) and certain types of package.

Tax on natural resources
The tax is payable on the value of extracted natural resources.

Branch income

A branch of a foreign company is defined as a structural subunit of a foreign company, which has an establishment in Lithuania and is entitled to engage in commercial activities in Lithuania as well as conclude contracts and undertake obligations according to the power of attorney issued to the branch by its founder. A branch does not have the status of a legal person. It is taxed in the same manner as a PE.

Income determination

Inventory valuation
Under domestic accounting legislation, stock used in the production and included in the cost of produced products is valued in the financial statements by the first-in, first-out (FIFO) method. The last-in, first-out (LIFO), weighted-average, progressive-average, actual-price, or another method that corresponds to the stocks' movement can also be used. However, the method used must be disclosed in the notes to the annual accounts, and, among other things, the note must report the profit that would have been calculated if the FIFO method of valuation had been used. For CIT purposes usage of other method than FIFO should be approved by the tax authorities.

Capital gains
Capital gains are taxed as part of the corporate profit of the enterprise.

Capital gains are treated as non-taxable income when they are derived from the transfer of shares in a company incorporated in the EEA or in a country with which Lithuania has a valid double taxation treaty and that pays CIT or an equivalent tax. This holds true if the Lithuanian holding company holds more than 25% of voting shares for a continuous period of (1) at least two years; or (2) at least three years when the shares were transferred in one of established forms of reorganisation. Certain restrictions apply.

Dividends
Dividends distributed by a resident company to another resident company are subject to a 15% corporate income tax, which is withheld by a distributing company.

The dividends are exempt from withholding tax if the recipient company has held not less than 10% of the voting shares in the distributing company for at least a 12-month period and the distributing entity is subject to 5% or 15% Lithuanian corporate income tax rate. However, this relief is not applied if the foreign entity (recipient) is registered or otherwise organised in blacklisted territories, as specified by the Ministry of Finance. Please note that the requirement of the 12-month holding period does not necessarily have to be fulfilled on the day of dividend distribution.

The receiving company may reduce its payable CIT for that period when dividends were received by the amount of CIT withheld from the received dividends. Any excess credit may be offset with other taxes payable.

Dividends distributed by a foreign entity are subject to a 15% withholding tax which is to be paid by the receiving Lithuanian entity.

Dividends are exempt from withholding tax if the distributing foreign entity is established in the EEA and related profit is properly taxed in the domiciled country.

The dividends are exempt from withholding tax if the recipient company has held not less than 10% of the voting shares in the distributing company for at least a 12-month period and the receiving entity is subject to 5% or 15% Lithuanian corporate income tax rate. This participation exemption satisfies the requirements of the EC Parent-Subsidiary Directive. The exemption also applies to dividends paid by non-EU foreign companies, except those registered or organised in blacklisted territories.

The receiving company does not include the dividends received from other entities in its taxable income.

Foreign income
Income is not subject to taxation in Lithuania if it was received from activities through a permanent establishment in a foreign country, which is in the EEA or which has a DTT with Lithuania, and if the income was subject to taxation there. Since income is not subject to taxation in Lithuania, costs related to the income cannot be deducted from income that is subject to taxation in Lithuania.

Deductions

Depreciation
Intangible and tangible assets may be depreciated using a directly proportional (straight-line) depreciation method, a production depreciation method or a double-declining-balance depreciation method. Depreciation may not exceed maximum rates established by the law.

Net operating losses
Operating losses may be carried forward for an indefinite period provided that certain requirements are met.

Current year operating losses incurred after 1 January 2010 can be transferred to another legal entity of the group if certain conditions are met.

Losses incurred due to the transfer of securities and/or derivative financial instruments may be carried forward for five years.

Taxes
All taxes, fees and other compulsory payments to the state budget are deductible for corporate income tax purposes, except:

Lithuania

- VAT paid to the budget (with exceptions indicated in the following);
- Corporate income tax; and
- Social tax (temporary tax that was applicable only in 2006 and 2007).

VAT can be treated as deductible for corporate income tax purposes only if:

- Input or paid import VAT which is non-refundable for VAT purposes.
- This input or paid import VAT is calculated on deductible expenses.

Other significant items

Allowable deductions include all the usual costs that an entity actually incurs for the purpose of earning income or receiving economic benefit unless the law on CIT provides otherwise.

Limited deductible expenses are:

1. Depreciation or amortisation expenses of fixed assets (for tax purposes assets cannot be depreciated faster than indicated in the CIT law);
2. Maintenance, repair and reconstruction expenses of tangible fixed assets (however, if the repair or reconstruction increase the service period and improve the qualities (useful characteristics of the fixed assets), the value of repair or reconstruction shall be added to the acquisition value of the tangible fixed assets);
3. Business travel expenses (deductible with restrictions);
4. Advertising and representation expenses (75% of representation expenses are deductible);
5. Natural losses (not more than 1% of turnover);
6. Taxes (deductible with restrictions);
7. Bad debts (deductible only if proved and specific criteria met, provisions are non-deductible);
8. Contributions and expenses for the benefit of employees (deductible with restrictions);
9. Special provisions of credit institutions and insurance companies;
10. Sponsorship (the double amount deductible but only if provided to registered recipients and only up to 40% of taxable result before deduction of sponsorship and utilisation of tax losses carried forward); and
11. Membership fees, contributions and premiums (deductible with restrictions);
12. Losses of previous tax periods (losses can be carried forward for indefinite period if certain requirements are met), etc.

Non-deductible expenses:

1. VAT payable to the budget and corporate income tax;
2. Default interest (forfeit), fines and late interest paid to the state budget as well as other sanctions imposed for violations of laws and regulations of the Republic of Lithuania;
3. Interest or any other indemnity paid due to non-performance of contractual obligations by related parties;
4. Amount of the limited deductible expenses in excess of the established limits;
5. Expenses attributed to allowable deductions more than 18 months past, although the payments for goods or services supplied by the entities registered or otherwise organised in blacklisted territories have not been made;

6. Sponsorship and gifts that do not correspond to the requirements of CIT law;
7. Payments to blacklisted territories if they are not verified and payments are not subject to withholding tax;
8. Indemnification for damages inflicted by the entity;
9. Dividends or otherwise distributed profits;
10. Other expenses not related to the deriving of income and not attributed to operating activities of the entity as well as the expenses that are not considered allowable deductions under the law;
11. Amounts resulting from adjustments and corrections of errors of previous tax periods;
12. Expenses related to revaluation of fixed assets and securities;
13. Social tax (applicable for CIT calculation in 2006 and 2007);
14. Deductible or limited deductible expenses attributed to non-taxable income; and
15. Expenses related to income from certain international maritime activities, if a maritime entity chose to apply a fixed CIT.

Group taxation

Group taxation legislation and regimes are not available in Lithuania. Each Lithuanian entity is regarded as a separate taxpayer and may not deduct tax losses of any other group entity.

However, recent amendments to CIT law allowed transfer of current year operating tax losses incurred as of 1 January 2010 to the entity of the same group of companies if certain requirements are met.

Tax incentives

The rate of corporate income tax on certain maritime activities is 15%, with the base set by reference to the functional capacity of the ship. This fixed corporate income tax could be applied to maritime entities that fulfil certain conditions indicated in the law. An election must be made to the tax authorities to apply this regime.

Entities with fewer than 10 employees and less than LTL 500,000 (approximately EUR 145,000) gross annual revenues can benefit from a reduced corporate income tax rate of 5% (the standard rate is 15%).

Entities involved in an investment project are able to reduce their taxable profits up to 50% by the actually incurred acquisition costs of the long-term assets meeting certain requirements. Please note that depreciation (amortisation) expenses of such assets shall be deducted in common manner.

Taxable profits can be reduced by costs incurred in 2009 – 2013.

The costs exceeding the above mentioned 50% limit can be carried forward for four years. Consequently, the entity incurring losses in 2009 may benefit from the tax relief in subsequent periods.

There are certain criteria defining what could be considered an investment project. The project should be precisely described to meet the criteria allowing it to use the tax relief and the tax authorities should be properly notified about the project.

Lithuania

Moreover, entities that invest in Lithuanian free economic zones are entitled to partial or complete CIT relief (depending on the investment amount), relief of tax on real estate and 50% relief of land lease tax.

In addition, local authorities are entitled to grant reliefs on real estate tax or land lease tax.

Withholding taxes (WHT)

Domestic legislation

Income of a foreign entity in Lithuania not derived through a PE is deemed to be Lithuanian-source income:

- Interest on any type of debt obligations including securities (10% WHT rate);
- Proceeds from the sale, transfer (with title) or lease of immovable property located in Lithuania (15% WHT rate);
- Income derived from sports activities or performers' activities (15% WHT rate);
- Income from distributed profits (15% WHT rate);
- Royalties (10% WHT rate);
- Annual payments (tantiems) to the members of the board or supervisory board (15% WHT rate); and
- Indemnities received for the infringement of copyrights or neighbouring rights (10% WHT rate).

The EC Interest and Royalty Directive have been implemented in the Lithuanian domestic tax law. However, Lithuania was granted a transitional period of six years. Withholding tax on royalties paid to related parties meeting requirements of the EC Interest and Royalty Directive is 10% until 30 June 2011 and from 1 July 2011 the rate will be reduced to 0%. Notwithstanding this, according to local tax legislation, Lithuanian withholding tax on interest paid to the entities, EU or DTT tax residents, is 0% as of 1 January 2010.

Furthermore, withholding tax is not applied on government securities issued on international financial markets, interest accumulated and paid on deposits, and interest on subordinated loans which meet the criteria established by legal acts adopted by the Bank of Lithuania.

Blacklisted territories

Blacklisted territory means a foreign country or territory that is included on the list of offshore territories established by the Minister of Finance and meeting at least two of the following criteria:

1. Similar tax rate in such territory is below 75% of that set in the Lithuanian CIT law;
2. In such territory different rules for levying a similar tax are applied, depending on the country where the parent company (controlling entity) is registered or otherwise organised;
3. In such territory different rules for levying a similar tax are applied, depending on the country where the business is conducted;
4. The company (the controlled taxable entity) has entered into agreement with the tax administrator of that territory with regard to the application of a tax rate or tax base;
5. There is no effective exchange of information in such territory; and

6. There is no financial and administrative transparency in such territory, the tax administration rules are not quite clear and the application thereof is not communicated to tax administrators of other countries.

A list of 58 offshore territories has been published. With certain exceptions specified in the law, all payments to offshore companies or their branches for any work or services, commodities, interest on funding, insurance premiums, guarantees, etc., are non-deductible for corporate income tax purposes unless the Lithuanian entity provides evidence to the state tax authorities that:

1. The payments are related to usual activities of the paying and the receiving business entities;
2. The receiving foreign business entity manages the property necessary to carry out such usual activities; and
3. There is a connection between the payment and the economically grounded business operation.

Tax treaties
Where a treaty for the avoidance of double taxation and prevention of fiscal infringement with the country in question contradicts the local regulations, the treaty provisions prevail. Lithuania has now signed 48 double taxation treaties with foreign countries.

Reduction of, or exemption from, withholding taxes under a double taxation avoidance treaty may be obtained if a special residence certificate (request for a reduction or exemption from the Lithuanian withholding tax withheld at source (Form DAS–1)) is completed and approved by the tax authorities before a taxable payment is transferred. If a payment that would have been subject to a tax treaty has already been made and withholding tax at the local rate was withheld, it is possible to obtain an appropriate refund (reduction) by completing a special claim for a refund of the Lithuanian tax withheld at source (Form DAS–2) and obtaining the approval of the tax authorities.

In addition, the tax authorities may require completion of a special certificate giving information about income received and taxes paid in Lithuania (Form DAS–3).

Tax administration

Returns
Corporate income tax
Corporate income tax returns must be submitted by the first day of the tenth month of the following tax period (October 1 for companies using the calendar year).

If corporate income tax is calculated based on activity results for the previous year, the advance corporate income tax return for the first nine months of the tax period is to be submitted by the last day of the first month (usually January) of the tax period. The return for the remaining months of the tax period is to be submitted by the last day of the tenth month (usually October) of the tax period. If the taxpayer has chosen to pay the advance amount based on the projected amount of corporate income tax for the current year, the return must be submitted not later than the last day of the first month of the tax period.

Lithuania

Withholding tax on payments other than dividends
A tax-withholding entity must submit to the tax authorities a special form of a return reporting the amounts paid and taxes withheld during the calendar month no later than 15 days after the end of the month in which the amounts were paid.

Withholding tax on dividends
A tax-withholding entity must submit to the tax authorities a special form of a return reporting the dividends paid and tax withheld within 10 calendar days after the end of the month of the dividend payment.

Payment of tax
Corporate income tax
Based on the activity results for the previous year, the advance amount of corporate income tax for the first nine months of the tax period is calculated based on the actual corporate income tax amount for the tax period before the previous tax period. For example, the corporate income tax for the first nine months of 2010 would be calculated based on the appropriate portion of the actual amount of corporate income tax for 2008. The advance amount for the remainder of the tax period is based on the actual amount of corporate income tax for the previous period, for example, tax for the last three months of 2010 would be based on the appropriate portion of the actual amount of corporate income tax for 2009. Thus, the advance corporate income tax amount for each quarter would be equal to one-fourth of the actual tax amount calculated for the tax periods discussed.

The taxpayer may choose to pay the advance amount based on the projected amount of corporate income tax calculated for the current year. The advance tax (one-fourth of the advance corporate income tax) must be paid no later than the last day of the respective quarter, and for the last quarter by the twenty-fifth day of the last month of the quarter.

If the amount of tax indicated in the return exceeds the amount actually paid during the tax period, the taxpayer is obliged to transfer the additional amount no later than the return submission deadline. Overpaid tax is refunded in accordance with the law on tax administration.

Withholding tax on payments other than dividends
Withholding tax is to be calculated, withheld and remitted by a Lithuanian company or a permanent establishment of a foreign company no later than the return submission deadline.

Withholding tax on dividends
Withholding tax is to be calculated, withheld and remitted by a Lithuanian company that pays dividends within 10 calendar days after the end of the month of the payment.

Corporate taxes in Luxembourg

For more information, contact:

Wim Piot
PricewaterhouseCoopers S.à r.l.
400, Route d'Esch
B.P. 1443 L-1014 Luxembourg
Tel: +352 49 48 48 1
Email: wim.piot@lu.pwc.com

Significant developments

The Research, Development and Innovation Act

As of 1 July 2009, a new legislation has been enacted in order to promote research, development and innovation within Luxembourg. Many research and development (R&D) incentives can be granted. Together with the 80% exemption regime applicable to IP rights, these incentives position Luxembourg as a highly attractive location for R&D activities, as well as IP *(see "Tax incentives")*.

The circular on Islamic Finance

On 12 January 2010, the Luxembourg tax authorities issued a circular on Islamic Finance providing guidance on the Luxembourg corporate direct tax treatment of some of the common Shariah compliant financial instruments (i.e., Murabaha and Sukuk instruments), which further confirmed the compatibility of Luxembourg tax framework with Islamic Finance requirements.

Exchange of information

As of May 2010, Luxembourg has signed 24 double tax treaties (DTTs) or amendments to comply with OECD principles on exchange of information. The country is on the OECD "white" list having "substantially implemented the internationally agreed tax standards".

Value-added tax (VAT) package

The Luxembourg VAT law has implemented as from 1 January 2010, the new rules introduced by the so-called "VAT package" in the European VAT directive 2006/112/EC. These new rules extend the principle of taxation in the country where the recipient is established in "Business to Business" transactions. Some transactions taking place in a Business to Consumer framework are also impacted. "Business" means a taxable person who performs, even partially, an economic activity or non-taxable legal person identified for VAT purposes. The reverse charge mechanism is also extended. The new rules set forth an additional VAT reporting obligation: Most of services exchanged in an European cross-border situation need to be reported as such in an "European Sales Listing", unless they are VAT exempt in the county of the recipient. Another change came for the procedure on VAT refund in countries where an European company is not established and suffered local VAT (8th directive refund claims).

End of the 1929 Holding tax regime

As announced in 2006, the phasing-out period for 1929 Holding Companies will end on 31 December 2010. Hence, it is recommended to make a tax review of the business organisation by this date for remaining 1929 Holding Companies.

L

Luxembourg

Taxes on corporate income

Corporate income tax
Businesses with taxable income lower than EUR 15,000 are subject to tax at a rate of 20%. The corporate income tax rate is currently 21% for companies with a taxable income in excess of EUR 15,000. Additionally, a 4% solidarity tax is imposed on the corporate income tax amount.

Taking into account the 4% solidarity tax, the aggregate corporate income tax rate is 21.84%.

The corporate income tax does not apply to tax exempt entities (e.g., 1929 Holding Companies that benefit from grandfathering rules, see *"Tax incentives"*), or to tax transparent entities (e.g., general or limited partnerships or European Economic Interest Grouping).

Municipal business tax on income
Municipal business tax is levied by the communes and varies from region to region. As of 1 January 2006, the municipal business tax for Luxembourg City has been reduced to 6.75%. No change in the rate has occurred since 2006 in Luxembourg City.

Aggregate rate
The effective combined corporate income tax rate for Luxembourg City (i.e., both corporate income tax and municipal business tax) is 28.59% for 2010.

Corporate residence

Without regard to double tax treaty provisions, a company is considered to be resident of Luxembourg, if either its registered office or place of central administration is located in Luxembourg. The registered office is designated as such in the company's articles of incorporation. The place of central administration generally is defined as the centre from which the company's activities are directed.

Luxembourg taxes its corporate residents on their worldwide income.

Other taxes

Net wealth tax
Both Luxembourg resident companies and branches of foreign companies generally are subject to net wealth tax levied at a rate of 0.5% on their net wealth, based on prescribed valuation methods. In general, assets are taken into account at market value (except for real estate, which is subject to a special regime). Shareholdings qualifying for the participation exemption (see "Income determination") generally are exempt from net wealth tax.

Resident companies and branches of foreign companies may claim a reduction of their net wealth tax liability by making an allocation to a special reserve before the closing of the tax year following the year for which the net wealth tax reduction is claimed. To this end, an amount corresponding to five times the net wealth tax that should have become payable must be kept in this special reserve for the five years following the year in which it was allocated. The reduction, however, may not be higher than the taxpayer's corporate income tax liability, before tax credits, for that same year.

Value-added tax (VAT)

Proceeds of sales and services, which are deemed to take place in Luxembourg, are subject to VAT at the standard rate of 15% (lowest standard VAT rate in the European Union) or, on certain transactions, at 12% (e.g., wine, advertising pamphlets), 6% (e.g., supply of gas or electricity), or 3% (e.g., food except alcohol beverages, pharmaceutical products, books, radio and television broadcasting services except adult entertainment). Some transactions, such as export and related transport, are zero-rated.

Taxpayers whose activities are subject to VAT are entitled to offset against their VAT payable the amount of such tax charged to them by their suppliers or reverse charged (i.e., self-accounted) by them on import or acquisitions of goods or services from abroad.

Banking, financial, insurance and reinsurance generally are exempt activities. The VAT paid on costs made for these transactions cannot be recovered except when related to services performed for persons established outside the European Union. VAT on expenses made in the context of "passive" holding activities, which are considered as outside the scope of VAT, are not recoverable.

Excise duties

In addition to the VAT, some products are subject to specific excise duties. In Luxembourg these products are electricity, mineral oils, manufactured tobaccos and alcohols.

Excise duties are not based on the sale price of the products but on the quantity. Excise duty becomes chargeable at the time, and in the European Union Member State, of release for consumption. This means any of the following:

a. The departure of excise goods from a duty suspension arrangement;
b. The holding of excise goods outside a duty suspension arrangement where excise duty has not been levied pursuant to the applicable provisions of Community law and national legislation;
c. The production of excise goods outside a duty suspension arrangement; or
d. The importation of excise goods, including irregular importation, unless the excise goods are placed, immediately upon importation, under a duty suspension arrangement.

Subscription tax

Certain holding companies and investment funds are subject to subscription tax (at various rates) on their market or net asset values. 1929 Holding Companies, which benefit from grandfathering rules, are subject to a 0.2% subscription tax on the value of the shares issued, with a minimum amount of EUR 48.

For investment funds, the subscription tax is applied to the total net assets evaluated at the last day of each quarter. Institutional funds and monetary funds are subject to an annual rate of 0.01%, and the other funds to an annual rate of 0.05%. Funds of institutional funds and monetary institutional funds are exempt from subscription tax.

General registration taxes

General registration taxes (inclusive of the transcription tax) are levied at 7% on the market value of real estate purchased or transferred (10% in the commune of

Luxembourg

Luxembourg City for some categories of properties) and 1% on mortgages on real estate. The taxes are deductible for income tax purposes.

Capital duty has been abolished as of 1 January 2009. As a consequence, the general registration duty regime governs all transactions previously falling within the scope of the capital duty law. The general registration duty regime has also been slightly modified as follows:

- A fixed registration duty of EUR 75 is levied on certain transactions involving Luxembourg entities (i.e., incorporation, amendment to the articles of association and transfer of seat to Luxembourg).
- For Luxembourg real estate assets, contribution made to a company remunerated by shares are now subject to a proportional registration duty of 0.6% (but 0.9% for Luxembourg City for some categories of properties) and a transcription tax of 0.5%. Contribution remunerated by means other than shares remain subject to a proportional registration duty of 6% (but 9% for some categories of properties located in Luxembourg City) and a transcription tax of 1%. Transfer made within the framework of a corporate reorganisation may be exempt from any proportional registration duty under certain conditions.

Special income tax
"Billionaire" and "financial" holding companies, which benefit from grandfathering rules, are subject to a special income tax applied at varying percentage rates to interest expenses on bonds and similar negotiable debt-claims, payments to non-resident directors, and dividends distributed to shareholders. The minimum annual tax is EUR 48,000 *(see "Other incentives/holding companies" under "Tax incentives" for further information)*.

Commune (municipalities) real estate tax
Communes (municipalities) levy a real estate tax, the basis of which is the unitary value of real estate, which represents its estimated value in 1941. The basic rate varies from 0.7 to 1% of the unitary value, according to the category of property, and is multiplied by a coefficient, which varies with communes and different types of property. For commercial properties, the coefficient in Luxembourg City is 750%, which should be applied to 1% of the unitary value. The tax is deductible for income tax purposes.

Branch income

Branch income generally is taxed at corporate income tax rates. However, the municipal business tax generally only applies, if the branch is carrying on commercial activity within Luxembourg.

Income determination

Inventory valuation
Inventories generally are valued at the lower of actual or market cost. There is no statutory specified method. In general, the FIFO (first-in, first-out), the LIFO (last-in, first-out) and the weighted-average costs methods of inventory valuation are acceptable for income tax purposes, provided the method accords with the facts.

Inter-company dividends

Dividends received by a Luxembourg fully taxable resident company (or by a domestic permanent establishment in certain cases) should, in principle, be subject to corporate income tax and municipal business tax at the aggregate rate of 28.59% (for Luxembourg city).

However, dividends received may be tax exempt in Luxembourg under certain conditions, according to the so-called "participation exemption" regime, if the conditions described below are satisfied:

1. The distributing company is:
   - A collective entity falling under article 2 of the amended version of the EU Council directive of 23 July 1990 (90/435/EEC), hereafter the "Parent Subsidiary Directive";
   - A Luxembourg resident joint-stock company, which is fully taxable and does not take one of the forms listed in the appendix to the paragraph 10 of article 166 of the Luxembourg Income Tax Law (LITL) *(see "Withholding taxes – Note 2" for a detailed list of the entities)*; or
   - A non-resident joint-stock company that is fully liable (in its state of residence) to a tax corresponding to the Luxembourg corporate income tax (i.e., as a general rule, it is required that the foreign tax is compulsory levied at an effective rate of at least 10.5%, on a basis similar as the Luxembourg one); and
2. The beneficiary company is:
   - A Luxembourg resident collective entity, which is fully taxable and takes one of the forms listed in the appendix to the paragraph 10 of article 166 LITL;
   - A Luxembourg resident joint-stock company, which is fully taxable and does not take one of the forms listed in the above-mentioned appendix;
   - A domestic permanent establishment of a collective entity falling under article 2 of the amended version of the Parent-Subsidiary Directive;
   - A domestic permanent establishment of a joint-stock company that is resident in a country with which Luxembourg has concluded a double tax treaty; or
   - A domestic permanent establishment of a joint-stock company or of a cooperative society, which is a resident of a European Economic Area (EEA) member state (other than a EU member state); and
3. At the date on which the income is made available, the beneficiary has been holding or undertakes to hold, directly, for an uninterrupted period of at least 12 months a participation in the share capital of the subsidiary of at least 10% or with an acquisition price of at least EUR 1.2 million.

Capital gains

Capital gains (and losses) generally are taxed as ordinary income (or losses). It is possible to defer the taxation on gains on certain fixed assets where the gain is used to acquire replacement items. Under certain conditions, exempted capital gains and hidden reserves may be unrealised in a merger or another form of reorganisation of resident companies or other EU companies.

In general, capital gains on the disposal of qualifying shareholdings held by entities eligible to the participation exemption regime *(see "Inter-company dividends")* are tax exempt, provided: (1) the total shareholding constitutes at least 10% of total ownership or an acquisition price of at least EUR 6 million; and (2) the disposing company has held or intends to hold the qualifying shareholding for at least 12 months.

Luxembourg

A recapture system exists, under which the exempt amount of the gain is reduced by the sum of expenses connected with the participation (e.g., financing cost and write-downs in the value of the participation), to the extent that they have reduced the taxable base of that year or previous years. Basically, the effect of this rule is that the capital gain realised will become taxable up to the amount of the aggregate expenses and write-downs deducted during the respective and previous years in relation to the participation.

The purpose of the system is to avoid a taxation vacuum, which could result if the deductibility of expenses and write-downs connected to the participation were allowed, while the income arising from the participation was tax exempt. This system should, in principle, remain tax neutral as the company should have available carryforward losses for an equivalent amount (unless previously used to offset other taxable income).

Transparent entities
From a Luxembourg tax perspective, a transparent entity is seen as having no legal personality distinct from the one of its partners (those transparent entities are commonly referred to as "partnership") for a corporate income tax and net wealth tax. Provided that the partnership carries out a commercial activity, it will however be liable to municipal business tax on its own. The tax transparent entity may however be regarded as a separate legal entity from a civil/corporate law point of view.

Foreign income
A Luxembourg tax resident company is liable for corporate income tax on its worldwide income, whether derived from Luxembourg or from foreign sources (subject to the provisions of double tax treaties, if any). Dividends from foreign subsidiaries are taxed when received, except where exempt as mentioned above. Profits of a foreign branch which are not exempt by the mean of a double tax treaty may however benefit from a foreign tax credit. Any taxes paid in excess of the tax credit are deductible as expenses. Luxembourg is however using the exemption method in most of its double tax treaties.

Thin capitalisation
No thin capitalisation ratio is specifically provided by the Luxembourg tax law.

In practice, the tax authorities apply an 85/15 debt-to-equity ratio for the intra-group financing of participations. Should the 85/15 ratio not be complied with by the taxpayer, the surplus of interest could be requalified by the tax authorities as a hidden distribution and therefore non-deductible and potentially subject to a 15% withholding tax.

Deductions

Depreciation
Depreciation rates must be consistent with economic reality. The depreciation must be calculated on the total acquisition cost, bearing in mind the normal life of the asset and the estimated residual value. Depreciation normally is calculated using the straight-line method. However, the declining-balance method is permitted for fixed assets, other than buildings and intangible assets. The depreciation rate may not, however, exceed three times the rate applicable according to the straight-line method, or 30% (in the case of assets used exclusively for scientific and technical research, four times the applicable rate, or 40%).

It is permissible to change from the declining-balance method to the straight-line method, but the converse is not allowed. Tax depreciation must be reflected in the financial accounts prepared for commercial purposes.

In the event of a sale of a depreciated asset, the net book value at the moment of the disposal must be compared with the sale price of that asset. If this comparison indicates a profit, corresponding income tax may be due unless the sale price is reinvested in eligible assets. Capital losses are deductible.

Under certain conditions, fixed assets with a value of less than EUR 870 or a life that is not in excess of one year can be expensed fully in the year of acquisition. Special accelerated depreciation on 60% of the cost of fixed assets is available for assets that protect the national environment, save energy in Luxembourg, or permit the development of workplaces for handicapped workers, under certain conditions.

Shareholdings
Expenses linked to a shareholding qualifying for the participation exemption, including write-downs in the value of the shareholding booked as a consequence of a dividend distribution, are not deductible up to the amount of the exempt dividend. Recapture rules may apply in the event of disposal of the shareholding. Basically, the effect of this rule is that capital gain realised will become taxable up to the amount of the aggregate expenses and write-downs in relation to the participation, deducted during the year of disposal and the previous years. The qualifying shareholding is exempted for net wealth tax. The excess portion of a debt linked to the qualifying shareholding (i.e., portion above the value of the exempted shareholding) is deductible from the taxable basis *(see "Inter-company dividends")*.

Net operating losses
Net operating losses can be carried forward for an unlimited period but cannot be carried back.

Payments to foreign affiliates
Royalties, management service fees, and interest charges paid to foreign affiliates by a Luxembourg company are deductible items, provided they are equal to what the company would pay an unrelated entity for comparable services.

Taxes
Several taxes are deductible in determining income subject to corporate income tax, including the registration duties and real estate tax. Also, certain taxes are credited against the computed amount of income tax owed, including taxes withheld from Luxembourg dividend income, tax withheld abroad from dividend and interest income received by a Luxembourg corporation (subject to limitations), and investment tax credits *(see "Tax incentives")*.

The main non-deductible taxes are corporate income tax, municipal business tax, net wealth tax as well as interest for late payment of said taxes.

Gifts
Gifts for scientific, charitable or public purposes and to institutions in the general interest are deductible, subject to a maximum of 20% of the net income or up to an amount of EUR 1,000,000 (the minimum being EUR 120) with a possibility to spread the deduction over two years.

Luxembourg

Group taxation

Tax unity

Luxembourg permits tax unity. Generally, the conditions to qualify for tax unity include that:

1. Each company is a fully taxable company that is resident in Luxembourg (the top entity may be a Luxembourg PE of a fully taxable non-resident company);
2. At least 95% of each subsidiary's capital is directly or indirectly held by the parent company;
3. Each company's fiscal year starts and ends on the same date; and
4. Tax unity is requested jointly by the top company and each of the subsidiary that becomes member of the Group.

The tax unity lasts for a five-year period and taxable income/loss is computed on the consolidated result. Tax losses that occurred before the consolidation period may be offset only against tax profits of the company that incurred the loss. Tax losses that are sustained by a group member during the consolidation period is compensated with the tax profits of the other group members. Tax losses arising during the consolidation period that exist after the consolidation period are attributed to the parent company.

Transfer pricing

No detailed rules with respect to the determination and documentation of transfer pricing in company groups have been currently implemented in Luxembourg law.

However and as a member of the OECD, Luxembourg applies the OECD transfer pricing guidelines.

Tax incentives

Inward and capital investment

Luxembourg tax law provides for various incentives with specific requirements, in the areas of risk-capital, audiovisual activities, environmental protection as well as research and development, professional training and recruitment of unemployed persons.

The most commonly used incentives are the investment tax credits. Luxembourg tax law provides for two types of investment tax credits.

First, a tax credit which amounts to 12% on the increase in investment in tangible depreciable assets made during the concerned year. The increase in investment of a year is computed as the difference between the current value of all qualifying assets and the reference value allocated to the same type of assets.

Independently, the company may benefit from a 6% tax credit on the first EUR 150,000 of qualifying new investments, and a 2% tax credit on the amount of new investments exceeding EUR 150,000 in tangible depreciable assets as well as investments in sanitary and central heating installation in hotel buildings and investments in buildings used for social activities. The above 6% and 2% rates are increased up to 8% and 4% for investments eligible for special depreciation (i.e., investments favouring the protection of the environment, the realisation of energy savings and the creation of employment for handicapped workers). However certain investments are excluded from the credit calculation, including investments in real property, intangible assets, and vehicles (unless specifically stated by the law).

Intellectual property (IP) regime

An IP regime has been introduced by the law of 21 December 2007 and is applicable to qualifying IP rights acquired or developed after 31 December 2007. This regime provides for an 80% tax exemption of the net income and gains deriving from the use and the right to use qualifying IP rights, under certain conditions. Qualifying IP rights include patents, trademarks, design, domain names, models and software copyrights.

An 80% deduction of net deemed income is available also under certain conditions for self-developed patents, which are used internally by the taxpayer.

The net capital gain realised upon disposal of the qualifying IP rights also benefits from the 80% exemption.

Finally, qualifying IP rights may be tax fully exempt for net wealth tax purposes under certain conditions.

Research and development (R&D) incentives

Effective as of 1 July 2009, a new legislation has been introduced in order to promote research, development and innovation within Luxembourg.

Luxembourg entities involved in innovative and R&D activities can benefit, in addition to the specific IP tax regime and general tax incentives, from financial support (e.g., cash grants or interest subsidies).

Innovation loans may be granted by the Société Nationale de Crédit et d'Investissement and may carry a fixed interest rate lower than the market rate. Financial support may also be granted, in the form of cash grants or interest subsidies.

R&D projects or programmes receive support up to a maximum eligibility (percentage of costs eligible for the incentives) depending on the size of the beneficiary (private research companies or organisations):

- Large (25% to 100% depending on the investment);
- Mid-size (35% to 100%); or
- Small (45% to 100%).

These incentives are available for:

- Experimental development;
- Experimental development and cooperation;
- Industrial research;
- Industrial research and cooperation; or
- Fundamental research.

Innovation in process and organisation and investment in innovation pools can benefit from support between 15% and 35% (50% for public research companies).

Promotion and development of innovation pools can benefit from support up to:

Luxembourg

- 50% for private organisations; or
- 75% for public research companies.

Research regarding technical feasibility if prior to experimental development can benefit from support of up to 40% or 50% and up to 65% or 75% if prior to experimental research.

Other incentives
Other incentives include the following:

1. Holding companies: Holding companies set up under the law of July 31 1929 (so called 1929 Holding Companies) generally are exempt from income taxes (corporate income tax, municipal business tax) and withholding tax on dividends paid. These holding companies are subject to the previously described annual subscription tax and to the general registration duty regime. Luxembourg generally provides for three types of 1929 Holding Companies: ordinary (as described above); billionaire holdings, which require minimum capitalisation of EUR 24 million and provide for further tax exemptions; and financial holdings, which provide for greater flexibility for intra-group financing. Due to a European Commission decision, Luxembourg has repealed the 1929 Holding Companies tax regime. Nevertheless, subject to certain conditions, 1929 Holding Companies established before 20 July 2006 (including billionaire holdings and financial holdings) are permitted to keep the benefits of this favourable tax regime until the end of 2010.
2. Investment funds: Investment funds resident in Luxembourg generally are exempt from corporate income tax, municipal business tax, and withholding tax on dividends. These investment funds are subject to the previously described subscription tax and to the general registration duty regime.
3. Financial participation company (Soparfi): A Soparfi ("Société de Participation Financière") is not a specific type of company, rather it is a special tax regime for a resident company that holds and manages the shareholdings of subsidiaries. Unlike the 1929 holding company regimes, a Soparfi is not tax exempt, however, it does benefit from Luxembourg's double tax treaties, EU Directives (e.g., Parent-Subsidiary Directive), the domestic participation exemption on dividends received and capital gains on qualifying participations (as discussed above).
4. Société de gestion du Patrimoine Familial" (SPF). The SPF has been tailored to enter the private sphere of individuals for the purpose of wealth management. Its corporate objective is restricted to the acquisition, holding, management and disposal of financial assets, to the exclusion of any commercial activity. As a general rule, an SPF is exempt from Luxembourg taxation on income and wealth tax in Luxembourg. A yearly subscription tax of 0.25% is due on the basis of paid-up capital, share premium and excessive debts. It, however, is capped at EUR 125,000. No withholding tax applies on dividends distributed by an SPF. Non-resident investors are not taxed in Luxembourg on dividends paid by a SPF or on capital gains realised on shares in a SPF.
5. Securitisation companies, which are incorporated under the law of 22 March 2004, are subject to normal corporate taxation. A securitisation company is a company which carries out securitisation activities or which participates in securitisation transactions. Securitisation companies are taxed based on their net accounting profit (i.e., gross accounting profits minus expenses). However, the commitment to remunerate the security holders (both capital and debt) issued by the securitisation

company qualifies as interest on debt even if paid as return on equity. Securitisation companies are not subject to net wealth tax in Luxembourg.

6. Financial services companies: Banks, securities depositaries, insurance and reinsurance companies as well as other financial service companies may benefit from preferential regulations when establishing their taxable basis for corporate income tax (e.g., provision for the neutralisation of unrealised exchange gains; general banking risk provision; provision for guarantee of deposits; mathematical reserves; and/or catastrophe reserves).

7. Shipping companies: Luxembourg-resident shipping companies are not subject to municipal business tax, and can benefit from investment tax credits and accelerated depreciation (even for used assets).

Withholding taxes

Dividends paid by a Luxembourg fully taxable company to its corporate shareholders resident in a treaty country, which hold or commit themselves to hold a participation of at least 10% in the Luxembourg company (or shares with an acquisition price of at least EUR 1.2 million) for an interrupted period of at least 12 months may be exempt from withholding tax (see "Note 2" for more details).

The following taxes are withheld on payments made. The withholding tax due on dividends paid to residents of a treaty country cannot exceed the non-treaty rate.

Recipient	Portfolio (1) %	Substantial Holdings %	Interest (3) %	Royalties (4) %
Resident corporations	15	0 (2)	–	–
Resident individuals	15	15	10 (5)	–
Non-resident corporations and individuals:				
Non-treaty	15	15/0 (2)	–	–
Treaty (2,6):				
Austria	15	5/0 (7)	–	–
Azerbaijan	10	5/0 (8)	–	–
Belgium	15	10/0 (9)	–	–
Brazil	25	15/0 (10)	–	–
Bulgaria	15	5/0 (7)	–	–
Canada	15	5/0 (20)	–	–
China, P.R. (11)	10	5/0 (7)	–	–
Czech Republic	15	5/0 (7)	–	–
Denmark	15	5/0 (7)	–	–
Estonia	15	5/0 (7)	–	–
Finland	15	5/0 (13)	–	–
France	15	5/0 (13)	–	–
Georgia	10	5/0 (23)	–	–
Germany	15	10/0 (21)	–	–
Greece	7.5	7.5/0	–	–
Hungary	15	5/0 (7)	–	–
Hong Kong	10	0 (11)	–	–

Luxembourg

Recipient	Portfolio (1) %	Substantial Holdings %	Interest (3) %	Royalties (4) %
Iceland	15	5/0 (7)	–	–
India	10	0	–	–
Indonesia	15	10/0 (7)	–	–
Ireland, Rep. of	15	5/0 (21)	–	–
Israel	15	5/0 (22)	–	–
Italy	15	0	–	–
Japan	15	5/0 (16)	–	–
Korea, Rep. of	15	10/0 (7)	–	–
Latvia	10	5/0 (7)	–	–
Lithuania	15	5/0 (7)	–	–
Malaysia	10	5/0 (17)	–	–
Malta	15	5/0 (7)	–	–
Mauritius	10	5/0 (10)	–	–
Mexico	15	5/0 (10)	–	–
Moldavia	10	5/0 (24)	–	–
Mongolia	15	5/0 (17)	–	–
Morocco	15	10/0 (7)	–	–
Netherlands	15	2.5/0 (7)	–	–
Norway	15	5/0 (7)	–	–
Poland	15	5/0 (7)	–	–
Portugal	15	15/0	–	–
Romania	15	5/0 (7)	–	–
Russia	15	10/0 (18)	–	–
San Marino	15	0 (10)	–	–
Singapore	10	5/0 (19)	–	–
Slovak Republic	15	5/0 (7)	–	–
Slovenia	15	5/0 (7)	–	–
South Africa	15	5/0 (7)	–	–
Spain	15	5/0 (7)	–	–
Sweden	15	0 (10)	–	–
Switzerland	15	5/0 (7)	–	–
Thailand	15	5/0 (7)	–	–
Trinidad and Tobago	10	5/0 (10)	–	–
Tunisia	10	10/0	–	–
Turkey	20	5/0 (7)	–	–
United Arab Emirates	10	5/0 (10)	–	–
United Kingdom	15	5/0 (15)	–	–
United States	15	5/0 (14)	–	–
Uzbekistan	15	5/0 (7)	–	–
Vietnam	15	10/5/0 (12)	–	–

Notes

These notes are not extensive. The full text of the double tax treaty should be checked for a comprehensive view on the conditions of applications of reduced rates.

The numbers in parentheses refer to the notes below:

1. Dividends paid by Luxembourg 1929 Holding Companies benefiting from grandfathering rules or investment funds are exempt from withholding taxes.
2. Under Luxembourg domestic law (i.e., so called "participation exemption" regime), no withholding tax is levied on dividends paid by a Luxembourg qualifying subsidiary to an entity which is:
   - A collective entity falling under article 2 of the amended version of the Parent-Subsidiary Directive;
   - A Luxembourg resident joint-stock company, which is fully taxable and does not take one of the forms listed in the appendix to the paragraph 10 of article 166 of the Luxembourg income tax law;
   - A permanent establishment of a collective entity falling under the previous categories;
   - A collective entity that is resident in a State with which Luxembourg has concluded a double tax treaty and which is fully liable to a tax corresponding to the Luxembourg corporate income tax, or a domestic permanent establishment of such an entity; or
   - A Swiss resident joint-stock company that is subject to Swiss corporate income tax without benefiting from any exemption;
   - A joint-stock company or a cooperative society which is resident in a EEA Member State (other than a EU Member State) and is fully liable to a tax corresponding to the Luxembourg corporate income tax; or
   - A permanent establishment of a joint-stock company or of a cooperative society which is resident in a EEA Member State (other than a EU Member State), and at the date on which the income is made available, the beneficiary has been holding or undertakes to hold, directly, for an uninterrupted period of at least 12 months, a participation of at least 10%, or with an acquisition price of at least EUR 1.2 million in the share capital of the income debtor.

Qualifying shareholders need to be fully taxable collective entities subject in their country of residence to a tax similar to the one imposed by Luxembourg. As a general rule, this requirement is met if the foreign tax is compulsory levied at an effective rate of at least 10.5%, on a basis similar to the Luxembourg one. The term of "collective entities" has replaced "capital company" as of 2005 to take into account that the participation exemption is not restricted to capital companies.

The entities listed in appendix to the paragraph 10 of article 166 Luxembourg Income Tax Law are the following:

a. Companies under Luxembourg law known as "société anonyme", "société en commandite par actions", "société à responsabilité limitée","société coopérative", "société coopérative organisée comme une société anonyme", "association d'assurances mutuelles", "association d'épargne-pension", "entreprise de nature commerciale, industrielle ou minière de l'État, des communes, des syndicats de communes, des établissements publics et des autres personnes morales de droit public", as well as other companies constituted under Luxembourg law;
b. Companies under German law known as "Aktiengesellschaft", "Kommanditgesellschaft auf Aktien", "Gesellschaft mit beschränkter Haftung", "Versicherungsverein auf Gegenseitigkeit", "Erwerbs- und Wirtschaftsgenossenschaft", "Betriebe gewerblicher Art von juristischen Personen des öffentlichen Rechts";
c. Companies under Austrian law known as "Aktiengesellschaft", "Gesellschaft mit beschränkter Haftung", "Versicherungsvereine auf Gegenseitigkeit", "Erwerbs- und Wirtschaftsgenossenschaften", "Betriebe gewerblicher Art von Körperschaften des öffentlichen Rechts", "Sparkassen";
d. Companies under Belgian law known as "société anonyme"/"naamloze vennootschap", "société en commandite par actions"/"commanditaire vennootschap op aandelen", "société privée à responsabilité limitée"/"besloten vennootschap met beperkte aansprakelijkheid", "société coopérative à responsabilité limitée"/"coöperatieve vennootschap met beperkte aansprakelijkheid", "société coopérative à responsabilité

L

Luxembourg

illimitée"/"coöperatieve vennootschap met onbeperkte aansprakelijkheid", "société en nom collectif"/"vennootschap onder firma", "société en commandite simple"/"gewone commanditaire vennootschap", as well as public undertakings which have adopted one of the abovementioned legal forms;

d'. Companies under Bulgarian law known as "събирателното дружество", "командитното дружество", "дружеството с ограничена отговорност", "акционерното дружество", "командитното дружество с акции", "неперсонифицирано дружество", "кооперации", "кооперативни съюзи", "държавни предприятия";

e. Companies under Cypriot law know as "εταιρείες";

f. Companies under Danish law known as "aktieselskab" et "anpartsselskab";

g. Companies under Spanish law known as "sociedad anónima", "sociedad comanditaria por acciones", "sociedad de responsabilidad limitada", as well as public law bodies which operate under private law;

h. Companies under Estonian law known as "täisühing", "usaldusühing", "osaühing", "aktsiaselts", "tulundusühistu";

i. Companies under Finnish law known as "osakeyhtiö/aktiebolag", "osuuskunta"/"andelslag", "säästöpankki"/"sparbank" and "vakuutusyhtiö"/"försäkringsb olag";

j. Companies under French law known as "société anonyme", "société en commandite par actions", "société à responsabilité limitée", "société par actions simplifiée", "société d'assurance mutuelle", the "caisses d'épargne et de prévoyance", the "coopératives" and "unions de coopératives", as well as industrial and commercial public establishments and undertakings ;

k. Companies under Greek law known as "ανώνυμη εταιρεία", "εταιρεία περιορισμένης ευθύνης (Ε.Π.Ε.)";

l. Companies under Hungarian law known as "közkereseti társaság", "betéti társaság", "közös vállalat", "korlátolt felelősségű társaság", "részvénytársaság", "egyesülés", "szövetkezet";

m. Companies incorporated or existing under Irish law, bodies registered under the Industrial and Provident Societies Acts, building societies incorporated under the Building Societies Acts and trustee savings banks within the meaning of the Trustee Savings Banks Act, 1989;

n. Companies under Italian law known as "società per azioni", "società in accomandita per azioni", "società a responsibilità limitata", "società cooperative", "società di mutua assicurazione", as well as private and public entities whose activity is wholly or principally commercial;

o. Companies under Latvian law known as "akciju sabiedrība", "sabiedrība ar ierobežotu atbildību";

p. Companies incorporated under the law of Lithuania;

q. Companies under Maltese law known as "Kumpaniji ta' Responsabilita' Limitata", "Soċjetajiet en commandite li lkapital tagħhom maqsum f'azzjonijiet";

r. Companies under Dutch law known as "naamloze vennnootschap", "besloten vennootschap met beperkte aansprakelijkheid", "Open commanditaire vennootschap", "Coöperatie", "onderlinge waarborgmaatschappij", "Fonds voor gemene rekening", "vereniging op coöperatieve grondslag" and "vereniging welke op onderlinge grondslag als verzekeraar of keredietinstelling optreed";

s. Companies under Polish law known as "spółka akcyjna", "spółka z ograniczoną odpowiedzialnością";

t. Commercial companies or civil law companies having a commercial form and cooperatives and public undertakings incorporated in accordance with Portuguese law;

t'. Companies under Romanian law known as "societăţi pe acţiuni", "societăţi în comandită pe acţiuni", "societăţi cu răspundere limitată";

u. Companies incorporated under the law of the United Kingdom;

v. Companies under Slovak law known as akciová spoločnosť", "spoločnosť s ručením obmedzeným", "komanditná spoločnosť";

w. Companies under Slovenian law known as "delniška družba", "komanditna družba", "družba z omejeno odgovornostjo";

x. Companies under Swedish law known as "aktiebolag", "försäkringsaktiebolag", "ekonomiska föreningar", "sparbanker", "ömsesidiga försäkringsbolag";

y. Companies under Czech law known as "akciová společnost", "společnost s ručením omezeným"; and

z. Companies incorporated under Council Regulation (EC) No 2157/2001 of 8 October 2001 on the Statute for a European company (SE) and Council Directive 2001/86/CE supplementing the Statute for a European company with regard to the involvement of employees and cooperative societies incorporated under Council Regulation (EC) No 1435/2003 of 22 July 2003 on the Statute for a European Cooperative Society (SCE) and Council Directive 2003/72/CE of 22 July 2003 supplementing the Statute for a European Cooperative Society with regard to the involvement of employees.

3. Interest paid to non-residents generally is not subject to withholding tax in Luxembourg. However, interest that represents a right to profit participation on a bond may be assimilated as a dividend and subject to withholding tax. Further analysis should be made to determine the applicable reduced rate on the basis of the treaty (i.e., pursuant to dividend or interest clause) The withholding tax that may be due as a consequence of the EU Savings Directive (Council Directive 2003/48/EC dated June 3 2003) is not mentioned.

4. Royalties paid to non-residents are not subject to withholding tax in Luxembourg without considerations whether the companies are associated or not.

5. Since 1 January 2006, a withholding tax of 10% is withheld on defined interest income paid by a Luxembourg paying agent to resident individuals. Interest indirectly cashed through investment funds are out of the scope of this withholding tax.

6. Double tax treaties have been concluded with Albania, Argentina (limited scope), Armenia, Bahrain, Barbados, Cyprus, Kazakhstan, Kuwait, Kyrgyzstan, Lebanon, Liechtenstein, Macedonia, Monaco, Pakistan, Qatar, Serbia and Montenegro, Syria and Ukraine, but are not yet in force.

7. The recipient company holds at least 25% of the Luxembourg company's capital. In some rare cases a holding period requirement may have to be met as well (e.g., Spain, Switzerland).

8. The recipient company owns at least 30% of the company's capital and the equivalent of an acquisition price of USD 300,000.

9. The recipient company owns a 25% investment or the equivalent of an acquisition price of EUR 6,197,338. The investments may be held by several Belgian companies, provided one owns at least 50% of the shares of each of the others. The investment must be held since the beginning of the financial year of the recipient of the dividends.

10. The recipient company holds at least 10% of the Luxembourg company's capital. A holding period requirement has to be met for Sweden and San Marino.

11. Hong Kong is not covered by the Luxembourg–P.R. China double taxation treaty. A double tax treaty between Hong-Kong and Luxembourg was signed on November 2007 and has entered into force on January 2009. For dividends paid to Hong Kong companies, no withholding tax is levied if the recipient company holds at least 10% of the Luxembourg company's capital or a participation of a least EUR 1.2 million.

12. The rate of 5% of withholding tax on the gross amount of the dividends applies where the effective recipient company owns directly or indirectly at least 50% of the share capital of the paying company or has contributed more than USD 10 million or the equivalent in Luxembourg or in Vietnamese currency, in the capital of the company paying the dividends; the rate of 10% of withholding tax on the gross amount of the dividends applies where the beneficial owner is a company which holds directly or indirectly at least 25% but less than 50% of the capital of the company paying the dividends and has contributed not more than USD 10 million, or the equivalent in Luxembourg or Vietnamese currency, in the capital of the company paying the dividends.

13. The recipient company owns directly or indirectly 25% of the company's capital. Indirect participation includes the holding through several treaty resident companies located in the same country provided one owns more than 50% of the shares of each others.

14. The substantial holding is taxable at 5% where the recipient US company owns at least 10% of the voting stock of the paying company. No withholding tax is levied when the US company has held during an uninterrupted period of two years a direct shareholding of at

Luxembourg

least 25% of the voting power of the paying company and certain conditions regarding the nature of activities performed by the distributing company are met.

15. The recipient company owns directly or indirectly 25% of the company's voting rights. Indirect participation includes the holding through several treaty resident companies located in the same country provided one owns more than 50% of the voting rights of each others.

16. The recipient company holds at least 25% of the Luxembourg company's voting shares during the period of six months immediately before the end of the accounting period in which the distribution of profits takes place.

17. The dividends are taxable at a rate of 5% if the beneficial owner is a company that holds directly at least 10% of the capital of the company paying the dividends. No withholding tax is levied when the beneficiary company has held during the 12 preceding months a direct shareholding of at least 25% of the capital of the paying company. The holding period must be met before the date of distribution of the dividend. Furthermore, certain conditions regarding the nature of activities performed by the company must be met.

18. The recipient company holds at least 30% of the Luxembourg company's capital and the acquisition price reaches at least EUR 75,000 (or equivalent).

19. The recipient company holds at least 10% of the Luxembourg company's capital. Dividends paid to the Government of Singapore are exempt.

20. The beneficial owner is a company (other than a partnership) which controls directly or indirectly at least 10% of the voting power in the company paying the dividends.

21. The recipient company holds at least 25% of the Luxembourg company's voting shares (Germany/Luxembourg) or company's voting power (Ireland/Luxembourg).

22. The rate of 5% of withholding tax on the gross amount of dividends applies where the recipient company holds at least 10% of the Luxembourg company's capital.

23. The rate of withholding tax is 5% if the beneficial owner is a company that holds directly at least 10% of the capital of the company paying the dividends and made an investment in the capital of the paying company of more than EUR 100,000 or the equivalent in Georgian currency. No withholding tax is levied when the beneficiary company holds directly at least 50% of the capital of the company paying the dividends and made an investment in the capital of the paying company of more than EUR 2,000,000 or the equivalent in Georgian currency.

24. The recipient company holds at least 20% of the Luxembourg company's capital.

Tax administration

Returns

Companies must file their tax returns at the latest on 31 May of each year following the calendar year during which the income was earned.

Assessments are issued after the end of the tax year and normally can be finalised within five years, although the delay may extend to 10 years, if the declaration is found to be incomplete or inexact, with or without the intention of fraud. Once issued, the tax assessment notice is in principle final (unless new facts come to light).

From 1 January 2009, tax offices also may issue a tax assessment based on the tax return filed by the taxpayer, without having to perform an immediate review of the file. The tax office will then have a five year period to perform a tax audit and issue a final tax assessment, if required.

Payment of tax

Quarterly tax advances must be paid. These payments are fixed by the tax administration on the basis of the tax assessed for the preceding year, or on the basis of the estimate for the first year. This estimate is given by the company pursuant to the request of the Luxembourg tax authorities.

For more information, contact:

Pat Wong
PricewaterhouseCoopers (Macau) Limited
Avenida Doutor Mario Soares
Bank of China Building
29/F
Macau, SAR
Tel: +853 8799 5122
Email: pat.lk.wong@hk.pwc.com

Significant developments

Protocol to the People's Republic of China/Macau double taxation arrangement (DTA)

The Central Government of the People's Republic of China (the PRC) and the Government of the Macau Special Administrative Region (SAR) signed the Protocol (Protocol) to the PRC/Macau DTA on 15 July 2009. The Protocol will be effective upon completion of the necessary ratification procedures by both parties, and will be applicable to income arising from the 1st of January of the year following the year in which the Protocol will become effective.

The PRC/Macau DTA was signed in 2003. Some of the provisions of the PRC/Macau DTA are less favourable than those of the PRC/Hong Kong DTA. Under the Protocol, the treaty-based rates for withholding tax on dividends, interest, and royalty will be reduced. Further, the criteria for determination of a service permanent establishment and certain criteria for capital gains exemption under the PRC/Macau DTA will be clarified. In summary, the Protocol will bring the PRC/Macau DTA broadly in line with the PRC/Hong Kong DTA. This will no doubt increase the competitiveness of the Macau SAR and provide added incentives for Macau companies to do business or invest in the PRC. Nevertheless, as Macau adopts a worldwide taxation system in its domestic tax regime, consideration should be given as to whether the use of a Macau company as a holding company for investments in the PRC is favourable from a tax perspective.

Exchange of information

On 11 August 2009 the Legislative Assembly passed Law 20/2009, which governs the exchange of information by the Macau SAR with other tax jurisdictions within the scope of bilateral tax treaties or arrangements. Law 20/2009 is effective from 15 September 2009 and its objective is to promote the transparency of the Macau tax administration and to demonstrate the Macau SAR's willingness to cooperate with treaty partners in combating tax avoidance or tax evasion activities.

The information to be exchanged under Law 20/2009 is strictly confined to information collected for tax purposes only, and includes the following:

- Information collected within the jurisdiction of the Macau Finance Bureau (MFB); and
- Information collected by the MFB from financial institutions that are governed by the Macau Financial System Act and offshore institutions that are governed by the Macau Offshore Law (the Institutions).

M

Macau

At present, the only bilateral tax arrangements/treaties entered into by the Macau SAR which have come into effect are with the PRC and Portugal. However, in response to the Organisation for Economic Co-operation and Development's (OECD) request for cooperation in combating tax avoidance or evasion activities, and to prevent the Macau SAR from being viewed as a tax haven, it is believed that more comprehensive tax arrangements/treaties or tax information exchange agreements (TIEAs) will be signed between the Macau SAR and other tax jurisdictions in the near future.

As the information of a Macau taxpayer is becoming more transparent under comprehensive tax arrangements/treaties or TIEAs, it is important for Macau companies with cross-border transactions to perform periodic tax health checks to ensure that tax planning arrangements, if any have been put in place in the past, remain technically defensible. As Macau offshore companies continue to be a focus of investigations for many tax jurisdictions, it is important to ensure that such companies have adequate commercial substance in Macau and the companies' transfer pricing policies are supported by appropriate transfer pricing documentation and transfer pricing studies.

Taxes on corporate income

Complementary income (corporate) tax is imposed on the total income earned by Macau registered entities, irrespective of where their residence or headquarters are situated, and irrespective of the nature of the income. The exception to the foregoing is rental income from leasing of immovable properties located in Macau, which is taxed separately under the Property Tax Regime.

According to the Macau Complementary Tax Law, complementary tax is imposed on a progressive rate scale ranging from 3% to 9% for taxable profits below or equal to Macau Pataca (MOP) 300,000 and 12% for taxable profits over MOP 300,000. Taxable profits below MOP 32,000 are exempt from tax.

According to the Budget for the financial year 2010, which has already been approved by the Legislative Assembly (2010 Approved Budget), the tax-free income threshold for Macau Complementary Tax has been increased from MOP 32,000 to MOP 200,000 for income derived in the financial year 2009 (the next MOP 100,000 of taxable income is taxed at 9% and taxable income in excess of MOP 300,000 is taxed at 12%). Such increase in the tax-free income threshold has been granted since the tax year 2007. While it is generally believed that the direction of the Macau government policy would remain stable at least for several years, the changes in tax-free income threshold and the tax brackets beyond the tax year 2009 are subject to approval by the Legislative Assembly on an annual basis, unless such amendments are written into the relevant tax laws.

Types of taxpayers
Group A taxpayers
Taxpayer entities whose registered capital reached MOP 1,000,000 or more, or whose average taxable profits reached MOP 500,000 per year in three consecutive years will automatically become Group A taxpayers in the fourth year. A taxpayer entity can also elect to become a Group A taxpayer by filing a Group A declaration form. Profits are assessed based on the actual accounting income after making necessary tax adjustments.

M

Group B taxpayers

Group B taxpayers refer to any individual or any other form of companies not mentioned above and those taxpayers that do not keep detailed accounting records. Profits are assessed on a deemed basis if the reported income is below the internal parameters set by the Macau Finance Bureau for taxpayers in similar industries.

Corporate residence

Corporate residence is generally determined by reference to the place of establishment. The exception to the foregoing is a Macau offshore company or a Macau offshore financial institution that is established under Law 58/99/M. Such a Macau offshore company or financial institution is not considered as a Macau tax resident in the context of the comprehensive tax arrangement/agreement entered into between the Macau SAR and the PRC and Portugal, respectively.

There is no specific definition of permanent establishment in the Macau Complementary Tax Law. Technically speaking, there are two major criteria for determining whether a foreign entity should be subject to Macau Complementary Tax and the key phrases are "engaging in commercial/industrial activities" and/or "rendering services in Macau". These phrases are again not defined. Generally, if an overseas company is engaged in commercial/industrial activities in Macau, the resultant gain from such commercial/industrial activities will be subject to Macau Complementary Tax.

Other taxes

Property tax

Property tax is imposed on the owner of buildings situated in Macau. This is first payable after acquiring a property or upon the expiry of the property tax exemption period, if applicable. Different exemption periods are granted, depending on the location of the property. Additional exemption periods may apply in special cases. For leased properties, property tax is charged at 16% on the actual rental income. For self-use properties, property tax is charged at 10% on the official rateable value as established by the appointed committee of the MFB. A surcharge of 5% is levied on the tax payable in both cases. If the property is not occupied, the owner can apply for an exemption from property tax, the approval of which is entirely at the discretion of the MFB. Rental income derived from leasing of real estate is not subject to complementary tax, and therefore related expenses are not deductible.

A deduction of up to 10% of the rental income or actual repair and maintenance expense, whichever is the lesser, shall be allowed upon approval by the MFB to cover repairs and maintenance expenses incurred by the taxpayer.

According to the 2010 Approved Budget, there is a standard MOP 3,500 reduction in the property tax liabilities assessed in the financial year 2010 for both self-used and rental properties.

Annual industrial tax

All commercial or industrial operations carried out in Macau are subject to industrial tax at the beginning of each year. The amount taxed is dependent upon the nature of the business. For example, according to the Industrial Tax Code, the tax amounts applicable to various operations are shown below.

Macau

Type of business	Tax (MOP)
Commercial banks	80,000
Construction companies	500
Hotels	500
Insurance companies	500
Textile companies	500

The above annual industrial tax has been exempted since 2002. This exemption, if extended, will be published by the Macau Government on an annual basis. The exemption has been extended for 2010.

Special gaming tax
Special gaming tax is levied at 35% on the gross gaming revenue derived by gaming concessionaires authorised to carry on the operation of games of chance in the Macau SAR under Law 16/2001.

Tourism tax
Tourism tax is imposed at the rate of 5% on bill of services, excluding telecommunication and laundry services, and service charges of up to 10%, rendered in Macau by establishments such as hotels, guest houses, dancing halls, night clubs, massage/sauna parlours, gymnasium, karaoke and the like. Such tax is generally borne by consumers.

Tourism tax for restaurants has been exempted since 2002. This exemption, if extended, will be published by the Macau Government on an annual basis.

Consumption tax (excise duty)
Consumption tax is imposed only on specific goods entering into Macau, as follows:

* Tobacco; and
* Spirits.

There are two methods for determining the amount of consumption tax payable, by quantity or by value. The former method of assessment is based on the weight or volume of goods and the latter is based on the price of the goods imported into Macau. The rate of consumption tax varies depending on the classification of the imported goods.

Motor vehicle tax
Motor vehicle tax is imposed on the sale of new motor vehicles to consumers and the importation of new motor vehicles for self-use. Exemptions are available to certain persons and organisations and for certain specific usages. Generally, motor vehicle tax is levied based on the listed selling prices as registered with the MFB. The rate of motor vehicle tax varies depending on the type of motor vehicle and its value.

Stamp duty
Stamp duty is payable on certain types of documents and stampable transactions at a small fixed amount, or at rates ranging from 0.1% to 10% on the value represented by the documents and transactions. The charge to stamp duty has been extended to property transfers and the irrevocable transfer of certain assets. Stamp duty at progressive rates ranging from 1% to 3% is payable on transfer of immovable property

with a surcharge of 5% on the duty payable, resulting in effective stamp duty rates of 1.05% to 3.15%. Where the transfer of the immovable property is preceded by a private sale and purchase agreement that is not registered and hence not legally enforceable, an additional 0.5% stamp duty on the transfer consideration is payable. The irrevocable transfer of certain assets without consideration is subject to a 5% stamp duty.

Stamp duty for insurance policies written or renewed and stamp duty for banking transactions have been exempt since 2005. This exemption will continue to be available in the financial year 2010.

According to the 2010 Approved Budget, an adult who holds a Macau permanent resident identity card and who does not own any properties other than one car-parking space is eligible to enjoy exemption on stamp duty levied on the purchase of a residential property for self-use purposes for the first MOP 3 million of the transfer consideration. The transfer consideration in excess of MOP 3 million will be subject to stamp duty. The stamp duty exemption has a three-year lock-in period, such that unless the residential property so purchased is transferred as part of a deceased estate, the purchaser will have to pay back the stamp duty that was originally exempt on the purchased property if such residential property is sold within three years after the stamp duty exemption granting date.

The stamp duty on admission tickets for performances, exhibitions, and any kind of entertainment programmes has been exempted for the tax year 2010. This exemption, if extended, will be published by the Macau Government on an annual basis.

Land rent
According to the 2010 Approved Budget, land rent below MOP 100 shall not be collected by the Macau Finance Bureau in the financial year 2010. However, any such amount already collected shall not be refunded.

Branch income

Branch income is subject to tax at the same rate as that for corporations. The taxable income is ascertained based on branch accounts.

Income determination

The paragraphs below describe the tax acceptable treatments under the prevailing Complementary Tax Law and are for reference only.

Inventory valuation
Inventory should be stated at actual cost, and conformity between book and tax reporting is required. Market selling price or replacement cost is allowed only in special circumstances and prior approval of the Director of the MFB is required for adoption of such inventory valuation methods. The write-down of inventory values is not permitted.

Capital gains
Gains or losses from the realisation of capital assets of a corporation taxpayer are treated as current revenue or expense items for complementary tax purposes.

Macau

Inter-company dividends

Dividends from all sources are subject to complementary tax in the hands of a recipient incorporated in Macau unless the dividends were paid out of profits that have been taxed at the corporate level in Macau. Where dividend to shareholders is paid out of profits of a Macau entity that have not been taxed in Macau, complementary tax will technically be charged on the dividend distribution to the shareholders, except for distribution of tax exempt profits of approved offshore institutions, where complementary tax, in practice, has not been charged by the MFB to date.

Foreign income

Companies incorporated in Macau are subject to complementary tax on all income, wherever received or credited. Currently, double taxation relief is available under the respective avoidance of double taxation agreement/arrangement that Macau has with Portugal and the People's Republic of China.

Deductions

Depreciation and depletion

An initial allowance of 20% is granted on buildings. The rates of tax depreciation are detailed in Decree-Law No.4/90/M, dated 5 March 1990. The Decree-Law prescribes the maximum annual tax depreciation rates and the number of years of asset life for different asset classes under the straight-line method. For illustration, the maximum depreciation rates and the maximum useful life currently applicable to the general types of assets are set out below.

	Maximum annual percentage rate	Maximum number of years
Tangible assets:		
Industrial buildings	4	50
Office and residential buildings	2	100
Machinery and installations, air conditioning, elevators, equipment	10–20	20–10
Tools	20–33.3	10–6
Laboratory, telex and interior telephone equipment, furniture, filing systems, typewriters, and accounting machines	16.66–25	12–8
Computer hardware	25	8
Office installations	14.29	14
Trucks	14.29	14
Automobiles	20	10
Intangible assets, pre-operating expenses incurred prior to commencement of business	33.33	6
Deferred expenses arising in connection with increases in share capital, changes in form of business enterprises, issuance of debentures, marketing and other studies, and financial expenses incurred for the acquisition or own production of fixed assets prior to completion	33.33	6
Patents	10	20
Manufacturing licences, concessionary agreements, and similar rights	*	*
Trademark	*	*

* At the discretion of the authorities.

In the case of commercial and industrial buildings, depreciation is not allowed for the value attributable to the cost of the freehold land. Where the value of the freehold land cannot be determined from the total cost of land and buildings, a portion equal to 20% is deemed to be attributable to the land value for the purpose of determining the value of buildings to be depreciated.

Depreciation can be claimed either on a prorated basis in accordance with the prescribed annual rates for assets that are not acquired at the beginning of the financial year or on an annual basis.

The cost of repairs and maintenance exceeding 10% of the acquisition cost of the asset in a given year is deemed to be expenses of a capital nature, and should be capitalised and depreciated over the remaining life of the asset.

Net operating losses
Agreed tax losses can be carried forward for three consecutive years for Group A taxpayers. Group B taxpayers are not allowed to carry their tax losses forward to future years.

Payments to foreign affiliates/foreign firms
The regulations make no specific mention of royalties, interest, and service fees paid to foreign affiliates. The MFB generally monitors the deductibility of such payments. Payments to foreign service providers for consulting services or construction-related services are not deductible if such consulting contracts are not properly registered in Macau.

Other significant items
- The amount provided against doubtful trade receivables is an allowable tax deduction, but the provision cannot exceed 2% of the total receivables except in the case of banks, where the minimum provisions required under the local banking regulations are fully tax-deductible.
- Debts considered uncollectible may be written off only when adequate proof can be shown, usually by way of bankruptcy court proceedings.
- An amount provided against stock obsolescence of up to 3% of the total stock value at year-end is allowed as a tax deduction.
- A deduction of up to 0.2% of the company's turnover is allowable for donations to charitable organisations recognised by the tax authorities.
- Staff social welfare expenses paid for the benefit of employees, for example canteens and libraries, are fully tax-deductible.
- The employer's contribution to the staff provident fund legally registered in Macau is fully tax-deductible up to 15% of the employees' basic salary.
- Tax fines are not deductible.
- Losses arising from insurable risks are not allowable as a tax deduction.

In addition to the above, the assessor is empowered to disallow any business expenses, for example entertainment, and travelling, where the amount incurred is considered to be excessive.

M

Macau

Group taxation

There is no provision for group taxation in Macau.

Tax incentives

Capital investment
A 50% reduction in complementary tax and stamp duty on certain transactions, as well as exemptions from annual industrial tax and property tax (up to periods prescribed by the MFB) are allowable for taxpayers in the manufacturing industry (as defined in the Decree Law) whose capital investment is aimed at the introduction of new products or high technology, improvement of productivity, and increase in exports of goods to new markets.

Where profits are retained in reserves and reinvested in installation of new equipment within the following three financial years, the reinvested reserves can be deducted from taxable profits, provided that the reinvested reserves are attributable to profits earned from normal business operations and the investment is considered to be beneficial for the economic development of Macau.

Offshore services business
Profits derived by approved offshore institutions from prescribed offshore service-related activities are exempt from all forms of taxes, such as complementary tax, annual industrial tax (currently exempt for all taxpayers) and stamp duties. By application, the executives, staff at a supervisory level and/or specialised technicians who have obtained a residency permit in Macau are exempt from professional tax for three calendar years from the date the exemption application is approved.

Investment in touristic facility
Additional incentives such as an extended property tax exemption period, exemption from annual industrial tax, reduction in stamp duty, as well as acceleration of depreciation for complementary tax purposes are available to owners of facilities that qualified as touristic facilities.

Withholding taxes (WHT)

Currently, there is no provision in the tax regulations to withhold taxes for any payments made by domestic corporations to overseas companies.

Tax treaties
A comprehensive DTA was entered into between the Macau SAR and the PRC Government on 27 December 2003. Subsequently, a Protocol to the DTA was signed on 15 July 2009. The Protocol will be effective upon completion of the necessary ratification procedures by both parties, and will be applicable to income arising from the 1st of January of the year following the year in which the Protocol will become effective. The following are some of the features of the DTA:

* Withholding tax on dividends is generally levied at a rate of 10% and the rate will be reduced to 5% pursuant to the Protocol where the beneficial owner is a company directly owning at least 25% of the capital of the company that pays the dividend.

- Withholding tax on interest is generally levied at a rate of 10% and the rate is reduced to 7% for payments made to general banks or financial institutions, or 0% for payments made to recognised banks or financial institutions. Pursuant to the Protocol, the rate will be reduced to 7% for general cases and 0% for payments made to recognised banks or financial institutions.
- Withholding tax rate on royalties is 10% and will be reduced to 7% pursuant to the Protocol.
- Gains arising from the alienation of shares representing a participation of not more than 25% of the shares in a non-real property company which is a resident of one contracting state will be taxable only in the state in which the alienator is a resident. In other words, there is an exemption in the investee country for gains arising from the sale of portfolio investments situated in that country.
- The DTA also covers business profits, income from dependent and independent personal services, income of artists or athletes, teachers, researchers, students and apprentices, as well as income for government services.

In addition, a DTA is in effect between Macau and Portugal. DTAs with Belgium and Mozambique have been signed but are not effective until the necessary ratification procedures are completed.

The Macau SAR also entered into a Closer Economic Partnership Arrangement (CEPA) with the PRC Government on 17 October 2003, which came into effect on 1 January 2004. Supplements I to VII to CEPA have been promulgated subsequently to broaden or update the original CEPA. The content of the Macau SAR/PRC CEPA is similar to the CEPA between the Hong Kong SAR and the PRC Government.

Tax administration

Returns
Assessments are made by the MFB upon review of the tax returns, which must be lodged before 31 March or 30 June of each year for Group B or Group A taxpayers, respectively. The Macau tax year is on a calendar-year basis.

Payment of tax
A provisional tax payment calculated based on the declared taxable profit for a Group A taxpayer or final assessed profits for a Group B taxpayer is payable in two equal instalments in September and November. However, if the amount is not greater than MOP 3,000, payment would be requested in one lump sum amount in September. For Group A taxpayers, a final tax assessment would be issued upon the completion of tax assessment by the MFB.

Statute of limitation
The statute of limitation period is five assessment years from the relevant year of assessment for both Group A and Group B taxpayers.

M

Macau

Other issues

Choice of business entity

An investor conducting business in Macau is obligated to set up a legal establishment, which could be in the form of a company or a branch.

There are two types of Macau companies: companies limited by shares and companies limited by quotas. The capital and corporate governance requirements for a company limited by shares are higher than a company limited by quotas, and in general, a company limited by quotas is used by investors that are not in regulated industries.

Corporate taxes in Macedonia

For more information, contact:

Paul Tobin
PricewaterhouseCoopers
9-11 Maria Louisa Blvd., 8th Floor
1000 Sofia
Bulgaria
Tel: +359 2 9355 200
Email: paul.tobin@bg.pwc.com

Significant developments

Starting from 1 January 2009, important changes to profit tax legislation were introduced as part of the government's measures in response to the financial crisis.

Under the amendments, any income realised by a corporate taxpayer will be exempt from corporate income tax (CIT) on the condition that such income is not distributed in the form of dividends (i.e., kept as retained earnings). In accordance with this, any profit distributions will be subject to CIT in the year of payment.

Effective from 1 January 2009, amendments were also made regarding tax treatment of capital revenue. The article that previously provided a tax exemption for dividends realised with participation in the capital of another resident taxpayer of Macedonia, on condition the dividends were taxed at the dividend payer, was abolished. In line with the profit tax exemption for undistributed profits, the dividends are taxable upon payment.

Capital gains
As of 1 January 2009, capital gains are fully included in the taxable base of the company. Since under the latest amendments the profits of a company are not taxable until distributed, such profits are not subject to corporate income tax before that time.

Loss carryforwards
Loss carryforwards are not allowed under the Macedonian legislation.

Taxes on corporate income

Generally, all resident and non-resident companies operating through a permanent establishment (PE) are liable to pay CIT in Macedonia. Computation and payment of the tax is performed by companies. The CIT rate is 10%.

The basis for computation of the tax is the result determined in the tax return. There are two types of returns:

- Annual returns – relating to expenses, which are non-deductible for tax purposes; and
- Returns related to profit distributions – with respect to distribution of profits accumulated by a Macedonian company.

Macedonian resident entities are taxed on their worldwide income. Non-resident entities are taxed on their Macedonian-source income. Non-business organisations (including governmental bodies) are taxed on income from their business activities.

M

Macedonia

The Macedonian Trade Companies Law provides for the following types of entities:

- General partnerships;
- Limited partnerships;
- Limited liability companies;
- Joint stock companies;
- Limited partnerships by shares; and
- Foreign business entities may register a branch office in Macedonia.

Corporate residence

A company is resident in Macedonia for tax purposes if it is established or maintains its headquarters in the territory of Macedonia. Foreign legal entities with headquarters abroad are non-residents for tax purposes, but their Macedonian branches are liable for tax on any profit generated in the territory of Macedonia.

Permanent establishment (PE)
In 2006, the profit tax law introduced the concept of a PE. Generally, a PE is a fixed place of business through which the business of an enterprise is wholly or partly carried on, either directly or through a dependent agent.

More specifically, the domestic law provides that a PE may include a place of management, a branch office, a factory, a workshop, mining activities, or any other place of extraction of natural resources.

A building site or construction or installation project may constitute a PE if it lasts longer than six months.

Furthermore, the provision of services, including consulting services, is deemed to give rise to a PE if such activities last longer than 90 days within a 12-month period.

Other taxes

Value-added tax (VAT)
VAT was introduced on 1 April 2000. In general, the VAT regulations are in line with the provisions of the sixth VAT European Union directive.

The standard VAT rate is 18%. This rate applies to overall turnover and imports of goods and services. A lower rate of 5% applies to supplies of certain goods, including foods, drinking water from public supply systems, and publications such as books, pamphlets, newspapers, and other printed material, except for publications mainly used for advertising purposes.

All taxpayers whose total turnover for the previous calendar year exceeded MKD 1.3 million or whose total supplies, as projected at the beginning of the business activity, will exceed this amount, are liable to register for VAT purposes.

Residents that do not meet the criteria above may voluntarily register for VAT purposes at the beginning of each calendar year.

The standard VAT period is one calendar month. However, if the total turnover in the previous calendar year did not exceed MKD 25 million, the tax period is the calendar quarter. The tax period for voluntarily VAT registered taxpayers is the calendar year.

A taxpayer is obliged to submit a VAT return for each tax period within 15 days following the end of the relevant tax period.

Excise duties
Excise duties are levied with respect to a limited number of goods. Petroleum products, alcohol and alcoholic beverages, and tobacco products are subject to an excise duty at a flat or percentage rate.

The excise duty for passenger motor vehicles, which was cancelled on 31 December 2003, was reintroduced as of 1 January 2005. The tax is based on engine capacity and the purchase value of the car. It ranges from MKD 0 to MKD 550,000.

Property tax
Property tax is paid on the ownership of real estate, including land (agricultural, construction, forest and pastures) and buildings (residential buildings or flats, business buildings and business premises, administrative buildings and administrative premises, buildings and flats for rest and recreation, and other construction facilities, as well as installations constructed on the buildings or below and permanently attached to the buildings).

The tax liable person is the legal entity or the individual owner of the property. If the owner is not known or cannot be reached, the tax liable person is the user of the property. A property taxpayer may also be the taxpayer who usufructs the property, and if the property is owned by several persons, each of them is a property taxpayer proportionately for the portion owned. A property taxpayer is also the legal entity or physical person user of the real estate owned by the state and the municipality.

The property tax base is the market value of the real estate. For the purpose of determining the market value of the real estate, Municipal Council, Municipal Council of the City of Skopje and the Council of the City of Skopje establish a commission. Market value is determined according to the methodology for determining the market value of real estate.

Property tax rates are proportional and range from 0.10% to 0.20%. The rates are determined on the basis of the type of property. Thus, property tax rates on agricultural land not used for agricultural production may be increased from three to five times in relation to the basic rates.

The amount of the rates is decided by the Municipal Council, Municipal Council of the City of Skopje and the Council of the City of Skopje pursuant to the Law on the City of Skopje.

The taxpayer paying property tax for a residential building or flat in which he/she lives with family members is entitled to a reduction of the calculated tax by 50%.

Transfer tax
The sale of real estate is subject to transfer tax. A sale is defined as the transfer by compensation of the right to ownership of real estate, the replacement of one piece

M

Macedonia

of real estate with another, as well as other means of acquiring real estate with compensation between legal entities and/or physical persons. In addition, the transfer of securities on the basis of compensation is subject to transfer tax.

The tax liable person is a legal entity or an individual who sells real estate. As an exception, a taxpayer may also be a legal entity or physical person who buys real estate, if the sale and purchase agreement states that the buyer is to pay the tax. When replacing real estate, the taxpayer is the participant that replaces the real estate of greater value.

If the right to ownership of real estate is transferred on the basis of a lifelong support agreement, the receiver of the real estate (i.e., the heir) is the taxpayer.

When selling real estate in bankruptcy and executive procedure, as well as when realising agreements on mortgage, the taxpayer may be the buyer of the real estate.

The tax base is the market value of the real estate at the moment of the establishment of the liability.

When replacing real estate, the tax base is the difference between the market values of the real estate being replaced.

When selling real estate in bankruptcy and executive procedure, the tax base is the attained selling price.

Tax rates are proportional and range from 2% to 4%.

Garbage collection fee
A garbage collection fee is payable for immovable property depending on the type of property and on the surface area used. It is calculated on the basis of a tariff. It is collected together with the bills for water usage.

Companies and individuals are liable for paying communal taxes for usage of certain rights and services (mainly for usage of the urban space in the municipalities, posting commercials, etc.).

Branch income

Branch offices are registered in the Trade Registry. Branches are subject to tax in accordance with the general statutory provisions. The foreign parent company is fully liable for the obligations of its established branch office in Macedonia.

A foreign company that is entitled to carry out commercial activities pursuant to its national legislation may establish a commercial representative office in Macedonia. Representative offices are not legal entities and may not carry out any commercial activities. Representative offices are not subject to CIT.

Income determination

Effective from 1 January 2009, taxpayers are not subject to tax on undistributed profits.

Undistributed profits is the difference between total revenue and total expenditures of the taxpayer, in amounts determined according to the accounting regulations and accounting standards, decreased by the paid tax determined in the tax return.

Starting from 1 January 2009, distributions of dividends and other types of profit are subject to profit tax. The distributed amount, regardless of whether in monetary or non-monetary form, is taxed at the time of payment. In addition, on an annual basis tax is payable on the non-deductible expenses.

Monthly advanced payments of profit tax for 2010 are calculated from the amount of tax computed on the basis of the non-deductible items on the 2009 tax return, decreased by tax credits and other tax incentives stated in the return.

Addbacks

Tax-deductible expenditures, for the purposes of determining the taxable base, are solely those incurred by the taxpayer within its business activity. The CIT law provides further guidance on this issue:

- The calculated gross salaries of employees are tax-deductible up to the amount paid. Salaries include employees' income paid based on the business success of the employer as well as food and transportation allowance.
- The personal income of the managing and supervisory board members is tax-deductible up to 50% of the amount paid.
- Employees' related expenditures such as organised transportation to/from work, organised food (cantina), business trip allowance, field allowance, family separation allowance, one-off severance payment, retirement allowance, annual holiday allowance, anniversary awards, etc. are tax-deductible up to the amount prescribed by law and collective agreement.
- The depreciation taken on intangible and tangible assets is recognised as expenditure in the tax return up to the amount calculated on the procurement value of such assets, by applying depreciation rates within the limits set by the law. Once determined, the depreciation method is used until the final depreciation of the asset or group of assets.
- The interest on credits received for the purposes of conducting a company's business activities is fully tax-deductible, provided the interest does not fall under the thin capitalisation rules effective from 1 January 2009. Under these rules, the interest is not tax-deductible if the credit received from a shareholder who holds at least 25% of the capital in the company (which is not a bank or a financial organisation) exceeds the amount of three times its share in a tax period.
- The costs for research and development (R&D) incurred within a company's own R&D centres or through independent scientific and research institutions are fully tax-deductible.
- The premiums paid for insurance of the taxpayer's business property and all kinds of compulsory non-life insurance determined by law are tax-deductible.
- Property tax, fees, and other paid public duties not depending on operating performance, except withholding taxes, are tax-deductible.
- The costs for economic propaganda and marketing for the purpose of improving the taxpayer's business are tax-deductible in the amount of actual costs suffered.
- The outlays for donations is recognised as expenditures in the tax return in the amount of 5% of the overall revenue, and sponsorship outlays in the amount of 3% of the overall revenue, pursuant to the manner, the conditions and the procedure set in the law on donations and sponsorships in public activities.

Macedonia

- The revenue realised on the basis of the funds that are strictly earmarked for performance of the taxpayer's activity (budgets, funds) is fully tax-deductible.
- The value of the supplies from the uncompleted production, intermediate products, and final products is estimated at a maximum of the full cost.
- Transfer prices between related parties have to be market-based.

Deductions

Dividends
Effective from 1 January 2009, amendments were made regarding the tax treatment of capital revenue. The article giving tax exemption for dividends realised with participation in the capital of another taxpayer-resident of the Republic of Macedonia, on condition they are taxed at the dividend payer level, was abolished. In line with the profit tax exemption for undistributed profits, dividends are taxable upon payment only.

Capital gains
Capital gains are treated as ordinary income of the taxpayer and are included in its general taxable base.

Loss carryforwards
Loss carryforwards are not permitted by Macedonian legislation.

Group taxation

Tax consolidation provisions were abolished starting from 1 January 2009.

Tax incentives

A taxpayer that is a registered user within a technological industrial development zone is exempt from profit tax payment for a period of 10 years from the commencement of the performance of the activity in the zone under terms and conditions and according to a procedure determined with the law on technological and industrial development zones.

A taxpayer that is obliged, in accordance with the law on registration of cash payments, to introduce and use approved equipment for registering cash payments is granted reduction of the calculated corporate tax for up to 10 procured fiscal machines in the amount of their value.

Simplified tax regime for small companies
Companies that perform economic activity (except banking, financial, insurance activities and games of chance and entertainment games) and have not earned overall revenue from any source exceeding MKD 3 million on an annual level in any of the past three years may calculate and pay annual tax on total revenue in the amount of 1% of the amount of earned total revenue presented in the annual income statement for the previous calendar year.

Withholding taxes (WHT)

WHT on income paid to foreign legal entities was introduced on 1 January 2006.

Macedonia

All domestic legal entities and domestic physical persons that are registered for carrying out an activity, as well as foreign legal entities or physical persons that are non-residents but have a PE in Macedonia when paying certain types of income to a foreign legal person, are obliged to withhold tax and to pay the tax withheld to a respective suspense account simultaneously with the payment of the income.

The WHT rate is 10% and is applied on the following forms of incomes payable abroad:

- Dividends;
- Interest from residents;
- Interest from non-residents with a PE in Macedonia;
- Royalties paid by residents;
- Royalties paid by non-residents with a PE in Macedonia;
- Income from entertainment or sporting activities in Macedonia;
- Income from management, consulting, financial services, or services related to R&D;
- Income from insurance or reinsurance premiums;
- Income from telecommunications services between Macedonia and a foreign country; and
- Income from the lease of immovable property in Macedonia.

As an exception, WHT is not applicable to the following forms of income:

- The after-tax profit of a PE transferred to its foreign headquarters;
- Interest from bonds issued or guaranteed by the government;
- Interest on deposits in banks located in Macedonia; or
- Income from transactions in state securities on the international financial markets.

If a double taxation avoidance agreement is in place, WHT shall be payable in accordance with the treaty provisions.

The Republic of Macedonia has signed double taxation avoidance agreements with 33 countries: Netherlands, France, Italy, Sweden, Denmark, Finland, Switzerland, Hungary, Croatia, Turkey, Yugoslavia, Poland, People's Republic of China, Russia, Ukraine, Slovenia, Bulgaria, Egypt, Albania, Iran, Romania, Belarus, Spain, Czech Republic, Moldova, United Kingdom of Great Britain and Northern Ireland, Ireland, Qatar, Austria, Latvia, Lithuania, Estonia, Slovakia, and Germany.

Additionally, Macedonia has adopted agreements with Malaysia, Norway, and Belgium, that were concluded by the former Yugoslavia.

Tax administration

The taxable period for which profit tax is determined covers one calendar year.

Taxpayers are obligated to calculate and pay tax on the basis of a tax return form, which must be submitted to the public revenue office together with the annual financial statements.

Taxpayers pay profit tax during the year in monthly advance payments by filing a monthly tax return form within 15 days of the end of each month.

M

Macedonia

The monthly advanced payment is determined as one-twelfth of the CIT computed in the annual CIT return for the previous year, increased by the percentage of the growth of the retail prices in the country.

Monthly advanced payments of profit tax for 2010 are calculated from the amount of tax computed on the basis of the non-deductible items of the 2009 tax return decreased by tax credits and other tax incentives stated in the return.

The difference between the advance payments and the final tax liability is paid within 30 days of the deadline for submitting the annual financial statement.

Interest is due on late payments.

A request for refund of overpaid tax may be made, and the refund should be made within 30 days of submitting the request. If the requested refund is not made, the overpaid amounts will be considered as advance payment for the following period.

Corporate taxes in Madagascar

For more information, contact:

Dominique Taty
Fidafrica SA
Immeuble Alpha 2000
20th Floor
Rue Gourgas – Plateau
Abidjan 01
Côte d'Ivoire
Tel: +225 20 31 54 67
Email: d.taty@ci.pwc.com

Significant developments

The most significant changes of the past three years are:

- The corporate tax decreased from 25% in 2008 to 24% in 2009 and once again to 23% in 2010.
- Tax loss may be carried forward for five years instead of three years.
- The increase in the corporate tax rate for a Madagascar branch of a foreign company was cancelled.

Taxes on corporate income

A corporate entity or individual person registered in Madagascar and having an annual turnover exceeding MGA 20,000,000 is subject to corporate income tax (CIT) at a rate of 23%.

The tax payable cannot be less than 5/1000 of turnover plus a fixed amount of MGA 100,000 for taxable persons carrying on agricultural, artisan, transportation, industrial, hotel, or mining activities. The minimum tax cannot be less than 5/1000 of turnover plus MGA 320,000 for other activities.

Revenue of foreign businesses that do not have a permanent establishment (PE) in Madagascar is subject to withholding income tax of 10% of any income realised in Madagascar.

Corporate residence

Companies are considered resident in Madagascar if they are registered in Madagascar or have a legal existence in Madagascar. Companies usually are required to have a legal existence when they carry out business in Madagascar or have revenue from ownership of assets in Madagascar.

Other taxes

Value-added tax (VAT)
VAT is applicable to all transactions realised in Madagascar by a VAT vendor. Services are considered to be performed in Madagascar if such services are used in Madagascar or invoiced to a taxpayer established in Madagascar.

Madagascar

Any corporate entity or individual person who realises an annual turnover exceeding MGA 200,000,000 is a VAT vendor. For a business realising annual revenue less than MGA 200,000,000, VAT vendor registration is an option.

A foreign company that has no permanent establishment in Madagascar but renders services to a Madagascar taxpayer must appoint a tax representative to collect and pay VAT on its behalf. Otherwise, the beneficiary of the services must collect and pay VAT on behalf of the foreign supplier.

The VAT rate is 20%, and the VAT rate on export is 0%. VAT input is recoverable under certain conditions.

Registration fees

Registration fees are applicable to transfers of title ownership (sales, donations) of movable and immovable assets, to transfers of interests, to share capital increases and to lease agreements.

Registration fee rates are 0.5% to 6%, depending on the nature of the transaction.

Payroll tax

Salary taxes are levied at a rate of 23% on the total taxable remuneration of employees, including salaries, allowances, and benefits in kind.

Real estate ownership tax

Real estate ownership tax is imposed annually at the rate of 5% to 10% on the rental value of the property. Land ownership is also taxable at a rate depending on the nature of the land.

Tax on insurance contracts

All insurance or life annuity conventions concluded with a company, insurance firm, or with any other Madagascan or other insurer are subject to an annual tax on insurance contracts at a rate of 3% to 20% levied on the insurance premiums.

Social security contributions

Employers must contribute to Caisse Nationale de Prévoyance Sociale (Madagascar's national social security fund, which includes pensions and accident insurance). The contribution is capped at 13% of eight times the legal minimum salary per employee.

Health contributions

Employers must contribute to the health system assessment at a rate of 5% of the total amount of taxable remuneration of its employees.

Branch income

The tax on branch income is the same as for corporate income.

Income determination

Inventory valuation

There are no provisions for valuing inventories or determining inventory flows. The tax treatment will follow the accounting treatment.

Madagascar

Capital gains

There is no provision for capital gains in Madagascar except for capital gains on the sale of real estate by an individual. Capital gains made by a company on the sale of assets and interests are considered as normal business income, subject to income tax.

Inter-company dividends

Dividends received by a company are considered as business income subject to income tax. No withholding tax applies on payment of dividends.

Foreign income

Foreign income is considered as normal business income subject to income tax, unless a tax treaty is established and indicates otherwise.

Stock dividend

Stock dividends are unusual, but they are considered as business income, subject to income tax.

Deductions

Deductible wages

Salaries and wages that are not submitted to salary income tax or not declared to "Caisse Nationale de Prévoyance Sociale" are not deductible.

Depreciation

The amount of deductible depreciation should not exceed the amount that is calculated according to the rates of depreciation provided by the law:

- Industrial buildings: 5%;
- Plant and machinery: 10%;
- Mining exploration and development: (licence): 33%;
- Transportation: (car) 20%; (utility cars, vans, trucks) 25% ;
- Computers: 25%; and
- Electricity generators: 10%.

With the exception of buildings, it is also possible to practise a graduated depreciation. In this case, the annual depreciation corresponds to 30% of the net book value of the asset.

In case of loss, depreciation of assets can be deferred and carried forward to the next financial years until absorption.

Payments to foreign affiliates

For branches, the deductible amount of overhead that the head office can charge to the branch is limited to 1% of the turnover of the branch.

Interest on inter-company loans: Only interest calculated on twice the amount of the share capital at a rate practised by the Central Bank plus two points is deductible.

Net operating losses

Accumulated loss can be carried forward for the next five financial years following the period in which the loss occurs.

Other significant items

To be tax-deductible, provisions must relate to existing liability or loss. Fines and third-party taxes borne by the company are not tax-deductible.

Madagascar

Group taxation

There is no provision regarding group taxation in Madagascar.

Tax incentives

The general tax legislation does not provide tax incentives with the exception of microfinance activity, which is exempt from income tax during the first five years. After this period, the microfinance company is subject to income tax at a rate of 23%.

The following activities benefit from a special tax and customs regime:

- Free-zone law for industrial and other service providers that export all products. They can be eligible under the free-zone law, which provides income tax exemption during the first two to five years and a reduced income tax of 10% after this period, and exemption from customs duties on importation.
- Big investment mining. The big investment mining law provides a minimum income tax exemption, and a reduced income tax rate for the transformation entity, exemption from custom and importation duties, and VAT reimbursement on local purchased equipment and investments.
- Petroleum code. The petroleum code provides custom and importation duties exemption for hydrocarbon research, exploration, and exploitation activities.
- Leasing law. The leasing law provides that leasing activities can benefit from income tax exemption and reduction during the first four years.

Withholding taxes (WHT)

WHT are levied as follow:

- Impôt sur les revenues des capitaux mobiliers (IRCM): Withholding tax on interest of 23% is applicable on financial loan interest. However, interest paid to banks, financial institution, and foreign financial organisation is exempt.
- Withholding tax of 23% is applicable on remuneration of a member of a board of directors or a single director.
- Income tax for non-resident entity: Management fees, royalties, technical and assistance fees, licence fees, equipment rental fees, and any income realised by foreign suppliers is subject to income tax of 10%.

Tax administration

Corporate income tax is payable bimonthly in provisional instalments. The balance is payable before 15 May each year for companies whose financial year ends at 31 December, and before 15 November each year for companies whose financial year ends at 30 June.

Withholding tax on foreign services is payable to the tax authorities within one month of the date of payment.

Withholding tax on interest and on payments to members of boards of directors are payable at 15 May or 15 November, depending on the financial year-end.

Corporate taxes in Malawi

For more information, contact:

Misheck Msiska
PricewaterhouseCoopers
1st House
Corner Glyn Jones Road and Chilembwe Avenue
Blantyre, Malawi
Tel: +265 1 820 322
Email: misheck.msiska@mw.pwc.com

Significant developments

From 1 July 2005:
- Losses carried forward from trading operations are restricted to a period of six years. Manufacturers may carry forward losses indefinitely.
- Provisional tax is payable 30 days after the end of each quarter.
- Minimum tax on turnover is abolished.

From 1 July 2006:
- There is a 100% allowance on mining expenditures in the first year of assessment.
- No capital gain is recognised if the gain on disposal is used to acquire a replacement asset within 18 months.

From 1 July 2007:
- Consumer price indices are used for calculating the basis upon disposal of fixed assets for capital gains tax purposes.
- There is a 100% allowance on plant and machinery and industrial buildings for taxpayers in the manufacturing industry.

From 1 July 2009:
- A turnover tax is introduced for businesses with a turnover between MWK 2 million and MWK 6 million.
- Corporate tax self-assessment is introduced.
- Transfer pricing regulations and an additional tax anti-avoidance provision on transactions between related parties are introduced.
- Penalties increase for late submission of returns from MWK 30,000 to MWK 200,000.

Taxes on corporate income

Malawi does not have separate legislation for taxation applicable to the income of different types of legal persons or types of transactions such as corporate tax, personal tax, and the taxation of capital gains. All are included in the Taxation Act.

Summary of corporate tax rates

	Note	Rate
Corporate tax		
Locally incorporated companies	(1)	30%
Branches of companies not incorporated in Malawi		35%
Companies in export processing zones	(2)	0%

Malawi

	Note	Rate
Companies in priority industries	(3)	
– Either for a period not exceeding 10 years		0%
– Or in all other cases for companies incorporated in Malawi		15%
– Or in all other cases for Malawi branches of external companies		20%
Personal tax		
First MWK 120,000		0%
Next MWK 36,000		15%
Thereafter		30%

Notes

1. In the case of a mining company, an additional resource rent tax of 10% is levied on profits after tax if the company's rate of return exceeds 20%. The basis for calculating rate of return has not been defined.
2. An Export Processing Zone Appraisal Committee was established in 2000. A company in the manufacturing category may submit an application, in the prescribed manner, for the Minister's approval for its business premises to be declared an Export Processing Zone and for its products to be declared export products.
3. Priority industries have not been defined.

Corporate residence

A corporate entity is considered a resident for tax purposes in Malawi if it has a permanent establishment (PE) in Malawi. There have been no recent changes to this legislation.

Definition of a permanent establishment
The Taxation Act defines a PE as "an office or other fixed place of business through which business activity is carried on."

This short definition is wide in scope. Care must be exercised when considering this definition in situations that may be affected by a double tax agreement. Each agreement contains a specific and far more detailed definition of what constitutes a PE.

Other taxes

Miners pay resource rent tax of 10% on after tax profits if the rate of return exceeds 20%.

Non-resident tax is payable on income due to a non-resident at the rate of 15% of the gross income.

Summary of other tax rates

Other taxes	Note	Rate
Ecclesiastical, charitable and educational institutions of a public character and trusts of a public character		0%
Discretionary trusts		25%
Other trusts	(1)	See note
Life insurance business		21%
Clubs formed or operated for pleasure or recreation	(2)	30%

Other taxes	Note	Rate
Dividend withholding tax	(3)	10%
Non-resident tax	(4)	15%
Fringe benefits tax	(5)	30%

Notes

1. The income of these trusts is aggregated with that of the beneficiaries and taxed at the personal tax rates.
2. Clubs formed or operated for pleasure or recreation are taxed at the rate applicable to locally incorporated companies on 6.25% of their total receipts from sales of goods, cinematography, performances, stage plays, and gambling machines.
3. Dividend withholding tax (WHT) is a final tax. The dividend is not included in the taxpayer's taxable income, and the WHT is not deducted from the taxpayer's tax liability.
4. Taxable income is determined by deducting from assessable income expenses that are not expenses of a capital nature and are incurred wholly, exclusively, and necessarily in the production of the income or for the purposes of the trade.
5. The fringe benefits tax expense is borne by the employer and is not a tax-deductible expense for the employer.

Branch income

There is a 35% tax on taxable income of a branch of a foreign company. Locally incorporated companies pay tax at the rate of 30%.

No dividend WHT is applicable on repatriation of profits.

Income determination

Inventory valuation
Inventory is stated at cost.

Capital gains
The tax basis for capital gains is the cost of the asset adjusted by the applicable consumer price index (inflation index). Once determined, the taxable gain is subjected to corporate tax at the rate applicable to the particular entity.

Inter-company dividends
A 10% WHT is applicable on the declaration of an inter-company dividend.

Foreign income
Generally, income whose source is not Malawi is not taxable in Malawi (see Income deemed to arise in Malawi).

Stock dividends
The conversion of shares into stock has been prohibited in Malawi since the 1984 Company's Act.

Assessable and taxable income
Section 11 of the Taxation Act defines income as the total amount in cash or otherwise including any capital gain received by or accrued to or in favour of the person in any year or period of assessment from a source within or deemed to be within Malawi. The taxpayer's assessable income excludes any amount exempt from tax under this act.

M

Malawi

Taxable income is calculated by deducting allowable items from assessable income. Section 28 of the Taxation Act defines tax-allowable deductions as any expenditures and losses (not being of a capital nature) wholly, exclusively, and necessarily incurred by the taxpayer for the purpose of his trade or in the production of income.

Income deemed to arise in Malawi
The liability for Malawi tax is based on the source of the income rather than residence of the person. Certain transactions may be deemed to be from a source within Malawi even if effected outside Malawi. Section 27 of the Taxation Act limits the income that may be deemed to have arisen in Malawi to the following:

* Remuneration for services rendered or work performed in Malawi;
* Pensions or annuities arising from services rendered or work performed in Malawi;
* Pensions or annuities arising from services rendered outside Malawi to the government, a local authority, or a statutory corporation where the person is resident outside Malawi solely for the purpose of rendering those services;
* Remuneration for services rendered or work performed in or out of Malawi where the amount may be claimed as a tax-deductible expense by a PE in Malawi;
* Pensions payable to pensioners of the government of the former Federation of Rhodesia and Nyasaland (reference should be made to the Twelfth Schedule of the Taxation Act for definitions of which pensioners are affected);
* Interest paid by the government to a member of its permanent pensionable staff for a loss of career or concomitant expense;
* Amounts incurred, claimed, or claimable in connection with a PE in Malawi;
* Realised exchange gains and losses arising in connection with a PE in Malawi or foreign exchange assets and liabilities held in Malawi; and
* Capital gains and losses realised with respect to tangible property located in Malawi and interests in companies incorporated in Malawi.

Tax-exempt income
The following are common examples of tax exempt income:

* The income of agricultural, mining, and commercial institutions or societies not operating for private pecuniary profit or gain of the members;
* The income of clubs, societies, and associations formed, organised, and operated solely or principally for social welfare or civic improvement or other similar purpose provided that the income of such bodies may not be divided among or used for the benefit of the members or shareholders;
* The income of ecclesiastical, charitable, and educational institutions of a public character and trusts of a public character;
* War disability or war widows' pensions;
* Interest up to MWK 10,000 received by or accrued to or in favour of an individual;
* Capital gains arising from the disposal of personal and domestic assets not used in connection with trade;
* Capital gains arising on the transfer of assets between spouses, former spouses, to a spouse from the estate of a deceased spouse, and to a child from the estate of a deceased parent;
* A capital gain arising from the disposal of a taxpayer's principal residence;
* Capital gains arising from the sale of shares traded on the Malawi Stock Exchange where they have been held for at least one year;
* Redundancy pay of up to MWK 50,000, excluding notice pay or commutation of leave;

- Contract gratuity of up to MWK 40,000 with prior approval from the Commissioner General; and
- Dividends, however they are subject to a 10% dividend WHT, which is a final tax. (Although the word "final" has not been defined, it is applied as meaning that dividend WHT suffered may not be offset against an income tax liability.)

Domestic consumption, gifts, and sales below market value
The value of trading stock taken by the taxpayer for private or domestic consumption is determined as follows:

- In the case of non-farming stock, the value is equal to the cost price to the taxpayer or the market selling value at the time the stock was taken, whichever the taxpayer elects.
- In the case of farming stock, the value is the amount the Commissioner General accepts to be fair and reasonable at the time the stock was taken.
- If a taxpayer disposes by sale, gift, or otherwise of property being trading stock, standing, or growing crops or trees that have been planted and tended for the purpose of sale and: (a) the property constitutes or constituted the whole or part of the assets of a business which is or was carried on by the taxpayer; and (b) the disposal was not in the ordinary course of carrying on that business, then the value of that property is the market selling value at the date of disposal. The purchaser of that property is deemed to have acquired it at this market selling value.

Commissioner General's power to increase taxable income
The Commissioner General is empowered to increase the taxable income and liability of a taxpayer where he is of the opinion that the main purpose or one of the main purposes of a transaction was the avoidance or reduction of tax or where the main benefit that might have been expected to accrue from a transaction was the avoidance or reduction of tax.

Farming operations
Farming operations receive a 100% allowance with respect to expenditures incurred during any year of assessment on:

- Stumping, leveling, and clearing of land;
- Work in connection with the prevention of soil erosion;
- Boreholes;
- Wells;
- Aerial and geophysical surveys;
- Water control work, including any canal, channel, dyke, furrow, and any flood control structure, whether or not of a permanent nature; and
- Water conservation work, meaning any reservoir, water dam, or embankment constructed for the impounding of water. In the case of water conservation work, the Taxation Act limits the amount deductible to amounts actually paid, where the farmer incurs a liability in terms of any law relating to natural resources.

Where a farmer derives taxable income from growing timber, the farmer may elect that the taxable income is determined in accordance with the following rules:

- Carry forward the cost of planting the timber until the timber reaches maturity.
- Add annually to the cost of planting the timber an amount calculated as 5% of the cost of planting the timber until the timber reaches maturity.

Malawi

- When the timber is sold, a proportionate amount of the total of (a) and (b) is deducted from the proceeds.
- In each year of assessment, the amount calculated under (b) above is treated as taxable income in the hands of the farmer.

A farmer may not claim as a deductible any expenditures that have been recovered through a subsidy or as capital allowances any assets where the expenditures have been recovered through a subsidy.

Mining operations

Mining operations receive a 100% allowance with respect to mining expenditures incurred during any year of assessment. Mining expenditures are defined as capital expenditures incurred in Malawi by a person carrying on or about to carry on mining operations in Malawi:

- In searching for or in discovering and testing or in winning access to deposits of minerals.
- In the acquisition of or of rights in or over such deposits, other than the acquisition from a person who has carried on mining operations in relation to such deposits.
- In the provision of plant and machinery and industrial buildings that would have little or no value to such person if the mine ceased to work.
- On the construction of any buildings or works that would have little or no value if the mine ceased to be worked.
- On development, general administration and management prior to the commencement of mining operations.

Persons engaged in mining operations are not entitled to claim the export tax allowance on non-traditional exports or the 25% transport tax allowance on international transport costs for non-traditional exports.

Other special trades and cases

The Taxation Act contains provisions specific to cooperative agricultural societies, consumer cooperative societies, non-life insurance business, and hire purchase or other agreements providing for postponement of ownership and approval of pension or provident funds. The detail of these provisions has not been included there.

Pre-operating expenditures

A manufacturer may claim as a deduction any expenditure incurred in the course of establishing the business provided that the following are true:

- The expenditure was incurred not more than 18 months before commencing business.
- The expenditure would have been allowed as a deduction if it had been incurred after commencing business.

Capital gains and losses

A capital gain or loss is calculated as the difference between the disposal proceeds of an asset and its adjusted cost. Capital gains are included in income and taxed at the rate applicable to the taxpayer. The determination of adjusted cost depends on whether capital allowances have previously been claimed in respect of the asset.

Asset on which capital allowances have been claimed
The adjusted cost is the tax written-down value of the asset. The whole of the excess of disposal proceeds over tax written-down value is treated as taxable income. There is no limitation to the recoupment of allowances previously claimed.

Asset on which no capital allowances have been claimed
An asset on which no capital allowances have been claimed is termed a "qualifying asset".

The cost of the asset is adjusted by using the consumer price indices at the date of the disposal of the asset and applicable to the year in which the purchase or the construction of the asset was effected or completed, or the 1992 index where a 1992 valuation was registered. Adjustment by reference to the consumer price indices is the legal requirement.

Rollover relief
If a business asset is sold and the taxpayer acquires a qualifying replacement asset, the taxpayer may claim rollover relief. This means that the taxpayer does not immediately pay the tax on the gain. Instead, the cost of the replacement asset is reduced by the amount of the gain. The taxpayer must declare this in the tax return.

A qualifying replacement asset is an asset similar to, or related in service or use to, the asset disposed of. The replacement asset must be acquired within 18 months of the disposal giving rise to the gain.

Transactions exempt from tax on capital gains
No capital gain or loss is to be determined with respect to the following:

* The disposal of a taxpayer's principal residence.
* Qualifying involuntary conversion of an asset or property (excluding motor vehicles) if the gain has been used to acquire a qualifying replacement asset similar to or related in service to the asset so disposed. (In such cases, any taxable gain is restricted to the excess, if any, of the proceeds of involuntary conversion over the cost of the replacement asset. The replacement asset must be acquired within two years of the year of assessment in which the gain is realised.)
* Dealings in a company's equity shares following a qualified reorganisation. (Such a reorganisation must be pursuant to a written plan undertaken for valid business purposes and not have as its purpose tax avoidance by any person who is a party to the reorganisation. While advance approval of the plan by Malawi Revenue Authority is not required by the legislation, taxpayers may wish to obtain written confirmation from Malawi Revenue Authority that the plan is tax exempt in order to avoid potential misunderstandings and disputes.
* The disposal of personal and domestic assets not used in connection with trade.
* Dealings in shares quoted on the Malawi Stock Exchange provided that the shares have been held for more than one year.
* Transfers of capital assets between spouses, or former spouses, to a spouse from the estate of a deceased spouse, and to children from the estate of a deceased parent.

Notes on capital allowances
On disposal, assets are subject to balancing charges (capital gains) or balancing allowances (capital losses).

M

Malawi

If an asset is subject to extensive use, such as machinery working double shifts, so that its expected economic life is reduced, the commissioner general may agree to increase the rates of annual allowances.

1. The 100% investment allowance is available only on new and unused qualifying assets belonging to and used by a manufacturer or farmer. The rate for used qualifying assets is 40%. The investment allowance is claimable only in the first year of use.
2. Where an investment allowance is claimed, the initial allowance is not allowed on the same asset. The initial allowance is claimable when an expenditure is incurred.
3. Annual allowances at the above rates are on cost less investment/initial and annual allowances previously claimed. Assets qualifying for the 100% investment allowance are not eligible for the annual allowance.
4. Investment allowance on plant and machinery excludes motor vehicles intended or adapted for use on roads.
5. A 20% annual allowance is standard, but the Commissioner General may vary the amount.
6. No initial allowance is granted on private passenger motor vehicles. These include saloons, sedans, station wagons, and double cabin pickups. However, the restriction does not apply where the motor vehicle is used for hiring purposes.
7. The allowances for computer equipment are claimed on a straight-line basis. In a budget speech, the Minister of Finance announced that the annual allowance on computer equipment would be increased from 20% to 40%. The procedures for implementing this have not yet been followed. However, Malawi Revenue Authority has accepted computations claiming a 40% allowance. Taxpayers claiming a 40% allowance may wish to obtain written confirmation from Malawi Revenue Authority to prevent potential disputes.
8. The building must be newly constructed at a cost of no less than MWK 100,000,000.

Foreign exchange gains and losses

Foreign exchange gains realised on foreign currency assets or liabilities are taxable.

Foreign exchange losses realised on foreign currency assets or liabilities are tax deductible.

Unrealised gains and losses are carried forward until realised and then included in income or allowable expenditure. The maintenance of records that accurately track unrealised exchange rate adjustments from year to year is necessary to ensure correct tax computations. This, however, can prove difficult for some taxpayers.

Export allowances

Exporters, including those manufacturing in bond, are entitled to claim additional tax allowances for nontraditional exports:

a. On the export of nontraditional products, there is a 12% tax allowance. From the introduction of the allowance in 1988 until recently, Malawi Revenue Authority accepted that the allowance was calculated as 12% of export sales. It now states that the calculation is to be 12% of net profit derived from export sales. Malawi Revenue Authority also has recently stated that the export incentive allowances are not claimable when the taxpayer is in a tax loss situation. This is subject to dispute.

b. There is a 25% transport tax allowance on international transport costs for nontraditional exports. Traditional exports are tea, coffee, cane sugar, and unmanufactured tobacco and tobacco refuse. Export allowances may not be claimed in respect of exports from mining operations.

Lease, patent, trademark, and copyright premium
The tax-deductible amount of a premium paid for the right of use or occupation of land or buildings, plant or machinery, patent design, trademark, copyright, or any other property of a similar nature is one of the following:

*   The amount of premium or consideration divided by the number of years for which the right of occupation or use is granted
*   Where the period for which the right of occupation or use is granted exceeds 25 years, the deduction is one-twenty-fifth of the premium or consideration

The premium is tax deductible only where the asset or right with respect to which the premium or consideration is paid is used for the generation of income. If a taxpayer acquires ownership of the asset or right, no further deduction of the premium or consideration is allowed from the date ownership is acquired.

Pension contributions
The tax-allowable amount of ordinary pension contributions made by an employer to an approved pension fund is subject to limitations. The limit with respect to each employee is the lowest of one of the following:

*   The actual contribution;
*   24% of the employee's compensation; or
*   MWK 9,000 per annum.

No allowance is available if an employee is entitled to a tax-free gratuity. Employees, self-employed individuals, and nonemployed individuals may not claim tax relief on pension contributions. Tax relief on such individuals is available only to an employer.

Training costs
Taxpayers training a Malawi citizen to obtain a degree, diploma, or other certificate receive an additional allowance equal to 50% of the actual costs incurred.

Donations
Donations to approved charities and approved nonprofit institutions formed for the purpose of social welfare, civic improvement, educational development, or other similar purposes are allowable for tax. The minimum individual donation allowable is MWK 500. The minimum donation for other approved charities is MWK 250. In both cases, there is no maximum donation.

Controlled foreign companies
There is no controlled foreign company regime in Malawi.

Deductions

Depreciation and depletion
Depreciation allowances (capital allowances) applicable as stipulated in the Taxation Act at various rates:

Malawi

Capital allowances, which are available to companies and individuals in business, are:

Asset	Initial	Investment	Annual	Note
		Allowances		
Industrial and farm buildings, hotels and docks	10%	100%/40%	5%	1, 2, 3
Staff housing	10%	–	5%	3
Plant, machinery and equipment	20%	100%/40%	20%/10%	1, 2, 3, 4
Furniture and fittings	20%	–	10%	3
Motor vehicles	20%	–	20%	3, 4, 5, 6
Commercial buildings	–	–	2½%	7

Note

1. The 100% investment allowance is available only on new and unused qualifying assets as indicated above, belonging to and used by a manufacturer or farmer. The rate for used qualifying assets is 40%. The investment allowance is claimable only in the first year of use. Prior to the 2008 tax year, the rates were 40% and 20%, respectively.
2. Where an investment allowance is claimed, the initial allowance is not allowed to be claimed on the same asset. The initial allowance is claimable only in the first year of use.
3. Annual allowances at the above rates are based on cost less investment and initial and annual allowances previously granted. Assets qualifying for 100% investment allowance are not eligible for annual allowance.
4. Investment allowance on plant and machinery excludes motor vehicles intended or adapted for use on roads.
5. A 20% annual allowance is standard, but the Commissioner General may vary the amount.
6. No initial allowance is granted on private motor vehicles. These include saloons, sedans, station wagons, and double cabin pickups. However, the restriction does not apply where the motor vehicle is used for hiring purposes.
7. This allowance was introduced in the 2005-2006 tax year. The building must be newly constructed at a cost of no less than MWK 100,000,000.

On disposal, assets are subject to balancing charges (capital gains) or balancing allowances.

Net operating losses
Current taxable income may be offset against net operating losses brought forward and current operating losses may be increased by net unexhausted trading losses brought forward. Manufacturers and taxpayers in the agricultural industry may carry losses forward indefinitely, while other taxpayers may carry losses forward for only six years. Net operating losses may not be carried back.

Payments to foreign affiliates
A deduction for payments to foreign affiliates if such payments are expended wholly, exclusively, and necessarily for the production of income or for the purposes of trade, and it can be demonstrated that the transaction is at arm's length.

Research and development
Research expenditures are fully allowable as a deduction if it is "experiments and research relating to trade".

Allowable deductions
For corporate tax purposes, an expense is allowable if it is not of a capital nature and incurred wholly, exclusively, and necessarily for the production of income or for the purposes of trade.

Group taxation

Group taxation is not permitted.

Tax incentives

There is a 100% investment allowance on plant and machinery and industrial buildings for taxpayers in the manufacturing industry.

There is a 100% capital allowance on mining expenditures in the first year of assessment.

There is a 100% allowance on farming expenditures, which includes expenditures which would ordinarily be capital in nature and not allowable as a deduction in determining taxable income.

Withholding taxes

WHT rates

Nature of payment	Rate %
Royalties	20
Rents	10
Payment of more than MWK 60,000 per annum for any supplies to traders and institutions	
Food stuff	7
Other	10
Commission	20
Payment for carriage and haulage	10
Payment of more than MWK 60,000 for tobacco and other farm products	7
Payment to contractors and subcontractors in the building and construction industries	4
Payment for public entertainment	20
Payment of more than MWK 500 for casual labour or services	20
Bank interest in excess of MWK 10,000	20
Fees	10

Tax administration

Returns
Income tax returns are due within 180 days after the end of the financial year.

Payment of tax
Tax is payable in two instalments at 30 November and 30 January, with the balance of the tax being paid on 30 April.

Corporate taxes in Malaysia

For more information, contact:

Chuan Keat Khoo
PricewaterhouseCoopers
Level 10, 1 Sentral
Jalan Travers
Kuala Lumpur Sentral
50470 Kuala Lumpur
Malaysia
Tel: +60 3 2173 1368
Email: chuan.keat.khoo@my.pwc.com

Significant developments

Real property gains tax, which was not applicable on disposals of properties on or after 1 April 2007, is reimposed on gains from disposals of properties from 1 January 2010 at the rate of 5% on gains arising from disposals of chargeable assets in respect of real properties that are disposed within five years of their acquisition.

Taxes on corporate income

Income tax
For both resident and non-resident companies, the income tax is imposed on income accruing in or derived from Malaysia at a flat rate of 25% for the year of assessment (YA) 2010. As a concessionary treatment for resident companies with paid-up capital from ordinary shares of MYR 2.5 million or less, the rate of tax is 20% on the first MYR 500,000 of chargeable income, and 25% on any income in excess of MYR 500,000 (for YA 2010). However, with effect from YA 2009, if a company meets the above capital requirement, but controls or is being controlled directly or indirectly by another company which has a paid-up capital of more than MYR 2.5 million in respect of ordinary shares, it will not be eligible for the concessionary tax rate.

Assessment of income is on a current-year basis. A company is taxed on income from all sources (whether business or non-business) arising in its financial year ending in the calendar year which coincides with that particular year of assessment. For example, a company that closes its accounts on 30 June of each year is taxed on income earned during the financial year ending on 30 June 2010 for the year of assessment 2010.

Self-assessment for companies was implemented from the year 2001. Under the self-assessment system, companies are required to submit a return of income within seven months from the date of closing of accounts. Particulars required to be specified in the return include the amount of chargeable income and tax payable by the company. An assessment is deemed to have been made on the company upon submission of the return. The return is deemed to be a notice of assessment that is deemed to be served on the company upon the date the return is submitted.

Petroleum income tax
Petroleum income tax is imposed at the rate of 38% on profits from petroleum operations in Malaysia. No other taxes are imposed on income from petroleum operations.

Corporate residence

A company is tax resident in Malaysia in a basis year if, at any time during the basis year, the management and control of its affairs are exercised in Malaysia. Generally, a company would be regarded as resident in Malaysia if at any time during the basis period for a year of assessment, at least one meeting of the Board of Directors is held in Malaysia concerning the management and control of the company.

Other taxes

Real property gains tax
Real property gains tax (RPGT) is charged upon gains from disposals of real properties (referred to as "chargeable assets") situated in Malaysia, including shares of a real property company (RPC). A real property company is a controlled company that owns real property or RPC shares with a defined value of not less than 75% of its total tangible assets. However, disposals of real properties or RPC shares between 1 April 2007 and 31 December 2009 were not subject to RPGT. From 1 January 2010, RPGT is reimposed at the rate of 5% on gains arising from disposals of chargeable assets in respect of real properties that are disposed of within five years of their acquisition.

Sales tax and service tax
A single-stage ad valorem tax (sales tax) at rates ranging from 5% to 10% is imposed on all goods imported into or manufactured in Malaysia, unless specifically exempted.

Service tax is imposed at the rate of 5% on the value of taxable services sold or provided by taxable persons. A list of "taxable persons" and "taxable goods" is found in the Service Tax Regulations, 1975.

Goods and services tax
The GST Bill 2009 was tabled in Parliament for a first reading on 16 December 2009. The second and subsequent readings of the Bill were scheduled for March 2010. However, the tabling of the Bill for a second reading has been delayed to a date yet to be announced. The Goods and Services Tax (GST) of 4% was originally expected to be implemented in mid 2011. The reason reported for the delay in tabling the Bill was to allow the government more time to engage with the public in order to gather feedback on the implementation of the GST. Nevertheless, the introduction of the GST is included in the New Economic Model unveiled by the Prime Minister on 30 March 2010, as a key component of fiscal reforms aimed at transforming Malaysia into a high income nation.

GST, when implemented, will replace the sales tax and services tax currently imposed and collected under the Sales Tax Act 1972 and the Services Tax Act 1975. Companies with revenue below a certain threshold (to be gazetted separately, and expected to be MYR 500,000) are exempted from imposing GST.

Windfall profit levy
A levy is imposed on crude palm oil and crude palm kernel oil at a maximum of MYR 50 per ton where the price exceeds MYR 2,000 per ton. From 10 March 2009, the threshold has been increased to MYR 2,500 per ton in Peninsula Malaysia, and MYR 3,000 per ton in the states of Sabah and Sarawak.

Malaysia

Contract levy
A levy of 0.125% on contract works having a contract sum above MYR 500,000 is imposed on every registered contractor by the Construction Industry Development Board (CIDB).

Human resource development (HRD) levy
Employers engaged in the manufacturing and services sectors that employ more than a specified number of employees must contribute to the Human Resource Development Fund (HRDF). The levy required to be paid is at the rate of 1% of the employees' monthly wages on a monthly basis. From 1 April 2009, all employers who contribute to the HRDF, except those in the textile industry and the electronics and electrical industry, will make levy payments at the reduced rate of 0.5% until March 2011. Employers in the textile industry and electronics and electrical industry were exempted from payment of the HRD levy for six months from February 2009, and will make payments at the rate of 0.5% from August 2009 until March 2011.

Branch income

Tax rates on branch profits of a company are the same as those on corporate profits. No tax is withheld on transfer of profits to a foreign head office.

Income determination

Inventory valuation
Inventories are generally stated at the lower of cost or net realisable value. Cost for this purpose may be determined by using one of several possible bases, such as unit cost, average cost or the first-in, first-out (FIFO) method, as long as the basis used is consistent from one year to another.

Capital gains
Generally, gains on capital assets are not subject to tax, except for gains arising from the disposal of real properties. Gains arising from the disposal of real property (which include the disposal of shares in a real-property company) situated in Malaysia is subject to RPGT *(see Other taxes)*, but for disposals of real properties or RPC shares between 1 April 2007 and 31 December 2009, RPGT was not applicable. From 1 January 2010, RPGT is reimposed at the rate of 5% on chargeable gain arising from disposals of properties which are sold within five years of acquisition.

Inter-company dividends
A single-tier system of taxation came into force on 1 January 2008 which replaced the previous full imputation system. There is a six-year transitional period (until 31 December 2013) for all companies to migrate into the single-tier system.

Under the previous (full-imputation) system, dividends received from Malaysian companies are taxed at gross in the hands of shareholders (whether corporate or individuals). Companies distributing dividends are required to deduct tax at source at the prevailing corporate tax rate, from gross dividends payable, but the income tax deducted or deemed deducted from the dividends is available as a credit (deducted) against the income tax liability of the shareholder. If a dividend is paid by a company which was subjected to tax at the rate of 20% *(see Taxes on corporate income)*, tax is to be deducted or is deemed to be deducted from the dividend at the normal corporate tax rate (25% for YA 2010).

Under the single-tier tax system, dividends are exempt in the hands of shareholders. Companies are not required to deduct tax from dividends paid to shareholders, and no tax credits will be available for offset against the recipient's tax liability. Corporate shareholders receiving exempt one-tier dividends can, in turn, distribute such dividends to their own shareholders who are also exempt on such receipts.

Foreign income

Under the Income Tax Act, 1967 (ITA) a Malaysian tax-resident corporation and a unit trust are not taxed on their foreign-sourced income, regardless of whether such income is received in Malaysia. However, income of a resident company from the businesses of banking, insurance and air or sea transport is assessable on a global basis, except for income attributable to a Labuan business activity of the branch or subsidiary of a Malaysian bank in Labuan which is subject to tax under the legislation applicable to Labuan entities in Labuan (Labuan Business Activity Tax Act 1990). From YA 2008, a Labuan entity may also make an irrevocable election to be taxed under the ITA in respect of its Labuan business activity.

In respect of Malaysian-owned banks, insurance companies and takaful (Islamic insurance) companies, the profits of newly established branches overseas or remittances of new overseas subsidiaries are tax exempt for five years, provided that the applications to establish overseas branches or subsidiaries are received by the Central Bank of Malaysia no later than 31 December 2015.

Relief from double taxation is available by means of a bilateral credit if there is a governing tax treaty or unilateral relief where there is no treaty. The relief is restricted to the lower of Malaysian tax payable or foreign tax paid if there is a treaty, or one-half of the foreign tax paid if there is no treaty.

Undistributed income of foreign subsidiaries is not taxable.

M

Stock dividends

A Malaysian corporation may distribute bonus shares tax-free to shareholders.

Deductions

Depreciation and depletion

Tax depreciation (called capital allowance) on machinery, equipment, and industrial buildings is available at specific rates for all types of businesses. Locally acquired machinery and equipment qualify for an initial allowance of 20%, while imported heavy machinery (used in building and construction, mines, plantation, and timber industries) qualifies for 10% when the expenditure is incurred and the asset is in use. An annual allowance ranging from 10% to 20% is calculated on cost for every year during which the asset is in use for the purposes of the business. An accelerated capital allowance (ACA) is available for certain types of plant and machinery, such as computers, information technology equipment, environmental protection equipment, waste recycling equipment, and plant and machinery used in the business of plantation companies. Small-value assets costing less than MYR 1,000 each are entitled to 100% capital allowance, subject to a maximum total cost of MYR 10,000. Under the Economic Stimulus Package presented on 10 March 2009, qualifying expenditure on plant and machinery incurred from 10 March 2009 to 31 December 2010 is given ACA, which allows the cost to be fully claimed within two years. This allowance was made

Malaysia

to encourage businesses to continue investing in plant and machinery. The incentive is available from YA 2009.

Depreciation recapture on the sale of plant is taxable as ordinary income. Tax depreciation is not required to conform to book depreciation.

A depletion allowance is available on natural-resource properties.

Net operating losses

Up to YA 2005, the carryforward of business losses and capital allowances is unlimited in time. From YA 2006, the law has been amended so that the carryforward of business losses and capital allowances would not be available for deduction in subsequent years of assessment if the company does not meet the conditions of a shareholders' continuity test. However, a recent guideline issued by the Ministry of Finance states that the rule restricting the carryforward of losses and capital allowances based on the shareholder continuity test would apply only to dormant companies.

Current-year business losses may be utilised against all sources of income. Set-off of unutilised carried-forward losses is restricted to income from business sources only. Utilisation of tax depreciation is also restricted to income from the same underlying business source. There is hitherto no provision for loss or tax depreciation carryback to previous tax years. However, under the Stimulus Package presented in Parliament on 10 March 2009, a taxpayer (including a company) may make an irrevocable election for the current-year loss for YA 2009 or YA 2010 to be carried back for set-off against income of the immediately preceding year, up to a maximum loss of MYR 100,000.

Payments to foreign affiliates

A Malaysian corporation can claim a deduction for royalties, management service fees, and interest charges paid to affiliates, provided that these are made at arm's length (i.e., the amounts it would pay if it was dealing with an unrelated entity).

To enhance transparency of tax treatment relating to transfer pricing and thin capitalisation cases, a new provision was introduced, effective 1 January 2009, which empowers the Director General of Inland Revenue (DGIR) to make adjustments on transactions of goods and services if the DGIR is of the opinion that the transactions were not entered into on an arm's-length basis. With regard to thin capitalisation, the portion of the interest charge that relates to the amount of financial assistance which is excessive will be disallowed a deduction. This would cover related-party transactions within a domestic group of companies. However, the specific rules to be made under this provision have yet to be issued.

Taxes

Taxes on income are generally not deductible, whereas indirect taxes, such as sales tax and service tax, are deductible.

Group taxation

From YA 2006, group relief is available to locally incorporated, resident companies. A company that qualifies may surrender a maximum of 70% (with effect from YA 2009) of its adjusted loss for a year of assessment to one or more related companies, if the following conditions are met:

1. Both the claimant and surrendering companies must each have paid-up capital of ordinary shares exceeding MYR 2.5 million at the beginning of the basis period for that particular year of assessment, and must have the same (12-month) accounting period.
2. The companies must be "related" throughout the period that forms the basis period for a particular year of assessment as well as the 12 months preceding that basis period. "Related company" is defined by law and involves the application of a two-tier test. The first test relates to the proportion of one company's ownership in the ordinary share capital of the other company (at least 70%), or at least 70% ownership of the surrendering and claimant companies' shares by a third company. The other test is based on the proportion of distributable profits and assets on winding up to which the holding company is entitled (at least 70%).

Companies that wish to avail themselves of group relief must make an irrevocable election to surrender or claim the tax loss in the return to be filed with the Inland Revenue Board for that year of assessment.

Tax incentives

Inward investment
Pioneer status (PS)
Corporations in the manufacturing, agricultural, hotel and tourism sectors, or any other industrial or commercial sector that participate in a promoted activity or produce a promoted product, may be eligible for PS. This incentive is given by way of exemption from income tax on 70% of the annual profits for five years. The remaining 30% of the profits is taxed at the prevailing corporate income tax rate. The profits exempted from tax are available for distribution as tax-free dividends.

In the following cases, the general rule of tax exemption and period of incentive is varied:

a. Corporations undertaking a project of national and strategic importance involving heavy capital investment and high technology will be granted full exemption on its profits. The tax-relief period may be extended for a further five years. Projects recognised to be of national and strategic importance include forest plantation activities, projects with Multimedia Super Corridor (MSC) status, and production of electronic wafers.
b. High-technology companies engaging in a promoted activity or in the production of a promoted product in areas of new and emerging technologies, as well as companies participating in an industrial linkage programme (only in respect of applications received before 31 December 2010), may be granted PS, which entitles them to full exemption on profits for a period of five years.
c. Corporations with projects eligible for PS that are located in the eastern corridor states of Peninsular Malaysia, Sabah, and Sarawak will be granted exemption on 85% of their profits for five years. However, for applications made on or after 13 September 2003, the incentive is enhanced to an abatement of 100% for a period of five years. An existing pioneer or ex-pioneer corporation that undertakes an expansion programme through a subsidiary or controlled company in the eastern corridor states of Peninsular Malaysia, Sabah, Sarawak and Labuan, and the state of Perlis (with effect from 2 September 2006) that involves the same promoted activities or promoted products is eligible for a second round of PS or investment

tax allowances if certain conditions are satisfied. The eastern corridor states include Kelantan, Trengganu, and Pahang, and the district of Mersing in Johor.

d. Existing locally owned companies reinvesting in production of heavy machinery, machinery and equipment are to be granted exemption on 70% of the increased statutory income arising from reinvestment for five years.

e. New and existing companies utilising oil palm biomass and reinvesting to produce value-added products are to be entitled to full exemption on profits for a period of 10 years.

f. Small companies that meet with specified conditions are entitled to full exemption on profits for a period of five years.

g. A second round of PS is available for hotel and tourism companies which invest in expansion, modernising and renovation, as well as for companies providing cold-chain facilities and services for perishable agricultural produce.

A company granted PS which intends to reinvest before the expiry of its PS is eligible for reinvestment allowance provided that it surrenders its pioneer status *(see section on Reinvestment allowance below)*.

Deduction for export expenses

Resident corporations in the manufacturing, hotel, tourism, and service sectors are entitled to double deduction for expenditure incurred on the promotion of exports, such as overseas advertising, free samples, export market research, participation in trade exhibitions, preparation of tenders, travel, participation in virtual trade shows, participation in trade portals for promotion of local products, and maintenance of overseas sales offices and warehouses. For promotion of export of services, expenses such as feasibility studies for overseas tender projects, participation in a trade or industrial exhibition in Malaysia or overseas, airfares, and sustenance are entitled to double deduction. Expenses incurred by pioneer companies are aggregated and setoff against post-pioneer (taxable) profits.

Capital investment

Incentives for capital investment are as follows:

a. Investment tax allowance (ITA)
    A corporation may be granted an ITA of 60% of capital expenditure incurred on a factory or plant and machinery used for purposes of an approved manufacturing, agricultural, hotel, tourist, knowledge-intensive or other industrial or commercial activity (other than one granted PS). ITA is granted on capital expenditure incurred for a period of five years. For an integrated agricultural activity, ITA may be granted for both the agricultural and the processing activities for five years each.

    The amount of ITA to be utilised for each year of assessment is restricted to a maximum of 70% of the profits, while the balance of 30% of the profits is taxed at the prevailing corporate income tax rate. Unutilised allowances may be carried forward indefinitely for set-off against future profits of the business. Dividends paid out of exempt profits are exempt from tax in the hands of shareholders.

    The ITA incentive is enhanced for the following types of projects:

    • A corporation undertaking a project of national and strategic importance may be granted ITA at a rate of 100% and would be able to utilise the amount of ITA granted for set-off against 100% of profits each year, without restriction.

- A high-technology company or a company participating in a promoted activity or producing a promoted product in an industrial linkage programme may be granted ITA at the rate of 60%, and the amount of ITA would be available for set-off against 100% of profits. This incentive is an alternative to PS (effective only for applications received before 31 December 2010). *(See Pioneer status (b) under Inward investment.)*
- A company granted ITA in respect of a project located in the eastern corridor states of Peninsular Malaysia, Sabah, Sarawak, and Labuan, and the state of Perlis (with effect from 2 September 2006), would be granted ITA at a rate of 80%, and the amount of ITA that could be utilised for each year would be restricted to a maximum of 85% of the profits. However, for applications made on or after 13 September 2003, the incentive is increased to a rate of 100%, and the amount of allowance can be setoff against 100% of its profits for each year. An existing ITA or ex-ITA company that undertakes an expansion programme through a subsidiary or controlled company in the eastern corridor states of Peninsular Malaysia, Sabah, Sarawak, and Labuan involving the same promoted activities or promoted products is eligible for a second round of ITA or pioneer status if certain conditions are satisfied.
- A company that provides technical and vocational training or science courses in biotechnology, medical and health, molecular biology, material sciences and food sciences in Malaysia may be granted ITA of 100% of qualifying capital expenditure incurred within a period of 10 years, and the maximum amount of ITA that could be utilised each year would be restricted to 70% of profits.
- Existing locally owned companies reinvesting in production of heavy machinery, machinery, and equipment are granted ITA at the rate of 60% on additional qualifying expenditure incurred for a period of five years.
- New and existing companies utilising oil palm biomass to produce value-added products that reinvest are granted ITA at a rate of 100%, and would be able to utilise the amount of ITA granted for set-off against 100% of profits each year, without restriction.
- A second round of ITA is available for hotel and tourism companies which invest in expansion, modernising and renovation, as well as companies providing cold-chain facilities and services for perishable agricultural produce.
- Companies upgrading an existing testing laboratory for testing medical devices, may be granted ITA of 60% on qualifying expenditure incurred within a period of five years to be off-set against 100% of profit for each year of assessment.

b. Reinvestment allowance
   A corporation that embarks on a programme to expand, modernise, automate, or diversify its existing manufacturing or processing business is entitled to a reinvestment allowance. The amount of reinvestment allowance is 60% of qualifying capital expenditure incurred within a period of 15 years on a factory or plant and used for expansion, modernisation, automation, or diversification activity. The reinvestment allowance will be withdrawn if the asset for which the reinvestment allowance is granted is disposed of within five years. The amount of reinvestment allowance that can be utilised each year is limited to 70% of profits after deduction of capital allowances. The remaining 30% is taxed at the normal corporate income tax rate. Unutilised reinvestment allowances may be carried forward indefinitely for set-off against future profits of the business. The 70% restriction does not apply to projects that achieved the level of productivity as prescribed by the Minister of Finance and to projects located in the eastern corridor

M

Malaysia

states of Peninsular Malaysia, Sabah, Sarawak, and Labuan, and the state of Perlis (with effect from 2 September 2006). A reinvestment allowance is also extended to:

- A tax-resident company undertaking an approved agricultural project that incurs qualifying capital expenditure for the purposes of expanding, modernising, or diversifying its cultivation and farm businesses
- Those who rear chickens and ducks and who reinvest to transform the chicken/ duck-rearing business from an open-house to a closed-house system (verified by the Minister of Agriculture), or those who reinvest to expand the closed-house system in existing or new locations approved by the Ministry of Agriculture (available until 2010 only)

Dividends paid out of exempt profits are not taxable in the hands of shareholders.

Venture capital company

A company investing in approved venture companies in the form of start-up or seed capital is given a deduction equivalent to the value of the investment. To qualify for the deduction, the investment must not be in a company that is listed on a stock exchange, and it should not be in a company related to the investing company at the point of first investment. Alternatively, tax exemption for 10 years on income from all sources, other than interest income from savings or fixed deposits, is available if at least 50% of its funds are invested in venture companies (reduced to 30% in respect of applications received by the Securities Commission from 30 August 2008 to 31 December 2013).

Other incentives

Operational headquarters company (OHQ)

An OHQ company that provides qualifying services to its offices and related companies may be granted approved OHQ status.

The income (business income, interest, and royalties) derived by an approved OHQ from the provision of qualifying services is exempt from income tax for a period of 10 years. This includes income from services provided to related companies in Malaysia, provided such income does not exceed 20% of the OHQ income. Dividends distributed from exempt income are exempt in the hands of shareholders. Expatriates working in an OHQ are taxed only on the portion of chargeable income attributable to the number of days they are in Malaysia. An OHQ is also granted special facilities, including the following:

- Approvals for expatriate posts are based on the requirements of the OHQ.
- Credit facilities in foreign currency can be obtained from licensed commercial banks in Malaysia, without approval of the Central Bank of Malaysia.
- There is no restriction on investments in foreign securities and lending to related companies outside Malaysia.
- A single or foreign currency account may be opened with licensed commercial banks in Malaysia or offshore banks in Labuan.

International procurement centre (IPC)

An IPC is a company incorporated in Malaysia, whether local or foreign owned, that is engaged in the procurement and sale of raw materials, components, and finished products to its group companies in Malaysia or abroad.

Tax incentives include:

- Exemption for 10 years on income from qualifying activities in respect of export sales after deduction of tax-depreciation allowance (subject to conditions).
- Dividends paid from exempt income are exempt from tax in the hands of shareholders.
- Goods brought into free zones, bonded warehouses, or licensed manufacturing warehouses for repackaging or cargo consolidation and integration before distribution to final consumers are exempt from customs duties.

To qualify, an IPC must serve as a collection and consolidation centre for finished goods, components, and spare parts from overseas or within the country to be distributed to the dealer, importer, or its subsidiary or associated company within or outside the country.

In addition, other available non-tax incentives include:

- Approval for expatriate posts based on the requirements of the IPC.
- Ability to maintain more than one foreign currency account for the retention of export proceeds with any licensed commercial bank and without any limit on the balance in the accounts.
- Permission to enter into foreign exchange forward contracts with a licensed commercial bank to sell forward export proceeds based on projected sales.
- Exemption from foreign equity ownership restrictions.

International trading companies
Companies that obtained approval as "international trading companies" are exempt for five years on income equivalent to 20% of increased export value, up to a maximum of 70% of statutory income. To qualify for the incentive, the company must meet the following three conditions:

1. It must be incorporated in Malaysia, with 60% Malaysian ownership;
2. Achieve minimum annual sales of MYR 10 million, not more than 20% of which may be derived from the trading of commodities; and
3. Use local services (banking, finance, and insurance) and infrastructure (local ports and airports) in its operations.

Regional distribution centre
A regional distribution centre (RDC) is a collection and consolidation centre for finished goods, components and spare parts from overseas or within the country to be distributed to the dealer, importer, or its subsidiary or associated company within or outside the country. Among the activities involved are bulk breaking, repackaging, and labelling. Incentives accorded to an RDC include:

- Exemption for 10 years on income from qualifying activities in respect of export sales, after deduction of tax depreciation allowance (subject to conditions).
- Dividends paid from exempt income are exempt from tax in the hands of shareholders.
- Import duty and sales tax on goods for distribution are tax exempt.

M

Malaysia

Other non-tax incentives include:

* 100% equity holding by the promoter is allowed.
* Approval for expatriate posts based on requirement of the RDC.
* Eligibility to open one or more foreign currency accounts with any licensed commercial bank to retain their export proceeds, without any limit imposed.
* Permission to enter into foreign exchange forward contracts with any licensed commercial bank to sell forward export proceeds, based on projected sales.

Multimedia Super Corridor status companies
The MSC is Malaysia's initiative for the global information technology industry and is designed to be the research and development (R&D) centre for industries based on information technology (IT). Conceptualised in 1996, the MSC has grown into a thriving information communication technology (ICT) hub, hosting multinational corporations, foreign-owned, and home-grown Malaysian companies focused on multimedia communications products, solutions services, and research and development. The Malaysian government has equipped core areas in the MSC with high-capacity global telecommunications and logistics networks. The MSC is also supported by secure cyber laws, strategic policies and a range of financial and non-financial incentives for investors.

The Multimedia Development Corporation (MDeC) was established to develop and manage the MSC. The MDeC is a fully empowered "one-stop shop" that acts as approving authority for companies applying for MSC-company status.

MSC status is awarded to both local and foreign companies that develop or use multimedia technologies to produce or enhance their products and services as well as for process development. Companies awarded MSC status are eligible for incentives which include the following:

* PS for five years (extendable up to five additional years) or investment tax allowance of 100% for five years for a new company or an existing company on its additional income.
* Eligibility for R&D grants (for majority Malaysian-owned, MSC-status companies).
* Exemption from indirect taxes on multimedia equipment.
* Unrestricted employment of local and foreign knowledge workers.
* Freedom to source funds globally for investments.
* Protection of intellectual property and cyber laws.
* No censorship of the Internet.
* MSC-status companies located within the MSC will enjoy globally competitive telecommunication tariffs and services guarantees, world-class physical and IT infrastructure, and excellent R&D facilities, including the region's first Multimedia University.

Biotechnology industry
Companies undertaking biotechnology activity with approved bionexus status from Malaysian Biotechnology Corporation Sdn Bhd are eligible for 100% income tax exemption for 10 years from the first year in which the company derives profit or ITA of 100% on qualifying capital expenditures incurred for a period of five years. Dividends distributed from exempt income are tax exempt for the recipient. Double deduction is available for expenditures incurred on R&D and on promotion of exports.

The following incentives are also available:

- A company or individual investing in a bionexus company is given a tax deduction of an amount (approved by the Minister of Finance) equal to the value of investment for the purpose of financing activities at seed capital stage or early stage of a new business.
- Stamp duty and real property gains tax exemption is granted to a bionexus company undertaking a merger and acquisition with a biotechnology company within a period of five years until 31 December 2011.
- Accelerated industrial building allowance is given (over 10 years) on qualifying building expenditures for buildings used by a bionexus-status company for the sole purpose of its new business or expansion project.

Also included in the 2007 budget is a proposal to tax income from qualifying activities at the reduced tax rate of 20% for 10 years upon expiry of the tax-exempt period.

Unit trusts
Gains from the realisation of investments are not regarded as taxable income of a unit trust. Interest received by unit trusts from certain bonds and securities, as well as interest credited by banks and other financial institutions licensed under the Banking and Financial Institutions Act 1989 or the Islamic Banking Act 1983, are exempt from tax. Distributions from such gains are tax exempt to the unit holders.

Capital allowance in respect of plant and machinery used for the purpose of the letting of properties is allowed at the rate of 10% per annum against the rental income of a property unit trust.

Research and development (R&D)
Companies that provide R&D services to third parties are eligible for PS with full exemption of their profits for a period of five years. A second round of PS incentive is available for another five years. As an alternative, such companies may be granted ITA at the rate of 100% of qualifying capital expenditure incurred within a period of 10 years and a further 10 years for a second round of ITA. The ITA incentive may also be granted to companies undertaking R&D for their group.

Companies undertaking in-house R&D projects are eligible for ITA at the rate of 50% of the qualifying capital expenditure incurred within a period of 10 years.

A company that has made an investment for the sole purpose of financing a project on commercialisation of R&D findings (which must be R&D findings in the resource-based industry, wholly owned by a public research institute or public institute of higher learning in Malaysia) is given a deduction equivalent to the value of that investment.

Double deduction is granted for expenses incurred on approved research and development projects, as well as for payments made to defined R&D companies. Local universities are recognised as approved research institutes for the purposes of claims for the double-deduction incentive by companies making cash contributions or payments for the use of the services of such universities for R&D activities.

Buildings used for approved R&D activities qualify for the industrial building allowance at the normal rate.

Malaysia

Training
There is a double deduction for approved training expenditures incurred to train employees under an approved training programme. Manufacturing corporations with 50 or more Malaysian employees registered with the Human Resources Development Fund are not eligible for this incentive. These corporations are, however, eligible to seek financial assistance from the fund for training their employees.

Preoperating training expenses are also available as a double deduction to small- and medium-scale manufacturing companies that are not registered with the Human Resources Development Fund. The normal deduction for preoperating training expenses may also be available to certain resident companies.

Training expenses incurred by employers for employees who complete certain courses, including aircraft maintenance engineering courses and post-graduate courses in ICT, are given double deduction (for YA 2009–2012).

Approved service projects
A resident company undertaking a project in the service sector in relation to transport, communications, utilities, or other approved subsectors may elect to apply for an investment allowance or for an income tax exemption for a period of five years. The mechanisms for tax exemption and investment allowance are similar to those for PS and ITA, respectively.

For projects located in Sabah, Sarawak, and the eastern corridor states of Peninsular Malaysia, the rate of tax exemption is increased to 85% and the rate of investment allowance is increased to 80%. Service projects of national and strategic importance qualify for tax exemption of 100% for a period of 10 years or for an investment allowance of 100%.

Dividends paid out of exempt profits are exempt in the hands of shareholders.

Buildings used solely for the purposes of approved service projects qualify for an industrial building allowance.

Foreign fund management company
A foreign fund management company providing fund management services to foreign clients is taxed at a concessionary rate of 10% in respect of the income derived from the management of foreign funds, while income arising from services rendered to clients in Malaysia is taxed at the prevailing corporate tax rate. Its income after deduction of tax at 10% may be distributed as tax-exempt dividends to its shareholders.

A foreign fund management company is a Malaysian incorporated company licensed under the Securities Industry Act 1983. Its activities are regulated by the Securities Commission.

Shipping
Tax-resident corporations and individuals carrying on shipping business are exempt from tax on income derived from the operation of Malaysian ships. Dividends distributed by a company qualifying for this incentive are exempt from tax in the hands of the shareholders.

Export incentives
Partial tax exemption is granted at various rates for export-oriented companies. Manufacturing companies are eligible for exemption on profits after deduction of tax depreciation allowances on 10% (or 15%) of the value of the increase in the company's exports, provided it attains at least 30% (or 50%) value added. Companies exporting fruits and cut flowers or exporting selected services also enjoy an exemption on profits, after deduction of tax depreciation allowances, equivalent to 10% of the value of the increase in exports. Companies engaged in export of selected services are eligible for exemption on profits on 50% of the value of increased exports.

Effective from YA 2003, a Malaysian-owned manufacturing company may be granted exemption on profits, after deduction of tax depreciation allowance of an amount equal to 30% of the value of increased export value, provided it achieves a significant increase in exports. The rate is increased to 50% of the value of increased export for a company that succeeds in penetrating new markets. Full exemption on increased export value is granted if the company achieves the highest increase in export.

Resource-based industries
Malaysian companies that are engaged in the manufacture of rubber-, oil palm- and wood-based products that are of export potential, may be granted the following tax incentives when they incur capital expenditures for the purpose of an expansion:

- Companies located outside promoted areas:
  - PS for five years (exemption is restricted to 70% of statutory income); or
  - ITA of 60% of qualifying capital expenditure incurred within five years (ITA is restricted to 70% of statutory income).
- Companies located within promoted areas:
  - PS for five years (exemption is restricted to 85% of statutory income); or
  - ITA for five years (ITA is restricted to 85% of statutory income).

Manufacturing-related services
Companies providing integrated logistics, marketing support, and utility services may be given the following incentives:

- Income tax exemption of 70% of statutory income for five years. The rate of exemption is increased to 100% of statutory income for projects located in areas designated as the "Eastern Corridor of Peninsula Malaysia, Sabah and Sarawak;" or ITA of 60% of qualifying capital expenditure (QCE) incurred within five years of the date upon which QCE was first incurred, to be offset against 70% of statutory income. This ITA incentive is enhanced to 100% of QCE, to be offset against 100% of statutory income for projects in the Eastern Corridor of Peninsula Malaysia, Sabah and Sarawak.
- Exemption from import duty and sales tax on equipment in the related projects.

Offshore trading through websites in Malaysia
Income received by companies undertaking offshore trading (comprising the buying and selling of foreign goods to non-residents) via websites in Malaysia is to be taxed at a reduced rate of 10% for a period of five years. The approval of the Minister of Finance must be obtained.

M

Malaysia

Islamic banking and other Islamic financing activities
To further the government's objective of developing Malaysia into a leading international Islamic financial centre, the following incentives are available:

- Tax deduction is allowed for expenses incurred in the issuance of Islamic securities approved by the Securities Commission or by the Labuan Financial Services Authority. (Effective from YA 2010 for securities approved by the Securities Commission and from YA 2011 for those approved by the latter authority and available until YA 2015 only.)
- Full income tax exemption for 10 years is granted to Islamic banks licensed under the Islamic Banking Act 1983 on income from Islamic banking business conducted in international currencies, and to takaful (Islamic insurance) companies on income from the takaful business conducted in international currencies. (Effective from YA 2007 until YA 2016.)
- Full income tax exemption on management fees received by local and foreign companies for managing funds of foreign and local investors established under Syariah principles is granted (effective from YA 2008 until YA 2016). Such funds must be approved by the Securities Commission.
- A special-purpose vehicle (SPV) established solely for the purpose of Islamic financing approved by the Securities Commission or one established under the Offshore Companies Act 1990, is not subject to income tax and is not required to comply with administrative procedures under the tax law. Deduction for the cost of issuance of Islamic bonds is allowed for the company that established the SPV, which is also deemed to be the recipient of income received by the SPV and taxed accordingly.
- Expenses incurred prior to the commencement of an Islamic stock-broking company is allowed to be deducted, provided the company commences business within two years from the date of approval. (Available for applications to establish such a company that is received by the Securities Commission before 31 December 2015.)
- Double-tax deduction is granted for specified expenses incurred for the purpose of its business in promoting Malaysia as an international Islamic financial centre for the years of assessment 2008 to 2015.

Real estate investment trusts (REITs)
REITs or property trust funds (PTFs) approved by the Securities Commission are exempted from income tax on chargeable income distributed to unit holders whereas its undistributed chargeable income is taxed at 25% (from YA 2009 onwards). However, with effect from YA 2007, REITs/ PTFs are exempted from tax on all income, provided that at least 90% of their total income is distributed to unit holders. If the 90% distribution condition is not complied with, all income is taxed at the prevailing income tax rate and tax credit is claimed by the unit holders. Unit holders are taxed as follows:

Unit holders	Income tax
Individuals (whether resident or non-resident), body of persons, or other unincorporated persons	Withholding tax of 15% (reduced to 10% from 1 January 2009 to 31 December 2011)
Non-resident company	Withholding tax at 25% (from YA 2009 onwards)
Resident company	No withholding tax (income to be included in annual tax return)

Unit holders	Income tax
Institutional investor (pension fund, collective investment scheme, or other person approved by the Minister of Finance)	Withholding tax at 20% (reduced to 10% from 1 January 2009 to 31 December 2011)

Other incentives available are:

* Real property gains tax exemption on disposal of real property to a REIT/PTF
* Stamp duty exemption on transfer of real property to REIT/PTF
* Tax deduction given for consultancy, legal and valuation service fees incurred on the establishment of a REIT

Development corridors

As part of the Malaysian government's plan for national economic advancement through regional development and growth acceleration in various strategic locations by promotion of domestic and foreign investments, the following "development corridors" were launched during the period from the end of 2006 to early 2008:

Economic region	Location	Year of launch
Iskandar Malaysia (renamed in April 2008 and formerly known as "Iskandar Development Region") www.idriskandarmalaysia.com.my	Southern Johor	2006
Northern Corridor Economic Region www.ncer.com.my	States of Perlis, Kedah, Penang, and northern Perak	2007
East Coast Economic Region www.ecerdc.com	States of Kelantan, Trengganu, Pahang, and district of Mersing in Johor	2007
Sabah Development Corridor www.sdc.gov.my	Western, central, and eastern regions of Sabah	2008
Sarawak Corridor of Renewable Energy www.sarawakscore.com.my	Central Sarawak	2008

Basic to the strategy for promotion of investments in these development corridors is the provision of all necessary infrastructure (financial and non-financial) for the creation of a business-friendly environment, including tax and other financial incentives. Apart from existing incentives which are available for promoted activities and products provided under the Promotion of Investments Act 1986 (PS, ITA etc.) and the Income Tax Act 1967 (outlined above), special incentives customised for the purpose of each development corridor have been (or will be) developed. So far, however, special legislation has been enacted only in respect of Iskandar Malaysia (IDR) to grant the following exemptions/incentive:

* Income tax exemption for an approved IDR-status company in respect of income from the provision of qualifying services to a person situated within designated nodes in the IDR or outside Malaysia, for 10 years, provided that these operations commence before 31 December 2015.
* Income tax exemption for non-residents in respect of income from technical fees, interest, or royalties received from approved developers in designated nodes in the

Malaysia

IDR, or IDR-status companies. Withholding tax requirements are also waived in respect of such payments.

- Income tax exemption for an approved developer on income from the disposal of rights over land or buildings in designated nodes in the IDR or rental from such buildings until 2020. Exemption is also granted to an approved development manager on income from the provision of management, supervisory, and marketing services to such developers until 2020.
- Knowledge workers residing in Iskandar Malaysia are taxed at the rate of 15% on chargeable income in respect of a qualified activity (green technology, biotechnology, educational services, healthcare services, creative industries, financial advisory and consulting services, logistics services, or tourism) from an employment in Iskandar Malaysia (from YA 2010).

Information pertaining to each development corridor, including incentives available, may be obtained from the corridor's website, the address of which is provided above.

Other incentives granted under the 2010 Budget
The following are some incentives included under the 2010 Budget:

Healthcare service providers – Granted tax exemption on statutory income equivalent to 100% of the value of increased exports, but limited to 70% of statutory income in a year. Any unutilised allowance can be carried forward indefinitely for deduction in the future. Export income is income derived from providing healthcare services to foreign clients.

Buildings awarded Green Building Index (GBI) Certificate – Incentives are given to the following:

- Owners – Granted tax exemption equivalent to 100% of additional capital expenditures incurred to obtain GBI Certificate which can be setoff against 100% of statutory income for each year (for new buildings and upgrading of existing buildings).
- Buyers who purchase the building from property developers – Granted stamp duty exemption on instruments of transfer of ownership on the additional cost incurred to obtain the GBI certificate (only given once to the first owner).

Forest plantations – The following incentives for forest plantations (deemed to have taken effect from 21 May 2003) are available only for applications received no later than 31 December 2011.

- Alternative (1)
  - A company investing in a subsidiary that is engaged in forest plantation activities ("investor company") – Granted a tax deduction equivalent to the amount of investment in the subsidiary.
  - For the subsidiary – Granted exemption of 100% of statutory income for 10 years commencing from the first year in which profit is derived.
  - The same exemption is given to an existing forest plantation company that reinvests for purposes of expansion of the forest plantation project, but only for five years commencing from the first year the company derives profit.
  - Any losses incurred before and during the tax-exempt period can be carried forward for deduction in the post-exempt years until fully utilised.

- Alternative (2)
  - For the investor company – Granted group relief on losses incurred by the subsidiary before it records any profit.
  - For the subsidiary – Granted exemption of 100% of statutory income for 10 years commencing from the first year in which profit is derived.
  - Any amount of loss that is not surrendered to the investor company prior to and during the exempt years of assessment may be carried forward for deduction in the post-exempt years until fully utilised.

Export of financial services – Income tax exemption is granted to Malaysian banks, insurance companies, and takaful companies on profits of newly established branches overseas or income remitted by new overseas subsidiaries. The exemption period, which is five years, may commence from a date to be determined by the company but should not be later than the third year of operations. (Applications to establish new branches or subsidiaries overseas should be received not later than 31 December 2015.)

Small and medium enterprises (SMEs) – Expenses incurred by SMEs on the registration of patents and trademarks are allowed a deduction of these expenses against business income. The term SME must come within the definitions provided in specified legislation.

Withholding taxes (WHT)

Corporations making payments of the following types of income are required to withhold tax at the rates shown in the table below. *See Note (7) for other types of income.*

Recipient	Dividends (1)	Interest (2)	Royalties and certain rentals [--] (3) (4) (5)
	%	%	%
Resident corporations	Nil	Nil	Nil
Resident individuals	Nil	Nil or 5	Nil
Non-resident corporations and individuals:			
Non-treaty	Nil	Nil or 15	10
Treaty:			
Albania	Nil	Nil or 10	10
Australia	Nil	Nil or 15	Nil or 10
Austria	Nil	Nil or 15	10
Bahrain	Nil	Nil or 5	8 [10]
Bangladesh	Nil	Nil or 15	Nil or 10
Belgium	Nil	Nil or 10 or 15	10
Bosnia & Herzegovina*	Nil	Nil or 10	8 [10]
Brunei*	Nil	Nil or 10	10
Canada	Nil	Nil or 15	Nil or 10 [10] (6)
China, P.R.	Nil	Nil or 10	10
Chile	Nil	15	10 [5]
Czech Republic	Nil	Nil or 12	10
Croatia	Nil	Nil or 10	10

Malaysia

Recipient	Dividends (1)	Interest (2)	Royalties and certain rentals [--] (3) (4) (5)
	%	%	%
Denmark	Nil	Nil or 15	Nil or 10
Egypt	Nil	Nil or 15	10
Fiji	Nil	Nil or 15	10
Finland	Nil	Nil or 15	Nil or 10
France	Nil	Nil or 15	Nil or 10
Germany	Nil	Nil or 15	Nil or 10
Hungary	Nil	Nil or 15	10
India (new agreement)	Nil	Nil or 10	10
Indonesia	Nil	Nil or 15	10
Iran	Nil	Nil or 15	10
Ireland, Rep. of	Nil	Nil or 10	8 [10]
Italy	Nil	Nil or 15	Nil or 10 (6)
Japan	Nil	Nil or 10	10 (6)
Jordan	Nil	Nil or 15	10
Kazakhstan*	Nil	Nil or 10	10
Korea, Rep. of	Nil	Nil or 15	Nil or 10
Kuwait	Nil	Nil or 10	10
Kyrgyzstan	Nil	Nil or 10	10
Lebanese Republic	Nil	Nil or 10	8 [10]
Luxembourg	Nil	Nil or 10	8
Malta	Nil	Nil or 15	10
Mauritius	Nil	Nil or 15	10
Mongolia	Nil	Nil or 10	10
Morocco	Nil	Nil or 10	10
Myanmar	Nil	Nil or 10	10
Namibia	Nil	Nil or 10	5
Netherlands	Nil	Nil or 10	Nil or 8
New Zealand	Nil	Nil or 15	Nil or 10
Norway	Nil	Nil or 15	Nil or 10 (6)
Pakistan	Nil	Nil or 15	Nil or 10
Papua New Guinea	Nil	Nil or 15	10
Philippines	Nil	Nil or 15	Nil or 10
Poland	Nil	Nil or 15	Nil or 10
Qatar	Nil	Nil or 5	8
Romania	Nil	Nil or 15	Nil or 10
Russian Federation	Nil	Nil or 15	10
Saudi Arabia	Nil	Nil or 5%	8 [10]
Singapore	Nil	Nil or 10	8 [5]
Sri Lanka	Nil	Nil or 10	10
Seychelles Republic	Nil	Nil or 10	10
Spain	Nil	Nil or 10	7 [5]
South Africa	Nil	Nil or 10	5
Sudan	Nil	Nil or 10	10

Recipient	Dividends (1)	Interest (2)	Royalties and certain rentals [--] (3) (4) (5)
	%	%	%
Sweden	Nil	Nil or 10	8
Syria	Nil	Nil or 12	10
Switzerland	Nil	Nil or 10	Nil or 10
Thailand	Nil	Nil or 15	Nil or 10 (6)
Turkey	Nil	Nil or 15	10
Turkmenistan	Nil	Nil or 10	10
United Arab Emirates	Nil	Nil or 5	10
United Kingdom	Nil	Nil or 10	8
Uzbekistan	Nil	Nil or 10	10
Venezuela	Nil	Nil or 15	10
Vietnam	Nil	Nil or 10	10
Zimbabwe	Nil	Nil or 10	10

Notes

Rate for certain rentals is shown in parenthesis […] if different from royalty rate.

* Treaties pending ratification

Restricted tax treaties dealing with taxation of specific transport operations in international traffic have also been signed with Argentina and the United States.

The numbers in parentheses refer to the notes below:

1. A single-tier system of taxation came into force on 1 January 2008 which replaced the previous full imputation system. There is a six-year transitional period (until 31 December 2013) for all companies to migrate to the single-tier system.
    Under the previous imputation system, dividends are franked with (deemed to be paid net of) the tax paid by corporations. If any dividend-paying corporation has not paid sufficient tax to cover the total tax deemed deducted from dividends, it must pay the balance of the tax to the tax authorities.
    Under the single-tier system, dividends are exempt in the hands of shareholders. Malaysia, at present, has no withholding tax on dividends in addition to tax on the profits out of which the dividends are declared. Some treaties provide for a maximum withholding tax on dividends should Malaysia impose such a withholding tax in the future.
2. Interest on loans given to or guaranteed by the Malaysian government is exempt from tax. Interest paid to a non-resident by a commercial or merchant bank operating in Malaysia is also exempt from tax.
3. Approved royalty payments under certain treaty provisions are exempt from withholding tax.
4. Other income:
    a. Effective 21 September 2002, contract payments made by a person (including a partnership) to non-resident contractors (including professionals) in respect of services under a contract project are subject to a 13% deduction of tax (10% on account of the contractors' tax liability and 3% on account of their employees' tax liability). This deduction of tax at source does not represent a final tax, which is determined upon the filing of the tax return.
    b. Payments made to non-residents in respect of the provision of technical services performed in Malaysia and rental of movable properties are subject to a 10% withholding tax (unless exempted under statutory provisions for purpose of granting incentives).

M

5. Royalty income received by non-resident franchisors under franchised education scheme programmes approved by the Ministry of Education is exempted from tax.
6. Royalty income does not include royalty paid in respect of motion picture films or tapes for television or broadcasting or of the operation of a mine, oil well, quarry, or any other place of extraction of natural resources or of timber or other forest products.
7. From 1 January 2009 withholding tax is also applied in respect of income of a non-resident from sources other than the following:
   - Sources shown in the preceding table;
   - A business source; and
   - An employment source.

   The rate of withholding tax on such income is 10%. This is applicable on payments made to residents of all the treaty partners previously listed, except for Germany and Jordan, where the respective double taxation agreements have provided for such type of income to be taxed only in the contracting state in which the recipient is resident.

Tax administration

Returns

Returns of income for the year 2008 will be issued to companies as follows:

Accounting year-end in	Return form issued in
January, February, March 2010	April 2010
April, May, June 2010	July 2010
July, August, September 2010	October 2010
October, November, December 2010	January 2011

Returns are to be submitted within seven months after the closing of accounts.

"E-filing" or online filing of tax returns via the Internet is available. E-filing is not compulsory, although it is preferred by the Inland Revenue Board.

Payment of tax

Tax payable under an assessment upon submission of a return is due and payable by the "due date." The "due date" is defined as the last day on expiry of seven months from the date upon which the accounts are closed.

Companies are required to furnish estimates of their tax payable for a year of assessment no later than 30 days before the beginning of the basis period. However, from the year of assessment 2008, a newly established company with paid-up capital of MYR 2.5 million or less that meets with certain specified conditions is exempted from this requirement for two years, beginning from the year of assessment in which the company commences operation. A revised estimate can be submitted in the sixth and ninth months of the basis period for a year of assessment.

Companies are then required to pay tax by monthly instalments (based on the estimates submitted) commencing from the second month of the company's basis period (financial year).

From year of assessment 2011, a company commencing operations in a year of assessment is not required to furnish estimates of tax payable or to make instalment payments if the basis period for the year of assessment in which the company commences operations is less than six months.

Corporate taxes in Malta

For more information, contact:

Kevin Valenzia
PricewaterhouseCoopers
167 Merchants Street
Valletta VLT1174, Malta
Tel: +356 2564 6601
Email: kevin.valenzia@mt.pwc.com

Significant developments

A number of changes to Maltese tax legislation have been published during the first half of 2010.

In a Maltese domestic context, the new tax provisions introduce a number of anti-abuse provisions as well as some new taxing provisions. Many of these provisions target mainly transactions in immovable property situated in Malta and companies owning such property. However the new amendments also cover a number of other important aspects from a Maltese domestic tax perspective.

Some other rules dealing with international tax matters have also been introduced. The main purpose of these rules is to further facilitate the use of Malta as a financial services centre, thus demonstrating Malta's continuing commitment to remaining an attractive jurisdiction of choice for investors.

The new innovative provisions include among others the following:

- An option for a step-up in the cost of acquisition of assets situated outside Malta owned by persons (including companies) effecting a change in domicile or residence or being Maltese companies resulting from cross-border mergers.
- An exemption is being introduced on royalties derived from qualifying patents with respect to inventions and satisfying the applicable conditions, which are to be set out in regulations.
- Provisions are being introduced in Maltese tax legislation in order to facilitate the use of Malta for international aviation activities.
- The Maltese tonnage tax regime has been extended to cover also qualifying non-Maltese-flagged vessels and ship management activities.

The exchange of information provisions under Maltese tax law have been extended in order to be more in line with those contained in the Organisation for Economic Co-operation and Development (OECD) Model Tax Convention.

The Value-added tax (VAT) Act has been amended in line with the provisions of Council Directive 2008/8/EC. Such amendments became effective as from 1 January 2010.

_M_

Malta

Taxes on corporate income

Income tax
Companies are subject to tax at a flat rate of 35%. There is no corporation tax structure separate from income tax.

Petroleum profits tax
Petroleum profits tax is levied as income tax, but taxable profits are computed in a special way, including on a production-sharing basis. Profits with respect to production sharing contracts signed after 1 January 1996 are taxed at 35%. Other petroleum profits are taxed at 50%.

Insurance profits tax
Insurance profits tax is levied as income tax and imposed at the same rate as other corporate profits, but the tax is computed in a special way. In the case of non-resident companies, the computation is applied with reference only to business carried on in or from Malta.

Corporate residence

All companies incorporated in Malta are considered to be both domiciled and resident in Malta. Other bodies of persons (including companies incorporated overseas) are considered to be resident in Malta when the control and management of their business are exercised in the country.

Other taxes

There are no other corporate taxes.

VAT
Supplies of goods and services in Malta are subject to VAT at the standard rate of 18% (5% on accommodations in hotels and licensed premises, supply of electricity, works of art, collector's items and antiques, certain confectionery, medical accessories, printed matter, and items for exclusive use by the disabled). Exports to outside the EU, food, and certain other goods and services are exempt from VAT and provide a right to credit of VAT suffered.

Customs and excise duties
Goods imported from outside the EU may be subject to customs duties. A Customs Code provides for customs procedures and concepts, which are based on European Community requirements. Excise duties are chargeable on certain energy products, certain alcoholic drinks, certain manufactured tobacco products, and mobile telephony services.

Employer's social security contributions
Employers are obliged to pay social security contributions at the rate of 10% of the individual employee's salary, and at fixed rates of EUR 32.91 per week for annual salaries exceeding EUR 17,115.

Stamp duty
Stamp duty is charged on, among other transactions, transfers of immovable property (5% for both residents and non-residents) and marketable securities (2%; 5% in the

case of transfers of shares in property companies). Furthermore, in the event that the market value of shares held by a person is reduced following a change in the company's issued share capital or voting rights and the value shifts onto the other shareholders, the transferor would be deemed to have transferred the said value to the transferee(s) and such value shifting may be subject to a stamp duty liability (although certain exceptions/exemptions may apply).

There could be the possibility of a stamp duty exemption subject to the satisfaction of certain conditions.

Branch income

The tax rate on branch income is the same as that for resident companies. Other than the tax charged on a branch's income, no tax is withheld on transfers of profits to the head office.

Income determination

Inventory valuation

Stock valuations are generally made at the lower of cost or market value. The last-in, first-out (LIFO) method is not accepted for taxation purposes. In general, the book and tax methods of inventory valuation will conform. Obsolescence is accepted where proved, but there are no provisions to take into account monetary inflation effects on the inventory valuation.

Capital gains

Tax is chargeable on capital gains realised on the transfer of immovable property (real estate), shares and other securities, business, goodwill, business permits, copyrights, patents, trade names, trademarks, and beneficial interests in a trust. In the case of transfers of immovable property, a final withholding tax of 12% on the transfer value applies as from 1 November 2005 (there are certain cases where the 12% final withholding tax on the transfer value may not apply – in many instances such cases would be subject to the normal tax on capital gains regime with the chargeable profit being taxed at the taxpayer's applicable rate(s)).

No tax is levied on investments that yield a fixed rate of return. A tax exemption applies in certain instances and subject to the satisfaction of certain conditions on the capital gain arising on the transfer of shares in a company listed on a recognised stock exchange other than shares held in certain collective investment schemes. If the capital gain arsing on the transfer of listed shares is subject to tax, then special rules apply with respect to the calculation of the gain and such gain would be subject to tax separately at the rate of 15%.

Subject to the satisfaction of certain conditions, if the asset is transferred between group companies, no loss or gain is deemed to arise from the transfer. A provision has been introduced to bring to charge the transfer of shares in property companies (as specifically defined) that were originally subject to intra-group tax deferral, when the transferor and the transferee cease to be members of the original group within six years from the date of such intra-group transfer.

Gains realised from the transfer of other assets fall outside the scope of the tax. Gains arising outside Malta and derived by a company that is either not domiciled

M

Malta

or not ordinarily resident in Malta are not subject to tax. There are also a number of exemptions provided in the law. For example, capital gains realised by non-residents on transfers of units in collective investment schemes, similar investments relating to linked long-term insurance business and shares, or securities in companies (except for companies holding certain Maltese immovable property) are exempt from tax.

Rollover relief
Group relief and reorganisation relief (subject to certain specific conditions) are granted.

Inter-company dividends
Dividends received by one resident company from another, whether or not a subsidiary, are taxable on the gross amount in the recipient's hands. If the distributed profits have been taxed, no further tax should be chargeable to the recipient company. However, for resident shareholders, if the corporate rate of tax in the year in which the profits are earned is lower than that in the year in which they are distributed, an amount equivalent to the difference in rates (topping up) is payable. If the distribution is made from untaxed income, the dividend would be tax-free in the hands of the recipient company.

Dividends and gains on disposal of shares received by a corporate investor from a non-resident company (or from a non-resident limited partnership) may qualify for a participation exemption in Malta, subject to the satisfaction of certain statutory conditions.

The participation exemption has also been extended to gains upon the disposal of equity holdings in Maltese-resident entities (previously the exemption applied only to transfers of shares in companies or limited partnerships resident outside Malta); distributions of taxed income by Maltese-resident companies are not subject to further tax under the full imputation system.

Foreign income
A company is taxable on its worldwide income when it is ordinarily resident and domiciled in Malta. A company that is either not ordinarily resident or not domiciled in Malta is taxable on its foreign income only insofar as such income is remitted to/received in Malta. Foreign tax is relieved by way of tax credits. This may occur under the terms of a double taxation treaty. Where no treaty exists, the foreign tax can be relieved through a system of unilateral relief. Relief for underlying tax is also granted with respect to dividend income, either in terms of a double taxation treaty or as unilateral relief. Such reliefs may be available if, among other things, evidence of tax paid abroad is produced.

Profits of Malta resident companies are subdivided for tax purposes into five accounts: the Immovable Property Account, the Final Tax Account, the Maltese Taxed Account, the Untaxed Account, and the Foreign Income Account. The last of these includes, among other things, taxable profits of Maltese-resident companies resulting from foreign investments; profits of a foreign permanent establishment; and profits resulting from foreign investments, assets, or liabilities of an onshore bank licensed in Malta. Income allocated to the Foreign Income Account for which no evidence of tax paid abroad is available can qualify for a flat-rate foreign tax credit of 25%.

The Immovable Property Account would include profits and income derived directly or indirectly from immovable property situated in Malta. The Final Tax Account would include, among other items, profits that have been subject to a final tax at source or were exempt from tax and such exemption is extended to shareholders upon a distribution of such profits. The Maltese Taxed Account would include any other taxed profits while the Untaxed Account would represent the difference between the distributable profits and the profits allocated to the other taxed accounts.

Under Malta's system of taxation of dividends, shareholders receiving distributions from the Maltese Taxed Account and/or the Foreign Income Account may be entitled to a tax refund of part or the full tax paid by the distributing Maltese company on such profits being distributed. The tax refund may be either a six-sevenths refund, a five-sevenths refund, a two-thirds refund, or a full refund of the tax suffered by the Maltese distributing company on the distributed profits. The type of the tax refund depends on the nature of the income to be distributed.

No anti-controlled foreign company/Subpart F type rules or legislation are applicable in Malta.

Stock dividends
A Maltese company may distribute bonus shares from profits, whether of an income or capital nature, and from share premium and capital redemption reserves. When bonus shares represent a capitalisation of profits, they are deemed to be dividends for tax purposes. Such bonus shares are subject to tax in the recipients' hands, gross of any tax paid at the corporate level on the relative profits, but tax credits equivalent to the gross-up of tax are available to stockholders.

Deductions

Income tax deductions
The basic condition for deductibility of expenses is that deductions are allowable only with respect to expenditures which are wholly and exclusively incurred in the production of the income.

The Income Tax (Deductions) Rules of 2001 provide for specific conditions on deductions with respect to the use of cars and the payment of employee compensation. The cost on which capital allowances on certain motor vehicles may be claimed is restricted to EUR 7,000 (increased to EUR 14,000 as from year of assessment 2011). Deductions for lease payments on cars are restricted in a manner that corresponds with the stated restriction of EUR 7,000 (increased to EUR 14,000 as from year of assessment 2011) that applies to capital allowances on owned cars. With respect to payment of employee compensation, the Deduction Rules require that in order for employee compensation to be allowed for tax purposes in the hands of the employing company, they must have been duly accounted for, in particular, the employee compensation must have been reported on the appropriate forms and within the statutory time limit to the Office of Inland Revenue. The rules also provide for restrictions on deductibility of emoluments with respect to the payment of certain fringe benefits to employees.

Depreciation and depletion
Tax depreciation is computed on the straight-line method. The rate of depreciation on plant and machinery varies according to the category of the plant and machinery

M

Malta

in question. The wear and tear rate on industrial buildings and structures (including hotels) may not exceed 2% per annum. New acquisitions of industrial buildings and structures are entitled to a concurrent extra 10% allowance in the year of acquisition. Tax depreciation is not required to conform to book depreciation.

The total allowances over the asset's useful life may not exceed 100% of its cost. If on disposal of a tax-depreciated asset a surplus arises, it is either added to the year's income or utilised to reduce the cost of any replacement. If the asset has been under-depreciated, a balancing allowance is granted.

No deduction is available for the depletion of natural resources.

The rules on tax deductions for wear and tear of plant and machinery provide for certain specific treatment in particular situations including, among other things, the following:

- To establish the cost of an asset when it is transferred between related companies, the lower of the actual cost of the asset or the tax written-down value adjusted by any balancing charge or allowance incurred by the transferring company should be applied.
- Deductions for wear and tear are allowed only where proper records and documentation have been kept that support the cost of the respective assets.
- A proportional deduction is allowed where an asset is used partly in the production of income and partly for other purposes.

Net operating losses
Net operating losses may be carried forward indefinitely until absorbed. There is no carryback of losses, not even in terminal years. Unabsorbed capital allowances may be carried forward only against the same underlying source of income. Where the source ceases to exist, any remaining balance is lost.

Payments to foreign affiliates
There are no restrictions on the deductibility of royalties, interest, and service fees paid to foreign affiliates as long as the particular expenses are considered to be incurred in the production of the particular income and satisfy the applicable statutory conditions. Interest, discount, premium, or royalties derived by non-residents are exempt from tax, subject to the applicable statutory requirements.

Taxes
A credit for foreign taxes may be applied against the Maltese tax charge. *(See Foreign income in the Income determination section.)*

Other significant items
Capital expenditures on scientific research, patents, and intellectual property rights are written off over a number of years. In the case of scientific research, a deduction may be granted at 150% of the expenditure. Certain pre-trading expenses are allowed as a deduction (subject to the satisfaction of certain statutory conditions).

Group taxation

Two companies that for tax purposes are resident exclusively in Malta, where one company is a 50% plus subsidiary of the other or both are 50% plus subsidiaries of a third Malta-resident company, qualify as members of a group of companies. Allowable losses may be surrendered by a company to another company within the group where both companies have concurrent accounting periods and form part of such group throughout the entire basis year for which this relief is claimed; however, such surrendering of losses may not occur where the surrendering or claimant company is carrying on the business of insurance. Each company must file a separate tax return, and no combined grouping or consolidated returns are permitted.

Tax incentives

Inward investment
Investments by foreigners may be readily repatriated together with profits.

The Malta Enterprise Act and other related legislation provide a comprehensive package of incentives. These incentives are reserved for enterprises carrying on certain activities in Malta, mainly manufacturing activities. The accent is on high-value-added activities. Approval of a project's eligibility for benefits by the Malta Enterprise may be required. In general, eligibility does not depend on whether the company produces for the local or for export markets. The main tax incentives include the following:

- Enterprises carrying out qualifying activities qualify for investment tax credits whereby a percentage of up to 30% (50% in the case of small-sized enterprises and 40% in the case of medium-sized enterprises) of qualifying expenditure is set-off against the tax charge (not against taxable income). Any unused credits are carried forward and added to the credits for subsequent years. The amount carried forward is increased by a percentage rate which is based on EU parameters as updated from time to time.
- Certain tax credits and special incentives may be available, subject to certain conditions, as from basis tax year 2003. These tax credits are calculated on the basis of specific expenditures incurred by a company while the special incentives grant tax exemptions on all or part of the chargeable income in specified circumstances.
- Investment allowances of up to 50% of qualifying expenditure may be granted (subject to certain capping rules) over and above tax depreciation in the year of acquisition of plant and machinery or industrial buildings/structures.
- No further tax is charged on distributions from profits that had previously been taxed at a reduced rate. This benefit is also extended to amounts that were not subject to tax on account of the investment allowance, investment tax credits, and specific tax credits/special incentives.
- The tax rate applicable to profits reinvested in the enterprise, pursuant to a project approved by the Malta Enterprise, is set at 15.75%.
- The combination of certain tax treaties and Maltese domestic law lowers the Maltese tax rate on certain companies receiving certain industrial assistance to 15%.

Capital investment
In the case of qualifying companies, an investment allowance *(also referred to in the previous section under point 3)* of 50% on plant and machinery and of 20% on industrial buildings and structures may be available (subject to certain capping rules), bringing the total allowances granted during the lifetime of the assets up to 150% and 120%, respectively. Apart from the investment allowances, normal allowances for wear and tear are also available on such assets as set out under the heading *Depreciation and depletion in the Deductions section*.

M

Malta

Shipping profits

A tonnage tax regime is applicable under Maltese law. Such regime covers profits from shipping activities as defined under the applicable regulations which are derived by qualifying Maltese-flagged and EU/EEA vessels as well as non-EU/EEA vessels satisfying certain additional rules. Furthermore, qualifying ship management activities are also entitled to the benefits of the tonnage tax regime. Profits qualifying under the tonnage tax regime may also be distributed tax-free. The related company shares are exempt from the provisions of the Duty on Documents and Transfers Act (stamp duties).

International business profits

Tax benefits are available for shareholders with respect to distributions by such companies of specified types of income. A beneficial tax regime is also available in respect of collective investment schemes.

The Maltese fiscal implications relative to trusts vary, depending on a number of circumstances including: (i) the particulars of the parties involved (e.g., domicile or residence of the trustees or beneficiaries); (ii) the act or event under review (e.g., the settlement of property, transfers of beneficial interests, distributions of trust assets, etc.); and (iii) the nature of the trust assets. Furthermore, in certain circumstances, tax transparency provisions are set out in the law, particularly so as to allow, among other things, the application of tax exemptions that would have applied to beneficiaries if there was no trust relationship.

Withholding taxes (WHT)

Domestic corporations paying certain types of income are subject to deduction of tax-at-source obligations as follows:

Recipient	Dividends (1)	Interest	Royalties
	%	%	%
Resident corporations	35	35 (2)	Nil
Resident individuals	35	25 (2)	Nil
Non-resident corporations:			
Non-treaty	35	Nil (3)	Nil (3)
Non-resident individuals:			
Non-treaty	35	Nil (3)	Nil (3)
Non-resident corporations and individuals:			
Treaty	(4)	Nil (3)	Nil (3)
Albania	35		
Australia	35		
Austria	32.5		
Barbados	35		
Belgium	35		
Bulgaria	30		

Recipient	Dividends (1)	Interest	Royalties
	%	%	%
Canada	35		
China, P.R.	35		
Croatia	35		
Cyprus	35		
Czech Republic	35		
Denmark	35		
Egypt	35		
Estonia	35		
Finland	35		
France	35		
Germany	35		
Georgia	35		
Greece	35		
Hungary	35		
Iceland	35		
India	35		
Ireland	35		
Italy	35		
Korea, Rep. of	35		
Kuwait	10/15		
Latvia	35		
Lebanon	35		
Libya	15		
Lithuania	35		
Luxembourg	35		
Malaysia	35		
Montenegro	35		
Morocco	35		
Netherlands	35		
Norway	35		
Pakistan	35		
Poland	35		
Portugal	35		
Qatar	35		
Romania	30		
San Marino	35		
Singapore	35		
Slovakia	35		
Slovenia	35		
South Africa	35		
Spain	35		
Sweden	35		
Syria	35		
Tunisia	35		

M

Malta

Recipient	Dividends (1) %	Interest %	Royalties %
United Arab Emirates	35		
United Kingdom	35		

Notes

Treaties relating to international air and shipping traffic are in force with Switzerland and the US.

The numbers in parentheses refer to the following notes:

1. Malta makes no distinction between portfolio and substantial holdings. The tax at source is not a withholding tax because no additional tax is imposed on distributions other than the tax charged on the company with respect to distributed profits. Under Malta's full-imputation system of taxation of dividends, the corporate tax is assimilated with the personal income tax of the shareholder with respect to the dividend. In the shareholder's hands, the dividend is taxed at the gross amount, and the relevant amount of corporate tax offsets the shareholder's tax liability on income from all taxable sources. Special provisions exist for taxation of distributions from income that would not have suffered tax at the corporate level.
2. Withholding of tax may be required only where the interest is debenture interest or interest on any other loan advanced to a corporation for capital purposes. The withholding tax is in effect a prepayment of the recipient's final liability because a reassessment on income is made upon the submission of returns. Any resulting overpayment is refunded.
3. Interest and royalty income derived by non-residents is exempt from tax in Malta as long as certain conditions are complied with (e.g., they are not effectively connected to a PE of the recipient situated in Malta).
4. Under its treaties, Malta retains the right to tax dividends at a rate not exceeding that paid by the company in question on the profits out of which the dividends are distributed. This rate is currently 35% (in certain treaties, for example those with Austria, Bulgaria, Kuwait, Libya, and Romania, the maximum tax is set at a lower rate). In a number of treaties the rate of deduction and of tax is reduced to 15% in the case of companies enjoying certain tax incentives. *See also Note 1 with respect to Malta's full-imputation system of taxation of dividends.*

Tax administration

Returns
An income tax return for income earned during the previous year must be filed for every year of assessment. The year of assessment is a calendar year, but a company may obtain authorisation from the Maltese Revenue to have a different year end (i.e., other than 31 December). Companies pay tax in the currency in which their share capital is denominated. The tax return for a company must be submitted by the later of nine months following the end of the financial year or by 31 March following the year of assessment (however, in recent years the Commissioner of Inland Revenue has provided concessionary extensions to such statutory deadlines in the case where the tax return is submitted electronically). Penalties are incurred on late filing of returns. The tax return submitted by the company is a self-assessment and the Commissioner of Inland Revenue will not raise an assessment unless he does not agree with the self-assessment.

Payment of tax

During the basis tax year, a company is in general required to make provisional tax (PT) payments every four months. In general, the PT payments are based on the last self-assessment filed by the company and payments are divided into three instalments of 20%, 30% and 50%, respectively. Any tax liability that is still due at the tax return date after deducting all tax credits must be settled immediately with the submission of the return. Interest at 0.75% per month is charged on any unpaid tax.

In certain instances, especially for companies with mostly international operations, PT may not be payable and the tax payment is normally paid on the earlier of the date profits are distributed or 18 months after the end of the relative accounting period.

The employer is required to withhold income tax and social security contributions from employees' salaries and pass on such tax/contributions to the Office of Inland Revenue. This system of withholding tax at source is referred to as the Final Settlement System (FSS) and the employer is legally required to operate such a system. The salary from which the withholding is to be effected should also include the value of any taxable fringe benefits. There are three main categories of fringe benefits: (i) use of motor vehicles; (ii) use of other assets including accommodation; and (iii) other benefits. The method of valuation in each case varies and the employer is required to refer to the Fringe Benefits Regulations (and also to the fringe benefits guidelines) so as to calculate the correct value of any fringe benefits being provided to the employees and to deduct the right amount of tax accordingly.

M

Corporate taxes in Mauritius

For more information, contact:

Anthony Leung Shing
PricewaterhouseCoopers
3rd floor
HSBC Centre
Ebène Cybercity
Mauritius
Tel: +230 404 5071
Email: anthony.leung.shing@mu.pwc.com

Significant developments

From the year of assessment commencing 1 January 2011, Mauritius-source royalties payable to a non-resident will be subject to a tax deduction at the rate that is the lower of 15% or the rate specified in the double taxation convention in place between Mauritius and the foreign country where the payee is resident. The withholding tax will be deemed to be the final tax payable in Mauritius. This does not apply to companies holding a category one global business licence.

The submission date for companies with a due date of 31 December for advance payment system statements or final tax returns has now been brought forward by two working days prior to 31 December.

Taxes on corporate income

Income tax is payable on total net income before distribution at the following rates:

Tax rates	%
Companies holding a Category 1 Global Business Licence (GBC1) and offshore trusts (see below)	15
Private Freeport developers and operators carrying activities other than processing	Exempt (until June 2011)
Third-party Freeport developers and operators carrying processing activities	15
All other companies	15

Companies holding a Category 2 Global Business Licence (GBC2) incorporated under the laws of Mauritius are exempt from income tax.

Under local tax law, a company may offset any foreign tax paid on any foreign-source income against the Mauritius tax on the same income. Further, where the foreign tax paid is greater than the Mauritius tax liability, the Mauritius tax would be reduced to nil.

A GBC1 may, in the absence of evidence of payment of foreign tax, claim as tax credit (presumed tax credit) an amount equal to 80% of the Mauritius tax chargeable on the foreign-source income. The presumed tax credit may also be claimed by a bank against the tax payable by it on income derived from banking transactions with non-residents and with GBC1s and GBC2s.

In the case of dividends received from abroad, a tax credit in respect of underlying tax is also available, provided that the Mauritian shareholder holds at least 5% of the share capital of the company paying the dividend. Mauritius also allows a tax-sparing credit under its local tax legislation.

Companies paying or declaring dividends must either pay tax computed in accordance with normal rules or pay an alternative minimum tax (AMT), whichever is higher.

Corporate residence

A company incorporated in Mauritius is resident in Mauritius for tax purposes.

A company not incorporated in Mauritius is resident in Mauritius only if it has its central management and control there. A GBC2 is not considered a resident in Mauritius for the purposes of double taxation treaties (DTT).

Other taxes

Local income taxes
Local income taxes leviable by local administration, such as urban councils, do not exist in Mauritius.

Morcellement tax
A capital gains (morcellement) tax is payable by every landowner who makes a parcelling of land. The tax is calculated on the excess, if any, of the sale price over the aggregate of the amounts of purchase price and the cost of infrastructure works.

Land development tax
Land development tax is payable by every person who makes a parcelling of land.

Value-added tax (VAT)
VAT is charged by VAT-registered entities at the standard rate of 15% on all goods and services supplied by them, other than exempt supplies. A person should register for VAT if his/her turnover exceeds MUR 2 million a year. However, certain persons like accountants and auditors, attorneys and solicitors, consultants, surveyors, valuers, etc., should register for VAT irrespective of their turnover.

Branch income

Tax rates on branch income are the same as on corporate profits. No tax is withheld on the remittance of profits to a head office.

Income determination

Inventory valuation
Inventories should be valued at the lower of historical cost or net realisable value. The last-in, first-out (LIFO) basis of valuation is not allowed for tax purposes.

Conformity is required between book and tax reporting. Where the revenue authority is not satisfied that the basis of valuation is acceptable, for example, where the LIFO basis has been applied, it will make such adjustment as it believes is appropriate to determine the profits arising from the business carried on.

M

Mauritius

Capital gains

There is no tax on capital gains. Gains realised from the sale of any property or interest in property acquired in the course of a business, the main purpose of which is the acquisition and sale of property as part of a profit-making undertaking or scheme, are taxable as ordinary income. Where a transaction is in the nature of trade, the revenue authority may take the view that it is an ordinary trading transaction and assess the gains derived as income. Any profit from dealings in units and securities, however, are exempt from tax.

Inter-company dividends

Companies, whether resident or not, are exempt from tax on dividends received from resident companies.

Foreign income

Resident corporations are taxed on their worldwide income with the following qualifications:

1. Generally, double taxation is avoided by means of a unilateral credit relief for foreign tax paid. The net amount of foreign income that has borne tax is grossed up at the foreign rate of tax, and the foreign tax paid is allowed as a credit against the Mauritius tax payable. However, the tax credit cannot exceed the Mauritius tax referable to the relevant foreign income. Unused credit is not refunded. In the case of foreign dividends, the tax credit includes foreign tax imposed on the profits out of which the dividends are paid (underlying tax), provided that the shareholding in the foreign company is at least 5%.
2. Regarding foreign income derived from countries with which Mauritius has treaties for the avoidance of double taxation, tax credit is given for foreign tax in accordance with the treaties. There are clauses in the double taxation conventions that provide that income arising from certain specified foreign sources is to be exempt from Mauritius tax. Mauritius has signed double taxation conventions with Barbados, Belgium, Botswana, the People's Republic of China, Croatia, Cyprus, France, Germany, India, Italy, Kuwait, Lesotho, Luxembourg, Madagascar, Malaysia, Mozambique, Namibia, Nepal, Oman, Pakistan, Rwanda, Seychelles, Singapore, South Africa, Sri Lanka, Swaziland, Sweden, Thailand, Uganda, the United Kingdom, Tunisia, United Arab Emirates, Senegal, and Zimbabwe. Double taxation treaties with Bangladesh, Malawi, Nigeria, Qatar, Russia, Vietnam, and Zambia have been signed and are awaiting ratification. Treaties with Canada, Czech Republic, Greece, Portugal, Egypt, and the Republic of Iran are under negotiation.

    Undistributed income of foreign subsidiaries is not subject to any special taxation. The income of the foreign subsidiary before distribution must not be included in the accounts of the local parent company. Dividends paid by the foreign subsidiary to the local parent company will, however, be taxable to the latter, whether or not such dividends are actually received in Mauritius. However, dividends received from outside Mauritius by a company holding a regional development certificate are tax-exempt.

Stock dividends

A resident company can distribute stock dividends (bonus shares) proportionately to all its shareholders. Stock dividends per se or convertible into cash are not taxable in the hands of the recipient. Dividends in kind are treated as taxable benefits.

Other significant items

A corporate owner of a foreign vessel registered in Mauritius or of a local vessel registered in Mauritius is exempt from tax on its income derived from the operation of such vessel. In the case of a local vessel, the exemption is limited to income derived from deep-sea international trade.

Deductions

Depreciation and depletion

Annual allowance – At rates varying between 5% and 50% of base value (unless stated otherwise), as follows:

* 5% on industrial and commercial buildings and buildings used for education and training (on cost);
* 20% on ships and aircraft, furniture and fittings;
* 35% on plant or machinery generally, 25% on motor vehicles, 30% on hotel buildings, and 25% on agricultural improvements and scientific research;
* 50% on electronic and high-precision machinery, computer hardware and peripherals, and computer software;
* 100% on aircraft leased by a company engaged in aircraft leasing (on cost); and
* 100% in respect of plant or machinery costing MUR 30,000 or less.

Tax depreciation need not conform to book depreciation. Depreciation is generally recaptured on disposal or sale when balancing charges or allowances are computed.

Net operating losses

Losses made in an accounting year are carried forward for a maximum of five years, provided the corporation can demonstrate a 50% continuity of shareholding between the year of loss and the year of claim. Losses resulting from capital allowances can be carried forward indefinitely. Loss carrybacks are not permitted.

Where a sugar factory operator that is not also a sugar cane planter incurs a loss, such loss to the extent it is unrelieved may be transferred in the income year in which it is incurred to a planter related to the operator.

Where a company takes over another company engaged in manufacturing activities, any unrelieved loss of the acquiree may be transferred to the acquirer in the income year in which the takeover takes place, on such conditions relating to safeguard of employment as may be approved by the minister of finance.

Payments to foreign affiliates

Royalties, interest, and service fees payable to foreign affiliates are allowed as expenses, provided they correspond to actual expenses incurred, are reasonable and do not exceed what would be paid under an arm's-length agreement. There are certain limitations if the recipient of the interest is not liable to Mauritius tax. Royalties paid to non-residents by GBC1s, banks out of their foreign-source income as defined in the Income Tax Act, and trusts are tax-exempt.

Taxes

Taxes paid are not normally deductible; however, municipal taxes relating to buildings that are let are deductible.

M

Mauritius

Other significant items

A bank or an approved financial institution may claim as deductions any irrecoverable loans due by a company in liquidation in respect of which winding-up procedures have started or by a company in receivership.

Group taxation

There are no group provisions in the Mauritius tax legislation other than the transfer of losses by tax incentive companies, sugar factory operators, subsidiaries located in the Island of Rodrigues, and manufacturing companies upon their take-over.

Tax incentives

Inward investment

Owners of foreign vessels registered in Mauritius are exempt from income tax on income derived from such vessels. Owners of local vessels registered in Mauritius are also exempt to the extent that the income is derived from deep-sea international trade.

Capital investment

Capital allowances are allowable on capital investment. Investment allowance is not deducted in computing written-down or residual values.

Withholding taxes (WHT)

There is no WHT in Mauritius for payments to non-residents not carrying out any business in Mauritius made by GBCs. A non-resident company receiving service fees or interest from Mauritius is liable to tax thereon at the corporate rate of 15% through a self-assessment system. Interest is either exempt from tax or taxed at reduced rates under certain tax treaties. *For dividends see Inter-company dividends.*

Since 1 October 2006 tax deduction at source has been applicable on the following:

- Interest – 15% (to be deducted by banks and deposit taking financial institutions only and for individual accounts only);
- Royalties payable to residents – 10%;
- Royalties payable to non-residents – 15%;
- Rent – 5%;
- Payments to providers of specified services – 3% (in the construction industry); and
- Payments to contractors and sub-contractors – 0.75% (in the construction industry).

Tax administration

Returns

Companies are assessed for a year beginning 1 January and ending 31 December on their income for the preceding year ending 31 December. Where a company closes its accounts at a date other than 31 December, it may elect to adopt as a basis year the accounting year ending in the 12-month period preceding the year of assessment.

Every company, both taxpayer and non-taxpayer, must file a return of its income on the basis of the income year preceding the year of assessment. Where the accounting (basis) year ends on 31 December, the return must be filed six months from the financial year-end.

Payment of tax

If timely payment is not made, a penalty representing 5% of the amount of tax due is payable. In addition, interest at the rate of 1% of the tax unpaid for each month or part of a month is payable until the tax is paid. A penalty of MUR 2,000 for each month or part of a month is also prescribed for failure to file a return, subject to a maximum of MUR 20,000.

M

Corporate taxes in Mexico

For more information, contact:

Mauricio Hurtado
PricewaterhouseCoopers
Mariano Escobedo No. 573
Col. Rincón del Bosque
CP 11580 México, DF
México
Tel: +52 55 5263 6045
Email: mauricio.hurtado@mx.pwc.com

Carlos Montemayor
PricewaterhouseCoopers
Mariano Escobedo No. 573
Col. Rincón del Bosque
CP 11580 México, DF
México
Tel: +52 55 5263 6066
Email: carlos.montemayor@mx.pwc.com

Significant developments

The Mexican tax reform for 2008 generated a number of important changes, including the introduction of the "flat tax" (referred to as "IETU", its Spanish acronym).

After two years of adaptation to the flat tax, the Mexican Congress approved other significant changes in the tax laws for 2010, mainly dealing with temporary income tax rate increases and a reduced timing benefit under the tax consolidation regime, as well as a 1% increase in Mexican value-added tax (VAT).

Taxes on corporate income

Federal income tax

The federal corporate income tax rate for the period 2010 to 2012 will be 30%. As from 2013 the rate will drop to 29% and back to 28% (as in force until 2009) as from 2014. There are no state taxes on corporate net income.

All corporate entities, including associations of a civil nature, branches, etc. are subject to the tax rules (unless specifically ruled out, such as not-for-profit organisations) applicable to Mexican corporations.

The income tax rate applicable to taxpayers engaged exclusively in agriculture, livestock, fishing, and forestry activities is currently 21%.

Provisions to recognise the effects of inflation for tax purposes in the areas of monetary assets and liabilities (annual monetary adjustment) and depreciable assets are provided in the income tax law, even though recent inflation rates have been decreasing.

Once a corporation has paid its income tax, after-tax earnings (i.e., earnings arising from the after-tax earnings account, "Cuenta de Utilidad Fiscal Neta", or CUFIN) may be distributed to the shareholders with no tax charge at the corporate level and without income tax withholding regardless of the tax residence of the recipient.

Nonetheless, if a corporation makes a distribution out of earnings that for any reason have not been subject to corporate income tax, such as distributions of book earnings (i.e., not yet recognised for tax purposes in Mexico), the corporation will be subject to corporate tax on the grossed-up distributed earnings (gross-up factors are: 1.4286 from 2010 to 2012, 1.4085 in 2013, and 1.3889 as from 2014).

Tax paid on dividends distributed in excess of CUFIN can be credited against the corporate income tax of the year or in the following two fiscal years further to the year in which the tax on the non-CUFIN distributions was paid. The CUFIN of the tax years in which the credit is applied must be reduced by an amount equal to the grossed-up dividend distribution.

Federal flat tax

The new flat tax was effective from 1 January 2008 and replaced Mexican asset tax. The flat tax applies to Mexican resident taxpayers' income from worldwide sources, as well as to foreign residents on the income attributed to their permanent establishments located in Mexico. As from 2010 a flat tax rate of 17.5% (16.5% in 2008 and 17% in 2009) is applied to the flat tax base.

In general, the flat tax base is the excess of income actually collected relating to: (i) the sale or disposal of property, (ii) the provision of independent services, and (iii) the granting of temporary use or enjoyment of assets (i.e., rental income and unrelated party royalty income) over amounts actually paid for: (i) the acquisition of assets, (ii) the receipt of independent services and (iii) the temporary use or enjoyment of assets, as well as certain (iv) other cash expenses, with the exceptions noted below.

Even though there are no tax losses for flat tax purposes, a tax credit (with similar results than the application of NOLs) may be available where flat tax deductions exceed income in a fiscal year, provided certain conditions are met. This credit may be used against flat tax liabilities for the subsequent 10 years.

Salaries and wages, employer contributions to the social security system, non-taxable employee benefits, most interest income, and royalties received from related parties for the temporary use or enjoyment of intangible assets are not included within taxable income under the flat tax legislation. Accordingly, payments in respect of these types of expenses are non-deductible items. Nevertheless, the employer can obtain a flat tax credit on "taxable" wages paid and social security contributions made, which is generally equivalent to deducting these two items.

Certain taxpayers are exempt from flat tax, principally those that are not considered taxpayers under the Mexican income tax law.

The flat tax operates as a supplemental tax to the income tax, to the extent the flat tax due is higher than the income tax due for the fiscal year. Hence, the initial flat tax triggered is reduced by a "credit" for an amount equal to the income tax of the fiscal year plus any income tax on distributions exceeding the balance of the after-tax earnings account (i.e., non-CUFIN distributions).

Flat tax is computed on a cash-flow basis (with certain exceptions) and determined per calendar year. Nevertheless, advanced monthly flat tax payments are made based on the year-to-date flat tax gross income, minus the authorised deductions in that same period.

Depreciation and amortisation are not deductible for flat tax purposes. However, a transitional rule allows the deduction of certain deferred charges and expenses acquired and paid between 1 September 2007 and 31 December 2007. Also, a flat tax credit is available for depreciable assets acquired in the period from 1998 through

M

Mexico

2007. Any payments for these types of investments made as from 2008 are deductible in-full at the time of payment.

The flat tax law also provides a transitional regime for items such as: asset tax credits carried-forward inventories and net operating losses carried forward as of 31 December 2007.

Maquiladoras (factories importing duty free materials for processing and re-exporting) are subject to specific provisions that can significantly reduce their effective flat tax rates, to the extent certain conditions are satisfied.

Financial sector entities are subject to flat tax on their financing intermediation margin, less certain cash expenses paid, pursuant to specific rules applicable to these entities in the flat tax law.

State taxes
There are no state taxes on corporate net income.

Financial system
Financial institutions must comply with reporting requirements regarding payments made to resident individuals, including the disclosing of information on the type of investment, investor identity, and the amount of interest paid.

Shares sold through the stock market
In certain specific cases the sale of shares is exempt from income tax when such shares are disposed of by individuals and residents abroad through authorised stock markets to the extent that certain requirements are met.

Interest
Income tax withholding on interest paid by financial institutions to Mexican resident investors is generally set at 0.6% of the invested capital.

To simplify the calculation of interest income from loans entered into with financial institutions, a new procedure has been proposed based on cash flow which would enter into force on 1 January 2011.

Through this procedure, financial services taxpayers would be relieved from the requirement to withhold the corresponding income tax on the principal of the loan. Income tax withheld would be considered as a final payment for individuals and an advance payment for corporations.

Corporate residence

The federal tax code provides that corporations are deemed residents in Mexico if the principal centre of administration or the effective place of management is located in Mexico. A specific definition of "tax resident" in any tax treaty overrides domestic law definitions, if the taxpayer is eligible to apply the treaty.

When a company ceases to be Mexican resident in terms of the Mexican federal tax code or any tax treaty, it is deemed to be liquidated for tax purposes. In such cases, a notification is required at least 15 days before the change and the income tax return must be filed with the Mexican tax authorities within 15 working days following the date on which the change of tax residency takes place.

Other taxes

Value-added tax (VAT)

VAT is payable at the general rate of 16% (from 2010) on sales of goods and services, as well as on lease payments and imports of goods and services, except in the border zones, where the 11% VAT rate generally applies (except on the sale of construction and developed real estate which is subject to the general rate). Until 2009 these rates were 15% and 10% for the general border zone, respectively. The sale of medicines, as well as the sale of most food products, is zero-rated. The principal VAT-exempt transactions are the sale of land, credit instruments (including equity shares), residential construction, interest paid by banks, medical services, education, salaries and wages, rentals of residential property, and the sale of non-amortisable participation certificates on real estate investment trusts, provided specific requirements are satisfied.

The sale in Mexico of temporarily imported goods by non-residents to (i) other non-residents, (ii) Maquiladoras or (iii) companies in the automotive industry is also VAT-exempt under certain circumstances.

The 0% VAT rate, which generally means that no VAT is payable, is applicable to a substantial number of transactions, including the sale of books, magazines and newspapers published by the taxpayer, the exportation of goods and certain services (including some Maquiladora activities intended for exportation), the sale of certain basic foodstuffs, agricultural goods and services, sales and rentals of farm machinery and equipment, and other specified transactions.

Taxes paid by business enterprises on their purchases and expenses related to VAT taxable activities (including activities subject to the 0% VAT rate), may usually be credited against their liability for VAT they collect from customers on their own sales, services rendered, etc. The input VAT credit on goods or services of a general nature, or those not specially identified with either taxable or exempt activities for VAT purposes, is computed based on a VAT ratio proportional to the VAT taxable versus VAT exempt activities carried out by the taxpayer. Creditable VAT paid on purchases and expenses in excess of VAT collected from customers is recoverable via either a refund or a credit against subsequent VAT liabilities.

VAT is a "cash basis" tax, with few exceptions (e.g., VAT on some types of interest must be paid on an accrued basis), therefore only the receipt of payment for goods or services triggers the output VAT liability, and an input VAT credit may be claimed only when the taxpayer pays VAT to its providers of goods and services. VAT is calculated for each calendar month as a final tax. In addition, VAT overpayments may be used to offset the tax liabilities arising from other federal taxes.

VAT must generally be withheld by Mexican residents acquiring or leasing tangible goods from non-residents, if such foreign residents do not have a permanent establishment in the country to which income is attributed. Mexican business entities are required to withhold VAT on payments to individuals or entities for services consisting of ground transportation of goods. Mexican corporations must also withhold

M

Mexico

VAT on commissions paid to individuals, as well as on independent services rendered by Mexican individuals, and on tangible goods leased from individuals.

Compulsory profit sharing
Although not a tax, every business unit with employees (irrespective of the type of organisation) is required to distribute a portion of its annual profits among all employees, except directors and the general manager. The amount distributable to the employees in most cases is 10% of taxable income, adjusted to eliminate income or deductions that relate to the recognition of inflation and include dividend income. Special rules apply to a limited number of specific businesses.

No profit sharing is paid during the first year of operations. Also, special rules apply for personal service entities and for entities deriving their income from rental activities, both of which can limit their profit sharing payment to the equivalent of one month of regular salary.

The profit sharing amount paid out is a deductible item for income tax purposes provided certain requirements are met.

Excise tax
The excise tax law ("Impuesto Especial Sobre Producción y Servicios", or IEPS) levies substantial federal excise rates on the importation and/or sale of certain taxable items, such as gasoline (% variable), beer (26.5%), wine (26.5% to 30%), spirits (53%), and cigarettes and other tobacco products (160% plus an additional quota), and on certain services related to these activities, such as commission, mediation and distribution of excise taxable items as well as services for raffles and gambling (30%). Additionally, from 2010 excise tax is also applicable to certain telecommunications services (3%).

In general terms, goods are exempt from IEPS when exported. However, since the input IEPS paid by exporters on their purchases is not creditable, that tax becomes an additional cost.

IEPS is payable (output tax) and creditable (input tax) on a cash basis. It is payable on the date that the charge invoiced is collected from the client and can be credited when the respective payment is made to the supplier. On imports, IEPS is creditable when paid at the customs offices.

In certain cases, the IEPS legislation allows taxpayers that are not subject to this tax to credit IEPS paid on the acquisition and/or the importation of certain goods, such as alcohol and semi-processed and fluid syrups (as a raw material), against income tax payable.

There is a specific procedure to calculate the tax for beer producers, bottlers and importers, however the tax can never be lower than 26.5%.

Among other obligations, IEPS taxpayers must file information regarding their 50 main clients and suppliers before the Mexican Tax Administration on a quarterly basis.

Vehicle taxes
Taxes are levied yearly on the ownership of motor vehicles, as well as on the acquisition of new vehicles. These two taxes are payable in addition to the VAT on the purchase. Note that some vehicles considered as "hybrid" (e.g., battery assisted vehicles) will not

be subject to the new vehicle acquisition tax and ownership tax will be levied at the 0% rate.

Tax on Cash Deposits (IDE)

As from 2010, IDE is applicable at 3% on monthly cash bank deposits exceeding MXP 15,000 or its equivalent in foreign currency. This tax can be credited against certain taxes, including income tax.

Branch income

Mexican branches of foreign corporations (i.e., permanent establishments or PEs) are generally subject to the same tax rules as Mexican corporations, with some exceptions. Such exceptions include that branches may deduct pro rata allocations of home office expenses, provided certain requirements are complied with (such as the existence of an applicable tax treaty and a comprehensive agreement for the exchange of tax information between the relevant territory and Mexico), but may not deduct remittances to their home offices, even when such remittances are classified as royalties, fees, commissions, services, or interest.

In general terms, distributions to the head office (other than those regarded as a return to the head office of the capital invested into the branch) either in cash or in kind from branches or other PEs are subject to the statutory corporate tax rate on the grossed-up distribution, unless the remittance is made from the CUFIN account balance (i.e., the after-tax earnings account).

The income tax law considers a PE to be any place in Mexico where business activities or services are carried out or rendered by non-residents, such as agencies, offices, mining exploration sites, or any other place of exploration, extraction, or exploitation of natural resources, regardless of the length of time involved.

A foreign insurance company could also be considered as having a PE when it engages in activities consisting of insuring risk or collecting premiums (with the exception of reinsurance activities) in Mexico through a party other than an independent agent.

Sites used for display, storage or purchasing facilities, inventories imported in-bond to be processed by a third party, short-term construction services, offices to carry out auxiliary or preliminary activities and information gathering or scientific research are not considered to create a PE in Mexico. A PE is taxed as a branch. Non-residents may also keep merchandise in bonded warehouses (including merchandise delivered for importation into Mexico) without being considered as having a PE.

A non-resident is not considered to have a PE in Mexico as result of the legal or economic relationships maintained with companies carrying out certain inventory processing activities (i.e., Maquiladoras) which normally process goods or merchandise maintained in Mexico by the non-resident by using assets provided by the non-resident or any related party, as long as certain requirements are met.

The requirements to avoid the creation of PE in Mexico include the conditions that the non-resident is a resident in tax treaty country and that the Maquiladora complies with the transfer pricing provisions provided in the law.

M

Mexico

Maquiladoras under shelter programmes may not be considered creating a PE in Mexico, when assets of foreign residents are involved and certain information is provided to the Mexican Tax Administration in relation to the gross revenues earned and income taxes paid by its non-Mexican related party. This duration of benefit (in force until 2011) is expected to be extended by the Mexican Tax Administration.

A definition of "permanent establishment" in any tax treaty overrides domestic law definitions where the taxpayer is eligible to apply the corresponding tax treaty.

Income determination

Recognition of income
Income is generally recognised on an accrual basis. However, the service revenues of civil entities that render professional services (e.g., law and accounting firms) are reported on a cash basis.

Inventory valuation
In order to determine the cost of goods sold for income tax purposes, inventories must be determined based on the valuation methods provided in the Law (e.g., first-in, first-out (FIFO), last-in, last-out (LIFO), averages, identifiable costs, retail, etc).

Capital gains
Capital gains are taxed as follows:

Securities
Gains are included in regular taxable income. There are two different procedures for computing the tax basis of a Mexican company's shares, depending on the period for which the shares are held (i.e., whether less or more than 12 months).

The tax basis of shares of Mexican corporations sold may be increased by the inflation adjustment applicable for the holding period.

In the case of shares with a holding period of more than 12 months, there are certain items to be considered when computing the tax basis, such as: (i) the movement in the after-tax earnings account (CUFIN) of the issuing company (including the possible negative CUFIN effects), as adjusted for inflation, (ii) the unamortised prior years' tax losses at the date of the sale, (iii) tax losses arising prior to the date on which the shares were acquired and amortised during the holding period, and (iv) any capital reductions of the issuing company.

When the sum of: (i) the CUFIN balance at the date of acquisition of the shares, (ii) the capital reductions paid, (iii) the unamortised prior years' tax losses at the date of the sale, and (iv) the negative CUFIN balance of the issuing corporation is higher than the sum of: (i) the CUFIN balance at the date of the sale and (ii) the tax losses arising prior to the date on which the shares were acquired and amortised during the shares' holding period, the difference must be subtracted from the tax basis of the shares to be disposed (potentially resulting in the shares' tax basis being equal to zero).

When the aforementioned difference exceeds the tax basis of the shares disposed, this excess (restated by inflation) must be subtracted from the tax basis of the shares in any subsequent share sale by the same taxpayer, even if the shares are issued by a different company.

The aforementioned procedure allows the average cost (tax basis) of the shares to be determined, which is then updated and considered as the acquisition cost for future sales.

A different but simpler procedure applies for computing the tax basis of shares held during a period of 12 months or less.

Deduction of losses arising from the sale of shares is limited to the value of gains from similar transactions in the same or the following five fiscal years. Losses may not be deducted by non-residents selling shares.

A gain from the sale of shares is considered Mexican source income when the transferred shares are issued by a Mexican resident or when more than 50% of their book value arises directly or indirectly from immovable property located in Mexico, including cases where the shareholding is structured in different levels.

In general terms, the sale by non-residents of shares issued by a Mexican company is subject to a 25% withholding tax applicable to the gross amount of the transaction (i.e., without deductions). However, there may be the option for gains realised by non-residents on the sale of shares issued by a Mexican company to be taxed by applying the statutory 30% rate to the net gain (i.e., the value of the transfer less the tax basis of the shares). The tax rate for these purposes is the same as that applicable to corporate taxpayers in each year, as mentioned above. Hence, in 2013 the rate will be reduced to 29% and to 28% as from 2014.

This net income election is available only if the foreign shareholder is resident of a country that is not considered a "preferred tax regime jurisdiction" (tax haven) or a country with a territorial tax system. The non-resident seller must have previously appointed a representative in Mexico, and have a public accountant assigned to issue a statutory tax audit report on the transfer of shares. The public accountant issuing the respective report must specify the accounting value of the shares sold and explain the factors used in determining the sales price and the market value of the shares if shares are sold between related parties.

The representative is jointly liable for the tax on the sale of shares, even when the statutory report is issued by a public accountant.

The tax authorities may authorise the deferral of taxes that would otherwise be triggered by the transfer of shares in a group reorganisation (the authorisation must be obtained prior to the share transfer). The price used on the transaction must be at arm's length. The tax deferred adjusted for inflation is due upon the sale of the originally transferred shares outside the same interest group. An interest group consists where shareholders have over 50% common voting stock of the companies.

In principle, authorisations for tax deferral are not granted if the party acquiring or selling the shares is resident in a tax haven, or of a country that has not signed a broad exchange of information agreement with Mexico. However, in the latter case, an authorisation may still be granted if the taxpayer provides documentation to the Mexican tax authorities stating that the taxpayer has authorised the foreign tax authorities to provide information to the Mexican authorities regarding the operation in question.

Mexico

If the share sale qualifies as an exempt reorganisation under tax treaty rules, the non-resident must appoint a legal representative in Mexico prior to the sale and file a notice with the Mexican Tax Administration informing them of such appointment and the details of the reorganisation process intended to be carried out. Additionally, certain formal requirements are established in the regulations of the Mexican income tax law that must be satisfied when carrying out this type of transaction.

Tax treaty rules (optionally) override domestic law rules when the seller resides in a tax treaty country.

Real estate
In determining the taxable gain, the cost basis of the land and buildings may be adjusted (i.e., increased) for tax purposes on the basis of the period of time for which the assets have been held. This adjustment is performed by applying inflation adjustment factors to the net undepreciated balance. Similar rules apply to non-residents electing to pay tax on net income by appointing a legal representative in Mexico. The rate of tax on the net gain is 30% (in 2013 the rate will be reduced to 29% and to 28% as from 2014). Otherwise, the 25% final withholding tax on gross income applies to non-residents.

Machinery and equipment
Gains or losses from the disposal of machinery, equipment, and other fixed assets are also calculated after adjusting the basis in these assets, by applying inflation factors to the net undepreciated balance.

Inflationary gain or loss
Taxpayers are required to calculate an adjustment for inflation (resulting in additional taxable income or deductible expense) on an annual basis by applying the percentage increases in the National Consumer Price Index (NCPI) to the value of essentially all liabilities reduced by monetary assets, including bank balances, investments (except in shares), and some debt and receivables.

Inter-company dividends
Dividends received by Mexican corporations from other Mexican corporations need not be included in gross income. However, dividend income is subject to the 10% compulsory profit sharing, and must be included within the recipient corporation's CUFIN.

No further taxes apply on dividends distributed out of the CUFIN. However, non-CUFIN distributions (i.e., distributions that for any reason have not been subject to corporate income tax) are generally subject to tax at the level of the distributing company at the general income tax rate on the grossed-up distribution.

Foreign income
A Mexican corporation is taxed on foreign-source income when earned. Double taxation is reduced, or possibly avoided, by means of foreign tax credits. However, the undistributed profits of a foreign subsidiary are not subject to Mexican tax until dividends are paid, with the exception of companies with investments in entities located in a tax haven ("income subject to preferred tax regimes"), in which case income is generally taxable even if no distributions are received from those entities.

Investments in tax havens (income subject to preferred tax regime)

Investments in tax havens include those made directly or indirectly in entities, branches, real property, shares, bank accounts, or investment accounts, and any kind of participation in entities, trusts, joint ventures, or investment funds, as well as in any other similar legal entities created or incorporated in accordance with foreign law and located in a tax haven, and including those that are carried out through an intermediary.

A business, entity, trust, or joint venture is considered to be located in a tax haven when it has a physical presence, an address, a post office box, or effective management in a tax haven, or when its bank account is held in or through financing entities located in a tax haven.

Unless it can be demonstrated that the taxpayer does not have management control of the foreign investments, the taxpayer must include the income generated through such entities or foreign vehicles in the proportion that corresponds to their direct or indirect participation in the capital of the entity or vehicle.

Income and profits subject to preferred tax regimes (PTR) are taxed separately. This income cannot be combined with other taxable income or losses and it is not considered for purposes of making advance income tax payments. Tax applicable to this type of income is payable together with the corporate annual tax return.

The classification of a PTR is not based on the location of the investment but on the tax effectively paid on the income generated abroad. An investment is considered subject to a PTR if the income tax paid abroad is less than 75% of the income tax that would have been incurred and paid in Mexico, if the income had been taxed under Mexican rules.

In general, interest income and the annual inflationary adjustment made to liabilities of the investment in the tax haven are included in taxable income without subtracting the annual inflationary adjustment on receivables.

However, the annual inflationary adjustment on receivables may be subtracted from interest income earned, provided an information return is filed.

Tax on investments in a PTR is determined by applying the general corporate income tax rate to taxable income. Additionally, net operating loss carryforwards associated with an investment in a PTR may be amortised against the tax profit of the following tax years arising from investments in PTR, and tax deductions related to the investment may also be applied, as long as accounting records pertaining to those investments are available and the annual information return on the investments is filed on time.

Undistributed income from investments in entities located in a PTR need not be immediately included in taxable income under the above provisions in certain particular cases (e.g., income arising from activities that qualify as active business activities in accordance with the applicable legislation and in the case of indirect investments in a tax haven when certain strict conditions are met).

Income earned in a PTR will be exempted where the PTR income arises from a business activity. This exemption will not be applicable, however, if income such as interest,

M

Mexico

dividends, royalties, certain capital gains, and rents (i.e., passive income) represents more than 20% of the total income generated.

Other specific exemptions may remain applicable in the case of share transfers within the same group and for income derived from royalties and interest that do not represent a tax deduction for Mexican tax residents to the extent that certain specific requirements are fulfilled.

Maquiladoras

Companies operating under an IMMEX programme (Maquiladoras/In bond processing companies) are considered to not have a PE in Mexico for the non-resident principal who owns the equipment and inventory to the extent they are residents of a country that has a tax treaty with Mexico in force, that all the terms and requirements of the treaty are complied with, and that the mutual agreements of Mexico and its treaty partner are satisfied. This relief applies only if the Maquiladora complies with any of the following options stated by the domestic law.

1. Maintenance of documentation on transfer pricing in accordance with the applicable legislation, adding to the Maquila fee 1% of the net book value of the machinery and equipment owned by the foreign related company and used by the Maquiladora in its activities.
2. Reporting of a taxable income margin of a minimum of the higher of:
    * 6.9% of the value of assets used in the Maquila activity (including the inventories and fixed assets owned by the foreign related party); or
    * 6.5% of the value of the operating costs and expenses of the Maquiladora.
3. Maintenance of documentation on transfer pricing using the transactional net margin method (TNMM) and considering a return on the net book value of machinery and equipment owned by the foreign related company used by the Maquiladora in its activities, adjusted by financing terms.

Maquiladoras that apply option 1 or option 3 may request an advanced pricing agreement (APA) from the Mexican tax authorities. However, this APA is not mandatory to obtain the PE exemption.

Maquiladoras that apply any of the three options above are not required to file an annual information return on transactions with foreign related parties. This exemption is only available in respect of the Maquila activity.

If the Maquiladora renders services other than exported Maquila services (including domestic sales), specific transfer pricing requirements apply and potential PE issues must be evaluated.

In general terms, the Maquiladoras receive a significant reduction on their effective income tax and flat tax rates to the extent certain conditions are satisfied.

The Mexican Tax Administration has recently initiated a detailed review of the Maquiladora programme, hence it is expected that significant tax reforms will be approved in the coming years.

Deductions

General rule
The applicable deduction requirements must be complied with no later than the last day of the tax year to which the deduction applies, although the invoice supporting the expense may be provided up to the date on which the tax return for the period in question is filed (or comes due). An expense invoice must contain a date within the year for which the deduction is claimed.

Deductions for certain business expenses are limited in the case of business meals and use of company owned cars.

Cost of goods
The costing system to be used will be the incurred cost system, based on historic costs or pre-determined costs. If the requirements provided on the regulations of the income tax law are met, the direct cost system (based on historical costs) may be used.

Inventory may be determined by any of the following methods:

- First-in, first-out (FIFO);
- Last-in, first-out (LIFO);
- Identifiable costs;
- Average cost; or
- Retail.

The FIFO and LIFO methods must be applied to each type of merchandise and each movement. The monetary FIFO and LIFO methods may not be used. Taxpayers selling goods that are identifiable by serial numbers, at a cost exceeding MXP 50,000, must determine their inventory by the identifiable cost method.

Once elected, a method is compulsory for five years and can be changed only if the requirements established in the regulations of the income tax law are fulfilled. The monetary results of the change in method are amortised over the following five years.

For accounting purposes, different methods and certain variations can be adopted. However, a record of the differences must be maintained, and such difference will not be taxable or deductible.

The cost of imported goods may be deducted (and included in the cost of goods sold) only if it can be supported that the goods were legally imported into the country.

Depreciation, amortisation and depletion
Straight-line depreciation is permitted at the rates specified in the law, and the deduction may be increased by applying the percentage increases in the NCPI from the month in which the asset was originally acquired. When an asset is disposed of or becomes useless, the remaining undepreciated historical cost may also be deducted, after application of the appropriate inflation adjustment factor to the undepreciated historical cost.

Mining exploration and development expenses incurred prior to the commencement of operations and the cost of mining claims may be amortised at 10% per year, after

M

Mexico

applying inflation adjustment factors, unless the taxpayer elects to deduct these costs as incurred.

Intangible assets for the exploitation of goods that are in the public domain, or for rendering public services under concession, are considered deferred assets (i.e., not deducted as incurred). Therefore, these assets are subject to amortisation for income tax purposes.

Specific annual depreciation rates are established for goods used in certain industries.

Tax losses
Subject to certain limitations, losses incurred in prior years by a business may be carried forward and deducted from income earned over a subsequent 10-year period.

Losses carried forward may be increased by the percentage increase in the NCPI between the seventh and twelfth months of the fiscal year in which they are incurred, and thereafter up to the sixth month of the fiscal year in which they are applied.

Tax loss carryforwards are non-transferable; however they can be used by the surviving entity, in a merger with certain restrictions. In the case of a spin-off, tax loss carryforwards can be divided between the surviving entity and the spun-off entities in proportion to the following:

1. Inventories and accounts receivable transferred in the case of commercial entities; or
2. Fixed assets transferred, in all other cases.

Current tax legislation limits the utilisation of tax losses in changes in ownership. The rule provides that changes in ownership representing more than 50% of the voting shares, prevents the utilisation of tax losses against income obtained in the same trade of business ("giro"), with certain exceptions.

Payments to foreign affiliates
Taxable income and authorised deductions must be determined on the basis of prices that would be agreed with independent parties in comparable transactions (arm's-length values).

For this purpose, taxpayers must secure and maintain contemporaneous documentation supporting transactions with related parties residing abroad, demonstrating that income and deductions are based on market values. This documentation must be prepared per type of transaction, and must include all operations carried out with related parties.

Domestic transactions must also be supported by the application of a recognised transfer pricing method selected in accordance with the ordering preferred methods determined in the legislation.

Payments made to residents of tax havens (or PTRs described above) are considered non-deductible, unless it can be demonstrated that the price of the transaction is the same that would have been set between or among unrelated parties in comparable transactions. Unless the contrary is demonstrated, it is assumed that operations with companies, entities, or trusts resident in a PTR are carried out between or among related parties, and that prices are not set as they would be in comparable operations between or among independent parties.

The sales price of shares (other than publicly traded shares) sold to a related party must be set at market value and the transaction must be supported by the corresponding contemporaneous transfer pricing documentation.

In order to be deductible, payments of technical assistance fees and for the transfer of technology or royalties must be made directly to companies with the required technical capabilities to provide the corresponding service, and should correspond to services actually received.

Payments to non-residents of a prorated portion of expenses (i.e., allocations of expenses) are not deductible for Mexican corporations.

Thin capitalisation

Interest generated by excess debt lent by a related party is non-deductible for income tax purposes. Excess debt is defined as more than three times the value of shareholders' equity (i.e., a 3-to-1 debt-to-equity ratio) as per the taxpayer's Mexican GAAP balance sheet.

In principle, all liabilities are considered in determining the annual average liabilities for purposes of calculating the ratio and thereby the disallowed interest expense amount. However, certain liabilities incurred for construction, operation, or maintenance of the productive infrastructure associated with the strategic areas of Mexico may be excluded from this computation.

Taxpayers may also be able to obtain a ruling from the Mexican Tax Administration in order to apply a higher financial leverage (i.e., not the 3-to-1 debt-to-equity ratio), owing to the characteristics of their activities. Also, the thin capitalisation rules do not apply to the financial sector.

In addition, taxpayers are entitled to use instead of shareholders' equity, the sum of the average balances of the capital contributions account (CUCA) and the after-tax earnings account (CUFIN) to determine the 3-to-1 debt-to-equity ratio. Taxpayers that opt for this tax equity computation must continue to use it for at least five years. This alternative computation is mandatory for those taxpayers that do not account for capital following Mexican Generally Accepted Accounting Principles.

Specific provisions dealing with the disallowance of interest expenses for debt financing structured though back-to-back loans should also be closely observed.

Taxes

In general, all federal, state, and local taxes levied on a company (not including those required to be withheld from other parties) represent deductible expenses for income tax, with the following exceptions.

1. Federal income tax.
2. Flat tax.
3. Federal VAT and excise tax when the company is entitled to credit the tax.
4. Taxes on acquisitions of fixed assets and real estate, which must be capitalised and deducted as part of the total cost of such assets to be depreciated.

M

Mexico

Donations

The maximum amount for deductible donations is limited to 7% of the taxable income of the previous year.

Group taxation

The income tax law contains a chapter that allows certain holding companies to file a consolidated income tax return with their majority-owned subsidiaries. Tax consolidation is applicable for income tax purposes, but not for other taxes (e.g., flat tax and VAT) or compulsory employee profit sharing.

The principal requirements for a company to qualify as a holding company for fiscal consolidation are that it must be a Mexican tax resident with no more than 50% of its shares owned by other companies, regardless of their country of residence. Shares that qualify as placed among the general investing public and non-voting shares are not considered for this purpose.

Where more than 50% of the holding company's shares are held by a foreign corporation, the above qualifying rule precludes the possibility of filing a consolidated return for a Mexican group, for companies that would otherwise qualify. However, there is an exception in cases where the foreign corporation that owns the shares of the Mexican holding company is a resident in a country that has executed a comprehensive agreement for the exchange of tax information with Mexico.

At present, Australia, Belgium, Brazil, Canada, Chile, the Czech Republic, Ecuador, Finland, France, Germany, Israel, Italy, Japan, New Zealand, the Republic of Korea, the Netherlands, Norway, Romania, Singapore, Spain, Sweden, the United Kingdom, and the United States have agreements of this nature with Mexico, and other agreements or tax treaties that might contain such an agreement are awaiting ratification or being negotiated.

The Mexican Tax Administration must authorise the application of the consolidation regime and financial statements and written consent of the legal representative must be filed before August 15 of the year prior to the first year of consolidation. There is a minimum five-year period of fiscal consolidation and special consolidated tax accounts should be prepared by the consolidated group.

There are some entities that are non-qualifying entities for inclusion in the consolidation regime, such as non-profit entities, credit institutions, insurance corporations, trusts, auxiliary credit institutions, stock exchange entities, foreign exchange houses and capital investment companies, non-resident companies, companies in liquidation, civil or social associations, and cooperatives.

In general terms, the consolidation regime allows certain benefits, such as:

- Individual company loss offset against profits of other companies in the same group during a deferral period.
- Deferral of tax on dividends in excess of the individual CUFIN, to the extent that the dividend flow remains within the consolidation group.
- Capital losses in the holding company from the sale of subsidiaries deducted as an ordinary loss in the year.

Prior to 2010, these deferral benefits are subject to recapture, which can generally be triggered upon:

- A member of the consolidated group leaves the group.
- A reduction in the ownership percentage.
- Deconsolidation of the group.
- Expiration of certain carryforward limitations (i.e., tax loss and capital loss recapture is required if any of the above three events occur during the 10-year period).

The significant 2010 tax reforms introduced important modifications to the consolidation regime, including a reduction of the recapture period from ten to five years in the case of tax losses and capital losses. Moreover, the introduction of new rules now trigger for excess dividends over the CUFIN balance and other recapture items after five years while these deferrals were often considered indefinite before the reform, as long as the same group remained in the consolidation with the same ownership percentages.

As a result, most of the consolidated benefits will be reversed in five years and the deferred income tax will be payable with the submission of the tax return starting from "Year six", as follows:

- 25% in each of years six and seven;
- 20% in year eight; and
- 15% in each of years nine and 10.

Similar transitional rules have also been implemented for the recapture and repayment of certain consolidated benefits obtained in years prior to 2010.

Tax incentives

Inward investment
Tax incentives for inward investment are as follows.

1. Duty-deferral programmes: A deferral programme is an authorisation provided by the Mexican Ministry of Economy to those companies importing raw materials and fixed assets on a temporary basis to manufacture finished products within Mexico that will be exported.

    In addition to the benefits described for corporate tax purposes in the *Income determination section*, IMMEX companies (known as Maquiladoras - i.e., entities with a Manufacturing, Maquila and Export Service Program in force) are entitled to the following customs benefits:

    - No payment of import duties and VAT for temporarily imported raw materials, as long as they are exported.
    - Sales of temporarily imported goods to other Maquila companies at a 0% VAT rate.
    - Temporary import of fixed assets without paying VAT.

    Another programme allowing preferential duty rates is the Program of Sectoral Promotion (known as PROSEC) which allows manufacturers to apply lower duty

Mexico

rates on the permanent import of raw materials and machinery required for its productive processes, regardless of their country of origin and regardless if they are for the Mexican market or for export. These programmes were created by the federal government in order to establish competitive tariff conditions for Mexican manufacturers needing to import raw materials and fixed assets from non-NAFTA countries due to the changes made in 2001, where non-originating merchandise exported to NAFTA countries must pay duties.

The Ministry of Economy also provides a Registry for High Export Companies (known as ALTEX) which provides the following benefits:

- The company can obtain the refund of its favourable VAT balances in a shorter period of time.
- The company is exempted from the second customs review of its exports which expedites the customs clearance process.

Companies in Mexico which had formerly performed import operations with values from MXP 200 million to MXP 400 million per semester could take advantage of significant customs and administrative benefits if registered into the "Certified Company Registry" (authorised by the Ministry of Finance).

In general terms, the main benefits provided by the Certified Company Registry are the following:

- Permission to perform import customs clearance through any customs office.
- Reduction in time and number of reviews when clearing goods at customs facilities.
- Permission to perform clearance of goods for export at the company's own facilities.
- Possibility to amend information contained within the import-export documents (including origin), fines reductions, and self-correction.
- In the event of an "Administrative Customs Process Review", the obligation to comply with non-tariff regulations can be met within 60 days of receiving notification from the Customs Authority, without the seizure of the imported goods. For 2010, 58.15% of 10,900 tariff items are exempt from import duties, and for the remaining tariff items the average import duty rate is 5.34%.

2. Investments in certain new fixed assets outside Mexico City, Guadalajara, and Monterrey are entitled to an accelerated depreciation deduction considering a present value discounted rate of the future stream of depreciation. Some taxpayers may benefit from this deduction in the aforementioned cities if they can show that their business operations do not contribute to pollution and do not require the intensive use of water.
3. An income tax incentive for taxpayers involved in certain technological research and development projects carried out during the year allows a cash subsidy to be yearly determined by the tax authorities, based on a budget to be approved by the Mexican Congress.
4. Another incentive offers a credit equivalent to 100% of the income tax corresponding to the salary paid to workers/employees with certain types of disabilities.

5. A limited credit is applicable for investments in movie production activities through an immediate tax credit which is capped at 10% of the total income tax of the prior year.
6. Taxpayers investing in specific regions of Mexico considered to be "marginal scarcely inhabited zones" (less than 50,000 inhabitants) can receive certain tax benefits, such as 100% exemption on Social Security contributions to the extent certain requirements are met and financing benefits for the development of industrial facilities according to the guidelines and limitations provided by the Ministry of Economic Affairs in Mexico.
7. Several tax benefits exist for qualifying real estate investments (i.e., Mexican REITs such as FIBRAS, SIBRAS, etc.) in Mexico.

Capital investment

There are certain incentives to encourage risk capital investments in Mexico.

Other incentives

Certain other specific and limited tax incentives are available for taxpayers engaged in certain activities (e.g., those engaged in air or sea transportation of goods or passengers with respect to aircraft and ships with a federal government commercial concession or permit; in the agricultural and forestry sectors; and in bond warehouses with respect to real property used for the storage, safeguarding, or conservation of goods or merchandise).

Withholding taxes (WHT)

Payments to Mexican residents

Payments to resident corporations and permanent establishments in Mexico are generally not subject to withholding taxes.

Payments by resident corporations to resident individuals are subject to withholding tax as follows:

Withholding tax	Percentage of income tax to be withheld
1. Wages, salaries and other remuneration	0-30
2. Fees:	
(i) Members of boards of directors and advisory boards	30
(ii) Other professional fees	10
3. Lease payments on real property	10
4. Interest on securities (1)	0.6
5. Interest on nonqualified securities	20
6. Dividends	Nil
7. Miscellaneous types of income of individuals, usually sporadic payments	20

Notes

1. This withholding tax is currently calculated on the total amount of the capital invested.

M

Mexico

Payments to non-residents

Income tax must usually be withheld from payments to non-resident corporations and individuals. In the case of non-tax treaty countries, the statutory withholding rates are as noted below.

Income tax of 40%, with no deductions, must be withheld on most payments made to foreign related parties located in tax havens, in lieu of the tax provided in the domestic law for non-tax haven residents. This is not applicable in certain cases, such as on income not subject to Mexican taxation in accordance with the regular provisions for income earned by non-residents from a source of wealth located in Mexico, income from dividends and certain types of interest, including interest payments made to foreign banks. In these cases, the regular provisions of the domestic law should be applied to determine the income tax withholding.

Additionally, revenues for intermediation services, including commissions for brokerage, agents, distribution, and assignment and generally all income from the negotiation of third-party interests are also subject to 40% withholding tax when paid to tax haven residents.

Non-residents' wages and salaries are taxed on the basis of a 12-month earnings period at the following income tax withholding rates:

Taxable income		
From	**To**	**%**
0	MXP 125,900	Nil
MXP 125,901	MXP 1,000,000	15
MXP 1,000,001	and above	30

The above mentioned rates are also applicable to retirement fund payouts.

However, no tax arises on compensation (wages, salaries, or fees other than board fees) paid by a non-resident with no establishment in Mexico (even if not subject to tax) to which the services relate, provided the individual remains in Mexico for fewer than 183 days (consecutive or not) in any 12-month period.

The tax, when applicable, is withheld if the income is paid by a resident (or a non-resident with a permanent establishment in Mexico). Otherwise, the tax is generally payable within 15 working days of the associated payment, by the party earning the Mexican-sourced income.

Statutory withholding rates (not mentioned above) under local legislation are as follows:

Withholding tax rates	%
1. Professional fees for services rendered in Mexico	25
2. Lease payments:	
2.1 Lease of real property	25
2.2 Lease of containers, airplanes, and ships authorised by the Mexican Government to be commercially exploited in the transportation of goods or persons	5
2.3 Lease of personal property	25

Withholding tax rates	%
3. Time-sharing services (1)	25
4. Charter agreements	10
5. Sales:	
5.1 Real property located in Mexico (1)	25
5.2 Shares of Mexican companies (1, 2)	25
5.3 Transfers of ownership of Mexican public debt by other than the original creditors (intended to cover debt-for-equity swaps) (1)	25
6. Derivative transactions:	
6.1 On capital (1)	25
6.2 On debt (3)	Same rates applicable to interest
7. Interest (4):	
7.1 Paid to foreign government financing entities, to duly registered foreign banks and other entities that provide financing with funds obtained by issuing publicly traded debt instruments abroad, registered with the Ministry of Finance (5)	10
7.2 Interest on debt instruments placed abroad (6)	4.9
7.3 Interest payments to specific foreign financial institutions (7)	4.9
7.4 Other interest payments (not otherwise included above) paid by Mexican financial institutions to residents abroad	21
7.5 Paid to foreign suppliers of machinery and equipment, to others to finance purchases of such assets or inventory or working capital loans, if the lender is duly registered	21
7.6 Paid to reinsurance entities	15
7.7 Other interest payments (11)	30
7.8 Financial leases (on the portion deemed to qualify as interest or finance charge)	15
8. Dividends	Nil
9. Royalties (8):	
9.1 For the use of railroad cars	5
9.2 For the use of copyrights on scientific, literary, or art works, including motion pictures and radio and television recordings, as well as software and payments for the transmission of video and audio signals via satellite, cable, optic fibre, and similar media	25
9.3 On patents, invention or improvement certificates, trademarks, brand names, and advertising (11)	30
9.4 For the use of drawings or models, plans, formulas, or procedures, and of scientific, commercial, and industrial equipment; on amounts paid for information regarding scientific, commercial, and industrial experience; and for technical assistance	25
10. Short-term construction, and the respective installation, maintenance, technical direction or supervision (9)	25
11. Reinsurance premiums	2
12. Income obtained by athletes and artists (1)	25
13. Income derived from prizes (e.g., lottery tickets or raffles) (10)	1, 21
14. Other income (forgiven debts, indemnifications, rights to participate in business, investments, etc.) (11)	30

M

Mexico

Notes

1. The non-resident may elect to pay tax at a rate of 30% in 2010 (*see note 11 below for the rate applicable thereafter*) on the net taxable profit, in the case of (i) time-sharing services, (ii) share sales, (iii) sales of real property, (iv) activities of sportsmen/artists, and (v) derivative stock and debt transactions provided that the non-resident recipient of the income has a legal representative resident in Mexico and to the extent that the following specific requirements are met:

   i. For time-sharing services, the resident legal representative must keep the audited financial statements of the taxpayer available for inspection by the Mexican Tax Administration.

   ii. For share sales, a tax opinion issued by a registered public accountant is required.

   iii. For shares and debt-for-equity swap transactions, this election is available only where the foreign taxpayer is not a resident of a country classified as a tax haven or a country with a territorial tax system.

   It should be noted that there is an option to defer Mexican income tax arising from the sale of shares within the same group due to a corporate reorganisation provided certain conditions are met and that no legal representative is required for sales of real property by public deed.

2. The sale of shares through the Mexican Stock Exchange and government securities are exempt from income tax withholding provided certain rules are satisfied.

3. The applicable withholding rate (based on the withholding tax rates for interest) for debt-derivative transactions is applied on a net basis, that is, gross income less authorised deductions. However, if the transaction is liquidated in kind, the applicable withholding rate (on the same net basis) is 10%.

4. Interest payments to non-residents are exempt from Mexican income tax when they are paid on the following.

   i. Loans to the federal government or to the Bank of Mexico (Central Bank) or bonds issued by the latter organisation to be acquired and paid abroad.

   ii. Loans for three or more years granted or guaranteed by duly registered financial entities that promote exports through special financing.

   iii. Preferential loans granted or guaranteed by foreign financial entities to institutions authorised to receive tax-deductible donations in Mexico, provided these institutions are properly registered and use the funds for purposes consistent with their status.

   iv. Loans derived from bonds issued by the Federal government or the Bank of Mexico placed on a recognised national stock exchange, to the extent the beneficial owner is a foreign resident.

5. In 2010, 4.9% (such rate has been extended for another year) is applicable when the interest is paid to registered banks resident in countries with which Mexico has signed a tax treaty.

6. The 4.9% withholding rate applies provided the placement is handled through banks or brokerage firms resident in a country with which Mexico has signed a tax treaty, if there is compliance with the information requirements established in the general rules issued by the Ministry of Finance. If there is failure to comply with these requirements, the 10% withholding rate applies. The 4.9% and 10% withholding rates mentioned in the preceding paragraphs do not apply, and instead a 30% (*see note 11 below for the rate applicable thereafter*) withholding rate is applicable to interest, when the direct or indirect beneficiaries of the interest, either individually or jointly with related parties, receive more than 5% of the interest arising from the instrument in question, and are either (a) holders of more than 10% of the voting shares of the issuing company, either directly or indirectly, either individually or jointly with related parties, or (b) business entities holding more than 20% of their shares, either directly or indirectly, either individually or jointly with parties related to the issuer.

7. The 4.9% tax withholding rate is applicable to interest payments made to foreign financial institutions in which the Mexican federal government or the Mexican Central Bank has an equity participation.

8. The withholding tax rate is applied to the gross amount of the payment.

9. The non-resident taxpayer may elect to pay 30% in 2010 through 2012 *(see note 11 below for the rate applicable thereafter)* tax on the net profit, if the taxpayer has a resident legal representative and so advises the customer, who then makes no withholding. When business activities last for more than 183 days, the foreign taxpayer is deemed to have a permanent establishment in Mexico for tax purposes and is taxed in the same manner as a local resident corporation or branch.
10. The 21% federal rate is applied only in the case of non-qualifying prizes (i.e., income derived from prizes that is subject to a state taxation that exceeds a rate of 6%).
11. A 30% income tax withholding rate is applicable for the period 2010 to 2012. As from 2013 the rate will reduce to 29% and back to 28% as from 2014. The statutory withholding rates mentioned above may be reduced by applying tax treaty provisions. During the last decade, Mexico has embarked on a policy of negotiating a network of tax treaties with its principal trading and investment partners.

As of 30 April 2010, the following treaties are pending ratification, in process of compliance of specific formalities by the respective governments in order to become effective, have not been published yet in the Official Gazette or are under negotiation: Colombia, Hungary, Kuwait, Latvia, Lebanon, Malaysia, Morocco, Nicaragua, Panama, Slovenia, South Africa, Thailand, Ukraine, Uruguay, and Venezuela. The treaty with India has been signed and published. However, its reduced withholding tax rates are not yet in force.

Note that the tax treaties in force with Austria, Luxembourg, Switzerland, and the UK are being renegotiated. Although, they have not been published yet in the Official Gazette, they are expected to be applicable as from 2011 (subject to certain formalities), in which case some of the rates displayed below may have to be updated.

Tax treaties with Australia, Austria, Barbados, Belgium, Brazil, Canada, Chile, China, the Czech Republic, Denmark, Ecuador, Finland, France, Germany, Greece, Iceland, Indonesia, Ireland, Israel, Italy, Japan, the Republic of Korea, Luxembourg, the Netherlands, New Zealand, Norway, Poland, Portugal, Romania, Russia, Singapore, the Slovak Republic, Spain, Sweden, Switzerland, the United Kingdom, and the United States have been published in the Official Gazette, and are in force.

M

The tax rates are as follows:

	Dividends			
	Portfolio	Substantial holdings	Interest	Royalties
	%	%	%	%
Australia	15	0 (1)	10, 15 (25)	10
Austria	10	5 (4)	10	10
Barbados	10	5 (1)	10	10
Belgium	15	5 (2)	10, 15 (16)	10
Brazil	15	10 (6)	15	10, 15 (27, 29)
Canada	15	5 (4)	10	10
Chile	10	5 (6)	5, 15 (26)	5, 10 (29, 30)
China	5 (7)	5 (7)	10	10
Czech Republic	10 (7)	10 (7)	10	10
Denmark	15	0 (3)	5, 15 (17)	10
Ecuador	5 (7)	5 (7)	10, 15 (16)	10

Mexico

	Dividends			
	Portfolio	Substantial holdings	Interest	Royalties
	%	%	%	%
Finland	Nil	Nil	10, 15 (24)	10
France	0, 5 (9)	0, 5 (9)	5, 10 (29, 17)	10 (29)
Germany	15	5 (1)	5, 10 (18)	10
Greece	10 (7)	10 (7)	10	10
Iceland	15	5 (1)	10	10
Indonesia	10 (7)	10 (7)	10	10
Ireland, Rep. of	10	5 (4)	5, 10 (17, 29)	10
Israel	10	5 (10)	10	10
Italy	15 (7)	15 (7)	10 (29)	15
Japan	15	5 (8)	10, 15 (25)	10
Korea, Rep. of	15	0 (1)	5, 15 (17)	10
Luxembourg	15	8 (11)	10	10
Netherlands	15	Nil (12)	5, 10 (21)	10 (28)
New Zealand	15 (7, 13)	15 (7, 13)	10	10
Norway	15	Nil (3)	10, 15 (16)	10
Poland	15	5 (3)	10, 15 (19)	10
Portugal	10 (7)	10 (7)	10	10
Romania	10 (7)	10 (7)	15	15
Russia	10 (7)	10 (7)	10	10
Singapore	Nil	Nil	5, 15 (17)	10
Slovak Republic	Nil (14)	Nil (14)	10	10
Spain	15	5 (3)	5, 10, 15 (21, 22, 29)	10
Sweden	15	5 (5)	10, 15 (16)	10
Switzerland	15	5 (3)	10, 15 (16)	10
United Kingdom	Nil	Nil	5, 10, 15 (21, 23)	10
United States	10	5 (4, 15)	4.9, 10, 15 (23, 20)	10

Notes

The numbers in parentheses refer to the following numbered Notes. The applicable tax rates on dividends paid abroad in accordance with the tax treaties executed by Mexico are detailed below. Dividends paid to parties resident abroad are not subject to withholding tax in Mexico under domestic law.

There are certain specific cases of interest paid to parties resident abroad that might be exempted by certain tax treaties (e.g., interest paid to a pension fund or paid by a bank, interest paid on certain loans granted or guaranteed by certain entities for exports under preferable conditions, etc.), which are not detailed in the information below.

As previously mentioned it should be noted that under the local law, there is no withholding tax on dividends paid to parties resident abroad, regardless of their tax residency.

1. This rate applies when the recipient corporation that is the beneficial owner of the dividend (except for civil partnerships) directly owns at least 10% of the capital of the distributing corporation. In the case of Bermuda the specific exclusion of civil partnerships is not included.

2. This rate applies where the company that is the beneficial owner of the dividends directly or indirectly owns at least 25% of the capital of the distributing company.
3. This rate applies where the company that is the beneficial owner of the dividends (except for civil partnerships) directly owns at least 25% of the capital of the company distributing dividends. In the case of Norway, the taxation is limited to the country of residence of the party receiving the dividends, provided the aforementioned substantial holding rule is satisfied.
4. This rate applies where the recipient corporation that is the beneficial owner of the dividend owns at least 10% of the voting shares of the paying corporation. The Mexico-US tax treaty contains a most favoured nation clause.
5. This rate applies where a company that is the beneficial owner of the dividends (except for civil partnerships, although limited liability partnerships are included) directly owns at least 10% of the voting shares of the company distributing the dividends.
6. This rate applies where a company that is the beneficial owner of the dividends owns at least 20% of the voting shares of the company paying the dividends.
7. This is the maximum withholding rate for dividends, with no distinction for substantial holdings. In the case of Ecuador, the tax payable on dividends paid to residents in Mexico must not exceed a limit established in the treaty.
8. The 5% rate applies when a company that is the beneficial owner of the dividends owns at least 25% of the voting shares of the company paying dividends during the six months prior to the end of the tax period in which dividends are paid. Under certain particular rules and provided this ownership requirement is complied with, dividend payments are only subject to tax in the country of residence of the recipient of the dividends.
9. No withholding applies when more than 50% of the shares of the recipient corporation are owned by residents of France or Mexico or when the beneficial owner of the dividend is a resident individual. Accordingly, withholding tax applies to dividends when more than 50% of the recipient corporation's shares are owned by residents of other countries. However, the tax withholding must not exceed 5% when the party receiving the dividend is the effective beneficiary of said dividend.

   Dividends paid by a company resident in France to a resident of Mexico, other than a company which directly or indirectly holds at least 10% of the capital stock of the first-mentioned company, may also be taxed in France, in accordance with the law of France, but if the recipient of the dividends is the beneficial owner, the tax thus charged must not exceed 15% of the gross amount of the dividends.
10. The 5% rate applies where the company that is the beneficial owner of dividends directly or indirectly owns at least 10% of the capital of the company distributing the dividends. There is a 10% tax rate that applies when these same ownership requirements are complied with, but the company paying dividends is a resident of Israel (provided dividends are paid from earnings taxed in Israel at a tax rate lower than the regular corporate tax rate in Israel).
11. The applicable tax rate on the gross amount of the dividends when the recipient company (beneficial owner) (except for civil partnerships) directly holds at least 10% of the capital of the corporation paying the dividend must not exceed 5% in the case of Luxembourg, and 8% in the case of Mexico.

    The protocol of the Mexico-Luxembourg tax treaty states that this rate might be reviewed in the future by the contracting states if withholding tax is not fully creditable, and can be adjusted under the principle of avoiding double taxation, provided the adjusted withholding rate is not lower than 5%.
12. Dividends paid by a company resident in Mexico to a company resident in the Netherlands (which is the beneficiary of said dividends) are subject to a maximum tax of 5% on the gross amount of the dividends, if the beneficial owner is a company that directly or indirectly owns at least 10% of the capital of the company paying said dividends. However, as long as a company resident in the Netherlands is not subject to Dutch income tax on dividends received from a company resident in Mexico in the terms of the Dutch income tax law and any future amendments thereto, the dividends mentioned in the preceding paragraph may only be taxed in the Netherlands (not in Mexico).
13. The Mexico-New Zealand tax treaty contains a most favoured nation clause that may be applicable in the future.

M

14. The exemption on dividend withholding tax is not applicable in the case of deemed dividends.
15. To the extent certain requirements provided in the Protocol are met, the withholding tax may be reduced to 0%.
16. The 10% rate applies to loans from banks.
17. The 5% withholding tax rate is applicable to interest paid to banks.
18. The 5% rate applies to interest on loans from banks, insurance companies, and retirement and pension plans.
19. The 10% rate applies to interest on loans from banks, insurance companies, and securities regularly and substantially traded on a recognised national stock exchange.
20. The 4.9% rate applies to interest on loans from banks and insurance companies and to interest on securities regularly and substantially traded on a recognised national stock exchange.
21. In the case of the Netherlands the 5% rate applies to interest on loans from banks and to interest on securities regularly and substantially traded on a recognised national stock exchange. In the case of Spain and the UK the 5% rate extends to interest paid to insurance companies.
22. The 10% rate applies to interest paid by financial institutions and interest paid to the original seller of machinery and equipment.
23. The 10% rate on interest applies in the case of interest paid to the original seller of machinery and equipment and interest paid by banks.
24. The 10% rate applies to interest on loans from banks and to interest derived from bonds or securities that are regularly and substantially traded on a recognised securities market, as well as to interest paid by the purchaser of machinery and equipment to a beneficial owner that is the seller of the machinery and equipment.
25. The 10% rate applies to interest on loans from banks and insurance companies, to interest on securities regularly and substantially traded on a recognised national stock exchange, to interest paid to the original seller of machinery and equipment in a sale on credit and to interest paid by banks.
26. The 5% rate is applicable to interest on loans granted by banks and insurance companies, securities traded on a recognised securities market, and the sale on credit of machinery and equipment.
27. It is understood that the definition of royalties applies to any type of payment received for the provision of technical assistance services. The 15% rate applies to royalties arising from the use of, or the right to use, trademarks.
28. The original rate is 15%, but has been reduced to 10%, as long as the Netherlands does not impose a withholding tax.
29. Reduced withholding rate resulting from the application of the most favoured nation clause.
30. The 5% rate applies to industrial, commercial, and scientific equipment.

Tax administration

Returns

Corporate taxpayers are required to file annual income and flat tax returns for the preceding calendar year by 31 March, and/or to pay any balance of tax shown as due at that time. Holding companies in the tax consolidation regime are required to file an annual consolidated tax return within four months of the end of the tax period (i.e., usually by 30 April). Thereafter, the taxpayer is generally required to obtain the certification of tax compliance by an independent auditor and to file the related tax compliance opinion by the end of June. This certification process covers all federal taxes other than customs duties.

Employees' profit sharing payments are generally due by 31 May of the year following that in which the corresponding profit was obtained.

Payment of tax

Corporate taxpayers are required to make estimated payments of income tax by the seventeenth day of each month based on their estimated taxable income at the end of the previous month and calculated principally by applying the profit factor to the cumulative monthly gross income (the profit factor is determined by dividing the taxable profit by gross income shown in the annual return for the preceding year, or, if no profit factor is to be found in that annual return, the factor appearing in the year preceding that and so on, up to five years, with certain adjustments). For this purpose, gross income includes nominal income, excluding inflationary adjustments.

Definitive monthly VAT payments and flat tax advance payments are also required by the seventeenth day of the immediately following month.

Special procedures are provided for computing advance income tax payments, and for obtaining authorisation to reduce the amounts of monthly advances after the sixth month of the year. No advance payments or adjustments thereto are required in the first year of operations.

Information returns must be filed no later than 15 February each year, reporting on, amongst others, the following activities performed in the immediately preceding year:

1. Payments made to parties resident abroad;
2. Loans received from or guaranteed by non-residents;
3. Transactions conducted through a business trust;.
4. Parties to which the taxpayer makes payments and withholds income tax;
5. Parties to which the taxpayer has made donations;
6. Parties to which the taxpayer has paid dividends, and the value of such payments;
7. Taxpayers making salary payments are also required to file information returns reporting salaries paid and salary credit paid in the immediately preceding calendar year;
8. An annual information return must be filed on investments made or held in a tax haven. This must be filed in February of the immediately following year;
9. An information return on transactions carried out with non-resident related parties must be filed together with the corporate annual tax return (no later than March of the following year);
10. An information return related to the VAT taxable activities carried out by the taxpayer, must be filed on a monthly basis;
11. Transactions carried out with suppliers and clients, either local or overseas; and
12. Monthly informative returns disclosing items used in the flat tax computation.

M

Statute of limitations

In general, the right of the tax authorities to collect taxes, review tax returns, or claim additional tax expires five years after the date the respective return is filed. However, in cases where the taxpayer has not secured a federal tax registration number, has no accounting records, has failed to keep accounting records for the required five-year period, or has not filed a tax return, the statute of limitations expires in 10 years. Similarly, the period for claiming a refund of overpaid tax expires after five years.

Mexico

Other issues

Transfer pricing

Mexican transfer pricing legislation has been significantly developed as a result of Mexico's admission to the Organisation for Economic Co-operation and Development (OECD) in 1994. This development has resulted in the implementation of transfer pricing guidelines that are in line with the global economy and market liberalisation.

In general terms, from a Mexican transfer pricing perspective all related party transactions (including certain joint-venture relationships) must be reported at arm's-length prices.

Local legislation allows the selection of both traditional methods and profit-based methods consistent with the OECD guidelines. However the legislation requires a strict ordering for the application of a method.

Mexican legislation is generally "form over substance" oriented and therefore contractual terms remain relevant when defining the economic substance of the transactions subject to the transfer pricing analysis.

Reliable financial information is not always publicly available for Mexican entities. Hence, reliance is often placed on foreign information, which is then adjusted to properly reflect local market conditions and render the transactions in question more comparable.

International Financial Reporting Standards (IFRS) adoption

Business taxpayers meeting certain size criteria or belonging to a group that as a whole meets these criteria must file a tax-compliance audit report on an annual basis with the Mexican Audit Administration. This report consists of audited financial statements and detailed schedules, together with a report by the auditor stating that no irregularities were observed in respect of the taxpayer's compliance with its federal tax liabilities. These reports must be filled electronically and the auditor must be an independent CPA registered with the Mexican Audit Administration. Since 2008, the amount of detailed information required to be filed, and the auditor's responsibility in connection therewith, have increased significantly.

All companies listed on the Mexican Stock Exchange are required to submit annual consolidated financial statements accompanied by the opinion of a Mexican independent CPA. Commencing in the year ending 31 December 2012, these financial statements must be prepared in conformity with International Financial Reporting Standards (IFRS) and cover three years. Financial institutions and insurance companies must file audited financial statements with the appropriate regulatory agency.

The adoption of IFRS in Mexico presents companies with great challenges and opportunities. Changing from Mexican Financial Reporting Standards (MFRS) to IFRS requires companies to review their financial reporting procedures. Major changes in the requirements often have a ripple effect, impacting many aspects of a company's information reporting organisation.

Nevertheless, the benefits to Mexican companies in reporting under IFRS are numerous. Among the greatest of these is the opening up of the Mexican Stock Market to overseas investors. By adopting IFRS investors are able to compare two companies on different sides of the world with greater ease, and thus it is hoped that the change will encourage investment in Mexican companies.

Adoption of IFRS is not a straightforward process, and it will require time and effort on the part of the adopting entities to be able to ensure a smooth transition from MFRS to IFRS and ensure that the changes and benefits from this transition are duly implemented.

Corporate taxes in Moldova

For more information, contact:

Mihaela Mitroi
PricewaterhouseCoopers
Opera Center
1-5 Costache Negri Street
050552 Bucharest
Romania
Tel: +40 21 202 8717
Email: mihaela.mitroi@ro.pwc.com

Significant developments

Corporate income tax

The corporate income tax (CIT) rate applicable in 2010 is 0%. However, taxpayers are still liable to calculate the taxable base for CIT purposes and to submit CIT returns. Moreover, the Moldovan Tax Authorities (MTA) are entitled to apply a fine of 15% of the amount by which a taxpayer under-reported its taxable income.

Value-added tax (VAT)

Various amendments were made to the Moldovan VAT legislation, which entered into force on 1 January 2010, including the following:

- An updated list of operations that are out of the VAT scope. The list also includes free of charge supplies of goods and services for advertising purposes and/or promotion of sales, in the amount of 0.1% of the net revenues registered during the year before the year in which the current supplies are made.
- An express provision that a property transfer within the reorganisation of a company is out of the VAT scope.
- An increase in the VAT rate from 5% to 6% for import / local supply of natural and liquefied gas.
- The introduction of a reduced 8% VAT rate for certain goods produced and supplied on the Moldovan territory.
- The due date for payment of VAT in the case of imports of services is the date the service is provided, indicated on the document that confirms the completion of such services (previously, the date of the external payment of the related service fees).
- Implementation of the possibility to compensate VAT refundable amounts with the tax liabilities administered by customs authorities due by economic agents (or by their creditors, if an assignment of receivable is performed).
- Express specification of the place of supply of certain services (e.g., for marketing services (residence of the beneficiary of these services), for services in science domain, or entertainment (place these services are actually rendered), etc.).

Excise duties

Among the most important amendments enforced in 2010 with respect to excise duties are the following:

- Implementation of the possibility to compensate refundable excise duties with import duties administered by customs authorities and due by the economic agents (or by their creditors, if an assignment of receivable is performed).

- Changes of the excise duties rates for a number of excisable goods (e.g., alcoholic beverages, cigarettes, gasoline / diesel fuel, perfume, jewellery, etc.).
- Expansion of the list of goods subject to excise duties (e.g., crystal objects, lighting devices).
- New excise duty compliance rules applicable for businesses supplied by other persons (both individuals and legal entities) with articles of jewellery of precious metals and precious stones, for further sale and with no documents confirming the payment of excise duties, etc.

Customs duties

Among the most important changes brought to the Customs Code is the modification of regulations applicable to the determination of import duties that are due for an object of cross-border leasing (i.e., being in Moldova under the temporary admission customs regime).

Taxes on corporate income

The CIT rate applicable in 2010 is 0%. However, taxpayers are still liable to calculate the taxable base for CIT purposes and to submit CIT returns. Moreover, the MTA are entitled to apply a fine of 15% to the amount by which a taxpayer under-reported its taxable income.

Individual entrepreneurs and farming enterprises are also subject to the 0% CIT rate in 2010. CIT deductibility rules applicable for individual entrepreneurs and farming enterprises generally follow the same rules as are applicable for legal entities.

If an MTA tax inspection, applying indirect methods, re-assesses the income amount compared to the declared gross income, a 15% CIT rate may be applied to the excess amount.

In addition, from 2010, taxpayers that apply the nil CIT rate have to compute and pay a 15% tax of the value of the following:

- Free of charge payments to parties and other social political organisations; and
- Donations to individuals, which are tax exempt for the individual and are treated as non-deductible expenses for the taxpayer, from the perspective of CIT.

In addition, the application of this tax is maintained on any amount exceeding the deductibility limit for charity and sponsorship expenses.

Corporate residence

According to Moldovan tax law, a tax resident is a legal entity organised or managed in Moldova or that has its main place of business in Moldova. In practice, tax residency is determined by the place of incorporation.

M

Moldova

Other taxes

VAT

VAT rates

Under Moldovan VAT legislation, the standard VAT rate is 20%. It is applied on the VAT-able amount of local supplies of goods and services, as well as on the VAT-able amount of goods subject to import and services subject to the reverse charge mechanism.

Certain types of supplies are subject to reduced VAT rates (e.g., 8% on local supplies of bread and milk, certain bakery and diary products, import/supplies of sugar produced from sugar beets, and drugs and certain pharmaceutical products, and 6% on natural and liquefied gas imported in or supplied on the territory of Moldova).

A number of supplies are subject to the nil VAT rate (i.e., VAT exempt with the right to an input VAT credit), including exports of goods or services, international transportation, etc., as well as VAT exemptions without the right to a deduction, including sale or rental of dwellings, land, financial services, etc.

An entity may be registered as a VAT payer if input VAT related to specific capital investments performed starting with 1 January 2008 exceeds a certain threshold (i.e., VAT registration available for VAT refund purposes).

Input VAT deductibility rules

Input VAT incurred on the acquisition of goods or services may be deducted, provided it is incurred by a VAT payer for performing VAT-able supplies within its business activity.

If input VAT relates to acquisitions used for performing VAT exempt supplies, such input VAT would be a cost/expense for the company, except for cases of contributions in kind to the statutory capital (i.e., VAT exempt operation), when input VAT should be fully deductible at the level of the contributor.

Input VAT related to acquisitions of goods / services not used for business purposes may not be deducted and shall be treated as cost/expense.

If input VAT relates to acquisitions destined for performing both VAT-able and VAT exempt supplies without a direct allocation by type of supplies, the company is entitled to deduct input VAT based on a prorata mechanism.

The temporary prorata ratio is computed monthly by taking revenues obtained from VAT-able supplies over revenues obtained from both VAT-able and VAT-exempt operations, both amounts being computed by backing out prepayments received. The final prorata amount is computed according to the same ratio above, but based on yearly amounts of the respective indices. Related differences are correspondingly recorded in the VAT return for December.

VAT liabilities settled by a Moldovan company for services provided to it by non-resident suppliers and subject to the reverse charge mechanism may be deducted under the same conditions above.

VAT refund
Under the VAT law, the deductible input VAT exceeding the output VAT may be partially refunded, provided the company carries out any of a range of specific business activities (e.g., exports of goods or services, international transportation services, production of bakery and diary products, leasing activity). Otherwise, the recoverable VAT amount may be carried forward only to the following months, offsetting against the Company's future output VAT liabilities.

Additionally, VAT payers performing capital investments in Moldova, except for Chisinau and Balti, are entitled to refund the recoverable VAT related to investments made starting with 1 January 2008 (with few exceptions). Specific conditions shall be met for such purposes.

VAT compliance
The fiscal period for VAT purposes is considered the calendar month.

Every VAT payer (sometimes also non-registered entities for VAT purposes) must submit VAT returns and must settle related payable VAT liabilities by the end of the month following the reporting month (except for VAT on services supplied by non-residents, but which are VAT-able in Moldova).

VAT payers are also required to keep detailed records in VAT ledgers of acquisitions and supplies performed according to a set of specific rules.

VAT payers must properly document supplies of goods or services performed (i.e., generally by issuing VAT invoices on VAT-able supplies). Under certain conditions, VAT payers are allowed to issue customised VAT invoices (i.e., with the particulars of the company in question).

VAT invoices for supplies of goods generally must be issued on the date of the supply (i.e., on the date of their transfer to customers, with certain exceptions). VAT invoices for VAT-able supplies of services are issued, under the law, upon the provision of the services. No VAT invoice is issued for pre-payments received (except for a list of specific supplies) or for export supplies.

Specific VAT invoicing requirements which are provided under the VAT law should also be considered.

Taxation of services with VAT
Under Moldovan tax law, services provided by non-resident suppliers to either residents or non-residents of Moldova, whose place of supply is in Moldova, are deemed as being imported.

The place of services supply depends on their specific nature. Therefore, if the place of supply is in Moldova (e.g., consultancy, supply of staff, legal or marketing services), 20% import VAT must be settled by the recipient company at the date the services are supplied, duly confirmed by the corresponding supporting documentation (i.e., previously, VAT was due at the date the external invoice for the respective service was settled). Otherwise, (if the place the services are supplied is outside of Moldova), no Moldovan VAT is due.

M

Moldova

Custom duties

Moldova's current customs framework is regulated by the Customs Code, Law on Customs Tariff, International Agreements concluded by Moldova to date and by other legal acts.

In general, any kind of goods and means of transport may enter and leave the territory of Moldova without any restriction. However, certain limitations specifically provided by the legislation are in force, which cover goods and means of transport crossing the border by breaching state security, public order, environment, etc.

Customs tariff and duties

The Law on Customs Tariff establishes standard customs duty rates applicable upon import of goods into Moldova, depending on their specific customs tariff classification code. The Moldovan Customs Tariff is based on the Harmonised Commodity Description and Coding System.

Customs duty rates are generally indicated as percentages to be applied to the customs value (i.e., *ad valorem* duty rates) of goods imported into Moldova. The maximum *ad valorem* standard customs duty rate is 25%. There are also specific customs duty rates established, as well as combined rates.

Customs valuation

Under Moldovan customs legislation, the customs valuation is generally performed in accordance with the customs valuation principles in the General Agreement on Tariffs and Trade (GATT).

The customs value is determined based on one of the six provided valuation methods (i.e., transaction value, transaction value of identical goods, transaction value of similar goods, deductive value, computed value, and reserve method). If the first method is not applicable, then the second method should be applied and so forth.

Preferential tariff treatment

A preferential tariff treatment presumes a reduction of or exemption from customs duty, which may also be applied within a specific quota (settled either as value or quantity).

The preferential tariff treatment is granted for specific categories of goods depending on their origin and in accordance with the free trade arrangements (FTAs) to which Moldova is a party.

Moldova has concluded FTAs to date with most of the Commonwealth of Independent States (CIS) countries and is also a Central European Free Trade Agreement (CEFTA) contracting state.

From 1 March 2008 until 31 December 2012, Moldova benefits from Autonomous Trade Preferences (ATP) from the European Union, which allows unlimited duty-free access to the EU market for all products originating in Moldova, except for certain agricultural products. Such agricultural products are accepted for import into the EU either with exemptions from customs duties within the limits of specific tariff quotas (e.g., fresh, chilled and frozen meat of bovine animals, dairy products, common wheat, barley, maize, white sugar) or with exemption of the *ad valorem* component of the import duty (e.g., tomatoes, grapes, apples).

Moldova

To benefit from these preferential terms for imports of goods into the EU, compliance with origin and certification requirements has to be observed.

Favourable tariff treatment
A favourable tariff treatment presumes a reduction or an exemption from customs duty upon import of specific goods into Moldova, depending on their type or final destination, according to domestic customs law or international agreements to which Moldova is a party.

Moldovan customs law provides the following exemptions, among others, from customs duty:

- Goods imported by individuals for personal use not exceeding a specific threshold;
- Fixed assets aimed at being contributed in kind to the statutory capital;
- Goods released in Moldova under transit, bonded warehouse regimes;
- Moldovan goods previously exported and released back within a three-year term in the same status, as well as compensatory products obtained under outward processing relief;
- Certain movable goods imported by legal entities carrying out leasing activities for the purpose of paying off their contractual liabilities derived from lease agreements concluded with Moldovan individuals or legal entities; and
- Goods imported by legal entities for noncommercial purposes whose customs value does not exceed EUR 50.

Customs regimes
Definitive and suspensive customs regimes are provided under Moldovan law.

Definitive customs regimes refer to import and export, while suspensive customs regimes comprise: transit, bonded warehouse, inward processing relief (with suspension), processing under customs control, temporary admission, and outward processing relief.

Of these customs regimes, the following are deemed to have economic impact: bonded warehouse, inward processing relief, processing under customs control, temporary admission, and outward processing relief.

Citizens of Moldova, as well as foreigners, are allowed to move any goods in or out of Moldova under a simplified customs regime, provided these goods are not used for business or commercial purposes. Individuals are exempt from the payment of customs duties on goods whose customs value does not exceed EUR 200 and which are not used for entrepreneurial or commercial purposes.

Note that there are specific environmental pollution tax-related regulations importers should observe.

Excise duties
The following are liable to taxation with excise duties:

- Any individual or legal entity producing and/or processing excisable goods on the territory of Moldova; and
- Any individual or legal entity importing excisable goods, unless there is no specific exemption provided.

Moldova

Businesses or individuals that produce and/or process excisable goods in the territory of Moldova (or intend to do so) must possess excise duty certificates, which must be granted by the tax authorities before these operations are actually carried out. It is mandatory for individuals or businesses, upon submitting the relevant applications to the tax authorities, to attach the details of the excise premises.

Excise duty rates are set either as fixed amounts per unit of goods, as a percentage of the customs value of goods or as a combined rate. Under certain circumstances, excise duty exemptions may apply. Some excise-liable goods are subject to mandatory excise stamp marking and labelling.

Local taxes

Moldovan tax law also provides for location taxation in the form of taxes and duties, such as: real estate tax, tax on natural resources, tax on immovable property and tax on advertising placement, among others.

Local taxation in Moldova refers to the application of the following types of taxes and duties:

- Real estate tax (i.e., building tax and local tax).
- Tax on the following natural resources:
  - Water;
  - Mineral exploration;
  - Geological exploration;
  - Mining operations;
  - Usage of underground areas for the construction of underground structures not related to mining operations;
  - Exploitation of underground structures within the performance of entrepreneurial activity, not related to mining operations; and
  - Standing wood.
- Tax on immovable property.
- Duty for the right to perform local auctions and lotteries.
- Tax on advertising placement.
- Fee for the right to use local symbols.
- Parking tax.
- Hotel room occupancy tax.
- Resort fee, etc.

Tax on immovable property

Tax on immovable property is a local tax paid on real estate (land and/or construction on the land) by the proprietor or owner of material rights. Residents and non-residents owning real estate located in the territory of Moldova have similar obligations.

The following are subject to taxation: immovable property, including land located within or outside the municipal area, and/or improvements to the land (buildings, apartments, etc.).

The maximum tax rate on immovable property used for entrepreneurial activity (i.e., due by legal entities) is 0.1% of the property's estimated value, while the maximum tax rate on property used for agricultural activities is 0.1% of the property's book value.

The land tax rate for a legal entity is established in monetary value (i.e., MDL), depending on its destination (e.g., land for agriculture usage) and location.

The tax on immovable property is paid quarterly by legal entities and in equal instalments by individuals, by 15 August and 15 October of the current year. However, if individuals settle tax on immovable property by 30 June then a 15% tax reduction may be requested.

Branch income

Branches
Moldovan tax law does not distinguish between branches of non-resident companies and local companies established by a foreign investor. As such, a non-resident's branch is registered in Moldova as an enterprise fully owned by the foreign investor, and is subject to the same tax regime as local incorporated companies.

Representative offices
Representative offices are often established as a first step to operating in Moldova. According to the tax law, a representative office can engage only in auxiliary or preparatory activities. A representative office can perform only a limited range of activities without being considered a permanent establishment of the non-resident.

All representative offices must submit by 31 March of the year following the reporting year the required Tax Reporting Statement on the activity conducted during the year concerned.

Income determination

Resident legal entities are taxed on their worldwide income, while non-resident entities are taxed on their Moldovan-source income.

Taxable income is computed as accounting income adjusted in accordance with tax legislation.

Inventory valuation
Moldovan law provides for the following inventory valuation methods: standard cost method, retail method, weighted average cost, first-in, first-out (FIFO), and last-in, first-out (LIFO).

Assets are generally valued at their acquisition cost, production cost, or market value.

Capital gains
The capital gains rule applies to Moldovan companies selling capital assets on an occasional basis and whose ordinary activity does not include transactions with land, buildings and shares. Shares and other investment assets (e.g., land, property) are treated under the tax law as capital assets. The income earned from the sale of capital assets is deemed to be a capital gain in the amount of 50% of the difference between the purchase price (i.e., including all costs related to the acquisition of capital assets) and the sale price. This capital gain must be included in the total gross amount of income for the year in which the shares were sold. This amount is subject to CIT. For 2010, the CIT rate is set at 0%.

Moldova

Capital gains may be decreased by capital losses registered in previous years.

Dividends

Dividends received by Moldovan legal entities both from Moldovan or foreign legal entities are taxed in Moldova with the applicable CIT rate (i.e., in 2010, the 0% CIT rate is in force).

Moldovan legal entities performing dividend payouts to resident individuals apply a 15% final withholding tax on the dividend amount, except those related to the fiscal periods prior to 1 January 2008.

Starting with 1 January 2010, a 15% withholding tax applies to amounts withdrawn from share equity, related to previously increased share equity, upon the distribution of net profit and/or other sources recorded in owner's equity between shareholders (associates), according to the participation share in the equity.

Exchange gains and losses

Foreign exchange losses are CIT deductible in the period they are incurred. Revenues obtained from foreign exchange differences are to be included in the taxable income.

In certain circumstances (e.g., high depreciation of the national currency), foreign exchange differences should be capitalised to the value of assets in relation to which the expenses were incurred.

Non-taxable revenues

Moldovan tax law provides for the following main types of non-taxable revenues:

- Contributions to the capital of an entity.
- Income earned while benefiting from an income tax exemption.
- Monies received from special funds and which are used in accordance with fund destination.
- Interest derived by legal entities on bank deposits with a period exceeding three years, as well as the interest derived from corporate securities issued in the form of bonds for a period exceeding three years, is tax exempted until 1 January 2010.
- Interest derived from state bonds (up to 1 January 2015).

Deductions

Deductible expenses

As a general rule, expenses incurred by a company are deductible for CIT purposes only if these expenses are deemed as ordinary and necessary, aimed at deriving taxable income, and justified with adequate supporting documentation.

Among others, the following expenses are CIT deductible:

- Depreciation of fixed assets calculated under the diminishing balance method;
- Amortisation of intangible assets computed under the straight-line method;
- Research and development expenses incurred during the fiscal year as current expenses, should certain conditions be met;
- Business trip expenses, representation expenses, and expenses on insurance of business entities, within the limits approved by the government;

- Waste, spoilage, and expiration expenses, within the annual limitation established by the company's manager;.
- Bad debts, under certain conditions;
- Charity and sponsorship expenses borne for the benefit of specific beneficiaries, up to 10% of taxable income; and
- Interest payable, in specific cases.

Depreciation

Fixed assets are subject to CIT depreciation under the diminishing-balance method if their useful economic life exceeds one year and acquisition costs exceed MDL 3,000.

According to the fiscal law, fixed assets are divided into five categories. These categories are set out according to specific rules, mainly on the assets' useful life (i.e., the number of years during which the assets' utilisation generates economic advantages; the useful life for each type of depreciating asset is regulated by governmental decision). The depreciation rates vary as follows:

- First category – 5%;
- Second category – 8%;
- Third category – 10%;
- Fourth category – 20%; and
- Fifth category – 30%.

Intangible assets are subject to CIT depreciation according to the straight-line method.

Thin capitalisation rules

Different CIT deductibility rules apply for interest on loans used for carrying out operational activities and for loans used for investment activities performed on an occasional basis.

As a general rule, deductions for interest and foreign exchange losses are allowed for CIT purposes, provided such expenses are deemed as ordinary and necessary for carrying out the activities of the business. Expenses should also be incurred for the purposes of obtaining taxable income and justified by adequate backup documentation.

If the interest paid by a Moldovan company relates to its operational or day-to-day activities, the related expenses are CIT-deductible. A few other provisions should also be considered, namely the following:

- Starting in 2010, interest expenses incurred, for the benefit of individuals and legal entities (except financial institutions and micro-financing organisations), by businesses are CIT deductible limited to the base rate (rounded to the next whole percentage), established by the National Bank of Moldova in November of the previous fiscal year, and applied to short-term monetary policy transactions (i.e., the limit is 5%).
- If the loan is obtained to acquire/build fixed assets, the related interest expense should be capitalised to the initial fiscal value of assets until they are commissioned. The deductibility of this expense would be capped at the above limit. The excess difference is treated as a CIT non-deductible expense for that fiscal year.

M

Moldova

- If interest relates to an investment activity, the interest expense is CIT-deductible within the limit of the income derived from the investment.

Fiscal losses
Fiscal losses may be carried forward in five equal instalments for five consecutive years following the year the losses were incurred, provided the company records taxable income. If the company recorded fiscal losses for more than one year, such losses are carried forward in the order in which they arose. Fiscal losses are recorded on off-balance-sheet accounts.

The carryforward of the fiscal losses of previous years does not represent a tax advantage in the view of the current 0% CIT rate applicability.

Transfer pricing (TP)
TP regulations are currently at the initial stage of development, as the law does not list any specific TP methods. Moreover, taking into account that Moldova is not currently an Organisation for Economic Co-operation and Development (OECD) member country, there is no possibility of applying the OECD TP Guidelines.

According to the law in force, transactions carried out between related parties should observe the arm's-length principle. Transactions that do not follow this rule are disregarded for tax purposes.

In accordance with Moldovan tax law, a company is considered the taxpayer's related party if it controls the taxpayer, is controlled by the taxpayer or both the company and the taxpayer are under the common control of a third party.

From a tax perspective, control is the ownership (either directly or through one or more related parties) of 50% or more in value of the capital or voting power of one of the companies. In this case, an individual is treated as owning all equity interest owned directly or indirectly by members of his or her family.

Two individuals are related parties if they are spouses or relatives up to the fourth degree.

Losses incurred in dealing between related parties carried out directly or through intermediaries are treated as non-deductible for CIT purposes. The Moldovan government foresees implementing TP provisions into Moldovan tax law, which will comply with the OECD TP Guidelines for Multinational Enterprises and Tax Administrations.

Group taxation

Moldovan tax law does not provide for group consolidation of gains or losses. No group taxation is envisaged under Moldovan tax law.

Tax incentives

Investment related CIT incentives
CIT incentives provided under the tax law are suspended during the period of applicability of the nil CIT rate.

Tax incentives for IT companies

CIT incentives are available to legal entities performing certain software development activity businesses up to 2012. In addition, their employees may also benefit from a personal income tax exemption for employment salaries earned from such companies, if certain conditions are met.

Free Trade Zones

Free entrepreneurial zones (FEZ) are territories where domestic and foreign investors can carry out entrepreneurial activities on preferential terms (i.e., favourable tax, customs, visa and other regimes). There are currently seven FEZ in Moldova.

The following types of activities may be carried out in a FEZ:

*   Production of goods preferentially for export (supply of goods in the territory of Moldova does not exceed 30% of the total amount of goods and services supplied within one year);
*   Sorting, packing, marking, and other similar operations of goods transiting the customs territory of Moldova; and
*   Other supportive activities.

According to the customs provisions, goods are introduced into the FEZ with no VAT or customs duty and are not subject to economic policy measures, according to specific criteria. However, certain taxes in specific situations might be incurred by residents of the FEZ. Investors in the FEZ are guaranteed and protected from changes in legislation for a general period of up to 10 years, while under certain conditions this period may be extended to 20 years.

Withholding taxes (WHT)

Residents

Resident legal entities making payments to individuals must withhold and pay WHT to the budget at the following rates:

*   5% preliminary withholding of payments made for the benefit of resident individuals, unless such payments are tax exempt or are computed as employment salaries. The beneficiary deducts (i.e., recovers) the 5% WHT from his/her annual income tax due.
*   10% final withholding of an individual's income derived from leasing, rent, usufruct of movable and immovable property, advertising campaign (according to certain specific rules), or gambling activities.
*   15% final withholding of dividends paid out to individuals, except those related to the fiscal periods prior to 1 January 2008.
*   15% preliminary withholding from royalties and interests; the beneficiary deducts (i.e., recovers) the 15% WHT from his/her annual income tax due.
*   18% final withholding from gambling revenues.

Further to the applicability of the 0% CIT rate in 2010, the WHT is not applied to payments between resident legal entities.

Non-residents

Under the 2010 domestic tax provisions, the following WHT rates apply upon payments to non-residents:

Moldova

- 15% for dividend payouts;
- 15% for (non)monetary payments whose amount is non-deductible for CIT purposes for the payer thereof; and
- 15% for other revenues.

Double tax treaties (DTT)
The DTTs in force between Moldova and other countries may provide for more favourable tax rates than those provided by the local provisions. For their application, the foreign beneficiary of such income should provide the paying entity with its fiscal residency certificate before the payments are actually made.

Operational DTTs to which Moldova is a party are outlined below:

State	Dividends	Interest	Royalties
Albania	5/10	5	10
Armenia	5/15	10	10
Austria	5/15	5	5
Azerbaijan	8/15	10	10
Byelorussia	15	10	15
Belgium	15	15	0
Bosnia and Herzegovina	5/10	10	10
Bulgaria	5/15	10	10
Canada	5/15	10	10
China	5/10	10	10
Croatia	5/10	5	10
Czech Republic	5/15	5	10
Cyprus	5/10	5	5
Estonia	10	10	10
Finland	5/15	5	3/7
Germany	15	5	0
Greece	5/15	10	8
Hungary	5/15	10	0
Israel	5/10	5	5
Japan	15	10	0/10
Kazakhstan	10/15	10	10
Kyrgyzstan	5/15	10	10
Latvia	10	10	10
Lithuania	10	10	10
Luxembourg	5/10	5	5
Macedonia	5/10	5	10
Montenegro	5/15	10	10
The Netherlands	0/5/15	5	2
Oman	5	5	10
Poland	5/15	10	10
Romania	10	10	10/15
Russian Federation	10	0	10
Serbia	5/15	10	10

State	Dividends	Interest	Royalties
Slovakia	5/15	10	10
Slovenia	5/10	5	5
Spain	0/5/10	5	8
Switzerland	5/15	10	0
Turkey	10/15	10	10
Tajikistan	5/10	5	10
Ukraine	5/15	10	10
Uzbekistan	5/15	10	15
United Kingdom	0/5/10	0/5	5

Tax administration

Returns

An annual corporate income tax return must be submitted to the MTA by 31 March of the year following the reporting year. For new business entities, the fiscal year is considered the period beginning with the registration date until the end of the calendar year.

The law also provides for various reporting deadlines for payments of withholding tax and VAT.

For WHT and VAT purposes, the fiscal period is the calendar month starting the first day of the month. WHT and VAT liabilities must be declared and settled monthly by the end of the month following the reporting month.

Individual entrepreneurs and farming enterprises with an annual average number of employees not exceeding three and not registered as VAT payers must submit a unified tax return, if certain conditions are met.

Moldovan tax law provides for a specific procedure for taxpayers submitting adjusted tax returns (after the taxpayer identifies previous errors) within a limited period of time.

Payment of tax

Taking into account that, as of 1 January 2008, the nil CIT is applied in Moldova, no income tax needs to be paid.

Still, legal entities that exceed the legally allowable limit on sponsorship expenses must declare and pay the applicable CIT by 31 March of the year following the reporting year.

Fines and penalties

From 1 January 2010, the MTA is entitled to apply a fine of 15% to the amount by which a taxpayer under-reported its taxable income for CIT purposes.

Taxpayers who settle amounts as assessed by the MTA within three business days and have no other outstanding liabilities qualify for certain tax incentives (i.e., 50% reduction of fines).

M

Moldova

In addition, certain special provisions regarding tax evasion apply. Tax evasion is assessed on a case-by-case basis but usually assumes the insertion into financial statements, tax returns, and accounting documents of false information on revenues and expenses. In addition, hiding other taxable income may also be considered tax evasion.

Under tax law, the MTA is entitled to apply a fine in the amount of the undeclared tax if this is a result of tax evasion.

Should the amount of the tax due exceed MDL 50,000, the tax evasion is regarded as a criminal offence. According to the Moldovan Criminal Code, legal entities can be punished for tax evasion with a fine up to MDL 120,000 and preclusion from performing certain activities or winding-up.

In 2010, the daily penalties for failing to pay social security contributions is 0.1%; for health insurance contributions, 0.1%; and for other taxes, 0.027%.

Rulings
The law does not provide for the possibility of obtaining binding rulings. However, taxpayers that inadequately computed tax liabilities due to incorrect written explanations issued by the MTA may not be subject to sanctions (i.e., fines and late-payment penalties). Tax liabilities may still be recomputed by the MTA. Written explanations are issued by the MTA free of charge and may remain valid for an indefinite period of time, unless cancelled by new legislation or other rulings. Such explanations are generally issued by the Moldovan competent authorities during a period of up to one month.

Corporate taxes in Mongolia

For more information, contact:

Richard Bregonje
PricewaterhouseCoopers Audit LLC
Sukhbaatar Square, SBD-8
Central Tower Office Building
Level 6, Suite 601
Ulaanbaatar 210620a
Mongolia
Tel: +7 727 298 0448
Email: richard.bregonje@kz.pwc.com

Significant developments

The loss carryforward provisions were amended on 25 August 2009. Previously the loss carryforward period for all business sectors was two years. Now, companies operating in the infrastructure and mining sectors can carry their net operating and capital losses forward for a four-eight year period depending upon the exact nature of their business. In other sectors, losses are still allowed to be carried forward for two years.

Taxes on corporate income

Mongolian corporate income tax (CIT) is levied at the following rates, using a progressive-rate scale that ranges from 10% to 25%, as follows:

- 10% applies to the first MNT 3 billion of annual taxable income; and
- 25% applies to any excess of MNT 3 billion of annual taxable income.

However, certain types of income are taxed at different tax rates:

Source of income	Applicable tax rate
Dividends	10%
Royalties	10%
Interest	10%
Gambling, betting games and lotteries	40%
Sale of immovable property (gross)	2%
Sale of rights	30%

Corporate residence

Residents and non-residents

A resident legal entity is an economic entity formed under the laws of Mongolia or a foreign economic entity that has its headquarters (place of effective management) in Mongolia.

A non-resident company is a foreign economic entity that conducts its business activities in Mongolia through a permanent establishment (PE) or a foreign economic entity that derives income from Mongolia in forms other than a PE.

Mongolia

A PE includes the following that partially or wholly conduct business activities of a foreign economic entity in Mongolia:

- Branches;
- Plants;
- Trade and services providers; and
- Oil and natural gas wells or mines.

As yet, the concept of a PE is not well developed.

Other taxes

Value-added tax (VAT)
VAT at the rate of 10% is imposed on the supply of taxable goods and services in Mongolia and on imports into Mongolia.

VAT is levied on the following:

- Goods sold in Mongolia;
- Work performed and services rendered in Mongolia;
- All goods imported into Mongolia to be sold or used; and
- Goods exported from Mongolia for use or consumption outside Mongolia.

Excise tax
Excise tax is levied on goods manufactured in or imported into Mongolia, such as tobacco, alcohol, gasoline and diesel fuel, and passenger vehicles. Excise tax is also levied on the physical units of special-purpose technical devices and equipment used for betting games and gambling, and activities of individuals and legal entities that conduct such activities.

Immovable property tax
An immovable property tax is levied at 0.6% of the value of the immovable property. For tax purposes, the value used is the value registered with the government registration authority. If the property is unregistered, the insured value is used. In the absence of either a registered or insured value, the accounting value is used.

This tax does not apply to property owned by persons and financed through the state budget, or to all dwelling houses and buildings and constructions for public use.

Stamp duty
Under the Law of Mongolia on State Stamp Duties, stamp duties are imposed on the following:

- Monitoring of and decisions on matters of legal status by a court of law;
- Registration of business entities and organisations;
- Permission to register business entities with foreign investment and allowing persons to be employed with representative offices of foreign organisations;
- Permission to carry out services and carry out production which requires special permission or expertise;
- Grant of certification for copyright, patent, or trademarks;
- Registration of copyrights;

- Granting of permission to carry out activities with respect to securities and registration of securities, and for authorisation to issue and register securities; and
- Other services.

The amount of duty varies according to the type of services involved.

Customs duty

A flat customs tariff of 5% applies with respect to goods imported into Mongolia, except computer technology devices, medical equipment and livestock. Heavy machinery and equipment purchased and imported by entities investing in priority sectors with foreign-sourced funds are exempt from the customs tariff.

Export duties apply to certain exported goods, such as waste iron, aluminium, copper, brass, and indentured cashmere.

Windfall profits tax

A windfall profits tax is imposed on the sale of gold and copper ore and concentrate if the prices exceed a certain base price. The tax is levied at the rate of 68% on gold and copper profits when profits reach USD 850 per ounce and USD 2,600 per ton, respectively. Note that windfall profits tax is to be annulled from 1 January 2011.

Branch income

The repatriation of profits from branches of foreign legal entities is subject to branch profits tax at a rate of 20%.

Income determination

Mongolian legal entities are taxable on aggregate annual income earned worldwide. Non-resident legal entities carrying out business activities in Mongolia are taxable on the income earned in the territory of Mongolia.

Common tax adjustments:

- Finance lease payments (except for interest); and
- Fines and penalties.

Any other expenses not specifically stated as deductible by the Mongolian Tax Code.

Bribes, kickbacks, illegal payments

Tax law is silent on these matters. However, per anti-corruption law, monetary amount involved for such payments will be confiscated and criminal proceedings will be applied.

Capital vs. ordinary transactions

Tax treatment is same for both types of transaction except immovable property sales income which is subject to income tax of 2%.

Dividend income

Dividend income earned by Mongolian resident entity is subject to income tax of 10%. Dividend income to be remitted out of country to foreign tax resident is subject to

Mongolia

withholding tax at 20%, but which may be reduced by an applicable double taxation treaty (DTT).

Foreign investment
Tax stability and other incentives are available for investments of a certain level.

Foreign income (anti-deferral regime, unremitted earnings)
Unremitted earnings have same tax treatments as ordinary earnings. Mongolia does not have an anti-deferral regime with regard to condition or countries.

Interest income
Interest income is subject to a special income tax of 10%.

Inventory valuation
There is no specific provision in the tax law on this matter.

Partnership income
Partnership income has same tax treatment as CIT.

Rents/royalties income
Rents/royalties income is treated as an income and, therefore, subject to tax implication. Rent income is included in taxable income for tax determination whereas royalty income is taxed at a special rate of 10%.

Stock transactions
Capital gains on stock transactions are taxable income.

Unrealised exchange gains/losses
Unrealised exchange gain/loss does not have a tax implication.

Deductions

Expenses mostly associated with generating aggregate annual income are deductible for corporate income tax purposes (provided proper documentation is in place). However, there are limits with respect to the deductibility of interest expense.

The corporate income tax law stipulates that finance lease payments (except interest) and fines and penalties are not deductible for tax purposes.

Common tax deductions
Interest expense, meals, and officers' compensation from which the social insurance and personal income tax is deducted are tax-deductible whereas entertainment expenses are not deductible for tax purposes. As life insurance is not in practice in Mongolia, tax law is silent on this issue.

Accrued expenses
Accrued expenses are tax-deductible.

Bad debt
Bad debt is not tax-deductible.

Charitable contributions
Charitable contributions are not tax-deductible except donations to the fund of vocational training.

Contingent liabilities
Contingent liability is not tax-deductible.

Depreciation of fixed assets/amortisation of intangibles
Depreciation of fixed assets/amortisation of intangibles is tax-deductible.

Goodwill
There is no specific provision in the tax law on this matter.

Organisational and start-up expenses
Organisational and start-up expenses are tax-deductible.

Payments to foreign affiliates
Deductibility depends on the nature of the payment:

- Interest payment – deductible but with restrictions.
- Dividend payment – non-deductible.
- Technical assistance service payment – deductible.
- Other services – deductible.

Pension expense
Compulsory pension insurance premium paid to Social Security Authority of Mongolia is deductible. Additional voluntary insurance premiums are tax-deductible but shall not exceed 15% of taxable income. Pension provision or internal pension fund expense is not tax-deductible.

Payment for directors
If a payment for directors is a salary payment from which the social insurance and personal income tax is deducted, it is considered as deductible.

Net operating losses
Net operating losses generally may be carried forward for up to two years. However, the annual amount of loss deductible from taxable income may not exceed 50% of the taxable income in the tax year.

Starting 1 January 2010, legal entities involved in the infrastructure and mining industries may carryforward 100% of their losses for up to four to eight years, depending on their investment period and based on government regulations.

Group taxation

There are no rules permitting grouping for tax purposes in Mongolia.

Tax incentives

A 50% tax credit is available for an economic entity that produces or plants the following products:

Mongolia

- Cereal, potatoes, and vegetables;
- Milk;
- Fruits and berries; and/or
- Fodder plants.

A 10% investment credit may be available for certain types of industries.

Withholding taxes (WHT)

Domestic inter-company dividends are exempt from WHT. Dividends, interest, and royalties paid; goods sold; and work/services provided to non-residents are subject to withholding tax at a 20% rate. Dividends, interest, and royalties paid to resident individuals are subject to withholding tax at a 10% rate.

Double taxation treaties (DTT):
Current
Austria – Mongolia
Belgium – Mongolia
Bulgaria – Mongolia
Canada – Mongolia
China (P.R.C.) – Mongolia
Czech Republic – Mongolia
France – Mongolia
Germany – Mongolia
Hungary – Mongolia
India – Mongolia
Indonesia – Mongolia
Kazakhstan – Mongolia
Korea (R.O.K.) – Mongolia
Kuwait – Mongolia
Kyrgyzstan – Mongolia
Luxembourg – Mongolia
Netherlands – Mongolia
Poland – Mongolia
Russia – Mongolia
Singapore – Mongolia
Switzerland – Mongolia
Turkey – Mongolia
Ukraine – Mongolia
United Kingdom – Mongolia
Vietnam – Mongolia

Pending
Belarus – Mongolia
Egypt – Mongolia
Italy – Mongolia
North Korea – Mongolia
Thailand – Mongolia
United Arab Emirates – Mongolia

•

Tax administration

Tax returns and assessment

The tax year is the calendar year. Companies must submit a quarterly return by the twentieth day of the month following the end of each quarter.

An economic entity or organisation that has withheld tax from a payment of dividends, royalties, sale of rights or a payment of income to a participant should transfer the withholding tax to the budget within seven working days. Tax withheld relating to the sale of immovable property should be transferred to the budget within 10 working days. A withholder must prepare and submit a quarterly return of the tax deducted by the twentieth day of the first month of the following quarter and an annual return by 10 February after the end of the tax year.

Payment of tax

Tax is paid in advance by the twenty-fifth day of each month. In practice, the Mongolian tax authorities allow concessions as follows:

A company with annual taxable income of less than MNT 500,000 may pay tax on a quarterly basis.

Where total tax paid exceeds the tax liability, the excess may be credited against other taxes due or credited against future tax payments. The overpayment also may, theoretically, be refunded, however, the practice of refunding in Mongolia is less clear and consistent.

M

For more information, contact:

Peter Burnie
PricewaterhouseCoopers Consulting d.o.o.
Airport City Belgrade
88a Omladinskih brigada st.
11000 Belgrade, Serbia
Tel: +381 11 3302 138
Email: peter.burnie@rs.pwc.com

Significant developments

The most recent changes to the corporate profit tax (CPT) law, effective from 1 January 2010, introduced taxation of 100% rather than 50% of capital gains. The amendments reduced a number of tax incentives, including abolishing tax deductions for newly employed staff and tax incentives for investment in efficient production of energy.

Taxes on corporate income

The taxable profit of the entities operating in Montenegro is taxed at 9%. This tax is levied at a state level and no local corporate income taxes exist.

Corporate residence

A legal entity is considered to be a tax resident if it is incorporated in Montenegro. In addition, a foreign corporation may also be deemed a Montenegrin tax resident if the corporation has a place of effective management in Montenegro.

Other taxes

Value-added tax (VAT)
VAT replaced the previous sales tax system in April 2003. The main principles of the Montenegrin VAT are in line with the European Union Sixth Directive guidelines. Taxable supplies are subject to a general 17% VAT rate; however, certain supplies are taxed at reduced 7% and 0% rates.

Taxable amount
In principle, consideration (in cash, goods, or services) received for supplies, including taxes except VAT (e.g., customs, excise duty), and direct costs (commissions, cost of packing, transport) comprises the VAT base.

If the consideration is not paid in cash, or if an exchange of goods for services takes place, the tax base will be the market value of the goods or services received at the time of supply.

Registration
Registration for VAT in Montenegro may be either as voluntary or mandatory. Voluntary VAT registration is possible for small taxpayers who have not realised turnover exceeding EUR 18,000 in the last 12-month period. Once registered, a company may not apply for deregistration for at least three years.

VAT registration is mandatory for an entity that realises turnover exceeding the EUR 18,000 threshold in any 12-month period.

VAT liability
A calendar month is the period for which VAT is calculated and paid (i.e., a VAT return must be submitted and VAT liability cleared monthly). VAT calculated on imports is paid along with custom duties.

Payroll tax
Employment income includes all receipts paid or given to an individual based on employment (salaries, pensions, benefits in kind, insurance premiums, benefits and awards above the non-taxable thresholds).

Income generated through other types of personal engagements similar to employment (temporary jobs and similar) is also considered employment income.

Employees are the taxpayers, however, the employer is responsible for calculating and withholding personal income tax on behalf of its employees.

The taxable base is gross salary, including fringe benefits.

Employment income is subject to withholding tax at a flat rate of 9% from 1 January 2010.

Social security contributions
Social security contributions are calculated and withheld by an employer from the salary paid to an employee. Unlike two other types of social security contributions, only pension and disability insurance contributions are subject to a specific annual cap (EUR 31,015.60 for 2010). These contributions are payable by the employer and employee at different rates. The amount borne by the employer is treated as an operating cost, while the portion payable by the employee is taken from the gross salary.

M

The rates are as follows:

* On behalf of employee:
  * Pension and disability insurance 15%;
  * Health insurance 8.5%; and
  * Unemployment insurance 0.5%.
* On employer's behalf:
  * Pension and disability insurance 5.5%;
  * Health insurance 3.8%; and
  * Unemployment insurance 0.5% .

Excise duty
Legal entities that are importers or producers of the following products are subject to the excise duty:

* Alcohol and alcohol beverages;
* Tobacco products; and
* Mineral oils, their derivatives and substitutes.

Montenegro

When excise is paid for the mentioned products, there is no difference with respect to the origin of the product (local and imported). Excise duty can be prescribed as a fixed amount and/or as a certain percentage (*ad valorem*).

Environmental charges
Legal entities are subject to environmental charges for the following:

* Use of firing or electrical feed equipment with power greater than 1MW;
* Import of substances harmful to the atmosphere;
* Production or deposit of dangerous waste; and
* Tax for use of road vehicles (Vignettes).

Property tax
Property tax is payable by legal entities who own or have user rights over real estate located in Montenegro. The tax is levied at proportional rates, ranging from 0.08% to 0.8% on the market value of assets as of 1 January of the current year. A taxpayer is obliged to submit a tax return to the tax authorities within 30 days from the acquisition date. Tax is payable in two instalments, based on decisions issued by the tax authorities.

Property transfer tax
Transfer tax is payable on the acquisition of ownership rights over immovable property at a 3% rate.

The taxable base is the market value of the immovable property at the time of the acquisition. A taxpayer (i.e., the acquirer of immovable property) is obliged to submit a tax return within 15 days from the contract date. The liability is payable within 15 days from the receipt of the tax administration decision.

Branch income

Non-residents carrying out business in Montenegro through a permanent establishment (PE) are taxed on their Montenegrin source income at a rate of 9%. A branch is considered to be a PE.

Income determination

Taxable profit is calculated by adjusting the accounting profit (determined in accordance with IFRS and accounting legislation) in accordance with the provisions of the CPT law.

The following expenditures are recognised for corporate profit tax purposes up to the prescribed threshold:

* Depreciation computed in accordance with tax legislation;
* Expenses for health care, scientific, educational, humanitarian, religious, environment protection and sports-related purposes, up to 3.5% of total revenue;
* Entertaining expenses up to 1% of total revenue;
* Membership fees paid to chambers of commerce and other associations (except political parties) up to 0.1% of gross revenue;
* Provisions for redundancy payments and jubilee awards recognised as expenditures up to the amount prescribed by the labour law;

- Provisions made by banks and insurance companies will be deductible as expenditures for CPT purposes in an amount not exceeding the amount prescribed by the legislation that regulates operation of these entities;
- Provisions for special risks of brokers and dealers up to amount prescribed by the securities law; and
- Provisions for renewable natural resources, the warranties for the sale of goods and service (guarantee period) and the expected loss from court process (delicate agreements) if accounted for in accordance with the accounting legislation.

Provisions and write-offs

Write-offs and provisions for doubtful debts are considered deductible, provided that:

- Written-off/provided receivables were previously included in taxpayer's revenues;
- Doubtful debts were written-off/provided as uncollectible; and
- Proof of unsuccessful collection of these debts exists.

Inventory valuation

The cost of materials and of goods sold is tax-deductible up to an amount calculated by applying the average-weighted-cost method or the first-in, first-out (FIFO) method. If another method is used, an adjustment for tax purposes should be made.

Capital gains

Capital gains realised by the sale or transfer of real estate or other property rights, as well as shares and other securities, are subject to the 9% CPT rate. Recent law changes, applicable from January 2010, levy tax on capital gains at 100% rather than 50% of the capital gains amount.

Capital gains may be offset against capital losses occurring in the same period. A capital loss may be carried forward for five years.

Inter-company dividends

Dividend income of the recipient is exempt from corporate taxation in Montenegro if the distributor is a Montenegrin corporate taxpayer.

Foreign income

Resident taxpayers are entitled to a tax credit for up to the amount of corporate tax paid in another state on income realised in that state. This tax credit is equal to the tax paid in another country, but may not exceed the amount of the tax that would have been paid in Montenegro.

Deductions

Depreciation and depletion

Depreciable assets are tangible and intangible assets with a useful life of at least one year and an individual acquisition value of at least EUR 300.

Intangible and fixed assets are divided into five depreciation groups, with depreciation rates prescribed for each group (I – 5%, II – 15%, III – 20%, IV – 25%, and V – 30%). A straight-line depreciation method is prescribed for assets classified in the first group (real estate), while a declining-balance method is applicable for assets classified in the other groups.

M

Montenegro

Net operating losses
The taxpayer is entitled to carry losses incurred in an accounting period forward over the following five years.

Payments to foreign affiliates
In general, no specific restrictions apply for payments made to foreign entities.

Supplies of goods or services from a foreign group entity not established in Montenegro to a Montenegrin entity must be valued at arm's length. Excess expenses recorded over market value are treated as non-deductible expenses.

With respect to payment of charges of a PE, CIT law provides that administrative costs charged by the non-resident head office are non-deductible for CIT at the level of PE.

Taxes
The basic deductibility rule is that business expenses incurred for business purposes are CIT deductible. Following that rule, CIT law provides for full deductibility of taxes. However, penalty interest for late payment of taxes is not CIT deductible.

Group taxation

Tax consolidation is permitted for a group of companies in which all of the members are Montenegrin residents and the parent company directly or indirectly controls at least 75% of the shares in the other companies. Each company files its own tax return and the parent company files a consolidated tax return for the entire group.

Each company is taxed based on its contribution to the consolidated taxable profit (or loss) of the group.

Tax consolidation is binding for at least five years.

Tax incentives

The CPT law provides only two tax incentives related to businesses in non-developed municipalities and nongovernment organisations. The amendments to the CPT law greatly reduced the incentives available, including abolishing the tax incentives for newly employed staff and energy-efficient production.

Tax exemption/tax credit for newly established business in non-developed municipalities
Newly established production companies located in non-developed municipalities are entitled to a three-year tax exemption on the profits attributable to operations in these municipalities. The exemption period starts from the year in which production began.

Tax exemption for non-governmental organisations
Non-governmental organisations (NGO) registered for business activity are permitted to decrease the corporate tax base by EUR 4,000 with the condition that this money is used for realisation of the main goals of an NGO.

Withholding taxes (WHT)

Montenegrin CPT law imposes WHT on income distributed to a non-resident realised from a Montenegrin source.

The scope of the withholding tax applies to dividends and profit distribution, capital gains, interest, royalties, intellectual property rights fees, and rental income, as well as fees for consulting, marketing, and audit services.

Exceptionally, distributions of dividends and share of profits are subject to withholding tax if the recipient is a Montenegrin resident or non-resident (both individual or legal entity).

The general withholding tax rate is 9%.

Application of a double-tax treaty may reduce or eliminate Montenegrin withholding tax. To qualify for the beneficial rates prescribed by the treaty, a non-resident must prove tax residency of a relevant treaty country and beneficial ownership over the income. No further guidance has been issued up to date.

Tax administration

Returns
The tax year in Montenegro is the calendar year. Tax returns and supplementary documents (e.g., tax depreciation form) must be filed with the tax authorities by the end of March of the following year.

Payment of tax
Amendments to the corporate profit tax applicable from 1 January 2010 abolished monthly advance payments of the corporate tax and introduced annual payment of tax.

M

Corporate taxes in Mozambique

For more information, contact:

João Martins
PricewaterhouseCoopers, Lda
Pestana Rovuma Hotel
Centro de Escritòrios, 5th floor
Rua de Sé 114
Maputo, Mozambique
Tel: +258 21 350 400
Email: joao.l.martins@mz.pwc.com

Significant developments

Mozambique has been undergoing major tax reform since the beginning of 2003, which has consisted of replacing the existing corporate income tax and strengthening the tax administration by improving collection procedures and increasing enforcement capacity. Effective as from 1 January 2003, a new Corporate Income Tax Code ("Código do Imposto Sobre o Rendimento das Pessoas Colectivas", or CIRPC) came into force and was further amended on 1 January 2008. In September 2009 the Corporate Income Tax Code was further again to accommodate the introduction of IFRS rules in Mozambique.

Mozambique also introduced, with effect from 1 July 2002, a new Code of Fiscal Benefits, replacing the general tax benefits conceded under the previous Code as well as sectarian incentives granted under specific legal diplomas. In January 2009, the referred Code was amended by changing and, in some situations reducing, some of the customs and tax incentives granted under the previous Code.

Taxes on corporate income

Corporate tax is payable on corporate income at the rate of 32%. For tax years prior to 2010, income arising from agricultural or cattle breeding activities was subject to a reduced rate of 10%.

Capital gains are considered as profit and, therefore, taxed as normal income of the company jointly with other income earned during a certain year at the general tax rate of 32%.

Undocumented expenses as well as illicit or confidential expenses are taxed separately at a rate of 35%.

Corporate residence

Corporate residence is determined on the basis of a company's place of incorporation or effective management. Thus all companies with headquarters in Mozambique are considered tax residents, as well as any permanent establishments (PE) of non-resident entities.

Other taxes

Value-added tax (VAT)
VAT is chargeable on the sale of most goods and services as well as on imports. The standard rate is 17%. Usually, VAT is recoverable by corporate entities, except for those engaged in special business activities (e.g., financial and insurance operations, leasing (exemption with restrictions), sale of immovable property, some exempt activities, etc).

Property transfer tax
In Mozambique this tax is charged on transfers of real estate excluding the land, which is owned by the State. The rate of tax is 2% of the selling price of the building.

Gifts and inheritance tax
This tax is payable on transfers of all movable and immovable property by way of gift or bequest to persons resident in Mozambique or with respect to possessions situated in Mozambique. The tax is payable by the beneficiary and the rates vary from 0% to 15%, depending on the extent of the relationship between the donor and donee and the value of goods or rights transferred.

Stamp tax and service charges
Various documents require the payment of stamp duties. Service charges are payable for the performance of certain services for official purposes, such as those rendered by public notaries. These duties have been recently amended and vary generally from 0.03% to 50% on the amount of the transaction supported by the document to be stamped. In some other cases, the stamp tax comprises fixed amounts, ranging from MZN 0.50 to MZN 5,000.

Municipality taxes
Municipality taxes that should be considered for corporate purposes include:

M

- Municipality tax on real estate – This tax replaces the Property Tax on Buildings on immovable property situated within the municipality. It is levied on the value of immovable assets owned or possessed by corporate entities. Effective tax rates range from 0.2% to 1% of the building value, depending on the decision of each municipality.
- Municipality tax on economic activities – Levied on commercial or industrial activities carried out within the municipal territory. The tax depends on the activity being carried out, adjusted by coefficients, which are based on the zone and total area of the premises in square metres. In Maputo, this tax is calculated based on the following formula:

Rate = Basis rate x Index of location x Index of area occupied

Where,

- The basis rate varies from MZN 2,000 to MZN 4,000, depending on the nature of the activity carried out:
  - MZN 2,000 for industry;
  - MZN 2,500 for commerce;
  - MZN 3,000 for services in general; and
  - MZN 4,000 for hotels.

Mozambique

- The index of the location varies from 1 to 1.5 depending on the location of the premises within the municipality.
- The index of the area occupied varies from 1 to 1.5 depending on the nature of the activities and the space occupied by the premises (per m2).
- The tax payable is the amount resulting from applying the basic tax due on certain coefficients that are based on both the location and total area of the premises in square metres.

- Municipal surtax – This local surtax (called Derrama) may be imposed by the municipalities at a rate up to 15% of the following taxes: (i) corporate tax; and (ii) tax on real estate.

The local surtax is levied in relation to profits derived from activities carried out in the territory of each municipality.

When the municipalities decide to impose the surtax, the final corporate taxation will be increased by adding the surtax (at a rate of up to a maximum of 15%) to direct taxes (e.g., corporate tax). For example, normal corporate tax (32%) + municipal surtax (15%) = 32% + 4.8% = 37.25%, final corporate tax rate.

Branch income

From a tax perspective, branches are liable for Mozambican corporate tax as a separate entity and, therefore, the regime is the same that would apply to a Mozambican resident company. However, on the grounds that branches do not distribute dividends, no withholding tax would apply to the after-tax profits arising in Mozambique.

Income determination

Inventory valuation
Special rules regarding valuation of inventories are waiting for approval from the Minister of Finance. In the meantime, all inventory valuation methods generally accepted and according to international accounting principles are permitted for tax purposes, provided that the method is:

- Used by the taxpayer consistently; and
- Based on arm's-length prices duly documented and effectively exercised.

Based on the above assumptions, last-in, first-out (LIFO) and first-in, first-out (FIFO) methods are allowed. Write-downs and depreciation of inventories are not allowed. Conformity between book and tax reporting is required.

In principle, large companies will adopt IFRS beginning in 2010. New legislation in this regard is being currently prepared.

Capital gains
Capital gains less any capital losses derived from the sale or disposal of tangible fixed assets, including insurance indemnities received in case of accident, are taxed as part of normal income. If a taxpayer reinvests the sale proceeds within three tax years following the year of sale, the gain may be deferred until the end of the third year. A four-year reinvestment period may be accepted provided a prior application is submitted to the Minister of Finance. However, if the taxpayer does not realise the

reinvestment, the corporate tax that was not assessed during the three-year period will be assessed, along with compensatory interest.

Inter-company dividends
In the case of resident companies, income arising from dividends is excluded from taxable income, provided that the shares that a resident company holds in another resident company represents at least 25% of the total capital and are held for at least two consecutive years (or with an undertaking to hold the shares for this period). The same applies to income arising from risk capital companies and holding companies (Sociedade Gestora de Participações Sociais (SGPSs)) or from subsidiaries as a result of the application of technical reserves in insurance companies. However, in the case of holdings, the percentage of share capital decreases to 10% and shares should be held for at least one year.

If the shareholding falls outside the parameters indicated above, the tax withheld (20%) constitutes a payment on account. A tax credit corresponding to 60% of the corporate tax is attributable to the gross-up dividend.

Foreign income
Mozambican resident companies are taxed on the total income earned on a worldwide basis. Double taxation treaties allow tax paid abroad to offset Mozambican corporate tax. Mozambique has signed double tax treaties (DTT) with Portugal, Mauritius, Italy, the United Arab Emirates, South Africa, and Macau.

Other significant items
Companies generally may create specific provisions for doubtful or bad debts and also for depreciation of stock, which are allowed as tax-deductible costs.

Deductions

Depreciation and depletion
Depreciation is a deductible cost for corporate tax purposes, according to the regulations of the Corporate Income Tax Code, subject to restrictive and specific rules. Depreciation rules are contained in a specific legal diploma, which is Portaria nº 20 817, of 27 January 1968, which established the rates and limits legally allowed for depreciation purposes.

The main legal principles regarding depreciation are as follows:

- The establishment of the applicable rates falls under the competence of the Ministry of Finance.
- The calculation is carried out on a straight-line basis in accordance with the rates applicable.

The main depreciation rates are:

Depreciation rates	%
Tangible assets:	
Industrial buildings	4%
Office and residential buildings	2%
Machinery and installations, air conditioning, and telephone equipment	10%

M

Mozambique

Depreciation rates	%
Lifts	8.33%
Tools	25%
Laboratory equipment	12.5%
Telex and interior equipment	10%
Furniture and filing systems	10%
Typewriters and accounting machines	14.28%
Computer hardware	16.66%
Warehouse and filing installations:	
Of concrete	5%
Of wood	6.66%
Of steel	8.33%
Trucks	20%
Automobiles	25%
Intangible assets:	
Pre-operating expenses incurred prior to the commencement of business	33.33%
Deferred expenses arising in connection with increases in share capital, changes in form of business enterprises; issuance of debentures; marketing and other studies; financial expenses incurred for the acquisition or own production of fixed assets prior to completion	33.33%
Patents	10%
Manufacturing licenses, concessionaire agreements and similar rights	5% (1)
Trademark or premium of taking over leases of real estate (2)	

Notes

1. Subject to certain conditions set forth by the tax authorities.
2. Depreciation allowed in cases of effective reduction of value within the limits regarded as reasonable by the tax authorities.

Net operating losses
Carryback of losses is not allowed in Mozambique. On the other hand, losses may be carried forward for a period of five consecutive years.

Payments to foreign affiliates/related companies
Any payments to non-residents are allowed as deductible expenses provided that the amount does not exceed normal rates and that the taxpayer is able to prove that a business transaction was carried out with the non-resident company. The tax authorities may redetermine taxable income if, due to a special relationship between the Mozambican and non-resident companies, certain conditions existed that allowed a calculation of profit that differed from the profit that would have been calculated without the existence of such relationship (i.e., the arm's-length principle).

Where loans from related foreign corporations exceed twice the corresponding equity in the borrowing Mozambican corporation, the interest on the excess borrowing is not tax-deductible. Thin capitalisation rules are in force.

Taxes
Taxes paid in relation to the activities of a company are tax-deductible, excluding the corporate tax itself.

Mozambique

Group taxation

There are no group taxation provisions available in Mozambique. Each member of a group of companies preparing consolidated accounts for accounting purposes must file separate tax returns in order to be taxed on its profits on a stand-alone basis.

Tax incentives

Inward investments
In addition to the guarantees of ownership and remittance of funds abroad, the Mozambican government also guarantees the concession of tax and customs incentives. The incentives vary depending on whether a company is starting a new venture or rehabilitating one, and also on the nature of the project to be developed. The incentives discussed in this section are the generic benefits applicable to standard projects. Certain specific benefits also may be applicable depending on the activities of the industry for the investment project (e.g., industry, agriculture, tourism, science and technology, etc.).

Exemption of import duties
An exemption from customs duties and VAT applies upon the importation of capital equipment, listed in Section "K" of the Customs Tariff Schedule.

Tax credit for investment
Investments in new fixed tangible assets used in the operations of an enterprise within the Mozambican territory may benefit from an investment tax credit equal to 5% of the total investment realised, for a period of five years. This investment tax credit is offset against corporate income tax, up to the total amount of the tax assessment. This incentive does not apply when the investment in tangible fixed assets is with respect to the construction, acquisition, restoration or extension of buildings, passenger vehicles, furnishings and articles of comfort and decoration, leisure equipment, advanced technology or other assets not directly associated with the production activity carried out by the enterprise. When the project is located outside Maputo City, this tax credit is increased to 10%.

Accelerated depreciation
New immovable assets, used for the furtherance of the business, may be depreciated by increasing to 50% the normal depreciation rates approved by law. This benefit is also granted to rehabilitated immovable assets, machinery, and equipment used in agro-industrial activities.

Deduction from taxable income
The amount invested in specialised equipment classified as advanced technology, during the first five years from the date of commencement of activity, may be deducted from taxable income for purposes of calculating the corporate income tax up to a maximum of 10% of taxable income. Also, investment expenditures for professional training of Mozambican workers shall, up to a maximum amount of 5% of the taxable income (10% in case of professional training related to new/high technology equipment), be deductible from taxable income for the purposes of calculating the Corporate Income Tax during the first five years from the date of the commencement of such activities.

M

Mozambique

During a period of five years counting from the date of exploration, the following expenditure may be treated as deductible expenditures for purposes of calculating the corporate income tax:

- In the case of undertakings carried out in the City of Maputo, 110% of the value of expenditures for the construction and rehabilitation of roads, railways, airports, telecommunications, water supply, electric energy and other works of public utility, is deductible for tax purposes;
- In the case of undertakings carried out in the rest of the Provinces, an amount equal to 120% of the expenditures referred to in the paragraph above is deductible for tax purposes; and
- In the case of expenditures for the acquisition for personal ownership of works of art and other objects that are representative of Mozambican culture, as well as activities that contribute to the development of such works, 50% of the expenditures is deductible for tax purposes.

Withholding taxes (WHT)

Any non-resident entity carrying out economic activities in Mozambique, without being registered as a taxpayer, is liable to a final and definitive 20% withholding tax that is applied on all income earned. An exception exists for telecommunications and international transport as well as the respective installation and assembly of equipment made by those same entities, which are subject to a 10% withholding tax rate.

Both Mozambican resident and non-resident recipients are liable to tax on dividends at a tax rate of 20%.

Tax treaties
Mozambique has double tax treaties in force with Portugal, Mauritius, Italy, the United Arab Emirates, South Africa, and Macau. In accordance with these DTTs, the following tax rates will be applicable to dividends, royalties, and interest:

	Portugal	Mauritius	Italy	Macau	Dubai	South Africa
Dividends	15%	8% – If the recipient of the dividends is a company which has more than 25% of the share capital in the company that distributes the dividends.	15%	10%	0%	8% – If the recipient of the dividends is a company which has more than 25% of the share capital in the company that distributes the dividends.
		10% – If the recipient is a company, which has less than 25% of the share capital in the company that distributes the dividends.				15% – In all other cases.
		15% – In all other cases.				
Interest	10%	8%	10%	10%	0%	8%
Royalties	10%	5%	10%	10%	5%	5%
Capital Gains on shares	10%	0%	0%	0%	0%	0%

Tax administration

Returns

The tax year is, as a general rule, the calendar year. A different tax year may be applied (if previously authorised by the Ministry of Finance) for companies that carry out activities that justify a different year or non-resident companies with a permanent establishment in Mozambique.

Corporate tax assessment must be prepared by the companies on annual returns, based on the accounting records and on adjustments prescribed by the tax regulations.

The submission of the annual tax return is due by the last working day of May for companies using the calendar year as their tax year. For companies with a tax year that is not coincident with the calendar year, the presentation of the tax return is due by the last day of the fifth month subsequent to the respective year-end.

Payments

Mozambican companies and non-resident companies with a permanent establishment in Mozambique must pay corporate tax as follows:

- In three advance on account payments (based on 80% of the preceding tax year's corporate income tax), due in May, July, and September of the respective tax year; or if the tax year chosen is not coincident with the calendar year, on the fifth, seventh, and ninth months of the respective tax year; and
- In three special advance on account payments (0.5% of the preceding year's turnover less the advance on account payments made in previous years, which cannot be less than MZN 30,000 or more than MZN 100,000) due in June, August, and October of the respective tax year or if the tax year chosen is not coincident with the calendar year, on the sixth, eighth, and tenth months of the respective year.

M

For more information, contact:

Stéfan Hugo
PricewaterhouseCoopers
344 Independence Avenue
Windhoek, Namibia
Tel: +264 61 284 1000
Email: stefan.hugo@na.pwc.com

Significant developments

The latest annual budget speech was held on 30 March 2010. No tax changes were announced for the coming year. However, in the 2009 budget speech, presented by the Minister of Finance, Saara Kuugongelwa-Amadhila, amendments were proposed. Some of these amendments have since been promulgated but those that have not yet been promulgated are not yet effective.

Some of the announcements are summarised as follows.

Environmental taxes

An environmental levy was announced on disposable products that are harmful to the environment. No further details are available and this amendment has not yet been promulgated.

Value-added tax (VAT)

The zero-rating of essential basic items, such as milk and sugar, became effective on 1 May 2010. VAT will thus be levied at a rate of 0% on these products and registered vendors may claim input VAT paid on products acquired in the course of selling such essential products (provided that it is not denied input tax credit or subject to apportionment where both taxable and tax exempt supplies were made).

Medical services, previously exempt from VAT, are now zero-rated. VAT, will thus, be levied at a rate of 0% on these products and registered vendors may claim input VAT paid on products acquired in the course of selling such essential products (provided that it is not denied input tax credit or subject to apportionment where both taxable and tax exempt supplies were produced).

Income tax

The corporate tax rate for companies (other than mining companies, but including branches) was reduced from 35% to 34%, effective for financial years beginning on or after 1 January 2009.

The reduction in the corporate tax rate also affects the following taxpayers and tax rates:

- Long-term insurance companies are taxed at 40% of gross investment income multiplied by the corporate tax rate. The effective rate has now been reduced from 14% (40% x 35%) to 13.6% (40% x 34%).
- The withholding tax on royalties or similar payments is reduced from 10.5% (30% x 35%) to 10.2% (30% x 34%).

Transfer duty

It was announced that transfer duty will be payable on the transfer of membership interest in a close corporation or shareholders' interest in a company in terms of the 2008 budget speech of the Minister. No legislation in this regard has been promulgated.

Transfer duty rates have been amended, effective 1 May 2010, as follows:

Natural person: Non-agricultural

Value of property (NAD)	Transfer duty payable
0–400,000	Nil
400,001–800,000	1% of the value exceeding NAD 400,000
800,001–1,500,000	NAD 4,000 + 5% of the value exceeding NAD 800,000
1,500,001 and above	NAD 39,000 + 8% of the value exceeding NAD 1,500,000

Natural persons: Affirmative Action Loan Scheme for commercial farmland

Value of property (NAD)	Transfer duty payable
0-500,000	Nil
500,001-1,000,000	1% of the value exceeding NAD 500,000
1,000,001 and above	NAD 5,000 plus 3% of the value exceeding NAD 1,000,000

Rates for other persons

Value of property (NAD)	Transfer duty payable
Any value	12%

Taxes on corporate income

Namibia has a source-based tax system, which means that income from a source within Namibia or deemed to be within Namibia will be subject to tax in Namibia, unless a specific exemption is available.

Income earned by foreign companies from a source within or deemed to be within Namibia will be subject to tax in Namibia. In such case, the foreign entity must determine whether it is obliged to register a local entity or branch. A company is required to register a branch if it has established a place of business in Namibia. A local subsidiary company may be registered as an alternative to a branch.

In the event that Namibia has entered into a double tax agreement with the country where the foreign company resides, such entity will only be taxable in Namibia if it has established a permanent establishment (PE) in Namibia. A PE includes, in most cases, a fixed place of business and the establishment of a local entity or branch will most often create a PE; however, the provisions of the related tax treaty should be considered. If a PE exists, only the portion of income attributable to the PE will be subject to tax in Namibia.

Namibia, Republic of

Non-residents that do not have a place of business in Namibia may, however, be subject to withholding tax. *(See Withholding taxes.)*

No capital gains tax is payable in Namibia.

Calculation of taxable income

Gross income	The total amount, in cash or otherwise, received by or accrued to any person from a source within, or deemed to be within Namibia, excluding receipts of a capital nature (provisions for specific inclusions in gross income and amounts deemed to be from a Namibian source exist).
Less exemptions	The Income Tax Act provides for certain amounts to be specifically exempt from tax.
= Income	
Less: Deductions	Expenditures and losses actually incurred to generate income may be deducted, provided that these expenses are not of a capital nature.
	The Income Tax Act specifically provides for certain expenditures to be deductible and allows a deduction for capital allowances.
	Only expenses incurred to generate 'income' may be deducted. Expenses incurred to generate income exempt from tax are not deductible. Apportionment should be considered when expenses are incurred to generate both taxable income and tax exempt income.
Taxable income	Taxable income is taxed at the corporate tax rate as set out under the tax rate section below.

Tax rates

The corporate tax rates can be summarised as follows:

Entity	Current tax rate
Domestic companies and close corporations (excluding entities mentioned below)	34%
Branches of foreign companies	34%
Registered manufacturers (only applicable for the first 10 years of registration)	18%
Diamond mining companies and companies that render services to such companies in connection with diamond mining	55%
Mining companies (other than diamond mining companies) and companies that render services to such companies in connection with mining	37.50%
Long-term insurers (the rate is applied to gross investment income)	13.6%
Petroleum income tax rate	35%

Anti-avoidance

Note that the Income Tax Act, Act 24 of 1981 (Act), contains an anti-avoidance section, Section 95, that enables the Receiver of Revenue to disregard the implications of a transaction or scheme if it can be proven that:

i.   Such transaction or scheme had been entered into to avoid or postpone the payment of any duty or levy imposed by the Act; and

ii. Such transaction or scheme was entered into or carried out by means or in a manner that would not normally be employed in the entering into or carrying out of a transaction, operation or scheme of the nature of the transaction, operation or scheme in question, or has created rights or obligations that would not normally be created between persons dealing at arm's length under a transaction, operation or scheme of nature of the transaction, operation or scheme in question; and

iii. Such transaction or scheme was entered into or carried out solely or mainly for the purposes of the avoidance or the postponement of liability for the payment of any tax duty or levy.

The Receiver of Revenue can, at its sole discretion, impose Section 95 on any transaction or scheme, which will place the onus on the taxpayer to prove that any/all of the requirements noted above will not be applicable to the transaction or scheme.

Transfer pricing

Namibia introduced transfer pricing legislation on 14 May 2005. The legislation was aimed at enforcing the arm's-length principle in cross-border transactions carried out between connected persons. On 5 September 2006, the Directorate of Inland Revenue issued Income Tax Practice Note 2 of 2006 that contains guidance on the application of the transfer pricing legislation. The Practice Note is based on guidance set out by the Organisation for Economic Co-operation and Development (OECD) Transfer Pricing Guidelines for Multinational Enterprises and Tax Administrations.

The objective of this practice note is to provide taxpayers with guidelines regarding the procedures to be followed in the determination of arm's-length prices, taking into account the Namibian business environment. It also sets out the Minister of Finance's views on documentation and other practical issues that are relevant in setting and reviewing transfer pricing in international agreements.

Transfer pricing legislation is essentially aimed at ensuring that cross-border transactions between companies operating in a multinational group are fairly priced and that profits are not stripped out of Namibia and taxed in lower tax jurisdictions. The legislation achieves this by giving the Minister of Finance (who essentially delegates to the Directorate of Inland Revenue) the power to adjust any non-market related prices charged or paid by Namibian entities in cross-border transactions with related parties to arm's-length prices and to tax the Namibian entity as if the transactions had been carried out at market-related prices.

In terms of the normal penalty provisions of the Income Tax Act, the Directorate of Inland Revenue may levy penalties of up to 200% on any amount of underpaid tax. Consequently, the Directorate of Inland Revenue may invoke such provisions in the event that a taxpayer's taxable income is understated as a result of prices that were charged in transactions, not carried out at arm's length. Further, interest will be charged on the unpaid amounts at 20% per annum.

Thin capitalisation

The Minister may, if any amount of financial assistance provided by a foreign connected person is excessive in relation to a company's fixed capital (being share capital, share premium, accumulated profits, whether capital or not), disallow the deduction for income tax purposes of any interest or other charges payable by the Namibian person on the "excessive portion" of the financial assistance provided by the foreigner.

Namibia, Republic of

There is no guidance that provides a definition for "excessive". Therefore, each case should be considered on the basis of the facts provided. The 3:1 ratio is applied by the Bank of Namibia for exchange control purposes and this guideline is therefore deemed suitable, until otherwise determined by the Directorate of Inland Revenue.

Treaty relief

Namibia has entered into double tax agreements with the following countries:

- Botswana;
- France;
- Germany;
- India;
- Malaysia;
- Mauritius;
- Romania;
- Russian Federation;
- South Africa;
- Sweden; and
- United Kingdom.

Namibia has negotiated tax treaties with the following countries, but these treaties have not yet been signed:

- Singapore;
- Zimbabwe; and
- Canada.

The following treaties are in negotiation:

- Belgium;
- Seychelles; and
- Zambia.

Corporate residence

The Namibian tax system is based on source and not on residency. Income derived or deemed to be derived from sources within Namibia are subject to tax.

The source is determined as the place where income originates or is earned, not the place of payment. If goods are sold pursuant to a contract entered into within Namibia, the source of income is deemed to arise in Namibia, regardless of the place of delivery or transfer of title.

Certain types of income arising outside Namibia may, in the hands of a domestic company, be deemed to arise in Namibia and be taxed as such. Examples are interest and certain copyright royalties arising outside Namibia.

Otherwise, and except for the PE concept embodied in the tax treaties, corporate residence is of little tax significance.

Other taxes

VAT

VAT is a transaction tax and the implications will vary for different transactions. Some transactions are taxed at a rate of 15% or 0% while other transactions are exempt from VAT. Input tax deductions may be claimed, subject to certain provisions.

VAT is levied on every taxable supply by a registered person. A taxable supply means any supply of goods or services in the course or furtherance of a taxable activity.

A taxable activity means any activity that is carried on continuously or regularly in Namibia, which involves the supply of goods or services for consideration.

VAT is payable on all imports for home consumption in Namibia, subject to certain exemptions (e.g., in terms of a technical assistance agreement, donations to the State, goods of which the local supply is zero-rated, etc).

Import VAT is payable on the greater of the free on board (FOB) value plus 10%, or the market value. The payment may be deferred in terms of an import VAT account registered with the Directorate of Inland Revenue to the twentieth day of the month following the month of importation. Penalties of 10% per month or part of a month and 20% interest on outstanding import VAT, according to the Customs Asycuda reports on import VAT account numbers, are levied by the Directorate of Inland Revenue.

A company/branch is required to register for VAT if it supplies goods or services on a regular basis for consideration and if their taxable supplies (standard rated and zero-rated supplies) exceed NAD 200,000 in any 12-month period.

Registered vendors are required to levy VAT on all taxable supplies at the standard rate of 15%.

A registered VAT vendor is entitled to deduct input tax credits paid in the course of taxable supplies made to such person, provided that a tax invoice is available to support the input tax deduction. It is also important to take note of deemed input tax deductions, and prohibited input deductions. Import VAT paid may be deducted only as input tax if the import was in furtherance of a taxable activity and the required documentation (e.g., stamped customs entries) is held by the importer.

Customs and excise

Namibia is a member of the Southern African Customs Union (SACU) and customs duties are not levied on intra SACU trade (i.e., between Botswana, Lesotho, Namibia, South Africa and Swaziland).

Customs duties are payable according to the Common Customs Tariff of SACU on imports from outside SACU. Preferential duty rates apply on imports from Southern African Development Community (SADC) countries while goods may be imported free of customs duties from Zimbabwe in terms of the Namibia-Zimbabwe Free Trade Agreement.

Excise duties are levied on local production of excisable products and are included on most excisable products imported from another SACU country in terms of the Duty at source procedures. Identical excise duty rates are applied throughout the SACU.

Namibia, Republic of

Importation of excisable products from outside the SACU is subject to customs duties and specific customs duties. *Ad valorem* duties are levied on certain products (e.g., motor vehicles, perfumes, etc.) in addition to the normal customs duties.

Fuel levies are payable on petrol, diesel and illuminating kerosene and may be claimed back for certain non-road operations (e.g., mining, farming, and construction).

Security is required by customs on all temporary importations to cover import VAT and customs duties (if applicable).

It is possible to import goods that are subject to customs duties into registered customs bonded warehouses, where goods are kept for later use. In this case, the payment of duties may be deferred until the goods are taken out of the bonded warehouse for home consumption or acquitted if the goods are subsequently exported.

Annual duty
Annual duty is levied in terms of the Companies Act at an amount of NAD 4.00 for every NAD 10,000 (or part thereof) of the issued share capital of a company, with a minimum duty of NAD 80.00 per annum. Issued shares include ordinary shares, share premium, and preference shares.

Since a branch does not issue share capital, the issued share capital of the head office will be used to calculate the annual duty payable in Namibia.

Stamp duty
Certain transactions may attract stamp duty. The amount of stamp duty payable differs and is based on the nature of every individual transaction.

The basic transactions can be summarised as follows:

Transaction	Stamp duty
Agreements or contracts (other than those where duty is specifically provided for in the Act)	NAD 5.00
Lease agreement or lease	The stamp duty will be based on lease payments, together with additional considerations specified in the lease agreement
Transfer or issue of marketable securities and other share transactions	Between NAD 2.00 and NAD 5.00 for every NAD 1,000 or part thereof of the value/consideration, depending on the specific transaction

Transfer duty
Transfer duty is payable on the acquisition value of property acquired.

Transfer duty is normally payable by the buyer but the agreement for the sale of the property may determine the person liable to pay these costs.

Exchange control
The Exchange Control Regulations in Namibia are administered by the local banking institutions.

Foreign exchange transactions that involve the transfer of funds to countries outside the Rand Common Monetary Area (RCMA) are subject to Bank of Namibia approval. Countries within the RCMA are South Africa, Namibia, Lesotho and Swaziland.

The issuance of shares to countries outside the RCMA will involve the transfer of funds to these countries once dividends are declared. Bank of Namibia approval is thus required prior to the issuance of the related shares.

Bank of Namibia approval is also required if funds are transferred to countries outside the RCMA.

Branch income

Branch income that is received or accrued from a source within or deemed to be within Namibia is taxable in Namibia based on the normal corporate tax rules.

A branch is regarded as an extension of its foreign head office. A branch may, therefore, not deduct fees paid to its foreign head office (unless a tax treaty provides for such a deduction), as it is argued that a branch cannot transact with itself. Reimbursement of actual expenses may, however, be deducted, subject to the normal deduction rules.

Transfer pricing rules apply between a branch and its foreign head office or other cross-border related parties.

Income determination

Please refer to the Taxes on corporate income section.

Deductions

Capital allowances
The cost (including finance charges) of machinery, equipment, and other articles used by the taxpayer to generate income is deductible in three equal annual allowances. No apportionment is required where an asset is held for less than 12 months.

Buildings used by the taxpayer to generate income qualify for an initial allowance of 20% of erection costs in the year they are first brought into use. Thereafter, an annual allowance of 4% is deductible for each year following the year of erection. Additions to existing buildings (not alterations or repairs) qualify for the same 20% and 4% deductions. Note that the allowance is calculated on the cost of erection and not the cost of acquisition. The allowance is also only calculated for a period of 21 years from the date of erection.

Mining exploration expenditures incurred before commencement of production are deductible in full in the first year that income is generated from the mine. Subsequent developmental expenditures are written off in three equal annual allowances.

Capital allowances may also be deducted with respect to patents, trademarks, leasehold improvements, etc.

A recovery or recapture of allowances previously claimed should be included in the gross income of a taxpayer in the event that the allowance is recovered or recaptured by way of disposal, withdrawal from trade for non-trade purposes, or removal from Namibia. The recapture is calculated at the market value of the asset.

Trading losses

Assessed tax losses may be carried forward indefinitely provided the company continues to trade. Tax laws do not allow losses to be transferred to other members of a group and anti-avoidance provisions may be triggered by transactions designed to transfer or exploit assessed losses.

If a company ceases to trade for a full fiscal year, its assessed losses are forfeited, regardless of subsequent activities. Assessed losses are also reduced in the event of a compromise agreement with creditors.

Group taxation

No taxation of combined operations is allowed in Namibia where operations are conducted by more than one company.

Tax incentives

Manufacturing

The following is a high-level summary of tax incentives available for the manufacturing industry and does not consider the specific conditions that should be met in order for these incentives to be utilised.

	Tax treatment for normal taxpayers	Tax incentive for manufacturers
Building allowance	A building allowance is deductible with respect to buildings used for purposes of trade.	
	The allowance is calculated as 20% of the cost of erection in the year in which the building is put into use and 4% during the 20 years that follow the year of erection.	The allowance is calculated as 20% of the cost of erection in the year in which the building is put into use and 8% during the 10 years that follow the year of erection.
Employee allowances	Expenditure for remuneration and training of employees are deductible for tax purposes.	
		An additional allowance of 25% of remuneration and training of employees that are directly engaged in the manufacturing process are deductible.
Export expenditure allowance	Export expenditure incurred is deductible for tax purposes.	
		An additional allowance of 25% of costs incurred in an export country, in order to export Namibian manufactured goods to such country, may be deducted.

	Tax treatment for normal taxpayers	Tax incentive for manufacturers
Export allowance	Any taxpayer that derives income from the export of manufactured goods, excluding meat or fish, may deduct an export allowance equal to 80% of the taxable income derived from the export of manufactured goods.	
	Gross profit derived from the export of manufactured goods as a percentage of total gross profit should be used to determine the percentage of taxable income that is used to calculate the export allowance.	
Transport allowance	Land-based transport costs (i.e., transport by road or rail) are deductible for tax purposes.	
		An additional allowance of 25% of land-based transport costs in respect of material and components used in the manufacturing process or equipment imported for direct use in the manufacturing process may be deducted.
Preferential tax rate	The normal tax rate for companies other than mining companies or registered manufacturers is 34%.	The tax rate for a registered manufacturer for taxable income with respect to the manufacturing activity for which they are registered is 18%. This preferential rate is applicable for a period of 10 years from registration as a manufacturer.

Note that only the building allowance and preferential tax rate (as set out above) may create or increase a tax loss.

Export processing zones (EPZ)

In order to become an export processing zone company, a particular entity must register with the EPZ governing body and obtain approval from the Directorate of Inland Revenue.

An EPZ company qualifies for the following benefits:

- The company is exempt from income tax;
- No VAT is payable on the sale of goods or services rendered in a zone;
- No VAT is payable on goods imported or manufactured in the zone;
- No customs or excise duty is payable on goods imported into the zone;
- No stamp duty or transfer duty is payable in relation to the transfer of movable or immovable property in a zone;
- A 75% refund of expenditures incurred in training Namibian citizens; and
- Some of the provisions in the Labour Relations Act do not apply in a zone.

Enterprises must comply with the following requirements in order to qualify for EPZ status:

- Goods must be exported to countries other than countries in the SACU;
- Industrial employment must be created or increased; and

Namibia, Republic of

- Namibia's export earnings must be increased as a result of manufactured goods exported.

EPZ companies may not be involved in retail business operations.

Withholding taxes (WHT)

WHT are applicable where dividends and royalties or similar payments are declared or distributed to non-Namibian residents.

Dividends
Dividends declared by a Namibian company to a non-resident holding company are subject to non-resident shareholders tax (NRST), a WHT. NRST is payable at a rate of 10% unless treaty relief is available. NRST is payable within 30 days after declaration of a dividend.

Royalties or similar payments
WHT on royalties are payable when a Namibian company pays a royalty to a non-resident. WHT is levied at a rate of 10.2% (30% of the corporate tax rate of 34%) and is payable within 14 days after the end of the month during which the liability for payment is incurred.

A royalty includes payment for the use or right to use any patent or design, trademark, copyright, model, pattern, plan, formula, process, property rights, or right of a similar nature. A royalty also includes the imparting of any scientific, technical, industrial or commercial knowledge, or information for use in Namibia. The nature of fees payable should therefore be carefully considered in order to determine whether the relevant amount represents a royalty.

Interest
A WHT of 10%, calculated on the gross amount of interest, is payable on interest accruing to any person, other than a Namibian company, from a registered Namibian banking institution or unit trust scheme.

The tax withheld is a final tax and the financial institution is responsible to withhold the tax.

Namibian companies are however taxed on interest at the corporate tax rate.

It is the obligation of the financial institution to withhold the tax and pay such tax to the revenue authorities.

Summary of WHT payable
The WHT rates and treaty relief for Namibian double tax agreements can be summarised as follows. Note that the tax treaties contain certain requirements that should be met before the reduced tax rate may be applied.

The definitions of dividends, royalties, and interest in the various treaties should also be considered.

Country	Dividends	Royalties	Interest
Namibian tax legislation	10%	10.2%	10%**

Country	Dividends	Royalties	Interest
Botswana	10%	10%	10%
France	5%	10%	10%
Germany	10%	10%	0%
India	10%	10%	10%
Malaysia	5%	5%	10%
Mauritius	5%	5%	10%
Romania	N/A	5%	10%
Russian Federation	5%	5%	10%
South Africa	5%	10%	10%
Sweden	5%	5%	10%
United Kingdom	5%	5%	N/A

** Namibian companies are taxed at the corporate tax rate on interest received.

N/A means that the provisions of the tax treaty limited the rate to a rate that is higher than the local Namibian rate. It should be noted that a treaty may only provide tax relief and cannot impose a higher tax rate.

Mining royalties

The Minerals (Prospecting and Mining) Act levies a royalty on minerals won or mined by a licence holder in Namibia, based on the table below:

Group of Minerals	Percentage of market value of minerals leviable as a royalty
Precious metals	3%
Base and rare metals	3%
Semi-precious stones	2%
Nuclear fuel minerals	3%*
Industrial minerals	2%
Non-nuclear fuel minerals	2%

* Applicable to all licence holders on nuclear fuel minerals, except Rössing Uranium Mine Ltd where a 6% royalty is applicable.

Tax administration

The due date for filing of returns can be summarised as follows:

Tax return submission

Return	Due date
Income tax return	Within seven months after the financial year-end of the company
Provisional tax return – first payment	Within six months from the commencement of the respective tax year
Provisional tax return – second payment	On/before the last day of the respective tax year
Provisional tax return – top-up payment	Within seven months after the financial year-end of the company or tax year-end of the business individual

Namibia, Republic of

Return	Due date
Employees' tax return (PAYE return)	Within 20 days following the month to which the PAYE relates
PAYE reconciliation return	Within 30 days from the tax year-end for individuals (i.e., 30 March each year)
VAT return	Within 25 days following the month to which the VAT relates
Import VAT	Within 20 days following the month to which the VAT relates
WHT on dividends	Within 30 days after declaration of the dividend
WHT on royalties or similar payments	Within 14 days after the end of the month during which the liability for payment of the royalty was incurred

Corporate taxes in The Netherlands

For more information, contact:

Sytso Boonstra
PricewaterhouseCoopers
Westgate, Thomas R. Malthusstraat 5
1066 JR Amsterdam
The Netherlands
Tel: +31 8879 23470
Email: sytso.boonstra@nl.pwc.com

George de Soeten
PricewaterhouseCoopers
Fascinatio Boulevard 350
P.O. Box 8800
3009 AV Rotterdam
The Netherlands
Tel: +31 8879 23671
Email: george.de.soeten@nl.pwc.com

Significant developments

After the fundamental changes in the Dutch Corporate Income Tax Act as of 1 January 2007, the Ministry of Finance proposed major amendments at the end of 2008, followed by a more detailed set of possible proposals in June 2009 laid down in a consultation document. The Ministry of Finance has indicated that a bill for amending the Corporate Income Tax Act will be submitted in 2010. It currently would appear that the primary focus lies on the limitation of interest deduction for takeover companies and the exclusion of permanent establishment losses from the Dutch tax base.

This reform must be seen as a reaction to a series of developments which have negatively impacted the competitive position of the Netherlands relative to other member states of the European Union (EU). Therefore, it is necessary to improve the Dutch international position from a fiscal perspective. The potential amendments should make substantially lower corporate income tax rates possible.

In this respect, the 2010 Tax Package, as published by the Dutch government on 15 September 2009, already provides for an important liberalisation of the participation exemption regime in the corporate income tax and a further expansion of the patent box (now "innovation box") as of 1 January 2010.

Since 2008, the government has taken several measures, including tax measures, in order to deal with the consequences caused by the worldwide economic crisis. New temporary provisions provide for accelerated depreciation up to 50% a year of the value of qualifying assets bought and investments made in 2009 and 2010, under certain conditions. Furthermore, for the years 2009 and 2010 the first corporate income tax bracket has been extended substantially. Finally, corporate taxpayers may opt for a temporary extension of the carryback period of losses.

The 2009 Tax Package, which was announced in September 2008, included some minor amendments. The most important change, which was retroactive to 1 January 2008, provided for a substantial extension of the first corporate income tax bracket for the years 2008, 2009 and 2010. Other relevant amendments were related to the Dutch tonnage tax regime, making the Netherlands more attractive for ocean shipping, and to the regime for investment companies, removing some bottlenecks for those investment companies that exploit real estate in separate subsidiaries. Finally, the 2009 increase of the Dutch main value-added tax (VAT) tariff from 19% to 20% announced in 2007 was cancelled, mainly to protect the consumer purchasing power, to strengthen the economy and to restrict inflation.

The Netherlands

Most discussed in 2008 was the Government's plan to tax so called "excessive" remuneration suggesting on the one hand an employer levy on certain qualifying severance payments and past service pension premiums, and on the other hand taxation on carried interest arrangements qualifying as "lucrative investments". Both provisions became effective as of 1 January 2009.

As of 1 January 2009, the provisions of the amended tax treaties with Ghana and South Africa to avoid double taxation on income became applicable. As of 1 January 2010, the tax treaties with Azerbaijan, Bahrain and Qatar came into force.

Several tax bills are pending, including a proposal to create the possibility for partnerships to opt for legal personality, which will also will consequences for, among other things, the Dutch real estate transfer tax.

Taxes on corporate income

Standard corporate income tax rate
The Dutch standard corporate income tax rate has been reduced significantly over the past years. While it is 25.5% for the years 2007 to 2010, it was 31.5% in 2005 and 29.6% in 2006. The Dutch corporate income tax rate is determined based on taxable income brackets. The tax rate on the first bracket is 20%. For 2009 and 2010 the upper limit of the first bracket was extended to a taxable amount of EUR 200,000. For 2008 the upper limit of the first bracket was retroactively extended to EUR 275,000.

Fiscal investment fund regime
In general terms, under the existing regime, the corporate income tax rate for fiscal investment funds is 0%, provided that their profit is made available to the shareholders and holders of certificates of participation no later than eight months after year end. This regime was amended on 1 August 2007. One of the main amendments is the possibility for fiscal investment funds to invest in real estate development (or redevelopment) activities, provided that these activities take place through a subsidiary subject to Dutch corporate income tax and the development (or redevelopment) activities are exercised for the benefit of real estate that is (or will be) forming part of the fund's own portfolio, an affiliated fiscal investment fund's portfolio, the portfolio of a company in which the fund or the affiliated fund has a substantial interest, or for the benefit of the subsidiary's own portfolio. The amended law applies to fiscal book years ending after 1 August 2007.

As of 1 January 2009, the regime for investment companies has been changed in order to remove some bottlenecks for those investment companies that exploit/hold real estate in separate subsidiaries.

Exempt investment fund regime
On 1 August 2007, a new tax exempt investment fund regime became effective. In accordance with this regime, if an investment fund is (or considered as) a public interest entity or a mutual investment fund subject to the Dutch Financial Supervision Act ("Wet op het financieel toezicht"), and further conditions are met, such investment fund can request an exemption from corporate income tax. Apart from the exempt status for corporate income tax purposes, the exempt investment fund will not be obliged to withhold dividend withholding tax with regard to profit distributions to its shareholders. The exempt investment fund regime can be applied to fiscal book years starting on or after 1 August 2007. In March 2008, the Ministry of Finance

issued a decree with, among other things, directives to determine whether or not the investment fund is considered open-ended.

As of 1 January 2009, the definition of the notion "financial devices" has been extended to include bank credits (e.g., current, savings or deposit accounts).

Innovation box regime

As of 1 January 2007, a special regime applies with respect to profits, including royalties, derived from a self-developed intangible asset by the taxpayer developed after 31 December 2006. In this so called "patent box", the taxpayer may opt, under certain conditions, for the application of a 10% effective rate on taxable profits derived from these intangible assets. This patent box is applicable provided that at least 30% of the profits have been originated by the patent. However, the 10% rate applies only to a maximum of four times the production costs of the intangible asset included in the patent box (pre-2010). As of 1 January 2008, this regime has been expanded in a substantial way. Companies which have incurred certain qualified research and development (R&D) costs for the development of intellectual property for which no patent was granted are also entitled to the favourable effective tax rate. The extension of the scope is subject to the condition that these qualified R&D assets become part of the company's assets after 31 December 2007.

As of 1 January 2010, the patent box is further expanded and renamed as "innovation box". The effective tax rate is lowered to 5%. Furthermore, the different limits that apply to patented assets and R&D assets are cancelled, resulting in a widening of the scope of the regime and an equal treatment of all innovative activities. In addition, the lower effective tax rate of 5% only applies to positive income, allowing innovation losses to be taken into account in full. Based upon a favourable decree, the latter has also been approved for innovation losses arising in 2009.

Other corporate/business taxes

There are no provincial or municipal corporate income taxes.

Corporate residence

In the Netherlands, corporate residence is determined by each corporation's circumstances. Management and control are important factors in this respect. Companies incorporated under Dutch law are deemed to be residents of the Netherlands (although, not with respect to certain provisions, such as participation exemption and fiscal unity).

Other taxes

Value-added tax (VAT)

Known in Dutch as the BTW ("Belasting over de Toegevoegde Waarde"), VAT is payable on sales of goods and on services rendered in the Netherlands as well as on the importation of goods and on the "intra-European" acquisition of goods. There are three VAT rates, which are 19%, 6% and 0%.

The main VAT rate remains at 19%. The proposed increase announced in 2007 from 19% to 20% has been cancelled.

The Netherlands

The reduced VAT rate (6%) is on certain prime necessities (and as from 2 July 2009, also on certain energy-saving insulation activities on houses).

The special VAT rate (0%) is applicable mainly to intra-European Union supplies, exports, imports stored in bonded warehouses, services rendered in connection with the above, and certain other services.

The following are exempt from VAT:

- The supply of immovable property two years after putting it into use and lease. However, if the lessee's use of the immovable property is 90% or more for input VAT-deductible purposes, the lessor and lessee may opt to be subject to VAT on rent, in which case the lessor may deduct the VAT charged in respect of the property;
- Medical, cultural, social, and educational services. The medical exemption has been changed slightly as of 1 January 2009;
- Services provided by banks and other financial institutions in connection with payment transactions and the granting of credit facilities;
- Insurance transactions; and
- Transactions in shares.

Transfer tax on immovable property
Acquisition of economic or legal ownership of immovable property in the Netherlands is subject to 6% transfer tax on market value. Some exemptions are available.

Capital tax
The capital tax was abolished as of 1 January 2006. Transactions within the scope of the capital tax that occurred prior to the date of abolishment are still subject to capital tax.

Other indirect taxes
An insurance tax of 7% is payable on insurance premiums if the insured is a resident of the Netherlands or if the insured object is in the Netherlands. Several exemptions are available.

Municipalities impose immovable property tax on the owners of the immovable property. The rates depend on the municipality. The taxable basis is the market value of the immovable property. Please note that the (assessment of the) value as of 1 January 2007 also is of importance for corporate taxation, as depreciation might be limited based on this value (see Deductions section and specifically, Limited depreciation of immovable property).

An excise tax is levied on certain consumer goods (e.g., cigarettes, cigars, mineral oils, alcoholic products, etc.). If the goods are used solely as raw materials, no excise tax is levied. The excise tax is refundable if the article is exported.

Environmental charges on packaging
As of 1 January 2008, producers or importers have to pay taxes on packaging. The tariff depends on the type and method of packaging. An exemption is granted to companies that bring less than 15,000 kilos of packaging materials a year on the market. In the summer of 2008, the Ministry of Finance declared a simplification of the rules after consulting with the business community. For example, it is now possible to arrange a special agreement with the Dutch tax authorities, the number of tariffs

on packaging has been reduced, and the definition of "packaging" has altered. Most changes became effective as of 1 January 2009, however, some of the new rules have retroactive effect to 1 April 2008 or even to 1 January 2008.

The threshold for liability to the packaging tax has increased from 15,000kg to 50,000kg as of 1 January 2010. On the other hand, the tax rates have risen by more than 8%. Further, a refund of the packaging tax for indirect export also is available to foreign entrepreneurs as of 1 January 2010.

Branch income

Rates for branch profits are the same as for other corporate profits, but no tax is withheld on transfers of profits to the head office. The tax-base is in principle calculated on the same rules as for Dutch resident companies.

Income determination

Inventory valuation
In general, stocks/inventory are stated at the lower of cost or market value. Cost may be determined on the basis of first-in, first-out (FIFO), last-in, first-out (LIFO), base stock, or average cost. The LIFO system can be used for commercial/financial and tax purposes.

There is no requirement of conformity between commercial/financial and tax reporting.

Capital gains
Capital gains are taxed as ordinary income. However, capital gains realised on disposal of shares qualifying for the participation exemption are tax exempt *(see Inter-company dividends section)*.

The gain on disposal of depreciable assets may be carried over to a special tax deferral reinvestment reserve but must then be deducted from the acquisition cost of the later acquired assets. Except in special circumstances, the reserve cannot be maintained for more than three consecutive years. If the reserve has not been fully applied after three years, the remainder will be liable to taxation.

Capital losses are deductible, unless attributable to the disposal of a shareholding qualifying for the participation exemption.

Inter-company dividends
Subject to meeting the conditions for the participation exemption, a Dutch company or branch of a foreign company is exempt from Dutch tax on all benefits connected with a qualifying shareholding, including cash dividends, dividends in kind, bonus shares, hidden profit distributions, and capital gains.

In general, the participation exemption will apply to a shareholding in a Dutch company, if the holding is at least 5% of the investee's capital. Due to the amendments of the participation exemption, the non-inventory requirement is not applicable after 1 January 2007. When the shareholder's interest is a portfolio investment in a company, that is not subject to a tax rate that is considered adequate (meaning subject to a profit

N

The Netherlands

tax that equals at least an effective tax rate of 10% over a taxable base according to Dutch tax standards) the exemption cannot be applied.

Whether or not a shareholder's interest in a company is a portfolio investment is determined solely by the assets of that company (participation exemption regime 2007-2009). If the company's assets consist predominantly (more than 50%) of portfolio investments, the interest in the company is considered a passive participation. A distinction in this respect is made between portfolio investments held by a company in its line of business and free portfolio investments. Only the presence of free portfolio investments can lead to the qualification of a portfolio investment participation. Portfolio investments held by a company in its line of business are qualified as good assets. Assets that are used for more than 50% for intra-group financing activities are deemed to be held as free portfolio investments. This applies, unless credible evidence to the contrary can be given. In that case, the participation exemption could apply. Furthermore, participations whose assets consist of at least 90% real estate (real estate participation) are not considered low taxed portfolio investment participations, which means that the participation exemption applies.

In February 2008, the Ministry of Finance issued an important decree stating, among other things, several commitments regarding the asset test, the subject-to-tax requirement and the real estate participation.

As of 1 January 2010, the participation exemption regime has been further liberalised. As a general rule, the participation exemption is applicable as long as the participation is not held as a portfolio investment. The intention of the parent company, which can be based on particular facts and circumstances, is decisive as of 1 January 2010. Regardless the company's intention, the participation exemption also is applicable if the new sufficient tax test, which is if the income is subject to a real profit tax of at least 10%, or the revised asset test, which has been relaxed in comparison to the asset test of the participation exemption regime 2007-2009, as discussed above, is met.

For portfolio investment participations not qualifying for the participation exemption, double taxation will be avoided by applying the tax credit method, unless the portfolio investment shareholding effectively is not subject to tax at all. For EU shareholdings, it is optional to credit the actual underlying tax.

Dividends not qualifying under the participation exemption are taxable in full at the ordinary corporate income tax rate.

Interests of 25% or more in a company of which the assets consist (nearly) exclusively of portfolio investments should be annually valued – as an asset – at the fair market value.

Costs related to the acquisition and disposal of a participation, such as legal fees, compensations, notary fees, are not deductible for corporate tax.

Losses arising from the liquidation of a (foreign) subsidiary are deductible for corporate tax, subject to certain conditions. This regime has been changed slightly as of 2008 to make it more in-line with EU directives.

Profits derived from a company that was created by converting a foreign permanent establishment, only qualify for the participation exemption after they exceed the losses from the permanent establishment during the previous years, insofar as those losses reduced the taxable profits in the Netherlands. Under certain circumstances, such as the alienation of (part of) the shares of the company, all non-recaptured losses will be added to the profits of the Dutch parent company at once. As of 9 March 2007, the scope of these anti-abuse provisions has been extended by including situations in which a foreign intermediate holding company is interposed.

Foreign income

A Dutch resident company is subject to corporate tax on its total worldwide income.

Double taxation of certain foreign-source income, including foreign branch income, is avoided by reducing Dutch tax by the ratio of foreign income (subject to a foreign income tax and/or covered by certain tax treaty provisions) to total income, the so-called exemption method. Currency exchange profits or losses on the head office's investment in its foreign branch are not considered "foreign income" for the purposes of these relief provisions.

Unilateral relief from double taxation for income from foreign financing branches is provided by means of a credit of 17.5% of the passive financing income for foreign taxes deemed paid or the foreign tax actually paid. However, the exemption method will apply only if the taxpayer can demonstrate that the foreign branch is actively engaged in intra-group financing activities.

Double taxation of foreign dividends, interest and royalties is relieved by a tax credit provided by Dutch tax treaties or unilaterally, if the payer of the income streams is a resident of a developing country, designated by Ministerial Order. If no treaty or unilateral relief applies, a deduction of the foreign tax paid is allowed in computing the net taxable income.

However, relief by exemption is given for dividends from foreign investments qualifying for the participation exemption, as discussed above. In that case, there is no Dutch tax to credit against taxes withheld in the subsidiary's country of residence.

In most circumstances the foreign dividend is exempt for Dutch corporate tax under the participation exemption, as previously discussed. As a consequence, foreign withholding taxes cannot be credited, and thus, withholding taxes constitute a real cost for the companies concerned. A credit of the foreign withholding tax is granted against Dutch dividend withholding tax due on the distribution to foreign parents of the Dutch company. The credit amounts to a maximum of 3% of the gross dividend paid, to the extent that it can be paid out of foreign-source dividends received that have been subject to at least a 5% withholding tax and the foreign company is liable for corporate tax. This tax credit does not result in taxable income for corporate income tax purposes.

Stock dividends

Stock dividends are taxed as dividend income to the extent that they are paid out of earned surplus. They are not taxable if paid out of share premium ("agio"), provided the share premium account was not created pursuant to a share-for-share merger, in which only Dutch companies were involved. In the case of a share-for-share merger, in which shares in foreign subsidiaries were contributed to a Dutch company, the Dutch company can distribute the difference between the fair market value and the paid-in capital of the subsidiaries being contributed as a stock dividend without triggering

The Netherlands

Dutch dividend withholding tax (step-up in basis), provided certain requirements are met.

Work in progress
As of 2007, the rules with regard to work in progress have changed. Up to 2007 for tax purposes it was allowed to postpone the realisation of taxable profit until a project was fully completed ("completed contract method"). However, as of 1 January 2007, this method, in principle, is no longer permitted as profit should be accounted based on the percentage of completion of a project. Moreover as of 2007, all project costs should be recognised as opposed to the previous rules that allowed certain costs to be deducted in the year the costs occurred.

Deductions

Depreciation and depletion
To meet companies' urgent need for cash due to the worldwide credit crunch a temporary provision has been introduced, allowing accelerated depreciation of certain assets in 2009 and 2010. This temporary provision is discussed under "Accelerated depreciation" below.

Generally, depreciation may be computed by a straight-line or a reducing-balance method or, in accordance with any other sound business practice on the basis of historical cost. Depreciation is applied from the date the asset comes into use. As of 1 January 2007, Dutch tax law includes specific rules that potentially limit the depreciation of assets (e.g., immovable property, goodwill and other fixed assets).

Limited depreciation of immovable property
For immovable property the legislation of 1 January 2007 introduced special provisions, which, in principle, limited depreciation. A distinction is made between immovable property held for investment purposes and buildings used in a trade or business.

The investment property cannot be depreciated to an amount lower than the official property's fair market value for tax purposes, which is known as WOZ-waarde. In other words, a property will not be subject to depreciation unless the carrying amount of the building and the land on which it is located is higher than its value for tax purposes. This value is determined by the municipal tax authorities annually. As this value is based on the assumption that the property is free of lease, the value for tax purposes of commercial real estate may be lower than fair market value.

Alternatively, the depreciation of buildings employed in a trade or business will be limited to 50% of the property's value for tax purposes. It should still be possible to value immovable property at fair market value, if this is demonstrably lower than the current book value. In addition, anti-abuse measures apply to prevent the division of land and buildings into separate legal entities or to related individuals. A limited transitional provision for recent investments in buildings allows depreciation according to pre-2007 rules for a period of three years. The reinvestment reserve (*see Capital gains under Income determination section*), will remain applicable.

These changes are mitigated since maintenance costs continue to qualify for tax relief and any maintenance-related value increase does not lead to a compulsory upward revaluation of the property. Moreover, a property is not required to be revaluated as its value increases due to market developments.

Depreciation of land is not permitted.

The sale of depreciated assets triggers tax on the difference between the sale price and the depreciated book value unless a reinvestment reserve is set up *(see Capital gains under Income determination section)*.

Limited depreciation of goodwill and other fixed assets

Besides the introduction of rules limiting the depreciation of immovable property after 1 January 2007, rules entered into force that limit the depreciation of goodwill and other fixed assets. With regard to goodwill, the period of depreciation is reduced to 10 years. Therefore, depreciation of goodwill in five years, which was common practice under the pre-2007 rules, is no longer permitted.

Furthermore, the depreciation period of other fixed assets (i.e., inventory, equipment) is reduced to five years. The rules also affect fixed assets acquired before 1 January 2007 and certain transitional rules are applicable.

Accelerated depreciation

The law provides for accelerated depreciation of several specific assets. Accelerated depreciation applies to investments in assets, at least 30% of whose environment-improving results accrue to the Netherlands and that appear on the so-called VAMIL ("Vervroegde Afschrijving Milieu-investeringen") list. In March 2009, the Dutch government increased the budget for the execution of this provision of accelerated depreciation (along with the budget for the deduction regarding investments in certain new environmental assets, *discussed in Investments in environmental assets under the Tax incentives section)* to stimulate the economy.

Accelerated depreciation of production costs of qualifying Dutch films was abolished after 1 July 2007.

Accelerated depreciation also is available for certain other designated assets, for example, investments of starting entrepreneurs.

Investment costs minus residual value of sea-vessels that are operated mainly from the Netherlands may be depreciated straight-line over five years. Instead of accelerated depreciation these taxpayers may choose immediate taxation *(see Tonnage tax regime under Tax incentives section)*.

As a temporary provision to stimulate the economy, companies may depreciate under certain conditions, the value of assets bought and investments made in 2009 and 2010 in two years (or more), provided that the assets are not used formerly and the assets are not meant to be mainly put at the disposal of third parties, directly or indirectly. Further, the asset has to be brought into use before 1 January 2012 and 1 January 2013, respectively.

The temporary possibility for accelerated depreciation, however, is prohibited for among other things buildings; ground, road and hydraulic works; cars (except environmentally very clean and efficient cars); and intangible fixed assets. It is possible to depreciate up to 50% of the asset's value in the year of investment (2009 or 2010).

N

The Netherlands

The remainder may be depreciated, without the 50% limitation, in subsequent year(s). The annual amount to be depreciated is limited to the payments or investments made in a year.

A depletion allowance for natural resources may be granted for tax purposes, when it conforms to sound business practice and is appropriate for accounting purposes.

Net operating losses

As of 1 January 2007, the tax loss carryback has been reduced from three years to one year. A tax loss carryforward, which was not subject to time limitations, up to and including 2006, is limited to nine years. This also applies to start-up losses.

With regard to losses arising in the years 2009 and 2010, corporate taxpayers may opt for a temporary extension of the carryback period for losses from one to three years. This option, however, also means that the maximum period for loss carryforward will be limited to six years (instead of nine). Furthermore, the extended measure is limited to EUR 10 million loss carryback per extra year.

Complex rules may prohibit the utilisation of net operating losses after a change of 30% or more of the ultimate control in a company. Furthermore, limitations exist on loss utilisation for holding/finance companies. Based on these rules, losses incurred by a mere holding or group finance company can be offset only against holding or finance income in preceding and following years, provided that certain strict conditions are met. These conditions are meant to counter tax planning, whereby, the Dutch company concerned acquires (e.g., by way of equity contribution or exchange) other assets that enhance its income streams, and therefore, its capacity to make use of the losses. Companies carrying out significant other activities (with 25 or more employees) are, in principle, unaffected by these loss relief restrictions.

Payments to foreign affiliates

A Dutch corporation generally can claim a deduction for royalties, management service fees, and interest charges paid to foreign affiliates, to the extent that the amounts are not in excess of what it would pay an unrelated entity (i.e., arm's-length principle). Dutch companies are obliged to produce transfer pricing documentation describing the calculation of the transfer price and the comparability of the transfer price with third party prices.

Taxes

Certain taxes, such as the tax on insurance transactions, are deductible. Tax paid on the transfer of immovable property must be included in the cost price and taken into account in the course of normal depreciation.

Other deductions

Deduction of certain expenses (e.g., costs for food, drink, and entertainment) paid by employers for employees are not deductible, in part. The non-deductable portion is 0.4% of the total taxable wages of all employees but never less than EUR 4,200 per year. Alternatively, the employer may choose to deduct only 73.5% of the actual expenses.

Anti-abuse rules regarding interest and loans

Due to existing anti-abuse rules, the deduction for interest paid on intra-group debts relating to certain transactions is disallowed. However, if the taxpayer provides credible evidence of overriding commercial reasons for the transaction as well as the loan, or of effective taxation of the interest in the hands of the recipient that is comparable to Dutch taxation as far as the base and rate of taxation are concerned, the interest may be deductible.

Furthermore, interest paid on certain profits depending on participating loans, will be qualified as a dividend, and thus, will not be tax deductible. Interest received upon these loans may meet the definitions for the participation exemption if the creditor also holds a qualifying participation in the debtor. Intra-group conduits may be denied a credit of foreign withholding tax with respect to royalties or interest received if no economic risk is deployed.

Until 2007, interest due on a loan from a group company related to an acquisition of a company from outside the group, which was included in a fiscal unity, was deductible only as far as the acquiring company had its own profits. Full deductibility was granted only eight years after the acquisition. This 2007 interest provision is replaced by the regular inter-company interest deduction limitations. If the interest payment to a group company relates to a loan, which is directly or indirectly, granted by a group company in order to finance an acquisition or capital contribution, the interest will be deductible only if the loan and the underlying transaction are based predominantly on sound business considerations or if the interest received is effectively and sufficiently taxed.

When the debt ultimately is financed externally (outside the group) and a direct relationship exists between the internal debt and the ultimate external financing, it can be substantiated that there are sound business reasons for the loan. Furthermore, the use of tax losses or similar relief claims by the recipient of the inter-company interest, may affect adversely the deductibility of the interest paid. Also the law states that the interest deduction related to indebted dividend distributions, paid back capital and capital contributions is not only possible in case of sound business reasons but also if the interest is taxed in the hands of the creditor at an effective tax rate that is considered adequate by Dutch standards. The latter requirement means that the interest needs to be subject to an effective tax rate of at least 10% over taxable profits determined according to Dutch standards. For the determination of "a taxable base according to Dutch tax standards" the tax base limitation for the patent box is not taken into account.

As of 1 January 2008, a change of law has entered into force with regard to this limitation of deduction of intra-group interest payments. If the taxpayer makes a reasonable case that the interest is taxable at a tax rate of at least 10%, the tax authorities, nevertheless, have the option to substantiate that either the liability or the corresponding transaction is not based on sound business reasons. The tax authorities also have the option to substantiate that the liability is incurred in order to compensate losses or other rights that were formed in that year or that will be formed shortly thereafter. The change also is applicable to existing loans.

Thin capitalisation rules

Thin capitalisation rules, which limit the deductibility of interest paid on intra-group debts, were introduced as of January 2004. These rules apply to all Dutch companies that are part of a domestic or international group of companies. The allowed debt-to-equity ratio is 3:1, based on the average of the tax equity at the beginning and at the end of the year. A higher ratio may apply at the request of the taxpayer, if the group to which the Dutch company belongs has, according to the financial statements, a higher, worldwide debt-to-equity ratio. Interest paid on loans exceeding the 3:1 ratio, are disallowed only to the extent it exceeds inter-company interest received. The deduction of interest paid on genuine third party loans is not limited by the thin capitalisation rules.

Limited deductibility of costs relating to remuneration by way of shares

Any remunerations by way of shares, profit-sharing certificates, option rights on shares or similar rights are not deductible as of January 2007. However, grandfathering rules exist for situations where option rights have been granted to employees before 24 May 2006.

As of 1 January 2009, costs related to so called stock appreciation rights for employees that earn an income which exceeds EUR 500,000 are not deductible, as a result of the tax legislation on "excessive" remuneration. However, grandfathering rules apply for situations where stock appreciation rights were granted before 1 January 2009.

Group taxation

Fiscal unity regime

A parent company and its Dutch-resident subsidiaries (if the parent owns at least 95% of the shares) may, under certain conditions, file a tax return as one entity (fiscal unity). Group taxation is available for companies having their place of effective management in the Netherlands, both for Dutch tax and treaty purposes.

The main feature of the fiscal unity is that profits of one company can be set off against losses of another company forming part of that fiscal unity. Furthermore, inter-company transactions are eliminated.

In the summer of 2008, the Dutch Supreme Court referred a question to the European Court of Justice (ECJ) whether the "place of effective management" condition is allowed under the EU Treaty. In February 2010, the ECJ decided that the Dutch fiscal unity regime does not violate EU law (the freedom of establishment), insofar as it disallows a cross-border fiscal unity. However, the ECJ has not yet explicitly dealt with the effects of the fiscal unity regime, other than cross-border loss utilisation, such as the transfer of assets between group companies without immediate taxation and the use of "final losses". The Dutch Supreme Court will possibly deal with those issues at a later stage (the case has been referred back to this Court for final judgment).

Transfer pricing rules

Based on a general transfer pricing provision in the corporation tax, all transactions between related parties must be at arm's length. Furthermore, a specific transfer pricing provision exists with respect to the transactions of an interest and royalty conduit company. Dutch companies are obliged to produce transfer pricing documentation describing the calculation of the transfer price and the comparability of the transfer price with third party prices. If a transaction between related parties is not at arm's length, the taxable income may be corrected by the tax authorities. Moreover, transactions that do not meet the arm's-length test may constitute a contribution of informal capital or a hidden profit distribution.

On the basis of a decree of the State Secretary for Finance regarding transfer pricing, companies may request an advance tax ruling (ATR) and an advance pricing agreement (APA). An ATR may be requested on the classification of activities and an

APA may be required on the classification of activities and the arm's-length character of the transfer price.

Tax incentives

Small investments
A system of allowances for small investments is in place. To calculate this annual allowance, investments of more than EUR 450 each are totalled to determine the percentage of the allowance. Under the system, a deduction of 28% of the value of the total annual investments from corporate income is granted on investments exceeding the amount of EUR 2,200 up to and including EUR 54,000. On investments exceeding EUR 54,000 up to and including EUR 100,000, a fixed deduction of EUR 15,120 is granted. On investments exceeding EUR 100,000 up to and including EUR 300,000, the deduction is EUR 15,120 minus 7.56% of the amount exceeding EUR 100,000. If the investments total more than EUR 300,000 in a year, no allowance is given.

Investments in energy-efficient assets
For investments in energy-efficient assets, there is a deduction from corporate income of 44% of the value of the total annual amount of investments exceeding EUR 2,200 up to and including EUR 115,000,000. From 1 June 2009 until 1 December 2010, this deduction is possible in case of certain energy-saving investments in existing rental houses limited to a total investment of EUR 15,000.

Investments in environmental assets
For investments in certain new environmental improving assets exceeding EUR 2,200 per calendar year (with a maximum of EUR 25 million per asset), a deduction from corporate income of 40%, 30% or 15% exists, depending on the ministerial classification of the assets. In March 2009, the Dutch government decided to increase the budget for this deduction (and also for the execution of the provision of accelerated depreciation of environment-improving assets, the so-called VAMIL, *see Depreciation and depletion under Deductions section*), in order to stimulate the economy. If additional conditions are met, the deduction for investments in new environment improving assets may be increased to 60%, 50% or 30%.

New technology
R&D of applied new technology are subsidised by a reduction of wage tax to be paid on wages of employees engaged in research and development of technologically new products. The subsidy accrues to the employer when the employee is credited for the normal amount of wage tax. The benefit for each employer (or group of companies) may not exceed EUR 14,000,000 per year, being the amount substantially raised for the purpose of the years 2009 (retroactively) and 2010 to stimulate the economy.

To obtain the relief under the R&D incentive programme, taxpayers must file an application with the Ministry of Economic Affairs. The budget for this subsidy is fixed, so the amount of the subsidy is dependent on budget availability. As of 2009, self-developed and utilised software falls within the scope of the R&D incentive under certain conditions.

Tonnage tax regime
In order to stimulate entrepreneurs engaged in ocean shipping, a favourable regime (known as the Dutch tonnage tax regime) may be available to certain shipping companies. Under this regime the taxable profit of a sea-going vessel is based on its

N

registered net tonnage multiplied by a fixed amount of deemed profit per ton, instead of the actual profits from the exploitation. The regime only applies to the calculation of the profit related to the qualifying shipping activities. These activities include operating vessels in international traffic (including transportation for the purpose of the exploitation of natural resources at sea), towing and dredging and connected activities. The tonnage tax regime applies upon request and for a fixed period of 10 years or multiples of the 10-year period.

The Dutch government has proposed to expand the tonnage tax regime as of 1 January 2010, by including the transportation activities of sea-going ships involved in cable- and pipe-laying and the transportation activities of research and crane ships. The European Commission needs to approve this proposal. Further, adding a fifth bracket to the current four bracket degressive scale system with retroactive effect as of 1 January 2009, and introducing a significant lower amount of deemed profit per ton for large vessels with a net tonnage of more than 50,000, has been proposed.

Withholding taxes (WHT)

Domestic corporations are required to withhold taxes as follows:

Recipient	Dividends (stock/cash)	Interest (1)	Royalties and certain rentals (1)	Personal services (1)
	%	%	%	%
Resident corporations	15 or Nil	Nil	Nil	Nil
Resident individuals	15	Nil	Nil	Nil
Non-resident corporations and individuals:				
Non-treaty situations	15	Nil	Nil	Nil
Treaty:				
Albania	15, 5 or Nil (30)			
Argentina	15 or 10 (2)			
Armenia	15, 5 or Nil (3)			
Aruba	15, 5, 7.5 or 8.3 (21)			
Australia	15 (5)			
Austria	Nil (6)/15 or 5 (3, 7)			
Azerbaijan	10 or 5 (38)			
Bahrain	10 or Nil (8)			
Bangladesh	15 or 10 (8)			
Barbados	15 or Nil (8)			
Belarus	15, 5 or Nil (2, 9)			
Belgium	Nil (6)/15 or 5 (8)			
Bosnia Herzegovina	15 or 5 (2, 4)			
Brazil	15 (5)			
Bulgaria	Nil (6)/15 or 5 (2)			
Canada	15 or 5 (5, 10)			
China, P.R.	10 (5, 11)			
Croatia	15 or Nil (8)			
Czech Republic	Nil (6)/10 or Nil (2)			
Denmark	Nil (6)/15 or Nil (8)			

Recipient	Dividends (stock/cash)	Interest (1)	Royalties and certain rentals (1)	Personal services (1)
	%	%	%	%
Egypt	15 or Nil (2)			
Estonia	Nil (6)/15 or 5 (2)			
Finland	Nil (6)/15 or Nil (37)			
France	Nil (6)/15 or 5 (2, 5)			
Georgia	15, 5 or Nil (31)			
Germany	Nil (6)/15 or 10 (5, 12)			
Ghana	10 or 5 (8)			
Greece	Nil (6)/15 or 5 (2)			
Hungary	Nil (6)/15 or 5 (2)			
Iceland	15 or Nil (8)			
India	15 – 10 (32)			
Indonesia	10 (2)			
Ireland, Rep. of	Nil (6)/15 or Nil (13)			
Israel	15 or 5 (2)			
Italy	Nil (6)/15, 10 or 5 (14)			
Japan	15 or 5 (5, 15)			
Jordan	15 or 5 (8)			
Kazakhstan	15, 5 or Nil (17)			
Korea, Rep. of	15 or 10 (2, 5)			
Kuwait	10 or Nil (8)			
Kyrgyzstan	15 (5, 24)			
Latvia	Nil (6)/15 or 5 (2)			
Lithuania	Nil (6)/15 or 5 (2)			
Luxembourg	Nil (6, 18)/15 or 2.5 (2, 18)			
Macedonia	15 or Nil (8)			
Malawi	15 (19)			
Malaysia	15 or Nil (7)			
Malta	Nil (6)/15 or 5 (2)			
Mexico	15, 5 or Nil (16, 33)			
Moldavia	15, 5 or Nil (20)			
Mongolia	15 or Nil (8)			
Montenegro	15 or 5 (2, 4, 5)			
Morocco	15 or 10 (2)			
Netherlands Antilles	15, 5, 7.5 or 8.3 (21)			
New Zealand	15			
Nigeria	15 or 12.5 (8)			
Norway	15 or Nil (2)			
Pakistan	15 or 10 (2)			
Philippines	15 or 10 (8)			
Poland	Nil (6)/15 or 5 (8)			
Portugal	Nil (6)/10			
Qatar	10 or Nil (39)			

N

The Netherlands

Recipient	Dividends (stock/cash)	Interest (1)	Royalties and certain rentals (1)	Personal services (1)
	%	%	%	%
Romania	Nil (6)/15, 5 or Nil (22)			
Russian Federation	15 or 5 (23)			
Serbia	15 or 5 (2, 4, 5)			
Singapore	15 or Nil (7)			
Slovak Republic	Nil (6)/10 or Nil (2)			
Slovenia	Nil (6)/15 or 5 (2)			
South Africa	10 or 5 (16)			
Spain	Nil (6)/15 or 5 (25)			
Sri Lanka	15 or 10 (2)			
Surinam	15 or 7.5 (2)			
Sweden	Nil (6)/15 or Nil (2)			
Switzerland	15 or Nil (2, 5, 36)			
Taiwan	10			
Tajikistan	15 (24)			
Thailand	15 or 5 (34)			
Tunisia	15 or Nil (8)			
Turkey	15 or 5 (2, 5)			
Turkmenistan	15 (5, 24)			
Uganda	15, 5 or Nil (35)			
Ukraine	15, 5 or Nil (26)			
United Kingdom	Nil (6)/15 or 5 (5, 13)			
United States	15, 5 or Nil (27)			
Uzbekistan	15, 5 or Nil (28)			
Venezuela	10 or Nil (2)			
Vietnam	15, 7 or 5 (29)			
Zambia	15 or 5 (2)			
Zimbabwe	15 or 10 (2)			

Notes

1. A nil withholding tax rate applies to payments to a resident corporation when its shareholding qualifies for the participation exemption and the shares form part of a company whose activities are carried on in the Netherlands. However, dividend withholding tax may be levied on certain profit participating loans.
2. The lower rate applies if the foreign company owns directly at least 25% of the capital of the Dutch company.
3. The 5% rate is applicable if the foreign company directly owns 10% of capital of the Dutch company. The 0% rate is applicable if the dividend originates from ordinary taxed profits and the dividend is tax exempt in the hands of the recipient.
4. Based upon the treaty concluded with former Yugoslavia.
5. Negotiations on (revisions of) tax treaties are currently pending with Algeria, Australia, Barbados, Brazil, Canada, China, Costa Rica, Cyprus, Cuba, France, Germany, Iran, Japan, Kenya, Kyrgyzstan, Lebanon, Libya, Peru, Republic of Korea, Serbia and Montenegro, Slovak Republic, Tanzania, Turkey and Turkmenistan. Revised (new) tax treaties with Switzerland (26 February 2010) and the United Kingdom (26 September 2008) have been signed, but are not yet in force. New tax treaties (with new countries) that have

been signed but not yet effective: Hong Kong (22 March 2010), Oman (5 October 2009), Saudi Arabia (13 October 2008) and United Arab Emirates (8 May 2007).

6. Indicates member state of the EU. The EU Parent/Subsidiary Directive applies from January 1 1992. According to the Directive, dividends paid by a Dutch company (BV or NV) to a qualifying parent company resident in another EU member state must be exempt from Dutch withholding tax, provided certain conditions are met. Among other things, the EU parent company must hold at least 15% (from 2009, to the EU parent must hold 10%) of the Dutch dividend-paying company's capital (or, in certain cases, voting rights) for a continuous period of at least one year. A provisional exemption from dividend withholding tax will apply from the start of the one-year holding period. The exemption will be cancelled retroactively if, following the dividend distribution, the one-year holding requirement is not actually met. The Dutch dividend-distributing company must provide to the Dutch tax authorities a satisfactory guarantee for the payment of dividend withholding taxes that, but for the provisional exemption, would be due. The exemption is also applicable if the parent company is a resident of a EU member state and owns at least 10% of the (voting) shares in the Dutch company but only on the basis of reciprocity (Finland, Germany, Greece, Luxembourg, Spain, and United Kingdom). Should the withholding tax exemption not be available under the EU Parent/Subsidiary Directive the treaty rate(s) set out in the right-hand side of the same column (following "/") will apply.

7. The lower rate applies if the foreign company owns, directly or indirectly, at least 25% of the capital of the Dutch company.

8. The lower rate applies if the foreign company directly owns at least 10% of the capital of the Dutch company.

9. The nil rate applies if the foreign company directly owns at least 50% of the capital of the Dutch company, or invested more than EUR 250,000 in the Dutch company or owns directly 25% of the capital of the Dutch company and has a statement indicating that the investment in Dutch capital is, directly or indirectly, guaranteed by the government of Belarus.

10. The 5% rate applies if the foreign company owns, directly or indirectly, at least 25% of the capital or at least 10% of the voting rights in the Dutch company.

11. The treaty is not applicable for Hong Kong and Taiwan.

12. The lower rate applies if the foreign company owns at least 25% of the voting shares of the Dutch company.

13. The lower rate applies if the foreign company owns at least 25% of the voting rights in the Dutch company.

14. The 5% rate is applicable if the Italian company owns at least 50% of the voting shares in the Dutch company for a continuous period of at least 12 months prior to the date chosen for distribution of a dividend. The 10% rate is applicable if the Italian company owns at least 10% of the voting shares in the Dutch company for the continuous period mentioned above. In other cases, the dividend withholding tax rate is 15%.

15. The lower rate applies if the foreign company owns at least 25% of the voting shares of the Dutch company for a continuous period of at least six months immediately before the end of the book year to which the dividend distribution relates.

16. The lower rate applies if the foreign company owns, directly or indirectly, at least 10% of the capital of the Dutch company.

17. The zero rate is applicable if the foreign company owns, directly or indirectly, at least 50% of the capital of the Dutch company or if it has invested more than USD 1 million in the Dutch company, insofar as the government of Kazakhstan has guaranteed the investment; the 5% rate applies if the recipient company owns at least 10% of the capital of the paying company.

18. These rates do not apply to dividend payments to Luxembourg "1929" holding companies.

19. The dividend article of the treaty is not applicable anymore. The national withholding tax rate is applicable.

20. The zero rate is applicable if the foreign company owns, directly or indirectly, at least 50% of the capital of the Dutch company and invested more than USD 300,000 in the Dutch company. The 5% rate is applicable if the foreign company owns directly 25% or more of the capital of the Dutch company. The 15% rate is applicable on portfolio investments.

N

The Netherlands

21. The rate is 15% unless the dividend is paid to an Antillean company holding at least 25% of the paid-up capital in the Dutch company. In this latter case, the withholding tax rate will be reduced to:
    a. 5% if the dividends received are subject to Antillean profits tax of at least 5.5% on the dividend; or
    b. 7.5% if the profits tax is less than 5.5%.

    The combined Netherlands Antilles corporate income tax and Dutch dividend withholding tax for participations of at least 25% must not exceed 8.3%. Depending on the tax percentage levied in the Netherlands Antilles, the Dutch dividend withholding tax will be restituted accordingly.
22. The 5% rate is applicable if the recipient of the dividend is the beneficial owner and directly owns 10% of the capital of the Dutch company. The zero rate is applicable if the recipient of the dividend is the beneficial owner and directly owns at least 25% of the capital of the Dutch company.
23. The 5% rate is applicable if the recipient of the dividend is the beneficial owner and directly owns at least 25% in the capital of the Dutch company with a minimum investment of at least EUR 75,000.
24. The Netherlands applies the treaty with the former Soviet Union unilaterally to Kyrgyzstan, Tajikistan and Turkmenistan.
25. The lower treaty rate applies if the Spanish company owns 50% or more of the capital of the Dutch company, or if the Spanish company owns 25% or more of the capital of the Dutch company and another Spanish company also owns 25% or more of that capital.
26. The zero rate is applicable if the foreign company owns, directly or indirectly, at least 50% of the capital of the Dutch company or invested more than USD 300,000 in the Dutch company. The 5% rate is applicable if the foreign company owns directly 20% or more of the capital of the Dutch company.
27. The lower rate applies if the foreign company owns directly at least 10% of the voting rights in the Dutch company. On 8 March 2004, the Netherlands and the United States signed a protocol amending the applicable tax treaty. Based on this protocol, the withholding tax on dividends will be reduced to 0% if the receiving company owns 80% or more of the voting power of the distributing company, provided that certain other conditions are also met. This reduction of the dividend withholding tax has taken effect as of 1 January 2005.
28. The 5% rate is applicable if the foreign company owns directly 25% or more of the capital of the Dutch company. The zero rate is applicable if the dividend for that company qualifies for the participation exemption in the Netherlands. The 15% rate is applicable to portfolio dividends.
29. The 5% rate is applicable if the foreign company owns, directly or indirectly, at least 50% of the capital of the Dutch company or invested more than USD 10 million in the Dutch company. The 7% rate applies to the foreign company owning, directly or indirectly, at least 25% of the capital of the Dutch company.
30. No dividend withholding tax is due provided the share in the participation is at least 50% and at least USD 250,000 capital is paid in, in the participation. A dividend withholding tax of 5% is due if the share in the participation is at least 25%.
31. A dividend withholding tax of 5% is due if the share in the participation is at least 10%. No dividend withholding tax is due provided the share in the participation is at least 50% and at least USD 2,000,000 capital is paid in, in the participation.
32. Based upon most-favoured nation principle.
33. In case the dividend is not taxed in the Netherlands due to the application of the participation exemption, a zero dividend withholding tax is applied.
34. In case a Thai company holds at least a 25%-share in a Thai company, the Dutch dividend withholding tax rate is 5%.
35. If a share of at least 50% is held by a company, no dividend withholding tax is due. If the share the company holds is less than 50%, 5% dividend withholding tax is due.
36. As per 29 December 2004 Switzerland and the EU concluded a treaty in the light of the EU savings directive. The treaty, amongst others, contains a clause that no dividend tax is withheld if certain requirements are met. The main requirements are that a shareholding of at least 25% is held directly for a period of at least two years and both corporations

are not subjected to a special tax regime. Please note that even though the treatment of dividend appears to be equal to the treatment on the basis of the EU-parent subsidiary directive, the directive is in fact not applicable to Switzerland.

37. The zero rate applies if the foreign company owns directly at least 5% of the capital of the Dutch company.
38. The 5% rate applies if the foreign company owns directly at least 25% of the capital of the Dutch company with a minimum investment of at least EUR 200,000 in the Dutch company.
39. The nil rate applies if the foreign company directly owns at least 7.5% of the capital of the Dutch company.

Tax administration

Returns
Tax returns must be filed either every calendar year or every financial year. The Dutch tax authorities generally make a provisional assessment before issuing the final assessment after a full examination of the return.

Payment of tax
The corporate tax assessed must be paid within two months of the date of the assessment. In addition, provisional assessments are issued for the current tax year on the basis of the prior year's taxable income.

N

For more information, contact:

Steve Vanenburg
PricewaterhouseCoopers
Julianaplein 38
Willemstad, Curaçao
Netherlands Antilles
Tel: +599 9 4300000
Email: steve.r.vanenburg@an.pwc.com

Significant developments

Amendments to the profit tax
The Parliament of the Netherlands Antilles has approved several changes to the profit tax. These changes impact provisions to the participation exemption, the exempt companies and foreign subsidiaries.

Participation exemption
The participation exemption has been changed as follows:

- The exemption for foreign participations is extended from 95% to 100%.
- An activity and a subject-to-tax clause have been introduced.
- A definition of "dividend" has been included.
- The minimum cost price limit for participations less than 5% is reduced to ANG (Netherlands Antilles guilder) 890,000.

Please see the section on Income determination for more information on changes to the participation exemption.

Exempt company and foreign subsidiaries
The possible use of an exempt company has been expanded. In addition to investments in debt instruments, securities and deposits, relevant amendments to the profit tax have been added to include the licensing of intellectual and industrial property rights and other comparable property and usage rights as permitted activities.

A new limitation requires that no more than 5% of the revenues of the exempt company may consist of dividends from subsidiaries that are not subject to a tax regime comparable to that of the Netherlands Antilles. A profit tax regime is comparable to that of the Netherlands Antilles if the foreign tax regime provides for a profit tax rate of at least 15% (50% of the Netherlands Antilles tax rate, excluding island surcharges). The subject-to-tax requirement is also met if the foreign tax regime appears on a list of comparable tax regimes issued by Ministerial Decree.

Based on the amount and kind of dividends received, the Inspector may issue a notification that the company no longer meets the requirements for exempt status. The exempt status will then terminate starting the first day of the year following the year in which the notification becomes final.

Entry into force

The new regime became effective in December 2009 and was made retroactive to 1 January 2009. According to a transitional clause, a taxpayer may elect to continue the application of the old regime up to and including the tax year 2010. The request must be filed with the Inspectorate of taxes before the end of March 2010.

Compliance with sound international fiscal standards

In recent years, the Netherlands Antilles has complied with international standards as set forth by the Organisation for Economic Co-operation and Development (OECD) and the European Union (EU). There is, for example, no distinction in the fiscal treatment of offshore and onshore taxpayers. Well-known incentives such as a participation exemption comparable to that applied in the Netherlands and Luxemburg apply to all taxpayers, as well. The Netherlands Antilles does not have bank secrecy laws, and has in recent years concluded tax information exchange agreements (TIEAs) with several countries.

Tax treaties

The Netherlands Antilles currently has tax treaties in effect with the Netherlands, Aruba and Norway. A double tax agreement (DTA) has recently been negotiated with Jamaica.

Furthermore, the Netherlands Antilles has signed TIEAs with several countries, including Australia, Canada, Denmark, Mexico, Spain, Sweden, New Zealand and the United States. As a result, the Netherlands Antilles has been moved to the white list of the OECD Global Forum.

Transitional legislation

In 2001, the old offshore legislation was abolished. Qualifying offshore companies incorporated before 1 January 2002 may continue to apply the old regime until 2019, provided that certain conditions are met.

Latest political developments

The Netherlands Antilles consists of five islands: Curaçao, Bonaire, St. Maarten, Saba and St. Eustatius. Together with Aruba and the Netherlands, the Netherlands Antilles belong to the Kingdom of the Netherlands.

An agreement between the Netherlands and the Netherlands Antilles has been reached, which will result in the dissolution of the Netherlands Antilles. Maintaining two levels of government has been burdensome and not cost effective; therefore, the central (federal) level of government will be abolished and the Netherlands Antilles, as such, will cease to exist. Bonaire, Saba and St. Eustatius (the BES islands or the BES) will become a public body of the Kingdom of the Netherlands. St. Maarten and Curaçao have each chosen to become autonomous states within the Kingdom of the Netherlands. This means that each of the islands will remain within the Kingdom of the Netherlands structure, but the ties between the islands will be loosened. Defence and foreign affairs will remain within the province of the government of the Kingdom of the Netherlands. Also, the judiciary system will remain an integral part of the Kingdom of the Netherlands. The change is scheduled to become effective fourth quarter 2010.

In November 2009, a draft of the new tax system for the islands of Bonaire, St. Eustatius and Saba was introduced to Parliament. The system will deviate substantially from the systems that currently apply to the Netherlands Antilles and to the

Netherlands Antilles

Netherlands, respectively. The new tax system proposes to replace the profit tax with two new taxes.

One of these taxes is levied on the revenue from real estate. Taxable revenue is computed as 4% of the market value of the real estate. This amount would be taxed at a rate of 20%. The second new tax is on all revenue derived from legal entities. This applies, for example, to dividends and interest, as well as to payments to beneficiaries by a trust or private foundation. The tax rate in this case is 5%.

The new tax system will also apply to legal entities that are sufficiently connected to the BES islands. As a general description, a legal entity is said to be sufficiently connected to these islands in cases where more than 50% of its assets are employed locally, or the entity employs at least three local citizens and owns an office there.

Please note, the dissolution of the Netherlands Antilles is planned to take effect in fourth quarter 2010. Accordingly, the new tax laws are expected to take effect starting January 2011.

Taxes on corporate income

General
Resident corporations are taxed on worldwide income. Non-resident companies are taxed on the following Antillean-source income:

- Income attributable to a permanent establishment;
- Income from real property situated in the Netherlands Antilles; and
- Interest on loans secured by a mortgage on property situated in the Netherlands Antilles.

Capital gains are not differentiated from operating income and are subject to the same applicable rates. Corporations are taxed on their income as reflected in their profit and loss account, less certain deductible items.

Companies are generally taxed at a flat rate of 34.5% (consisting of a 30% profit tax rate and a 15% municipal surtax) as per 1 January 2000.

Special minimum rates apply to the taxable income of certain companies:

Type of company	Rate (%)
E-zone companies	2
New industries and hotels	2
Land development companies	2

Shipping business
Shipping companies are subject to the general profit tax rate of 34.5%. Shipping companies can however apply for the tonnage regime. If applicable, their profit is calculated based on the rates in the table below. If a shipping company applies the tonnage regime, the actual profits or losses are not taken into account, regardless of whether they are regular profits or capital gains.

The calculated profit based on the table below is subject to the general tax rate of 34.5%.

Over	Not over	Per net ton
0	10,000	ANG 2.00
10,000	25,000	ANG 1.35
25,000		ANG 0.60

Exempt company

Please see the section on Tax incentives for more information on exempt companies.

Companies under transitional offshore rules

The transitional rules distinguish three types of offshore companies.

1. Offshore companies which, on the last day of the financial year that ended before 1 January 2002, had all (or almost all) investments in or revenues from portfolio investments, royalties, holding companies, finance companies, or technical support will be grandfathered through the last day of the financial year of the company that starts before 1 July 2019.
2. Offshore companies which, on the last day of the financial year that ended before 1 January 2002, had all (or almost all) their profit subject to the tax rates of the Guarantee Ordinance Profit Tax (GOPT) 1993 (i.e., 15%, 24% to 30% and 2.4% to 3%) and which had a valid ruling with the tax inspector (e.g., trading companies, banks, captives commissions and fee-earning companies) on the aforementioned date or for which a request for (extension of) such a ruling had been filed on that date, will be grandfathered through the last day of the financial year of the company that starts before 1 July 2019.
3. Companies that, on the last day of the financial year that ended before 1 January 2002, had invested all (or almost all) investments in or revenues from real estate property or rights connected thereto, located outside the Netherlands Antilles. For profit tax purposes these companies will be grandfathered through the last day of the financial year of the company that starts before 1 July 2019.

Specific rules are applicable to companies that were incorporated after 30 June 1999 but before 31 December 2001. These companies may also qualify for the aforementioned transitional rules provided that these companies have been active in a meaningful way. In principle, a company will not be considered to have been active in a meaningful way if the assets of the companies consist predominantly of deposits or receivables on shareholders or affiliated parties.

The grandfathering period continues until 2019.

Corporate residence

Corporate residence is, in principle, determined by the place of incorporation. However, other factors may also determine residence. For example, a foreign company with effective management in the Netherlands Antilles is considered to be a resident. A company that has been established in the Netherlands Antilles will always be considered a resident of the Netherlands Antilles.

Offshore entities in the Netherlands Antilles must have a local managing director. This function is easily provided by one of the many trust companies established in the Netherlands Antilles.

N

Netherlands Antilles

Transfer of legal seat

Legislation has been enacted under which a Netherlands Antilles company is allowed to transfer its legal seat to another jurisdiction (if permitted under the laws of the outside jurisdiction), and allows a foreign company to migrate to the Netherlands Antilles.

Other taxes

Turnover tax

In Curaçao and Bonaire, a turnover/sales tax is levied on the revenue derived from services and deliveries rendered by an entrepreneur or company in the relevant territory. A limited number of services and deliveries are exempt, such as:

- Exports;
- Certain services to non-residents;
- Medical services;
- Services at the airport or in the harbour regarding imported or exported goods or goods in transit; and
- Advisory and management services provided to or by offshore companies and offshore banks.

An entrepreneur liable to turnover/sales tax must file a declaration, with the Tax Inspectorate before the sixteenth day of month following the month concerned, at the Tax Collector's office. The turnover tax rate is 5%.

In St. Maarten, Saba and St. Eustatius the applicable turnover tax rate is 3%.

Land and property taxes

The transfer of Netherlands Antilles-located immovable property is subject to a 4% transfer duty. A land tax is levied on real estate located in the Netherlands Antilles at an annual rate of 0.3% on the value of the land.

Dividend withholding tax

Dividend tax is not applicable.

Branch income

The Netherlands Antilles has adopted a definition of a branch (permanent establishment/permanent representatives) that is in line with the definition in the OECD Model Double Taxation Convention on Income and Capital.

The profits of a permanent establishment in Aruba or the Netherlands are tax exempt based on the tax arrangement with the Kingdom of the Netherlands. In the case of a permanent establishment outside the Kingdom of the Netherlands (the Netherlands, the Netherlands Antilles and Aruba), the income realised through the permanent establishment, after deduction of foreign taxes, is tax exempt. In the case of a foreign loss, this is not deductible.

Foreign real estate is always deemed to be part of a permanent establishment and, as such, is fully tax exempt.

The current regime became effective in December of 2009, and was made retroactive to 1 January 2009. Changes were also introduced to the participation exemption and the exempt company.

A taxpayer may elect to continue to apply the old regime for up to two years, until 2010. If the election is made, then it must be made for all the corporate tax amendments. It is not possible, for example, to continue to use the old regime for branch income but apply the new regulations for the participation exemption.

Income determination

Inventory valuation
Both the last-in, first-out (LIFO) and first-in, first-out (FIFO) methods of inventory valuation are permitted provided the chosen method conforms to sound commercial practice. Conformity of book and tax reporting is not required. However, occasions or situations for differences are very rare.

Capital gains
Capital gains or losses are, in principle, considered ordinary income and subject to standard corporate rates. An exemption from profit tax is granted for advantages (dividends and capital gains) from a qualifying participation (*see Inter-company dividends*).

Under the transitional regime for offshore companies (investment, holding, finance and patent holding companies), capital gains and losses are tax exempt.

Inter-company dividends
In December 2009, an amendment to the profit tax entered into force retroactively from 1 January 2009. Based on this amendment, the participation exemption applies as follows:

- In general, a full participation exemption applies to all local as well as foreign participations. The exemption applies for dividends as well as for capital gains. However, it is now required that dividends be derived from an active participation (non-portfolio investment) or a participation that is subject to tax.
- Expenses incurred in connection with a qualifying participation (including capital losses) are not deductible, unless it can be demonstrated that these are indirectly incurred to realise profits that are subject to tax in the Netherlands Antilles.

Non-portfolio investment clause
A participation is deemed to be active if the gross income of that participation consists of not more than 50% of dividends, interest or royalties received other than from an enterprise of that participation.

Subject-to-tax clause
A participation is deemed to be subject to tax if it is subject to a tax rate of at least 10%.

If at least one of these clauses has been met, the 100% participation exemption will apply. If none of these clauses are met, the participation exemption is limited to 70% of dividends. Consequently, the dividends would be subject to an effective tax rate of 10.35% (30% * 34.5% regular tax rate).

Netherlands Antilles

The 100% exemption also applies to income other than dividends, such as capital gains derived from qualifying participations.

Immovable property
The aforementioned clauses do not apply to dividends from a participation that (almost) exclusively (directly or indirectly) holds immovable property. The 100% participation exemption applies to these dividends.

New definition of dividend
A dividend is defined as a distribution of profits on shares or profit-sharing notes, paid from statutory profits or profit reserves. Dividends shall not be considered payments for the purchase of own shares or profit-sharing notes, distributions on shares upon liquidation, repayment of paid-up capital, or the distribution of bonus shares.

Minimum cost-price threshold for participations
The minimum cost-price threshold for shareholdings, profit-sharing notes or voting rights of less than 5% is reduced from the current ANG 1 million to ANG 890,000.

Under the old regime, a foreign participation was exempt for 95%. The same applied to a participation in an exempt company. However, the non-portfolio investment clause and the subject-to-tax clause are new amendments provided under the current regime.

Transitional regulation
A taxpayer may elect to continue to apply the old regime for up to two until 2010. This also applies to the amendments with regard to the exempt company and foreign branch income. The request for the continuation of the old regime must be filed with the Inspectorate of Taxes before the end of March 2010.

Foreign income
A Netherlands Antilles corporation is taxed on foreign interest and other income as earned, and on foreign dividends when received. Except as provided in treaty arrangements, there is no general provision in the tax law allowing credits for foreign taxes paid. Undistributed income of foreign subsidiaries is not taxable.

The profit of a permanent establishment is tax exempt. Foreign losses would not be deductible.

Deductions

Depreciation and depletion
Depreciation of tangible fixed assets, excluding land, is taken over the estimated useful life of the asset. The depreciable base includes purchase price, customs duties, shipping costs and installation costs, less residual value, if any. The straight-line method is customary, but the declining-balance method is also acceptable. In addition, an accelerated deduction of one-third of the assets' depreciable basis may be taken. The assets' remaining cost basis (two-thirds) is depreciated using one of the acceptable methods.

The cost basis of certain intangible assets, such as patents, trademarks and copyrights, can be amortised over their expected useful lives. Goodwill and other intangibles resulting from the excess of purchase price over the cost basis of assets purchased are amortised over three to five years.

Net operating losses

Losses may be carried forward for a period of 10 years. Start-up losses during the first four years for companies having tax holidays may be carried forward indefinitely. Carrybacks are not permitted.

Payments to foreign affiliates

The Corporate Tax Act provides for specific limitations for deduction of interest in certain cases of restructuring and refinancing involving the creation of artificial flows of interest payments to persons who are tax exempt or subject to lower taxes in their jurisdiction.

Taxes

Taxes, other than the corporate tax itself, incurred in the course of doing business are deductible.

Other significant items

Charitable donations to qualifying entities within the Kingdom of the Netherlands may be deducted to the extent that they exceed 1% of net income and ANG 100 after utilisation of tax loss carryforwards. The maximum deduction is 3% of net income.

Group taxation

Fiscal unity

The Corporate Tax Act provides for fiscal unity treatment for corporate income tax purposes. Resident companies with wholly owned resident subsidiaries could qualify for this regime. The parent company is entitled to submit one consolidated income tax return on behalf of the entire fiscal unity group. As a result, only the parent company is assessed.

Within certain limitations, losses of one company can be offset against the profits made by another company in the fiscal unity group. No profits need to be recognised on inter-company transactions, as these are disregarded for tax purposes. The fiscal unity applies for profit tax purposes only; the participating entities remain separate and identifiable under civil law.

Fiscal unity relief is confined to companies organised under the laws of the Netherlands Antilles, the Netherlands or Aruba. The companies which invoke this relief must have their place of management in the Netherlands Antilles.

On the basis of the non-discrimination provision of a relevant tax treaty, entities established under the laws of a tax treaty party may also be admitted to the fiscal unity regime provided that they are resident in the Netherlands Antilles.

Mergers

The Corporate Tax Act provides for a tax facility for business mergers. In a business merger, a company acquires all or a substantial part of the trade or business of another company with a view towards combining the business operations of the two companies into a permanent financial and economic organisation. If the business is transferred as part of a business merger, the gains realised by the transferor are not subject to profit tax if certain conditions are met.

N

Netherlands Antilles

Although there is no specific provision in the Corporate Tax Act with regard to legal mergers, legal split-ups and reincorporations, the Tax Inspectorate has announced that when certain conditions are met, a tax facility also applies in these cases.

Tax incentives

Inward investment and capital investment
There are tax incentives or holidays for the establishment of new economic enterprises and hotels with a predetermined minimum employment and capital investment. Special provisions relate to the taxation of shipping and insurance companies.

Investment allowance
For a minimum investment of ANG 5,000, an 8% investment allowance on acquisitions and improvements (for new buildings,12%) is permitted as a deduction from taxable profit in the year of investment and in the subsequent year, for businesses operating within the Netherlands Antilles.

Accelerated depreciation and tax rollover reserve
An accelerated deduction of one-third of the assets' depreciable basis may be taken. If a profit results at the time of sale of capital assets with the intention to replace that asset, the profit may be placed in a tax rollover account

Tax exempt company
It is possible to elect tax-exempt status for a private limited company (Besloten vennootschap or NABV). To qualify for the exemption, a number of conditions must be met, including (but not limited to) the disclosure of beneficiaries, management, financials, and the activities (only investment and financing activities) of the company. Recently, the licensing of intellectual and industrial property rights and other comparable property and usage rights have been added to the list of allowed activities.

Another condition has been added that requires that no more than 5% of the revenues of the exempt company consist of dividends from subsidiaries that are not subject to a tax regime comparable to that of the Netherlands Antilles. A profit tax regime is comparable to that of the Netherlands Antilles if the foreign tax regime provides for a profit tax rate of at least 15% (50% of the Netherlands Antilles tax rate, excluding island surcharges).

The subject-to-tax requirement is also met if the foreign tax regime appears on a list of comparable tax regimes. The list that has been issued includes all EU and OECD member states and all jurisdictions with which the Netherlands Antilles has a tax treaty. According to the list, the subject-to-tax requirement is also met in the case of a jurisdiction that is included in the white list issued by the OECD, provided that no special tax regime is applicable.

Independent expert
Currently, an independent expert is required to certify that the exempt company meets the requirements for exempt status. If more than 5% of the revenues of the exempt company consist of dividends from subsidiaries that are not subject to a tax comparable to that of the Netherlands Antilles, the independent expert must inform the Inspectorate of Taxes. The inspector notifies the company that it no longer meets the requirements for exempt status. The exempt status is then terminated starting the first day of the year following the year in which the notification becomes final.

Other incentives
Ocean shipping companies
These companies are taxed on a fixed profit per net ton of ANG 0.60 up to ANG 2.00 (or per 10 net ton in case of management and control). International aviation companies may apply a reduced tax rate against 80% of their profit, as their profits are deemed to be gained outside of the Netherlands Antilles. As a result, the overall effective tax rate is 9.66%.

E-zone companies
E-zone companies are subject to a minimum 2% corporation tax until 1 January 2026. They will be granted special facilities regarding turnover tax and will not be subject to import or export duties. The e-zone area also includes a full free processing zone and an international service centre (e.g., repair and maintenance of machinery situated outside the Netherlands Antilles and other export services are now allowed).

New industries and hotels
These are granted partial exemption from profit tax and a minimum 2% tax rate for a period of five to 11 years. They are afforded an exemption from import duties on materials and goods necessary for construction and initial equipment and from land tax for a period of 10 years. A minimum investment is required. Losses incurred during the first four years of operations may be used to offset taxable income for an indefinite period of time.

Land development companies
Land development companies are granted a tax holiday and exemption from import duties on materials and goods used in development/construction activities. They are exempt from tax on profits realised on the sale of the developed land. A minimum investment of ANG 1 million is required. Activities should be expected to enhance the economic development of the Netherlands Antilles.

Private foundations
The "private" foundation is a variant of the long-existing "common" foundation. The most important difference is that the purposes of a common foundation may not include making distributions (other than distributions of an idealistic or social nature). This restriction does not apply to private foundations, whose purpose may include making distributions to the founders and others. A private foundation may not run a business or enterprise for profit. Acting as a holding company or investment company is not considered running a business. Private foundations are exempt from Netherlands Antilles profit tax, and their distributions are exempt from Netherlands Antilles gift tax, as are contributions of assets to the foundation by a non-resident. Gift tax in the contributor's country may be applicable. The private foundation is intended to be an alternative to the Anglo-Saxon trust, especially in civil law jurisdictions.

Mergers, split-ups and reincorporations
In cases of a business merger, relief is granted under certain circumstances. Although there is no specific provision in the Corporate Tax Act with regard to legal mergers, legal split-ups and reincorporations, the Tax Inspectorate has announced that when certain conditions are met, a tax facility also applies in these cases.

Fiscal unity treatment
Fiscal unity treatment is available for corporate income tax purposes.

N

Netherlands Antilles

Exchange controls

In general, exchange control regulations are very liberal for offshore companies. Offshore companies established in the Netherlands Antilles can obtain non-resident status for exchange control purposes, which basically provides for total exemption from exchange controls. Onshore companies are subject to slightly stricter rules. These companies are subject to a licence fee of 1%.

Withholding taxes (WHT)

Although a dividend WHT was approved in 1999, it has been decided that for the foreseeable future this tax will not enter into force. If it is decided that the tax will enter into force, there is a mandatory transitional period during which the tax will not be applicable to legal entities resident at that time in the Netherlands Antilles.

Tax treaties

The Netherlands Antilles currently has tax treaties in effect with the Netherlands, Aruba and Norway. A double tax agreement (DTA) has recently been negotiated with Jamaica. Furthermore, the Netherlands Antilles has signed TIEAs with several countries including Australia, Canada, Denmark, Mexico, Spain, Sweden, New Zealand and the United States. As a result, the Netherlands Antilles has been moved to the white list of the OECD Global Forum.

Tax arrangement for the Kingdom of the Netherlands Antilles (TAK)

As part of the Kingdom of The Netherlands, the Netherlands Antilles is party to a federal tax agreement with The Netherlands and Aruba (TAK). Subject to this treaty, dividends, interest, and royalties paid out to the Antilles company may qualify for reduced rates of withholding taxes in the subject countries.

Dutch dividend withholding taxes are 15% if the Antilles company owns less than 25% of the Dutch company. In the Netherlands Antilles, only 5% of these dividends are taxed, at a rate of 34.5%, which results in an effective profit tax rate of 1.725%.

If the Antilles company's interest is 25% or more, Dutch withholding tax can be reduced to 8.3%. This tax is then paid, under a special procedure to the Netherlands Antilles tax authorities. These dividends are fully exempt from profit tax in the Netherlands Antilles.

Capital gains derived from shareholdings in Netherlands' corporations are fully exempt from profit tax in the Netherlands Antilles, provided that the shareholding amounts to at least 25% interest in the corporation. If the shareholding amounts to less than 25%, the capital gain is tax exempt for 95%.

The withholding tax regime in the TAK also applies to the old Netherlands Antilles offshore companies.

The TAK is to be revised.

Tax administration

Returns

Profit tax is levied by way of a self-assessment system. Returns are to be filed on a calendar-year basis. Non-resident corporations may file their returns based on a calendar year basis or on a different book-year. On request, this may also apply, for example, when a resident company is the subsidiary of a foreign parent company (i.e., only a local company must request for a different tax year end).

A provisional return must be filed within three months after the end of the book-year. A final return must be filed within six months after the end of the book-year.

Payment of tax

Payment is to be made at the time of filing and in a lump sum on the basis of the self-assessment.

In general, at the time of filing the provisional return, an amount equal to the profit tax of the previous year must be paid; the remaining balance due for the year for which the return is filed must be paid at the time of filing the final return.

For example, if the tax due for the year 2007 was 100, then at the time of filing the provisional return for 2008, that same amount must be declared and paid. If there is reason to believe that the amount for the year 2008 will be lower than for 2007, upon request, the estimated lower amount may be paid at the time of filing the provisional return.

At the time of filing the final return for the year 2008, the balance due must be paid, or if the total amount is less than the amount already paid up, a repayment will follow.

N

Corporate taxes in New Zealand

For more information, contact:

Tony Gault
PricewaterhouseCoopers New Zealand
PricewaterhouseCoopers Tower
188 Quay Street
Auckland
New Zealand
Tel: +64 9 355 8000
Email: tony.gault@nz.pwc.com

Significant developments

Corporate tax rate reduced
The Taxation (Budget Measures) Act 2010 enacted in May 2010 reduces the company tax rate from 30% to 28% with effect from the beginning of the 2011/2012 income year, which for most companies is 1 April 2011. The reduced rate applies to all resident and non-resident companies, including branches.

There will be a two year transition period to allow tax paid at 30% to be imputed or credited to dividends at a rate of 30%.

Portfolio investment entity rates reduced
From 1 October 2010, the top portfolio investment entity (PIE) tax rate is also reduced to 28%. At the same time, the other PIE rates will also be reduced to align with the new lower levels of personal taxes. From 1 October 2010, the current PIE rates of 12.5% and 21% will reduce to 10.5% and 17.5%, respectively.

Increase in goods and services tax (GST)
The recently enacted Taxation (Budget Measures) Act 2010 increases the GST rate to 15% (currently 12.5%) from 1 October 2010.

For transactions spanning 1 October 2010, the GST rate is equal to the rate applicable at the "time of supply". The "time of supply" is generally the earlier of an invoice being issued or any payment being received. For recurring or successive supplies, the time of supply may be triggered upon each payment being made or falling due.

Changes to the thin capitalisation threshold
The recently enacted Taxation (Budget Measures) Act 2010 reduces the safe harbour threshold for the inbound thin capitalisation rules from 75% to 60% effective from the beginning of the 2011/2012 income year.

Broadly, New Zealand's inbound thin capitalisation rules limit the scope for non-residents to fund New Zealand operations with debt and thereby reduce taxes paid in New Zealand. Under the existing rules New Zealand taxpayers controlled by non-residents may be denied an interest deduction in New Zealand to the extent that their debt percentage (total group debt/total group assets) exceeds both 75% and 110% of the worldwide group's debt percentage. Under the change announced in the government's 2010 budget, the 75% safe harbour will decrease to 60%.

Removal of depreciation (on certain buildings and loading rates)

The Taxation (Budget Measures) Act 2010 removes the 20% depreciation loading on new plant and equipment for assets purchased after 20 May 2010.

The depreciation rate for buildings with an estimated useful life of 50 years or more (regardless of when they were purchased) will also reduce to 0% from the 2011/2012 income year.

Changes to qualifying companies and loss attributing qualifying companies

The government announced changes to the tax treatment of qualifying companies, including loss attributing qualifying companies (LAQCs) in the May 2010 budget.

Shareholders in qualifying companies (including LAQCs) are currently able to deduct losses at their marginal tax rate but have their profits taxed at 30%.

The government announced that, from 1 April 2011, all qualifying companies (including LAQCs) will become proper "flow-through" entities for tax purposes. This means that income and losses will flow through to shareholders in proportion to their interest in the qualifying company. As such, shareholders will be taxed at their marginal tax rate on profits.

An Officials' Issues Paper released May 2010, sets out how this change could be implemented. One option is to treat qualifying companies and LAQCs as partnerships. Submissions close on 5 July 2010.

Capital contributions

Capital contributions are contributions made to fund the acquisition of a capital asset.

Many recipients of capital contributions currently treat the contribution as a capital receipt and depreciate the full cost of the resulting capital asset. For capital contributions made after 20 May 2010, recipients can either:

- Exclude the capital contribution from the tax cost of the resulting depreciable asset; or
- Amortise the capital contribution as income over 10 years.

Changes to prevent GST phoenix fraud

In the 2010 budget, the government also announced that it will introduce rules to prevent GST fraud through "phoenix" arrangements. These schemes typically involve a purchaser claiming GST refunds, but no GST being paid by a vendor.

From 1 April 2011, transactions between GST registered persons involving the transfer of land will be zero-rated for GST.

International tax rules

The Taxation (International Taxation, Life Insurance, and Remedial Matters) Act 2009 (the Act), which was enacted on 6 October 2009, includes new rules which change fundamentally the way in which income derived from investments in foreign subsidiaries is taxed.

The new rules apply for all income tax years beginning on or after 1 July 2009.

N

New Zealand

A key feature of the reform is the exemption from New Zealand income tax for active income derived by New Zealand residents from interests in controlled foreign companies (CFCs). Passive income (such as dividends, interest, royalties and rents) is taxed on an attribution basis.

For CFCs that pass an "active business" test, no income from the CFC is attributable to the New Zealand shareholders. A CFC passes the active business test if its passive income is less than 5% of gross income. The active business test replaces the previous grey list exemption. However, an exemption from attribution of income is retained for CFCs in Australia.

The Act provides CFCs that are insurance companies with the opportunity to apply to the Commissioner for a determination qualifying them for the active income exemption. This exemption has not been extended to other financial institutions that may also actively derive "passive income".

The Act also:

- Extends the current thin capitalisation rules to New Zealand companies that are controlled by New Zealand residents and have interests in CFCs. However, the new rules do not apply where the New Zealand resident has 90% or more of their assets in New Zealand, or less than NZD 250,000 of interest deductions;
- Amends the definitions of "debt" and "assets" for thin capitalisation purposes by treating fixed rate shares issued by a foreign company to New Zealand taxpayers as debt, excluding equity investments in CFCs from assets and aligning the definition of debt for the worldwide group with that for the New Zealand group;
- Abolishes the ability to claim conduit tax relief;
- Exempts most foreign dividends received by New Zealand companies from domestic tax, unless the dividends are received on fixed rate shares and for which the CFC has received a tax deduction in its home jurisdiction or the dividends are from portfolio foreign investment funds (FIFs) (i.e., interests under 10%) that are exempt from the FIF rules (e.g., interests in Australian listed companies); and
- Repeals the foreign dividend payment (FDP) and underlying foreign tax credit (UFTC) rules.

The government is also considering:

- Special rules to extend the active income exemption to non-portfolio FIFs; and
- A relief mechanism for non-resident withholding tax (NRWT) on dividends paid to non-resident shareholders if those dividends represent distributions of active offshore income.

A discussion document asking for input on extending the active income exemption to non-portfolio FIFs was released in March 2010.

"Associated persons"
The Act introduces significant changes to the definitions and conditions of associated persons in the Income Tax Act 2007, including:

- A standardised definition of associated person;
- Tests associating a trustee and a beneficiary, a trustee and a settlor, a settlor and a beneficiary, and the trustees of two trusts that have the same settlor;

- Tighter rules for aggregating the interests of associates;
- A tripartite test associating two persons if they are each associated with the same third person;
- Limiting the associated persons test for relatives to two degrees of relationship instead of four degrees; and
- A new definition of "settlor" that excludes a person who provides services to a trust for less than market value.

The new standardised definition is modified in some respects under the land sales context. The application of the tripartite test is limited in certain circumstances.

The new rules apply generally from the 2010/2011 income year. In the land context, the new rules apply to land acquired on or after 6 October 2009.

Life insurance
The Taxation Act introduces comprehensive changes to the taxation of life insurance businesses. Income from a life insurer's business will be separated into shareholder income (income earned by the equity owners of the company) and policyholder income (income earned by policyholders from life insurance savings products).

Under the new rules, shareholder base income will be taxed at the corporate tax rate in a similar manner to other businesses. The current portfolio investment entity (PIE) rules will apply to policyholder income, allowing savers in life products to be taxed on their investment income at a maximum rate of 30%.

The new rules apply generally from 1 July 2010.

Australia – New Zealand (NZ) double tax agreement (DTA)
On 19 March 2010 a new DTA between Australia and New Zealand came into force.

The new DTA lowers withholding tax rates on dividends, interest and royalties.

The standard withholding tax rate on dividends stays at 15% in the new agreement but is reduced to 5% for an investing company that has at least 10% of the voting power or shareholding in the company paying the dividend. The rate reduces to 0% if the investing company holds 80% or more of the shares in the other company and meets other criteria.

The withholding tax rate on interest stays at 10% in the new agreement but is reduced to 0% if it is payable to eligible financial institutions (subject to the 2% approved issuer levy).

The withholding tax rate on royalties is reduced from 10% to 5%.

The DTA provides that pensions exempt in the person's home country are exempt in the other country. Lump sum payments are to be taxed only in the country where the pension is sourced and not in the country in which the pensioner has retired.

For withholding taxes, the new DTA applies from 1 May 2010. For other taxes it applies in New Zealand to income years commencing on or after 1 April 2010.

N

New Zealand

Singapore – NZ DTA

On 21 August 2009, New Zealand and Singapore signed a new DTA replacing the DTA dating from 1973.

The key changes to the DTA include amendments to the withholding tax rates on dividends, interest and royalties.

The standard withholding tax rate on dividends is 15% reduced to 5% for an investing company that has at least 10% of the voting power or shareholding in the company paying the dividend.

The withholding tax rate on interest is reduced from the current 15% to 10%.

The withholding tax rate on royalties is reduced from 10% to 5%.

Other changes include:

- Revising the treatment of interest paid between associated persons. The interest Article in the 1973 DTA does not limit the rate of tax applicable to interest paid to an associated person. The 15% rate is a minimum rate of tax, which means that the net income (after deducting expenses) must be included in the non-resident's New Zealand tax return along with all other New Zealand sourced income. The new DTA removes the associated persons restriction. Consequently, all interest paid will benefit from the 10% rate;
- Amending the definition of a "permanent establishment" to include a building site, a construction, installation or assembly project if the project lasts more than 12 months, instead of six months as found under the current DTA; and
- Incorporating the new internationally agreed upon standard for the exchange of information between tax authorities.

The new DTA will come into force once both parties have given it legal effect, which in New Zealand's case will occur through an Order in Council.

In New Zealand, the DTA will apply for withholding taxes on interest, profits, or gains paid or credited on or after the first day of the second month following the date on which the DTA enters into force.

In respect of all other taxes the DTA will apply in New Zealand for any income year beginning on or after 1 April following the date the DTA enters into force.

US – NZ DTA

The US and New Zealand Governments have signed a protocol updating the double tax agreement between the two countries. The key changes include a reduction in withholding tax rates on dividends, interest and royalties.

The Protocol also makes changes to the Business Profits article and Limitation of Benefits article.

The changes will come into effect after the Protocol has been ratified in both countries and both governments have formally notified each other that their ratification procedures have been satisfied.

The withholding tax provisions will apply in both countries on the first day of the second month following the Protocol's entry into force. In the US, other provisions will apply from the 1 January following the Protocol's entry into force. In New Zealand the other provisions will apply from the 1 April following the Protocol's entry into force.

Changes to FITC regime

The recently enacted Taxation (Consequential Rate Alignment and Remedial Matters) Act 2009 brings an end to the general availability of supplementary dividend tax credits.

The foreign investor tax credit (FITC) regime ensures that foreign investors are not taxed at more than the New Zealand corporate tax rate. Foreign investors are allowed a FITC equalling the non-resident withholding tax (NRWT) that they would have had to pay on their New Zealand-sourced investment income.

The new double tax agreements with US, Australia and Singapore all reduce the NRWT rate on dividends paid to corporate shareholders that hold voting power of 10% or more of a New Zealand company from 15% to 5% or 0%. Consequently, in some circumstances, there will no longer be a need for the FITC regime in its current form.

The changes are as follows:

- Only portfolio investors (i.e., those with less than 10% voting power) with NRWT rates of at least 15%, and supplementary dividend holding companies, will qualify for relief under the supplementary dividend rules;
- A zero rate of NRWT applies to dividends paid to non-portfolio shareholders (i.e., shareholders with more than 10% voting power) and to any other dividends subject to lower tax rates, to the extent they are fully imputed; and
- These changes will apply from 1 February 2010.

The supplementary dividend regime will cease to apply to holding companies from the 2013/14 income tax year.

The changes affect provisional tax calculations for taxpayers who take into account their anticipated FITC in calculating their provisional tax. Taxpayers should also consider the need to impute dividends where a tax treaty applies to reduce the NRWT rate.

Stapled securities

The Act introduces new rules so that certain stapled securities are treated as equity for tax purposes – meaning that no deductions are available for interest payments.

The new rules apply from 25 February 2008.

Research and development (R&D) tax credits

The Taxation (Urgent Measures and Annual Rates) Act 2008 repealed the R&D tax credit regime. However, businesses are still able to lodge R&D credit claims for the 2008/2009 income year.

New R&D funding measures were announced in the 2010 budget. Broadly, NZD 321 million of targeted funding has been allocated to research, science and technology activities over the next four years.

New Zealand

The most significant measure is NZD 189.5 million of funding for technology development grants. These grants will be available to medium to large research-intensive businesses that can show that their activities result in wider benefits for New Zealand. The government will contribute 20% of these businesses' expected R&D expenditure for three years, up to a set maximum. The grants will not be administered through the tax system.

KiwiSaver
The Taxation (KiwiSaver) Act 2007 introduced compulsory employer contributions to KiwiSaver from 1 April 2008. Compulsory employer contributions are capped at 2% of an employee's gross salary or wages from 1 April 2009. A tax credit for employers that reimburses them partially for their contributions to KiwiSaver (capped at NZD 20 per week per employee) was discontinued from 1 April 2009.

Employer contributions to KiwiSaver (or other qualifying registered superannuation schemes) are exempt from employer superannuation contribution tax (ESCT) capped at 2% of compulsory employer contribution from 1 April 2009 (previously 4%).

Approved issuer levy and bonds
Officials are seeking feedback on possible changes to the approved issuer levy (AIL) and NRWT rules.

An Officials' Issues Paper examines whether AIL should apply at a zero rate, rather than the usual 2%, on interest paid to non-residents on corporate bonds that meet widely-held or stock exchange tests.

The Officials' Issues Paper suggests that AIL could apply at a zero rate to interest paid on qualifying bonds. A "qualifying bond" would include a debt security that belonged to a group of identical debt securities that satisfied a widely held test or a stock exchange test. The proposed widely held test would require:

* The debt securities to be held by at least 100 unassociated investors; and
* No person (or group of associated persons) to hold more than 10% of the debt securities (disregarding an underwriter for the first year).

The issuer would be required to apply the test annually to ensure the thresholds are still satisfied. The proposed stock exchange test requires the debt securities to be listed on a recognised stock exchange.

A debt security would not be a qualifying bond if it:

* Is issued through a private placement that is limited to a select group of investors;
* Is not openly advertised to the target market during the book-build process; or
* Is an asset-backed security, i.e., a security where the interest payments are financed by cashflows from a pool of financial assets.

GST: Accounting for land and other high-value assets
The government has released a discussion document which proposes to introduce a domestic reverse charge (DRC) on business-to-business transactions for land, going concerns and high value transactions (NZD 50 million or more); and to change the rules on recovering GST (which will mainly affect taxpayers who cannot fully recover GST).

Legal expenditure
From the 2009/2010 income tax year onwards, taxpayers with business-related legal expenditures of NZD 10,000 or less are able to deduct the full amount of the expenditure in the year it is incurred, whether or not it is capital in nature.

Profit distribution plans
The government is considering legislation to ensure that bonus issuances of shares distributed under profit distribution plans (PDPs) are taxed in the same way as shares issued under other dividend reinvestment plans.

Under standard dividend reinvestment plans shareholders choose between receiving cash dividends or shares. Both are taxed as dividends and are subject to the imputation regime. Under a PDP a company declaring a dividend makes a bonus issuance of shares to all shareholders, which can be sold back to the company for cash. When the shareholder chooses to retain shares, the receipt of the shares may not be taxable as a dividend. For certain taxpayers, this could provide a tax advantage relative to the treatment of standard dividend reinvestment plans.

Until legislation is enacted, the taxation of dividend reinvestment plans will continue to be governed by the existing tax rules including the anti-avoidance rules.

Relocation expenditure and overtime meal allowances
The Act provides that most relocation costs and overtime meal allowances paid by employers to employees are exempt from income tax and fringe benefit tax. The changes apply retrospectively from 1 October 2001.

Tax information exchange agreements (TIEAs)
New Zealand has signed tax information exchange agreements with the Cook Islands, Dominica, Guernsey, Jersey, Isle of Man, Cayman Islands, British Virgin Islands, Gibraltar, Bahamas, St Vincent and the Grenadines and St Kitts and Nevis.

The new TIEAs come into force once the countries involved in each agreement have given legal effect to them.

Taxes on corporate income

Income tax
From the beginning of the 2008/2009 income year, resident and non-resident companies (including branches) are subject to income tax at a flat rate of 30% (previously 33%).

From the beginning of the 2011/2012 income year, the 30% rate is reduced to 28%.

There are not state and municipal income taxes.

Corporate residence

Residence is determined by place of incorporation, location of head office or centre of management, or by directors' exercising control of the company in New Zealand.

N

New Zealand

Other taxes

Accident compensation levy

A statutory-based scheme of accident insurance is funded in part by premiums payable by employers and employees.

Premiums paid by employers (including the self-employed) fund insurance for work-related accidents. Employers are liable to pay a residual claims levy and an employer levy.

Excise duty

Excise duty is levied on petroleum products, tobacco and alcohol.

Goods and services tax (GST)

GST is a form of value-added tax. It applies to most supplies of goods and services. The rate applied to taxable supplies is currently 12.5% or 0%, with the 12.5% rate increasing to 15% from 1 October 2010. The 0% rate applies to a few supplies, including exports and financial services supplied to other registered businesses. There is also a "reverse charge" mechanism that requires the self assessment of GST on the value of certain services imported by GST registered persons.

Refer to Significant developments – GST: Accounting for land and other high-value assets for changes proposed in a recent discussion document.

Fringe benefit tax

Employers are subject to a tax-deductible fringe benefit tax (FBT) on the value of non-cash fringe benefits provided to their employees. Employers can elect to pay FBT at flat rates (for the 2010/2011 income year, 55% on attributed benefits and 46% on pool benefits, i.e., those benefits which cannot be attributed to a particular employee) applied against the value of the benefit, or can attribute fringe benefits to individual employees and pay FBT based on each employee's marginal tax rate. Under the attribution option, the applicable FBT rate depends on the net remuneration (including fringe benefits) paid to the employee. The attribution calculation treats the fringe benefit as if it was paid in cash and calculates FBT as the notional increase in income that otherwise would have arisen.

From 1 April 2011, the 55% and 46% FBT rates are reduced to 49% and 43%, respectively.

The multi rates for the 2009/2010 income tax year are:

2009-2010

Net remuneration	FBT rate
	%
NZD 12,250 or less	14.29
NZD 12,251 – NZD 39,110	26.58
NZD 39,111 – NZD 52,850	49.25
>NZD 53,851	61.29

The multi rates for the 2010/2011 income tax year are:

2010-2011	
Net remuneration	**FBT rate**
	%
NZD 12,250 or less	12.99
NZD 12,251 – NZD 39,110	23.84
NZD 39,111 – NZD 52,850	45.99
>NZD 53,851	55.04

The multi rates for the 2011/2012 income tax year are:

2011-2012	
Net remuneration	**FBT rate**
	%
NZD 12,250 or less	11.73
NZD 12,251 – NZD 39,110	21.21
NZD 39,111 – NZD 52,850	42.86
>NZD 53,851	49.25

Fringe benefits include motor vehicles available for private use, loans at below prescribed interest rates, contributions to medical insurance schemes, and employer contributions to superannuation schemes.

In relation to motor vehicles, employers can value a vehicle on an annual basis either using 20% (previously 24%) of the cost price or market value (GST inclusive) of the vehicle (depending on whether the vehicle is owned or leased by the employer) or 36% of the vehicle's tax written down value (GST inclusive). In each case, the FBT value must be reduced proportionately for whole days when the vehicle is not available for private use at any time.

FBT is also applicable to benefits received by an employee from a third party where there is an arrangement between the employer and the third party, and where the benefit would be subject to FBT if it had been provided directly by the employer.

Employer superannuation contribution tax (ESCT)
Employers' contributions to an approved superannuation fund (excluding foreign schemes) are subject to ESCT, formerly known as "specified superannuation contribution withholding tax." Employer contributions made to a KiwiSaver scheme or a superannuation scheme that has comparable lock-in requirements will be exempt from ESCT (up to the lesser of the employee's contributions or 2% of the employee's gross salary or wages)

Fund withdrawal tax (FWT)
The FWT provisions make the superannuation fund liable to income tax at a rate of 5% on amounts withdrawn from a superannuation fund prior to retirement, to the extent they include employer contributions since 1 April 2000 (and earnings thereon). FWT applies where the superannuation fund member's income is above NZD 70,000.

New Zealand

Branch income

A New Zealand corporation is taxed on foreign branch income as earned. Double taxation with respect to all types of taxable income, including interest, rents and royalties, is avoided by foreign tax credits.

Income determination

Inventory valuation
Inventory must be valued by a cost-valuation method or, where market-selling value is lower than cost, may be valued at a market-selling value. If the inventory is shares, it must be valued at cost. Cost is determined under generally accepted accounting principles. Acceptable cost flow methods are first-in, first-out (FIFO) or weighted-average cost. Some valuation concessions are available to small taxpayers.

Capital gains
There is no capital gains tax. However, the income tax legislation specifically includes various forms of gain that would otherwise be considered a capital gain within the definition of "income." Taxable income includes gains on the sale of real estate in certain circumstances and on personal property where the taxpayer acquired the property for resale or deals in such property or where a profit-making purpose or scheme can be deemed or imputed.

Inter-company dividends
Dividends derived from resident companies are exempt where there is 100% common ownership and the companies have the same balance date.

Previously, dividends paid by non-resident companies were exempt from income tax, but subject to a Foreign Dividend Payment (FDP) at the corporate tax rate.

However, new rules exempt most foreign dividends received by New Zealand companies from domestic tax and repeal the FDP and underlying foreign tax credit rules *(refer to Significant developments – International tax rules)*.

The foreign investor tax credit (FITC) regime effectively eliminates NRWT on fully imputed dividends. The FITC regime provides that total New Zealand tax paid on a non-resident investor's earnings through a New Zealand company can be limited to 30%. It does not operate by exemption from NRWT. Rather, where a dividend is imputed, the paying company qualifies for a reduction in its income tax if it pays a supplementary dividend. The amount of reduced company income tax is equal to the supplementary dividend. The combination of reduced income tax plus NRWT on both dividends can result in total New Zealand tax on the earnings of 30%. Deemed dividends may arise from transactions between related companies where the transactions are not at market value.

The Taxation (Consequential Rate Alignment and Remedial Matters) Act 2009 introduced significant changes to the FITC regime *(refer to Significant developments – Changes to FITC regime)*.

Foreign income
A New Zealand corporation is taxed on foreign income as earned. Double taxation with respect to all types of taxable income, including interest, rents and royalties, is

avoided by foreign tax credits. Foreign dividends received are exempt from income tax but may be subject to the foreign dividend withholding payment. New rules exempt most foreign dividends received by New Zealand companies from domestic tax and repeal the foreign dividend payment and underlying foreign tax credit rules *(refer to Significant developments – International tax rules)*.

Controlled foreign companies (CFCs)

Previously, New Zealand residents were taxed on deemed income derived from an interest in a non-resident company, foreign investment fund or foreign trust. New Zealand tax was imposed on residents with income interests of 10% or more in certain CFCs on the notional share of income attributable to their interest in the CFC. The regime applied to all types of income but did not apply to CFCs resident in "grey list" countries, except where the CFC derived exempt income from carrying on a business outside its country of residence. Grey list countries included Australia, Canada, Germany, Japan, Norway, Spain, the United Kingdom (UK) and the United States.

Previously no distinction was made between passive and active (business) income. However, there is now an exemption from New Zealand income tax for active income derived by New Zealand residents from interests in CFCs. Passive income (such as dividends, interest, royalties and rents) is taxed on an attribution basis. An "active business" test replaces the current grey list exemption (except in relation to Australia) *(refer to Significant developments – International tax rules)*.

Foreign investment funds (FIFs)

The FIF regime, an extension of the CFC regime, subjects persons with interests in certain foreign entities (which are not CFCs) to New Zealand tax. This regime also applies in cases where the investor does not have a sufficient interest in a CFC.

Examples of investment vehicles that are commonly classified as FIFs include foreign companies (including unit trusts), foreign superannuation schemes and life insurance policies issued by foreign entities not subject to New Zealand tax.

Generally, however, a New Zealand resident does not have an interest in a FIF when:

- The foreign entity in which the interest is held is a company or unit trust resident in a "grey list" country – this exemption does not apply to portfolio FIF interests or interests in foreign superannuation schemes or life insurance policies;
- The total cost of FIF-type interests held by an individual does not exceed NZD 50,000;
- The interest is an "employment-related foreign superannuation scheme";
- The interest is a "qualifying foreign private annuity";
- A natural person acquired interests in foreign life insurance policies or foreign superannuation schemes before first becoming resident in New Zealand – these interests will be exempt from the FIF regime for the rest of the initial income year in which the individual first became resident and for the following three income years; and
- Certain other limited exceptions apply.

The exemption includes interests in foreign employment-related superannuation schemes, interests held by returning residents as well as new migrants arriving in New Zealand from 1 April 2006. A permanent exemption is provided for interests that a person acquired before he/she became a New Zealand resident and interests acquired within the first five years of New Zealand residence.

New Zealand residents with an interest in a FIF are required to include in their New Zealand gross income, the amount of FIF income calculated using one of the following six methods:

- The fair dividend rate (FDR) method (available for portfolio interests only);
- The comparative value method;
- The cost method (for portfolio interests only);
- The deemed rate of return method;
- The branch equivalent method; or
- The accounting profits method.

The choice of method is restricted by the nature of the interest held and the availability of information.

Where an interest is exempt from the FIF rules (e.g., the interest is a certain pension or annuity provided by a foreign entity), distributions will be taxed on a receipts basis in accordance with normal principles.

Interests in FIFs must be disclosed by taxpayers in their annual tax returns. Failure to provide disclosure gives rise to potentially stringent penalties.

Offshore portfolio equity investments
The key features of the taxation of offshore portfolio equity investments are:

- The "grey list" does not apply to investments that fall within the new regime;
- Individual and family trust investors are taxable on the lower of the actual return (all gains and dividends) from their investments or 5% (the "fair dividend rate" or FDR) of the opening market value of the investments each year;
- Shares in certain Australian resident listed companies are excluded from the rules;
- Temporary exclusions apply to holdings in Guinness Peat Group (GPG) and the New Zealand Investment Trust;
- If an individual's non-excluded investments have an aggregate cost of NZD 50,000 or less, the entire portfolio is excluded from the new rules and is taxed in accordance with ordinary principles; and
- Distributions from all investments excluded from the new rules (either permanently or temporarily) are taxed on a receipts basis in accordance with ordinary principles.

These rules impact investors with a shareholding or interest of less than 10% in a foreign company, unit trust, certain foreign superannuation schemes or any life insurance policies.

Portfolio investment entities (PIEs)
A collective investment vehicle (e.g., a managed fund) that meets the eligibility requirements and elects to become a PIE is taxed on its investment income at the marginal tax rates of its investors – currently capped at 30% (and reduced to 28% from the 2011/2012 income year). The rules align the tax treatment of investments made through PIEs with the tax treatment of direct investments made by individuals. PIEs

are not taxable on the capital gains and losses they make on New Zealand shares and certain Australian shares.

Conduit tax relief

Previously, the conduit tax relief (CTR) regime provided relief for non-resident investors who invested in non-New Zealand companies through a New Zealand subsidiary (the "conduit" company). The regime was complex but effectively deferred New Zealand tax on the non-resident shareholder's share of the New Zealand company's conduit income that was not distributed by the New Zealand company. NRWT was imposed on dividend income distributed by the New Zealand company to the non-resident shareholder. However, new rules enacted recently abolish the conduit tax relief regime *(refer to Significant developments – International tax rules)*.

Stock dividends

Bonus issues can be taxable or non-taxable. With a taxable bonus issue, the amount capitalised becomes available for tax-free distribution upon a subsequent share cancellation. With a non-taxable bonus issue, the amount capitalised is not available for tax-free distribution upon a subsequent share cancellation.

Other significant items

Financial instruments/Income or expenditure (including foreign exchange gains and losses) from financial arrangements must be recognised on an accrual basis (generally, yield to maturity or other commercially acceptable method). These rules do not apply to the income or expenditure of a non-resident if the financial arrangement does not relate to a business carried out in New Zealand *(see also Deductions – Financial arrangements, and Other issues – International Financial Reporting Standards)*.

The government is considering legislation to ensure that bonus issues of shares distributed under profit distribution plans (PDPs) are taxed in the same way as shares issued under other dividend reinvestment plans *(see also Significant developments – Profit Distribution Plan)*.

Deductions

Depreciation and depletion

For tax purposes, depreciation of property can be computed under the diminishing value (DV) method, the straight-line (SL) method or a pooling method. The rates of depreciation depend on the following factors:

1. Type of asset; and
2. Whether the asset is acquired new or second-hand (i.e., used).

Taxpayers must use the economic depreciation rates prescribed by the Inland Revenue Department (IRD), together with a 20% uplift in the case of new assets (other than buildings and imported motor vehicles) purchased on or before 20 May 2010 (the 20% uplift has been removed for assets purchased after this date). Fixed-life intangible property (including the right to use land and resource consents) is depreciable on a straight-line basis over its legal life. Any depreciation recovered on the sale of an asset (up to its original cost) is taxable in the year of sale.

The double-declining-balance (accelerated) method applies to most plant and equipment. Under the double-declining-balance method, equipment with an estimated

New Zealand

useful life of 10 years results in DV depreciation deductions of 20% per annum (i.e., double the straight-line rate of 10% over the equipment's 10-year life). Buildings, certain motor vehicles, high-residual-value property, fixed-life intangible property and property acquired prior to the introduction of the new rules cannot be depreciated under the double-declining-balance method.

The depreciation rate for buildings with an estimated useful life of 50 years or more (regardless of when they were purchased) is reduced to 0% from the 2011/2012 income year pursuant to the Taxation (Budget Measures) Act 2010.

Entertainment expenditure
Entertainment expenditures are generally only 50% deductible; however, entertainment expenditures incurred overseas are 100% deductible.

Legal expenditure
Legal expenditure is deductible if the expenditure is:

*   Incurred in deriving assessable or excluded income; or
*   Incurred in the course of carrying on a business for the purpose of deriving assessable or excluded income.

However, the expenditure is not deductible if it is of a capital, private or domestic nature.

The Taxation (Business Tax Measures) Act 2009 provides that from the 2009/2010 income tax years, taxpayers with business-related legal expenditure of NZD 10,000 or less will be able to deduct the full amount of the expenditure in the year it is incurred, whether or not it is capital in nature.

Interest
Generally, interest incurred by most companies is deductible, subject to thin capitalisation rules.

New rules have extended the thin capitalisation rules to New Zealand companies that are controlled by New Zealand residents and have interests in CFCs *(refer to Significant developments – International tax rules)*.

Net operating losses
Losses may be carried forward indefinitely for offset against future profits, subject to the company maintaining 49% continuity of ownership. Carryback of losses is not permitted. A legislative amendment in 2002 ensures that losses of a subsidiary are preserved on a spinout (i.e., when shares in the subsidiary are transferred to shareholders of its parent company).

Payments to foreign affiliates
A New Zealand corporation can claim a deduction for royalties, management service fees and interest charges paid to non-resident associates, provided the charges satisfy the arm's-length principle which forms the basis of New Zealand's transfer pricing regime.

Research and development (R&D)

R&D costs, which are expensed under New Zealand's Financial Reporting Standard (FRS)–13: Accounting for research and development activities, are tax-deductible. Expenses written off as immaterial and not tested against the asset-recognition criteria in FRS–13 are not automatically deductible for tax purposes.

From the 2008/09 income year businesses that met certain criteria were eligible for a 15% tax credit for qualifying research and development expenditure. The Taxation (Urgent Measures and Annual Rates) Act 2008 repealed the R&D tax credit regime. Businesses are able to lodge R&D tax credit claims for the 2008/09 income year.

New funding for R&D was announced in the 2010 budget. The most significant measure is NZD 189.5 million of funding for technology development grants over the next four years. These grants will be available to medium to large research-intensive businesses that can show that their activities result in wider benefits for New Zealand. The government will contribute 20% of these businesses' expected R&D expenditure for three years, up to a set maximum. The grants will not be administered through the tax system.

Taxes

Fringe benefit tax is deductible, as is GST payable on the value of fringe benefits.

Financial arrangements

For income tax purposes specific timing rules apply to the recognition of income and expenditure in relation to financial arrangements, applicable to New Zealand residents or entities carrying on business in New Zealand.

A number of changes to the financial arrangements rules have been enacted to ensure that taxpayers who adopt International Financial Reporting Standards (IFRS) can continue to use tax rules that rely on the financial arrangement rules. For other taxpayers, the existing tax spreading methodologies continue to apply but without the option of using the financial reporting method.

The new rules include a combination of compulsory methods and elective methods that are available subject to the taxpayer meeting certain qualification criteria. Two new methods (the expected value method and the equity-free fair value method) have been introduced to assist in reducing exposure to volatility that might otherwise arise under IFRS fair value accounting.

Group taxation

Companies that are 66% or more commonly owned constitute a "group." Group companies are able to offset losses by election as well as by subvention payment. A subvention payment is a payment made by the profit company to the loss company and is equal to the amount of loss to be offset. The payment is deductible to the profit company and assessable to the loss company. Certain companies subject to special bases of assessment (e.g., mining companies other than petroleum extraction companies) are excluded from the grouping provisions. Branches of non-resident companies may be included, provided they continue to carry on business in New Zealand through a fixed establishment.

N

New Zealand

Groups of resident companies that have 100% common ownership may elect to be subject to the consolidated group regime. The group is effectively treated as a single company and transfers of assets, dividends, interest, and management fees among members of the group are generally disregarded for tax purposes. The group files a single return and is issued a single assessment. Group members are jointly and severally liable for tax purposes.

Losses incurred by a dual-resident company are not available for offset by election or subvention payment.

Tax incentives

Inward investment
There are limited specific tax incentives designed to encourage the flow of investment funds into New Zealand.

Legislation enacted in 2004 encourages foreign venture capital investment into unlisted New Zealand companies. Gains derived by certain non-residents from the sale of shares (held on revenue account and owned for at least 12 months) in New Zealand unlisted companies that do not have certain prohibited activities as their main activity, are exempt from income tax. The rules apply to foreign investors who are resident in all of the countries with which New Zealand has a DTA (except Switzerland) and who invest into New Zealand venture capital opportunities.

Capital investment
Investment allowances on fixed assets are not available.

Trans-Tasman imputation
Elective rules allow trans-Tasman groups of companies to attach both imputation credits (representing New Zealand tax paid) and franking credits (representing Australian tax paid) to dividends paid to shareholders.

Withholding taxes (WHT)

Resident corporations paying certain types of income are required to withhold tax on gross income, as shown in the table below.

Recipient	Dividends	Interest	Royalties
	%	%	%
Resident corporations	33 (1)	33 (1)	Nil
Resident individuals	33	33	Nil
Non-resident corporations and individuals	(2)	(3)	
No treaty	30 (4)	15 (5)	15
Treaty:			
Australia	15, 5 or 0 (12)	10 (12)	10 (12)
Austria	15	10	10
Belgium (15)	15	10	10
Canada (14)	15	15	15
Chile	15	10 (6)	10

Recipient	Dividends	Interest	Royalties
	%	%	%
China, P.R.	15	10	10
Czech Republic (7)	15	10	10
Denmark	15	10	10
Fiji	15	10 (5)	15
Finland	15	10	10
France	15	10	10
Germany	15	10	10
India	15	10	10
Indonesia	15	10	15
Ireland, Rep. of	15	10	10
Italy	15	10	10
Japan	15	15 (5)	15 (8)
Korea, Rep. of	15	10	10
Malaysia	15	15 (5)	15
Mexico	15	10	10
Netherlands	15	10	10
Norway	15	10	10
Philippines	15	10	15
Poland	15	10	10
Russian Federation	15	10	10
Singapore (13)	15	15 (5)	15
South Africa	15	10	10
Spain	15	10	10
Sweden	15	10	10
Switzerland	15	10	10
Taiwan	15	10	10
Thailand	15	10	10 (9)
United Arab Emirates	15	10	10
United Kingdom (10)	15	10	10
United States (11)	15 (11)	10 (11)	10 (11)

Notes

Numbers in parentheses refer to the notes below:

1. Resident withholding taxes apply to both interest and dividends. Unless the recipient corporation holds an exemption certificate, and if the recipient provides a tax file number, the default rate of the interest withholding tax is 33% (reducing to 28% from 1 April 2011). Recipients can elect for the rate of interest withholding to be 38%. The rate of interest withholding tax is 38% where the recipient does not provide a tax file number.
   To align the RWT rate on interest paid to companies with the new 30% company tax rate, an optional RWT rate of 30% is available to payers of interest for the 2010/2011 income year. This rate is reduced to 28% to align with the company tax rate from 2011/2012.
   The rate of withholding tax on dividends paid is 33%, but the tax is reduced by the aggregate imputation and withholding payment credits attached to the dividend or taxable bonus share. Interest and dividends paid between group companies and in certain other limited circumstances are exempt from the withholding tax.

N

New Zealand

2. Non-resident investors – the foreign investor tax credit and conduit tax relief regimes provide relief to companies paying dividends to non-resident investors. However, the Taxation (International Taxation, Life Insurance, and Remedial Matters) Act 2009 introduces new rules which abolish the conduit tax relief regime *(refer to Significant developments – International tax rules)*.
    The Taxation (Consequential Rate Alignment and Remedial Matters) Act 2009 amended the FITC regime *(refer to Significant developments – Changes to FITC regime)*.
3. Resident corporations paying interest to non-associated non-resident corporations and individuals need not withhold tax if they have approved-issuer status and the security under which interest is payable is registered with the IRD. In this case, the resident corporation pays a 2% levy (tax-deductible) on the interest payments instead of the withholding tax otherwise applicable.
4. NRWT is imposed on dividends at the following rates regardless of the jurisdiction to which the dividends are paid:
    *   0% – Fully imputed dividends paid to a shareholder holding 10% or more of the direct voting interests in the company and fully imputed non-cash dividends;
    *   15% – Fully imputed cash dividends paid to a shareholder holding less than 10%; or
    *   30% – In most other cases, subject to any relief available under a DTA.
5. Net interest income is subject to reassessment at the company tax rate where the payer and the recipient are "associated persons," but withholding tax is the minimum liability. Non-resident withholding tax is not imposed where the recipient of the interest has a fixed establishment in New Zealand.
6. 10% if the interest received is derived from loans granted by banks or insurance companies. In all other cases, 15%.
7. Net income from industrial royalties is subject to reassessment at the company tax rate, but withholding tax is the minimum liability.
8. 10% if the interest is received by a financial institution or relates to indebtedness arising from a credit sale between non-associated persons. In all other cases, 15%.
9. 10% or 15%, depending on the type of royalty.
10. The government has announced that it is re-negotiating New Zealand's DTA with the UK.
11. A Protocol to update the DTA between the United States and New Zealand was signed on 1 December 2008. The key changes include amendments to the withholding tax rates on dividends, interest and royalties:
    *   The withholding rate on dividends is reduced from 15% to a maximum of 5% for an investor who holds at least 10% of the shares in the company that pays the dividend, and to 0% if the investor holds 80% or more of the shares in the company and meets other criteria;
    *   The withholding tax on royalties is reduced from 10% to 5% and the definition of "royalties" will be revised to exclude payments for leased equipment; and
    *   The rate on interest will generally remain at 10%, although it will drop to 0% for interest paid to lending or finance businesses, provided that the 2% approved issuer levy is paid on New Zealand-sourced interest *(refer to Significant developments – US – NZ DTA)*.
12. The new DTA that applies to withholding tax from 1 May 2010 lowers withholding tax rates on dividends, interest and royalties *(refer to Significant developments – Australia – NZ DTA)*.
13. On 21 August 2009, New Zealand and Singapore signed a new double tax agreement (DTA) replacing the current DTA dating from 1973.
    The key changes to the DTA include amendments to the withholding tax rates on dividends, interest and royalties *(refer to Significant developments – Singapore – NZ DTA)*.
14. The government has announced that the DTA with Canada will be re-negotiated.
15. The government has signed an amending Protocol which updates the 1981 double tax agreement between New Zealand and Belgium.

Tax administration

Returns

Tax returns are based on the fiscal year ending 31 March, although other fiscal year-ends are possible if permission is obtained. The system is one of self-assessment, under which the corporation files an income tax return each year. For those not linked to a tax agent, returns must be filed by 7 July for March balance dates, or by the seventh day of the fourth month following a substituted balance date. Those linked to a tax agent with a substituted balance date have extensions of time for filing their tax returns.

Payment of tax

The terminal tax due date is extended by two months for taxpayers linked to a tax agent.

Where provisional tax paid is less than the amount of income tax deemed due on that instalment date, interest is imposed. If provisional tax is overpaid, interest is payable to the taxpayer. Interest is deductible for tax purposes by business taxpayers, and interest earned on overpaid provisional tax is gross income for tax purposes. From 29 June 2009, the interest rate for unpaid tax is 8.91%, while the rate for overpaid tax is 1.82%.

Calculating provisional tax

Provisional taxpayers have four options available for calculating their provisional tax for the 2009/2010 income year (i.e., year ending 31 March 2010).

These options are:

- Where the 2008/2009 return of income has been filed, 2009/2010 provisional tax can be based on 100% of the 2008/2009 residual income tax;
- Where the 2008/2009 return of income has not been filed, due to an extension of time for filing, 2009/2010 provisional tax can be based on 105% (previously 110%) of the 2007/2008 residual income tax, but only for the first two instalments or for companies and other 30% rate taxpayers, 95% of the 2007/2008 residual income tax. The final instalment must be calculated based on the first option above; or
- Provisional tax can be based on a fair and reasonable estimate of 2009/2010 residual income tax or the GST ratio option.

For the 2010/2011 income year (i.e., year ending 31 March 2011), provisional taxpayers have the following options:

- Where the 2009/2010 return of income has been filed, 2010/2011 provisional tax can be based on 105% of the 2009/2010 residual income tax;
- Where the 2009/2010 return of income has not been filed, due to an extension of time for filing, 2010/2011 provisional tax can be based on 110% of the 2008/2009 residual income tax, but only for the first two instalments. The final instalment must be calculated based on the first option above; or
- Provisional tax can be based on a fair and reasonable estimate of 2010/2011 residual income tax or the GST ratio option.

For the 2011/2012 income year (i.e., year ending 31 March 2012), provisional taxpayers have the following options:

N

New Zealand

- Where the 2010/2011 return of income has been filed, 2011/2012 provisional tax can be based on 100% of the 2010/2011 residual income tax;
- Where the 2010/2011 return of income has not been filed, due to an extension of time for filing, 2011/2012 provisional tax can be based on 105% (previously 110%) of the 2009/2010 residual income tax, but only for the first two instalments. The final instalment must be calculated based on the first option above; or
- Provisional tax can be based on a fair and reasonable estimate of 2011/2012 residual income tax or the GST ratio option.

The GST ratio method has been introduced to enable smaller taxpayers to align their provisional tax payments with their cash flow and reduce their exposure to use of money interest. The option is intended to benefit those taxpayers with declining, seasonal or fluctuating income. This option calculates provisional tax by reference to the taxpayer's GST taxable supplies in the relevant provisional tax instalment period.

Taxpayers can also make voluntary payments. Such payments can be made to minimise exposures to assessed interest. A taxpayer choosing to estimate residual income tax is required to take reasonable care when estimating.

When the taxpayer's return of income for the year is furnished, the provisional tax paid for that year is credited against the tax assessed. This results in either a refund or further tax to pay by way of terminal tax.

Tax pooling
Taxpayers are able to pool their provisional tax payments with those of other taxpayers through an arrangement with a commercial intermediary. Tax pooling allows underpayments to be offset by overpayments within the same pool and vice versa.

Tax penalties
An initial late payment penalty of 1% applies if a tax payment is not made on the due date. A further 4% late payment penalty applies if the payment is not made within seven days of the due date. An incremental late payment penalty of 1% is then imposed monthly until payment is made.

Inland Revenue (IR) is required to notify a taxpayer the first time their payment is late rather than imposing an immediate late payment penalty. If payment is not made by a certain date, a late payment penalty will be imposed. Taxpayers will be entitled to one notification every two years. After receiving a first warning, the IR will not send further notifications for two years and an initial late payment penalty will be imposed in the normal manner.

Shortfall penalties
Shortfall penalties, calculated as a percentage of the tax shortfall resulting from the action or position taken by the taxpayer in a tax return, may also apply.

There is a 50% discount on certain penalties where the taxpayer has a past record of "good behaviour" and, in certain circumstances, a cap of NZD 50,000 on shortfall penalties for not taking reasonable care or for taking an unacceptable tax position.

Other issues

International Financial Reporting Standards (IFRS)

The relationship between statutory accounting and taxable income is quasi-dependent.

The year of final adoption was 2007.

The impact of IFRS adoption on significant areas of tax law is as follows.

Comments on tax regime
New Zealand's determination of taxable income starts with the statutory accounts' accounting profit and then specific tax adjustments are made based on rules for revenue recognition and deductible expenditure in the tax legislation. Changes have been made to the tax treatment of 'financial arrangements' (a defined tax legislative term) to allow for the alignment to the accounting recognition of fair values on such arrangements in specific cases.

Year of adoption cash impact
Mandatory adoption of NZ IFRS accounting standards for most entities (except for small & medium enterprises) applied for balance dates beginning 1 January 2007. Depending on the specific IFRS adoption adjustment, the resulting income or expenditure is taken into taxable income based on the ordinary statutory tax provisions. The key areas which were changed for tax under IFRS adoption are the trading stock provisions (which align tax with accounting standards subject to some provisions) and the financial arrangement rules. These rules are very broad and deal with the tax treatment of accrual income or expenditure on debt instruments, debt type instruments, derivatives, etc.

Thin capitalisation
The thin capitalisation rules work on a debt over assets percentage. It relies mostly on the tax legislative definition for debt and the amount disclosed in the financial statements under generally accepted accounting practice as assets (although there are some other measurement alternatives).

Debt versus equity classifications
The classification of debt and equity instruments for tax is dependent on the tax legislative definitions for specific purposes (such as the spreading of any deductions or income where the financial arrangement rules apply, thin capitalization, etc). Tax applies legal form and does not strictly rely upon the classification applied under IFRS.

Lease versus sale determinations
There are specific tax provisions dealing with finance leases.

Distributable reserves
The level of distributable reserves is based on the company law requirements of solvency and not specifically on the amounts shown as reserves in the financial statements.

Transfer pricing determination
There have been no specific comments released yet by the New Zealand Revenue Authority on the adoption of IFRS impact for transfer pricing.

Corporate taxes in Nicaragua

For more information, contact:

Ramon Ortega
Edificio Bank of Nova Scotia
3rd Floor
Avenida John F Kennedy, Esquina con Avenida Lope de Vega
Santo Domingo, Dominican Republic
Tel: +809 567 7741
Email: ramon.ortega@do.pwc.com

Significant developments

Equity Tax Law Reform No. 712 and Decree No. 93-2009 on Regulation of Equity Tax Law Reform were recently made effective.

Significant modifications include:

- Dividends and profits remitted abroad are subject to a definitive 10% withholding tax. Interests obtained by a loan that are provided by non-resident financial institutions are subject to a 10% definitive withholding tax.
- Interest earned on government bonds and the equivalent is considered taxable income subject to a 10% definitive withholding tax.
- 1% definitive minimum tax is applied to gross taxable income.
- Excise tax on tobacco cigarettes will apply on imports. It will not be a creditable tax.

Taxes on corporate income

Income taxes are levied only on domestic-sourced income at a flat rate of the higher percentage of:

- 30%, applied to net taxable income (gross taxable income less allowed deductions by law); or
- 1% definitive minimum tax on gross income obtained during the fiscal year.

The law establishes exceptions to the 1% definitive minimum tax, as follows:

- First three fiscal periods of recently incorporated entities;
- Taxpayers whose sales are controlled by government; and
- Taxpayers that ceased operations on account of force majeure.

Corporate residence

Corporate residence is determined by the place of incorporation.

Other taxes

Real estate municipal tax
This annual tax is levied at a rate of 1% on 80% of cadastral/surveyed value, as recorded by the government. If the cadastral/surveyed value is not available, the cost or fiscal appraisal value could be used.

Value-added tax (VAT)

VAT is imposed at 15% rate on the:

* Sale of goods;
* Rendering of services;
* Grant of use of assets; and
* Import of goods.

VAT liquidation is determined by subtracting VAT debts (sale of goods or rendering services), from VAT credits paid on transactions needed to generate taxable income for VAT purposes. VAT credits are applicable or allowed when related to goods/services subject to VAT. VAT paid on transactions to generate non-taxable income for VAT purposes are not allowed as VAT credits but may be proportionally applied.

VAT exemptions include:

* Medicine;
* Real estate transfer;
* Sale of used goods;
* Basic food products;
* Credit instruments;
* Tuition; and
* Textbooks and educational supplies.

Selective consumption tax

It is applied to goods that are considered to be nonessential. The tax base is the CIF price for imported items, and the tax is levied and paid only at that stage.

Municipal sales and services tax

A monthly 1% tax is levied on all sales of goods and rendering of services in each of the municipalities of the country.

Municipal registration tax

An annual 2% tax is levied on the average gross income received during the last trimester. In the case of the incorporation of new establishment or enterprise, municipal registration tax is 1% of the capital invested.

Branch income

Income received is subject to corporate income tax.

Income determination

Inventory valuation

LIFO (last-in, first-out) and FIFO (first-in, first-out) as well as average methods are accepted. Tax Authorities shall authorise the change of a valuation method.

N

Nicaragua

Capital gains and losses

Capital gains and losses are treated as ordinary taxable corporate income. Capital gain transactions that require any annotation in public registry (real state, vehicles, other) will be subject to withholding tax depending on the amount of transaction, as follows:

Good Value (USD)		Percentage applicable
From	Through	
0.01	50,000.00	1%
50,000.01	100,000.00	2%
100,000.01	A más	3%

Foreign income

Business enterprises are subject to income tax only on Nicaraguan source income.

Stock dividends

Stock dividends paid by Nicaraguan entities to resident or non-resident shareholders are subject to 10% definitive withholding tax.

The Equity Tax Law Reform regulations define "stock dividends" as stock dividends paid as well as remittance of net income after income tax made by branches to headquarters and any payments considered as advance net income remittance abroad or locally.

Other significant items

Interest earned on government bonds and equivalent certificates are taxable subject to a 10% definitive withholding tax.

Deductions

Depreciation

Depreciation must be computed by the straight-line method. Depending on the type of construction and the estimated life of fixed assets, annual rates for depreciation are as follows:

	%
Buildings	3, 5, 10
Vehicles	12.5, 20
Plant and equipment	10, 15, 20
Other assets	10, 20

Alternative method of depreciation

Taxpayers under the Temporary Admission for Active Processing (TAP) regimen could, at their convenience, request a different depreciation rate (accelerate depreciation) from tax authorities. Used fixed assets acquired abroad could also be subject to a different depreciation rate.

Net operating losses

Carryforward losses are deductible in the following three fiscal periods in which they were incurred.

Payments to foreign affiliates

Payments made from affiliates to foreign related parties are deductible for income tax purposes provided the requirements below are met:

- The expense (royalties, interest, and services) is needed to generate taxable income.
- This expense is duly supported (agreement, invoices, payment receipts).
- The expenses are incurred within the fiscal period.
- The withholding tax is applied and paid to Tax Authorities.

Taxes

In principle, income tax expense is not deductible for income tax purposes. Municipal or local taxes (real estate tax, monthly income tax, annual registration tax) are deductible for income tax. Many types of penalties or charges made by tax, customs, Social Security or municipal authorities are not deductible for income tax purposes.

Group taxation

Section 3 of Equity Tax Law recognises "Unite Economy" as a taxpayer formed by many entities of one Group.

Tax incentives

Inward investment

Under present law and on a case-by-case basis, new companies with tourist activities may request and the government may grant, during the facilities' construction phase, total exemption of customs duties and, for income tax law, partial or total exemption for a maximum period of 10 years.

The renewable energy sector is covered by a special law with tax benefits or exemptions in corporate income tax, VAT, customs duties and municipal tax.

Free Trade Zone industries have a special law with tax benefits or exemption in tax and duties customs in imports and corporate income tax, VAT and municipal taxes.

Withholding taxes (WHT)

Payments to residents

Dividend payments to residents or non-resident shareholder (corporations or individuals) are subject to 10% income tax withholding.

Payments of royalties to resident individuals or corporations are subject to 2% withholding income tax.

Interest paid to a resident or non-resident individual or legal entity is subject to 10% definitive withholding tax.

Payments on the local acquisition of goods and services are subject to 1% withholding tax.

N

Nicaragua

Payments to non-residents

Payments of royalties, interest, dividends and technical service fees to non-resident individuals and corporations are subject to withholding tax, as follows:

	Taxable income	Tax rate
	%	%
Royalties	70	21
Dividends	–	10
Technical assistance, generally	35	10.5
Interest:		
Non-financial companies	–	10
Financial companies	0	10

Present administrative taxing procedure requires that taxable income for technical assistance be determined on a case-by-case basis by the Tax Authorities.

Tax administration

Returns

Without exception, all corporations and individuals are required to file tax returns for a fiscal year within the following three months after the fiscal year end, which commonly ends on 30 June; however, companies can obtain authorisation from tax authorities in order to change or have a different year-end: March, September or December.

Payment of tax

Corporations shall pay fiscal-year income tax in monthly advanced payments. The monthly payable amount is calculated as 1% of gross income.

Corporate taxes in Nigeria

For more information, contact:

Kenneth Aitken
PricewaterhouseCoopers
Plot 252E Muri Okunola Street
Victoria Island
Lagos, Nigeria
Tel: +234 1 271 1700
Email: ken.aitken@ng.pwc.com

Significant developments

There are a number of ongoing reforms in the Nigerian tax environment including administrative and legislative changes. One of the key reforms is the recently approved national tax policy, which seeks to establish a set of principles, rules, regulations and guidelines necessary to create a modern tax system in Nigeria. The necessary legislative processes are now being initiated to give effect to the provisions of the policy.

Other key changes include the ongoing legislative process to combine 16 different national petroleum laws into a single document called the Petroleum Industry Bill. The bill aims to ensure transparency, make industry participation more equitable and maximise government revenue through increased royalty rates and rationalisation of tax incentives.

Taxes on corporate income

Income tax

The corporate income tax rate is 30% assessed on a preceding year basis, i.e., tax is charged on profits for the accounting year ending in the preceding year of assessment.

N

For small companies in the manufacturing industry and wholly export-oriented companies with turnover not exceeding NGN 1 million, the corporate tax rate is 20% in the first five calendar years of operation.

Minimum tax was introduced effective 1 January 1990. The tax is payable by companies having no taxable profits for the year or where the tax on profits is below the minimum tax. However, companies in the first four calendar years of business, companies engaged in the agriculture business or companies that have foreign equity capital of at least 25%, are exempt from minimum tax.

Minimum tax payable is calculated as follows:

1. Where the turnover of the company is NGN 500,000 or below, minimum tax is the highest of:
   a. 0.5% of gross profits;
   b. 0.5% of net assets;
   c. 0.25% of paid up capital; or
   d. 0.25% of turnover of the company for the year.

Nigeria

2. Where the turnover is higher than NGN 500,000, minimum tax is the highest of the calculations noted in (1), plus 0.125% of turnover in excess of NGN 500,000.

There is a tax on distributions where a company pays a dividend in excess of its taxable profit. Such a company will be charged tax on the dividend paid as if the dividend is the taxable profit of the company for that year of assessment.

Non-resident companies are subject to tax on the income or profit derived from Nigeria. The revenue authorities often assess non-resident companies on a deemed income basis. This is done by applying 20% of turnover as deemed profit and charging 30% corporate tax, resulting in an effective tax rate of 6% on turnover.

Corporate residence

A company is considered resident in Nigeria if such a company is registered or incorporated under the Companies and Allied Matters Act. This means that a company formed outside Nigeria under the laws in force in the foreign territory will be considered a non-resident company for tax purposes.

Other taxes

Education tax
The tax is levied on every Nigerian company at the rate of 2% of the assessable profit for each year of assessment. The tax is payable within two months of an assessment notice from the revenue authority. In practice, many companies pay the tax on a self-assessment basis along with their corporate income tax.

For companies subject to the petroleum profit tax, the education tax is to be treated as an allowable deduction. For other companies, income/profit taxes are not deductible in arriving at taxable income. Non-resident companies and unincorporated entities are exempt from the education tax.

Capital gains
Gains accruing to a chargeable person (individual or company) on the disposal of chargeable assets shall be subject to tax under the capital gains tax (CGT) Act at the rate of 10%. There is no distinction between long-term and short-term gains and no inflation adjustment to cost for CGT purposes. All forms of assets including options, debts and foreign currency, other than those specifically exempt, are liable for capital gains tax.

The gains on the disposal of shares are exempt from capital gains tax.

CGT is applicable on the chargeable gains received or brought into Nigeria in respect of assets situated outside Nigeria.

Capital losses are not allowed as an offset against chargeable gains accruing to a person from the disposal of any assets.

Information technology levy
The National Information Technology Development Agency (NITDA) Act No. 27 was introduced in 2007 and took effect beginning from the 2008 year of assessment. The act stipulates that a company with an annual turnover of NGN 100 million or more is

required to pay 1% of its profit before tax as information technology tax. This levy is tax-deductible when paid (typically in the year of assessment following that in which the payment was made).

This tax is applicable to companies in:

- Banking and other financial activities including capital and money market operators, mortgage institutions and micro-finance banks;
- Insurance activities including brokerage;
- Pension fund administration, pension management and related services;
- Global system for mobile communications (GSM) services providers and telecommunication companies; and
- Cyber and internet services providers.

Value-added tax (VAT)

VAT has been in effect since 1994.The standard rate is 5% but there is a proposal to increase the rate to 10%. Some of the latest amendments include the re-introduction of zero-rated products covering non-oil exports, goods and services purchased by diplomats, and goods and services purchased for use in humanitarian donor-funded projects. Exempt items include plants and machinery for use in export processing zones or free trade zones, basic food items, medical and pharmaceutical products.

Effective since 1 September 2007, oil and gas companies are required to deduct VAT at the source and remit it to the tax authority.

VAT is payable in the currency of the transactions.

Petroleum profit tax (PPT)

The petroleum profit tax as amended is a tax on the income of companies engaged in upstream petroleum operations.

The PPT rates vary as follows:

1. 50% for petroleum operations under Production sharing contracts (PSC) with the Nigerian National Petroleum Corporation (NNPC).
2. 66.75% for non-PSC operations in its first five years during which the company has not fully amortised all pre-production capitalised expenditure.
3. 85% for petroleum operations carried out under a joint venture (JV) arrangement with the NNPC after the first five years.

Tax is payable on the actual year basis.

The estimated tax returns must be filed within two months of the fiscal year (which runs from 1 January to 31 December). Actual tax returns should be filed within five months after the end of the accounting period, that is, not later than 31 May.

Payments in any accounting period of 12 months are made in 12 instalments, with a final thirteenth instalment (if there is an underpayment). The first instalment for the year is due by the end of March.

N

Nigeria

Late submission of returns attracts an initial penalty of NGN 10,000 and NGN 2,000 for each day such failure continues while late payment of tax attracts a penalty of 5% of the tax not paid.

Branch income

Except in rare circumstances, it is illegal for a foreign company to operate through a branch in Nigeria. The income of a foreign corporation derived from Nigeria, where applicable, is taxable at the corporate tax rate of 30%.

Income determination

Inventory valuation
The first-in, first-out (FIFO) valuation method is commonly used. Average and standard cost methods are also allowed but last-in, first-out (LIFO) is not permitted. Other than the accounting requirement in the local generally accepted accounting principles (GAAP), there are no special statutory provisions for inventory valuation.

Inter-company dividend
Other than withholding tax (WHT), a dividend received from a Nigerian company by a foreign investor is exempt from further tax in the hands of the recipient company.

The rate of WHT on a dividend is 10%. This tax is also the final tax for resident investors.

Dividends received by a Nigerian company from another Nigerian company are not subject to further tax. Also, dividends distributed by unit trusts are tax-exempt and are not subject to further WHT.

Foreign income
A Nigerian company is taxable on its worldwide income. On the other hand, a foreign company is subject to tax only on income derived from Nigeria.

Dividends, interest, rents and royalties earned abroad and brought into Nigeria through Government approved channels are exempt from Nigerian tax. Government approved channels means the Central Bank of Nigeria and any bank or financial institution authorised to carry out foreign exchange transactions.

The WHT rate on dividends, interest and royalties payable to beneficiaries under the double taxation treaty (DDT) agreements with Nigeria is 7.5%.

Stock dividend
Stock dividends (bonus shares) are not taxable at source or included in the taxable income of the recipient company.

Taxable income
The following income is taxable in Nigeria under corporate tax:

1. Profits accruing in, derived from, brought into, or received in Nigeria in respect of any trade or business;
2. Dividends, interest, royalties, discounts, charges or annuities;

3. Rent or any premium arising from the right granted to any person for the use or occupation of any property, where applicable;
4. Any source of annual profits or gain not falling within the preceding categories;
5. Any amount deemed to be income with respect to any benefit arising from a pension or provident fund, of the Personal Income Tax Act;
6. Fees, dues and allowances (wherever paid) for services rendered; and
7. Any amount of profits or gains arising from the acquisition or disposal of short-term money instruments like federal government securities, treasury bills, treasury or savings certificates, debenture certificates and treasury bonds.

Deductions

Depreciation and depletion

Capital allowances are calculated on a straight-line basis. Capital allowances claimable in any year are restricted to 66.67% of assessable profits for all companies except companies in the manufacturing and agricultural sectors, which are excluded from this restriction.

The following are the capital allowance rates on fixed assets (qualifying expenditures):

Qualifying expenditure	Initial allowance	Annual allowance
	%	%
Building (industrial and non-industrial)	15	10
Furniture and fittings	25	20
Plant expenditure (1)	95/50	Nil/25
Mining expenditure	95	Nil
Plantation equipment	95	Nil
Motor vehicle (2)	50/95	25/Nil
Ranching and plantation expenditure	30	50
Housing estate expenditure	50	25
Research and development	95	Nil

Notes

1. 95% initial allowance for plant used in agricultural production; others 50%.
2. 95% initial allowance is granted for motor vehicles used for public transportation if the company has a fleet of at least three buses; all other motor vehicles 50%.

The initial allowance is first deducted and the balance is written off on a straight-line basis over a fixed period, depending on the rates of annual allowance. There is a requirement that assets not yet disposed of cannot be fully written off in the books. A nominal amount of NGN 10 per asset must be retained in the books until the assets are disposed. However, where 95% has been claimed as an initial allowance, the 5% balance is the value that must be maintained on the books until the final disposal of the asset.

When assets are sold, the proceeds over the tax written-down value are taxed at 30% to the extent of the allowances already claimed.

Nigeria

Expenses

Expenses are deductible for tax purposes if they are wholly, reasonably, exclusively and necessarily incurred for the business or trade. Some such expenses are:

- Sum payable by way of interest on capital borrowed;
- Rent for the period;
- Expenses incurred in respect of salary and wages;
- Expenses incurred for repair of assets;
- Bad debt incurred in the course of trade;
- Liability incurred for purpose of trade
- Research and development costs; and
- Donations subject to the provisions of the law.

Net operating losses

Losses can be carried forward indefinitely except for insurance companies where losses can only be carried forward for four years. Losses made from one line of business cannot be relieved against another line of business. Loss carryback is not permitted.

Group taxation

There are currently no provisions for group taxation, group relief or group filing of tax returns in Nigeria. Each legal entity within a group is treated as distinct and separate for tax purposes.

Payments to foreign affiliates

Payments considered to be artificial are not deductible for tax purposes. Royalties, management and technical fees require the approval of the National Office for Technology Acquisition and Promotion (NOTAP) for exchange control purposes and for tax deduction. NOTAP approved royalties and technical fees are limited to a range of 1% to 5% of net sales, while management fees are limited to a range of 2% to 5% of profit before tax and consultancy fees are limited to 5% of total project cost. Technical fees are limited to approved man-hour rates.

Trademark fees are disallowed where the trademark owner has more than 75% equity participation in the local company.

Tax incentives

Nigeria has various tax incentives intended to encourage investment in key sectors of the economy as follows:

Pioneer companies investing in specified industrial activities may, on application, be granted a tax holiday for a maximum period of five years. Examples of economic activities that may be granted a tax holiday include: glass and glassware manufacture, manufacture of fertilisers, steel manufacture, etc.

A new company that engages in the mining of solid minerals is exempt from tax for the first three years of its operation.

Certain incentives are available to companies located in rural areas. The incentives take the form of tax reductions at graduated rates for enterprises located at least 20 kilometres from available electricity, water and tarred roads.

Interest accruing on deposit accounts of a non-resident company is tax-exempt, provided the deposits are made by transfer of funds to Nigeria on or after 1 January 1990 and the depositor does not become non-resident after making the deposit while in Nigeria.

Interest on foreign-currency domiciliary accounts is also tax exempt.

A company engaged in an approved manufacturing activity in the export processing zone (EPZ) and incurs expenditure in its qualifying building and plant equipment is entitled to 100% capital allowance in that year of assessment.

In addition, a company that is 100% export oriented but located outside an EPZ will enjoy a three year tax holiday, provided the company is not formed by splitting up or reconstruction of an already existing business and the export proceeds form at least 75% of its turnover.

Profits of companies whose supplies are exclusively inputs to the manufacture of products for export are exempt from tax. Such companies are expected to obtain a certificate of purchase of the input from the exporter in order to claim tax exemption.

Where plant and machinery are transferred to a new company, the tax written-down value of the asset transferred must not exceed 25% of the total value of plant and machinery in the new company. The company should also repatriate at least 75% of the export earnings to Nigeria and place it in a Nigerian domiciliary account in order to qualify for a tax holiday.

Profits of any Nigerian company in respect of goods exported from Nigeria are exempt from tax, provided that the proceeds from such exports are repatriated to Nigeria and are used exclusively for the purchase of raw materials, plant, equipments and spare parts.

For companies engaged in gas utilisation, they are entitled to:

- A tax-free period for up to five years;
- Accelerated capital allowance after the tax-free period; and
- Tax-free dividend during the tax-free period.

25% of the income derived from tourism by hotels in convertible currencies is exempt from tax if such income is put in a reserve fund to be utilised within five years for expansion or construction of new hotels and other facilities for tourism development.

Interest on any foreign loans, and interest on any loan granted by a bank for the purpose of manufacturing goods for export are exempt from tax as follows:

Repayment period	Moratorium	%
Over 7 years	Not less than 2 years	100
5-7 years	Not less than 1.5 years	70
2-4 years	Not less than 1 year	40
Under 2 years	Nil	Nil

N

Nigeria

Interest on any loan granted by a bank to a company engaged in agricultural trade, fabrication of local plant and machinery or as working capital to any cottage industry is 100% tax-free if the loan has a moratorium of not less than 18 months and the rate of interest is not more than the base lending rate.

An investment allowance of 10% on the cost of qualifying expenditures in respect of plant and machinery is available as a deduction from assessable profits in the year of purchase. There is no restriction to the full claim of capital allowance in any year of assessment for companies in the mining, manufacturing and agricultural sectors.

Double tax treaties (DTT)
Nigeria now has tax treaties with South Africa and China. The treaty with South Africa was signed in 2000, ratified in 2008 and came into effect on 1 January 2009 while the treaty with China was signed in 2002, ratified in 2009 and came into effect on 1 January 2010.

Nigeria also has tax treaties with other countries including: Belgium, Canada, Czech Republic, France, the Netherlands, Pakistan, Philippines, Romania, Slovak Republic, and the United Kingdom.

The provisions of Nigeria's tax treaty allows a reduced WHT rate of 7.5% on dividends, royalties and interest payable to a beneficiary resident in a treaty country, compared to 10% for non-treaty residents.

Withholding taxes (WHT)

The principal legislation governing WHT in Nigeria is the Company Income Tax Act 2007 (Section 60 – 64), the Personal Income Tax Act (Section 68 – 72), and the WHT regulations and rules. Guidelines are normally issued by the Federal Inland Revenue Service (FIRS) through information circulars.

WHT is applicable on specified transactions as follows:

Types of Payment	Applicable for rates	
	Companies	Individuals
Dividends, interest and rents	10%	10%
Directors fees	N/A	10%
Hire of equipment	10%	10%
Royalties	10%	5%
Commission, consultancy, technical, service fees	10%	5%
Management fees	10%	5%
Construction/building	5%	5%
Contracts other than sales in the ordinary course of business	5%	5%

The period for filing WHT is 21 days after the duty to deduct arose (previously 30 days) for deductions from companies, while for non-companies WHT is due within 30 days.

The penalty for failure to deduct or remit tax is now 10% (previously 200%) of the amount not deducted/remitted.

Companies are permitted to carry unutilised tax credits forward to future periods.

Effective September 2008, companies are required to submit in electronic form a schedule of all their suppliers for the month showing the tax identification number (TIN), address of the suppliers, the nature of the transaction, WHT deducted and invoice number.

Tax administration

Returns

Companies are required to register for tax and file their audited accounts and tax computations with the Federal Inland Revenue Service (FIRS or the Revenue) within six months of their financial year-end on a self-assessment basis or 18 months after incorporation (whichever comes first). A company may file an application for extension of filing tax returns for up to two months at the discretion of the FIRS.

Upon registration, a company is issued a TIN which will serve as the company's file number for all federal taxes and future correspondence with the Revenue authority.

The company must file the following documents with the tax authority:

- Tax computation for the relevant year of assessment;
- The audited financial statements for the respective period (this should be in conformity with the local GAAP);
- A duly completed and signed self-assessment form for company income tax; and
- Evidence of remittance of the income tax liability (partly or in full).

Assessment

Nigerian companies file their tax returns based on a self-assessment system where the taxpayer prepares its annual returns and determines its tax liability. However, the FIRS may apply a best of judgment (BOJ) assessment where it is of the opinion that the tax returns filed are deliberately misstated or where no returns are filed within the stipulated period.

Payment of tax

Companies are required to pay provisional tax of an amount equal to the tax paid in the preceding year, within three months from the commencement of each assessment year. This amount must be paid in one lump sum.

Provisional tax payment is not applicable to companies that file self-assessment returns. Tax charged by an assessment is payable within two months after service of the notice of assessment on the company. However, where the notice of assessment is served within the approved period of payment of provisional tax, the tax is to be paid within two months after the end of the approved period and, in any case, not later than 14 December of the assessment year.

A company that files its self-assessment within six months after the accounting year-end could apply to the revenue authority in writing to pay its income tax in instalments. The maximum number of instalments the Revenue authority may approve is six. Evidence of the first instalment has to accompany the tax returns filed in order to qualify for the instalment payment. However, all payments have to be made on or before 30 November of the year of assessment.

Nigeria

Assessments are made on a preceding year basis. This means that the financial statements for a period ended in 2009 will form the basis for the 2010 year of assessment.

Late payment of taxes attracts a 10% penalty and interest at commercial rate.

A company that files its annual tax return late or fails to submit its accounts by the due date is liable to a nominal penalty.

Corporate taxes in Norway

For more information, contact:

Bård Ivar Koppang
Advokatfirmaet PricewaterhouseCoopers DA
Forus Atrium
Vassbotnen 15
N-4313 Sandnes
Norway
Tel: +47 95 26 11 72
Email: baard.koppang@no.pwc.com

Significant developments

As part of the measures against the financial crises, tax losses incurred in 2008 and 2009 may be used to offset profits earned in the previous two income years. The deduction is limited to NOK (Norwegian Krone) 20 million per year. Furthermore, machinery, equipment and cars acquired or upgraded in 2009 may, in addition to the regular annual depreciation of 20%, be depreciated an additional 10%.

Taxes on corporate income

Income tax
Corporate tax is assessed at a rate of 28%.

Petroleum tax regime
All upstream activity on the Norwegian Continental Shelf (NCS) is taxable to Norway.

Taxation is based on net income at a marginal tax rate of 78%. The income tax is comprised of the ordinary 28% corporate tax rate, and the 50% special tax. All income is subject to the 28% corporate tax, while only income from offshore production and pipeline transportation of petroleum from the NCS (offshore tax regime) is subject to the additional 50% special tax. Income is taxable when the right to the benefit is earned, and costs are deductible when the liability to cover the cost is imposed on the taxpayer. Actual payment is not relevant.

Upstream activity on the NCS is consolidated within the company. There is no ring fence per oil field. Tax consolidation against other activity is limited. Crude oil sales from most of the fields are taxed at a predetermined market price set by an official board (i.e., the norm price). A norm price may be imposed on gas sales, but this has not been implemented. Investments in installations for exploitation and production of petroleum as well as investments in pipelines are depreciated linearly over six years.

An investment-based "supplementary depreciation" ("uplift") of 30% (7.5% per year for four years) is granted on investments in installations for exploitation and production of petroleum as well as investments in pipelines. The uplift is deducted against the special tax base. Loss and unused uplift may be carried forward indefinitely with an annual interest. If the upstream activity on the NCS ceases, the tax value of loss carryforward and unused uplift may either be sold or compensated by the Norwegian state. Exploration costs are tax deductible as incurred. If a loss is created due to exploration cost, the taxpayer may claim the tax value of such loss repaid in the year following the income year in which the loss was created.

Norway

Special rules apply as to the deductibility of net interest cost in the offshore tax regime (78%). Upstream activity on the NCS is exempt from VAT. A CO_2 tax is calculated on petroleum that is flared and natural gas emissions to air, as well as on CO_2 that is separated from petroleum and emitted into the air, on installations used for production or transportation of petroleum. The CO_2 tax is regarded as a normal operating cost for income tax purposes and is a fully deductible cost both for corporate and special tax calculations.

Hydro power tax regime

The hydro power tax regime is applicable on taxation of income derived from production, sales, transfer or distribution of hydro power.

Taxation is based on net income at a marginal tax rate of 58%. The income tax is comprised of the ordinary 28% corporate tax rate, and a 30% resource rent tax.

All income is subject to the 28% corporate tax, while only income from hydro power production is subject to the additional 30% resource rent tax.

The resource rent is calculated per hydro power plant. The gross income is, with some exceptions, calculated based on spot market price per hour multiplied with actual production. Deductible costs will be the same as for the corporate income tax (CIT); that is, expenses related to the power plant except for interest expenses, which are not deductible. Special rules apply to depreciations of investments in hydro power plants. Effective from 2008, tax consolidation is mandatory within the company and, provided the conditions for group taxation are fulfilled, available on a group level. Losses (negative resource rent) on a company (eventually on a group) level will be compensated by the Norwegian state. Transitional rules apply for losses derived before 2007.

In addition, a NOK 0.013 per kWh natural resource tax will apply, based on 1/7 of the produced kWh for the income year in question and the six previous years. The natural resource tax is creditable against the 28% ordinary corporate tax.

Hydro power producers also have to pay a 0.2–0.7% (decided by the local municipality, usually 0.7%) property tax on the hydro power plant's capitalised value.

Corporate residence

Companies incorporated in Norway in accordance with Norwegian law and registered in Norway are, as a general rule, regarded as a resident in Norway. If management at the board/director level is carried out outside Norway, the residency in Norway for tax purposes may cease, and the company may be subject to liquidation for tax purposes. Note that several factors should be considered in order to determine whether the residency has been moved.

Foreign corporations will be regarded as resident in Norway if the place of effective management is in Norway. The place of effective management will, for example, be deemed to be in Norway if the board of directors makes its decisions in Norway.

Other taxes

Value-added tax (VAT)

The general VAT rate is 25% and applies to all supplies of goods and services not qualifying for another rate or an exemption. A reduced rate of 14% applies to supply of food and beverages, excluding tobacco, alcohol, medication and water from waterworks. The reduced rate is not applicable to the supply of food and beverages consumed in restaurants and other food establishments.

A reduced rate of 8% applies to the television licence fee charged for broadcasting services provided by the Norwegian Broadcasting Company (NRK), domestic passenger transport services and procurement of such services, domestic ferry services related to transport of vehicles, accommodation services and cinema tickets.

Exemptions with credit (zero-rated) include but are not limited to:

* Export of goods and services;
* Goods and services for Norwegian offshore and non-resident ships;
* Transfer of a going concern; and
* Supply of newspapers and books to recipients.

Exemptions without credit include but are not limited to:

* Supply of works of art owned by the artist;
* Health services;
* Social services;
* Financial services including banking, insurance and the sale of shares;
* Educational services;
* Lease of real estate (accommodation and lease of parking lots are taxable); and
* Services supplied by cultural and entertainment institutions.

Exemptions, whereby an option to tax is available, include the letting of immovable property to VAT liable lessees following a specific VAT registration with the VAT authorities.

The registration threshold is met when VAT taxable supplies (including self-supplies) exceed NOK 50,000 during a 12-month period. For charitable and public utility institutions and organisations, the threshold is set at NOK 140,000.

Net wealth taxes

Private limited companies (AS) and public limited companies (ASA) are not liable to net wealth tax or other capital taxes.

Branch income

Branch income is taxed at the corporate rate of 28% (the same as Norwegian companies). Branches of foreign companies are taxed more or less in the same way as Norwegian limited liability companies.

Norway

There is no branch profit tax or other repatriation taxes. However, if assets and/
or liabilities are transferred from a permanent establishment (PE) in Norway to the
head office or another foreign PE of the same company, this may trigger exit taxation.
As before, a transfer of assets, etc. to another corporate entity is subject to regular
taxation.

Branches of foreign limited liability companies are not subject to net wealth tax.

Income determination

Inventory valuation
Inventory is valued at cost. Cost is normally determined using the first-in, first-out
(FIFO) method. The last-in, first-out (LIFO) method is not acceptable for tax purposes.
Conformity between book and tax reporting is not required.

Capital gains
Capital gains realised in the course of a business activity are almost always regarded
as taxable income. Gains resulting from real estate transactions are taxed, regardless
of whether they are incurred in connection with business activity. Losses may be offset
against the taxpayer's other income.

Capital gains realised on both business-related and non-business-related securities
are, in principle, taxable. In general, any capital gains realised on bonds at maturity
are regarded as taxable income. Correspondingly, realised losses will be eligible
for deductions.

Tax exemption rules for corporate shareholders
Under the tax-exemption rules, corporate shareholders will be exempt from tax
on dividends received and capital gains on all shares and on derivatives where the
underlying object is shares, regardless of the level of the holding or the time for which
shares have been held. Losses on shares will accordingly not be tax-deductible. All
expenses related to exempt income from shares are fully tax-deductible. In order to
limit the benefit of these deductions, the tax-exemption method is limited to 97%
of the relevant income, and the remaining 3% is taxable for Norwegian corporate
shareholders (at a 0.84% effective tax rate). The 3% taxable income is calculated
on dividends and net gains/losses in the income year. Unused losses may not be
carried forward.

In addition, an investment in a company resident in a low-tax country in the European
Economic Area (EEA) has to fulfil certain substance requirements to qualify for the
tax-exemption rules. These requirements are intended to be in line with the substance
requirements of the European Court of Justice's (ECJ's) decision in the *Cadbury
Schweppes* case. A country is considered a low-tax country if the level of effective
taxation is less than two-thirds of the tax that would have been due had the foreign
company been resident in Norway. This is the same test used for the controlled foreign
company (CFC) regime, which means that a comparison shall not be made on a
year-by-year basis, but rather that an overall comparison is required. The Directorate
of Taxes has published a non-exhaustive list of low tax jurisdictions (black list) and
non-low tax jurisdictions (white list).

However, for investments outside the EEA, the exemption would apply only if a
shareholder holds 10% or more of the share capital and the voting rights of the foreign

company for a consecutive period of two years or more. To be able to deduct losses on realisation of shareholdings outside the EEA, the shareholder and/or a related party may not hold 10% or more of the share capital and the voting rights of the foreign company in a two-year period prior to the realisation. For dividends, the holding period of two years would not have to be met when dividends are distributed but may be met after the ex-dividend date.

Shareholdings in low-tax countries (*see above*) outside of the EEA do not qualify for the tax-exemption rules.

Acquisition and sales-related costs (e.g., broker fees, etc.) must be activated (i.e., added to the cost price of the shares for tax purposes). Costs incurred to manage acquired tax-exempt shares are, however, tax-deductible.

Norway's internal tax rules do not allow taxation of a non-resident's capital gain on disposal of financial instruments including, among others shares in Norwegian companies, unless the non-resident has a PE to which the financial instrument may be allocated.

Foreign income
A Norwegian resident company is subject to corporate tax on its worldwide income. Double taxation of foreign-source income including foreign branch income and CFC income, is avoided either through tax treaties or domestic tax provisions. A deduction for foreign tax may either be claimed as an expense or as a credit against Norwegian tax payable on that income. In most circumstances the foreign dividends are exempt according to the tax-exemption rules. As a consequence, foreign withholding taxes may not be credited, and therefore constitute a real cost for the companies concerned.

Controlled foreign companies (CFCs)
Norwegian residents (individual or company) will be taxed directly for their allocable part of the profits from a CFC's income if the company is resident in a low-tax country, irrespective of whether income is distributed to the Norwegian investor. A low-tax country in this respect is a country where the assessed foreign income tax on the company's profits is less than two-thirds of assessed taxes calculated according to Norwegian tax rules as if the company had been a resident in Norway. A condition for such taxation is that 50% or more of the foreign company's shares or capital is held or controlled, directly or indirectly, by Norwegian taxpayers (alone or together), based on ownership status at the beginning and end of the income year in question.

The control requirement is, as mentioned, fulfilled if at least 50% of the shares or capital is controlled directly or indirectly by Norwegian taxpayers both at the beginning and end of the income year. However, if Norwegian taxpayers own or control more than 60% of the shares or capital at the end of the income year, Norwegian control exists irrespective of the level of control at the beginning of the year. Norwegian control ceases to exist if Norwegian taxpayers own or control less than 50% of the shares or capital at both the beginning and end of the income year or less than 40% of the shares or capital at the end of the income year.

On condition that Norway has signed a tax treaty with the country involved and the company in question is covered by the treaty, the CFC rules will be applicable only if the income of the entity in question is mainly of a passive nature. Furthermore, CFC taxation may also be prohibited if the company in question is resident within the EEA

Norway

and cannot be deemed as a wholly artificial arrangement as outlined in the ECJ's decision in the *Cadbury Schweppes* case. Hence, CFC taxation will be avoided for EEA companies that fulfil certain substance requirements.

Stock dividends
Stock dividends (bonus shares) are not taxable on receipt, provided that the dividends have been distributed in accordance with the Limited Liability Company Acts and distributed in proportion with the ownership level of the shares.

Exit tax
The exit rules levy taxes upon the migration of assets or liabilities. The tax is calculated by reference to the accrued but unrealised gains at the time of migration. Exit charges are levied if a company:

- Transfers its operational headquarters to another country.
- Has assets, etc. that are transferred to a PE that is tax-exempt pursuant to a double tax treaty (DTT).
- Has assets, etc. that are transferred from a Norwegian PE of a foreign company to the head office or a foreign PE of the same company.

Transfer of operational equipment to a PE in a country where the DTT in question is based on the credit method is, however, not regarded as a taxable event.

According to the rules, the tax treatment is different depending on the type of assets being transferred. Business-related operational equipment and financial assets being transferred out of Norwegian taxing jurisdiction are considered as taxable events, but the tax charges may be deferred if certain conditions are met. In addition, the tax charges may be completely avoided if the assets are not sold within five years after they are transferred out of Norway. Transfer of intangible assets and inventory would trigger immediate and unconditional exit charges.

Threshold rules apply when determining whether the exit tax may be levied. Exit tax on the transfer of tangible assets is applicable only if the unrealised capital gains exceed NOK 5 million. Exit tax on the transfer of other assets and liabilities is applicable only if the unrealised capital gains exceed NOK 1 million.

Exit charges at both the corporate and shareholder level will be triggered when companies migrate from Norway because these companies will be deemed to have liquidated.

Deductions

Depreciation and depletion
For depreciation, the declining-balance method is mandatory. The depreciation rates given below are the maximum rates.

There is a duty to capitalise if the value of an asset subject to declining-balance method of depreciation is NOK 15,000 or higher and has an economic life of at least three years.

Asset	%
Office machines, etc.	30

Asset	%
Acquired goodwill/business value	20
Trucks, lorries, buses, taxicabs, vehicles for persons with disabilities	20
Cars, tractors, other vehicular machinery, instruments, fixtures and furniture, etc.	20
Ships, vessels, offshore rigs, etc.	14
Aircraft, helicopters	12
Construction for transmission and distribution of electric power and electronic equipment in a power company	5
Buildings and construction, hotels, hostels, inns, etc.	4 (8)*
Office buildings	2
Fixed technical installations in buildings, including heating plant, cooling and freezing plant, electrical installation, sanitary installation, elevator, etc.	10

* The applicable rate would be 8% if, from the date of its erection, the structure has an economic life of 20 years or less.

Special depreciation rules apply to assets moved in and out of Norwegian jurisdiction to and from companies, etc resident outside the EEA.

Net operating losses
Losses may be carried forward indefinitely. Losses incurred in the year of ceasing business may be carried back for a period of two years. If a loss is incurred in the next to last year, it may be carried back to the preceding year.

Payments to foreign affiliates
Royalties and service fees paid to related foreign companies are fully deductible, provided they meet the arm's-length standard. There are no formal thin-capitalisation or income-stripping rules in Norway. In practice the tax authorities require that the entity in question is able to service its debts. In addition, any loan terms should be comparable to those that would have been agreed upon by unrelated parties. Interest on financing to the extent that these rules are not satisfied may be regarded as dividends and thus non-deductible and, in addition, may be subject to Norwegian withholding tax.

Taxes
Real estate tax, as well as foreign income and capital taxes paid by the taxpayer, is deductible in determining corporate income. Foreign taxes are deductible only if they have not been credited against Norwegian payable tax.

Goodwill
Acquired goodwill may be depreciated according to the declining-balance method at a maximum of 20% per annum. The tax authorities have, however, on several occasions recently questioned the allocation to goodwill and claimed that a part of the purchase price should be allocated to brand and firm names, etc. (which may, as a rule, not be depreciated unless it is of a time-limited nature). Other intangibles are depreciable on condition that they are subject to an evident loss in value or if they are time-limited.

These rules do not apply to companies engaged in oil- and gas-producing activities subject to the Petroleum Tax Act.

Norway

Thin capitalisation

There is no fixed debt to equity ratio in Norwegian tax law. However, if Norwegian income from the subsidiary is reduced due to the affiliation between the Norwegian company and a foreign company, adjustments may be made under the arm's-length provisions, cf. section 13-1 of the General Tax Act. Generally, these provisions apply only if the company has obtained a larger loan from a group company than an independent credit institution would have granted, or if the agreed level of interest is higher than an independent credit institution would have required. As a rule of thumb 25% to 30% equity is feasible. Naturally this analysis will vary based on the actual company's credit worthiness, which would consist of several elements such as the nature of the business, financial status, future income possibilities and group relationship, etc. The company must also be able to service its debts.

If a Norwegian entity is regarded as being thinly capitalised, part of the entity's interest and debts will be reclassified to dividend and equity. Such dividend will not be covered by the participation exemption rules as they are not distributed in accordance with the rules and regulations of the Limited Liability Companies Acts.

Group taxation

Income taxes are assessed on companies individually, not on a consolidated basis. This may be avoided through group contributions between Norwegian companies, provided common direct or indirect (including foreign) ownership and voting rights is more than 90%. Furthermore, the Norwegian group contribution rules are, under certain conditions, also applicable to branches of companies that are resident within the EEA. Group contributions are not deductible for companies engaged in oil- and gas-producing activities subject to the Petroleum Tax Act.

Assets may be transferred tax-free between group companies as defined above at tax book value for tax purposes and at market value for financial book purposes. Payment in this respect must equal market value of the assets transferred for tax and financial book purposes. The same applies to payment in shares. If the transferee loses the affiliation with the tax group while still owning the transferred assets, the transferor will be taxed for the difference between the tax book value and the market value of the assets.

Tax incentives

Shipping taxation rules

Effective for the income year 2007, a new tonnage tax model has been introduced in Norway. The new rules imply substantial changes to the taxation of shipping companies resident in Norway.

The new rules are in line with the tonnage tax rules found in other EU/EEA countries and imply that shipping income will be tax-exempt on a permanent basis. This is the main difference compared with the previous model that was based on deferral of the tax liability.

Norwegian tonnage-taxed companies are allowed to keep only certain kinds of assets inside the model (legal assets) and are not allowed to have income from non-tonnage-taxed activities except financial income. If the requirements are not fulfilled, the company would fall outside the scope of the model and be taxed at ordinary rates (28%).

Qualifying assets
A tonnage-taxed company must own at least one qualifying asset (i.e., a vessel, for example bulk, tankers, container vessels, car carriers, tugboats, and entrepreneurial vessels and auxiliary vessels for use in the petroleum industry) new building contracts, a 3% share in another tonnage-taxed limited company, or a 3% ownership interest in a partnership or CFC company.

Qualifying and legal business activities/income
Qualifying business income is income from operation of the company's own and chartered vessels. A tonnage-taxed company may, for example, charter vessels in and out on bareboat and time charter terms without limitations. Furthermore, gains upon disposal of vessels and new building contracts are exempt from taxation.

Income from related activities such as sales of goods and services onboard vessels, loading and discharging vessels or leasing out containers and operations of ticket offices is also exempt from taxation. The exemption also applies to income from the strategic and commercial management of the company's owned and chartered vessels, as well as vessels owned or operated by group companies (more than 50% joint ownership), and vessels operated according to a pool agreement. Pure management companies are not included (i.e., all companies must have at lease one qualifying asset).

Financial income is permitted except for income from shares in unlisted companies and ownership interests in partnerships that are not taxed under the tonnage tax system. The condition is that financial activities do not constitute a separate business.

Entrance into the tonnage tax system
Entry into the new tonnage tax system is optional and may take place with effect from 1 January every year provided that the company has fulfilled the conditions for application of the tonnage tax system from the beginning of the year. Newly established companies will have direct entry and may enter into the tonnage tax system from the date of incorporation. All qualifying companies within the same group should be obliged to make the same election (tonnage taxation or ordinary taxation) with effect from the income year 2009.

Upon entry into the tonnage tax system (from 2010) the difference between market value and tax value of the company's assets (including vessels, new building contracts, ownership interests in partnerships and shares in CFC companies/tax exempt assets) is taxed as a capital gain (28%). There is continuity for financial assets and assets covered by the tax-exemption rules (qualifying shares and derivatives).

Transitional rules applicable in 2007, 2008 and 2009
Companies that were taxed under the old tonnage tax system prior to 2007 had to elect between exit from the tonnage tax system or transition to the new tonnage tax system effective from 1 January 2007. Transition into the new tonnage tax system resulted in an income settlement that was based on the difference between book value and tax value of the company's tax-exempt assets (3/3). According to the transitional rules 2/3 of the gain was to be entered as income over 10 years (1/10 each year), while the tax liability related to the last 1/3 (optional) may be waived if the company invested an

Norway

amount equal to the tax amount in qualifying environmental measures (environmental fund). On 12 February 2010, the majority of the Norwegian Supreme Court concluded that the transitional rules are unconstitutional. The ruling implies that the gain (2/3) calculated upon entry into the new tonnage-taxed system may not be subject to taxation until untaxed profit is distributed to non-tonnage-taxed shareholders, or the company leaves the tonnage tax system. For the time being, companies that have offset 1/3 to an environmental fund may continue this fund.

An ordinarily taxed company could enter into the new system according to transitional rules effective from 1 January 2007, 2008 or 2009. Entry into the tonnage tax system resulted in an income settlement. The gain was calculated based on the difference between book value and tax value of the company's tax-exempt assets. The gain could be offset to the company's gain and loss account and be entered as income with 20% of net balance each year. If the company sells vessels or ownership interests in partnerships owned by the company at the time of entry into the tonnage tax system within three years after entry or exits the model within three years after entry, the difference between market value and book value upon entry into the system will be subject to taxation.

Exit from the tonnage tax system
A shipping company may exit the regime on a voluntary basis, or is obliged to do so after breaching specific requirements for companies within the tonnage tax system. As a starting point, no income settlement will have to be made when leaving the regime and the tax value on the company's assets will be adjusted to market value at the time of exit. However, a possible exit while the company has untaxed reserves calculated upon entry into the tonnage tax system could result in tax liability. The same applies if a company that was previously taxed under the ordinary tax regime exits the tonnage tax system during the first three years after it has benefited from the transitional rules applicable in 2007, 2008 and 2009 (or disposes of vessels or ownership interests in partnerships owned upon entry).

Lock-in period
Companies that enter into the tonnage tax system are subject to a formal 10-year lock-in period. If a company exits the tonnage tax system before the lock-in period expires, it will be excluded from the tonnage tax system until after the initial lock-in period has ended.

Withholding taxes (WHT)

Norway does not levy withholding taxes on payments of royalties and interest except interest derived from primary capital certificates ("No. grunnfondsbevis"). The internal withholding tax rate is 25%, which either may be reduced under the tax-exemption rules or an applicable tax treaty. To qualify for the tax-exemption rule, the recipient of the dividends has to be a corporate investor resident in an EEA country and also fulfil certain substance requirements. If these requirements are met, no dividends withholding tax is imposed.

Dividends

Recipient	Regular rate	Parent/subsidiary
	%	%
Non-treaty	25	25
Treaty:		

Recipient	Regular rate	Parent/subsidiary
	%	%
Albania	15	5 (1)
Argentina	15	10 (1)
Australia	15	0 (10) /5 (4)
Austria	15	0 (1)
Azerbaijan	15	10 (2)
Bangladesh	15	10 (3)
Barbados	15	5 (3)
Belgium	15	5 (1)
Benin	20	20
Bosnia and Herzegovina	15	15
Brazil	25	25 (9)
Bulgaria	15	15
Canada	15	5 (4)
Chile	15	5 (5)
China, P.R.	15	15
Croatia	15	15
Cyprus	5	0 (6)
Czech Republic	15	0 (3)
Denmark	15	0 (3)
Egypt	15	15
Estonia	15	5 (1)
Faroe Islands	15	0 (3)
Finland	15	0 (3)
France	15	5 (3) /0 (1)
Gambia	15	5 (1)
Germany	15	0 (1)
Greece	20	20
Greenland	15	5 (3)
Hungary	10	10
Iceland	15	0 (3)
India	25	15 (1)
Indonesia	15	15
Ireland, Rep. of	15	5 (3)
Israel	15	5 (6)
Italy	15	15
Ivory Coast (Côte d'Ivoire)	15	15
Jamaica	15	15
Japan	15	5 (5)
Kazakhstan	15	5 (3)
Kenya	25	15 (5)
Korea, Rep. of	15	15
Latvia	15	5 (1)
Lithuania	15	5 (1)
Luxembourg	15	5 (1)

N

Norway

Recipient	Regular rate %	Parent/subsidiary %
Malawi	5	0 (6)
Malaysia	0	0
Malta	15	15
Mexico	15	0 (1)
Morocco	15	15
Nepal	15	5 (1)/10 (3)
Netherlands	15	0 (1)
Netherlands Antilles	15	5 (1)
New Zealand	15	15
Nordic Treaty	15	0 (3)
Pakistan	15	15
Philippines	25	15 (3)
Poland	15	5 (1)
Portugal	15	10 (1)
Qatar	15	5 (3)
Romania	10	10
Russia	10	10
Senegal	16	16
Serbia (not Montenegro)	15	15
Sierra Leone	5	0 (6)
Singapore	15	5 (1)
Slovak Republic	15	5 (1)
Slovenia	15	0 (11)
South Africa	15	5 (1)
Spain	15	10 (1)
Sri Lanka	15	15
Sweden	15	0 (3)
Switzerland	15	0 (8)
Tanzania	20	20
Thailand	15	10 (3)
Trinidad and Tobago	20	10 (5)
Tunisia	20	20
Turkey	25	20 (1)
Uganda, Republic of	15	10 (1)
Ukraine	15	5 (1)
United Kingdom	15	5 (4)
United States	15	15
Venezuela	10	5 (3)
Vietnam	15	5/10 (7)
Zambia	15	15
Zimbabwe	20	15 (1)

Notes

1. 25% of the capital.
2. 30% of the capital and an investment of no less than USD 100,000.
3. 10% of the capital.
4. 10% of the voting rights.
5. 25% of the voting rights.
6. A total of 50% of voting the rights.
7. A total of 5% for 70% of the capital; 10% for 25% to 70% of the capital.
8. 20% of the capital.
9. Internal Norwegian withholding tax rate.
10. 80% of the voting rights provided certain conditions.
11. 15% of the capital.

Tax administration

Returns

The income tax year normally runs from 1 January to 31 December, with assessments being issued in the early fall of the following calendar year. Companies are liable for both advance payments and final settlements in the calendar year of assessment. Companies with a financial year other than the calendar year may, if they belong to a foreign group with a deviating accounting year, use the financial year of the group for tax purposes.

Companies are required to file their tax returns by the end of March in the year following their financial year. If filed electronically, the return must be filed by the end of May. Upon application, an extension of the time limit to file normally will be granted.

The annual assessment is made by various local tax assessment offices and independent, locally elected boards, which notify the taxpayer if taxable income is determined to deviate from what was submitted in the tax return.

Payment of tax

Companies are required to make advance payments of tax on 15 February and 15 April in the year following the income year. The two payments should together cover all of the expected corporate tax to be assessed. Any balance must be paid three weeks after the assessment has been made public (i.e., in early autumn of the year following the relevant accounting year).

Corporate taxes in Oman

For more information, contact:

Russell Aycock
PricewaterhouseCoopers
Hatat House
Suites 205-210
Wadi Adai, Muscat
Oman
Tel: +968 24 559 110
Email: russell.aycock@om.pwc.com

Significant developments

The new tax law titled "Income Tax Law of Oman" promulgated by Royal Decree 28/2009 became effective 1 January 2010.

The new tax law replaces the Company Income Tax Law No. 47/81 and the Profit Tax Law on Commercial and Industrial establishments No. 77/89.

The new tax law covers all taxable entities which include:

- Omani establishments;
- Omani companies; and
- Permanent establishments including branches of foreign companies.

The major changes introduced in the new tax law are highlighted below:

- Under the prior law, Oman followed a territorial concept of taxation, although in practice the tax authorities sought to tax income arising outside Oman. The new law has effectively replaced the territorial concept with a global basis of taxation. Under the new law, companies formed in Oman will now be taxed on their global (worldwide) income. Foreign taxes paid are allowed as a deduction (subject to limitation) under the new law.
- The definition of the term permanent establishment (PE) is expanded and now includes a stipulation that a stay of 90 days or more during any 12-month period is deemed to create a PE in Oman for persons (legal or natural) who render consulting or other services.
- Under the old law, branches of foreign companies were taxed at rates ranging from 5% to 30%. Under the new law, these branches are taxed at the same rates as Omani companies. This rate is 12% on taxable profits over OMR (Omani Rial) 30,000.
- New rates for calculating tax depreciation have been specified and the concept of "blocks of assets" has been introduced, in which assets falling under the same rates of depreciation are pooled together.
- Finance and leasing companies are treated as banks for purposes of allowing a deduction for loan loss provisions.
- Executive regulations to clarify positions on head office expenses, shareholders loans, thin capitalisation rules and related party transactions are expected to be issued by the end of 2010.

Taxes on corporate income

Effective 1 January 2010 (tax year 2010), the rate of tax has been made uniform for all types of business entities, regardless of whether it is a corporate entity and/or whether it is registered.

The tax rate is as follows:

Taxable profits	Rates %
First OMR 30,000	Nil
Over OMR 30,000	12

Special provisions are applicable to the taxation of income derived from the sale of petroleum. The tax rate specified for such companies is 55%. However, the tax rates are applied on income as determined by the individual Exploration and Production Sharing Agreement entered into between the government of Oman and the company engaged in the sale of petroleum. Under these agreements, the government pays the company's share of income tax from amounts withheld from the government's share of production. Therefore, the income tax is not actually borne by the company.

Corporate residence

The Income Tax Law (Royal Decree 28/2009) seeks to tax worldwide income of entities formed in Oman, and the Oman source income of branches and other forms of permanent establishments. The term "resident" is not defined in the tax law.

Permanent establishment (PE) is defined in very broad terms and includes places of sale, places of management, branches, offices, factories, workshops, mines, quarries, and building sites for construction. However, the mere use of storage or display facilities does not constitute a permanent establishment. The definition of PE references carrying on business in Oman either directly or through a dependent agent.

Additionally, the definition now stipulates that a total stay of 90 days during a 12-month period creates a PE in Oman. However this 90 day period would apply to rendering of consultancy services or other services only.

Under this definition, while the sale of goods into Oman will not be deemed to be a taxable activity, a contract for the supply and installation of equipment is likely to attract tax. By the same criterion, services rendered by personnel visiting Oman will be treated as taxable activities, applying the 90 day rule.

Other taxes

No other taxes are levied on sales or profits other than the withholding taxes discussed below.

There is no value-added tax or sales tax in Oman.

Customs duty of 5% of cost, insurance and freight (CIF) value applies to most non-Gulf Corporation Council (GCC) source goods. Exemptions apply for certain food items, medical supplies, etc.

Oman

Municipal taxes apply to the following items:

* Property rents (3%);
* Hotel occupancy (5%); and
* Leisure and cinema houses (10%).

Branch income

Branches of foreign entities (regardless of country) are subject to tax at the rate of 12% on income over OMR 30,000. The tax rate for branches is now the same as that for Omani legal entities. This change is effective 1 January 2010.

Rules for the deduction of head office expenses for branches are expected to be changed. New executive regulations providing guidance are expected shortly.

Income determination

Inventory valuation
Inventory should be valued using a method that complies with International Accounting Standards.

Capital gains
Gains on sales of securities listed on the Muscat Securities Market are exempt from taxation. A recent Supreme Court ruling held that gains on transfers of other assets are taxable as ordinary income.

Inter-company dividends
Dividends received from Omani entities are exempt from taxation. Foreign source dividends are taxable. Foreign source dividends are taxed as the same rates as corporate income.

Foreign income
Worldwide income of an entity formed in Oman is taxed in Oman. Credit for foreign taxes paid is given under the law; however this may not exceed the amount of Omani tax payable on such income.

Stock dividends
There are no provisions in the tax law which address stock dividends.

Illegal payments
Payment of bribes, kickbacks and other illegal payments is not deductible.

Capital or revenue
The law does not recognise a difference between capital receipt and a revenue receipt.

Interest, rent/royalty income
Interest income is taxable as business income. Similarly rental income and royalties are taxed as business income.

Unrealised gains or losses
Unrealised exchange gains are not taxable. Similarly any unrealised loss is not deductible from the total taxable income.

Deductions

Depreciation and depletion
Depreciation is taken on a straight-line basis on the following classes of assets at the annual rates shown.

Asset	Rate %
Permanent buildings	4
Semi-permanent buildings	15
Docks, sea barriers in ports, pipelines, roads and railway lines	10
Aircraft and ships	15
Hospital buildings, educational establishments and equipment for scientific research	100

The rate of depreciation allowed is doubled in the case of buildings used for industrial purposes.

The tax law now provides for calculation of depreciation on a net book value basis for the following class of assets. A "pooling" concept has been introduced, whereby assets subject to same rate of depreciation may be pooled together for purposes of depreciation.

	Rate %
1st pool comprising machinery and equipment, includes: computer software installations furniture & fixtures vehicles	33.33
2nd pool comprising drilling equipment	10
3rd pool comprising "other machinery and equipment" not included above	15

Net operating losses
Carryforward of losses is limited to five years except in the case of companies that incurred losses during a mandatory tax-exempt period, where the losses may be carried forward indefinitely for set-off against future profits.

Payments to foreign affiliates
Payments to foreign affiliates normally receive in-depth scrutiny from the tax authorities. Accordingly, proper documentation should be obtained in order to establish that these transactions are made at an arm's-length basis.

Social security payments
Social security contributions paid by employers in respect of employees may also be deducted. There are no other indirect taxes such as VAT or sales tax.

Start-up expenses
Expenses incurred before the commencement of business are allowed as a deduction in the first taxable year (or period).

Oman

Interest expenses

Deduction of expenses incurred for the purpose of earning income is generally allowed. Interest expense is allowed for loans from unrelated parties or on loans from banks. Interest paid to related parties is allowed only to the extent the loan terms are at arm's length.

Meals, entertainment, officers' compensation, etc.

All expenses incurred for the generation of gross total income are allowed. There are no specific restrictions on deduction for expenses like meals and entertainment, compensation for officers and life insurance payments for employees. There are limits on the deductibility of directors' fees.

Pension payments

The law provides a deduction for contributions towards pension funds, subject to the executive regulations that are expected to be issued shortly.

Fines and penalties

Civil fines and penalties are not deductible.

Other significant items/restrictions on allowable expenses

The Law has imposed restrictions on the deductibility of certain expenses. The principal items affected are the following:

- Sponsorship fees paid to Omani sponsors are restricted to 5% of net taxable income before sponsorship fees. Net taxable income is determined after setting off any losses carried forward.
- Charges or expenses allocated from the head office or other group companies are currently restricted to the lower of the following:
  - Expenses allocated to Oman operations;
  - Average of such expenses approved for the Oman operations during the three years immediately preceding the most recent taxable year subject to assessment; or
  - 3% of the total income derived from Oman operations during the year subject to assessment. This percentage is increased to 5% in respect of branches of foreign banks and insurance companies and to 10% in respect of operations of major industrial companies that use the latest and most advanced production techniques, pursue scientific research, provide technical assistance, or use patents that require exchange of information and technical assistance with their associates. The Minister of Finance has discretionary authority to increase this percentage above 10%, but such authority is exercised very rarely.
- Executive regulations on head office expenses are expected by the end of 2010. These regulations may change the treatment and percentages described above. Commissions paid by insurance companies are restricted to 25% of net premiums collected.
- Amounts charged to the profit and loss account for creating provisions in respect of bad debts, stock obsolescence, warranties, and similar types of contingencies are not tax deductible. Deduction is allowed only at the time of write-off. However provisions created by licensed banks in respect of bad debts are allowable within the limits approved/required by the Central Bank of Oman.
- Leasing companies are treated on par with banks as far as deduction for loan loss provision is concerned. Leasing companies are allowed deductions for loan loss provisions subject to the limits or recommendations of the Central Bank of Oman.

- Losses arising on sale of investments listed on the Muscat Securities Market are not allowed as a deduction from taxable income.
- Any expenses or costs which have been incurred to generate income exempted from tax are not allowed as a deduction from taxable income.
- Charitable donations are limited to specified institutions and organisations and are subject to an overall limitation of 5% of total income.
- Amounts paid as tax consultancy or advisory fees are disallowed.

Group taxation

Businesses are taxed as separate entities and the tax law does not recognise group taxation.

Transfer pricing regime

The new tax law proposes to issue executive regulations that would define the transfer pricing policies. Under prior law, there were no defined policies on transfer pricing, though the tax authorities by practice followed arm's-length principles in most cases.

Inter-company payments

All inter-company payments are scrutinised in detail to ensure that the profits are not transferred to avoid payment of tax.

Thin capitalisation

The new tax law proposes to issue executive regulations that will define the thin capitalisation rules. Under the previous law, there were no defined policies on thin capitalisation, though the tax authorities by practice did look into the terms of loans and interest payments in most cases.

Controlled foreign companies

There is no controlled foreign company regime.

Tax incentives

Exempt activities

Income from the principal activities listed below is exempt from tax, if an exemption is applied for and obtained:

- Industry and mining;
- Export of products manufactured or processed locally;
- Operation of hotels or tourist villages;
- Agriculture and animal husbandry and the processing of agricultural produce;
- Fishing and fish processing and aquaculture; and
- University education, college or institutes of higher studies, private schools, nurseries, training colleges and institutes.

Period of exemption

The exemption is valid for a period of five years from the date of commencement of production or the practice of activities and may be made subject to such conditions as the Minister of Commerce and industry may specify. The exemption is renewable for a period not exceeding five years, subject to approval by the Financial Affairs and Energy Resources Council.

Oman

Exempt incomes

- Dividends received from an Omani company.
- Profits or gains on disposal of securities listed on Muscat Securities Market.
- Omani marine companies, whether wholly owned by Omanis or with foreign and Omani ownership and registered in Oman, are exempt from tax. Foreign marine companies conducting activities in Oman through an authorised agent are exempted from tax with effect from the date of commencement of activity provided that reciprocal treatment is afforded by the country of the foreign company.
- Income realised by foreign airlines carrying on business through establishments in Oman is exempt from tax. This exemption is limited to the extent of the income from operating airplanes for international transport, provided reciprocal treatment is accorded in the airline's home country.
- Income realised by investment funds established in Oman under the Capital Market Authority Law or established overseas for dealing in shares and securities listed on Muscat Security Market is exempt.
- Foreign companies engaged in oil and gas exploration activities, while taxable under the law, normally have their tax obligations discharged by the government under the terms of the Exploration and Production Sharing Agreement.
- Foreign companies working for the government in projects deemed to be of national importance may be able to negotiate a tax protection clause whereby any tax paid by them is reimbursed by the government.
- Foreign taxes paid to a country with whom Oman has a double tax treaty are eligible for a credit to the maximum of the Oman tax that would have been payable on such income. The taxpayer is required to submit an application to the Secretariat General for Taxation to claim such credit.

Withholding taxes (WHT)

WHT was introduced under an amendment effective November 2 1996. The new tax law effective 1 January 2010 made certain changes to the categories that attract withholding taxes.

Foreign companies that do not have a PE in Oman for tax purposes and that derive income from Oman in the nature of the following are subject to withholding tax at 10% of gross income from such sources:

- Royalties;
- Consideration for research and development;
- Consideration for use of or right to use computer software; and
- Management fees.

Such withholding tax is required to be withheld by the Omani-based company and paid to the tax department within 14 days of the end of the month in which tax is deducted or payments are due or made to the foreign company.

There is no withholding tax on dividends and interest payments.

The term royalty has been defined under the law to include consideration for the use of intellectual property, including computer software, cinematography films, tapes, discs, or any other media, patents, trademarks, drawings etc. The term further includes consideration for using industrial, commercial or scientific equipment and consideration for information concerning industrial, commercial or scientific experience or consideration for granting rights to exploit mining or other natural resources.

Double tax avoidance agreements

At present, Oman has double taxation treaties with France, India, Tunisia, the United Kingdom, Mauritius, Pakistan, Algeria, Egypt, Lebanon, China, Yemen, South Africa, Russia, Seychelles, Singapore, Thailand, Vietnam, Canada, Korea, Iran, Turkey, Belarus, Moldova, Brunei, Belgium, Morocco and Uzbekistan. There are also agreements with various countries which are pending ratification.

Under the new tax law, in respect to international tax treaties, foreign taxes paid are eligible for a credit to the maximum of the Oman tax that would have been payable on such income. The taxpayer is required to submit an application to the Secretariat General for Taxation to claim such credit.

Tax administration

Returns

The tax year is the calendar year. Assessments can be made on the basis of a year-end other than 31 December, provided permission is granted in advance by the Omani tax authorities and the company then adheres to the year-end on a consistent basis.

A provisional declaration of tax must be submitted in the prescribed form within three months from the end of the accounting period to which it relates. The final annual return of income should be submitted in the prescribed format within six months from the end of the accounting period to which it relates. Reasonable time extensions can be sought and are normally provided for filing the provisional and annual returns of income but these do not defer payment of tax which will be subject to additional tax at 1% per month from the due date to the actual date of payment.

In the case of companies having a paid-up capital in excess of OMR 20,000, the annual return of income should be accompanied by audited accounts signed by an auditor registered in Oman. The law requires accounts to be drawn up in accordance with the International Financial Reporting Standards (IFRS) consistently applied. It specifically provides for accrual accounting unless prior permission of the Secretary General of Taxation (the Secretary General) has been obtained. The accounts must be submitted in local currency unless prior approval of the Secretary General has been obtained for submitting them in foreign currency.

Delay or failure in submitting the provisional or annual returns may attract a penalty of not less than OMR 100 and not more than OMR 1,000.

Failure to file the provisional or annual returns of income may result in an estimated profit assessment by the Secretary General.

Failure to submit audited accounts as required under the Law is deemed to result in an incomplete annual return of income and may attract an estimated profit assessment.

The law confers wide powers on the Secretary General for requesting information. Experience has shown that notwithstanding the presentation of audited accounts, the tax department requests very detailed information and supporting documentation relating to revenue and expenses. Failure to provide such information or the provision

O

Oman

of incorrect information can result in an additional assessment by the Secretary General and/or various penalties on the company and/or the officer responsible for providing the information.

Objections and appeals

A company has a right to object to any assessment issued by the Secretary General. The objection document should be prepared in writing (in English and in Arabic) and filed with the office of the Secretary General for Taxation within 45 days from the date of assessment. The Secretary General is required to give a judgment within five months extendable up to another five months at his discretion from the date of receiving the objection. The tax demanded may be kept in abeyance on request. No additional tax is payable until the Secretary General issues the judgment.

The company has the right to file a petition against the judgment of the Secretary General for Taxation with the Tax Committee at the Ministry of Finance within 45 days of the date of the judgment. The petition should be in Arabic, however, before filing the petition the company must pay the tax demanded or include a request to be granted dispensation from paying the additional tax demanded in the judgment. The Tax Committee may, when the company furnishes a bank guarantee, grant such dispensation. In practice the Tax Committee takes one to two years to issue its judgment.

The company has the right to appeal against the judgment given by the Tax Committee within 45 days of the date of the judgment. The appeal is to be filed with the Court of First Instance. The appeal should be in Arabic, and the company must be represented by an authorised lawyer. However, before filing the appeal, the company must pay the fee to the Secretariat of the Court.

The final judicial authority is the Supreme Court, and petitions can be filed with this court within 45 days of receiving a decision from the Court of First Instance. All proceedings in the above courts are in Arabic.

Maintenance of records

The Law requires accounting records and supporting documentation to be maintained for 10 years after the end of the accounting period to which these records relate.

Payment of tax

Any tax estimated to be payable in respect of an accounting period should be paid with the provisional assessment and "topped up" for any additional amount computed as payable following submission of the annual return of income. Failure to pay taxes by the due date attracts interest at the rate of 1% per month from the date on which such tax was due to the date of payment.

The difference between the amount paid and the amount assessed, subject to filing of an objection, should be paid within one month from the date of the assessment. The additional amount assessed attracts interest at the rate of 1% per month from the date on which such tax was due to the date of payment.

Under the Law, the Secretary General has the authority, with the approval of the Minister and the Tax Committee, to sequester and sell the assets of a taxable entity to recover the taxes due.

If decisive proof is presented to the Secretary General that any person has paid tax for any year exceeding the tax due and payable for such tax year as finally settled, such person has the right to recover the tax. However, if any tax has become payable by such person in respect of another tax year, the excess amount will be adjusted against the future tax liability. Any request for recovery must be presented within five years from the end of the tax year to which it relates.

Where the taxpayer fails to declare correct income in the tax return for any tax year, the Secretary General may impose a fine not exceeding 25% of the difference between the amount on the basis of the correct taxable income and the amount of tax as per the return submitted.

The tax authorities have a period of up to five years from the end of the year in which a tax return is submitted to complete the assessment for that tax year. However where the entity has not submitted any tax return, the tax authorities have a period of 10 years to complete the assessments.

Other issues

Exchange controls
There are no exchange controls on any payments made from Oman.

Choice of business entity
Basically there are two common forms of doing business in Oman:

* Subsidiary of a foreign company (up to 70% foreign holding); or
* Branch of a foreign company.

Mergers and acquisitions (M&A)
There are no provisions in the tax law concerning M&A. M&A law in general is not well developed.

O

For more information, contact:

Sohail Hasan
A.F. Ferguson & Co
State Life Building 1-C
Off: I. I. Chundrigar Road
Karachi 74000
Pakistan
Tel: +92 21 32419322
Email: sohail.hasan@pk.pwc.com

Significant developments

The following significant developments in corporate taxation occurred in Pakistan in the past two years:

- Remittance of profits by a branch of foreign company engaged in the exploration and production business are excluded from the definition of "dividend";
- Minimum tax on the revenue of resident companies is reintroduced;
- The administrative structure of Pakistan's tax authorities was amended – the Income Tax Ordinance 2001, Sales Tax Act 1990 and Federal Excise Act 2005 have been brought in harmony with each other;
- A first year allowance at the rate of 90% is allowed on the cost of plant, machinery and equipment installed for generation of alternate energy and put to use after 1 July 2009:
- Salaried taxpayers with income of more than PKR 500,000 are now required to e-file their returns: and
- Tribunal (second appellate forum) of income tax and sales tax are combined.

Taxes on corporate income

The federal corporate tax rates on taxable income for the tax year ending after 1 July 2007 onwards are as follows:

	%
Banking company	35
Public company other than a banking company	35
Any other company	35
Small company	20

The term "public company" implies a company listed on any stock exchange in Pakistan or one in which not less than 50% of the shares are held by the federal government or a public trust.

In the case of a modaraba (see Other significant items for a definition), except relating to trading activities, income is exempt from tax, provided that 90% of its profit is distributed to the certificate holders as cash dividends.

The final tax regime (FTR) for resident taxpayers, a presumptive tax scheme where taxes are withheld at the source on the sale of goods, execution of contracts or collected at the time of import (for other than industrial raw materials) is considered a final tax liability in respect of income arising from the sale, contract or import.

In the case of exports, tax collected at the time of realisation of foreign-exchange proceeds is treated as final tax for that income.

The FTR is also applicable to non-resident taxpayers, at their option. However, it is only applicable in cases of receipts on account of the execution of a contract for construction, assembly or installation, including a contract for the supply of management activities in relation to such project as well as, certain contracts for services and contract for advertisement services rendered by TV satellite channels.

Tax at the rate of 10% is payable on remittance of profits by a branch of a non-resident company to its head office, except for companies engaged in oil and gas exploration and production business.

Corporate residence

A company is resident in Pakistan if it is incorporated or formed by or under the law of Pakistan or if the control and management of its affairs is situated wholly in Pakistan in that year. The term "company" includes a trust, a co-operative society, a finance society or any other society established or constituted by or under any law, a corporate body incorporated outside Pakistan as well as any foreign association, incorporated or unincorporated, which the Central Revenue authorities may declare to be a company.

Other taxes

Value-added tax (VAT)
VAT (locally termed as "sales tax") is ordinarily levied at 16% on the value of goods, unless specifically exempt, after allowing related input credits. Federal excise duty is levied on certain types of manufacturing, import of goods and rendering of services (telecommunication services are levied at a VAT rate of 19.5%).

In the case of sale or transfer of immovable property, stamp duty is payable (with varying rates on the basis of location of the property) on the value of the property.

Branch income

The rates of tax for a branch of a company incorporated outside Pakistan are the same as those applicable on resident companies, other than public and banking companies. Tax at the rate of 10% is levied on the transfer of profits to the head office, with an exception for companies engaged in oil and gas exploration and production business.

Payments to a branch in Pakistan of a non-resident are subject to deduction of tax at the source, on the same basis as a resident in the case of sale of goods, rendering of professional services and execution of contracts. In other circumstances, a reduced/Nil withholding rate certificate can be obtained from the Commissioner of Income Tax.

Pakistan has signed agreements for avoidance of double taxation with over 60 countries.

Pakistan

Income determination

Inventory valuation
Inventories are to be stated at the lower of cost or market. The first-in, first-out (FIFO) and average methods are accepted. Conformity of methods used for book and tax reporting is desirable, and the method used should be consistently applied.

Depreciation is to be calculated on a reducing-balance method. Extra depreciation is also available in the first year of acquisition of capital asset. However, total depreciation is not to exceed the cost of the capital asset. Depreciation rates are discussed under "Deductions".

Capital gain
Capital gain on the sale of immovable property, on which depreciation is not allowed, is not taxable. Gain on the disposal of shares of a resident company or a non-resident company, whose assets wholly or principally consist of immovable property situated in Pakistan or rights to explore/exploit natural resources in Pakistan, shall be Pakistan-source income. Capital gains on the sale of shares of public companies or modaraba (profit sharing) certificates are exempt from tax up to the assessment year ending on or before 30 June 2010. Capital gain, other than on statutory depreciable assets, realised within one year of acquisition is fully taxed; after one year, 75% of such gains are taxed and 25% are exempt.

Capital gains on statutory depreciable assets (other than immovable property) are chargeable to tax as normal business income in the year of sale. Gains are measured as the difference between the sale proceeds and the tax written-down value of the relevant asset sold.

In the case of an asset disposal transaction that is on a non-arm's-length basis, fair market value of the asset shall be taken to be the consideration received by the seller, as well as the cost for the buyer.

Where assets are transferred outside Pakistan, the original cost is treated as the sale price, which means that the entire depreciation is recaptured at the time of export, except if the assets are used in oil or gas exploration, in which case only the initial depreciation is recaptured.

No gain or loss shall be taken to arise on disposal of an asset by a resident company to another resident company, if certain conditions are met. The required conditions include, inter alia, that the transferor is 100% owned by the transferee or vice versa or both companies are 100% owned by a third company, and the transferee income is not exempt in year of transfer. The scheme of arrangement must be approved by the Securities and Exchange Commission of Pakistan or State Bank of Pakistan.

Any distribution to the shareholders of a company to the extent that it relates to undistributed profits is treated as dividend.

Capital loss can be offset only against capital gains. Unabsorbed capital loss can be carried forward for adjustment against capital gains for six years.

Tax on dividend income

	%
Public company or an insurance company	10*
All other cases	10*

*Or lower treaty rate

The above deduction at source shall be a full and final discharge of tax liability on dividend income.

Foreign income
A resident company is taxed on its worldwide income and on its foreign income as earned. Double taxation of foreign income is avoided by means of foreign tax credits; this relief is allowed to the resident company on the doubly taxed income at the lower of the Pakistan or foreign tax rate. Undistributed income of a non-resident subsidiary is not subject to tax.

Stock dividends
Stock declared by resident companies is exempt.

Other significant items
Liabilities allowed as a tax deduction in a tax year and remain unpaid for three subsequent years are deemed to be income in the first tax year following the said three-year period. Such items are then allowed as a deduction in the year the liability is discharged.

Royalties received by non-residents are deemed to accrue or arise in Pakistan and are taxable if paid by a resident in Pakistan or borne by a permanent establishment (PE) of a non-resident in Pakistan.

Income from "fees for technical services" (FTS) is deemed to accrue or arise in Pakistan if paid by a resident in Pakistan or borne by a PE of a non-resident in Pakistan. FTS means any consideration for the rendering of any managerial, technical or consultancy services (including the provision of the services of technical or other personnel), but does not include consideration for any construction, assembly or like project undertaken by the recipient or consideration that would be income of the recipient chargeable under the head salary.

Withholding tax (WHT) on payments of royalty and FTS, when royalty or FTS are not attributable to a PE in Pakistan, is 15% or a lower treaty rate, of royalty or gross fees. The tax withheld would be deemed to be the final tax liability of the non-resident. In the case of a non-resident where royalty or FTS is attributable to a PE in Pakistan, the amount of royalty/FTS shall be chargeable to tax as normal income, and withholding on payments can be avoided subject to approval of the commissioner. If a reduced rate is available in a tax treaty, such rate would be applicable.

Modaraba (profit sharing) is a financing vehicle which enables a management company to control and manage the business of a modaraba company with a minimum of 10% equity participation. The management company is entitled to remuneration based on an agreed percentage (but not exceeding 10%) of annual profits of the modaraba business. A modaraba can be for a specific purpose or many purposes and for a limited or unlimited period. The income of a modaraba not relating to trading activity is free from tax, if 90% of its profits are distributed as a cash dividend.

Pakistan

Agricultural income is exempt from income tax.

Deductions

Pre-commencement expenditure
Expenditure incurred before the commencement of a business wholly and exclusively to derive income chargeable to tax can be deducted over a period of five years.

Intangibles
The cost incurred on acquisition of a patent, invention, design or model, secret formula or process, copyright, software, quota, license, intellectual property or other like property or rights and any expenditure that provides an advantage or benefit for a period of more than one year is allowed as deduction on a straight-line basis over the useful life of the asset, but not exceeding a period of 10 years.

Depreciation
Normal depreciation is allowed at the following prescribed rates by applying the reducing-balance method.

	%
Buildings	10
Furniture	15
Machinery and equipment, including motor vehicles and ships	15
Computer hardware, including monitors and printers	30
Aircraft and aero engines	30
Below-ground installation in mineral oil concerns	100
Offshore platform	20

All depreciable assets put into service for the first time in Pakistan during a tax year – other than road transport vehicles not plying for hire, furniture including fixtures, plant and machinery used previously in Pakistan or plant and machinery for which deduction has been allowed under another section of this ordinance, for the entire cost of the asset – shall be entitled to an initial allowance at 50% of the cost of the asset.

Book depreciation need not conform to tax depreciation. Unabsorbed tax depreciation not set-off against the income of the year is carried forward and added to depreciation of the assets of the same business in the following year. Tax depreciation can be carried forward without limit until fully absorbed.

Net operating losses
Operating loss may be carried forward and set-off against the profits of the succeeding six years of the same business in which the loss was incurred. Unabsorbed depreciation can be carried forward indefinitely.

Carried forward loss of an entity in the case of group relief cannot be utilised if the ownership of the holding company is reduced to less than 55% and 75% if one of the companies is a listed company or none of the companies is a listed company, respectively.

Business loss can be carried forward up to a period of six years in the case of the amalgamation of two companies, with the condition that the same business is continued for a minimum period of five years.

Carryback of loss is not permitted.

Taxes
Taxes on income are not deductible. Sales tax and excise tax are tax-deductible.

Other significant items
The deductibility of a head office expenditure of a non-resident taxpayer is limited to the same proportion of total head office expenditure as the Pakistan turnover has with the total world turnover. However, such domestic rules are overridden if the branch is a tax resident of a country having an agreement for avoidance of double taxation (treaty) and that treaty provides a different basis.

Expenditure on scientific research incurred in Pakistan wholly and exclusively for the purpose of deriving income chargeable to tax is an allowable expenditure.

Exchange gains and loss on foreign currency loans specifically obtained for acquiring an asset are adjusted against the depreciable cost of the asset.

Any lease rental incurred by a person in the tax year to a scheduled bank, financial institution, approved modaraba or approved leasing company shall be a deductible expense. However, financial charges paid for the above-mentioned leases are added back into the taxable income of the company.

Group taxation

A locally incorporated holding company and subsidiary of a 100% owned group may be taxed as one group by giving an irrevocable option for taxation as one fiscal unit. The relief is not available for losses prior to formation of the group. The group is available if the companies are designated as entitled to avail group relief by the Securities and Exchange Commission of Pakistan.

Any company that is the subsidiary of a holding company may surrender its loss for the year to its holding company or its subsidiary, or between another subsidiary of the holding company, provided that the holding company holds directly 55% or more capital of the subsidiary, if one of the companies is a listed company. However, if none of the companies is a listed company, the holding requirement is 75% or more. The loss can be surrendered for a maximum of three years and the required holding is for at least five years.

Tax incentives

Any tax relief from Pakistani income tax, which is provided in any other law and not provided for in the Income Tax Ordinance or the treaty, is not valid.

P

Pakistan

Inward investment and capital investment

Incentives are available as follows:

- Profits and gains derived from an electric power generation project set up in Pakistan are exempt;
- Profits and gains derived by a company from the export of computer software, IT services or IT enabled services are exempt through to 30 June 2016; and
- Profits and gains derived by a joint venture capital company registered under the Venture Capital Companies and Funds Management Rules 2000, between 1 July 2000 and 30 June 2007, are exempt.

Small companies

Incorporation of companies as small businesses is encouraged. A small company has been defined to mean a company which:

- Is registered on or after 1 July 2005 under the Companies Ordinance of 1984;
- Has a paid-up capital plus undistributed reserves not exceeding PKR 25 million;
- Has an annual turnover not exceeding PKR 250 million; and
- Is not formed by splitting up or the reconstitution of business already in existence.

Income is taxed at a special rate of 20%.

Withholding taxes (WHT)

Resident corporations paying certain types of income must withhold as follows:

Recipient (1, 2, 3)	Dividends %	Interest %	Royalties %
Resident individuals	10	10	N/A
Resident corporations	10	10	Nil
Non-resident individuals:			
Non-treaty	10 (10)	10	15
Treaty	10 (10)	(4)	(4)
Non-resident corporations:			
Non-treaty	10	(5)	15
Treaty:	(6)	(7)	
Austria	10	(8)	20
Bangladesh	10	15	15
Belgium	10	15	20, 15
Bosnia and Herzegovina	10	20	15
Canada	10	25	20, 15
China	10	10	12.5
Denmark	10	15	12
Egypt	15, 30	15	15
Finland	12, 15, 20	10, 15	10
France	10	30	(9)
Germany	10	10, 20	10
Hungary	10	15	15
Indonesia	10	15	15

Recipient (1, 2, 3)	Dividends %	Interest %	Royalties %
Ireland, Rep. of	10	(8)	(9)
Italy	(8)	30	30
Japan	3.75	0, 30	(9)
Kazakhstan	10	12.5	15
Korea, Rep. of	10	12.5	10
Kuwait	10	Nil, 10	10
Libya	(8)	(8)	(8)
Malaysia	10	15	15
Malta	10	10	10
Mauritius	10	10	12.5
Netherlands	10	10, 15, 20	15, 5
Nigeria	10	15	15
Norway	10	10	12
Oman	10, 12.5	10	12.5
Philippines	10	15	25
Poland	10	(8)	20, 15
Qatar	10	10	10
Romania	10	10	12.5
Singapore	10	12.5	10
Sri Lanka	10	10	20
Sweden	10	15	10
Switzerland	10	30	(9)
Thailand	10	10, 25	10, 20
Turkmenistan	10	10	10
Turkey	10	10	10
Tunisia	10	13	10
United Kingdom	10	15	12.5
United States	8.75	(8)	(9)
United Arab Emirates	10	10	12
Uzbekistan	10	10	15
Yemen	10	10	10

Notes

1. This table is a summary only and does not reproduce all the provisions that may be relevant in determining the application of WHT in each tax treaty.
2. Resident and non-resident imply tax status.
3. Individuals and companies are required to render annual returns of income and pay tax at the applicable rates. Credit is given for WHT deducted.
4. Withholding rates for interest and royalties given to non-resident corporations (treaty countries) also apply to non-resident individuals.
5. The withholding rate for companies would be 30%.
6. The following remarks for dividends should be noted:
   a. The intercorporate rate of tax on dividends received by a foreign corporation is 10%; corresponding, treaty withholding rates in excess of 10% have been specified;
   b. The rates given in the table for treaty countries relate to recipient corporations. The maximum rate, as stated above, in respect of intercorporate dividends is 10%. The lower rates are expressly provided in respect of dividends paid to a parent/associated

Pakistan

corporation that has a certain minimum holding in a Pakistan industrial undertaking. The level of holding are noted:

	%
Japan	33.33
United States	50

7. Certain treaties provide for tax exemption of interest paid to the government or the central bank of the contracting state and on foreign loans specifically approved by the federal government.
8. No concession is provided under the treaty.
9. A fair and reasonable consideration for royalties is exempt from tax, provided the recipient does not have a PE in Pakistan.
10. Intercorporate dividend where companies are entitled to group relief is exempt.

Tax administration

Returns and assessment

All companies are required to file an income tax return each year by 31 December for the preceding financial year (1 July through to 30 June) by accounting for business income on accrual basis. Tax authorities are empowered to approve a special year-end. If the special year ends on 31 December, then the tax return is required to be filed by 30 September following the year-end.

An across-the-board self-assessment scheme is in place whereby assessment is taken to be finalised upon filing of the return. The Commissioner, however, has powers to amend the assessment if he believes the ordinance has been incorrectly applied or otherwise has definite information that the assessment made is incorrect. These powers are to be exercised within a prescribed time frame. In the case of transactions between associates/related parties, the Commissioner can substitute the transaction value with the fair market consideration. The Commissioner is also empowered to determine tax liability according to the substance of the transaction, disregarding formal arrangements between the parties.

Payment of tax

Companies are required to pay advance tax on the basis of tax liability of the immediately preceding tax year in respect of their income (excluding capital gains and presumptive income). The advance tax is to be paid after adjusting the taxes withheld at source (other than the tax withheld relating to final tax regime).

Advance tax is required to be paid in four quarterly instalments on or before 15 October, 15 January, 15 April and 15 June in each financial year. Credit for tax paid in a tax year shall be allowed against tax liability of that year.

The total tax liability is to be discharged at the time of filing the return of income.

Advance taxes and taxes withheld are adjustable against the tax payable with the return of income.

Corporate taxes in Panama

For more information, contact:

Angel Dapena Lambridge
PricewaterhouseCoopers
Avenida Samuel Lewis y
Calle 55 E
Urbanización Obarrio, Panamá
Panama
Tel: +507 206 9200
Email: angel.dapena@pa.pwc.com

Significant developments

Significant developments on taxation issues, mostly initiated after the second quarter of 2009, have taken place under the new Panamanian government of President Martinelli's Administration.

Panama has totally changed its international taxation policy, and plans to sign 12 double taxation treaties in 2010. Currently, tax treaties with Mexico, Italy and the Netherlands have been signed.

The National Deputies Assembly also passed three laws amending tax matters: Law No. 49 of 2009, Law No. 69 of 2009 and Law No. 8 of 2010.

Taxes on corporate income

As of 1 January 2010, corporations are subject to income tax at a fixed rate of 27.5%. Beginning in 2011, this rate will be reduced to 25%. Certain businesses and the related parties that render services to them will be subject to a 30% tax rate until 31 December 2011. Beginning on 1 January 2012 this tax rate will be reduced to 27.5%, and from 1 January 2014 will be reduced even further to 25%.

The higher tax rate (i.e., the 30% rate) applies to either the generation or distribution of energy; telecommunication services in general; insurance; reinsurance; financial institutions regulated by Law No. 42 of 2001; cement industries; the operation and management of gambling games; mining in general and entities dedicated to banking activities in Panama.

For companies in which the State owns more than 40% of the stock the tax rate will remain at 30%.

The tax base (amount to which the tax rate will apply) for companies whose taxable income is greater than USD 1,500,000 will be the greater of:

- Net taxable income calculated on the normal basis, or
- 4.67% of the gross taxable income (excludes exempted and non-taxable income and foreign-source income) – this is called the Alternate Calculation of Income Tax ("Calculo Alternativo del Impuesto sobre la Renta" or CAIR).

P

Panama

If the entity's tax year results in a loss due to the alternative calculation, the taxpayer may request to the Tax Administration (the General Directorate of Revenues, i.e., DGI or "Dirección General de Ingresos") not to be subject to the CAIR.

The taxpayer may also request not to apply the CAIR if its effective income tax rate is higher than the applicable income tax rate.

The DGI has a six-month period within which to reach a decision on the request, otherwise the petition will be considered as granted.

Corporate residence

A company is considered as a tax resident when it has been incorporated in Panama, regardless of where the main office is located or whether central management is exercised in Panama or abroad. Entities incorporated abroad may also be registered with the Tax Administration in order to avoid withholdings.

Since the Panamanian income tax is levied based on the territoriality principle, Panamanian income is subject to taxation whether it is received by a resident or non-resident entity. Residency is only relevant to determine if the entity is subject to withholding or not.

Panama does not have permanent establishment rules.

Other taxes

Franchise tax
Franchise income tax must be paid by all corporations on an annual basis. The deadline for payment depends on the date of incorporation of the company. If the company was incorporated on any date between the first six months of the year, the due date for payment will be on 15 July of each year. If it was incorporated in the last six months, the due date will be 15 January of each year.

Non-profit organisations, cooperatives and civil partnerships are not subject to franchise tax.

Movable goods and services transfer tax (ITBMS)
The movable goods and services transfer tax (ITBMS) is the Panamanian value-added tax (VAT).

The general tax rate is currently 5% but will increase to 7% after 30 June 2010.

Alcoholic beverages are taxed at 10% and tobacco and tobacco-derived products are taxed at 15%.

ITBMS is calculated on the value-added through a method of tax credits (ITBMS paid on transactions to produce taxable transactions) and tax debits (ITBMS collected on transactions).

Exports are not taxed and the ITBMS paid to generate the exports may be refunded. The sale of goods such as medicines, foods, and certain products for babies are not taxed, and may allow the supplier to recover the ITBMS as an exporter if certain criteria is met.

Medical services and transportation among other services are not taxed, but do not produce ITBMS credit for the supplier.

Excise tax (selective consumption tax)
The selective consumption tax is applied to goods (jewellery, expensive automobiles, guns, tobacco, alcoholic beverages, etc.) and services that are considered as non-essential (mobile, cable TV or satellite TV). The tax base is the cost, insurance and freight (CIF) price plus import duties for imported items and sales price for all other activities. The tax is levied at only one stage: on the importation of the taxed products, the sale of taxed goods produced in Panama, and for services, it may be levied at the time when the service is invoiced, the service is completely rendered or upon receipt of advance payments, whichever first occurs.

Different tax rates apply depending on the type of service or good, with a minimum of 5% on sodas and 100% on tobacco products.

Custom duties
All goods introduced into the Panamanian territory from another country are subject to customs duties. The duty rates are provided by the Panamanian Customs and Tariffs Office.

Customs duties may only be assessed by authorised customs brokers.

Local municipal tax
Local municipal tax is charged, depending on the gross income generated by the business through the corresponding accounting period; it will also depend on the type of activity being conducted by the corporation. In most cases, it cannot exceed USD 1,000 per month for each activity performed.

Operations notice tax
The notice of operations is an annual tax on equity at a rate of 2%, with a minimum tax amount of USD 100 and a maximum tax amount of USD 60,000.

The tax base is the outcome from total assets less total liabilities (excluding liabilities with related parties abroad).

Stamp duty
Stamp duty is charged at a rate of USD 0.10 per USD 100 (or fraction thereof) of value on non ITBMS taxed transactions.

Branch income

For tax purposes, branches are considered separate entities from the Head Office and must therefore keep accounts separately and will have separate tax liability.

Branches located within the Panamanian territory must pay dividend tax through definitive withholding of 10% over 100% of net taxable income generated by the Panamanian branch, less all income taxes paid by the same corporation in Panama. This amount will be paid jointly on filing the corresponding income tax return.

Panama

Income determination

Tax base
Taxable income is determined by deducting from the Panamanian source income all costs, expenses and non-taxable income applicable and permitted by law. The deductibility of costs and expenses depend on the relation of such costs and expenses with the generation or preservation of income source. Special restrictions will apply to the following:

* Bad debts;
* Depreciation; and
* Donation.

Costs and expenses related to non taxable income are not considered as deductible. Thus, the taxpayer must split the expenses and costs related to taxable transactions from those related to non-taxable transactions. As of 1 July 2010 the expenses and costs allocated to taxed transactions may not exceed the amount from multiplying the portion of taxable income from the total income, by the total costs and expenses. The following deductions are not subject to the deductions cap: deductions on bad debts, donations to the State and non-profit organisations and education institutions (limited to 1% of the taxable income).

In the specific case of companies whose gross taxable income is greater than USD 1,500,000, the tax base will be the greater of the outcome of the aforementioned method or 4.67% of gross taxable income. The taxpayer may request not to pay based on his gross income, in which case the Tax Administration shall grant approval. *See corporate tax for CAIR exemption process.*

Inventory valuation
Inventory should be valued at the start of any business and subsequently at least once every accounting period. All assets must be put together, depending on their nature and indicate different aspects such as: the unit of measurement, the name of the asset, the price of the unit and the total value of units. It shall also include the reference to the accounting records.

Inventories are generally stated at cost and can be valued using the compound average cost method, first-in, first-out (FIFO) method, retailer method, or specific identification method. Since all entities must keep legal records, any adjustment resulting from using different methods of inventory valuation for tax purposes and financial purposes should be recorded and must be reported to the proper authorities. Once a taxpayer adopts a method, they must maintain it for up to five years.

Capital gains
The transfer of real estate property and securities is subject to withholding on the gross transactions amount, but the taxpayer may make a special income tax assessment to pay over the capital gain and may request a rebate of the difference between the withholding and the capital gain.

In the case of the transfer of real estate property the withholding rate is 3% (over the gross transaction amount, or the cadastral value, whichever is greater) and the tax rate on the capital gain is 10%. If the transfer of real estate properties is part of the taxpayer's business, there would only apply a 3.75% tax over the gross transaction or the cadastral value. An additional 2% property transfer tax (non income tax) applies on the gross transaction amount, or the adjusted cadastral value, whichever is greater.

The transfer of securities is subject to a 5% withholding and the tax rate on capital gain is 10%.

The sale of fixed assets is subject to 10% on the capital gain, and there is no withholding tax.

Inter-company dividends
The distribution of dividends derived from income received as dividends from other entities is not subject to income tax or dividend tax as long as the entity that paid the dividend in the first instance was exempt from withholding any dividend tax, or if it was required to, made the corresponding withholding.

Foreign income
As stated previously, Panamanian resident companies are taxed on their income generated within the Panamanian territory. Any other income generated abroad will be exempt from income tax payment, but may be subject to dividend tax.

Dividends
Panamanian legislation establishes that distribution of dividends is subject to definitive withholding, applied at the moment of distribution. Generally dividends are subject to income tax at a rate of 10% rate without taking into consideration the form of payment, types of stock, assets or money.

Dividend tax applies at a 5% rate on dividends paid from foreign source income, from income derived from exports, as well as exempt income from banking account interests and interests and earnings derived from securities issued by the government.

Free zone users are taxed at a 5% rate as well for local source income.

Notwithstanding the aforementioned, if the entity's shares are issued to bearer they will be subject to dividend tax at a rate of 20%.

Dividend tax is not levied if the entity meets one of the following: (a) does not require an operation permit to operate in Panama, (b) does not require an operation key to operate at the Colon Free Zone; (c) is not established in a Petroleum Free Zone; (d) is not established in a free zone or special zone; (e) does not produce Panamanian-source taxable income. Dividend tax also does not apply to dividends paid on income received as a dividend if the entity is not required to withhold dividend tax or if the entity withheld the tax.

A complementary tax applies each tax year that the entity distributes less than 40% of the net profits after income tax. The complementary tax is an advance payment of the dividend tax, calculated on the difference of the distributed dividends and 40% of the net profits after income tax and applies the corresponding tax rate. If complementary tax is paid, when the corresponding dividend is decreed, the entity may offset the paid complementary tax with the dividend tax.

P

Panama

Deductions

Depreciation and depletion

The straight-line and sum-of-the-years-digits methods of depreciation are allowed.

	% Straight -line
Buildings	3⅓% as maximum
Machinery and equipment	33% as maximum
Furniture and fixtures	33% as maximum
Vehicles	33% as maximum

In the case of mines, depletion will be deductible during its useful life or depending on the state contract methodology.

Net operating losses

Losses incurred by common taxpayers may be carried forward and deducted from the taxable profits for the following five years, at a rate of 20% each year, but limited to 50% of taxable income. Loss carrybacks are not allowed. And, losses are not allowed for estimated income tax purposes.

Payments to foreign affiliates

A payment to a foreign entity (including affiliates) in a foreign country will be subject to withholding tax, anytime it represents a cost or expense for the payer. The tax base will be 50% of the remittance and the income tax rate applicable is 27.5%.

Taxes

All income received by foreign entities or corporations located outside Panama, from the performance of any act or service which benefits any person located within the Panamanian territory, (which includes but is not limited to the following: copyrights, royalties, trademarks, patents, know-how, scientific and technological knowledge) will be considered as taxable income generated within the Panamanian territory. Any time these services have a direct effect on the generation of income in Panama, its value has been considered a deductible expense by the person who incurred the expense.

Under the territoriality principle, the following will not be considered as taxable income: all income produced outside Panama, all income generated from operations or services performed outside the Panamanian territory, distribution of dividends from income not generated within the Panamanian territory.

The tax will be calculated by multiplying the corresponding tax rate by 50% of remittances.

Group taxation

In Panama there is no group taxation.

Tax incentives

Free zones

Entities established in free zones may enjoy exemption from import duties on goods, income tax, sales tax, export tax, selective consumption tax derived from royalties on exportation and re-exportation activities. However these incentives may be affected by the World Trade Organization (WTO) rules.

Incentives for exporters

Export Process Zones: Special benefits exist for industries that import semi-manufactured materials for assembly in Panama and export finished products. Benefits consist of duty-free import of raw materials for subsequent export as manufactured products and exemption of income tax. Machinery for these industries may also be imported duty-free. However, these incentives may be affected by the World Trade Organization (WTO) rules.

Tourism, industry and agriculture allowances

The Incentive Law for Tourism Development grants several tax benefits, such as exemption from import duties on certain tourism services, related goods, and from property tax for companies dedicated to tourism, but only for those corporations with a signed tourism agreement with the government. Income tax exemptions may apply in special cases.

In general, income from individuals or corporations that engage in agricultural production activities will be exempted from income tax if annual gross income is lower than USD 250,000.

Forestry plantations are totally exempted from income tax payment until 2018 if the lot planted has been duly registered at the Forestry Registry of the Environmental National Authority and resolution with approval from this authority has been issued.

Special laws

The Panamanian government has enacted special laws regarding tax exemptions for certain activities performed in Panama such as call centres (Law No. 54 of 2001) and tax exemptions for certain appointed areas such as the Panama Pacific Economic Zone (Law No. 41 of 2004) and Law No. 41 of 2007 which creates a special regime for the establishment and operation of Regional Headquarters in Panama.

Withholding taxes (WHT)

Payment to entities abroad

Royalties and commissions on services paid to foreign entities are taxed through the application of the corresponding tax rate (generally 27.5%) over 50% of remittance under the concept of withholding tax (effective tax rate is 13.75%). The taxpayer may decide not to withhold taxes, and consequently not to deduct the expense.

Payment of interest is also subject to income tax on 50% of the interest paid to a beneficiary abroad on loans invested in the Republic of Panama, but the payer must proceed with the withholding even if he does not deduct the interest.

If the beneficiary is registered as a taxpayer in Panama before the Tax Administration, no income tax withholding may be required.

Recipient	Dividends %	Interest	Royalties
Foreign corporations	5%, 10%, 20%	13.75%	13.75%

Panama

Tax administration

Returns

The accounting period is the period for which the company makes its accounts. Returns shall be made upon completion of the accounting period and may not exceed 12 months. For most companies it is usually from 1 January to 31 December.

Payment of tax

Income tax payment shall be made depending on the income tax return, and shall be made no longer than three months after closing of the corresponding accounting period.

Additionally, taxpayers must pay estimated taxes (usually the same amount as generated income), at the sixth, ninth and twelfth month after the end of the corresponding accounting period.

As of 1 January 2011 no estimation will be made, but the taxpayer will have to pay 1% of its monthly gross income as an income tax advance payment. The taxpayer will have to file monthly income tax returns assessing the advance payment within the next 15 days following the end of the month. VAT on purchases may be offset against this advance payment if the taxpayer is a seller in the local market of pharmaceutical products or food and meets certain criteria.

Statutes of limitation

The statute of limitation depends on the type of tax. The Tax Administration may audit the income tax returns filed within the last three years from the last day of the year on which the tax return was filed. The statute of limitation for the ITBMS is five years.

For more information, contact:

David Caradus
PricewaterhouseCoopers
Credit House
Cuthbertson Street
Port Moresby, NCD 121
Papua New Guinea
Tel: +675 321 1500
Email: david.caradus@pg.pwc.com

Significant developments

Papua New Guinea's 2010 National Budget was handed down on 17 November 2009; however, no corporate taxation changes were announced.

It has been reported that Papua New Guinea (PNG) is in the process of entering into a double taxation treaty (DTT) with Indonesia, although the terms of the DTT are currently unknown.

Taxes on corporate income

PNG resident companies are liable for income tax on their income from all sources. Trading profits and other income of resident companies (except income which is specifically exempt) are liable for PNG income tax at the following rates:

Income other than income from mining, petroleum or gas operations	
– Resident company	30%
– Non-resident company	48%
Income from petroleum operations – existing projects	50%
Income from petroleum operations – new projects	45%
Income from petroleum operations – incentive rate projects	30%
Income from mining operations	
– Resident company	30%
– Non-resident company	40%
Income from gas operations	30%

Most resident companies are also liable for dividend withholding tax (DWT) at a rate of 17% on dividends paid by the company. This is reduced to 10% where a dividend is paid by a company carrying on mining operations. Dividends paid out of assessable income from petroleum or gas operations are not subject to DWT.

A foreign tax credit may be available to offset foreign tax paid against PNG tax payable. The foreign tax credit is limited to either the foreign tax paid or the average PNG tax payable on that foreign income, whichever is less.

Non-resident companies are generally taxed only on their PNG sourced trading income. A non-resident's PNG sourced passive income, including dividends, interest and royalties, is generally only subject to withholding tax. The payer of the dividend,

P

Papua New Guinea

interest or royalty must withhold the relevant amount of the tax and remit this to PNG's Internal Revenue Commission (IRC).

Companies are assessed for income tax separately whether or not they are part of a group of associated or related companies. Losses of one company within a group cannot be offset for tax purposes against the profits of another company within that group.

The Companies Act allows two or more companies to amalgamate and continue as one, and provisions are in place to allow this to occur without any adverse income tax consequences.

Corporate residence

A company is deemed a resident for income tax purposes if it is incorporated in PNG. A company incorporated outside PNG that trades in PNG and has its voting power controlled by resident shareholders, or has its central management and control in PNG is also considered a resident. What constitutes central management and control is a question of degree and fact, and it exists where the directors meet to do the business of the company. This may be divided between two places, in which case the company will be resident in both places.

Incorporation test
A company incorporated in PNG is automatically regarded as a PNG tax resident. However, the operation of the law of another country and a relevant tax treaty may result in a company also being treated as resident in another country.

Management and control test
A company is a PNG tax resident if it is managed and controlled in PNG, regardless of where it is incorporated. Generally, a company is managed and controlled in PNG if key decisions affecting the company are made at directors' meetings held in PNG.

An entity may be a tax resident of both PNG and another country by application of domestic legislation. A DTT entered into between PNG and another country may contain a tiebreaker test to determine the country of residence for the purposes of the DTT.

Other taxes

Goods and services tax
The goods and services tax (GST) rate is 10% and applies to most goods and services supplied in PNG. Exported goods and services attract a zero rate of GST. Goods and services, other than motor cars, supplied to mining, petroleum or gas companies are also zero-rated. Some goods and services are exempt, including medical, educational and financial services. Land is excluded from GST, but buildings and other improvements are subject to the tax.

Customs and import duties
The majority of manufacturing inputs (including plant and machinery) attract no duty and other duty rates are being progressively reduced. The remaining rates of duty are currently 15%, 25% and 40%. Although duty is now minimal in many cases, some goods – most notably motor vehicles – now attract excise tax. Private motor vehicles

generally attract excise at the rate of 60%, whereas work vehicles attract excise of 10%. Customs bonds may be issued for the temporary importation of goods that are to be re-exported within 12 months.

Export duty
Export duty on timber logs (not sawn timber) is based on US dollar values.

Stamp duties
Stamp duty applies at varying rates on documents and certain transactions. Of particular note is duty charged on the conveyance of property, which rises to a maximum of 5% where the value of the property being transferred exceeds PGK 100,000. The duty is payable by the purchaser and a 5% duty on the unencumbered value of land may also be payable where there is a transfer of shares in certain landholding companies.

Other dutiable transactions include share transfers (including some share buy-backs) which are subject to a rate of 1%. The Collector of Stamp Duties has the power to amend assessments and refund overpayments of stamp duty.

Stamp duty is payable on documents executed outside PNG which relate to property or matters done or to be done in PNG.

Gift duty/probate duty
There is neither gift nor probate duty in PNG. However, stamp duty may be levied on certain gifts.

Contributions to employee superannuation funds
Contributions to employee superannuation funds are compulsory for entities with 15 or more permanent employees. The employer's compulsory contribution is 8.4% of each employee's gross basic salary. The employee's minimum contribution is 6.0%.

Membership is generally compulsory for citizens. Non-citizens are currently exempt, although this exemption may cease to apply in May 2010 (but is under continuing review).

Contributions must be paid to an authorised superannuation fund. Contributions paid to an authorised fund are tax-deductible to the extent that they do not exceed 15% of the relevant employee's gross taxable salary. Contributions to non-resident funds are not tax-deductible.

Training levy
All businesses whose annual payroll exceeds PGK 200,000 are subject to a 2% training levy, calculated on the sum of the taxable salaries, including benefits, of all personnel. Qualifying expenses incurred in training PNG citizen employees are creditable up to the actual amount of the levy. The training levy, if payable, is not tax-deductible.

Land tax
Land tax is imposed by provincial governments on the unimproved value of the land. The power to levy land tax is vested exclusively with the provincial governments. In PNG, land tax is difficult to implement and faces major geographical and social problems.

P

Papua New Guinea

Departure tax
A departure tax is collected by airlines issuing tickets for persons departing PNG.

Gaming machine tax
PNG imposes a 74% tax on gross revenue from gaming machines.

Spice export levy
Levies are imposed from time to time on the export of specified spices (e.g., vanilla).

Resource project production levies
Production royalties of 2% are payable to the national government on the net smelter return from mining operations. These royalties are tax-deductible. A royalty, at the rate of 2% of the wellhead value, is payable from the production of petroleum and gas operations. Holders of new petroleum development licences are entitled to treat royalties as income tax paid. However, new petroleum projects will also pay a tax-deductible development levy calculated at the same rate of 2% of the wellhead value.

Mining projects are also required to pay a production levy to the Mineral Resources Authority calculated at a rate between 0.25% and 0.5% of the assessable income from production.

Branch income

Income derived by a non-resident contractor for services in PNG is usually subject to a withholding tax at the rate of 12% of the gross income. This amount is calculated on a deemed taxable income of 25% of the gross contract income, which is taxed at the foreign contractor tax rate of 48% (subject to tax treaties). The provisions extend to payments for the following:

- The installation, maintenance and use in PNG of substantial equipment or machinery;
- Construction projects;
- For the lease or charter of any industrial, commercial or scientific equipment or any machinery or vehicle; and
- Consultancy or management services.

Where the non-resident contractor rules do not apply, the non-resident company will be subject to income tax at the foreign contractor tax rate of 48% on its PNG sourced taxable income.

PNG branch remittances are not liable to DWT or any branch profits or similar tax.

Income determination

Taxable income is defined as the sum of assessable income minus the allowable deductions. In practice, profits are calculated for tax purposes by reference to the profits reported in the financial accounts. Accounts must be prepared in accordance with PNG accounting principles, which follow the International Financial Reporting Standards.

Inventory valuation

There is no form of stock relief or trading stock valuation adjustment to recognise the effects of inflation in PNG. There is a once-only option to adopt the lowest of the cost amount, the market selling value or the replacement value. Where the option is not exercised the value of the stock is deemed to be the cost price. However, in special circumstances the Commissioner General of Internal Revenue may accept a lower valuation.

Capital gains

There is no general capital gains tax in PNG. However, profits arising on the sale of property acquired for the purpose of resale at a profit, or from the carrying out of a profit-making scheme, are taxable as ordinary income.

Inter-company dividends

Dividends received by a resident company from other companies whether resident or non-resident, while being assessable to tax, are generally subject to a full tax rebate and are effectively received tax-free. However, where a company has losses on other activities or losses carried over from earlier years, those losses are applied against dividend income before the calculation of the dividend rebate.

Subject to the provisions of PNG's DTTs and the domestic law, DWT at the rate of 17% tax must be withheld from dividends paid by resident companies. The DWT applies to all dividends paid by a resident company, including dividends derived from sources outside PNG and certain deemed dividends. The rate is reduced to 10% where a dividend is paid by a company carrying on mining operations. Dividends paid out of assessable income from petroleum or gas operations are not subject to DWT.

The DWT on dividends received is available as a credit to the recipient company for up to seven years. Therefore, when an additional dividend is paid, no further withholding tax should be payable.

Foreign income

PNG resident companies are liable to income tax on their income from all sources (i.e., including foreign sourced income). A foreign tax credit may be available to offset foreign tax paid against PNG tax payable. The foreign tax credit is limited to the lesser of the foreign tax paid or the average PNG tax payable on that foreign income.

Stock dividends

In most cases, the payment of a dividend by way of the issue of shares is subject to the same taxation treatment as the payment of a dividend by way of cash or the distribution of other property.

Dividends paid wholly and exclusively out of profits arising from the sale or revaluation of assets not acquired for the purpose of resale at a profit where those dividends are paid by the issue of shares are exempt from income tax and DWT.

Deductions

General deduction provisions provide that all losses and outgoings, to the extent incurred in gaining or producing the assessable income or are necessarily incurred in carrying on a business for the purpose of gaining or producing that income, are allowable deductions. However, the general deduction provisions do not allow a

Papua New Guinea

deduction to the extent a loss or outgoing is an outgoing of capital, or of a capital, private or domestic nature, or incurred in relation to the gaining or production of exempt income.

Depreciation and depletion

Depreciation is allowed for equipment and other assets at prescribed rates. A taxpayer must use the diminishing value method unless an election is made to use the prime cost method. The applicable diminishing value rates are 150% of the prime cost rates.

Plant, machinery and equipment

Plant, machinery and equipment (including buildings) are depreciable at rates according to their estimated lives. A taxpayer other than a taxpayer who derives income from mining, petroleum or gas operations may elect to claim special accelerated depreciation rates for certain capital items. For example, flexible depreciation rates (up to 100%) may be claimed on new industrial plant with a life exceeding five years that is used for manufacturing purposes. Other new plant and articles used in manufacturing, construction, transport, storage, communication, and agricultural production are eligible for an accelerated deduction equal to 20% of cost price in the year of purchase. New plant and articles used for tourism are eligible for an accelerated deduction equal to 55% of cost price in the year of purchase.

Motor vehicles

Motor vehicles are generally depreciable at 20% prime cost. There is no upper limit in value for depreciation purposes.

Buildings

Buildings forming an integral part of plant, machinery and equipment are depreciable at a prime cost rate of up to 7.5% depending on the construction materials. Buildings housing plants eligible for the one-year write-off deduction *(see comments on new industrial plant above)* can be written off in the year of construction. Other income producing buildings may qualify for the accelerated deduction of 20% in the year of purchase.

Agricultural and fishing plants

Most items of new agricultural and commercial fishing plants qualify for 100% depreciation as do boats and ships, including ancillary equipment, used solely as dive boats or for scuba diving by accredited tour operators. Other new items having a life exceeding five years used by a person carrying on agricultural operations are eligible for accelerated depreciation in the initial year of use.

Net operating losses – domestic

Trading losses may be offset against all income received in the same accounting period or carried forward and offset against future trading profits. The limitation period on the carryforward of losses is generally 20 years. Losses may not be carried back against prior years' profits. Primary production losses and resource project losses may be carried forward without a time limitation, although again they may not be carried back. The carryforward of losses is subject to a 50% or more continuity of shareholding and control test, or a continuity of business test where there is a breach of the ownership test.

Net operating losses – foreign

Losses incurred by a resident taxpayer from a source outside PNG (other than in relation to export market development) are not deductible against assessable income derived within PNG. In practice, overseas losses can be carried forward and offset against overseas income for up to 20 years.

Payments to foreign affiliates

The deduction available to a taxpayer for management fees paid to an associated person is limited to the greater of:

1. 2% of assessable income derived from PNG sources by the taxpayer; or
2. 2% of the total allowable deductions, excluding management fees incurred by the taxpayer in PNG.

The limitation applies to both resident and non-resident taxpayers. Special rules apply to mining, petroleum and gas companies. These limits may not apply where the recipient of the management fee is resident in a country with which PNG has a DTT or where it can be demonstrated that the management fee arrangements do not have the purposes or effect of avoiding or altering the income tax payable in PNG.

PNG also has transfer pricing provisions that require transactions with foreign affiliates to be conducted on an arm's-length basis.

Taxes

A deduction is not allowable in respect of payments of income tax or training levy. Other taxes may be deductible subject to meeting the general principles for deductibility.

Double deductions

An additional amount equal to the actual amount of expenditure incurred is deductible in respect of certain expenditures (e.g., export market development costs, some staff training costs and certain donations). In other words, a "double deduction" is available in respect of these items.

Primary production

Outright deductions are allowed for certain capital expenditures including clearing, preparing or conserving land for agriculture, eradicating pests, providing labourers' accommodation and for the conservation and conveyance of water.

In addition, a 100% deduction is available for a new plant used directly for the purposes of agricultural production and an initial 20% accelerated depreciation deduction is allowed for a new plant with a life exceeding five years.

Losses incurred in carrying on a primary production business can be carried forward indefinitely; they are not restricted to the 20-year limit that generally applies to company tax losses.

A 150% deduction is available for expenditures on services provided free of charge to smallholder growers, including the provision of advice, training and technical assistance in relation to primary production to assist growers with production, processing, packaging and marketing issues.

P

Papua New Guinea

Research and development (R&D)
A 150% deduction is available for expenditures on R&D. The deduction is available to all sectors of the economy. Broadly, R&D expenditures are defined as systematic, investigative and experimental activities that involve innovation or a high degree of technical risk carried out for the purpose of acquiring new knowledge, or creating new or improved materials, products, devices, processes or services.

Group taxation

Companies are assessed for income tax separately regardless of whether they are part of a group of associated or related companies. Losses of one company within a group cannot be offset for tax purposes against the profits of another company within that group.

The Companies Act allows two or more companies to amalgamate and continue as one, and provisions are in place to allow this to occur without any adverse income tax consequences.

Tax incentives

Manufacturers' wage subsidy
Certain companies manufacturing new products are eligible for a subsidy based on a percentage of the relevant minimum wage of full-time citizen employees. The subsidy is taxable and available over a five-year period with a reduction in the relevant percentage each year.

Research and development (R&D)
A 150% deduction is available for expenditures on R&D. The deduction is available to all sectors of the economy. Broadly, R&D expenditures are defined as systematic, investigative and experimental activities that involve innovation or a high degree of technical risk carried out for the purpose of acquiring new knowledge, or creating new or improved materials, products, devices, processes or services.

Agricultural production extension services
A 150% deduction is available for expenditures on services provided free of charge to smallholder growers, including the provision of advice, training and technical assistance in relation to primary production to assist growers with production, processing, packaging and marketing issues.

Investment in primary production
Agricultural companies may transfer to their shareholders the benefit of the outright tax deduction available for many types of capital expenditures. The total deduction available to shareholders may not exceed the amounts paid on their shares.

Incentive rate primary production projects
As part of promoting investment in primary production, a 20% tax rate is prescribed in respect of "incentive rate primary production income" derived by a company (as opposed to the normal 30% tax rate for a resident company or 48% for a non-resident company). The 20% rate of income tax applies during the period commencing on the date that construction, clearing or planting was started and ending at the end of the tenth full tax year after the date of commencement.

Papua New Guinea

The "incentive rate primary production income" is income from primary production derived by a company from a new primary production development project that is:

- A project with a capital cost not less than PGK 1 million;
- Located in an area in which primary production of the crop or the livestock proposed was not previously carried out, or not previously carried out on a large scale;
- Not an extension or development of an existing primary production project; and
- A project that commenced construction, clearing or planting during the period 1 January 2004 to 31 December 2011.

Rural development incentive
Qualifying new businesses located in certain specified remote areas of the country are exempt from income tax on their income for 10 years after the commencing year. Any loss from this exempt activity is deductible against taxable income from another activity.

Large scale tourist accommodation facilities
A 20% tax rate applies to income derived by a taxpayer from the operation of a large scale tourist accommodation facility or a substantially improved large scale tourist accommodation facility. The rate applies for 14 years after the end of the year of income in which the taxpayer first derives income from the facility. There are four main requirements which must be satisfied:

1. The taxpayer must derive all its income from the operation of the tourist accommodation facility;
2. Construction of the facility or improvements thereto must be commenced between 1 January 2007 and 31 December 2011;
3. The amount expended on the construction or improvement must exceed USD 7 million; and
4. There must be 100 rooms or more for the purpose of temporary accommodation of people.

Export market development costs
Expenditures incurred in the promotion for sale outside PNG of goods manufactured in PNG or tourism promotion is eligible for double deduction. The total tax saving cannot exceed 75% of the expenditures incurred.

Export incentives
The net export income from the export sale of certain types of goods is exempt for the first four years of income, with a partial exemption in the following three years.

Staff training costs
Certain staff training costs, including the cost of full-time training officers and tourism training, are eligible for a double deduction. The total tax saving is limited to 75% of the expenditure incurred.

Solar heating
Expenditures on the acquisition and installation of a solar heating plant for use in deriving income are allowable as an outright deduction.

P

Papua New Guinea

Infrastructure development by agricultural, mining, petroleum and gas companies

A tax credit is available to agricultural, mining, petroleum, gas and certain tourism companies that incur expenditure on a prescribed infrastructure development. In the case of taxpayers engaged in mining, petroleum and gas operations, the credit is limited to 0.75% of the assessable income or the amount of tax payable for the year (in respect of that mining, petroleum or gas project), whichever is less. Excess expenditure over the 0.75% or tax payable may be included in the following year's rebate claim.

Unutilised credits or excess expenditures can generally only be carried forward for two years. In the case of taxpayers engaged in agricultural production, the credit is limited to 1.5% of the assessable income or the amount of tax payable for the year, whichever is less.

A prescribed infrastructure development includes a school, aid post, hospital road and other capital assets that have been approved as such by the Department of National Planning and the IRC. It cannot be an expenditure required under the Mining Act or the Oil and Gas Act.

Petroleum, mining and gas operations

Special incentives and rules apply to mining, petroleum and gas exploration, extraction and production activities. The main aspects are as follows:

Project basis of assessment

A project basis of assessment (ring-fencing) is adopted for all resource projects. This means losses from other operations, regardless of whether or not they are resource related cannot generally be offset against resource project income from a particular ring-fenced project. However, there are some concessions to the ring-fencing principle in respect of exploration expenditures and expenditures in respect of discontinued projects.

In general, all costs incurred in the exploration and development phases of the project are accumulated and amortised over the life of the project. Once production starts, an immediate deduction is allowed for "normal" operating and administration expenses. Capital expenditures incurred after the start of production are capitalised and amortised over the life of the project.

Rate of tax

The rates of tax in respect of income from a resource project are:

	Non-resident companies	Resident companies
Mining	30%	40%
Petroleum – existing projects	50%	50%
Petroleum – new projects	45%	45%
Petroleum – incentive rate	30%	40%
Gas	30%	30%

Interest deductions

Interest is not deductible prior to the commencement of a resource project. Following the issue of a resource development licence, a person carrying on a resource project or exploration in relation to a resource project may claim a deduction against resource income for interest on money borrowed for carrying on the relevant operations or exploration. This is subject to a number of conditions including maintaining a debt-to-equity ratio of 3:1.

Capital allowances
Allowable exploration expenditure (AEE) is amortised over the life of the resource project. The deduction is calculated by dividing the unamortised balance by either the remaining life of the project or four, whichever is less. The amount of the deduction is limited to the amount of income remaining after deducting all other deductions, other than deductions for allowable capital expenditure. In other words, the deduction cannot create a tax loss.

Allowable capital expenditure (ACE) is amortised over the life of the resource project. The ACE is split into two categories: capital expenditures with an estimated effective life of more than 10 years (long-life ACE) and capital expenditures with an estimated effective life of less than 10 years (short-life ACE).

The annual deduction for long-life ACE is claimed on a straight-line basis over 10 years.

Where the remaining life of the project is less than 10 years, the rate at which the deduction is allowed is calculated by referring to the remaining life of the project. For short-life ACE, the annual deduction is calculated by dividing the unamortised balance by either the remaining life of the project or four, whichever is less. For new mining projects the deductions for both long-life ACE and short-life ACE are calculated by dividing the unamortised balance by either the remaining life of the project or four, whichever is less.

The amount of the deduction for ACE is limited to the amount of income remaining after deducting all other deductions. In other words, the deduction cannot create a tax loss.

Off licence exploration expenditure
A major easing of the ring-fencing principle applies to taxpayers, which are involved in a producing project, where the taxpayer or a related party incurs exploration expenditures outside the area of the productive project. In this situation, the taxpayer can elect (whether or not it is currently involved in a producing project) to add such exploration expenditures to an exploration pool that can be amortised against income from the producing project.

The amount allowable as a deduction from this exploration pool in respect of resource operations carried on by the taxpayer or a related corporation is the lesser of:

1. 25% of the total undeducted balance of expenditures in the exploration pool; or
2. Such amount as reduces the income tax (other than additional profits tax) which would, but for this deduction, be payable by the taxpayer and its related corporations in respect of those resource operations for that year of income, by 10% (or 25% for mining projects).

Management fees
Once a resource project derives assessable income, the deduction for management fees is restricted to 2% of operating expenses other than management fees. During the exploration phase of a project, the amount of management fees which can be treated as allowable exploration expenditure is limited to 2% of the exploration expenditure

Papua New Guinea

other than management fees. Furthermore, during the development phase the amount of management fees which can be treated as allowable capital expenditure is limited to 2% of the allowable capital expenditure other than management fees.

Transfer of expenditures
When interests are transferred from one taxpayer to another, the vendor and purchaser can agree to transfer deduction entitlements for the unamortised balances of allowable exploration expenditure and allowable capital expenditure to the purchaser.

Liquefied natural gas (LNG) project
A number of provisions with specific application to the PNG LNG project have been included in the Income Tax Act, Stamp Duties Act, Goods and Services Tax Act, Customs Act and Excise Act.

Other provisions were added or amended at the same time as the PNG LNG project-specific provisions, the most notable being the re-introduction of additional profits tax for all designated gas projects.

Withholding taxes (WHT)

Interest, dividend, royalties and technical/management fees
The following withholding tax rates apply to interest, royalties, technical fees and dividends under PNG domestic law and tax treaties. PNG domestic legislation provides an exemption from withholding tax for interest and dividends in certain circumstances. The higher rates quoted are the maximum rates allowable under the treaties.

Recipient	Interest (%)	Dividends (%)	Royalties (%)	Technical fees (%)
Domestic law (non-treaty)				
Non-resident corporations and individuals	15	17	10/30	17
Treaty				
Australia	10	17	10	0
Canada	10	17	10	0
China	10	15	10	0
Fiji	10	17	15	15
Germany*	10	15	10	10
Korea, Republic of	10	15	10	0
Malaysia	15	15	10	10
Singapore	10	15	10	0
United Kingdom	10	17	10	10

* The treaty with Germany has not yet been ratified by Germany.

The rate of DWT on dividends paid by mining companies is 10%. Dividends paid to a resident or a non-resident out of income from petroleum or gas operations are exempt from income tax and are not subject to DWT.

Business income withholding tax
Income derived by local contractors in certain industries is covered by the business income withholding tax regime. The industries affected include:

– Building and construction	– Security
– Road transport	– Cleaning and maintenance
– Motor vehicle repairs	– Advertising
– Joinery and cabinet making	– Entertainment
– Architecture	– Consultancy
– Engineering	– Equipment hire
– Surveying	

Businesses affected are required to have a certificate of compliance and to produce it when entering into contracts with their customers. Payers are required to file an annual income reporting statement where either they make an eligible payment of PGK 500 or more in relation to one contract, or eligible payments for several contracts exceeding PGK 3,000 in the year of income in relation to a single payee. Payers are required to deduct a 10% withholding tax if payees do not produce a certificate of compliance.

Non-resident insurer withholding tax

Premiums paid to non-resident insurers in respect of insurance contracts on property situated in PNG or insured events which can only occur in PNG are subject to tax in PNG. The tax is calculated on a deemed taxable income equal to 10% of the gross premium, which is taxed at the non-resident tax rates of 48% (companies) or 30% (unincorporated associations). Tax treaties may limit the rate of tax applied.

Overseas shippers

Income derived by overseas shippers or charterers carrying passengers, livestock, mail or goods out of PNG is taxable in PNG. The tax is calculated on a deemed taxable income equal to 5% of the gross income which is taxable at the non-resident rate of 48% in the case of companies. The IRC may exempt the overseas shipper from tax if the shipper's home country exempts PNG shippers from a similar tax.

Tax administration

Returns

PNG operates on a full assessment basis and companies are required to lodge an annual income tax return showing the calculation of taxable income for the year. In addition, the return must provide detailed disclosures in relation to income derived and expenses incurred during the year of income.

The tax year is generally the period 1 January to 31 December; however, application may be made for a substituted tax year end. These will normally be granted where the substituted tax year end coincides with the accounting year end of an overseas holding company. A company's tax year does not need to be the same as its accounting period.

A company must file a tax return by 28 February in the year following the year of income to which the return relates. However, an automatic extension to 30 June applies where the company lodges its return through a registered tax agent.

Payment of tax

Corporate income tax is collected under a provisional tax system. Under this system, tax is paid in respect of a company's current year profits (i.e., payments made in the year of income are in respect of income derived in the same year as the payment is due).

P

Papua New Guinea

Provisional tax is assessed by the IRC based on the last return lodged. In the event that no tax was payable on the previous year's return, the Commissioner General has the right to estimate the amount of tax based on any other information available.

Provisional tax is payable in three equal instalments by 30 April, 31 July, and 31 October.

Applications may be made to reduce provisional tax assessed if the tax due for the year in question is expected to be lower than the provisional tax assessed. Where estimated provisional tax is less than 75% of the income tax ultimately assessed, additional tax may be levied. Additional tax at a rate of 20% will be assessed, based on the difference between the estimate lodged and the provisional tax originally determined, or the actual tax payable, whichever is less. The Commissioner General has the discretion to require payment of additional tax.

Mining, petroleum and gas companies are subject to advance payments tax, a system that broadly mirrors the provisional tax system in place for non-resource companies. The main difference for resource companies is they have the option to lodge an estimate of their taxable income for the year prior to 30 April, 31 July, and 31 October each year, which the IRC uses to assess each advance payments tax instalment.

Following the lodgement of the income tax return the IRC will serve a notice of assessment on the company. The balance of tax payable for a year of income, after the application of provisional tax (or advance payments tax in the case of a resource company) and other tax credits or rebates, is due to be paid within 30 days of the date of service of the notice of assessment.

Corporate taxes in Paraguay

For more information, contact:

Edgar Rubén Taboada
PricewaterhouseCoopers
General Díaz 521, 6th. floor
Edificio Internacional Faro
Asunción, Paraguay
Tel: +595 21 445 003
Email: ruben.taboada@py.pwc.com

Significant developments

In July 2004, Law 2421/04 introduced changes to the Tax Law (Law No. 125/91),
which remain in force with some emendates.

Taxes on corporate income

There are three tax systems, depending on the type of taxpayer (determined by
annual income).

- For income from commercial, industrial and service activities, the general income
  tax rate of 10% applies.
- For income from agricultural and cattle activities, the rate ranges from 2.5%
  to 10%.
- For those taxpayers with annual income of less than PYG 100 million, a single tax at
  a rate of 10% applies.

Corporate residence

Corporate legal residence is determined as the place where direction or central
management takes place, unless the corporation's charter states otherwise.

Other taxes

Tax on acts and documents
There is no longer a tax on acts and documents.

Value-added tax (VAT)
VAT applies to all corporations and to individuals or associations of individuals
rendering personal services.

The general VAT rate is 10%, but in 2006, a special VAT rate of 5% was introduced for
selling real state, basic groceries, farming products, pharmaceutical products, and
loans interest.

Real estate tax
Real estate tax is levied annually at 1% of the fiscal value of the property, which is
generally less than actual value. A tax rate of 0.5% applies if the area of rural property
is smaller than five hectares and is used for agricultural or cattle ranching. In certain
areas, an additional tax is levied on the fiscal value of vacant and semi-vacant land

P

Paraguay

when the area of the built-up portion falls within certain determined percentage limits. Large tracts of land in rural areas are subject to an additional tax determined on a percentage basis and to a proportional tax of 0.5% to 1% on the fiscal value of tracts with areas ranging from 10,000 to 60,000 or more hectares.

The 1992 Paraguayan Constitution established that municipalities and departments are entitled to the tax revenues directly related to real estate. Collection of these taxes is the responsibility of municipal governments.

Branch income

Branches are taxed at the same rate as domestic corporations. Profits transferred or credited to the head office are subject to a 15% withholding tax when remitted to the head office abroad.

Income determination

Inventory valuation

Taxpayers may adopt any method of inventory valuation, provided it is technically acceptable, according to Tax Administration criteria (e.g., first-in, first-out, average cost). The valuation must be applied consistently and may be changed only with the prior approval of the treasury minister.

Damaged, deteriorated and obsolete inventories may be written down to fixed values by the taxpayer. The tax administration can reject valuations that are not realistic.

Capital gains

Gains on all assets, tangible and intangible, are taxable as part of profits and subject to income tax at a rate of 10%.

Inter-company dividends

Dividends are not taxable income except when the recipient (or shareholder) is a non-resident, in which case a 15% withholding tax applies. An additional 5% tax is charged to local entities when the income or dividend is distributed to a local or foreign (non-resident) shareholder.

Foreign income

Foreign-source income is not taxable. Interest, commissions and capital gains are considered Paraguayan source when the investor is resident in Paraguay.

Stock dividends

Stock dividends are not taxable income, except when dividends represent more than 30% of the taxable income of an investor. In the case when dividends represent more than 30% of an investor's taxable income, a tax rate of 15% and an additional tax rate of 5% applies (see Inter-company dividends).

Deductions

Depreciation and depletion

The maximum allowable depreciation rates range from 2.5% for urban buildings to 25% for computer equipment. Depreciation is calculated by the straight-line method based on the useful life of assets, as determined by the Treasurer. The Treasurer may

Paraguay

also authorise the use of other depreciation or depletion methods that are deemed to be technically justified and generally accepted. Fixed assets must be revalued annually based on the increase of the price index. Capital gains derived from the revaluation of fixed assets are not taxable income.

Net operating losses
Tax losses incurred in one year were permitted to be carried forward and applied against taxable income in later years until 2005. Since 2005, net operating losses are no longer permitted to be carried forward and applied against future years.

However, Congress is considering amending the law to permit carrying forward of losses for three years.

Payments to foreign affiliates
There are no limits on the deductibility of payments to foreign affiliates, including management fees, research and development, and general and administrative expenses, provided that the taxpayer maintains corresponding legal documentation that includes the country of origin and applies appropriate withholding taxes. For the applicable withholding tax rates, *see Withholding taxes*.

Taxes
In general, all taxes mentioned under *Other taxes* are deductible. Income tax and any fiscal surcharges or fines are not deductible.

Other significant items
Special rules apply for the deduction of donations, extraordinary losses, deferred expenses, other taxes (such as VAT), bad debts, and executive remuneration. General provisions for expenses or other potential losses are not deductible.

Other special non-deductible items include:

- Interest on capital, loans or any other investment by an owner, partner, or shareholder in a business;
- Personal expenses of an owner, partner, or shareholder;
- Money drawn on account of future earnings;
- Amortisation of goodwill;
- Direct expenses incurred in earning non-taxable income; and
- Earnings from any fiscal period that are retained in the business as capital increases or reserve accounts.

Group taxation

Group taxation is not permitted.

Tax incentives

Inward investment
The framework of economic investment was established in the Law No. 60/90, which offers some special tax exemption benefits to foreign and local investors.

The benefits of the Law No. 60/90 may be available for the following investments:

Paraguay

- Cash, financing, provision of credit or other financial instruments, under the conditions established by the administration of the President of Paraguay and the corresponding ministries;
- Capital goods, raw materials and inputs for local industry for the fabrication of capital goods;
- Transfers of licensing rights with respect to trademarks, industrial processes and models and other technologies;
- Technically specialised services;
- Capital leases; and
- Other forms that the administration of the President of Paraguay and the corresponding ministries determined by law.

The investment incentives included in Law 60/90 that remain enacted after tax law modification (Law No. 2421/04) are the exemptions from certain fiscal, municipal and customs duties taxes.

When the amount of financing for an investment is greater than USD 5 million, it will be exempt from withholding taxes on interest, commissions and capital that have to be paid to financial or banking entities abroad. This benefit is for five years.

If the investment is at least USD 5 million and the project is approved for a term of at least 10 years, the dividends and profits derived from the project are tax exempt. In this case, the taxes on those dividends and profits would not be creditable in the country of origin.

Other incentives

Exports are exempt from certain customs duties and from VAT. A Capital Market Law (No. 1284/98) established incentives for companies listed on the Asunción Stock Exchange. In addition, Law 536/95 established incentives for forestry activities.

Withholding taxes (WHT)

Payments by a domestic corporation

Recipient	Portfolio (1) %	Substantial holdings (1) %	Interest (2, 3) %	Royalties (3, 4) %	Fees (3, 5, 6) %
Non-resident corporations	15	15	30	30	30
Non-resident individuals	10	10	30	10	10

Notes

1. Since 2006, local entities are required to pay an additional 5% withholding tax when the income or dividend is distributed.
2. The withholding tax on interest is based on 100% of the amount paid when remitted to the head office abroad. In other cases, when the payment is not directly made to the head office or shareholders that have control of the local subsidiary, the withholding tax is based on 50% of the amount paid. The tax rate is 30%.
3. VAT is withheld on interest, royalties and other services provided for non-resident corporations or individuals at a rate of 9.09%, except on fees for financing, which are withheld at a rate of 4.76%.
4. The withholding tax on royalties is based on 100% of the amount paid when remitted to the head office abroad. In other cases, when the payment is not directly made to the

head office or shareholders that have control of the local subsidiary, the withholding tax is based on 50% of the amount paid. The tax rate is 30%.

5. The withholding tax on fees is based on 100% of the amount paid when remitted to the head office abroad. In other cases, it is based on 50% of the amount paid. The tax rate is 30%.

6. Fees for personal services rendered by non-resident corporations are subject to withholding income tax at a rate of 50% on the amount paid. The tax rate is 30% (effective tax rate of 15%).

   Fees for personal services rendered by non-resident individuals are subject to withholding of the personal income tax at a rate of 50% on the amount paid. The tax rate is 20% (effective tax rate of 10%). Congress is considering suspending this tax.

Tax administration

Returns
Returns are submitted on a fiscal-year basis as a self-assessment.

Payment of tax
Income tax returns must be filed and income tax that is due must be paid by the fourth month following the end of the fiscal year. The tax is due on varying days in the fourth month, depending on the taxpayer ID number, according to a calendar established by the treasury ministry. Four equal advance payments are made throughout the year, calculated based on 100% of the tax due in the previous year. Payments must be made in May, July, September, and November of each year after the due date for filing the income tax returns accordingly to the calendar established by the tax authorities.

P

For more information, contact:

Miguel Mur
PricewaterhouseCoopers\Dongo-Soria, Gaveglio y Asociados Sociedad Civil
Av. Santo Toribio No. 143
Piso 8
Lima 27, Peru
Tel: +51 1 211 6500
Email: miguel.mur@pe.pwc.com

Significant developments

Several changes to corporate taxation legislation in Peru were applicable starting 1 January 2010, including the following:

- The financial transactions tax (FTT) rate for fiscal year (FY) 2010 was reduced to 0.05%.
- The tax unit for 2010 is PEN 3,600.
- The rate of the temporary net assets tax for FY 2010 was reduced to 0.4% (applicable to net assets in excess of PEN 1 million).
- Tax exemption on income from bank deposits in local banks remains in force until 31 December 2011.
- The exemption on capital gains derived from the sale of stocks through the stock exchange and on interest from deposits in local financial institutions is no longer in force.
- The general tax treatment on mutual funds and investment funds has been changed.
- The Free Trade Agreement with China is in force as of 1 March 2010.
- The double tax agreement with Brazil is in force as of 1 January 2010.

Taxes on corporate income

Companies incorporated in Peru are considered domiciled in Peru for tax purposes and thus subject to an income tax rate of 30% on worldwide net income.

For purpose of determining taxable income, such entities are allowed to deduct expenses to the extent that they are necessary to generate or maintain the source of taxable income. Requirements, limitations and/or caps may apply to the deduction of certain expenses (thin capitalisation rules), bad debt provisions, salaries, travel expenses, gifts, etc.

The Peruvian income tax law allows crediting for various payments against income tax, including income taxes paid in advance, amounts paid for certain other taxes and income taxes paid in foreign tax jurisdictions, provided that the foreign country's tax rate is not higher than the Peruvian corporate tax rate.

Dividends and any other types of profit distributions are taxed at a 4.1% rate, upon distribution, whether the distributions are made to domiciled individuals or non-domiciled companies (either individuals or legal entities). The entity distributing dividends or profits is liable for withholding tax at a rate of 4.1%. Nevertheless, enterprises are subject to an additional tax rate of 4.1% on every amount or payment in kind that, as result of a tax audit, is construed as taxable income to the extent that it is an indirect distribution of such income that is not susceptible to further tax control, including income that has not been declared.

Corporate residence

For income tax purposes, the following entities, among others, are considered as resident entities in Peru:

- Corporations duly incorporated in Peru;
- Branches, agencies and permanent establishments (PE) in Peru of non-domiciled individuals or entities (the Regulations of the Peruvian income tax law provide the cases in which a PE is deemed to be established in Peru); and
- Partnerships and limited liability companies.

Other taxes

Value-added tax (VAT)

The general rate of VAT is 19%, applicable to the following operations:

- Sale of goods within the country;
- Rendering or first use of services within the country;
- Construction contracts;
- The first sale of real estate made by construction firms; and
- Import of goods.

For all transactions, the vendor is subject to VAT, except in the case of importation of goods or services rendered abroad, but economically used within Peru, for which VAT is self-assessed by the importers and users, respectively.

The VAT law follows a debit/credit system, and input VAT may be offset by output VAT. Should excess input VAT be obtained in a particular month, it shall offset output VAT obtained during the following months, until it is exhausted. Cash refunds of excess input VAT may be made only if it is not possible to offset the excess input VAT related to the exportation of goods and services, as explained below, but not to domestic transactions.

The export of movable goods (including the sale of goods in the international zone of ports and airports) is not subject to VAT, nor is the exportation of certain services. Thus, VAT paid upon the acquisition of goods, performance of services, construction agreements and the importation of goods related to exported goods or services creates a positive VAT export balance.

The positive balance may offset (i) output VAT, (ii) income tax, or (iii) any other outstanding tax debt in favour of the central government. If the positive balance is not completely offset, as the amount of the aforementioned tax obligations is insufficient, the taxpayer may apply for a refund (which may be made in cash or by cheque).

Excise tax

The sale of specific goods, including fuel, cigarettes, beer, liquor, and vehicles, is subject to excise tax.

Peru

Excise tax rates depend on the type of goods or services.

Financial transactions tax (FTT)

Obligations that are fulfilled through cash payments exceeding PEN 3,500 must be made via bank account deposits, wire transfers, payment orders, credit cards, non-negotiable cheques or other means of payment provided by entities of the Peruvian financial system. Failure to use one of these payment methods when such an obligation exists will result in the disallowance of deductions for any expenses or costs for income tax purposes and the disallowance of a credit for the corresponding VAT.

Law No. 28194 also created the FTT applied at a rate of 0.05% on all debits and/or credits on bank accounts held by the taxpayers.

The following operations, among others, are exempted from the FTT:

- Operations made between accounts of the same holder;
- Credits to bank accounts for payment of salaries; and
- Credits and debits to bank accounts of diplomatic representations and international organisations recognised in Peru.

Payments of the FTT are deductible as expense for income tax purposes.

Temporary net assets tax (TNAT)

Companies subject to corporate income tax are obliged to pay the TNAT, except companies that are in preoperative stages or that commenced business on 1 January of the fiscal year in which the TNAT must be paid.

The taxable basis is the value of the assets set forth in the taxpayer's balance sheet as of 31 December of the year prior to that of the tax payment, adjusted for deductions and amortisations accepted by the Peruvian law.

Thus, the amount of the TNAT is determined by applying the following rates on the taxable basis:

- 0% – Up to PEN 1 million; and
- 0.4% – Excess of PEN 1 million.

The amount paid for the TNAT may be credited against the taxpayer's corporate income tax.

Branch income

Branches, agencies and PEs of non-domiciled companies or entities incorporated in Peru are subject to income tax at a 30% rate on their Peruvian-source income.

For tax purposes, branches or subsidiaries are subject to the same obligations applicable to all companies in Peru, including, income tax, VAT, FTT, filing of the corresponding income tax and VAT returns, issuance of invoices, etc.

Nevertheless, the following important differences between subsidiaries and branches domiciled in Peru must be taken into account:

Peru

- Branches are subject to the income tax only for their Peruvian-source income, while subsidiaries are subject to income tax on their global-source income (both Peruvian and foreign income).
- For branches, the 4.1% rate for distribution of dividends is applied from the date the annual income tax return is submitted. Subsidiaries are subject to the 4.1% rate on the earlier of the date in which the corresponding shareholders agreement took place or the date when the beneficiary has the right to use the dividends distributed by the subsidiary.

Income determination

Inflation accounting
As of 2005, no adjustments to balance sheet accounts for inflation apply.

Inventory valuation
The first-in, first-out (FIFO), average, specific-identification, retail, and normal or base-stock methods are allowed for inventory valuation. The last-in, first-out (LIFO) method is not permitted.

Capital gains
Capital gains are taxed as ordinary income.

Inter-company dividends
Cash dividends distributed to resident corporations are not subject to any taxes.

Foreign income
A Peruvian corporation is taxed on foreign source income. Double taxation may be avoided by means of foreign tax credits.

Deductions

Expenses derived from transactions entered into with entities domiciled in tax havens
Certain expenses are not tax-deductible, including expenses incurred with respect to transactions with (i) entities domiciled in tax havens on the list attached to the Peruvian Income Tax Law regulations, (ii) PEs located in tax havens, or (iii) entities that generate revenues or income through tax havens. Nonetheless, expenses incurred from the following transactions are excluded from the above-mentioned limitations: (i) interest on loans, (ii) insurance premiums, (iii) leases of aircraft or ships, (iv) maritime freight, and (v) fees for passing through the Panama Canal.

Depreciation

	%
Buildings	5
Cattle (both labour and reproduction) and fishing nets	25
Vehicles (except trains) and any kind of ovens	20
Machines and equipment used for mining, oil and construction activities; excluding furniture, household and office goods	20
Equipment for data processing	25
Machines and equipment acquired as of 1 January 1991	10

Peru

	%
Other fixed assets	10

There is a special depreciation regime applicable for years 2010 and 2011 for buildings and constructions that, provided certain requirements are met, can be depreciated at a 20% rate.

Loss carryovers

Tax losses may be offset according to either of the following systems:

- Against net income generated within the following four fiscal years after the year in which the loss was generated. Any losses that are not offset within such period may not be carried forward to any later years.
- Against 50% of the net income generated in the following fiscal years after the year in which the loss was generated. Under this system, there is no time limitation for carrying forward the losses.

After choosing one of the aforementioned systems, the taxpayers may not change the system until any accumulated tax losses from prior fiscal years are exhausted. Losses may not be carried back to years prior to the year in which the loss was generated.

Payments to foreign affiliates

Payment of royalties to non-domiciled affiliates is permitted and deductible from gross income.

Taxes

Other taxes assessable on properties and activities generating taxable income are deductible for income tax purposes.

Profit sharing

Entities with more than 20 employees and provided they obtain taxable income on the fiscal year must distribute a percentage (5%, 8% or 10% depending on the industry) of its profits (the basis is the tax profit of the fiscal year) among its employees, the amount of distribution for each employee depends on the effective working days during the year and annual remuneration.

Start-up costs

Organisation expenses, pre-operating expenses (including initial operations and further expansion of operations), and interest accrued during the pre-operating period may be expensed in the first period of operation or amortised using the straight-line method over a maximum of 10 years. However, once a company has elected to recover start-up costs via the straight-line method, it may revoke such election only upon receiving approval of the tax authorities. The total period may not exceed 10 years.

Employee's retributions and health insurance premiums

Employee's retributions paid during a fiscal year may be deducted in such year, provided the payments are made by the employer before the term to file its annual income tax return expires. Likewise, health insurance premiums for employees, their spouses and children are deductible.

Vehicle expenses deductions

Vehicle expenses may be deducted provided the vehicles are essential to a company's business activities and are continually used for such purpose. There is a limitation on the tax deductibility of car expenses, depending on the amount of income generated by the company. The number of company cars assigned to directors, managers and representatives of a company may not exceed five under any circumstances.

Vehicles subject to these limitations are those classified in categories as A2, A3 and A4, pursuant to the provisions of the Ministry of Transport.

Group taxation

Group taxation is not permitted.

Tax incentives

Early recovery of VAT
Companies in a preoperative stage with large projects in process may apply for early recovery of VAT prior to commencing operations. An investment agreement with the government (the Ministry of its sector) is required.

Stability agreement
Investors may enter into stability agreements with the government, either under the general regime or specific regimes (i.e., mining and petroleum).

Under the general regime, investors may enter into Juridical Stability Agreements that guarantee the following advantages for a 10-year period:

- Stability of the income tax regime in force at the time the agreement is entered into with respect to dividends and profit distribution;
- Stability of the Peruvian government monetary policy, according to which there is a complete absence of exchange controls, foreign currency can be freely acquired or sold at whatever exchange rate the market offers and funds can be remitted abroad without any previous authorisation; and
- Right of non-discrimination between foreign and local investors.

Under the mining regime, local mining companies may enter into stability agreements of guarantees and investment promotion measures that guarantee the following for 10 or 15 years:

- Stability of the overall tax regime;
- Stability of the overall administrative regime;
- Free disposition of funds (foreign currency) arising from export operations;
- No exchange rate discrimination;
- Free trade of products; and
- Stability of special regimes for tax refunds, temporary importation, etc.

Oil companies may enter into stability agreements that guarantee the following for the term of the contract:

- Stability of the overall tax regime;
- Free disposition of funds (foreign currency) arising from export operations;
- Free convertibility of its funds; and
- Free trade of products.

Peru

Investment promotion in the Amazon

As of 1 January 1999, certain tax benefits with regard to VAT and income tax have been established for taxpayers located in the area designated by the law as the "Amazon" and that are engaged in the following activities:

- Agriculture and livestock enterprises;
- Aquaculture;
- Fishing;
- Tourism; and
- Manufacturing activities linked to the processing, transformation and commercialisation of primary products originating in the activities listed above and in forest transformation, provided these products are produced in the area.

Special zones – Centres of Export, Transformation, Industry, Commercialisation and Services (CETICOS)

CETICOS are geographical areas duly delimited with custom primary zone status and special treatment, destined to generate development poles through industrial, maquila, assembling or storage activities. CETICOS are located in Paita, Ilo and Matarani cities.

Agribusiness and agro-exporting activities may be performed within a CETICOS. Agribusiness activity is primarily the transformation of agro-farming products produced in the country. Such transformation must be carried out at CETICOS.

Companies engaged in industrial, maquila or assembling activities, established or set up in the CETICOS, until 31 December 2012, are exempt from income tax, VAT, excise tax, municipal promotion tax, as well as from any other taxes, fees, contributions levied by the Central Administration and even taxes that require express exempt regulation.

Withholding taxes (WHT)

Domestic corporations are required to withhold income tax with respect to income paid to non-domiciled entities at the following rates:

	%
Interest on non-related party loans, provided certain requirements are fulfilled	4.99
Interest on related party loans	30
Interest paid by Peruvian financial entities or banks to foreign beneficiaries for credit lines used in Peru	1
Royalties	30
Digital services	30
Technical assistance, provided that certain requirements are met (otherwise 30%)	15
Lease of vessels or aircraft	10
Dividends or profit distributions	4.1
Other income	30

Note that domiciled taxpayers may not deduct the withholding tax of a third party, except in the case of loans provided by non-domiciled creditors, to the extent that the debtor has contractually assumed the obligation of bearing the withholding tax.

Capital gains derived from the sale of stocks through the stock exchange paid to a non-domiciled company have an income tax rate of 5% and are not subject to any withholding. In these cases, the income tax must be paid directly by the non-domiciled company.

Capital gains derived from the sale of stocks paid to domiciled individuals are subject of a 5% income tax rate, even though they are not sold through the stock exchange.

In the case of the services mentioned below that entail the execution of activities both in Peru and abroad, non-domiciled entities are only subject to tax on a percentage of gross income at the following rates:

	%
Insurance	7
Lease of vessels	80
Lease of aircraft	60
Air transport	1
Maritime transport	2
Telecom services	5
International news services	10
Distribution of movies, records and similar products	20
Rights for broadcasting live foreign TV shows within Peru	20

Tax treaties

Peru has entered into treaties with Canada, Chile and Brazil regarding double taxation on income tax (the last three entered into in accordance with the Organisation for Economic Co-operation and Development (OECD) Model). Recently, Peru has entered into a double-taxation treaty with Spain (also entered into pursuant to the OECD Model), but the treaty has not yet entered into force, as the Peruvian Congress ratification required for such purpose is still pending. In addition, Peru is a member of the Andean Community of Nations (ACN), which also includes Bolivia, Colombia and Ecuador.

Pursuant to the provisions of the tax treaties entered into in accordance with the OECD Model, income is taxable in the country of the service provider's residence, unless a PE is configured, in which case both countries are entitled to levy tax on income and the country of residence allows a credit for taxes paid in the other country.

On the other hand, according to the treaties with the ACN, income is taxable in the country in which its source is located, unless a PE is configured, in which case income tax is levied in the country where the PE is located. Thus, in transactions with entities resident from one of the member countries of the ACN, in certain cases income is taxable in Peru if the source of such income is located within Peru. For such purpose, the term "source" is defined as the place where the activity, right or goods that generates or will generate income is located.

P

Peru

Tax administration

Returns
The filing deadline for the income tax return is generally the first week of April. According to law, the fiscal year must coincide with the calendar year. The system is one of self-assessment, but the tax return filed with the tax authorities is subject to review.

Payment of taxes
Income tax is paid in advanced instalments calculated based on monthly revenue, either by applying a 2% rate or by a factor equivalent to the effective tax rate on net revenue of the prior year. Income tax is paid in 13 instalments (12 monthly payments and the annual income tax return). As noted, the first 12 payments must be made on a monthly basis and the last payment is due at the time that the annual tax return is filed. Late payment of interim or final instalments is subject to moratorium interest. Excess payments are subject to indexation up to the date of reimbursement or application to future taxes.

Tax authority
The tax authority in Peru is called "Superintendencia Nacional de Administración Tributaria" (SUNAT). SUNAT is responsible for administering all of the aforementioned taxes (income tax, VAT, etc.). Companies domiciled in Peru must be registered with the tax administration (Taxpayer's Registry).

The Tax Court (Tribunal Fiscal) is a specialised court of law that is given an administrative level from the Economics and Finances Ministry, but is otherwise autonomous regarding its specific functions. Its mission is to rule over tax contingencies that may arise between the Tax Administration and the taxpayers, by interpreting and applying the corresponding tax legislation, issuing mandatory observance jurisprudence, establishing homogenous criteria and providing legislation that continues to support the progress of the tax system.

Corporate taxes in the Philippines

For more information, contact:

Alex Cabrera
PricewaterhouseCoopers\Isla Lipana & Co.
29th Floor Philamlife Tower
8767 Paseo de Roxas
Makati City 1226
Philippines
Tel: +63 2 459 2002
Email: alex.cabrera@ph.pwc.com

Significant developments

Several laws were passed between 2005 and 2010 to address fiscal and other concerns of the government.

Excise tax rates imposed on alcohol and tobacco products were increased, effective 1 January 2005.

The Attrition Act of 2005 was passed to improve the revenue collection performance of the Bureau of Internal Revenue (BIR) and the Bureau of Customs (BOC). The Act created a rewards and incentives fund to reward BIR and BOC personnel if collection targets are exceeded. At the same time, a new Revenue Performance Evaluation Board was empowered to remove personnel from service if their collection falls 7.5% or more short of their collection target.

Republic Act (RA) No. 9337 made significant amendments to the value-added tax (VAT) law. The VAT rate increased from 10% to 12%. Several VAT exemptions were removed, the most notable being in the power and petroleum sectors. Payments on government contracts became subject to 5% final withholding VAT. Clearer invoicing and registration rules were introduced, and the registration threshold was increased from PHP 750,000 to PHP 1.5 million.

Two controversial provisions related to input tax credits were also introduced. Input VAT from the purchase or importation of capital goods must be spread over the lesser of five years or the depreciable life of an asset if the aggregate acquisition cost exceeds PHP 1 million (excluding VAT) in a calendar month. Creditable input taxes (other than those related to zero-rated sales) are also restricted to 70% of output tax for a quarter, although this 70% cap was removed by a subsequent enactment (RA No. 9361).

RA No. 9337 also amended some non-VAT provisions. The excise taxes on some petroleum products were reduced to mitigate the expected price effects from the imposition of VAT on power and petroleum. The corporate tax rate was, however, reduced to 30%, effective 1 January 2009.

The VAT rate increase took effect from 1 February 2006, while the other amendments were generally effective from 1 November 2005.

RA No. 9343 extended the period for establishing special purpose vehicles (SPVs), as originally provided for under the SPV Act of 2002, which grants certain tax exemptions and fee privileges to qualified SPVs that purchase non-performing loans under

Philippines

conditions therein provided. Under the amendatory law, new SPVs may be established within 18 months from 14 May 2006, the date of effectivity of RA 9343. SPV privileges for the transfer of non-performing assets from financial institutions to the SPVs shall be available within two years also, from 14 May 2006.

Finally, RA No. 9504 introduced the optional standard deduction of 40% of gross income, beginning 1 July 2008.

RA No. 9640 amended the Local Government Code of 1991 by reducing the amusement tax that a province or city may levy and collect from proprietors, lessees, or operators of theatres, cinemas, concert halls, circuses, boxing stadiums and other places of amusement from not more than 30% to not more than 10% of the gross receipts derived from admission fees. The Act lapsed into law on 21 May 2009 without the signature of the President.

RA 10001 (Act) reduced the rate of percentage tax on life insurance policies from 5% to 2% of the total premiums collected. This reduced rate of 2% will only apply to insurance policies issued after the effectivity of the Act, which will be within 15 days after its publication in a newspaper of general circulation. However, with respect to insurance policies taken out before the effectivity of the Act, carrying still outstanding unpaid premiums, the 2% rate will only apply to the remaining balance and for the remaining years. Moreover, it also provides for the following revised schedule of documentary stamp taxes (DST) rates on life insurance policies:

* Exempted if the amount of insurance does not exceed PHP 100,000;
* PHP 10 for amounts exceeding PHP 100,000 but not exceeding PHP 300,000;
* PHP 25 for amounts exceeding PHP 300,000 but not exceeding PHP 500,000;
* PHP 50 for amounts exceeding PHP 500,000 but not exceeding PHP 750,000;
* PHP 75 for amounts exceeding PHP 750,000 but not exceeding PHP 1 million; and
* PHP 100 for amounts exceeding PHP 1million.

Section 4 of the Act, however, which pertains to the exemption from premium tax and DST of life insurance policies, has been vetoed by the President. Congress, which is now in recess, has yet to act on this vetoed item of the revenue bill. A two-thirds vote to pass the Act in its entirety from both houses of Congress upon resumption of their session in May this year, would override the President's veto of Section 4.

Revenue Memorandum Circular No. 28-2010 dated 23 March 2010, circularises the full text of RA No. 10026 entitled "An Act Granting Income Tax Exemption to Local Water Districts" which amended Section 27(C) of the Tax Code. This RA exempts Local water districts (LWDs) from payment of income taxes. Moreover, it added another section i.e., (Section 289-A under Chapter II- Special Disposition of Certain National Internal Revenue Taxes) to the Tax Code which has the following features:

The amount saved by LWDs by virtue of their exemption from income taxes shall be used by them for capital equipment expenditure in order to expand water services coverage and improve water quality in the provinces, cities, and municipalities;

The LWDs shall adopt internal control reforms that would bring about their economic and financial viability. Further, they shall not increase by more than twenty percent (20%) a year their appropriation for personal services, as well as for travel, transportation or representation expenses and purchase of motor vehicles.

All unpaid taxes or any portion thereof due from a LWD for the period starting 13 August 1996 until the effectivity date of this Act are hereby condoned by the Government subject to the following conditions: (1) that the BIR, after careful review of the financial statements of a water district applying for condonation of taxes due, establishes its financial incapacity, after providing for its maintenance and operating expenses, debt servicing and reserved fund, to meet such obligations for the period stated herein; and (2) that the water district availing of such condonation shall submit to Congress of the Philippines a programme of internal reforms, duly certified by the local water utilities administration, that would bring about its economic and financial viability.

Taxes on corporate income

Domestic corporations

The following rates apply to domestic corporations:

	%
In general, on net income from all sources	30
Minimum corporate income tax (MCIT) on gross income, beginning in the fourth taxable year following the year in which business operations commence. MCIT is imposed where the corporate income tax at 35% is less than 2% MCIT on gross income	2
Proprietary educational institutions and non-profit hospitals:	
On net taxable income if gross income from unrelated trade, business and other activities does not exceed 50% of the total gross income from all sources	10
On total net taxable income if gross income from unrelated activities exceeds 50% of income	30
Non-stock, non-profit educational institutions (all assets and revenues used actually, directly and exclusively for educational purposes)	Exempt

Certain passive income from domestic sources is subject to final tax rather than ordinary income tax.

Improperly accumulated earnings tax

An improperly accumulated earnings tax of 10% is imposed on improperly accumulated income. The tax applies to every corporation formed or used for the purpose of avoiding income tax with respect to its shareholders, or the shareholders of any other corporation, by permitting earnings and profits to accumulate instead of being divided or distributed. Exceptions are made for publicly held corporations, banks and non-bank financial intermediaries, and insurance companies.

Resident foreign corporations

Resident foreign corporations are taxed in the same manner as domestic corporations (except on capital gains on the sale of buildings not used in business, which are taxable as ordinary income), but only on Philippine-source income. International carriers are subject to an income tax of 2.5% on their gross Philippine billings. Where there is a tax treaty, the preferential rate provided in it applies.

Philippines

Income of offshore banking units (OBUs) and foreign currency deposit units (FCDUs) of depository banks from foreign currency transactions with non-residents, other OBUs or FCDUs and local commercial banks (including branches of foreign banks) authorised by the Bangko Sentral ng Pilipinas (central bank) to transact business with OBUs and FCDUs, are exempt from all taxes except net income specified by the Secretary of Finance upon recommendation of the Monetary Board. Interest income from foreign currency loans granted to residents other than OBUs or local commercial banks shall be subject to a 10% final income tax.

Non-resident foreign corporations

In general, non-resident foreign corporations are taxed on gross income received from sources within the Philippines at 30%, except for reinsurance premiums, which are exempt, and on interest on foreign loans, which is taxed at 20%. Dividends from domestic corporations are subject to a final withholding tax at the rate of 15% if the country in which the corporation is domiciled does not impose income tax on such dividends, or allows a tax deemed paid credit of 15%. If the recipient is a resident of a country with which the Philippines has a tax treaty, the treaty rate applies, if lower. Otherwise, the normal corporate rates apply.

Rentals and charter fees payable to non-resident owners of vessels chartered by Philippine nationals on leases or charters approved by the Maritime Industry Authority are subject to a final tax of 4.5%. Rentals, charter fees, and other fees payable to non-resident lessors of aircraft, machinery and other equipment are subject to a final tax of 7.5%.

Regional or area headquarters of multinational corporations that do not earn or derive income from the Philippines, and that act as supervisory, communications and coordinating centres for their affiliates, subsidiaries or branches in the Asia-Pacific region and other foreign markets are not subject to income tax.

Regional operating headquarters pay a tax of 10% of their taxable income. A regional operating headquarters is a branch established in the Philippines by a multinational company that is engaged in any of the following services: general administration and planning; business planning and coordination; sourcing and procurement of raw materials and components; corporate finance advisory services; marketing control and sales promotion; training and personnel management; logistic services; research and development services and product development; technical support and maintenance; data processing and communication; or business development.

Corporate residence

A domestic corporation (i.e., one that is created or organised under Philippine laws) is subject to tax on its worldwide income. On the other hand, a foreign corporation is subject to tax only on income from Philippine sources. A foreign corporation that is duly licensed to engage in trade or business within the Philippines is referred to as a 'resident foreign corporation'.

Other taxes

Fringe benefits tax

A final tax of 32%, payable by the employer, is imposed on the grossed-up monetary value of fringe benefits, for example housing, expense accounts, vehicles of any kind, household personnel, interest on loans at lower than market rates (the current benchmark rate is 12%), membership dues for social and athletic clubs, foreign travel expenses, holiday and vacation expenses, educational assistance, insurance, and so on, furnished or granted to managerial or supervisory personnel by the employer. An exception is for fringe benefits required by the nature of or necessary to the trade, business or profession of the employer, or when the fringe benefit is for the convenience or advantage of the employer.

The following fringe benefits are not subject to the tax:

- Those authorised and exempted from tax under special laws;
- Contributions of the employer for the benefit of the employee to retirement, insurance and hospitalisation benefit plans;
- Those granted to rank-and-file employees (however, the employees may be subject to withholding tax on compensation); and
- Those of relatively small value or *de minimis* benefits.

The fringe benefits tax is payable on the calendar quarter basis, and is an additional deductible expense for the employer. Fringe benefits already subjected to fringe benefits tax will no longer be included in the employee's taxable income.

The grossed-up monetary value of the fringe benefit is generally computed by dividing the actual monetary value of the benefit by 68%.

Value-added tax (VAT)
VAT applies to practically all sales of services and imports, and sales, barter, exchange, or lease of goods or properties (tangible or intangible). The tax is equivalent to a uniform rate of 12%, based on the gross selling price of goods or properties sold, or gross receipts from the sale of services. On importation of goods, the basis of the tax is the value used by the Bureau of Customs in determining tariff and customs duties plus customs duties, excise taxes, if any, and other charges. Where the valuation used by the Bureau of Customs is by volume or quantity, the VAT basis is the landed cost plus excise taxes, if any.

Certain transactions are zero-rated or exempt from VAT. Export sales by VAT-registered persons are zero-rated. Certain sales of services exempt from VAT, including services provided by financial intermediaries, are subject to percentage taxes based on gross sales, receipts or income. A 3% percentage tax also applies to persons who are not VAT-registered because their annual sales or receipts do not exceed PHP 1.5 million.

Other national taxes
Aside from income tax and VAT, other internal revenue taxes include excise tax, documentary stamp tax and percentage taxes.

Local government taxes
Local government units impose local (business) taxes and permit fees, which are generally based on the prior year's gross sales or gross receipts, and real property taxes, which are levied on the basis of a fixed proportion of the value of the real property.

Philippines

Branch income

The income tax rate on branch profits is the same as on corporate profits. In general, profits remitted abroad by a branch office are subject to a 15% tax rate, based on the total profits applied or earmarked for remittance, without any deduction for the tax component thereof. A lower rate may apply under certain tax treaties. Profits from qualified activities remitted by a branch registered with the Philippine Economic Zone Authority (PEZA) are exempt.

Income determination

Inventory valuation

Inventories are generally stated at cost or at the lower of cost or market. LIFO is not allowed for tax purposes. Generally, the inventory valuation method for tax purposes must conform to that used for book purposes.

Capital gains

Capital gains arise from the sale or exchange of 'capital assets'. Capital assets are property held by the taxpayer (whether or not connected with its trade) other than the following:

1. Inventories or property held primarily for sale to customers in the ordinary course of business;
2. Real property or depreciable property used in trade or business; and
3. Property of a kind that would be included in the inventory of the taxpayer if on hand at the close of the taxable year.

Capital losses are deductible only to the extent of capital gains.

There are no holding period requirements for capital assets of corporations. A 6% final tax is imposed on the higher of the gross selling price or fair market value upon the sale, exchange or disposition of land or buildings not actually used in the business of a corporation. The tax is withheld by the buyer at the time of sale. Net capital gains derived from the sale, exchange, transfer, or similar transactions of shares of stock not traded through a local stock exchange are taxed at 5% of gains not over PHP 100,000, and 10% of gains in excess of PHP 100,000. Sales of shares of stock listed and traded on a local stock exchange, other than the sale by a dealer in securities are subject to a stock transaction tax of 0.5%, based on the gross selling price.

Capital gains from the sale of bonds, debentures or other certificates of indebtedness with a maturity of more than five years are exempt from tax.

A tax is levied on every sale, barter, exchange, or other disposition through an initial public offering (IPO) of shares of stock in closely held corporations. A 'close corporation' is any corporation of which at least 50% in value of the total outstanding capital stock, or at least 50% of the total combined voting power of all classes of stock entitled to vote, is owned directly or indirectly by, or for, not more than 20 individuals. The tax rates provided hereunder are based on the proportion of the gross selling price, or gross value in money, of the shares of stock sold, bartered, exchanged, or otherwise disposed of to the total outstanding shares of stock after listing on the local stock exchange.

	%
25% or less	4
Over 25% but not over 33¹/₃%	2
Over 33¹/₃%	1

Inter-company dividends

Dividends received by a domestic or resident foreign corporation from another domestic corporation are not subject to tax. These dividends are excluded from the taxable income of the recipient.

Dividends received by a non-resident foreign corporation from a domestic corporation are subject to a final withholding tax at the rate of 15% if the country in which the corporation is domiciled either does not impose income tax on such dividends, or allows tax deemed paid credit of 15%. If the recipient is a resident of a country with which the Philippines has a tax treaty, the treaty rate applies if lower. Otherwise, the normal corporate income tax rate of 30% applies.

Foreign income

A Philippine (domestic) corporation is taxed on its worldwide income. A domestic corporation is taxed on income from foreign sources when earned or received, depending on the accounting method used by the taxpayer. Double taxation is generally relieved through a credit for foreign taxes. However, a taxpayer can take a deduction for foreign taxes instead, if that leads to a more favourable outcome.

Stock dividends

A Philippine corporation can distribute stock dividends tax-free, proportionately to all shareholders.

Other significant items

Interest on bank savings, time deposits and money market placements, and royalties received by domestic or resident foreign corporations from a domestic corporation, are subject to a final tax of 20%. Interest income of domestic or resident foreign corporations from FCDU deposits is subject to a final tax of 7.5%. Such income is excluded from gross income reportable in corporate income tax returns. Interest on loans granted to residents by OBUs and FCDUs, and income from foreign currency transactions with local commercial banks (domestic), and branches of foreign banks and other FCDUs, are subject to a 10% final tax, while income derived from foreign currency transactions with non-residents is exempt from tax.

Other non-taxable items include proceeds of life insurance policies; return of policy premium; gifts, bequests and devises; interest on certain government securities; income exempt under a treaty; gains from sale, exchange or retirement of bonds, debentures or other certificates of indebtedness with maturities of more than five years; and gains from redemption of shares of stock in mutual fund companies.

Deductions

Depreciation and depletion

Depreciation is generally computed on a straight-line basis, although any reasonable method may be elected if the aggregate amount of depreciation, plus salvage value at the end of the useful life of the property, will equal the cost of the property. Gain

Philippines

on the sale of depreciated property is taxable as ordinary income. Generally, book depreciation should conform to tax depreciation, unless the latter includes incentives. Properties used in petroleum operations may be depreciated over a period of 10 years using the straight-line or declining-balance method, at the option of the service contractor. Properties used in mining operations with expected life of more than 10 years may be depreciated over any number of years between five years and their expected life.

A cost depletion allowance is available as follows:

1. For oil and gas wells – Based on actual reduction in flow and production ascertained not by flush flow, but by the settled production or regular flow; and
2. For mines – An amount not to exceed the market value as used for purposes of imposing the mining *ad valorem* taxes on the products mined and sold during the year.

Net operating losses
A net operating loss for any taxable year immediately preceding the current taxable year, which had not been previously offset as a deduction from gross income, may be carried over as a deduction from gross income for the next three consecutive taxable years immediately following the year of this loss (except losses during the period when the taxpayer was tax-exempt), provided there has been no substantial change in the ownership of the business or enterprise. For mines other than oil and gas wells, a net operating loss calculated without the benefit of incentives provided for under Executive Order (EO) No. 226, or the Omnibus Investments Code of 1987, as amended, incurred in any of the first 10 years of operation may be carried over as a deduction from taxable income for the next five years immediately following the year of such loss. Loss carrybacks are not allowed.

Payments to foreign affiliates
A Philippine corporation can claim a deduction for royalties, management service fees and interest charges paid to foreign affiliates, provided such amounts are equal to what it would pay an unrelated entity, and the appropriate withholding taxes are withheld and remitted. The registration of licensing and management agreements, now known as technology transfer arrangements (TTAs), has been liberalised. Only TTAs not conforming to certain provisions of the Intellectual Property Code require approval by, and registration with, the Documentation, Information and Technology Transfer Bureau of the Intellectual Property Office (formerly Bureau of Patents, Trademarks and Technology Transfer) to render the contracts enforceable.

Taxes
Corporate taxpayers can claim a deduction for all taxes paid or accrued within the taxable year in connection with their trade or business, except for the following:

1. Philippine income tax;
2. Income taxes imposed by authority of any foreign country, unless the taxpayer elects to take a deduction in lieu of a foreign tax credit;
3. Estate and donor's taxes; and
4. Taxes assessed against local benefits of a kind tending to increase the value of the property assessed.

In the case of a foreign corporation, deductions for taxes are allowed only if they are connected with income from sources within the Philippines.

Special deductions

A resident foreign corporation is allowed to claim allocated head office expenses as a deduction, subject to compliance with certain requirements.

Other significant items

The deduction for charitable contributions ordinarily may not exceed 5% of taxable income. However, contributions to certain institutions are 100% deductible, subject to certain conditions. Special deductions are allowed for certain businesses, for example insurance, mining and petroleum. The allowable deduction for interest expense is reduced by an amount equal to 33% of interest income that is subject to final tax. Entertainment, amusement and recreation expenses should not exceed 0.5% of net sales for taxpayers engaged in sale of goods or properties, or 1% of net revenue for taxpayers engaged in sale of services, including professionals and lessors of properties.

Effective 1 July 2008, corporate taxpayers are given the option to avail of the optional standard deduction computed at 40% of gross income. The optional standard deduction shall be in lieu of the itemised operating expenses.

Group taxation

Group taxation is not permitted.

Tax incentives

Inward investment

See *Capital investment*.

Capital investment

Tax incentives available to export enterprises registered with the Board of Investments (BOI) are as follows:

1. Income tax holiday giving full exemption from corporate income tax for six years for pioneer firms and those locating in less-developed areas, and four years for non-pioneer firms from the date of commercial operation, or target date of operation, whichever is earlier. Expanding export-oriented firms are given three years. If prescribed conditions are met, an income tax holiday may be extended by up to three years. In no case, however, can an income tax holiday exceed eight years. Subject to certain exceptions, new and expansion projects located in the National Capital Region (NCR) or Metro Manila are no longer entitled to the income tax holiday;
2. Tax and duty exemption on imported spare parts and supplies for export producers with a customs bonded manufacturing warehouse exporting at least 70% of annual production, if foreign-owned or 50%, if Filipino-owned;
3. Full deduction of the cost of major infrastructure undertaken by enterprises in less-developed areas;
4. Additional deduction of 50% of the incremental labour expense if the prescribed ratio of capital assets to annual labour is met, and 100% of the incremental labour if located in less-developed areas within five years from date of registration (this incentive cannot be availed of simultaneously with the income tax holiday);

P

Philippines

5. Ten-year exemption from taxes and duties on importation of breeding stock and genetic materials;
6. Tax credit on domestic breeding stocks and genetic materials (10 years);
7. Exemption from wharfage, any export tax, duty, impost, or fees; and
8. Tax credits equivalent to taxes and duties paid on purchases of raw materials, supplies and semi-manufactured products forming part of the products for export.

Other incentives

Other incentives available are as follows:

Export and free-trade enterprises, information technology (IT) enterprises, and special economic zone developers/operators (including IT buildings located in Metro Manila and IT parks) registered with PEZA are entitled to an income tax holiday of six years for pioneer firms, and four years for non-pioneer firms. Foreign articles brought into the zones will be exempt from import duties and taxes. Local purchases of goods from VAT-registered suppliers outside the economic zones are zero-rated. After the lapse of the income tax holiday incentives, enterprises registered and operating within special economic zones/export processing zones will pay only 5% final tax on gross income earned, in lieu of paying all local and national taxes. A regional or area headquarters established in the country as a supervisory, communications and coordination centre for a corporation's subsidiaries, affiliates and branches in the Asia-Pacific region, and whose headquarters do not derive income from the Philippines, are not subject to any income tax nor value-added tax, and are entitled to certain non-tax incentives. Regional operating headquarters (ROHQ) that are allowed to derive income in the Philippines by performing qualifying business services to its affiliates, subsidiaries, or branches in the Philippines, in the Asia-Pacific Region and other foreign markets may avail itself of the following incentives:

1. Income tax at the preferential rate of 10% of its taxable income;
2. Exemption from all kinds of local taxes, fees, or charges imposed by a local government unit, except real property tax on land improvements and equipment;
3. Tax and duty-free importation of equipment and materials for training and conferences, which are needed and used solely for its functions as ROHQ and which are not locally available, subject to the prior approval of the BOI;
4. Importation of new motor vehicles, subject to the payment of corresponding duties and taxes; and
5. Exemption from travel tax, specific immigration fees and requirements, subject to certain conditions.

The following are the incentives granted to exporters under the Export Development Act (Republic Act No. 7844):

1. Exemption from Presidential Decree No. 1853 (requiring 100% of Letter of Credit), provided that the importation shall be used for the production of goods and services of export;
2. Tax credit for incremental export performance. The tax credit for increase in current export revenues shall be computed as a percentage to be applied on the incremental export revenue converted to pesos at the current rate. The percentages or rates are as follows:

    *   For the first five percent (5%) increase in annual export revenues over the previous year – 2.5%;

- For the next 5% increase – 5.0%;
- For the next 5% increase – 7.5%; and
- In excess – 10.0%.

(This incentive, however, is not available for exporters enjoying ITH or VAT exemption or whose local value-added tax is below 10%.)

3. In addition to the above incentive, all existing incentives being enjoyed by the enterprise if registered with the BOI, PEZA, SBMA, CDC, or other ecozone regulating agencies.

Withholding taxes (WHT)

Corporations and individuals engaged in business and paying certain types of income to non-residents are required to withhold the appropriate tax, which generally is 30% in the case of payments to non-resident foreign corporations, or 25% for non-resident aliens not engaged in trade or business. For withholding taxes on resident corporations, *see the discussions under the Income determination section*.

Tax treaty rates
For countries with which the Philippines has concluded tax treaties, the taxes to be withheld are as follows:

As of April 2010:

Country	Dividends (1) %	Interest (2) %	Royalties %
Australia	15/25 (3) (4)	10/15 (5)	15/25 (6)
Austria	10/25 (3) (7)	10/15 (5, 8)	10/15 (6, 9)
Bahrain	10/15 (7)	10	10/15 (10)
Bangladesh	10/15 (11)	15	15
Belgium	10/15 (7)	10	15
Brazil	15 /25	10/15 (5)	15/25 (12)
Canada	15/25 (3) (7)	10/15 (5)	25 (9)
China, P.R	10/15 (7)	10	10/15 (13)
Czech Republic	10/15 (7)	10	10/15 (14)
Denmark	10/15 (11)	10	15
Finland	15 (3) (7)	10/15 (5)	15/25 (15)
France	15/25 (3) (7)	10/15 (5)	15
Germany	10/15 (11)	10/15 (5, 16, 17)	10/15 (13)
Hungary	15/20 (3) (11)	15	15 (9)
India	15/20 (3) (7)	10/15 (5, 17)	15/35 (6)
Indonesia	15/20 (3) (11)	10/15 (5)	15/25 (6)
Israel	10/15 (7)	10	15 (9)
Italy	15	10/15 (5)	15/25 (6, 9, 18)
Japan	10/25 (3) (11)	10/15 (19)	10/15/25 (6, 20)
Korea, Rep. of	10/25 (3) (11)	10/15 (5)	10/15 (6)
Malaysia	15/25	15	15/25 (6)
Netherlands	10/15 (7)	10/15 (5, 16, 17)	10/15 (6)
New Zealand	15/25	10/15 (5)	15/25 (6)

Philippines

Country	Dividends (1) %	Interest (2) %	Royalties %
Norway	15/25 (3) (7)	15	7.5/10/25 (9, 21)
Pakistan	15/25 (3) (11)	10/15 (5)	15/25 (6)
Poland	10/15 (11)	10	15
Romania	10/15 (11)	10/15 (5, 16, 17)	10/15/25 (22)
Russia	15	15	15
Singapore	15/25 (3) (23)	10/15 (5)	15/25 (6, 18)
Spain	10/15 (7)	10/15 (5, 16)	10/15/20 (24)
Sweden	10/15 (11)	10	15
Switzerland	10/15 (7)	10	15
Thailand	15/35	10/15/25 (5)	15/25 (6, 18)
United Arab Emirates	10/15 (7)	10	10
United Kingdom	15/25 (3) (7)	10/15 (5)	15/25 (6, 20)
United States	20/25 (3) (7)	10/15 (5)	15/25 (6, 9)
Vietnam	10/15 (11)	15	15

Notes

1. The lower rate generally applies if the beneficial owner of the dividends is a company with a substantial ownership in the dividend paying company.
2. Interest derived by a foreign government or its agencies is typically exempt from Philippine tax. Many treaties also contain special rules for both Philippine and home country taxation of interest paid on instruments secured by a government agency of one of the countries. Such provisions have been excluded from the analysis.
3. A 15% rate applies under domestic law if the home country exempts the dividend from tax or permits a 20% or greater credit for corporate taxes paid by the company paying the dividend.
4. Entitlement to the lower rate depends on how the dividend will be taxed in Australia.
5. The 10% rate applies to interest paid in respect of the public issues of bonds, debentures, or similar obligations.
6. The lower rate applies to royalties paid by an enterprise registered with the Philippine Board of Investments and engaged in preferred areas of activity.
7. The threshold for substantial ownership is 10%.
8. The 10% rate also applies to interest paid by a company registered with the Board of Investments and engaged in preferred pioneer areas of investment in the Philippines.
9. The treaty also contains a most-favoured-nation rule, limiting the Philippine tax on royalties to the lowest rate of Philippine tax that may be imposed on royalties of the same kind paid in similar circumstances to a resident of a third state.
10. The 15% rate applies to royalties arising from the use of, or the right to use, any copyright of literary, artistic, or scientific work including cinematograph films or tapes for television or broadcasting.
11. The threshold for substantial ownership is 25%.
12. The 25% rate applies to royalties arising from the use or the right to use trademarks and cinematographic films, films or tapes for television or radio broadcasting. The 15% applies to any other royalties.
13. The 10% rate applies to the use of, or the right to use, any patent, trademark, design or model, plan, secret formula or process, or from the use of, or the right to use, industrial, commercial, or scientific equipment, or for information concerning industrial, commercial, or scientific experience. Strictly, application of the rate is generally at the discretion of the Philippine Competent Authorities, but the BIR has never raised this as an issue.
14. The 10% rate applies to royalties arising from the use of, or the right to use, any copyright of literary, artistic, or scientific work (other than copyright of cinematograph films), any patent, trademark, design or model, plan, secret formula or process, or from the use

of, or the right to use, industrial, commercial, or scientific equipment, or for information concerning industrial, commercial, or scientific experience.

15. The 15% rate applies to royalties paid by an enterprise registered and engaged in preferred areas of activities, and to royalties in respect of cinematographic films or tapes for television or broadcasting, and for the use of, or the right to use, any copyright. The 25% rate applies to other royalties.
16. The 10% rate also applies to interest paid in connection with the sale on credit of any industrial, commercial, or scientific equipment.
17. The 10% rate also applies to interest paid on any loans granted by a bank.
18. The 15% rate also applies to royalties in respect of cinematographic films or tapes for television or broadcasting.
19. The 10% rate applies to interest paid on government securities, or bonds or debentures. The 15% rate applies to any other interest income.
20. The 15% rate applies to royalties paid for the use of, or the right to use, cinematographic films and films or tapes for radio or television broadcasting.
21. The 7.5% rate applies to the lease of containers. The 10% rate applies to royalties paid by an enterprise registered with the Board of Investments. The 25% rate applies to other royalties.
22. The 10% rate applies to royalties paid by an enterprise registered with the Board of Investments and engaged in preferred pioneer areas of activity. The 15% rate applies to rentals from cinematographic films and tapes for television or broadcasting. The 25% rate applies to all other royalties.
23. The threshold for substantial ownership is 15%.
24. The 10% rate applies to royalties paid by an enterprise registered with the Board of Investments and engaged in preferred pioneer areas of activity. The 20% rate applies to rentals from cinematographic films and tapes for television or broadcasting. The 15% rate applies to all other royalties.

Tax administration

Returns
Corporations should file their returns and compute their income on the basis of an accounting period of 12 months. This accounting period may be either a calendar year or a fiscal year. With prior approval of the Commissioner of Internal Revenue, corporations may change their accounting period from calendar year to fiscal year, or vice versa. Corporate taxpayers file self-assessing returns. Electronic filing and payment of taxes are available under the Electronic Filing and Payment System (EFPS) of the BIR.

Payment of tax
Every corporation files cumulative quarterly income tax returns for the first three quarters, and pays the tax due thereon within 60 days after each quarter. A final adjustment return covering the total net taxable income of the preceding taxable year must be filed on the fifteenth day of the fourth month following the close of the taxable year. The balance of the tax due after deducting the quarterly payments must be paid, while the excess may be claimed as refund or tax credit. Excess estimated quarterly income taxes paid may be carried over and credited against estimated quarterly income tax liabilities for succeeding taxable years. Once the option to carry over has been made, such option is irrevocable for that taxable period, and no cash refund or tax credit certificate (TCC) is allowed.

P

Corporate taxes in Poland

For more information, contact:

Iwona Smith
PricewaterhouseCoopers
International Business Centre
Aleja Armii Ludowej 14
00-638 Warszawa, Poland
Tel: +48 22 523 4000
Email: iwona.smith@pl.pwc.com

Significant developments

At the end of 2009, Poland adopted the law to implement three major European Union (EU) Directives on VAT (VAT Package). The law came into force as of 1 January 2010, and set new rules related to the following areas:

- Place of the supply of services;
- VAT refund (eased procedures related to cases where a business is entitled to a claim VAT refund from a foreign country belonging to the EU); and
- Reporting requirements aimed at preventing tax evasion.

On 1 July 2009, new rules came into force with respect to withholding taxes on interest and royalties paid to related companies based in the EU. Before that date, such payments were subject to a 10% preferential withholding tax rate provided that specified conditions were met. Starting from 1 July 2009, the specified conditions remained the same, however, the preferential withholding tax rate was cut to 5%.

Taxes on corporate income

The corporate income tax (CIT) is the only tax levied on corporate income. The CIT rate is 19%.

The CIT applies to all legal entities (including, but not limited to, corporations), which are companies under organisation and "organisational entities without corporate status" (with the exception of partnerships), which run business activities. Partnerships are regarded as "transparent entities," which means that partnerships are not taxpayers. Instead, the income generated by partnerships is allocated to and taxed in the hands of the partners.

Further to these rules, the CIT applies to companies with foreign participation. Such companies may be set up as either limited liability companies or joint-stock companies. There is no limitation on the percentage of foreign participation. Both types are subject to the general CIT rules, including the 19% tax rate. The same rate applies to branches of foreign companies *(see the "Branch income" section for more information)*.

Corporate residence

A company is considered to be a resident if its registered office or management is located in Poland. Polish residents are subject to tax on their worldwide income. Non-residents are taxed only on their Polish-sourced income.

The tax authorities' right to tax a non-resident is further limited if the non-resident's home country concluded a double-tax treaty with Poland. In this case, the Polish tax authorities are entitled to tax only the portion of the non-resident's income that is derived through a permanent establishment (PE) located in Poland. The exceptions relate to specific types of income such as royalties, interest, dividend and capital gains that are taxed based on special treaty rules.

Other taxes

Value-added tax (VAT)

Polish VAT applies to the following activities:

- Supplies of goods and services within the territory of Poland;
- Exports of goods outside the territory of the EU;
- Imports of goods from countries that do not belong to the EU;
- Intra-community acquisitions of goods (imports from countries belonging to the EU); and
- Intra-community supplies of goods (exports to the countries belonging to the EU).

VAT rates

The VAT rates are 22% (standard rate), 7%, 3%, 0% and exemption. The standard 22% VAT rate generally applies to the supply of all goods and services, except for those that are covered by special VAT provisions that provide other rates or treatments. Supplies covered by a reduced rate of 7% include, among others, supplies of pharmaceutical products and passenger transport services. Supplies of certain agricultural products will be subject to VAT at a rate of 3% until the end of 2010 (a 7% rate will apply from 2011). Zero-rated activities include, among others, exports of goods to countries outside the EU. VAT-exempt supplies include, among others, certain financial, insurance and educational services.

Basic calculation rules

In general, the VAT due equals the VAT on outputs decreased by the VAT on inputs (in other words, input VAT is deducted from output VAT). Input VAT may be deducted from output VAT when a business (with a VAT payer status) receives an invoice for goods or services purchased. Input VAT may not be deducted unless a purchased supply is linked to the VAT-able activities. Furthermore, the deductibility of input VAT is restricted by the VAT law with respect to the purchase of certain goods and services. In addition, subject to numerous conditions, output VAT may be reduced when receivables, resulting from VAT-able sales, become uncollectible.

VAT refunds

The Polish VAT law allows direct refunds when input VAT (available for deduction) exceeds output VAT. A Polish business may also be entitled to the VAT refund owed by another country under certain circumstances. If such country belongs to the EU, the procedure is substantially simplified due to the EU Directive 2008/9/EC. The same directive provides favourable rules for businesses based in other EU countries that are seeking VAT refunds in Poland. This directive was implemented in Poland as of 1 January 2010.

Reporting rules

Generally, the VAT reporting period is one month. VAT returns should be submitted by the twenty-fifth day of the month following the VAT reporting period. From 1 January

Poland

2009, all taxpayers may opt for a quarterly, instead of monthly, reporting period. Note that businesses involved in intra-community acquisitions or supplies of goods are obliged to submit additional VAT returns with respect to these particular transactions.

International services
The treatment of international services largely depends on the place of supply, since it is determinative of whether particular services are subject to the Polish VAT. The Polish VAT applies only to those services that are supplied within Poland. If a Polish entity provides such services, it should invoice the recipient based on general rules (i.e., rules that are equally applicable to purely domestic services). If a Polish business receives services that are supplied in Poland (and such services are rendered by a foreign provider), such Polish business should recognise "import of services," and as a result, should report output and input VAT of the same amount (equal to the value of the services multiplied by the applicable VAT rate). Therefore, in most cases, the import of services is VAT-neutral. Finally, taxpayers should consider circumstances in which a Polish business renders services outside of Poland. In this case, as previously mentioned, the services are not subject to the Polish VAT, however, the business in question is entitled to deduct input VAT paid in relation with these activities.

The rules determining the location where international services are provided changed on 1 January 2010, following the implementation of the EU Directive 2008/8/EC. Generally, the place of supply depends on the recipient of services. If the recipient is a business entity, the place of supply is determined to be the recipient's country; if the recipient is a private person, the place of supply is determined to be the service provider's country. However, these general rules are subject to several exceptions.

Excise duties
Excise duties are levied on the production, sale, import and intra-community acquisition of "excise goods," which are listed in the excise duty law and include (among others) alcohol, cigarettes, energy products (e.g., petrol, oils, gas etc.), passenger cars and electricity.

Depending on the excise goods in question, one of four methods of calculating excise tax may be applicable:

- A percentage of the taxable base;
- An amount per unit;
- A percentage of the maximum retail price; or
- An amount per unit and a percentage of the maximum retail price.

The excise rate for car petrol is PLN 1,565 per 1,000 litres.

Passenger cars are subject to the following excise rates:

- 3.1% for cars with engine cubic capacity that does not exceed 2000cm^3; and
- 18.6% for cars with engine cubic capacity that exceeds 2000cm^3

Notwithstanding the above, Polish excise duty law provides for a wide system of excise duty exemptions as well as 0% taxation. Under specified circumstances such preferential treatment may apply to, specified goods that are otherwise taxed based on general rules. This concerns, for example, specific energy products used for other purposes than as a fuel or for heating.

Property tax

Property tax rates are fixed by municipalities within limits set in the Law on Local Taxes and Fees. In 2010, land used for business purposes is subject to a rate limit of PLN 0.77 per square metre. Buildings used for business purposes are subject to a rate limit of PLN 20.51 per square metre.

Capital tax

A share capital increase is subject to a 0.5% capital tax, payable by a company that receives a capital contribution. This tax applies equally to limited liability companies as well as joint-stock companies. A merger, division, or transformation of a company into another company is no longer subject to capital tax, even if the transaction results in a share capital increase for any party. A similar exemption applies to a capital increase resulting from an in-kind contribution, including a whole business or a branch thereof.

Branch income

Foreign businesses are allowed, under certain conditions, to establish their branch offices (exclusively within the scope of their "foreign" business activity) and representative offices (exclusively with regard to promotion and advertising) in Poland.

A branch office almost always has PE status in Poland. Once a branch is established, the foreign company pays CIT at the standard rate of 19%, based on the income attributable to the operations of the Polish branch. For this purpose, as well as for accounting purposes, a branch is obliged to keep accounting books that include all the data necessary to establish the taxable base. In this respect, general income determination rules relevant to Polish companies apply to branches as well. In the few cases in which a branch can demonstrate, based on a double-tax treaty, that its business presence in Poland does not amount to a PE, its profits are not subject to Polish corporate income tax.

Income determination

Tax base

The tax base is the overall income, which is a difference between aggregated taxable revenue and aggregated tax-deductible costs. A tax-deductible cost is defined as a "cost incurred in order to generate revenue" as well as the cost incurred to "protect a source of revenue."

Subject to numerous exemptions, the tax base includes all sources of income. Consequently, there is no special treatment for income such as capital gains or interest.

In practice, taxable income is calculated by adjusting the profit reported for accounting purposes. The relevant adjustments are necessary due to differences between tax and accounting treatment of numerous revenue and cost items. As a result, the taxable base is usually higher than the accounting profit.

Inventory

Generally, the value of lost inventory may be included as a tax-deductible cost. Other write-offs in the value of inventory are not recognised for tax purposes until the inventory in question is sold.

Poland

When inventory is lost or sold, a tax deduction is allowed for the costs incurred when the inventory was purchased. The methods acceptable for inventory valuation for tax (and accounting) purposes are standard cost, average (weighted) cost, first-in, first-out (FIFO), and last-in, first-out (LIFO).

Capital gains
There is no separate capital gains tax. Capital gains or losses are aggregated with an entity's other taxable income or losses. Capital losses are tax-deductible.

Domestic dividends
Dividends received from Polish residents (domestic dividends) are excluded from overall income. Instead, such dividends are subject to a 19% tax, which is withheld and remitted to the tax office by the payer of dividends.

However, based on the participation exemption, which was introduced and effective from 1 January, 2007, domestic dividends are no longer subject to the 19% tax, provided that the Polish beneficiary holds at least a 15% share in the paying company for at least two years.

Foreign income
Resident corporations are taxed on their worldwide income unless there is an applicable double-tax treaty in place between Poland and the relevant foreign state that provides that the foreign income shall be exempt from taxation in Poland. In all other cases (in particular, when the income is not covered by any treaty), Poland uses the credit method to avoid double taxation. Therefore, a Polish resident is liable for income tax imposed on its worldwide income, but the tax is proportionately reduced by the income tax paid abroad.

Dividends from abroad
Generally, dividends collected by a Polish corporate tax resident, if paid by a non-resident, are treated as regular income and taxed at the standard CIT rate. Corporate tax on such dividends paid in other countries may be credited proportionately against Polish CIT. The CIT law also provides for an "underlying tax credit," which is related to the CIT paid by a foreign subsidiary under a foreign tax jurisdiction, subject to a number of conditions. Specifically, a double-tax treaty between Poland and the subsidiary's country of residence should be in place and the Polish recipient of the dividend should hold at least 75% of the shares in the foreign subsidiary.

Much more favourable rules apply to dividends received from subsidiaries having their residences in EU countries or in Iceland, Liechtenstein, Norway or Switzerland. Such dividends are CIT-exempt (i.e., participation exemption) provided that the Polish recipient holds at least 10% of the shares in the paying company for at least two years (with respect to the Swiss subsidiaries, the minimum shareholding is 25%).

Transfer pricing
Transactions between related parties should be conducted in accordance with the arm's-length principle. The tax authorities may increase the taxable base if the pricing used between related parties differs from what would have been used between unrelated parties in a similar business transaction and the difference results in income being shifted from a Polish taxpayer to another entity (whether a Polish resident or not). Similar rules apply to transactions between Polish residents and the residents

of tax haven countries. These transactions may be subject to the transfer pricing principles even if the parties thereto are not related. The CIT law also contains detailed requirements for transfer pricing documentation.

Taxpayers can reduce the transfer pricing risk by applying for an advance pricing arrangement (APA). An APA decision shall be issued by the Minister of Finance in response to a taxpayer's application. An APA will oblige a taxpayer to follow a specified methodology when calculating the transfer prices applicable to transactions between related entities. In exchange, the tax authorities may not challenge the agreed upon methodology.

Deductions

Tax depreciation

Depreciation is treated as a tax-deductible cost. Generally, depreciation allowances are calculated based on the straight-line method and the maximum rates provided in the CIT law. If this is the case, a taxpayer deducts equal annual write-offs, calculated by multiplying the maximum rate of depreciation by the asset's initial value until the total value of write-offs equals the initial value (typically, the initial value equals the purchase price).

For certain categories of machinery and vehicles (but not passenger cars) the reducing-balance depreciation method may be applied. Under this method, the tax depreciation may be accelerated during the initial period of the asset's use by multiplying the statutory maximum rate by two. The rate is then applied to the net value of fixed assets (i.e., initial value reduced by earlier annual write-offs). The reducing-balance method is applied until the annual depreciation write-off equals the hypothetical write-off that would be made under the straight-line method. From this point, the depreciation allowance is taken based on the straight-line method for its remaining useful life.

The main categories of assets and the related statutory annual tax depreciation rate:

	%
Various buildings and constructions	1.5–10.0
Machinery and equipment (general)	7.0–20.0
Machinery for road building and construction	18.0–20.0
Machinery for paper industry	14.0
Office equipment	14.0
Computers	30.0

Apart from the above, the Polish CIT law includes provisions for accelerated depreciation (within specified limits) for assets used in deteriorated conditions and for second-hand assets.

Tax losses

A tax loss reported in a tax year may be carried forward over the next five consecutive tax years; however, in any particular tax year, the taxpayer may not deduct more than 50% of the loss incurred in the year in which it was reported. For example, a taxpayer that incurred PLN 100 annual loss in 2010 may carry it forward to 2011-2015. However

Poland

the maximum loss deduction in any of these years may not exceed PLN 50 (assuming that there are no other losses available for deduction).

Payments to foreign affiliates

Deductions may be claimed for royalties, management services and interest charges paid to foreign affiliates. However, note that interest expenses are subject to the thin capitalisation restrictions *(see the following section)*. Furthermore, note that transactions with related companies should be made according to the market conditions. Where a company shifts income to another entity (especially a foreign entity), the tax authorities may adjust the taxable base upward *(see Transfer pricing section)*.

Thin capitalisation

A portion of the interest paid by a Polish company on a loan granted by a qualified lender (a qualified shareholder or a qualified sister company) will not be considered a tax-deductible cost if the value of the Polish company's overall debt from the shareholders and other affiliates mentioned in the tax law exceeds three times the value of the Polish company's share capital (3:1 debt-to-equity ratio). A qualified shareholder is defined as a holder of 25% or more of the voting power of a Polish company. A qualified sister company is a company of which a shareholder holds at least 25% of the value of the shares.

Taxes

Income tax and, in most cases, VAT are not deductible. However, VAT is deductible for CIT purposes if it cannot be offset against the company's output VAT. Other taxes, if paid in the course of business activities, are generally deductible in full.

Business expenses

Generally, a tax-deductible cost is defined as a cost incurred in order to generate taxable revenue or to "protect a source of income". The last element of the definition of a tax-deductible cost was added a few years ago to reduce uncertainties surrounding the deductibility of business expenses that do not directly generate revenue.

The CIT law provides a list of items that are not deductible for tax purposes, even if the items meet the general conditions described above. This list contains over 60 items including, among others, the following:

1. Written-off, lapsed accounts receivable;
2. Entertainment costs;
3. Accrued but unpaid interest;
4. Accounting and comparable provisions;
5. Tax penalties and penalty interest;
6. A portion of the insurance premium paid on a passenger car – the portion calculated on the excess of the car value over EUR 20,000; and
7. A portion of the depreciation write-offs made on a passenger car – the portion calculated on the excess of the car value over EUR 20,000.

Furthermore, expenses incurred in connection with the acquisition of fixed and intangible assets (e.g., licenses, trademarks, know-how) are not deductible directly. Instead, the acquired assets are subject to depreciation. If such assets are sold, a business is entitled to deduct the net value (cost of acquisition reduced by the overall value of the tax depreciation allowances made). Similar treatment relates to the acquisition of shares or land, except that these particular assets are not depreciable. Therefore, the full cost of an acquisition of shares or land may be deducted when such assets are sold.

Group taxation

The CIT law includes provisions on group taxation (i.e., in theory, a group of companies) if it meets certain conditions and can be treated as a single taxpayer. However, the required conditions are extremely demanding and as such, very few taxpayers of this type exist.

Tax incentives

Polish legislation provides investment incentives related to business activities carried out in 14 zones defined as Special Economic Zones. A business entity can benefit from tax incentives offered by a Special Economic Zone, provided that the entity obtains a permit from the Ministry of the Economy to conduct business activities there and meets other legal requirements.

Most of the Special Economic Zones offer income tax exemption of up to 50% of the investment expenditure. In other words, the annual CIT due is reduced by 50% of the investment expenditure. If the amount available for deduction exceeds the annual CIT due, the excess may be utilised in the following years. Furthermore, entities classified as small- or medium-sized may be granted income tax exemptions of up to 65% of their investment expenditure. Consequently, in the case of significant investments, it is possible for businesses that run activities in the Special Economic Zones to enjoy total exemption from income tax for a considerable period.

Withholding taxes (WHT)

Domestic provisions: General rules
The general WHT rate for dividends is 19%. Other types of income, such as income from the redemption of shares or liquidation of a company, are taxed at the same 19% rate. The general WHT rate on interest and royalties paid to non-residents is 20%. These WHT rates may be reduced by double-tax treaties.

There is also a 20% WHT on payments made to non-residents as consideration for intangible supplies (such as consulting services). However, if a payment is made to a country that has a double-tax treaty with Poland, this tax may be avoided with the completion of certain minimal administrative formalities.

Special treatment: EU directives
The CIT law provisions and certain EU directives provide special treatment for dividends, royalties and interest paid to numerous European countries. Dividends paid to corporate residents of EU countries as well as Iceland, Liechtenstein, Norway and Switzerland are exempt from WHT, subject to certain conditions specified in the CIT law. The basic requirement is that the foreign beneficiary holds at least 10% of the shares in the Polish company for a minimum of two years. This exemption also applies to income resulting from the redemption of shares or the liquidation of a company.

When joining the EU, Poland was granted a transitional period to phase out the WHT on interest and royalty payments paid by Polish corporate residents to associated EU

P

Poland

companies. Starting from 1 July 2009, the WHT rate on these payments is 5%. Starting from 1 July 2013, a full exemption will apply. In general, the transitional rules, as well as the full exemption after 1 July 2013, only apply to interest and royalty payments between associated companies (parent-subsidiary relationships or sister-sister relationships) in which capital involvements are significant.

Treaty rates

If EU special rules do not apply, Polish companies are required to withhold tax on payments of dividends, interest and royalties based on domestic CIT Law provisions. However, the domestic withholding tax (WHT) rates can be decreased by a double-tax treaty concluded between Poland and the payment recipient's country of residence.

The following table lists the WHT rates as provided in the treaties concluded by Poland. Notably, the following table shows only rates that result from general treaty provisions; the treaties themselves occasionally include special provisions (applicable in special circumstances or to special entities) that provide lower WHT rates than the ones listed.

Furthermore, if a treaty rate is higher than a domestic one, the latter should apply.

Recipient	Dividends	Interest	Royalties
	%	%	%
Non-treaty	19	20	20
Treaty:			
Albania	10	10	5
Armenia	10	5	10
Australia	15	10	10
Azerbaijan	10	10	10
Austria	15	5	5
Bangladesh	15	10	10
Belarus	15	10	0
Belgium	15	5	5
Bosnia and Herzegovina (Yugoslavian Treaty)	15	10	10
Bulgaria	10	10	5
Canada	15	15	10
Chile	15	15	15
China, P.R.	10	10	10
Croatia	15	10	10
Cyprus	10	10	5
Czech Republic	10	10	5
Denmark	15	5	5
Egypt	12	12	12
Estonia	15	10	10
Finland	15	0	0
France	15	0	10
Georgia	10	8	8
Germany	15	5	5
Greece	Domestic rate	10	10
Hungary	10	10	10

Recipient	Dividends	Interest	Royalties
	%	%	%
Iceland	15	10	10
India	15	15	22.5
Indonesia	15	10	15
Iran	7	10	10
Ireland, Republic of	15	10	10
Israel	10	5	10
Italy	10	10	10
Japan	10	10	10
Jordan	10	10	10
Kazakhstan	15	10	10
Korea, Republic of	10	10	10
Kyrgyzstan	10	10	10
Kuwait	5	5	15
Latvia	15	10	10
Lebanon	5	5	5
Lithuania	15	10	10
Luxembourg	15	10	10
Macedonia	15	10	10
Malaysia	0	15	15
Malta	15	10	10
Mexico	15	15	10
Moldova	15	10	10
Morocco	15	10	10
Mongolia	10	10	5
Montenegro (Yugoslavian Treaty)	15	10	10
Netherlands	15	5	5
New Zealand	15	10	10
Norway	15	0	10
Pakistan	15	0	20
Philippines	15	10	15
Portugal	15	10	10
Romania	15	10	10
Russia	10	10	10
Serbia (Yugoslavian Treaty)	15	10	10
Singapore	10	10	10
Slovak Republic	10	10	5
Slovenia	15	10	10
South Africa	15	10	10
Spain	15	0	10
Sri Lanka	33.33	10	10
Sweden	15	0	5
Switzerland	15	10	10
Syria	10	10	18
Tajikistan	15	10	10

P

Poland

Recipient	Dividends	Interest	Royalties
	%	%	%
Thailand	20	10	15
Tunisia	10	12	12
Turkey	15	10	10
Ukraine	15	10	10
United Arab Emirates	5	5	5
United Kingdom	10	5	5
United States	15	0	10
Uzbekistan	15	10	10
Vietnam	15	10	15
Zimbabwe	15	10	10

Tax administration

CIT settlements
The annual CIT return should be submitted to the tax office within three months following the end of the tax year. The same deadline applies to the settlement of the annual CIT liability. In financial terms, the final settlement is not significant, since most of the annual liability is paid by CIT advances throughout the tax year. The CIT advances should be paid for each month by the twentieth day of the following month. The CIT advances do not need to be reported and thus, the annual return is the only tax return associated with the CIT.

Entities that started business activities (except for companies organised as a result of certain transformations) and entities whose gross sales revenue (including VAT) in the prior tax year did not exceed EUR 1,200,000 are entitled to opt to make advance settlements on a quarterly basis (instead of a monthly basis).

VAT settlements
Similar to the CIT, the VAT reporting period is a month. VAT returns should be submitted by the twenty-fifth day of the following month. However, starting from 1 January 2009, all taxpayers are entitled to opt for filing VAT returns on a quarterly basis. Taxpayers choosing a quarterly reporting period should submit VAT returns by the twenty-fifth day of the month following the last month of the quarter being reported. Payment of the VAT due should be made by the same deadline as the one provided for filing the monthly (or quarterly) VAT return.

Finally, businesses involved in intra-community acquisitions or supplies of goods (cross-border sale transactions within the EU), are obliged to submit additional VAT returns that report these particular transactions.

Corporate taxes in Portugal

For more information, contact:

Jaime Esteves
PricewaterhouseCoopers
Palácio Sottomayor
Rua Sousa Martins, 1 – 2°
1069-316 Lisbon
Portugal
Tel: +351 213 599 601
Email: jaime.esteves@pt.pwc.com

Significant developments

2010 state budget

Given the elections in September 2009 and the change of government, the state budget for 2010 was published on the 28 April 2010. The most significant amendments regarding corporate income tax are summarised below.

Bonuses and other variable remuneration paid to managers or board members
These are now subject to autonomous taxation at the rate of 35%, when the respective amount (i) corresponds to more than 25% of the annual salary and (ii) exceeds EUR 27,500; no taxation arises if not less than 50% of the payment is deferred for at least three years and the company has positive results during the same period; in 2010, the rate increased to 50% in case of managers or board members of banks and financial institutions.

Tax losses carryforward
The period to carryforward tax losses has been reduced from six to four years.

Limitation to tax benefits
The corporate income tax assessed after the deduction of tax benefits or derived from special tax regimes cannot be lower than 75% (formerly 60%) of the amount that would be assessed if no deductions would apply.

Elimination of double taxation on dividends distributed by European Economic Area (EEA) subsidiaries
Portuguese parent companies are now exempt from taxation on dividends received from subsidiaries resident in a Member State of the EEA; this means that besides the 27 European Union (EU) Member States, Iceland, Liechtenstein and Norway now benefit from this regime; additionally, no withholding tax is levied on dividends paid by a Portuguese subsidiary to a parent company resident or to a permanent establishment located in a EEA member state, provided the conditions foreseen in the EU Parent/Subsidiary, as transposed by Portugal, apply (at least 10% ownership or EUR 20 million acquisition value and at least one year holding period); since Liechtenstein is black-listed, the regime will apply after the conclusion of agreements on exchange of information.

P

Portugal

Relief from taxation on capital gains under the reinvestment regime
The reinvestment of the sales proceeds arising from the sale of shares no longer provides for a relief from a taxation on the capital gains realised, in case the reinvestment is made in Portuguese State bonds; this measure aims to harmonise with the EU law, as the regime did not apply in case of acquisition of foreign State bonds. The regime is still in force in case of reinvestment in other securities or tangible assets (conditions apply).

The Stability and Growth Programme for 2010-2013
In March 2010, the Portuguese Government presented to the Parliament the Stability and Growth Programme for 2010-2013 (PEC – "Programa de Estabilidade e Crescimento"). PEC is the Portuguese Government's strategy to reduce public deficit, reducing tax benefits and increasing tax revenues, while at the same time aiming a structural reform towards modernisation and competitiveness of the Portuguese economy.

The measures proposed in the PEC focus in particular on the period 2010 through 2013. These are, among others, an autonomous taxation that will apply to fringe benefits, namely daily allowances, use of company car and other benefits in kind; salaries and other remuneration received by board members, directors or shareholders of loss-making companies shall be subject to autonomous taxation, above certain limits yet to be defined.

On 12 May 2010, additional measures within PEC were announced – an additional corporate income tax (CIT) of 2.5% will apply on taxable profit above EUR 2 million.

A new accounting system
The adoption of International Accounting Standards (IAS) in the EU had an important impact in Portugal, leading to the adoption of a new accounting system – "Sistema de Normalização Contabilística" (SNC). This also had a significant impact on the CIT Code and other legislation – the main changes are as follows:

- Republication of the CIT Code and publication of a new depreciation regime, which adjusts the tax terminology to the accounting terms;
- Greater independence between the accounting and tax rules (partial dependence);
- New rules for CIT assessment; and
- New and more detailed obligations at the level of the tax file ("Dossier Fiscal").

From 1 January 2010 onwards, new tax rules are in force, including:

- Depreciation and amortisation are allowed as tax-deductible expenses to the extent they are accounted for as current year costs or costs incurred in previous tax years (formerly only tax-deductible if accounted for in the current tax year);
- Different depreciation methods, besides straight-line method and declining-balance method, may be applied without previous approval from the Portuguese Tax Authority (annual depreciation cannot exceed the depreciation resulting from using either the straight-line or declining-balance methods);
- Upon authorisation from the Tax Authorities, it is possible to change the depreciation method during the lifetime of the asset;
- Depreciation of light vehicles and capital losses realised are disallowed as a tax-deductible cost in the amount that exceeds an amount to be defined by Decree (previously EUR 40,000; EUR 29,927.87 in 2009 and previous tax years);

- Assets with an acquisition cost not exceeding EUR 1,000 (formerly EUR 199.52) are allowed as a tax cost of the year;
- Costs incurred with loans are included in the acquisition or production value of inventories with a useful life of more than one year;
- Advertising campaigns – It is no longer possible to deduct the costs over three years, except for campaigns launched prior to 2010;
- Impairment losses on depreciable assets disallowed as tax-deductible expenses are deductible over the remaining lifetime of the asset or until the period immediately prior to its transfer;
- The provision for guarantees to clients, under certain conditions, is acceptable for tax purposes;
- The criteria used for measuring provisions for accounting purposes (present value) is acceptable for tax purposes;
- The last in, first out (LIFO) inventory method is disallowed; and
- New rules have been issued for financial instruments.

Certain transitional adjustments resulting from the adoption of the new accounting system with tax impact are treated as follows:

- Adjustments in equity with tax relevance are considered for CIT purposes over a five-year period; and
- Supplementary contributions to pension funds required to cover the increase of responsibilities as a consequence of the adoption of the SNC are deductible over a five-year period.

Taxes on corporate income

Two thresholds of taxable income determine the application of the following tax rates:

- Up to EUR 12,500, the tax rate is 12.5%.
- The standard tax rate of 25% is applied to the remaining taxable income.

It should be noted that under the Stability and Growth Programme a new additional taxation of 2.5% (State surtax – "Derrama estadual") will apply on the excess of taxable profits above EUR 2 million.

The CIT rate is increased in most cases by a municipal surcharge ("Derrama") of up to 1.5%, computed on the taxable profit before the deduction of tax losses from previous years.

Special rates apply to income generated in Portugal that is attributable to non-residents, *see Withholding taxes section.*

Corporate residence

Tax is assessed on the worldwide income of business entities with their head office or effective management in Portugal. Tax is also applicable to income attributable to a permanent establishment of a non-resident company in Portugal.

Portugal

Other taxes

Surcharges
The following surcharges, self-assessed with the corporate tax, are levied on:

- Representation and entertainment expenses: 10%;
- Company car expenses: 10%; 5% for low-pollution vehicles (not applicable for electrical vehicles);
- Mileage allowance: 5%;
- Per diem allowance: 5%;
- Non-documented payments: 50% (70% for partially or fully exempted taxpayers);
- Company car expenses for which acquisition cost exceeds a limit to be determined by Decree (formerly, EUR 40,000): 20% for taxpayers in a tax loss position;
- Dividends distributed to exempt taxpayers regarding participations held for less than one year: 20%;
- The total amount of the expenses incurred with any compensation paid as a result of the termination of functions of managers or board members, if not related to the productivity targets previously established under the existing labour relation; or the amount that exceeds the remuneration that would be received by the manager or the board member until the term of the labour agreement, in case of redundancy prior to that term; or in all cases if the liability for the payment is shifted to another entity: 35%; and
- The total amount of the expenses incurred with bonuses paid to managers or board members if the respective amount corresponds to more than 25% of the annual salary and exceeds EUR 27,500; at 35%. In 2010, the rate increased to 50% in case of managers or board members of banks and financial institutions.

Value-added tax (VAT)
VAT closely follows the EU Counsel Directive 2006/112/EC, dated 28 November, and is assessed at the normal rate of 20% (14% in the Autonomous Regions of Madeira and the Azores), at an intermediate rate of 12%, and at a reduced rate of 5%.

On 12 May 2010, it was announced that all the VAT rates will be increased by 1%, with effect from 1 July 2010 – the standard rate will increase to 21% (15% in the Autonomous Regions of Madeira and the Azores), the intermediate to 13% and the reduced rate to 6%. In principle these shall be transitory measures, in force until 2011.

Restaurant services, basic canned foods, fruit jellies, fats, honey, coffee, natural water, fruit juices, decorative flowers, petroleum and diesel fuel for equipment for agricultural and fishing activities and certain ecological equipment, are subject to the 12% rate. Food, books, some pharmaceutical products, milk products and certain services are assessed at 5%. Exports and intra-EU-transfer of goods are zero-rated.

The transposition of Council Directive 2008/8/EC led to significant changes of the national VAT legislation on the deemed place of supply of services, defining two general rules as of 1 January 2010.

As of 1 January 2010, the general rule for taxation of business-to-business (B2B) services is the place where the customer is established or has a permanent establishment, permanent address or where he usually resides. Whereas for business-to-consumer (B2C) services, the general rule remains the place where the supplier is established. Note that on 1 January 2011; 1 January 2013; and 1 January 2015, additional adjustments to the VAT rules will become effective.

In addition, as of 1 January 2010, the existing procedure for obtaining a VAT refund in another EU member state other than the member state of establishment has been replaced by a new electronic procedure, as indicated in Council Directive 2008/9/CE.

Finally, as of January 2010, the provisions of Council Regulation 143/2008 are in force regarding administrative cooperation and exchange of information concerning the place of supply of services, the special scheme and the refund procedures.

Stamp tax

Stamp duty is payable on a wide variety of transactions and documents, at rates that may be set in specific amounts or on a percentage basis. Important examples include the following:

Item	%
Loans (on the principal)	
– With determined term, over 1 year	0.5–0.6
– With undetermined term or under 1 year	0.04 per month
Guarantees	
– Over 1 year	0.5–0.6
– Under 1 year or with undetermined term	0.04 per month
Bank interest and fees	4
Insurance premiums	3–9
Incorporation of companies (on the share capital) – expected abolishment, as foreseen in 2010 State Budget Proposal	0.4
Real estate purchases and sales	0.8
Donations and inheritances	10
Sale of business as a going concern	5

Property tax

"Imposto Municipal sobre Imóveis" (IMI) is a municipal tax upon which taxable basis is calculated by reference to a formula based on objective criteria, such as the construction cost per square metre, area, age, construction quality and comfort indexes.

The property tax is levied in addition to corporate or individual tax assessed on actual income generated by real estate.

Tax rates	%
Urban real estate	0.4–0.7
Urban real estate (valued under the new rules)	0.2–0.4
Rural real estate	0.8

The tax rate of municipal tax on properties owned by entities resident for tax purposes in a blacklisted territory is 1%.

Portugal

Property transfer tax

"Imposto Municipal sobre as Transmissões Onerosas de Imóveis" (IMT) is a municipal tax payable in Portugal on the onerous transfer of local real estate. The tax is levied on the purchaser, and the taxable basis is the same as for IMI, or the price agreed upon by the contracting parties, whichever is higher.

The IMT rates are set at 5% for rural real estate and 6.5% for urban real estate and land for construction. For non-residents located in blacklisted jurisdictions, the rate is 8%.

The transfer of residential property is subject to IMT at marginal and progressive tax rates from 1% up to 8%. An exemption is available for a taxable basis not higher than EUR 90,418, applicable to situations where the residential property is the permanent residence of the acquirer. Taxable basis higher than EUR 561,960 (EUR 557,500 in 2009) is subject to a 6% flat rate, in case the residential property is the permanent residence of the acquirer.

Branch income

Branch profits are taxed on the same basis as corporate profits. Income remitted by a branch to the head office is not subject to taxation.

Income determination

Taxable income is based on the accounting income adjusted according to the specific provisions of the tax legislation, when applicable.

Inventory valuation

Inventories are valued at the lower of the following values: cost or net realisable value. The first-in, first-out (FIFO) and average-cost methods of valuation are accepted.

Inventory adjustments are deductible for tax purposes on the amount accounted for in the tax year, capped at the difference between the acquisition or production value and, if lower, the net realisable value (duly documented) with reference to the balance sheet.

Capital gains

The positive net difference between capital gains and capital losses arising from the disposal of fixed assets or shares, held for more than one year, is taxed as part of normal income.

Capital gains and capital losses are determined by the difference between the sales proceeds, deducted from any related cost, and the acquisition value, deducted from impairment losses and tax-deductible depreciations or amortisations, adjusted by the inflation index (in case of at least two years ownership).

Only half the amount of the negative difference between capital gains and capital losses arising from the disposal of shares or other negative net worth variations related to participations or other parts of the equity of a company, such as supplementary capital contributions, are considered for purposes of assessing the taxable income.

In certain circumstances, only 50% of the net gains on disposal of tangible fixed assets or shares are taxed, provided the sales proceeds are reinvested.

Capital losses regarding shares owned for less than three years when acquired from related companies, offshore companies or companies subject to a privileged taxation regime are not deductible. Capital losses are also not tax-deductible if the shares are transferred to related parties, offshore companies or entities subject to a privileged taxation regime.

Capital gains/losses realised by holding companies ("Sociedade Gestora de Participações Sociais", or SGPS) are not taxed/deductible, if the underlying shares have been held for more than one year (or three years if the shares were acquired from related parties, offshore companies or entities subject to a special tax regime).

Inter-company dividends

For Portuguese-resident companies holding shares in other Portuguese companies, or in companies resident in Portuguese African Speaking countries, or in companies resident in the EU or the EEA (meeting the p/Subsidiary Directive 90/435/CEE), 100% of the dividends distributed are excluded from the taxable income. In case of Portuguese, EU and EEA subsidiaries, the shares should represent at least 10% of total capital, or have an acquisition value not lower than EUR 20 million, and if it has been held for at least one year (this minimum holding period should be met before or after distribution). For holding companies or SGPS, the deduction requires only the fulfilment of the shareholding period.

This also applies to regional development corporations ("Sociedades de desenvolvimento regional"), investment companies, securities dealers and insurance companies (where technical reserves are concerned) regardless of the proportion of capital or the period held.

Foreign income

A Portuguese company is taxed on all its foreign income. Taxes paid abroad can be offset against corresponding Portuguese tax capped at the lower of a) the tax liability corresponding to the foreign income or b) the foreign tax paid. In both cases it is limited to the foreign tax as foreseen in the applicable double-taxation treaty. No carryforward of foreign tax is allowed.

Other significant items

Impairment losses on doubtful debts are deductible for tax purposes when an insolvency or recovery has been requested or the credits have been claimed in court.

The annual amount of accumulated impairment losses on doubtful debts due for more than six months with evidence that measures towards its perception were taken is capped at the following percentages of the debts:

Accumulated impairment loss caps	%
More than 6 and less than 12 months	25
More than 12 and less than 18 months	50
More than 18 and less than 24 months	75
More than 24 months	100

Amounts guaranteed by insurance or mortgage, or due or secured by the state, autonomous regions or municipalities, or due by related parties (e.g., 10%

Portugal

shareholding) are not considered as doubtful debts and the respective impairment loss is disallowed for tax purposes.

The ageing of bills of exchange is calculated from the date when the respective payment is due.

Uncollectable debts are allowed as tax-deductible costs if supported under insolvency, recovery enforcement or in an out-of-court conciliation procedure for the viability of insolvent companies or companies in difficult economic situation (mediated by the Institute for the Support of Small and Medium-sized Enterprises – IAPMEI). This rule applies to the amount of the uncollectable debts which were not deducted for tax purposes as impairment losses (or for which the amount was insufficient).

Deductions

Depreciation and depletion
The qualifying cost of an asset for tax purposes is the acquisition or production cost.

Depreciation must be computed by using the straight-line method or the declining-balance method. The latter cannot be applied to buildings, passenger vehicles, furniture, social welfare equipment or second-hand assets. Straight-line rates of depreciation are normally consistent with rates privately used by business and industry and are increased, for the purposes of applying the declining-balance method, by coefficients of:

- 1.5 if assets have a useful life of less than five years;
- 2 if useful life is five or six years; and
- 2.5 for useful lives in excess of six years.

Different depreciation methods may be applied without previous approval from the Tax Authorities (annual depreciation cannot however exceed the depreciation resulting from using either the straight-line or declining-balance methods).

Rates can be reduced by 50% in any one year at the taxpayer's option. If the reduction is more than 50%, the difference is allowed for tax purposes at a future date. Any depreciation in excess of the maximum allowed must be subsequently adjusted in the accounting records to be allowed for tax purposes in future years. A total of 60% of additional depreciation on revaluation of fixed assets, as permitted by law from time to time, is allowed for tax purposes.

Depreciation rates of tangible assets may be increased by 25% in case of companies with a schedule of two shifts (for three shifts, 50%), given the faster deterioration of those assets.

Assets with an acquisition value lower than EUR 1,000 can be depreciated in the acquisition year, unless the assets are part of a set of elements that should be depreciated as a whole.

Depreciation of yachts and airplanes that are not essential for business activities, and depreciation on the excess of a limit to be defined by Decree (formerly EUR 40,000) for passenger cars and certain other vehicles, is not allowed as a cost for tax purposes.

Start-up and research expenses are deductible for tax purposes in the respective tax year. Transitional adjustments of remaining start-up expenses incurred prior to the adoption of the new accounting system should be written off the balance sheet against equity and are deductible over a five-year period.

Development expenses, patents, trademarks, licenses and similar rights may be depreciated for tax purposes if acquired for a limited period of time.

Expenses relating to assets generated internally are deductible for tax purposes in the tax year in which the cost is incurred.

Goodwill cannot be depreciated for tax purposes (unless subject to an effective economic depreciation approved by the Portuguese tax authorities).

Some examples relating to the maximum straight-line depreciation rate are as follows:

Type of asset	Rate %
Office building	2
Industrial building	5
Electronic equipment	20
Computers	33.33
Ordinary tools & paintings	25
Engines & machine tools	12.5
Office equipment	20
Furniture	12.5
Software	33.33
Light passenger vehicles	25

Tax losses
As of 2010, tax losses can be carried forward for four years (previously six years). Carryback of losses is not allowed. The tax losses carried forward are lost if one of the following situations occurs:

- Change in direct ownership of the company of at least 50% shareholding or voting rights; or
- Change in the scope of the business as stated in the articles of association or, regardless of any formal change, if the nature of the activity carried out by the company is substantially modified.

In special cases of economical merits, the Ministry of Finance may authorise the use of tax losses upon a request filed by the taxpayer before those changes occur.

Payments to foreign affiliates
A Portuguese corporation is allowed to deduct royalties, interest and other costs paid to foreign affiliates, provided the amounts are at arm's length. Service fees paid are allowed if there is adequate proof that the service was effectively rendered, has economic substance and qualifies as indispensable for the generation of taxable revenue, as well as if the amount is at arm's length.

P

Portugal

Interest on shareholder loans

If the rate applicable to interest and other compensation regarding loans provided by the shareholders to the company is higher than the Euro Interbank Offered Rate (EURIBOR) 12-month rate rounded up with a spread of 1.5% (at the date the loan was granted), the amount paid in excess is not tax-deductible. This rule does not apply when the shareholder is resident of a tax treaty country or when the interest rate is at arm's length under the transfer pricing provisions.

Transfer pricing

The tax authorities are entitled to adjust taxable income if the taxpayer and another individual or entity, due to their special relationship, have established particular conditions which diverge from the conditions normally agreed upon between independent entities and distort the results that would arise if those relations were at arm's length. For tax years starting on or after 1 January 2002, Portugal has implemented detailed transfer pricing legislation which broadly follows the Organisation for Economic Co-operation and Development (OECD) guidelines.

An Advance Pricing Agreement (APA) mechanism has been introduced for taxpayers and Portuguese Tax Authorities (PTA) to establish agreements on taxpayers' future transfer pricing policy. This aims to guarantee compliance with the arm's-length principle. This regime applies to transactions carried out with related parties and between a permanent establishment and the respective head office.

The conclusion of an APA implies the payment of a charge calculated with reference to the taxpayer's turnover, capped at EUR 35,000. This charge is reduced by 50% in the case of a renewal or revision of an existing APA.

The assessment of an APA procedure takes 180 days for unilateral APAs, and 360 days for bilateral or multilateral APAs. This period is reduced to 100 business days for APAs concluded in connection with a relevant investment project in Portugal, as foreseen in the Tax Investment Code ("Código Fiscal do Investimento").

For the Portuguese Tax Authority (PTA) to confirm compliance of the transfer pricing method(s) with the terms and conditions set out in the APA, the taxpayer must prepare an annual report. The report must be made available to PTA before the last business day of May in the year following that in which the transactions took place (i.e., when the tax year corresponds to the calendar year). Failure to comply invalidates the APA.

Thin capitalisation

Where loans from non-EU-resident related parties exceed twice the parties' capital in the borrowing Portuguese entity, the interest on the excess borrowing is not tax-deductible. This rule may not apply if the company (as long as it is not resident in a blacklisted territory) proves, under a safeguard clause, that takes into account the type of activity, the sector in which it operates, the dimensions and other relevant criteria, to determine if it would be possible to obtain the same loan on similar terms from an independent entity.

Anti-avoidance

A general anti-avoidance provision is in force, pursuant to which contracts and other acts are ineffective whenever it is demonstrated that they were tax driven to reduce taxation that would be due under contracts bearing a similar economic effect, in which case taxation would be based on the latter.

Controlled foreign corporations

Profits derived by an affiliate resident in a blacklisted offshore jurisdiction or in a jurisdiction where it is subject to an effective tax rate equal to or lower than 60% of the Portuguese corporate tax rate, are imputed to the Portuguese shareholder, provided it holds, directly or indirectly, a minimum holding participation of 25% (10% if more than 50% of the capital is held by Portuguese shareholders). Upon distribution of the profits, a deduction is available for previously imputed income.

Taxes

All taxes other than corporate tax and municipal surcharge constitute a normal business expense.

Vacation accrual

Vacation pay and vacations subsidies are tax-deductible in the year in which the benefit accrues, regardless of the year in which payment is made.

Other significant items

Pension, invalidity and health schemes are tax-deductible up to 15% of annual staff expenses, provided they are available to all employees and the management and disposition of the benefits are outside the control of the taxpayer, such as under an insured scheme with vested benefits.

A specific regime applies for deduction of the additional (mandatory) contributions made to pension funds by insurance companies as a result of the adoption of the new accounting system (SNC). These contributions are not considered for purposes of computing the maximum annual amount accepted as a cost, but are considered as a cost in accordance with an annual instalment plan, during a term of five years that began in 2008.

The costs borne from the acquisition of social passes are regarded as tax-deductible costs to the extent the employer attributes them on a general basis.

Uninsured losses, including indemnities to third parties, are disallowed unless the risk could not be insured.

Donations to authorised charitable institutions are allowable up to 0.8% of turnover, with the possibility of the cost being raised up to 150%. Donations to authorised cultural institutions are allowable up to 0.6% of turnover, with the possibility of the cost being raised up to 130%.

Donations to the state, municipalities, foundations where the state or municipalities participate in the initial capital are fully deductible, with the possibility of the cost being raised up to 140%. Special application may be made by certain entities in order to be included under the referred regime.

Donations of computers, software equipment, training and consultancy in the area of computers granted to the state, municipalities, foundations, museums as well as to authorised charitable and cultural institutions are allowable up to 0.8% of turnover, with the possibility of the cost being raised up to 140%.

Non-documented expenses are not tax-deductible and are subject to a 50% tax surcharge for fully taxable entities.

P

Portugal

Group taxation

The taxation of group income can be obtained by presenting a special form to the tax authorities for companies with a head office and effective management in Portugal. Such group taxation may apply, provided one of the companies, directly or indirectly, holds 90% or more of the statutory capital of the others and more than 50% of the voting rights. Tax grouping generally enables the group companies to offset losses incurred by one company against profits of another company. Tax losses obtained prior to the beginning of the tax grouping can be carried forward only against the particular company's taxable income.

To be taxed under this regime, the group companies must meet the following conditions:

* Must be tax resident in Portugal;
* Must be subject to the normal regime of taxation at the highest corporate tax rate;
* Must maintain a minimum holding participation of 90%;
* All companies must be held by the parent company for more than one year (excluding newly incorporated companies);
* Cannot be dormant for more than one year;
* Cannot be dissolved or insolvent;
* Cannot have tax losses in the three years prior to the regime application, unless the companies have been held by the parent company for more than two years; and
* Cannot have a tax period different from that of the parent company.

Additionally, the parent company:

* Should not be controlled by any other Portuguese-resident company that fulfils the requirements to be the parent company; and
* Should not have renounced to the application of this regime in the three previous years.

When the regime comes to an end or when one company ceases to qualify for this regime, the tax losses obtained during the regime cannot be carried forward and deducted against future individual taxable income of the companies.

Tax incentives

General tax benefits and incentives
Contractual tax incentives
Relevant investment projects up to 2020 (minimum investment of EUR 5,000,000) that qualify for strategic economic interest and promote the creation of jobs are eligible for tax incentives, as foreseen in the Tax Benefits Code and the Investment Tax Code.

These are granted on a case-by-case basis under a government contract for a period not exceeding 10 years and include a tax credit of 10% to 20% of the investment and exemptions or reductions from property transfer tax, property tax and stamp duty.

Investment funds
- Other investment funds
  Portfolio investment funds are taxable at the following final rates:

Portfolio investment funds	%
Capital gains (net of capital losses) on shares held < 12 months	10
Capital gains (net of capital losses) on shares held > 12 months	–
Other income:	
- Earned in Portugal	20/25
- Earned abroad	20/25

- Real estate investment funds
  These funds are subject to corporate tax at the following rates:

Real estate investment funds	%
Rents (net of expenses)	20
Real estate capital gains (net of capital losses)	12.5
Capital gains (net of capital losses) on shares held < 12 months	10
Capital gains (net of capital losses) on shares held > 12 months	–
Other income	See Other investment funds above.

Income paid by the two aforementioned investment funds to individuals is not subject to taxation. Income paid to companies is taxed as normal income and taxes paid by the fund are considered as payment on account against the final corporate tax due.

- Funds of funds
  Income paid by investment funds is exempt from CIT. Other income is subject to the same taxation as investment funds. Income received by individuals is not subject to further taxation. Income received by companies is taxed at the standard corporate tax rate on 40% of the respective amount as normal income.

Pension funds
Are exempt from corporate tax and real estate transfer tax.

Contractors for NATO infrastructures
These contractors are exempt from corporate tax.

Net young employment creation
150% of the costs related to the net increase job creation, under labour contracts without term, for employees up to 35 years (including) of age and for long-term unemployed individuals may be deducted from taxable income. For this purposes, these costs should be considered the fixed remunerations paid and the contributions made by the employer to the social security. The maximum amount of annual increase on deductible costs for each eligible employee is 14 times the national minimum retribution (EUR 450 in 2009; expected EUR 475 in 2010).

This tax benefit is not cumulative with any other tax benefit concerning the same employee and it is applicable only once for each employee.

Portugal

This deduction applies for a period of five years for each employee.

Inland region investment
Companies pursuing an economic activity of industrial or service-rendering nature in inland regions have the following tax benefits:

*   A reduced CIT rate of 15%;
*   In case of establishment of new entities in the referred regions, the income tax rate is reduced to 10%, during the first five years of activity;
*   Tax losses can be carried forward for seven years;
*   Depreciation and amortisation concerning investment expenses up to EUR 500,000 (excluding land acquisition and passenger cars), can be deducted, with an increase of 30%; and
*   Social security costs, concerning net employment creation, can have an increase of 50%.

Research and development (R&D)
Portuguese tax resident companies carrying out commercial, industrial or agricultural activities, and non-resident companies with a permanent establishment in the Portuguese territory, are allowed to deduct from the corporate tax due, up to the respective amount, the value of eligible expenses incurred with R&D, in a double percentage as follows:

*   Base rate: 32.5% of the R&D expenses incurred in the tax;
*   Incremental rate: 50% of the difference between the R&D expenses made in the tax year and the average amount of the R&D expenses made in the previous two years, up to the limit of EUR 1,500,000; and
*   The expenses that, due to insufficient tax due, cannot be deducted in the tax year they were incurred can be carried forward for six years.

Dividends from entities resident in the Portuguese speaking African countries (PALOP's) and in Timor-Leste
These are not subject to CIT at the level of the Portuguese parent provided that:

i.   The entity in Portugal is subject and not exempt to CIT;
ii. The entities in the PALOP and in Timor-Leste are subject and not exempt to a corporate tax;
iii. The entity in Portugal holds a direct participation in the share capital of the subsidiary not less than 25% for at least two years; and
iv. Dividends distributed have been taxed in at least 10% and do not arise from a determined type of income expressly mentioned in the law.

Loan interest and lease rentals on imported equipment
When paid by the State, regional authorities and public services, loan interest and lease rentals on imported equipment can qualify for partial or full exemption from tax upon an appropriate application.

Real Estate Investment Fund for Residential Lease (REIFRL)
The regime is applicable: (i) both to REIFRL and to Real Estate Investment Companies for Residential Lease (REICRL) incorporated in accordance with the Portuguese law within a term of five years following the entering into force of the State Budget for 2009; and, (ii) to the real estate properties acquired by those entities during that same term, i.e., from 1 January 2009 until 31 December 2014.

The incorporation of the REIFRL will be done in accordance with the provisions applicable to the Real Estate Investment Funds (REIFs) laid down in the Portuguese law. The REIFRL portfolio is required to be comprised in at least 75% by real estate properties located in Portugal destined for the lease of permanent residences.

The following tax regime and benefits are established:

- CIT exemption on income obtained by REIFRLs;
- Personal income tax (PIT) and CIT exemption for the income obtained by participation unit holders, except for the capital gains arising from the sale of such participation units;
- Capital gains obtained by a property owner that sells its real estate to a REIFRL are exempt from PIT, provided that the taxpayer maintains the residential lease agreement in place and that the property owner exercises the option to acquire the real estate property;
- At personal income tax level, 30% of the rents borne by the lessees as a result of the conversion of a real estate property holding right into a lease right of the same real estate property are deductible to the annual taxable income up to a maximum amount of EUR 586;
- Local property tax exemption established for the real estate properties destined for the lease of permanent residences that integrate the REIFRL;
- Municipal property transfer tax exemption on real estate property acquisition made within this regime by the REIFRL, as well as the acquisitions arising from the option for the acquisition by the lessees, until 2020, of the real estate properties that integrate the assets of the REIFRL;
- Stamp duty exemption is established for the acts arising from the transfer of the real estate properties by means of the conversion of holdings rights in real estate properties into a lease right with the option of acquisition in respect of the same real estate property by the lessee; and
- The above-referred tax regime and respective exemptions will not be applicable to entities resident in a country or jurisdiction with a more favourable taxable regime included in the Decree-Ruling published by the Ministry of Finance.

Incentives to urban rehabilitation
These incentives are applicable to real estate property covered by rehabilitation projects undertaken between 1 January 2008 and 2020.

Real estate investment funds incorporated between 2008 and 31 December 2012 may benefit from:

- CIT: the income obtained by real estate investment funds is tax exempt when the funds are incorporated in accordance with the Portuguese law, and respective assets are comprised of at least 75% of real estate subject to rehabilitation projects in qualifying areas.

P

Portugal

- Property transfer tax: urban property (buildings or autonomous units) destined for permanent residence and located in a rehabilitation area may benefit from an IMT exemption on the first transfer of such urban property upon undertaking of rehabilitation works. The granting of this exemption depends on a decision in this respect of the municipality of the area of the real estate property.
- Property tax: the IMI exemption granted in respect of urban properties subject to rehabilitation works is extended from eight to 10 years (it is granted for a five-year term and renewable for an additional five-year period). Again, the granting of this exemption depends on a decision in this respect of the municipality of the area of the real estate property.
- Personal income tax:
  - The real estate property owner may deduct, up to the limit of EUR 500, 30% of the expenses incurred with the rehabilitation works of the urban property eligible for the application of this regime; and
  - Rental income and capital gains arising from urban properties eligible for the application of the rehabilitation regime and obtained by resident individual taxpayers are subject to taxation at the rate of 5%.

Tax benefits and incentives for non-resident corporate entities
- Capital gains on the sale of shares and quotas held in a Portuguese company by a non-resident company may be tax exempt. However, there are some important exceptions, such as:
  - Where the more than 25% of a non-resident shareholder is held, directly or indirectly, by a Portuguese resident company;
  - Where the non-resident shareholder is located in a country that is included in a blacklist from the Ministry of Finance; and
  - Where the assets of the company sold consist mainly of immovable property.
- Interest and capital gains on government and corporate bonds are tax exempt (where held by entities not located in blacklisted offshore jurisdictions) under certain conditions.
- Interest paid by resident credit institutions to non-resident financial companies deriving from loans as well as gains arising from swap transactions are tax exempt.
- Interest obtained by non-resident credit institutions deriving from term deposits held on resident entities authorised to receive such deposits are tax exempt.

Madeira and Azores international business centre
Qualifying industrial, shipping, international services (e.g., holding and trusts) and financial entities licensed in Madeira or in the Santa Maria Island (Azores) international business centres before 31 December 2000, are eligible for a CIT exemption until 31 December 2011.

The European Commission extended the existing regime and approved a new regime for entities licensed to operate in the Madeira International Business Centre (MIBC) in the period 2007-2013, which is applicable until 31 December 2020.

The 2007 MIBC special tax regime provides, besides full exemptions from taxation to non-resident shareholders and service providers, for the following reduced CIT rates for these entities, on their qualifying foreign source income, based on thresholds of income and subject to job creation requirements:

- 4% between 2010 to 2012; and
- 5% from 2013 to 2020.

Portugal

Azores and Madeira international business centre based companies generally benefit from Portugal's network of double taxation agreements. EU laws and regulations apply to Azores and Madeira.

Companies licensed under the previous regime will have the same benefits, but will not be tax exempt on their qualifying foreign source income, being subject to the reduced rates mentioned above (and subject to the same requirements).

Withholding taxes (WHT)

General withholding tax rates:

Recipient	Residents (1)	Non-residents (1)
	%	%
Dividends	20 (2)	20 (3)
Interest:	15	20
Royalties	15	15
Interest & royalties (EU Directive)	N/A	5 (4)
Banks deposits	20	20
Property income	15	15 (1)
Service charges	0	15 (5)
Other	15	20

Notes

The numbers in parentheses refer to the following numbered notes:

1. For residents, tax withheld constitutes a payment on account of final corporate or individual income tax due. For non-residents, tax withheld is the final tax unless in case of property income, in which it is a payment on account.
2. Not subject in the case of holdings of at least 10% or if the acquisition value was not lower than EUR 20 million.
3. Not subject if the parent/subsidiary directive applies.
4. This withholding tax rate will be in force until 30 June 2009; from 1 July 2009 until 30 June 2013, the applicable rate will be reduced to 5% and will be nil from 1 July 2013 onwards.
5. Not subject if a tax treaty is applicable.

Tax treaty rates

Tax treaties reduce the above-mentioned rates as follows:

Recipient	Dividends	Interest	Royalties
	%	%	%
Algeria (3)	15 (10)	15	10
Austria (1, 2)	15	10	10 (5)
Belgium (2)	15	15	10
Brazil (3)	15 (10)	15	15
Bulgaria (3)	15 (10)	10	10
Canada (3)	15 (10)	10	10
Cape Verde	10	10	10
Chile (3, 9, 10)	15 (10)	15 / 5 / 10	10 (5)
China, P.R.	10	10	10
Cuba (3)	10 (5)	10	5

P

Portugal

Recipient	Dividends	Interest	Royalties
	%	%	%
Czech Republic (3)	15 (10)	10	10
Denmark (2)	10	10	10
Estonia	10	10	10
Finland (2, 3)	15 (10)	15	10
France (2, 4, 5)	15	12 (10)	5
Germany (2, 6)	15	15 (10)	10
Greece (2)	15	15	10
Hungary (3)	15 (10)	10	10
Iceland (3)	15 (10)	10	10
India (3)	15 (10)	10	10
Indonesia (4)	10	10	10
Ireland, Rep. of (2)	15	15	10
Israel (11)	15 (10) (5)	10	10
Italy (2)	15	15	12
Korea, Rep. of (3)	15 (10)	15	10
Latvia	10	10	10
Lithuania	10	10	10
Luxembourg (2, 6)	15	15 (10)	10
Macau	10	10	10
Malta (3)	15 (10)	10	10
Mexico	10	10	10
Mozambique	10	10	10
Morocco (3)	15 (10)	12	10
Netherlands (2)	10	10	10
Norway (3)	15 (10)	15	10
Pakistan	15 (10)	10	10
Poland (3)	15 (10)	10	10
Romania (3)	15 (10)	10	10
Russia (3)	15 (10)	10	10
Singapore	10	10	10
Slovakia (3)	15 (10)	10	10
Slovenia (3)	15 (5)	10	5
South Africa (3)	15 (10)	10	10
Spain (2, 3)	15 (10)	15	5
Sweden	10	10	10
Switzerland (3)	15 (10)	10	5
Tunisia	15	15	10
Turkey (3, 8)	15 (5)	15 (10)	10
Ukraine (3)	15 (10)	10	10
United Kingdom (2, 3)	15 (10)	10	5
United States (3)	15 (5)	10	10
Venezuela (7)	10	10	12 (10)

Notes

1. The rate in parentheses applies to royalties when the beneficiary holds 50% or less of the paying company's share capital.
2. There is no withholding tax on dividends if the EU Parent/Subsidiary Directive applies.
3. The rate in parentheses applies to dividends when the beneficiary directly holds 25% or more of share capital. Depending on each DTT, a two-year holding period may be required.
4. The rate in parentheses applies to interest on debentures raised in France after January 1 1965 or on significant loans or debentures raised in Portugal or abroad under major development projects listed in the treaty annex.
5. The rate in parentheses applies to bank loans, but if interest is payable from Portugal, bank loans must qualify as being of economic or social interest or fall under an approved development plan.
6. The rate in parentheses applies to interest received by financial institutions.
7. The rate in parentheses applies to technical assistance.
8. The rate in parentheses applies on interest related to loans with a minimum maturity of two years.
9. The rate of 5% regarding interest applies to bonds interest or other securities transacted in the stock market. The rate of 10% applies to loans from banks or insurance companies or credit selling of equipment.
10. The rate of 5% regarding royalties applies to equipment lease.
11. The rate of 10% applies if the company which is paying the dividends is a resident of Israel and the dividends derive from profits which are subject to tax in Israel at a rate which is lower than the normal rate of Israel company tax. The rate of 5% applies if the beneficial owner is a company which holds directly at least 25% of the capital of the company paying the dividends.

Tax administration

Tax returns

The tax year is, as a general rule, the calendar year, and the annual corporate tax return must be submitted by electronic data transmission by the last day of May of the year following the year of income.

A different tax year is allowed in the case of companies obliged to the accounting consolidation and of permanent establishments of non-resident entities, which can adopt the tax period of the non-resident company. If this option is taken, the new tax period must be maintained for a minimum of five years.

Other entities may apply for a different tax period based on economic grounds. In these situations (i.e., whenever the tax year ends on a date other than 31 December, the annual corporate tax return shall be submitted by electronic data transmission by the last day of the fifth month following the year-end.

The system is one of self-assessment.

Payment of tax

Tax is paid in four instalments. The first three correspond to 90% of the previous year's corporate tax assessment (for taxpayers with a turnover above EUR 498,797; 70% if below this amount). A reduction of the amount of these payments is expected. The first three instalments are paid on 15 July, 15 September, and 15 December of the year in which taxable income arises. The fourth instalment is paid (or received) through self-assessment upon filing the annual tax return in May of the following year.

Portugal

If the tax year ends on a date other than 31 December, interim payments take place in the seventh, ninth and twelfth months of the tax year. Filing of the annual tax return together with the final payment is in the fifth month following the close of the tax year. Given the expected introduction of a State surtax of 2.5% on the excess of taxable income above EUR 2,000,000, an additional payment on account of the State surtax will also be due, on the same months as the interim payments.

Payments on account are not required if the previous year's corporate tax assessment is less than EUR 199.52, and may be suspended upon declaring that no further tax is due in respect of the current year. However, interest is assessed at a rate of 4% if this results in postponing more than 20% of the tax that would otherwise have been paid.

In particular situations, a special payment on account is due of a minimum of EUR 1,000 up to EUR 70,000, paid in March, or in March and October (the third or the third and tenth month of the tax year if it ends on a date other than 31 December).

The statute of limitation period is four years, but this period can be extended in case of tax losses.

Corporate taxes in Puerto Rico

For more information, contact:

Victor Rodríguez
PricewaterhouseCoopers
254 Munoz Rivera Avenue
BBVA Building
Suite 900
San Juan, Puerto Rico 00918
Puerto Rico
Tel: +1 787 772 7958
Email: victor.rodriguez@us.pwc.com

Significant developments

Act 194 of 22 December 2009 (Act 194)

Automatic extension to file individual and corporate income tax returns – The act amended section 1053 of the Puerto Rico Internal Revenue Code (PRIRC) to increase the automatic extension of time for individuals to file an income tax return from 30 days to a three-month period. The standard three month extension applies to individuals, corporations, partnerships, trusts and estates. The Act 194 also eliminated the use of a specific number of dates and established the use of months to calculate the new filing date.

This is applicable for taxable years commenced after 31 December 2008.

Estimated tax payments by corporations and partnerships – The Act 194 amended section 1062 of the PRIRC to eliminate the filing requirement of an estimated tax declaration by corporations and partnerships. Furthermore, corporations and partnerships are allowed to reduce their estimated tax liability by income tax overpayments from prior years or any tax credits allowed by the PRIRC or special laws.

The effective date of this provision is for taxable years commenced after 31 December 2009.

Additions to the tax for failure to pay estimated tax by corporations and partnerships – The Act 194 amended sections 6069 and 6070 of the PRIRC to simplify the calculation of Schedule T (i.e., additions to the tax, or penalty for the underpayment of estimated taxes). The act states that the penalty for the failure to timely pay any estimated tax instalment would be 10% of such instalment (it was 20% before the enactment of Act 194). The effective date of this provision is for taxable years commenced after 31 December 2008.

Sales and use tax – The Act 194 amended section 2301 of the PRIRC to provide an exemption from sales and use tax for services rendered by a registered tax specialist. A registered tax specialist, as defined by section 6170 of the PRIRC, is a natural or juridical person that prepares or reviews declarations and request refunds pursuant to the PRIRC or the US Internal Revenue Code. The effective date of this provision is for taxable years commenced after 31 December 2009. Furthermore, the annual sales and use tax return (Form SC 2935) is no longer required to be filed for taxable years commenced after 31 December 2008.

Puerto Rico

Penalties for failure to file certain information returns and reconciliation statements – The Act 194 amended section 6071 of the PRIRC to limit the penalty for not filing certain information statements (i.e., Form 480.6B1 and Form 480.30) to USD 100. The penalty for not filing the quarterly payroll tax return is also limited to USD 100 for each return. The effective date of this provision is 22 December 2009.

Act 164 of 16 December 2009 (Act 164)
Annual reports – Articles 15.01 and 15.03 of Act 164, which is the current Puerto Rico General Corporation Law (PRGCL), modified the volume of business threshold to submit audited balance sheet along with the corporate annual report. The volume of business threshold was increased from USD 1 million to USD 3 million. In the event the volume of business does not exceed USD 3 million, a balance sheet prepared under generally accepted accounting principles (GAAP) by a person with a general knowledge in accounting has to be submitted along with the corporate annual report. This current volume of business requirement applies to domestic and foreign corporations. The audited balance sheet is still required when gross income exceeds USD 3 million.

This provision and the other discussed below are effective on 1 January 2010 and covers the 2009 annual report filings.

New expeditious procedure for certificate of good standing – Article 15.06 of the PRGCL provides that in order to issue a certificate of good standing, the secretary of state will review compliance with the annual reports filing requirement for the five years prior to the date the certificate is being requested. Once the certificate of good standing is issued, the secretary of state will not impose a penalty for any non-compliance attributable to years prior to the five years period mentioned above.

Penalty for failure to file an annual report – Amnesty Period – Article 22.08 establishes that the secretary of state will grant a five-month period during which any unfiled annual reports may be filed without imposing a late filing penalty.

However, the filling fee for the annual reports will apply as follow:

- Not-for-profit corporations will pay two times the amount required for the standard annual filing fee – (i.e., USD 20); and
- For-profit corporations will pay three times the amount required for the standard annual filing fee – (i.e., USD 300).

A detailed guidance of the filing procedures and the amnesty period will be covered in the regulations to be issued by the Secretary of State.

New extended due date for corporate annual report – The PRGCL authorises the Secretary of State to grant an extension of time to file the corporate annual report for up to 90 days from the original due date. As such, the Secretary of State granted a 60 days extension to file the 2009 corporate annual report, and the current extended due date is 15 June 2010. However, an additional extension of time of 30 days is available upon request in which case the final extended due date is 15 July 2010.

Act 7 of 9 March 2009 (Act 7)
The Act 7 provides for several temporary and permanent amendments or additions to the PRIRC that will affect various taxpayers, including domestic and foreign corporations doing business in Puerto Rico, insurance companies, credit and savings

cooperatives (or credit unions), insurance cooperatives, etc. The following provisions have also been updated to include the amendments from Act 15 of 23 April 2009 and Act 37 of 10 July 2009.

Temporary provisions

Alternative minimum tax on corporations, partnerships, LLCs and LLPs – For taxable years commenced after 31 December 2008 and before 1 January 2012, no deduction for expenses paid or incurred for services performed outside of Puerto Rico by a related party (as defined by sections 1221(a)(3) or 1231(a)(3) of the PRIRC) will be allowed for purposes of determining the alternative minimum tax to the extent the recipient is not subject to tax under the PRIRC. It is expected that the above adjustment will significantly increase the alternative minimum net income of those affected companies that receive a substantial amount of management or service fees' allocations from their parent companies, home office, or related entities located outside Puerto Rico.

A 5% surtax over the tax liability – A 5% additional tax will be imposed on the income tax liability determined (not on the taxable income) for those corporations, partnerships and trusts whose gross income exceeds USD 100,000. This provision will be effective for taxable years commenced after 31 December 2008 and before 1 January 2012.

A 5% tax imposed on insurance cooperatives and credit and savings cooperatives (or credit unions) with net taxable income in excess of USD 250,000 – Cooperatives are generally exempt organisations not subject to income taxes. Nevertheless, these types of organisations will be required to pay a 5% tax on their "taxable income" for years commenced after 31 December 2008 and before 1 January 2012. Taxable income for this purpose will be determined in accordance with the PRIRC. In the case of insurance cooperatives, the net income will be determined in accordance with subchapter G of the PRIRC (i.e., similar to insurance companies). In the specific case of life cooperative insurance companies, such net income, as a general rule, would be the gain on sale of capital assets.

A 5% tax imposed on cooperative banks (credit unions) – Similarly, cooperative banks will be required to pay a 5% special tax on their "taxable income" determined under the PRIRC for years commenced after 31 December 2008 and before 1 January 2012.

A 5% tax imposed on international banking entities (IBEs) & international insurance companies – A 5% tax upon IBEs net income will be imposed for every taxable year commenced after 31 December 2008 and before 1 January 2012. IBEs operating as a branch will be subject only to the 5% tax on income otherwise not previously subject to regular tax, computed under the provisions of the PRIRC. The same provision will apply to international insurance companies.

Deferral of tax credits – For taxable years commenced after 31 December 2008 and before 1 January 2012 certain tax credits may not be claimed against Puerto Rico income taxes. The tax credits covered by this moratorium are:

- Purchase of products manufactured in Puerto Rico for local sale and consumption (Section 1040E of the PRIRC).
- Waste Disposal Credits Law (authorised under article 21 of Act 70 of 23 June 1978).
- Puerto Rico Capital Investment Funds Act of 1999 (article 14 of Act 46 of 28 January 2000).

Puerto Rico

- Act that created a Theatrical District (from Bolivar Street to Ernesto Cerra Street in Santurce – article 11 of Act 178 of 12 August 2000).
- Conservation Law (Act 183 of 27 December 2001).
- Urban Center Revitalization Law (article 4.03 and 4.04 of Act 212 of 29 August 2002) – Some exceptions may apply.
- Tax Credits Act for Investment in New Construction or Rehabilitation of Social Interest Housing (article 3 of Act 140 of 4 October 2001).
- Tax Credits Act for Investment in Housing Infrastructure (article 4 of Act 98 of 10 August 2001).
- Credits for Investment in the Constructions or Rehabilitation of Rental Housing projects for low or moderate income families (Act 140 of 4 October 2001).
- Credits for the Investment in projects for Tourism Activities (Act 78 of 10 September 1993) – Some exceptions may apply.
- Credits for investment in Housing Projects for the Elderly, among others (Act 7 of 9 March 2009) – Some exceptions may apply.

Credits that were acquired by purchase before 4 March 2009 will not be subject to this limitation. Also, taxpayers will be required to file an informative return on or before 31 August 2009 to properly inform the Secretary of the Treasury the amount of credits that were previously granted in order for the Secretary to evaluate the economic and tax impact of these credits. In addition, other tax credits issued by other laws (Tourism Development Act of 1993, Tax Incentives Acts of 1997 and 2008, etc.) will need to be included in the informative return.

Deferral of tax credits to financial institutions – Act 37 modified the Housing Tax Credits generated by financial institutions and contained in Sections 1040K and 1040L of the PRIRC. Those financial institutions that have obtained tax credit certificates from the Secretary of the Treasury of Puerto Rico and that have not been able to use them against their tax responsibility (or have not sold, ceded or transferred them) will be able to request such tax credits as a refund within the period established in the tax credit certificate. Such refund request will be based on the procedures to be established by the Secretary through Regulations or Administrative Determinations. However, the Secretary will not be authorised to issue tax refunds under section 1040K or 1040L before 1 January 2011 unless the financial institution had requested such refund before 9 March 2009.

Permanent provisions
Sale and use tax – The Act 7 significantly changed the requirements of the sales and use tax, particularly in the case of retailers. The act created two groups of taxpayers for purposes of the exemption certificate and also changed the due date to remit the sales and use tax to the corresponding Puerto Rico tax agencies and to file the monthly sales and use tax returns.

- Two groups of taxpayers for purposes of the exemption certificate:

  Those merchants with an annual gross income equal or in excess of USD 500,000 (including new merchants with a reasonable estimate of annual gross income equal or in excess of USD 500,000) and that have acquired taxable articles for retail, will be entitled to request an exemption certificate on SUT subject to the requirements to be established by the secretary. On the other hand, those merchants with annual sales volume of less than USD 500,000 will be entitled to the exemption certificate if they are in good standing with the provisions of the PRIRC and comply with the requirements to be issued by the secretary. In this regard, merchants with less than USD 500,000 in annual gross income must comply with the following requirements in order to obtain an exemption certificate: (i) should not have any pending tax liability with the P.R. Treasury Department, (ii) need to be in good standing with respect to all tax filings, including but not limited to, income tax and sales and use tax, and (iii) need to submit a volume of business declaration showing the payment of municipal license tax in all the municipalities where the merchant has operations.

- Changes in the due date of the sales and use tax filings and payments:

  The act accelerates the sales and use tax due date from the twentieth day to the tenth day of the following month after the tax is collected. For returns and payments filed by mail, the postmark will continue to support the proof of filing. When the due date falls on Saturday, Sunday or official holiday, the due date for filing and payment will be the next business day. In the case of electronic filings (including payments), the due date will always be the tenth day of the following month, unless otherwise specified by regulations.

The Secretary is also authorised to issue municipal exemption certificates to merchants for the 1% sales and use tax to be collected by municipalities to the extent merchants are also registered with the P.R. Treasury Department and they are entitled to the exemption certificate.

Credit for purchases of locally manufactured products to be exported – Corporate taxpayers will not be entitled to claim a credit against the sales and use tax for those purchases of locally manufactured products that will eventually be exported. The act provides that this credit may still be used against the taxpayer's income tax liability.

Increase in excise taxes applicable to cigarettes and alcoholic beverages – Effective on 1 June 2009, the excise tax on cigarettes increased from USD 6.15 to USD 11.15 per 100 cigarettes or fraction thereof. Similarly, the act provides for an excise tax increase applicable to wine and beer. In the case of beer, the excise tax will increase by USD 0.30 on each gallon or fraction thereof for those that are imported and by USD 0.46 on each gallon or fraction thereof for those manufactured in Puerto Rico. The increase in the excise tax corresponding to wine will range between USD 0.35 and USD 0.70 on each gallon or fraction thereof, depending on its classification.

Excise tax on motorcycles and ATV vehicles – Act 37 states that every vehicle, truck, ATV vehicle (four tracks) and motorcycles will be exempt from the sales tax established in Subtitle BB of the PRIRC. Motorcycles and ATV vehicles will be subject to an excise tax of 10% of the taxable price in Puerto Rico effective on 1 August 2009. Furthermore, the inventory of motorcycles and ATV vehicles as of 1 August 2009 will be considered as introduced into Puerto Rico for purposes of this excise tax.

Act 73 of 28 May 2008 (Incentives Act or Act 73)
Act 73 of 28 May 2008, known as the "Tax Incentives Act for the Puerto Rico Economic Development", attempts to create a new economic environment with the goal of developing the local industry, maintaining current investments and promoting the direct investment from the US and other countries. Act 73 changes the fixed income tax rates applicable to industrial development income (IDI), yet introduces certain credits

Puerto Rico

to reduce the income tax determined, when applicable. The act does not provide an expiration date; therefore, it is effective until a new act replaces it.

The following are the most significant differences from the previous tax incentive act (Puerto Rico Tax Incentives Act of 1998):

1. Income tax scenarios that exempt entities may elect:
   - General scenario: 4% income tax rate with a withholding tax rate on royalty payments of 12%.
   - Alternate scenario: 8% income tax rate with a withholding tax rate on royalty payments of 2%.
2. Special deductions are eliminated, except for the capital investment in buildings, structure, machinery and equipment, and the net operating losses carryforward.
3. Credits include a credit for purchases of products manufactured in Puerto Rico, a credit for every incremental job applicable to exempt businesses, a credit for the eligible investment in research and investment activities, a credit for the eligible investment in the acquisition of machinery and equipment for the creation of energy, a credit for payments made to the Puerto Rico Power Authority during the corresponding taxable year, a credit for payments made to resident entities for the use of intangible property in Puerto Rico, a credit for the eligible investment in strategic projects, and a credit available to persons engaging in an eligible business investment.

Any exempt business with a tax-exemption grant under any of the prior acts can request to renegotiate its tax decree under this act. Such renegotiation would be possible provided certain requirements of minimal increase in investment and employment are met. The exemption period is 15 years. This act became effective on 1 July 2008.

Act 181 of 10 December 2007
Act 181 of 10 December 2007 introduced amendments to the income tax law related to capital gains tax rates for corporations. Long-term net gains (holding period of more than six months) from the sale of capital assets taking place after 30 June 2007 may be subject to a preferential tax rate of 15%.

Act 168 of 9 November 2007
Act 168 of 9 November 2007 extended up to 30 June 2008 the period within which an application for exemption pursuant to the Puerto Rico Tax Incentives Act of 1998 shall be received by the Office of Industrial Tax Exemption in order to qualify for exemption. Act 168 was enacted to give a multisector committee additional time to draft a new tax incentives legislation that will provide for the social economic development of Puerto Rico.

Act 117 of 14 July 2006
Act 117 of 14 July 2006, known as the Puerto Rico Tax Reform, enacted new sales and use tax legislation. In general terms, the sales and use tax system replaced the general excise tax system with the exception of certain articles (i.e., cigarettes, fuels, crude oils, vehicles, alcoholic beverages, cement, sugar and plastic products), which are presently subject to a special excise tax. The aggregate sales and use tax is 7% and includes two components: 1.5% for municipalities and 5.5% for the central government, effective 1 July 2006 and 15 November 2006, respectively.

Puerto Rico

Act 98 of 16 May 2006

Act 98 of 16 May 2006 imposed a special tax, known as the extraordinary tax, of 5% on net taxable income to corporations with gross income (as defined in the regulations) in excess of USD 10 million. The tax is computed based on the taxable income for taxable years ended on/or before 31 December 2005. Generally, the extraordinary tax may be claimed as a credit against the income tax liability over a four-year period commencing after 31 July 2006.

Act 89 of 13 May 2006

Act 89 of 13 May 2006 enacted a transitional additional tax of 2% on financial institutions (e.g., corporations operating according to the Puerto Rico Banking Act) for taxable years beginning after 31 December 2005 and on/or before 31 December 2006.

Act 41 of 1 August 2005

Act 41 of 1 August 2005 imposed a transitional additional tax of 2.5% on corporations with taxable income of USD 20,000 or more. This act was recently amended to be effective for taxable years commenced after 31 December 2004 and before 1 January 2007. Therefore, corporations will be subject to this tax for a period of two consecutive years.

Taxes on corporate income

The current corporate income tax rate comprises a 20% normal tax and a graduated surtax (computed on the "surtax net income") up to a maximum combined and effective tax rate of 39%. The "surtax net income" is basically the net taxable income subject to regular tax less a surtax credit in the amount of USD 25,000.

If the net income subject to surtax is (in USD):	The tax shall be (in USD):
Not over USD 75,000	5%
Over USD 75,000 but not over USD 125,000	USD 3,750 plus 15% of the excess over USD 75,000
Over USD 125,000 but not over USD 175,000	USD 11,250 plus 16% of the excess over USD 125,000
Over USD 175,000 but not over USD 225,000	USD 19,250 plus 17% of the excess over USD 175,000
Over USD 225,000 but not over USD 275,000	USD 27,750 plus 18% of the excess over USD 225,000
Over USD 275,000	USD 36,750 plus 19% of the excess over USD 275,000

If the net income subject to regular tax exceeds USD 500,000, a 5% tax will be imposed over the excess. Nevertheless, the total tax determined shall not exceed 39%.

Act 98 of 16 May 2006 imposed a special tax, known as the extraordinary tax, of 5% on net taxable income to corporations with gross income (as defined in the regulations) in excess of USD 10 million. The tax was computed based on the taxable income for taxable years ended on/or before 31 December 2005. Generally, the extraordinary tax may be claimed as a credit against the income tax liability over a four-year period commencing after 31 July 2006. The amount of the credit for each taxable year cannot exceed 25% of the extraordinary tax paid.

Puerto Rico

For taxable years beginning after 31 December 2008, corporations whose total income does not exceed USD 5,000,000 may opt to pay a normal tax rate of 25% to the extent it maintains an average of seven or more employees during the taxable year, or pay a 30% in the event that the taxpayer does not comply with the employee requirement. If the taxpayer opted for the normal tax rate, it will not be subject to the surtax of 5% to 19%.

Temporary provision – 5% surtax over the tax liability
A 5% additional tax will be imposed on the income tax liability determined (not on the taxable income) for corporations, partnerships, and trusts whose gross income exceeds USD 100,000. This provision will be effective for taxable years commenced after 31 December 2008 and before 1 January 2012. This 5% surtax, which is not creditable against the tax liability of future years, will be treated as a separate tax. The special surtax will also apply upon the tax on capital gains. For those corporate taxpayers in the maximum tax bracket, this special surtax will increase effective tax rate from 39% to 40.95%.

A domestic corporation is taxable in Puerto Rico on its worldwide income. Corporations resident in Puerto Rico are subject to tax on Puerto Rico-source income and on non-Puerto Rico-source income that is effectively connected with their trade or business in Puerto Rico. The net taxable income is generally defined as gross income from sources within Puerto Rico (including Puerto Rico effectively connected income) less the allowed deductions. Subject to certain limitations, taxes paid abroad on foreign-source income can be claimed as a foreign tax credit. Note that partnerships and limited liability companies (LLCs) are taxed in Puerto Rico as a corporation, which is first taxed at the entity level (at regular graduated rates up to 39%) and it is taxed again at the shareholders level (10%).

Generally, a corporation is required to prepay 90% of the actual tax for the year or, in the case an income tax return was filed by the corporation in the preceding year, 100% of such tax liability through estimated tax payments in four equal instalments.

Corporate residence

A corporation organised or created under the laws of the Commonwealth of Puerto Rico is a domestic corporation. A domestic corporation is a resident corporation even if it does not conduct business operations in Puerto Rico.

A foreign corporation engaged in trade or business in Puerto Rico is taxed at the regular corporate tax rates on income from Puerto Rico sources that is effectively connected income and at a 29% tax rate on its Puerto Rico source gross income not effectively connected with that business.

Other taxes

In addition to the regular Puerto Rico income tax, the following taxes may apply:

Net capital gains preferential rate
Net gains from the sale of capital assets having a holding period of more than six months may be subject to a preferential tax rate of 15%.

Alternative minimum tax

Alternative minimum taxes are applicable to all corporations and partnerships taxed as corporations except for not-for-profit organisations, corporations eligible for Industrial Incentives Act tax exemptions (only to the extent of the exemption) and certain investment companies. The tax is 22% of the amount to which the alternative minimum net income (AMNI) exceeds the exemption amount of USD 50,000. The AMNI is computed by adjusting the corporation's regular taxable income by certain tax preference accounting items such as accelerated depreciation, instalment sales, long-term contract accounting, and deductions for interest expense related to exempt interest income.

Tax on improper accumulation of income

A surtax of 50% is imposed on corporations that improperly accumulate earnings to prevent the imposition of tax on shareholders or partners, rather than paying the earnings out as dividends. The tax is not imposed on accumulated earnings and profits but on the net income for the year computed without taking capital loss carryover or net operating loss carryover deductions, and reduced by the following items: Puerto Rico income taxes paid or accrued, disallowed net capital losses, and charitable contributions in excess of the deductible amount. The net income does not include industrial income exempted from income taxes under Industrial Incentives Acts. However, an exempt business can be subject to the penalty tax on non-exempt income.

Special partnerships

A partnership that meets certain requirements (i.e., mainly engaged in the construction and rental businesses, among others) may elect not to be taxed as a regular partnership but instead as a special partnership. Note that partnerships in Puerto Rico are taxed as corporations, which mean that partnerships are first taxed at the entity level and again at the shareholders level. By electing to be a special partnership, income or loss will flow through and will only be taxed to its partners.

For the partnership to qualify as a special partnership, it must satisfy certain tests regarding its source of income and must conduct a trade or business in specified industries. In addition, at least 70% of the gross income of the special partnership must be derived from sources within Puerto Rico during the year of the election.

Corporation of individuals

Domestic corporations (including partnerships) and US corporations engaged in a trade or business solely in Puerto Rico with no more than 75 shareholders and that meets certain requirements may elect not to be taxed as a regular corporation but instead as a Corporation of individuals (COI). If the COI election is made, income or loss flows through and will only be taxed to the corporation's individual stockholders.

To qualify as a COI, the corporation needs to make an election on or before the fifteenth day of the fourth month of the taxable year for which the election is to be effective. The COI status is similar to the S corporation concept established in the US Internal Revenue Code.

Municipal license tax

Every corporation is required to file an annual volume-of-business declaration with each of the municipalities in which it establishes or conducts business operations during the year. The declaration must indicate the actual volume of business (i.e., net sales, gross income from any service rendered and other gross receipts) attributable

Puerto Rico

to each municipality. When a business operates in more than one municipality, but does not receive income in all of them, the license tax shall be computed based on a distribution of sales apportioned to each municipality by square feet of the building used in each municipality.

For a non-financial business, the license tax payment varies from a minimum of 0.20% to a maximum of 0.50% depending on each municipality. The payment must be made in two equal instalments on or before 15 July and 15 January, on the basis of the volume of business generated by the entity during its accounting year ended within the immediately preceding calendar year before the due date of the declaration. A 5% discount its available when the tax is fully paid on the declaration due date (on or before five working days after 15 April of each year).

For the first six months after a new business is established, the new company is generally exempt from the municipal license tax, provided that the business informs the municipality that it has established a new business in the municipality within the first 30 days of operations and request the provisional license tax as established in each municipality. A copy of the municipal license is generally requested as a perquisite for obtaining other licenses and permits in Puerto Rico.

Personal property taxes

Every corporation engaged in a trade or business in Puerto Rico which on 1 January of each year owns personal property used in its trade or business within Puerto Rico, whether it is leased to another entity or not, is subject to tax on such property. The tax is self-assessed by the corporation and it is paid together with the filing of an annual return. The tax ranges between 5.08% and 8.23% depending on the municipality. A 5% statutory discount is available if payment is made in full on the return due date (15 May of each year).

In general, all personal property not specifically exempted, including cash, finished goods inventory, supplies, and depreciable property, is subject to the tax. The personal property tax is generally based on the book value of the asset as of 1 January. Finished goods inventory, however, is assessed on the average of the monthly balances for the 12-month period preceding 1 January of each year.

The valuation of the personal property subject to tax is determined by multiplying the book value of such property by the applicable tax rate determined by the municipality in which the property is located. If the book value of depreciable property is below its estimated residual value, the property should be assessed at its estimated residual value.

Real property taxes

The property tax system is administered by the Municipal Revenue Collection Center (MRCC). The tax on real property is directly assessed by the MRCC and may be paid in two instalments. The tax, (which varies from a minimum of 7.80% to a maximum of 10.23% depending on the municipality), is applied to an amount based on the hypothetical fair market value (FMV) of the relevant property in the year 1957. In general terms, this hypothetical FMV normally ranges between 40% and 50% of the cost of the property.

Puerto Rico

Sales and use tax

A sales and use tax was introduced in Puerto Rico on November 2006, eliminating, for the most part, the general excise tax regime. As a general rule, the SUT shall be applied, collected, and paid on all transactions of taxable items in Puerto Rico. Taxable items consist of tangible personal property, taxable services, admissions, and what is known as bundled transactions. Excluded from this definition are: professional associations and certain membership fees; stamps issued by professional associations, the Commonwealth of Puerto Rico or the federal government; human blood, tissue and organs; maintenance fees paid to resident associations; air and maritime tickets; real property; and bingos, raffles and lottery. Other transactions that are exempt from the sales and use tax include: export transactions; duty-free stores located at airport or maritime ports; prescription medicines; insulin; taxable items acquired for certain manufacturing operations (e.g., raw materials); and food and ingredients for food (except for prepared food, diet supplements, sweets and carbonated beverages).

The sales and use tax is imposed at the state level at a 5.5% and an additional 1.5% at the municipal level, for an aggregate tax of 7%. The 7% tax should be remitted to the PR government as follows: 6% to the Puerto Rico Treasury Department ("PRTD") and the remaining 1% to the corresponding municipality. However, there are some municipalities that have entered into an administration agreement with the PRTD by which the PRTD will collect the entire 7% of the sales and use tax from merchants and remit the 1% to the municipality (collected on the municipality's behalf).

Every natural or juridical person who does or wishes to do business of any kind in Puerto Rico shall request registration in the Merchant's Registry of the PRTD at least 30 days before starting operations. Registration in the Merchant's Registry shall be done by filling out Form AS 2914.1: Application for Merchant's Registration Certificate and Exemption Certificate. Once this application is filled out and approved, the Secretary of Treasury will grant a Merchant's Registration Certificate. This certificate constitutes the merchant's authorisation to do business in Puerto Rico, and confirms the merchant's obligation as a withholding agent. The Merchant's Registration Certificate shall be displayed, at all times, in a visible place for the general public in the commercial establishment for which it was issued. The PRTD issues two kinds of merchant registration certificates: a certificate to indicate that the merchant is a person who collects sales tax (green certificate), or a certificate that indicates that the merchant is not a collector agent (red certificate). Please note that if a merchant is doing business in one or more of the 78 municipalities in Puerto Rico, the merchant only needs to register with the PRTD.

Unless specifically exempted, all persons selling taxable items are required to file a monthly tax return. This return shall be delivered to the PRTD no later than the tenth day of the calendar month following the month during which the sales occurred. If the merchant wishes to claim any exemption corresponding to taxable items, the merchant needs to file the monthly return and claim the exemption in it.

Excise taxes

Although the sales and use tax replaced the excise tax system; there are certain articles that continue to be subject to a special excise tax such as cigarettes, fuels, crude oils, vehicles, alcoholic beverages, cement, sugar and plastic products.

Puerto Rico

Annual report

Every corporation is required to file an annual corporation report with the Puerto Rico Department of State. This annual report must be filed by the fifteenth day of April along with a USD 100 annual fee and a balance sheet as of the close of operations of the prior year. If the volume of business exceeds USD 3 million the annual report must be accompanied by a balance sheet certified by a certified public accountant (CPA) licensed in Puerto Rico. In the event that the volume of business does not exceed USD 3 million, a balance sheet prepared under generally accepted accounting principles (GAAP) by a person with a general knowledge in accounting has to be submitted along with the corporate annual report. An extension of 60 days for filing the annual report can be obtained if timely requested. An additional 30 day period may also be requested. The Secretary of State is authorised to impose a penalty for failure to timely or accurately file the annual corporate report that would be between USD 100 and USD 1,000 if a non-profit corporation, and between USD 500 and USD 2,000 if a for-profit corporation.

Branch income

Corporations operating in Puerto Rico as a branch may be subject to a 10% tax on the dividend equivalent amount (commonly known as the branch profit tax or BPT). The BPT should be determined and paid along with the corporate income tax return. There would not be an income tax withholding at source at the time cash transfers are made by the Puerto Rico branch to its home office outside of Puerto Rico.

Income determination

Business profits
The gross income of a corporation generally includes business income, profits from the sale of property, interest, dividends, and income derived from any source unless specifically exempted by law.

Accounting period
The annual accounting period may be on the basis of the calendar year, a fiscal year ending on the last day of a month or a 52/53 week year.

Accounting methods
A corporation's net income is generally calculated in accordance with the method used for financial statement purposes, except for various items of income and expenses, which are treated differently. For example, the cash method of accounting may not be used by a corporation with inventory or with an average annual gross income in excess of USD 1 million. Long-term contract methods and the instalment method can be used for regular tax calculations.

Inventory valuation
In general, inventory is valued at the lower of cost or market. Retail merchants can use the retail method of accounting.

Capital gains
Tax-advantaged treatment is provided for net long-term gains (holding period of more than six months) from the sale of capital assets. For corporations, net long-term capital gains, reduced by any short-term capital losses, are subject to an alternative tax in lieu

of the regular corporate tax rates. For transactions conducted after 30 June 2007, the alternative (preferential) tax is 15%.

Other income
Interest income is generally taxable, except interest from obligations of the federal government or any state, or territory or political subdivisions; the District of Columbia; and the Commonwealth of Puerto Rico or any of its instrumentalities or political subdivisions.

Dividends from a corporation that derives 20% or more of its profits from sources within Puerto Rico are taxable in Puerto Rico. However, a dividend-received deduction may apply.

Royalties from property located in Puerto Rico or from any interest in such property are included in gross income.

Service fees are generally taxable as ordinary income.

Deductions

Business expenses
All ordinary and necessary expenses paid or incurred during the taxable year in carrying on any trade or business are deductible by corporations operating in Puerto Rico.

Depreciation and depletion
A reasonable depreciation allowance is deductible for the exhaustion, wear and tear, and obsolescence of property used in business. The most common depreciation method used by corporations is the straight-line method. Nevertheless, any other consistent method may be used in lieu of the straight-line method as long as it is in accordance with the recognised trade practice. In addition, a corporation (other than one that is exempt under an Industrial Incentives Act) can elect an accelerated depreciation method for new or used tangible property acquired by purchase, on taxable years commencing after 30 June 1995.

Inter-company charges
Management fees paid to a foreign affiliate are deductible to the extent that they are reasonable compensation for the services rendered. However, the Secretary of the Treasury has the authority to reallocate items of income and expense to properly reflect the Puerto Rico taxable income.

Employee remuneration
Corporations may deduct payments of reasonable salaries or other compensation for services actually rendered.

Insurance premiums
Insurance premiums paid or accrued on risks related to a trade or business are deductible as well as premiums on group life policies covering employees, where the beneficiary is not the corporation. No deduction is allowed for premiums paid to an insurance company not authorised to provide insurance in Puerto Rico, or through an agent or broker not authorised to operate in the Commonwealth of Puerto Rico.

P

Puerto Rico

Net operating losses

All corporations are generally entitled to the net operating loss deduction in computing their tax. Net operating losses may be carried over for seven years (there are no carryback provisions). Also, losses from sales or exchanges of capital assets are allowed only to the extent of gains from such sales or exchanges. The carryforward period is, however, five years.

Dividends-received deduction

All corporations engaged in trade or business in Puerto Rico are entitled to an 85% deduction on dividends received from a domestic corporation but not in excess of 85% of the net income of the corporation. A 100% dividend-received deduction applies for dividends received from taxable controlled domestic corporations (if ownership in a corporation is 80% or more).

Other significant items

Deductions for allowed charitable contributions are limited to 5% of net income, computed regardless of the contributions.

The cost of incidental repairs (not adding value to the property) is deductible as business expenses.

Subject to certain limitations, savings and retirement plans for the benefit of the employees are deductible, if qualified by the Secretary of the Treasury.

A corporation is allowed a deduction for taxes paid (except for Puerto Rico income tax), including income tax paid to the United States, its other possessions and any foreign country. The deduction is in lieu of claiming a foreign tax credit.

Corporations are entitled to a rent expense deduction if the rented property is used in the business.

Meals and entertainment expenses are deductible, subject to a 50% limitation. Travelling expenses are fully deductible if the trip is for business purposes.

Group taxation

Puerto Rico does not have group taxation rules. In other words, corporations can not file a consolidated return for Puerto Rico tax purposes.

Thin capitalisation

There are no specific thin capitalisation rules in Puerto Rico.

Tax incentives

A corporation engaged in specific eligible activities may apply for a reduced income tax rate through the request of a Tax Exemption Grant to the Puerto Rico Office of Industrial Tax Exemption. On 28 May 2008, Act 73 was enacted into law to create a new Incentives Act in an attempt to create a new economic environment with the goal of developing the local industry, maintaining current investments, and promoting the direct investment from the United States and other countries. Act 73 (the new act) replaces the Puerto Rico Tax Incentives Act of 1998 (the 1998 Act) which expired on 30 June 2008. The new act changed the fixed income tax rates applicable to industrial development income (IDI) and introduced certain credits to reduce the income tax determined, when applicable. The new act does not provide an expiration date; therefore, it is effective until a new act replaces it.

Any exempt business with a tax-exemption grant under any of the prior acts can request to renegotiate its tax decree under this act. Such renegotiation would be possible provided certain requirements of minimal increase in investment and employment are met. The exemption period is 15 years. This new act became effective on 1 July 2008.

Tax rate
Exempt entities may elect one of the following two scenarios:

General scenario: 4% income tax rate with a withholding tax rate on royalty payments of 12%. Under this scenario, the amount of withholding taxes on the royalty payments is creditable against the 4% income tax.

Alternate scenario: 8% income tax rate with a withholding tax rate on royalty payments of 2%. Under this scenario, the withholding tax on royalty payments is creditable against the 8% income tax rate.

Companies may elect one of these scenarios at the time of applying for the benefits under the new act. However, there are other possibilities:

- 4% fixed income tax rate on IDI, excluding income from certain investments provided by section 2(j).
- Existing exempt businesses currently taxed at a rate of 2% to 4% under the 1998 Act may continue to enjoy the same tax rate under the new act when it is determined by the Secretary of the Puerto Rico Economic Development (the Secretary) that said tax rate is in the best interest of Puerto Rico and the existing business complies with an employment commitment of at least 80% of its average employment during the three preceding years before the application of exemption under the new act. Note that the secretary could require a minimum income tax payment equal to the average income tax paid during said period.
- Pioneer industries are eligible for a 1% income tax rate.
- Activities for the development in Puerto Rico of intangible property are eligible for a 0% income tax rate.
- Any exempt business having operations at a municipality located in a "low or intermediate development zone" may reduce its income tax rate by an additional 5%.
- Any exempt business having operations in Vieques and Culebra may be totally exempt from income taxes during the first 10 years of operations as established in the new act. The remaining years covered by its tax decree may qualify for a 2% income tax rate.

Special deductions
Special deductions are eliminated, except for capital investment in buildings, structure, machinery and equipment and the net operating losses carryforward.

P

Puerto Rico

Credits

Credit for purchases of Puerto Rico manufactured product: Subject to certain limitations, the credit for purchases of products manufactured in Puerto Rico will remain at 25% (35% in the case of recycled products).

Job creation credit: There is a credit for every incremental job applicable to exempt business starting operations after 1 July 2008. The amount of the credit (maximum of USD 5,000 per each employment) depends upon the location of the industrial development zone.

Research and development investment credit: 50% credit granted for the eligible investment in research and investment activities including operational expenditures, clinical trials, infrastructure, renewable energy or intellectual property.

Energy investment credit: 50% credit granted for the eligible investment in the acquisition of machinery and equipment for the creation of energy.

Energy cost credit: There is also a 3% credit (which could be increased up to 10% if certain employment requirements are met) for payments made to the Puerto Rico Power Authority during the corresponding taxable year. This credit will be available for a 10-year period starting on 1 July 2008. Additional credits (for the purpose of reducing the cost of energy) may be available to industrial units subject to certain limitations.

Technology transfer credit: 12% credit (2% in the case of exempt businesses that opted for the alternate tax) for payments made to resident entities for the use or privilege of using intangible property in Puerto Rico.

Strategic projects investment credit: There is a 50% credit for eligible investment in strategic projects including activities for the design, development and construction of dams.

Industrial investment credit: There is a 50% credit, up to a maximum of USD 8,000,000, for cash invested in the purchase of 50% or more of the stock or operating assets of an exempt business that is in the process of shutting down operations, amount used to start-up small or medium exempt business, or amounts used for a substantial expansion of an exempt business.

Several of the above mentioned credits were also made available to entities operating under prior tax incentives acts.

Property taxes

Similar to the previous incentives laws, the current act allows for a 90% property tax exemption on personal and real property. However, the current act introduced a methodology for the classification and assessment of real property owned by the exempt businesses. Under the provisions of the current act, a taxpayer can self-assess his real property tax responsibility (similar to the current personal property tax system) and remit the related tax liability due along with a real property tax return (to be issued by the MRCC) by 15 May of each year. The self-appraisal method is only applicable to real property that has not been appraised by the MRCC and is mainly limited to machinery and equipment classified as real property. Note that this method is not available for assets such as land, building and building equipment.

Municipal license tax and other municipal taxes

The current act did not introduce many changes regarding treatment of exempted businesses for municipal license tax purposes. The tax exemption remains at the same 60% as it was under the 1998 Act. Exempt businesses operating in Vieques or Culebra will be 90% exempt; small or medium exempt businesses will be 75% exempt; and central or regional corporate headquarters providing managerial services to affiliated companies will be 100% exempt during the first five years after becoming eligible for the exemption.

Withholding taxes (WHT)

Corporations not engaged in a trade or business in Puerto Rico are subject to a 29% withholding tax at source on certain gross income items (considered fixed or determinable annual or periodical (FDAP)) from Puerto Rico sources.

FDAP income may include interests received from a related person, rents, royalties, salaries, annuities, compensation, remuneration, and net capital gains. However, if the payment received is from dividends and partnership profits, a 10% withholding tax should apply.

The payer, as a withholding agent, is responsible for the deduction and remittance of the 29% (10% in the case of dividends) to the Puerto Rico Treasury Department. Such tax is due on or before the fifteenth day of the month following the receipt of the income by the non-resident corporation and it is reported in Form 480.31 "Deposit Slip of Nonresidents Income Tax Withheld at Source". An annual informative return is also required to be filed (Form 480.30 "Nonresidents Annual Return of Income Tax Withheld at Source") no later than 15 April of the following year.

Tax administration

Returns

The Puerto Rico tax system is based on the principle of self-assessment. A corporate taxpayer is required to file an annual return (generally Form 480.20) by the fifteenth day of the fourth month following the close of its tax year. In general terms, a taxpayer can obtain an additional extension of three months to file its tax return. Failure to timely file can result in penalties.

Payment of tax

A corporation must substantially satisfy its annual income tax liability, if any, through estimated income tax payments. The amount of estimated income taxes should be paid on equal instalments on the fifteenth day of the fourth, sixth, ninth and twelfth month of the taxable year of the corporation. The estimated payments should equal or exceed 90% of the actual tax for the year or, in the case an income tax return was filed by the corporation in the preceding year, 100% of such tax liability. Failure to pay the tax by the due dates indicated above may result in a penalty of 10% of the instalment due.

Other issues

Foreign currency restrictions

As a territory of the United States, Puerto Rico's currency is the United States dollar.

Puerto Rico

Furthermore, there are no foreign currency regulations and/or treaties between foreign countries and Puerto Rico. However, the Puerto Rico Supreme Court has recognised that, although Puerto Rico is generally not a signatory party to a treaty entered into by the United States, if an international treaty does not explicitly exclude Puerto Rico, the treaty would be applicable to Puerto Rico.

Audited financial statements

Accounting records must be prepared in accordance with the general accepted accounting principles (GAAP) followed in the United States. Domestic corporations (i.e., incorporated in the Commonwealth of Puerto Rico) with volume of business of more than USD 3 million must include with their income tax return audited financial statements of the Puerto Rico operations for the accounting year ended on or before the preceding 31 December. The financial statements should be submitted with an audit report issued by a CPA licensed in Puerto Rico. Nevertheless, foreign corporations with volume of business of more than USD 1 million must include with their income tax return audited financial statements of the Puerto Rico operations.

With respect to the municipal license and personal property tax filings, the threshold amount for the audited financial statements requirement is gross revenues of more than USD 3 million regardless the corporate residency (i.e., foreign or domestic).

Corporate taxes in Qatar

For more information, contact:

Ian Clay
PricewaterhouseCoopers
3rd Floor Al Emadi Business Centre
C – Ring Road
Doha, Qatar
Tel: +974 4675581
Email: ian.clay@qa.pwc.com

Significant developments

Qatar Financial Centre (QFC)

The government of Qatar established an onshore financial centre, the Qatar Financial Centre (QFC), in 2005, mainly aimed at regulated organisations operating in the financial services sector. However, the QFC law permits certain other non-regulated activities to be carried out as well, for example, acting as a holding company or providing group treasury functions.

Although the QFC tax law has been drafted, it has not yet been approved. It is expected that the QFC tax law will be enacted during 2010 and will be retroactively applied from 1 January 2010. The guidance provided in other sections therefore relates only to the law applied outside the QFC. The draft QFC tax law previously circulated contained a flat corporate tax rate of 10%.

New Qatar corporate tax law

A new tax law, Law No. 21 of 2009, came into force with effect from 1 January 2010 and replaced the previous tax law, Law No. 11 of 1993. Key highlights of the new law include the reduction of the tax rate to a flat tax rate of 10%, the elimination of progressive tax rates (with the top rate of 35% under the previous tax law), a shift to a "source based taxation" from an "activity based test" and the introduction of withholding tax.

Detailed regulations containing the implementation rules and guidelines have not yet been issued by the Qatar tax authorities.

Taxes on corporate income

The tax law with respect to QFC-based entities has not yet been enacted. Accordingly, the information provided in this section is directed towards other entities with Qatar source income.

An entity that is wholly or partially foreign owned and that derives income from sources in Qatar is subject to income tax in Qatar. In the case of a joint venture, the tax liability of the joint venture is dependent upon the foreign partners' share of the joint venture's profit. Currently, no corporate income tax is levied on a corporate entity that is wholly owned by Qatari nationals. Following the introduction of the new tax law with effect from 1 January 2010, the tax treatment with respect to corporate entities owned by Gulf Cooperation Council (GCC) nationals may vary from country to country.

Q

Qatar

Unless specifically exempt from tax, an entity will be taxable in Qatar if it has generated Qatar source income, regardless of the place of its incorporation. Even if an entity has been granted exemption from tax, the entity is required to submit a tax return.

Taxable income generally is subject to a flat corporate income tax rate of 10%, with certain exceptions available. In prior periods, tax was levied at differing rates on different portions of income, with the first QR 5 million of income being taxed at an average rate of 24% and any income in excess of QR 5 million being taxed at 35%.

Since 1 January 2010, the following tax rates apply in the specific circumstances noted:

* If a special agreement has been reached with the Government of the State of Qatar prior to 1 January 2010, the rate specified in the agreement continues to apply. If no rate is specified in the agreement, a rate of 35% will be used.
* The rate applied with respect to oil operations, as defined in Law No. 3 of 2007, may not be less than 35%.
* Payments made to non-residents with respect to certain service activities not connected with a permanent establishment (PE) in Qatar are subject to withholding tax. *(See Withholding taxes.)*

The amount of tax payable is reduced for companies that are partly foreign owned, depending on the extent of local ownership.

Corporate residence

It is important to recognise that residence is not the basis used to determine whether an entity is taxable in Qatar. Accordingly, a tax exposure in Qatar may arise even if a company is not resident in Qatar. Residence is therefore primarily relevant when considering whether withholding tax will apply on payments received rather than the typical form of corporate taxation on taxable income.

A company is resident in Qatar if it is incorporated in accordance with Qatar laws, its head office is situated in Qatar or its place of effective management and control is in Qatar.

Other taxes

Qatar currently imposes no sales tax or value-added tax (VAT) on operations in Qatar. Customs duties are applied to goods with an origin outside the GCC countries, normally at a rate of 5%, but sometimes are applied at higher rates for specific types of goods, such as tobacco products. Temporary import exemptions are sometimes available.

Branch income

The profits of a branch owned by a foreign parent entity are subject to the same tax rules as apply to other forms of taxable entity, although a reduction for partial local ownership is not available.

Income determination

General principles
Corporate income tax is levied on a company's Qatar source income. Some examples of Qatar source income include:

- Income derived from an activity carried on in Qatar;
- Income derived from contracts wholly or partially performed in Qatar;
- Income from real estate situated in Qatar, including income from the sale of shares of companies with assets consisting of mainly real estate situated in Qatar;
- Income from shares in companies resident in Qatar or listed on Qatar's stock market;
- Interest arising in Qatar; and
- Bank interest realised outside Qatar if it results from the taxpayer's activity in Qatar.

Capital gains
Any chargeable gains on the sale of capital assets are taxed as ordinary income.

Exemptions
A number of exemptions have been specified in the Qatar tax law, including the income generated by Qatar-based companies that are wholly owned by Qatari nationals.

Dividends are exempt from tax if the dividends are paid from profits that were either subject to tax in Qatar or distributed by a company that is exempt from tax in Qatar.

Losses
Losses may be deducted from net income during the year. Losses may not be carried forward for more than three years after the year in which they were incurred. Losses may not be carried back.

Self-employed contractors
While the Qatar sourced income of self-employed contractors is subject to taxation in Qatar, employment income is outside the scope of Qatar tax.

Deductions

Taxable income is determined after deducting all expenditures, costs and losses incurred to generate gross income, particularly the following:

- Interest on loans used in the activity;
- Employee costs (including salaries, wages, gratuities, and other end of service benefits);
- Tax depreciation of fixed assets;
- Losses resulting from the sale of assets;
- Bad debts approved by the tax authorities in accordance with the criteria set out in the tax law; and
- Donations, gift aid and subscriptions to charitable, humanitarian, scientific, cultural or sporting activities paid in Qatar to government authorities or public bodies, provided the value does not exceed 5% of net profit in the year in which the deduction is claimed. A deduction is usually available for expenses that are

Qatar

considered ordinary rather than "capital" in nature and incurred in generating Qatar source revenue.

Depreciation and depletion
Depreciation should be calculated in accordance with rates specified by the Qatar tax law and regulations.

Allocations of overheads to branches
The branch's share of the head office expenses (i.e., indirect or allocated overheads) generally is deductible only up to a certain limit. The deduction is capped at 3% (1% for banks) of the total revenue less certain other costs under the previous tax law. This threshold may be altered by the executive regulations, which are expected to be published later in 2010.

Group taxation

There is no definition of a "group" for Qatar tax purposes and therefore, there is no concept of group taxation.

There are no specific rules on transfer pricing, thin capitalisation, or controlled foreign companies. However, there is a broad anti-avoidance provision in the tax law that gives the tax department wide powers including that of restatement.

Tax incentives

Qatar Science and Technology Park
Qatar has established the Qatar Science & Technology Park (QSTP), which was aimed at entities with research and development activities. QSTP entities may be exempt from Qatar tax, however, tax exempt entities are required to file tax returns.

Other tax exemptions
An application for a tax exemption may be made for certain projects that are considered to be strategically significant to the Qatar economy. The exemptions are generally granted for a period of three or six years (reduced from five or 10 years under the previous tax law). Applications for an exemption are assessed based on certain criteria set out in the Qatar tax law. Notwithstanding the fact that an exemption is granted, an entity that is exempt is still required to file a tax return under the Qatar tax law.

Withholding taxes (WHT)

Mechanics of the withholding tax system
Withholding tax was introduced in Qatar for the first time on 1 January 2010 by the new tax law. Withholding tax is levied on certain payments made to non-residents in relation to royalties and technical services (the applicable rate is 5%) and on interest, commissions, brokerage fees, directors' fees, attendance fees and any other payments for services carried out wholly or partly in Qatar (the applicable rate is 7%). Withholding tax on interest is currently suspended until further notice; however, this is expected to be a temporary measure.

The company that makes the payment to its foreign supplier is required to withhold the tax and remit to the tax department the funds that were withheld by the sixteenth day of the following month. In the event that the company does not make a payment to the tax department, the company will be liable for a penalty equal to the amount of unpaid tax due, in addition to the withholding tax.

Withholding tax in Qatar may be reduced under the terms of a double tax treaty.

Retention system

Pursuant to circulars issued by the tax department, a retention system is in place whereby certain final contract amounts are required to be retained from payments made by Qatari entities to foreign entities in connection with work performed in Qatar. However, a practice has developed over time whereby 5% to 10% of each payment is retained rather than the final contract payment. All ministries, government departments, public, semi-public and private establishments and Qatar tax payers are required to retain these amounts until the recipient entity provides a final tax clearance, which is obtained from the Qatar tax authorities. Where withholding tax is not deducted, the retention system may continue to apply.

Tax treaties

Qatar has a growing network of double tax treaties with around 25 double tax treaties currently in force.

Tax administration

Returns and payment of tax

The tax year is generally the same as the calendar year, although advance approval may be sought from the Qatar tax authorities to use a company's accounting year-end.

The tax return is due within four months from the date of a company's tax filing period. The tax payable is based on the tax declaration and should be paid on the same day that the tax return is due.

Late filing penalties

The Qatar tax law contains a penalty regime, which imposes a penalty for the late filing of a tax return. In addition, a penalty applies where there is a late payment of tax.

Objection and appeals process

It is possible for a taxpayer to initially object directly to the tax department regarding a decision related to a tax position. If the objection is unsuccessful with respect to altering the tax department's decision, an appeal may be made by the taxpayer to the Tax Appeals Committee. Based on the Tax Appeals Committee's decision with respect to the appeal, a final appeal may be made by either the tax department or the taxpayer to the administrative chamber of the court. The law prescribes time limits for each stage of the appeal process.

Accounting and audit requirements

A company's corporate income tax return is required to be accompanied by audited financial statements if the company's capital or profit exceeds QR 100,000, or the head office is situated outside Qatar. The audit report must be signed by a locally registered auditor.

Q

Qatar

Qatar tax law requires accounts to be prepared in accordance with International Financial Reporting Standards (IFRS). It is possible to seek approval from the Qatar tax authorities for an alternative accounting basis.

Accounting record retention

All accounting books, registers and documents relating to activity in Qatar are required to be retained in Qatar for a 10-year period.

Other issues

The tax law in relation to QFC-based entities is yet to be enacted. Accordingly the guidance in this section is directed towards other entities with Qatar source income.

Anti-avoidance provisions

A new anti avoidance provision was introduced by the new tax law, which gives the Qatar tax authorities very wide powers to counteract transactions that have been carried out with a tax avoidance purpose. These powers include substituting an arm's-length value or recharacterising transactions.

Corporate taxes in Romania

For more information, contact:

Peter de Ruiter
PricewaterhouseCoopers
Lakeview Building
301-311 Barbu Vacarescu Street
RO-020276, Bucharest 2
Romania
Tel.: + 40 21 225 3500
Email: peter.deruiter@ro.pwc.com

Significant developments

Given the current economic environment, it is expected that the Government will enact during 2010 fiscal measures with significant impact. Among others, these measures may consist of widening the tax base for income tax, through the inclusion of the incomes from interest, capital gains, meal tickets, and compensation payments.

The Government also intends to introduce effective payment of value-added taxes (VAT) for intra-community acquisitions of certain products with high tax fraud risk (e.g., meat, fish, grains, vegetables, fruits). On the other hand, the companies that acquire such products from the Romanian market will no longer need to pre-finance the VAT, the payment being borne only by the final customer.

Taxes on corporate income

The standard profit tax rate is 16%, for Romanian companies and foreign companies operating through a permanent establishment in Romania. Starting 1 May 2009, all active companies pay the higher of the 16% corporate income tax (CIT) or the minimum tax. The minimum tax is determined based on the revenues reported on 31 December of the previous year. The annual minimum tax ranges from EUR 500 to EUR 10,000, depending on the businesses' turnover in the prior year. Start ups are exempted from minimum tax for the tax year of their incorporation.

The profit tax liability due from nightclubs and gambling operations cannot be less than 5% of the revenue obtained from such activities.

Corporate residence

A company is considered resident in Romania if it was set-up under Romanian law, or has its place of effective management in Romania.

Starting in 2010, the tax code introduced the concept of "legal person set-up in accordance with European legislation." Such legal persons become tax residents if they establish (or transfer) their registered office in Romania. As a result, such entities are subject to the same tax treatment as Romanian legal persons for taxation of profits and dividends.

Permanent establishment (PE)
PE is defined as being the place through which the activity of a non-resident is conducted, fully or partially, directly or through a dependent agent. Once a PE is

Romania

created, Romania has the right to tax the profits of the foreign enterprise derived from the activity performed on its territory.

The Romanian legislation explicitly states three conditions that should be met simultaneously in order to trigger a PE:

1. A place of business must exist (e.g., premises, machinery or equipment);
2. The place of business must be fixed (i.e., must be established at a distinct place with a certain degree of permanence); and
3. The activity should be carried out through this fixed place of business (i.e., there are people dependent on the enterprise and conducting its business in the state where it is located).

The registration, filing and payment requirements are similar to those for a Romanian company.

Other taxes

Value-added tax (VAT)
The standard VAT rate is 19% and is applied to all supplies of goods and services that do not qualify for an exemption (with or without credit) or for the VAT reduced rate (this includes imports).

The reduced VAT rate is 9%, and is applicable to admission fees at museums, historical monuments, architecture and archaeological monuments, zoos and botanical gardens, fairs and exhibitions, cinema tickets, supply of school manuals, books, newspapers and periodicals, supply of prostheses and orthopaedic products (except for dentures), medicine for human and veterinarian use, accommodation in hotels or in areas with a similar function.

Some operations are exempt with credit (i.e., deduction right) for input VAT, including: export of goods, transport and related services, intra-community supply of goods, international transport of passengers, certain operations performed in free-trade zones and free warehouses, supply of goods to a bonded warehouse, a VAT warehouse and related services, supply of foreign goods which are placed under suspensive customs regimes, supply of services in connection with goods placed under customs suspensive regimes, supply of goods and services to diplomatic missions, international organisations and North Atlantic Treaty Organisation (NATO) forces.

VAT exemption applies to a range of activities, including banking, finance and insurance. However, some financial services are also subject to a 19% VAT (e.g., factoring, debt collection, managing and depositing certain equity papers).

VAT on imported goods continues to be paid at customs until 1 January 2012, save for taxable persons registered for VAT purposes that obtain an import VAT deferment certificate from the customs authorities. For these taxpayers, the VAT is not paid at customs but is shown in the VAT return as both input and output VAT.

The rules for establishing the place of supply of goods and services (and therefore the place of VAT taxation) are fully aligned with the Recast of the EU Sixth VAT Directive.

Services provided by offshore entities to Romanian companies with deemed place of supply in Romania are subject to Romanian VAT.

The reverse-charge mechanism applies for services performed by offshore entities and the place of supply is where the beneficiary is established or has a fixed establishment (e.g., consultancy, marketing services, telecommunications and electronically supplied services). This is possible provided the suppliers are not established in Romania for VAT purposes. Under the VAT reverse-charge mechanism, VAT is not actually paid, but only shown in the VAT return as both input and output tax, provided the beneficiary is registered for VAT purposes.

As a general rule, the fiscal period is the calendar month. For taxable persons registered for VAT purposes whose previous year-end turnover did not exceed EUR 100,000, the fiscal period is the calendar quarter.

Customs regulations

The customs value is determined and declared by importers in accordance with the provisions of the WTO Customs Valuation Agreement (i.e., the Agreement pertaining to the implementation of Article VII of the General Agreement on Trade and Tariffs (GATT)).

For chain transactions with goods intended for import, the customs value may be determined, under certain conditions, based on the price in any of the transactions in the chain ("first sale principle"). This way, the customs value can be determined based on a price lower than that paid or payable by the importer (e.g., based on the price of the first transaction in the chain).

The customs value can be modified within 12 months of the acceptance of the customs declaration for the release of the goods for free circulation, in specific cases (e.g., in the case of defective goods).

Under specific conditions, determining customs value upon import is possible, even if certain elements that need to be added to the customs value are not quantifiable on the importation date (e.g., licence fees, royalties) or are missing.

The customs authorities may inspect the customs value either during the customs clearance or during a post-import audit (the customs authorities are entitled to perform such an audit during a five-year period following the date of import).

It is also possible to amend or invalidate the customs declaration, as follows:

- Amendment of the customs declaration before the customs clearance is obtained;
- Invalidation of the customs declaration within 90 days of the customs clearance being obtained; or
- Amendment after the customs clearance is obtained, which can be performed at the request of the traders within three years of the customs clearance date.

The customs duties are those specified in the EU Common Customs Tariff.

Customs duties are expressed as a percentage applied to the customs value (i.e., *ad valorem* taxes), or as a fixed amount applied to a specific quantity (i.e., specific taxes).

R

Romania

Agricultural products (i.e., products from chapters 1–24 of the EU Common Customs Tariff) are subject to specific taxation.

In certain cases (e.g., meat), the customs duty rate is established with regard to the cost, insurance and freight (CIF) or the entry price of the products. In other cases, the customs duty rate is established by adding to the *ad valorem* tax additional duties such as agricultural components.

Legal entities established in non-EU states can declare goods by indirect representation. The indirect representation can be used for customs regimes such as transit or temporary importation.

Moreover, legal entities established in non-EU states can occasionally declare goods on their own through direct representation, provided that the customs authorities consider this to be justified.

Customs brokers can be authorised to use the local customs clearance procedure or to submit simplified customs declarations for the companies they represent (either directly or indirectly). Any Romanian legal person can act as an indirect representative for a sole person using the simplified customs clearance procedures.

Operators that obtain Authorised Economic Operator (AEO) status benefit from simplifications regarding customs inspection, obtaining customs authorisations and performing customs formalities.

Moreover, through the AEO certificate, the holder is recognised by the customs authorities as a reliable person, giving comfort as regards observance of the safety and security standards.

Companies can obtain rulings ("binding tariff information" or BTI) from the Romanian customs authorities on the tariff classification of imported goods that are binding for the customs authorities for a six-year period, whenever goods identical to those described in the BTI are imported.

A similar type of ruling can also be obtained regarding the origin of goods (binding origin information BOI). The BOI is valid for a three-year period.

Property taxes

For buildings owned by individuals, the tax rate is 0.1% and is levied on the taxable value of the building, determined depending on the surface, zoning and locality rankings. Various adjustments to the taxable base are provided for dwellings, older buildings, etc. The tax increases depending on the number of buildings owned.

For buildings owned by companies, the building tax rate is set by the Local Council at between 0.25% and 1.5% of the entry value of the building, adjusted with the value of reconstruction, consolidation, modification and extension works and the revaluation, if applicable. If the building has not been revaluated in the previous three years, the tax rate is increased by the Local Council to between 5% and 10%. The taxable value of fully depreciated buildings is reduced by 15%.

Building tax is paid twice a year, by 31 March and 30 September, in equal instalments. As a general rule, if the building tax due for the entire year is paid in advance by 31 March, a reduction of up to 10% may be granted by the Local Council.

Owners of land are subject to land tax established at a fixed amount per square metre, depending on the rank of the locality where the land is located and the area or category of land use, in accordance with the classification made by the local council.

Companies are not subject to land tax on land where buildings are sited.

Similar to building tax, land tax is paid twice a year, in equal instalments, by 31 March and 30 September. A 10% reduction is granted for full advance payment of this tax by 31 March.

Social expenses
Employers must pay social security contributions, calculated on the gross salary costs as follows: 20.8%, 25.8% or 30.8%, depending on working conditions.

Other contributions payable by employers for employees are as follows:

- 0.85% – Contribution for medical leaves;
- 5.2% – Health fund;
- 0.5% – Unemployment fund;
- 0.25–0.75% – Commission for Labour Office;
- 0.25% of the salary fund – Guarantee fund; and
- 0.15%–0.85% – Work accidents insurance fund.

Excise duties
Harmonised excisable products
The following products are subject to harmonised excise duties: ethyl alcohol and alcoholic beverages, tobacco products, energy products (e.g., unleaded petrol, diesel oil and coal) and electricity. Excise duties are due when excise goods are released for consumption (e.g., imported into Romania, taken out of an excise duty suspension regime). Excisable products can be produced, transformed, held and received under a duty suspension arrangement only in a tax warehouse, which should have prior approval from the tax authorities.

Such excisable products can also be received from within the EU under excise duty suspension arrangements by registered consignees.

Romanian tax warehouse keepers are deemed authorised for the intra-community movement of excisable products under excise duty suspension arrangements.

Excisable products can also be dispatched under duty suspension arrangements after being released for free circulation by the registered consignor (this also applies for the holder of a single authorisation for a simplified customs clearance procedure).

The movement of these excisable products under a duty suspension arrangement has to be made based on the accompanying administrative document (AAD). From 1 April 2010 the paper AAD procedure will be replaced by the computerised system for monitoring the movement of excise goods under suspension of duty.

R

Romania

The production, holding and movement of excisable products under duty suspension arrangements are subject to a guarantee.

Ethyl alcohol and other alcoholic products are exempt from the payment of excise duties if they are denatured, used in nutritional, pharmaceuticals or cosmetics industry. From 1 April 2010 there will be exemptions for ethyl alcohol and other alcoholic beverages when used in a manufacturing process provided that the final product does not contain alcohol or as samples for analysis, for necessary production tests, or for scientific purposes.

The excise duty exemption for alcohol products and energy products can in some cases be granted directly based on an end-user licence or indirectly through reimbursement/compensation.

Some energy products subject to movement control can be purchased to be used for the purposes excepted from excise duty, provided that an end-user authorisation is obtained and the payment of excise duties is secured.

From 1 April 2010 the guarantee required for movement under duty suspension arrangements may be lodged by the transporter or carrier, by the owner of excise goods or by the consignee; or jointly by two or more persons involved in the movement of the excise goods (e.g., the consignor and the transporter of the goods).

In some cases, traders can claim a refund of the excise duties paid (e.g., excise duty paid for goods released for consumption in Romania, but intended for consumption in other Member States; excise duties paid for goods released for consumption and then returned to the production tax warehouse for recycling, reprocessing or destruction; excise duties paid for goods acquired from the EU or imported and then returned to the suppliers).

Before being released for consumption in Romania, spirit-based beverages and tobacco products have to be marked with duty stamps. The responsibility for such marking lies with the tax warehouse keepers, registered consignees and importers releasing such goods for consumption.

Companies selling fuel in gas stations have to register with the tax authorities.

Other excisable products
From 1 April 2010 the other excisable products are green coffee, roasted coffee (including coffee with substitutes) and soluble coffee (including blends with soluble coffee).

The excise duty for coffee will be decreased to nil by 2011.

Excise duties are due when the actual reception takes place, for the excisable products received from EU.

For imports of excisable goods, the importers holding single European authorisations for simplified customs clearance procedures issued by another EU Member State have to file a VAT and Excise Duties declaration with the customs authorities. Excise duties will be due on the date the import declaration is registered.

Excise duty exemption applies in this case, provided the excisable products are exported or placed under a suspensive customs regime.

Companies performing exports or intra-community supplies of coffee may benefit from the refund of the excise duty paid for the coffee used as raw materials.

Traders purchasing coffee are entitled to a refund of the excise duties paid, if the products are exported, supplied to another EU Member State or returned unchanged to the supplier.

Branch income

Branch
A foreign company can set up a branch in Romania.

Profits derived by the branch are taxed at the standard profit tax rate of 16%, but as of 1 May 2009, the tax due is the higher of the 16% CIT and a minimum tax. The annual minimum tax ranges from EUR 500 to EUR 10,000, depending on the businesses' turnover in the prior year.

Branches can operate only in the same field of activity as their parent companies.

Representative offices
Representative offices are often established as a first step to operating in Romania. A representative office can undertake only auxiliary or preparatory activities, cannot trade in its own name and cannot engage in any contractual activity. A representative office can perform only a limited range of activities without being considered a permanent establishment for profit tax purposes.

Representative offices are subject to a yearly flat tax of EUR 4,000 (payable in local currency, i.e., the Romanian New Leu – RON). It has to be paid in two instalments by 20 June and 20 December. If a representative office is set up or closed down during a year, the tax due for that year is prorated on the basis of the number of months the representative office operated in that fiscal year.

Income determination

The taxable profit of a company is calculated as the difference between the revenue derived from any source and the expenses incurred for the purpose of obtaining taxable incomes, during a fiscal year, out of which non-taxable incomes are deducted and non-deductible expenses are added.

Inventory valuation
The methods permitted for inventory valuation under Romanian law are standard cost; detail sale price; average (weighted) cost; first-in, first-out (FIFO); and last-in, first-out (LIFO).

Assets are generally valued at their acquisition cost, production cost or market value. Fixed assets could be revalued at certain points in time for various purposes.

R

Romania

Capital gains

Capital gains earned by a Romanian resident company are included in ordinary profits and are taxed at 16%. Capital losses related to sale of shares are, in general, tax-deductible. Capital gains obtained by non-residents from real estate property located in Romania or the sale of shares held in a Romanian company are also taxable in Romania. However, the income may be subject to treaty protection.

Dividends, interest, royalties

Dividends received by a Romanian company from another Romanian company are not subject to the profit tax, but are subject to a final withholding tax of 10%.

Dividends received by a Romanian company from a foreign company are taxed at the normal CIT rate in Romania. Credit is available for tax paid abroad.

Moreover, as Romania joined the European Union (EU) in 2007, dividends received from a foreign or Romanian legal person from a member state of the EU are not taxable if the Romanian legal person has held a minimum of 15% of the shares in the foreign legal person for an uninterrupted period of at least two years on the date when the dividend is paid. Starting with 2009, these rules apply to companies from all member countries of the European Economic Area (EEA).

Interest and royalty payments by Romanian companies to other Romanian companies are taxable income in the hands of the beneficiary with ordinary corporate income tax.

Foreign income

Resident companies are taxed on worldwide income, unless a double-tax treaty between Romania and the said treaty stipulates otherwise.

Deductions

From the deductibility standpoint, expenses fall into three categories: deductible expenses, limited deductibility expenses and non-deductible expenses.

Deductible expenses

As a general rule, expenses are deductible only if incurred for the purpose of generating taxable income.

The following expenses are considered as being incurred for the purpose of generating taxable income:

- Expenses incurred for marketing, market research, promotion within existing or new markets, participation in fairs and exhibitions, business missions and publishing of own brochures;
- Advertising expenses incurred in promoting the company, products or services, based on written contracts, as well as costs associated with the production of the materials necessary for broadcasting advertisements, including goods granted as samples, for product testing at selling units, as well as other goods and services granted to stimulate sales;
- Research and development expenses that do not meet the requirements to be recognised as intangible assets for accounting purposes;
- Expenses incurred for environmental protection and resource conservation;

- Expenses incurred for improvement of management, information technology (IT), the introduction, maintenance and development of quality management systems, and obtaining quality compliance confirmation;
- Bad debts expenses in any of the following cases: the bankruptcy procedure of the debtor was closed based on a court decision; the debtor is deceased and the receivable cannot be recovered from the heirs; the debtor is dissolved or liquidated; the debtor has major financial difficulties affecting its entire patrimony;
- Travel and accommodation expenses related to business trips in Romania or abroad by employees and directors, and also individuals assimilated to these positions (directors based on mandate and secondees whose costs are covered by the Romanian company); this also includes transport of personnel to/from the workplace;
- Expenses incurred from professional training and development of employees;
- Expenses incurred in relation to work safety, prevention of work accidents and occupational diseases, the related insurance contributions and professional risk insurance premiums;
- Expenses incurred from acquisition of packaging during their useful life; and
- Fines, interest, penalties and other increased payments due under commercial contracts.

Companies can benefit from an additional deduction of 20% from the eligible expenses in respect of research and development activities they perform. Moreover, accelerated depreciation may be applied for devices and equipment used in the research and development activity.

Limited deductibility expenses
The deductibility of certain expenses is limited as follows:

- Interest and foreign exchange losses under thin capitalisation rules;
- Depreciation of assets under fiscal depreciation rules;
- Perishable goods capped as set by the relevant central administration bodies;
- Protocol expenses, up to the limit of 2% of the difference between total taxable revenue and total expenses related to taxable revenue, except for protocol and profit tax expenses;
- Daily allowances for expenses from domestic and foreign travel by employees, up to the level of two and a half times the ceiling set for public institutions;
- Social expenses up to 2% of salary expenses, including maternity allowances, expenses for nursery tickets, funeral benefits and allowances for serious or incurable diseases and prostheses, as well as expenses for the proper operation of certain activities or units under taxpayers' administration (e.g., kindergartens, nurseries, health services supplied for occupational diseases and work accidents prior to admission to health establishments, canteens, sports clubs, clubs); expenses incurred under a collective labour agreement, such as holiday tickets granted to employees;
- Health insurance premiums for employers, up to the limit of EUR 250 per year, per person; private pension insurance premiums, up to the limit of EUR 400 per year, per person;
- Taxes and contributions paid to non-governmental organisations and professional associations related to the taxpayer's activity, up to the limit of EUR 4,000 per year; and

R

Romania

* Expenses from operation, maintenance and repair of vehicles used by individuals in company leadership and management positions, within the limits of one vehicle per person.

Non-deductible expenses

Expenses which are specifically non-deductible include, among others, the following:

* Domestic profit tax and profit tax paid in foreign countries;
* Expenses related to non-taxable revenues (Note that revenues from dividends have no corresponding expenses);
* Expenses related to withholding tax supported by Romanian taxpayers on behalf of non-residents;
* Interest, fines and penalties due to Romanian or foreign authorities;
* Expenses incurred from management, consultancy, assistance or other supply of services if no contracts or any other lawful agreements are entered into and the beneficiary cannot justify the supply of such services for the activities performed and their necessity;
* Sponsorship and patronage expenses and expenses for private scholarships; however, taxpayers are granted a fiscal credit up to 0.3% of turnover and 20% of the profit tax due, whichever is lower;
* Other salary and/or similar expenses (if not taxed at the level of the individual), except for those specifically exempted from individual income taxation;
* Expenses incurred from insurance premiums unrelated to company assets or business, save for those regarding goods which are bank collateral on loans used to conduct the activity for which the taxpayer is authorised or those used under rental or leasing contracts;
* Bad debt expenses in excess of the deductible provision *(see below);*
* Expenses recorded without "justifying" documents;
* Expenses in favour of shareholders, other than those related to goods or services provided by the shareholders at market value;
* Expenses incurred from fixed assets impairments (i.e., losses in value defined as provisory adjustments by the accounting regulations transposing European Accounting Directives);
* During the period 1 May 2009 to 31 December 2010, fuel expenses for company vehicles weighing under 3,500kg and with fewer than nine passenger seats (including the driver's seat) and used exclusively for passenger transport – exceptions are vehicles used in the following activities:
  * Intervention, repair, safety and security, courier services, transporting staff to and from the work place, TV vans, cars used by sales agents and recruitment agents;
  * Paid transportation services and taxi activities;
  * Rental; and
  * Driver schools.

Thin capitalisation rules

If the company's equity is negative or the debt-to-equity ratio is higher than 3:1, all the interest expenses and the net losses from foreign exchange differences related to credits or loans with a reimbursement period longer than 12 months are non-deductible in the year in which they are booked. These expenses are carried forward to the following fiscal years, and they will become deductible at once when the debt-to-equity ratio becomes lower than 3:1.

The interest expenses and the net losses from foreign exchange differences related to loans from Romanian or foreign banks, leasing companies and other entities expressly mentioned by law are fully deductible, without being limited by the debt-to-equity ratio.

Loans contracted directly or indirectly from Romanian or foreign banks, leasing companies, mortgage companies and other entities expressly mentioned by the law are no longer taken into account when computing the debt-to-equity ratio.

From 2010 the tax deductibility threshold for interest on foreign currency loans from non-financial institutions is 6%.

Depreciation

Romanian law distinguishes between fiscal and accounting depreciation. Companies should maintain a separate record to reflect the separate computation of the fiscal and the accounting depreciation. Any accounting revaluations of fixed assets are not taken into account in computing the tax depreciation.

Assets are generally depreciated using the straight-line method. However, accelerated or digressive depreciation methods may be used to determine fiscal depreciation, while the accounting depreciation method may be different.

Accelerated depreciation (50% deduction from the book value in the first year of operation) can be used for technological equipment and other tools, installations, computers and related peripherals.

The useful lives to be used for tax purposes are the ones stated in the Official Fixed Assets Catalogue, published under government decision. Ranges are provided for classes of fixed assets, from which the taxpayers can choose the useful life (e.g., office and housing buildings: 40–60 years, commercial buildings: 32–48 years, commercial furnishings: nine–15 years, and automobiles: four–six years).

Land cannot be depreciated.

Net operating losses

Companies are allowed to carry forward fiscal losses as declared in the yearly profit tax returns for a period of seven years based on a FIFO method. No related adjustment for inflation is allowed.

For foreign legal persons, this rule (i.e., carryforward of losses) applies only to revenues and expenses attributable to their permanent establishment in Romania, and only for a period of five years.

Fiscal losses

Profit tax is not deductible, nor are late payment interest and fines related to tax liabilities or social security obligations.

Provisions and reserves

Amounts used for setting up or increasing reserves or provisions are deductible as follows:

- Setting up or increasing the legal reserve fund to a limit of 5% of the yearly accounting profit before tax (with adjustments) until it reaches 20% of the share capital;
- Provisions for doubtful debts recorded after 1 January 2006, up to the limit of 30% if the related receivables meet the following conditions simultaneously:
  - Booked after 1 January 2004;
  - Not collected for a period exceeding 270 days from the due date;
  - Not guaranteed by another person;
  - Due by a person not affiliated with the taxpayer; and
  - Included in the taxable income of the taxpayer.
- Bad debt provisions, if all the following conditions are met:
  - Receivables are booked after 1 January 2007;
  - The debtor is a company declared bankrupt by a court ruling;
  - Receivables are not guaranteed by another person;
  - The debtor is not a related party; and
  - Receivables were included in the taxable income of the taxpayer.
- Provisions for receivables recorded before 1 January 2004, within the limit stipulated by the Fiscal Code for provisions established for receivables recorded after 1 January 2006. Two additional conditions must be met to set up a provision for receivables: bankruptcy proceedings against the debtor must be opened and no tax-deductible provisions can be previously set up for such receivables;
- Specific provisions established by credit institutions, non-banking financial institutions and other similar entities;
- Technical reserves set up by insurance and reinsurance companies, in accordance with their regulatory legal framework except for the equalisation reserve; and
- Risk provisions for transactions carried out on financial markets, in accordance with the rules issued by the National Commission of Movable Assets.

The reduction or cancellation of any provision or reserve deducted from the taxable profit, due to changing the destination of the provision or reserve, distribution towards shareholders in any form, liquidation, spin-off, merger or any other reason, is included in the taxable revenues and taxed accordingly. The reconstruction of the legal reserve is also non-deductible.

Group taxation

There is no tax consolidation or group taxation in Romania. Members of a group must file separate returns and therefore are taxed separately. No provision exists for offsetting the losses of group members against the profits of other group members.

Transfer pricing

Transactions between related parties should observe the arm's-length principle. If transfer prices are not set at arm's length, the Romanian Tax Authorities have the right to adjust the taxpayer's revenues or expenses so as to reflect the market value. Traditional transfer pricing methods (comparable uncontrolled prices, cost plus and resale price methods), as well as any other methods that are in line with the Organisation for Economic Co-operation and Development (OECD) Transfer Pricing Guidelines (i.e., transactional net margin and profit split methods) may be used for setting transfer prices. Domestic legislation expressly stipulates that when applying transfer pricing rules, the Romanian tax authorities will also consider the OECD Transfer Pricing Guidelines. There are five methods for assessing the performance of transactions at arms' length, as follows:

1. Comparable uncontrolled price method;
2. Resale price method;
3. Transactional net margin method;
4. Profit split method; and
5. Cost plus method.

Transfer pricing documentation

Taxpayers engaged in related-party transactions have to prepare and make available upon the written request of the Romanian Tax Authorities their transfer pricing documentation file.

The content of the transfer pricing documentation file has been approved by order of the president of the National Agency for Tax Administration. The Order is supplemented by the OECD Transfer Pricing Guidelines and the Code of Conduct on transfer pricing documentation for associated enterprises in the EU (EUTDP).

The deadline for presenting the transfer pricing documentation file will not exceed three calendar months, with the possibility of a single extension equal to the period initially established.

Failure to present the transfer pricing documentation file or presenting an incomplete file following two consecutive requests may trigger estimation of transfer prices by the tax authorities, based on generally available information, as the arithmetic mean of three transactions considered similar.

The transfer pricing audit activity has significantly increased during the past year and requests for presenting the transfer pricing documentation file have started to become common practice. We are aware of recent cases where the Romanian tax authorities adjusted the taxable result of a local taxpayer in accordance with the applicable regulations.

Advance pricing agreement (APA)

Taxpayers engaged in transactions with related parties can request that the National Agency for Tax Administration issue an APA. These taxpayers can also schedule a pre-filing meeting to discuss the feasibility of the APA.

The request for an APA is filed together with the relevant documentation and payment evidence of the fee (ranging between EUR 10,000 and EUR 20,000). The required documentation is based on the EUTPD and suggests up-front the content of the APA.

The term provided by the Fiscal Procedural Code for issuance of an APA is 12 months for unilateral APAs and 18 months for bilateral and multilateral APAs. The APA is issued for a period of up to five years. In exceptional cases such as long-term agreements, it may be issued for a longer period.

APAs are opposable and binding on the tax authorities as long as there are no material changes in the critical assumptions. In this view, the beneficiaries are obliged to submit an annual report on compliance with the terms and conditions of the agreement.

If taxpayers do not agree with the content of the APA, they can notify the National Agency for Tax Administration within 15 days. In this case, the agreement does not produce any legal effects.

R

Romania

Tax incentives

Research and development (R&D) incentives
Companies can benefit from an additional deduction of 20% from the eligible expenses in respect of their R&D activities. Moreover, accelerated depreciation may be applied for devices and equipment used in the R&D activity.

Corporate income tax exemption for reinvested profits
The incentive is available from 1 October 2009 until 31 December 2010 and applies to reinvested profits used for the production or acquisition of new (meaning not previously used) technological equipment used in the business. Note that the amount for which the incentive is applied is deducted from the fiscal value of the equipment produced or acquired, meaning the tax deduction for depreciating the equipment will be reduced in the future (thus, in effect, this incentive represents only a deferral of tax). Other important conditions imposed in connection with the application of this incentive are:

- Reinvested profit is to be allocated for the creation of a reserve, and release of such reserve in the future might have unintended tax consequences.
- The assets created or acquired in relation to the incentive must be kept for at least half their normal useful life. If the assets are disposed of prior to this time, profit tax is recalculated and delay penalties are due from the date the exemption was granted (assets transferred in the reorganisation process, under certain conditions, and assets disposed of due to liquidation or insolvency are exempt from this penalty).

Dividend tax exemption for reinvestments
Distributed dividends are exempted from taxation as of 1 January 2009 if they are invested in the same or in another Romanian company's share capital.

To benefit from this exemption, dividends must be reinvested to preserve and increase the number of employees and to boost existing lines of business.

Reduced VAT rate of 5% for sale of buildings
Companies selling buildings can apply a reduced VAT rate of 5% in the following cases:

- If the buildings are part of a social policy, such as homes for the elderly, retirement homes, orphanages, rehabilitation centres for children with disabilities
- The building is supplied as housing to an individual or family and has a maximum useful surface of 120 square metres and a value of less than RON 380,000 (exclusive of VAT)

Local tax exemptions for business located in industrial parks, and scientific and technological parks
Industrial parks
No property tax is due for buildings and constructions located in an industrial park. Also, land within industrial parks is exempt from land tax.

Scientific and technological parks
The incentives granted for the set-up and development of scientific and technological parks include:

- Lower taxes on tangible assets and land used by the park;
- Exemption of specific taxes on land;
- Deferred payment of VAT for materials, equipment and connection to the public utilities networks during the investment period, until the park is put into operation;
- Development programmes for infrastructure, investments and equipment endowments granted by the local and central public administration, companies and foreign financial assistance; and
- Donations, concessions and structural funds for development.

The companies operating within the park benefit from:

- Various services offered by the park administrator free of charge or with reduced fees; and
- Advantageous conditions with regard to location, use of the infrastructure and communications of the park, with payment in instalments.

Withholding taxes (WHT)

Domestic dividend tax

Dividend payments by a Romanian company to another Romanian company are subject to 10% dividend tax.

From 2009 distributed dividends are exempt from taxation if they are invested in a Romanian company to preserve and increase the number of employees and boost activity.

As of 1 January 2007, the provisions of the EU Parent-Subsidiary Directive are applicable. Consequently, the dividends received by a Romanian company from another Romanian company are not taxed if the beneficiary has held at least 10% of the Romanian company's shares for a continuous period of at least two years by the date of dividends payment.

Withholding tax for non-residents

Non-resident companies are subject to a 16% withholding tax rate on other revenues derived from Romania, such as interest, royalties, revenues from services performed in Romania, dividends, revenues obtained from management and consultancy, services (irrespective of where the services are performed), commissions, and revenues derived from liquidation of a Romanian legal entity.

Certain specific provisions and exceptions apply to the above rates, as follows:

- The withholding tax rate applicable to dividends received by non-residents from Romania is 10%, for EU/EEA member states' companies.
- As Romania is an EU member state, the provisions of the Parent-Subsidiary Directive are applied. Thus, dividends paid by Romanian companies to companies resident in one of the EU/EEA member states are exempt from withholding tax if the dividend beneficiary has held a minimum of 10% of the shares of the Romanian company for a continuous period of at least two years by the date of dividends payment.

As of 2010, the tax treatment of investment income of pension funds established in European Economic Area is harmonised with the treatment applicable to domestic

R

Romania

pension funds. Thus, dividend and interest income obtained from Romania by EEA registered pension funds will be exempt from withholding tax.

Romania has implemented the EU Interest and Royalties Directive with a transitional period for the application of this directive until 2010. Until 31 December 2010, a 10% withholding tax applies on payments of interest and royalties made by Romanian companies to companies resident in EU/EEA member states and holding at least 25% of the share capital of the Romanian company for a continuous period of at least two years prior to the date of payment of interest or royalties. Such payments are exempt from withholding tax from 1 January 2011, under the same conditions as stated above.

A 20% withholding tax applies on gambling proceeds obtained by non-residents.

To comply with European legislation, non-residents are required to present the certificate of tax residence and a declaration stating compliance with the necessary requirements, including that they are the beneficial owner of the income.

The following categories of income derived from Romania by non-residents are exempt from withholding tax:

- Bonds issued and/or guaranteed by the Romanian government;
- Revenues derived from interest on demand deposits or current accounts, as well as interest from term deposits or other types of saving instruments;
- Revenues from consultancy, technical assistance and similar services financed by means of non-reimbursable funds and loans granted to the Romanian state, or loans guaranteed by the Romanian state, provided that the interest rate for such loans is below 3% per annum;
- Revenues from international transportation and accessory services;
- Prizes paid from public funds; and
- Income obtained from a partnership constituted in Romania by a non-resident company. Such income is to be taxed under title II of the Fiscal Code, with corporate income tax.

Tax administration

Corporate tax returns
In Romania, the fiscal year is the calendar year.

Annual profit tax returns should be submitted to the tax authorities together with annual financial statements if the company has not chosen to submit the annual profit tax return on 25 February. Certain returns should be submitted monthly (e.g., the return on tax liabilities due to the consolidated general budget, the VAT return and social security contribution returns).

Annual profit tax returns have to be filed with the Romanian tax authorities by 25 April of the following year.

The Government postponed the introduction of the advance payments of profit tax (this system would have been applied to most taxpayers from 2010) until 2012. Until then, taxpayers (excluding banks) have to declare and pay quarterly profit tax.

Non-resident companies

Non-resident companies deriving income from real estate property located in Romania or the sales of shares held in a Romanian company are obliged to declare and pay the related profit tax. Non-residents may appoint a tax agent to fulfil this requirement. However, if the payer of the income is a Romanian company or a permanent establishment, they have the obligation to pay and declare the profit tax.

For capital gains tax declaration and payment, the Romanian legislation requires the following tax returns to be submitted as follows:

* Quarterly statements, starting the twenty-fifth day of the month following the quarter in which the non-resident first earned capital gains taxable in Romania; an annual profit tax return.
* The quarterly statements and annual return must be submitted during the entire period of time the non-resident is registered with the Romanian tax authorities, even if it no longer carries out transactions generating taxable revenues in Romania.

Late-payment penalty
Starting 1 July 2010 the late-payment interest is reduced from 0.1% to 0.05% for each day of delay and, in addition, the following late-payment penalties are due:

* 5% of the fiscal liabilities, if the payment is made after 30 days but before the expiry of the 90 days from the due date; and
* 15% of the remaining unpaid fiscal liabilities, if the payment is made after 90 days from the due date.

Late-payment penalties for the fiscal claims due to local budgets are owed in the amount of 2% of the fiscal claims, calculated for each month or part thereof.

VAT compliance
Fiscal period
As a general rule, the fiscal period is the calendar month. For taxable persons registered for VAT purposes whose previous year-end turnover did not exceed EUR 100,000, the fiscal period is the calendar quarter.

Invoicing
Companies are not required to use standard pre-printed fiscal invoices. Instead, they can issue invoices containing the minimum information required by law.

Taxable persons are also allowed to issue summary invoices or invoices on behalf of the supplier, and to issue and store invoices electronically. From a VAT perspective, the signing and stamping of invoices is no longer mandatory.

Ledgers and returns
Taxable persons must keep complete and detailed records for calculation of VAT liabilities.

VAT returns should be submitted to the tax authorities by the twenty-fifth day of the month following the end of the fiscal period; the VAT is due by the same date. The VAT return should be submitted using an electronic carrier (e.g., floppy disk).

Romania

Taxable persons not registered for VAT purposes are required to pay VAT and to submit a special VAT return on services rendered by non-residents, which have a deemed place of supply in Romania. These obligations must be fulfilled by the twenty-fifth day of the month following that in which the services are performed.

Taxable persons are required to file twice yearly for acquisitions and supplies of goods and services performed on Romanian territory.

VAT refund

If a company is in a VAT refundable position, it must tick the VAT refund box on the VAT return to claim the refund. Alternatively, the balance can be carried forward against VAT liabilities reported in future returns. The refund claims must be processed by the tax office within 45 days of being submitted.

Large taxpayers (as classified by law) are entitled to refund on request, with a subsequent inspection (i.e., a "fast refund"). Other taxpayers may be entitled to a "fast refund" (i.e., without a prior inspection), but only after a complex risk analysis.

If the VAT is not reimbursed within the legal term (i.e., 45 days), taxable persons are entitled to claim interest, currently set at 0.1% per day of delay.

Refund to non-residents

Taxable persons established in the EU and taxable persons established outside the EU (under reciprocity conditions) are entitled to VAT reimbursement from Romania, if certain conditions are fulfilled.

Other issues

Mergers, spin-offs, transfers of assets and exchanges of shares between two Romanian companies should not trigger capital gains tax.

In the case of a relocation of the registered office of a European Company (SE) and European Cooperative Society (SCE) from Romania to another EU Member State, if certain conditions are met there is no tax on the difference between the market value of the transferred assets and liabilities and their fiscal value. There will also be no tax on such movements at the shareholder level and, thus, in the case of Romanian shareholders a tax basis step-up may be achieved.

If a Romanian company has a permanent establishment in another Member State, and the Romanian company is dissolved as a result of a cross-border reorganisation, the Romanian tax authorities will not have the right to tax the former permanent establishment.

Corporate taxes in the Russian Federation

For more information, contact:

David John
PricewaterhouseCoopers
White Square Office Center
10 Butyrsky Val
Moscow, Russia
125047
Tel: + 7 495 967 60 00
Email: david.c.john@ru.pwc.com

Significant developments

Tax law changes

From 1 January 2010, the Unified Social Tax (UST) is replaced with insurance contributions. The assessment rates are a flat 26% in 2010, which is equal to the maximum UST rate. In 2010, the UST is applied on the first RUB 415,000 of individual's salary per year. One tax base is established for contributions to all funds.

From 2011, the overall assessment rate will reach 34%, and the ceiling will be adjusted according to an annual index. The provisions relating to the following key elements for the new insurance contribution system (payers, tax base, assessment procedures, reporting periods, and timeframes for making contribution payments) generally coincide with the relevant UST provisions.

The Russian Government has adopted a new model tax treaty that incorporates anti-abuse concepts similar to those in the OECD, US, and UN models. According to the new treaty, domestic thin capitalisation rules may be applied by contracting states to interest payments. It is not expected that effective double tax treaties will be revised in accordance with the new model tax treaty.

Expected tax law changes in 2010

New transfer pricing legislation passed the first of three readings in the Duma (the lower house of the Russian Parliament). If adopted, the legislation will come into force on 1 January 2011. The new version of transfer pricing legislation contains the following provisions:

- A significant reduction in the list of transactions for which the Russian tax authorities may control prices for tax purposes;
- Expansion of the list of related parties;
- The introduction of the arm's-length principle as the fundamental principle of Russian transfer pricing rules;
- Formally introducing functional analysis as one of the comparability factors;
- The introduction of new methods for determining market prices;
- The introduction of reporting and transfer pricing documentation requirements; and
- The introduction of unilateral and multilateral advance pricing agreements (APAs) for companies registered as "large" taxpayers (but not earlier than 2012).

The draft law on consolidated taxpayers has been published by the Ministry of Finance. If adopted, it will come into force on 1 January 2011. After two years of discussions, the draft law framework and the majority of its provisions remain unchanged.

R

Russian Federation

In particular, the consolidated taxpayer regime can apply still only to profits tax. Compared to the previous version of the draft law (posted on the same Russian Ministry of Finance website in April 2008), the new version contains criteria values for creating a consolidated taxpayer (including the total revenue and the total assets of a group). The criteria are rather high – only a limited number of Russian companies will be able to satisfy them.

Customs and duties changes
The foundation of and deeper integration processes within the Customs Union among Russia, Belarus and Kazakhstan (Customs Union) resulted in significant developments of the customs legislation. The Customs Union proposes the united customs territory, within which no customs duties or economic restrictions will be applied. These countries should apply unified customs tariffs and customs valuation methodology, general rules of non-tariff regulation, uniform technical regulations, etc. Certain provisions of the legislation on the Customs Union took effect on 1 January 2010, in particular the Common Customs Tariff (CCT) and the Agreement on Rules of Licensing in Foreign Trade. A number of other documents, which constitute the legal framework for the Customs Union, including the Customs Code of the Customs Union (CU Customs Code) are effective as of 1 July 2010. It is worth mentioning that the CU Customs Code prevails over the domestic customs legislation within the Customs Union.

Expected customs and duties changes in 2010
Given that several provisions of the CU Customs Code refer to the domestic laws, decisions of the Customs Union Committee and the Eurasian Economic Community (EurAsEC) Interstate Council, a large number of regulatory documents governing imports, exports and customs clearance of goods have already been adopted or will be adopted in the near future (e.g., uniform templates of customs documents, a procedure for amending the customs declaration after the release of goods).

Taxes on corporate income

Profits tax
Corporations and their shareholders are taxed separately. The maximum profit tax rate for all taxpayers in the Russian Federation has been established at 20% from 1 January 2009. The amount payable to the budgets of constituent regions may be reduced by such regions, so the minimum tax rate may be 15.5% for taxpayers located in certain regions.

Corporate residence

The tax system in Russia distinguishes between Russian and foreign legal entities on the basis of their law of incorporation.

Russian legal entities pay tax on their worldwide income (credit relief is available for foreign tax paid up to the amount of the Russian tax liability that would have been due on the same amount under Russian rules). Foreign legal entities pay tax on income derived through a permanent establishment (at the rate of 20%) and are also subject to withholding tax on income from Russian sources not related to a permanent establishment (at rates varying from 10% to 20%, depending on the type of income and the method used to calculate it).

All taxpayers are required to obtain tax registration and be assigned a taxpayer identification number, irrespective of whether their activities are subject to Russian taxation.

Other taxes

Value-added tax (VAT)

The VAT system, while not originally based on the EU model, gradually is moving towards it. VAT applies to the value added by each element in the chain of production, from producer to consumer. The standard rate is 18% (with a lower rate of 10% for certain basic foodstuffs, children's clothing, medicines and medical goods, and printed publications). The same VAT rates are applied for the import of goods into Russia. Exports and related services are taxed at a zero rate of VAT.

The list of exempt goods and services includes basic banking and insurance services, educational services by certified establishments, the sale of certain essential medical equipment, passenger transport, and certain other socially important services. Most accredited offices of foreign legal entities (as well as the accredited employees of these offices) may be exempt from VAT on property rental payments. The majority of exemptions from VAT carry no right to input credit in Russia, instead input VAT is, in most cases, deducted for profits tax purposes.

Most taxpayers are on an EU-type input-output VAT system, whereby, a VAT payer accounts for VAT on its full sales price, and deducts VAT incurred on inventory costs and other related expenses. VAT should be calculated on an accrual basis only.

The export of goods to destinations outside Russia, including the Commonwealth of Independent States (CIS) countries, transport and other services related to the export of goods from and import of goods into Russia, international passenger transport, sales to diplomatic functions, and certain other transactions are zero-rated with a right to offset input VAT. To apply the 0% rate and achieve input credit for exported goods, there must be proof available of the actual export. A significant number of documents must be submitted to the tax authorities.

Under the reverse-charge mechanism, a Russian company must account for VAT on any payment it makes to a non-tax registered foreign company, if the payment is connected to the sale of goods or services in Russia. The VAT withheld is eligible for normal input VAT credit by Russian payers. Foreign suppliers are allowed only to offset VAT collected through the reverse-charge mechanism against Russian VAT paid on imported and domestically acquired supplies by registering for taxes in Russia. There is no special VAT registration.

Russian VAT law contains an EU-type set of place-of-supply rules for determining where services are supplied for VAT purposes. These rules divide all services into different categories for determining where they are deemed to be supplied for VAT purposes. For example, certain services are deemed to be supplied where they are performed, some where the "buyer" of the services is located, and others where certain property is located.

Uniform invoicing for VAT purposes applies to all Russian-registered taxpayers that provide goods and services. Standard invoices are to be issued within five days after a supply of goods or services. A duplicate copy of the invoice is registered in a sales

R

Russian Federation

journal, and incoming invoices are recorded in a purchase book. Compliance with invoicing procedures is critical to the supplier's ability to recover input VAT.

From 1 January 2007, VAT returns are due on a quarterly basis. VAT must be paid to the Russian Government after the end of each quarter in three instalments not later than the twentieth day of each of the three consecutive months following the quarter.

Import VAT
A limited range of goods is granted exemption from import VAT. The list of such goods includes, for example, humanitarian aid and goods designated for diplomatic corps. Relief from import VAT is available on certain machinery and equipment and their components and spare parts.

Import duties
In addition to VAT, customs duties are levied on assets imported into the Russian Federation. The rate varies according to the tariff code of the goods imported and the country of origin (generally the rate varies from zero to 20% of the customs value of imported goods). There is special relief from customs duties for qualifying goods contributed to the charter capital of Russian companies with foreign investments.

Excise duty
Excise taxes apply to the production and import of cars, tobacco, alcohol, petrol and lubricants. Special excise rates for each type of excisable goods are established in the tax code. The rates are widely variable and are based on multiple factors.

Customs processing fee
Goods transported across the Russian Federation customs border are subject to a customs processing fee with a flat rate. The fee depends on a customs value of transported goods. Generally the fee is not significant.

Property tax
The property tax base includes only the book value of fixed assets recorded on the taxpayer's balance sheet (including property leased out). Intangible assets, inventories, work-in-progress, and financial assets are not subject to property tax in Russia. The maximum property tax rate is 2.2%, and regional legislative bodies have the right to reduce this rate. Certain types of property are exempt from the tax. The relief is also available to a limited number of categories of taxpayers.

Transport tax
A transport tax is imposed on certain types of land, water and air transport registered in Russia. Fixed rates apply (per unit of horsepower, gross tonnage, or unit of transport), which are differentiated based on engine capacity, gross tonnage, and type of transport. The actual rates in the regions may be subject to a maximum 10-fold increase/decrease by the legislative bodies of Russian Federation constituent subjects. Reporting and payment rules are established by regional legislative authorities.

Branch income

Foreign legal entities pay tax on profits attributable to a permanent establishment (PE). A PE is broadly defined as "a branch, division, office, bureau, agency, or any other place through which a foreign legal entity regularly carries out its business activities in Russia". Russia's various double taxation treaties may define a PE differently, which could in some cases result in tax relief. Conducting business through an agent also may create a taxable PE in Russia.

A PE's profits are computed on substantially the same basis as Russian legal entities, including the composition of tax-deductible expenses. The tax code does not provide specifically for the deductibility of expenses incurred abroad by a head office with respect to its PE in Russia (including a reasonable allocation of administration costs), although most double tax treaties provide for such an option. If a foreign legal entity conducts free-of-charge preparatory and/or auxiliary services for the benefit of third parties, a PE is considered to have been formed, and the tax base is calculated as 20% of its expenses relating to such activities.

Foreign legal entities operating in Russia through a PE are to follow the filing and payment schedules established for Russian legal entities, although they do not make monthly advance payments, but pay profits tax on a quarterly and annual basis only.

Income determination

The accounting period in Russia is a calendar year. Different periods are not permitted. The taxable base is calculated on an accrual basis (only small-scale taxpayers are still allowed to use the cash basis).

Taxable income is to be computed following the rules and principles established in the tax code. Taxpayers must maintain tax accounting registers. Statutory accounts may be used for computing tax items for which accounting methods are the same. In practice, most taxpayers use statutory accounts as a basis and apply adjustments to arrive at the taxable income.

Inventory valuation
Inventory can be valued using one of the following methods: first-in, first-out (FIFO), last-in, first-out (LIFO), average cost and individual unit cost methods.

Capital gains
Capital gains are subject to the same 20% rate and are added to ordinary income to arrive at the taxable income. An exception applies to gains/losses from securities (e.g., shares, bonds, notes) and financial instruments, which are generally taxed separately.

Gains from the sale of fixed assets and other property equal the difference between the sale price and their net book value for tax purposes. Losses resulting from the sale of fixed assets should be deducted in equal monthly instalments during the period, defined as the difference between their normative useful life and the actual time of use.

Dividends
Dividends received by Russian legal entities from Russian or foreign legal entities are taxed in Russia at a 9% flat rate.

Dividends received from "strategic investments" are exempt from Russian income tax. An investment is considered strategic when:

- The owner (recipient of dividends) owns at least 50% of the capital of the payer of dividends, or owns depository receipts entitling it to receive at least 50% of the total amount of paid dividends;

Russian Federation

- The share or depository receipts have been owned for at least 365 calendar days on the day dividends are declared; and
- The value of the investment is at least RUB 500 million (This requirement will be abolished from 2011).

Dividends from companies residing in "offshore" zones with preferential tax regimes will not be eligible for the tax exemption. The list of the offshore zones is established by the Ministry of Finance.

Tax on dividends from abroad withheld in the source country may be credited against Russian tax, if a special provision exists in the relevant tax treaty.

The standard 15% tax rate is applicable to dividends paid by Russian legal entities to foreign legal entities. The tax should be withheld by the Russian legal entity paying dividends. The tax may be reduced based on a relevant double tax treaty (typically to 10% or 5%).

Interest
Interest income is taxed on the accrual basis. A standard tax rate of 20% is applied to interest income, except for interest on state and municipal securities, which is taxed at 0%, 9% or 15%, depending on the type of security. The rate may be reduced (typically to zero) based on a relevant tax treaty.

Foreign income
Russian legal entities pay tax on their worldwide income. Credit relief is available for foreign taxes paid up to the amount of the Russian tax liability that would have been due on the same amount under Russian rules.

Exchange gains and losses
Foreign exchange gains and losses are recognised for tax purposes on the accrual basis. However, gains and losses from settlements in a local currency of amounts denominated in (tied to) a foreign currency are taxable (deductible) on payment.

Deductions

General
Expenses generally are deducted on the accrual basis. The main criteria for the deductibility of expenses is that the expense is (a) incurred in the course of an income-generating activity, (b) properly documented, (c) not mentioned in the tax code as non-deductible for tax purposes.

Loss carryforward
Tax losses may be carried forward 10 years without limitations (i.e., they can be used to offset the entire taxable profit before a loss carryforward deduction). Carryback of losses, however, is not allowed. Losses from the sale of securities can be credited only to the future income from the sale of the same type of securities (either listed or non-listed). Losses from the sale of fixed assets are recognised evenly during the remaining useful life.

Interest

Period	Debt obligation in RUB	Debt obligation in a foreign currency
From 1 January 2010 to 31 December 2010 (except as indicated below)	The refinancing rate of the Central Bank of Russia increased 1.8 times	15%
From 1 January 2011 to 31 December 2012	The refinancing rate of the Central Bank of Russia increased 1.8 times	0.8 of the refinancing rate of the Central Bank of Russia
From 1 January 2010 to 30 June 2010 for debt obligations arising before 1 November 2009	The refinancing rate of the Central Bank of Russia increased 2 times	15%

Under the tax code, interest on loans received from foreign shareholders (as well as their Russian affiliates, or loans guaranteed by foreign shareholders or their Russian affiliates) owning more than 20% of capital is deductible provided the loans do not exceed by three times the equity allocable to the shareholder (12.5 times for banks and leasing companies). If the loans exceed this limit, the excess part of interest on the loans will be reclassified for taxation purposes as dividends paid to foreign shareholders. Such dividends are not deductible for profit tax purposes and are subject to withholding income tax at the rate of 15% (treaty benefits may apply to reduce the rate).

Doubtful (bad) debt reserve

Losses in the form of bad debts written off generally are deductible. Companies may create a bad debt reserve. The method of accrual for a bad debt reserve for tax purposes may differ from that in financial accounting because it is based only on the overdue payment period: if the delay exceeds 90 days, the full amount of the account receivable is charged to the reserve. Generally, a debt written off is recognised as a taxable income for a debtor. The debts usually are written off where a debtor disappeared or became bankrupt.

Insurance premiums

Expenses related to all types of obligatory insurance are deductible subject to state tariff limitations, where established. Voluntary insurance expenses are deductible to the extent that they relate to the insurance of damage and losses related to certain classes of assets, and the insurance of construction activity risks. Contract liability insurance expenses are deductible to the extent that such insurance is required by an international treaty to which Russia is a party or a generally accepted international trade custom.

Long-term life and pension insurance is deductible within a limit of 12% of the payroll fund. Voluntary medical insurance is deductible within a limit of 6% of the payroll fund.

Research and development (R&D) expenses

R&D expenses (including R&D with a negative result) are deductible within one year after completion. From 1 January 2009, certain R&D expenses may be deducted using a coefficient of 1.5. The list of such types of R&D is established by the government.

Russian Federation

Depreciation

Two methods of depreciation are allowed: the straight-line method and the declining balance method. The useful life of assets for tax purposes is established in the Classification of Fixed Assets adopted by the Russian Government. Accelerated depreciation is permitted for leased property – a special ratio of up to three may be applied (with some exceptions).

From 2008, an upfront premium is allowed, which means that a taxpayer has the right to deduct 10% (from 1 January 2009: 30% for certain categories of fixed assets) of the cost of fixed assets purchased (or constructed) in the month when the depreciation started. The balance is depreciated over the useful life of the asset. A premium must be recaptured if a relevant asset is sold within five years of its acquisition.

Intangible assets are amortised over their useful life (or over 10 years if their useful life cannot be established).

Payments to foreign affiliates

There are no special tax provisions regarding deductibility of payments to foreign affiliates for services provided. They may be deducted in full if the general deductibility criteria are met. Charges with respect to administrative support provided by foreign affiliates may be deductible, but due care should be taken with regard to documentary support.

Group taxation

At present, Russia does not allow any group relief.

Legislation introducing the option to file a consolidated profits tax return is being considered by the government and is expected to be adopted in 2010 (with effect from 2011). According to the draft law, a consolidated taxpayer regime (CT) may be established provided that all companies meet the following conditions:

- The total amount of federal taxes accrued and recorded in the tax return for the calendar year preceding the year in which the CT is created exceeds RUB 15 billion;
- The total revenue from the sale of goods, products, work and services, and operating income in the financial reports of the calendar year preceding the year in which the CT is created exceeds RUB 100 billion;
- The total assets value reported as of the first day of the calendar year in which the CT is created exceeds RUB 1 trillion;
- The limit on a share in a direct or indirect holding in CT companies is 90%;
- The holding company must be a Russian legal entity; and
- CT participants cannot have foreign representative offices.

The limits are rather high and it is expected that only a few groups of companies will be able to apply the CT regime and, accordingly, the provisions in the law to exempt intra-group transactions from transfer pricing control from the tax authorities.

Tax incentives

At present, the following types of incentives exist in Russia:

- Regional incentives granted by regional or local authorities with respect to taxes paid to their budgets;
- Special tax regimes in special economic zones (SEZ); and
- Research and development incentives.

The incentives briefly are described as follows:

a. Regional incentives in the form of reduced tax rates for taxes payable to regional budgets (primarily profits tax and property tax) are granted to certain classes of taxpayers (typically large investors or entities operating in specific industries). The extent of regional incentives and the willingness of regional authorities to grant them have been diminishing over time.
b. The following types of SEZ are established in Russia:
    - Technical research and implementation zones for scientific projects;
    - Industrial production zones to develop industrial production;
    - Tourism-recreation zones for the development and effective use of Russian tourist resources; or
    - Port zones.
   SEZ residents may take advantage of different combinations of benefits, such as reduced profits tax, exemption from property tax and land tax, and in some cases exemption from customs duty and VAT.
c. The following R&D incentives are available to taxpayers in Russia:
    - Certain R&D services are exempt from VAT;
    - Certain R&D service-related expenses, as listed by the government, are deductible using a coefficient of 1.5; and
    - Fixed assets used in the sphere of science and technology may be amortised with an accelerated coefficient of 3.

Tax accounting
Since 1 January 2002, tax accounting has been mandatory. Tax accounting may be based on statutory accounting records (where accounting methods are the same).

Withholding taxes (WHT)

In accordance with the general provisions of the tax code, income received by a foreign legal entity and not attributed to a PE in Russia is subject to withholding income tax in Russia (to be withheld at source). Withholding income tax rates are as follows:

- 15% on dividends and income from participation in Russian enterprises with foreign investments;
- 10% on freight income;
- 20% on some other income from Russian sources, including royalties and interest; or
- 20% of revenue or 20% of the margin on capital gains (from the sale of immovable property located in Russia, or shares in Russian subsidiaries where the immovable property located in Russia represents more than 50% of assets).

Taxation of the margin (rather than the gross amount of income received from the above sales) may be applied only if proper documentary support of expenses is available.

R

Russian Federation

Tax should be withheld by the tax agent and paid to the Russian Government. Income tax withholding rates may be reduced under a relevant double taxation treaty, whose provisions may be applied based on confirmation of tax residence, to be provided by a foreign company to the Russian tax agent prior to the date of payment (no advance permission from the Russian tax authorities is required), and also provided general conditions are fulfilled (proof of beneficial ownership, etc.).

The Russian tax authorities recognise the terms of former USSR treaties until they are renegotiated by the Russian Government, and the tax treaty network is continuously updated. The list below is current as of 15 April 2010, and indicates the withholding tax rates stipulated in the treaties.

Country	Treaty benefits available from	Dividends (%)	Interest (%)	Royalties (%)	Construction site duration (months)
Albania/RF	1 January 1998	10	10	10	12
Algeria/RF	1 January 2009	5 or 15	0* or 15	15	6 and an aggregated period of more than 3 months in any 12-month period for furnishing services
Armenia/RF	1 January 1999	5 or 10	0	0	18
Australia/RF	1 January 2004	5 or 15	10	10	12
Austria/RF	1 January 2003	5 or 15	0	0	12
Azerbaijan/RF	1 January 1999	10	0* or 10	10	12
Belarus/RF	1 January 1998	15	0* or 10	10	no special provisions in the relevant DTT, local tax legislation provisions should apply
Belgium/RF	1 January 2001	10	0* or 10	0	12
Botswana	(***)	5 or 10	0* or 10	10	6
Brazil	1 January 2010	10 or 15	0* or 15	15	9
Bulgaria/RF	1 January 1996	15	0* or 15	15	12
Canada/RF	1 January 1998	10 or 15	0* or 10	0 or 10 (0% applies to specific types of rights)	12
China/RF	1 January 1998	10	0* or 10	10	18
Croatia/RF	1 January 1998	5 or 10	10	10	12
Cyprus/RF	1 January 2000	5 or 10	0	0	12
Czech/RF	1 January 1998	10	0	10	12
Denmark/RF	1 January 1998	10	0	0	12 and an aggregated period of more than 365 days in any 18-month period for a drilling rig

Country	Treaty benefits available from	Dividends (%)	Interest (%)	Royalties (%)	Construction site duration (months)
Egypt	1 January 2001	10	0* or 15	15	12 and an aggregated period of more than 6 months in any 12-month period for furnishing services
Finland/RF	1 January 2003	5 or 12	0	0	12 and 18-month period for particular types of construction works
France/RF	1 January 2000	5 or 10 or 15	0	0	12
Germany/RF	1 January 1997	5 or 15	0	0	12
Greece/RF	1 January 2008	5 or 10	7	7	9
Hungary/RF	1 January 1998	10	0	0	12
Iceland/RF	1 January 2004	5 or 15	0	0	12
India/RF	1 January 1999	10	0* or 10	10	12 (may be extended on agreement with the competent authorities)
Indonesia/RF	1 January 2003	15	0* or 15	15	3
Iran/RF	1 January 2003	5 or 10	0* or 7,5	5	12
Ireland/RF	1 January 1996	10	0	0	12
Israel/RF	1 January 2001	10	0* or 10	10	12
Italy/RF	1 January 1999	5 or 10	10	0	12
Japan/USSR	1 January 1987	15	0* or 10	0 or 10 (0% applies to specific types of rights)	12
Kazakhstan/RF	1 January 1998	10	0* or 10	10	12
Korea, Democratic People's Rep/ RF	1 January 2001	10	0	0	12 and an aggregated period of more than 6 months in any 12-month period for furnishing services
Korea, Rep./RF	1 January 1996	5 or 10	0	5	12 (may be extended up to 24 months upon agreement with the competent authorities)

R

Russian Federation

Country	Treaty benefits available from	Dividends (%)	Interest (%)	Royalties (%)	Construction site duration (months)
Kuwait/RF	1 January 2004	0 or 5 (0% rate applies to dividends paid to governmental agencies or financial institutions)	0	10	6
Kyrgyzstan/RF	1 January 2001	10	0* or 10	10	12
Lebanon/RF	1 January 2001	10	0* or 5	5	12
Lithuania/RF	1 January 2006	5 or 10	0* or 10	5 or 10	9
Luxembourg/ RF	1 January 1998	10 or 15	0	0	12
Macedonia/RF	1 January 2001	10	10	10	12
Malaysia/USSR	1 January 1989	0 or 15 (15% rate applies to profits received from joint-venture by resident of Malaysia)	0* or 15	10 or 15 (depending on the type of rights)	12 and more than 6-month period for installation or assembly projects
Mali/RF	1 January 2000	10 or 15	0* or 15	0	no special provisions in the relevant DTT, local tax legislation provisions should apply
Mexico/RF	1 January 2009	10	10	10	6
Moldova/RF	1 January 1998	10	0	10	12
Mongolia/RF	1 January 1998	10	0* or 10	rates in accordance with local legislation	24
Montenegro/RF	1 January 1998	5 or 15	10	10	18
Morocco/RF	1 January 2000	5 or 10	0* or 10	10	8
Namibia/RF	1 January 2001	5 or 10	0* or 10	5	9 and more than 6-month period for furnishing of services and installation projects
Netherlands/RF	1 January 1999	5 or 15	0	0	12
New Zealand/ RF	1 January 2004	15	10	10	12
Norway/RF	1 January 2003	10	0* or 10	0	12
Philippines/RF	1 January 1998	15	0* or 15	15	183 days and an aggregate period of more than 183 days in any 12-month period for furnishing of services

Country	Treaty benefits available from	Dividends (%)	Interest (%)	Royalties (%)	Construction site duration (months)
Poland/RF	1 January 1994	10	0* or 10	10	12 (may be extended up to 24 months upon agreement with the competent authorities)
Portugal/RF	1 January 2003	10 or 15	0* or 10	10	12
Qatar/RF	1 January 2001	5	0* or 5	0	6
Romania/RF	1 January 1996	15	0* or 15	10	12
Saudi Arabia	(***)	0 or 5	0* or 5	10	6
Serbia/RF	1 January 1998	5 or 15	10	10	18
Singapore/RF	1 January 2009	5 or 10	0* or 7,5	7,5	6 and an aggregated period of more than 3 months in any 12-month period for furnishing services
Slovakia/RF	1 January 1998	10	0	10	12
Slovenia/RF	1 January 1998	10	10	10	12
South Africa/ RF	1 January 2001	10 or 15	0* or 10	0	12
Spain/RF	1 January 2001	5 or 10 or 15	0* or 5	5	12
Sri Lanka/RF	1 January 2003	10 or 15	0* or 10	10	6 and an aggregated period of more than 183 days in any 12-month period for furnishing services
Sweden/RF	1 January 1996	5 or 15	0	0	12
Switzerland/RF	1 January 1998	5 or 15	0** or 5 or 10	0	12
Syria/RF	1 January 2004	15	0* or 10	4.5 or 13.5 or 18 (depending on type of rights)	6
Tajikistan/RF	1 January 2004	5 or 10	0* or 10	0	12 (may be extended on agreement with the competent authorities)
Thailand/RF	1 January 2009	15	0* or 10	15	6 and an aggregated period of more than 3 months in any 12-month period for furnishing services
Turkey/RF	1 January 2000	10	0* or 10	10	18

R

Russian Federation

Country	Treaty benefits available from	Dividends (%)	Interest (%)	Royalties (%)	Construction site duration (months)
Turkmenistan/RF	1 January 2000	10	5	5	12
UK/RF	1 January 1998	10	0	0	12
Ukraine/RF	1 January 2000	5 or 15	0* or 10	10	12
USA/RF	1 January 1994	5 or 10	0	0	18
Uzbekistan/RF	1 January 1996	10	0* or 10	0	12
Venezuela	1 January 2010	10 or 15	0* or 5 or 10	10 or 15	9
Vietnam/RF	1 January 1997	10 or 15	10	15	6 and more than 12-month period for furnishing services

*   In general a 0% tax rate applies to interest payments to the governments of contracting states, and to payments guaranteed by the government.

**   A 0% tax rate may be applied provided such interest is paid (a) in connection with the sale on credit of any industrial, commercial or scientific equipment, or (b) in connection with the sale on credit of any merchandise by one enterprise to another.

*** The Federal Law ratifying the Convention was signed by the Russian President in November 2009. There is currently no official information on the date when the Convention enters into force.

Tax administration

Payments
Companies pay advance profits tax payments on a monthly basis. The final payment for the year is due by 28 March of the following year. The mechanism of paying other taxes may differ.

Returns filing
Companies are required to file tax returns with the tax authorities on a monthly, quarterly or annual basis, depending on the particular tax. Some taxes (i.e., profits tax, property tax, etc.) are paid in monthly, quarterly or annual instalments, with a final adjustment made when annual tax returns are submitted. An annual profits tax return must be filed by 28 March of the year following the end of the reporting year.

Corporate taxes in Saudi Arabia

For more information, contact:

Kenny Hawsey
PricewaterhouseCoopers Al Juraid
King Faisal Foundation Building
10th Floor – North Tower
King Fahad Road, Olaya
Riyadh
Saudi Arabia
Tel: +966 1 456 4240
Email: kenny.b.hawsey@sa.pwc.com

Significant developments

The Saudi Arabian tax law was completely re-written, as of 30 July 2004, for all taxpayers whose financial year starts after this effective date. The withholding tax regulations took effect as of 30 July 2004, irrespective of when the financial year started for the taxpayer.

The tables below outline the main features of the revised tax law.

Persons subject to taxation

Item	Law
Persons subject to taxation	A resident capital company to the extent of its non-Saudi shareholding
	A resident non-Saudi natural person who conducts business activities in the Kingdom of Saudi Arabia (Kingdom)
	A non-resident person who carries out activities in the Kingdom through a permanent establishment (PE)
	A non-resident person who has other income subject to tax from sources within the Kingdom
	A person engaged in natural gas investment fields
	A person engaged in oil and other hydrocarbon production

Types of tax and tax rates

Item	Law
Tax on companies	Flat rate of 20%
	30% for those engaged in natural gas investment (where the rate of internal return exceeds 8%, graduated tax rates up to 85% will be applied).
	85% for those engaged in oil and hydrocarbon production
Tax on individuals	Flat rate of 20%

S

Saudi Arabia

Item	Law
Withholding tax	The following rates apply (although they may be reduced where a relevant double tax treaty is in force):
	20% on management fees
	15% on royalties or proceeds; payments for services to a head office or related company
	5% on rent, technical or consultant services, air tickets or air freight or, international telecommunication services, dividends, loan interest, insurance or reinsurance premiums
	15% on other payments

Applicable tax penalties

Item	Law
Non-registration	From SAR 1,000 to SAR 10,000 (Saudi Riyal – SAR)
Failure to file the tax return	From 5% to 25% of the unpaid tax
Delay payment	1% of the unpaid tax for each 30 days of delay
Evasion	25% of the unpaid tax

Treatment of certain expenses for tax purposes

Item	Law
Salaries and benefits paid to the partners	Non-deductible expense, as this is considered a distribution of profit
Repair expenses	Deductible expense subject to certain terms and limits
Reserves and provision	Non-deductible expense except provisions made for doubtful accounts in the banking sector and certain provisions in the insurance sector
Depreciation	Deductible expense as per declining balance method applied on each group of assets
Tax accounting standards	Specific standards are provided under the law
Filing tax return and payment of taxes	Within 120 days from the financial year-end

Loss carryforwards

Item	Law
Loss carryforwards	Allowing loss carryforwards for indefinite years subject to certain terms and limits

Procedures for payment of taxes

Procedure description	Law
Advance payments of tax	Each taxpayer whose tax in previous year exceeded SAR 2 million
Refund of tax overpayments	Allowed with a compensation for delay
Collection of taxes	Specific procedures are provided under the law

Appeals

Appeals against assessments issued by the tax authority are heard by the Preliminary Appeal Committee. Appeals against a decision by the Preliminary appeal committee are heard by the High Appeal Committee. A 60 day time limit applies for making the appeals, as noted in the tables below:

Preliminary appeal committee	Law
Appeal statutory date	Within 60 days from the date the final assessment is received
Committee ruling	Final unless appealed to the high appeal committee
Formation of the committee	Resolution from the Ministry of Finance

High appeals

Preliminary appeal committee	Law
High appeal statutory date	Within 60 days from the date the preliminary appeal ruling is received
Committee ruling	Final unless appealed to the Board of Grievances
Formation of the committee	Resolution from the Council of Ministers

Swap transactions

The Department of Zakat and Income Tax (DZIT) introduced new rules on the taxation of swap transactions in early 2009 for Swaps that have been approved as qualifying swap transactions under the Capital Markets Authority rules.

Taxes on corporate income

The rate of income tax is 20% of the tax adjusted profits. Withholding tax rates are between 5% and 20%. Zakat, an Islamic assessment, is charged on the company's zakat base at 2.5%.

Only non-Saudi investors are liable for income tax in Saudi Arabia. In most cases, Saudi citizen investors (and citizens of the Gulf Cooperation Council (GCC) countries, who are considered to be Saudi citizens for Saudi tax purposes) are liable for Zakat. Where a company is owned by both Saudi and non-Saudi interests, the portion of taxable income attributable to the non-Saudi interest is subject to income tax, and the Saudi share goes into the basis on which Zakat is assessed.

Capital gains are subject to tax or zakat, as appropriate, at the normal tax or zakat rate.

According to the income tax law, the following persons are subject to tax:

- A resident capital company to the extent of its non-Saudi shareholding;
- A resident non-Saudi natural person who carries on activities in the Kingdom;
- A non-resident person who carries on activities in the Kingdom through a PE;
- A non-resident person who has other income subject to tax from sources within the Kingdom;
- A person engaged in natural gas investment fields; and
- A person engaged in oil and other hydrocarbon production.

S

Saudi Arabia

Corporate residence

A company is considered a resident company if it meets any of the following conditions:

1. It is formed under the Saudi Arabian Regulations for Companies; and/or
2. If the headquarters is situated within the Kingdom.

Other taxes

Social insurance tax
Social insurance tax is paid monthly based on the monthly basic salary plus housing with an upper limit of SAR 45,000 and is computed at 2% for non-Saudi employees and paid by the employer. For Saudi employees, the rate is 20% and is paid by both the employees (9%) and the employer (11%).

Withholding tax
There are withholding tax regulations (see section titled "Withholding taxes").

Value-added tax (VAT)
There is currently no VAT system in Saudi Arabia.

Other taxes
There is no form of stamp, transfer, excise, sales, turnover, production, real estate or property taxation except in so far as they may fall within the scope of Zakat, which is applicable only to Saudi nationals.

Branch income

Taxable income from a branch of a non-Saudi based corporation is taxed at 20%. Certain charges incurred by the headquarters are not deductible on the branch tax return.

Income determination

Inventory valuation
The weighted average-cost method is used for valuing inventory under Saudi tax law.

Capital gains
Gains on the disposal of non-listed shares are taxed at a rate of 20%.

Stock dividends
Stock dividends distributed to the non-resident recipient shareholders are subject to a 5% withholding tax.

Foreign income
The gross income of any company carrying on its business activities both inside and outside Saudi Arabia is considered to include all the income that the company receives locally from any source within Saudi Arabia, as well as the income that the company derives from outside Saudi Arabia.

Other significant items – imports and supply contracts

Saudi tax law provides that no profit will be considered to arise from a contract for the supply of goods to Saudi Arabia, provided delivery of the goods is either free on board (FOB) or cost, insurance and freight (CIF) to a Saudi port. However, should the contract provide for the delivery and/or installation of materials at a point inside Saudi Arabia, the supplier may be considered to be carrying on business within Saudi Arabia, and, as a consequence, the contract may be subject to Saudi taxation as follows:

- If the material cost was identified in the supply contract separately from the cost of work performed in the Kingdom, then taxes will be assessed on the work that will be performed in the Kingdom on a deemed-profit basis at a minimum of 15% of the total value of such work.
- If the supply contract indicates a total cost for the supply and other activities in the Kingdom, then the work performed in the Kingdom will be assigned a value equal to 10% of the contract value for each type of activity, and a deemed profit of a minimum of 15% of the estimated work will be computed, which will be subject to tax according to Saudi tax regulations.

Deductions

General

All expenses that are necessary and normal to the business, paid or accrued, are allowable deductions, provided the expense meets the following conditions:

- It is an actual expense, supported by a verifiable document or other qualifying evidence;
- It is related to the generation of taxable income;
- It is related to the subject tax year; and
- It is of a non-capital nature.

Loan charges (interest expenses)

The deduction is limited to the lower of the loan charge incurred during the tax year, if related to income that is subject to tax, or the result of the following formula, whichever is less.

The taxpayer's total income from loan charges, plus 50% of (a minus b) as below:

a. Equals income subject to tax other than income from loan charges.
b. Equals expenses allowed under the law other than loan charge expenses.

Banks are not subject to this formula.

Bad debt

Bad debts, provided they meet the following conditions, are deductable:

- The bad debt was previously declared in the appropriate year's income;
- The debt resulted from sale of goods or services;
- The company holds a certificate from the taxpayer's certified public accountant certifying that the debt has been written off in the taxpayer's books and records, based on a decision by the taxpayer at the appropriate management level;

Saudi Arabia

- Serious efforts have been exerted by the taxpayer to collect the debt with no success and the inability of the debtor to pay has been proved based on a judicial ruling or bankruptcy;
- The debt is not from a related party; and
- There is a commitment by the taxpayer to reinstate, as income, any written-off debt whenever collected.

Allocations and reserves

Allocations and reserves formed during the year as follows:

- Bank allocations to a reserve fund for doubtful debts are allowable deductions. However, a bank must submit a certificate from the Saudi Arabian Monetary Agency (SAMA) stating the amount of doubtful debts and the amount of doubtful debts collected during the year, which should be reinstated in the tax base of the year of collection.
- Insurance/reinsurance companies may deduct, based on industry standards, a reserve for unearned premiums and for unexpired risks, provided that it is reported in the tax base of the following year.
- A reserve for unearned premiums means a part of premium amounts collected or stated in books that covers risks related to the future tax year(s). A reserve for unexpired risks means the amount of compensation claimed or reported, but for which the payment process falls short of completion during the tax year.
- A taxpayer may reduce its book profit by the amount of reserves used during the year that had been readjusted when made, to increase income or decrease expenses in the year of formation. Examples of such reserves are end-of-service awards, doubtful debt, and drops in prices. Such amounts are allowed, provided the following conditions are met:

  - The used amount was paid or accrued during the year, and it is supported by documentation; and
  - The reserve had been adjusted in the year of formation to increase the tax base.

School fees

School fees paid by taxpayers for their employees' children are deductible expenses, provided they meet the following conditions:

- They are paid to a local licensed school; and
- This benefit is stated in the employment contract.

Pension fund

Employers' contributions to employees' pension funds or savings funds established under the Kingdom's rules and regulations are deductible, provided that such contribution, one payment or in aggregate, is not in excess of 25% of the employee's income before the employer's contributions and that the fund meets the following:

- The fund is established according to special provisions that clearly stipulate conditions of subscription and rights of subscribers;
- Such obligation is stated in the employment contract or in the Articles of Association of the establishment; and
- The fund has a character independent of the establishment and has separate accounts audited by an independent certified public accountant.

Research and development (R&D)

A deduction is allowed for R&D expenditure incurred during the tax year in connection with the generation of income that is subject to tax. Such expenditure relates to technical, scientific and engineering experiments, computer systems or similar research. This provision does not apply to the acquisition of land and facilities, or to equipment used for research. Such facilities and equipment are subject to depreciation under the law.

Depreciation

Depreciation deduction under the following limitations as stipulated by the law:

- The asset is not intended for resale and is to be used, in full or in part, for the entity's purposes;
- The asset is of a depreciable nature that loses value because of use or because of wear and tear and obsolescence and which has a value extending beyond the end of the taxable year;
- The asset is owned by the business, as per the ownership document for buildings, and contracts and invoices for other assets; and
- The asset depreciation is allowed even if the asset becomes inoperational during the tax year.

The depreciation for tax purposes is calculated as follows, based on the following five categories of depreciable tangible or intangible assets, other than land:

Category/Asset	Depreciation rate (%)
1) Fixed buildings	5
2) Industrial and agricultural movable buildings	10
3) Factories, machines and equipment, and computer application programs, passenger cars and cargo vehicles	25
4) Expenditures for geological surveying, drilling, exploration, and other preliminary work to exploit and develop natural resources and their fields	20
5) All other tangible or intangible assets not included in previous categories, such as furniture, planes, ships and trains, and goodwill	10

The declining balance method of depreciation according to the above rates should be followed for tax purposes.

There are also rules for depreciation relating to assets either acquired or disposed. Essentially, 50% of the allowable acquisition price or disposal proceeds is added to or subtracted from the asset pool in the first year, and the remaining 50% in the following year.

Assets under build own transfer (BOT), and build, own, operate, and transfer (BOOT) are allowed to be depreciated over the contract period. This presumes, although it is not clear, that assets under the BOT and BOOT schemes actually will have a separate grouping in addition to the above prescribed groups

Non-deductible expenses

The following expenses are non-deductible:

Saudi Arabia

- Wages, salaries and whatever is so deemed, in cash or in kind, paid to an owner, partner or shareholder, or to a member of their families, being a parent, spouse, sons/daughters and siblings (this provision does not apply to stockholders in a stock company).
- Compensation in cash or in kind paid to a partner, shareholder, or to a family member including a parent, spouse, sons/daughters and siblings for a property or service to the extent that the compensation is higher than the fair market value of such property or service at time of transaction.
- Entertainment expenses incurred for events such as parties, sports competitions, entertainment trips and activities, etc.
- Expenses of a natural person for personal consumption, such as personal withdrawals, dependents' cost of living or education.
- Income tax and related fines and penalties paid or payable to the Kingdom or to other countries.
- Financial fines or penalties paid or payable to any party in the Kingdom, such as traffic fines, or fines for causing damage to public utilities.
  This does not include fines or penalties paid for breach of contractual obligations, such as fines on delayed or defaulted completion of contracts. Such fines are deductible, provided they are documented by the contracting party and the income from such penalties is reported in the year of recovery.
- Any bribe or similar payment which is considered an illegal practice in the Kingdom, even if paid abroad.
- Insurance commission in excess of 3% of total premiums collected in the Kingdom through an agent or others and regardless of whether or not the agent is a partner.
- Employer contributions to their employees' legal pension fund, social insurance or savings funds.
- Payments made to headquarter offices located abroad by wholly owned local subsidiaries or branches, such as:
  a. Royalties or commissions;
  b. Loan charges (interest expense) or any other financial fees; and
  c. Indirect administrative and general expenses allocated on an estimated basis.
- The value of goods or services delivered to the taxpayer by related parties to the extent that it is in excess of an arm's-length value.

Group taxation

There is currently no concept of taxation on a consolidated basis, or group relief, for related companies in Saudi Arabia, other than for wholly owned subsidiaries of Saudi/Gulf Cooperation Council owned companies that are subject to Zakat. However, an entity operating in the Kingdom that has undertaken more than one project under the same commercial registration is required to consolidate the results of such projects into the financial statements of that entity and subject them to taxation as a single operation.

Tax incentives

Inward investment
The Saudi Arabian government lists the following as incentives potentially available to qualifying companies:

- There are no restrictions on repatriation of profits, fees, capital, salaries, or other monies.

- The government of Saudi Arabia has granted tax concessions to six less-developed regions in the Kingdom, with the intention of attracting more investment. These tax privileges are granted for a period of 10 years from the start of any project. The tax cuts will be offered in the following regions:
  - Ha'il;
  - Jazan;
  - Najran;
  - Al-Baha;
  - Al-Jouf; and
  - Northern territory.

  The qualifying investing company's annual tax bill can be reduced by:
  - Half the annual training expenditure on Saudis.
  - Half the annual salaries paid to Saudis.
  - More deductions are granted if investment capital for any project exceeds SAR 1 million and if more than five employees of Saudi nationality have jobs of a technical or administrative nature with contracts of at least one year.
  - There have been indications recently that incentives may be extended to research and development expenditure but no details have been forthcoming.

- An exemption from customs duties is available on machinery and raw materials that are required for approved projects, provided that they are not available in the local market. Such exemptions should be applied for prior to their importation and are subject to certain terms.

Capital investment

No specific incentives are available for capital investment other than those listed under the section titled *Inward investment*.

Withholding taxes (WHT)

Payments made from a resident party or a PE to a non-resident party for services performed are subject to withholding taxes. The rates vary from 5%, 15% and 20% based on the type of service and whether the beneficiary is a related party.

The withholding tax should be paid within the first 10 days of the month following the month during which the payment was made.

The domestic rate for withholding tax is 5% on dividends, 15% on royalties and 5% on interest.

Tax treaties

Saudi Arabia has entered into tax treaties with several countries including France, India, Pakistan, China, Austria, Malaysia, South Africa, South Korea, Turkey, Italy and United Kingdom.

There are a number of other treaties not yet in force (i.e., Greece, Russia, The Netherlands, Uzbekistan, Germany and Belarus) and negotiations with some 20 other countries are in progress.

S

Saudi Arabia

Double tax treaties have not yet been effectively tested in Saudi Arabia. However, they generally follow the Organisation for Economic Co-operation and Development (OECD) model treaty and may provide certain relief, including withholding tax on dividends, royalties and interest.

Tax administration

Returns

Tax filings are based on the company's fiscal-year. Returns are due to be filed with the DZIT and tax due must be paid within 120 days after the taxpayer's year-end. The system is one of self-assessment.

Advance tax payments are required to be made for a current tax year under the following conditions:

- The taxpayer has earned income during the year;
- An advance payment is 25% of the amount resulting from the taxpayer's tax; liability based on the previous year return minus the withheld tax;
- The computed payment is at least SAR 500,000;
- Three equal advance payments of tax on the last day of the sixth, ninth and twelfth months of the tax year; and/or
- Late payment of an advance payment is subject to a delay penalty of 1% of the amount due for every 30 days of delay.

Corporate taxes in Senegal

For more information, contact:

Pierre Michaux
PricewaterhouseCoopers Tax & Legal
3 Place de l'Indépendance
Immeuble SDIH
Dakar, Senegal
Tel: +221 33 849 05 00
Email: pierre.michaux@sn.pwc.com

Significant developments

In 2009 amendments were introduced into law that increased excise duty rates on certain products, notably: 15% to 20% for cigarettes; 30% to 45% for other kinds of tobacco; and 30% to 40% for alcoholic drinks. These measures were aimed at reducing the consumption of alcohol and tobacco.

Additionally, a 2% tax on telecommunication use and access was introduced in 2009. To offset the tax, the purchase of mobile telephones (and other types of telephones) are no longer subject to value-added tax (VAT) and customs duty.

Taxes on corporate income

Branches and companies are liable for 25% corporate income tax (CIT). A minimum CIT is due in case of lack of profits and the amount depends on the annual turnover:

- XOF 500,000 in case of an annual turnover up to XOF 250,000,000;
- XOF 750,000 if the annual turnover ranges from XOF 250,000,000 to XOF 500,000,000; and
- XOF 1,000,000 in case of an annual turnover over XOF 500,000,000.

Corporate residence

Companies are considered as Senegalese residents if they have a registered fixed establishment. Nonetheless, foreign companies that are not registered locally may be deemed to have a permanent establishment (PE) in Senegal in relation to their local activity, and be subsequently subject to tax liabilities. The general criteria of a PE deriving from the General Tax Code are close to the Organisation for Economic Co-operation and Development (OECD) standards. Double tax treaties can be applicable and can provide specific definitions. These double tax treaties are based on the OECD model in most cases.

Senegal has concluded such treaties with Belgium, Canada, France, Italy, Morocco, Mauritania, Norway, Qatar, Tunisia and state members of the West African Economic and Monetary Union (UEMOA) including: Benin, Burkina-Faso, Côte d'Ivoire, Guinea-Bissau, Mali, Niger and Togo.

S

Senegal

Other taxes

Value-added tax (VAT)

Subject to certain exclusions, most commercial operations are subject to an 18% VAT duty. A 17% special tax on banking operations is applicable instead of VAT.

Business licence tax

Annual duty is constituted by a fixed annual payment (fixed duty) and a proportional duty calculated in most cases on the basis of the rental value of premises used. The amounts and rates of these taxes are fixed according to the type and size of the activity carried out.

Tax on built real estate (land with buildings and/or industrial equipment fixed thereon)

It applies to owners of buildings, factories, industrial premises or equipment fixed on the land. The tax rate is 5% for common buildings and 7.5% for factories and industrial premises. It is applied on the basis of the rental value of the lands, buildings, etc.

Tax on non-built real estate

It applies to owners of land without buildings, factories, industrial premises or equipment fixed on the land. The tax rate is fixed at 5%. It is applied on the basis of the rental value of the land.

Stamp/registration duties

There are many stamp and/or registration duties depending on the operations. For example:

- 1% registration duty applicable to the incorporation of a company and the increase in cash of the share capital;
- 1% registration duty applicable to transfer of stocks;
- 1% registration duty applicable to transfer of debts;
- 15% registration duty applicable to sale of business;
- 15% registration duty applicable to transfer of real estate; and
- 5% registration duty applicable to rent agreements.

Tax on vehicles

An owner of a motor vehicle (car, truck or motorbike) must pay an annual registration tax ranging from XOF 18,000 to XOF 200,000 per vehicle, depending on its nature and horsepower.

Company tax on vehicles

In addition to the tax on vehicles, companies owning or renting vehicles (more than 15 days a year) must pay a specific annual tax on them. Rates range from XOF 50,000 to XOF 200,000, depending on the nature and horsepower of the vehicle.

Branch income

In general, the tax on branch income is similar to that of corporate income. Nonetheless, a 10% duty is automatically applied to profits generated after corporate income tax. It corresponds to an automatic application of the 10% tax on payment of dividends applicable to a company.

Senegal

Income determination

Inventory valuation
Inventory is generally stated at the lower of cost or market value. Last-in, first-out (LIFO) and first-in, first-out (FIFO) are permitted. Book and tax conformity is required.

Capital gains
Regarding companies, capital gains deriving from the transfer of assets are subject to the 25% corporate income tax. There is no basket system. The taxable base will be reduced to one-third if the transfer of assets arises due to a cessation of activity. However, if the transfer of assets is made less than five years after the start of the business, a one-half reduction of the taxable base will be applicable.

Sales of stocks by a non-resident are liable to the 25% corporate income tax, subject to the application of a double tax treaty.

Inter-company dividends
If a parent company domiciled in Senegal owns 20% of the subsidiary (main condition for the application of the parent-subsidiary corporation special taxation status), a 95% reduction on the dividends received is applicable for corporate income tax purposes.

Foreign income
In general, profits generated in Senegal are taxed under Senegal's income tax law. Profits generated outside Senegal and constituting a permanent establishment in the relevant country are not taxed in Senegal. Profits generated outside Senegal and constituting a permanent establishment in the relevant country are not taxed locally. A double tax treaty can provide different rules.

Stock dividends
Stock dividends are unusual in Senegal. However, this kind of distribution would be taxable at the general withholding tax rate of 10% on the basis of its real value.

Deductions

Depreciation and depletion
The rates of depreciation are not provided by the law. The rate is determined on the normal and predictable duration of use of the asset by taking into account normal wear and tear. In practice, there are standard rates for common assets. Accelerated depreciation can be applicable, subject to conditions.

Net operating losses
Tax losses may be carried forward to the next three years. The carryback procedure does not exist. Losses corresponding to the depreciation of assets can be forwarded indefinitely.

Payments to foreign affiliates
Reasonable royalties, interest, and management service fees paid to foreign parent companies are tax-deductible. Supporting documents (invoices, contracts, etc.) will be necessary to prove that these expenses are justified. Transfer pricing issues are rare.

Senegal

Other significant items

Interest paid to shareholders may be deducted when it relates to loans with an amount inferior or equal to the amount of the share capital and whose rate is inferior or equal to the base rate of the Central Bank of West African States plus two points.

Provisions are deductible if they correspond to a risk or a probable cost that is more than possible and leads to a decrease of the assets. Provisions for paid holidays and retirement compensation are not deductible.

Payments made to specific chartered organisations are deductible at a rate of up to 0.2% of turnover.

Headquarter expenses, which are a proration of the worldwide office expenses, may be allocated to the Senegal branch. This proration is based upon a ratio of the local turnover of the branch and the worldwide turnover of the parent company. It applies to the total amount of headquarters' expenses incurred by the company. In addition, the deductibility of headquarters expenses is limited to 20% of the accounting profits before the deduction. This limitation does not apply to other types of services provided by headquarters such as technical assistance.

Fines, penalties and foreign taxes are not deductible.

Group taxation

Group taxation is not permitted.

Tax incentives

The Investment Code

The Investment Code applies to investments over XOF 100,000,000 (mainly production, processing, industrial, tourism, agricultural and complex trade). Advantages: Customs duties exemption, suspension of VAT payment for three years, corporate income tax limitation applicable, etc.

The status of the free export company

Agriculture, industry and telecommunications companies that have an exporting potential amounting to at least 80% of their turnover may qualify for the free export company status. Advantages: corporate income tax rate of 15%, exemption of dividend tax, exemption of business license tax, exemption of taxes on real estate, and exemption of registration duty for incorporation or bylaws change purposes.

Miscellaneous incentives

There is a wide range of investment laws for investments higher than XOF 250,000,000,000 (negotiation of a derogatory tax regime), including the mining code and the petroleum code, among others.

Withholding taxes (WHT)

Senegal has various withholding taxes. The primary ones are:

- A 20% withholding tax on remuneration paid for services rendered by a foreign individual or foreign company;
- A 10% withholding tax on dividends distributed;
- A 13% withholding tax on bond interest;
- An 8% withholding tax on deposits or guaranteed interest on accounts with a bank; and
- A 16% withholding tax on other revenues, notably interest on loans.

These withholding taxes may be limited by double tax treaties.

Tax administration

Returns

Companies must file corporate income tax returns by 30 April of the year following the tax year (calendar one) for corporate income tax purposes.

VAT returns must be filed monthly.

Business license tax and taxes on real estate are due annually.

Payment of tax

Corporate tax must be paid in two instalments (each equal to one-third of the previous year's tax) by 15 February and 30 April. The outstanding balance payment amount of the tax due must be paid by 15 June.

For the first financial year of a newly incorporated company, no instalment is due; the new company pays the whole corporate income tax before 15 June of the following year.

S

Corporate taxes in Serbia

For more information, contact:

Peter Burnie
PricewaterhouseCoopers Consulting d.o.o.
Airport City Belgrade
88a Omladinskih brigada st.
11000 Belgrade
Serbia
Tel: +381 11 3302 138
Email: peter.burnie@rs.pwc.com

Significant developments

The Corporate Profit Tax (CPT) law was introduced in April 2001. Amendments to the CPT law were enacted on 27 March 2010 and apply to determination of the CPT liability for fiscal year 2010.

A new customs law has been adopted and is effective as of 4 May 2010. This law represents a significant step forward in the process of aligning Serbian customs legislation with the European Union (EU) Community Customs Code.

Taxes on corporate income

The rate of corporate profit tax is 10%.

Corporate residence

A legal entity is considered to be a resident of Serbia if it is established or has its place of effective management and control in the territory of the Republic of Serbia. Residents are taxed on their income generated in the territory of the Republic of Serbia, as well as on their worldwide income. Non-residents are taxed only on their income sourced through a permanent establishment (PE) on Serbian territory. A PE is any permanent place of business through which a non-resident conducts its business.

Other taxes

Value-added tax (VAT)
The VAT was introduced on 1 January 2005 and generally follows the EU's Sixth Directive.

A taxpayer for VAT purposes is a person who independently, and in the course of its business activities, undertakes the supply of goods and services, or import of goods. Business activity is defined as the permanent activity of a manufacturer, salesperson or service provider for the purpose of gaining income. A branch or other operating unit can be a taxpayer.

A non-resident without a head office or PE within Serbia cannot register for VAT purposes.

The VAT rates are as follows:

- The standard VAT rate – 18% (for most taxable supplies); and
- A reduced VAT rate – 8% (for basic food stuffs, daily newspapers, utilities etc.).

In addition to these tax rates, there is a 0% tax rate with the right of deduction of the input VAT which applies to the export of goods, transport and other services directly related to exports, international air transport, etc.

A 0% tax rate without the right of deduction of the input VAT applies to trading in shares and other securities, insurance and reinsurance, and the lease of apartments, business premises, etc.

The VAT law requires taxpayers to file VAT returns and pay VAT within 10 days of the end of each taxable period. The usual taxable period is a calendar month, but if a taxpayer's total turnover (for the last 12 months) is less than RSD (Serbian dinar) 20 million or is forecast (for the next 12 months) to be so, the taxable period is three calendar months.

Customs duties

Goods imported into Serbia are subject to customs duty rates provided in the Law on Customs Tariff. These rates are *ad valorem* (the only exception is related to the importation of other cigarettes containing tobacco, where a combined *ad valorem* and specific customs duty rate is prescribed) and applies to goods originating in countries which have a most favoured nation (MFN) status in trading with Serbia. Goods originating in other countries are subject to MFN duty rates increased by 70%.

At the moment, the only trading partner with Serbia that does not have MFN status is Taiwan.

Customs duty rates in Serbia range from 0% to 57.6% with most being under 30%. At the moment, the 57.6% rate only applies to cigarettes containing tobacco – tariff code 2402 20 90 00.

Excise duties

Excise duties are levied on producers and importers of the following goods:

- Oil derivatives;
- Tobacco products;
- Alcoholic beverages; and
- Coffee (green, roasted, ground and coffee extracts).

Excise duty in Serbia is specific (for oil derivatives, alcoholic beverages, cigars and cigarillos), *ad valorem* (for coffee and pipe tobacco), and combined (for cigarettes – specific + *ad valorem* on retail price).

Excise duties stated in Serbian currency are adjusted on a half-year basis according to variations of the consumer price index (CPI) declared by relevant government bodies in charge of statistics. For oil derivatives, government can modify the specific excise duty amounts during the year according to changes in prices of crude oil on the market.

S

Serbia

Property tax

Property tax is payable in Serbia by all legal entities and individuals who own or have rights over real estate located in the Republic of Serbia, such as:

- Ownership rights;
- Right of occupancy;
- Tenancy rights over an apartment or a building for a period longer than one year or for an indefinite period; and
- Urban land usage right (municipal, public and other state-owned land) larger than 10 acres in area.

Where the taxpayer keeps books, the property tax on real estate is levied at a flat rate which cannot exceed 0.40%.

Branch income

Non-residents carrying on business in Serbia through a branch are taxed on their Serbian sourced income at a rate of 10%. A branch is considered to be a PE.

Income determination

Taxable profit is determined by adjusting the accounting profit as stated in the profit and loss statement (determined in accordance with International Financial Reporting Standards (IFRS) and local accounting and audit legislation) and in accordance with the provisions of the CPT Law.

For taxpayers who, according to local legislation, are not obliged to apply IFRS, taxable profit is determined according to the special guidelines prescribed by the ministry of finance.

The following expenses are not recognised for corporate profit tax purposes:

- Non-documented expenses;
- Provisions for receivables from the entities that are creditors at the same time;
- Presents provided to political organisations;
- Presents provided to related parties;
- Penalty interest for late payment of taxes;
- Expenses related to forced collection of taxes and other liabilities;
- Fines and penalties (both commercial and the one charged by the authorities);
- Contractual fines and penalties;
- Non-business related expense;
- Calculated but unpaid redundancy payments (deductible when paid);
- Impairment of assets (deductible in tax period in which asset is disposed or used);
- Direct write-off of receivables (under certain conditions); and
- Long-term provisions (except those for renewal of natural resources, expenses within warranty period and other mandatory long-term provisions).

The following expenses are recognised for corporate profit tax purposes only up to a certain limit:

- Depreciation in the amount computed in accordance with the tax legislation;
- Advertising and promotional expenses up to 5% of total revenues;

- Representation expenses up to 0.5% of total revenues;
- Expenses for health care, scientific, educational, humanitarian, religious, ecological, cultural and sport related purposes up to 3.5% of total revenues; and
- Membership fees paid to chambers of commerce and other associations (except political parties) up to 0.1% of gross revenue.

Valuation of inventory

Cost of materials and the purchase value of merchandise are tax-deductible up to an amount calculated by applying the average weighted cost method or the first-in-first-out (FIFO) method. If another method is used, an adjustment for tax purposes should be made.

Capital gains

Capital gains are generated by the sale or other transfer of real estate, rights related to industrial property, as well as shares, stocks, securities, certain bonds and investment units. A capital gain is determined as the difference between the sale and purchase price of the asset concerned, determined in accordance with the provisions of the Law. If the amount is negative a capital loss results.

Capital gains are taxed separately from the trade or business income. Consequently, capital gains/losses cannot be used to offset business losses/gains.

However, capital gains can be offset with capital losses occurring in the same period. A capital loss can be carried forward for five years.

The capital gains tax rate is 10%.

Foreign income

Companies resident in Serbia are taxed on their worldwide income.

When profit generated in another country is taxed in the foreign country, a company has the right to decrease its tax liability by claiming a tax credit from the tax authorities in Serbia. This tax credit is equal to the tax paid in the foreign country, but it cannot exceed the amount of the tax that would have been paid in Serbia.

A Serbian entity is entitled to a tax credit for the withholding tax paid on distributed dividends and underlying CPT paid abroad (by its non-resident subsidiary). The tax credit cannot exceed the amount of corporate tax that would have been paid in Serbia. Non-utilised tax credit can be carried forward by the parent company for five years. The parent company is required to own not less than 25% of a non-resident subsidiary for at least one year before filing the tax return.

A resident taxpayer also has the right to decrease its tax liability for withholding tax paid abroad by its non-resident subsidiary on interest and authorship fees.

Deductions

Intangible and fixed assets are divided into five groups, with depreciation rates prescribed for each (Group I: 2.5%; II: 10%; III: 15%; IV: 20%; and V: 30%). A straight-line depreciation method is prescribed for the first group, which includes real estate, while a declining balance method is applicable for assets in the other groups.

S

Serbia

Assets subject to tax depreciation are all tangible and intangible (except goodwill) assets with useful life longer than one year and acquisition value above the average monthly gross salary published in Serbia at the moment of acquisition.

Transfer prices
A transfer price is the price of transactions between related parties. Related parties exist if there is a possibility of control or influence over business decisions between them. Ownership of 50% or more of shares is considered as potential control. Influence over business decisions exists when an associated party holds 50% or more or individually holds the greatest portion of votes in the taxpayer's management bodies. If the same persons participate in the management or control of both companies, a connection between them will be deemed to exist.

A company should disclose transactions with related parties separately at transfer prices and at arm's-length prices in its corporate tax calculation. Positive difference between these prices (adjustments of expenses) and negative difference (adjustments of revenues) is included in taxable profit.

Thin capitalisation
The old thin capitalisation rule has been changed considerably. It is our understanding that interest and related expenses arising in related-party loans are now deductible up to four times the taxpayer's net assets (10 times for banks). In addition, the carryforward of non-deductible interest due to the application of the thin-cap rule is no longer available.

Tax loss
The taxpayer has the right to carryforward and utilise tax losses incurred over the following five years.

Group taxation

Tax grouping/consolidation is allowed to a group of companies where all members are Serbian residents and one company directly or indirectly controls at least 75% of the shares in another company. Each company files its own tax balance sheet and the parent company files a consolidated tax balance sheet for the whole group.

In the consolidated tax balance sheet, losses of one or more companies are offset by the profits of other related companies. Each company is liable for the portion of tax attributable to its share of the group's taxable profit.

Once approved by the ministry of finance, tax grouping/consolidation applies for at least five years.

Tax incentives

Profit earned on the basis of a concession is tax exempt for a period of five years.

Tax credits

The minimum investment in property, plant and equipment (PPE) required to qualify for the 10-year tax holiday is RSD 800 million. To qualify for the credit, a taxpayer must employ at least 100 new workers for an indefinite period. The tax holiday is available for the 10-year period in proportion to the investment made. The number of employees employed in the tax period in which the taxpayer qualified for the tax holiday must be retained throughout the whole tax holiday period.

A five-year tax holiday is available for companies conducting business in undeveloped regions that invest at least RSD 8 million in fixed assets. In addition, the company is obliged to employ at least five new workers for an indefinite period. The tax holiday is available for the five year period in proportion to the investment made.

A tax credit of 20% (40% for small enterprises) is available for qualifying investments in fixed assets. The credit is limited to 50% (70% for small enterprises) of the assessed corporate profit tax liability in the current tax period. Unused tax credits can be carried forward for 10 years.

Taxpayers generating profit in a newly established operating unit in an underdeveloped region may claim tax credits for a period of two years in an amount proportional to the profit generated by that unit.

Taxpayers classified into one of the following industries: agriculture, fishing, production of textile yarn and fabrics, garments, leather, base metals, standard metal products, machines, office machines, electrical machines, radio, TV and communication equipment, medical instruments, motor vehicles, recycling and video production are entitled to receive a tax credit in the amount of 80% of investments made in fixed assets which were not previously in use in Serbia. Unused tax credits can be carried forward up to 10 years.

Withholding taxes (WHT)

Withholding tax is calculated and paid at the rate of 20% on payments such as dividends/share in profit, royalties (including neighbouring authorship rights and intellectual property rights), interest income, capital gains, lease payments for real estate and other assets made to a non-resident, unless a Double Tax Treaty (DTT) applies to provide a reduced rate.

Withholding tax is also payable on a non-resident's income realised on the basis of performing entertaining, artistic, sports and similar programmes in Serbia, which is not taxed as income of an individual (performer, musician, sportsman etc.).

Capital gains realised by non-residents (both from residents or other non-residents) are subject to Serbian withholding tax. Non-residents should appoint a fiscal representative in Serbia who should submit a tax return within 15 days from the realisation of capital gain. Based on the tax return, Tax Authorities will issue a decision assessing tax liability (if any).

In order to benefit from application of a relevant DTT, non-residents (i.e., the income recipient) must provide a tax residency certificate on the form prescribed by the Serbian Ministry of Finance stamped by the relevant body from the non-resident's country of residence.

S

Serbia

Withholding tax rates envisaged by applicable DTTs are provided in the following table.

Country	Dividends (1)	Interest	Royalties	Applicable from
Albania	15/5	10	10	2006
Austria (3)	15/5	10	10/5 (4)	N/A
Belgium	15/10	15	10	1982
Belorussia	15/5	8	10	1999
Bosnia and Herzegovina	10/5	10	10	2006
Bulgaria	15/5	10	10	2001
China	5	10	10	1998
Croatia	10/5	10	10	2005
Cyprus	10	10	10	1987
Czech Republic	10	10	10/5 (4)	2006
North Korea	10	10	10	2002
Denmark (2)	15/5	0	10	1983
Egypt	15/5	15	15	2007
Estonia (3)	10/5	10/0 (6)	10/5 (4)	N/A
Finland	15/5	0	10	1988
France	15/5	0	0	1976
Ghana (3)	15/5	10	10	N/A
Germany	15	0	10	1989
Greece (3)	15/5	10	10	N/A
Hungary	15/5	10	10	2003
Italy	10	10	10	1986
Iran (3)	10	10	10	N/A
Ireland (3)	10/5	10/0 (6)	10/5 (4)	N/A
India	15/5	10	10	2009
Kuwait	10/5	10	10	2004
Latvia	10/5	10	10/5 (4)	2007
Libya (3)	10/5	10	10	N/A
Lithuania (3)	10/5	10	10	N/A
Macedonia	15/5	10	10	1998
Malaysia	0 (5)	10	10	1991
Malta (3)	10/5 (7)	10/0 (6)	10/5 (4)	N/A
Moldova	15/5	10	10	2007
Netherlands	15/5	0	10	1983
Norway	15	0	10	1986
Poland	15/5	10	10	1999
Qatar (3)	10/5	10	10	N/A
Romania	10	10	10	1998
Russia	15/5	10	10	1998
Slovak Republic	15/5	10	10	2002
Slovenia	10/5	10	10/5 (4)	2004
Spain (8)	10/5	10/0 (6)	10/5 (4)	N/A
Sri Lanka	12.5	10	10	1987
Sweden	15/5	0	0	1982

Country	Dividends (1)	Interest	Royalties	Applicable from
Switzerland	15/5	10	10	2007
Turkey	15/5	10	10	2008
Ukraine	10/5	10/0 (6)	10	2002
United Kingdom	15/5	10	10	1983
Zimbabwe (3)	15/5	10	10	N/A

Notes

1. If the recipient company owns/controls at least 25 percent (25%) of the equity of the paying company, the lower of the two rates applies.
2. A new double taxation treaty was signed with Denmark in 2009, but it is not applicable yet. Meanwhile, the old treaty is still applicable.
3. The treaty has not been ratified by one of the parties.
4. A tax rate of five percent (5%) will be applicable to literary and scientific works of art, films and works created like films, or other source of reproduction tone or picture. A tax rate of 10 percent (10%) will be applicable to: patents, petty patents, brands, models and samples, technical innovations, secret formulas or technical procedure.
5. Only in cases when dividends are to be paid to Serbian residents. If paid to Malaysian residents, they are taxable at 20 percent (20%) in Serbia.
6. A zero percent rate (0%) is applicable in cases when the income recipient is the government or government-owned banks.
7. Withholding rate refers solely to dividends distributed from Serbia. In Malta, withholding tax cannot be higher than corporate tax on profit before dividend distribution.
8. Will become applicable from 1 January 2011.

Tax administration

The tax period in Serbia is the calendar year. However, entities have a possibility to opt for a different tax period other than the calendar year (subject to the approval of the ministry of finance), but still 12 months long. Once approved, such tax period must be applied for at least five years.

Tax returns together with all supporting documents (e.g., tax depreciation and tax credit forms) must be filed with the tax authorities by 10 March of the following year.

A newly established company needs to register with the tax authorities within 15 days of registration with the court.

Corporate profit tax is payable monthly in advance instalments by the fifteenth of the following month for the prior calendar month. The amount of payable advances is determined on the basis of a company's corporate tax calculation for the previous year.

S

Corporate taxes in Singapore

For more information, contact:

See Tiat Quek
PricewaterhouseCoopers Services LLP
8 Cross Street, 17-00
PwC Building
Singapore 048424
Tel: +65 6236 3218
Email: see.tiat.quek@sg.pwc.com

David Sandison
PricewaterhouseCoopers Services LLP
8 Cross Street, 17-00
PwC Building
Singapore 048424
Tel: +65 6236 3675
Email: david.sandison@sg.pwc.com

Significant developments

The Economic Strategies Committee, which was tasked with developing strategies for Singapore's future economic growth, recommended improving skills, innovation and productivity as the basis for sustaining economic growth. The 2010 Budget was announced on 22 February 2010 and the changes proposed were generally consistent with these recommendations.

Corporate tax changes relate mainly to the introduction of incentives for productivity and innovation, mergers and acquisitions, the maritime sector and international legal services. In addition, certain income tax, goods and services tax (GST) and stamp duty incentives for real estate investment trusts, listed registered business trusts, aircraft rotables and donations that expired or are due to expire this year were renewed. There were also changes to the incentives for offshore insurance and the Financial Sector Incentive and the replacement of industrial building allowances with a new Land Intensification Allowance.

Taxes on corporate income

Tax on corporate income is imposed at a flat rate of 17% for the year of assessment 2010 (i.e., for income derived in accounting periods ending in 2009). This is a one percent reduction in the rate from the prior year. There is an exemption of up to SGD 152,500 out of the first SGD 300,000 of chargeable/taxable income.

For qualifying start-up companies, a three-year tax exemption on the first SGD 100,000, and a further exemption of up to SGD 100,000 on the next SGD 200,000 of chargeable/taxable income is available.

Singapore adopts a one-tier taxation system, under which all dividends are tax exempt in the shareholder's hands.

Corporate residence

In Singapore, the tax residence of a corporation is determined by the place where the central management and control of its business is exercised. This is taken generally to mean the place where the directors meet to exercise de facto control, although the Inland Revenue Authority of Singapore (IRAS) has recently set out further qualifying criteria.

Other taxes

Goods and services tax (GST)
GST is charged at 7% on the supply of goods and services made in Singapore by a taxable person in the course or furtherance of business.

The only exemptions from GST are prescribed financial services (including life insurance) and the sale or rental of residential properties. Zero-rating only applies to the export of goods and international services (defined).

GST is also levied on imports of goods, at the time of importation. However, there are reliefs available to ease the cash-flow burden of import-export traders by suspending GST at the time of importation. GST is not currently charged on imports of services.

A taxable person is one who is, or is required to be, registered for GST as his taxable turnover exceeds SGD 1 million per year. Voluntary registration is permitted if the taxable turnover is below the registration limit, subject to conditions.

A supply of goods is made in Singapore if the goods are in Singapore at the time of supply, and a supply of services is made in Singapore, if the supplier belongs in Singapore. Generally, a person belongs in Singapore if he has a business (including carrying on a business through a branch or agency) or fixed establishment in Singapore.

A taxable person is allowed to offset the input GST paid on taxable purchases against the output GST chargeable on supplies made by him. However, certain purchases are specifically denied an input GST deduction. These include supplies of goods and services such as non-business expenses, club subscription fees, family benefits, car rental expenses, motor vehicle expenses, medical expenses and transactions involving betting, sweepstakes, lotteries, fruit machines or games of chance.

A non-resident is not entitled to GST refunds except by appointing a resident tax agent to act on his behalf. The resident tax agent can then recover import GST paid on behalf of the non-resident business, but will be required to account for output GST on any subsequent supply of the non-resident's goods in Singapore.

Foreign workers' levy
In certain industries a levy not exceeding SGD 500 per month is assessed for each foreign employee. It was announced in the 2010 Budget that levy rates will be gradually increased over the next three years.

Property tax
Property tax is levied at 4% on the annual value of owner-occupied residential premises and at 10% on the annual value of all other houses, land, buildings, or tenements. A property tax rebate of up to SGD 100 per year was given in 2008 and 2009 each for owner-occupied residential property. In addition, a 40% rebate (after other existing rebates) was given for 2009 for owner-occupied residential property and commercial and industrial property.

Stamp duties
Stamp duties are levied on written documents relating to stocks and shares at 0.2%, and relating to immovable property in Singapore at graduated rates of up to 3%.

Singapore

Leases with annual rents not exceeding SGD 1,000 are exempt from stamp duty.

Branch income

Tax rates on branch profits are the same as on corporate profits. There is no branch profits remittance tax on the repatriation of profits to the head office.

Income determination

Inventory valuation
There are no special rules as to which valuation basis should be adopted for inventories (stock-in-trade) in the case of a continuing business, as long as the basis is consistent from one year to another. However, the last-in, first-out (LIFO) basis of valuation is not permitted for tax purposes. Generally, tax reporting conforms to book reporting.

Capital gains
There is no tax on capital gains. Where there is a series of transactions or where the holding period of an asset is relatively short, the tax authorities may take the view that a business is being carried on and attempt to assess the gains as trading profits of the corporation. The UK Badges of Trade, which are used in judicial decisions to distinguish capital and revenue transactions, are generally applied in determining this issue. They include the existence of a profit seeking motive, the number of transactions, the nature of the asset, the existence of similar trading transactions or interests, changes to the asset, the way the sale was carried out, the source of finance, the interval of time between purchase and sale and the method of acquisition.

Inter-company dividends
There are no special concessions for Singapore inter-company dividends. Singapore dividends are exempt in the hands of the recipient.

Foreign income
A corporation, whether resident in Singapore or not, is taxed on foreign income when it is received in Singapore. Legislative provisions govern the basis of treating foreign income as received in Singapore. There are no special rules for taxing the undistributed income of foreign subsidiaries. Where income is earned from treaty countries, double taxation is avoided by means of foreign tax credit granted under those treaties. For non-treaty countries, unilateral tax credit is given in respect of foreign tax on all foreign-sourced income, effective as of the year of assessment 2009 (i.e., for income derived in accounting periods ending in 2008). Foreign dividends, foreign branch profits and foreign service fee income remitted to Singapore are exempt from tax subject to certain conditions. A temporary tax amnesty was introduced in the 2009 Budget for all foreign-sourced income, but this expired on 21 January 2010.

Stock dividends
Stock dividends generally are not taxable. However, certain distributions could be treated as deemed dividends in certain circumstances.

Deemed dividends
Certain distributions to shareholders under a capital-reduction scheme, a share buy-back or a share redemption exercise may be treated as dividends paid by the company. Under the one-tier taxation system, this is not a significant issue unless the transaction is not correspondingly treated as a dividend in the hands of the

shareholder. In which case, the gain may be taxable if it is in respect of a trade or business.

Deductions

Depreciation and depletion
Tax depreciation is allowable at specified rates on buildings used in qualifying industry sectors, subject to conditions. However, during the 2010 Budget, industrial building allowances were replaced by a Land Intensification Allowance. The latter provides for faster depreciation, but is subject to approval as it is allowed as a tax incentive. Transitional provisions for industrial building allowances are available for taxpayers who committed to qualifying capital expenditure before the Budget announcement.

Tax depreciation is available on machinery and equipment on a straight-line basis over their specified working life for all types of business. In lieu of the straight-line basis, accelerated tax depreciation allowances can be claimed by all businesses on all machinery and equipment in equal instalments over three years.

For machinery and equipment purchased during the accounting periods ending in 2009 and 2010 (years of assessment 2010 and 2011), tax depreciation may be claimed over two years instead of three, with 75% of the claim allowed in the first year of assessment and the remainder allowed in the second.

A 100% depreciation allowance is available on capital expenditure incurred on computers, robots, standby generators, pollution control and energy-efficient equipment, certain diesel-driven vehicles and prescribed automation equipment.

Writing down allowances on a straight-line basis over five years is allowable on the cost of acquisition of intellectual property, subject to certain conditions, while a 100% writing down allowance is allowed for capital expenditure on approved research and development cost-sharing arrangements entered into on or after 17 February 2006.

Gains on tax depreciable property (that is, the excess of proceeds over tax base) are taxed as ordinary income to the extent that tax depreciation has been allowed; that is, any clawback of tax depreciation on the disposal of the asset is taxed.

Net operating losses
Loss carryover, including unutilised tax depreciation allowances, is unlimited, provided shareholdings in the loss-making corporation have not changed beyond 50% of the issued and paid-up capital. Additionally, for tax depreciation allowances to be carried forward, the same trade needs to be continued. The tax authorities may exercise discretion to allow carryover of tax losses and unutilised tax depreciation even when there has been a change in shareholding beyond 50%, absent any tax avoidance motives. Losses of up to SGD 100,000 incurred by the company in the current year can be carried back for one year. For the years of assessment 2009 and 2010 (income years 2008 and 2009) the amount allowed to be carried back was increased to SGD 200,000 and the period for which the losses can be carried back was increased to three years.

Payments to non-residents, including foreign affiliates
These payments are deductible, provided they are fair and reasonable, are revenue in nature and can be seen to be relevant to earning the payer's income. Unless a lower treaty rate applies, interest on loans and rentals from movable property are subject

Singapore

to withholding tax at 15%. Royalty payments are subject to withholding tax at 10%. The tax withheld represents a final tax, and applies only to non-residents who are not carrying on any business in Singapore or who have no permanent establishment in Singapore. Technical assistance and management fees for services rendered in Singapore are taxed at the prevailing corporate rate. However, this is not a final tax. Royalties, interest, rental of movable property, technical assistance and management fees can be exempt from withholding tax in certain situations, or subject to reduction in tax rates applicable, usually under fiscal incentives, or double taxation agreements.

Payments made to public entertainers and non-resident professionals who perform services in Singapore also are subject to a final tax of 15% on the gross income. For public entertainers, this appears to be a final tax unless they qualify to be taxed as Singapore tax residents. However, non-resident professionals may elect to be taxed at the prevailing tax rate for non-resident individuals of 20% on net income if this results in a lower tax cost. The withholding tax rate on payments to non-resident entertainers has been reduced to 10% from 22 February 2010 to 31 March 2015.

Taxes
Income taxes are not deductible generally in determining corporate income. However, irrecoverable GST is deductible under certain circumstances. The foreign workers' levy and property taxes are deductible to the extent they are incurred wholly and exclusively in the production of income.

Other significant items
Private automobile expenses are not deductible.

Donations are deductible only if they are made in cash or another prescribed form and to an approved recipient. The deduction allowed for qualifying donations is generally 200% of the value of the donation. However, the deduction is increased to 250% of the value of qualifying donations made in 2009 and 2010.

The tax deduction for medical expenses is limited to 2% of total payroll if the employer implements certain portable medical insurance or benefit schemes. Otherwise, the amount deductible will be limited to 1% of total payroll. Where the company is exempt or taxed at a reduced rate, the expenses disallowed are taxed at the prevailing corporate rate.

A tax deduction for employee share-based remuneration (stock award or stock option schemes) is allowed only if treasury shares are purchased to fulfil such obligations. The deduction is restricted generally to the actual outlay incurred.

Borrowing costs incurred on capital employed in the production of income will be allowed a tax deduction effective as of the year of assessment 2008, if the costs are incurred as a substitute for interest or to reduce interest costs.

Effective as of the year of assessment 2009 (i.e., for income derived in accounting periods ending in 2008), expenses incurred in respect of R&D carried out in Singapore qualify for a tax deduction of 150% of the R&D expenses incurred.

Group taxation

A company is allowed to transfer excess current year trade losses, current year tax depreciation, and current year approved donations to another company within the same group if certain conditions are satisfied.

Broadly, to qualify for group relief, companies must be incorporated in Singapore, belong to the same "75%" group of companies such that there must be at least a 75% ownership relationship between claimant and transferor, and have the same accounting year-end. In addition, a group must comply with certain prescribed set-off and apportionment rules.

Tax incentives

There are various tax incentives available to taxpayers involved in specified activities or industries identified as being beneficial to Singapore's economic development.

Inward investment
Incentives are available to pioneer industries, high-value-added or expanding industries and to export services.

Corporations manufacturing approved products with high technological content, providing qualifying services or engaging in countertrade activities may apply for tax exemption for five to 15 years under the pioneer tax incentive. Corporations may apply for their post-pioneer profits to be taxed at a reduced rate under the Development and Expansion Incentive as discussed below.

Under the Development and Expansion Incentive, corporations engaging in new high-value-added projects, expanding or upgrading their operations, or undertaking incremental activities after their pioneer or post-pioneer period may apply for their profits to be taxed at a reduced rate of not less than 5% for an initial period of up to 10 years. The total tax relief period is subject to a maximum of 20 years (inclusive of the post-pioneer relief period previously granted, if applicable).

An approved enterprise providing selected export services with respect to overseas projects is given tax exemption for 90% of the qualifying export income. The exemption is given for a period of five years, with provision for an extension.

Capital investment
The various incentives include investment allowances and the merger and acquisition allowance.

Under the investment allowance, a tax exemption is granted on an amount of profits based on a specified percentage (of up to 100%) of the capital expenditure incurred for qualifying projects or activities within a period of up to five years (up to eight years for assets acquired on hire-purchase on or after 15 February 2007).

The merger and acquisition allowance allows a write-off over five years of 5% of the value of qualifying merger or acquisition deals executed between 1 April 2010 and 31 March 2015, subject to a cap of SGD 5 million per year of assessment. This incentive is available only to companies that are incorporated, tax resident and carrying on a business in Singapore.

S

Singapore

Financial services
Various incentives include:

1. Financial sector incentive (FSI) scheme – This scheme covers approved bond intermediaries, Asian currency units, approved derivative traders, approved fund managers, equity capital market intermediaries, operational headquarters, syndicated offshore credit and underwriting facilities, providers of high-value-added processing services supporting financial activities, futures members of the Singapore Exchange Limited and members of the Singapore Commodity Exchange Limited. High growth, high-value-added activities such as services and transactions relating to the bond market, derivatives market, equity market (i.e., futures, securities trading, which includes sale of stocks, shares, bonds and other securities, and extends to brokerage, nominee and custodian services in relation to securities trading), credit facilities syndication and Islamic finance will be exempt from tax or taxed at 5%, whilst other broader range financial activities will only qualify for a 12% tax rate. The tax incentive period may vary from five, seven or 10 years subject to certain conditions being met.
2. Finance and treasury centre (FTC) – Income derived by an FTC from approved finance and treasury centre activities is taxed at a reduced rate of 10%. Approved activities include regional and international treasury and fund management activities, corporate finance and advisory services, economic and investment research and analysis, and credit control and administration.
3. Debt securities – A package of tax exemptions and reduced tax rates is available to various players in the Singapore bond market, including certain Islamic financing arrangements.
4. Offshore insurance – Approved insurance companies engaged in the business of insuring and reinsuring offshore risks are taxed at 10% on qualifying income arising from offshore risks business, and at 5% on qualifying income arising from writing offshore Islamic insurance (takaful) and reinsurance (retakaful) business. Tax exemption is available for qualifying income from the writing of both onshore and offshore marine hull and liability risk insurance and offshore specialised risk insurance, and for qualifying income of approved offshore captive insurance companies. In addition, a concessionary tax rate of 10% is available to qualifying insurance and reinsurance brokers on income derived from the provision of insurance broking and advisory services to non-Singapore based clients.
5. Real Estate Investment Trusts (REITs) – Distributions made to foreign non-individual investors by a listed REIT out of rental from Singapore real estate are subject to a reduced tax rate of 10%, subject to certain conditions. Listed REITs investing in foreign properties can apply for tax exemption for certain foreign income received in Singapore. Distributions out of this income similarly are exempt. Stamp duty relief is available upon the transfer of immovable Singapore property to a REIT, and GST concessions are available with respect of overseas non-residential properties and special purpose vehicles or sub-trusts.
6. Islamic financing arrangements – The income tax, stamp duty and GST treatment of (a) Islamic financing arrangements based on (i) the cost-plus (Murabaha) concept, (ii) the investment-partnership (Mudaraba) concept, (iii) the leasing-with-option-to-purchase (Ijara Wa Igtina) concept for mortgage financing; and (b) Islamic debt securities (Sukuk) is aligned with conventional financing contracts that they are economically equivalent to, subject to certain conditions. In addition, concessionary tax rates are available for certain activities relating to Islamic financing *(see FSI scheme and Offshore insurance above)*.

7. Maritime Finance Incentive (MFI) – Approved ship investment managers are taxed at 10% on their qualifying management-related income. Approved ship investment vehicles are tax exempt on their qualifying vessel lease income. Approved container investment enterprises are taxed at 5% or 10% on qualifying income from container-leasing. Approved container investment management companies are taxed at 10% on qualifying management fees.
8. Infrastructure Project Finance – Tax exemption is available for interest income earned from qualifying investments in qualifying infrastructure projects/assets. FSI companies that provide project finance advisory services related to qualifying projects/assets pay tax at 5% on their qualifying income, and companies that provide management services to qualifying business trusts and funds pay tax at 10% on their qualifying income. Stamp duty relief is available also on the transfer of such projects/assets to listed companies.

Other incentives
Other incentives include:

1. Headquarters (HQ) schemes – Approved regional headquarters in Singapore are taxed at a concessionary rate of tax of 15% on qualifying overseas income. Approved international headquarters can negotiate for various tax incentives, including tax exemption or concessionary tax rates on qualifying income.
2. Incentives for not-for-profit organisations, international arbitration, shipping companies, investment holding companies, oil traders, international traders, general insurance companies, leasing companies, trust companies, cyber traders, international freight and logistics operators and the provision of international legal services include tax exemptions or concessionary tax rates of 10% for qualifying income. The concessionary tax rate for liquefied natural gas (LNG) trading, aircraft leasing, qualifying oil traders and international traders is further reduced to 5%.

Withholding taxes (WHT)

Domestic corporations paying certain types of income are required to withhold tax, as shown in the following table. The numbers in parentheses refer to the notes below.

Recipient	Dividends (1)	Interest (2)	Royalties (2)
	%	%	%
Resident individuals	Nil	Nil	Nil
Resident corporations	Nil	Nil	Nil
Non-resident corporations and individuals:			
Non-treaty	Nil	15	10
Treaty:			
Australia	Nil	10	10 (4a)
Austria	Nil	5 (3b, d)	5
Bahrain	Nil	5 (3b)	5
Bangladesh	Nil	10	10 (4a)
Belgium	Nil	5 (3b, d)	5/3 (4b)
Brunei	Nil	10/5 (3a, b)	10

Singapore

Recipient	Dividends (1)	Interest (2)	Royalties (2)
	%	%	%
Bulgaria	Nil	5 (3b)	5
Canada	Nil	15	10
Chile (5b)	Nil	15	10
China, P.R.	Nil	10/7 (3a, b)	10/6 (4b)
Cyprus	Nil	10/7 (3a, b)	10
Czech Republic	Nil	Nil	10
Denmark	Nil	10 (3b)	10
Egypt	Nil	15 (3b)	10
Estonia	Nil	10 (3b)	7.5
Fiji Islands, Rep. of	Nil	10 (3b)	10
Finland	Nil	5 (3b)	5
France	Nil	10/Nil (3b, c)	Nil (4a)
Germany	Nil	8 (3b)	8
Hong Kong (5c)	Nil	15	10
Hungary	Nil	5 (3b, d)	5
India	Nil	15/10 (3a)	10
Indonesia	Nil	10 (3b, e)	10
Israel	Nil	7 (3b)	5
Italy	Nil	12.5 (3b)	10
Japan	Nil	10 (3b)	10
Kazakhstan	Nil	10 (3b)	10
Korea, Rep. of	Nil	10 (3b)	10
Kuwait	Nil	7 (3b)	10
Latvia	Nil	10 (3b)	7.5
Lithuania	Nil	10 (3b)	7.5
Luxembourg	Nil	10 (3b)	10
Malaysia	Nil	10 (3b, f)	8
Malta (5d)	Nil	10/7 (3a, b)	10
Mauritius	Nil	Nil	Nil
Mexico	Nil	15/5 (3a, b)	10
Mongolia	Nil	10/5 (3a, b)	5
Myanmar	Nil	10/8 (3a, b)	10
Netherlands	Nil	10 (3b)	Nil (4a)
New Zealand	Nil	15	10
Norway	Nil	7 (3b)	7
Oman	Nil	7 (3b)	8
Pakistan	Nil	12.5 (3b)	10 (4a)
Papua New Guinea	Nil	10	10
Philippines	Nil	15 (3e)	10
Poland	Nil	10 (3b)	10
Portugal	Nil	10 (3b, f)	10
Qatar	Nil	5 (3b)	10
Romania	Nil	5 (3b)	5
Russian Federation (5d)	Nil	7.5 (3b)	7.5

Recipient	Dividends (1)	Interest (2)	Royalties (2)
	%	%	%
Saudi Arabia (5a)	Nil	15	10
Slovak Republic	Nil	Nil	10
South Africa	Nil	Nil	5
Sri Lanka	Nil	10 (3a, b)	10
Sweden	Nil	15/10 (3b, c)	Nil (4a)
Switzerland	Nil	10 (3f)	5 (4a, e)
Taiwan	Nil	15	10
Thailand	Nil	15/10 (3a, b)	10
Turkey	Nil	10/7.5 (3a, b)	10
Ukraine (5d)	Nil	10 (3b)	7.5
United Arab Emirates	Nil	7 (3b)	5 (4f)
United Kingdom	Nil	10 (3b)	10
United States (5c)	Nil	15	10
Uzbekistan (5d)	Nil	5	8
Vietnam	Nil	10 (3b)	10/5 (4c)

Notes

1. Singapore has no withholding tax on dividends over and above the tax on the profits out of which the dividends are declared. However, some treaties provide for a maximum withholding tax on dividends should Singapore impose such a withholding tax in the future.
2. The non-treaty rates (a final tax) apply only to non-residents who do not carry on business in Singapore or have a permanent establishment in Singapore. This rate may be further reduced by tax incentives.
3. Interest:
    a. Lower rate or exemption if received by a financial institution.
    b. Exempt if paid to the government.
    c. Lower rate or exemption if paid by an approved industrial undertaking.
    d. Exempt if paid by a bank and received by a bank.
    e. Exempt if paid to a bank but linked to a government loan agreement or paid to specific financial institutions/banks.
    f. Exempt if paid in respect of an approved loan or indebtedness.
4. Royalties:
    a. Royalties on literary or artistic copyrights, including film royalties, are taxed at the non-treaty rate.
    b. Lower rate for payments in connection with industrial, commercial or scientific equipment.
    c. Lower rate for payments in connection with patents, designs, secret formulas/ processes, or industrial, commercial or scientific equipment/experience.
    d. Exempt if paid to the government.
    e. Exempt for approved royalties.
    f. Lower rate or exemption for industrial royalties in accordance with domestic laws.
7. Treaties:
    a. Treaty with Saudi Arabia covers only international air transport.
    b. Treaty with Chile covers only international ship operations.
    c. Treaties with Hong Kong and the United States cover only shipping and air transport activities.
    d. Treaty applies from 1 January 2010.

S

Singapore

Tax administration

Returns
Tax is computed for each tax year based on the income earned in the preceding year (the tax basis period). The tax basis period is the calendar year; however for business profits, the accounting year would be adopted generally. The corporation files a return of income, and the tax is assessed by the Comptroller of Income Tax. There is no fixed date for the issue of assessments.

Payment of tax
Assessed tax is payable within one month after the service of the notice of assessment, whether or not a notice of objection to the assessment has been lodged with the tax authorities. Application may be made to the Comptroller to pay estimated tax liabilities on a monthly basis. However, the Comptroller is under no obligation to grant such an application.

Late payment of tax will attract penalties up to a maximum of 17% of the outstanding tax.

Other issues

Transfer pricing
The Income Tax Act contains provisions that may be used in a transfer pricing context to effectively allow IRAS to challenge and revise inter-company transactions, and specific transfer pricing provisions were introduced in 2009 which define the arm's-length principle and provide the IRAS a right to make transfer pricing adjustments in cases where taxpayers do not comply with the arm's-length principle.

The IRAS has also issued transfer pricing guidelines to supplement the provisions in the Income Tax Act and the various treaties signed by Singapore. The guidelines cover the application of the arm's-length principle and documentation requirements relating to all related party transactions, including local related party transactions. The intention of the guidelines is to help taxpayers substantiate their transfer prices with their related entities by maintaining adequate documentation to mitigate the risk of tax adjustment by the IRAS and to safeguard them from potential economic double taxation. The IRAS has also provided guidance on matters relating to Mutual Agreement Procedures (MAP) and Advance Pricing Arrangements (APA).

In 2009, the IRAS also issued guidance on the application of the arm's-length principle to related party loans and services.

Although Singapore's income tax rates are traditionally lower than the majority of its trading partners, the IRAS is increasing its focus on transfer pricing issues.

Adoption of International Financial Reporting Standards (IFRS)
Companies incorporated in Singapore and Singapore branches of foreign companies are required by the Companies Act to prepare and present financial statements that comply with the Singapore Financial Reporting Standards (SFRS). In Singapore, the Accounting Standards Council (ASC) has the statutory authority to issue SFRS for adoption.

Singapore

The SFRS is principally based on and substantially similar to the International Financial Reporting Standards (IFRS) that are issued by the International Accounting Standards Board (IASB). The SFRS will converge with IFRS by 2012 for use by listed companies. For unlisted companies, the development of IFRS for small and medium-sized entities is being observed and evaluated.

Companies are required to submit financial statements as part of their tax return filing. The IRAS generally accepts financial statements prepared for statutory filing, although companies that have been allowed to prepare their financial statements using standards other than SFRS, such as IFRS or the Generally Accepted Accounting Principles (GAAP) adopted by the United States, may be required to explain and/or account for any differences and make the necessary tax adjustments, if any.

In relation to financial instruments, the Income Tax Act was amended to align the tax treatment with the accounting treatment prescribed by SFRS 39 (Financial Instruments: Recognition and Measurement).

Sample corporate tax calculation
Fiscal year ended 31 December 2009 (year of assessment 2010).

	SGD	SGD
Net profit before tax per accounts		5,857,500
Less:		
Singapore dividend (exempt)	1,500	
Foreign-sourced dividend (exempt)	2,200	
Foreign-sourced interest (exempt)	1,600	
Profit on sale of fixed assets	34,000	
Capital exchange gain	6,750	(46,050)
		5,811,450
Add:		
Depreciation	550,000	
Foreign pension contribution	100,000	
Medical expenses (non-deductible)	500	
Legal fees (capital in nature)	15,500	
Automobile expenses	33,500	
Donations	9,000	
Penalties and fines	2,000	
Depreciation	100,485	810,985
Adjusted profit before capital allowances		6,622,435
Less:		
Unutilised capital allowances brought forward	1,152,000	
Capital allowances (current year)	3,000,000	

Singapore

	SGD	SGD
Balancing charge	(7,700)	(4,144,300)
Adjusted profit after capital allowances		2,478,135
Less: Unutilised losses brought forward		(67,500)
Adjusted profit after capital allowances and unutilised losses brought forward		2,410,635
Less: Approved donations (250% deduction)		(22,500)
Chargeable income before partial exemption		2,388,135
Less: Partial exemption		
75% of first SGD 10,000	7,500	
50% of the next SGD 290,000	145,000	(152,500)
Chargeable income after partial exemption		2,235,635
Tax thereon at 17%		380,057.95

For more information, contact:

Todd Bradshaw
PricewaterhouseCoopers Tax, k.s.
Námestie 1. mája 18
815 32 Bratislava
Slovak Republic
Tel: +421 2 59 350 111
Email: todd.bradshaw@sk.pwc.com

Significant developments

The tax legislation in the Slovak Republic (Slovakia) was significantly amended 1 January 2004. The legislation is subject to frequent amendments and new official interpretations. Therefore, it is advisable to contact PricewaterhouseCoopers Bratislava for up-to-date information. The latest amendment recently approved by the Slovak Parliament is effective from 1 January 2010. Thus, the information included in this summary applies from 1 January 2010 unless otherwise stated.

Taxes on corporate income

As a member state of the Organisation for Economic Cooperation and Development (OECD), the Slovak Republic's system of corporate taxation generally follows OECD guidelines and principles.

Slovakia has a flat corporate income tax (CIT) rate of 19%, and does not have local, state or provincial CIT.

Corporate residence
A company is a resident in the Slovak Republic if it has its registered seat or effective place of management in the Slovak Republic. A foreign company may create a permanent establishment (PE) if its employees (or persons working for it) are present and providing services in the Slovak Republic on behalf of the foreign company where this activity meets the definitions of permanent place of business; or if the employees conclude and negotiate agreements on the foreign entity's behalf; or if the foreign entity establishes a building site within the territory of the Slovak Republic.

Other taxes

Value-added tax (VAT)
A basic VAT rate of 19% applies to all taxable supplies with certain exceptions, medical products and printed materials have a VAT rate of 10%, and certain food products (such as meat, raw milk, eggs, and honey) placed on the market by entities producing small quantities, have a VAT rate of 6%. Exempt supplies without credit entitlement include postal services, financial and insurance services, education, public radio and TV broadcasting services, health and social services, the transfer and leasing of real estate (with exceptions), and lottery services. There are also other VAT-exempt transactions without credit entitlement as well as exempt taxable supplies with credit entitlement.

S

Slovak Republic

VAT grouping is possible if certain conditions are met.

Stamp taxes
There are no special stamp taxes in Slovakia

Excise tax
Excise tax is charged on the release to free tax circulation or import of tobacco products, wine, spirits, beer and mineral oil. In addition, effective 1 July 2008, excise tax is also charged on electric energy, coal and natural gas.

Immovable property tax
Immovable property tax is governed by the Act on Local Taxes, and is divided into: land tax, building tax and tax on apartments. Immovable property tax is calculated based on the area of the real estate, its location and its type, as well as the tax rate of each self-governing region.

Real estate transfer tax was abolished effective 1 January 2005, and there are no stamp duties or similar taxes on share or other property transfers, although small administrative fees are payable to register such transactions.

Transfer taxes
Transfer taxes are not applicable for Slovakia.

Turnover taxes
Turnover taxes are not applicable for Slovakia.

Registration taxes
Registration taxes are not applicable for Slovakia.

Customs duties
- Goods imported from non-EU countries are subject to import customs clearance.
- Goods exported from the EU customs territory have to be declared for export customs clearance.
- The person responsible for paying the customs debt is the declarant.
- The declarant is the person making the customs declaration in his own name, or the person in whose name the customs declaration is made.
- The custom declaration should be made in the prescribed form and manner (in writing or by another action).
- Import or export duties are customs duties and other charges payable on the import or export of goods (import VAT, excise duties and charges under the common agricultural policy).
- The customs authorities require declarants to provide a deposit to cover the customs debt in the event that a customs debt arises. Such a deposit may be in cash, or may be provided by a guarantor.

To communicate with the customs offices, each person must have an Economic Operator Registration and Identification Number (EORI), which is registered by the customs authorities on request. EORI registration is mandatory for customs clearance.

Motor vehicle tax
Vehicle tax applies to vehicles that are used for business purposes in the Slovak Republic, regardless of where they may be registered. The taxpayer is the entity that

uses the vehicle for business purposes. The tax rate depends on engine capacity, vehicle size and the decision of each self-governing region.

Inheritance tax and gift tax
Inheritance tax and gift tax were abolished from 1 January 2004.

Branch income

A foreign company may trade through a Slovak branch, which must be registered in the Slovak Commercial Register. The taxable income of the branch may not be lower than that which an independent entity (e.g., a Slovak company) would achieve from carrying out similar activities under similar conditions. If the branch's taxable income cannot be assessed based on its income less costs, as adjusted for tax purposes, certain other methods may be used. A taxpayer may ask the tax authorities in writing to approve such a method. A Slovak tax resident entity is able to deduct from its tax base a tax loss made by its taxable PE (e.g., branch) outside Slovakia.

Income determination

The tax base is generally the accounting result as determined under Slovak statutory accounting rules, adjusted for tax purposes. Under the transfer pricing rules, the tax base should be increased by the difference in prices charged between a Slovak entity and its foreign related parties compared with those that would be charged between independent parties. Slovak tax law generally reflects OECD rules with respect to transfer-pricing methods.

Capital gains from the disposal of assets are included in the CIT base. The tax treatment of capital losses depends on the type of asset on which they arose.

Dividends paid out of profits earned on or after 1 January 2004, and liquidation surpluses and settlement amounts to which shareholders became entitled on or after 1 January 2004, are not subject to tax. Income received by inheritance or donation, and income from acquiring new shares due to an increase in share capital from retained profits or mergers and demergers within Slovakia or the European Union (EU), is also not subject to tax.

Companies resident in the Slovak Republic are taxed on their worldwide income, including income of its foreign branches. Credit relief is available for foreign tax paid under most of Slovakia's double tax treaties (DTTs). Alternatively, exemption of foreign income taxed abroad from taxation in Slovakia may apply.

The taxpayer may decide whether to include unrealised foreign exchange differences relating to unsettled payables and receivables in the tax base in the tax period when they are accounted for or in the tax period when they are realised. However, the decision to exclude these differences must be made in writing to the Tax Office before the start of the tax period. Any subsequent decision to revert back to including these differences must be made before the end of the tax period concerned.

Reserve fund
When a joint-stock company is incorporated, it must create a reserve fund of at least 10% of its share capital. The statutory reserve fund must be increased annually by an

S

Slovak Republic

amount set out in the company's Articles of Association, but not less than 10% of its net profit, up to a total of 20% of the share capital.

A limited liability company must create a reserve fund following the first year in which it reports a profit, at the latest. The minimum contribution is then 5% of the net profit each year (or more if specified in the company's Articles of Association) up to a total of at least 10% of the company's share capital.

A branch of a foreign company is not required to set up a reserve fund.

A reserve fund may be used to cover prior year losses of the company, and, in certain other limited situations, but it is not distributable.

Business combinations

Two alternative tax treatments may be used for business combinations including in-kind contributions to a company's share capital, mergers and demergers.

Under the first alternative, the taxpayer should value assets for tax purposes using their current market values, and the revaluation difference must be reflected in the appropriate company's tax returns within seven years of the transaction. Under the second alternative, the taxpayer should continue to use the original tax book values of the assets, and revaluation difference is not taxable/tax deductible.

When selling a business as a going concern, the purchaser must include goodwill or negative goodwill, acquired as part of the purchase, in its tax base within seven tax periods.

Deductions

Depreciation

Tax depreciation is calculated on an asset-by-asset basis using a straight-line or reducing-balance method at statutory rates, and is generally available for expenditure incurred on tangible fixed assets. The tax depreciation of intangible fixed assets equals the accounting depreciation. Some types of assets are excluded from depreciation, such as land, artwork and national monuments. Tangible fixed assets are classified into tax depreciation groups to which different depreciation periods apply, as follows:

Depreciation group	Depreciation (years)	Examples
1	4	Motor vehicles, office machines and computers, tools and implements
2	6	Engines, most production line equipment, furniture
3	12	Buildings made of metal, turbines, air-conditioning systems, ships
4	20	Buildings of a permanent nature

Taxpayers do not have to depreciate an asset every year. Tax depreciation may be interrupted in any year and continued in a later year without a loss of the total tax depreciation available.

A lessee can depreciate a tangible fixed asset held under a financial lease. For tax purposes, the depreciation period equals the leasing period, and the tax depreciation base equals the acquisition value of the leased asset without VAT and financing costs, plus expenses related to acquisition of the leased asset that the lessee incurred before the asset was put into use.

The value to be used as the basis for tax depreciation depends on how the asset is acquired and is usually based on one of the following:

- Acquisition costs (the price for which the asset was acquired); or
- The taxpayer's own costs incurred, if the asset is acquired or produced internally.

Losses
A company or branch may carryforward and utilise a tax loss for a period of up to five years following the year in which the loss arose, and for up to seven years for tax losses reported after 31 December 2009. Each year's tax loss should be considered separately, and can be utilised over its own five- or seven-year period.

Carryback of losses is not available in Slovakia.

Bad debt provisions
Provisions for unsecured receivables from loans created by banks, and bad debts of regular commercial companies, are fully tax-deductible (subject to certain conditions) once the debt has been overdue for more than 1,080 days (20% of the bad debt is tax-deductible when it has been overdue for more than 360 days, and 50% after 720 days). Tax deductions already taken for bad-debt provisions created before 1 January 2008 had to be adjusted to bring them in line with the above rules and included in the CIT base equally over 2008 and 2009 tax periods.

Charitable contributions
Charitable contributions are treated as gifts which are not tax-deductible.

Non-deductible expenses
Expenses are generally tax-deductible if incurred to generate, secure and maintain the entity's taxable income. However, certain costs are specifically not tax-deductible. These include entertainment costs, penalties and fines, various provisions, and certain expenses in excess of statutory limits (e.g., employee travel expenses and meal allowances).

Fines and penalties
Contractual penalties and late payment interests are generally tax-deductible on a cash basis; however, other penalties are not tax-deductible.

Goodwill
Depreciation of goodwill is not tax-deductible, with the exception of goodwill that arose as of 2010 at the purchase of business as a going concern, or at the contribution of business as a going concern under fair value alternative.

Start-up expenses
Start-up expenses are tax-deductible in the period when incurred.

Slovak Republic

Pension expenses
Contributions to supplementary pension savings made by the Slovak employer on behalf of the employee, up to 6% of the gross salary of the employee participating in these plans, are tax-deductible.

Group taxation

There is no concept of group CIT in the Slovak Republic. Each company in a group is taxed individually.

Treatment of inter-company items
Dividends are not treated as taxable costs as they are paid out of the profit after tax.

Royalties, commissions and other payments paid to foreign related parties are tax-deductible provided they would be taxable if paid to a third party, and if the charges are in line with transfer pricing rules.

Related party transactions
Under the transfer pricing rules, prices in transactions between a Slovak company and its foreign-related parties should be at arm's length, which means the prices should be at rates similar to those that would be charged between unrelated parties for the same or similar transactions under comparable conditions.

If transactions between the related parties are not made at arm's length, and this results in a reduction in the Slovak entity's corporate tax base, then the tax authorities can adjust the corporate tax base to that which it would have been achieved if arm's-length prices had been used.

Thin capitalisation rules
There are no thin capitalisation rules in Slovakia.

Tax incentives

There are several types of investment incentives potentially available, including corporate tax credits, discounts on the price of publicly owned real estate, and financial support for creating jobs or for training employees. All of these are treated as state aid.

Various conditions must be met in order for a company to qualify for state aid. These include a minimum amount of investment in fixed assets, the amount depends mainly on the type of project and where it is located.

Investment incentives
Investment incentives (including tax credits) are potentially available for projects in the following areas:

- Industry;
- Technology centres;
- Shared services centres; and
- Tourism.

The granting of a tax relief is subject to approval of the Slovak authorities. If certain conditions are met, a taxpayer may apply tax relief in the five subsequent years following tax period in which the relief was granted.

Research and development (R&D) incentives
R&D incentives currently available under Slovak law are as follows:

- Subsidies for research and development projects from the state budget; and
- Income tax relief – at the amount incurred for research and development.

Types of projects which can be granted investment incentives:

- Fundamental research projects;
- Experimental development projects;
- Applied research projects;
- Feasibility studies;
- Protection of intellectual and industrial property; and
- Staffing of research and development functions.

Withholding taxes (WHT)

The following payments are subject to withholding tax when made by Slovak companies to foreign parties. However, a DTT may reduce or eliminate the rate:

	%
Management fees for services provided in the Slovak Republic	19
Royalties*	19
Interest on loans and deposits**	19

* Royalties paid to related EU-resident companies are not subject to withholding tax if certain conditions are met.

** Interest paid to related EU-resident companies is not subject to withholding tax if certain conditions are met.

Dividends paid out of profits arising in 2004 and later years are not subject to Slovak withholding tax.

Withholding tax should be paid to the Tax Office no later than 15 days from the end of the calendar month following that in which the payment was made. The withholding obligation lies with the Slovak resident taxpayer. If the tax is not properly withheld, the unpaid tax becomes the Slovak tax resident's tax liability, and a penalty may be assessed.

Double tax treaties (DTT)
This table showing countries with which Slovakia has entered into DTT.

Treaty recipient	Interest (%)		Royalties (%)	
Australia	10		10	
Austria	0		0/5	(1)
Belarus	0/10	(3)	5/10	(1)

Slovak Republic

Treaty recipient	Interest (%)		Royalties (%)	
Belgium	0/10	(2a)	5	
Bosnia and Herzegovina	0		10	
Brazil	0/10/15	(2) (3)	15/25	(1b)
Bulgaria	0/10	(3)	10	(6)
Canada	0/10	(14)	0/10	(1)
China, P.R.	0/10	(4)	10	
Croatia	10		10	
Cyprus	0/10	(3)	0/5	(1)
Czech Republic	0		0/10	(1)
Denmark	0		0/5	(1)
Egypt 17	n/a		n/a	
Estonia	0/10	(15)	10	
Finland	0		0/1/5/10	(8)
France	0		0/5	(1)
Germany	0		5	
Greece	0/10	(3)	0/10	(1)
Hungary	0		10	
Iceland	0		10	
India	0/15	(4)	30	
Indonesia	0/10	(3)	10/15	(5)
Ireland	0		0/10	(1)
Israel	2/5/10	(9)	5	
Italy	0		0/5	(1)
Japan	0/10	(4)	0/10	(1)
Kazakhstan	0/10	(3)	10	
Korea	0/10	(4) (11)	0/10	(1)
Latvia	0/10	(4)	10	
Libya 18	n/a		n/a	
Lithuania	0/10	(4)	10	
Luxembourg	0		0/10	(1)
Macedonia	0		10	
Malta	0		5	
Mexico	0/10		0/10	
Moldavia	10		10	
Mongolia	0		0	
Montenegro	10		10	
Netherlands	0		5	
Nigeria	0/15	(3)	10	
Norway	0		0/5	(1)
Poland	0/10	(4)	5	
Portugal	10		10	
Romania	0/10	(4)	10/15	(1a)
Russia	0		10	
Serbia	10		10	
Singapore	0		10	

Treaty recipient	Interest (%)		Royalties (%)	
Slovenia	10		10	
South Africa	0		10	
Spain	0		0/5	(13)
Sri Lanka	0/10	(12)	0/10	(1)
Sweden	0		0/5	(13)
Switzerland	0/10	(7) (11)	0/5/10	(1) (10)
Syria	0/10	(3)	12	
Tunisia	0/12	(3)	5/15	(1)
Turkey	0/10	(3)	10	
Turkmenistan	0/10	(3)	10	
Ukraine	10		10	
United Kingdom & Northern Ireland	0		0/10	(1)
United States	0		0/10	(1)
Uzbekistan	10		10	
Vietnam	0/10	(3)	5/10/15	(16)

Notes

(1) The lower rate applies to cultural royalties.

(1a) The rate of 10% applies to royalties in respect of the use of trademarks, patents or know-how. The higher rate applies in any other cases.

(1b) The rate of 25% applies to royalties for the use of trademarks. The lower applies in other cases.

(2) The lower rate applies to interest on loans and credits granted by a bank for at least 10 years in connection with the sale of industrial equipment; with the study, installation or furnishing of industrial or scientific units; or with public works.

(2a) The zero-rate applies to interest: on certain commercial debt-claims, loans guaranteed by public entities for export promotion, accounts/loans between banks/public institutions of the two states and interest paid to another state or political subdivision of a local authority.

(3) The zero-rate applies if the interest is received by the government/the central bank/other state institutions (see the respective treaty for exact wording).

(4) The zero-rate applies if the interest is received by the government or the central bank or other state institutions, or if the receivables on which the interest is paid are guaranteed / financed / indirectly financed by the government/governmental institutions (see treaty for exact wording).

(5) The rate of 10% applies to royalties for cinematography/TV broadcasting/ radio broadcasting, and to giving up rights related to royalties. The higher rate applies in other cases.

(6) This rate also applies to payment for services.

(7) Withholding tax is nil on bank loans.

(8) The zero-rate applies to copyrights, 1% applies to finance lease of equipment, 5% applies to equipment rental and royalties for software/cinematography/TV and radio broadcasting, 10% applies to payments for the use of trademarks and know-how.

(9) The rate of 2% applies to state bonds and obligations, and loans insured or guaranteed by the National Bank of Slovakia/Israel, Slovak Society for Insurance of Foreign Credits and Loans, or Israel Society for Insurance of Foreign Trade; 5% applies if interest is received by a financial institution; 10% applies in all other cases.

(10) Slovakia can apply the rate of 5% to royalties for the use of trademarks, patents or know-how paid from Switzerland to Slovakia, if Switzerland does not apply the 10% rate.

(11) The zero-rate applies to interest on loans and credits in connection with the sale of industrial, business or scientific equipment, or the sale of goods.

Slovak Republic

(12) The zero-rate applies if the interest received is related to loans (monetary or non-monetary) provided to the government of the other contracting state corporation or any other institution with state shareholding or to loans provided to a bank institution under a governmental approval.

(13) The zero-rate applies to copyrights.

(14) The zero-rate applies to interest received by a resident of one state in respect of indebtedness of the other state government or political subdivision/local authority, or in respect of a loan made/guaranteed by the other state government in respect of imports/exports.

(15) The zero-rate applies if the interest is received by the government or the central bank or other state institutions, or if the receivables on which the interest is paid are guaranteed/financed/indirectly financed by the government/governmental institutions (see treaty for exact wording).

(16) The rate of 5% applies to royalties for the use or the right to use of patent, draft or model, plan, confidential formula or procedure, for information related to industrial or scientific experience and for the use or the right to use of an industrial, business or scientific device. The rate of 10% applies to royalties for the use or the right to use of trademark or for information related to business experience. The rate of 15% applies to royalties, other than those stated above.

(17) Slovakia is waiting for Egypt to announce its approval of DTT.

(18) Slovakia is waiting for Libya to announce its approval of DTT.

Tax administration

The standard fiscal year is a calendar year, but a Slovak entity may opt to change this to a different 12-month period. A corporate tax return must be filed together with the entity's financial statements within three months following the fiscal year-end. A three-month extension to the filing deadline may be used. Also, if part of the income to be reported in the tax return is from sources abroad, the taxpayer may extend the filing deadline by up to six months. To extend the filing deadline, the taxpayer has to notify the tax office before the normal filing deadline. After notification, the deadline is automatically extended.

The balance of tax due for a fiscal year is payable by the filing deadline.

Advance payments of corporate tax must be paid monthly or quarterly during the current tax period. Instalments are usually based on the last known tax liability of the entity. It is not necessary to pay tax advances if the last tax liability did not exceed EUR 1,659.70. After the tax return for the preceding tax period is filed, and the final tax liability is known, any outstanding tax is paid and a new schedule for paying advances for the current year is made.

Statue of limitations

A tax may not normally be assessed or additionally assessed more than five years (10 years when DTT treaty was applied, including transactions with foreign related parties) after the end of the year during which the obligation to file a tax return arose, or during which the taxpayer was obliged to pay the tax. If a tax inspection is undertaken within this five-year period, another five-year period commences from the end of the year in which the taxpayer was notified of this action.

If a tax payer utilises a tax loss reported as of 2010, a tax or additional tax cannot be assessed more than seven years after the end of the year in which the obligation to file a tax return in which a tax payer reported the tax loss arose

However, tax may be assessed, or additionally assessed, no later than 10 years after the end of the year during which the obligation to file a tax return arose, or during which the taxpayer was obliged to pay the tax.

Other issues

International Financial Reporting Standards (IFRS) adoption
Slovakia has adopted most of the principles of IFRS in its accounting law. However, there are still some differences between IFRS and Slovak accounting standards.

Obligation to prepare statutory financial statements according to IFRS
Financial institutions (banks, insurance companies, etc.) must prepare their statutory financial statements according to IFRS. In addition, a company which fulfils two or more of the following conditions, in two consecutive accounting periods, must prepare its statutory financial statements according to IFRS:

* The total value of assets is more than EUR 165,969,594;
* Net turnover exceeds EUR 165,969,594; and/or
* The average number of employees in the individual accounting period exceeds 2,000.

If the Slovak taxpayer is obliged to prepare its financial statements under IFRS, the tax base is derived from either:

* The profit before tax under IFRS, adjusted for tax purposes using the "IFRS Tax Bridge" issued by the Slovak Ministry of Finance; or
* The profit before tax under Slovak statutory accounting standards.

Transfer pricing documentation
All Slovak taxpayers must keep sufficient transfer pricing documentation to justify prices charged by or to their foreign related parties. The Slovak Ministry of Finance has issued a guideline setting out detailed requirements for transfer pricing documentation (the Guideline) for entities which are obliged to prepare their financial statements under IFRS.

Slovak tax inspectors may require transfer pricing documentation during a tax inspection, and without such documentation transfer pricing adjustments (increased tax base) are much more likely to be imposed. In addition, entities reporting under IFRS may be specifically penalised for not keeping transfer pricing documentation or for non-compliance of their documentation within the Guideline requirements.

S

Corporate taxes in Slovenia

For more information, contact:

Clare Moger
PricewaterhouseCoopers
Cesta v Klece 15
SI-1000 Ljubljana, Slovenia
Tel: +386 1 58 36 058
Email: clare.moger@si.pwc.com

Significant developments

Tax relief for investments in the Pomurje region

In 2010 a new decree came into effect that enables entities based in the Pomurje region of Slovenia to benefit from additional employment incentives and additional tax relief for investments. These extra benefits are available for 2010 to 2015. As a result, provided certain conditions are met, entities with their seat in Pomurje are entitled to a 70% tax allowance for investments in equipment and intangible assets as well as to certain employment allowances.

Other changes to corporate tax

The Slovene Corporate Income Tax (CIT) Act, which became effective on 1 January 2007, was amended twice during 2009 introducing further changes.

The main purpose of the amendments was to harmonise the provisions in the CIT Act with the provisions in the European Union (EU) Treaty and European Economic Area (EEA) Agreements. The amendments provide tax relief on donations made both in cash and, in certain cases, contributions in-kind made for specific purposes, not only to residents of Slovenia and EU member states, but also to member states of the EEA.

There have also been changes to the CIT Act with respect to withholding tax and amendments that provide a general tax allowance for investments in equipment and intangible assets. The section on *"Withholding taxes"* includes the effects of these changes.

Taxes on corporate income

The corporate tax rate was reduced from a flat rate of 21% in 2009 to a flat rate of 20% for 2010 and thereafter.

A special tax regime is granted for certain economic zones where additional tax allowances for investment and employment may be available.

Taxpayers, such as non-profit or charitable organisations, associations, foundations, etc., are exempt from corporate taxation on their non-profit-making activities.

Investment funds as well as pension funds, pension insurance companies and venture capital companies may be taxed at a rate of 0% if certain conditions are met.

There are no state or local taxes on income.

Corporate residence

A legal entity is considered to be a Slovenian tax resident, provided that the entity:

- Has its statutory (registered) seat in Slovenia; or
- Has its place of effective management located in Slovenia.

The preceding conditions do not exclude a society or any association of persons, including an association under civil or foreign law that does not have legal identity, from also being considered to be a Slovene tax resident.

Slovenian tax residents are liable to pay tax on their worldwide income. Slovenian tax non-residents are taxed only on income from sources in Slovenia, including income earned through permanent establishments (PE) in Slovenia.

Other taxes

Tonnage tax
In July 2007, the Slovene Tonnage Tax Act came into force. The tonnage tax is an alternative to the CIT and applies as of 1 January 2008.

A company may request to be subject to tonnage tax instead of CIT if it meets certain conditions (i.e., it operates in maritime transport in international shipping) and notifies the tax authorities in advance.

Value-added tax (VAT)
A basic VAT rate of 20% applies to all taxable supplies.

A lower VAT rate of 8.5% generally applies to foodstuffs; live animals; seeds; plants; water supplies; medicines; medical equipment; transport of passengers; books; admission fees; royalties for writers and performers; certain works of art; certain residential properties; hotel accommodation; use of sport facilities; burial and cremation services; public hygiene services; minor repairs of bicycles; shoes and clothing; domestic care services; hairdressing services.

Exempt supplies without credit entitlement include financial and insurance/reinsurance services, rent and lease of immovable goods (with exceptions), tax and court stamps, lottery services, trade of land, health and social services, etc. There are also other VAT-exempt transactions without a credit entitlement as well as exempt taxable supplies with a credit entitlement.

VAT grouping is not possible within Slovenia.

Excise tax
Excise tax is charged on the release into free tax circulation or import of tobacco products, alcohol and alcohol drinks, fuel and mineral oils, and electricity.

Real estate tax
Real estate tax of 2% is charged on real estate transfers and leases, unless VAT has been charged on the transaction.

S

Slovenia

Customs duties

- Goods imported from non-EU countries are subject to import customs clearance.
- Goods exported from the EU customs territory have to be declared for export customs clearance.
- The person responsible for paying the customs debt is the declarant.
- The declarant is the person making the customs declaration in his own name, or the person in whose name the customs declaration is made.
- The customs declaration should be made in the prescribed form and manner (in writing or by another action specified by law).
- Import or export duties are customs duties and other charges payable on the import or export of goods (import VAT, excise duties, environmental tax and motor vehicle tax).

For purposes of communication with the customs offices, each person has to be identified by an EORI number (Economic Operator Registration and Identification Number), which is registered by the customs authorities on request. EORI registration is mandatory for customs clearance.

Environmental tax

Environmental tax is charged on carbon dioxide emissions, waste disposal, lubricating oils and fluids, and used motor vehicles.

Motor vehicle tax

Motor vehicle tax applies to all vehicles, which are registered for the first time in the territory of the Republic of Slovenia. The taxpayer is the entity that imports the vehicle from EU or non-EU countries. The tax rate depends on fuel range and emission of CO_2 and ranges from 0.5% to 31%.

Insurance premium tax

This tax is levied on insurance premiums and paid by insurance companies. The tax rate is 6.5%.

Branch income

If a branch meets the conditions, as set out in the tax legislation and relevant double-tax treaties, to be treated as a PE, then it will be liable to pay tax in Slovenia on profits that are attributable to the PE.

The profit that is attributed to a PE is determined broadly in line with Organisation for Economic Co-operation and Development (OECD) principles. Generally, the attributable profit is the profit that would be expected to be earned by the PE if it were an independent taxpayer performing the same or similar activities and/or business.

A branch whose activities do not create a PE is not subject to corporate tax in Slovenia.

Income determination

General rules

Taxable profits are assessed in accordance with Slovenian Accounting Standards 2006 or International Financial Reporting Standards (IFRS) and modified for certain revenues and certain expenses, which are partly or wholly tax non-deductible.

Generally, business expenses that are necessary to generate taxable revenues are tax-deductible.

Dividend income received

Dividends and similar income received by a Slovenian taxpayer are generally 95% exempt from taxation as long as the distributor was subject to Slovenian corporate tax or to a comparable profits tax. The exceptions to this are where dividends represent untaxed reserves of the distributor, or where the distributor is tax resident in a country that:

- Is outside the EU;
- Has a corporate tax rate less than 12.5%; and
- Is included in a list published by the Ministry of Finance.

Capital gains exemption

Under certain circumstances, the gains made by a Slovenian taxpayer on the disposal of an equity shareholding are 47.5% exempt from taxation. Similarly, 47.5% of a loss arising on the disposal of such a shareholding would not be deductible for corporate tax. The above treatment applies to the disposal of shareholdings of at least 8% that have been held for at least six months and where the taxpayer disposing of the holding employed at least one person during the six-month holding period.

The above treatment is not available for the disposal of a shareholding of a company which is resident in a country that:

- Is outside the EU;
- Has a corporate tax rate less than 12.5%; and
- Is included in a list published by the Ministry of Finance.

Related party transactions

Prices between a Slovenian entity and its related parties must be set, for tax purposes, at fair market value using the arm's-length principle. Broadly speaking, taxpayers are related by direct or indirect or common shareholdings of over 25%; through a participation in management; or by control through other means including through contractual terms.

For transactions between two related Slovenian tax residents, provided neither is in an "advantaged" position, (advantaged usually means having unutilised tax losses), there is, no actual requirement for the companies to adjust their tax returns to reflect an arm's-length price.

Taxable persons must prepare transfer pricing documentation. The Slovenian rules regarding such documentation follow the EU Code of Conduct on transfer pricing documentation for associated enterprises in the European Union (EU TPD).

Deductions

Depreciation and amortisation

There are eight tax depreciation groups, with maximum annual depreciation or amortisation rates for each. Any depreciation charges in excess of these rates are not tax-deductible in the period incurred, but may be deductible in subsequent tax periods, until the asset is fully depreciated or disposed of.

Slovenia

In general, if goodwill is impaired for accounting purposes, then the impairment cost may be treated as tax-deductible. The amount that may be treated as tax-deductible in any one tax period is limited to 20% of the initial value of the goodwill.

Net operating losses

Tax losses may be carried forward to reduce taxable profits indefinitely, but loss carrybacks are not permitted. Loss relief may not exceed the amount of current taxable income. Generally, losses that are generated in multiple tax years are absorbed chronologically. The right to carry losses forward may be forfeited if the ownership of the capital or voting power of the taxpayer claiming the loss carryforward changes by more than 50% within the tax period and the taxpayer either has not performed business activities for two years prior to the change of ownership or substantially changes its business activity two years prior to or after the change in ownership.

Treatment of tax losses mentioned in the preceding paragraph does not apply for those losses that are generated in the year of the change of ownership or prior tax periods.

Business-related expenses

In general, business expenses which are necessary to generate taxable revenues are fully tax-deductible. The following expenses are considered unnecessary for the generation of taxable revenues and are not deductible for tax purposes:

- Expenses which are not directly necessary for performing business activities or are not incurred as a consequence of a business activity;
- Expenses of a private character; and
- Expenses which do not correspond to standard business practice.

Salaries and other payments relating to employment (e.g., wage compensation, holiday allowances, employer's social security contributions, long-service awards, severance benefits paid upon retirement, solidarity assistance and reimbursement of business related expenses) are generally fully tax-deductible.

The costs of benefits in kind are also tax-deductible if such benefits are taxed for the individual under the Personal Income Tax Act.

Some of the most common non-deductible expenses include:

- Penalties and the cost of bribes;
- Input VAT that could have been reclaimed in accordance with the VAT act;
- Donations, although a tax incentive may be available. *Please see the Tax incentives section for more information*;
- Entertainment costs, which are only 50% tax-deductible;
- Costs relating to the supervisory board, which are only 50% tax-deductible; and
- Legal and other costs of incorporation, which may be deductible for the parent company, but not for the entity being incorporated.

Related-party interest

Companies may deduct interest expense on loans from their owners or other associated parties up to a maximum of the amount calculated by using the prescribed interest rate published by the Ministry of Finance. Taxpayers must increase taxable profits by the amount of any excess interest expense, unless they can prove that they could have received the loan on comparable terms from an unrelated party.

Thin capitalisation

Interest payments on loans granted, or guaranteed, by a related party (a party which directly or indirectly owns at least 25% of the shares or voting rights in the taxpayer) are not tax-deductible to the extent that the loan amount exceeds the thin capitalisation threshold specified in law. This does not apply to loan recipients who are banks or insurance companies. Generally speaking the thin capitalisation threshold would be exceeded if the debt-to-equity ratio exceeds 6:1.

The debt-to-equity threshold ratio will decrease as follows:

- 6:1 for 2010;
- 5:1 for 2011; and
- 4:1 for 2012.

Provisions

Certain provisions are only 50% tax-deductible when accrued, with the remaining 50% being treated as tax-deductible when the provision is utilised. The provisions which are subject to this treatment are provisions for warranties granted when selling products or providing services, reorganisations/redundancies, anticipated losses from onerous contracts, pensions, long-service bonuses and severance payments on retirement.

Bad debt provisions

Bad debt provisions are only tax-deductible if the amount does not exceed the lower of:

- The arithmetic mean of the bad debts written-off in the past three tax periods, under certain conditions specified in the tax law; and
- The amount corresponding to 1% of taxable revenues of the tax period.

In order to take advantage of this deduction, a company must be able to calculate amounts for both tests and then take the lower of the two amounts so calculated. If the company is not able to determine the amount for either, the cost of the bad debt provision is not tax-deductible until the provision is utilised.

Costs of bad debts are tax-deductible when the debt is finally written-off, provided there is a finalised court procedure or the creditor can demonstrate that it would cost more to pursue the debtor than the debt is worth, or that it has done everything required by good business practice to try to recover the debt.

Group taxation

Group tax returns were abolished with the introduction of the CIT Act from 1 January 2007. However, special provisions allow a group of taxable persons to continue to file a group tax return, until the period for which approval was granted to file a group tax return expires, in accordance with CIT Act.

Tax incentives

Investment allowances

As of 1 January 2007, general investment allowances have been abolished; however, a tax allowance for investment in equipment and intangible assets is available for investments made after 1 January 2008. The tax allowance is limited to the lesser of 30% of the value of the assets acquired or EUR 30,000.

Slovenia

Research and development (R&D) allowances
A 20% investment allowance is granted for investments in R&D within the tax period. Such an investment tax allowance may be obtained for expenditure on:

- Internal R&D activities within the company; and
- The purchase of R&D equipment from related or unrelated parties or from a private research institution.

In addition, the following higher investment allowances can be available for companies that are established in certain regions in Slovenia, which have lower GDP rates than the state average:

- 30% investment allowance for investments in locations where the average regional GDP rate ranges between the state average and 15% lower than the state average; and
- 40% investment allowance for investments in locations where the average regional GDP rate is more than 15% below the state average.

Allowances for employing certain individuals
A taxpayer that employs trainees or students to undertake practical work may reduce its taxable profits by an additional 20% of the average monthly payment paid to such persons, for every month the person carries out the work.

A taxpayer that employs disabled persons may decrease its taxable profits by an additional 50% of the salary paid to such persons. A taxpayer that employs a disabled person or a person with a combination of total hearing loss and speech impairment may reduce its taxable base by an additional 70% of the salary paid to such person.

Donations
A taxpayer may claim a reduction of its taxable profits for donations made for humanitarian, disabled, charitable, scientific, educational, medical, sports, cultural, ecological and religious purposes to residents of Slovenia or of EU or EEA member states, up to 0.3% of the taxable person's taxable revenues. An additional allowance of 0.2% of the taxpayers' taxable revenues is available for payments made for cultural purposes and to voluntary organisations that work for the public interest to protect the public from natural and other disasters.

A taxpayer may decrease its taxable base for payments made to political parties and representative trade unions, up to an equal to three times the average monthly salary per employee of the taxpayer.

Pension allowances
Under certain conditions, a tax-deductible allowance for voluntary supplementary pension insurance may apply, of up to 24% of compulsory contributions for pension and disability insurance for insured employees, but may not exceed EUR 2,390 annually per employee.

Withholding taxes (WHT)

In Slovenia, tax must be calculated and withheld on the payments made by residents and non-residents on Slovenian-sourced income to recipients outside Slovenia.

Payments to which the withholding tax rules apply include payments for dividends, interest, copyrights, patents, licences, leases on real estate situated in Slovenia, services of performing artists and services charged from low-tax jurisdictions. As of 1 January 2007, a rate of 15% of withholding tax applies.

If a double-tax treaty exists, the withholding tax rate may be reduced in line with the provisions of the treaty. Similarly for payments of interest, royalties and dividends within Europe, the Interest and Royalties directive and the Parent Subsidiary directive, respectively, may also reduce this withholding tax rate to zero.

Furthermore, WHT is not deducted on dividends paid to a parent company in another EU Member State if those dividends are subject to an exemption from tax in the hands of the recipient, provided certain conditions are met.

Recipient	Dividends*	Interest**	Royalties
	%	%	%
Austria	5,15	5	5
Belgium	5,15	10	5
Bosnia and Herzegovina	5,10	7	5
Bulgaria	5,10	5	5,10
Canada	5,15	10	10
Croatia	5	5	5
Cyprus	10	10	10
Czech Republic	5,15	5	10
Denmark	5,15	5	5
Estonia	5,15	10	10
Finland	5,15	5	5
France	15, 0	5	5
Germany	5,15	5	5
Greece	10	10	10
Hungary	5,15	5	5
India	5,15	10	10
Ireland	5,15	5	5
Israel	5,10,15	5	5
Italy	10	10	10
Korea	5,15	5	5
Latvia	5,15	10	10
Lithuania	5,15	10	10
Luxembourg	5,15	5	5
Macedonia	5,15	10	10
Malta	5,15	5	5
Moldova	5,10	5	5
Netherlands	5,15	5	5
Norway	0,15	5	5
People's Republic of China	5	10	10
Poland	5,15	10	10
Portugal	5,15	10	5

Slovenia

Recipient	Dividends* %	Interest** %	Royalties %
Romania	5	5	5
Russian Federation	10	10	10
Serbia/Montenegro	5,10	10	5,10
Slovakia	5,15	10	10
Spain	5,15	5	5
Sweden	5,15	0	0
Switzerland	5,15	5	5
Thailand	10	10,15	10,15
Turkey	10	10	10
Ukraine	5,15	5	5,10
United Kingdom and Northern Ireland	15, 0	5	5
USA	5,15	5	5

* Under certain treaties, the withholding tax rate depends on whether, and to what extent, the recipient participates in the capital of the distributor. Generally, if the recipient holds a participation of more than 25% in the distributing company, the dividends are subject to a lower 5% withholding tax rate. The higher withholding tax rate is, however, normally due when the participation is less than 25%.

** Some double-tax treaties include specific provisions whereby interest payments are subject to a 0% withholding tax rate, if certain conditions are met.

Tax administration

The tax period should be the calendar year. However, a tax period may differ from the calendar year, but may not exceed a period of 12 months. In this case, the tax authorities must be informed about the chosen tax period, and the taxable entity will not be allowed to change its tax period for the following three years.

A tax return must be submitted to the tax authorities by the end of the third month following the end of the tax year.

Tax is paid in advance in monthly instalments (if the amount of prepayment exceeds EUR 400 per month) or in quarterly instalments (if the amount of prepayment is less than EUR 400 per month) determined on the basis of the previous year's assessment.

For more information, contact:

Paul De Chalain
PricewaterhouseCoopers Inc
2 Eglin Road
Sunninghill 2157
South Africa
Tel: +27 11 797 4260
Email: paul.de.chalain@za.pwc.com

Mark Badenhorst
PricewaterhouseCoopers Inc
2 Eglin Road
Sunninghill 2157
South Africa
Tel: +27 11 797 4641
Email: mark.badenhorst@za.pwc.com

Significant developments

After the switch from the source-based taxation to the worldwide taxation of South African (SA) residents in 2000, and the introduction of capital gains tax in 2001, the SA tax system has not undergone fundamental changes. Smaller reforms, however, are ongoing. In 2008, the most significant changes introduced by the government included: a reduction of the corporate tax rate from 29% to 28%, the introduction of industrial tax incentives, the introduction of an electricity levy coupled with incentives for renewable-source energy, and the introduction of a special tax package in terms of which very small businesses may elect to pay a presumptive, turnover-based tax instead of normal income tax.

In the 2009 Budget, there were several more announcements. These included the implementation of the electricity levy announced in the 2008 budget, reduction of the current *ad valorem* excise duty rate on the sale of new motor vehicles and an introduction of an additional excise duty component to take into account carbon dioxide emissions. From an administrative perspective, the 2009 Budget included a provision that the lodging (filing) of an objection will no longer suspend payment of the taxes due and a final set of amendments to support the dividends tax reform.

Secondary tax on companies reform

The Secondary Tax on Companies (STC) is a tax borne by the company on any dividends declared and paid to shareholders. A reform of STC that was launched in 2007 will likely culminate in the latter part of 2010 with the introduction of a withholding tax on dividends. This tax will replace the current STC in an attempt to align the SA system of taxing the corporate profits with the worldwide practice.

Administrative developments

In 2009, administrative developments include employer reconciliations of employee's tax (withheld by the employer on the employee's remuneration) to be submitted more than once per year and employer reconciliations to extend to the Skills Development Levy (SDL) and Unemployment Insurance Fund contributions (UIF). Furthermore, 2008 and later income tax returns for companies and trusts can be filed via the South African Revenue Service (SARS) e-filing on the internet. Previously, e-filing with SARS was possible only for individual income tax returns.

S

South Africa

Taxes on corporate income

Normal tax
In South Africa, the tax rate applicable for corporate income of companies for tax years ending between 1 April 2008 and 31 March 2010 is a flat 28%. In the three previous years the tax rate was 29%.

Close corporations, which are essentially a simplified form of company, are taxed at the same rate as companies and are subject to the same taxation rules.

An employment company, (i.e., a company that provides certain services that are performed by persons who have an interest in the company) is taxed at 33% of its taxable income. Similarly, a branch of a company with its effective place of management outside SA (i.e., a non-resident company) is taxed at 33%.

Small business corporations (i.e., a company with only natural persons as members/ owners and with gross income of not more than ZAR 14 million) are taxed at 0% on the first ZAR 54,200 of taxable income earned, 10% on the amount above ZAR 54,200, but not exceeding ZAR 300,000, and 28% on the amount exceeding ZAR 300,000.

To reduce the compliance costs for very small companies, a turnover-based presumptive tax is effective after 1 March 2009. Companies with a turnover of less than ZAR 1 million per year can elect to pay this tax instead of normal corporate income tax, at a rate ranging from 0 to 7.5%, depending on the turnover.

Special rates apply in certain industries, such as insurance and mining.

Secondary tax on companies (STC)
STC is levied at a rate of 10% (12.5% for dividends distributed before 1 October 2007) on the net dividends declared by SA resident companies. The net dividend amount is calculated by deducting dividends accrued from dividends declared during the dividend cycle. The company declaring the dividend, not the recipient, is liable for payment of the tax. Branches of foreign companies are exempt from STC but subject to a higher statutory income tax rate.

STC is in the process of being replaced with a withholding tax on dividends, which will be charged at the rate of 10%. In the case of foreign shareholders, the rate may be reduced by an applicable double taxation agreement. It is anticipated that the switch from STC to a withholding tax will become effective in the latter part of 2010. As part of the change, all dividend credits (i.e., dividends accrued to the company that currently can be set-off against dividends declared) will expire.

Capital gains tax
Although the capital gains tax forms part of income tax, the two taxes are not fully integrated. Gains realised by companies are taxed at the normal corporate income tax rate. However, only 50% of gains are included in the taxable income, bringing the effective rate for gains down to 14% (starting from the 2008/9 tax year).

Mining companies
There are two formulae: one for gold-mining companies that have elected to be exempt from secondary tax on companies (STC) and the other for such companies that are subject to STC. The formula for gold-mining companies subject to STC will, from the

12-month period ending 31 March 2010, be Y = 34 – 170/x, and for those exempt from STC, Y = 43 – 215/x. For these formulae, the following applies.

x = the ratio, expressed as a percentage, is calculated as follows:

$$\frac{\text{Taxable income from gold mining}}{\text{Total revenue (turnover) from gold mining}}$$

and

y = calculated percentage which represents the rate of tax to be levied

The maximum tax rate, which applies only to companies income from specified oil and gas activities is capped at 28% as from the 2008/9 tax year and the companies are entitled to enter into so-called fiscal stabilisation agreements with the SA government to "lock in" this rate. The agreement will not prevent the company from benefiting from any possible rate reduction in the future.

The rate of STC for the companies engaged in SA oil and gas activities is 5%. Where, however, a company was engaged in oil and gas activities under the so-called OP 26 right (a right to mine oil and gas), it is completely exempt from STC. The normal STC rate of 10% will apply, if the company is engaged in refining.

The branches of foreign companies engaged in SA oil and gas activities are taxed at a maximum rate of 31%.

Long-term insurance companies
Life insurance companies are obliged to follow the "four-fund approach", with policies divided into four funds, depending on the nature of the beneficiary. Each fund is then allocated assets according to the risk carried by the fund. Funds are treated as separate taxpayers and taxed at four separate rates. These rates are 30% for individual policyholder funds, 0% for untaxed policyholder funds, 28% for company policyholder funds, and 28% for corporate funds.

Corporate residence

A SA resident company is subject to tax on its worldwide income, irrespective of source. Non-residents are taxable on SA actual or deemed source income.

A company is resident in SA, if it is incorporated, established or formed in SA, or has its place of effective management in SA. However, a company that is deemed to be exclusively resident in another country by the terms of a double taxation agreement is excluded from SA residency.

The place of effective management is, in terms of the Interpretation Note issued by the SARS, interpreted as the place where the operational management of the company is carried out. Where a double taxation agreement entered into by SA and a foreign country presumes a different interpretation, such as a place of directors' meeting, it is believed that SA will have to adopt such different interpretation. However, such approach has not yet been tested by the courts.

S

South Africa

Royalties and know-how payments made to non-residents for the use of or right to use intellectual property rights in SA are deemed to be from an SA source. The payer of the royalty or know-how payment is obliged to deduct a withholding tax of 12% of this payment, which is a final tax payable by the recipient of such income. The 12% withholding tax may be reduced by the terms of the relevant tax treaty.

If one or more residents together hold more than 50% of the voting or participation rights in a foreign company then it is a "controlled foreign company" (CFC) in relation to those residents. The income of a CFC is imputed to the controlling holders in proportion to their holdings, subject to certain exclusions and tax credits where applicable.

Foreign dividends are, in principle, taxed in SA, except for the exemptions applicable to "qualifying" dividends. A qualifying foreign dividend requires a holding by the recipient of at least 20% of the total equity share capital and voting rights in the company declaring the dividend.

Other taxes

Value-added tax (VAT)

VAT is an indirect tax, which is largely directed at the domestic consumption of goods and services and at goods imported into SA. The tax is designed to be paid mainly by the ultimate consumer or purchaser in SA. It is levied at two rates, namely a standard rate (currently 14%) and a zero rate (0%).

All suppliers of goods and services having an annual turnover currently exceeding ZAR 1,000,000 are obliged to register as VAT vendors and to charge output VAT. Other vendors may elect to register as VAT vendors provided their annual turnover exceeds ZAR 50,000. If they do not register, they are prohibited from charging VAT on goods or services they supply and claiming an input tax (rebate of VAT paid) on goods and services which they acquire.

Supplies which are charged with tax at a zero rate are primarily supplies of goods or services which are exported from SA. Standard rated and zero rated supplies are known as taxable supplies. Other supplies are known as exempt and non-supplies. Very few business transactions carried out in SA are not subject to VAT. The tax is collected by businesses which are registered as vendors with SARS on all taxable supplies throughout the production and distribution chain. Sales or supplies by non-vendors are not subject to VAT. Under the VAT system, vendors normally pay VAT on expenses (input tax) and charge VAT on supplies made (output tax). This mechanism, therefore, ensures that only the so-called 'added-value' is taxed. Due to VAT being a self-assessment system, the output tax collected may be reduced by input tax paid. Thereafter, the net amount is payable to, or refundable by, the SARS. The self-assessment returns are due regularly within prescribed periods (tax periods).

An invoice-based VAT system has been in force since 30 September 1991. The VAT system is similar to those used in Western Europe and New Zealand.

Vendor: A vendor is a person who is registered or is required to be registered as a vendor. There are two criteria for registration: the carrying on of an enterprise and the value of taxable supplies. A person who does not carry on an enterprise cannot register as a vendor. An enterprise is any enterprise or activity carried on continuously or regularly within or partly within SA in the course of which goods or services are supplied for a consideration, whether or not for a profit. Included are certain activities of public authorities, local authorities, welfare organisations and share block companies. Specifically excluded are the activities of a permanent, independent branch located outside SA, services rendered by an employee to his employer and activities involving the making of exempt supplies.

If a person (company, individual, trust, or partnership) carries on an enterprise and has a taxable supplies turnover for a past or future 12-month period in excess of ZAR 1,000,000, it must register as a vendor. Taxable supplies include supplies at the standard rate or the zero rate but exclude (for registration purposes) exempt supplies and certain abnormal turnover (e.g., that are attributable to the cessation of an enterprise).

If the value of taxable supplies of a person carrying on an enterprise is less than this amount, the person may voluntarily register as a vendor in certain circumstances.

Once registered, vendors pay VAT on taxable supplies made to them for the purpose of their enterprise and charge VAT on the taxable supplies made by them in the course or furtherance of their enterprise. If the VAT the vendor pays exceeds the VAT the vendor charges in a tax period, the vendor obtains a refund of the excess from the Receiver of Revenue. If the VAT charged exceeds the VAT paid by a vendor in a tax period, the vendor pays the excess to the receiver. Depending on the value of taxable supplies and the vendor's choice, a vendor will have a one, two, or four (calendar) month tax period. Farmers may (subject to certain turnover requirements) elect to have a six calendar month tax period. For each tax period a vendor must submit a VAT return together with the payment of any VAT liability. The return also activates a refund of VAT in appropriate cases.

Goods and services: For a liability for VAT to exist, there must be a supply or importation of goods or services. Goods are corporeal movable things, fixed property and real rights in such things and property. The meaning of "services" is very broad and includes the granting, assignment, cession, or surrender of any right or the making available of any facility or advantage.

Imports: Services imported by a vendor and utilised or consumed by the vendor for the making of taxable supplies are not subject to VAT. In addition, the VAT Act has a schedule that lists goods that are exempt from VAT on importation, whether by a vendor or an unregistered person.

Zero-rated supplies: The VAT Act contains a list of the supplies of goods or services that are taxed at the zero rate. Most of the items refer to exports and international transport, but other specified goods utilised for farming purposes, the sale of an enterprise as a going concern, fuel subject to the fuel levy and deemed supplies by welfare organisations are also zero-rated.

A zero-rated supply made by a vendor is subject to VAT but at a rate of 0%. Under a zero-rated supply a vendor does not charge VAT on the consideration for the supply and obtains a refund or credit for the VAT paid on taxable supplies utilised in the making of the zero-rated supplies.

South Africa

Exempt supplies: In addition to zero-rated supplies, the VAT Act contains a list of the supplies of goods or services that are exempt from VAT. From 1 October 1996 all fee-based financial services are subject to VAT. The charging of interest remains exempt. Other exempt supplies include residential rentals, basic foodstuffs, non-international passenger transport by road or rail and educational services. Under exempt supplies by vendors, the vendors do not charge VAT on the supply, and they are not entitled to a deduction or credit for the VAT paid by them on goods and services supplied to them for the making of the exempt supply. Accordingly, vendors treat the VAT paid by them, and for which they do not obtain a deduction or credit, as another cost and recover it in the consideration they charge for the making of the exempt supply.

Skills development levy (SDL)
The Skills Development Levy (SDL) is a compulsory levy to fund the education and training as envisaged by the Skills Development Act. The levy is payable by an employer and cannot be deducted from the remuneration payable to an employee. Small employers with an annual payroll of less than ZAR 500,000 are exempt from the levy. SDL is levied at the rate of 1% of payroll. It is payable monthly, together with income tax that the employer has withheld on its employees' salaries.

Unemployment insurance fund (UIF) contributions
Employers are required to contribute on behalf of their employees on a personalised basis to the UIF. The rate of contributions is 1% of gross remuneration payable to an employee, however, the monthly cap of ZAR 124.78 applies. Another 1%, subject to the same cap, is payable by the employee and withheld by the employer.

Compensation for occupational injuries and diseases (COIDA) fund
Employers are liable for making annual contributions to the COIDA Fund. COIDA contributions are a payroll cost that cannot be deducted from the employee's salary. The rates vary depending on the employer's industry, for example, a rate of 1.62% is applied to the salaries of employees involved in the manufacture of pottery up to a maximum salary band of ZAR 214,305 per annum.

Donations tax
Donations tax is payable by the resident companies at a flat rate of 20% on the donations made. An annual exemption of ZAR 10,000 is available.

Public companies, comprising mostly listed companies, are exempt from donations tax. Also, an exemption is available for donations made to certain charities and other non-profit organisations. Disposal of assets below their market value is a donation and, at least theoretically, subject to donations tax.

Securities transfer tax (STT)
Stamp duty and uncertified securities tax has been abolished and replaced by securities transfer tax (STT). STT came into effect on 1 July 2008 and applies to the transfer of listed and unlisted securities on or after 1 July 2008. The tax rate is 0.25%, which is applied to the taxable amount in respect of the transfer of a security. The taxable amount is usually the consideration for which the security is purchased or the market value of the security, if the consideration declared is less than the market value or if no consideration was paid. STT will be payable by the company that has issued the shares in question. However, the company can recover the tax from the person acquiring the shares.

Transfer duty
A transfer duty is levied on the sale or transfer of immovable property. The rate applicable to companies is 8%, calculated on the higher of purchase price or market value. Transfers of immovable property subject to VAT are exempt from transfer duty.

Customs duties
Customs duties are charged on importation of goods into SA. The import duties may include anti-dumping and countervailing duties. No customs duties are charged on trade between SA and Botswana, Lesotho, Namibia and Swaziland, as these five countries constitute a Southern African Customs Union.

Excise duties
Excise duty is levied on certain locally manufactured goods as well as their imported equivalents. A specific duty at a pre-determined amount is levied on tobacco and liquor, and an *ad valorem* duty (calculated as a percentage of price) on cosmetics, televisions, audio equipment, and automobiles. Relief from excise duty is available for exported products and for certain products produced in the course of specified farming, forestry and (limited) manufacturing activities.

Fuel levy
A fuel levy is charged on petroleum fuel sold. From 1 April 2009, the levy is 150 cents per litre of petrol and 135 cents per litre of diesel.

Electricity levy
Due to the inability of the national electricity provider, Eskom, to meet the growing demand for electricity, SA has experienced what may be called an energy crisis. To support energy efficiency, the government has implemented a 2 cents/kWh levy on electricity generated from non-renewable sources. The levy is collected at the source by the electricity producer. The levy is effective from 1 July 2009.

Air passenger tax
Passengers departing on international flights pay air passenger tax at the rate of ZAR 80 on flights to Botswana, Lesotho, Namibia and Swaziland, and ZAR 150 on other flights. The tax is added to the price of the ticket.

Branch income

SA branches of foreign companies are not considered to be separate legal entities for tax purposes and no tax is withheld on transfers of profits to the head office. Branches of foreign companies are taxed at a rate of 33% for tax years ending on or after 1 April 2008. For the three previous tax years, the companies are taxed at the rate of 34% and are exempt from STC.

However, a branch must register as a taxpayer and submit tax returns. Separate financial statements must be drawn up for the SA trading operations. For all practical purposes, the SARS will treat the branch as a separate entity. For example, inter-branch cost recoveries levied by the head office incurred in the production of SA income normally will be allowed as a deduction by the branch.

In terms of double taxation agreements, the taxation of branches is limited to cases where the branch constitutes a permanent establishment.

S

South Africa

Income determination

Inventory valuation
Inventories generally are stated at the lower of cost or net realisable value. Write-downs of inventory for slow-moving and obsolete items must be justified, and a general policy on a percentage basis is not permitted. LIFO (last-in, first-out) is not accepted for tax purposes.

Capital gains
A total of 50% of net capital gains realised on the disposal of capital assets is included in taxable income from 1 October 2001 for companies and trusts other than special trusts. Special trusts and life assurance individual policyholder funds will include 25% of the realised net capital gains in taxable income. Currently, capital gains tax does not apply to retirement funds.

Inter-company dividends
Dividends, other than foreign dividends, are not subject to tax in the hands of companies, but the company declaring the dividend is liable for STC. Qualifying foreign dividends are also not subject to tax where they are received by resident shareholders holding in excess of 20% of the equity share capital and voting rights of the company declaring the dividend. Dividends received by residents holding less than 20% of such capital will be taxable in SA subject to a tax credit for foreign withholding taxes payable by the recipient shareholder.

Foreign income
Foreign income received by a SA resident company is subject to tax in SA. Double taxation may be avoided under certain double taxation agreements or by way of unilateral credit for foreign tax payable on foreign income.

Section 6quat of the South African Income Tax Act makes provision for a rebate against normal SA tax in respect of foreign taxes pain on *foreign sourced income* or a deduction against income of foreign taxes paid on SA *sourced income*. In both instances the taxpayer must be a SA resident, the income must be included in their taxable income and is not exempt and that income was subject to a foreign which is not recoverable. The rebate is limited to the total normal tax payable calculated by applying the ratio of the total taxable income attributable to the foreign tax to the total taxable income. The deduction, however, may not exceed the income on which the foreign tax was levied.

Stock dividends
Stock dividends (capitalisation issues of shares) are not subject to tax or STC, until the stock is realised.

Other significant items
Transfer pricing: Transfer pricing legislation has been in SA law since 1995, however it has only been in recent years that SARS has focussed on this area of taxation. The rules require those liable to tax in SA to follow arm's-length principles in their dealings with inter alia connected persons that are not tax residents of SA.

Section 31 of the South African Income Tax Act of 1962 combines transfer pricing and thin capitalisation (explained below) measures. Section 31(2) provides the commissioner the power to adjust the consideration of a transaction to an arm's-length price for the purposes of computing the South African taxable income of a taxpayer.

This rule applies to both goods and services as well as to direct and indirect financial assistance.

Section 31 is a discretionary section which means that whilst the taxpayer can place some comfort on the fact that the commissioner must have applied due care and reasonableness in raising a transfer pricing adjustment, the onus of proof for rebutting such adjustments rests squarely with the taxpayer.

Thin capitalisation rules: The thin capitalisation rules may be applied by SARS where financial assistance, such as a loan, advance or debt, or the provision of any security, is granted by a non-resident investor to a resident investee who is either a connected person, or a corporate entity in which the investor has a direct or indirect interest entitling it to participate in not less than 25% of the dividends, profits, capital or votes.

The thin capitalisation rules, when applied, disallow the deductibility of interest paid by the SA resident to the foreign lender, to the extent that such interest is considered to be excessive by the SARS. The excessive interest is determined in terms of the formula:

$$A = B \times [(C-D)/C]$$

Where:

A = Disallowable interest, limited to interest incurred in respect of financial assistance granted on or after 19 July 1995

B = Total interest incurred during the year in respect of all financial assistance in existence during the year

C = The weighted average of all interest-bearing financial assistance in existence during the year

D = The greater of: three times the fixed capital of the SA company; or the weighted average of all interest-bearing financial assistance granted prior to 19 July 1995 which existed during the year.

In broad terms, the rules will not be applied if the debt-to-equity ratio falls within a safe haven ratio of 3:1. In other words, where the financial assistance granted by the non-resident investor does not exceed three times the fixed capital (being essentially share capital, share premium and accumulated profits) of the resident investee and the interest rate does not exceed the weighted average of prime plus 2% for SA Rand denominated loans, or the relevant weighted average interbank rate plus 2% for loans denominated in other currencies.

These rules do not apply to financial assistance granted by a "parent" company to its branch operating as an external company in SA.

Deductions

Depreciation and depletion
A depreciation (wear and tear) allowance may be deducted on movable assets used for the purpose of trade. There are no statutory provisions relating to rates of wear and tear, but SARS has published a table of periods over which the assets may be written

South Africa

off, in the absence of evidence to support a different write off period. The rates of wear and tear, based on the cash cost, are calculated either according to the straight-line or diminishing balance method *(see Capital investment in the Tax incentives section)*

New and unused machinery used in the process of manufacture or in a similar process is depreciable at the rate of 40% in the first year of use and 20% in the three following years. If the machinery is not new and unused, an allowance of 20% per year over five years is available.

An accelerated depreciation schedule (50% in the first year of use, 30% in the second and 20% in the third year) applies to the machinery and articles used in farming, production of biodiesel or bio-ethanol and production of energy from renewable sources.

Buildings and other permanent structures may not be depreciated, apart from an annual allowance for each of the following:

1. Buildings used in a process of manufacture or a process similar to a process of manufacture – For buildings erected before 1 January 1989 a 2% per year rate applies. For buildings erected after 1 January 1989, a 5% rate applies. However, buildings erected between 1 July 1996 and 30 September 1999 are subject to an accelerated depreciation rate of 10% per year;
2. Hotel buildings – For hotel buildings erected from 4 June 1988 a 5% rate applies. For buildings built prior to 4 June 1988 the rate of 2% applies. Improvements within the existing building framework that commenced on or after 17 March 1993 are depreciated at the rate of 20%;
3. Agricultural cooperative storage buildings – Buildings erected on or after 1 January 1989 are subject to a 5% rate. Buildings built prior to 1 January 1989 are subject to a 2% rate;
4. Housing projects of not less than five units – Housing projects of not less than five units of residential accommodation, which consist of more than one room and the erection of which commenced on or after 1 April 1982 and before 21 October 2008, are subject to a 2% rate of depreciation. After 21 October 2008, a new allowance of 5% is available on this type of property. The 5% depreciation rate is available to the taxpayer provided that the unit is used by the taxpayer solely for trade purposes, the unit is situated in SA and the taxpayer owns at least five units in SA used for the purposes of trade. An additional allowance will be available for a low-cost residential unit. Additionally, from 21 October 2008, taxpayers also are granted relief for the transfer of ownership on a contract for deed basis of employer provided low cost residential units to employees;
5. Buildings in urban development zones – *More discussion can be found in "Capital investment in the tax incentives section*;
6. Specific allowances are also provided for pipelines, transmission lines, railway lines, airport property, ships, mining operations, and other qualifying industrial assets;
7. Buildings used and specifically equipped for certain research and development activities can be depreciated 50% in the first year of use, 30% in the second and 20% in the third year; and
8. Commercial buildings – The cost to the taxpayer of any new and unused building owned by the taxpayer, or any new and unused improvement to any building owned by the taxpayer, if that building or improvement wholly or mainly is used by the taxpayer for trade purposes, other than the provision of residential

accommodation is subject to a 5% rate of depreciation. This allowance is applicable to any building or improvement contracted for on or after 1 April 2007 and the construction of which commenced on or after 1 April 2007.

An allowance for assets disposed of or scrapped during a year of assessment is determined by reference to the cost less allowances already granted and the proceeds on disposal (if any). Recoupments of allowances granted are taxable where disposal proceeds exceed the tax basis at the time of sale. Such recoupments cannot exceed the cost of the asset. Proceeds above cost will be taxed as a capital gain.

Book depreciation does not need to be consistent with tax depreciation.

No cost or percentage depletion is available for natural resources.

Net operating losses
Losses may be carried forward indefinitely, provided an active trade or business of a similar nature is carried on without interruption. There is no loss carryback in SA.

Payments to foreign affiliates
Deductions may be claimed for royalties, managerial service fees and interest charges paid to foreign affiliates, provided such amounts approximate those that would be paid to an unrelated entity in an arm's-length transaction.

Interest deductions may be limited where the paying company is thinly capitalised *(refer to the Thin capitalisation rules)*.

Specific provisions apply for "bullet interest" (bullet interest is a once off upfront lump sum payment of interest). Any interest expenditure must be spread over the life of the interest-bearing arrangement on the compounding accrual basis.

Taxes
Payroll taxes are deductible from taxable income for the corporation.

Research and development (R&D)
To encourage innovation, the current costs related to certain R&D activities carried on in SA are 150% deductible. The cost of machinery and other capital assets acquired for the purposes of research and development may be depreciated 50% in the first year of use, 30% in the second and 20% in the third year.

Inventory
The cost of inventory is, in principle, deductible as soon as the inventory is acquired. However, at the end of each year the cost of the inventory still on hand has to be added to the company's income. Then in the next year, it can be deducted again. This has the effect of timing the deduction of the cost of inventory to match the time of its realisation.

Assets acquired for shares issued
When current assets are acquired by a company in return for the shares or debt instruments issued to the seller, the purchaser of the assets may deduct the lesser of the market value of the assets immediately after acquisition or the market value of the shares immediately after acquisition.

S

South Africa

Group taxation

Group taxation generally is not permitted in SA. However, relief is given for transactions between group companies to allow for reorganisations, provided certain requirements are met.

In general, the relief will only apply to transactions between companies within the same group. A group of companies is defined as a controlling company and one or more controlled companies in relation to that controlling company. A controlling company means a company holding directly or indirectly at least 70% of the equity of any other company. After 1 October 2007, non-resident companies cannot form part of a group of companies.

Corporate rollover relief is available for company formation, asset-for-share transaction, amalgamation transaction, intra-group transaction, unbundling transaction, and a transaction relating to liquidation, winding-up and deregistration.

The relief may cover the capital gains tax arising from the disposal of capital assets, income tax arising from the disposal of a depreciable asset, income tax arising from the disposal of trading stock, donations tax arising from the disposal of an asset, STC and transaction taxes.

Tax incentives

Inward investment
Cash grants, received within the terms of a Government Incentive Scheme (see Other incentives) by taxpayers with manufacturing operations or similar processes are exempt from income tax on such grants.

Capital investment
The available capital incentives are as follows:

1. For assets brought into use after 15 December 1989, a 20% annual rate of depreciation applies to plant and machinery used in a process of manufacture or in a similar process or to machinery and equipment used in the hotel trade. An accelerated rate of 33⅓% per year is applicable for new and unused plant and machinery acquired and placed in service in a manufacturing process under an agreement executed during the period commencing on 1 July 1996 and ending on 30 September 1999. Plant and machinery brought into use on or after 1 March 2002 that was acquired in terms of an agreement concluded after 1 March 2002, will qualify for a 40% allowance in the first year and a 20% allowance in the following three years. Machinery and equipment used for farming are depreciated at the rate of 50% in the first year, 30% in the next year and 20% in the final year;
2. Residential buildings, initial allowance – If construction commenced prior to 21 October 2008, housing projects of not less than five units may qualify for an initial depreciation allowance of 10% of the cost in the year in which they are completed and rented for the first time; and
3. Buildings in urban development zones – Improvements to an existing building in an urban development zone, here the existing structural or exterior framework is preserved and brought into before 31 March 2014, qualify for an accelerated allowance of 20% per year. Buildings that are erected, extended or added to in an urban development zone on or after 21 October 2008 and which are not covered

by the first mentioned allowance qualify for a 20% allowance in the first year and a 8% allowance in the following 10 years. From 21 October 2008, new and unused low-income residential units located in urban development zone demarcations will be subject to an additional annual depreciation allowance. The rate will be 25% in the first year, 13% in the succeeding five years and 10% in the year following the last year. Improvements will be subject to a depreciation allowance of 25% over a period of four years.

Other incentives

Taxpayers may also obtain the following incentives:

1. The Critical Infrastructure Fund is a cash grant for projects that are designed to improve critical infrastructure in SA. The incentive covers up to 30% of the development costs in qualifying infrastructure;

2. The Foreign Investment Grant is available to registered, incorporated foreign investors in new manufacturing businesses in SA. It covers up to 15% of the costs to a limit of ZAR 3 million of moving new machinery and equipment from abroad to a manufacturing location in SA;

3. The Skills Support Programme is a cash grant for skills development with the objective of encouraging greater investment in training and creating opportunities for the introduction of new advanced skills;

4. Industrial policy projects – In 2008, a ZAR 2 billion incentive package for investors in energy efficient projects over three years was announced. The incentive is available for industrial projects participating in the manufacturing sector (other than alcohol or alcohol related products, tobacco or tobacco related products, arms and ammunition and bio-fuels, which have a negative impact on food security). Companies are divided into those with a qualifying status and those with a preferred status. The status is determined in terms of a point system. The proposed project must either be a "brownfield project" (expansion or upgrade of an existing industrial project) or a "greenfield project" (a wholly new industrial project, which uses new and unused manufacturing assets). Approved projects may be granted a tax allowance known as an additional investment allowance equal to: 55% of the cost of any manufacturing asset used in an industrial policy project with preferred status; or 35% of the cost of any manufacturing asset used in any other approved industrial policy project.
   However, the additional investment allowance may not exceed ZAR 900 million in the case of any greenfield project with a preferred status, or ZAR 550 million in the case of any other greenfield project; or ZAR 550 million in the case of any brownfield project with a preferred status, or ZAR 350 million in the case of any other brownfield project.
   In addition to the above, a company may also claim a deduction known as an additional training allowance; and

5. Venture capital companies – In order to assist small- and medium-sized businesses to raise capital to finance businesses, a tax incentive for investors in small- and medium-sized enterprises through venture capital companies has been introduced. This incentive became effective on 1 July 2009 and will last for 12 years.
   A deduction will be allowed from the income of an individual, a listed company (or a controlled group company in relation to a listed company) in respect of expenditure actually incurred by that person with respect of shares issued to that person by a venture capital company. A company may deduct its entire expenditure in respect of shares, provided that the shares held by that company and other companies within the same group do not constitute more than 10% of

S

South Africa

the equity shares of the venture capital company. The deduction available to an individual is capped at ZAR 750,000. A venture capital company is essentially a holding company deriving its income from equity investments in small and medium companies that, in turn, derive their income from active trade within SA. A venture capital company has to be specifically approved by SARS.

Incentives are also available for industrial export.

Withholding taxes (WHT)

Resident corporations
No withholding taxes, other than payroll taxes, are levied against payments to resident corporations.

Royalties payable to non-residents
The accruals and receipts by non-residents of South-African sourced royalties are subject to withholding taxes, as follows:

	Rate %
All countries other than those listed below	12
Austria, Belgium (1), Cyprus (1), Denmark (1), Finland (1), France (1,2), Germany (2), Hungary (1), Ireland (1), Israel (2,3), Luxembourg (1), Malawi (2), Mauritius (1), The Netherlands (1,2), Norway (1), Russia, Swaziland (2), Sweden (1,2), Switzerland (1), United Kingdom (2), United States (1), Zambia (2) and Zimbabwe (2)	0
Australia (1,2), Croatia, Greece (1,2), Mozambique (1,2), Singapore (1) and Spain (1,2)	5
Italy (1) and Canada (4)	6
Nigeria (1,2)	7.5
Oman (1,2)	8
Algeria (1), Belarus (1,2,6), Botswana (1,2), Brazil (1,2,7), Bulgaria (1,2,6,8), Canada (1), People's Republic of China (5), Czech Republic (1), Ghana (1,2), India (1), Indonesia (1), Iran (1), Japan (1), Republic of Korea (1), Kuwait (1,2), Lesotho (1), Malta (1), Namibia (1), Portugal (1,2), New Zealand (1), Pakistan (1), Poland (1), Saudi Arabia (1,2), Slovak Republic (1), Taiwan (1), Tanzania (1,2), Tunisia (1), Turkey (1,2), Ukraine (1) and Uganda (1)	10
Egypt (1), Romania (1) and Thailand (1)	15
Ethiopia (1,2)	20

Notes

1. Recipient is the beneficial owner of the royalty.
2. Royalty is subject to tax in recipient country.
3. 15% is levied on royalties for cinematographic or television films.
4. The maximum rate for copyright royalties, royalties for use of computer software and patents concerning industrial, commercial and scientific experience is 6% of the royalties paid, otherwise 10%.
5. Maximum rate of 10% of the adjusted amount (being 70% of the gross royalties) for use of industrial, commercial or scientific equipment.
6. The 5% rate applies to royalties for the use of a copyright. A 7% rate applies to royalties for the use of patents, trademarks, designs, models, etc.
7. In respect of right to use industrial, commercial or scientific equipment and transport vehicles a 10% rate applies.
8. Maximum rate of 15% on royalties arising from the use of, or the right to use trademarks.

As of 6 March 2010 the following information holds:

- The treaty with the United Kingdom extends to Grenada and the Seychelles;
- Comprehensive agreements have been ratified by SA with the Democratic Republic of Congo, Gabon, Rwanda and Sudan;
- Comprehensive agreements have been signed but not ratified with Germany and Mexico;
- Comprehensive agreements or amendments to current agreements have been negotiated or renegotiated but not signed with Bangladesh, Chile, Cuba, Cyprus, Estonia, Ireland, Kenya, Kuwait, Lesotho, Latvia, Lithuania, Madagascar, Malawi, Malta, Morocco, Namibia, Oman, Qatar, Serbia, Seychelles, Singapore, Sri Lanka, Sweden, Syria, United Arab Emirates, United Kingdom, Zambia, Zimbabwe and Vietnam; and
- There is a limited sea and air transport agreement with Brazil.

Non-resident entertainers and sportspersons

A withholding tax at the rate of 15% applies to all payments made to non-resident entertainers and sports persons in respect of their activities exercised in SA. This tax applies in respect of all activities exercised on or after 28 July 2006.

Tax administration

Returns

The corporate fiscal year is the same as the company's financial year. It may be changed upon application showing reasonable cause. Annual income tax returns must be submitted within one year from the end of the company's fiscal year.

Payments

Payments are made with provisional returns filed at six-month intervals from the fiscal year-end and are generally based on the last issued assessment. Interest is charged on any underpayment outstanding for more than six months after the fiscal year-end except in the case of February year-ends, in which case it is seven months. Any balance (together with interest) is then paid following assessment.

S

Corporate taxes in Spain

For more information, contact:

Santiago Barrenechea
Landwell, Abogados y Asesores Fiscales
Torrelaguna, 75
28027 Madrid, Spain
Tel: +34 915 684 400
Email: santiago.barrenechea@es.landwellglobal.com

Significant developments

Over the past 12 months, the following significant amendments have been made to Spanish law on direct taxation of companies:

- A Royal Decree law passed on 9 April 2010 (RDL 6/2010) approves certain measures to boost economic recovery. The measures laid down in this legislation include, most notably, the extension until 2012 of free depreciation (a method to depreciate the assets can be chosen that may result in an effective depreciation higher than that which results from established methods) for new tangible fixed assets and investments in real estate used for business activities which can be availed of by companies if they maintain or increase their staff levels. This tax relief introduced with Law 4/2008 was initially applicable for tax years commencing in 2009 and 2010 and has now been extended to tax years 2011 and 2012.
- A law passed on 1 March 2010 (Law 2/2010) incorporates certain European Union (EU) directives on indirect taxation into Spanish law amending Spain's non-residents' income tax law.
  This law increases the types of expenses which are tax deductible when determining taxable income for non-residents' income tax levied on Spanish non-residents with tax residence in the EU and no Permanent Establishment (PE) in Spain. For this tax, deductible expenses now include all expenses stated in personal income tax law which are directly related to income earned in Spain and directly and inseparably linked to an activity carried out in Spain.
- The state general budget law for 2010 (Law 26/2009) was passed on 23 December 2009. The most notable amendments made with this law are as follows:
  1. Increase of the tax rate levied on savings income and certain capital income and gains to 19%.
  2. Increase of (i) the general rate of withholding for corporate income tax, (ii) the non-residents' income tax rate levied on sums transferred by a PE to its head office, and (iii) the non-residents' income tax rate levied on dividends, interest and capital gains generated on transfers of assets, to 19%.
  3. The corporate income tax rate for companies which maintain or increase their staff levels and comply with certain requirements is reduced for tax years commencing in 2009, 2010 and 2011 as follows:
     a. For taxable income up to EUR 120,202.41, the tax rate is 20%; and
     b. For taxable income over EUR 120,202.41, the tax rate is 25%.
- A law passed on 26 October 2009 (Law 11/200) introduces a special regime for publicly traded real estate investment trusts (REITs) into Spanish law.

Taxes on corporate income

The general corporate income tax rate in Spain is currently 30%. Other tax rates (ranging from 25% to 35%) may apply depending on the type of company which is taxed and the type of business which is carried out.

Small companies (i.e., companies with a turnover under EUR 8 million in the preceding tax year) are taxed at the following rates:

- Taxable income up to EUR 120,202.41 is taxed at a 25% tax rate; and
- The part of the taxable income which exceeds this threshold is taxed at the general tax rate of 30%.

The tax rate levied on companies forming part of a group depends on the total amount of the corporate group's turnovers. The general 30% tax rate is levied when the sum of the group companies' turnovers exceeds EUR 8 million.

A new regulation came into force in Spain as of December 2009 which establishes lower tax rates for companies which maintain or increase their staff levels. These rates are as follows:

- Taxable income up to EUR 120,202.41 is taxed at a 20% tax rate.
- The part of the taxable income which exceeds this threshold is taxed at the tax rate of 25%.

These lower rates of 20% and 25% apply retroactively to tax years commencing after 1 January 2009 until tax years commencing in 2011 and are applicable on the compliance of, amongst others, the following requirements: (i) the income generated all the company's business activities does not exceed EUR 5 million; (ii) the company's total staff is not more than 25 employees; and (iii) the company's average number of employees during the twelve-month period following the commencement of the tax year in question is not less than one employee and not less than the company's average number of employees during the twelve-month period prior to the commencement of the tax year in question.

For PEs in Spain of foreign companies, non-residents' income tax is chargeable on their taxable income at a 30% tax rate. Non-residents' income tax is levied on non-established foreign companies/individuals which obtain income in Spain *(see section on Withholding tax)*.

Corporate residence

A company is resident in Spain and subject to corporate income tax on its worldwide income when:

- It has been incorporated in accordance with Spanish law;
- Its registered office is in Spain; and/or
- Its "effective" head office is in Spain.

Under Spanish law a company's "effective" head office is in Spain when its business activities are managed and controlled from Spain.

S

Spain

Companies established in a country or territory where no tax is levied or which is a tax haven are deemed to be tax resident in Spain in the following cases:

- When the company's main assets consist, directly or indirectly, of property located or rights fulfilled or exercised in Spain; and/or
- When the company's core business activity is carried on in Spain.

This presumption may be refuted by the company if it can prove that it is effectively administered and managed in the country or territory in which it is established and that it was incorporated and operates for valid economic and business reasons and not merely for the purpose of managing securities or other assets.

Other taxes

Value-added tax (VAT)
Spanish VAT is payable on supplies of goods and services carried out in Spanish VAT territory and on imports/intra-European Union acquisitions of goods and services. There are three rates for the different types of goods and services, which are as follows:

1. Ordinary rate of 16%, to be increased to 18% in July 2010, applied on regular supplies of goods and services.
2. Reduced rate of 7%, to be increased to 8% in July 2010, applied on basic necessities (e.g., food and agricultural products not included in the "super reduced" 4% rate (4%), dwellings, and other qualifying services).
3. Super reduced rate of 4% applied on basic necessities other than those classified under the reduced rate (e.g., bread, milk, books, medicine, etc.).

In the Canary Islands, a specific tax is applied in lieu of VAT, called the Canary Island General Indirect Tax (IGIC). The ordinary IGIC rate is 5% and the other IGIC rates are 0%, 2%, 9% and 13% (20% or 35% for tobacco). IGIC is similar to VAT but it has some significant differences, such as the exemption established for telecommunications services. Imports of tangible goods into the Canary Islands are subject to this tax. In Ceuta and Melilla, sales tax is applied instead of VAT.

Transfer tax
A transfer tax of 6 % or more frequently 7%, depending upon the region, is generally levied on *inter vivo* transfers, including real estate transfers and real estate leases that are exempt from VAT.

Second and ulterior transfers of buildings are exempt from VAT and thus, they are in principle, subject to transfer tax.

Residential leases are exempt from VAT and therefore subject to transfer tax.

Transfers of quoted or unquoted (listed or unlisted) securities are, in principle, exempt from both transfer tax and VAT, except in the following cases:

- Transfers of securities of a company whose real estate assets in Spain represent more than 50% of its total assets, or whose assets include securities in another company whose real estate assets in Spain represent at least 50% of its total assets are subject to and not exempt from transfer tax if the acquirer gains control of the real estate company as a result of the transfer; and

- Transfers of securities received in exchange for real estate contributions carried out on the incorporation of a company or on the execution of a subsequent capital increase are also subject to and not exempt from transfer tax provided that not more than three years have elapsed between the date on which the contribution was made and the date on which the securities are transferred.

In addition, acquisitions of assets by new businesses in the Canary Islands are exempt from transfer tax on the compliance of certain requirements.

Capital duty
A 1% capital duty applies to incorporations of companies and capital increases, reductions and contributions by shareholders. Capital duty is incompatible with transfer tax and stamp duty in certain cases, but it is compatible with VAT.

Stamp duty
A stamp duty is mostly levied on notarial instruments and records documenting transactions which have an economic value and need to be registered in public registries (e.g., company, land and industrial property registries). A stamp duty is incompatible with transfer tax and capital duty, but compatible with VAT. The general rate is between 0.75% and 2% depending on the region of Spain and the taxable event.

Stamp duty is also levied on certain commercial documents (e.g., bills of exchange, promissory notes), court and administrative documents.

Tax on non-resident companies owning real estate in Spain
Non-resident companies which own real estate or hold real property rights in Spain are subject to a special levy accrued on 31 December and declared and paid in January of the following year in the place and manner established by law. The tax is 3% of the assessed value of the real estate. This special levy is not applicable for companies resident in a country which has signed a tax treaty, which includes an exchange-of-information provision, with Spain if the ultimate shareholders of such companies are resident in Spain.

In addition, some other exceptions are established for this levy.

Business and professional activities tax
The business and professional activities tax is a local direct tax levied annually on the operation in Spain of business, professional or artistic activities, regardless of whether they are carried out in a particular premises or not. The tax payable depends on different factors such as the type of activity carried out and the location and size of the premises where the activity is carried out.

Corporate income taxpayers and non-resident companies carrying on an activity in Spain through a PE are exempt from this tax if their net turnover for the tax year of the last corporate/non-residents' income tax return filed prior to the date of accrual of the local tax (1 January) was less than EUR 1,000,000.

Others
In addition to the taxes stated above, other taxes may be charged on companies such as (i) real estate tax, levied annually by local authorities on the ownership of real estate; (ii) a local tax levied on the increase of the value of urban land, chargeable when urban real estate is sold; (iii) motor vehicle tax, charged on the ownership of vehicles; (iv) tax

S

Spain

on constructions, installations and building works, charged on the cost of certain works which require town planning licences; and (v) waste collection fees.

Branch income

Income obtained by a company resident in Spain through a branch located outside Spain is treated as income generated by the head office and taxed accordingly. A tax exemption regime is applicable in this case on the compliance of certain requirements.

Income obtained by a branch in Spain of a non-resident company is taxed at the standard corporate income tax rate of 30% for tax years commencing after 1 January 2008 and, in most cases, the regulations established by tax law for resident companies are applicable.

Payments made by a branch to its head office or other PE of its head office for royalties, interest, commissions or technical assistance fees are not tax deductible. Management and general administrative expenses incurred by the foreign head office which can be allocated to the branch are tax deductible, if the payments of these expenses are made following a criteria of continuity and rationality and provided that certain documentary requirements and other formalities are complied with.

Under Spanish law, income obtained by a branch which is repatriated to its head office is taxed at source at general withholding tax rate of 19%. This tax is not chargeable in the case of a PE of a company resident in the EU (unless the company is resident in a tax haven). Most tax treaties signed by Spain do not establish any provisions on this matter and in these cases, it is generally understood that no tax is chargeable on income repatriated by branches. Some tax treaties such as the treaties with the US, Canada and Indonesia, expressly establish a tax on income repatriated by branches. For example, US head offices are taxed at a 10% rate on the repatriated profits of a Spanish branch under the US/Spanish tax treaty.

Income determination

General rules
The general rule for determining income for corporate income tax purposes is that accounting rules should be followed unless tax law establishes otherwise. In order to maintain this consistency, corporate income tax/PE Non-residents' income tax returns include pages in which the company's accounting/commercial balance sheet and profit and loss account figures should be entered.

In Spain, the tax authorities are authorised to modify accounting results exclusively for the purpose of determining tax results if they observe that a company's accounting results have not been calculated in accordance with Spanish GAAP.

Inventory valuation
Inventory is valued at acquisition price or production cost under the average and first-in, first-out (FIFO) valuation methods (the replacement and base stock valuations methods may only be used in exceptional cases). Again since there are no specific tax rules for determining taxable income, accounting rules are also applicable for calculating valuation and obsolescence provisions for inventory.

Spain

Capital gains

Capital gains are taxable in the tax year in which they arise. They are treated as normal income and taxed at the standard corporate income tax rate of 30% (in the case of gains from real estate after taking into consideration an increase in the cost base for tax indexation purposes).

If the proceeds of the sale of qualifying tangible fixed assets and intangible assets or shares in companies are reinvested in similar assets within the time period established by law (from one year before the sale up to three years after the sale), the taxpayer may be eligible for a tax credit of 12% of the capital gain obtained from the sale (i.e., in this case, the effective capital gain taxation would be 18%). In the case of a sale of shares of a company, to be eligible for this tax credit, the interest in the company should be a minimum of 5% and should have been held for more than one year prior to the sale.

Inter-company domestic dividends

The amount of dividends included in the calculation of taxable income should be the gross amount. Upon meeting certain requirements, companies may be eligible for a tax credit for dividends equal to the tax rate applied by the company on the dividends received. This tax credit is generally allowed for the total dividends received from taxable domestic companies when the interest of the company receiving the dividend in the other company is 5% or more and such interest has been held for at least one year. This one-year holding period is deemed to be complied with if it is completed after the dividend is distributed.

This tax regime is to some extent the same as a tax exemption regime. When an interest in a company is less than 5% or is held for less than one year, the tax credit is 30% of half of the amount of the dividends received.

In addition, taxation on capital gains arising from the sale of shares by a company with at least a 5% interest in the subsidiary held for at least one year prior to the sale can be reduced by means of a tax credit for the tax rate applicable on the undistributed part of the subsidiary's profits generated during the company's holding period. The reason for this tax relief is that this capital gain is understood to be an underlying dividend.

Foreign income

Resident companies are taxed on their worldwide income. For foreign-source income, total or partial tax relief in the form of tax credits or exemptions is given if tax is levied on the income in both Spain and the foreign country where the income has been generated.

This tax relief may be available for:

- Economic double taxation, which is when the same income is taxed in the hands of two different taxpayers. For example another government taxes a foreign company on the income earned in that country and a Spanish resident shareholder is taxed on the dividends that it receives from the foreign company or the capital gains from transfers of its shares.
- Juridical double taxation, which is when the same income is taxed in two countries in the hands of the same taxpayer. For example the income is taxed (via a withholding tax) in the country where the income is generated and again in the other country where the recipient is resident.

S

Spain

The main characteristics of double tax relief are discussed below:

Dividends or profit-sharing income received by a Spanish company from a foreign company are tax exempt on the compliance of the following requirements:

a. The Spanish company has at least a 5% interest in the foreign company during the entire tax year prior to the tax year in which the dividend is paid. This one-year holding period is deemed to be complied with if it is completed after the dividend is distributed.
b. The foreign company is subject to a similar tax to Spanish corporate income tax and is not resident in a tax haven. The foreign tax is deemed to be similar to Spanish corporate income tax if the foreign company is resident in a country with which Spain has signed a tax treaty which establishes an exchange-of-information provision.
c. The income out of which the dividend is paid is generated from the business activities of the foreign company carried out abroad stipulated in corporate income tax law.

Capital gains arising from the sale of shares in foreign companies also qualify for a tax exemption provided that the requirements stated above are complied with during the holding period and the acquiring company is not resident in a tax haven. Tax exemption is limited in certain cases.

As an alternative to this "tax exemption" regime and applicable for dividend distributions only, a tax credit based on imputation is established. This tax credit allows the crediting of the foreign tax paid abroad on the income from which the dividends are paid and the foreign withholding tax paid on the profit distribution, up to the limit of the tax that would have been paid on the gross amount in Spain. The only requirement for the application of this "tax imputation" regime is that the Spanish company has at least a 5% interest in the foreign company during the twelve months prior to the date on which the dividend is due and payable. This one-year holding period is deemed to be complied with if it is completed after the dividend is distributed. The tax relief of this point may be carried forward for up to ten years.

Spanish international legislation provides for corporate income tax relief on "juridical" double taxation by applying the "tax imputation" regime. With this regime, gross foreign income (including foreign withholding tax paid) is considered for Spanish tax calculation purposes and a tax credit for the foreign withholding tax paid is applicable up to the amount of the corporate income tax that the company would have paid if such gross income had been obtained in Spain. The tax credit can be carried forward for up to 10 years, but the rate applicable will be the rate applicable at the moment when the tax credit is applied.

Under Spanish tax treaties and implemented EU tax directives, several methods have been established to avoid double taxation. The main one is the traditional deduction of a tax credit from the tax effectively paid. However, some treaties establish a tax exemption or the exclusive right to tax. Also, a tax-sparing clause is included in some treaties which allows for the deduction of not only the tax actually paid but a higher amount of tax.

Stock dividends

Corporate income tax is not levied on bonus shares (shares partially or totally given to shareholders in a capital increase charged against distributable reserves) although they should be taken into account when calculating the average cost of shares held for the levying of tax when the shares are sold.

Other significant items

The following items, amongst others, are excluded or deferred from taxable income:

- Distributed dividends corresponding to profits obtained by companies in tax years in which the flow-through tax regime (internal and international) has been applied; and
- Assets written up in accordance with revaluation laws and tax-protected restructuring transactions involving accounting capital gains.

Deductions

Depreciation (amortisation)

All assets, except land, are depreciable for tax purposes. Guideline tables of tax depreciation rates are established which state maximum per annum rates and maximum number of years of useful life for each asset type classified according to business sector. The straight-line depreciation method is normally used which is calculated over the asset's useful life and applied on the asset's cost or written-up value (if such write-up is acceptable for tax purposes). Off-book adjustments should be included in tax assessments if accounting depreciation exceeds tax depreciation/amortisation.

Qualifying assets with a useful life of more than one year can also be depreciated by one of the following declining-balance methods:

- By applying a constant percentage on the carrying amount of the asset multiplied by 1.5, 2, or 2.5 depending on the useful life of the asset (below five years, between five and eight years and over eight years, respectively); or
- By using the sum-of-digits method: The asset's acquisition price is multiplied by the ratio between the number of the years in which it is depreciated/amortised in a descending order (e.g., in a three-year useful life, 3 for the first year, 2 for the second and 1 for the third) and the total numbers for the years of the asset's useful life (1 + 2 + 3 = 6 for 3 years of useful life).

Buildings, furniture and fittings cannot be depreciated by the declining-balance methods.

Special depreciation plans for new assets can be approved by the tax authorities upon request, when they are subject to wear-and-tear at a higher rate than the normal rate applicable.

Recorded depreciation is fully tax deductible, even when it is higher than the depreciation which would result on applying any of the tax depreciation methods stated above, if the taxpayer is able to justify that the depreciation is real.

Mining assets and assets used for research and development, amongst others but not including buildings, can be freely depreciated/amortised for tax purposes.

Spain

Depletion is allowed for mining companies and companies involved in exploring/investigating natural oil resources as established in applicable legislation.

A 50% reduction may be applied for income obtained from licensing certain intangible assets on the compliance of certain requirements (the effective tax on this income would be 15%).

As from 2008, goodwill cannot be amortised under Spanish GAAP. However, it can be amortised for tax purposes at an annual rate of 5% on the compliance of certain requirements (e.g., it is acquired for consideration from a non-related party in accordance with the provisions of Section 42 of the Spanish Commercial Code and an obligatory non-distributable reserve is established).

New tangible fixed assets and property investments used for business activities and at the company's disposal in 2009, 2010, 2011 and 2012 can be freely depreciated, provided that the company's average number of staff during the year prior to the moment when the assets/property investments are at the disposal of the company is maintained during the following two years. Depreciation is fully tax deductible in this case even if it is not recorded in the company's profit and loss account.

Intangible assets with a specific useful life may be amortised and such amortisation is tax deductible even if it is not recorded in the company's profit and loss account, when the company complies with the following requirements: (i) the assets are acquired for consideration and (ii) the company does not form part of a group as defined in Section 42 of the Spanish Commercial Code. The tax deduction of the amortisation is up to 10% per annum; unless a lower useful life can be justified. If the two requirements stated above are complied with, amortisation on intangible assets which do not have a specific useful life is also tax deductible up to the 10% annual limit, regardless of whether they are amortised under Spanish GAAP or not.

Assets leased under financial lease contracts may be eligible, on the compliance of certain requirements, for the application of a special tax regime which enables accelerated depreciation (the part of the lease payments which corresponds to the recovery of the cost of the assets is tax deductible up to the limit of twice the straight-line tax depreciation rate).

Tax-loss carryforwards
Tax losses may be carried forward for 15 years but they cannot be carried back. There are no tax loss "baskets" (operating/capital) under Spanish law.

Complex rules may limit the use of tax losses of a company dissolved as a result of a restructuring operation and, in certain circumstances, when it has a change of shareholders.

Payments to foreign affiliates
Supplies of goods or services by a company not established in Spain to a Spanish group company should be valued at arm's length. If recorded expenses for such goods/services exceed arm's-length price, the tax deductibility of the excess amounts could be challenged in a tax inspection. The tax deductibility of expense charges received from tax havens is fully disallowed unless proper evidence of an actual service valued at arm's length can be provided.

For tax periods commencing after 1 January 2007, management services received from outside Spain and recorded as distribution of costs of a group centre do not have to be documented in a written agreement entered into before the commencement of the services to ensure the tax deductibility of the expenses (as previously was the case), although it would be recommendable to have such an agreement. For any other types of services, an agreement recorded before a notary public is not obligatory under Spanish law, but it is advisable.

As regards the taxation in Spain of the foreign company which supplies the services, the withholding tax rate to be applied on the gross income obtained by the company is 24%. Dividends, interest and capital gains generated as a result of a transfer of assets are taxed at a 19% withholding tax rate. If management services, technical assistance or the performance of studies are solely used outside Spain and are linked to business carried on abroad, then no withholding tax is applicable. In addition, under most tax treaties signed by Spain, "business profits" obtained in Spain by non-residents are exempt from withholding tax. However, "business profits" is a miscellaneous residual category. For instance, if the amount obtained qualifies as a royalty payment, withholding tax would apply at the reduced tax treaty rates if the foreign company can obtain a document from the tax authorities of its country of residence certifying its tax residence. If no tax treaty applies, then the above 24% withholding tax rate is applicable (see section on Withholding tax).

Taxes

Taxes, other than corporate income tax that are recorded as an expense due to their nature (e.g., business and professional activities tax or capital duty levied on the incorporation of a company, but not, for example, withholdings) are tax deductible expenses. In some cases, indirect taxes such as non-deductible VAT or transfer tax could be added to the value of assets for depreciation purposes.

However, penalties imposed for failure to pay taxes and surcharges for late filing/payment or for other tax infringements are not tax deductible.

Late payment interest recorded as an expense is, in principle, tax deductible.

Group taxation

Tax groupings for corporate income tax purposes

Under Spanish tax law, companies can form a group and apply a special tax consolidation regime for corporate income tax purposes. Companies forming a tax group should formally pass a resolution agreeing to do so before the beginning of the first tax year in which the tax consolidation regime will be applied.

To apply the tax consolidation regime, the controlling company of the tax group should hold a 75% or higher interest, either directly or indirectly, in the companies forming the tax group at the beginning of the first tax year in which the tax consolidation regime is applied and this interest should be maintained during the year unless the controlling company is dissolved. For tax years commencing after 1 January 2010, the interest requirement is 70% for companies listed on the Stock Exchange.

The main characteristics of the tax consolidation regime are as follows:

S

Spain

- The taxable income of the tax group is the sum of the taxable incomes of each of the companies forming the group;
- The tax losses of any of the companies forming the group can be offset against the tax profits of any of the other group companies;
- For the calculation of consolidated taxable income, the tax profits(losses) generated from transactions carried out between group companies are eliminated and only included in consolidated taxable income when (i) they are carried out with third parties, (ii) a group company participating in the internal operation ceases to form part of the tax group and (iii) the tax consolidation regime is no longer applied by the group for whatever reason;
- Specific limitations apply regarding the offsetting of tax losses or the application of tax credits generated by the group companies before they formed part of the tax group. Such tax losses/credits may be offset (applied) by the tax group up to the limit of the tax profits/tax liability of the company which generated the losses/credits; and
- No withholding tax is chargeable over payments made between companies of the tax group, e.g., interest, dividends, etc.

Tax groupings for VAT purposes

As from 1 January 2008, groups of companies may also choose to be taxed under a special tax consolidation regime for VAT purposes. This special regime is optional but once it has been opted for, it should be applied for a minimum of three years which is extendible unless it is expressly waived by the companies.

The VAT consolidation regime may only be applied by groups resident in Spanish VAT territory which do not form part of any other VAT grouping.

The controlling company of the group should be a legal entity or PE which is not dependent on any other entity established in Spanish VAT territory and it should hold at least a 50% interest in the subsidiary companies of the group for the entire calendar year.

With the application of the VAT consolidation regime, there are two different options for taxation:

- The aggregation system, where the balances of the VAT returns of the individual companies of the group are totalled. The right to a tax deduction is exercised by the individual companies; or
- The consolidation system, where, in addition, an individual company can opt to reduce the VAT taxable income for inter-company operations; which is limited to the "external" cost.

Tax incentives

Tax relief

No specific tax relief is established in Spanish law for foreign investors. However, relief may be availed of by Spanish and foreign-owned companies alike. The types of tax relief available under corporate income tax law in Spain are described below.

Spain

Tax relief for business activity or place of business activity includes
- 50% tax credit on corporate income tax levied on income obtained in Ceuta and Melilla through companies established and carrying on activities during a full business cycle in these enclaves;
- 99% tax credit on the corporate income tax levied on income obtained from the supply of local public services, except when the state company in question is owned, partially or wholly, by a quoted/non-quoted company or individual; and
- 50% tax credit on the corporate income tax levied on income obtained from exports of films, books and similar cultural items, if profits are reinvested in the acquisition of assets used for such activities. This tax credit will be gradually reduced over the coming years and eliminated in 2014.

Tax relief for promoting certain investments
Many current tax credits for promoting certain investments are to be reduced and finally eliminated.

However, the largest tax credits for promoting investments (tax credit for the reinvestment of extraordinary profits and tax credit for research and development (R&D)) as well as tax credits to prevent internal and international double taxation are maintained.

R&D
A 25% tax credit is available for expenses incurred from R&D activities. If the expenses are higher than the average expenses incurred by the company during the previous two years, the tax credit is 42% for the excess amount.

An additional tax credit of 17% is available for staff expenses incurred for staff exclusively carrying out and qualified to carry out R&D activities.

An 8% tax credit is available for investments made in tangible fixed assets (excluding buildings) and intangible assets which are exclusively assigned to R&D activities.

Innovation
An 8% tax credit is available for expenses incurred from technological innovation activities.

Reinvestment of extraordinary profits
A 12% tax credit is available for sales of assets which are used for the company's business activities when the amount obtained from the sale is reinvested in similar types of assets during a four-year period (as from one year prior to the sale up to three years after the sale). This tax credit therefore reduces the effective tax levied on sales of certain assets to 18%. The asset in which the reinvestment is made must be maintained for five years (three in the case of movable assets) unless its useful life is shorter.

The following tax credits will be eliminated in 2011:
- Tax credit for the promotion of information and communications technologies (3%);
- Tax credit for investments in vehicle navigation and tracking systems, adaptation of vehicles for the disabled and nursery school fees for staff's children (2%);
- Tax credit for environmental investments (2%);
- Tax credit for staff training costs (1-2%);

S

Spain

- Tax credit for contributions made by employers to certain staff pension schemes (2%);
- Tax credit for export activities (3%); and
- Tax credit for expenses incurred in, or related to, financing staff continuing education programmes (1% to 2%). This tax credit can also be availed of for expenses incurred by companies to familiarise staff in the use of new technologies. These expenses are not a benefit in kind for the staff.

The tax credit for film productions (18%) will be eliminated in 2012.

The tax credit for investments in heritage assets (8%) and book editing (3%) will be eliminated in 2014. As from 2007, the rates applicable will be reduced by 12.5% each year.

Other tax relief
As an incentive to create employment, the following reduced tax rate is available for companies for tax years commencing on 1 January 2009 up to tax years commencing in 2011 if the company maintains or increases its staff and meets other requirements:

- Taxable income up to EUR 120,202.41 will be taxed at a 20% tax rate
- The part of the taxable income that exceeds such threshold will be taxed at the general tax rate of 25%

(See section Taxes on income generated by companies for further details)

A tax credit can be applied for increases in the number of disabled workers contracted per year on a permanent and full-time basis (EUR 6,000 per worker contracted). This increase is calculated by taking the average number of company workers meeting these requirements in the tax year in question and comparing it with the company's average number of staff in the previous tax year.

As from 2008, goodwill cannot be amortised under Spanish GAAP but it can still be amortised for tax purposes at an annual rate of 5% on the compliance of some requirements (e.g., it is acquired for consideration from a non-related party in accordance with Section 42 of the Spanish Commercial Code, an obligatory mandatory reserve is established).

In addition to the tax relief stated above, other tax relief which may be availed of is commented in section *Deductions*.

Special tax regimes
Special tax regimes are applicable in the following cases:

- For Spanish and European Economic Interest Groupings.
- For joint ventures.
- For restructuring transactions. In this case, the special tax regime is a tax neutrality regime implemented under the EU Directive 90/434. As a general rule, under this regime, asset transfers carried out in these transactions do not have any tax implications (either from a direct, indirect or other Spanish tax perspective) for the parties involved (transferor, beneficiary and shareholder) until a subsequent transfer which is not protected by this regime.

The transactions that can be taxed under this regime are mergers, global transfers, spin-offs of business units/majority interests, splits, share-to-share transactions, contributions of business units and contributions of assets (this last transaction is not fully tax-protected). Each of them should comply with a series of requirements for the application of the regime.

Brief outline of some significant features of this regime
The tax credit position of a company dissolved as a result of a tax-protected restructuring transaction is "acquired" in full by the beneficiary company in the case of universal succession.

The "acquired" tax credits would only be those tax credits which are given in relation to assets transferred in transactions where the transferor is not dissolved or the succession is not a full succession for Spanish commercial purposes.

Regarding tax losses, the Spanish tax authorities hold the view that tax losses may not be transferred when the transferring company is not dissolved. When the transferring company is dissolved, the tax losses may be applied by the beneficiary company up to certain limits and with certain restrictions.

Financial goodwill arising in a merger transaction is amortised for tax purposes at a maximum annual rate of 5% by the Spanish beneficiary company of the merger if the seller of the shares which gives rise to the "merger" goodwill has been actually taxed for the equivalent capital gain in Spain or any other EU country (excluding tax havens) and has met certain other requirements. Depreciation of financial goodwill does not have to be recorded in the profit and loss account for it to be tax deductible although an annual amount should be charged to a non-distributable reserve (either from annual profits or from freely available reserves) which should be at least the tax deductible amount.

Under an EU anti-abuse clause, this tax regime cannot be applied if the transaction is done for the purpose of tax fraud or evasion. An additional anti-abuse clause in Spanish law similar to the EU clause provides that the tax regime can be applied only if it is for valid economic reasons, such as streamlining of activities or group restructuring to gain efficiency, but not to merely obtain a tax benefit. The tax authorities should be notified of the application of this tax regime.

- Tax transparency (international controlled foreign company rules). Not applicable for companies resident in the EU.
- Industrial development companies.
- Venture capital companies and funds and collective investment institutions.
- Lease transactions.
- Spanish holding companies of foreign companies. Spanish resident companies whose corporate purpose includes the holding and management of foreign companies' shares are granted some tax benefits on complying with certain requirements.

The tax authorities should be notified of the application of this tax regime.

Companies taxed under this tax regime are granted a tax exemption on dividends and capital gains *(tax exemption stated in the section on Foreign income above)*

Spain

when they have a 5% direct interest or, if their interest is less than 5%, when the acquisition value of their interest is at least EUR 6 million.

In addition, the distribution of profits by the holding company to non-resident companies or individual shareholders is not taxable in Spain (unless the profits are distributed to a tax haven). Resident company shareholders are now entitled to an internal tax credit on dividends under Spanish law.

Contributions of shares in foreign subsidiaries qualifying for a tax exemption on dividends and capital gains made to a Spanish holding company have full tax neutrality under the tax neutrality regime applicable for restructuring transactions.

- Small and medium-sized companies are eligible for tax relief such as accelerated depreciation or more favourable bad debt provision treatment. Accelerated depreciation can be applied for assets acquired with amounts obtained from sales of trading assets. To be eligible for this relief, turnover should not exceed EUR 8 million (in the case of a group, the turnover of all companies should be considered for this purpose).

A reduced corporate income tax rate of 25% is levied on the first EUR 120,202 of annual tax profits.

Small and medium-sized businesses are eligible for a tax credit of 3% of investments made and expenses incurred to improve their capabilities in Internet access and business information management to improve the efficiency of their internal processes. This tax credit may be carried forward for a period of 15 years.

Special economic and tax regime of the Canary Islands

Due to the distance and isolation of the Canary Islands, they have traditionally enjoyed a special economic and tax regime with specific economic and tax measures different to those established for the rest of Spain.

Regarding direct taxes, the Canary Islands economic and tax regime establishes the following tax benefits for companies and businesses domiciled in the Canary Islands or with a PE in the Canary Islands:

- Up to 90% of annual undistributed accounting profits can be allocated to a special investment reserve and not taxed providing that they are invested within a four-year period (including the period during which the profits are obtained) in qualifying assets in the Canary Islands, certain public debt securities or shares in other companies operating in the Canary Islands which invest in qualifying assets.
- Most Spanish corporate income tax relief is 80% higher for companies and businesses located in the Canary Islands regarding both the relief granted. A 25% tax credit can be availed of for investments in new tangible fixed assets and, on the compliance of certain requirements, second-hand assets.
- A 50% tax credit of the corporate income tax liability is granted for taxable income generated from the production of tangible goods on carrying out agricultural, farming, industrial and fishing activities.
- A 90% tax credit of the corporate income tax liability is granted for profits of shipping companies generated from ships registered in the Canary Islands Special Ships and Shipping Companies Register. For sailors of such ships a 50% tax exemption can be applied on the personal income tax levied on their employment

income and a 90% reduction on the part of their social security contributions paid by their employers.

Regarding indirect taxes, in addition to a lower taxation with the Canary Islands general indirect tax (IGIC at the general rate of 5%) compared to VAT and specific IGIC exemptions, the following should be noted:

- Companies domiciled in the Canary Islands which are Corporate Income taxpayers and which are newly incorporated, start new activities or improve their existing ones may benefit from the following tax relief:
  - Exemption from transfer tax and stamp duty on their incorporation and any capital increases made if the increase of capital is allocated to the acquisition of new assets.
  - Exemption from IGIC on supplies and imports of capital goods if the company has the right to offset 100% of IGIC borne.
- Shipping companies qualify for an exemption from transfer tax for any contracts related to ships registered in the Canary Islands Special Ships and Shipping Companies Register.
- Custom Free areas are available. Upon EU demand, there are restrictions on the application of some tax relief (special investment reserve, tax credits for production and new businesses' indirect taxes relief) for the following industrial sectors: shipbuilding, synthetic fibres, automobile, iron, steel and coal.

Canary Islands Special Zone tax regime

In January 2000 a special Canary Islands Special Zone tax regime was approved by the EU. The main regulations of this regime established by the Spanish government are as follows:

- New companies may qualify for the application of this tax regime and, on the approval of the tax authorities, may be registered up to 31 December 2013 (applying the tax regime up to 31 December 2019). This may be extended by the EU.
- To qualify for the application of the tax regime, the company should:
  1. Covenant to make an investment in fixed assets for at least EUR 100,000 in Gran Canaria or Tenerife or EUR 50,000 in Fuerteventura, Lanzarote, La Palma, El Hierro or La Gomera, within the first two years of their business activity;
  2. Covenant to create at least five new jobs in Gran Canaria or Tenerife or three in the other islands;
  3. Provide a description of the business activities which will be carried out which justifies the company's solvency, viability, international competitiveness and its contribution to the economic and social development of the Canary Islands;
  4. Establish its registered office and place of effective management in the Special Area;
  5. Have at least one company director who resides in the Canary Islands; and
  6. Carry out one of the qualifying business activities.
- The territory where this tax regime can be applied includes all the Canary Islands except for companies which intend to carry out industrial or commercial activities involving tangible goods, which must be located in specific controlled areas.
- Companies applying the tax regime may operate outside the Canary Islands through branches if separate accounting books are kept but the tax regime will not be applicable for such branches' activities.

S

Spain

- Activities for which the tax regime can be applied include a wide range of industrial and commercial activities, most services and holdings. Credit and insurance entities are excluded and no stock exchanges are allowed.
- Companies applying the tax regime are subject to corporate income tax in Spain at a 4% rate for companies authorised from 1 January 2007 onwards and at a variable rate of between 1% and 5% for companies authorised before this date. The special 4% rate shall be levied on a maximum amount of the taxable income which will depend on the number of jobs created and the type of activity carried out by the company. The general corporate income tax regime establishes a 30% tax rate for Spanish companies applicable as from 2008. For small companies, the tax rate is 25% for the first EUR 120,202 of profits and 30% for remaining profits.
- Under this tax regime, companies can avail of large tax exemptions for IGIC, transfer tax and stamp duty and large reductions and simplified regulations for local taxes.
- Interest and some other returns from movable goods paid by companies under this tax regime are exempt from Spanish Non-Residents' Income Tax, except when paid to residents in tax havens.
- Benefits established in the EU Parent-Subsidiary Directive are extended to non-EU residents. These benefits are not applicable when the income is paid to residents in tax havens.
- A fee of EUR 732.51 is payable to be registered as a company which applies this tax regime and an annual fee of EUR 1,098.76 is payable to continue to be registered as qualifying for the tax regime.

Finally, Spanish Parliament has recently proposed some amendments to the law regulating the Canary Islands Special Zone tax regime including, amongst other tax benefits, a reduction of the special corporate income tax rate for companies which apply the regime to 1% for the first tax base segment.

Withholding taxes (WHT)

Introduction
Ordinarily, withholding tax is the mechanism by which the Spanish tax authorities collect the final tax levied on non-residents. In the case of resident beneficiaries, however, it is simply an advance payment of a tax that is then normally self-assessed by the resident taxpayer in the final annual tax return.

The advance payment system of withholding tax for resident beneficiaries referred to above also applies if non-resident companies/individuals not established in Spain sell their ownership in Spanish real estate. In this case, the acquirer of the real estate should levy a 3% withholding tax on the sale price on account of the 19% tax chargeable on the seller on its capital gain. Other capital gains (for instance, from a sale by a non-resident of a substantial interest in a Spanish company where neither a tax treaty nor internal rules establish a tax exemption) are taxed in the hands of the non-resident transferor, but the mechanics of levying the tax are not those of a withholding tax. In this case, the non-resident's tax is paid directly, through its representative or by the depositor or manager of the assets in question, if any.

The following table states the general withholding tax rates on income obtained by resident/non-resident companies. The most significant peculiarities regarding the rates for the type of income are stated in footnotes to the table.

Withholding tax rates table

Recipient	Dividends %		Interest %		Royalties %	
Resident corporations and individuals	19%	(1)	19%	(2)	19%	(3)
Non-resident corporations and individuals:						
Non-treaty	19%	(4)	19%	(5a)	24%	(5b), (6)
Treaty (*):						
Algeria	5%	(7)	5%	(8), (9), (10), (11)	7%	(12)
Argentina	10%	(13)	12.5%	(8), (9), (10), (14)	15%	(15)
Australia	15%		10%		10%	
Austria	10%	(4), (16)	5%	(5a)	5%	(5b)
Belgium	15%	(4), (18), (32)	10%	(5a), (17), (32)	5%	(5b), (32)
Bolivia	10%	(13)	15%	(8), (9), (10), (11)	15%	(19)
Brazil	10%	(59)	15%	(9), (20), (21)	12.5%	(22)
Bulgaria	5%	(4), (23)	Nil	(5a)	Nil	(5b)
Canada	15%	(24)	15%	(24)	10%	(19)
Chile	5%	(25)	15%	(26)	10%	(27)
China	10%		10%		10%	(28)
Columbia	5%	(29)	10%	(30)	10%	
Croatia	0%	(13), (32)	8%	(31), (32)	8%	(31), (32)
Cuba	5%	(13)	10%	(33)	5%	(19)
Czech Republic	5%	(4), (23)	Nil	(5a)	5%	(5b), (35)
Denmark (34)	15%	(4), (18)	10%	(5a)	6%	(5b)
Ecuador	15%		10%	(36)	10%	(37)
Egypt	12%	(38)	10%	(39)	12%	
El Salvador	12%	(40)	10%	(41)	10%	
Estonia	5%	(4), (13), (32)	10%	(5a), (9), (10), (32)	10%	(5b), (27), (32)
Finland	10%	(4), (13)	10%	(5a)	5%	(5b)
France	15%	(4), (42)	10%	(5a), (43)	5%	(5b), (44)
Germany	10%	(4), (13)	10%	(5a), (45)	5%	(5b)
Greece	5%	(4), (46)	8%	(5a), (47)	6%	(5b)
Hungary	5%	(4), (13)	Nil		Nil	
Iceland	5%	(13), (32)	5%	(32)	5%	(32)
India	15%		15%	(9), (48), (49)	20%	(50)
Indonesia / Timor Oriental	10%	(13)	10%	(9), (51), (52)	10%	
Iran	5%	(53)	7.5%	(8), (9), (10), (11)	5%	

Spain

Recipient	Dividends %		Interest %		Royalties %	
Ireland	15%	(4), (32)	10%	(5a), (52)	10%	(5b), (32), (54)
Israel	10%	(32)	10%	(32), (55)	7%	(32), (56)
Italy	15%	(4)	12%	(5a), (9)	8%	(5b), (57)
Jamaica	5%	(46), (58)	10%	(41), (58)	10%	(58)
Japan	10%	(59)	10%		10%	
Latvia	5%	(4), (32), (46)	10%	(5a), (9), (10), (32)	10%	(5b), (27), (32)
Lithuania	5%	(4), (32), (46)	10%	(5a), (9), (10), (32)	10%	(5b), (27), (32)
Luxembourg	10%	(4), (60)	10%	(4), (5a), (9), (61)	10%	(5b), (62)
Macedonia	5%	(7)	5%	(63)	5%	
Malaysia	5%	(32), (64)	10%	(9), (32)	7%	(32), (65)
Malta	5%	(4), (66)	Nil		Nil	
Mexico	5%	(13)	15%	(67)	10%	(19)
Moldova	0%	(68)	5%	(41)	8%	
Morocco	10%	(13)	10%		10%	(37)
Netherlands	15%	(4), (69)	10%	(5a)	6%	(5b), (70)
New Zealand	15%		10%		10%	
Norway	10%	(13)	10%	(9), (10)	5%	(62)
Philippines	10%	(71)	15%	(72)	15%	(73)
Poland	5%	(4), (59)	Nil	(5a)	10%	(5b), (19)
Portugal	10%	(4), (13)	15%	(5a)	5%	(5b), (19)
Romania	10%	(4), (13)	10%	(5a), (74)	10%	(5b)
Russian Federation	15%	(75)	5%	(9), (76)	5%	
Saudi Arabia	5%	(66)	5%	(8), (9)	8%	
Serbia	5%	(13)	10%	(9)	10%	(77)
Slovakia	5%	(4), (23)	Nil	(5a)	5%	(5b), (35)
Slovenia	5%	(4), (13), (32)	5%	(5a), (8), (9), (32)	5%	(5b), (32)
South Africa	5%	(13), (32)	5%	(32), (78)	5%	(32)
South Korea	10%	(13)	10%	(9), (79)	10%	
States of the former URSS (Except Russia)	18%		Nil		5%	
Sweden	10%	(4), (16)	15%	(5a)	10%	(5b)
Switzerland	15%	(87)	10%	(91)	5%	(88)
Thailand	10%		15%	(80)	15%	
Trinidad and Tobago	nil	(68)	8%	(8), (9), (61), (79)	5%	
Tunisia	5%	(85)	10%	(86)	10%	
Turkey	5%	(13)	15%	(84)	10%	
United Arab Emirates	5%	(9), (90)	Nil		Nil	
United Kingdom	10%	(4), (7)	12%	(5a)	10%	(5b)
United States	10%	(13)	10%	(9), (63)	10%	(54)

Recipient	Dividends		Interest		Royalties	
	%		%		%	
Venezuela	nil	(46)	10%	(83)	5%	
Vietnam	7%	(32), (89)	10%	(9), (32), (61)	10%	(32)

Notes

The rates above are for income obtained by non-residents which is not related to any PEs which they may have in Spain.

Aside from these Tax Treaties, the following Tax Treaties are not yet in force as they are currently being negotiated or are not yet approved or published: Albania, Armenia, Barbados, Bosnia and Herzegovina, Costa Rica, Georgia, Kazakhstan, Kuwait, Namibia, Nigeria, Pakistan, Panamá, Peru, Senegal, Syria and Uruguay.

1. If a corporate taxpayer, as shareholder, is entitled to full tax relief on the dividend received, no withholding tax would be levied. As a general rule, corporate shareholders with at least a 5% interest held for at least one year are granted full tax relief.
2. The 19% withholding tax rate does not apply if, amongst other cases, the recipient is a resident bank or savings or other financial institution subject to corporate income tax, provided that this income is not portfolio income. In addition, no withholding tax is levied on interest arising between companies taxed under the tax consolidation regime.
3. A 19% withholding tax rate is levied on income generated under royalty and technical assistance agreements, from leases or from the granting of rights when ownership is not transferred, except when such income constitutes the habitual business activity of the recipient. A 24% rate is levied on fees received by a company for the transfer of rights to an image or consent or authorisation to its use.
4. Implementation of the EU Parent-Subsidiary Directive in Spanish law gives EU shareholders a withholding tax exemption on dividends from Spanish companies on the compliance of certain requirements. Luxembourg recipients of income which are companies under paragraph 1 of the protocol to the tax treaty with Spain (holding companies) are not allowed this exemption. Recipients of Luxembourg income, as companies regulated under paragraph 1 of the protocol to the tax treaty with Spain (holding companies), are not allowed this exemption.
5a. Spanish law establishes a withholding tax exemption on interest obtained by EU lenders not established in Spain on the compliance of certain requirements.
5b. The EU Interest and Royalties directive is applicable when appropriate.
6. The taxable income for supplies of services, technical assistance or assembly/installation work under engineering contracts, provided or carried out by non-resident companies with no PE in Spain does not follow the general rule of gross income. In such cases, total income can be reduced by related staff costs, certain supplies (water, electricity, telephone, etc.) and materials used for the services/work, provided that, in the case of staff costs, evidence can be provided that they were actually taxed in Spain. For royalties paid to EU lenders, a reduced tax rate of 10% is levied on the compliance of certain requirements.
7. Levied if the recipient is a company holding at least a 10% interest in the paying company; otherwise, a 15% rate is levied.
8. Interest paid by certain public institutions is tax exempt.
9. Interest paid to certain public institutions is tax exempt.
10. Interest arising from the acquisition of commercial, industrial or scientific equipment is tax exempt.
11. Interest paid on any loans granted by a bank or other financial institution is tax exempt.
12. For royalties for any copyright of literary work (including cinematograph films, and films or tapes for radio or television broadcasting), the rate levied is 14%.
13. Levied if the recipient is a company holding at least a 25% interest in the paying company; otherwise, a 15% rate is levied.

S

Spain

14. No withholding tax is levied on interest when both contracting states agree this and the loan is for no less than five years.
15. A 3% withholding tax rate is levied on royalties for the use of or right to use news. A 5% withholding tax rate is levied on royalties for any copyright of literary work (including cinematograph films, and films or tapes for radio or television broadcasting).
    A 10% withholding tax rate is levied on royalties for the use of or right to use copyright of industrial property, know-how or scientific, commercial or industrial equipment.
16. Levied if the recipient is a company holding a direct interest of at least 50% in the paying company for at least one year; otherwise a 15% rate is levied.
17. A tax exemption can be availed of for interest arising from commercial loans, loans guaranteed by public bodies for the promotion of exports and for interest arising from current accounts in banks or nominative advances between banks of both contracting states.
18. No withholding tax is levied if the requirements laid down in internal law which transposes the EU Parent-Subsidiary Directive are complied with.
19. Royalties for any copyright of literary, theatrical, musical or artistic work (with some exceptions such as films and TV programmes) are exempt from withholding tax.
20. The maximum withholding tax is 10% for interest paid to financial institutions for loans and credits granted for a minimum term of 10 years for the purchase of capital equipment.
21. Interest arising from securities issued by a contracting state is exempt from withholding tax.
22. A 10% withholding tax rate is levied on royalties on copyright of any literary, theatrical, musical or artistic work (including films and TV programmes).
23. Levied if the beneficial owner is a company (excluding partnerships) with at least a 25% interest in the paying company held directly or indirectly; otherwise a 15% rate is levied.
24. A reduced withholding tax rate is only levied if the income is taxed in Canada; otherwise the general rate is levied.
25. Levied if the recipient is a company with at least a 20% interest in the paying company held directly or indirectly; otherwise a 10% rate is levied.
26. Interest arising from bank or insurance company loans, bonds, some securities that are regularly negotiated on stock markets and credit sales of industrial equipment are taxed at a 5% tax rate.
27. A 5% withholding tax rate is levied on royalties for the use of industrial, commercial or scientific equipment.
28. Withholding tax is levied on 60% of gross royalties for the use of industrial, commercial or scientific equipment.
29. A 0% withholding tax rate is levied if the recipient is a company with at least a 20% interest in the paying company held directly or indirectly.
30. No withholding tax is levied if: (i) the beneficiary is a contracting state, one of its political subdivisions or one of its local entities; or (ii) interest is paid in connection with the sale on credit of merchandise or equipment to a company of a contracting state; or (iii) interest is paid on a loan granted by a bank or financial institution resident in a contracting state.
31. A 0% withholding tax rate will be levied from 20 April 2011.
32. Reduced withholding tax rates or exemptions are not levied/applied if the income is paid to a company resident in a contracting state whose shares are directly or indirectly held, by more than 50%, by non-residents. This clause will not apply if the company can prove that it carries out important industrial or commercial activities and does not merely manage or hold shares.
33. No withholding tax is levied if: (i) the beneficiary is a contracting state, one of its political subdivisions or one of its local entities; or (ii) interest is paid in connection with the sale on credit of merchandise or equipment to a company of a contracting state; or (iii) interest is paid on a long-term loan (five or more years) granted by a bank or financial institution resident in a contracting state.
34. Denmark has terminated its tax treaty with Spain. The tax treaty ceased to have effect on 1 January 2009.
35. Royalties on copyright of any literary, theatrical, musical or artistic work, excluding films and TV programmes, are tax exempt if the recipient is resident in the other contracting state and taxed on such income in such state.

36. A 5% withholding tax rate is levied on interest arising from the sale of industrial, commercial or scientific equipment, the sale of merchandise from one business to another business, or the financing of construction, installation or assembly works.
37. A 5% withholding tax rate is levied on royalties on copyright of any literary, theatrical, musical or artistic work (excluding films and TV programmes).
38. A 9% withholding tax rate is levied on the gross amount of the dividends if the beneficiary owner is a company (other than a partnership) which has at least a 25% direct interest in the company paying the dividends.
39. Withholding Tax is not levied on interest if the recipient is a contracting state, one of its political subdivisions or one of its public bodies or local authorities or if the interest is paid to the Central Bank of the other contracting state.
40. No withholding tax is levied if the recipient is a company with at least a 50% direct interest in the company paying the dividends, provided that the dividends are distributed from profits taxed in Spain.
41. No withholding tax is levied on interest if: (a) the recipient is the other contracting state, its central bank or its political divisions; (b) the payer is a contracting state or its political divisions; (c) the interest arises from a loan or credit granted or guaranteed by a contracting state or its political divisions; (d) the recipient is a financial institution depending on a contracting state or its political divisions; or (e) the recipient is a pension fund qualifying for tax purposes in a contracting state and the income from such fund is tax exempt in the contracting state paying the dividend.
42. No withholding tax is levied if the French company has at least a 10% direct interest in the company distributing the dividend.
43. No withholding tax is levied if the French company receives interest; (i) from the other contracting state or any of its political divisions; or (ii) from a resident in the other contracting state from an underlying commercial or industrial activity; or (iii) in connection with a credit sale of industrial, commercial or scientific equipment; or (iv) for a loan granted by a financial institution.
44. No withholding tax is levied on royalties on copyright of any literary or artistic work (excluding films and TV programmes) if the recipient is the beneficiary owner.
45. No withholding tax is levied on interest paid to "Deutsche Bundesbank" or "Kreditanstalt für Wiederaufbau".
46. Levied if the recipient is a company with at least a 25% direct interest in the paying company; otherwise; a 10% rate is levied.
47. No withholding tax is levied on interest if: (i) the interest is paid by a contracting state, one of its political subdivisions or one of its local entities; or (ii) the interest is paid to the other contracting state, one of its political subdivisions, or one of its local entities or to a body (including financial institutions) of such contracting state; or (iii) the interest is paid to another body (including financial institutions) in relation to loans granted by virtue of an agreement between both contracting states.
48. No withholding tax is levied on interest paid to the Central Bank of the other contracting state.
49. No withholding tax is levied on interest paid to companies in the other contracting state if the operation that generates the debt has been authorised by the government of the state where the company paying the interest is resident.
50. A 10% withholding tax rate is levied on royalties for the use or cession of use of industrial, commercial or scientific equipment. The general 20% withholding tax rate is levied on technical services and other royalties.
51. No withholding tax is levied on interest if the recipient is a contracting state, one of its political subdivisions or one of its local entities or if the interest is paid to the Central Bank or a financial institution controlled by the other contracting state, its political subdivisions or its local entities.
52. No withholding tax is levied on interest arising from the credit sale of industrial, commercial or scientific equipment.
53. Levied if the recipient is a company with at least a 20% interest in the paying company; otherwise a 10% rate is levied.
54. Royalties for copyright on literary, theatrical, musical or artistic work are taxed at a 5% withholding tax rate. Royalties on films or other means of audio or video transmission,

S

Spain

for the use or right to use industrial, commercial or scientific equipment or over scientific works or under agreements between both states are taxed at an 8% rate.

55. A 5% withholding tax rate is levied on interest arising from the sale of industrial, commercial or scientific equipment, the sale of merchandise from one business to another business or a loan granted by a financial institution.

56. A 5% withholding tax rate is levied on royalties for copyright on literary, theatrical, musical or artistic work (excluding films and TV programmes).

57. A 4% withholding tax rate is levied on royalties for copyright on literary, theatrical, musical or artistic work (excluding films and TV programmes).

58. Reduced withholding tax rates are not levied when more than 75% of shares of the recipient company resident in a contracting state are owned directly or indirectly by non-residents and the income generated by the paying company is not taxed in its country of residence.

59. Levied if the recipient is a company with at least a 25% interest in the paying company with voting rights; otherwise a 15% rate is levied.

60. Levied if the recipient is a company with at least a 25% interest in the paying company for at least one year; otherwise a 15% rate is levied.

61. No withholding tax is levied on interest arising from a loan guaranteed by a contracting state.

62. Consideration received for renouncing, either totally or partially, the use or right to use goods or rights is considered to be a royalty.

63. No withholding tax is levied on interest paid in connection with the sale on credit of merchandise or equipment to a company of a contracting state or on interest paid on a long-term loan (five or more years) granted by a bank or credit institution resident in a contracting state.

64. No withholding tax is levied if the recipient is a company with at least a 5% direct interest in the paying company.

65. A 5% withholding tax rate is levied on royalties for technical services.

66. No withholding tax is levied on dividends paid to a shareholder resident in the other contracting state of the company distributing the dividend with at least a 25% interest.

67. A 10% withholding tax rate is levied on interest received by a bank (beneficial owner).

68. Levied if the recipient is a company with at least a 50% direct interest in the paying company. A 5% withholding tax rate is levied if the recipient is a shareholder with at least a 25% direct interest; otherwise a 10% rate is levied.

69. Withholding tax is reduced to 10% if the recipient is a Dutch company with at least a 50% direct interest in the paying company or if the recipient holds 25% of this capital and another Dutch company holds at least the other 25%.

70. No withholding tax is levied on capital gains from sales of assets/rights when they are considered to be a royalty.

71. Levied if the recipient is a shareholder of the paying company with voting rights with at least a 10% direct interest; otherwise a 15% rate is levied.

72. A 10% withholding tax rate is levied on interest paid for bonds or similar securities generally offered to investors and related to transfers of industrial, commercial or scientific equipment. No withholding tax is levied on interest from bonds or similar securities issued by the state or a local entity, or from loans given or guaranteed by either of the two contracting states, Central Banks or financial institutions as agreed between the contracting states.

73. A 20% withholding tax rate is levied on royalties for films, audio or TV tapes.

74. No withholding tax is levied on interest from loans granted or guaranteed by a contracting state.

75. If the recipient has invested more than EUR 100,000 in the company that pays the dividend or the dividend is tax exempt in its country of residence, the withholding tax rate levied is 10%. If both of these requirements are complied with, the rate applicable is 5%.

76. Interest from loans with a maturity period of over seven years is tax exempt.

77. A 10% withholding tax rate is levied on any patents, trademarks, designs or models, plans, secret formulae or processes and computer software, or for the use of, or the right to use, industrial, commercial or scientific equipment, or for information concerning industrial, commercial or scientific experience. A 5% withholding tax rate is levied on any

copyright of literary, artistic or scientific work, excluding computer software and including cinematographic films or tapes used for radio or television broadcasting.

78. No withholding tax is levied on interest paid to a contracting state, one of its political subdivisions or one of its local entities, interest paid in connection with the sale on credit of merchandise or equipment to a company of a contracting state or interest paid on any long-term loan (seven years minimum) granted by a bank resident in a contracting state.

79. No withholding tax is levied on interest arising from the credit sale of industrial, commercial or scientific equipment or merchandise.

80. A 10% withholding tax rate is levied on interest received by financial and insurance entities. No withholding tax is levied on interest from loans granted by the government, Central Bank or certain institutions.

81. A 5% withholding tax rate is levied on royalties for copyright (excluding films), whilst an 8% withholding tax rate is levied on fees for leases of industrial, commercial or scientific equipment.

82. A 4.95% withholding tax rate is levied on interest received by financial institutions.

83. No withholding tax is levied on interest if: (a) the recipient is the other contracting state, its central bank or its political divisions; (b) the interest is paid by one contracting state or its political divisions; (c) the interest arises from a loan or credit granted or guaranteed by a contracting state to promote exports and development; (d) the recipient is a pension fund qualifying for tax purposes in a contracting state and the income generated from the fund is tax exempt in the contracting state paying the dividend; (e) the interest is paid in relation to the credit acquisition of industrial, commercial or scientific equipment.

84. The withholding tax rate is 10% if the interest arises from a loan granted by a bank or is related to a credit acquisition of merchandise or equipment.

85. Levied if the recipient is a shareholder of the paying company with at least a 50% interest.

86. A 5% withholding tax rate is levied for long-term loans (more than seven years).

87. No withholding tax is levied on dividends when they are paid to a shareholder with at least a 25% interest held for at least two years, provided that the company distributing the dividends is effectively taxed.

88. No withholding tax is levied if the royalties are paid between associated companies, affiliated by at least a 25% direct interest held for at least two years or both held by a third company with at least a 25% interest in both companies and corporate income tax is levied on all of the companies.

89. Levied if the recipient is a shareholder of the paying company with at least a 50% interest. A 10% withholding tax rate is levied if the recipient is a company with at least a 25% direct interest; otherwise a 15% rate is levied.

90. Levied if the recipient is a shareholder of the paying company with at least a 10% interest; otherwise a 15% rate is levied.

91. No withholding tax is levied on interest paid to a bank resident in Switzerland on a long-term loan (over five years).

Tax administration

Tax returns
The tax system in Spain is a system of self-assessment and tax returns may be inspected by the tax authorities. The tax year for corporate income tax purposes is the company's accounting year. The tax year cannot exceed 12 months and therefore commencement, termination or change of a tax year can give rise to a period of less than one year.

Payment of corporate income tax
For corporate income tax, three on-account payments of the annual tax payment should be made during the first 20 calendar days of April, October and December. Large companies should calculate these advance payments as a percentage (21%) of their annual tax profits or each period, i.e., at 31 March, 30 September and 30 November. Some allowances and the tax year's advance payments can be credited against this percentage of tax profits. Small companies can opt to calculate their

Spain

advance payments in the same way as large companies or to apply a rate (currently 18%) on their last corporate income tax liabilities paid for the previous period (on 1 April, 1 October or 1 December).

Annual corporate income tax returns should be filed and the tax paid within 25 calendar days following the six months subsequent to the end of the tax year (i.e., if the tax year coincides with the calendar year, the return should be filed between 1 July and 25 July of the following calendar year).

Other issues

Special tax regime applicable in the Basque country
The three provinces that make up the region of the Basque country (Alava, Guipúzcoa and Vizcaya) have an "economic agreement" with Spain's central government (laid down and regulated by Law 12 of 23 May 2002) in accordance with which these regions are granted the right to regulate their own tax regimes.

There are certain provisions in this law regarding corporate income tax, which make this area of Spain more attractive for companies.

General tax rate
The general tax rate is 28%.

Lower tax rates
A reduced rate of 24% is levied on small companies. From 1 January 2010, a small company is considered to be a company which meets the following requirements in the year prior to the application of the special tax regime:

- Carries on an economic business activity;
- Its net turnover or assets are under EUR 10 million;
- Its average number of staff is under 50; and
- An interest of 25% or more in the company is not held, directly or indirectly, by a company that does not meet the previous requirements.

A 20% rate (24% in Guipúzcoa) is levied on real estate companies which comply with the following requirements:

- Their share capital is wholly owned by individuals during the whole tax year;
- More than half of their assets are securities or more than half of their assets are not used for economic business activities during at least 90 days of the tax year; and
- Al least 90% of their profits are generated from investment income and capital gains.

A 21% rate is levied on companies that are floated on the Bilbao Stock Exchange and for brokerages and cooperatives. Companies that are floated on the Bilbao Stock Exchange are taxed at this rate for three years, as long as they are in the compliance of certain requirements.

Tax-loss carryforwards
Tax-losses may be carried forward for the following 15 years in Guipúzcoa. In Vizcaya and Alava, there is no time limit for the offsetting of tax losses.

Tax deductibility of amortisation of goodwill and intangible assets
Amortisation recorded for intangible assets (irrespective of whether they have a specific useful life or not), including goodwill, is tax deductible up to a maximum annual limit of 20% on the compliance of the following requirements:

- The assets have been acquired for consideration; and
- The acquiring and transferring companies are not associated parties.

Financial goodwill
Financial goodwill is tax deductible over a period of five years when at least a 5% interest is acquired in the company and these shares are not quoted on a Stock Exchange or if they are quoted on a Stock Exchange, they are shares of group or associated companies.

If the company from which the shares have been acquired has an interest in another company, the equity, assets and rights recorded in the group's consolidated annual accounts should be taken into consideration for the purpose of calculating the amount of the financial goodwill.

If the company from which the shares have been acquired is a non-resident company, in addition to the requirements stated above, the following requirements should be complied with:

- The company is taxed in its country of residence by a tax which is identical or similar to Spanish corporate income tax; and
- The company carries on business activities abroad.

If the shares are not acquired on a stock market, the company which acquires the shares should not be in any of the situations provided for in Article 42 of the Spanish Commercial Code in relation to the transferring company.

Depreciation periods
The depreciation periods for assets are shorter than those under state corporate income tax law.

Reinvestment of extraordinary income
Income obtained from the sale of tangible fixed assets or intangible assets can be deducted from taxable income on the compliance of the following requirements:

- The amount obtained from the sale is reinvested in similar types of assets within a four-year period (as from one-year prior to the sale up to three years after the sale);
- The asset in which the reinvestment is made is maintained for five years (three in the case of movable assets) unless its useful life is shorter; and
- For sales of shares in other companies when the interest held is at least 5% and it is has been held for a period of one year prior to the date of the sale, 60% of the income obtained from the sale can be deducted from taxable income.

S

Spain

Income generated from intellectual or industrial property
30% of the income obtained from the transfer of intellectual or industrial property
rights can be deducted from taxable income on the compliance of certain requirements,
and 60% if the company has created the intellectual or industrial property itself. There
are no quantity limits to be complied with for the application of this deduction.

Tax credits
Investments in new tangible fixed assets
A 10% tax credit can be availed of for investments made in new tangible fixed assets
on the compliance of certain requirements. The minimum depreciation period for the
assets, excluding computer equipment, is five years.

The total amount of the investment is over EUR 60,100 and the investment complies
with at least one of the following requirements:

- Exceeds 10% of the carrying amounts (minus depreciation/amortisation) of the
  company's tangible fixed assets, buildings and software during the previous year;
  and/or
- Exceeds 15% of the carrying amount of the same type of tangible fixed assets of the
  company during the previous year.

Special reserve for investments in production
A tax credit can be applied for the distribution of profits to a special reserve for
investments in production on the compliance of the following requirements:

- The company invests the amount distributed to the reserve in new tangible fixed
  assets during the following two years;
- These assets are maintained by the company during a five-year period or during
  their useful life if it is less than five years; and
- The company's shareholder's equity is increased by the amount distributed to the
  reserve and this increase is maintained for a five-year period as from the date on
  which the investment was made.

The tax credit is 10% of the profits distributed to the reserve.

Research and development (R&D)
A 30% tax credit can be availed of for expenses incurred from R&D activities. If the
expenses are higher than the average expenses incurred by the company during the
previous two years, the tax credit is 50% for the excess amount.

An additional tax credit of 20% can be availed of for the following expenses:

- Staff expenses incurred for staff exclusively carrying out and qualified to carry out
  R&D activities; and
- Expenses incurred for projects contracted from certain universities and
  public organisations.

A 10% tax credit can be availed of for investments made in tangible fixed assets
(excluding buildings) and intangible assets which are exclusively assigned to
R&D activities.

Technological innovation
A 20% or 15% tax credit can be availed of for certain expenses incurred for technological innovation.

Expenses incurred for environmental conservation and improvement and for conservation of energy
Companies are eligible for a 30% tax credit for investments made in the equipment listed in the Basque List of Environmental Technologies on the compliance of certain requirements.

Companies may also qualify for a 15% tax credit for investments made and expenses incurred in tangible fixed assets on the compliance of certain requirements.

Export investments (e.g., foreign advertising, formation of companies and branches abroad)
This tax credit is the same as the credit available under State corporate income tax law.

Staff training
A 10% tax credit can be applied for expenses incurred in staff training. If the expenses are higher than the average expenses incurred by the company during the previous two years, the tax credit is 15% for the excess amount.
A tax credit can also be applied for expenses incurred for the obtaining of the OHSAS 18001 certificate and for training staff in new technologies.

Job creation
For tax years commencing during the period 1 January 2010 to 31 December 2011, the following tax credits can be availed of for job creation on the compliance of the requirements stated:

- EUR 4,600 for each job created provided that a permanent employment contract is signed with the employee;
- EUR 8,600 for each job created provided that a permanent employment contract is signed with the employee and a person who has special difficulties in finding employment is contracted; and
- The company's average number of staff with permanent employment contracts should be increased by at least the same number of contracts that generated the tax credit and this increase should be maintained by the company for two years.

Time limits for the application of tax credits
In Guipúzcoa, tax credits can be carried forward for a period of 15 years as from the date on which the company qualifies for them. In Vizcaya and Alava there is no time limit for the application of tax credits.

Limits of the amount of tax credit applied
The combined sum of all investment tax credits, excluding those for R&D and technological innovation, may not exceed 45% of the company's corporate income tax liability.

S

Corporate taxes in Sri Lanka

For more information, contact:

Yudhishtran (Yudy) Kanagasabai
PricewaterhouseCoopers
P O Box 918,
No. 100, Braybrooke Place
Colombo 02
Sri Lanka
Tel: +94 11 4719838 ext. 502
Email: yudhishtran.kanagasabai@lk.pwc.com

Significant developments

As of 1 May 2009, a 3% Nation Building Tax (NBT) is payable on the "liable turnover" by every person (a person includes any company, body of persons or any partnership) who imports any article, carries on the business of manufacture or carries on the business of providing a service of any description.

Taxes on corporate income

Resident companies and public corporations are liable for income tax on their worldwide taxable income. The rate of tax in general is 35% (33⅓% for any quoted public company, for five years from the year in which it becomes a quoted public company, and 15% for any company other than a holding company, a subsidiary company or an associate company of a group of companies, of which the taxable income does not exceed Sri Lankan Rupee (SRL) 5 million). A lower rate of 15% applies to profits from exports, fisheries, tourism and construction. The 15% rate applicable to the construction industry is restricted to resident companies only.

Public corporations are also subject to tax of an additional amount, the excess (if any) of 25% of the balance of profits left after deduction of the income tax payable at 35% or 15% over the amount of gross dividends distributed out of profits on which taxable income is computed.

In addition, income tax is payable at 10% of the gross dividends distributed by a resident company, other than such dividends distributed out of any dividend received from another resident company (and few other exceptions).

Deemed dividend tax at 15% is payable by any resident company in any tax year commencing from the tax year 2007 to 2008, if the said company has, in the preceding tax year, distributed dividends of less than 25% of the distributable profits (duly defined) for that preceding tax year.

Unit trusts and mutual funds are treated like resident companies for income tax purposes. Units of investment are treated like company shares, and returns thereon to investors are treated like company dividends. The tax rate is 10% on the profits derived by any unit trust or mutual fund.

The tax rate applicable to venture capital companies is 20%.

Non-resident companies are liable to income tax at 35% (or 15%, if the taxable income does not exceed SRL 5 million) of their Sri Lanka-source taxable income. Where profits are remitted in a tax year, tax is also payable in an amount equal to 10% of the remittances.

Corporate residence

Where a company has its registered or principal office in Sri Lanka or where the control and management of its business are exercised in Sri Lanka, the company is treated as resident for tax purposes.

Other taxes

Economic service charge (ESC)
The ESC is payable quarterly by every person (a person includes a company) and every partnership in respect of the aggregate turnover of the trade, business, profession or vocation at the rates varying from 0.05% to 1%, depending on the business activity, if the total turnover exceeds SRL 7.5 million for that quarter. ESC so paid is deductible from the income tax payable for that year of assessment. ESC is not refundable but could be carried forward for four immediately succeeding tax years and set-off against the income tax payable for those four tax years. Maximum ESC payable for any quarter is SRL 30 million.

Social responsibility levy
Social responsibility levy is payable by every company on the amount of income tax, dividend tax, deemed dividend tax and remittance tax chargeable at 1.5%. The payment should be made at the time of payment of income tax, dividend tax, deemed dividend tax and remittance tax.

Nation building tax (NBT)
NBT is chargeable from every person (person includes any company, body of persons or any partnership) who imports any article on the "liable turnover" from such importation, and who carries on the business of manufacture of any article or carries on the business of providing a service of any description on the liable turnover of the relevant quarter at the rate of 3% (1.5% rate is applicable to the "liable turnover" of rice manufactured from locally produced paddy). Certain specified articles or services are exempt from NBT.

Liable turnover means:

- In the case of importer; the value of any article ascertained under section 6 of the Value Added Tax Act for the purpose of importation.
- In the case of manufacturer; the proceeds receivable whether received or not from the manufacture and sale in Sri Lanka.
- In the case of service provider; the proceeds receivable whether received or not.

Bad debts, VAT and excise duty should not include to the liable turnover.

Construction industry guarantee fund levy
Construction industry guarantee fund levy is payable by each construction contractor or subcontractor on their contract value arising from any contract entered into,

calculated at the rates varying from 0.25% to 1%, depending on the value of the construction contract.

Tourism development levy

Tourism development levy is payable by tourist hotels and institutions licensed under the Tourist Development Act on the turnover of such institution at the rate of 1%.

Employees' provident fund

Employers and employees are required to contribute specified percentages (employer, 12%; employee, 8%) of each employee's monthly emoluments/salary to the Employees Provident Fund (EPF) established by the Government. Alternatively, employers and employees must contribute to certain private provident funds approved by the labour authority.

Employees' trust fund

Employers are also required to contribute a specified percentage (currently 3%) of each employee's monthly emoluments/salary to the Employees Trust Fund established by the government.

Turnover tax

In terms of the Provincial Council Statutes, turnover tax at rates varying from 1% to 5% of turnover continues to be charged on any person who buys and sells articles in any area of Sri Lanka.

Value-added tax (VAT)

VAT is payable on imported goods and on the supply of goods (excluding in particular the supply to merchants who purchase goods locally) and services in Sri Lanka. Provisions are made for filing returns monthly or quarterly, based on specified criteria. Even where returns could be filed quarterly, the tax payments are required to be made on a monthly basis. Certain specified imports and domestically supplied goods and/or services are exempt.

The tax is payable on the prescribed valuations of imports and domestic supplies at a standard rate of 12%. There is also a higher rate of 20% for luxury items. Exports and certain specified international services are zero-rated. No registration for VAT is necessary if the total value of taxable supplies in a quarter is SRL 650,000 or less, or SRL 2,500,000 or less in a year. The input tax paid on the imports and supplies of goods (including capital goods) and services in a month, and used in the business of making taxable supplies in that month can be deducted from the tax payable (output tax) on such supplies, subject to a limitation of lesser of 85% of output tax or the actual input tax paid.

Refunds of excess tax paid are available to zero-rated supplies, to suppliers who are qualified to issue suspended tax invoices and to new businesses registered under Section 22 (7) of the VAT Act.

Excise duties

Excise duties and special excise levies are charged on tobacco, cigarettes, liquor, motor vehicles, selected petroleum products, paints, air conditioners, dishwashers, household washing machines and other products.

Stamp duty

Stamp duty is payable on specified instruments and documents at rates prescribed in the Gazette.

Share transaction levy

The Share transaction levy at the rate of 0.2% is chargeable from the buyer and from the seller on the sale of listed shares.

Local taxes

Taxes (more usually called rates) are currently assessed and collected annually from the owners of land and premises by the local authorities of the areas in which the properties are located. These authorities also charge and collect annual licence fees from certain businesses as well.

Branch income

Foreign companies are permitted to register a place of business in Sri Lanka or to be registered as an overseas company under local company law, where the business carried on conforms to the stipulations made under the exchange control law.

In addition to paying the standard corporate income tax, branches are subject to a 10% tax on remittance to a foreign head office.

The Sri Lanka-source income of foreign companies from a local 'place of business' is taxed at the non-resident company rates mentioned above. However, under most double-taxation-avoidance treaties that Sri Lanka has entered into, the income of a turnkey or service project will not be liable to income tax if its duration is less than a period specified in the treaty concerned. Where branch or project income is liable to income tax but the income is not readily ascertainable, the tax authority may prescribe that the income be computed on a fair percentage (not less than 6%) of the branch or project turnover in Sri Lanka.

Income determination

Business accounting for income tax purposes should, unless otherwise specified by the tax statute, conform to Sri Lanka Accounting Standards, which have been given statutory force by legislation enacted in 1995.

Inventory valuation

Inventories should be measured at the lower of cost and net realisable value.

Capital gains

There is no capital gains tax.

Capital gains from transfer of property are exempt from income tax.

S

Sri Lanka

Dividends

Resident company dividends paid on shares held by resident or non-resident persons are not assessable on the recipients if income tax is withheld on such dividends (see below), or the dividends are exempt from income tax, or the dividends are paid out of dividends received from resident companies.

Stock dividends (or bonus shares, in local parlance) are not taxable in the hands of a shareholder at the time of issue, but where such shares are capitalised out of company profits and there is a return of this capital to the shareholder within six years from the date of issue, the amount of capital returned to the extent of the paid-up value of the bonus shares is treated by definition as a dividend and is taxable in the hands of the shareholder. However, if the shareholder is a company, this dividend may not be assessable, as explained above.

Deemed dividend

Deemed dividend tax at 15% is payable by any resident company for every tax year on or before 30 October of that tax year, provided that 25% or more of its distributable profits (duly defined) for the immediate preceding year has not been distributed as dividends on or before 30 September of that year.

Deductions

In ascertaining the total income liable to income tax from the financial accounts filed by a company, deductions from revenue are permitted for outgoing and matching expenses incurred in producing the income, including special deductions.

Depreciation

An allowance for depreciation for wear and tear, calculated at:

- 33⅓% for ships if owned by a company for a period of three years;
- 25% of the cost of any information technology and machinery used for the construction industry for a period of four years;
- 20% for a period of five years of the cost of acquisition of any motor vehicle or furniture;
- 12.5% for a period of eight years of the cost of any other plant and equipment; and
- 6⅔% for a period of 15 years of the cost of any qualified building.

The cost of renewal of any capital asset, if no allowance exists, is deductible for depreciation of that asset.

Bad debts and doubtful debts

In the case of a bank or financial institution, deductibility of a specific bad debt provision is restricted to the lesser of the actual amount of the provision or 1% of the aggregate debts as at the end of the period for which profits are ascertained.

Interest

Interest paid or payable on borrowings for purposes of business, subject to the thin capitalisation rules pursuant to which, interest payments made between members of a group of companies, including holding companies, will be restricted to the debt equity ratio of 3:1 for manufacturing companies and 4:1 for other companies.

Turnover tax

Turnover tax payable at the provincial level is tax deductible.

Formation or liquidation expenses of a company

Termination gratuities paid to employees on cessation of business and annual payments made to an approved fund, held for payment under compulsory legislation of gratuities to employees upon termination of their services are deductible.

Foreign taxes

Taxes paid in a foreign country that does not have a tax treaty with Sri Lanka may be deducted.

Non-deductible expenses

Deductions not permitted for certain expenses or allowances, in the determination of total income are itemised below:

- Foreign travel expenses incurred in connection with a business, other than those expenses incurred solely in connection with the promotion of the export trade, or the provision of any services for payment in foreign currency or in carrying out an approved programme for the promotion of tourism;
- Business entertainment expenses incurred or entertainment allowances paid to executive officers;
- Any expenditure of a capital nature or any loss of capital, including book depreciation of capital assets;
- Sri Lanka income tax payable or any income tax or other similar tax payable in any country with which Sri Lanka has a double-taxation-avoidance treaty, other than the excess of the foreign-country tax on doubly taxed income over the maximum amount of the credit allowed in the foreign country for the Sri Lanka income tax on that income;
- Any other prescribed tax or levy;
- Depreciation allowances or rentals or annual payments or renewals in respect of vehicles used for purposes of business travel, or capital assets provided for the use of employees at their places of residence, other than motorcycles or bicycles used by non-executive staff and motor coaches used to transport employees to and from their places of work;
- The excess of management fee paid over SRL 1 million or 1% of turnover, whichever is lower, or such amount as may be determined by the tax authority. This restriction does not apply to a venture capital company, unit trust or mutual fund; and
- Input VAT, which is creditable against output VAT.

Contribution

Relief is still available as a deduction from assessable income, for contributions in money to an approved charity and contributions in money or in kind to the Government of Sri Lanka. The deduction for the former is subject to a ceiling of one-fifth of the assessable income of the company. In the case of the latter, there is no limit to the deduction and any un-recouped excess of such contributions over the assessable income is available for carryforward deduction from the following year's assessable income and so on.

S

Sri Lanka

Interest

Deductions from the total income from all sources of a company are allowed for any interest payable on loans used for the construction or purchase of any building or the purchase of any site for construction of a building; or for any annuity, ground rent or royalty payable; or for a business loss other than a loss incurred in any business of life insurance and any business of finance leasing, including any loss current or brought forward from a previous year, up to a maximum limit of 35% of the total statutory income in determining the residual balance income, which would be assessable for income tax. Where such deductions exceed the total income, any unrelieved excess is carried forward for deduction in the succeeding tax year from its total statutory income for that year of assessment and so on.

Royalties

No deduction is allowed for a royalty payable by a person outside Sri Lanka to another person outside Sri Lanka.

Losses

No deduction from total income is allowed in a tax year for a business loss if at any time in that year more than one-third of the issued share capital of the loss-making company is held by persons who did not hold such share capital at any time in the year in which the loss was incurred. In such circumstances, the loss is deferred for deduction only from profits of the particular business in which the loss was incurred.

Any loss incurred in any business of life insurance could be deducted to the extent of any profits from such business included in such total statutory income. Similarly, any loss incurred in any business of finance leasing could be deducted to the extent of any profits from such leasing business included in such total statutory income.

Losses incurred in the creation of a trade or business may be carried forward indefinitely but only up to 35% of statutory income. Carryback of losses is not permitted.

Group taxation

There are no special provisions for taxation of companies in a group. Each company is taxed independently of others in the group.

Tax incentives

A tax holiday is available to companies engaged in:

1. Agriculture, agro processing, industrial and machine tool manufacturing, machinery manufacture, electronics, export of non-traditional products, or information technology and allied services.
2. Any designated project.
3. An undertaking for large-scale infrastructure development.
4. Small-scale infrastructure undertakings for generation of power, tourism, recreation, warehousing and cold storage garbage collection or disposal, construction of houses or hospitals.

The period of the tax holiday will be determined by reference to the nature of the undertaking and the amount invested in the project.

- A tax holiday is available to any company that carries on any specified agricultural undertaking until 31 March 2011.
- A five year tax holiday is available to a new venture capital company satisfying specified criteria.
- A tax holiday is available to companies that commence new undertaking located outside the districts of Colombo and Gampaha and investing not less than SRL 30 million before 1 April 2009 in plant, machinery, furniture or building (and on land if such undertaking is an agricultural undertaking).
- Exemption from income tax is granted for profits from relocated undertakings in relation to any company that has relocated outside the districts of Colombo and Gampaha and, which prior to 1 November 2005, was being carried on in a location within the districts of Colombo or Gampaha.
- A five-year tax holiday is granted for the profits from the new undertaking of a company that is engaged solely in research and development in the field of science or technology with the object of using the results thereof for the production or improvement of products with a minimum investment of SRL 2 million.
- Exemption from income tax is granted on the profits and income earned in foreign currency, remitted to Sri Lanka net of expenses (considered reasonable by the tax authority), by a resident company in respect of services (including a construction project) rendered outside Sri Lanka (previously, these profits were taxable at 15%).
- Exemption from income tax is granted on the profits and income earned in foreign currency by any resident company, any resident individual or any partnership in Sri Lanka from the services rendered in or outside Sri Lanka in respect of any profession or vocation as is specified by the Commissioner General by notice published in the Gazette, if such profits and income (less such amount, expended outside Sri Lanka as is considered by the Commissioner General to be reasonable expenses) are remitted to Sri Lanka through a bank.
- Exemption from income tax is granted on the profits and income for the period from 1 April 2009 to 31 March 2011 earned in foreign currency by any resident company, resident individual, or any partnership in Sri Lanka, from any service rendered in or outside Sri Lanka to any person or partnership outside Sri Lanka if such profits and income (less such amount expended outside Sri Lanka as is considered by the Commissioner General to be reasonable expenses) are remitted to Sri Lanka through a bank.
- Exemption from income tax is granted in respect of dividends or interest received on the investment made outside Sri Lanka, provided that dividends and interest are remitted to Sri Lanka through a bank.
- New or existing companies that export non-traditional goods are entitled to be taxed on the profits from these exports or services at a concessionary rate of 15% for a period of 20 years, ending on 31 March 2014 and 2015, respectively. Dividends paid by such companies out of profits earned from the exports of non-traditional goods, which are taxed at 15%, are in turn liable to tax of 10% in the hands of corporate shareholders where the income tax is already withheld from the dividends (see below).
- Corporate profits from fisheries, construction and tourism are taxed at 15%. A company that produces or manufactures non-traditional goods and supplies these to a company for export or for use in the production or manufacture of goods for export by the latter company is entitled to be taxed on the profits from such supplies at a concessionary rate of 15%, provided the exporting company to which the goods are supplied is entitled to be taxed as mentioned above and the tax authority is satisfied that the goods supplied have been exported.

S

Sri Lanka

- Exemption from income tax is granted on the profits arising from trading in shares, rights to any share, bonus or share warrants in respect of which the share transaction levy has been charged.
- Exemption from income tax is granted on an amount equal to the interest or the discount paid or allowed to any non-resident person or to any licensed commercial bank in Sri Lanka by the issuer of any sovereign bond denominated in foreign currency, issued on or after 21 October 2008, by or on behalf of the government of Sri Lanka and on the profits and income from the sale of such sovereign bond.
- Exemption from income tax is granted on an amount equal to the interest or the discount paid or allowed to any person on or after 1 April 2009, on any Sri Lanka Development Bond denominated in United States dollars, issued by the Central Bank of Sri Lanka and on the profits and income from the sale of such Sri Lanka Development Bond.
- Exemption from income tax is granted on the profits and income derived by or accruing to any person or partnership from investment in Economic Resurgence Certificates, utilising money lying to credit of any account opened in any commercial bank or in any specialised bank with the approval of the Central Bank of Sri Lanka from and out of monies deposited in such account on or after 1 February 2009.
- Tax holidays outside the purview of the tax statute are also available in specified areas of investment to companies that enter into agreements with the Board of Investment of Sri Lanka (BOI). The specified areas include non-traditional export-oriented manufacturing and thrust industries, export-oriented services, large-scale projects of which the project cost exceeds SRL 500 million. Generous waiver of import duties on specified imports and other concessions are also available for these companies.

Withholding taxes (WHT)

Resident companies are entitled to withhold income tax at 10% of gross dividends payable to any shareholder that is chargeable with income tax, excluding any dividend received from another resident company and any dividend that is exempt from income tax.

Any person in Sri Lanka who pays or credits to a person or partnership outside of Sri Lanka any sum due as interest, rent, ground rent, royalty, or annuity is required to withhold income tax at a rate of 20% of the sum, but the requirement to withhold income tax does not apply to interest not sourced in Sri Lanka, or to interest on any loan or advance made by a banker or to interest paid on foreign currency held in an account with a foreign currency banking unit.

In particular instances, the tax authority may prescribe that income tax be withheld at a rate other than 20%, or the rate may be reduced for sums falling due as interest or royalties in respect of persons resident in countries with which Sri Lanka has double taxation treaties in force. Sri Lanka-source income from loan interest or royalties accruing to a non-resident company is taxed at a flat 20%, in the absence of a lower rate in the tax treaty with the home country of the non-resident.

Every bank and financial institution is required to withhold income tax at 10% on the amount of any interest paid on any sum of money deposited with it. The depositor is entitled to receive a certificate setting out the gross amount of interest, the amount of tax withheld and the net amount of interest paid. With respect to Treasury bills and

Treasury bonds issued by the Central Bank, the withholding tax rate of 10% applies to an investor from any country.

Every person or partnership that pays a fee to another person or partnership in consideration for services rendered by the latter in the course of any business, profession, vocation or activity of an independent character is required to withhold income tax at 5% of such fee and furnish a certificate to the payee similar to that described above. The withholding requirement is extended to any commission, brokerage fee or other income of a like nature, and also to any payment for supply of an article on contract through a tender or quotation.

Treaty countries	Dividends	Interest	Royalties
	%	%	%
Australia	15	10	10
Bangladesh	15	15	15
Belgium	15	10	10
Canada	15	15	10
China	10	10	10
Denmark	15	10	10
Finland	15	10	10
France	15	10	10, 0 (1)
Germany	15	10	10
Hong Kong (4)			
India	15	10	10
Indonesia	15	15	15
Iran	10	10	8
Italy	15	10	10
Japan	15	-2	(3), 0(1)
Korea, Rep. of	15, 10	10	10
Kuwait (4)			
Malaysia	15	10	10
Mauritius	15, 10	15, 10	10
Nepal	15	10, 15	15
Netherlands	15, 10	15, 10	10
Norway	15	10	10, 0 (1)
Oman (4)	–	–	–
Pakistan	15	10	20
Poland	15	10	10
Qatar	10	10	10
Romania	12.5	10	10
Russia	10, 15	10	10
Saudi Arabia	–	–	–
Singapore	15	10	15
Sweden	15	10	10
Switzerland	15, 10	10	10
Thailand	15	10	15
United Arab Emirates	10	10	10

S

Sri Lanka

Treaty countries	Dividends	Interest	Royalties
	%	%	%
United Kingdom	15	10	10
USA	15	10	–
Vietnam	–	–	

Notes

The numbers in parentheses refer to the notes below.

1. 0% for copyright royalties.
2. 0% in certain circumstances.
3. 50% of normal tax.
4. These treaties are limited to the avoidance of double taxation of income from international transport by air.

Tax treaties with the following countries, which are in different stages of negotiation or finalisation, await entry into force: Austria, Bulgaria, Jordan, Lebanon, New Zealand, the Philippines, Egypt, South Africa and Cyprus.

New proposals from Croatia, Ukraine, Saudi Arabia and Luxembourg were received.

Tax administration

A tax year is any period of 12 consecutive months reckoned from 1 April in any calendar year to 31 March of the following year.

Sri Lanka has a pay-and-file system under which the income tax payable for each tax year is required to be paid in four instalments, on or before 15 August, 15 November and 15 February of the tax year and the 15 May immediately following the end of the tax year. If each instalment is not less than one-quarter of the income tax payable for the tax year immediately preceding, the balance of any income tax payable may be paid on or before 30 September immediately following the end of the tax year without incurring penalties.

For more information, contact:

Jefferson Hunte
PricewaterhouseCoopers
Cnr. Bank Street & W. Independence Sq.
P.O. Box 1038
Basseterre, Saint Kitts
Tel: +1 869 466 8200
Email: jefferson.hunte@ag.pwc.com

Significant developments

In April 2010, the Government of the Federation of St. Kitts and Nevis (St. Kitts-Nevis) released a white paper on value-added tax (VAT) which it proposes to introduce in November 2010.

Taxes on corporate income

Corporate tax is currently imposed at a rate of 35% on all companies except exempt companies or enterprises that have been granted a tax concession. A company which carries on business exclusively with persons who are not resident in the Federation is exempt from all income, capital gains and withholding taxes. Companies registered under the Condominium Act are governed by that act and are not required to pay corporate tax.

Corporate residence

A corporation is deemed to be resident if it is incorporated in St. Kitts-Nevis or if it is registered as an external company doing business in St. Kitts-Nevis under the Companies Act.

Other taxes

Life insurance premium tax
A premium tax of 5% is levied on the premium income of all life insurance companies, whether resident or non-resident. In addition, a registration fee of East Caribbean dollar (XCD) 2 per XCD 1,000 or XCD 30, whichever is less, must be paid to the Comptroller of Inland Revenue.

General insurance premium tax
A premium tax of 5% is levied on the premium income (net of agent's commission) of all general insurance companies, whether resident or non-resident.

Stamp duty on the transfer of property
Stamp duty is levied on the consideration for the sale or the value of the property as assessed by the Property Valuation Officer, whichever is higher.

The vendor is responsible for the payment of all stamp duty on property transfers on the following basis:

St. Kitts and Nevis

a. Transfer of property for consideration in money or value in kind of not less than the value of the property	12%
b. Transfer of property for consideration in money or value in kind of less than the value of the property	12%
c. Transfer of property without consideration in money or value in kind	6%
d. Transfer of property in any Special Development Area other than the South East Peninsula	14% (on the consideration or market value)
e. Transfer of property situated in the South East Peninsula	18.5%
f. Transfer of property other than stock or debenture stock or funded debt or land	2%
g. Transfer of property between husband and wife and between parents and children and vice versa	XCD 100
h. Transfer of land by will or by similar instrument	XCD 100
i. Transfer of registered condominium units	5%

Where a developer has obtained concessions in connection with a house or building constructed on the land being transferred, the developer will be required to pay stamp duty on the same basis as noted in a., b. and c. above.

Where a developer has obtained concessions in connection with a house or building to be constructed on the land being transferred, then the developer will be required to pay stamp duty initially on the land on the same basis as noted in a., b. and c. above. However, when the house or building is subsequently constructed on the land with the aid of the concession, the owner of the building shall pay stamp duty on the house or building as provided in a., b. and c. above as if the concessions or any part thereof had not been utilised.

Where a developer has not obtained concessions in connection with a house or building constructed on the land being transferred, the developer will be required to pay stamp duty on the same basis as noted in a., b. and c. in respect of the land only.

Stamp duty on the transfer of shares
Stamp duty is levied on the value of the consideration for the sale of shares or debentures issued by or on behalf of a company or at the value assessed by the Property Valuation Officer, whichever is higher. The stamp duty is levied at a rate of 2%. If the company owns property and its value exceeds 50% of the value of the company's assets then the stamp duty would be calculated using the applicable rate on the transfer of property.

Stamp duty on mortgages
Stamp duty is levied on the total amount secured and is applicable to both the registration and discharge of the mortgage. The standard rate is 1% and, for amounts secured in relation to a Special Development Area, the rate is 2%.

Stamp duty on bank loans to aliens
Stamp duty is levied on the total amount of the loan. The standard rate is 2.5% and, for loans to finance development in a Special Development Area, the rate is 5%.

Alien land holding licenses

To hold property as an owner, a non-citizen must first obtain an alien land holding licence and pay 10% of the market value of property or XCD 750, whichever is greater.

A non-citizen is required to obtain a licence to hold shares in a company which owns land, to vote at shareholders meetings of the company and to be a director of the company. Each licence costs XCD 250.

If a non-citizen purchases property in the Frigate Bay area then there is no requirement to obtain a licence and only a minimal fee of XCD 50 is payable.

If a non-national wishes to purchase land in the South-East Peninsula the non-national is required to obtain a licence prior to purchasing the property however, the payment of the 10% licence fee would be waived.

Property Tax – St. Kitts

Property tax is levied at varied rates on the basis of the market value of the real property (including land and building as assessed by the Chief Valuation Officer) and its class.

Property classes and rates of tax are as follows:

Residential use property	0.2%
Commercial use property	0.3%

Annual allowances and tax rebates are available as follows:

1. Residential use property and condominium allowance of XCD 80,000 from the taxable value.
2. No property tax will be assessed on any buildings, condominiums etc. that are under construction.
3. New residential use property and condominiums are exempt from tax for one year from the date certified by the valuation officer.

Properties located in the South East Peninsula are assigned values based on fixed rates for land (XCD 20 per square ft.) and building (XCD 300 per square ft.). Property tax is then applied at a rate of 0.2%.

Where property situated in the South East Peninsula area is not developed within five years, a surcharge can be assessed at the rate per annum of 1% of the assessed market value and increased annually at the rate of 1% per annum thereafter until it reaches a maximum rate of 5% of the assessed market value while the property remains undeveloped. If property is less than one acre and undeveloped and owned by a resident for the purpose of erecting a house, such property shall be exempt from the surcharge upon application in writing to the Comptroller of Inland Revenue.

Property tax is payable on or before 30 June of each year. Tax is deemed to be in default if not paid within 30 days of becoming due. Interest is charged at a rate of 12% per annum on the unpaid taxes.

S

St. Kitts and Nevis

Property tax – Nevis

Property tax is levied at varied rates on the basis of the market value of the real property (including land and building as assessed by the Chief Valuation Officer) and its class.

Property class and rates are as follows:

Residential

Building	0.156%
Land	0.075%

Commercial

Building	0.3%
Land	0.2%

Accommodation

Building	0.3%
Land	0.2%

Certified farming

Building	0%
Land	0.01%

Institutional

Building	0.2%
Land	0.15%

Accommodation use property is defined as property for short term accommodation and includes a guest house.

Commercial use property is defined as property which does not include accommodation use property or property used for certified farming operations.

Annual allowances and tax rebates are available as follows:

1. Residential use property and condominium allowance of XCD 80,000 from the taxable value.
2. No property tax will be assessed on any buildings, condominiums etc. that are under construction.

Property tax is payable on or before 30 June of each year. Tax is deemed to be in default if not paid within 30 days of becoming due. Interest is charged at a rate of 12% per annum on the unpaid taxes.

Value-added tax (VAT)

There is currently no VAT. However, legislation is being drafted to introduce VAT in November 2010.

Hotel accommodation and restaurant tax

Hotel and restaurant tax is levied on the room revenue and revenue from food as follows:

- Hotel and accommodation and restaurant tax: 7%; and
- Island enhancement fund: 2%.

This tax is paid monthly and must be remitted to the Inland Revenue Department by the 15th of the following month. Interest at a rate of 1.25% per month or 15% per annum is charged on unpaid taxes in default.

These taxes will be repealed when VAT is introduced.

Branch income

Branch income is taxed on the same basis and at the same rate as the income of a corporation. Recharges of expenses from head office to the branch will be subject to withholding tax at a rate of 10%; however the recharges have to be justified and cannot be based on a percentage allocation.

A resident branch of a foreign company shall be regarded as a separate company and shall be taxed on the same basis as that of a locally registered corporation.

Income determination

Inventory valuation
Inventories are generally stated at the lower of cost or net realisable value. The first-in, first-out (FIFO) and average cost methods of valuation are generally used for book and tax purposes. However, the Comptroller of Inland Revenue will normally accept a method of valuation that conforms to standard accounting practice in the trade concerned. The last-in, first-out (LIFO) method is not permitted for tax or book purposes.

Capital gains
Capital gains tax will be imposed if an asset is sold within one year of the date of acquisition. The maximum rate of tax will be one half the corporation tax rate, which is 35%. Assets sold after one year will not attract capital gains tax.

Inter-company dividends
Dividends received by a company resident in St. Kitts-Nevis from another company resident in St. Kitts-Nevis are taxed at source at the rate of 35%. Credit is given to the recipient for the tax on the dividend in computing the tax liability.

Foreign income
A St. Kitts-Nevis corporation is taxed on foreign branch income when earned and on foreign dividends when received. Double taxation is avoided by means of foreign tax credits where active tax treaties exist and through deduction of foreign income taxes in other cases (the United Kingdom (UK), and the Caribbean Community (CARICOM)).

Deductions

Depreciation and depletion
Depreciation allowed for tax purposes is computed by the diminishing-balance method at prescribed rates. An initial allowance of 20% is granted on industrial buildings or structures and in respect of capital expenditure incurred on plant and machinery by a person carrying on a trade or undertaking, as defined. In addition, an annual

S

St. Kitts and Nevis

allowance of 2% – 5% is allowed on all buildings constructed after 1 March 1994. Concrete buildings are depreciated at a rate of 2% while the rate varies for other buildings depending on the type of material used in construction. Conformity between book and tax depreciation is not required. Any gain on the sale of depreciated assets is taxable as ordinary income up to the amount of tax depreciation recaptured. Initial allowances and annual allowances cannot reduce the tax that would have been otherwise payable by more than 50%. Any initial allowance or annual allowance not utilised may be carried forward indefinitely.

Contributions to a pension fund
Contributions made by an employer to a pension fund (approved by the Comptroller) on behalf of its employees up to a maximum of 5% of annual earnings of the employee or a maximum of XCD 2,000. Application should be made to the Ministry of Finance or to the Pension Fund Committee.

Net operating losses
Income tax losses may be carried forward for five years following the year in which the loss was incurred. However, the chargeable income of a company after deducting initial and annual capital allowances in any one income year may not be reduced by more than 50% by losses brought forward. No carryback of losses is permitted.

Payments to foreign affiliates
A company incorporated in St. Kitts-Nevis may claim a deduction for royalties, management fees and interest charges paid to foreign affiliates, provided the payments are equal to or less than what the corporation would pay to an unrelated entity. The deductibility of any payments to a foreign affiliate will be subject to an arm's-length test and withholding tax would be payable at a rate of 10%.

Non-deductible expenses – restriction on compensation
Salaries, wages, leave pay, fee, commission, bonus, gratuity, or any other perquisite or such other payment which an employee of a company receives in the course of his employment or the value of any benefit to such employee or to any member of his family in excess of XCD 60,000 per annum would not be allowed as a deduction from chargeable profit.

Non-deductible expenses – restriction on bad debts
Specific bad or doubtful debts in excess of 5% of total trade receivables will not be allowed as a deduction.

Group taxation

Group taxation is not permitted.

Tax incentives

Inward investment and capital investment
Tax incentives are currently available under the following legislation.

Income Tax Act, No. 17 of 1966
The Act provides that if a hotel is licensed under the Hotel Aids Ordinance and constructs a hotel with in excess of 30 bedrooms, the hotel will receive an exemption from income tax for a period of 10 years beginning on the day it is first open for

business. If the hotel has less than 30 rooms then it would be entitled to a five year tax holiday. During the tax holiday period no initial deductions or annual capital allowance deductions shall be allowed. Thereafter, only the annual allowance would be allowed and will be computed on the total capital expenditure incurred during the holiday period less any assets sold. The net losses arising during the tax holiday period (i.e., the excess of accumulated tax losses over total profits) may be carried forward and reduced against profits following the expiration of the tax holiday in accordance with the normal rules for set-off of losses.

The Income Tax Act also provides that if a licence is granted to a pioneer manufacturer under the Pioneer Industries Act the manufacturer is entitled to a five year tax holiday or for such period up to 10 years or as provided in the licence.

Hotel Aids Act
The Act provides that a licence may be granted to any person who desires to construct or extend an existing hotel to import building material and equipment as specified in the licence for use in the construction of the hotel and to furnish and equip the hotel. The holder of a licence may not dispose of any hotel equipment within three years of being imported free of duties and taxes. Permission must be received from the Comptroller of Customs to dispose of any building material and hotel equipment within the three year period.

Fiscal Incentives Act
The Act provides that if a company is declared to be an approved enterprise to manufacture certain approved products then the manufacturer would be entitled to a tax holiday period of between 10 and 15 years depending on the classification of the approved enterprise. The net losses arising during the tax holiday period (i.e., excess of all losses over all profits) may be carried forward and set-off against profits of the approved enterprise for the five year period following the tax holiday period.

Other incentives
Approved manufacturing, agricultural, and tourist ventures are permitted to import building material and equipment free of customs duties.

A Memorandum of Understanding (MOU) between the government and small hotel operators provides for certain conditions under which small hotel operators will be eligible for duty free concessions on the refurbishment of their facilities every seven years, and on food and wine for their restaurant facilities where applicable. For the purposes of this new incentive package, a small hotel is defined as a hotel consisting of at least 10 rooms and not exceeding 99 rooms.

Withholding taxes (WHT)

A WHT at the rate of 10% should be withheld from payments made to non-residents in respect of the following:

- Dividends;
- Interest, annuity, premium, and discount;
- Rent, lease, contract, and royalty payments;
- A natural resource payment;
- Commissions, remuneration, fees, and licences;

St. Kitts and Nevis

- Charges for the provision of personal services, commercial advice, and managerial skills;
- Administration, management, or head office expenses;
- Profit;
- Technical, professional, vocational, and any other service fees;
- Accounting, actuarial, legal, and audit expenses;
- Non-life insurance premiums; or
- Any other annual or periodic payment or distribution.

Tax treaties

There is a tax treaty with the UK and a double taxation agreement between member states of CARICOM.

Tax administration

Returns

Taxes are assessed on a fiscal-year basis. The taxpayer must file an information return on Form CIT–01 by the fifteenth of the fourth month after the fiscal year end with the financial statements. The authorities either accept the self-assessment or issue a revised assessment. If a return is not filed on a timely basis the authorities have the power to issue estimated assessments. There is a 2.5% penalty for late filing (minimum of XCD 1). The taxpayer can object to assessments raised within one month and ask the Comptroller of Inland Revenue to review and revise. In the event that the objection is unsuccessful, the taxpayer may appeal to the Commissioners of Income Tax. Assessments may be reviewed and revised by the comptroller within the year of assessment or within six years of the expiration of the assessment year.

Payment of tax

Advance tax is payable in quarterly instalments on 15 March, 15 June, 15 September and 15 December of each year and is ordinarily based on the tax chargeable and assessed in the previous fiscal year. The standard amount of each instalment is determined as one-fourth of the tax chargeable in the previous fiscal year. If the assessment for the prior year has not been finalised the Comptroller of Inland Revenue can raise an assessment based on his best judgment.

The balance of tax due after the final assessment is issued, as notified in the assessment, is payable on or before the fifteenth of the fourth month after the fiscal year end. If the Comptroller of Inland Revenue revises the assessment then payment of the balance of taxes due is due one month after the date of issue of the revised assessment.

Tax is deemed to be in default if not paid by the fifteenth of the fourth month after the fiscal year end or within one month of the date of the notice of assessment, whichever is later. Interest of 1% per month or 12% per annum is charged on unpaid taxes in default.

For more information, contact:

Richard Peterkin
PricewaterhouseCoopers
Pointe Seraphine
Castries, St. Lucia
Tel: +1 758 456 2600 Ext. 2626
Email: richard.n.peterkin@lc.pwc.com

Significant developments

In its annual budget address in April 2010, the government announced its intention to introduce tax reforms, which include the reintroduction of withholding tax on interest paid or accrued to non-residents, an increase in the tax on the use of cellular phones, a change in the property tax regime from the annual rental values to an open market valuation system for assessing residential properties, and an increase in the current rate of stamp duty for the conveyance and transfer sale or otherwise of a debenture, stock, debt or shares in a company. If enacted, the withholding tax rate on interest will be 15%; the tax on the use of cellular phones will increase from 10% to 15%; the property tax rate will change from 5% of the annual rental values to 0.25% of the open market valuation for residential properties; and an increase in the stamp duty from 2% of the nominal value of the shares to 0.5% of the net asset value of the company on a proportional basis. Some of these proposed tax changes have not been enacted to date, and are being reviewed. The following tax reforms that have been enacted are as follows:

1. Effective 1 May, 2010 a tax on the use of cellular phones is now 15% from 10%; and
2. Effective 14 June 2010, all persons making interest payments to non-residents should deduct withholding tax at a rate of 15%.

Taxes on corporate income

Income tax
Resident companies are subject to tax at a flat rate of 30% on taxable income. Companies that, prior to 2003, had tax in arrears, or had not complied with the requirements of the Income Tax Act (Act) were subject to tax at 33.33% until the arrears were paid and the company was compliant. Associations of underwriters are taxed at 30% on 10% of the gross premium arising in St. Lucia, and life insurance companies are taxed at 30% on 10% of the gross investment income arising in St. Lucia.

Corporate residence

Companies are regarded as resident if they are incorporated in St. Lucia, or managed and controlled through a permanent establishment (PE) in St. Lucia. A PE is defined as a fixed place or premises through which the business is wholly or partly carried on.

S

St. Lucia

Other taxes

Value-added tax (VAT)
VAT may be implemented in 2011, at the earliest.

Consumption tax
Consumption tax is levied on goods manufactured and on a wide range of imported goods. Rates range between 5% and 15%. For manufactured goods, the tax is charged on their open market value. For imported articles, consumption tax is charged as a percentage of the Cost, Insurance and Freight (CIF) value plus customs duty.

Stamp tax
Stamp tax is charged on any document that evidences a legal or contractual relationship between two or more parties. Additionally, many types of commercial and legal documents must be stamped, denoting the payment of taxes, which may be either at a fixed rate or at an *ad valorem* rate, depending, for example, on the value of the property transferred.

Stamp duty payable on the conveyance or transfer sale of immovable property, if paid by the purchaser is 5% *ad valorem*; if paid by the vendor where the vendor is not a citizen of St. Lucia or is a foreign company is 10% ad valorem; where the vendor is a citizen of St. Lucia or is a local company: (a) 2.5% ad valorem from XCD 50,000 to XCD 75,000 (b) 3.5% *ad valorem* from XCD 75,001 to XCD 150,000 and (c) 5% *ad valorem* from XCD 150,001 and over. The current rate of stamp tax under the stamp duty regulations for the conveyance, transfer sale of the debenture, stock, debt or shares of a company is 0.5% of the net asset value of the company, on a proportional basis.

The current regulations do not specify who pays the stamp duty on the transfer of shares, but the current practice is that the purchaser pays the 0.5% based on a recent balance sheet of the company. The government now proposes that the stamp duty on the sale of a company that owns immovable property would be the greater of 0.5% of the net asset value of the company, or the current stamp duties on the sale of the immovable property.

Commercial property tax
Commercial property tax is currently assessed at 0.25% of the open market value of the property. The owner is required to obtain a commercial valuation assessing the open market value of the property. All new commercial properties completed after 1 April 2001 can benefit from a three-year tax exemption from commercial property tax. The government now proposes an increase in the tax rate from 0.25% to 0.4% but no change to the current system has been enacted.

Residential property tax currently is charged on the annual rental value of property at the rate of 5%. Certain exemptions exist for new homeowners. The government now intends to change the property tax regime to an open market valuation system. Under the new regime, the rate will change to 0.4% of the open market valuation.

Transfer tax
Transfer tax is not applicable.

Turnover tax
Turnover tax is not applicable.

Registration tax
Registration tax is not applicable.

Custom duty tax
Customs duties are charged on a wide range of imported goods. Exemptions are granted for raw materials and plant and machinery used in manufacturing and for certain items imported by hotels under construction, extension or refurbishing projects.

Excise tax
Excise taxes are imposed on home-produced goods, mainly liquor, beer and cigarettes. ECD 1.44 per litre of liquid applies to beer in glass bottles and ECD 3.50 per liquid gallon applies to beers in metal cans. There is also an excise tax on fuel when fuel is imported by a wholesaler. Tax is included on the price of fuel paid at the gas pump. The tax rate formula is based on the current price provided by the supplier and regulated price at the gas pump.

Branch income

The tax rate on branch income is the same as that on income earned by resident companies. No additional tax is withheld on transfers of profits to the head office.

A proposal was announced by the government in 2009 to tax at a rate of 10% of after tax income of foreign owned branches and subsidiaries. If this proposal is enacted, withholding tax of 10% will be assessed on branch profits after tax, whether or not the profits are transferred to the head office. Some relief will be granted where branch profits are reinvested in new local property, plant and equipment, or other qualifying investments. This has not been enacted to date, and is being reviewed.

Income determination

Inventory valuation
Stocks generally are valued at the lower of cost or market value. Obsolescence is permitted where it occurs, but there are no provisions to account for monetary inflation on inventory valuation.

Capital gains
There is no tax on capital gains except in instances where such gains comprise a portion of the income-earning activities of the business; in this instance, the corporate rate applies.

Inter-company dividends
Inter-company dividends and dividends paid to individuals are not subject to tax.

Foreign income
Resident companies are taxed in St. Lucia on income earned outside St. Lucia. Reciprocal understandings exist with some countries for the avoidance of double taxation, and foreign tax is allowed as a credit against tax charged in St. Lucia. St. Lucia has no tax treaties with other countries, except for the member states that make up the

S

St. Lucia

Caribbean Community (CARICOM). There is an agreement among the governments of CARICOM for the avoidance of double taxation. Where no agreement exists, the foreign tax offset is the lesser of the foreign tax paid or the tax payable on that income in St. Lucia.

Stock dividends
A bonus issuance of shares out of distributable earnings or out of a capital surplus on the sale of fixed assets of a company is not taxable. Distributions to shareholders on the reconstruction or winding-up of a company are not subject to withholding tax, and are not subject to tax in the hands of shareholders.

If the proposals announced by the government in 2009 are enacted, distributions to non-resident shareholders will be subject to withholding tax of 10%.

Partnerships
Partnerships are not subject to tax since they are treated as conduits; the individual partners are taxed on their share of the partnership income based on a tax table that ranges from 10% to 30%.

Interest income
The corporate tax rate of 30% applies to interest income. However, interest income accrued to a company on treasury bills, bonds, debentures and income earned on securities issued by member governments of the Eastern Caribbean Central Bank are exempt income.

Royalty and rental income
The corporate income tax rate of 30% also applies to royalty and rental income. However, rental income from a residential accommodation shall be exempt from tax, if certain requirements as defined by regulations are met.

Unrealised exchange gains/losses
Unrealised exchange gains/losses are not taxable.

Common tax adjustments
Some of the common tax adjustments in St. Lucia are:

*   Depreciation expense – added back to income per the profit and loss account, but capital allowances are available.
*   Uncovenanted donations – added back (this deduction is allowed if there is a deed of covenant for a period of at least three years in favour of any religious, charitable, medical or educational institution or sporting body or fund of a public character approved by the Cabinet, if the donation is made to the St. Lucia National Trust. However, the donation may not exceed 25% of the assessable income of the claimant company).
*   Unrealised gains/losses – deducted/added back.
*   Exempt income, such as government securities and bonds – deducted.

Bribes, kickbacks, illegal payments
Bribes, kickbacks and illegal payments received by a company are includible in taxable income.

Deductions

Depreciation and depletion

The following capital allowances are available:

- An initial allowance of 20% is granted on the acquisition of industrial, agricultural and commercial buildings (except for hotels and rental properties); on plant and machinery, including motor vehicles and furniture; and on fixtures and equipment.
- Thereafter, annual allowances for wear and tear, ranging from 10% to 33.33%, are granted on the reducing-balance method, except for industrial and agricultural buildings, which are allowed an annual rate of 5% and commercial buildings (except for hotels and rental properties), which are allowed an annual rate of 2.5%.

Gains on disposal are taxable as ordinary income to the extent of depreciation recovered, and any proceeds in excess of the cost of the asset are treated as a capital gain, which is not subject to tax. Where the proceeds on disposal are lower than the tax written-down value of the asset, a balancing allowance is granted for the shortfall.

Net operating losses

Net operating losses may be carried forward for up to six years if the losses have not been fully absorbed earlier. Losses may not be carried back. In carrying losses forward, the amount that can be claimed in any subsequent year is restricted to one-half of the assessable income of that year.

Payments to foreign affiliates

There are no restrictions on the deductibility of interest paid to foreign affiliates, if the transaction is carried out at arm's length and at the commercial rates. However, deductions for management charges, allocations of head office expenses, royalties, and other charges that are subject to 25% withholding tax, are restricted to the lesser of the aggregate of those charges or 10% of all allowable business deductions, excluding cost of sales.

Taxes

Consumption taxes paid on goods imported or purchased, and sold in the ordinary course of business, are deductible for tax purposes. Property taxes are deductible where the property is used in producing assessable income. Income taxes, penalties and interest on tax in arrears are not deductible.

Other significant items

Foreign exchange gains or losses arising from foreign exchange transactions on trading items are assessable or deductible as realised gains or losses, if settled within normal credit terms. Gains or losses on other instruments, including inter-company loans, are recognised only when actually realised.

Interest expense

Interest on any loan, including interest payable on debentures, is an allowable deduction to the extent that the amount of such loan was used for the purpose of producing assessable income.

Accrued expenses

Accrued expenses are deductible as long as they are business related.

St. Lucia

Bad debt
Bad debt expense is deductible provided it has been brought to account in generating the company's assessable income for any income year.

Charitable contribution/donation
Charitable contributions/donations are an allowable deduction when the contributions/donations are made under a deed of covenant for a period of not less than three years to any religious, charitable, medical, or educational institution or sporting body or fund of a public character, approved by Cabinet, if such contributions/donations are made to the St. Lucia National Trust. However, the deduction with respect to such contributions/donations shall not exceed 25% of the assessable income of the company for that income year.

Contingent liabilities
Contingent liabilities are deductible expenses once they are recognised in the book of accounts.

Organisational and start-up expenses
All expenditures incurred in connection with incorporation costs for the establishment of a new small business enterprise are allowable deductions. A small business enterprise is an enterprise incorporated during the year of income and (i) is wholly owned by citizens of St. Lucia who have not been owners of previously incorporated businesses in St. Lucia; (ii) employs not more than 50 persons; (iii) has gross income that does not exceed ECD 1 million; (iv) engages in an activity on the listing of preferred business activities as approved by the Minister; and (v) satisfies the provision of any law in force with respect to micro or small scale business.

Pension expense
Current annual contributions to an approved pension fund are deductible expenses. However, where a special payment is made to an approved pension fund, in relation to a period of service by an employee prior to the setting up of the approved pension fund, or to meet any actuarially ascertained insufficiency in the resources of the approved pension fund to meet its obligations to its employees, such amount shall be allowed as follows: (i) where the special payment does not exceed the current annual contribution, such amount is wholly allowed; (ii) where the special payment exceeds the current annual contribution, such payment is an allowable deduction in such year of income, not exceeding five years; (iii) where under (ii) above, annual deductions are allowable over a number of years of income, the first such deduction is allowable for the income year for which the special payment is made.

Goodwill
Neither the amortisation of impaired goodwill nor the related write-off of it is an allowable deduction.

Other deductions
Meals and entertainment, officer's compensation/life insurance and payment to directors are deductible expenses, provided they are wholly and exclusively incurred by a company during that year of income for the purpose of producing its assessable income.

Group taxation

Consolidation/Group taxation rules

Group tax filing is not allowed in St. Lucia; however, group tax relief is available to allow the trading losses, excluding the current loss, of a resident company within a group to offset the profits of another resident company within the same group.

Treatment of inter-company items

Inter-company dividends are not subject to tax however, there is a proposal to withhold 10% tax on dividends paid or accrued to non-residents. Inter-company royalties, management charges and commissions paid to non-residents are subject to a 25% withholding tax. If the recent proposals announced by the government are enacted, inter-company interest payments to non-residents will be subject to a 15% withholding tax.

Related party transactions

Related party transactions are accepted if they are made on an arm's-length basis. The Inland Revenue has the power under the Income Tax Act to make any adjustment deemed necessary to place such transactions at arm's length.

Tax incentives

Inward investment

Income tax incentives and other fiscal concessions are provided under the Fiscal Incentives Act, the Tourism Incentives Act, the Special Development Areas Act and other concessions granted by the Cabinet of Ministers. The extent of the incentives and concessions granted are specific to the legislation or Cabinet conclusions, and depend on the impact that the investment would have on local employment, exports and the generation of foreign exchange earnings. The incentives granted include the following:

- Duty-free importation of raw materials, machinery, components, and spare parts and other inputs used in manufacturing, and the duty-free importation of construction materials, equipment and other inputs used in the construction and operation of hotels and other hospitality products;
- Income tax waivers of up to 100% of the taxable income of companies engaged in manufacturing, tourism and agriculture and other employment generating activities, for periods of up to 15 years;
- Whole or partial waivers of property tax, stamp duties, Alien Landholding License fees, withholding taxes and consumption taxes with respect to investments in specific areas, or in specific industries and activities;
- Guaranteed repatriation of capital, dividends and interest; and
- Export allowances for goods manufactured in St. Lucia and exported.

Capital investment

The Income Tax Act provides an initial allowance of 20% on the cost of property, plant and equipment, on which capital allowances may be claimed, in the year in which they are acquired. The Comptroller of Inland Revenue may also grant, on application, a higher rate for annual allowance for assets that have higher or abnormal wear and tear.

Other incentives

Tax incentives are also available in the Income Tax Act for hiring university graduates (additional 25% of salaries), hiring persons in the offshore financial services industry

S

with skills not available in St. Lucia, and complete or partial waivers of income tax on the taxable profits of companies engaged in providing services to the offshore financial services industry.

Foreign taxes paid

Where income has accrued to a resident and has been taxed in a foreign country with which there is no double tax agreement, or is income to which a double tax agreement, if there is one, does not relate, credit for tax on such income is allowed for the lesser of: the tax payable in the foreign country or the tax charged under St. Lucia tax law.

Tax holiday

Tax holidays are available for manufacturing companies. The incentives are aimed at increasing the manufacturing base of St. Lucia, the level of exports, and the use of local materials and labour in production. An approved manufacturing enterprise will be granted a tax holiday up to a maximum of 15 years. In determining the length of the tax holiday, account is taken of the extent of the local value added to approved products. Special tax concessions are available for capital construction in the hotel industry. Capital expenditures on the construction of a hotel may offset profits for up to 15 years.

Withholding taxes (WHT)

Domestic corporations and persons that make certain payments of an income nature to residents or non-residents are required to withhold tax on these payments as follows:

Recipient	%
Resident corporations:	
Payments to contractors	10
Equipment hire	10
Non-resident corporations	10
Interest	15
Royalties	25
Management fees	25
Commissions or fees (not by way of employment)	25
Income of a trust	25
Premiums, including insurance premiums	25
Any other payment of an income nature	25

Tax administration

Returns

Tax returns must be filed within three months of the company's fiscal year-end. Returns must cover a 12-month period, which may be changed only with the Comptroller's permission.

Payment of tax

Tax is payable in instalments on 25 March, 25 June and 25 September in each year of income, based on the preceding year's income. Any remainder is payable within three months of the end of the financial year.

Audit cycle

Every locally incorporated company and any other company that has carried on business in St. Lucia in an income year are required to file an income tax return. The returns are due three months after the end of the company's fiscal period. An extension of the filing date may be obtained. Financial statements must be submitted with the returns, together with a schedule reconciling taxable income with book income and various other schedules of additional information.

Assessments

The system is one of self-assessment. Upon receipt of the returns, the Inland Revenue Department examines the information provided and issues a notice of assessment at any time, subject to the statute of limitations. The Revenue Department may also issue assessments in the absence of returns.

Appeals

Within 30 days after the date of service of a notice of assessment or reassessment, the taxpayer may submit a written objection to the Revenue Department on any matters in such assessment or reassessment. If the Revenue Department confirms its assessment, the taxpayer may file an appeal with the Appeal Commission, which comprises seven persons appointed by the Minister of Finance. A decision by that body may be further appealed to the St. Lucia High Court within 30 days. An appeal against an order from this Court may be made to the Court of Appeal.

Tax audits

The Inland Revenue Department carries out audits of a selection of tax returns, usually at the taxpayer's place of business. Audits may be carried out at any time prior to the expiration of the statute of limitations, whether or not notices of assessment have been issued. The Revenue Department has wide powers in determining the information it requires for these audits.

Penalties and interest

The following civil penalties and interest, which are non-deductible, are imposed:

- For late filing or for failure to file – 5% of the tax charge at filing date;
- For late payment – 10% of the unpaid tax at the due date;
- On tax and penalties unpaid – monthly interest at a rate of 1.04% ; and
- Tax knowingly evaded or sought to be evaded – 100% of the tax.

Statute of limitations

Assessments are not final until six years after the end of the income year, within which period assessments may be made at any time. In cases of misrepresentation or failure to disclose any material fact, a reassessment can be made at any time.

Other issues

The Income Tax Act, Chapter 15.02, became effective on 31 December 2001. The main purpose of this Act was to consolidate amendments that had been made to the previous Income Tax Act in the previous 12 years. There have been a number of amendments since 2001, mainly to reduce corporate tax rates and provide other relief and incentives granted in annual government budgets. Regional and national committees have made recommendations for tax reform but no major changes have been implemented or proposed.

S

Corporate taxes in Swaziland

For more information, contact:

Theo Mason
PricewaterhouseCoopers
MTN Office Park
Old Tavern Hotel Site
Karl Grant Street
Mbabane, Swaziland
Tel: +268 404 2861
Email: theo.mason@sz.pwc.com

Significant developments

There have been no recent significant developments in corporate taxation
in Swaziland.

Taxes on corporate income

The corporate income tax rate is 30%.

Corporate residence

Income tax is levied on all income derived from sources generated within or deemed to
be generated within the country, irrespective of whether the recipient of the income is
actually resident in Swaziland.

Other taxes

There are no capital gains taxes or estate taxes.

Sales tax is levied at a rate of 14% (25% for liquor and cigarettes) on goods imported
into Swaziland and on the first sale of goods manufactured for sale in Swaziland.
Customs and excise duties are also imposed on such goods. A 14% tax is applicable to
most professional services.

Branch income

Income tax on registered branch profits is calculated as for a resident company.
In practice, branches are rare, as most foreign companies incorporate local
subsidiary companies.

Income determination

Inventory valuation
Inventory valuation is not specific but is effectively at the lower of cost (first-in, first-out
(FIFO) or average cost) and net realisable value.

Capital gains
Capital gains are not subject to income tax, provided it can be demonstrated that the
gains are of a capital and not an income nature (i.e., recurring transactions).

Inter-company dividends
Inter-company dividends are not subject to income tax. *(See Withholding taxes section.)*

Foreign income
Foreign income is not subject to income tax unless it is deemed to be from a Swaziland source.

Stock dividends
Stock dividends are paid out of taxed profits. Such dividends are not subject to income tax when received by a local company, but are subject to taxation in the hands of local individual taxpayers at the rate of 10%.

Deductions

Depreciation
Depreciation (wear-and-tear) allowances calculated by the net-reducing-balance method are available as follows:

Asset	Rate (%)
Aircraft	25
Casino equipment	15
Construction equipment	25
Computer hardware	33.33
Computer software	33.33
Furniture and fittings	10
Hotel soft furnishings, including carpets	10
Legal and professional libraries	5
Lifts and elevators	25
Motor vehicles:	
Buses	33.33
Cars	20
Light delivery vehicles	25
Lorries	33.33
Office equipment	10
Plant and machinery	10
Sound and projection equipment	20
Television sets	20
Tractors	25
Trailers	20
Video recorders	33.33
Videotapes	25

For the first year after the addition of an asset, the wear-and-tear allowance is calculated on a monthly basis. With respect to leased assets, the lessor's claim for wear-and-tear allowance is usually spread over the lease period.

An initial allowance of 50% is granted for plant and machinery used in a manufacturing process, including hotel equipment. An initial allowance of 50% is

S

Swaziland

granted for industrial buildings used for manufacturing purposes and hotels, together with a 4% annual allowance.

Net operating losses
Losses may not be carried back but may be carried forward for as long as trading continues. If any break in trading occurs, the losses are forfeited.

Payments to foreign affiliates
Deductions may be claimed for payments of management service fees, interest and royalties to foreign affiliates, provided the payments are made under a written agreement, are reasonable and receive exchange control approval for transfers outside the rand monetary area. This approval is routinely given without any significant delay for bona fide transactions.

Group taxation

There is no specific group taxation legislation. All companies are assessed on individual profits and losses.

Tax incentives

Tax holidays
Tax holidays are no longer available.

Development enterprises
The Minister of Finance, along set guidelines and with prior consent of the Cabinet, may nominate a business as a developmental enterprise (i.e., a business the Minister deems to be beneficial to the development of the economy) for a grant of a Development Approval Order. If approved, the business generally will be granted tax concessions, for example, a lower corporate tax rate.

Training expenditure
Approved training schemes resulting in a 150% tax deduction of salaries is no longer available.

Withholding taxes (WHT)

Non-resident taxes are levied as follows.

Dividends
Tax is payable at the rate of 15% (12.5% for companies registered in Botswana, Lesotho and the Republic of South Africa). Variations may occur under certain double taxation agreements. Non-resident shareholders' tax is payable within 30 days of the date on which the dividend is payable.

Interest
Tax is payable at the rate of 10% on interest. Non-resident tax on interest is payable within 14 days of the date of the accrual of the interest.

Entertainers and sportsmen

Tax is payable at the rate of 15% on income earned in Swaziland by entertainers and sportsmen. This tax relates only to public entertainers and sportsmen not ordinarily resident in Swaziland. The payer is required to deduct the tax and pay it within 15 days.

Contractors or professionals

Tax is payable at the rate of 15% on services provided by contractors or professionals in Swaziland (materials are not taxed to the extent that materials are incidental to the overall charge). The Commissioner of Taxes must be notified of any agreement relating to construction operations or professional services under which payments are made to non-resident persons within 30 days after entering into the agreement. It is required that the tax be paid within 15 days from the date of payment.

Tax administration

Returns

The tax year runs from 1 July to 30 June. Companies are required to have a 30 June year end, unless another year end date is approved by the Commissioner of Taxes; such approval is routinely given. Income tax returns should be submitted within 30 days of 30 June, unless an extension of time for submission is granted, which also is routinely given.

Payment of tax

Notice of the date of payment is usually given on the tax assessment.

Provisional tax

With respect to companies, provisional tax is payable in two instalments: one payment is due within six months of the company's financial year-end and the other payment is due no later than the last day of the company's financial year.

The estimate of taxable income for provisional tax purposes should not be less than the taxable income assessed for the latest preceding year of assessment, for which an assessment has been issued not less than 21 days before the date the estimate is made. This rule does not apply if the taxpayer can convince the Commissioner of Taxes that the taxable income for the current year will be less than the taxable income for the preceding year.

A provisional taxpayer becomes liable to pay a penalty if the estimate for taxable income for the second payment of provisional tax is both found to be less than 90% of the taxable income as finally determined and is less than the taxable income as assessed for the immediately preceding tax year.

S

For more information, contact:

Magnus Johnsson
PricewaterhouseCoopers
Torsgatan 21
SE-113 97 Stockholm
Sweden
Tel: +46 8 555 331 72
Email: magnus.johnsson@se.pwc.com

Gunnar Andersson
PricewaterhouseCoopers
Torsgatan 21
SE 113 97 Stockholm
Sweden
Tel: +46 8 555 338 60
Email: gunnar.andersson@se.pwc.com

Significant developments

The Swedish corporate tax rate has been reduced from 28% to 26.3%, partly to be financed by the interest deduction restrictions. The new tax rate is applicable for financial years commencing on or after 1 January 2009.

In 2009, Sweden enacted anti-debt push down provisions under which a deduction is not allowed for interest payments on any intra-group loans for the acquisition of shares from an affiliate, unless the creditor is taxed on the interest income at a rate of at least 10% (tax rate comparison), or it is shown that the share transfer and the debt is based on commercial reasons. Note that also for loan agreements that may have been signed years ago, the interest payments are covered by these new provisions.

In 2010, shares in partnerships (tax transparent entities) were included in the Swedish participation exemption regime for capital gains (thus, making capital losses non-deductible). This also includes capital gains from qualifying indirect holdings via a partnership. The provision requires that partners restore negative acquisition costs on the partnership share for taxation.

Taxes on corporate income

State (national) income tax
Taxable income is subject to tax at the rate of 26.3% for financial years commencing on or after 1 January 2009. The previous rate was 28%. All income of corporate entities is treated as business income.

Resident legal entities are liable for tax on their worldwide income unless tax treaties or special exemptions apply. Non-resident entities are taxed on income that is deemed to have its source within Sweden.

Corporate residence

A company is considered to be tax resident of Sweden, if it is incorporated in Sweden.

Other taxes

Value-added tax (VAT)
The Swedish VAT system is harmonised with the European Community rules. The general VAT rate is 25% and chargeable on most goods and services. Reduced rates apply to a few goods and services, such as food that is taxed at the rate of 12% and

transport of passengers that is taxed at the rate of 6%. Certain financial and insurance services are exempt from VAT.

Stamp duty
Stamp tax at 3% is payable on a transfer of real estate. The tax base consists of the highest of the purchase consideration or the tax assessed value of the real estate. Stamp tax on an intra-group transfer of real estate may be deferred as long as the real estate remains within the group.

Social fees
Mandatory social security charges payable by employers on remuneration to employees (or by the self-employed) are levied at approximately 31%. Reduced rates apply for young or old people. Social security charges are deductible for corporate tax purposes.

Pension benefits beyond the mandatory system are customary amongst most Swedish employers. A special salary tax is levied at approximately 24% on these additional pension premiums/commitments. The tax is deductible for corporate tax purposes.

Real estate tax
Buildings are divided into business premises and apartments. The tax rate on business premises is 1% of the tax assessed value. For industrial property, the tax rate is 0.5%. The tax rate on apartments has been lowered to SEK 1,272 per apartment but no more then 0.4% of the tax assessed value as of 1 January 2009.

Branch income

Branch income (permanent establishment income) is taxed at the corporate tax rate of 26.3% and general corporate tax rules apply for branch offices in Sweden. No withholding tax is levied on the outbound repatriation of taxed profits.

The term permanent establishment (PE) is defined as a fixed place of business through which the business is carried on from a specific establishment, such as a place of management, branch, office, factory, or workshop. Places where entrepreneurial work is carried on are also regarded as PEs as well if an agent or a representative who is dependent upon the foreign company habitually exercises his authority in Sweden.

The receipt of Swedish source royalties or fees for use of tangible or intangible assets by a foreign resident is also (subject to treaty) regarded as PE income.

Income determination

Inventory valuation
Inventories (stock-in-trade) are valued at acquisition cost or market value, whichever is lower. As an alternative, inventories may be valued at 97% of the total acquisition cost, which is determined on a FIFO (first-in, first-out) basis. LIFO (last-in, first-out) is not permitted. Generally, inventories should be stated at the same amount for tax and accounting purposes.

Capital gains
The abolishment of the capital gains taxation for corporations has under the participation exemption provisions made Sweden a favourable holding company location. The capital gains tax exemption applies for Swedish corporate entities on gains related to the disposal of shares held for business reasons.

S

Sweden

Shares in Swedish corporations as well as in foreign companies can qualify as shares held for business reasons. Unquoted/unlisted shares will always be considered as held for business reasons. Quoted/listed shares are considered held for business reasons, provided that the company has a holding corresponding to at least 10% of the voting rights, or the shares are held in the course of the business. An additional condition regarding quoted/listed shares is that the shares must be held for a period of at least one year.

As of 2010, participation in partnerships (tax transparent entities) became included in the capital gains tax exemption regime (making losses non-deductible), including qualifying indirect holdings via a partnership.

An exception from the capital gains tax exemption applies for the sale of shares in a "shell company", that is, a company or partnership where the market value of cash, shares and other marketable instruments (other than shares held for business reasons) and similar assets exceeds 50% of the consideration paid for the shares. The sale of a shell company results in harsh taxation of the gross consideration. Provided certain formalities are fulfilled it is, however, possible to avoid such taxation.

A consequence of the participation exemption is that capital losses on shares or participations held for business reasons are not deductible.

Capital losses on portfolio holdings of shares, share options, convertible debentures, and similar financial instruments are allowed only as an offset to capital gains on the same group of financial instruments. Certain special rules apply to computation of capital gains and losses on real estate.

Inter-company dividends
Participation exemption will apply for dividends received on shares held for business reasons *(see above)*, and on qualifying holdings via partnerships. The requirement of a minimum holding period for a holding of quoted/listed shares can be fulfilled retroactively.

Foreign income
Companies resident in Sweden are taxed on their worldwide income. Non-resident entities are taxed on income that is deemed to have its source within Sweden.

A Swedish corporation is taxed on foreign branch income. Double taxation normally is avoided by means of either a deduction for foreign tax, or a foreign tax credit.

Dividends and capital gains from foreign subsidiaries are generally exempt from taxation according to the domestic provisions (tax exemption for dividends on shares held for business reasons, *see above*).

Controlled foreign corporations (CFC) legislation
Sweden's CFC provisions aim at taxing a Swedish resident shareholder for shareholdings in low-taxed foreign entities. A Swedish resident shareholder with a holding in a CFC-entity will annually be taxed for its ownership portion of the income, according to provisions applicable to a Swedish corporation. For a corporation, the portion will be taxed at the Swedish corporate tax rate. Only holdings, direct or indirect through other foreign entities, corresponding to at least 25% (capital or voting rights) in the foreign entity could lead to CFC taxation. A foreign company is

considered lowly taxed, if the income in the company, calculated in accordance with Swedish provisions, is taxed at a rate below 14.47%. However, if the foreign entity is resident in an "approved country", CFC taxation should not arise. Approved countries appear in an official "black/white" list. Active European Economic Area entities are under certain circumstances excluded from CFC taxation.

Deductions

Depreciation and depletion
The following allowances are available:

Depreciation on fixed assets
Land improvements may be depreciated at the rate of 5% per year of the acquisition cost. The maximum allowance is 100% of the tax basis of the improvement.

Buildings may be depreciated at rates between 2% and 5% per year of the taxable basis, depending on type and usage of the building. The maximum allowance is 100% of the tax basis of the building.

Machinery, equipment, motor vehicles, patents, leaseholds, and goodwill: The depreciation for tax purposes should correspond to the depreciation charged in the books and accounts, as long as the total net value of the assets is not less than the 70% of net value in previous accounts plus additions less proceeds of sales (i.e., 30% declining balance depreciation); or cost less 20% per year (i.e., 20% straight-line depreciation on remaining assets).

Currently deductible
The cost of assets having an expected life of not more than three years and the cost of assets not exceeding certain levels, depending on size of operations may be deducted immediately. Certain costs for repairs, maintenance and modifications of buildings may also be deducted immediately.

Mines and quarries
The entire cost of mines and quarries may be depleted over their expected exploitation period. These depletion amounts may be deducted annually but are limited to 100% of the acquisition cost of the mine or quarry.

Net operating losses
Tax losses may be carried forward indefinitely, subject to restrictions or forfeiture upon ownership changes, mergers and demergers, dispositions with creditors and certain other reorganisations.

Payments to foreign affiliates
Transactions with an affiliate not liable for tax in Sweden must be at arm's length.

Formal transfer pricing documentation requirements apply since 1 January 2007.

Taxes
Generally, Swedish taxes are not deductible for tax purposes. However, specific taxes, fees and foreign taxes may be deductible. Recoverable VAT is not treated as an expense or cost.

Sweden

Group taxation

Swedish companies are not taxed on a consolidated basis. However, it is for qualifying groups (i.e., a holding of greater than 90% of the capital which must have been owned during the whole fiscal year) possible effectively to offset operating losses of one Swedish company against operating profits of another Swedish company by way of group contributions, which is tax deductible for the contributor and taxable for the recipient. European Economic Area (EEA) companies are regarded as Swedish companies for these purposes, if the recipient is taxable in Sweden.

Tax incentives

There are no specific tax incentives in Sweden for corporations. However, some generally applicable regimes exist.

First, machinery and equipment is subject to accelerated depreciation at a maximum 30% of declining balance rate.

Second, Sweden has an accrual income reserve account regime. The accrual income reserve regime allows for a tax-deductible appropriation for corporations of 25% of the taxable profit before appropriation to a reserve. Each year's appropriation forms a separate reserve that must be reversed to income no later than the sixth year following the appropriation. However, a standardised interest income is imposed on former years' appropriations with 72% of the interest rate on governmental debt notes.

Third, interest on any debt is deductible as long as it meets an arm's-length requirement, and the anti-debt push down provisions are not applicable. There is no outbound interest withholding tax. There are also no thin capitalisation rules for tax purposes.

Withholding taxes (WHT)

There are no Swedish taxes on interest and service fees paid to non-resident corporations or individuals. Such payments to resident corporations and individuals are taxed as ordinary income. Domestic withholding tax is due on various payments to resident individuals. Withholding taxes on dividends, royalties and certain rentals vary according to domestic law and tax treaties, as shown below.

Apart from the highlighted treaties, Sweden has concluded agreements on exchange of information in tax matters and partial tax treaties with many tax haven jurisdictions.

Recipient	Cash dividends (1) (2)	Royalties, certain rentals (3)
	%	%
Resident corporations	Nil (4)	Nil (5)
Resident individuals	30 (4)	Nil (5)
Non-resident corporations and individuals:		
Non-treaty	30	Nil (5)
Treaty:	(6)	
Albania	15/5	5

Recipient	Cash dividends (1) (2)	Royalties, certain rentals (3)
	%	%
Argentina	15/10 (7)	3/5/10/15 (7)
Australia	15	10
Austria	10/5 (6)	10/Nil (8)
Bangladesh	15/10	10
Barbados	15/5	5/Nil (9)
Belarus	10/5/Nil	10/5/3 (10)
Belgium	15/5 (6)	Nil
Bolivia	15/Nil	15
Botswana	15	15
Brazil	25/15	25/15
Bulgaria	10	5
Canada	15/10/5	10/Nil (11)
Chile (12)	10/5	5/10
China, P.R (13)	10/5	10
Cyprus	15/5 (6)	Nil
Czech Republic (14)	10/Nil (6)	5/Nil (9)
Denmark (15) (16)	15/Nil (6) (16)	Nil (16)
Egypt	20/5	14
Estonia	15/5 (6)	10/5 (17)
Faroe Islands (15) (16)	15/Nil (16)	Nil (16)
Finland (15) (16)	15/Nil (6)	Nil
France	15/Nil (6)	Nil
Gambia	15/5/Nil	12.5/5 (18)
Germany	15/Nil (6)	Nil
Greece	Nil (6)	5
Hungary	15/5(6)	Nil
Iceland (15) (16)	15/Nil (16)	Nil (16)
India	10	10/Nil
Indonesia	15/10	15/10 (19)
Ireland, Rep. of	15/5 (6)	Nil
Israel	15/5	Nil
Italy	15/10 (6)	5
Jamaica	22.5/10	10
Japan	15/5/0	10
Kazakhstan	15/5	10
Kenya	25/15	20
Korea, Rep. of	15/10	15/10 (20)
Latvia	15/5 (6)	10/5 (17)
Lithuania	15/5 (6)	10/5 (17)
Luxembourg	15/Nil (6)	Nil
Macedonia	15/Nil	Nil
Malaysia (12)	15/Nil	8
Malta	15/Nil (6)	Nil
Mauritius	15/5	15

S

Sweden

Recipient	Cash dividends (1) (2) %	Royalties, certain rentals (3) %
Mexico	15/5	10
Namibia	15/5/Nil	15/5 (21)
Netherlands	15/Nil (6)	Nil
New Zealand	15	10
Norway (15) (16)	15/Nil (16)	Nil (16)
Pakistan	30/15	10
Philippines	15/10	15
Poland (12)	15/5 (6)	5
Portugal	10/Nil (6)	10
Romania	10	10
Russia	15/5	Nil
Singapore	15/10	Nil
Slovak Republic (14)	10/Nil (6)	5/Nil (9)
South Africa	15/7.5/Nil	Nil
Spain	15/10 (6)	10
Sri Lanka	15	10
Switzerland	15/Nil	Nil
Taiwan	10	10
Tanzania	25/15	20
Thailand	30/20/15	15
Trinidad and Tobago	20/10	20/Nil (22)
Tunisia	20/15	15/5 (23)
Turkey	20/15	10
Ukraine	10/5/Nil	10/Nil
United Kingdom	5/Nil (6)	Nil
United States	15/5/0	Nil
Venezuela	10/5	10/7 (24)
Vietnam	15/10/5	15/5 (25)
Yugoslavia (former) (26)	15/5	Nil
Zambia	15/5	10
Zimbabwe	20/15	10

Notes

1. According to domestic law there is no withholding tax on dividends to a foreign company on shares held for business reasons (for the definition of shares held for business reasons, *see above*), provided that the foreign company is similar to a Swedish limited liability company (and some other legal entities) and is subject to income tax at similar level to that imposed on a Swedish company. Further, there is no tax liability for a legal entity of a member state of the EU if the entity owns 10% or more of the share capital in the distributing company and fulfils the conditions of the Directive (90/435) regarding parent company and subsidiaries.
2. The reduced rate shown after a stroke (/) refers to payments to corporations having requisite control. Where appropriate, the particular treaty should be consulted to see whether the reduced rate is applicable. For dividends to a foreign company on shares held for business purposes (*see Note 1*).
3. Swedish source royalties and certain rental fees are treated as a special form of PE, taxable at the corporate tax rate, subject to treaty reduction or waiver. Royalties paid

from Sweden to a company within the EU should not be taxed in Sweden if one of the companies holds at least 25% (capital) of the other, or where there are two companies concerned, at least 25% are held by another company within the EU. Indirect participation does not benefit from the legislation. Both the payer and the recipient must be legal entities under the EU directive.

4. Payments to resident corporations and individuals are taxed as ordinary income. Only resident banks and similar entities are required to withhold tax on payments of cash dividends to resident individuals.

5. Royalties and certain rentals paid by Swedish licensees are treated as business income taxable in Sweden and do not incur withholding taxes *(see Note 3)*.

6. Note also the domestic provision stating a 0% withholding tax on dividends distributed on shares held for business reasons to qualifying entities *(see Note 1)*.

7. Dividends – 10% of the gross amount if the company receiving the dividends owns at least 25% of the foreign company's capital. Royalties – Of the gross amount paid for the use of, or the right to use:
   a. News – 3%;
   b. Copyright of literary, dramatic, musical, or other artistic work – 5%;
   c. Any patent, trademark, design or model, plan, or secret formula or process; industrial or scientific equipment or information concerning industrial, commercial or scientific experience; payments for the rendering of technical assistance – 10%; and
   d. All other cases – 15%.

8. Royalties are normally taxable only in the recipient's home country. However, where the royalty is paid by a Swedish legal entity that is more than 50% owned by one Austrian recipient, entity or individual, the tax in Sweden is a maximum of 10%.

9. Literary, artistic or scientific royalties – Nil; other royalties – 5%.

10. Royalties for use of industrial, commercial or scientific equipment – 5%; with respect to patents, secret formulas or processes or for information concerning industrial, commercial or scientific experience – 3%; other royalties – 10%.

11. Royalties for use of copyright and literary, dramatic, musical, and artistic royalties – nil. Other royalties – 10%. (Treaty should be consulted).

12. The treaty has effect on income derived on or after 1 January 2006.

13. The double taxation treaty does not include Hong Kong.

14. The same treaty is applicable to the Czech Republic and the Slovak Republic.

15. According to the Nordic multilateral tax treaty.

16. Dividends are exempt from tax if the recipient of the dividends is a company directly owning at least 10% of the capital of the company paying out the dividends. Certain rentals are subject to tax if there is a permanent establishment in a state other than the home state and the claim is connected with the business carried on from the permanent establishment. Concerning Iceland, dividends are normally exempt from tax for companies, but the tax rate is 15% if the dividends have been deducted from the income of the distributing company.

17. Royalties for the use of industrial, commercial or scientific equipment – 5%; other royalties – 10%.

18. Royalties with respect to patents, secret formulas or processes or for information concerning industrial, commercial or scientific experience – 5%; other royalties – 12.5%.

19. Royalties for the use of industrial, commercial or scientific equipment or for information concerning industrial, commercial or scientific experience – 10%; other royalties – 15%. (Treaty should be consulted.)

20. Literary, artistic or scientific royalties including films – 15%; other royalties – 10%. (Treaty should be consulted.)

21. Royalties with respect to patents, secret formulas or processes or for information concerning industrial or scientific experience – 5%; other royalties – 15%.

22. Commercial royalties, including films – 20%; copyright, literary, dramatic, musical, or artistic royalties – Nil.

23. Commercial royalties, including films – 15%; literary, dramatic, musical, or artistic royalties – 5%.

24. Literary, artistic, scientific, or film royalties – 10%; other royalties – 7%.

S

Sweden

25. Royalties with respect to patents, designs or models, secret formulas or processes or for information concerning industrial or scientific experience or for the use of industrial, commercial or scientific equipment involving a transfer of know-how – 5%; other royalties – 15%.
26. The treaty is applicable to all republics and autonomous provinces of the former Yugoslavia with the exception of Macedonia, with which Sweden has concluded a bilateral treaty.

Tax administration

Returns
The tax year corresponds to the calendar year. If the income is derived from business, the basis for tax assessment is the financial year. The year-end for a company may be fixed at any of the following dates: 30 April, 30 June, 31 August, or 31 December. Another year-end can be used if special permission by the tax agency is requested and granted. Swedish subsidiaries of foreign parents are generally permitted to adopt the same year-end as the parent company, provided it ends on the last day of the month.

Every corporate entity or registered branch must file an annual corporate income tax return, which generally should be filed by 2 May each year, covering the financial year-ending during the preceding calendar year. Extension may be available. The annual assessments are made by the local tax offices during the calendar year following the income year, and should be completed by end November. VAT returns and employer (employee PAYE and employer withholding) returns are normally due on a monthly basis.

Income tax payments
Income taxes are collected during the year in which the income is earned, under a preliminary tax system. A corporate entity's preliminary tax liability is determined by a preliminary tax assessment based either on the latest available final tax assessment or on a preliminary tax return filed by the company. The preliminary taxes are payable in monthly instalments. Interest surcharges on underpayment of preliminary taxes however, generally apply from 12 February the year after the financial year (the assessment year). Any balance owed by the taxpayer is payable in 90 days after the assessment has been made. Normally, any balance owed to the taxpayer is refunded in December of the assessment year.

Tax penalty
A taxpayer that submits incorrect or insufficient information in a tax return is charged a penalty amounting to up to 40% of the tax which, if the incorrect information had been accepted, would have been imposed or credited. The penalty and the rate may vary depending on the type of the incorrect information given.

Tax administration
Taxes are assessed by the tax agency. Depending on the circumstances, reassessments and/or appeals generally can be initiated within one and five years after the assessment year. Appeals can be made to the administrative court, and onwards to the administrative court of appeal, and in case of granted trial dispensation, onwards to the supreme administrative court.

Corporate taxes in Switzerland

For more information, contact:

Andreas Staubli
PricewaterhouseCoopers AG
Birchstrasse 160
8050 Zurich
Switzerland
Tel: +41 58 792 4400
Email: andreas.staubli@ch.pwc.com

Significant developments

The Corporate Tax Reform II enacted on 24 February 2008 by Swiss voters included many favourable changes for entrepreneurial activity and investment. In summary, the main benefits of the reform from a Swiss corporate tax perspective are:

- Extension of participation relief on dividend income (effective from 1 January 2011): The limits to obtain participation relief on dividend income after the effective date of 1 January 2011 are reduced to a participation of at least 10% from the existing 20% of capital or a market value of at least CHF 1 million, instead of the existing CHF 2 million limitation.
- Extension of participation relief on capital gains on the sale of investments (effective from 1 January 2011): After the effective date of 1 January 2011, limited companies and cooperatives desiring the participation relief on capital gains must sell an interest of at least 10%, instead of the existing 20% requirement. The minimum holding period of one year remains unchanged.
- Introduction of the capital contribution principle (effective from 1 January 2011): The change from the nominal principle to the capital contribution principle allows repayment of shareholders' capital contributions without liability for Swiss withholding tax. In general, this also applies for premiums, additionally paid-in capital and contributions into the reserves of a company without increasing the nominal share capital. Specific transition rules apply. Shareholders' capital contributions accumulated prior to 31 December 1996 are still subject to withholding tax. Effective from 1 January 2011, shareholders' capital contributions contributed after 31 December 1996 are withholding tax exempt provided that they meet all necessary requirements and in particular that the correct recordings in the books of the company. As a matter of principle, Swiss withholding tax exempt distributions will also be income tax exempt at the level of the Swiss individual shareholder (holding the shares in his private assets), whereas the tax treatment of a corporate shareholder (or an individual shareholder holding the shares in his business assets) should be further analysed. Additional details should be clarified in the expected guidelines to be published by the Swiss tax administration.
- Imputation of income tax against capital tax: The cantons may impute corporate income tax against capital tax as of 1 January 2009.
- Extension of asset replacement (effective from 1 January 2011): The tax exempt transfer of undisclosed reserves in the case of an asset replacement is facilitated after the effective date of 1 January 2011.

S

Switzerland

In 2009, a new Swiss value-added tax (VAT) law was approved by the Swiss Parliament and put in force effective from 1 January 2010. The new VAT law features a noticeable simplification of the system, enhances transparency, is more customer-friendly and aims at providing more legal certainty.

Further, as from 1 January 2011, the VAT rates will be increased in order to support the solvency of the disability insurance. The increase is limited to seven years. The normal rate will increase by 0.4% to 8%, the privileged rate by 0.1% to 2.5% and the special rate by 0.2% to 3.8% *(see VAT section)*.

Taxes on corporate income

- Federal level: The Swiss Federation levies a direct federal income tax at a flat rate of 8.5% on profits after tax (i.e., taxes are deductible from the tax basis in Switzerland, the tax rate on income before taxes amounts to approximately 7.83%). At a federal level, no corporate capital tax is levied.
- Cantonal/communal level: In addition to the direct federal income tax, each canton has its own tax law and levies cantonal and communal (municipal) income and capital taxes at different rates. Therefore, the tax burden of income (and capital) varies from canton to canton. Some cantonal and communal taxes are imposed at progressive rates.
- General rule: As a general rule, the approximate range of the maximum effective income tax rate on profit for federal, cantonal, and communal taxes is between 12.5% and 24%, depending on the company's location.

Corporate residence

A company is considered resident in Switzerland if its place of incorporation is in Switzerland. Residency is also linked upon the place of effective management, which may be the centre from which day-to-day activities are directed or the place from which managerial decisions are made.

Other taxes

Capital tax
Corporate capital tax is only levied at a cantonal and not at a federal level. It is based on the corporation's equity (the taxable equity corresponds to the sum of nominal capital, paid in surplus, retained earnings, other equity reserves and − according to Swiss thin cap rules − potential deemed equity). Tax rates vary from 0.001% to 0.5288%. Reduced rates are applicable for companies subject to a special cantonal tax regime (e.g., holding companies, mixed trading companies).

Value-added tax (VAT)
In 2009, a new Swiss VAT law was approved by the Swiss Parliament and put in force effective from 1 January 2010. The new VAT law features a noticeable simplification of the system, enhances transparency, is more customer-friendly and aims at providing more legal certainty.

As a matter of principle, proceeds of sales and services conducted in Switzerland are subject to VAT at the standard rate of 7.6%. However, goods for basic needs are subject to VAT at the rate of 2.4% and services in connection with the provision of lodging are subject to VAT at the rate of 3.6%. The registered taxpayer generally is entitled to offset the amount of VAT charged by suppliers or paid on imports against the VAT payable.

As from 1 January 2011, the VAT rates will be increased in order to support the solvency of the disability insurance. The increase is limited to seven years. The regular rate will be increased by 0.4% to 8%, the privileged rate by 0.1% to 2.5% and the special rate by 0.2% to 3.8%.

Issuance stamp tax

Issuance stamp tax (often known as capital duty) on the issue and increase of the equity of Swiss corporations is levied at the rate of 1% on the fair market value of the assets contributed, with an exemption on the first CHF 1 million of capital paid in, whether it is made in an initial or subsequent contribution.

A tax ruling may be obtained to exempt a multitude of transactions from issuance stamp tax. In particular, special rules allow for most reorganisations to take place on a tax neutral basis.

In addition, generally, an existing foreign company may transfer assets to Switzerland without incurring Swiss issuance stamp tax. However, if the company was formed abroad and redomiciled to Switzerland exclusively or mainly in order to avoid Swiss stamp taxes the issuance stamp tax may apply.

Issuance stamp tax is further payable with respect to the following instruments:

- Bonds, which are defined for the purposes of this tax as bonds, promissory notes issued in sequence and similar paper, discount paper and any other evidence of indebtedness in the form of a debt security or traded as if there were a debt security which is intended for public placement as well as participations in loans granted to Swiss debtors.
- Money market papers, which are identical instruments to bonds with a fixed term of not more than 12 months, issued by a Swiss body.

The following tax rates apply:

- 0.12% of the nominal value for each year or part thereof up to the maturity of a bond.
- 0.06% each year on the same basis for sub-participations and medium term bonds.
- 0.06% each year on commercial paper with the face value calculated at 1/360th for each day on which such paper is outstanding.

Securities transfer stamp tax

Swiss securities transfer stamp tax (often called securities turnover tax) is levied on the transfer of Swiss and foreign securities in which Swiss securities dealers participate as contracting parties or as intermediaries. The ordinary tax rate of Swiss securities transfer stamp tax is 0.15% for securities issued by a tax resident of Switzerland and 0.3% for securities issued by a tax resident of a foreign country.

Swiss securities dealers are defined as any person professionally engaged in the buying or selling of securities for his own account or for another person, including Swiss banks and other Swiss bank-like institutions. But also companies holding taxable securities whose book value exceeds CHF 10 million and remote members of a Swiss stock

S

Switzerland

exchange with regard to Swiss titles, which are quoted on the Swiss stock exchange, are considered as Swiss securities dealers.

Taxable securities include, but are not limited to, shares (including participations) and bonds. Options and many other derivative instruments are not subject to Swiss securities transfer stamp tax. However, the exercise of such financial instruments or derivatives may result in a taxable transfer of a security.

Various transactions are exempt from Swiss securities transfer stamp tax. With the enactment of the Swiss merger law in 2004, no Swiss securities transfer stamp tax is in general levied in the case of a merger or a reorganisation in which a Swiss securities dealer is involved and taxable securities (including participations) are transferred. Furthermore, the merger law also states an exemption from Swiss securities transfer stamp tax in case of a replacement of a participation. This is particularly important for holding companies, which qualify as Swiss securities dealers, as the law provides for a much more flexible basis than under prior law in transferring shares tax neutrally.

Branch income

The same tax principles apply for foreign corporations, provided that transactions with the head office or other branches are at arm's length. There is no withholding tax on profit transfers to the head office.

Income determination

Resident companies are subject to corporate income tax on their worldwide income. Income attributable to permanent establishments or immovable property located abroad is, however, excluded from the Swiss tax base and only taken into account for rate progression purposes in the cantons that still apply progressive tax rates.

The statutory accounts of a Swiss company (or in the case of a foreign company, the branch accounts) serve as the basis for determining taxable income. There are generally very few differences between statutory profit and taxable profit apart from the participation relief for dividend and capital gains income (described below), adjustments required by tax law as well as the usage of existing tax loss carry forwards.

Participation relief

The participation relief is the name generally attributed to the tax relief received for qualifying dividend and capital gains income of a company. The participation relief is not an outright tax exemption, but rather a tax abatement mechanism. It is, therefore, also commonly referred to as "participation deduction" or "participation relief".

The participation relief is computed as follows:

$$\frac{\text{Net participation income}}{\text{Taxable income}} = \% - \text{age relief as a deduction from a company's income taxes}$$

Net participation income consists of the gross participation income from qualifying dividends and qualifying capital gains income less related administration and financing costs and any depreciation of the participation that is linked to the dividend distribution. In most cases, the participation relief results in a full exemption of participation income from federal income tax or one close thereto. At a cantonal/

municipal level, cantonal tax regimes often are more favourable than the participation relief (the latter usually also granted by the cantons). The participation relief may be diluted in certain cases, for example if loss carryforwards are set off.

Participation relief: Dividend income
Dividends qualifying for the participation relief are those from participations representing at least 20% (after 1 January 2011: 10% of the share capital or 10% of profits and reserves) of the share capital of another company or those having a market value of at least CHF 2 million (after 1 January 2011: CHF 1 million). There is neither a minimum holding period nor a requirement that the dividend paying subsidiary is liable to income tax in its jurisdiction of residence.

Participation relief: Capital gains income
Capital gains derived from the disposal of a qualifying participation are entitled to participation relief, if the following conditions are cumulatively met:

- The participation sold was owned by the company for a period of at least one year; and
- The amount sold constitutes at least 20% (after 1 January 2011: 10% of the share capital or 10% of profits and reserves while partial sales of residual holdings of less than 10% are possible, provided their market value at the beginning of the year still amounted to at least CHF 1 million) of the share capital of the underlying subsidiary.

It is noteworthy that capital gains are only entitled to participation relief to the extent the sales price exceeds the original investment costs of the participation (whereas recaptured depreciations are taxable).

Foreign income

Swiss tax resident corporations are basically taxed on their worldwide income. However, income attributable to a foreign permanent establishment outside Switzerland is not taxed in Switzerland but may be taken into account only to determine the rate of tax applicable to taxable income. The same rule applies for income from real estate situated abroad.

Dividends, interest, and royalties from Swiss or foreign sources are included in assessable income. However, in certain cantons, special methods of assessment may apply for dividend and other income originating outside Switzerland. For dividend income, a relief generally is available at a federal income tax level as well as at a cantonal level (*see the section Participation relief*). The irrecoverable portion of foreign withholding taxes of most treaty countries can be credited against the related Swiss income taxes on the same income. Foreign withholding taxes of all non-treaty countries generally are not creditable, but they are deductible for income tax purposes.

There are no controlled foreign corporation (CFC) rules in Switzerland. Consequently, undistributed income of foreign subsidiaries is usually not taxed in Switzerland.

S

Switzerland

Deductions

As stated above, the statutory accounts of a Swiss company are the basis for determining taxable income. To be tax-deductible, an expense has to be booked in the statutory accounts accordingly.

In principle, it can be said that all business expenses that are booked in the statutory accounts are tax-deductible assuming they are economically justified from a tax perspective. If an expense is not a justifiable business expense in the sense of the tax law, it will be added back to taxable income. Examples typically include excessive depreciation, non-justified payments to related parties (e.g., hidden profit distributions), etc.

Guidelines for the most common deductions are set forth on the following pages.

Interest expense
Interest paid by a corporation to a third party is a deductible business expense. Interest paid to related parties (affiliates or shareholders) has to reflect the fair market rate and is subject to limitations.

With respect to related parties, the Federal Tax Administration annually issues safe harbour interest rates to be used on loans in CHF on the one hand and in foreign currencies on the other hand. The corporation may deviate from these safe harbour rates as long as it can prove that the rates used are at arm's length and more appropriate in the present case.

The safe harbour rules for loans denominated in CHF applicable from 1 January 2010 are as follows:

For loans made to related parties (in CHF)	Minimum interest rate
Financed from equity	2¼%
Financed from debt (actual costs plus at least):	
– On amount up to CHF to 10,000,000	½%
– On amounts of more than CHF 10,000,000	¼%
– But in all cases at least	2¼%

For loans made to related parties (in CHF)	Maximum interest rate	
Type of loan	Home construction / agriculture	Industry and business
Real estate loans - a loan up to the amount possible for mortgage (i.e., 2/3 of the market value of the real estate)	2¼%	2¾%
Real estate loans - other**	3%	3½%
Operational loans - made to trading and production companies	–	4½%*
Operational loans - made to holding and asset administration companies	–	4%*

* In calculating the amount of the maximum interest permissible from a tax perspective, any potentially existing hidden equity has to be considered. Reference is hereby made to Circular No. 6 for direct federal tax purposes of 6 June 1997, which is also applicable for withholding tax and stamp tax purposes.

** Whereby the following maximum interest rates for debt are applicable: land, villas, residences, vacation houses, and business premises, up to 70% of the market value and other real estate up to 80% of market value.

Depreciation

Maximum depreciation/amortisation rates allowed for tax purposes are issued by the Federal Tax Administration. Higher depreciation/amortisation is allowed for tax purposes, if the taxpayer can prove that such higher depreciation/amortisation is required from a statutory accounting perspective. Some cantons follow the federal guidelines, whereas some cantons apply and/or publish their own (more liberal) applicable depreciation/amortisation rates.

The following summary of the rates specified by the Federal Tax Administration provides the general range of allowable depreciation:

	Depreciation rates (from 2007)	
	Declining balance	Straight-line
Commercial buildings		
– Buildings alone	4%	2%
– Buildings and land combined	3%	1.5%
Equipment		
– Office furniture and equipment	25%	12.5%
– Computer hardware and software	40%	20%
Other assets		
– Motor vehicles	40%	20%
– Intangible assets	40%	20%

Some cantons (such as Zurich and Basel-City) take a more liberal approach and even permit a write-down of certain assets (including fixed assets) to 20% or nil of the purchase price in the first year, provided that such write-downs do not, in the aggregate, result in a drastic decline in taxable income or even a tax loss and are commercially justified. For this accelerated depreciation to be tax-deductible, it must be booked in the statutory accounts. As the cantonal tax authorities are responsible for assessing not only cantonal/communal income taxes, but also federal income taxes, the accelerated depreciation usually will be accepted for federal income tax purposes as well.

Royalties

Royalty payments are generally deductible for tax purposes as long as the royalty rate is at arm's length.

Management and service fees

Management and services fees paid by a Swiss company to a related party are deductible as long as the fees are at arm's length.

Switzerland

Bad debt provision
Based on a longstanding but not published practice, it is admissible in Switzerland to set up an accounting provision for specific impaired debts, which will be accepted for tax purposes. Unlike most other countries, it is also possible in Switzerland to set up an additional ("lump sum") bad debt provision of 5% on all domestic and 10% on all foreign receivables (i.e., after deduction of specific impaired debts), except for inter-company receivables and receivables to the public, enabling the taxpayer to defer the related tax liability until this provision has been released. Some cantons, such as Zurich, accept an even higher reserve (i.e., 10% on domestic and 20% on foreign receivables). This additional bad debt provision may have the character of a "hidden" (undisclosed) reserve and is possible to build because the Swiss accounting standards favour prudence over true and fair view accounting principles.

Inventory provision
Similarly to the bad debt provision, it is also possible to build a "hidden" (undisclosed) reserve on a company's inventory. This provision, which has also to be booked in the statutory accounts, is accepted for tax purposes (similar to the bad debt provision). Specifically, a company may build a provision for obsolete inventory as well as a hidden reserve on 33.3% of the inventory value after deduction of the obsolete inventory.

Tax expenses
Corporate income and capital taxes paid to the Swiss Federation as well as to the cantons and the municipalities are tax-deductible.

Foreign exchange losses
Realised foreign exchange gains and losses are included in the tax basis of a corporation as taxable/tax-deductible. Based on a recent federal court decision – for which applicability for a specific case has to be reviewed – unrealised gains or losses resulting from the translation of financial statements in a foreign (functional) currency to CHF may not be taxable/tax-deductible.

Costs of employee share plans and stock option plans
The cost of employee share plans and stock option plans are generally deductible, assuming the employees eligible for the plan are employed by the Swiss company. The same holds true for the recharge of costs for plans covering local employees.

Goodwill
Only acquired goodwill (derivative goodwill) may be capitalised in the statutory accounts and depreciated. Depreciation is generally allowed over five years.

Group taxation

Tax is levied on each corporation as a separate entity, that is a parent company and its Swiss subsidiaries are taxed separately, and only the dividends from, but not the profits of, the subsidiaries are taxed in the parent company's hands and form the basis of relief.

Tax incentives

Business incentives
Many cantons offer a great variety of incentives for newly established companies or for expansion investments, such as tax holidays or significant tax relief for cantonal and

communal tax purposes for up to 10 years. In some cantons or for specific regions, a tax holiday even for federal tax purposes may be granted if certain conditions are met.

Privileged cantonal tax regimes
Many cantons offer privileged corporate tax regimes. Usually, an up-front confirmation for such privileged tax regime can be obtained by way of an advance tax ruling with the cantonal tax authorities. Such ruling process usually takes at least four to six weeks.

A special tax status is granted for an unlimited period of time and can be relied upon unless the Swiss company's circumstances change materially.

Holding company tax regime
The holding company tax status is available to companies, which meet the following conditions:

- The primary purpose of the company must be to hold and manage long term equity investments in affiliated companies and this purpose must be stated in the bylaws;
- The company must not be engaged in a commercial activity in Switzerland; and
- The company must pass an alternative asset or income test, whereby either two thirds of the company's assets must consist of substantial shareholdings or participations or two thirds of total income of the company must consist of participation income (dividend income or capital gains) from such shareholdings and participations.

A qualifying holding company is exempt from all cantonal/communal income tax (with the exception of income from Swiss real estate which is subject to tax after deduction of typical mortgage expenditures on such real estate).

Consequently, a holding company is in principle only subject to an effective tax rate of 7.83% (i.e., federal income tax rate) prior to participation relief for qualifying dividends and capital gains. A reduced capital tax at cantonal/communal tax level usually applies.

A tax ruling may be obtained prior to forming the holding company from the cantonal tax authorities in the proposed canton of residence in order to confirm eligibility for the holding company status.

Domicile company tax regime
The domicile company tax status is available for companies, which only carry out administrative functions in Switzerland and no commercial activities.

Insofar as a company fulfils the above mentioned criteria, it may apply to the cantonal tax authorities in the proposed canton of residence for a tax ruling entitling it to the following taxation:

- A modest portion of foreign source income (i.e., from 0% – 15%) is subject to tax in accordance with the importance of the administrative function in Switzerland;
- Income from qualifying participations (including dividends, capital gains and re-evaluation gains) is usually tax exempt (whereas losses deriving from qualifying participations usually are non-tax-deductible);
- All income from Swiss sources is taxed at ordinary rates;

S

Switzerland

- Expenditures which are justified for business purposes are deductible from the income to which they have a business correlation; and
- Reduced capital tax rates usually are applicable.

The conditions to qualify as a domicile company vary from canton to canton. This is particularly the case with regard to determining the percentage of income from foreign sources subject to tax in Switzerland and to the definition of exactly what type of income is considered foreign source income.

A domicile company can be expected to be subject to an effective tax rate of 7.83% – 11% on foreign source income.

Administrative/auxiliary/mixed company tax regime
This tax status, which is very similar to the domicile company tax status, has been given different names by the cantons. Internationally it is most often referred to, however, as the "Mixed company" tax status.

In contrast to the pure domicile company status, it is permissible for a mixed company to undertake limited commercial activity in Switzerland. As a general rule, at least 80% of the income from commercial activities of a mixed company must be derived from non-Swiss sources (i.e., a maximum of 20% of income may be linked to Swiss sources). Many cantons additionally require that at least 80% of costs must be related to activities undertaken abroad.

Insofar as a company fulfils the above-mentioned criteria, it may apply to the appropriate cantonal tax authorities for a tax ruling entitling it to tax treatment analogous to the rules set forth above for domicile companies. Depending on the concrete Swiss activity and infrastructure, the portion subject to cantonal and communal income tax generally varies from 5% to 25% of the foreign source income and is generally higher than is the case for domicile companies. The exact portion needs to be clarified with the responsible cantonal tax authorities in the tax ruling.

The additional related statements set forth above for domicile companies are applicable.

Withholding taxes (WHT)

The statutory rate of Swiss withholding tax is 35%. Relief, if any, generally is granted by refund. Since 1 January 2005 a notification procedure is applicable upon request on dividends paid by a Swiss company to foreign shareholders with a substantial shareholding. The following table shows the residual/remaining tax for the recipient. Credit for the unrelieved portion of Swiss withholding tax may be available in the country of the recipient.

Treaties in force (per 1 January 2010)
The following table does not cover Swiss withholding taxes on interest payments based on mortgage loans with respect to Swiss located real estate.

Recipient	Dividends			Interest (1)	Royalties (2)
	Portfolio	Substantial holdings			
			Min. shareholding		
	%	%	%	%	%
Resident corporations and individuals	Nil (3)	Nil	(4)	Nil (1)	Nil
Non-resident corporations and individuals:					
Non-treaty	35	35		0/35 (1)	Nil
Treaty:					
Albania	15	5	25	5	Nil
Algeria	15	5	20	10 (5)	Nil
Argentina	15	10	25	12 (5)	Nil
Armenia	15	5	25	10 (5)	Nil
Australia	15	15	Not applicable	10	Nil
Austria*	15	Nil	20	Nil	Nil
Azerbaijan	15	5 (17)	20 (17)	10 (5)(8)	Nil
Bangladesh	15	10	20	10 (5)	Nil
Belarus	15	5	25	8 (5)(8)	Nil
Belgium*	15	10	25	10 (5)	Nil
Bulgaria*	15	5	25	10 (5)	Nil
Canada	15	5	10	10 (5)	Nil
China	10	10	Not applicable	10 (5)	Nil
Croatia	15	5	25	5	Nil
Czech Republic*	15	5	25	Nil	Nil
Denmark*	Nil	Nil	Not applicable	Nil	Nil
Ecuador	15	15	Not applicable	10 (5)	Nil
Egypt	15	5	25	15 (5)	Nil
Estonia*	15	5	20	10 (5)(15)	Nil
Finland*	10	Nil	20	Nil	Nil
France*	15	0/15 (6)	10	Nil	Nil
Germany*	15	Nil (20)	20	30/0 (19)	Nil
Ghana	15	5	10	10 (5)	Nil
Greece*	15	5	25	10	Nil
Hungary*	10	10	Not applicable	10	Nil
Iceland	15	5	25	0	Nil
India	10	10	Not applicable	10 (5)	Nil
Indonesia	15	10	25	10	Nil
Iran	15	5	15	10 (5)(13)	Nil
Ireland*	15	10	25	Nil	Nil
Israel	15	5	10	10 (5)(7)(8)	Nil
Italy*	15	15	Not applicable	12.5	Nil
Ivory Coast	15	15	Not applicable	15	Nil
Jamaica	15	10	10	10 (5)	Nil
Japan	15	10	25	10 (5)	Nil
Kazakhstan	15	5 (9)	10	10 (5)	Nil

S

Switzerland

Recipient	Dividends			Interest (1)	Royalties (2)
	Portfolio	Substantial holdings			
			Min. shareholding		
	%	%	%	%	%
Korea (South)	15	10	25	10 (5)	Nil
Kuwait	15	15	Not applicable	10	Nil
Kyrgyzstan	15	5	25	5	Nil
Latvia*	15	5	20	10 (5)	Nil
Lithuania*	15	5	20	10 (5)	Nil
Luxembourg*	15	5/Nil	25	10	Nil
Macedonia	15	5	25	10 (5)	Nil
Malaysia	15	5	25	10	Nil
Mexico	15	5	25	15 (5)	Nil
Moldova	15	5	25	10 (5)(13)	Nil
Mongolia	15	5	25	10 (5)(13)	Nil
Montenegro	15	5	20	10	Nil
Morocco	15	7	25	10	Nil
Netherlands*	15	Nil	25	5	Nil
New Zealand	15	15	Not applicable	10	Nil
Norway	15	Nil	20	Nil	Nil
Pakistan	20 (22)	10 (22)	20 (22)	10 (22)	Nil
Philippines	15	10	10	10	Nil
Poland*	15	5	25	10	Nil
Portugal*	15	10	25	10	Nil
Romania*	10	10	Not applicable	10 (5)	Nil
Russia	15	5 (18)	20 (18)	10 (5)(8)(12)	Nil
Serbia	15	5	20	10	Nil
Singapore	15	10	25	10	Nil
Slovakia*	15	5	25	10 (5)(13)	Nil
Slovenia*	15	5	25	5	Nil
South Africa	15	5	20	5	Nil
Spain*	15	Nil (16)	25 (16)	Nil (16)	Nil
Sri Lanka	15	10	25	10 (8)	Nil
Sweden*	15	Nil	25	5	Nil
Thailand	15	10	10	15 (5)(10)	Nil
Trinidad and Tobago	20	10	10	10	Nil
Tunisia	10	10	Not applicable	10	Nil
UK*	15	Nil	10	Nil	Nil
Ukraine	15	5	20	10 (5)(13)	Nil
USA	15	5/0 (11)	10	Nil	Nil
Uzbekistan	15	5	20	5 (5)(13)	Nil
Venezuela	10	Nil	25	5 (5)(14)	Nil
Vietnam	15	10/7 (21)	20/50 (21)	10 (5)	Nil

Notes

1. In Switzerland, there is no withholding tax on interest deriving from regular loan agreements. In general, withholding tax is only levied on interest paid by banking institutions (or paid by entities tax-wise qualified as "banking institutions") to non-banks, interest on bonds, bond-like loans. In Switzerland, a withholding tax may be levied on interest paid on mortgage loans with respect to Swiss located real estate; however, this is not covered in the table above.
2. There is no withholding tax on royalties, licenses, and similar fees payable by Swiss individuals or corporations (provided that the dealing at arm's-length principle is met).
3. The statutory withholding tax rate of 35% is levied but refunded, provided that the respective earnings are declared as income for tax purposes.
4. No withholding tax is levied between Swiss group companies; tax liability may be met by notification procedure. For this purpose, a substantial holding is a participation of at least 20% in the capital or a market value of at least CHF 2 million. Effective from 1 January 2010, these thresholds will be lowered to 10% respectively CHF 1 million.
5. Certain types of interest payments income deriving from several countries are exempt from withholding tax (e.g., because only taxable in the resident state of the recipient). However, it is assumed that this is of only marginal relevance for Swiss tax purposes.
6. 15% residual tax for French companies with more than 10% shareholding if fulfilling the following requirements: i) no predominant shareholder of the company is EU or Swiss resident and ii) the shares are not traded at a stock exchange (neither the shares of the receiving nor of the distributing company).
7. Full relief of the withholding tax on interest paid for a loan granted by the Israel Government (including political subdivisions and local corporate bodies) or granted by the Israel Central Bank.
8. Interest on bank loans is 5%.
9. Full relief if certain requirements are met.
10. Interest on bank loans is 10%.
11. Full relief for certain dividend payments to certain US pension funds.
12. Full relief on certain categories of interest.
13. Interest on bank loans is 0%.
14. According to the territorial principle of Venezuela only certain persons can benefit from the tax relief.
15. Interest on bank loans to corporations 0%.
16. 0% withholding tax rate on dividends of participations of at least 25% as well as on interest payments is granted effective from 1 June 2007.
17. 20% minimal shareholding plus foreign investment of minimal USD 200,000.
18. 20% minimal shareholding plus foreign investment of minimal CHF 200,000.
19. 30% only on income bonds and on profit participating loans.
20. 5% for specific power houses.
21. 10% withholding tax for shareholdings between 20% and 50%; 7% withholding tax for shareholdings of more than 50%.
22. Rates effective from 1 January 2009.

*Bilateral Agreements respectively Art. 15 Savings Tax Agreement (STA) between Switzerland and the European Union (EU) apply as from 1 July 2005 and provide the following benefits:

- Upon request, Swiss withholding tax on dividends paid by a Swiss subsidiary company to its EU parent company may be reduced to nil (0%) (reduction at source) and are only subject to a notification procedure, if the following conditions are cumulatively met:
  - Direct minimum holding of 25% of the subsidiary's capital for at least two years; and
  - Both companies are subject to corporate income tax.
- Upon request, withholding tax on interest and royalty payments made between associated companies or their permanent establishment resident respectively situated in Switzerland and the EU may be reduced to nil (0%) (reduction at source) in the source state, if the following conditions are cumulatively met:

S

Switzerland

- Direct minimum holding of 25% for at least two years (parent/subsidiary), or direct holding by a third company of minimum 25% in the capital of both companies for at least two years (sister companies); and
- Both companies are subject to corporate income tax.
- Transition periods/rules:
  - Greece, Latvia, Poland and Portugal: withholding tax rate on interests is 10% at maximum as of 1 July 2005 to 30 June 2009; as from 1 July 2009 to 30 June 2013, the maximum withholding tax rate is 5%, afterwards 0% (Nil rate).
  - Lithuania: withholding tax rate on interests is 10% at maximum as of 1 July 2005 to 30 June 2009; as from 1 July 2009 to 30 June 2011, the maximum withholding tax rate is 5%, afterwards 0% (Nil rate).
  - Specific transition rules applied in relation to Spain until 31 May 2007.
  - The above mentioned transition rules only cover the Swiss outbound perspective. Further transition rules may apply for Swiss inbound payments (e.g., for royalties paid to a Swiss company), e.g., with respect to Czech Republic, Estonia, Slovakia, Spain.
- Double Tax Treaties between Switzerland and EU Member States with more favourable tax treatment of dividend, interest and royalty payments remain unaffected. In turn, the Bilateral Agreements between Switzerland and the European Union (EU) apply also in case there is no bilateral Double Tax Treaty with Switzerland and an EU-country (as is for example the case for Malta and Cyprus).
- In general, the Bilateral Agreements between Switzerland and the European Union (EU) is also binding with respect to new member states of the EU.
- The application of the Bilateral Agreements is subject to domestic and STA misuse conditions.

New treaties
Various treaties are subject to re-negotiations.

Tax administration

Overview
The tax year is the business year. Thus, the basis for corporate taxation is the applicable accounting period, which may end at any date within a calendar year.

The tax system is based on taxpayers' declarations, with subsequent assessments being issued by the tax authorities on the basis of the tax returns filed. Companies are initially assessed on a provisional basis, the final assessments being issued after the tax base has been either the subject of a tax audit or declared final by the authorities.

Payment of tax
Unless payments on account are specifically requested, federal, cantonal, and communal taxes on income and capital are, in most cantons and for federal tax purposes, payable only upon receipt of a demand based on a provisional or final assessment. However, cantonal exemptions apply: as an example, based on the date of maturity of the respective tax year (30 September), the canton of Zurich levies late payment interest to the extent that the full (final) tax amount had not been paid in time (independent from any earlier provisional tax invoices). About one month before the due date, a (provisional) tax bill based on the latest tax return filed or the assessment of the preceding period is sent to the taxpayer. Payment is usually in two or three instalments. If the entire amount is paid up front, a discount may be granted.

Other issues

Transfer pricing

Switzerland is of the opinion that transfer pricing matter cannot be addressed by legislation, and therefore, has no plans to issue any domestic provisions on transfer pricing in the near future. There is, however, an increasing awareness of the issue and concern on the part of the Swiss tax authorities that taxpayers may transfer profits without economic justification to countries with strict transfer pricing rules and documentation requirements in order to avoid challenges by the respective local tax authorities. In this context Swiss tax authorities take an increasing interest in a company's transfer pricing position in order to defend their own position. Some cantonal tax authorities are starting to focus on low risk/low profit entities located in Switzerland.

Switzerland follows the OECD Guidelines as closely as possible and recognises the arm's-length principle based on interpretation of actual legislation. To clarify transfer pricing issues, Switzerland offers an informal procedure for agreeing pricing policies in advance.

Corporate taxes in Syria

For more information, contact:

Wadih AbouNasr
PricewaterhouseCoopers
SNA Building, 5th Floor
Tabaris Square
Beirut
Lebanon
Tel: +961 1 200577 ext. 1610
Email: wadih.abounasr@lb.pwc.com

Significant developments

There have been no significant developments in corporate taxation in Syria in the last year.

Taxes on corporate income

General income tax rates (including branches of foreign companies)
Except for the special cases listed below, common corporate income tax rates (including branches of a non-resident entity) vary between 10% and 28% of profits, as follows:

Taxable profit (in SYP – Syrian pounds)	Tax rate (%)
Up to 200,000	10
From 200,001 to 500,000	15
From 500,001 to 1,000,000	20
From 1,000,001 to 3,000,000	24
Over 3,000,000	28

Depending on the location of the taxpayer, an additional local administration surtax of 4% to 10% (of the tax amount) will apply.

Joint-stock companies with more than 50% shares offered to the public
Joint-stock companies offering more than 50% of their shares to the public are subject to a flat income tax rate (on profits) of 14%. In this case, the 4% to 10% administration surtax does not apply.

Other joint-stock and limited liability companies and projects included under investment encouragement laws
Joint-stock companies offering less than 50% of their shares to the public, limited liability companies and projects signed with Syrian companies included under the investment encouragement laws are subject to a flat income tax rate of 22% on profits. In this case, a 4% to 10% local administration surtax applies.

Hotels, restaurants, and recreational establishments
International standard, first- and second-class hotels, restaurants, lodging houses, related services, and all recreational establishments are subject to tax based on their turnover. The tax rate is 3%, and it covers both income tax and salary tax.

Contracts with public sector, oil companies and non-residents

A Syrian company contracting with the public sector and/or with an oil company or with a non-resident entity will be subject to a withholding tax based on the contract value (on that specific contract only) rather than income tax on real profits.

The same tax rate applies to non-resident contractors operating directly from abroad; they are subject to a 1%, 2%, 4%, 7% or 10% tax on the value of the contract.

The applicable rates vary according to the nature of the contract and the customer. The non-resident tax covers both income tax and salary tax of the foreign and local employees working on the contract.

Corporate residence

The following entities are considered Syrian residents for tax purposes:

- An entity whose principal activities are administered in Syria;
- An entity that adopts the Syrian Arab Republic as its headquarters; and
- Branches or offices of foreign companies in Syria.

Tax is levied on all corporeal and incorporeal persons, residents and non-residents, on all profits generated in Syria. The main premise for considering profits to have been realised in Syria is whether they occurred from efforts exerted in Syria, irrespective of the taxpayer's identity or place of residency.

Other taxes

Stamp duty

Stamp duty generally is imposed on transactions such as the formation of corporations or the execution of documents, licenses, contracts, etc., at a rate ranging from 0.4% to 0.7%.

Branch income

The taxes on branch income are the same as taxes on corporate income (tax rate varies between 10% and 28%). *See Taxes on corporate income section.*

Income determination

Capital gains

Capital gains are considered taxable income, and are taxed at the normal corporate income rates (10% to 28%).

Capital gains include dividends, interest, revenue, premiums, and other cash income sources.

Inter-company dividends/stock dividends

Dividends paid by Syrian corporations on previously taxed income are not subsequently subject to tax upon distribution.

S

Syria

Foreign income
Income from any source, domestic or foreign, received by a company in Syria is subject to the applicable tax rate on profits.

Deductions

Depreciation and depletion
Depreciation of property, plant, and equipment (at rates fixed by the law) is deductible.

Net operating losses
Losses may be carried forward for five years. The carryback of losses is not available.

Payments to foreign affiliates
Payments to foreign affiliates are considered normal payments because Syria has no transfer pricing rules. However, the payments may be subject to withholding taxes.

Deductible expenses
The following expenses are deductible:

- Cost of goods sold;
- Cost of services rendered;
- Rent paid for the business premises (or rent value if the taxable entity owns the property);
- Salaries and incentives paid to employees/workers;
- Payments representing employer's portion of social security contributions;
- Indemnities and allowances (end of service…) paid according to the labour law;
- Depreciation accepted according to each kind of profession and industry except depreciation of real estate;
- Taxes and duties levied during the year except the tax on profits; and
- Grants paid by taxable persons against official receipts for known public or private entities on condition the grants do not exceed 3% of net profits.

Non-deductible expenses
The following expenses are not deductible:

- Expenses leading to the increase of the value of fixed assets (capital expenditures);
- Personal expenses considered by the business owner (or/and his partner) as personal compensation; and
- Compensations for partners in some business entities.

Group taxation

There is no group taxation in Syria.

Tax incentives

Incentives are granted under other non-tax laws for certain industrial projects and for tourism.

Withholding taxes (WHT)

Interests
The income, revenue, and interest earned from accounts opened at Syrian banks and from treasury bonds are subject to an 8.25% withholding tax.

Royalties
Royalties paid to non-residents are subject to a 5% withholding income tax as well as a 2% withholding payroll tax.

Resident contractors
When a Syrian company performs contracts with the public sector and/or with an oil company, or with a non-resident entity, it will be subject to a withholding tax based on the contract value (on that specific contract) rather than income tax on real profits.

Non-resident contractors
Revenue earned by non-resident contractors in Syria is subject to a withholding tax based on the contract value (of that specific contract) rather than income tax on real profits.

Double taxation treaties (DTTs)
The table below shows the treaty and non-treaty withholding taxes:

	Interest	Dividends	Royalties
	%	%	%
Non-treaty:	7.5	0	7
Treaty:			
Algeria	10	10	18
Armenia	10	10	12
Bahrain	10	(a)	18
Bulgaria	10	10	18
Cyprus	10	15	10
Egypt	15	15	20
India	10	(b)	10
Iran	10	7	17
Italy	10	(c)	18
Korea	10	10	18
Kuwait	10	(a)	20
Lebanon	10	5	18
Malta	10	(d)	18
Pakistan	10	10	(e)
Poland	10	10	18
Romania	7.5	(a)	(f)
Russia	10	15	(g)
Tunisia	10	0	18
Turkey	10	10	(h)
Ukraine	10	(a)	18
United Arab Emirates	10	(a)	18

Syria

Notes

a. Taxed only in the dividend beneficiary's jurisdiction (when the beneficiary is owner of the shares).

b. Tax should not exceed:
   - 5% of the gross amount of the dividends if the beneficial owner is a company (other than a partnership) that owns at least 10% of the shares of the company paying the dividends; or
   - 10% of the gross amount of the dividends in all other cases.

c. Tax should not exceed:
   - 5% of the gross amount of the dividends if the beneficial owner is a company that has owned at least 25% of the capital of the company paying the dividends; or
   - 10% of the gross amount of the dividends in all other cases.

d. Total Malta or Syrian tax on the profits of a company and the dividends distributed by such company, as the case may be, shall not exceed the maximum tax chargeable on the company's profits out of which the dividends are paid.

e. Tax should not exceed:
   - 18% of the gross amount for any patent, trademark, design or model, plan, secret formula or process, industrial or scientific equipment, or for information concerning industrial or scientific experience;
   - 15% of the gross amount paid for any copyright of literary, artistic or scientific work; or
   - 10% of the gross amount paid for any copyright of cinematographic films, or tapes for television or radio broadcasting.

f. Tax should not exceed:
   - 10% of gross amount paid for cinematographic films, magnetic films and tapes for television and radio; or
   - 15% of the sum paid for any copyright of a literary, artistic or scientific work, including cinematographic films and films and recordings for other forms of radio transmission or television transmission; any patent, trademark, design or model, plan, secret formula or secret process, as well as for the use or right to use industrial, commercial or scientific equipment and for information related to experience in the industrial, commercial or scientific area.

g. Tax should not exceed:
   - 18% of the gross amount of royalties paid for any patent, trademark, design or model, plan, secret formula or process, any computer software program, or for information concerning industrial, commercial or scientific experience;
   - 13.5% of the gross amount of royalties paid for any copyright of literary, artistic or scientific work; or
   - 4.5% of the gross amount of royalties paid for cinematographic films, programmes and recordings for radio or television broadcasting.

h. Tax should not exceed:
   - 15% of the gross amount of royalties paid for any patent, trademark, design or model, plan, secret formula or process, or for information concerning industrial, commercial or scientific experience; or
   - 10% of the gross amount of the royalties for the use of or the right to use any copyright of literary, artistic or scientific work including cinematographic films and recordings for radio and television.

Tax administration

Returns
The tax year in Syria is the calendar year.

Taxpayers in Syria shall comply with the following requirements:

- Tax returns must be filed by 31 May for limited liability and joint-stock companies and 31 March for other types of companies. Payment is due at the time of filing; and
- Payroll withholding tax should be submitted by the employer on a semi-annual basis.

Payment of tax
Penalties
A penalty is assessed for late payments 30 days after the filing date at a rate of 10%, up to the amount of the tax liability.

Statute of limitations
In Syria the statute of limitations with respect to tax is five years.

Permanent and temporary exemptions
Investment encouragement regulations allow foreign investors to benefit from customs exemptions for the imports used in the investment.

Permanent exemptions
Physical and moral persons and associations exempted from income tax either through the real profit or lump-sum profit method are the following:

- Types of consumers and investors' cooperative associations;
- Farmers harvesting and selling crops; this exemption includes animals and livestock bred on their farming lands;
- Facilities in which stocks are bred or where poultry farming is exercised; subject to income tax according to the real-profit tax;
- Persons engaged in the following activities: composition, playing music, drawing, painting and other artistic practices;
- Day-care centres;
- Institutes and associations taking care of people with special needs;
- 75% of the yearly net profits for air and maritime transportation; and
- 50% of net profits of stock breeding and poultry farming facilities.

Corporate taxes in Taiwan

For more information, contact:

Lily Hsu
PricewaterhouseCoopers
International Trade Building,
27F, 333 Keelung Road, Section 1
Taipei 110, Taiwan
Tel: +886 2 2729 6207
Email: lily.hsu@tw.pwc.com

Significant developments

Most tax incentives previously offered under the Statute for Upgrading Industries (SUI) expired at the end of 2009 and have been replaced by a new Statute for Innovating Industries (SII). Under the SII, research and development (R&D) credits are available up to 15% of qualified R&D expenses incurred, with the maximum amount of tax credit capped at 30% of the tax payable for the year in which the expenses are incurred. In addition to R&D credits, subsidies are also available for certain qualified activities. *See the Tax incentives section.*

On May 28 2010, the Legislative Yuan passed the third reading for amending the current corporate income tax rate from 20% to 17%. The reduced tax rate applies to the taxable year 2010 and onward. *See Income tax section.*

Taxes on corporate income

Income tax
Income is taxed as follows:

Taxable income	Tax thereon
Up to NTD 120,000	Exempt
NTD 120,001 and over	17% of total taxable income

To help improve Taiwan's investment environment and boost foreign investors' interest in injecting money into Taiwan, the current corporate income tax rate has been reduced from 20% to 17% effective to the taxable year 2010 and onward.

Taxation of interest
Interest received on commercial paper, treasury bills and certain other interest-bearing financial instruments are subject to withholding tax rates of 10% and 15% for resident and non-resident taxpayers, respectively. However, such income is not subject to any other form of income tax and is effectively taxed separately from other income referred to above.

Tax on retained earnings
For earnings accumulated on or after 1 January 1998, an additional 10% profit retention tax will be imposed on any current earnings that remain undistributed by the end of the following year.

Imputation tax system

Taiwan operates an imputation tax system to eliminate double taxation on earnings of a corporation. The corporate income tax and 10% profit retention tax already paid by the company can be distributed to the domestic individual shareholders as tax credits to offset their individual income tax. However, the tax credits distributable to shareholders are subject to certain limitations.

Non-resident shareholders may credit the 10% profit retention tax previously paid by the investee company against the dividend withholding tax where the dividends are distributed from retained earnings that have already been subject to the 10% profit retention tax. Please note that credit for profit retention tax from withholding tax is calculated based on a prescribed formula.

Income Basic Tax Act

Effective from 1 January 2006, all Taiwan resident companies, as well as foreign companies with a fixed place of business or business agent in Taiwan, should calculate income basic tax if they earn certain income that is tax-exempt or enjoy certain tax incentives. The basic income of a company shall be the amount calculated in accordance with a formulae stipulated by the government, with a deduction of NTD 2,000,000. Currently, the income basic tax rate is 10%. If the basic income tax amount is greater than the regular income tax amount, taxpayers have to pay income tax based on regular income tax amount plus the difference between the basic tax amount and the regular income tax amount. On the other hand, if the regular income tax amount is greater than the basic income tax amount, no special action is required.

Corporate residence

According to Taiwan's Company Act, the principal office of a company must be registered with the government. Corporate residence is determined by the place of registration, which normally is the place of central management.

Other taxes

Business tax

All sales of goods and services in Taiwan, as well as the importation of goods into Taiwan, are subject to business tax. The sellers and service providers are generally obligated to pay business tax for the sales of goods or services within Taiwan unless the law provides otherwise. For importation of goods, the business tax will be paid by the goods receivers or buyers via customs. For importation of services sold by foreign companies to Taiwanese buyers, business tax shall be paid by the service buyers. However, the service buyer will not be required to pay business tax if it adopts the value-added tax system, and is exclusively engaged in taxable transactions. There are two types of business tax systems: value-added tax and gross business receipts tax.

Value-added tax (VAT)

VAT is applicable to general industries, and the VAT rate is 5%. Under the VAT system, each seller collects output VAT from the buyer at the time of sale, deducts input VAT paid on purchases from output VAT, and remits the balance to the tax authority.

Gross business receipts tax (GBRT)

GBRT is applicable to specified industries, e.g., financial institutions, small businesses, etc. For banks, insurance companies, investment trust companies, securities and

T

Taiwan

futures firms, short-term commercial paper enterprises, and pawnshops, the rate is 2%. For re-insurance enterprises, the rate is 1%.

Stamp tax

Stamp taxes are imposed on each copy of the following documents executed within the territory of Taiwan (with the following respective tax rates):

1. Monetary receipts must have a revenue stamp of 0.4% of the amount received per piece. However a receipt for the money deposited by the bidder requires a revenue stamp of 0.1% of the amount received per piece.
2. Contract or deed for the sale or purchase of movable property must have revenue stamp of NTD 12 per piece.
3. Contractual agreement under which one party agrees to complete a specific piece of work for the other party for consideration must have a revenue stamp of 0.1% of the contract price.
4. Contract for the sale, transfer and partition of real estate must have a revenue stamp of 0.1% of the contract price.

Commodity tax

Commodity tax (excise duty) is levied on certain commodities, as specified in the Commodity Tax Act (including rubber tyres, beverages, cement, flat-glass, oil and gas, electrical appliances and vehicles), at the time when such goods are dispatched from a factory or when imported. Different rates of commodity tax apply to different types of commodities based on the value of the goods or the volume in specific circumstances.

Property tax

A tax is levied on property annually. At present, the rate for business properties is 3% of the assessed value and the rate for houses for private residence, private hospitals, professional offices and the premises of non-profit civil organisations is 1.2% or 2% of the assessed value.

Securities transaction tax

Tax is levied on securities transactions at the rate of 0.3% on gross proceeds from the sale of stocks. Trading in corporate bonds and financial bonds is temporarily exempt from securities transaction tax assessment.

Customs duties

Taiwan uses the Customs Cooperation Council Nomenclature (CCCN) to classify goods and set duty rates. The customs duty is payable by the consignee or the holder of the bill of lading for imported goods, and is based on the dutiable value or the volume of goods imported.

Branch income

A foreign company whose head office is located outside of Taiwan must keep separate books for each branch within Taiwan. A head office or regional headquarters' general and administrative expenses may be allocated to the branch under certain conditions. Income tax is assessed only on the branch's profits. A Taiwan branch should complete an annual income tax return. *The applicable rates of taxation are shown under "Taxes on Corporate Income"*. A Taiwan branch of a foreign company may remit after-tax profits to its head office without further taxation due.

Motion picture leasing

A foreign motion picture's branch in Taiwan can deem 45% of its revenue from leasing of motion pictures as cost. However, if a foreign enterprise with no branch office in Taiwan leases motion pictures through agents, 50% of the revenues can be deemed as cost.

Foreign company

A foreign company with no fixed place of business or business agent in Taiwan is subject to withholding tax at source on its Taiwan-sourced income. Withholding tax rates on dividends, interest and royalties may be reduced if the recipient is a tax resident of a tax treaty country and the relevant treaty provides for a reduced rate.

A foreign company which is engaged in international transportation, construction contracting, provision of technical services, or machinery and equipment leasing, within Taiwan, and where the cost and expenses are proven to be difficult to calculate, may apply for an advance approval from the National Tax Administration (NTA) to adopt the deemed profit method to determine the taxable income as 10% or 15% of the gross revenues. This will effectively reduce corporate tax rate on gross revenues once the approval is obtained from the NTA (assuming the corporate tax rate is 17%).

Income determination

Taiwan-sourced income

The company is taxed on its net income, which is defined as gross annual income after deduction of costs, expenses, losses and taxes. Except for certain exempt items, income from all sources is subject to corporate income tax. Article 8 of the Income Tax Act and related guideline define the types of income that should be regarded as sourced in Taiwan.

The Guideline issued by the Ministry of Finance (MOF) on 3 September 2009 clarifies the scope of Taiwan-sourced income for the existing income categories. For example, fees received by a foreign company for service performed entirely outside of Taiwan are exempt from income tax assessment, subject to supporting evidentiary documents. This opens up opportunities for foreign companies to reassess whether their cross-border service charges are wholly or partially non-Taiwan-source income, and to claim associated costs and expenses as reduction.

The Guideline further provides clearer tax treatment on R&D cost sharing (so called "cost contribution arrangement"). When a Taiwanese company enters into a joint technical cooperation and development agreement with other foreign companies and certain required criteria is met, the payment of R&D costs thus allocated shall not be deemed as Taiwan-sourced income.

The guideline is effective on the date of issuance, and does not apply retroactively based on the tax authority's current viewpoint, unless a case is undergoing tax remedy procedures.

Inventory valuation

Inventory must be valued at cost. If cost exceeds market price, the latter may be used as the valuation basis except where the last-in, first-out (LIFO) method is used. Cost may be determined by the LIFO, first-in, first-out (FIFO), moving-average, weighted-average

Taiwan

methods, specific identification method, or any other method approved by the tax authorities. Conformity between financial and tax reporting is not required.

Capital gains
Gains on the disposal of fixed assets are taxable as current-year income of the company, with the exception of gains on the sale of land. The capital gains tax on marketable securities is currently exempt. Instead, securities transaction tax is levied on the sales proceeds *(see Other taxes above)*. However, if a foreign company has a fixed place of business or business agent in Taiwan, capital gains on the sale of marketable securities may trigger income basic tax for the foreign shareholder.

Inter-company dividends
Starting 1 January 1998, dividends received from local investee companies by a domestic corporate shareholder are not included in taxable income. In addition, the imputation tax credit derived from the dividend income of the investee corporation can be distributed to the domestic corporate shareholders, but this tax credit cannot be used to offset the domestic corporation's income tax liability. The tax credits must be recorded in a separate book to be treated as tax credits available to the individual shareholders of the domestic corporate shareholders.

Dividends received from foreign subsidiaries are taxable, but credits are given for the withholding tax paid offshore, limited to the incremental tax liability that would result if the dividends were added to the Taiwan corporate shareholder's taxable income and taxed at the Taiwan corporate income tax rate.

Foreign income
Foreign income received by a Taiwan corporation is taxed. Double taxation is avoided by means of foreign tax credits.

Deductions

Depreciation and depletion
Straight-line, fixed percentage on diminishing book value, sum-of-years-digit, unit-of-production and working-hour methods are acceptable depreciation methods to the tax office. With the approval of the tax authority, a company may revalue its fixed assets each time the government's wholesale price index increases by 25% over the base period. A company's base period is established at the time of purchase of fixed assets or at such time when a company revalues its fixed assets. Any increase in fixed assets may then be depreciated for tax purposes.

Net operating losses (NOLs)
Based on Article 39 of the Income Tax Act amended on 21 January 2009, effective from 23 January 2009, a company's NOLs can be carried forward for 10 years instead of five years. This extension applies to NOLs incurred in 2003 and onwards.

Payments to foreign affiliates
Royalties, interest, and service fees paid to a foreign affiliate are subject to withholding tax. Royalties or service fees paid to a foreign entity may be tax-exempt if certain requirements are met and prior approval is obtained.

Taxes

All taxes other than income tax are generally deductible, unless where such taxes are related to tax-exempt income. However, tax penalties are not deductible. The tax associated with the acquisitions of real properties (such as taxes on the purchase of land) should be included in the cost of the land or building.

Other significant items

If a company invests in a foreign entity and holds at least 20% equity ownership (this limitation does not apply if special approval is obtained from the Executive Yuan), the company can attribute 20% of the investment amount to a "reserve for foreign investment loss."

Group taxation

As a result of a qualified merger, acquisition and spin-off, a company may choose to file a single consolidated corporate income tax return with its subsidiaries if the company continuously holds over 90% of the shares of the subsidiaries for 12 months in a tax year.

Transfer pricing

The Taiwan MOF announced the Assessment Rules for non-arm's-length transactions by Profit-seeking Enterprises (TP Assessment Rules) on 28 December 2004. The transfer pricing regulations were established to constrain multinational corporations from leaving their profits in countries with lower tax rates. For applicable companies, the disclosure of related party transactions in the corporate income tax return filing and the preparation of transfer pricing report will be required. Upon request, the transfer pricing report will have to be submitted to the Taiwan tax authority within one-month of notice. The transfer pricing report must demonstrate the company's good faith effort to comply with the assessment rules. Without proper reason, failure to comply with such rules will result in additional tax payable and financial penalties. The types of transactions governed by these regulations include the following: transfer of tangible assets; use of tangible assets; transfer of intangible assets; use of intangible assets; rendering of services; use of funds; and other types of transactions prescribed by the MOF.

Tax incentives

Certain tax incentives are provided to investors if they are located in prescribed areas such as science parks, economic processing zones, free trade zones and so on. Other tax credits are granted to qualifying companies that invest in specific businesses or industries promoted by the government, such as biotech.

Most tax breaks were previously offered under the Statute for Upgrading Industries (SUI), which expired at the end of 2009 and has been replaced by a new Statute for Innovating Industries (SII). Additional tax incentives are available under the Business Mergers and Acquisitions Act, the Financial Institutions Merger Act and other laws and regulations.

Notwithstanding the expiry of the SUI, companies can still apply for tax incentives under this statute if the requisite approvals had already been obtained from the government before the expiry date.

T

Taiwan

R&D tax incentive

Under the SII, R&D credits will be available up to 15% of qualified R&D expenses incurred, with the maximum amount of tax credit capped at 30% of the tax payable for the year in which the expenses were incurred. The unutilised R&D credits will be forfeited, and cannot be carried back or carried forward.

Tax concessions on merger

Under the Business Mergers and Acquisitions Act, a merger or consolidation of companies can be exempt from stamp tax, deed tax, securities transaction tax and business tax incurred from the merger or consolidation, if certain conditions are met. After the merger or consolidation, any tax concession previously enjoyed by the merged entities will continue to be applicable to the surviving company (or new company) after the merger or consolidation. However, the surviving company is required to manufacture the same products or provide services which were approved by the Ministry of Economic Affairs (MOEA) for tax concessions engaged by the merged entities in order to continue the concessions obtained previously.

The unexpired and unutilised NOLs of the participating entities prior to the merger or consolidation may be carried over to the surviving or newly-created entity according to the percentage of shareholding in the surviving or newly-created entity held by all shareholders of the participating entities.

Free-trade-zones

According to Act for the Establishment and Management of Free-trade-zones, foreign companies or their branch companies in Taiwan that apply for establishment or delegate free-trade-zone companies to store and/or perform simple processing in free-trade-zone and sell the products within and outside of Taiwan shall be exempted from corporate income tax. In the event that the annual domestic sales exceed 10% of the total annual domestic and foreign sales, the portion in excess shall not be exempted from corporate income tax.

Withholding taxes

Domestic corporations paying certain types of income are required to withhold as follows:

Recipient	Dividends	Interest	Royalties
	%	%	%
Resident corporations and individuals	N/A	10	10
Non-treaty	20	15/20 (1)	0/20 (2)
Treaty:			
Australia	15/10 (3)	10	12.5
Belgium	10	10	10
Denmark	10	10	10
Gambia	10	10	10
Indonesia	10	10	10
Israel	10	7/10 (4)	10
Macedonia	10	10	10
Malaysia (5)	12.5	10	10

Recipient	Dividends	Interest	Royalties
	%	%	%
Netherlands	10	10	10
New Zealand	15	10	10
Senegal	10	15	12.5
Singapore	(6)	Not prescribed	15
South Africa	15/5 (7)	10	10
Swaziland	10	10	10
Sweden	10	10	10
United Kingdom	10	10	10
Vietnam	15	10	15

Notes

The numbers in parentheses refer to the following notes:

1. For non-resident enterprises, a 15% withholding tax applies to interest income derived from short-term bills, securitised certificates, corporate bonds, government bonds or financial debentures, as well as interest derived from repurchase transactions involving these bonds or certificates. The rate in all other cases is 20%, unless reduced under a tax treaty.
2. Royalties received by foreign enterprises that are specially approved in advance by the government are exempt from income tax.
3. A rate of 10% for shareholders that are companies (other than partnerships) with at least a 25% shareholding.
4. 7% of the gross amount of the interest arising in a territory and paid on any loan of whatever kind granted by a bank of the other territory.
5. The withholding tax rate on technical service fee payments is reduced to 7.5%.
6. The total tax burden of corporate income tax and dividends tax is not to exceed 40% of the total profits of the company.
7. A rate of 5% for shareholders with at least a 10% shareholding.

Tax treaties
Double taxation treaties entered into with the following countries: Australia, Gambia, Belgium, Denmark, Senegal, United Kingdom, Sweden, Indonesia, Israel, New Zealand, Netherlands, Singapore, South Africa, Swaziland, Macedonia, Malaysia, and Vietnam relate to corporate and individual income tax. Treaties with Canada, the European Union, Germany, Israel, Japan, Korea, Luxembourg, Netherlands, Norway, Sweden, Thailand, Macau, and the United States relate to certain earnings from the operation of ships and/or aircraft.

Tax administration

Returns
The tax year in Taiwan runs from 1 January to 31 December. Tax returns are filed on a self-assessment basis. Businesses may request approval from the local collection authority to file income tax returns using a fiscal year-end other than 31 December. Income tax returns are due no later than five months after the end of the tax year.

Payment of tax
Tax is paid on a self-assessment basis in two instalments. The first payment is based on 50% of the tax liability of the prior year's tax return and is made in the ninth month of the enterprise's fiscal year. However, if the taxpayer meets certain requirements,

T

Taiwan

it may self-assess the provisional tax based on the taxable income of the first half of the current fiscal year. The second payment is made at the time of filing the annual tax return. The returns are subsequently reviewed by the tax authorities, and a final assessment is issued.

Effective from 21 January 2009, any overpaid tax as a result of the tax collection authority's mistake, shall be refunded to the taxpayer within two years of acknowledgement of such mistake and shall not be subject to the original five-year period for applying for refund where the taxpayer is responsible for the mistake. The revised regulations shall apply retroactively to all overpaid taxes resulting from mistakes attributable to the tax collection authority without regards to the original five-year limitation.

Corporate taxes in Tajikistan

For more information, contact:

Richard Bregonje
PricewaterhouseCoopers
29/6 Satpaev Avenue
Hyatt Regency Office Tower, 4th Floor
Almaty 050040
Republic of Kazakhstan
Tel: +7 727 298 0448
Email: richard.bregonje@kz.pwc.com

Significant developments

Changes were introduced to the Tajikistan tax code (Law No. 571 dated 3 December 2009) effective 1 January 2010. The major changes with respect to the taxation of corporations include:

- Increase of the vehicle tax rates, newly enacted tax rate is 2.5% – 13.75% of calculation index; and
- A double tax treaty (DTT) with Latvia became effective 1 January 2010.

Taxes on corporate income

Generally, all Tajik legal entities are subject to taxation in Tajikistan. Tax is computed by applying the statutory 15% rate to taxable income (25% for enterprises operating in transport, communication, banking and service sectors), which is calculated as gross income decreased by allowed deductions and losses carried from previous periods. In Tajikistan, there is a minimum income tax on company income at the rate of 1% of aggregate annual income. Corporate income tax (CIT) is taken into account for minimum income tax. If CIT is less than minimum income tax on company income, then CIT should not be paid. Only a positive difference between CIT and minimum income tax should be paid. Nonetheless, minimum income tax should be paid in full amount.

Corporate residence

Legal entities formed under Tajik law, as well as legal entities whose effective control (management) is in Tajikistan, are recognised as residents for corporate tax purposes.

Other taxes

Value-added tax (VAT)
VAT is generally assessed on taxable turnover, which includes goods and services. The current VAT rate is 18%. Individuals and businesses are required to register as VAT payers when the established threshold of taxable turnover is exceeded. Generally, the tax code exempts the following from VAT: goods and services that are not provided in Tajikistan under the place of supply rules, sale, transfer or rent of real property, financial services, medical services, publishing, and certain other goods and services.

For goods, the place of supply is determined as the initial point of transportation. Services are generally considered to be provided at the place of business of the service

T

Tajikistan

provider or the actual place where services are rendered. However, for certain types of services, such as consulting and accounting, the services are considered to be provided at the location of the buyer.

A VAT refund is generally available for qualified exporters if input VAT exceeds assessed VAT.

VAT returns, together with issued and received invoices, are filed monthly, not later than the fifteenth day of the month following the reporting month. Payments are due by the same date.

Excise taxes
Excise tax is assessed on beverages, tobacco products, fuel, tires, passenger automobiles, and jewellery. Excise tax rates are established by the government.

Social tax
The employer is obliged to make social tax payments assessed on salary at the rate of 25%.

Road tax
The formula for calculating road tax is total deductions of the reporting year multiplied by the 2% tax rate (0.5% for trade companies). If actual deductions do not exceed 70% of gross income, the tax base for road tax would be 70% of gross income.

Land tax
Land tax is paid based on the area of the land plot and varies depending on the location.

Real estate tax
Real property tax applies to immovable real property such as buildings, houses and flats. The tax rate is calculated by multiplying the land tax rate by a relevant coefficient, which depends on the purpose of real property.

Vehicle tax
Vehicle tax is computed as a percentage of the calculation index applied for horse power of the vehicle engine. The percentage ranges from 2.5% to 13.75%.

Customs duties
Tariff rates:

- *Ad valorem* rate – calculated as a percentage of the customs value of the declared goods;
- Specific rate – calculated based on a specified statutory amount per one unit of the declared goods; and
- Combined rate – contains both types of rates.

The applicable rates established by the government range from 0% to 15%.

Tajikistan is signatory to several free trade agreements, primarily among the following Commonwealth of Independent States (CIS) countries: Russia, Belarus, Kazakhstan, and Kyrgyzstan.

Customs fees

A customs processing fee of 0.15% of the declared value of the goods is assessed during customs clearance.

Branch income

In addition to income tax, permanent establishments (PEs) are subject to branch profit tax at the rate of 8% of net profit after income tax, unless a lower rate is prescribed by an applicable DTT.

Income determination

Generally, all Tajik legal entities are subject to taxation in Tajikistan. Tajik residents are taxed on their worldwide income. Non-residents are subject to income tax in Tajikistan only on Tajikistan source income. Non-residents operating through a PE are generally subject to the same income tax provisions. Income tax is assessed on taxable income, which is the difference between gross income and allowed exemptions and deductions.

Inventory valuation

Inventory accounting for tax purposes generally follows inventory accounting for financial reporting purposes.

Capital gains

Capital gains on securities in general are taxed as business profits.

Inter-company dividends

Inter-company dividends are exempt from income tax.

Foreign income

Tajik residents are taxed on their worldwide income. Non-residents are subject to income tax in Tajikistan only on Tajikistan source income.

Deductions

In general, all business expenses (materials, payroll, etc.) are allowed as a deduction if the expenses are connected with the earning of income, not of a capital nature, and supported by proper documentation.

Depreciation

The deduction for costs related to fixed assets generally is made through depreciation and amortisation at rates ranging from 7% to 20%, using the declining balance method.

Net operating losses

Net operating losses may be carried forward for three years but may not be carried back.

Interest deductibility

Interest deductibility is generally limited to three times the refinancing rate of the National Bank of Tajikistan (currently 8%). For certain entities, additional limitations may apply.

T

Tajikistan

Charity contributions
Charity contributions are limited to 10% of taxable income.

Taxes
Taxes paid to the budget of Republic of Tajikistan and other states are deductible except for:

- Income tax from individuals;
- Income tax from legal entities; and
- Penalties and fines.

Other significant items
Among other deductions specifically mentioned in the tax code are research and development, repair expenses, and geological and geophysical expenses.

Non-deductible expenses
Non-deductible expenses, specifically mentioned by the tax code, include fines and penalties, meals and entertainment, personal expenses, passenger vehicles, and non-business expenses.

Group taxation

There are no rules permitting grouping for tax purposes in Tajikistan.

Tax incentives

Tax incentives include tax-free special economic zones and an exemption from income tax for taxpayers that have made a certain amount of investments.

Withholding taxes (WHT)

Tajikistan source income of nonresidents is subject to WHT at its source at the rates shown in the following table:

Types of income at a source of payment	Tax rate
Dividends and interest	12%
Insurance and reinsurance premiums	4%
International transport and telecommunications	4-6%
Royalties, rent, lease income, management fees, and other income	15%

In accordance with the DTTs as of 1 January 2010, the rate of WHT may be reduced as follows:

Recipient	Dividends %	Interest %	Royalties %
No treaty	12	12	15
Armenia	10	10	10
Azerbaijan	10	10	10
China	5/10 (1)	8	8
Czech Republic	5	7	10
Germany	5/15 (2)	–	5

Recipient	Dividends %	Interest %	Royalties %
Kazakhstan	10/15 (3)	10	10
Kyrgyzstan	5/15 (4)	10	10
Latvia	0/5/10 (5)	7	5/10 (6)
Moldova	5/10 (7)	5	10
Pakistan	5/10 (8)	10	10
Poland	5/15 (9)	10	10
Russia	5/10 (10)	10	15
Turkey	10	10 (11)	10
Turkmenistan	10	10	10
Ukraine	10	10	10

Notes

1. A rate of 5% of the gross amount of the dividends if the recipient is the enterprise (except a partnership) and directly holds at least 25% of the capital of the company paying the dividends; 10% of the gross amount of the dividends in all other cases.
2. A rate of 5% of the gross amount of the dividends if the beneficial owner is a company (other than a partnership) that holds directly at least 10% of the capital of the company paying the dividends; 15% of the gross amount of the dividends in all other cases.
3. A rate of 10% of the gross amount of the dividends if the beneficial owner is a legal entity and directly holds no less than a 30% stake in the company paying the dividends; 15% of the gross amount of the dividends in all other cases.
4. A rate of 5% of the gross amount of the dividends if the beneficial owner is a company that holds at least 50% of the share capital of the company paying the dividends; 15% of the gross amount of the dividends in all other cases.
5. A rate of 0% of the gross amount of the dividends if the beneficial owner is a company (other than a partnership) that holds directly at least 75% of the capital of the company paying the dividends; 5% of the gross amount of the dividends if the beneficial owner is a company (other than a partnership) that holds directly at least 25% of the capital of the company paying the dividends; 10% of the gross amount of the dividends in all other cases.
6. A rate of 5% of the gross amount of the royalties paid for the use of or the right to use software, or industrial, commercial or scientific equipment; 10% of the gross amount of the royalties in all other cases.
7. A rate of 5% of the gross amount of the dividends if the beneficial owner is a company (other than a partnership) that holds directly at least 25% of the share capital of the company paying the dividends; 10% of the gross amount of the dividends in all other cases.
8. A rate of 5% of the gross amount of the dividends if the beneficial owner is a company (other than a partnership) that holds directly at least 25% of the share capital of the company paying the dividends; 10% of the gross amount of the dividends in all other cases.
9. A rate of 5% of the gross amount of the dividends if the beneficial owner is a company (other than a partnership) that holds directly at least 25% of the share capital of the company paying the dividends; 15% of the gross amount of the dividends in all other cases.
10. A rate of 5% of the gross amount of the dividends if the beneficial owner is a person who holds directly at least 25% of the share capital of the company paying the dividends; 10% of the gross amount of the dividends in all other cases.
11. Interest arising in Tajikistan and paid to the government of Turkey or to the Central Bank of Turkey shall be exempt from Tajikistan tax; interest arising in Turkey and paid to the government of Tajikistan or to the National Bank of Tajikistan shall be exempt from Turkish tax.

T

Tajikistan

Tax administration

Returns
The tax code prescribes a calendar year as the tax year. Annual CIT declarations are due by 1 April in the year following the tax year-end.

Taxpayers are required to submit their estimated calculation of monthly advance payments of CIT.

Payment of tax
With respect to CIT, the advance payments are due every fifteenth day of the month, except individual entrepreneurs. Payment of any outstanding income tax liabilities is required within 10 calendar days following submission of the annual income tax declaration.

Reporting periods vary for other taxes.

Fines and interest penalties
The fine for failure to file a tax return ranges from a minimum amount of 1 calculation index (CI), which is currently TJS 35, to a maximum fine of 100 CI, or TJS 3,500. The amount of the fine depends on the taxpayer's category and should be assessed based on each 10 days of delay. In the absence of tax returns, the tax authorities are entitled to assess taxes based on any information available.

Fines may be assessed in the amount of 10% to 20% of the understated tax liabilities. In severe cases, a violation may be considered a criminal offence.

A fine for failure to withhold and remit tax may be assessed in the amount of 3 to 200 CI (approximately TJS 1,225 – 7,000) of the tax not withheld.

Interest penalties may apply to late tax payments in the amount of 0.08% of the underpaid tax amount, for each day of tax underpayment.

Statute of limitation
Taxpayers are allowed to make changes to prior period tax returns within the statute of limitations (three years). No fines should apply to corrections in this case.

Other issues

Accounting system
In accordance with the governmental Resolution of the Republic of Tajikistan concerning International Standards of Financial Statements, the Ministry of Finance of the Republic of Tajikistan shall adopt the International Financial Reporting Standards (IFRS) through a step-by-step approach.

Accounting policies and practices are being revised in light of the legal requirement that companies adopt IFRS and International Accounting Standards. Such revised accounting policies should be adopted by companies' boards of directors and disseminated to all the accounting units with clear instructions on how to introduce and follow the new policies and procedures.

Corporate taxes in Tanzania

For more information, contact:

David Tarimo
PricewaterhouseCoopers
International House, Sixth Floor
Shaaban Robert Street/Garden Avenue
Dar-es-Salaam, Tanzania
Tel: +255 22 2192201
Email: david.tarimo@tz.pwc.com

Significant developments

The most significant recent changes in relation to income tax on corporations are the introduction of a concessionary income tax rate for companies newly listed on the Dar es Salaam Stock Exchange (DSE), and the introduction of an alternative minimum tax (AMT). Details on these changes are discussed below.

Taxes on corporate income

Income tax is charged at a rate of 30% on income of a resident corporation and of a permanent establishment (PE) of a non-resident corporation.

A reduced corporate tax rate of 25% applies for three consecutive years for companies newly listed on the DSE. To qualify, at least 30% of the company's shares must be issued to the public.

A new AMT applies at a rate of 0.3% of the gross turnover of a company that is in "perpetual loss status" for a period of at least three consecutive years as a result of tax incentives. The practical application of this tax is unclear but it has been provided that this new tax will apply to income years ending on or after 31 July 2008.

Non-residents are also subject to tax on income sourced in Tanzania. Certain payments to non-residents are subject to tax at the relevant non-resident withholding tax (WHT) rate *(see section on Withholding taxes for the relevant rates)*. Income from the disposal of investments in Tanzania is subject to income tax if such investments fall within the source rules, and in such a case the income will be taxed at a rate of 30%.

Corporate residence

A company is tax resident if it is incorporated or formed under the laws of Tanzania or if the management and control of its affairs is exercised in Tanzania.

Other taxes

Value-added tax (VAT)

VAT is chargeable on all taxable goods and services supplied in, or imported into, mainland Tanzania. For imported goods, VAT is payable at the time of importation together with any customs and excise duties. For imported services, VAT is accounted for by registered businesses through a "reverse charge" mechanism. The standard rate of VAT is currently at 18% but the export of goods and certain services is eligible for zero rating. Businesses with an annual taxable turnover of more than TZS 40 million must register for VAT.

The Commissioner for VAT has the discretion to register as intending traders, investors whose projects have not commenced production, but who wish to be VAT registered in order to reclaim the tax they incur on start-up costs. VAT payable with respect to capital goods (as defined), which are imported or purchased in Tanzania, may be permanently deferred, subject to certain procedures being followed.

Supplies of certain goods and services are exempt from VAT. A business that produces only exempt supplies is unable to register for VAT and consequently unable to recover the VAT incurred on inputs. However, businesses in this category that import taxable services with a value over the registration threshold must register for VAT to account for the VAT on such services.

Certain goods and services supplied to specified entities are eligible for "special relief" from VAT. The "special relief" provisions enable supplies, which would otherwise be chargeable with VAT, to be made VAT free provided certain administrative requirements are followed.

Registered businesses must submit VAT returns, with any tax due, on a monthly basis.

Businesses entitled to VAT refunds can claim any remaining credit six months after a refund first became due, subject to all intervening returns being rendered. Any claim for a VAT refund must be supported by an auditor's certificate. Businesses in a consistent refund position (e.g., exporters) can apply for approval to lodge their refund claims on a monthly basis.

Zanzibar has its own VAT Act but it is similar to the Mainland Tanzania Act.

Customs duties
Tanzania is a member of the East African Community, which became a Customs Union with effect from 1 January 2005 on the implementation of the East African Customs Union Protocol. This protocol provides for: a Common External Tariff (CET), elimination of internal tariffs, rules of origin, anti-dumping measures, a common Customs law, and common export promotion schemes.

The customs duty rates applicable under the CET are as follows:

Category	Rate
Raw materials, capital goods, agricultural inputs, pure-bred animals, medicines	0%
Semi-finished goods	10%
Finished final consumer goods	25%

Tanzania is also a member of the Southern African Development Community (SADC). Where goods are subject to a lower rate of duty from another trade bloc such as SADC, the lower duty rate applies until such a time as the trading arrangements between the trading blocs are harmonised.

Excise duties

Excise duty rates apply as follows:

Excise duty rates

Item	Rate for FY 2009/10
Sugared mineral water and aerated waters	TZS 58.00/= per litre
Other, including club soda	TZS 58.00/= per litre
Carbonated soft drinks	TZS 58.00/= per litre
Lemonade and flavoured minerals or aerated waters	TZS 58.00/= per litre
Malt beer	TZS 354/= per litre
Clear beer (from unmalted barley)	TZS 209/= per litre
Wine with more than 25% imported grapes	TZS 1,132/= per litre
Wine with domestic grapes content exceeding 75%	NIL
Spirits	TZS 1,678/= per litre
Cigarettes without filter containing more than 75% domestic tobacco	TZS 5,749/= per 1,000
Cigarettes with filter containing more than 75% domestic tobacco	TZS 13,564/= per 1,000
Other cigarettes not mentioned above	TZS 24,633/= per 1,000
Cut rag/filler	TZS 12,441/= per kg
Satellite and cable television broadcasting	7%
Airtime for mobile phones	10%
Disposable plastic bags	120%
Liquefied petroleum gas (LPG)	0
Motor car with cylinder capacity exceeding 1000cc but not exceeding 2000cc	5%
Motor vehicle with engine size greater than 2000cc	10%
Old motor vehicles (10 years or more)	20%
Motor spirit (gasoline) premium	TZS 339/= per litre
Motor spirit (gasoline) regular	TZS 339/= per litre
Gas oil (diesel)	TZS 314/= per litre
Jet fuel	NIL
Illuminated kerosene	TZS 52/= per litre
Other medium oil and preparation	TZS 9.32/= per litre
Industrial diesel oil	TZS 392/= per litre
Heavy furnace oil	TZS 97/= per litre
Lubrication oil	TZS 500/= per m3
Lubrication greases	TZS 0.75 per kg

Fuel levy

Fuel levy is charged on petroleum products at a rate of TZS 200 per litre.

Payroll taxes

Payroll taxes, including skills and development levy; is imposed at 6% of payroll cash costs, and also includes a 20% social security contribution. Whereby in general, 10% is borne by employers with the other 10% deducted from employee pay.

T

Stamp duty

Examples of instruments giving rise to stamp duty obligations include conveyances, leases, share transfers, issue and transfer of debentures. The current rate is 1% of the transaction value.

Local taxes

The local government levies property tax based on the value of premises. The rates vary depending on the value and location of the property. The local government is also entitled to charge a 0.3% service levy based on turnover generated in the relevant district. For agricultural produce and livestock, there is a cess tax, currently capped at 5% of the producer price.

Branch income

The income tax liability of a person with a PE in Tanzania is calculated as if the person and the PE are independent but as if the PE is resident in Tanzania. The income of the PE is taxed at the normal income tax rate for entities, namely 30%. The PE is also subject to a tax on "repatriated income," which applies at a rate of 10% (being the same rate as a company would withhold on dividends). In certain circumstances, business activities of the head office may be attributed to the branch. Arrangements between a PE and head office generally are not recognised other than the transfer of an asset or liability between the two. Amounts derived/payments received and expenditures incurred/payments made that relate to assets held by, or liabilities owed by, the business of the PE, are attributed to the PE.

Income determination

Subject to any provision to the contrary in the Act, income is to be calculated in accordance with generally accepted accounting principles. Corporations must apply an accrual basis of accounting.

Transactions between related parties

With respect to transactions between related parties, there is an obligation to "quantify, apportion and allocate amounts" for income tax purposes on an arm's-length basis. If the Commissioner considers that a person has failed to comply with this requirement, he may make such adjustments as he thinks appropriate.

The Commissioner has the power to make counteractive adjustments to a person's tax liability, where he considers that an arrangement is a tax-avoidance arrangement.

Anti-avoidance

Other anti-avoidance provisions include the following:

- A change in the underlying control of an entity, accompanied by some change in the conduct of the business;
- Controlled foreign trusts and corporations;
- Income or dividend stripping arrangements; and
- Income splitting.

Controlled foreign trusts and corporations

Certain provisions relate to the treatment of unallocated income of controlled foreign trusts and corporations, however, in practice, this is more of academic interest as there is limited outward investment from Tanzania.

Deductions

In calculating taxable profit, deductions are allowed for revenue expenditures incurred wholly and exclusively in the production of income, with some statutory exceptions. For capital expenditures, there are specific tax depreciation allowances.

Special rules apply with regard to the valuation of trading stock and long-term contracts and in relation to the treatment of instalment sales and finance leases.

In certain circumstances, there is a restriction on the amount of deductible interest for what are termed "exempt-controlled resident entities," whereby there is a deferral of relief for interest to the extent that the interest cost exceeds the sum of (a) interest income and (b) 70% of income before net interest income/expense.

In order to claim relief for bad debts it is necessary to demonstrate that all reasonable steps have been taken to pursue payment and that there is a reasonable belief that the debt claim will not be satisfied. Financial institutions, however, should normally be able to claim relief for provisions made in accordance with the standards established by the Bank of Tanzania.

Depreciation allowances – overview

The categories of depreciable assets and their tax depreciation rates are set out in the table below.

Expenditures on plant and machinery are generally written off on a reducing balance basis at rates of 37.5%, 25% or 12.5%, depending on the category of the asset. Certain plant and machinery for manufacturing, fish farming and tourist hotels benefits from a 50% allowance in the first year, with the normal rates applying to the remaining balance in subsequent years. There is an immediate write-off of expenditures on plant and machinery used in agriculture.

Expenditures on buildings qualify for a depreciation allowance of 5% per year on a straight-line basis. For intangible assets, the write-off is over the useful life of the asset.

Apart from the immediate write-off of plant and machinery, agricultural businesses also benefit from the immediate write-off of agricultural improvement expenditures (including the costs of clearing land and excavating irrigation channels, and planting perennial crops or tree bearing crops). Buildings, structures, dams, water reservoirs, fences and similar works of a permanent nature used in agriculture, livestock or fish farming are written off on a straight-line basis over five years.

Mining companies are entitled to a 100% capital deduction with respect to capital expenditure on exploration and development.

T

Tanzania

Depreciation allowances – rates

Class	Rate %	Depreciable assets
1	37.5	Computers and data handling equipment together with peripheral devices; automobiles, buses and minibuses with a seating capacity of less than 30 passengers, goods vehicles with a load capacity of less than seven tonnes; construction and earth-moving equipment.
2	25	Buses with a seating capacity of 30 or more passengers, heavy general purpose or specialised trucks, trailers and trailer-mounted containers; railroad cars, locomotives, and equipment; vessels, barges, tugs, and similar water transportation equipment; aircraft; other self-propelling vehicles; plant and machinery (including windmills, electric generators and distribution equipment) used in manufacturing or mining operations; specialised public utility plant and equipment; and machinery or other irrigation installations and equipment.
3	12.5	Office furniture, fixtures and equipment; any asset not included in another class.
4	20	Natural resource exploration and production rights and assets referred to in subparagraph (3) in respect of natural resource prospecting, exploration and development expenditure. (However, note that Income Tax Act 2004 does provide for predecessor capital deduction provisions in the Income Tax Act 1973 to continue for the holders of mining rights.)
5	20	Buildings, structures, dams, water reservoirs, fences and similar works of a permanent nature used in agriculture, livestock farming or fishing farming.
6	5	Buildings, structures and similar works of permanent nature other than those mentioned in class 5.
7	1 divided by the useful life of the asset in the pool and rounded down to the nearest half year	Intangible assets other than those in class 4.
8	100	Plant and machinery (including windmills, electric generators and distribution equipment) used in agriculture.

Tax losses

There is no limit on the carryforward period for tax losses. However, there is ring-fencing of tax losses as follows:

- Losses from agricultural business can only be offset against profits derived from agricultural business.
- Foreign source losses can only be offset against foreign source profits.
- Losses on investments can only be offset against investment income.
- Foreign source losses on investments can only be offset against foreign source investment income.

In certain circumstances, tax losses may be forfeited on a change in the underlying control of an entity.

Foreign tax credits

A credit is automatically given for foreign tax paid by a resident on foreign income, but such credit may not exceed the Tanzanian tax rate applicable to that income. Any unrelieved amount of foreign tax credit may be carried forward (subject to the "change of control" provisions). An election also may be made to claim relief as an expense instead of as a credit.

Group taxation

There are no provisions for tax consolidation or group relief.

Tax incentives

Agriculture, manufacturing, mining and tourism

Tax incentives by way of generous capital deduction provisions are given for specific sectors, namely agriculture, manufacturing, mining and tourism. *See the section on Deductions for further details*.

Export processing zones, special economic zones

There are special benefits for export processing zones (EPZ) and special economic zones (SEZ). Included in the benefits availed to a person licensed to carry on business in an EPZ, as well as to SEZ investors selling in export markets, are a 10-year income tax holiday and WHT holiday, subject to a requirement to export at least 80% of production.

Withholding taxes (WHT)

Withholding tax rates

Payment	Resident	Non-resident
	%	%
Dividend:		
– To a company controlling 25% or more of the voting power and holding 25% or more of the shares	0	10
– From a DSE listed company	5	5
– Otherwise	10	10
Interest	10	10
Rent:		
– Land and buildings	10	15
– Aircraft lease	0	0
– Other	0	15
Royalty	15	15
Natural resource payment	15	15
Service fees		
– Technical services provided to mining companies	5	15
– Other	0	15
Insurance premium	0	5
Payments by government to residents without a tax identification number certificate	2	n/a

Tanzania

Double tax treaties (DTTs)
DTTs are in force with Canada, Denmark, Finland, India, Italy, Norway, South Africa, Sweden, and Zambia. In certain circumstances, these may reduce the WHT rates.

Tax administration

While the year of income for tax purposes is the calendar year, an entity may apply to use its own accounting period rather than the calendar year.

Taxable income and deductible expenditure is quantified in Tanzanian shillings. The Commissioner does have the power by notice in writing to permit quantification in a foreign currency convertible to Tanzanian shillings.

Returns
A statement of estimated tax payable containing an estimate of the chargeable income and the tax payable thereon is due for submission within three months from the beginning of the accounting period. A final tax return must be furnished within six months from the end of the accounting period. WHT returns must be submitted every half year. A late filing penalty applies monthly at an amount equal to the higher of (a) TZS 100,000 and (b) 2.5% applied to unpaid tax. If estimated tax is significantly underestimated, a penalty may also apply.

Payment of tax
Instalment tax is payable in four equal instalments not later than three months, six months, nine months, and twelve months from the beginning of the accounting period. Final tax is payable on the date on which the final return is due for submission, namely six months after the end of the accounting period. WHT is due seven days after the month of deduction. Interest on late payment is charged at the Bank of Tanzania discount rate.

Corporate taxes in Thailand

For more information, contact:

Thavorn Rujivanarom
PricewaterhouseCoopers Legal & Tax Consultants Ltd.
15th Floor, Bangkok City Tower
179/74-80 South Sathorn Road
Yannawa
Bangkok 10120
Thailand
Tel: +66 2 344 1000
Email: thavorn.rujivanarom@th.pwc.com

Significant developments

There have been no significant developments regarding tax on corporate income during the past year.

Taxes on corporate income

Corporate income tax (CIT) is generally paid at a flat rate of 30% on net taxable profits.

A reduction is given to companies listed on the Stock Exchange of Thailand (SET) and the Market for Alternative Investment (MAI), the trading board established by the SET. The rates are shown below.

i. Companies listed between 6 September 2001, and 31 December 2005:

Companies listed on the SET	25%
Companies listed on the MAI	20%

The reduced rate applies for five accounting periods commencing from the first accounting period that begins on or after the day the company has listed its securities on the SET or the MAI.

ii. Companies applying for listing between 1 January 2007, and 31 December 2008, and duly listed by 31 December 2009:

Companies listed on the SET	25%
Companies listed on the MAI	20%

These rates will apply for three accounting periods starting from the first accounting period beginning on or after the day the company listed its securities on the SET or MAI.

iii. Listed companies other than those described previously:

T

Thailand

Companies listed on the SET

Net profit	Rate
(a) THB 0 – 300,000,000	25%
(b) Over THB 300,000,000	30%

Companies listed on the MAI

Net profit	Rate
(a) THB 0 – 20,000,000	20%
(b) Over THB 20,000,000	30%

These rates apply for three accounting periods commencing from the accounting period beginning on or after 1 January 2008.

Companies listed on the SET or MAI between 6 September 2001, and 31 December 2005, and whose concession rate as noted under item (i) above has expired, will be able to enjoy the concession rate under item (iii) but not beyond the accounting period ending on or after 31 December 2010.

Small and medium enterprises (i.e., companies and partnerships with paid-in capital not exceeding THB 5 million at the end of any accounting period) are subject to CIT at these reduced rates:

Net profit	Rate
(a) THB 0 – 150,000	Nil
(b) THB 150,001 – 1,000,000	15%
(c) THB 1,000,001 – 3,000,000	25%
(d) Over THB 3,000,000	30%

Banks are subject to CIT at the rate of 10% with respect to profits derived from lending to non-Thai residents from foreign currency funds obtained from non-Thai sources (so-called "out-out business").

A special development zone has been established in five provinces in the far south of Thailand in which a company or juristic partnership located therein will be subject to CIT at the rate of 3% for the revenue earned from the manufacture or sale of goods or provision of services from the accounting period that begins on or after 1 January 2010, until the accounting period that ends on or after 31 December 2012.

Corporate residence

Corporate residence is determined by the place of incorporation. A company incorporated under the laws of Thailand is a resident company. A company incorporated abroad is subject to corporate income tax in Thailand if it is considered to be carrying on business in Thailand. The term "carrying on business in Thailand" is broad and, subject to the provisions of double taxation treaties, includes the presence of an employee, representative or go-between that results in a foreign corporation deriving income or gains in Thailand.

Thailand

Other taxes

Value-added tax (VAT)
VAT is levied at the rate of 10% (reduced to 7% until 30 September 2010, unless extended further), except on exports, which are zero-rated, and a number of exempt goods and services (e.g., basic groceries, education, health care, interest, leasing of immovable property and sale of real estate).

Specific business tax
Specific business tax is levied on the gross receipts of certain businesses. Among the more significant items are interest and foreign exchange gains of banks and other financial institutions, and dealings in real estate, where the rate of tax is 3%.

The rate of specific business tax has been reduced to 0.01% for certain revenue derived by commercial banks and finance, securities and *credit foncier* businesses as well as businesses with regular transactions similar to commercial banking.

Municipality tax
An additional 10% of the specific business tax is levied as municipality tax.

Local taxes
There are three major local taxes:

1. Household and land tax – 12.5% of assessable economic rental income;
2. Signboard tax – Rates vary according to size; minimum of THB 200 per annum; and
3. Local development tax – Rates range between 0.25% and 0.95% of the value of land assessed by local authorities. This tax does not apply if the property is subject to household and land tax.

Capital taxes
There are no capital taxes in Thailand.

Branch income

Branches of foreign corporations pay income tax at the corporate tax rate on locally earned profits only. Branch profits remitted to the foreign head office are subject to additional tax at the rate of 10%. However, this is a tax on disposition of profits abroad and is not limited to remittances. For example, a credit of profits to the head office account in the books is held to be a disposition of profits abroad even though no remittance of funds takes place.

Income determination

Inventory valuation
Inventory is valued at the lower of cost or market price. Any recognised method of ascertaining the cost price may be used, but a change in the method may be made only with the prior approval of the director-general of the Revenue Department. Conformity between book and tax reporting is required.

Capital gains
There is no specific legislation governing capital gains. All capital gains earned by a company are treated as ordinary revenue for tax purposes. Capital gains on the sale of

Thailand

investments derived from or in Thailand by a foreign company not carrying on business in Thailand are subject to a tax of 15%, withheld at source by the purchaser, unless otherwise exempt under a double tax treaty.

Gains from the sale of government bonds earned by a non-resident are exempt from income tax.

Exemptions
Certain types of income are exempt from corporate income tax. The exemptions cover interest on government bonds paid to a foreign company not carrying on business in Thailand, interest on foreign loans paid to financial institutions organised under specific law and wholly owned by a foreign government, dividends or share of profits paid by a joint venture to a Thai company or foreign company carrying on business in Thailand, etc.

Inter-company dividends
Dividends received from a Thai company by a company listed on the SET are exempt from tax. Dividends received by a non-listed company from other Thai companies are also exempt from tax, provided that the company receiving the dividends holds at least 25% of the total voting shares without any cross-shareholding. The tax exemption applies on the condition that the shares must be held for at least three months before and three months after the dividends are received.

In other cases, where one Thai company receives dividends from another Thai company, one half thereof is exempt from tax.

Dividends received from outbound investment are exempt from tax provided that the Thai company receiving the dividends holds at least 25% of the shares with voting rights of the company paying the dividends for a period of not less than six months before the date on which the dividends are received and the dividends must be derived from net profit in the foreign country taxed at a rate of not less than 15%. In the event that a "special law" in a particular foreign country provides a reduced tax rate or exemption for the net profit, the limited company which receives the dividends is still eligible for tax exemption.

Foreign income
Only Thailand incorporated companies are taxed on worldwide income. A foreign incorporated company is taxed on profits arising from or in consequence of business carried on in Thailand. A foreign company not carrying on business in Thailand is subject to a withholding tax on certain types of assessable income (e.g., interest, dividends, royalties, rentals and service fees) paid from or in Thailand.

The Revenue Code does not describe how foreign income received by a Thailand-incorporated company is taxed, but the Revenue Department regards foreign branch income as taxable when earned and foreign dividend income as taxable when received. Double taxation is relieved by way of a credit against the tax chargeable in Thailand.

Stock dividends
Stock dividends are taxable to the recipient as ordinary income.

Deductions

Depreciation and depletion

Deduction for wear and tear and depreciation is allowed as a percentage of cost. If the rate of deduction adopted by a company under its own accounting method is lower than the percentage of cost, deduction will be allowed only at the rate adopted by the company. The straight-line basis is the method most commonly used by companies, but any generally accepted basis, such as sum-of-the-years-digits method or double declining method, is permitted. Statutory rates are as shown:

	%
Buildings:	
Durable buildings	5
Temporary buildings	100
Cost of acquisition of depletable natural resources	5
Cost of acquisition of lease rights:	
If there is no written lease agreement or if there is a written lease agreement containing a renewal clause whereby continual renewals are permitted	10
If there is a written lease agreement containing no renewal clause or containing a renewal clause but restricting renewable periods to a definitely limited duration	Percentage rate equals 100 divided by the sum of years of the original and renewable lease periods
Cost of acquisition of the right in a process, formula, goodwill, trademark, business license, patent, copyright or any other right:	
If the period of use is unlimited	10
If the period of use is limited	Percentage rate equals 100 divided by the number of years of use
Other assets not mentioned above, excluding land and inventory	20

Special depreciation methods for certain assets may be applied as follows:

- Machinery for research and development (R&D) may initially be depreciated at a higher rate (e.g., 40%) of cost, and the remaining balance is then depreciated at the prescribed rate;
- Machinery and equipment may initially be depreciated at a higher rate (e.g., 40%) of cost, and the remaining balance is then depreciated at a maximum of 20% per annum. This method is valid for machinery and equipment acquired until 31 December 2010; and
- Computer hardware and software may be depreciated within three accounting periods.

T

Thailand

Special depreciation method for small and medium enterprises (SME)
SME are companies and juristic partnerships with fixed assets, excluding land, at a value of no more than THB 200 million and with no more than 200 employees. In addition to the special depreciation methods noted previously, SME are entitled to the following special depreciation methods:

- Machinery and equipment may initially be depreciated at a higher rate (e.g., 40%) of cost, and the remaining balance is then depreciated at the prescribed rate;
- Computer hardware and software may initially be depreciated at a higher rate (e.g., 40%) of cost, and the remaining balance is then depreciated within three accounting periods;
- Factory buildings may initially be depreciated at a higher rate (e.g., 25%) of cost, and the remaining balance is then depreciated at the prescribed rate; and
- Any assets not mentioned above acquired during an accounting period, excluding land and inventory, may be depreciated at 100% of cost but not exceeding THB 500,000. This special treatment will be available only until 31 December 2010.

Net operating losses
Losses may be carried forward for the following five accounting periods. Carryback of losses is not permitted.

Payments to foreign affiliates
A Thailand incorporated company may claim a deduction for royalties, management service fees and interest charges, provided they are expended exclusively for the purpose of generating profits or for the purposes of business in Thailand and do not exceed a reasonable amount.

Taxes
In general, all taxes are deductible except CIT and VAT together with fines, penalties and surcharges charged under the Revenue Code.

Other significant items
Deductions for allowable charitable contributions and certain other donations may not exceed 2% of net taxable profits. Deductions for educational support as approved by the Ministry of Education may be allowed at the rate of 200% of the actual expense, but not exceeding 10% of net profit before deductions of the allowable charitable contributions and certain other donations. Furthermore, deductions for the support of public recreational facilities may also be allowed at the rate 200% of the actual expense, but not exceeding 10% of net profit before deductions of the allowable charitable contributions and certain other donations after including the educational support expense.

Group taxation

Group taxation is not permitted.

Tax incentives

Tax incentives in certain industries eligible for promotion under the Investment Promotion Act and Board of Investment (BOI) announcements include the following:

- Exemption from or reductions of import duties on imported machinery;

- A reduction of up to 90% of import duties on raw or essential materials imported for manufacturing for domestic sale;
- Exemption from CIT equal to the amount of the investment, excluding the cost of land and working capital, for three to eight years;
- Exclusion from taxable income of dividends derived from promoted enterprises during the period of exemption from CIT; and
- Exemption of up to five years from withholding tax on goodwill, copyright or other rights according to the contract approved by the BOI. (In practice, this incentive will be granted at the BOI's discretion).

Additional incentives to encourage exports include the following:

- Exemption from import duties on raw materials and components imported for manufacturing for export;
- Exemption from import duties on the items imported for re-export; and
- The ability to deduct from corporate taxable income the amount equivalent to 5% of the increase in income derived from export over the previous year, excluding costs of insurance and transportation. (In practice, the BOI will not grant this incentive because of World Trade Organization regulations).

Additional incentives for enterprises located in an industrial estate or promotion zone include the following:

- Reduction of 50% of CIT for five years after the termination of a normal income tax holiday or from the date of earning income if no tax holiday is granted; and
- Double deduction from taxable income for the cost of transportation, electricity and water supply.

In 2009, the BOI granted exemption from CIT for eight years to a promoted company that has been granted approval for listing on the SET or MAI during the period in which the project still enjoys the incentive of CIT exemption. Applications for this privilege must be submitted by 31 December 2012 and the approval of the SET or MAI must be granted within the period of CIT exemption.

In January 2010, the BOI amended the incentives for SMEs in certain industries, retroactive to 16 November 2009, which include the following:

- Exemption from import duty on imported machinery regardless of location;
- Exemption from CIT for eight years, with no maximum amount, regardless of location;
- Permission to use used machinery in Thailand with a value not exceeding THB 10 million provided that the value of the investment in new machinery is not less than 25% of the total value of the used machinery; and
- Other rights and incentives will be granted according to the BOI announcement No. 1/2000.

Applications for this privilege must be submitted by 31 December 2011.

Capital investment
A Special Purposes Vehicle (SPV) for securitisation is granted tax exemption on income derived from a securitisation project approved by the Office of the Securities and Exchange Commission (SEC). Nevertheless, the operation and allocation of cash inflow

T

Thailand

for debt and expenses settlement must follow the plan approved by the SEC. Moreover, no dividends will be paid to shareholders of an SPV until all remaining assets and benefits have been transferred back by the SPV to the originator of the securitisation project and the SPV ceases to exist.

Regional operating headquarters (ROH)

Regional operating headquarters (ROH) means a company organised under the Thai law providing administrative, technical assistance or supporting services to its domestic or overseas affiliated enterprises or branches in at least three countries other than Thailand with a paid-in capital of at least THB 10 million on the last day of any accounting period. Income from the provision of services must comprise at least 50% of the ROH income (reduced to one-third for the first three years).

The following tax incentives are available:

* 10% CIT on income from affiliated enterprises and branches for services rendered, including administrative services, technical assistance, management, R&D or training;
* 10% CIT on interest income received as a result of re-lending to affiliated enterprises or branches funds borrowed by the ROH;
* 10% CIT on royalty income derived from affiliated enterprises and branches and which is generated from R&D work performed in Thailand;
* CIT exemption on dividends received from domestic and overseas affiliated enterprises and branches;
* Personal income tax exemption for expatriate employees for services undertaken outside Thailand, provided that the relevant employment costs are not deducted by the ROH or an affiliated enterprise in Thailand; and
* Expatriate employees may elect to pay personal income tax at a rate of 15% for consecutive periods not exceeding four years provided they forego entitlement to withholding tax credits on their interest and dividend income.

Withholding taxes (WHT)

Tax rate schedule

Country of Recipient	Dividends	Interest	Royalties
	%	%	%
Resident corporations	0/10 (1)	0/1 (2)	3
Resident individuals	10	15	Progressive rate (3)
Non-resident corporations and individuals:			
Non-treaty	10	15	15
Treaty:			
Armenia	10	10/15 (4)	15
Australia	10	10/15 (4)	15
Austria	10	10/15 (4)	15
Bahrain	10	10/15 (4)	15
Bangladesh	10	10/15 (4)	15
Belgium	10	10/15 (4)	5/15 (9)
Bulgaria	10	10/15 (4)	5/15 (5)

Country of Recipient	Dividends	Interest	Royalties
	%	%	%
Canada	10	10/15 (4)	5/15 (6)
China, P.R.	10	10/15 (4)	15
Cyprus	10	10/15 (23)	5/10/15 (7)
Czech Republic	10	10/15 (4)	5/10/15 (8)
Denmark	10	10/15 (4)	5/15 (9)
Finland	10	10/15 (4)	15
France	10	3/10/15 (10)	0/5/15 (11)
Germany	10	10/15 (4)	5/15 (9)
Hong Kong	10	10/15 (12)	5/10/15 (13)
Hungary	10	10/15 (4)	15
India	10	10/15 (4)	15
Indonesia	10	10/15 (4)	15
Israel	10	10/15 (4)	5/15 (14)
Italy	10	10/15 (4)	5/15 (9)
Japan	10	10/15 (4)	15
Korea, Rep. of	10	10/15 (4)	5/10/15 (25)
Kuwait	10	10/15 (4)	15
Laos	10	10/15 (4)	15
Luxembourg	10	10/15 (4)	15
Malaysia	10	10/15 (4)	15
Mauritius	10	10/15 (4)	5/15 (5)
Nepal	10	10/15 (4)	15
Netherlands	10	10/15 (4)	5/15 (9)
New Zealand	10	10/15 (24)	10/15 (15)
Norway	10	10/15 (4)	5/10/15 (16)
Oman	10	10/15 (17)	15
Pakistan	10	10/15 (4)	0/10/15 (18)
Philippines	10	10/15 (4)	15
Poland	10	10/15 (4)	5/15 (19)
Romania	10	10/15 (4)	15
Russia	10	10/15 (26)	15
Seychelles, Rep. of	10	10/15 (4)	15
Singapore	10	10/15 (4)	15
Slovenia	10	10/15 (4)	10/15 (20)
South Africa	10	10/15 (4)	15
Spain	10	10/15 (4)	5/8/15 (21)
Sri Lanka	10	10/15 (4)	15
Sweden	10	10/15 (4)	15
Switzerland	10	10/15 (4)	5/10/15 (8)
Turkey	10	10/15 (4)	15
Ukraine	10	10/15 (4)	15
United Arab Emirates	10	10/15 (4)	15
United Kingdom	10	10/15 (4)	5/15 (9)
United States	10	10/15 (12)	5/8/15 (22)

T

Thailand

Country of Recipient	Dividends	Interest	Royalties
	%	%	%
Uzbekistan	10	10/15 (4)	15
Vietnam	10	10/15 (4)	15

Notes

The numbers in parentheses refer to the following notes:

1. The zero rate applies to a recipient company listed on the SET.
2. The 1% rate applies to interest paid to all resident corporations other than banks or finance companies, except where interest arises from bonds or debentures.
3. The progressive rate is in accordance with the personal income tax schedule.
4. The 10% rate applies to interest paid to a recipient that is a bank or financial institution (including an insurance company).
5. The 5% rate applies to royalties paid for the use of any copyright of literary, artistic or scientific work excluding cinematograph films and films, tapes or discs for radio or television broadcasting.
6. The 5% rate applies to royalties paid for the production or reproduction of any literary, dramatic, musical or artistic work excluding royalties with respect to motion picture films and works on film or videotape for use in connection with television.
7. The 5% rate applies to royalties paid for the use of any copyright of literary, dramatic, musical, artistic or scientific work including software, cinematograph films or films or tapes used for radio or television broadcasting; and the 10% rate applies to royalties paid for the use of industrial, commercial or scientific equipment or for information concerning industrial, commercial or scientific experience.
8. The 5% rate applies to royalties paid for the alienation or the use of any copyright of literary, artistic or scientific work excluding cinematograph films or films or tapes used for radio or television broadcasting, and the 10% rate for the alienation of any patent, trademark, design, or model, plan, secret formula, or process.
9. The 5% rate applies to royalties paid for the use of any copyright of literary, artistic or scientific work.
10. The 3% rate applies to interest paid on loans or credits granted for a period of four years or more with the participation of a public finance organisation to a public authority or to an enterprise in France that are tied to the sale of plant and machinery or studies relating to the equipping or supply of industrial, commercial or scientific installations, as well as public works. The 10% rate applies to interest paid to any financial establishment in France.
11. The zero rate applies to royalties paid to a contracting state or state-owned company with respect to films or tapes, and the 5% rate to royalties for the alienation or the use of any copyright of literary, artistic or scientific work.
12. The 10% rate applies to (a) interest paid to a bank or financial institution (including an insurance company) and (b) interest paid under a sale on credit of any equipment, merchandise or services.
13. The 5% rate applies to royalties paid for the use or the right to use any copyright of literary, artistic or scientific work and the 10% rate for the use or the right to use any patent, trademark, design, or model, plan, secret formula, or process.
14. The 5% rate applies to royalties paid for the use of any copyright of literary, artistic or scientific work excluding cinematograph films or films, tapes used for radio or television broadcasting.
15. The 10% rate applies to royalties paid for the use of any copyright; or the use of, or the right to use, any industrial, scientific or commercial equipment; or the use of, or the right to use, any motion picture film, or film or videotape or any other recording for use in connection with television, or tape or any other recording for use in connection with radio broadcasting; or the reception of, or the right to receive, visual images or sounds, or both, transmitted to the public by satellite or, cable, optic fibre or similar technology; or the use in connection with television or radio broadcasting, or the right to use in connection with

television or radio broadcasting, visual images or sounds, or both, transmitted by satellite or cable, optic fibre or similar technology.

16. The 5% rate applies to royalties paid for the use of any copyright of literary, artistic or scientific work and the 10% rate applies to royalties paid for the use or the right to use industrial, commercial or scientific equipment.

17. The 10% rate applies to (a) interest paid to a bank or financial institution (including an insurance company) and (b) interest from a loan or debt claim that is guaranteed by the government.

18. The zero rate applies to royalties paid to a contracting state or a state-owned company with respect to films or tapes, and the 10% rate applies to royalties paid for the alienation or the use of any copyright of literary, artistic or scientific work.

19. The 5% rate applies to royalties paid for the alienation or the use or the right to use any copyright of literary, artistic or scientific work excluding cinematograph films or tapes used for television or broadcasting.

20. The 10% rate applies to royalties paid for the use of, or the right to use, any copyright of literary or artistic or scientific work including motion pictures, live broadcasting, film, tape or other means of the use or reproduction in connection with radio and television broadcasting, and for the use of, or the right to use industrial, commercial, or scientific equipment.

21. The 5% rate applies to royalties paid for the use of any copyright of literary, dramatic, musical, artistic or scientific work excluding cinematograph films or films or tapes used for radio or television broadcasting. The 8% rate applies to royalties in consideration of financial leasing for the use of, or the right to use, industrial, commercial, or scientific equipment.

22. The 5% rate applies to royalties paid for the use of any copyright of literary, artistic or scientific work including software, motion pictures and works on film, tape or other means of reproduction for use in connection with radio or television broadcasting. The 8% rate applies to royalties paid for the use of industrial, commercial or scientific equipment.

23. The 10% rate applies to interest paid (a) to a recipient that is a bank or financial institution (including an insurance company); (b) in connection with the sale on credit of any industrial, commercial or scientific equipment; or (c) in connection with the sale on credit of any merchandise by one enterprise to another enterprise.

24. The 10% rate applies to interest paid (a) to a recipient that is a bank or financial institution (including an insurance company); or (b) with respect to indebtedness arising as a consequence of a sale on credit of any equipment, merchandise or services, except where the sale was between persons not dealing with each other at arm's length.

25. The 5% rate applies to royalties paid for the use of or the right to use any copyright of literary, artistic or scientific work including software, and motion pictures and works on film, tape or other means of reproduction for use in connection with radio or television broadcasting and the 10% rate for the use of or the right to use any patent, trademark, design, or model, plan, secret formula or process.

26. The 10% rate applies to interest paid to the following recipients (a) in the case of a resident of Russia, any institution having a license to carry on banking operations; and (b) in the case of a resident of Thailand, any financial institution (including an insurance company).

Tax administration

Returns

The tax year for a company is its accounting period, which generally must have a duration of 12 months. However, the tax year may be less than 12 months in the case of the first accounting period after incorporation or after prior approval from both the revenue department and the business development department has been received for a change in the closing date.

The system is one of self-assessment. A company prepares and files its tax returns by the due dates and at the same time pays the taxes calculated to be due.

T

Thailand

Withholding tax returns

Withholding tax returns (except for the sale of immovable property) must be filed within seven days from the last day of the month in which income has been paid. The tax withheld can then be used as a credit against the corporate income tax payable of the payee.

Payment of tax

CIT is paid twice each year. A half-year return must be filed within two months after the end of the first six months of an accounting period. The tax to be paid is computed on one-half of the estimated profit for the full accounting period, except for listed companies, banks, certain other financial institutions and other companies under prescribed conditions where the tax is based on the actual net profit for the first six months. The annual tax return is filed within 150 days from the closing date of an accounting period, at which time the balance of the tax due is payable. Credit is given for the amount of tax paid at the half-year.

Sample corporate tax calculation		
Year ended 31 December 2010		
Net profit according to the income statement of the company		THB 1,000,000
Add – Items not allowed for deduction:		
Provision for inventory obsolescence	100,000	
Provision for doubtful debts	50,000	
Expenses of a personal character, gifts	15,000	165,000
		1,165,000
Less:		
Dividend from subsidiary company	100,000	
Bad debts written off (1)	40,000	
Inventory written off (1)	150,000	290,000
Taxable profit		THB 875,000
Tax thereon at 30%		THB 262,500
If the company qualifies as SME, tax thereon:		
150,000 @ Nil		
725,000 @ 15%		
		THB 108,750

Note

1. It is presumed that the bad debt and inventory write-off procedures are in accordance with the rules and conditions under the Revenue Code.

Corporate taxes in Trinidad and Tobago

For more information, contact:

Allyson West
PricewaterhouseCoopers
The PricewaterhouseCoopers Building
11-13 Victoria Avenue
Port-of-Spain
Trinidad and Tobago
Tel: +1 868 623 1361
Email: allyson.west@tt.pwc.com

Significant developments

There have been no significant developments in the last year.

Taxes on corporate income

With effect from 1 January 2006 the standard rate of tax was reduced to 25%, but this varies in the case of certain classes of companies (e.g., life insurance companies). The current tax rates are as follows:

	%
Ordinary companies	25
Petroleum related companies	35
Life insurance companies	15
Petroleum production companies (petroleum profits tax)	50

These taxes are payable by way of quarterly instalments on 31 March, 30 June, 30 September and 31 December in the year of income based on the tax liability of the immediately preceding year with any balance of tax being paid on/before 30 April. Where the estimate for the current year is higher than the preceding year, the instalments must be based on the prior year plus 80% of the estimated increase over the prior year.

Corporate residence

Corporate residence is determined by reference to the location of the central management and control of the business of a company. The place of incorporation is regarded as merely one of the factors to be taken into account in determining where central management and control are located.

Other taxes

Business levy
With effect from 1 January 2001, corporations are subject to a business levy at the rate of 0.2% of gross revenue or receipts where the levy exceeds the corporation tax liability. Exemption is available for certain companies, including petroleum companies and companies whose annual turnover is less than TTD 200,000. This levy is payable

T

Trinidad and Tobago

quarterly, and the taxpayer is entitled to a tax credit of corporate tax up to a maximum of the business levy liability. The levy is a non-deductible expense for tax purposes.

Green fund levy
Effective 1 January 2001, a green fund levy of 0.1% is applicable to companies and partnerships doing business in Trinidad and Tobago and having gross income or receipts in excess of TTD 200,000 per annum. This levy is payable quarterly and is neither a deduction in computing chargeable income nor a credit against corporation tax due.

Unemployment levy
Only petroleum companies remain liable to the unemployment levy, at the rate of 5% of taxable profits. No set-off of prior year losses is permitted in computing the liability.

Supplementary petroleum tax
The supplementary petroleum tax (SPT) is chargeable on the gross income (derived from the sale of crude oil) less royalties and over riding royalties paid on the crude oil sold. The tax is computed separately in respect of land and marine operations and with effect from 2005 is a quarterly tax based on the actual gross income for each quarter.

The SPT is deductible in arriving at profits subject to petroleum profits tax.

Value-added tax (VAT)
VAT is applicable to a wide range of goods and services. The standard rate applicable to commercial supplies is 15%.

Certain basic unprocessed foods and agricultural supplies are zero-rated, as are crude oil, natural gas and all exported goods and services. Effective 1 January 1995, hotel accommodations and yachting services to non-residents are zero-rated.

A number of services, including financial services, real estate brokerage, residential rentals, and educational services, are exempt. However, with effect from 1 January 1994, financial services (as specified) are subject to a transaction tax at a rate of 15%. From 1 January 1993, imported inputs of highly capital-intensive manufacturers are exempt from VAT.

Hotel accommodation tax
With effect from 1 January 1995, hotels are subject to a hotel accommodation tax at a rate of 10% of the value of the accommodation.

Insurance premium tax
Also effective 1 January 1995, a tax at the rate of 6% has been imposed on insurance premiums in respect of general insurance contracts. Life insurance and reinsurance premiums are exempt.

Branch income

A branch is subject to Trinidad and Tobago taxation on all income directly or indirectly accruing in or derived from Trinidad and Tobago. The tax rates applicable on branch profits are the same as on corporate profits. In addition, branch profits, after deduction of corporation tax and reinvestments, are subject to withholding tax annually at varying rates on after tax profits which are remitted/deemed remitted to the head office. The position noted may be varied by the provisions of any applicable double tax treaties.

Income determination

Income
A Trinidad and Tobago resident corporation is taxed on worldwide income. A non-resident company engaged in business in Trinidad and Tobago is taxed only on income directly or indirectly accruing in or derived from Trinidad and Tobago. Double taxation is avoided by means of foreign tax credits.

Inventory valuation
Inventories are generally stated at the lower of cost or market value. Cost may be determined by the first-in, first-out (FIFO) or the average-cost method. The last-in, first-out (LIFO) and base-stock methods are not generally accepted for tax purposes.

Capital gains
Gains on the disposal of chargeable assets within 12 months of acquisition are subject to tax at standard corporate rates. *(see Depreciation and depletion under Deductions).*

Inter-company dividends
Dividends received from both domestic subsidiaries and other domestic corporations are fully exempt from tax.

Stock dividends
A Trinidad and Tobago corporation can distribute tax-free a dividend of common stock (bonus issue) proportionately to all common stockholders.

Deductions

Depreciation and depletion
With effect from 1 January 1995, tax depreciation rates (wear-and-tear allowances) have been standardised by statute. Fixed assets are to be classified into one of four classes:

	%
Class A – Furniture and fittings, buildings and improvements	10
Class B – Motor vehicles	25
Class C – Heavy equipment, motor lorries, trucks, computer equipment	33.3
Class D – Extra heavy equipment	40

The allowance will be calculated at the rate applying to aggregate expenditure incurred on assets within the class acquired after 1 January 1995 on a declining-balance basis.

Companies currently enjoying benefits under the Fiscal Incentives Act and the Free Zones Act will be unable to claim the 10% wear and tear on buildings under this provision while petroleum companies are entitled to an initial allowance of 10% and annual allowance of 5% on a straight-line basis.

Accelerated tax depreciation is allowed to manufacturers in the form of an initial allowance at the rate of 75% on capital expenditure on plant and machinery. The

Trinidad and Tobago

allowance is to be claimed in the year that the asset is first brought into use. For those companies engaged in the production of sugar, petroleum, or petrochemicals or enjoying concessions under the Fiscal Incentives Act, the rate is 20%.

Gains on sale of tax-depreciable assets are taxable as ordinary income (i.e., a balancing charge) but only when the written down value of the assets of a Class goes into credit. Prior to this the proceeds of sale are credited to the particular Class thereby reducing the written down value of the Class. Tax depreciation is not required to conform to book depreciation.

A company engaged in petroleum production business is entitled to capital allowances on tangible costs and intangible drilling and development costs as follows:

- Tangible costs – Initial allowance (20%) and annual allowance (20% SL); and
- Intangible costs – Initial allowance (10%) and annual allowance (20% reducing balance basis).

Allowances in respect of petroleum operations are granted from the earlier of (a) the year following the year in which the expenditure was incurred or (b) the year in which commercial production commences save that in the case of exploration activity the allowances are to commence from the year incurred.

Net operating losses
A trading loss may be carried forward indefinitely to be set-off against future profits.

Loss carrybacks are not permitted.

Effective 1 January 1997, a limited form of group loss relief has been introduced, whereby current year losses may be surrendered to a claimant company within a Group, except that the claimant's tax liability cannot be reduced by more than 25%. Companies must be resident in Trinidad and Tobago. Only losses incurred after 1 January 1997 qualify for this relief.

Payments to foreign affiliates
A corporation engaged in business in Trinidad and Tobago may claim a deduction for royalties and interest charges paid to foreign affiliates, provided the amounts paid are at arm's length and the appropriate withholding tax is deducted and properly accounted. For interest to be deductible for tax purposes the funds borrowed must have been utilised in the production of income and the recipient must be subject to tax in Trinidad and Tobago or otherwise specifically exempt therefrom.

Deduction for management charges (as this term is defined) paid to a non-resident is restricted to the amount of the management charges or 2% (2005 – 1%) of outgoings and expenses exclusive of the charges, whichever is the lower. Tax depreciation allowances may not be treated as an expense for this purpose. Withholding tax may also be applicable to management charges.

Taxes
Other than the supplementary petroleum tax, taxes or levies are not generally deductible in arriving at taxable profit (see Other taxes above).

Other significant items

Charitable contributions under a deed(s) of covenant to approved charity/charities are deductible up to a maximum of 15% of total income.

From 1994, contributions by local insurance companies to Catastrophe Reserve Funds are deductible for tax purposes up to the value of 20% of net premium income from property insurance business.

Group taxation

There is no provision for group taxation in Trinidad and Tobago, but with effect from 1 January 1997 a limited form of group loss relief has been introduced (*see Net operating losses under Deductions*).

Tax incentives

Tax holidays
Incentives include:

- Fiscal Incentives Act, 1979: An approved enterprise, which must be a locally incorporated resident corporation, may be granted an exemption from corporation tax for a period of up to 10 years, depending on the category under which it is approved. Exemption may be total or partial. Subject to approval, profits may be distributed tax-free to shareholders except in the case of certain non-resident shareholders, where the relief is restricted to so much of the tax as exceeds their liability in their country of residence. Net losses during the tax holiday period (i.e., the excess of total losses over total profits) may be carried forward for set-off without limitation for five years from the end of the tax holiday period, after which the normal set-off provisions for losses apply. Effective 1 January 2007, the tax holiday in respect of corporate tax is no longer granted.
- Approved tourism projects: Under the Tourism Development Act 2000, approved tourism development projects including hotels are granted a tax holiday for periods of up to seven years. In addition, a carryover from a tax exemption period is permitted of any loss arising out of the operation or renting of an approved tourism project to be written off against profits in accordance with normal Income Tax loss provisions, subsequent to the tax holiday period. An approved tourism project means a project declared to be so by the government.
- Approved mortgage and other companies: The profits of an approved company are exempt from corporation tax. The exempt profits when distributed to shareholders are exempt from corporation tax and income tax. Expenses incurred in the course of the approved mortgage business remain fully deductible.
- Business expansion scheme: The business expansion scheme was introduced in 1988 to allow approved small companies carrying on business in a regional development area and companies carrying out certain approved activities a tax credit of 15% of their chargeable profit. This scheme is to be restructured to encourage both individual and corporate investors to invest in venture capital companies by allowing a "tax rebate" on their investment. Effective 2006, the tax credit has been removed and replaced by a five year tax holiday.
- Free Zone: The profits of an approved company operating in a designated Free Zone are free from corporation tax. In addition, payments to non-residents are free of withholding tax. Approved activities include manufacturing.

T

Trinidad and Tobago

Other allowances/incentives include:

- Promotional expenses – Promotional expenses incurred by local firms to promote the expansion of existing markets and/or the creation of new ones for the export of specified services or locally produced goods will be tax-deductible as an expense at 150% of the actual outlay. Tax-deductible promotional expenses are defined as those expenses incurred in respect of specified services or goods produced in Trinidad and Tobago. This includes such items as advertising in foreign markets and participation in trade fairs and missions.
- Scholarship allowance – From the year 2001 companies can deduct the actual expenses incurred in granting scholarships to nationals who are not employees, directors or associates of directors of the company for tertiary education.
- Market development grants – An Export Development Corporation was established to manage government export-development programme and also to do all things necessary and appropriate for the encouragement, promotion and expansion of export-oriented business. The Corporation was empowered to give financial assistance to exporters by way of market development grants. In 1994, the Tourism and Industrial Development Corporation was formed to incorporate in a single entity the functions of the Export Development Corporation, the Tourism Development Authority and the Industrial Development Corporation. This is now the authority responsible for administering the grants. These grants are not exempt from taxation unless (1) they have been made in respect of expenses incurred by an exporter prior to the export of the first commercial shipment of goods produced in Trinidad and Tobago and (2) the foreign market is not in a country specified as an "excluded country." Market development grants will be awarded to exporters that meet the criteria set out by the Corporation. Qualifying expenses include costs incurred in research in foreign markets, product design and testing abroad.
- Training – An allowance of up to 100% of expenses may be claimed in respect of expenses incurred in the training or retraining of staff.
- Production company allowance equal to 150% of actual expenses incurred in respect of the company's own audio, visual or video productions for educational or local entertainments or local culture up to a maximum of TTD 1.0 million:
  - Art and culture allowance;
  - Sportsman/sporting activity allowance; and
  - Audio, visual or video production allowance. Allowances are granted in respect of this activity (and the two aforementioned activities) based on the actual expenditure incurred but not exceeding TTD 1.0 million.
- Child care/home work facility – a deduction is allowed for the actual cost incurred in setting up a facility for dependents of employees who are minors up to a maximum of TTD 500,000 for each facility subject to an aggregate sum of TTD 3.0 million in any year.

Withholding taxes (WHT)

Withholding tax is imposed at varying rates up to 15%, depending on the nature of the payment, the status of the payee and the applicability of double taxation treaties. From January 1995, as a result of a reduction in the standard withholding tax rate, the tax treaty rate in some instances is now higher than the statutory rate. In such cases the lower statutory rate applies. The rates below have been adjusted to reflect these reductions:

Trinidad and Tobago

Recipient		Dividends		Interest
		Portfolio	Substantial holdings	
		%	%	%
Resident corporations and individuals		Nil	Nil	Nil
Non-resident corporations and individuals:				
Non-treaty	(1)	10	10	15
	(2)	5/10	5/10	15
Treaty:				
Canada (3)	(1)	15	15	15
	(2)	15	10	15
Caricom countries	(1)	0	0	15
	(2)	0	0	15
China	(1)	10	10	10
	(2)	10	5	10
Denmark	(1)	15	15	15
	(2)	15	10	15
France	(1)	15	15	10
	(2)	15	10	10/Nil (4)
Germany	(1)	15	15	10/Nil/15 (5)
	(2)	15	10	10/Nil/15 (5)
Italy	(1)	15	15	10
	(2)	15	10	10
India	(1)	10	10	10
	(2)	10	10	10
Luxembourg	(1)	10	10	10
	(2)	10	5	7.5/10
Norway	(1)	15	15	15
	(2)	15	10	15
Sweden	(1)	15	15	15
	(2)	15	10	10/Nil/15 (6)
Switzerland	(1)	15	15	10
	(2)	15	10	10
United Kingdom	(1)	15	15	10
	(2)	15	10	10
United States	(1)	15	15	15
	(2)	15	10	15/Nil/20 (7)
Venezuela	(1)	10	5	15
	(2)	10	10	15

T

Trinidad and Tobago

Recipient	Royalties		
	(8)	(9)	(10)
	%	%	%
Resident corporations, individuals	Nil	Nil	Nil
Non-resident corporations, individuals:			
Non-treaty			
Treaty:			
Canada	15	Nil	20
Caricom countries	15	15	20
China	10	10	20
Denmark	15	Nil	20
France	10	Nil	20
Germany	10	Nil	20
Italy	5	Nil	20
India	10	10	10
Luxembourg	10	10	20
Norway	15	Nil	20
Sweden	20	Nil	20
Switzerland	10	Nil	20
United Kingdom	10	Nil	20
United States	15	Nil	20
Venezuela	10	10	20

Notes

The numbers in parentheses refer to the notes below:

1. Individuals.
2. Corporations. The lesser rate applies to parent companies.
3. The lesser rate applies to companies, other than investment companies, which control at least 10% of the voting power.
4. The rate is 10% of the gross amount if interest is paid to a resident of France; it is nil if the interest is paid to the French government or to any agency or instrumentality of the French government.
5. The rate is 10% of the gross amount if the interest is paid to a bank that is a resident of Germany, nil where interest is paid to certain stated governmental institutions and 15% of the gross amount in all other cases.
6. The rate is 10% of the gross amount if the interest is paid to a bank that is a resident of Sweden, nil where interest is paid to certain specified governmental institutions and 15% of the gross amount in all other cases.
7. The rate is 15% of the gross amount if the interest is paid to a bank or financial institution in the United States that does not have a permanent establishment in Trinidad and Tobago, nil where the interest is paid to the US government or to any agency or instrumentality wholly owned by the US government, and 20% of the gross amount in all other cases.
8. The rate applies to patent royalties.
9. The rate applies to copyright royalties and similar payments.
10. The rate applies to royalties paid in respect of the operations of mines or quarries or of the extraction or removal of natural resources.

Tax administration

Returns
The taxpayer is required to file a tax return with the Board of Inland Revenue by 30 April following the end of the fiscal period. An automatic six-month grace period is allowed, following which a penalty is imposed (effective October 1995) of TTD 1,000 for every six months or part thereof that the return remains unfiled.

Payment of taxes
Corporation tax, business levy and green fund levy are payable quarterly in advance on 31 March, 30 June, 30 September, and 31 December. Instalments of corporation tax are based on an estimate of the current year's liability or tax based on the actual chargeable profits for the previous year, whichever is greater. The levy liabilities are based on the actual receipts for the quarter.

Corporate taxes in Turkey

For more information, contact:

Zeki Gündüz
PricewaterhouseCoopers
Suleyman Seba Cad. No:48
BJK Plaza B Blok K.9
Istanbul, Besiktas 34357
Turkey
Tel: +90 212 326 6060
Email: zeki.gunduz@tr.pwc.com

Significant developments

Corporate Income Tax Law No. 5520 replaced the former corporate income tax law as of 1 January 2006. The new law introduces extensive amendments, including formal clarification of issues such as transfer pricing and thin capitalisation in line with Organisation for Economic Co-operation and Development (OECD) guidelines and worldwide applications. It also includes new provisions such as controlled foreign company applications and anti-tax haven regulations.

Additionally, a new income tax law currently being prepared is expected to bring about significant changes in line with contemporary international tax practices.

Transfer pricing
The new corporate income tax law, includes considerable amendments to transfer pricing regulations, using OECD guidelines as a basis. If a taxpayer enters into transactions regarding the sale or purchase of goods and services with related parties, in which prices are not set in accordance with the arm's-length principle, the related profits are considered to have been distributed in a disguised manner through transfer pricing. Such disguised profit distribution through transfer pricing is not accepted as tax-deductible for corporate income tax (CIT) purposes. The methods prescribed in the law are the traditional transaction methods described in the OECD transfer pricing guidelines.

Controlled foreign corporation (CFC) rules
A CFC is established abroad, and at least 50% of the organisation is controlled directly or indirectly by tax-resident companies and real persons by means of separate or joint participation in the capital or dividends voting rights. A CFC also must meet certain conditions such as 25% or more of its gross revenue must comprise passive income, and it must be subject to an effective income tax rate lower than 10% for its commercial profit in its home country.

The CFC's profit may be included in the corporate income tax base of the controlling resident corporation in the fiscal period covering the month of year-end closing of the according CFC at the rate of the shares controlled, irrespective of whether it is distributed.

Thin capitalisation
According to the thin capitalisation regulation, if the ratio of the borrowings from shareholders or from persons related to the shareholders exceeds triple the shareholders' equity of the borrower company at any time within the relevant year, the

exceeding portion of the borrowing will be considered thin capital. Accordingly, under the new thin capitalisation regulation, the ratio of loans received from related parties to shareholders' equity must be no more than three to one in order to eliminate Turkish thin capitalisation issues.

Anti-tax haven provisions

According to the new law, various payments made to corporations (including branches of resident corporations) that are established or operational in countries that are regarded by the Council of Ministers to undermine fair tax competition (through taxation or other practices) will be subject to taxation in Turkey, irrespective of whether the payments in question are subject to tax, or whether the corporation receiving the payment is a taxpayer.

In this case, withholding tax (WHT) at the rate of 30% is envisaged to be levied over these payments.

The Council of Ministers has not yet determined which countries receiving payments are considered tax havens. It is expected that the council will publish a list in line with recent OECD studies.

Draft Turkish commercial code

The draft Turkish Commercial Code is before Parliament for approval and is expected to enter into force as of 2011, although this event is not certain. Among the reforms, it will enable the incorporation of a joint stock company (A.S.) and a limited liability company (Ltd.) with a single shareholder or partner, respectively. It will also, for the first time in Turkey, cover group companies, i.e., the relations between the parent company and subsidiaries subject to the same principles and policies and gathered under the same group management. In order to ensure transparency, each capital company must have an internet site, a certain part of which is specific to information for stakeholders. Joint stock companies will be allowed to hold online general assembly meetings. All administrative transactions of joint stock companies may be conducted online, which will create such options as online attendance for general assembly meetings, online submission of motions, online negotiations and online voting.

Portfolio investments

In line with the amendments made in the income tax law effective 1 January 2006, certain investment income (e.g., capital gains on listed equities acquired after 1 January 2006 and interest and capital gains from domestic government bonds or treasury bills issued after 1 January 2006) derived by non-resident corporations without having a permanent establishment (PE) in Turkey and by non-resident individuals (non-residents) is currently subject to 0% WHT at source, subject to certain documentation requirements.

For Turkish individuals and corporations, certain investment income (e.g., capital gains and interest income on treasury bills and domestic government bonds issued after 1 January 2006) is subject to 10% WHT. A 0% WHT is currently applicable to capital gains from listed equities purchased after 1 January 2006 (excluding the listed equities of securities investment trusts acquired after 1 January 2006) derived by Turkish residents. A further 15% WHT is applicable for interest income from reverse-repo transactions and time deposits for both residents and non-residents.

T

Turkey

The WHT will be applied by local intermediary banks, brokerage houses or local custodian banks, instead of the conventional self-declaration mechanism, and the WHT would be the final taxation in Turkey for non-residents and Turkish individuals.

Research and development (R&D) activities
In the local tax regulations, tax incentives are provided via two laws. Under the provisions of Corporate Income Tax (CIT) Law No. 5520, R&D-related expenditures of companies can be wholly regarded as a deduction for CIT purposes.

On the other hand, Law No. 5746 related to the support of the R&D activities became effective in 2008. With this new law, R&D and innovation-related expenses of technology centre enterprises, R&D centres and those incurred in specific R&D and innovation projects (listed in the law), can be continually regarded as a deduction for CIT purposes.

You will find further information about the incentives provided by the new law under Tax incentives.

E-invoicing
"E-invoicing" is the general term given to invoices presented as electronic documents, the exchange of which between parties is made in a secure and careful manner. The e-invoice is not a brand new document with additional legal features, rather it possesses the same legal features of a printed invoice. The general application of e-invoicing among all companies is envisioned. The Revenue Administration registers user accounts for companies with approved e-invoice applications. Users, whose applications are approved, have to meet the obligation to obtain an Electronic Fiscal Stamp. The Electronic Fiscal Stamp refers to the electronic certification infrastructure established by TÜBİTAK-UEKAE on behalf of the Revenue Administration. Following activation of the certificate, e-invoicing can commence without further requirements. Only users with approved registration applications for e-invoicing can use the system to issue and receive e-invoices. It is not possible to issue e-invoices to those lacking a user account on the system.

Issuing, sending and receiving e-invoice can be accomplished by either:

- Integrated IT system; or
- The e-invoice portal (http://www.efatura.gov.tr).

It is only possible to issue e-invoices to registered users willing to receive e-invoices. If they request a printed invoice, a company is required to provide the counterparty with a printed invoice rather than an e-invoice.

Taxes on corporate income

Corporations are liable to taxation as described.

Profits generated, as adjusted for exemptions and deductions and including prior-year losses carried forward are liable to CIT at a rate of 20%.

Dividend distributions to individual and non-resident corporate shareholders are subject to WHT at a rate of 15%. This rate might be reduced for foreign shareholders in the presence of a tax treaty. Please note that dividend distributions to resident entities and branches of non-resident entities are not subject to dividend WHT. Corporations are required to pay advance corporate tax based on their quarterly balance sheets and income statements at the rate of 20%. Advance corporate tax paid during the year is offset against the corporate tax liability calculated over the annual corporate tax return. The balance of advance tax can be refunded or used to offset other tax liabilities.

Turkish CIT legislation allows deduction of "all ordinary and necessary business-related expenses paid or incurred during the taxable year in carrying out any trade or business." The general principle for tax deductibility is that payment should be a necessary business expense and it should be properly documented in accordance with the relevant provisions of tax procedural law. In cases of charges from related parties, arm's-length pricing is also sought.

Tax losses may be carried forward for five years, but they may not be carried back.

Corporate residence

According to Turkish tax legislation, income taxation differs significantly based on the taxpayer's place of residence.

If both the legal and the business headquarters of a company are located outside Turkey, the company is regarded as a non-resident entity. If one of these headquarters is located within Turkey, the company is regarded as a resident entity. Resident entities are subject to tax on their worldwide income, whereas non-resident entities are taxed solely on the income derived from activities in Turkey.

Other taxes

Value-added tax (VAT)
Deliveries of goods and services are subject to VAT at rates varying from 1% to 18%. The general rate applied is 18%. VAT payable on local purchases and on imports is regarded as "input VAT" and VAT calculated and collected on sales is considered "output VAT." Input VAT is offset against output VAT in the VAT return filed at the related tax office. If output VAT is in excess of input VAT, the excess amount is paid to the related tax office. Conversely, if input VAT exceeds output VAT, the balance is carried forward to the following months to be offset against future output VAT. With the exception of a few situations such as exportation and sales to an investment incentive holder, there is no cash refund to recover excess input VAT.

Turkish VAT principles contain a "reverse-charge VAT mechanism," which requires the calculation of VAT by resident companies on payments to foreign countries. Under this mechanism, VAT is calculated and paid to the related tax office by the Turkish company. The local company treats this VAT as input VAT and offsets it in the same month. This VAT does not create a tax burden for the Turkish or non-resident company, except for its cash flow effect on the former if there is insufficient output VAT to offset there from.

Banking and insurance transactions tax (BITT)
Banks and insurance companies are exempt from VAT but are subject to BITT at a rate of 5%, which is due on the gains of such companies from their transactions. The

T

Turkey

purchase of goods and services by banks and insurance companies are subject to VAT, but this is considered as an expense or cost for recovery purposes.

Property taxes

Buildings and land owned in Turkey are subject to real estate tax at different rates.

Stamp tax (stamp duty)

Stamp tax applies to a wide range of documents, including but not limited to agreements, financial statements and payrolls. Stamp tax is levied as a percentage of the value stated on the agreements at rates varying between 0.165% and 0.825%. Salary payments are subject to stamp tax at the rate of 0.6% over the gross amounts paid, whereas an insignificant lump-sum stamp tax is calculated for some types of documents.

Special consumption tax (SCT)

There are four main product groups that are subject to special consumption tax at varying rates:

- Petroleum products, natural gas, lubricating oil, solvents and derivatives of solvents;
- Automobiles and other vehicles, motorcycles, planes, helicopters, yachts;
- Tobacco and tobacco products, alcoholic beverages; and
- Luxury products.

Unlike VAT, which is applied on each delivery, SCT is charged only once (except for some activities such as production).

Branch income

The branches are taxed solely on the income derived from activities in Turkey since they are regarded as non-resident entities for Turkish tax purposes. Branch profits are subject to Turkish corporate tax at the rate of 20%.

The branch profit transferred to headquarters is subject to dividend WHT at the rate of 15%, which might be reduced if a tax treaty applies.

Income determination

Turkish CIT legislation allows as a deduction for "all the ordinary and necessary expenses paid or incurred for the generation and sustenance of income during the taxable year in carrying on any trade or business." The general principle for tax deductibility is that payment should be a necessary business expense and it should be properly documented in accordance with the relevant provisions of tax procedural law.

The methods used in calculating the value of year-end stock or goods sold are weighted average and first-in, first-out (FIFO). Stock-count deficits are recorded as disallowable expenses, whereas stock-count surpluses are treated as income at year-end for corporate tax purposes. Necessary VAT adjustments should also be made accordingly.

Capital gains

No separate rules exist with respect to capital gains taxation in Turkey. Capital gains and losses are included in the determination of corporate income. For resident companies there is a tax-planning tool to reduce the effective corporate tax rate on capital gains to 5% (75% of income is exempt from corporate tax – 20% * 25% = 5%) arising from the disposal of real estate or participation shares under certain conditions.

Dividends

In dividend distribution's between Turkish resident companies, the dividend payer is exempt from WHT and the recipient is exempt from CIT.

Foreign-sourced income

In principle, foreign-sourced income is taxable in Turkey. However, foreign-sourced dividend income may also be subject to participation exemption, if certain conditions are fulfilled. A participation exemption for capital gains generated from a foreign subsidiary may also be available in Turkey, subject to certain conditions. Other foreign-source income such as royalties and interest is fully taxable in Turkey. Partial relief from taxation is granted insofar as the tax paid overseas does not exceed the rate of tax payable for the same income in Turkey.

Although undistributed income of foreign subsidiaries is not taxable in Turkey, CFC rules should be taken into consideration.

Income from foreign construction and repair activities

The profit from construction and repair activities carried out by Turkish corporations in foreign countries is exempt from corporate tax in Turkey according to Article 5(1)/h of the corporate tax law. It should be noted that if loss occurs from these activities, it is not possible to deduct this loss amount from income generated through domestic activities since deduction of a loss relating to foreign activities that are exempt from corporate tax in Turkey is unacceptable.

Stock dividends

A Turkish corporation may increase its paid-in capital via retained earnings. The recipient is not taxed for shares issued in this manner. In principle, a Turkish corporation is not allowed to hold its own shares.

Deductions

Depreciation and depletion

The application of depreciation has been amended as of 2004. Under these amendments, fixed assets acquired after 1 January 2004 are subject to depreciation at rates determined by the Ministry of Finance, based on their useful life. Fixed assets acquired before 1 January 2004 will continue to be depreciated using the former application, in which the maximum rate applicable is 20% per year. Depreciation can be calculated by applying either the straight-line or declining-balance method, at the taxpayer's discretion. The taxpayer may also change the option from declining-balance to straight-line (but not vice versa) at any time during the life of the asset. The applicable rate for the declining-balance method is twice the rate of the straight-line method, with 50% being the maximum applicable rate. Furthermore, in special cases the tax authorities may determine higher depreciation rates.

T

Turkey

Intangible assets are depreciated by the straight-line method over their estimated useful lives if objectively determinable.

Profits or losses on disposal of fixed assets (i.e., the difference between the proceeds and the written-down values) are included in taxable income in the year of disposal. If the renewal of disposed-of assets is considered necessary by the owners of the business concern, the profit accrued may be retained for up to three years without being taxed. After the purchase of new fixed assets, the profits may be offset against the depreciation of the new assets.

Losses

Corporate losses may be carried forward for five years. Losses may not be carried back.

Payments to foreign affiliates

Charges for royalties and interest by foreign affiliates may be deductible for tax purposes, provided that transfer pricing and thin capitalisation rules are followed. WHT and VAT implications should be considered.

Taxes

Essentially, CIT and VAT (with exceptions) are not deductible for CIT purposes. Fees and duties paid in relation to assets of the company are, in principle, deductible in determining taxable income.

Pensions and employee termination benefits

These expenses are deductible for CIT purposes only when they are paid, and are not subject to income withholding taxation beyond a certain limit.

Bad debts

Bad and doubtful accounts receivable are deductible under certain conditions. Amounts of the receivables collected afterwards are added to the profits of the year in which they are collected.

Group taxation

Consolidation of the accounts of group companies for tax purposes is not allowed in Turkey since each company is regarded as a separate taxpayer.

Tax incentives

The major income tax and VAT incentives available are as follows:

Participation exemption for dividends

There is an unconditional corporate tax and dividend WHT exemption for dividend income between Turkish companies. If a Turkish company has a shareholding in a foreign company this dividend income is exempt from corporate tax under certain conditions.

Capital gains exemption

For capital gains generated from the sale of shares in a Turkish company to another Turkish company, a 75% corporate tax exemption is applicable under certain conditions. In the event a foreign subsidiary is sold by a Turkish company, a corporate tax exemption at the rate of 100% is applicable under certain conditions.

Investment incentives

The Turkish government provides investment incentives (state aid) to eliminate inter-regional economic imbalance, facilitate a larger capital contribution by public and foreign investors to the capital build-up of the country and support activities that have a positive effect on employment. Generally speaking, state aid can be classified as either a tax or a non-tax incentive.

The principal prerequisite for benefiting from state aid, except investment allowance, is to obtain an Investment Incentive Certificate (IIC). The IIC is a document granted to investors for their investments by the Undersecretariat for the Treasury. It allows utilisation of the said benefits.

According to investment incentive legislation, in order to obtain an IIC, the minimum amount of total investment should be at least TRY 1,000,000.

The advantages of an IIC can be summarised as exemption from customs duty, RUSF and VAT. For example, the import of machinery and equipment (excluding raw materials, intermediate and operating products) is exempt from customs duty and Resource Utilisation Support Fund (RUSF) payments. In addition, VAT exemption is also applicable on the importation of eligible machinery and equipment.

On the other hand, from an income tax perspective, the legislation related to investment incentives has changed substantially. There are six main components of the new investment regulation:

1. Reduced corporate tax rate;
2. VAT exemption;
3. Exemption for social security premium (employer's portion);
4. Customs duty exemption;
5. Interest support; and
6. Allocation of land for investments.

Free trade zone

Free trade zones are special sites that lie geographically within the country, but are deemed to be outside the customs territory. In these regions, the normal regulations related to foreign trade and other financial and economic areas are either inapplicable, partly applicable or superseded by new regulations.

In general, activities such as manufacturing, storage, packing, general trading, banking, insurance and trade may be performed in Turkish free trade zones. Goods moving between Turkey and the zones are treated, for all purposes, as exports or imports. However, operations within the zones are subject to the supervision of the zone management (and customs authorities), to whom regular activity reports must be submitted. Consequently, there is a requirement for zone users to maintain full accounting records (in Turkish) with respect to their activities. These accounting requirements extend to inventory records. Customs duty is levied on any unexplained inventory losses as though the goods had been imported into the country.

The right to operate in a free zone is conferred by an operating licence obtained from the Undersecretariat for Foreign Trade, which reviews the application for conformity with the objectives and types of activity specified by the Economic Affairs Coordination Council.

T

Turkey

Portfolio investment income

Portfolio investment income derived by Turkish securities investment funds and securities investment trusts is exempt from corporate income taxation. The exempt corporate income of such securities investment funds and the securities investment trusts is subject to 0% corporate WHT. Certain income (e.g., interest and capital gains from domestic government bonds issued after 1 January 2006, capital gains derived from listed equities acquired after 1 January 2006) derived by these funds and trusts are subject to 0% withholding at source.

In line with the amendments made to the income tax law effective 1 January 2006, capital gains from listed equities of securities investment trusts acquired after 1 January 2006 and income from participation certificates of investment funds acquired after 1 January 2006 derived by non-resident corporations without a permanent establishment in Turkey and by non-resident individuals (non-residents) is currently subject to 0% income WHT at source, subject to certain documentation requirements. For individual and corporate residents, 10% rather than 0% WHT should be applicable to such gains and income. If certain conditions are satisfied, 10% WHT will not apply. The withholding will be applied by local intermediary banks, brokerage houses, or local custodian banks, instead of the conventional self-declaration mechanism and the WHT would be the final taxation in Turkey for non-residents and Turkish individuals.

Research and development (R&D) activities

In the last decade, the Turkish Parliament has enacted several regulations to provide incentives for R&D activities in Turkey. The three primary R&D incentives include significant advantages granted to investors planning R&D activities in science, software and technology in special zones known as "techno-parks", cash subsidies from the Scientific and Technological Research Council of Turkey (TUBITAK) and corporate tax deductions.

On April 2008, a new R&D law was enacted to broaden incentives. One of the objectives of the law is to attract foreign investors with significant R&D activities abroad to invest in Turkey, by enabling non-resident companies with a subsidiary or branch in Turkey to benefit from R&D tax incentives.

The main incentives introduced by the new R&D law are:

R&D deduction

All eligible innovation and R&D expenditures made in technology centres or R&D centres, which must employ at least 50 full-time equivalent R&D personnel, or R&D and innovation projects supported by foundations established by law or international funds, can be deducted from the corporate income tax base at a rate of 100%. The same expenditures can also be capitalised and expensed through amortisation over five years in the case of successful projects, whereas the R&D expenditure on failed projects can be expensed immediately.

Companies with separate R&D centres employing more than 500 R&D personnel can, in addition to the aforementioned deduction, may deduct half of any increase in R&D expenditures over similar money spent in the previous period.

Any unutilised R&D deduction can be carried forward for an unlimited period of time, indexed to the revaluation rate, which is an approximation of the inflation rate.

Income tax exemption
80% of the salary income of eligible R&D and support personnel is exempt from income tax. However, this rate is increased to 90% for personnel with a doctorate degree.

Social security premium support
The Ministry of Finance will pay half the employer portion of social security premiums for R&D and support personnel for five years.

Stamp tax (stamp duty) exemption
Documents prepared in relation to R&D activities are exempt from stamp tax.

Withholding taxes (WHT)

There is no WHT on payments to resident corporations by other resident corporations, except for a 3% WHT on progress payments to contractors, both domestic and foreign, within the scope of construction work spanning more than one calendar year.

The local WHT rates are as follows:

Income derived by non-resident individual or company not constituting PE in Turkey	%
Rental from immovable assets	20
Leasing of goods (within the scope of the conditions regulated under Turkish Financial Leasing Law No. 3226)	1
Royalties (e.g., on patents, copyrights, license, etc.)	20
Professional services	20
Petroleum services	5
Interest on loan arrangements	10
Interest on time deposits	15
Interest income derived from time deposits	15
Reverse-repo income	15
Wages and salaries	15-35
Capital gains from listed equities of securities investment trusts purchased after 1 Jan. 2006	0
Income derived by local income tax residents	**%**
Capital gains on Treasury bills and domestic government bonds issued after 1 Jan. 2006	10
Capital gains from listed equities purchased after 1 Jan. 2006 (excl. those purchased by securities investment trusts after 1 Jan. 2006)	0
Income derived by Turkish securities investment funds and securities investment trusts	**%**
Capital gains from domestic government bonds issued after 1 Jan. 2006	0*
Interest from domestic government bonds issued after 1 Jan. 2006	0*
Capital gains from listed equities purchased after 1 Jan. 2006	0*

*Final withholding taxation at source

Please refer to the following tables for local withholding taxation on interests; royalties and dividends, respectively:

Turkey

Turkish WHT on interest and royalties

Party state	WHT on interest %	WHT on royalties %
Albania	10	10
Algeria	10	10
Austria	5 or 10 or 15 (1) (2) (16)	10 (2)
Azerbaijan	10	10
Bahrain	10	10
Bangladesh	10	10
Belarus	10	10
Belgium	15 (1)	10
Bosnia Herzegovina	10	10
Bulgaria	10	10
China (People's Republic of)	10	10
Croatia	10	10
Czech Republic	10	10
Denmark	15 (1)	10
Egypt	10	10
Estonia	10	5 or 10 (13)
Ethiopia	10	10
Finland	15 (1)	10
France	15 (1)	10
Germany	15 (1) (15)	10 (15)
Greece	12 (1)	10
Hungary	10	10
India	10 or 15 (1) (6)	15
Indonesia	10	10
Iran	10	10
Israel	10	10
Italy	15 (1)	10
Japan	10 or 15 (1) (5)	10
Jordan	10	12
Kazakhstan	10	10
Korea, Republic of	10 or 15 (1) (3)	10
Kuwait	10	10
Kyrgyzstan	10	10
Latvia	10	5 or 10 (13)
Lebanon	10	10
Lithuania	10	5 or 10 (13)
Luxembourg	10 or 15 (1) (11)	10
Macedonia	10	10
Malaysia	15 (1)	10
Moldova	10	10
Mongolia	10	10
Morocco	10	10
Netherlands, The	10 or 15 (1) (4)	10
Northern Cyprus, Turkish Republic of	10	10

Turkey

Party state	WHT on interest %	WHT on royalties %
Norway	15 (1)	10
Pakistan	10	10
Poland	10	10
Portugal	10 or 15 (1) (11)	10
Qatar	10	10
Romania	10	10
Russia	10	10
Saudi Arabia	10 (17)	10
Serbia-Montenegro	10	10
Singapore	7.5 or 10 (8)	10
Slovakia	10	10
Slovenia	10	10
South Africa	10	10
Spain	10 or 15 (1) (9)	10
Sudan	10	10
Sweden	15 (1)	10
Syria	10	10 or 15 (14)
Tajikistan	10	10
Thailand	10 or 15 (1) (10)	15
Tunisia	10	10
Turkmenistan	10	10
Ukraine	10	10
United Arab Emirates (UAE)	10	10
United Kingdom	15 (1)	10
United States (US)	10 or 15 (1) (7)	5 or 10 (12)
Uzbekistan	10	10

Notes

1. The local rate of 10% will be applied in the event a higher rate is stipulated in the agreement.
2. Provisions for WHT at source are effective for amounts paid or credited on or after 1 January 2010.
3. A rate of 10% if the loan or other debt claim is for a period exceeding two years; 15% in all other cases (1).
4. A rate of 10% if the loan is taken for a period exceeding two years; 15% in all other cases (1).
5. A rate of 10% if the loan/credit is taken from a financial institution; 15% in all other cases (1).
6. A rate of 10% if the loan is taken from a bank or a financial institution; 15% in all other cases (1).
7. A rate of 10% if the credit/loan is taken from a bank, financial or savings institution, insurance company; 15% in all other cases (1).
8. A rate of 7.5% if the loan is taken from a financial institution; 10% in all other cases.
9. A rate of 10% if the interest is the result of a loan provided/given by a bank or if the interest is paid in return for an article of merchandise or equipment given to the contracting state on credit; 15% in all other cases (1).
10. A rate of 10% if the loan is taken from a financial institution, including insurance companies; 15% in all other cases (1).

T

Turkey

11. A rate of 10% if the loan is taken for a period exceeding two years; 15% in all other cases (1).
12. A rate of 10% for the use of, the right to use or the sale (contingent on the productivity, use or disposition) of any copyright of literary, artistic or scientific work, including royalties in respect of motion pictures and works on film, tape, or other means of reproduction for use in connection with radio or television broadcasting, any patent, trademark, design or model, plan, secret formula or process, or for information concerning, industrial, commercial or scientific experience; 5% for the use of or the right to use industrial, commercial, or scientific equipment.
13. A rate of 5% for the use of industrial, commercial or scientific equipment; 10% in all other cases.
14. A rate of 15% for patent, trademark, design or model, plan, secret formula or process, or for information concerning industrial, commercial or scientific experience; 10% for the use of or the right to use any copyright of literary, artistic or scientific work including cinematographic films and recordings for radio and television.
15. The treaty has been terminated by Germany. The termination will apply for the periods following 1 January 2011, and in this context the provisions of the agreement will remain in effect for the fiscal years 2009 and 2010.
16. A rate of 5% in respect of a loan or credit made, guaranteed or insured for the purposes of promoting export by the Oesterreichische Kontrollbank AG or a similar Turkish public entity the objective of which is to promote the export; 10% if the interest is derived by a bank; 15% in all other cases (1).
17. If the beneficial owner of the "income from debt claims" is a resident of Saudi Arabia, the tax so charged shall not exceed 10% of the gross amount of income.

Turkish WHT on dividends

Party state	Shareholding interest %	WHT rate %
Albania	If greater than / equal to 25	5
	In all other cases	15
Algeria		12
Austria	If greater than / equal to 25	5 (2) (7)
	In all other cases	15 (2) (7)
Azerbaijan		12
Bahrain	If greater than / equal to 25	10
	In all other cases	15
Bangladesh		10
Belarus	If greater than / equal to 25	10
	In all other cases	15
Belgium	If greater than / equal to 10	15 (2)
	In all other cases	20 (1) (2)
Bosnia Herzegovina	If greater than / equal to 25	5
	In all other cases	15
Bulgaria	If greater than / equal to 25	10
	In all other cases	15
China, People's Republic		10
Croatia		10
Czech Republic		10
Denmark	If greater than / equal to 25	15
	In all other cases	20 (1)
Egypt	If greater than / equal to 25	5
	In all other cases	15

Party state	Shareholding interest %	WHT rate %
Estonia		10
Ethiopia		10
Finland	If greater than / equal to 25	15
	In all other cases	20 (1)
France	If greater than / equal to 10	15
	In all other cases	20 (1)
Germany	If greater than / equal to 10	15 (6)
	In all other cases	20 (1) (6)
Greece		15
Hungary	If greater than / equal to 25	10
	In all other cases	15
India		15
Indonesia	If greater than / equal to 25	10
	In all other cases	15
Iran	If greater than / equal to 25	15
	In all other cases	20 (1)
Israel		10
Italy		15
Japan	If greater than / equal to 25	10 (4)
	In all other cases	15
Jordan	If greater than / equal to 25	10
	In all other cases	15
Kazakhstan		10
Korea, Republic of	If greater than / equal to 25	15
	In all other cases	20 (1)
Kuwait		10
Kyrgyzstan		10
Latvia		10
Lebanon	If greater than / equal to 15	10
	In all other cases	15
Lithuania		10
Luxembourg	If greater than / equal to 25	10
	In all other cases	20 (1)
Macedonia	If greater than / equal to 25	5
	In all other cases	10
Malaysia	If greater than / equal to 25	10
	In all other cases	15
Moldova	If greater than / equal to 25	10
	In all other cases	15
Mongolia		10
Morocco	If greater than / equal to 25	7
	In all other cases	10
Netherlands, The	If greater than / equal to 25	15 (2)
	In all other cases	20 (1) (2)
Northern Cyprus, Turkish Republic of	If greater than / equal to 25	15

Turkey

Party state	Shareholding interest %	WHT rate %
	In all other cases	20 (1)
Norway	If greater than / equal to 25	25 (1)
	In all other cases	30 (1)
Pakistan	If greater than / equal to 25	10
	In all other cases	15
Poland	If greater than / equal to 25	10
	In all other cases	15
Portugal	If greater than / equal to 25	5
	In all other cases	15
Qatar	If greater than / equal to 25	10
	In all other cases	15
Romania		15
Russia		10
Saudi Arabia	If greater than / equal to 20	5 (8)
	In all other cases	10
Serbia-Montenegro	If greater than / equal to 25	5
	In all other cases	15
Singapore	If greater than / equal to 25	10
	In all other cases	15
Slovakia	If greater than / equal to 25	5
	In all other cases	10
Slovenia		10
South Africa	If greater than / equal to 25	10
	In all other cases	15
Spain	If greater than / equal to 25	5 (5)
	In all other cases	15
Sudan		10
Sweden	If greater than / equal to 25	15
	In all other cases	20 (1)
Syria		10
Tajikistan		10
Thailand	If greater than / equal to 25	10
	In all other cases	15
Tunisia	If greater than / equal to 25	12
	In all other cases	15
Turkmenistan		10
Ukraine	If greater than / equal to 25	10
	In all other cases	15
United Arab Emirates (UAE)	If greater than / equal to 25	10 (3)
	In all other cases	12
United Kingdom	If greater than / equal to 25	15
	In all other cases	20 (1)
United States (US)	If greater than / equal to 10	15
	In all other cases	20 (1)

Party state	Shareholding interest %	WHT rate %
Uzbekistan		10

Notes

1. The local rate is 15% for dividends. Unless a lower rate is stated in the Agreement, the local rate is applied.
2. As per the provisions of the protocol amending the agreement the rate may be (partially or wholly) reduced;
   - For the Netherlands, to 10%, as long as, under the provisions of the Netherlands Company Tax Act and to the future amendments thereto, a company which is a resident of the Netherlands is not charged tax with respect to dividends the company receives from a company which is a resident of Turkey;
   - For Belgium: to 10%, under the provisions of the Belgian laws and of the future amendments thereto, a company which is a resident of Belgium is not charged to CIT with respect to dividends the company receives from a company which is a resident of Turkey, with respect to dividends paid by a company which is a resident of Turkey to a company which is a resident of Belgium;
   - For Austria: to 5%, if the beneficial owner is a company (other than a partnership) which holds directly at least 25% of the capital of the company paying the dividends, provided that such dividends are exempt from tax in Austria.
3. Subject to 5% of the gross amount of the dividends if the recipient is the government, or a public institution which is wholly owned by the government or its political subdivisions, or local authorities of the UAE.
4. The tax rate shall be 15% where the amount of the Turkish tax imposed on the income of the company paying dividends is less than 40% of such income derived in the accounting period ending immediately before the date when such dividends become payable.
5. The income should be subject to full corporate taxation in the hands of the Turkish tax-resident subsidiary.
6. The treaty has been terminated by Germany. The termination will apply for the periods following 1 January 2011, and in this context the provisions of the agreement will remain in effect for the fiscal years of 2009 and 2010.
7. The provisions for WHT at source are effective for amounts paid or credited on or after 1 January 2010.
8. If the beneficial owner of the dividends is a resident of Saudi Arabia, the tax so charged shall not exceed 5% of the gross amount of the dividends provided: (i) the beneficial owner is a company (other than a partnership) which holds directly at least 20% of the capital of the Turkish company paying the dividends, or (ii) the beneficial owner is a central bank or an entity which is wholly owned by the government.

Tax administration

A self-assessment system is used in Turkey.

All Turkish taxes are imposed under laws drafted by or with the involvement of the Ministry of Finance, and are promulgated by the Parliament. The central government, acting through the Ministry of Finance, imposes most of them, although local authorities have certain rights over some minor transaction charges. Tax procedures are governed by Tax Procedural Law No. 213.

Returns
Resident and non-resident entities having a PE are obliged to be registered for all taxes in Turkey (e.g., VAT, WHT, income tax, etc.) and file annual corporate income tax returns on a calendar-year basis unless permission to the contrary is specifically obtained from the Ministry of Finance.

Turkey

The last date of submission of the corporate income tax return is the twenty-fifth of the fourth month following the fiscal year-end.

Corporate income tax (CIT) certification

In Turkey, a special kind of tax audit arises called "tax certification." It is regulated under the provisions of Law No. 3568. A licensed tax auditor ("sworn financial advisor") audits the accounts of a taxpayer from a tax perspective and certifies the accuracy of the CIT return.

In 1995, the Ministry of Finance announced that taxpayers whose tax returns have not been certified by a sworn financial advisor (Yeminli Mali Musavir, YMM) and whose assets and/or net turnover does not exceed the thresholds defined by the Ministry of Finance may not be in the priority tax inspection list. This tax certification service is utilised by the majority of companies in Turkey because such process helps identify and take corrective measures against erroneous actions that may otherwise be detected only upon a tax investigation by the Ministry of Finance.

Payment of tax

Corporate income tax must be paid by 30 April of the year of filing; taxable income is declared on a quarterly basis as advance tax on the fourteenth of the second month following each quarter, and is payable on the seventeenth of the same period. Advance corporate tax paid is offset against the final corporate tax calculated in the annual tax return.

Corporate taxes in Turkmenistan

For more information, contact:

Abdulkhamid Muminov
PricewaterhouseCoopers
5, Ivlev Street
Yakkasaray District
Tashkent 100090
Uzbekistan
Tel: +998 71 120 4870
Email: abdulkhamid.muminov@uz.pwc.com

Significant developments

The Law on Hydrocarbon Resources of 20 August 2008 (the petroleum law) re-establishes a legal framework for the exploration, development and other activities related to the production of hydrocarbon resources in Turkmenistan.

The petroleum law regulates activities in the oil and gas sector conducted under subsurface-use agreements (production-sharing agreements (PSAs), royalty contracts, service contracts, etc.) between contractors and the Turkmenistan government. The petroleum law stipulates a preferential tax regime to contractors under the above agreements. This preferential tax regime extends to subcontractors under those agreements.

The petroleum law also provides a waiver from any licensing requirements for eligible subcontractors.

Taxes on corporate income

Branches of foreign legal entities are subject to a 20% corporate income tax (CIT), whereas Turkmen legal entities are subject to an 8% CIT. Companies involved in oil and gas operations are subject to a 20% CIT, irrespective of the legal status/ownership structure. The CIT base is determined as gross income less allowable deductions. Residents of Turkmenistan are taxed on worldwide income; non-residents are subject to CIT only in respect of their Turkmenistan sourced income.

Corporate residence

Legal entities are treated as residents for purposes of the CIT if they are established in accordance with Turkmenistan law or their place of effective management is located in Turkmenistan.

Other taxes

Special purpose duty for improvement of urban and rural territories
A special duty aimed at improving urban and rural territories is imposed on registered entities (e.g., legal entities and branches). The duty applies at 1% of the taxable base for profits tax purposes. Generally, contractors and subcontractors operating under the umbrella of the petroleum law may be exempt from this duty.

T

Turkmenistan

Property tax

Property tax in Turkmenistan generally applies at the rate of 1% on the average annual net book value of fixed assets and average annual value of tangible assets used for business purposes and located in Turkmenistan. Generally, contractors and subcontractors operating under the umbrella of the petroleum law may be exempt from this tax.

Subsurface-use tax

Subsurface-use taxpayers are legal entities and individual entrepreneurs extracting natural resources and using land or subsoil waters for the extraction of chemical products. This tax does not normally apply to contractors and subcontractors operating under the umbrella of the petroleum law. Taxable operations include the sale of natural resources extracted by taxpayers and utilisation of natural resources for consumption. Tax rates vary depending on the goods being extracted. Natural or associated gas extraction is taxed at 22%, and crude oil extraction is taxed at 10%. Tax rates for other mineral resources vary depending on profitability (internal rate of return).

Social security payments

Social security is payable by employers at 20% of the total remuneration provided to local employees. Income paid to expatriate employees should not be subject to the social security contribution.

Advertising levy

An advertising levy is imposed on the amount of expenses on commercial advertising and is to be paid quarterly at the rate of 3% to 5% depending on the location of the payer within Turkmenistan. Generally, contractors operating under the umbrella of the petroleum law may be exempt from this levy.

Value-added tax (VAT)

VAT is generally payable at the rate of 15%. A zero-rate applies to exports of goods (except for oil and gas) and international transport services. Generally, contractors operating under the umbrella of the petroleum law may be exempt from this tax.

The tax base is sales turnover including excise tax. If a sale is made by state-fixed prices then it is the respective sales turnover including VAT and excise tax. The amount of input VAT incurred could be offset against the amount of output VAT. The amount of input VAT related to capital expenditures should be capitalised.

Contributions to Agriculture Development and Ashgabat City Development Funds

The contributions to the Agriculture Development Fund and Ashgabat City Development Fund are outside of the general tax legislation (tax code) and are provided for by specific decrees. Permanent establishments/branches of foreign legal entities are subject to those contributions on the same terms as local legal entities. Contribution to the Ashgabat City Development Fund only applies to entities located in Ashgabat City. The base for the contributions comprises the accounting income. The contribution rates are as follows:

- Agriculture Development Fund – 3%; and
- Ashgabat City Development Fund – 0.5%.

Generally, contractors and subcontractors operating under the umbrella of the petroleum law may be exempt from these contributions.

Branch income

Branches pay CIT at the rate of 20%. Turkmenistan does not impose branch profits tax in addition to the CIT.

Branches are taxed on profits received from activities in Turkmenistan. The gross income is reduced for expenses incurred (both inside and outside of Turkmenistan) in relation to the activities in Turkmenistan. The procedure for determining the taxable base for branches is generally similar to the one for Turkmen legal entities.

Branches subject to the standard tax regime also pay and file returns with respect to the other taxes described above.

Income determination

Inventory valuation
Inventory is valued at cost, including costs relating to their acquisition. The law permits the use of the weighted average, first-in, first-out (FIFO) and last-in, last-out (LIFO) methods.

Capital gains
Capital gains are taxable as normal business income.

Inter-company dividends
The tax code provides for relief from economic double taxation of inter-corporate dividends.

Foreign income
A resident company is subject to tax on its worldwide income (including capital gains).

Deductions

In general, taxpayers may deduct expenses paid or accrued during the year in connection with their business and aimed at income generation. All expenses must be substantiated by documentary proof.

The deduction of certain expenses is subject to specific ceilings. Such expenses include representation expenses, which are deductible at up to 1% of gross income. Furthermore, deductible norms for business travel expenses are established periodically by the government.

Depreciation and depletion
The tax depreciation is based on accounting depreciation.

Generally, for the purposes of CIT, depreciation accrued is deductible. Fixed assets acquired free of charge as well as assets of non-commercial legal entities, budget organisations and public associations should be excluded from depreciable assets for CIT purposes, even if they are used for generating income.

Depreciation on rented assets shall be deducted by the lessor (landlord).

T

Turkmenistan

Net operating losses

Loss is defined as excess of allowable deductions over gross revenue. Losses shall be carried forward and deducted in subsequent tax (reporting) periods, but not for more than three years. Losses cannot be carried back.

Payments to foreign affiliates

Administrative and management expenses incurred by the head office of a branch in Turkmenistan are not deductible at the branch level.

Taxes

For CIT purposes the following taxes are deductible: property tax, subsurface-use tax and levies established by the tax code (except the special-purpose duty for the improvement of urban and rural territories), accrued amounts of VAT in selling goods, performing work, rendering of services and amounts of excise tax included in the price of sold excisable goods by manufacturers of such goods.

Other significant items

Expenditures for the repair of fixed assets allowed for deduction shall comprise the cost of spare parts and consumable materials used for repair, remuneration of employees carrying out the repairs and other expenditures associated with such repairs, including payments to third parties for the purpose of such repairs.

Research and development costs (including those that produced no positive result) shall be subject to deduction from gross revenue, except for costs associated with the purchase of fixed assets, their installation and other costs of a capital nature.

Group taxation

There is no group taxation.

Tax incentives

Tax and investment incentives may be negotiated on a case-by-case basis. The President has often issued special decrees granting taxation exemptions and other privileges to specific investors. However, since adopting a new edition of the tax code in 2004 such practice has been significantly reduced.

Withholding taxes (WHT)

Turkmenistan source income generated by a foreign legal entity that has no permanent establishment in Turkmenistan generally is subject to withholding tax at the source of payment at 15% (6% for income from the lease of sea vessels and aircrafts). Relief may be available for withholding tax if a foreign entity is a resident of a country that has a valid double tax treaty with Turkmenistan and if the foreign entity complies with certain administrative procedures.

Currently, Turkmenistan has only a few double tax treaties in force. Turkmenistan is a successor to a number of double tax treaties concluded by the USSR, while some treaties were concluded and ratified by the government of Turkmenistan. The countries listed below are considered to have valid tax treaties with Turkmenistan:

Austria*	Japan*
Armenia	Kazakhstan
Belarus	Pakistan
Belgium*	Russia
France*	Slovakia
Great Britain*	Tajikistan
Germany*	Turkey
Georgia	Ukraine
India	USA*
Iran	Uzbekistan

* USSR treaties honoured by Turkmenistan.

Tax administration

Returns
Reports are generally filed quarterly within the month following the reporting quarter. Annual declaration of branches of foreign legal entities is due by 15 March of the year following the reporting one.

Payment of CIT
Advance payments under the standard tax regime are made before the thirteenth and twenty-eighth days of each month (unless agreed otherwise with tax authorities). Final payments upon results of the first quarter, first half-year, nine months and tax year are made within five days from the reporting deadlines. Under the petroleum law tax regime the CIT is paid once annually.

Corporate taxes in Uganda

For more information, contact:

Francis Kamulegeya
PricewaterhouseCoopers
Communications House
10th Floor
1 Colville Street
Kampala
Uganda
Tel: +256 41 4 236 018
Email: francis.kamulegeya@ug.pwc.com

Significant developments

Significant proposed changes in 2009

The changes are contained in the Finance Act 2009 assented to on 3 November 2009 as well as statutory instruments issued during the year for value-added tax (VAT).

The VAT rate of 5% on the supply of residential dwellings was abolished by revocation order in 2009.

The supply of both goods and services for no consideration as part of business activities is now considered an application of the goods/services own use, which attracts VAT at market value. Previously, this section only applied to goods and not services.

The definition of a supply of goods was amended to include a lease of goods. Previously a supply of goods only included a sale of goods.

The list of exempt supplies has been expanded to include:

*   Insurance brokerage services;
*   Supply of specialised vehicles, plant and machinery, feasibility studies, engineering designs, consultancy services as well as civil works related to agriculture, education and health sector;
*   All computer parts and accessories; and
*   Supply of packing materials exclusively for use by the milling industry and diary industry for packing milled products and milk, respectively.

Other restrictions introduced include:

*   Importation into Uganda of used refrigerators, freezers, computers and television sets was prohibited effective 1 April 2010;
*   Importation, local manufacture, sale or use of polythene bags was prohibited effective on 1 April 2010; and
*   Exportation of all kinds of scrap metals is now prohibited.

The amendments to the Income Tax Act (ITA) include:

*   A deduction of 2% of income tax payable is granted to any employer who can prove to the Uganda Revenue Authority (URA) that at least 5% of their employees on full time basis are people with disabilities (PWDs);

- The threshold for tax depreciation for non-commercial vehicles has been doubled from UGX 30 million to UGX 60 million. This, in effect, doubles the capital allowances that can be claimed on non-commercial vehicles that are purchased after 1 July 2009;
- The income derived by a person from managing or running an educational institution is exempt;
- Allowances, reimbursements or per diems given to employees to pay for accommodations, meals or refreshments while on duty which do not exceed the cost incurred or likely to be incurred are not considered to be part of the employee's income;
- The income derived by any person from agro-processing, which is already exempt from income tax if the person satisfies several conditions, is no longer restricted to locations outside the capital city (Kampala);
- Agro-processing has been defined to include an industrial or manufacturing process that substantially transforms or converts raw agricultural produce into a different chemical or physical state; and
- Income derived by persons who intend or actually export finished consumer or capital goods is exempt from income tax, subject to conditions. The conditions include: at least 80% of goods produced must be exported, proper records must be maintained and annual returns together with the final return of income must be submitted. The exemption is valid for 10 years, is not transferable and may not apply in any year in which the person did not fulfil the set conditions.

Petroleum operations

Several amendments were introduced in the ITA to cater for taxation of upstream petroleum operations. The legislation is still new and some amendments are expected with time.

Taxes on corporate income

The income tax rate applicable to the chargeable income of companies is 30%, with the exception of:

- Mining companies;
- Non-resident air transport, shipping and telecommunications companies; and
- Companies whose turnover is less than UGX 50 million.

The chargeable income of the company would be its gross income for the year less the total deductions allowed under the ITA.

The income tax rate applicable to mining companies is calculated using a specified formula (70-1500/X) where x is the ratio of the company's chargeable income to the gross revenue for the year. However, the derived tax rate is subject to a minimum tax rate of 25% and a maximum tax rate of 45%.

A rate of one percent (1%) of turnover is used to determine tax payable by a resident taxpayer whose turnover is between UGX 20 million and UGX 50 million (approximately between USD 10,000 and USD 25,000), subject to certain thresholds.

However, on application to the Commissioner a taxpayer with a turnover of less than UGX 50 million may be taxed at 30%.

U

Uganda

Corporate residence

A company is resident in Uganda for a year of income if it:

- Is incorporated or formed under the laws of Uganda;
- Has its management and control exercised in Uganda at any time during the year of income; or
- Undertakes the majority of its operations in Uganda during a year of income.

A resident company is taxed on its income from all geographical sources where as a non-resident company is only subject to Uganda tax on income derived from sources in Uganda.

Company tax returns

All companies in Uganda (including branches) are under a self-assessment system. Companies are required to file a provisional tax return at the end of six months after the start of the accounting period, and pay 50% of the tax due for the year. The balance of the tax payable for the year is due at the end of the company's 12 month period (year-end date).

Final tax returns and any balance of the tax due (if any) for a year are filed with the URA six months after year-end. For example if the company's year-end date is 31 December 2009, it will be required to file its returns and pay the balance of the tax due by 30 June 2010.

Other taxes

VAlue-added tax (VAT)

VAT is governed by the VAT Act and administered by the URA. VAT is charged at the rate of 18% on the supply of most goods and services in the course of business in Uganda. Specified goods and services attract a zero rate of tax as well as exports to outside Uganda.

Some supplies are exempt from VAT, the main categories being Government subsidies, the supply of unprocessed foodstuffs, agricultural products and livestock, financial services, insurance services, unimproved land, leases and sale of certain residential properties, betting and gaming, education, medical and health services, social welfare services, pesticides, petroleum products subject to excise duty, machinery for processing agricultural or diary products, accommodation in hotels outside specified areas, computers, accessories and software. The supply of specialised vehicles, plant and machinery, engineering designs, feasibility studies, consultancy services and civil works related to hydro-power, roads and bridges' construction, public water works, agriculture, education and health sectors is also exempt.

Zero rating is preferable to exemption, because the VAT on costs incurred in making a zero-rated supply can be recovered, while that incurred in making an exempt supply cannot be recovered.

The annual threshold for VAT registration is UGX 50 million (approximately USD 25,000). Persons who make supplies that are VATable and whose turnover exceeds UGX 50 million are required to register for VAT with the URA. VAT registered persons are required to:

- Charge VAT whenever they make supplies that are VATable.
- File monthly returns before the fifteenth day of the month following the reporting month.

Credit for input tax

In cases where a person making exempt supplies also makes taxable supplies, such a person may not claim input tax fully.

A person making exempt, zero-rated and standard supplies can recover all the input VAT if the exempt supplies are less than 5% of the total supplies. However, if the exempt supplies are more than 5% but less than 95%, the person is required to recover only a portion of the VAT input tax corresponding to the percentage of the taxable supplies. If the exempt supplies exceed 95%, the person cannot recover any input VAT.

Imported services

The VAT Act defines a supply of service to mean any supply which is not a supply of goods or money, including the performance of services for another person.

An imported service is one provided by a person normally resident outside Uganda who is not required to register for VAT in Uganda. According to regulation 14 of the VAT Regulations 1996, any person who imports a service into the country must account for VAT on such a service. The Regulations require the person importing the service to account for the VAT at the time when performance of the service is completed, or when payment for the service is made, or when the invoice is received from the foreign supplier, whichever is earliest.

The tax on such imported services is supposed to be computed at the rate of 18% of the cost of the service. Companies are required to prepare self-billed tax invoices to account for the input VAT. Further if the importer of the services is not registered for VAT, the importer is required to calculate and pay the VAT to URA.

Although there is no effect on the cash flow position, preparation of a self-billed tax invoice is important as it is a requirement by law. Failure to do so is tantamount to lack of compliance with the law, and a penalty of 2% per month compounded may apply.

Pay as you earn (PAYE)

The chargeable income of an individual for a year of income is charged to tax at the rates shown in the tables below. The chargeable income of a person for the year of income is the gross income of the person for the year less total deductions allowed under the ITA for the year.

The tables show both rates applicable for the resident and non-resident individuals. The income tax rates applicable to resident individuals/employees are as follows:

Chargeable monthly Income	Tax rate
Not exceeding UGX 130,000	Nil
Exceeding UGX 130,000 but not exceeding UGX 235,000	10% of the amount by which chargeable income exceeds UGX 130,000
Exceeding UGX 235,000 but not exceeding UGX 410,000	UGX 10,500 plus 20% of the amount by which chargeable income exceeds UGX 235,000

U

Uganda

Chargeable monthly Income	Tax rate
Exceeding UGX 410,000	UGX 45,500 plus 30% of the amount by which chargeable income exceeds UGX 410,000

The income tax rates applicable to <u>non-resident</u> individuals/employees are as follows:

Chargeable monthly income	Tax rate
Not exceeding UGX 235,000	10%
Exceeding UGX 235,000 but not exceeding UGX 410,000	UGX 23,500 plus 20% of the amount by which chargeable income exceeds UGX 235,000
Exceeding UGX 410,000	UGX 58,500 plus 30% of the amount by which chargeable income exceeds UGX 410,000

Stamp taxes

Stamp duty is charged on a number of transactions at varying rates. Stamp duty is charged at 1% of the total value for a number of instruments, including: hire purchase agreements, composition deeds, leases, exchange of property, conveyance, transfers, share warrants, gifts and agreement relating to deposit of title deeds. Stamp duty of 0.5% is incurred on capital-raising activities such as increase of share capital; debentures, equitable mortgages, mortgage deeds. No stamp duty is charged on the increase of share capital where it is in fulfilment of a condition precedent for acquiring loan funds for a development project or where it is made on becoming public through the stock exchange. Stamp duty of UGX 5,000 is also charged in a number of various other instruments.

Excise taxes

Excise duties are imposed on goods considered luxuriant on importation and some selected goods locally produced. Examples include locally manufactured soft drinks, cigarettes, alcoholic drinks and spirits. A schedule of some of the rates is provided below:

Cigarettes	Between UGX 20,000 and UGX 50,000 per 1,000 sticks subject to the type of cigarette
Cigars and other smoking tobacco	150%
Beer made from malt	60%
Beer made from local raw material	20%
Beer produced from barley grown and malted in Uganda	40%
Spirits	60%
Wine produced from local raw materials	20%
Other wine	70%
Air time	12%
Fuel and oils	Between UGX 200 and UGX 720 per litre depending on the type of fuel/oil

Property taxes

Property taxes are administered by the local authorities.

Turnover taxes

Every promoter of gaming and pools promoted within Uganda and every principal agent of a promoter of gaming and pools promoted outside Uganda is liable to tax at 15% of the total amount of money received or the total amount of bets.

A tax of 5% is charged on gross income earned by non-resident persons carrying on the business of transmitting messages by cable, radio or optical fibre or satellite communication or provision of direct to home pay television services to subscribers in Uganda.

Registration taxes

Stamp duty of 0.5% applies on formation of a company or upon increase in shares. The stamp duty is payable by the purchaser and is payable to the Government of Uganda. Stamp duty of 0.1% applies on transfer of shares.

Customs duties

Many goods imported into Uganda are subject to customs duties. However, exemptions are available to various classes of plant and machinery imported into Uganda. The rates of duty are provided by the East African Community common external tariff code. Certain products imported from the East African community and the Common Market for Eastern and Southern Africa (COMESA) region enjoys special custom duty rates. Imported items are classified according to the nomenclature established under the international convention on the harmonised commodity description and coding system. Duty's range from 0% to 60% depending on the item imported.

Environmental taxes

Environmental levies are charged on every person who imports motor vehicles that are eight years old or older. Levies are also imposed on the importation of used household appliances. The levy on motor vehicles is 20% of the value of the vehicle as determined for customs duty purposes. Levies on electrical appliances range from UGX 20,000 to UGX 50,000 per item depending on the nature of the item.

Branch income

Tax is imposed on the income of a non-resident company derived from running a branch in Uganda. The chargeable income of a branch in Uganda is taxed at the corporation tax rate of 30% after deduction of tax allowable expenses. In addition to corporation tax, branches are subject to extra tax at a rate of 15% on any repatriated income for a year of income. The repatriated income is calculated using the A+ (B-C)-D. Where A is the net assets at the beginning of the year, B is the net profit for the year, C is the tax charge for the year and D is the net assets at the end of the year.

Income determination

In arriving at chargeable income (taxable income) one has to go through the process of adjusting profits by taking into account deductions allowed and deductions not allowed as per the general rule principle.

U

Uganda

Chargeable income of a person is defined under section 15 of the Income Tax Act Cap 340 (ITA) to mean the gross income for the year less total deductions allowed under the Act for the year.

Deductions

Deductibility of expenses
The ITA sets out the following conditions for deductibility of an expense.

* There must be an expenditure or loss;
* The expenditure or loss must be incurred by a person during the year of income; and
* The expenditure must be incurred in the production of income included in the gross income.

No deduction is allowed for the following expenditures:

* Any expenditure or loss of a domestic or private nature, for instance, the cost incurred in the maintenance of the person and the person's family or residence and the cost of commuting between the person's residence and the work place;
* Any expenditure or loss of a capital nature;
* Any expenditure or loss recoverable under insurance contract or indemnity;
* Income tax payable in Uganda or in a foreign country;
* Any fine or similar penalty paid to a government or its sub-division for breach of any law;
* Any contribution or similar payment made to a retirement fund by the employee or for the benefit of any other person for instance company National Social Security Fund (NSSF) contributions;
* Any premium or similar payment made in respect of a life insurance policy for the life of the person paying the premium or on the life of some other person;
* Any income appropriated to a reserve fund or capitalised in any way; or
* The amount of pension paid to any person.

Bad debts
Deduction is allowed only if the amount was included in the person's income in the year of income or if it is in respect of money that was lent in the ordinary course of business by a financial institution in the production of income or if the amount of the debt claim was in respect of a loan granted to any person by a financial institution for the purpose of farming, forestry, fish farming, beekeeping, animal and poultry husbandry or similar operations. For the bad debt to be deductible, the taxpayer must demonstrate to the URA that reasonable steps to collect the debt were taken, and the taxpayer failed to recover the debt. In relation to a financial institution, it should be a debt in respect of which a loss reserve held against presently identified losses or potential losses, and which is therefore not available to meet losses which subsequently materialise, has been made.

Meals, refreshments and entertainment
These are allowed only where the value is included in the employment income of the employees or is excluded owing to the fact that it is provided on equal terms to all workers.

Interest
This is allowed if the interest is incurred in respect of a debt obligation by the company in the production of income included in the company's gross income. Interest arising from non-trade-related debt obligation is not allowed.

Interest on loans for capital development
Interest charged before capital investment is put to use has to be capitalised. Interest incurred after capital investment is put to use is allowed as a deduction.

If the company is foreign controlled, then the interest arising from the loan in excess of two times the company's equity will not be allowed (*see Thin capitalisation*).

Charitable donations
These are allowed if made to amateur sporting associations, religious, charitable or educational institutions of public character, trade unions and other similar associations. The donations should not exceed 5% of the person's chargeable income.

Net operating and capital losses (carryback and carryforward period)
A deduction is allowed for any assessed tax losses carried forward from previous years of income. Such tax losses are carried forward and deducted against future taxable profit of the business in the subsequent years of income. The losses can be carried forward indefinitely. There is no ring-fencing of losses except in the following circumstances:

i.   Where, during a year of income, there has been a change of 50% or more in the underlying ownership of a company, as compared with its ownership one year previously, the company is not permitted to deduct an assessed loss in the year of income or in subsequent years, unless the company, for a period of two years after the change or until the assessed loss has been exhausted if that occurs within two years after the change:
   * Continues to carry on the same business after the change as it carried on before the change; and
   * Does not engage in any new business or investment after the change where the primary purpose of the company or the beneficial owners of the company is to utilise the assessed loss so as to reduce the tax payable on the income arising from the new business or investment.
ii. In cases where losses relate to farming the assessed farming loss can only be deducted from farming income of the taxpayer in the following year and not from any other income.

Depreciation
A deduction is allowed for the depreciation of the person's depreciable assets, other than minor assets, in accordance with the appropriate applicable rates as provided for under the ITA. Plant and machinery is pooled in four classes according to their nature. Capital allowances are granted at various rates on a reducing balance basis.

This has been discussed in detail under *Tax incentives*.

U

Accrued expenses
A taxpayer who is accounting for tax purposes on an accrual basis:

* Derives income when it is receivable by the taxpayer; and

Uganda

- Incurs expenditure when it is payable by the taxpayer.

An amount is treated as payable by the taxpayer when all the events that determine liability have occurred and the amount of the liability can be determined with reasonable accuracy, but not before economic performance with respect to the amount occurs. Economic performance occurs:

- With respect to the acquisition of services or property, at the time the services or property are provided;
- With respect to the use of property, at the time the property is used; or
- In any other case, at the time the taxpayer makes payment in full satisfaction of the liability.

Contingent liabilities
These are not tax-deductible.

Fines and penalties
These are not tax-deductible when used to pay for breach of law or subsidiary legislation.

Goodwill
No tax deduction is allowed for goodwill.

Start-up expenses
Start-up costs are deductible over four years on a straight-line basis beginning with the year of income in which the expenditure was incurred. This also applies to expenses incurred for the initial public offering at the stock market

Payment to foreign affiliates
These are deducted as long as they are incurred in the production of income.

Pension expenses
Employers are allowed a deduction for the contributions made to pension schemes on behalf of their employees. Employees, on the other hand do not get a deduction for the contributions they make to pension funds.

Payment for directors
Directors are treated as employees and therefore expenses incurred in respect of directors are deductible expenses.

Bribes, kickbacks, illegal payments
Non-business expenses are not tax-deductible, including those of a private nature.

Capital vs. ordinary transactions
Capital expenses are not fully deductible in the year in which they are incurred but capitalised and capital allowances claimable using the applicable rate to the class of asset for which they are capitalised.

Ordinary transactions which are of a revenue nature are fully tax-deductible in the year in which they are incurred.

Uganda

Foreign investment
Residents are taxed on worldwide income but a tax credit is available with respect to tax if outside Uganda.

Foreign income (anti-deferral regime, unremitted earnings)
Uganda does not have a controlled foreign company regime.

Interest income
Interest income is taxable as part of business income at a rate of 30%. However, interest income earned by financial institutions with respect to agricultural loans is not subject to tax. Also interest income earned by financial institutions with respect to government securities is subject to tax at 15% as final tax.

Interest is also subject to withholding tax at 15%. Every resident person who pays interest to another resident or non-resident person should withhold tax at 15%. The withholding of tax between two resident persons tax does not apply where interest paid by a natural person; interest paid by a company to an associated company; interest paid to a financial institution; or interest paid which is exempt in the hands of the recipient. Specific conditions apply for non-residents to qualify for an exemption from withholding tax on interest in Uganda.

Rent/royalties income
Rental income for individuals is taxed at a rate of 20% after a standard allowable deduction of 20%. The taxable amount is subject to a specified threshold equivalent to approximately USD 800. Rental income for companies is included in gross income and taxed at the 30% corporate tax rate.

Stock transactions
A taxpayer is allowed a deduction for the cost of trading stock disposed of during a year of income. For tax purposes, the closing value of trading stock the lower of cost or market value of trading stock on hand at the end of the year of income.

Unrealised exchange gains/losses
The gains are not taxable and the losses are not tax-deductible.

Permanent establishment (PE)
A PE (branch) means a place where a person carries on business, and includes:

- A place where a person is carrying on business through an agent, other than a general agent of independent status acting in the ordinary course of business as such;
- A place where a person has, is using, or is installing substantial equipment or substantial machinery; or
- A place where a person is engaged in the construction, assembly, or installation project for 90 days or more, including a place where a person is conducting supervisory activities in relation to such a project.

Group taxation

There are no specific provisions in the law covering groups and therefore companies in a group do not get any special treatment for tax purposes.

Uganda

Transfer pricing regime

Uganda does not have specific transfer pricing legislation. However, the anti-avoidance provisions contained in Sections 90 and 91 of the ITA require transactions between associates to be at arm's-length basis. These are the provisions that are often applied by the URA in instances where they are of the view that a non-resident person may be transferring profits from Uganda.

Treatment of inter-company items (dividends, royalties, commissions, payments, receipts)

Not relevant in the context of group taxation. Generally, dividend payments are not tax-deductible and dividend income is subject to tax at 30%. However, a dividend paid to a resident company, other than an exempt organisation, by another resident company is exempt from tax where the company receiving the dividend controls, directly or indirectly, 25% or more of the voting power in the company paying the dividend.

Royalties and commissions are tax-deductible.

Thin capitalisation rules in Uganda

Where a company intends to finance some of its Uganda operations by use of a foreign debt, the ITA provides for thin capitalisation rules in Uganda and the safe debt: equity harbour ratio is 2:1. The thin capitalisation rules are provided for in Section 89(1) of the ITA.

According to this Section, where a foreign controlled resident company which is not a financial institution has a foreign debt to foreign equity ratio in excess of 2 to 1 at any time during that year of income, a deduction is disallowed for the interest paid by the company during that year on that part of the debt which exceeds 2 to 1 ratio.

Tax incentives

Start-up costs

A company setting up business for the first time will be entitled to a tax deduction for all its start-up costs that are of capital nature which would otherwise not be tax-deductible under the ordinary tax rules. The start-up costs will be allowed as tax-deductible costs over a period of four years at a straight-line basis at the rate of 25% per annum.

The other tax incentives for investment in Uganda are mainly in the form of accelerated depreciation on capital plant and machinery for business. These are discussed in more detail below.

Capital allowances/depreciation

The ITA allows a taxpayer a deduction for the depreciation of their depreciable assets on a reducing balance basis. Depreciable assets are classified in four classes as follows:

Class	Assets included	Rate of tax depreciation
1	Computers and data handling equipment.	40%
2	Automobiles, buses and mini-buses with a seating capacity of less than 30 passengers, goods vehicles with a load capacity of less than 7 tonnes; construction and earth moving equipment.	35%

Class	Assets included	Rate of tax depreciation
3	Buses with a seating capacity of 30 or more passengers; goods vehicles designed to carry or pull loads of 7 tonnes or more; specialised trucks, tractors; trailer-mounted containers; plant and machinery used in farming, manufacturing or mining operations.	30%
4	Rail cars, locomotives and equipment; vessels, barges, tugs and similar water transportation equipment; aircraft, specialised public utility plant, equipment and machinery; office furniture, fixtures and equipment, and any depreciable asset not included in another class.	20%

Initial allowance

Where a taxpayer places an item of eligible property into service for the first time during the year of income they would qualify for a tax deduction for that year of income which is equal to 75% of the cost of the asset if the property is put into use outside Kampala, Entebbe, Namanve, Jinja and Njeru. However if the property is put into use in the above named areas the tax deduction would be equal to 50%.

Eligible property is defined to mean plant and machinery wholly used in the production of income included in the gross income but does not include goods or passenger vehicles, appliances of a kind ordinarily used for household purposes; or office or household furniture, fixtures and fittings.

Industrial building allowance

A company is eligible to an industrial building allowance on its industrial and commercial buildings at a tax rate of 5% per annum on a straight-line basis. The industrial building allowance will be granted on the actual cost incurred in constructing the buildings.

In addition to the above, a company is entitled to initial allowance at the rate of 20% on the industrial building in the first year the building is put to use. The industrial building allowance will be computed on the residual value after the initial allowance of 20% on the power plant building.

An industrial building is defined to mean any building which is wholly or partly used, or held ready for use by a person in manufacturing operations; research and development into improved or new methods of manufacture; mining operations; an approved hotel business; an approved hospital; or approved commercial buildings.

Computer hardware and software

There is VAT exemption on all computer hardware and software imported or bought locally.

Scientific research expenditure, training expenditure and mineral exploration expenditure

100% allowance for scientific research expenditure, training expenditure and mineral exploration expenditure in the year of expenditure.

U

Uganda

Exemption of plant and machinery from VAT

Plant and machinery is exempt from customs duty on importation. Also a VAT deferral facility is available where VAT is deferred on importation of plant and machinery and subsequently waived upon approval by the relevant authorities.

Other exemptions

- Exemption for income derived from exportation of finished consumer and capital goods.
- A tax holiday of 10 years is available to exporters who export at least 80% of their produce of finished goods subject to certain conditions.
- Exemption of income derived from agro processing subject to certain conditions.
- Business income derived by a person from managing or running an educational institution.
- Exemption from withholding tax on importation of plant and machinery.
- New investors may be granted Investment Trader Status where they can claim their input VAT before they start to make taxable supplies. This is subject to certain conditions as specified by the VAT Act.
- Foreign tax credit – A resident taxpayer is entitled to foreign tax credit for any foreign income tax paid by the taxpayer in respect of foreign-source income included in the gross income of the taxpayer. The foreign tax credit allowed is subject to the income tax rate in Uganda.

Withholding taxes (WHT)

According to Section 83(1) of the ITA, a tax is imposed on every non-resident person who derives any dividend, interest, royalty, rent, natural resource payment or management charge from sources in Uganda.

Withholding tax at a rate 15% therefore applies on gross dividend payments, interest, management fees and royalty payments in respect of non-treaty countries.

However, section 83(5) exempts interest paid by a resident company in respect of debentures, which:

- Were issued by the company outside Uganda for the purpose of raising a loan outside Uganda;
- Were widely issued for the purpose of raising funds for use by the company in a business carried on in Uganda or the interest is paid to a bank or a financial institution of a public character; and
- The interest is paid outside Uganda.

A debenture is defined in the ITA as any form of debt including debenture stock, mortgage stock, loan, loan stock, or any similar instrument acknowledging indebtedness, whether secured or unsecured.

The term "widely issued" was clarified by a practice note issued on 20 July 2006 to mean that; for interest paid by a resident person in respect of debentures to be exempt from tax, the "public offer test" needs to be met. This means that the debentures, debenture stock, mortgage, mortgage stock, loan, loan stock or similar instrument acknowledging indebtedness whether secured or not must have been issued:

- To a reasonable number of people operating in a capital market;
- To several investors with a history of previous acquisition of debt instrument or debentures;
- As a result of negotiations for the loan in a public forum used by financial markets dealing in debt instruments; or
- To a dealer, manager or underwriter for the purpose of placement of the debt instrument.

This therefore means that the issuance of debentures should be non-exclusive, and preferably in a capital market arrangement that caters for public involvement in order to fulfil the requirement of "widely issued".

Not withstanding the requirement of widely issued, section 83(5) (b) gives an alternative of the interest being paid to a bank or a financial institution of a public character being exempt from withholding tax. For such interest to be exempt the following conditions must be met:

- The loan must have been acquired by a resident company;
- The loan must have been raised outside Uganda;
- The funds should be raised purposely for carrying on business in Uganda;
- The interest on the loan should be paid to a bank or a financial institution of a public character; and
- And the interest should be paid outside Uganda.

This therefore means that if a company receives a loan outside Uganda from a bank or financial institution located outside Uganda for carrying on a business in Uganda, the interest which the company pays to the bank or financial institution of a public character will not be subject to withholding tax.

Double taxation agreements (DTA)
A taxpayer will also benefit from the provisions of the DTA where Uganda has DTAs with other countries. Please find below a table showing the countries with which Uganda has DTAs and the applicable tax rates on various categories of income.

According to section 88 (2) of the ITA, the terms of the international agreement to which Uganda is a party prevails over the provisions of ITA in case the terms of the international agreement are inconsistent with the provisions of the ITA.

Category of income	Dividend	Royalty	Management fees	Taxation of branch profits	Repatriation of branch profits
South Africa	10%	10%	10%	30%	15%
United Kingdom/ Great Britain	15%	15%	15%	30%	15%
Mauritius	10%	10%	10%	30%	15%
Netherlands	**15%	10%	15%	30%	15%
Norway	10%	10%	10%	30%	15%
Denmark	15%	10%	10%	30%	15%
India	10%	10%	10%	30%	15%

U

Uganda

Note:

**With respect to the Uganda/Netherland DTA, the rate applicable on dividends is **15% except where the investment is new or is an expansion of the current investment made after the DTA entered into (10 September 2006).

Tax administration

Audit cycle
The laws do not provide for this.

Statute of limitations
The ITA requires a taxpayer to maintain records for at least five years after the end of the year to which the records relate.

The VAT Act provides for records to be maintained for six years after the end of the tax period to which they relate.

Tax return due dates
The ITA provides for two provisional returns within a 12-month period (financial year). The first provisional return is due within the first six months of the accounting year while the second is due by the end of the twelfth month of the accounting year. The Self Assessment Return (SAR) is due by the sixth month after the end of the accounting year. THE SAR must be filed together with an original copy of signed original statutory accounts.

VAT is due by the fifteenth day of the month following the month in which the transactions occurred.

Payment of tax
For all companies, a system of provisional payments on account, based on estimated profits, is in place. The first payment is due in the sixth month of the accounting period and the second payment is due in the twelfth month. The balance is expected to be paid together with the SAR.

Topics of focus for tax authorities
The focus keeps shifting but is generally based on the risk analysis of the information availed to them. Currently, the focus is on transfer pricing.

Other issues

Exchange controls
Not applicable in Uganda.

Corporate taxes in Ukraine

For more information, contact:

Ron Barden
PricewaterhouseCoopers
75 Zhylyanska Street
Kyiv 01032
Ukraine
Tel: +380 44 490 67 77
Email: ron.j.barden@ua.pwc.com

Significant developments

Ukraine continues to develop its tax system. There are plans to introduce a comprehensive tax code during 2010, which should ease compliance and administration. This code has not passed the Ukrainian Parliament as of May 2010.

Taxes on corporate income

Ukraine's corporate profits tax, which has a uniform rate of 25%, applies to taxable profits earned by:

- Resident entities in Ukraine and abroad; and
- Non-residents with the source of such profits in Ukraine.

Reduced rates (0% and 3%) are applicable for income of insurance companies.

The corporate income tax (CIT) is levied at the state/national level; no CIT is levied at the regional or local level.

A withholding tax (WHT) at a rate of 15% applies for the majority of income payments for non-residents unless a relief is given under double taxation treaty (DTT) rules. Ukraine has 68 effective DTTs.

A unified tax is available for agricultural producers.

Corporate residence

Corporate residence is determined by the place of incorporation. Resident entities are taxed on their worldwide income. Non-resident entities are taxed on their Ukrainian-source income.

Other taxes

Other principal taxes and compulsory payments in Ukraine are value-added tax (VAT), personal income tax, pension fund charge, excise tax, land tax, tax on owners of motor vehicles, import duty and stamp duty. In addition, 14 local taxes may be levied at the discretion of local authorities.

U

Ukraine

Value-added tax (VAT)

Tax registration as a VAT payer is compulsory if the volume of an entity's taxable transactions exceeds the compulsory registration threshold. The current registration threshold is UAH 300,000 for the previous 12 months. An entity qualifying as a taxable entity should register with the tax authorities at the place of its location and obtain a VAT registration number. In addition, a voluntarily VAT registration is available.

Transactions that are subject to VAT include:

- The supply of goods and services when the place of supply is in Ukraine, including supplies made without consideration;
- The importation of goods and ancillary services (i.e., services costs of which are included in goods customs value) into Ukraine; and
- Exportation of goods.

Transactions that are not subject to VAT include:

- The issue, sale and exchange of securities;
- The provision of property by a lessor to a lessee under an operating lease and return of property upon expiry of the operating lease;
- Interest/commission element of lease payments under financial lease agreements in the amount of up to double interest rate of the National Bank of Ukraine;
- Provision of financial loans and bank guarantees;
- Insurance and re-insurance services supplied by licensed insurers and services of insurance/reinsurance agents and brokers;
- Payment of royalties;
- Transfer of a taxpayer's assets in the course of business transformation (practical issues exist); and
- Transit of cargo and passengers through Ukraine territory.

There are two VAT rates: 20% and 0%. The rate of 20% applies to almost all transactions subject to VAT except the export of goods and related services, which is taxable at 0%. The zero rate also applies to the supply of international transport services (part of transportation performed outside Ukraine) and toll manufacturing services. In practice, obtaining a VAT refund is difficult.

The provision of services to a non-resident is not considered zero-rated. Such services are either subject to 20% VAT or considered to be out of scope of VAT (effectively exempt with no right to claim input VAT).

Generally, VAT incurred by a registered entity on the purchase and/or importation of goods and services used for the purpose of its own business (except for VAT incurred in relation to exempt supply) may be recovered by way of a credit against output VAT. In the case VAT credit exceeds VAT output for two months, a VAT refund is available in form of cash payment or set-off against future VAT liabilities (subject to certain rules and limitations).

Excise tax

Excise tax applies to certain goods imported into, or produced in, Ukraine. Excisable goods include alcoholic beverages, beer, tobacco and tobacco products, cars and car bodies and petrol and diesel fuel.

Rates of excise tax can be *ad valorem* (in percentage to value of goods), specific (in monetary units per unit of goods' characteristic) and combined.

Import duty
Import duty is payable by the importer when goods are imported into Ukraine and applies in accordance with the customs tariff. Currently, there are two rates of duty: relieved and full rates. Relieved rates of duty apply to goods originating from World Trade Organization (WTO) countries and countries which have granted Ukraine "most favoured nation" trade status. Full rates of duty apply to goods originating from other countries.

Branch income

Permanent establishment (PE)
A foreign company may set up a representative office in Ukraine. This is similar to an unincorporated branch. A non-resident company operating via a representative office is deemed to carry out business in Ukraine through a PE and may be subject to 25% CIT unless protected by a DTT. When a foreign company conducts business in Ukraine through a PE, taxable income should be determined on the same basis as for domestic entities.

The Ukrainian definition of a PE is similar to the PE definition provided by majority of tax treaties.

In particular, a non-resident's PE is defined as a fixed place of business through which the business activity of a non-resident entity is wholly or partly carried on in Ukraine.

Ukraine has no special tax rules for non-commercial representative offices established to engage in liaison-type activities. Such offices are treated as a PE, but an exemption from income tax may be available under a relevant tax treaty if the activities of the representative office are not sufficient to constitute a PE for the foreign entity.

Income determination

Ukrainian legislation defines taxable profits as adjusted gross income (term used to depict taxable income) less allowable gross expenses (term used to depict deductible expenses) and depreciation charges. Gross income includes any sales and non-sales income received or accrued within a reporting period (i.e., quarter). Gross income is deemed to be received either on the date the goods/services are shipped/rendered, or the date the payment is received from the customer, whichever happens first.

Dividends
Dividends received by Ukrainian companies from foreign companies controlled by these Ukrainian companies (except for those having "offshore status") are exempt from corporate income tax. Dividends distributed by Ukrainian companies to the extent of dividends received from companies under their control are not subject to advance corporate income tax, which is usually paid when distributing dividends.

Interest
According to the tax law, which has not yet been adopted at the time of publishing, Ukrainian banks should recognise income from lending accrued from 1 January 2009, but not received as of 1 January 2010 on a cash basis. If, however, income from lending

accrued from 1 January 2009 through 1 January 2010 has already been included into the taxable income during 2009, cash basis should not apply.

Inventory
The book value of inventories should be revaluated at the end of each reporting period (i.e., quarterly). If the book value of stocks at the end of the reporting period is less than their book value at the beginning of the reporting period, the difference is included in the deductible expenses of the taxpayer in this reporting period. The excess book value of goods at the end of the reporting period over their value at the beginning is included in taxable income.

Inventories may be valued for tax purposes using any of the following methods:

* Identified value of the appropriate inventory unit;
* Weighted average value of uniform inventories;
* First-in, first-out (FIFO) value of inventories;
* Target expenses; and
* For inventories sold on a retail basis, the inventory sales price.

Deductions

Deductions - in general
Gross expenses include any expense actually incurred or accrued in respect of the taxpayer's business excluding non-allowable expenses specified by law. Generally, gross expenses are recognised either at the date of payment to a supplier (contractor) or at the date when goods, works or services were received, whichever occurs first. However, expenses incurred on purchase from non-residents or resident tax-exempt entities and entities that pay tax at reduced rates are recognised upon actual receipt of goods/services.

Starting from 1 January 2009, banks are entitled to a tax deduction of all loss provisions (including interest, commissions and in respect of all securities). After 1 January 2011, there will be a deduction limit of 80% of such provisions. Other financial institutions are entitled to a deduction of up to 80% of all loss provisions.

The draft law attempts to limit the deduction mentioned above. If approved banks will be entitled to claim a doubtful debt provision of only up to 40% until 1 January 2011, 30% – from 1 January 2011 until 1 January 2012 and 20% – starting from 1 January 2012. Other financial institutions are supposed to claim a doubtful debt provision of only up to 15% and 10% of debt claims, respectively.

Depreciation
Fixed assets costing more than UAH 1,000 with a useful life exceeding one year are required to be depreciated. Depreciation is determined on a quarterly basis, and is generally computed using the reducing-balance method at the following rates (separately presented for new assets purchased after 1 January 2004, and before that date):

Description of fixed assets	Depreciation rate (%)
Group 1 (buildings, constructions and premises)	2%
Group 2 (transport vehicles, furniture, office equipment, household equipment, optical electronic and electrical appliances)	10%

Description of fixed assets	Depreciation rate (%)
Group 3 (all other assets)	6%
Group 4* (computers, devices for automatic processing of information, software, devices for scanning and printing, other information systems, telephone sets including mobile, microphones and portable radio transmitters).	15% (purchased after 1 January 2003)

*Those assets purchased prior to 1 January 2003 belong to Group 2 assets and are depreciated at 6.25% rate.

Land value may not be depreciated unless the land plot is purchased together with a building (Group 1).

Intangible assets may be depreciated using the straight-line method over the asset's useful economic life up to a maximum of 10 years.

Effective January 2010, generous depreciation rates (up to 50%) may be applied to environmentally friendly new fixed assets not used before.

Main points of concern:

- In the current turbulent economic environment, most companies are experiencing a significant drop in revenue, and for many, claiming maximum tax depreciation rates may no longer provide a tax benefit.
- In certain cases, the utilisation of maximum rates may only increase the amount of tax loss.
- Ukrainian tax legislation provides for the possibility to apply for any depreciation rates up to the maximum quarterly rates set out by the law.
- During the crisis years it may be beneficial to apply reduced depreciation rates or not to apply them at all – such an election must be submitted together with the tax return for the first quarter of 2009 (i.e., by 10 May 2010).

Net operating losses
It is proposed by the draft tax law, not adopted at the date of publishing of this summary, that only 20% of accumulated loss carryforwards can be claimed to shelter taxable income in 2010. The remaining amount of the losses may be further carried forward without limitations.

Payments of interest
Interest paid is generally deductible for corporate profits for tax purposes if incurred for business needs. However, limitation for deductibility of interest expense applies if the borrower's capital for at least 50% belongs to non-residents and the interest is payable to non-residents (and related entities) that have holding on the borrower's capital. The same rule applies if the borrower is owned by tax-exempt entities and pays interest to them.

Exchange gains
Realised and non-realised foreign exchange gains and losses generally are treated as taxable/deductible if such gains or losses relate to the following types of indebtedness denominated in foreign currency:

- Principal amounts of loans and deposits;

U

Ukraine

- Interest accrued on financial loans and deposits that is overdue at the end of a reporting period; and
- Book value of debt securities.

The draft tax law proposes that only realised foreign exchange gains and losses related to indebtedness, originated starting from 1 January 2010, can be treated as taxable/deductible. However, this law is not adopted as of May 2010.

Non-deductible expenses

Deductible expenses include any expenses in cash or in kind incurred during acquisition of goods and services for further use in the taxpayer's business. Examples of non-deductible items include:

- Expenses that are not supported by relevant documents (e.g., contract, voucher, receipt, cheque, etc.);
- Expenses in relation to the financing of management bodies, including holding companies;
- Service fees paid to related entities unless there is documentation to prove that fees are paid in relation to services actually performed;
- Payments in respect of goodwill;
- Expenses in respect of car parking, 50% of expenses in respect of purchase of fuel and lubricants for cars and operating lease of cars;
- Expenses relating to the provision of employees with uniform, safety clothes and shoes as well as food, if the amount exceeds the norms established by the Cabinet of Ministers of Ukraine;
- Expenses relating to receptions, presentations, entertainment, sampling and provisions of goods and services free within the scope of an advertising campaign, if the amount exceeds 2% of the company's taxable profits for the previous year;
- Expenses in respect of warranty services if the amount exceeds 10% of the total value of the goods sold that have valid warranty terms;
- Insurance expenses (except for medical, pension and mandatory insurance) in the amount exceeding 5% of the total amount of deductible expenses incurred in the reporting period; and
- Payments for goods or services to foreign entities in listed jurisdictions operating offshore tax regimes (37 tax haven jurisdictions are listed by the Ukraine's Cabinet of Ministers) are deductible within 85% of payments, unless evidence is held that the foreign entity is subject to the ordinary tax rules of the respective foreign jurisdiction (i.e., it does not benefit from the offshore tax regime).

Group taxation

In Ukraine, each company is taxed individually. However, companies that have domestic unincorporated branches may pay consolidated corporate profits tax.

Tax incentives

Ukraine currently has few incentives, although some are available. The following businesses are entitled to benefit from them:

- The publishing and agricultural industries;
- Investment funds;

- Enterprises selling domestically produced energy-saving goods in Ukraine, enterprises adopting energy-saving projects (up to 50% of profits may be exempt);
- Starting January 2010, a tax exemption is available for producers of electric and heat energy-generated from bioenergy fuel as well as for producers of bioenergy-powered domestic equipment. Tax incentives are also available for producers of gas (methane); and
- Certain tax incentives are granted to the Union of European Football Associations (UEFA) and its companies during the hosting stage of 2012 UEFA European Football Championship in Ukraine and to specific segments of the tourism industry.

Withholding taxes (WHT)

WHT must be remitted to the authorities no later than the date when the payment is made to the income recipient.

Passive income (e.g., dividends, interest, royalties) from Ukrainian sources that is paid to non-resident entities is generally subject to 15% WHT.

Other payments, including engineering services, lease payments, agency and brokerage fees, are also subject to 15% WHT, but payments for most other services are not subject to withholding.

A 15% WHT applies to income on the sale of real estate and on profits from the sale of securities.

Payments for freight services (including sea freight) are subject to 6% WHT.

WHT rates may be reduced under a relevant tax treaty.

Payments to non-resident persons for advertising services performed in Ukraine are not subject to withholding. However, the resident payer is required to pay, from its own funds, a 20% tax based on the value of such services. As the taxes on advertising and insurance are levied on a resident party, they cannot be relieved using a tax treaty.

A resident payer is similarly required to pay, from its own funds, a 12% tax if a payment is made to a foreign insurer or reinsurer whose rating of financial reliability does not meet requirements set by the authorised state agency. A 0% rate applies otherwise.

Country	Dividends (%)		Interest (2) (%)	Royalties (3) (%)
	Non-portfolio (1)	Portfolio		
Domestic rates:				
Non-resident individuals	15	15	5 / 15 (4)	15
Non-resident corporations	15	15	15	15
Treaty rates:				
Algeria	5	15	10	10
Armenia	5	15	10	0
Austria	5	10	2 / 5 (5)	0 / 5
Azerbaijan	10	10	10	10
Belarus	15	15	10	15

Ukraine

Country	Dividends (%)		Interest (2) (%)	Royalties (3) (%)
	Non-portfolio (1)	Portfolio		
Belgium	5	15	2 / 10 (5)	0 / 10
Brazil	10	15	15	15
Bulgaria	5	15	10	10
Canada	5	15	10	0/10
China (PRC)	5	10	10	10
Croatia	5	10	10	10
Cyprus (6)	0	0	0	0
Czech Republic	5	15	5	10
Denmark	5	15	0 / 10 (7)	0 / 10
Egypt	12	12	12	12
Estonia	5	15	10	10
Finland	0 / 5 (8)	15	5 / 10 (7)	0 / 5 / 10
France	0 / 5 (9)	15	2 / 10 (5)	0 / 5 / 10
Georgia	5	10	10	10
Germany	5	10	2 / 5 (5)	0 / 5
Greece	5	10	10	10
Hungary	5	15	10	5
Iceland	5	15	10	10
India	10	15	10	10
Indonesia	10	15	10	10
Iran	10	10	10	10
Israel	5/10	15	5 / 10 (10)	10
Italy	5	15	10	7
Japan (6)	15	15	10	0 / 10
Jordan	10	15	10	10
Kazakhstan	5	15	10	10
Korea (ROK)	5	15	5	5
Kuwait	5	5	0	10
Kyrgyzstan	5	15	10	10
Latvia	5	15	10	10
Lebanon	5	15	10	10
Libya	5	15	10	10
Lithuania	5	15	10	10
Macedonia	5	15	10	10
Malaysia (6)	15	15	15	10 / 15
Moldova	5	15	10	10
Mongolia	10	10	10	10
Morocco	10	10	10	10
Netherlands	0 / 5 (11)	15	2 / 10 (5)	0 / 10
Norway	5	15	10	5 / 10
Poland	5	15	10	10
Portugal	10 / 15 (12)	15	10	10
Romania	10	15	10	10 / 15

Country	Dividends (%)		Interest (2) (%)	Royalties (3) (%)
	Non-portfolio (1)	Portfolio		
Russian Federation	5 (13)	15	10	10
Serbia and Montenegro	5	10	10	10
Singapore	5	15	10	7.5
Slovakia	10	10	10	10
Slovenia	5	15	5	5 / 10
South Africa	5	15	10	10
Spain (6)	15	15	0	0 / 5
Sweden	0 / 5 (14)	10	0 / 10 (5)	0 / 10
Switzerland	5	15	0 / 10 (5)	0 / 10
Syria	10	10	10	15
Tajikistan	10	10	10	10
Thailand	10	15	10 / 15 (10)	15
Turkey	10	15	10	10
Turkmenistan	10	10	10	10
United Arab Emirates	5	15	3	0 / 10
United Kingdom	5	10	0	0 (15)
USA	5	15	0	10
Uzbekistan	10	10	10	10
Vietnam	10	10	10	10

Notes

1. The ownership threshold for the non-portfolio rate is 10%, 20%, 25% or 50%, depending on the specific provisions in the treaty.
2. Several treaties contain a rate of 0% on interest paid to or guaranteed by a government or one of its agencies.
3. If more than one rate is shown, this means that the rate will depend on the type of royalties paid.
4. The lower rate applies to interest on current or deposit bank accounts, certificates of deposit, contributions to a credit union, and participatory and fixed-yield mortgage certificates.
5. The lower rate applies to interest paid on certain credit sales, and on loans granted by a financial institution.
6. The treaties with Cyprus, Japan, Malaysia and Spain were entered into by the USSR before it dissolved. Ukraine will continue to honour these treaties, unless they are superseded.
7. The lower rate applies to interest paid in connection with the sale on credit of any industrial, commercial or scientific equipment, unless the indebtedness is between associated enterprises.
8. The 0% rate applies if the investor holds at least 50% of the capital of the company paying the dividends and the capital invested is at least USD 1,000,000; the payer of dividend should not operate in the field of gambling, show business or intermediation business, or auctions).
9. The 0% rate will apply if a French company or companies hold directly or indirectly at least 50% of the capital of the Ukrainian company, and the aggregate investments exceeds EUR 762,245.
10. The lower rate applies to interest paid on any loan granted by a bank.
11. The 0% rate applies if the investor holds directly at least 50% of the capital of the company paying the dividends, and the capital invested is at least USD 300,000.

U

Ukraine

12. The 10% rate applies if the company receiving the dividend has, for an uninterrupted period of two years before the dividend is paid, owned at least 25% of the capital stock of the company paying the dividends.
13. The 5% rate applies if the capital invested is at least USD 50,000.
14. The 0% rate applies if the Swedish company holds directly at least 25% of the voting power of the company paying the dividends, and at least 50% of the Swedish company is held by Swedish residents.
15. The 0% rate applies only if the royalties are taxable in the United Kingdom.

Tax administration

Returns
Tax returns must be filed by the taxpayer on a monthly (VAT) or a quarterly basis. Monthly tax returns are due within 20 calendar days following the end of the reporting month, and quarterly returns are due within 40 calendar days following the last day of the reporting quarter.

Payment of tax
Taxes payable assessed on the basis of tax returns are due within 10 calendar days following the deadline for filing of relevant tax returns.

Tax accounting
According to the draft tax law, which is not adopted at the date of publishing of this report, all large companies with prior-year revenues of UAH 100 million or more, as per statutory books, should submit statutory reports to the tax authorities (in addition to tax reports).

It is also proposed that starting from 2011 such companies should compute temporary and permanent book-to-tax differences.

Corporate taxes in United Arab Emirates

For more information, contact:

Dean Rolfe
PricewaterhouseCoopers UAE
Dubai International Financial Centre (DIFC)
4th Floor, Building 5
The Exchange
Dubai
United Arab Emirates
Tel: +971 4 3043100
Email: dean.rolfe@ae.pwc.com

Significant developments

The United Arab Emirates (UAE) forms part of the Middle East region and is also a member of the Gulf Cooperation Council (GCC).

There is a growing trend of tax reforms in the Middle East region and this may result in changes to the tax laws in the UAE.

In particular, the UAE (along with the other GCC states) has committed to introduce a value-added tax (VAT) system. The UAE government has made significant progress toward the introduction of a VAT. While no formal legislative announcement date has been made, the introduction may be as early as 2012. PricewaterhouseCoopers has been engaged since late 2006 as the advisor to assist in the VAT implementation.

Advice should therefore be sought to confirm the current status of the UAE tax laws and reforms.

Taxes on corporate income

The UAE comprises of a Federation of seven Emirates namely, Dubai, Abu Dhabi, Sharjah, Al Ain, Ras Al-Khaimah, Umm Al-Quwain and Ajman. Currently, the UAE federation does not impose a federal corporate income tax in the Emirates. However, most of the Emirates constituting the UAE federation introduced income tax decrees in the late 1960's and taxation is therefore determined on an Emirate by Emirate basis.

Under the Emirate based tax decrees, corporate income taxes may be imposed on all companies (including branches and permanent establishments) at rates of up to 55%. However, in practice the corporate income tax is currently imposed only on oil & gas companies and branches of foreign banks having operations in the Emirate.

In addition, some of the Emirates have introduced their own specific banking tax decrees which impose tax on branches of foreign banks at the rates of 20%.

Corporate residence

Tax residence under the tax decrees of the various Emirates is based upon the French concept of territoriality. Basically, the French territoriality concept taxes profits based on territorial nexus, rather than taxing profits earned outside the country.

U

United Arab Emirates

Other taxes

Municipal tax

Most Emirates impose a municipality tax on annual rental payments. It is the tenants' obligation to pay the tax; however, the tenants' employer will typically pay the tax on behalf of the employee.

The municipality tax rates are currently 5% of residential rent and 10% of commercial rent.

Customs duty

Generally, a customs duty of 5% is imposed on the cost, insurance, freight (CIF) value of imports. Other rates may apply to certain goods such as alcohol and tobacco, and certain exemptions may also be available.

Hotel tax

Most Emirates impose a tax of 5 to 10% hotel tax on the value of hotel services and entertainment.

Branch income

As each Emirate has a different corporate income tax decree, the decree of each Emirate must be consulted to determine the treatment of foreign corporations.

Income determination

The tax decrees of the various Emirates levy taxation on financial accounting profits. The tax decrees may provide for additional adjustments in situations.

Deductions

Deductions are determined based on accounting principles and the tax decrees.

Group taxation

The UAE does not currently permit group taxation.

Tax incentives

The UAE offers numerous incentives including offering a range of free trade zones (FTZ). Currently, there are over 30 FTZs (and business parks) in the UAE each having its own regulations. Businesses (and their employees) established in FTZs are generally eligible for guaranteed tax holidays for 10 to 50 year (renewable) periods. The FTZ also offers exemption from customs duties. The laws granting these "holidays" and exemptions are not consistent among the various FTZ, and each FTZ therefore needs to be considered separately.

Withholding taxes

There are currently no withholding taxes in the UAE.

Tax treaty network

Taxpayers resident in the UAE have access to an extensive tax treaty network. Treaties currently in force are listed below. A number of other treaties are at various stages of negotiation.

Recipient	Dividends	Interest	Royalties	In force
Algeria	0	0	10	25 June 2004
Armenia	0 or 3	0	5	19 December 2004
Austria	0	0	0	1 September 2004
Azerbaijan	5 or 10	0 or 7	5 or 10	Pending
Belarus	5 or 10	5	5 or 10	1 January 2001
Belgium	0 or 5 or 10	0 or 5	0 or 5	6 January 2004
Bosnia & Herzegovina	0 or 5 or 10	0	5	Pending
Bulgaria	0 or 5	0 or 2	0 or 5	16 November 2008
Canada	5 or 10 or 15	0 or 10	10	25 May 2004
China	7	7	10	28 August 1994
Czech Rep.	0 or 5	0	10	2 August 1997
Egypt	0	0 or 10	10	16 July 1995
Finland	0	0	0	26 December 1997
France	0	0	0	1 July 1990
Germany (old treaty has expired)	–	–	–	New Treaty is under negotiation
Greece	N/a	N/a	N/a	Pending
India	10	0 or 5 or 12.5	10	22 September 1993
Indonesia	10	0 or 5	5	8 November 1996
Italy	5 or 15	0	10	5 November 1997
Jordan	N/a	N/a	N/a	Pending
Kazakhstan	N/a	N/a	N/a	Pending
Korea, Rep of	5 or 10	0 or 10	0	2 March 2005
Lebanon	0	0	5	21 May 1999
Luxembourg	5 or 10	0	0	1 January 2010
Malaysia	10	0 or 5	10	10 February 2000
Malta	0	0	0	18 May 2007
Mauritius	0	0	0	31 July 2007
Mongolia	0	0	10	Pending
Morocco	0 or 5 or 10	0 or 10	0 or 10	2 July 2000
Mozambique	0	0	0 or 5	15 April 2004
Netherlands	5 or 10	0	0	2 June 2010
New Zealand	15	0 or 10	10	29 July 2004
Pakistan	10 or 15	0 or 10	12	30 November 1994
Philippines	0 or 10 or 15	0 or 10	10	2 October 2008
Poland	0 or 5	0 or 5	5	21 April 1994
Romania	0 or 3	0 or 3	3	23 January 1996
Seychelles	0	0	5	23 April 2007
Singapore	5	0 or 7	5	30 August 1996
Spain	5 or 15	0	0	2 April 2007
Sudan	0	0	5	Pending

U

United Arab Emirates

Recipient	Dividends	Interest	Royalties	In force
Syria	0	0 or 10	18	In force
Thailand	10	10 or 15	15	28 December 2000
Tunisia	0	2.5 or 5 or 10	7.5	27 May 1997
Turkey	5 or 10 or 12	0 or 10	10	26 December 1994
Turkmenistan	0	0	10	Pending
Ukraine	0 or 5	0 or 3	0 or 10	9 March 2004
Uzbekistan	N/a	N/a	N/a	Pending
Vietnam	N/a	N/a	N/a	Pending
Yemen	0	0	10	Pending

Notes

1. The dirham (AED) exchange rate is currently fixed at US$1 = AED3.673.
2. N/a – Not available

Tax administration

Most companies operating in the UAE (except oil and gas companies and branches of foreign banks), are currently not required to file corporate tax returns in the UAE.

Other issues

The UAE has introduced a wage protection system (WPS) which has implications for all UAE employers, who have employees registered with the Ministry of Labour. This was introduced in the Cabinet Decree No.133/1 of 2007 and entered into force as of 1 September 2009.

The newly-introduced WPS involves the payment of salaries through a transfer to selected banks, financial institutions and bureau de change approved and authorised by the Government and imposes significant compliance obligations on UAE employers as well as penalties for non-compliance.

For more information, contact:

Barry Marshall
PricewaterhouseCoopers LLP
1 Embankment Place
London WC2N 6RH
United Kingdom
Tel: +44 20 7213 4764
Email: barry.j.marshall@uk.pwc.com

Significant developments

Several notable changes to the United Kingdom (UK) corporate tax system have been made and proposed in the past year, as discussed below. In addition, at the date of writing (21 May 2010), we are waiting for the new coalition Government to announce its Budget on 22 June 2010. The Government has stated that it intends to unveil a five-year road map for major reform of corporation tax. We currently have only a sparse indication of what this might involve, but it has been indicated that the corporation tax package will include:

- Measures to tackle tax avoidance (one of the members of the coalition supported the introduction of a general anti-avoidance rule (GAAR) in the election campaign, so this may be among the measures);
- The simplification of reliefs and allowances;
- A reduction in the headline rate of tax (paid for by the two measures above);
- The imposition of a bank levy;
- Reform of the complex controlled foreign companies (CFC) regime in such a way as to encourage MNCs to come to the UK, rather than to leave (a process that is already underway, as discussed below); and
- A refocusing of research and development tax credits on hi-tech companies, small firms and start-ups.

Changes that have taken effect in the past year

Following consultation on the taxation of foreign profits, a package of complex and far reaching measures has been introduced which impacts UK inbound, outbound and purely domestic businesses. It comprises:

- A tax exemption for most UK and non-UK dividends and other distributions received on or after 1 July 2009;
- The introduction of a "debt cap" restricting UK tax deductions for finance costs to the level of a group's external finance expense, which will apply to amounts payable in accounting periods beginning on or after 1 January 2010;
- The repeal of the Treasury Consent legislation (which required prior consent to be obtained for certain transactions involving foreign subsidiaries) and its replacement with a new biannual reporting requirement (rather than quarterly as originally proposed) for transactions undertaken on or after 1 July 2009; and
- The abolition of certain CFC exemptions for accounting periods starting on or after 1 July 2009, subject to transitional provisions (with a more radical overhaul of the regime in prospect that is currently the subject of further consultation, *see below*).

U

United Kingdom

Various changes have arisen over recent years as a result of challenges brought by taxpayers on the grounds that specific measures were in breach of one or more freedoms provided by EU law. Notably, in the last 12 months:

- The European Court of Justice (ECJ) has ruled that the UK's 1.5% stamp duty reserve tax (SDRT) "season ticket" charge on issuing shares into an EU clearance service is in breach. HM Revenue & Customs (HMRC) has therefore said that it will cease to apply that part of the SDRT rules and a number of claims are expected to clawback previous charges. It is as yet uncertain whether the ECJ decision will extend to American Depository Receipts and bearer instruments which also suffer a similar 1.5% charge; and
- The ECJ is considering the current restrictions on the ability of a UK resident parent company to claim group relief for income losses of a non-UK subsidiary resident in the European Economic Area (EEA) or which has incurred the relevant losses in a permanent establishment within the EEA.

For accounting periods beginning on or after 21 July 2009, large companies are required to notify HMRC of the identity of their senior accounting officer. This individual annually must certify that the company's accounting systems are adequate for the purposes of accurate tax reporting, and both the individual officer and the company will be subject to penalties if there is a careless or deliberate failure to meet these obligations.

A new temporary "bank payroll tax" (BPT) was introduced in relation to certain payments by banks and similar employers in the period 9 December 2009 to 5 April 2010, with anti-avoidance rules that might also catch payments that have been delayed to fall outside this period. Broadly speaking, it will arise in connection with bonus payments to banking employees, but there are complex rules governing what these terms mean for the purpose of the BPT. This levy is payable at a rate of 50% but it is not deductible when calculating the employer's taxable profits.

Following a period of consultation, HMRC has published a Code of Practice on Taxation for Banks (Code) with the aim of encouraging banks to comply with the spirit as well as the letter of the tax law. Adopting the Code is voluntary, but HMRC will consider whether a bank has adopted the policy (and, if so, how it is implementing it) as part of the risk-assessment process it undertakes in order to decide upon the level of attention it needs to pay the banks tax affairs. The Code was published on 9 December 2009 and, whilst HMRC accept that banks may require time to consider the implications of the document, they consider that adoption and implementation should take place soon after.

With effect from 22 April 2009, "disguised interest rules" were introduced to tax the return arising on certain shareholdings as if they arose on debts. This generally will be the case where the return is economically equivalent to interest, although there are various exclusions including straightforward group shareholdings and CFCs and arrangements entered into prior to 22 April 2009.

Changes enacted but not yet in force
Changes tightening the Disclosure of Tax Avoidance Schemes (DOTAS) (or Tax Avoidance Disclosure (TAD)) regime have been enacted but are not yet in force. These are intended to become operative in the autumn of 2010.

A further increase of 0.5% on employer's national insurance contributions (NICs) also has been enacted which will be applicable from 6 April 2011. This increase is in addition to the 0.5% increase previously announced from that date, making an aggregate increase of 1%.

Consultations and proposals

There are a number of consultations currently in progress, most significantly:

*   Regarding a radical overhaul of the CFC regime, with legislation not anticipated before Finance Bill 2011;
*   Reviewing the UK taxation of foreign branches, which it has been announced will be conducted alongside the reform of the CFC rules;
*   On the possibility of introducing a generic or principles-based rule to neutralise any UK tax advantage that arises as a result of "group mismatches", i.e., where intra-group transactions are treated differently for tax purposes in the individual group members concerned; and
*   Considering the possibility of a reduced 10% rate of corporation tax on UK patent income from a date to be confirmed in the future – otherwise to be known as the UK 'patent box'.

In addition, the Government have put taxpayers on notice that they are:

*   Considering extending the DOTAS/TAD regime (which currently covers corporation tax, income tax, capital gains tax, stamp duty, stamp duty land tax and national insurance contributions, with a similar scheme in place for VAT) to cover inheritance tax; and
*   Keeping under review whether to introduce an extension to the 'unallowable purpose' anti-avoidance rule for loan relationships and derivative contracts, along the lines of the measure they proposed as part of the package of measures arising from the taxation of foreign profits consultation but did not enact.

Taxes on corporate income

General corporation tax rates

The normal rate is 28% for the year ending 31 March 2011. This has been the rate since 1 April 2008, before which it was 30%, and applies to companies with profits in excess of GBP 1,500,000. For UK resident companies with tax-adjusted profits below GBP 300,000, a lower rate is generally applicable. This small companies' rate is 21%, and has been since 1 April 2008. Despite previous announcements that this rate would rise to 22% from 1 April 2010, it was announced in the 2009 Pre-Budget Report that this rise is deferred until 1 April 2011. (Previously it was 19% for several years and then increased to 20% from 1 April 2007.) For companies with tax-adjusted profits between GBP 300,000 and GBP 1,500,000, there is a sliding scale of tax rates. For corporate entities with associated companies, both profit limits are divided by the number of active companies worldwide. A 0% tax band existed for a number of years for companies with tax-adjusted profits below GBP 10,000 but this was withdrawn with effect from 1 April 2006.

Special corporation tax regimes

There are no special rates for, for example, financial concerns or manufacturing groups; in general all companies in all sectors are subject to the same corporate tax rates. There are however two exceptions to this general rule.

U

United Kingdom

Profits which arise from oil or gas extraction, or oil or gas rights, in the UK and the UK Continental Shelf "ring-fence profits", are subject to tax in the UK in accordance with rates applicable in 2006, i.e., a full rate of 30% and a small companies' rate of 19%. It should be noted that with effect from 17 April 2002, a supplementary tax charge applies to "adjusted ring-fence" profits in addition to normal corporation tax. The supplementary tax rate of 10% applied from 17 April 2002 to 31 December 2005, and subsequent to this date an increased rate of 20% applies.

Life insurance businesses are also taxed under a special regime, which effectively includes different corporate tax rates as well as special rules for quantifying profits.

Petroleum revenue tax (PRT)

A tax of 50% is levied on profits accruing from oil and gas extracted in the UK and in the UK territorial sea and continental shelf in respect of fields given development consent before 16 March 1993. PRT has effectively been abolished, together with associated relief and allowances, for fields that received development consent after 15 March 1993. PRT paid is deductible in computing corporation tax on the company's total profits.

Income tax for companies

A non-resident company is subject to UK corporation tax only on the trading profits of a UK permanent establishment *(as discussed further in the Corporate Residence section below)*. Any other UK source income received by a non-resident company is subject to UK income tax at the basic rate, currently 20%, without any allowances (subject to any relief offered by a double tax treaty if applicable). This charge most commonly arises in relation to UK rental income earnt by a non-resident landlord (NRL). The UK therefore operates a NRL Scheme which requires the NRL's letting agent or tenants to withhold the appropriate tax at source unless they have been notified that the NRL has applied and been given permission to receive rents gross.

Local taxes

There are no local or provincial taxes on income.

Local taxes (known as "rates") are levied on the occupiers of business property by reference to the property's deemed rental (or "rateable") value, subject to certain reliefs. The amounts paid are deductible for corporation tax purposes, provided they meet all the usual requirements for deductibility.

Corporate residence

Basic rules

UK incorporated companies generally are treated as UK resident. However, companies resident in the United Kingdom under domestic law, but treated as solely resident in a different country under that country's double taxation treaty with the UK, are no longer treated as UK resident for the purposes of UK domestic tax law.

Additionally, subject to the above exception, companies incorporated overseas are also treated as UK resident if their central management and control is situated in the UK, that is, the place of the highest form of control and direction over a company's affairs, as opposed to decisions on the day-to-day running of the business.

Direct tax liability

Tax residence is important because resident companies are taxable in the UK on their worldwide profits, while non-resident companies are subject to UK corporation tax only on the trading profits attributable to a UK permanent establishment, plus UK income tax (generally by way of withholding, though this is not the case with UK source rental profits) on certain UK source income.

For non-resident companies, the liability to corporation tax depends on the existence of any kind of permanent establishment (PE) through which a trade is carried on. The meaning of PE for UK tax purposes is set out in statute; it largely is based on the OECD Model Tax Convention definition, but is not identical in all respects. Subject to the terms of the relevant double taxation agreement, a non-resident company will have a PE in the UK if it either:

- Has a fixed place of business in the UK through which the business of the company is wholly or partly carried on; or
- An agent acting on behalf of the company has and habitually exercises authority to do business on behalf of the company in the UK.

A fixed place of business includes (but is not limited to) a place of management, a branch, an office, a factory, a workshop, an installation or structure for the exploration of natural resources, a mine, oil or gas well, quarry or other place of extraction of natural resources or a building or construction or installation project. A company is not however regarded as having a UK PE if the activities for which the fixed place of business is maintained or which the agent carries on are only of a preparatory or auxiliary nature (also defined in the statute).

Rules exist to explain how the PE's profits should be evaluated for UK tax purposes. Financing arrangements between the branch and head office must be disregarded. There are special rules for banks to stop under-performing loans being allocated to the UK branch in a way that is considered unacceptable and similar potential manipulations. However, a deduction is given for a proportion of head office costs.

Other taxes

Value-added tax (VAT)

The standard rate of 17.5% applies to most goods and services, apart from domestic fuel and power, and certain other reduced-rate supplies, which are subject to VAT at 5%.

Most exports, most food, most public transport, books and publications, and certain other essential goods and services are zero-rated. Some supplies are exempt, the main categories being the grant of certain interests in land, insurance, financial services, betting and gaming, education, certain sports services, cultural services and health and welfare. Zero-rating is preferable to exemption, because the VAT on costs incurred in making a zero-rated supply can be recovered, while that incurred in making an exempt supply cannot.

VAT is chargeable on the supply of most goods and services made in the UK by "taxable persons" in the course of business, when their taxable turnover exceeds the registration thresholds. Taxable persons include individuals, companies, partnerships, clubs, associations or charities.

U

United Kingdom

Taxable persons who are not normally resident in the UK, and do not have a business establishment in the UK and, in the case of companies, are not incorporated in the UK, but who make taxable supplies, sales to unregistered persons in the UK, or acquisitions of goods in the UK (above the relevant limits), may be required to register and account for VAT here.

If the value of taxable supplies is over a specified limit, registration for VAT is compulsory unless the taxable supplies made are wholly or mainly zero-rated, in which case it is possible to apply for exemption from registration.

The rules applying to VAT and territoriality are different to those applying to direct tax in that they derive from the principles of the place of supply in EU law, as enshrined in EC VAT Directives. Having determined that a supply of goods or services has taken place, the second condition to be determined, if the transaction is to fall within the scope of UK VAT, is whether the supply takes place within the UK. The place of supply rules are different for goods and for services. A person or business belonging outside the UK, with no place of business here may nevertheless be liable to UK VAT registration where the place of supply of those goods or services is in the UK.

From 1 January 2010, for services the basic rule is that services are treated as made where the customer "belongs" or is established for VAT purposes, and the customer is responsible for accounting for the VAT due via the reverse charge procedure. However, this is subject to a number of special rules and exceptions. Determining where a business is established for VAT purposes is based on EU law criteria. From 1 January 2010, for business to consumer (B2C) supplies, the basic rule is that services are treated as made where the supplier "belongs" or is established for VAT purposes. For goods the basic rule is that a supply of goods is taxable in the territory where those goods are physically located at the time of supply. Hence if goods are supplied in the UK by a non-established taxable person there will still be a liability for VAT purposes and the person must register for VAT in the UK if the taxable supplies exceed the current UK VAT registration thresholds.

Customs and excise duties

Many goods imported into the UK from outside the European Union are subject to customs duties. The rates of duty are provided by the EU's Common Customs Tariff and vary widely.

Excise duties are chargeable on most hydrocarbon oil products, alcoholic drinks and tobacco products imported into or produced in the UK. Purely as examples, most road fuels carry a duty of about 58p per litre, cigarettes duty of about GBP 114 per thousand (plus 24% of the retail price), tobacco of about GBP 124 per kg, most wines of about GBP 2.25 per litre, and spirits of about GBP 24 per litre of pure alcohol included.

Insurance premium tax (IPT)

IPT at 5% applies to premiums for most general insurance, such as for buildings and contents and motor insurance, where the insured risk is in the UK. Life assurance and other long term insurance remain exempt, though there are anti-avoidance rules surrounding long term medical care policies. As an anti-avoidance measure, the rate increases to 17.5% for insurance sold by suppliers of specified goods or services, e.g., mechanical breakdown insurance, travel insurance (irrespective of supplier), insurance sold with TV and car hire, and 'non-financial' guaranteed asset protection (GAP) insurance sold through suppliers of motor vehicles or persons connected with them. Further anti-avoidance rules were introduced with effect from 9 December 2009 affecting administration or similar fees connected with contracts of insurance, charged under separate contracts by brokers and other intermediaries.

Airport passenger duty

Individuals leaving the UK by air are obliged to pay a duty, which in practice is invariably included in the cost of the air ticket. For journeys after 1 November 2009, rates of duty are based on a system of geographical banding and class of travel, ranging from a reduced rate of GBP 11 for short haul destinations in the lowest class of travel, to GBP 110 for long haul destinations in higher classes of travel. These rates are due to increase to between GBP 12 and GBP 170 respectively from 1 November 2010.

Environmental taxes

There are several environmental taxes as below, that is, "landfill tax," "climate change levy" and "aggregates levy".

Landfill tax

This is a tax on waste disposal in landfill sites. The standard rate from 1 April 2010 is GBP 48 per tonne, increasing to GBP 56 per tonne from 1 April 2011. The reduced rate for inert waste is GBP 2.50 per tonne from 1 April 2008.

Climate change levy

This is a tax on energy used in the UK such as electricity, gas, coal and so on, and is charged at rates that depend on the nature of the fuel used. There are reduced rates and exclusions from the charge, for example, supplies to domestic or charitable users and to those who carry out specific energy-saving measures.

Aggregates levy

This tax is levied on the extraction or importation of sand, gravel and crushed rock for commercial exploitation in the UK. The rate of tax is GBP 2.00 per tonne from 1 April 2009, increasing to GBP 2.10 per tonne from 1 April 2011.

Stamp taxes

Stamp duty is charged at 0.5% on instruments effecting sales of shares. Agreements to sell shares usually attract stamp duty reserve tax (SDRT) at 0.5%. The liability to SDRT may be cancelled by paying the stamp duty due on a stock transfer form (or other transfer instrument) executed in pursuance of the agreement. Stamp duty is not usually charged on an issue of shares, but is charged at a higher rate of 1.5% on an issue of shares in bearer form. Issues or transfers of shares to clearance services or depositary receipt systems attract SDRT at 1.5%. (Stamp duty at 1.5% may be payable on instruments effecting transfers of shares to such services or systems.) However, following a recent ECJ ruling, the 1.5% SDRT charge is no longer collected where the clearance service or depositary receipt system is based within the EU.

Transfers of land and buildings are charged to stamp duty land tax (at graduated rates up to 4%). Grants of new leases are charged to stamp duty land tax at 1% of the net present value of the rents payable in excess of GBP 150,000 plus up to 4% on any premium paid.

U

United Kingdom

Employers' national insurance contributions

Employers are obliged to pay national insurance contributions based on a percentage of each employee's earnings. For the year ending 5 April 2010, the rate is 12.8% on all earnings above GBP 105, increasing to 13.3% from 6 April 2011. There is some reduction for employees "contracted out" of the state pension scheme into a private scheme.

Local municipal taxes

Local taxes are not based on income, but rather are levied on the occupiers of business property by reference to a deemed annual rental value for the property concerned. These taxes are administered by regional local government authorities rather than central government.

Landline duty

A new tax known as "landline duty" may be introduced on UK telephone landlines ("local loops") with effect from 1 October 2010. The duty (if introduced) will be charged at rate of 50 pence (GBP 0.50) per month on each "local loop". The new tax was dropped from the Finance Act 2010 because of the General Election on 6 May 2010; whether it is enacted or not will depend on the view of the incoming government.

The reason for the tax being introduced was said to be to help fund the roll-out of superfast "next generation" broadband.

Bank bonuses tax

A "one-off" levy was imposed on bonuses paid by banks and certain other financial concerns between 9 December, 2009 and 5 April 2010 (after which the higher rate of personal income tax rose to 50% from 40%). The levy was calculated at 50% of any excess of each bonus over a GBP 25,000 limit, was payable by the employer, and was not deductible in computing their UK profits. The levy raised far more tax than was anticipated so it is possible that a similar levy may be imposed again at some future date.

Branch income

Basic rules for UK branches

Tax rates on the profits of PEs are the same as for domestic corporations, except that the small profits rate is not available to non-UK resident corporations unless under the terms of a double taxation treaty.

There are specific rules setting out how the PE's profits should be evaluated for UK tax purposes, which broadly seek to treat the business as if it were a stand alone company. Financing arrangements between the branch and head office must be disregarded and there are special rules for banks to stop under-performing loans being allocated to the UK branch in a way that is considered unacceptable and similar potential manipulations. However, a deduction is given for a proportion of head office costs.

No tax is withheld on transfers of profits to the head office.

UK companies' branches

The UK taxes on a worldwide basis, so non-UK branch profits are computed and taxed in the normal way for UK tax resident companies. However, UK tax will generally be reduced by credit for local direct taxes paid, either under a treaty or via the UK's unilateral relief rules.

The Pre-Budget Report 2009 announcements included a commitment by HM Treasury to review the viability of a foreign branch exemption system in consultation with stakeholders. If a decision is made to take this forward, legislation would not be enacted before the CFC reform is completed (i.e., 2011) at the very earliest because of the interaction with those rules. It may also have to wait further, until after the consultation on the reform of chargeable gains for companies has also been completed.

Taxable income determination

Income determination – overview
A UK resident company is taxed on its worldwide total profits.

The UK tax system requires those total profits to be calculated by finding the aggregate of (a) the company's net income from each source and (b) the company's net chargeable gains arising from the sale of capital assets.

The main sources of income recognised by the legislation are (a) profits of a trade, (b) profits of a property business, (c) non-trading profits (or losses) from loan relationships, mainly interest receivable or payable, (d) non-trading gains (or losses) on intangible fixed assets, (e) non-exempt dividends or other company distributions. Determining income from the first four of these relies heavily on the company's accounts; determining income from the last does not, nor does calculating chargeable gains or income from lesser sources such as royalties.

The rules for determining the gross income in each category differ in certain respects according to the source concerned and are different again when calculating gains. Likewise there are also subtle differences in the rules concerning the deductions that are permissible in respect of different sources of income and in respect of gains. Because of this continuing reliance on taxing companies on a "source by source" basis, the UK system is not well suited to being analysed in terms of income determination and deductions as two wholly separate topics.

Basic rules for accounts-based sources
A company's trading profits are based on its worldwide profit before tax in its accounts. Adjustments are made for non-trading receipts (such as dividends from other companies and income from property) and non-deductible expenditure (such as capital expenditure or expenditure which is not incurred for the purposes of the trade). Depreciation for tax purposes (known as capital allowances) is calculated and substituted for the depreciation charged in the accounts. There are also a number of other statutory adjustments to be made; three important ones are that pension contributions and deferred pay are broadly deductible only when paid, that a deduction is available for the notional cost of certain share awards to employees, and that where acquired intangibles are not depreciated in the accounts a 4% flat-rate deduction can usually be claimed. There are, however, many others.

Similar principles apply in relation to the calculation of profits of a property business.

The profits from a company's trading and non-trading loan relationships and related matters are based on the accounts. For this source of income, the distinction between

U

United Kingdom

"capital" and "revenue" receipts and deductions is not relevant. All credits and debits in the accounts are aggregated in order to find the net profit or deficit. Certain statutory adjustments have to be made – from January 2010 these include an interest capping limitation. Broadly the same regime applies to income and expenses relating to intangibles including goodwill. For a trader these are therefore specific areas where capital amounts can be taxed or allowed.

For traders any profit or loss on loan relationships, and/or on intangibles, are generally included within the trading profits; they become a single source of profits. For loan relationships and intangibles not connected with a trade, the company has a separate source of profits or a separate class of loss.

Income losses

Where a loss arises in respect of a particular source of income, there are detailed rules regarding the possible offset of the loss. Carryback and sideways reliefs are often allowed within limits; carryforward is generally allowed and carried forward losses do not time expire.

More specifically, dealing with the main sorts of income losses,

i.   trading losses may be set off against any other source of profit (or gains) in the same year, or may be carried back one year against profits from the same trade only (three years on the cessation of the trade), or may be carried forward without time limit against profits of the same trade only;
ii. property losses may also be set off against any other source of profit (or gains) in the same year, or may be carried forward without time limit against profits of any sort; they cannot, however, be carried back; and
iii. non-trading deficits (i.e., financing losses) can again be set off against any other source of profit (or gains) in the same year, or may be carried back one year against non-trading credits (i.e., financing profits) or may be carried forward without time limit against non-trading profits.

Non-trading companies may deduct the (non-capital) management expenses incurred in managing its investments from its total profits. Any excess management expenses can be carried forward (without limit) to set against profits in future years.

While income losses can generally be offset against capital gains of the same accounting period, capital losses are never available for offset against any type of income.

Inventory

In general, the book and tax methods of inventory valuation will conform. In practice, inventories are normally valued for tax purposes at the lower of cost or net realisable value. A first-in, first-out (FIFO) basis of determining cost where items cannot be identified is acceptable, but not the base-stock or the last-in, last-out (LIFO) method.

Unrealised exchange gains/losses

Unrealised exchange gains and losses tend to arise on debts and derivatives. They are then taxed or allowed on an accounts basis in the same way as other debits and credits arising out of loan relationships. Where they arise on other payables or receivables to a trader or property investor, they will again generally be taxed or allowed on an accounts basis. For a trader the taxable or allowable amount will become simply part of the trading profit or loss; for other companies it will become a separate source of taxable profit (a "non-trading credit") or loss (a "non-trading deficit").

Where they arise on other capital assets they will not generally be taxable or allowable, although they may in effect become so where the asset is realised.

Dividends received

Dividends received from non-UK companies traditionally have been subject to corporation tax in the hands of the recipient company, with credit given for foreign tax paid under the double tax relief (DTR) rules. However, with effect from 1 July 2009, most foreign dividends received by UK companies will be exempt from corporation tax; one of several criteria has to be met, but these are widely drawn. DTR will continue to be available on a dividend by dividend basis for non-exempt foreign dividends (but has not been extended to non-exempt UK dividends), although certain aspects of the DTR regime have now been repealed.

Dividends received from other UK companies have normally been exempted from corporation tax. However, from 1 July 2009, the treatment of UK-UK dividends and overseas-UK dividends has been aligned. So UK source dividends could now become taxable, though the width of the exemptions makes this unlikely.

Capital assets

Gains on capital assets are taxed at the normal corporation tax rates. The chargeable gain (or allowable loss) arising on the disposal of a capital asset is calculated by deducting from gross proceeds the costs of acquisition and subsequent improvements, plus the incidental costs of sale and indexation allowance. Indexation allowance compensates for the increase in costs based on the percentage rise (if any) in the UK retail prices index to the date of disposal. Indexation allowance is however limited: it cannot create or increase a capital loss, it can only reduce or eliminate a chargeable gain. These calculations must be done in sterling, so any foreign exchange gains and losses will be taxed (or relieved) on disposal.

Special rules apply to assets held since 31 March 1982.

Most acquisitions and disposals between UK group companies are treated as made on a no gain no loss basis (i.e., at base cost plus indexation). Otherwise acquisitions from, or disposals to, affiliates are treated as made at fair market value, as are other acquisitions or disposals not at arm's length.

Capital losses are allowed only as an offset to capital gains. An excess of capital losses over capital gains in a company's accounting period may be carried forward without limitation but may not be carried back.

There is anti-avoidance legislation concerning the computation of chargeable gains, notably to stop losses being created or gains avoided where assets are depreciated by intra-group transactions, or where losses are 'bought in' from third parties.

Gains realised on certain types of assets can be deferred where all or most of the proceeds are reinvested in other assets of those types within a specified period (generally three years). The 'rolled-over' gain then crystallises as and when the latter assets are sold. At present the main asset categories qualifying for roll-over are land and buildings used for a trade.

U

United Kingdom

From 1 April 2002, most disposals by trading groups of shareholdings of 10% or more are exempt from tax. The main exceptions will be those of non-trading subsidiaries or subgroups, or of companies acquired within the previous year. As noted previously, gains on goodwill and other intangibles acquired after March 2002 will be taxed as income, not as capital gains.

Controlled foreign corporation (CFC)

Under the CFC regime, a UK resident company may be taxed on a proportion of the undistributed profits of certain UK-controlled non-resident companies in which the resident company has an interest.

No liability arises where one of a number of tests (e.g., the "exempt activities" test) can be satisfied. Until 1 July 2009 one of the exemptions available (the Acceptable Distribution Policy or ADP) was where virtually all of the CFC's profits were paid up to the UK by way of dividend. However that exemption was withdrawn when the rules regarding the taxation of dividends were changed, which resulted in most CFC dividends being exempt.

As a result of a ECJ decision that the EC Treaty allows intra-EU CFC charges only where the arrangements are "wholly artificial", an additional exemption (not written into the statute) is available to those CFCs that are actually established in an EEA state and carry on genuine economic activity there.

The Government currently is consulting on a radical overhaul of the CFC regime. This process is expected to continue well into 2010 and possibly beyond, with legislation not anticipated before Finance Bill 2011.

Double tax relief

The UK has an extensive network of double taxation treaties. Unilateral relief is generally available in any event to credit overseas tax paid on non-UK source profits against the UK tax on the same profits, so that while the relevant treaty might extend that relief, their main function for UK companies is to limit overseas withholding taxes that would otherwise be payable on passive income.

The UK has a complex regime allowing "underlying" tax relief in respect of foreign dividends, so that tax suffered at lower levels can be relieved (at least in part) where dividends flow to the UK via a chain of companies; but the importance of this regime reduced sharply in 2009 as almost all foreign dividends became exempt from tax.

Partnerships

In broad terms, if companies participate in UK partnerships (whether general partnerships, limited partnerships or limited liability partnerships) they will be taxed on a flow through basis. This will in broad terms mean that UK corporate partners will be taxed on trading, property or financing income as it arises in the partnership accounts, and on non-exempt dividends on a receipts basis.

When considering overseas entities, the UK authorities will not be bound by how the entity is classified in its country of origin. Case law has determined a number of matters that should be considered when establishing whether a non-UK entity should be taxed in the UK as if it were a company or a partnership. HMRC also maintains a public list of non-UK entities and the decisions it has previously made regarding their classification. However, if the parties have flexibility regarding the constitution of such entities then their classification may be viewed differently, either by HMRC or the courts. This area is complex and therefore specialist advice should be sought.

General rules for deductions

As noted in the income section above, the UK tax system requires taxable profits to be calculated by aggregating (a) the company's net income from each source and (b) the company's net chargeable gains arising from the sale of capital assets. This approach gives rise to a particularly complicated regime so far as deductions are concerned. Expenses are usually allocated to the source of income (or occasionally by reference to income generally) or to the particular gain to which they relate. The rules governing their deductibility differ according to whether the expense relates to a capital gain or to income, and indeed according to the particular source of income concerned. For example, there is a considerable difference in the manner in which tax relief is given for expenses incurred by companies trading in property as compared to those that invest in property. The regime also has a large number of specific regimes dealing with particular types of deductions which take priority over the more general rules for each type of income.

We have therefore set out the general rule for trading expenses, being the most common category and, following that analysis, considered some specific common exceptions.

General rules for trading expenses

A trading company is generally permitted to deduct expenses that are incurred wholly and exclusively for the purposes of the company's trade, provided those costs are not capital in nature and are charged to the profit and loss account. There is a significant amount of case law surrounding whether expenses have been incurred wholly and exclusively for the purposes of a company's trade or as expenses of managing a company's investment business, and whether they are capital or not.

Relief is generally given in the period they are accrued in the accounts, subject to some specific exceptions. In particular, contributions to a registered pension scheme are only allowed on a "paid" basis with some further provisions under which some contributions may be spread over a number of years; and bonuses and other staff costs are only allowed on a paid basis if paid out more than nine months after the end of the accounts in which they are accrued.

This general rule is made subject to a raft of specific statutory provisions, some of which allow deductions and others of which limit them; some of the more important of these are discussed below, but there are many others. There is, as one example, a bar to deducting the costs of business entertainment, except within strict limits.

Management expenses

Holding companies are permitted a deduction for expenses to the extent that they are expenses of managing the company's investment business and are not capital in nature. Such costs would typically include audit fees, directors' costs, rent, local rates, and office costs. These costs can be set against any sources of profit the company may have (such as financing income). For the top company of a listed group, such expenses can be substantial.

U

United Kingdom

If the company has inadequate income (given that most dividend income will not be taxable) the excess can be surrendered as group relief. Alternatively it can be carried forward to set against future income, with no time limit.

Many of the specific prohibitions on the deduction of trading expenses (though not all) are extended to create a similar bar on the deduction of such costs as management expenses for non-traders; conversely, many rules giving traders a specific deduction for certain costs are extended to allow non-traders similar relief. But this is not invariably the case. For example, traders cannot deduct costs not "wholly and exclusively" incurred for the purposes of the trade; there is no similar rule for management expenses. However, the two specific limitations on trading deductions referred to above (pension contributions and late-paid remuneration) are extended to management expenses.

Employee share schemes
A deduction is often available to an employing company for the deemed cost of providing shares to employees, on a formula basis rather than the accounts charge (if any); this depends on the nature of the share plan and of the shares provided. This regime will generally allow a deduction to a subsidiary company whose employees receive shares (or options over shares) in the parent company.

Fines, penalties and bribes
Any payments that would constitute a criminal offence (e.g., a bribe), or would do so if paid inside the UK, are expressly not deductible as trading expenses or management expenses. Likewise fines and penalties imposed for breaking the law are also not deductible, although a deduction is usually available for legal costs incurred in defending such an action. Civil penalties, interest and default surcharges (e.g., relating to certain VAT defaults) are also generally non-deductible, except for damages which are compensatory rather than punitive (e.g., damages for defamation payable by a newspaper company).

The rule that any amount paid by way of a penalty for breach of the criminal law derives largely from case law, and was explicitly said to be a policy rule. It is applied strictly; parking fines, and fines for breaches of regulations, or for e.g., price-fixing, are not deductible.

The rule does not however extend to compensatory payments which are not punitive. So settlements in relation to negligence which harms customers or patients, or for breach of contract, or with employees for wrongful dismissal, ought to remain deductible.

Bad debts, provisions, and reserves
A provision will be deductible for tax purposes if (or to the extent that) it:

- Is in respect of allowable revenue expenditure;
- Is made in accordance with acceptable accounting practice;
- Does not conflict with any statutory rule governing the timing of relief (e.g., in relation to payment of staff cots); and
- Is estimated with sufficient accuracy.

This rule extends to bad debts on trading account. Generally, however, bad debts are dealt with under the "loan relationships" rules for financing costs and financing income. The rules there, however, are broadly the same; if the bad debt can be identified specifically enough to allow a bad debt provision which satisfies UK accounting standards, it should be deductible.

Local taxes
There are no local taxes on income.

Local municipal taxes (business rates) may be deducted from taxable income. These rates are based on property values.

Funding costs
Funding costs (primarily fees and interest) are broadly deductible on an accounts basis, even if capital in nature, but subject to thin capitalisation constraints (with no explicit safe harbours) and, from 1 January 2010, an interest cap based on the group's external debt levels. This extends to foreign exchange deductions relating to debts owed and receivable.

Traders will take the deductions in computing trading income (which is also accounts based). Deductions relating to loans not used for trading purposes will give rise to "non-trading deficits" which, if not group relieved, can be offset against profits of the year generally, or carried back one year (against that year's funding profits), or carried forward indefinitely against non-trading profits.

Intangible fixed assets
A similar regime has applied to intangible assets, such as patent rights, know-how and trademarks, and including goodwill, since 2002. Royalties are generally deductible on an accounts basis, and except in relation to "grandfathered" assets owned by the group on 31 March 2002, the accounts amortisation is also deductible (with an option to take a flat 4% deduction on goodwill even if not amortised in the accounts). Traders will take the deductions in computing trading income; non-traders will create a "non-trading loss on intangible fixed assets" which can be relieved as a loss against any profits of the year, carried back one year, or carried forward indefinitely.

Other types of depreciation are seldom allowable, but instead the UK has a wide (though diminishing) range of "capital allowances" which are discussed separately below.

Income costs relating to research & development (R&D) would normally be deductible in any event, but there is a special incentive connected with R&D which generally allows an additional deduction or the payment of a tax credit – see *Tax Incentives section*.

Depreciation/amortisation
Depreciation of fixed assets (other than goodwill and other intangibles) is not allowable as a deduction from any source of income. However traders, and most non-traders, are instead allowed specified rates of deduction in respect of specified classes of assets, together referred to as "capital allowances", which are deducted in calculating trading income for traders, and (broadly) against income derived from the use of the fixed assets for non-traders.

In the period of expenditure, capital allowances are available, generally at 20% (25% prior to 1 April 2008) of the cost of machinery and equipment acquired for use in a

U

United Kingdom

trade or property rental business; thereafter, tax depreciation is taken generally at 20% per annum on the reducing balance basis. However, a temporary 40% first year allowance was available on certain qualifying expenditure incurred in the 12-month period beginning on 1 April 2009 which came to an end, as planned, on 31 March 2010. With some exceptions (notably cars, ships and machinery and equipment in offices and other non-industrial buildings), the rate of tax depreciation for machinery and equipment with an expected useful life when new of at least 25 years, and purchased after 25 November 1996, is reduced to 10% (6% prior to 1 April 2008). Since 1 April 2008, this 10% rate also applies to certain integral features in buildings and thermal insulation.

Small and medium businesses, as defined, may have been eligible for capital allowances at a faster rate for expenditure on plant and machinery prior to 1 April 2008. For subsequent periods, all businesses, regardless of size, can claim an annual investment allowance of 100% on the first GBP 50,000 of most qualifying expenditure, rising to GBP 100,000 for expenditure incurred on or after 1 April 2010. This is restricted to a single allowance for groups of companies or associated businesses.

Enhanced allowances, typically at a rate of 100%, are available for expenditure on certain energy saving plant and other specific categories. The products and technologies supported by this regime are reviewed annually and detailed changes will be made in the summer of 2010 to implement the latest review.

The rate of tax depreciation of most plant or machinery leased to non-residents is restricted, generally to 10% but in some cases to nil. However, HMRC now accept that in some circumstances these rules may be contrary to EU law and for leases finalised on or after 1 April 2006 where the lessee is resident in an EEA country which does not give the lessee relief broadly equivalent to the UK's capital allowances, HMRC will accept that the lessor is entitled to allowances at the normal 20% rate; in addition the 0% rate will not be enforced in the case of other EEA lessees.

New industrial buildings and certain hotels qualify for tax depreciation at 1% per annum from 1 April 2010 (previously 4% prior to 1 April 2008, 3% in 2008/9 and 2% in 2009/10) (straight-line basis) on cost. This allowance is withdrawn and will reduce to 1% from 1 April 2010 and 0% after 1 April 2011. No tax depreciation is normally allowed on other commercial buildings, apart from certain machinery and equipment embodied in the fabric of the buildings.

Tax depreciation of machinery and equipment, and of industrial buildings, can be disclaimed in whole or in part, thereby deferring allowances.

Depreciation allowances may also be available in respect of the cost of the acquisition of mineral assets and other qualifying expenditures relating to mineral extraction, generally at the rates of 10% and 25% respectively on the reducing balance basis; and in respect of various other types of capital expenditure, including the cost of ships, construction of public roads, and dredging.

Excess depreciation allowances are generally recaptured on disposal. This was done on an asset by asset basis for industrial buildings, but ceased to arise on disposals of industrial buildings on or after 21 March 2007. The recapture is calculated on a "pool" basis for most machinery and equipment in which case there is no recapture unless the sale proceeds exceeds the total tax written down value of the pooled assets. The rules concerning which pool an asset goes into can be complex; a large company will generally have several pools ranging from single asset pools to a single large pool for most of its plant and machinery.

Where assets are leased, capital allowances are generally available to the lessor rather than the lessee. However, this is an area of complexity, and in some situations (generally relating to finance leases), the allowances are only available to the lessee.

Losses

Income losses may be carried forward indefinitely, and, in general, set against any type of non-trading profits, but in contrast losses of a particular trade can be carried forward only against profits of the same trade. Unlimited loss carryback is available for trading losses against total profits of (normally) the previous 12 months (provided the same trade was being carried on in that period). In addition, there is now a limited ability to carryback losses generated in accounting periods ending in the period 24 November 2008 to 23 November 2010 up to three years. The amount that can be carried back to the preceding year remains unlimited but this extension now allows additional losses of up to GBP 50,000 for each 12 month accounting period to be carried back for offset against the profits arising in the earlier two years. There is a more limited facility to carryback certain non-trading losses, also normally for 12 months. Losses can also generally be surrendered to other group companies to set against their taxable profits for the same period.

Capital losses may also be carried forward indefinitely but may not be carried back. There is no ability to surrender capital losses to fellow group members but gains or losses arising on a particular asset can be allocated to another group member (by means of a joint election on an asset by asset basis) and therefore there is a limited ability for the capital losses of one company to be offset against the gains of a fellow group member in the same or subsequent period.

Group taxation

The basic rule

Each individual corporate group member is required to submit their own tax return on a stand-alone basis, with the exception of the election available with respect to VAT *(discussed below)*. However, there are a variety of ways in which their relationship with fellow group members is recognised in the UK tax system for the purposes of corporation tax, VAT and stamp duty.

Corporation tax

The corporation tax system includes a number of measures that advantage UK members of qualifying groups, all of which are subject to anti-avoidance measures.

Operating profits and losses arising in the same period can usually be offset between UK resident 75% affiliates within a worldwide group. This extends to offsetting the UK profits attributed to a UK PE of a non-UK resident group member. There are some restrictions, primarily where one of the two companies is not an economic 75% subsidiary of the group, or is subject to arrangements under which it might leave the group.

Intra-group transfers of capital assets between UK companies, including UK PEs, are normally tax-free, though the definition of group for these purposes is slightly different

U

United Kingdom

to the definition for group relief. This treatment is also extended to intra-group transfers of loan relationships, derivatives and intangibles. There is generally a "degrouping" charge if the transferee company leaves the group within six years.

There is no automatic offset of capital gains and losses where these arise in different group companies, but it is normally possible for offset to be arranged by the appropriate tax-free transfer of the asset being disposed of to the third party. Such a tax-free transfer can either be actually done (prior to the third party disposal) or notionally only (by election between the companies concerned).

With effect from 1 April 2006, a UK resident parent company has been able to claim group relief for income losses of a non-UK subsidiary which is resident in the EEA or which has incurred the relevant losses in a permanent establishment within the EEA, provided that all possibilities of non-UK relief for the losses have been exhausted and future relief is unavailable. The EC has referred the UK to the ECJ over this "all possibilities" test and the fact that it must be met immediately after the end of the accounting period in which the loss arises, together with the fact that this extension of loss relief only applies to losses incurred after 1 April 2006.

In addition, the corporation tax system has a number of measures that seek to prohibit groups unfairly manipulating the tax system by shifting profits between group members (either internationally or within the UK) in a way that is considered unacceptable.

Under the CFC regime, a UK resident company may be taxed on a proportion of the undistributed profits of certain UK-controlled non-resident companies in which the resident company has an interest. No liability arises where one of a number of tests (e.g., the "exempt activities" test) can be satisfied. The Government is currently consulting on a radical overhaul of the CFC regime.

There is a transfer pricing regime that applies to UK-to-UK transactions as well as cross-border transactions. UK taxpayers are required to self assess their compliance with its arm's-length principle and must therefore identify and make transfer pricing adjustments when submitting their tax returns. Thin capitalisation is addressed within this regime, with no explicit safe harbours. This regime is discussed in more *detail in the transfer pricing section*.

Where a UK company borrows from a connected party that is not subject to UK tax in respect of the corresponding interest receipt (and certain other limited circumstances), the UK tax deduction may move to a paid basis rather than the usual accruals basis. However this so called "late paid interest" rule has been modified in order to make it comply with the UK's obligations under the EC Treaty. It now only applies where the creditor is a company that is resident or effectively managed in a non-qualifying territory, broadly a tax haven. The revised rule applies to accounting periods beginning on or after 1 April, 2009, although a company may elect that it not have effect for the first accounting period (not ending after 31 March, 2011) to which it would otherwise apply.

A debt cap has been introduced, applicable to accounting periods beginning on or after 1 January 2010, which limits the cumulative UK tax deductions group members may claim for finance costs to the level of a group's external finance expense.

United Kingdom

Indirect tax

Group companies can, subject to certain requirements, elect to account for VAT as if they were one taxable person, and where this is done, no VAT is charged on intra-group supplies of goods or services. The registration is made in the name of the representative member, who is responsible for completing and rendering the single return on behalf of the group. All the companies are jointly and severally liable for any VAT debts. VAT grouping is subject to detailed anti-avoidance provisions.

Stamp duty and stamp duty land tax

Transfers of assets within worldwide 75% groups are generally exempt from stamp duty and stamp duty land tax. The relief can be retrospectively withdrawn in certain circumstances, primarily where the transferee leaves the group within three years of the transfer.

Tax incentives

A variety of tax incentives are given in the form of enhanced tax depreciation allowances (known as capital allowances, *see Deductions – depreciation*). Some of these incentives are given by reference to the expenditure concerned and others by reference to the size of the company incurring that expenditure.

For example, a full write-off can be claimed in the year of expenditure on a range of "green" products and technologies. The list of items supported in this way is reviewed annually. It currently consists of the following: designated energy saving equipment; designated environmentally beneficial plant and machinery incurred from 1 April 2003; cars with low emissions (although the qualifying conditions have recently been tightened); plant or machinery relating to gas stations for refuelling vehicles with natural gas or hydrogen fuel incurred between 17 April 2002 to 31 March 2013; and conversion or renovation of business premises in designated disadvantaged areas of the UK incurred from 11 April 2007.

For periods after 1 April 2008, all businesses, regardless of size, can claim an annual investment allowance of 100% on the first GBP 50,000 of most qualifying expenditure, rising to GBP 100,000 for expenditure incurred on or after 1 April 2010. This is restricted to a single allowance for groups of companies or associated businesses.

Since 2002 a deduction, currently equal to 130% (125% before 1 April 2008) of the qualifying expenditure on R&D can also be claimed by large companies. For small and medium companies, as defined, a deduction equal to 175% (150% before 1 August 2008) of the qualifying expenditure on R&D is given in the year in which it is incurred, which can be surrendered for a cash payment (at a rate of GBP 24.50 for each GBP 100 of qualifying R&D spend) by companies that are trading at a loss or have not yet started to trade.

From 2001 a deduction equal to 150% of the qualifying expenditure on the remediation of contaminated land was given in the year incurred, which can be surrendered for a cash payment (at a rate of GBP 16 for each GBP 100 of qualifying land remediation spend) by companies that are trading at a loss. This relief is extended to expenditure on the remediation of derelict land for expenditure incurred on or after 1 April 2009.

There are special tax reliefs available for certain expenditure on UK films.

U

United Kingdom

There are no tax holidays nor any foreign investment incentives.

Withholding taxes (WHT)

Introduction

The table below sets out the rates of WHT applicable to payments of dividends, interest and royalties under UK domestic law where such a liability arises and the reduced rates that may be available under an applicable double tax treaty.

Under UK domestic law, a company may have a duty to withhold tax (withholding tax or WHT) in relation to the payment of either interest or royalties (or other sums paid for the use of a patent). The circumstances in which such a liability arises are discussed below.

There is no requirement to deduct WHT from dividends. Therefore, dividends may always be paid gross, regardless of the terms of the applicable double tax treaty.

Please note however that this is not an exhaustive list of all the deductions that might be required to be made in respect of UK tax from payments made to or by companies. In particular, non-resident companies that are subject to UK income tax on UK source rental profits (*see further comment in Taxes on corporate income section above*) will find their letting agent or tenants are obliged to withhold the appropriate tax at source (currently 20% without any allowances) from their rental payments unless the recipient has first applied and been given permission to receive rents gross under the Non-Resident Landlord Scheme. Two other important examples are the UK's deduction at source regime for entertainers and sportsmen, and the scheme under which payments to unregistered subcontractors working on big building projects may need to have tax deducted at source.

Interest

As a general rule, UK domestic law requires companies making payments of interest to WHT at 20%. However, there are a number of exceptions to this general rule. The key exclusions are:

Payments of interest by UK resident companies if the beneficial owner of the interest is also a UK resident company, or a UK PE provided the interest concerned will be taxed in the UK as part of the PE's trading profits;

- Payments of interest on a quoted Eurobond;
- Payments of interest that qualify for exemption under the EU Interest and Royalties Directive;
- Payments of interest paid to or by a UK bank (or a UK branch of a foreign bank);
- Payments of 'short' interest. This is, broadly speaking, interest on loans that will not be in place for more than a year. However, the definition can be contentious, and detailed advice should be taken on this if intending to utilise this exemption; and
- Payments of interest that do not "arise" in the UK. Whether a payment constitutes UK source interest is a complex issue and specialist advice needs to be taken if seeking to use this exception.

If none of these exceptions apply, a payment of interest must be made after the deduction of WHT unless (or until) HMRC has given authorisation that the payment made be made gross (or with a reduced rate of WHT) because of the applicability of treaty relief for the recipient.

Royalties

UK domestic law requires companies making payments of patent, copyright and design royalties that arise in the UK to deduct WHT at 20%. In addition, there is also the possibility that other royalties that arise in the UK may also be subject to the same rate of withholding tax if they constitute 'qualifying annual payments', so specialist advice will be needed to clarify this. However certain types of royalties, such as film royalties and equipment royalties will generally not be subject to UK WHT.

Unlike the rule regarding interest, a company may make a royalty payment gross of WHT (or subject to a reduced rate of WHT under a treaty) without prior clearance having been given by HMRC if they reasonably believe at the time the payment is made that the payee is entitled to relief under the treaty. However, if that belief is later found to be incorrect, HMRC may direct that the payment must be made gross and the payer may be subject to interest and penalties in respect of the WHT that should have been withheld (even if their belief was reasonable).

Recipient	Dividends (1)	Interest (2)	Royalties (3)
	%	%	%
Resident corporations		20/Nil (4)	20/Nil (4)
Resident individuals		20	20
Non-resident corporations and individuals:			
Non-treaty		20	20
Treaty (5):			
Antigua and Barbuda		20	Nil
Argentina		12 (6,7)	15 (8)
Australia (47)		10 (6)	5
Austria (51)	*	Nil	Nil (41)
Azerbaijan (12)		10 (6)	10 (10)
Bangladesh		10 (6,11)	10
Barbados	*	15	Nil (42)
Belarus (12)		Nil	Nil
Belgium (13, 51)	(14)	15	Nil
Belize	*	20	Nil
Bolivia		15 (7)	15
Bosnia-Herzegovina (16)		10	10
Botswana	*	10 (6)(38)	10 (38)
British Virgin Islands		20	20
Brunei	*	20	Nil
Bulgaria		Nil	Nil
Burma (Myanmar)		20	Nil
Canada	* (14)	10 (6,7)	10 (37)
Channel Islands:			
Guernsey		20	20
Jersey		20	20

U

United Kingdom

Recipient	Dividends (1) %	Interest (2) %	Royalties (3) %
Chile		15 (39)	10 (23)
China, P.R		10 (6)	10 (22)
Croatia (16,47)	*	10	10
Cyprus	*	10	Nil (43)
Czech Republic (17)		Nil	10 (18)
Denmark		Nil	Nil
Egypt		15 (6)	15
Estonia (12)		10 (6)	10 (23)
Falkland Islands		Nil	Nil
Faroes (52)		Nil	Nil
Fiji	*	10 (7)	15 (15)
Finland		Nil (7)	Nil
France (50)		Nil	Nil
Gambia	*	15 (6)	12.5
Georgia (12, 51)		Nil	Nil
Germany (47)		Nil	Nil
Ghana		12.5 (6)	12.5
Greece		Nil	Nil
Grenada		20	Nil
Guyana		15 (6,7)	10
Hungary (47)		Nil	Nil
Iceland	*	Nil	Nil
India	* (9)	15 (6,7,19)	15 (20)
Indonesia	*	10 (35)	15 (34)
Ireland, Rep. of		Nil	Nil
Isle of Man		20	20
Israel (47)		15	15/Nil (21)
Italy	* (14)	10 (6,7)	8
Ivory Coast (Côte d'Ivoire)		15 (6)	10
Jamaica	*	12.5 (7)	10
Japan	*	10 (6)	Nil
Jordan		10 (6)	10
Kazakhstan (12)		10 (6,7)	10
Kenya	*	15 (35)	15
Kiribati	*	20	Nil
Korea, Rep. of		10 (6,7)	10 (36)
Kuwait		Nil	10
Latvia (12)		10 (35)	10 (23)
Lesotho		10 (7,35)	10
Libya (54)		Nil	Nil
Lithuania (12)		10 (6)	10 (23)
Luxembourg (51)	* (14)	Nil	5
Macedonia (16)	*	10	Nil
Malawi	*	Nil (24)	Nil (24)

Recipient	Dividends (1)	Interest (2)	Royalties (3)
	%	%	%
Malaysia (51)		10 (35)	8
Malta	*	10 (6)	10
Mauritius	*	20 (6)	15
Mexico (51)		15 (7, 25)	10
Moldova (12)	*	5 (6)	5
Mongolia		10 (7, 26)	5
Montenegro (16)		10	10
Montserrat (51)		20	Nil
Morocco		10 (6)	10
Namibia (13)		20	Nil (13)
Netherlands (51)	* (14)	Nil	Nil
New Zealand (47)	(9)	10 (6)	10
Nigeria		12.5 (35)	12.5
Norway		Nil	Nil
Oman (51)		Nil	Nil
Pakistan		15 (6)	12.5
Papua New Guinea		10 (6)	10
Philippines	*	15 (6,27)	25/15 (28)
Poland (46)	*	5 (6)	5
Portugal		10	5
Romania	*	10	15 (29)
Russian Federation (12)		Nil	Nil
St. Kitts and Nevis (aka St Christopher and Nevis)		20	Nil
Saudi Arabia (44)		Nil	8 (23)
Serbia (16)		10	10
Sierra Leone		20	Nil
Singapore (51)		10 (6)	10
Slovak Republic (17)		Nil	10 (18)
Slovenia (16)	*	5 (6)	5
Solomon Islands	*	20	Nil
South Africa		Nil	Nil
Spain (47)	*	12 (7)	10
Sri Lanka		10 (6)	10 (32)
Sudan	*	15	10
Swaziland		20	Nil
Sweden	* (14)	Nil	Nil
Switzerland (51)	* (14)	Nil	Nil
Taiwan		10 (6)	10
Tajikistan (12)		Nil	Nil
Thailand (47)	*	20 (6,30)	15 (31)
Trinidad and Tobago	*	10 (6)	10 (45)
Tunisia		12 (30)	15
Turkey		15 (6)	10
Turkmenistan (12)		Nil	Nil

U

United Kingdom

Recipient	Dividends (1)	Interest (2)	Royalties (3)
	%	%	%
Tuvalu	*	20	Nil
Uganda		15 (35)	15
Ukraine (12)		Nil	Nil
United States		Nil (49)	Nil
Uzbekistan (12)		5 (6,7,33)	5 (33)
USSR (former) (12)		N/A	N/A
Venezuela		5 (6)	7 (40)
Vietnam		10 (6)	10
Yugoslavia (former) (16)		N/A	N/A
Zambia	*	10	10
Zimbabwe	*	10 (6)	10
Treaties which have been signed but are not yet in force:			
Austria		Nil	Nil
Bahrain		Nil	Nil
Belgium		10	Nil
Cayman Islands		20	20
Georgia		Nil	Nil
Luxembourg		Nil	5
Malaysia		10	8
Mexico		15	10
Montserrat		20	Nil
Netherlands		Nil	Nil
Oman		Nil	8
Qatar		20/Nil	5
Singapore		10	10
Switzerland		Nil	Nil

Notes

1. A tax credit is available to UK resident individual shareholders on dividends received, as described above. Some double taxation treaties allow a half or full tax credit (less, normally, a 5% to 15% notional withholding tax) also to non-resident individuals and usually to corporate portfolio investors. Treaties that allow a payable credit are indicated by an asterisk (*). However, since 6 April 1999 the credit has been reduced from one quarter to one ninth, which has the result that unless note 14 below applies, the tax credit indicated by the asterisk is now in effect useless, since it is wholly eliminated by the (usually 15%) withholding tax allowed by the treaty.
2. Withholding tax applies only to "annual interest" (i.e., excluding interest on certain short-term loans). Banks and similar financial institutions are also normally able to pay annual interest to non-UK residents free of withholding tax. In addition, most of the UK treaties provide for a nil rate of withholding on interest paid to governmental and quasi-governmental lenders. Such exemptions are not separately indicated in the table below.
3. Some types of royalties are not subject to UK withholding tax, including film royalties and equipment royalties. Treaty provisions specifically relating to these are therefore not mentioned here.
4. From 6 April 2001, payments to any UK resident company (not just banks, as before) can be made free of withholding tax if the recipient is chargeable to tax on the interest or

royalty. Discussions continue as to whether this provision will be extended to recipients who are exempt from UK tax on the interest or royalty.

5. Where a reduced rate of withholding is allowed by any treaty, whether on interest or royalties, it is usual for this reduced rate to be stated not to apply to amounts which are in excess of a normal commercial rate of interest/royalty, or where the interest/royalty is effectively connected to a PE in the United Kingdom of the recipient or where the debt/license was created primarily to obtain the advantage of the treaty; such general limitations are not specifically indicated in the table below.

6. Nil on certain loans.

7. Treaty rate not applicable to certain loans held by tax-exempt holders and resold within three months of acquisition.

8. Lower rates, primarily of 3% on use of news, 5% on copyright royalties other than films and TV, and 10% on certain intellectual property, will in practice apply in almost all cases.

9. No repayable tax credit for companies.

10. A 5% rate on literary/artistic copyright royalties.

11. A 7.5% rate on interest paid to banks and other financial institutions.

12. The UK announced that the old UK/USSR treaty ceased to apply to certain former Soviet Republics on 5 April 2002 (such that from that date there was no treaty in force with any of those countries), whilst it continued to apply to others until new treaties were concluded. Treaties have subsequently been signed with a number of these states such that the old UK/USSR treaty currently only continues to apply to Tajikistan, Turkmenistan and Belarus (the last of which concluded a new treaty with the UK in 1995 which is not yet in force). The only remaining states without a treaty in force with the UK post 5 April 2002 are Armenia and Kyrgyzstan. Moldova signed a new treaty with the UK on 8 November 2007 which took effect in the UK from 6 April 2009.

13. A rate of 5% applies to patent royalties and no relief is given for motion picture film royalties, as provided by the 1962 treaty with South Africa that was extended to Namibia by an Exchange of Notes.

14. Half tax credit payable by the UK Exchequer to non-resident companies possessing 10% or more of the voting power of the paying company, subject to a notional withholding tax (which in current circumstances makes the actual repayment very small).

15. Nil on literary/artistic or scientific copyright royalties, excluding payments in respect of cinematograph films and films or tapes for radio or TV broadcasting.

16. The UK's treaty with the former Yugoslavia is regarded as still in force between the United Kingdom and Croatia, Montenegro, Serbia and Bosnia-Herzegovina. Macedonia signed a new treaty with the UK on 8 November 2006 which took effect for UK withholding tax purposes on 1 January 2008. A new treaty with Slovenia was signed on 13 November 2007 and came into effect in the UK in April 2009.

17. The independent states of the Czech Republic and the Slovak Republic have confirmed that they will honour the treaty between the UK and the former Czechoslovakia.

18. The 10% rate applies to royalties for use of industrial, commercial or scientific equipment or experience as well as royalties in respect of patent, trademarks and know-how. Nil on all other royalties.

19. A rate of 10% on certain bank loans.

20. A rate of 10% in certain cases.

21. A rate of 15% on film and TV royalties.

22. A rate of 7% on royalties for use of (or right to use) industrial, commercial, or scientific equipment.

23. A rate of 5% on royalties for use of industrial, commercial, or scientific equipment.

24. No relief is available if the payment concerned is made to a company controlling (directly or indirectly) more than 50% of the voting power of the paying company. In addition, no relief is available in respect of cinematograph film royalties or amounts paid in respect of the extraction of natural resources.

25. Nil on government and local authority loans. The rate is 5% where the beneficial owner is a bank or insurance company or the interest is derived from bonds and securities that are regularly and substantially traded on a recognised securities market. The rate is 10% where the beneficial owner is not a bank or insurance company but the interest is paid

U

United Kingdom

by a bank or by the purchaser of machinery and equipment to a person who sold that equipment on credit.

26. A rate of 7% on interest paid to banks.
27. A rate of 10% on interest on bonds issued to the public.
28. A rate of 15% on royalties on films, TV and radio broadcasting.
29. A rate of 10% on copyright royalties.
30. A rate of 10% on interest paid to banks and other financial institutions.
31. A rate of 5% on literary/artistic/scientific copyright royalties.
32. Full relief for copyright royalties.
33. Lower rate may be substituted to match any lower rate agreed in a treaty between Uzbekistan and a third Organisation for Economic Co-operation and Development (OECD) country.
34. A rate of 10% for royalties on industrial, commercial or scientific equipment.
35. Nil on certain government loans.
36. A rate of 2% for royalties on industrial, commercial or scientific equipment.
37. Nil on literary/artistic copyright royalties, patent royalties and royalties for use of industrial, commercial or scientific know-how and computer software.
38. New treaty effective for UK income tax (and therefore withholding tax) from 6 April 2007 reduced withholding tax on both interest and royalties to the rates shown in table. Prior to this the rate of withholding tax on interest and royalties was 15% in both cases (subject, in the case of interest, to note 7).
39. A rate of 5% applies to loans from banks and insurance companies, interest paid on securities quoted on a stock exchange and on some sales of machinery and equipment.
40. A rate of 5% on royalties for the use of a patent, etc. concerning industrial, commercial, or scientific experience.
41. A rate of 10% can be withheld if the recipient of the royalties controls more than 50% of the voting power of the payer.
42. A rate of 15% can be withheld on royalties in respect of cinematograph or television films.
43. A rate of 5% can be withheld on royalties in respect of cinematograph or television films.
44. A new treaty with Saudi Arabia was signed on 31 October 2007 and entered into force from 1 January 2009. It will be effective in the UK from 1 April 2010 for corporation tax and from 6 April 2010 for income tax and capital gains tax purposes, including withholding tax. The withholding tax rates were not changed by the new treaty and therefore the figures shown above are valid both before and after this date.
45. Full relief is available for literary, artistic or scientific copyright (excluding royalties on cinematograph films and films or tapes for TV or radio broadcasting). No relief is available for amounts paid in respect of the extraction or removal of natural resources.
46. A new treaty with Poland was signed on 20 July 2006 and entered into force on 27 December 2006. It took effect in respect of UK withholding taxes from 1 January 2007, changing the rates to those shown in the table above. The rates were previously nil in respect of interest and 10% in respect of royalties.
47. HMRC intends to progress negotiations on new treaties in the year ending 31 March 2010 with: Australia, Croatia, Ethiopia, Germany, Hungary, Israel, New Zealand, Spain and Thailand.
48. Nil if recipient is: the State; an individual; a company whose shares are substantially and regularly traded on a stock exchange; a company owned at least 75% by residents of Qatar; a pension scheme; or a financial institution independent of the payer.
49. Relief may be restricted to 15% in certain circumstances.
50. A new treaty with France was signed on 19 June 2008 and entered into force on 18 December 2009. It will take effect with respect to UK withholding taxes from 6 April 2010 but the rates remain as shown in the table above.
51. New tax treaties/protocols with the following states have been signed but have not yet entered into force: Netherlands (2008), Mexico (2009), Cayman Islands (2008), Belgium (2009), Qatar (2009), Luxembourg (2009), Singapore (2009), Switzerland (2009), Malaysia (2009), Austria (2009), Oman (2009), Montserrat (2009), Georgia (2010) and Bahrain (2010). These agreements will enter into force once both countries have completed the required Parliamentary procedures and exchange of diplomatic notes and will take effect on the dates set out therein.

52. Treaty effective in the UK for WHT purposes from 6 April 2009.
53. Reduced treaty rate only applicable if one of various conditions is met by either the beneficial owner or payer of the interest. This is to ensure that the benefit of the interest article can only flow to residents of the other treaty state.
54. The first tax treaty between the UK and Libya entered into force on 8 March 2010 and has effect in the UK for WHT purposes from 6 April 2010.

Tax administration

Direct tax

Companies are assessed by reference to accounting periods. Normally, the accounting period is the period for which the company makes up its accounts. However, an accounting period for corporation tax purposes cannot exceed 12 months so companies preparing statutory accounts for longer than 12 months need to prepare more than one corporation tax return. Companies must file their statutory accounts and tax return within one year from the end of the accounting period; the return must include a self-assessment of the tax payable, eliminating the need for assessment by HMRC (though HMRC retains assessing powers for certain cases where it is not satisfied with the return, or where the company fails to make a return).

For smaller companies, corporation tax is payable nine months after the end of the accounting period to which it relates (so before the return must be filed). For larger companies and groups, a system of quarterly payments on account (based on estimated profits) is in place, with the first payment being due in the seventh month of the accounting period concerned. A company will generally be considered large for this purpose in any accounting period in which it has taxable profits in excess of GBP 1,500,000 (that limit being reduced by reference to the number of companies under common control, where relevant).

There is generally a period of one year after submission of the tax return for the tax authorities to start an enquiry into any aspect of the return. This period is extended for returns submitted after the filing deadline, that are amended by the taxpayer, or where an issue is subsequently discovered that was not sufficiently disclosed within the standard period. This enquiry window was shortened for many companies for returns relating to accounting periods ending after 31 March 2008, and now runs for 12 months from the date the return was filed, rather than 12 months from the filing date. However companies which are members of a group that is not small will continue to be subject to the old rule.

The UK tax system can impose numerous penalties for failing to adhere to the self-assessment system. These include penalties for late filing of returns, failing to maintain appropriate records, submitting an incorrect return, making errors in certain documents sent to HMRC, unreasonably failing to report errors in assessments by HMRC and failing to respond to a notice of enquiry from the tax authorities within the specified time limit.

Requirements to file online and pay electronically are expected to be phased in for corporation tax from 2011.

For accounting periods beginning on or after 21 July 2009 large companies are required to notify HMRC of the identity of their senior accounting officer, who must certify annually that the accounting systems are adequate for the purposes of accurate

U

United Kingdom

tax reporting. Penalties are chargeable on the officer and the company for careless or deliberate failure to meet these obligations.

Indirect tax

VAT returns must be completed at preset intervals (usually every three months). Larger companies may be required to file monthly returns, or make monthly payments on account. From 1 April 2010, companies with an annual turnover of GBP 100,000 or more, and all newly-registered businesses (whatever their turnover) will be required to submit their VAT returns online and pay electronically. Smaller enterprises can apply for annual returns. VAT returns are usually required to be filed 30 days after the end of the period.

Annual accounting is available for taxable persons with annual turnover (taxable supplies, excluding VAT) not exceeding GBP 1,350,000.

Cash accounting is available for taxable persons with annual turnover (taxable supplies, excluding VAT) not exceeding GBP 1,350,000.

In addition a Flat Rate Scheme operates for small businesses and is intended to simplify VAT accounting procedures.

Other issues

Adoption of International Financial Reporting Standards (IFRS)

IFRS became mandatory for the consolidated financial statements of UK listed companies with accounting periods beginning on or after 1 January 2005.

Companies continue to have the choice of adopting IFRS or remaining on UK GAAP at entity level for all entities. Many groups therefore continue to apply UK GAAP in their entity accounts.

The UK Accounting Standards Board (ASB) is proposing a new 3-tier system of reporting going forward. It is proposed that all publicly accountable UK registered companies will have to report under IFRS (as endorsed by the EU) in accounting periods beginning on or after 1 January 2012. In addition, UK registered SMEs (broadly entities that do not have public accountability and publish general purpose financial statements for external users) must apply "IFRS for SMEs" (a simplified IFRS) from the same date. Finally, the Financial Reporting Standard for Smaller Entities (FRSSE) will still be an option for small companies or small groups as defined by the Companies Act 2006. However the options available to a company are subject to the requirements of the UK Company Law framework for consistency of GAAP within a group.

In our experience, many large groups are considering early adoption of EU-endorsed IFRS. However, under current UK law early adoption of IFRS for SMEs or FRSSE is not possible.

Transfer pricing

The UK has widely drafted transfer pricing rules that are intended to apply to almost any kind of transaction made or imposed between related parties that gives rise to a provision that:

- Differs from one that would have been made between third parties; and
- Gives rise to a UK tax advantage (potential or actual) to one or more of the parties.

These rules apply to UK-to-UK transactions as well as cross-border transactions.

This regime therefore applies not only to the provision of products and services but also to finance arrangements, including both the rate of return charged and the amount of loan principle (or equivalent) made available. It is therefore the mechanism by which the UK's revenue authorities address the issue of thin capitalisation. Unlike many other territories, the UK does not operate any "safe harbours" of any kind in relation to the amount of debt or interest (or equivalents) it considers demonstrate that a UK company or group is not thinly capitalised. (Note that the UK now also has a debt cap regime which limits the amount of finance expense for which a UK tax deduction will be available by reference to the worldwide group's external finance expense, as discussed in the *Significant developments section*).

Parties are considered related for this purpose where either one controls the other, or both are under common control. Control here is not confined to situations in which one party is the majority shareholder in the other. Effectively, control exists where one party has the power to ensure that the affairs of another party are conducted in accordance with the first party's wishes. The concept is also subject to two important extensions:

- The rules apply to many joint venture companies where two parties each have an interest of at least 40%; and
- There are attribution rules to trace control relationships through a number of levels in determining whether parties are controlled for the purposes of the transfer pricing rules.

In addition, the regime restricts interest deductions to an arm's-length basis where a financier, and persons who collectively control a company or a partnership, have "acted together" in relation to the financing arrangements of that company or partnership. The financier (usually a bank) can then be taken as controlling the company or partnership, and the loan becomes subject to transfer pricing limitations.

There are a number of exemptions which essentially exclude SMEs and dormant companies from the regime.

The effect of the rules is to require an arm's-length provision to be substituted for the actual one, thereby increasing the party's UK tax liability and cancelling out the UK tax advantage that would otherwise have arisen.

Where both parties to the transaction are UK taxpayers, the disadvantaged party will generally be entitled to claim a compensating adjustment (except where the transaction falls within the transfer pricing regime because of the "acting together" provisions), but only after the UK adjustment has been made. The legislation also provides that parties may make balancing payments to each other in such circumstances, of any amount up to the transfer pricing adjustment, which will neither be taxable for the recipient nor tax deductible for the payer.

Where the disadvantaged party is outside the UK tax net they can pursue a claim for relief under the relevant double tax agreement, if that provides a mechanism for

U

United Kingdom

such relief; where the adjustment in the UK is to reduce a deduction for an amount paid under deduction of UK tax, the compensating adjustment rules should allow the overseas party to reclaim any withholding tax paid on the disallowed amount.

UK taxpayers are required to self assess their compliance with this arm's-length principle. Companies and partnerships must therefore identify and make transfer pricing adjustments when submitting their tax returns. This is the case even where the disadvantaged party would be entitled to claim a compensating adjustment equal to the transfer pricing adjustment. An important implication of this approach is the potential for interest and penalties if the adjustment made is subsequently held to be wrong.

UK tax legislation

Announcements of new legislation generally occur twice each year. The main announcement is made on Budget Day (generally in March) when tax rates are set for the coming year. The other announcement is made in the Pre-Budget Report (generally in the period October to December). The new legislation is then included in an annual Finance Act, which is normally finalised in July. Much of the legislation introduced in recent years has been due to challenges under the EC treaty, or as a result of the tax planning being notified under the UK's tax avoidance disclosure regulations.

UK tax law is periodically consolidated. Until recently the latest consolidation Act dated from 1988, which covered both income tax and corporation tax. Over the last few years income tax and corporation tax legislation has been consolidated separately, and currently the latter is to be found in the Corporation Tax Acts 2009 and 2010, and the Taxation (International and Other Provisions) Act 2010.

Corporate taxes in the United States

For more information, contact:

J. Richard (Rick) Stamm
PricewaterhouseCoopers LLP
300 Madison Avenue
24th floor
New York, New York 10017
United States of America
Tel: +1 646 471 4000
Email: rick.stamm@us.pwc.com

Significant developments

On 30 March 2010, President Obama signed the Health Care and Education Reconciliation Act of 2010, which amended a law enacted on 23 March 2010 (the Patient Protection and Affordable Care Act), to provide comprehensive health care reform. The legislation contains major changes to laws governing health insurance practices, Medicare, Medicaid, and related tax provisions. The Joint Committee on Taxation (JCT) staff estimated that the tax provisions in the legislation will raise USD 437.8 billion over 10 years. Some of the important business tax provisions included in the healthcare reform are as follows:

- Under the legislation, a transaction is treated as having economic substance, which is a prerequisite to being respected for Federal income tax purposes, only if (1) the transaction changes in a meaningful way (apart from the Federal income tax benefits) the taxpayer's economic position, and (2) the taxpayer has a substantial purpose (apart from Federal income tax benefits) for entering into the transaction. The legislation creates a new 20% penalty for underpayments of tax attributable to any disallowance of claimed tax benefits by reason of the transaction lacking economic substance. If the relevant facts affecting the tax treatment of the transaction are not adequately disclosed, the penalty increases to 40%.
- For fuels sold or used after 31 December 2009, the legislation modifies the cellulosic biofuel producer credit to exclude certain "black liquor" fuels produced as a byproduct of the paper manufacturing process.
- For tax years beginning after 31 December 2010, the legislation requires an employer to report on each employee's annual Form W-2 the value of the employee's health insurance coverage provided by the employer.
- For payments made after 31 December 2011, the legislation broadly expands current reporting rules to require a business to file an information return for all payments that total USD 600 or more in the aggregate during a calendar year to a single business (other than to a tax-exempt corporation).
- Beginning in 2013, the legislation eliminates the deductibility of a subsidy under the Medicare Part D programme for companies that sponsor drug coverage meeting certain standards for their Medicare-eligible retirees.
- Beginning in 2014, the legislation imposes new penalties on firms with 50 or more full-time employees that have employees enrolled in subsidised coverage in the new health insurance exchange created under the legislation.
- Beginning in 2018, the legislation imposes a 40% excise tax on "high-value" health plans.

U

United States

Previously, on 18 March 2010, President Obama signed the Hiring Incentives to Restore Employment (HIRE) Act, which provides two tax benefits to employers that hire workers who previously were unemployed or working part time. Employers who hire unemployed workers after 3 February 2010 and before 1 January 2011 may qualify for a 6.2% payroll tax incentive, effectively exempting them from their share of Social Security taxes on wages paid to these workers. In addition, for each worker retained for at least a year, employers may claim an additional general business tax credit, up to USD 1,000 per worker, when they file their 2011 income tax returns.

Prior to that, on 6 November 2009, President Obama signed the Worker, Homeownership, and Business Assistance Act of 2009. This legislation included an extension and expansion of the homebuyer credit and an extension and expansion of the five-year carryback of net operating losses. These tax benefits were offset by a delay in the application of worldwide allocation of interest, an increase in the penalties for failure to file partnership and S corporation returns, and an acceleration of corporate estimated tax payments.

Taxes on corporate income

2009 taxable income

Over	But not over	Pay +	% on excess	of the amount over
$0	$50,000	$0	15%	$0
50,000	75,000	7,500	25	50,000
75,000	100,000	13,750	34	75,000
100,000	335,000	22,250	39	100,000
335,000	10,000,000	113,900	34	335,000
10,000,000	15,000,000	3,400,000	35	10,000,000
15,000,000	18,333,333	5,150,000	38	15,000,000
18,333,333	....		35	0

The US corporate income tax rate is based on a progressive rate schedule; however, an alternative minimum tax *see the Other taxes section* provides for a flat rate with fewer deductions. The 39% tax rate applies to taxable income between USD 100,000 and USD 335,000 to eliminate the benefit of the 15% and 25% rates, and the 38% tax rate applies to taxable income between USD 15,000,000 and USD 18,333,333 to eliminate the benefit of the 34% rate. Special rules apply to personal service corporations and personal holding companies.

Corporate residence

A corporation organised or created in the United States under the law of the United States or of any state is a domestic corporation. A domestic corporation is a resident corporation even though it does no business or owns no property in the United States. Resident corporations are taxed based on worldwide income. Generally, a foreign corporation engaged in a US trade or business is taxed at regular US corporate tax rates on income from US sources that is effectively connected with that business and at 30% on US source income not effectively connected with that business.

Other taxes

In addition to the regular federal income tax, the following taxes may apply:

Top rate on net capital gains
On current transactions, the long-term capital gains tax rate is the same as the tax rates applicable to ordinary income. Thus, the maximum rate is 35%, excluding the additional phase out rates. However, differences may arise where the alternative minimum tax is imposed.

Federal alternative minimum tax
An alternative minimum tax (AMT) is imposed on corporations other than S corporations *(see below)* and small C corporations (generally those with no three year average annual gross receipts exceeding USD 7.5 million). The tax is 20% of alternative minimum taxable income (AMTI) in excess of a USD 40,000 exemption amount (subject to a phase out). AMTI is computed by adjusting the corporation's regular taxable income by specified adjustments and "tax preference" items. Tax preference or adjustment items could arise, for example, if a corporation has substantial accelerated depreciation, percentage depletion, intangible drilling costs, or non-taxable income.

Accumulated earnings tax
Corporations (other than S corporations, domestic and foreign personal holding companies, corporations exempt from tax under Subchapter F of the Internal Revenue Code (the Code), and passive foreign investment companies) accumulating earnings and profits for the purpose of avoiding shareholder personal income tax are subject to a penalty tax in addition to any other tax that may be applicable. The accumulated earnings tax is equal to 15% of "accumulated taxable income." Generally, accumulated taxable income is the excess of taxable income with certain adjustments, including a deduction for regular income taxes, over the dividends paid deduction and the accumulated earnings credit. Note that a corporation can justify the accumulation of income, and avoid tax, based on its reasonable business needs.

Personal holding company tax
US corporations and certain foreign corporations that receive substantial "passive income" and are "closely held" may be subject to personal holding company tax. The personal holding company tax is 15% of undistributed personal holding company income and is levied in addition to the regular tax.

S corporations
Corporations with 100 or fewer shareholders, none of whom may be corporations, that meet certain other requirements may elect to be taxed under Subchapter S of the Code and are thus known as S corporations. S corporations are taxed in a manner similar, but not identical, to partnerships. Thus, S corporations generally are not subject to US Federal income tax.

Payroll taxes
Employers are subject to federal unemployment insurance tax (FUTA) of 6.2% on the first USD 7,000 of wages paid to employees meeting certain criteria. In addition, states impose workers' compensation insurance tax at varying rates depending on state law and the nature of employees' activities. Employers also are subject to social security contributions tax of 7.65% (including 1.45% Medicare tax) on the first USD 106,800

U

United States

(for 2009 and 2010) of wages paid to employees and 1.45% of Medicare tax on any wages in excess of USD 106,800.

State and municipal taxes
Corporate income tax rates vary from state to state and generally range from 1% to 12% (although some states impose no income tax). The most common taxable base is federal taxable income, which is modified by state provisions and generally is allocated to a state on the basis of a three factor formula: tangible assets and rental expense, sales and other receipts, and payroll. Other taxes that states may impose, in lieu of or in addition to taxes based on income, include franchise taxes and taxes on the capital of a corporation. State and municipal taxes are deductible expenses for federal income tax purposes.

Excise taxes
The federal and state governments impose excise taxes on a variety of goods. For example, a federal and state excise tax is imposed on gasoline and diesel fuel used for transportation. The excise taxes are levied item by item and lack any uniformity in rates.

Value-added tax (VAT)
No provisions exist for a VAT at the federal level. However, state and local governments may impose sales taxes.

Stamp tax
No provisions exist for a stamp tax at the federal level. However, state and local governments frequently impose stamp taxes at the time of officially recording the transaction based upon the value of the real estate.

Other
Most states and some cities impose sales or use taxes and a variety of property taxes on both real and personal property. The sales tax on real estate may be a stamp tax on the documents recording the transfer of the real estate.

Branch income

Tax rates on branch profits are the same as on corporate profits. The law also imposes a 30% branch profits tax in addition to US corporate level income taxes on a foreign corporation's US branch earnings and profits for the year that are effectively connected with a US business. The taxable base for the branch profits tax is increased (decreased) by any decrease (increase) in the US net equity of the branch. The branch profits tax on profits may be reduced or eliminated entirely if a relevant treaty so provides (subject to strict "treaty shopping" rules). The purpose of the branch profits tax is to treat US operations of foreign corporations in much the same manner as US corporations owned by foreign persons.

With certain exceptions, a 30% (or lower treaty rate) branch profits tax also will be imposed on interest payments by the US branch to foreign lenders. In addition, the tax will apply if the amount of interest deducted by the branch on its US tax return exceeds the amount of interest actually paid during the year.

Income determination

List of common book/tax adjustments
Tax and financial accounting typically have differing treatment for the following items:

- Research and development;
- Domestic manufacturing costs;
- Depreciation of fixed assets;
- Amortisation of intangibles;
- Meals and entertainment;
- Foreign taxes; and
- Fines/penalties.

Inventory valuation
Inventories generally are stated at the lower of cost or market on a first-in, first-out (FIFO) basis. Last-in, first-out (LIFO) may be elected for tax purposes on a cost basis only and generally requires book and tax conformity.

The tax law requires capitalisation for tax purposes of several costs allocable to the manufacturing process that frequently are expensed as current operating costs for financial reporting (e.g., the excess of tax depreciation over financial statement depreciation).

Capital gains
Gains or losses on the sale or exchange of capital assets held for more than 12 months are treated as long-term capital gains or losses. Gains or losses on the sale or exchange of capital assets held for 12 months or less are treated as short-term capital gains or losses. The excess of net long-term capital gain over net short-term capital loss is considered net capital gain. Capital losses are allowed only as an offset to capital gains. An excess of capital losses over capital gains in a taxable year may be carried back three years and carried forward five years to be used against (offset) capital gains.

For dispositions of personal property and certain non-residential real property used in a trade or business, net gains are first taxable as ordinary income to the extent of the depreciation/cost recovery, with any remainder generally treated as capital gain. For other trade or business real property, net gains generally are taxed as ordinary income to the extent that the depreciation or cost recovery claimed exceeds the straight-line amount, with any remainder treated as capital gain.

An exception to capital gain treatment exists to the extent that losses on business assets were recognised in prior years. A net loss from the sale of business assets is treated as an ordinary loss. Future gains, however, will be treated as ordinary income to the extent of such losses recognised in the five immediately preceding years.

Inter-company dividends
A US corporation generally may deduct 70% of dividends received from other US corporations. The dividends received deduction is increased from 70% to 80% if the recipient of the dividend distribution owns at least 20% but less than 80% of the distributing corporation. Generally, dividend payments between US corporations that are members of the same affiliated group (see the Group taxation section) are deferred or eliminated until a transaction with a third party occurs. With minor exceptions, a US corporation may not deduct dividends it receives from a foreign corporation.

U

United States

Foreign income (Subpart F income) of US taxpayers

Generally, a US corporation is taxed on its worldwide income, including foreign branch income earned and foreign dividends when received. Double taxation is avoided by means of foreign tax credits. Alternatively, a deduction may be claimed for actual foreign taxes that are paid. In the case of foreign subsidiaries that are more than 50% owned by US shareholders (commonly known as controlled foreign corporations or CFCs), certain types of undistributed income will be taxed currently to the US shareholders (Subpart F income). Generally, Subpart F income includes income that is easily transferred to a low-tax jurisdiction.

Income from certain passive foreign investment companies (where 75% or more of the income is passive or at least 50% of the assets held produce passive income) also is subject to current taxation. Current taxation occurs if the corporation elects to be a qualified electing fund (QEF) or there are actual distributions. If a QEF election is not made and the corporation makes an actual distribution, the distribution will be treated as an excess distribution to the extent it exceeds 125% of the average of the distributions made with respect to the stock over the three immediately preceding years. The excess distribution is spread over the taxpayer's holding period, and the amount allocated to each year in the holding period is subject to tax at the highest marginal tax rate in effect for that year. This deferred tax amount also is subject to an interest charge. The interest charge is designed to pay the benefit of the tax deferral that arises out of having an overseas investment that pays no US income taxes.

US income of foreign taxpayers

Generally, if a foreign entity engages in a US trade or business, all income from sources within the United States that is connected with conducting such trade or business is classified as Effectively Connected Income (ECI). There are also situations in which foreign source income could be ECI. ECI generally is subject to tax at the same rate as corporate profits. A 30% branch profits tax is levied in addition to the US corporate level income tax, which may be reduced or eliminated entirely if a relevant treaty so provides. Deductions are allowed against ECI.

Tax treaties between the United States and other countries may provide special rules for allocating taxing authority between the treaty partners. Tax treaties may provide that income earned by a foreign entity that would otherwise be considered ECI is only taxable in the United States to the extent the profits are attributable to a permanent establishment of the foreign entity in the United States. A permanent establishment is generally defined as a fixed place of business.

Foreign Investment & Real Property Tax Act (FIRPTA)

FIRPTA provides that the gain or loss of a foreign person from the disposition of a US real property interest should be taken into account as if the taxpayer were engaged in a US trade or business and such gain or loss were effectively connected with such business. In these situations, the party purchasing the US real property interest from the foreign party is required to withhold 10% of the amount realised.

Fixed, determinable, annual or periodical (FDAP) income

FDAP income includes all income except gains from the sale of real or personal property and income excluded from gross income, without regard to whether the owner of the income is a US or foreign entity. Some examples of FDAP income include dividends, interest, royalties, and commissions. The gross amount of FDAP income or gains from US sources that are not effectively connected with a US trade or business are taxed at a rate of 30%. Deductions against FDAP income are not allowed.

Certain kinds of FDAP income are treated as ECI by reason of statutory requirements, allowable elections, or meeting the requirements under either the Asset-Use Test or Business Activities Test.

Stock dividends

A US corporation can distribute a tax-free dividend of common stock proportionately to all common stock shareholders. If the right to elect cash is given, all distributions to all shareholders are taxable as dividend income whether cash or stock is taken. There are exceptions to these rules, and extreme caution must be observed before making such distributions.

Partnership income

The income (loss) of a partnership passes through to its partners so that the partnership itself is not subject to tax. Thus, each partner generally accounts for their distributive share of the partnership's taxable income.

Corporate reorganisations

In general, a corporate reorganisation involving a merger, acquisition, or consolidation is a taxable event under the general recognition provisions of the Code. However, a corporate reorganisation that meets certain statutory and judicial requirements may qualify as a tax-free transaction, with gain or loss generally not recognised or deferred to a later date.

Transfer pricing

Transfer pricing regulations govern how related entities set internal prices for the transfers of goods, intangible assets, services, and loans in both domestic and international contexts. The regulations are designed to prevent tax avoidance among related entities and place a controlled party on par with an uncontrolled taxpayer by requiring an arm's-length standard. The arm's-length standard generally is met if the results of a controlled transaction are consistent with results that would have been realised if uncontrolled taxpayers had engaged in a similar transaction under similar circumstances. If a company is not in compliance with the arm's-length standard, the Internal Revenue Service (IRS) may raise taxable income and tax payable in the United States. After a transfer pricing adjustment, a multinational company may face double tax, paying tax twice on the same income in two countries. Multinational companies may request competent authority relief from double taxation through a tax treaty.

In order to avoid potential transfer pricing penalties, one avenue available to companies may be to obtain an advance pricing agreement with the IRS, unilaterally, or with the IRS and another tax authority, bilaterally, covering inter-company pricing.

Other

Interest income, rents, and royalties generally are includible in the determination of gross income.

U

United States

Deductions

Depreciation

Depreciation deductions are allowances that may be taken for capital outlays for tangible property. For property placed in service after 1986, capital costs must be recovered by using the modified accelerated cost recovery system (MACRS) method. Depending on the type of tangible property, the general cost recovery periods are three, five, seven, 10, 15, 20, 27.5, and 39 years (31.5 years for property placed in service before 13 May 1993). The cost recovery methods and periods are the same for both new and used property. Most tangible personal property is in the three, five or seven year class. Property placed in the three, five, seven, or 10 year class is depreciated by first applying the 200% declining balance method and then switching to the straight-line method at such a time as when use of the straight-line method maximises the depreciation deduction. Property in the 15 or 20 year class is depreciated by using the 150% declining balance method and later switching to the straight-line method. An election may be made to use the Alternative Depreciation System (basically, the straight-line method over prescribed lives). Residential rental property generally is depreciated by the straight-line method over 27.5 years. Non-residential real property is depreciated by the straight-line method over 39 years (31.5 years for property placed in service before 13 May 1993).

An election to use the straight-line method over the regular recovery period or a longer recovery period also is available. Alternatively, taxpayers may elect to use the 150% declining balance method over the regular recovery period for all property other than real property. This method is required for alternative minimum tax purposes.

For most tangible personal and real property placed in service in the United States after 1980 but before 1 January 1987, capital costs were recovered by the Accelerated Cost Recovery System (ACRS), which applied accelerated methods of cost recovery over periods specified by statute. The general ACRS recovery periods were three, five, 10, 15, 18, and 19 years.

Special rules apply to automobiles and certain other "listed" property. Accelerated depreciation deductions can be claimed only if the automobile is used 50% or more for qualified business use as defined in related regulations. Further, for automobiles placed in service after 1986, the allowable yearly depreciation deduction cannot exceed specific dollar limitations.

Separate methods and periods of cost recovery are specified by statute for certain tangible personal and real property used outside the United States.

Rapid amortisation may be allowable for certain pollution control facilities.

Tax depreciation is not required to conform to book depreciation. Tax depreciation generally is subject to recapture on the sale or disposition of certain property, to the extent of gain, which is subject to tax as ordinary income.

Section 179 deduction

Corporations can elect to expense, up to a statutory amount per year, the cost of certain eligible property used in the active conduct of a trade or business. This is commonly referred to as a 179 deduction for the Internal Revenue Code (code or TRC) section that allows the deduction. The maximum annual expensing amount for tax years that begin in 2008 and 2009 is USD 250,000. For tax years beginning in 2010, the maximum annual expensing amount is USD 134,000. For tax years beginning in 2011 and thereafter, the maximum amount is USD 25,000. The maximum deduction amount is reduced dollar for dollar where the corporation places in service during the tax year qualified tangible personal property in excess of USD 800,000 for tax years that begin in 2008 and 2009. For tax years beginning in 2010, the investment limitation is USD 530,000.

For tax years beginning in 2011 and thereafter, the investment limitation is reduced to USD 200,000. In addition, the deduction under this election is limited to the taxable income of the business. The annual expensing limit is increased by an additional USD 35,000 for qualifying assets placed in service in certain distressed communities. The annual expensing limit also is increased for certain property placed in service in the Gulf Opportunity Zone or Kansas disaster area.

Bonus depreciation

A 50% special first year depreciation allowance (i.e., bonus depreciation) applies (unless an election out is made) for new MACRS property with a recovery period of 20 years or less, certain computer software, water utility property, and certain leasehold improvements acquired after 31 December 2007 and before 1 January 2010. The special allowance applies for regular income tax and AMT purposes. No AMT adjustment is made if the special allowance is used. The property must be placed in service before 2010 (before 2011 for certain longer lived property). The special allowance does not apply to property that must be depreciated using the Alternative Depreciation System or to "listed property" not used predominantly for business. The special allowance reduces basis before regular depreciation is figured. Additionally, claiming bonus depreciation on automobiles may affect the first year depreciation limits on such automobiles (as mentioned above).

Depletion

For natural resource properties other than timber and certain oil and gas properties, depletion may be computed on a cost or a percentage basis.

Cost depletion is a method of depletion applied to exhaustible natural resources, including timber, which is based on the adjusted basis of the property. Each year, the adjusted basis of the property is reduced, but not below zero, by the amount of depletion calculated for that year. The current year cost depletion deduction is based on an estimate of the number of units that make up the deposit and the number of units extracted and sold during the year.

Percentage depletion is a method of depletion applied to most minerals and geothermal deposits, and, to a more limited extent, oil and gas. Percentage depletion is deductible at rates varying from 5% to 25% of gross income, depending on the mineral and certain other conditions. Percentage depletion may be deducted even after the total depletion deductions have exceeded the cost basis. However, percentage depletion is limited to 50% (100% for oil and gas properties) of taxable income from the property (computed without allowance for depletion). Generally, percentage depletion is not available for oil or gas wells. However, exceptions exist for natural gas from geopressurised brine and for independent producers of oil and gas.

U

United States

Net operating losses

A net operating loss (NOL) is generated when business deductions exceed gross income in a particular tax year. Depending on current tax law, an NOL may be carried back to offset past taxes and possibly obtain a refund or carried forward to offset future tax liability. Generally, a loss may be carried back two years and, if not fully used, carried forward 20 years. For tax years beginning before 6 August 1997 a loss may be carried back three years and, if not fully used, carried forward 15 years. For state tax purposes, carryback and carryforward provisions are often similar to the federal provisions, except that several states do not permit any carrybacks or carryforwards.

Special rules surrounding NOLs may apply if a taxpayer is located in a qualified disaster area. Special rules also apply relating to specified liability losses.

Complex rules may limit the use of net operating losses after a reorganisation or other change in corporate ownership. Generally, if the ownership of more than 50% in value of the stock of the loss corporation changes, a limit is placed on the amount of future income that may be offset by losses carried forward.

With certain exceptions, taxpayers may elect to increase the carryback period for an applicable NOL to three, four, or five years from two years under the Worker, Homeownership, and Business Assistance Act of 2009, which was signed by President Obama on 6 November, 2009. Under this act, an applicable NOL is the taxpayer's NOL for any tax year ending after 31 December 2007, and beginning before 1 January 2010. Generally, an election may be made for only one tax year, but an eligible small business that made or makes an election under the Code as in effect before 6 November 2009, may make an election for two tax years.

Under this special provision of the Worker, Homeownership, and Business Assistance Act of 2009, the amount of an NOL that may be carried back to the fifth tax year before the loss year may not exceed 50% of the taxable income for that fifth preceding tax year, determined without consideration of any NOL generated in the loss year or during any tax year after the loss year. An NOL otherwise carried to tax years following the fifth preceding tax year is adjusted to take into account that the NOL may offset only 50% of the taxable income for that fifth preceding tax year. Note that the 50% limitation does not apply to an applicable 2008 NOL of certain eligible small businesses that made an earlier election.

The Worker, Homeownership, and Business Assistance Act of 2009 also suspends the 90% limitation on the use of any alternative tax NOL deduction attributable to the carryback of an applicable NOL for which the extended carryback period is elected. Transition rules prescribe how a taxpayer may revoke certain elections to waive the carryback period.

US manufacturing deduction

Over the last several decades, various tax incentive systems have been enacted in the United States to encourage exports and later repealed, including the extraterritorial income (ETI) regime, which was repealed as a result of a World Trade Organisation ruling that the ETI regime favoured US goods and violated the national treatment provisions of the General Agreement on Tariffs and Trade. In response, the United States enacted the American Jobs Creation Act of 2004, which introduced a phase-out repeal of ETI, and introduced the domestic production activities deduction under section 199, seeking to compensate US manufacturers for the loss of ETI benefits.

Under section 199, taxpayers are allowed a 9% deduction for qualified production activities (QPA) income (subject to a taxable income limitation), phased in at 3% in 2005 and 2006; 6% in 2007 through 2009 and 9% in 2010 and thereafter. The deduction is available to all taxpayers actively engaged in QPA. For corporate taxpayers, the deduction generally will mean a federal income tax rate of 33.95%, 32.90% and 31.85%, respectively, for the years in question, on QPA income. Importantly, the deduction also applies in calculating the alternative minimum tax. There is a limit on the amount of the deduction equal to 50% of W-2 wages allocable to QPA (subject to a specific effective date), and the deduction is not allowed for taxpayers that incur a loss from their production activities or have an overall loss (including a carryover loss) from all activities.

A taxpayer's QPA income is calculated using the following formula: domestic production gross receipts less the sum of cost of goods sold allocable to such receipts and other expenses, losses, or deduction which are properly allocable to such receipts.

Payments to foreign affiliates
A US corporation generally may claim a deduction for royalties, management service fees, and interest charges paid to foreign affiliates, to the extent the amounts are actually paid and are not in excess of what it would pay an unrelated entity, (i.e., are at arm's length). In addition, US withholding on these payments may be required.

Debt-to equity rules
Thin capitalisation rules may apply to disallow interest payments related to excess debt and recharacterise such payments as dividends. The interest expense deduction can be limited and suspended if more than 50% of the adjusted taxable income of a thinly-capitalised corporation (with similar rules for a corporate partner in a partnership) is sheltered by interest paid to a related party (or paid to a third-party but guaranteed by the related party) who is not subject to US tax on the income.

Employee benefit plans (pension plans and expenses)
Through the Code, the government provides incentives for employers to provide retirement benefits to workers, including employee benefit, qualifying profit-sharing, or stock bonus plans. Usually, the employer will be allowed a current deduction for any contributions made to the fund, and the employee's tax liability will be deferred until the benefit is paid. For profit, non-government employers generally have two types of available plans, which generally are subject to the reporting and disclosure requirements set forth under the Employee Retirement Income Security Act of 1974 (ERISA).

The first category of employee benefit plans is the defined benefit plan, or more commonly known as a pension plan, to which an employer contributes money, on an ongoing basis, to cover the amount of retirement income owed to retired employees under the plan (which will vary based on years of service, average salary, and/or other factors). Any investment gains or losses will not affect the amount of benefits paid to participants but will affect the amount an employer needs to contribute in order to cover its obligation.

The second category of employee benefit plans is the defined contribution plan, or more commonly known in the United States as a "401(k) plan", to which an employer's contributions (if any) are allocated amongst the separate accounts of participating employees, who also may contribute to their respective accounts. Investment gains or

U

losses and the history of contributions will affect the value of a participant's account at retirement but would not affect an employer's contributions since the employer is not obligated to ensure any specified level of benefit in the plan.

Non profits, including churches and government entities, have similar employee benefit plans, except different requirements apply. Small employers and self-employed individuals also have similar options available but are subject to different requirements.

Bribes, kickbacks, illegal payments
An amount paid, directly or indirectly, to any person that is a bribe, kickback, or other illegal payment is not deductible.

Taxes
See, for example, State and municipal taxes under the section on Other taxes.

Other significant items
* Deductions for allowable charitable contributions may not exceed 10% of taxable income computed without regard to certain deductions, including charitable contributions themselves. Deductions for contributions so limited may be carried over to the five succeeding years, subject to the 10% limitation annually, as noted above.
* Bad debt resulting from a trade or business may be deducted in the year the debt becomes worthless. Determining the date the debt becomes worthless may present difficulty.
* No deduction generally is allowed for a contingent liability until such liability is fixed and determinable.
* No deduction generally is allowed for fines or penalties paid to the government for violation of any law.
* The cost of goodwill and most other intangibles assets generally is capitalised and amortisable ratably over 15 years.
* Generally, start up expenditures must be amortised over a 15 year period; however, a certain taxpayer may elect to deduct some expenses in the tax year in which the trade or business begins.
* Costs incurred for entertainment must meet strict tests in order to be deductible. The deduction for business meal and entertainment expenses is 50% of the expenses incurred. There are also limitations on the deductibility of international and domestic business travel expenses.
* Royalty payments, circulation costs, mine exploration and development costs, and other miscellaneous costs of carrying on a business are deductible subject to certain conditions and limits.
* Depending on the taxpayer's tax accounting method, research and experimental expenditures may be deducted as incurred or treated as deferred expenses and amortised over a period of not less than 60 months; however, in general, the method used must be consistently applied.

Group taxation

An affiliated group of US "includible" corporations, consisting of a parent and subsidiaries directly or indirectly 80% owned, generally may offset the profits of one affiliate against the losses of another affiliate within the group by electing to file a consolidated federal income tax return. A foreign incorporated subsidiary may not be consolidated into the US group, except for certain Mexican and Canadian incorporated entities. A partnership may not be included in a consolidated return, even if it is 100% owned by members of an affiliated group, since a partnership is not a corporation. However, a member's earnings that flow through from a partnership are included as part of the consolidated group's taxable income or loss. Filing on a consolidated (combined) basis also is allowed (or may be required or prohibited) in certain states.

Sales, dividends, and other transactions between corporations that are members of the same group generally are deferred or eliminated until such time as a transaction occurs with a non-member of the group. Losses incurred on the sale of members of the group are disallowed under certain circumstances.

Tax incentives

Inbound investment

There generally are no specific incentives related to inbound investment at the federal level, other than certain portfolio debt and bank deposit exceptions. The portfolio debt exception enables non-residents and foreign corporations to invest in certain obligations (which must meet certain statutory requirements to qualify as "portfolio debt") in the United States without being subject to US income (or withholding) tax on the interest income. Certain state and local benefits may also be available.

General business credit

Various business credits are available to provide special incentives for the achievement of certain economic objectives. In general, these credits are combined into one "general business credit" for purposes of determining each credit's allowance limitation for the tax year. The general business credit that may be used for a tax year is limited to a tax based amount. In general, the current year's credit that cannot be used in a given year because of the credit's allowance limitation may be carried back to the tax year preceding the current year and carried forward to each of the 20 years following the current year.

In general, the current year business credit is a combination of the following credits: (1) the investment credit; (2) the work opportunity credit; (3) the alcohol fuels credit; (4) the research credit; (5) the low-income housing credit; (6) the enhanced oil recovery credit; (7) the disabled access credit for certain eligible small businesses; (8) the renewable electricity production credit; (9) the empowerment zone employment credit; (10) the Indian employment credit; (11) the employer social security credit; (12) the orphan drug credit; (13) the new markets tax credit; (14) the small employer pension plan startup cost credit for eligible employers; (15) the employer-provided child care credit; (16) the railroad track maintenance credit; (17) the biodiesel fuels credit; (18) the low sulfur diesel fuel production credit; (19) the marginal oil and gas well production credit; (20) the distilled spirits credit; (21) the advanced nuclear power facility production credit; (22) the nonconventional source production credit; (23) the new energy efficient home credit; (24) the energy efficient appliance credit; (25) a portion of the alternative motor vehicle credit; (26) a portion of the alternative fuel vehicle refueling property credit; (27) the Hurricane Katrina housing credit; (28) the Hurricane Katrina employee retention credit; (29) the Hurricane Rita employee retention credit; (30) the Hurricane Wilma employee retention credit; (31) the mine rescue team training credit; (32) the agricultural chemicals security credit for eligible businesses; (33) the differential wage payment credit; (34) the carbon dioxide sequestration credit; and (35) a portion of the new qualified plug-in electric drive motor vehicle credit for vehicles that will vary based on the date of purchase.

U

United States

Employment credits
A "work opportunity tax credit" is available for employment of certain types of workers who began work for an employer after 30 September 1996 and before 1 September 2011. "Creditable" wages generally are the first USD 6,000 of wages paid to each qualified employee for the year. The credit is 40% of creditable wages, for a maximum credit of USD 2,400.

Research and development (R&D)
A credit against the federal tax equal to 20% of the sum of qualified research expenses incurred prior to 31 December 2009 in excess of the base amount (as discussed below) and basic research payments (as discussed below) to a qualified organisation may be obtained for certain periods. The base amount cannot be less than 50% of the current year's qualified research expenditures. In tax years ending after 8 August 2005, the research expense credit also includes 20% of the taxpayer's expenditures on qualified energy research undertaken by an energy research consortium.

In addition, for taxable years ending after 2006 taxpayers may be able to use the new alternative simplified credit (ASC) that does not use a gross receipts factor. The ASC generally equals 12% (14% in 2009) of qualified research expenditures (QRE) for taxable years that exceed 50% of the average QRE for the three taxable years proceeding the credit determination year. Special transition rules apply to fiscal year 2006-2007 taxpayers.

Those taxpayers that, despite significant R&D investments, are unable to claim the standard R&D credit because their current R&D intensity is lower than during the credit's 1984–88 "fixed base" period may use an elective "alternative incremental research credit" (AIRC). Under the AIRC, a graduated rate system applies to the extent that the taxpayer's current year qualified research expenses (QREs) exceed a specified percentage of its average gross receipts for the prior four years (the "base amount"). This election to be subject to the alternative incremental credit regime applies to the tax year for which it is made and all later years unless the IRS consents to its revocation.

The deduction for R&D expenditures must be reduced by the entire amount of the credit unless an election is made to reduce the amount of the credit.

Puerto Rico
Puerto Rico is the most populous and politically significant US possession. Puerto Rico corporations are considered foreign for US tax purposes. In general, Puerto Rico corporations are liable to the US for tax on income effectively connected to a US trade or business and on passive income from US sources and on US branch profits. Tax paid to the United States may be eligible for a foreign tax credit against Puerto Rico tax liability.

US corporations operating in Puerto Rico may take a credit against income from Puerto Rico sources. The credit applies to income from operating an active trade or business in Puerto Rico or from the sale of substantially all the assets of such a trade or business. For tax years beginning after 1995, this credit is subject to limitations and generally is available only to existing claimants. All claimants may also take the credit on possession source investment income received or accrued before 1 July 1996. The credit is repealed for tax years beginning after 2005.

United States

Other US possessions
The American Samoa, Guam, the Commonwealth of the Northern Mariana Islands, and the US Virgin Islands have their own independent tax departments. Accordingly, they have their own rules in addition to special provisions in the US tax code.

Qualified private activity bonds
Interest income received on certain qualified private activity bonds generally is exempt from federal income tax. This enables a business enterprise to issue the bonds at a lower interest rate.

Foreign tax credit
Generally, in any year, a taxpayer can choose whether to take as a credit (subject to limitation) or as a deduction foreign income, war profits, and excess profit taxes paid or accrued during the taxable year to any foreign country or US possession. A foreign tax credit (FTC) reduces US income tax liability dollar for dollar, while a deduction reduces the US income tax liability at the marginal rate of the taxpayer. For taxpayers with net operating losses, the FTC is of no value in such year. However, a benefit might be received either in an earlier year (through a refund of previously paid taxes) or a later year (through a reduction of future taxes). It also should be noted that a taxpayer has an ability to switch from credit to deduction (or from deduction to credit) at any time in a 10-year period commencing when the foreign taxes were paid or accrued. Generally, a foreign tax credit may be carried back one year and, if not fully used, carried forward 10 years.

In addition, the FTC goes beyond direct taxes to include foreign taxes paid "in lieu of" a tax upon income, war profits, or excess profits, which would otherwise generally be imposed. It also includes deemed-paid (indirect) taxes paid for certain US corporate shareholders of non-portfolio foreign corporations when actual or deemed dividends are received. Furthermore, the FTC system has numerous limitations to mitigate the potential abuses of the credit by the taxpayer.

Other incentives
State and local governments provide numerous incentives to encourage business and, thus, employment in their jurisdictions.

Withholding taxes (WHT)

The US has entered into various income tax treaties with countries in order to avoid double taxation of the same income and to prevent tax evasion. The table below from IRS Publication 901 (April 2010) summarises the benefits resulting from these treaties.

Recipient	Interest paid by US obligors general	Paid by US corporations general (a)	Dividends qualifying for direct dividend rate (a,b)	Royalties
Australia	10(c,f,w)	15(c,x)	5(c,x,z)	0(c)/5(c)/5(c)
Austria	0(c,u)	15(c,k)	5(c,k)	0(c)/10(c)/0(c)
Bangladesh	10.5(c,m,u)	15(c,x)	15(c,x)	10(c)/10(c)/10(c)
Barbados	5(c)	15(c,k)	5(c,k)	5(c)/5(c)/5(c)
Belgium	15(c,u)	15(c,dd,ee)	5(c,z,dd,ee)	0(c)/0(c)/0(c)
Bulgaria	5(c,u,w,dd)	10(c,dd,ee)	5(c,dd,ee)	5(c)/5(c)/5(c)

U

United States

Recipient	Interest paid by US obligors general	Paid by US corporations general (a)	Dividends qualifying for direct dividend rate (a,b)	Royalties
Canada	0(c,u)	15(c,x)	5(c,x)	0(c)/10(c)/0(c)
China, People's Republic of	10(c)	10(c)	10(c)	10(c,j)/10(c)/10(c)
Commonwealth of Independent States	0(h)	30	30	0/0/0
Cyprus	10(c)	15(c)	5(c)	0(c)/0(c)/0(c)
Czech Republic	0(c)	15(c,k)	5(c,k)	10(c)/0(c)/0(c)
Denmark	0(c,v)	15(c,dd,ee)	5(c,z,dd,ee)	0(c)/0(c)/0(c)
Egypt	15(d)	15(d)	5(d)	0(d)/0(d)/15(c)
Estonia	10(c,v)	15(c,k)	5(c,k)	5(c,o)/10(c)/10(c)
Finland	0(c,v)	15(c,dd,ee)	5(c,z,dd,ee)	0(c)/0(c)/0(c)
France	0(c)	15(c,x)	5(c,x,z)	0(c)/0(c)/0(c)
Germany	0(c,u)	15(c,dd,ee)	5(c,z,dd,ee)	0(c)/0(c,p)/0(c)
Greece	0(d)	30	30	0(d)/30/0(d)
Hungary	0(c)	15(c)	5(c)	0(c)/0(c)/0(c)
Iceland	0(c,v)	15(c,q,x)	5(c,q,x)	0(c,e)/5(c)/0(c)
India	15(c,n)	25(c,k)	15(c,k)	10(c,o)/15(c)/15(c)
Indonesia	10(c)	15(c)	10(c)	10(c,o)/10(c)/10(c)
Ireland	0(c)	15(c,x)	5(c,x)	0(c)/0(c)/0(c)
Israel	17.5(c,n,s)	25(c,k)	12.5(c,k)	15(c)/10(c)/10(c)
Italy (new treaty)	10(c,y)	15(c,x)	5(c,x)	5(c)/8(c)/8(c,aa)
Italy (old treaty)	15(c)	15(c)	5(c)	10(c,i)/8(c)/5(c)
Jamaica	12.5(c)	15(c)	10(c)	10(c)/10(c)/10(c)
Japan	10(c,bb,cc,dd)	10(c,bb,dd,ee)	5(c,bb,dd,ee)	0(c,bb)/0(c,bb)/0 (c,bb)
Kazakhstan	10(c)	15(c,r)	5(c,r)	10(c,ff)/10(c)/10(c)
Korea, South	12(c)	15(c)	10(c)	15(c)/10(c)/10(c)
Latvia	10(c,v)	15(c,k)	5(c,k)	5(c,o)/10(c)/10(c)
Lithuania	10(c,v)	15(c,k)	5(c,k)	5(c,o)/10(c)/10(c)
Luxembourg	0(c,d)	15(c,gg)	5(c,k)	0(c)/0(c)/0(c)
Mexico	15(c,t)	10(c,x,o)	5(c,j,x,z)	10(c)/10(c)/10(c)
Morocco	15(c)	15(c)	10(c)	10(d)/10(c)/10(c)
Netherlands	0(c)	15(c)	5(c)	0(c)/0(c,p)/0(c)

Recipient	Interest paid by US obligors general	Paid by US corporations general (a)	Dividends qualifying for direct dividend rate (a,b)	Royalties
New Zealand	10(c)	15(c)	15(c)	10(c)/10(c)/10(c)
Norway	0(c)	15(c)	15(c)	0(c)/0(d)/0(c)
Pakistan	30	30	15(d)	0(d)/30/0(d)
Philippines	15(c)	25(c)	20(c)	15(c)/15(c)/15(c)
Poland	0(c)	15(c)	5(c)	10(c)/10(c)/10(c)
Portugal	10(c)	15(c,k)	5(c,k)	10(c)/10(c)/10(c)
Romania	10(c)	10(c)	10(c)	15(c)/10(c)/10(c)
Russia	0(c)	10(c,r)	5(c,r)	0(c)/0(c)/0(c)
Slovak Republic	0(c)	15(c,k)	5(c,k)	10(c)/0(c)/0(c)
Slovenia	5(c)	15(c,x)	5(c,x)	5(c)/5(c)/5(c)
South Africa	0(c,u)	15(c,k)	5(c,k)	0(c)/0(c)/0(c)
Spain	10(c)	15(c,k)	10(c,k)	8(c,l)/8(c,l)/5(c,l)
Sri Lanka	10(c,u)	15(c,hh)	15(c,hh)	0(c)/10(c)/10(c,i)
Sweden	0(c)	15(c,dd,ee)	5(c,z,dd,ee)	0(c)/0(c)/0(c)
Switzerland	0(c,u)	15(c,k)	5(c,k)	0(c)/0(c)/0(c)
Thailand	15(c,n)	15(c,k)	10(c,k)	8(o)/5/15(e)
Trinidad & Tobago	30	30	30	15(c)/30/0(c)
Tunisia	15(c)	20(c,k)	14(c,k)	10(c,o)/15(c)/15(c)
Turkey	15(c,g,n)	20(c,k)	15(c,k)	5(o)/10/10
Ukraine	0(c)	15(c,r)	5(c,r)	10(c)/10(c)/10(c)
United Kingdom	0(c,v,bb)	15(c,x,bb)	5(c,x,z,bb)	0(c,bb)/0(c,bb)/0(c,bb)
Venezuela	10(c,v,w)	15(c,x)	5(c,x)	5(c,o)/10(c)/10(c)
Other countries	30	30	30	30/30/30

Notes

* Please note the tax rates and associated footnotes appearing in the "Royalties" column in the table address three types of royalties, as denoted in the most recent IRS publication. These three are Industrial Royalties, Motion Picture and Television Copyright Royalties, and "Other" Copyright Royalties. The back slashes "/" between each figure and associated footnote(s) are meant to demarcate these three types of royalties, respectively.

a. No US tax is imposed on a dividend paid by a US corporation that received at least 80% of its gross income from an active foreign business for the three-year period before the dividend is declared.

U

United States

b. The reduced rate applies to dividends paid by a subsidiary to a foreign parent corporation that has the required percentage of stock ownership. In some cases, the income of the subsidiary must meet certain requirements (e.g., a certain percentage of its total income must consist of income other than dividends and interest). For Italy, the reduced rate is 10% to 50% of the voting stock (for a 12-month period) of the company paying the dividends. For Japan, dividends received from a more than 50% owned corporate subsidiary are exempt if certain conditions are met.

c. The exemption or reduction in rate does not apply if the recipient has a permanent establishment in the United States and the property giving rise to the income is effectively connected with this permanent establishment. Under certain treaties, the exemption or reduction in rate also does not apply if the property producing the income is effectively connected with a fixed base in the United States from which the recipient performs independent personal services. Even with the treaty, if the income is not effectively connected with a trade or business in the United States by the recipient, the recipient will be considered as not having a permanent establishment in the United States under IRC section 894(b).

d. The exemption or reduction in rate does not apply if the recipient is engaged in a trade or business in the United States through a permanent establishment that is in the United States. However, if the income is not effectively connected with a trade or business in the United States by the recipient, the recipient will be considered as not having a permanent establishment in the United States to apply the reduced treaty rate to that item of income.

e. For Thailand, the rate is 5% for royalties on the use of any copyright of literary, artistic, or scientific work, including software. For Iceland the rate is 5% for trademarks and any information for rentals of industrial, commercial, or scientific equipment.

f. Interest determined with reference to the profits of the issuer or one of its associated enterprises is taxed at 15%.

g. Contingent interest that does not qualify as portfolio interest is treated as a dividend and is subject to the rates under columns 2 and 3, as appropriate.

h. The exemption applies only to interest on credits, loans, and other indebtedness connected with the financing of trade between the United States and the C.I.S. member. It does not include interest from the conduct of a general banking business.

i. The rate for royalties with respect to tangible personal property is 7% (5% in the case of Sri Lanka).

j. Tax imposed on 70% of gross royalties for rentals of industrial or scientific equipment.

k. The rate in column 2 applies to dividends paid by a regulated investment company (RIC) or a real estate investment trust (REIT). However, that rate applies to dividends paid by a REIT only if the beneficial owner of the dividends is an individual holding less than a 10% interest (25% in the case of Portugal, Spain, and Tunisia) in the REIT.

l. Royalties not taxed at the 5% or 8% rate are taxed at a 10% rate, unless footnote (c) applies.

m. The rate is 5% for interest (a) beneficially owned by a bank or other financial institution (including an insurance company) or (b) paid due to a sale on credit of any industrial, commercial, or scientific equipment, or of any merchandise to an enterprise.

n. The rate is 10% if the interest is paid on a loan granted by a bank or similar financial institution. For Thailand, the 10% rate also applies to interest from an arm's-length sale on credit of equipment, merchandise, or services.

o. This is the rate for royalties for the use of, or the right to use, industrial, commercial, and scientific equipment. The rate for royalties for information concerning industrial, commercial and scientific know-how is subject to the rate in column 4 ("other royalties").

p. The exemption does not apply to cinematographic items, or works on film, tape, or other means of reproduction for use in radio or television broadcasting.

q. Amounts paid to a pension fund or employee benefit organisation that are not derived from the carrying on of a business, directly or indirectly, by the fund or organisation are exempt.

r. The rate in column 2 applies to dividends paid by a regulated investment company (RIC). Dividends paid by a real estate investment trust (REIT) are subject to a 30% rate.

s. An election can be made to treat this interest income as if it were industrial and commercial profits taxible under article 8 of this treaty.

t. The rate is 4.9% for interest derived from (1) loans granted by banks and insurance companies and (2) bonds or securities that are regularly and substantially traded on a recognised securities market. The rate is 10% for interest not described in the preceding sentence and paid (i) by banks or (ii) by the buyer of machinery and equipment to the seller due to a sale on credit.

u. The rate is 15% (10% for Bulgaria; 30% for Germany and Switzerland) for contingent interest that does not qualify as portfolio interest.

v. The rate is 15% for interest determined with reference to (a) receipts, sales, income, profits, or other cash flow of the debtor or a related person, (b) any change in the value of any property of the debtor or a related person, or (c) any dividend, partnership distribution, or similar payment made by the debtor to a related person.

w. Interest received by a financial institution is tax exempt. For Venezuela, the rate is 4.95% if the interest is beneficially owned by a financial institution (including an insurance company).

x. The rate in column 2 applies to dividends paid by a regulated investment company (RIC) or real estate investment trust (REIT). However, that rate applies to dividends paid by a REIT only if the beneficial owner of the dividends is (a) an individual holding not more than a 10% interest in the REIT, (b) a person holding not more than 5% of any class of the REIT's stock and the dividends are paid on stock that is publicly traded, or (c) a person holding not more than a 10% interest in the REIT and the REIT is diversified.

y. Interest paid or accrued on the sale of goods, merchandise, or services between enterprises is exempt. Interest paid or accrued on the sale on credit of industrial, commercial, or scientific equipment is exempt.

z. Dividends received from an 80%-owned corporate subsidiary are exempt if certain conditions are met.

aa. Royalties for the use of, or right to use, a copyright of literary, artistic, or scientific work (excluding royalties for software, motion pictures, films, tapes, or other means of reproduction used for radio or television broadcasting) are exempt.

bb. Exemption or reduced rate does not apply to amount paid under, or as part of, a conduit arrangement.

cc. Interest is exempt if (a) paid to certain financial institutions, or (b) paid on indebtedness from the sale on credit of equipment or merchandise.

dd. Amounts paid to a pension fund that are not derived from the carrying on of a business, directly or indirectly, by the fund are exempt. This includes amounts paid by a REIT only if the conditions in footnote ee are met. For Sweden, to be entitled to the exemption, the pension fund must not sell or make a contract to sell the holding from which the dividend is derived within two months of the date the pension fund acquired the holding.

ee. The rate in column 2 applies to dividends paid by a regulated investment company (RIC) or real estate investment trust (REIT). However, that rate applies to dividends paid by a REIT only if the beneficial owner of the dividends is (a) an individual or a pension fund holding not more than a 10% interest in the REIT, (b) a person holding not more than 5% of any class of the REIT's stock and the dividends are paid on stock that is publicly traded, or (c) a person holding not more than a 10% interest in the REIT and the REIT is diversified. Dividends paid to a pension fund from a RIC, or a REIT that meets the above conditions, are exempt. For Sweden, the pension fund must also satisfy the requirements in footnote dd.

ff. If the payments were for the use of, or the right to use, industrial, commercial, or scientific equipment, an election may be made to compute the tax on a net basis as if such income were attributable to a permanent establishment or fixed base in the US.

gg. The exemption does not apply if the recipient of the gain is an individual who is present in the United States for more than 119 days during the year.

hh. The rate applies to dividends paid by a real estate investment trust (REIT) only if the beneficial owner of the dividends is (a) an individual holding less than a 10% interest in the REIT, (b) a person holding not more than 5% of any class of the REIT's stock and the dividends are paid on stock that is publicly traded, or (c) a person holding not more than a 10% interest in the REIT and the REIT is diversified.

U

United States

Tax administration

Returns
The US tax system is based on the principle of self assessment. A corporate taxpayer is required to file an annual tax return (generally Form 1120) by the fifteenth day of the third month following the close of its tax year. A taxpayer can obtain an additional six month extension of time to file its tax return. Failure to timely file may result in penalties.

Important tax return due dates

Form No.	Title	Purpose	Due date
W-2	Wage and Tax Statement	Employers must provide employees with statements regarding total compensation and amounts withheld during year.	Must be sent to employees on or before 1/31.
1099 series	Various	Information returns to be provided to recipients of dividends and distributions, interest income, miscellaneous income, etc.	Must be sent on or before 1/31.
1120 series, including 1120S (for S Corps)	US Corporation Income Tax Return	Income tax returns for domestic corporations or foreign corporations with US offices.	3/15 (Form 7004 may be filed to obtain an automatic six month extension)
Schedule K-1	Partner's Share of Income (Loss) from an Electing Large Partnership	Information returns to be provided to partners by large partnerships.	3/15
1065	US Return of Partnership Income	Information returns to be filed by large partnerships.	4/15 (Form 7004 may be filed to obtain an automatic six month extension)
State tax returns	Various	Income tax returns for states where corporation carries on trade/business.	Varies – often 4/15

Payment of tax
A taxpayer's tax liability generally is required to be prepaid throughout the year in four equal estimated payments and fully paid by the date the tax return is initially due. For calendar year corporations, the tax instalment payments are due by the fifteenth day of April, June, and September, and the tax liability must be fully paid by the fifteenth day of December. For fiscal year corporations, the tax instalment payments are due by the fifteenth day of the fourth, sixth, and ninth months, and the tax must be fully paid by the fifteenth day of the twelfth month of the tax year. Generally, no extensions to pay are allowed. Failure to pay the tax by the due dates as indicated above can result in estimated tax and late payment penalties and interest charges.

The instalment payments must include estimates of regular corporate income tax, alternative minimum tax, environmental tax, and, for foreign corporations, the tax on gross transportation income. To avoid a penalty, corporations must calculate the instalment payments based on at least 25% of the lesser of (i) the tax shown on the current tax return or (ii) the prior year's tax liability, provided that the tax liability was a positive amount in the prior year and that such year consisted of 12 months. However, corporations with taxable income of at least USD 1 million (before use of NOLs or capital loss carryforwards) in any of the three preceding years are not permitted to calculate the instalment based payment on the prior year's tax liability, except in determining the first instalment payment. Instead, such corporations must calculate the instalment payments based on the tax shown on the current tax return.

Corporations with more than USD 1 billion in assets will be required to make estimated tax payments that are 100.25% of the amount otherwise due in July, August, or September of 2014. Such overpayments will be balanced out in October, November, or December of 2014 when payments of 99.75% of the amount otherwise due will be paid by corporations with more than USD 1 billion in assets.

Audit cycle
Generally, the US tax system is based on self-assessment; however, many large and midsize businesses are under continuous audit by the IRS and state tax authorities. The audits may include the entire list of taxes for which the business is liable. Smaller business and persons with lower incomes are generally subject to audit on a random basis.

Currently, the IRS is focused on abusive payments related to contribution to capital of a corporation, domestic manufacturing deduction, foreign earnings repatriation, foreign tax credit generators, repairs vs. capitalisation change in accounting method, research credit claims, transfer of intangibles/offshore cost sharing, withholding taxes, and employee classification.

Statute of limitations
The IRS generally has three years after an original return is filed to assess income taxes. A return will be deemed to have been filed on its due date, even if the return is actually filed on an earlier date.

Tax shelter
Treasury regulations require taxpayers to disclose transactions determined to be abusive or possibly abusive. Current information on these transactions, known as listed and reportable transactions, is available from the IRS website (www.irs.gov).

Tax accounting and internal controls
ASC 740, Income Taxes (formerly known as FASB Statement No. 109, Accounting for Income Taxes) addresses how companies should account for and report the effects of taxes based on income. ASC 740's principles and requirements apply to domestic and foreign entities in preparing financial statements in accordance with US generally accepted accounting principles (GAAP), including not-for-profit entities with activities that are subject to income taxes. This scope includes: 1) domestic federal (national) income taxes (US federal income taxes for US enterprises) and foreign, state, and local (including franchise) taxes based on income; and 2) an enterprise's domestic and foreign operations that are consolidated, combined, or accounted for by the equity method.

U

United States

In recent years, controls around the accounting for income taxes have been a critical source of material weaknesses in companies' internal controls over financial reporting. Accounting for income taxes also has been a primary reason for restating financial statements. Management should ensure that its judgments and estimates are reasonable (e.g., assessing the need for a valuation allowance on deferred taxes) and that the underlying internal control processes are reliable.

The adoption of International Financial Reporting Standards (IFRS) in the United States is set by the Securities and Exchange Commission (SEC). The timeline included in the SEC's roadmap provides for adoption of IFRS in the United States between 2014 and 2016. The SEC has stated that it will reassess the transition to IFRS in 2011.

Accounting for income taxes
For US federal tax purposes, the two most important characteristics of a tax method of accounting are (1) timing and (2) consistency. If the method does not affect the timing for including items of income or claiming deductions, it is not an accounting method and generally IRS approval is not needed to change it. In order to affect timing, the accounting method must determine the year in which an income or expense item is to be reported.

In general, to establish an accounting method, the method must be consistently applied. Once an accounting method has been adopted for federal tax purposes, any change must be requested by the taxpayer and approved by the IRS. Changes in accounting methods cannot be made through amending returns. The two most common methods of accounting are the accrual basis and cash basis methods.

Penalties
Civil and criminal penalties may be imposed for failing to follow the IRC when paying US taxes. The civil penalty provisions may be divided into four categories: delinquency penalties , accuracy-related penalties, information reporting penalties, and preparer, promoter, and protester penalties. Many, but not all, have exception provisions to cover reasonable cause. In addition many have provisions directing how the penalties interact with the other penalties.

These four main civil penalty categories may further be divided. First the delinquency penalties may be divided into failure to file, failure to pay, and failure to make timely deposits of tax. Failure to make timely deposits of tax applies to taxpayers required to make instalment payments and withholding tax payments.

Second, the penalties relating to the accuracy of tax returns are divided into the negligence penalty, the substantial understatement penalty, substantial overstatement of pension liabilities, substantial estate or gift tax valuation underestimate, and the valuation penalties. These penalties are also coordinated with the fraud penalty to eliminate any stacking of the penalties. Again, like other provisions, the fraud penalty is not intended to be imposed as a stacked penalty.

The third category of penalties is the information reporting penalties. These penalties may be imposed upon those who only have a duty to report information to the IRS.

The fourth and final major category of civil penalties are the preparer, promoter, and protester penalties. Currently the most notable of these is the return preparer penalty for which there is a penalty for a position on a return for which the preparer did not have substantial authority. Also included in this provision is a penalty for wilful or reckless attempt to understate the tax liability of another person. Additionally, return preparer penalties may be imposed for failure to furnish a copy of a return or claim for refund to the taxpayer, sign the return or claim for refund, furnish his or her identifying number, or file a correct information return.

Other promoter and protestor penalties include a penalty for promoting abusive tax shelters, aiding and abetting the understatement of tax liability, and filing frivolous income tax returns. Additionally, a court may award sanctions and costs if a person institutes or maintains a proceeding primarily for delay, takes a position that is frivolous, or unreasonably fails to pursue available administrative remedies.

In addition to these major civil penalties, international tax related penalties for failures other than timely and accurate filing (e.g., wilful failure to report international boycott activity, failure of an agent to furnish a notice of a false affidavit relating to the withholding tax on dispositions of US real property interests, failure of a US person to furnish information relating to controlled foreign corporations and controlled foreign partnerships, failure of a US person to report foreign bank accounts, etc.) exist. Pension and employee benefit related tax penalties exist that protect the policy reasons for the tax incentives including, most notably, early withdrawal of pension funds. Another group of specialised penalties apply to exempt organisations.

Criminal penalties exist for situations when the failures to stay within the tax system are more egregious. Although applicable to corporate taxpayers, they are applied more frequently to individuals.

In addition to the penalty provisions, interest at statutory rates generally applies to underpayments of tax.

Corporate taxes in Uruguay

For more information, contact:

Sergio Franco
PricewaterhouseCoopers
Cerrito 461
1st floor
Montevideo 11000
Uruguay
Tel: +598 2 916 0463
Email: sergio.franco@uy.pwc.com

Significant developments

Tax reform law and regulatory decrees, effective on 1 July 2007, have modified several aspects of the Uruguayan tax regime. The tax reform law eliminated 10 different taxes of limited scope and application which made up a small portion of the overall tax collection; combined three other taxes with similar characteristics; introduced an income tax on individuals and on non-residents; reduced the corporate income tax (CIT) statutory rate from 30% to 25%; and reduced the value-added tax (VAT) rate from 23% to 22%.

Additionally, the new tax legislation introduced transfer pricing rules and permanent establishment (PE) concepts following internationally accepted standards and modified the application of withholding (WHT) and capital taxes.

Also, the Uruguayan tax regime maintains certain rules and benefits such as the source principle for levying taxes (i.e., the territorial system of taxation). Accordingly, Uruguay taxes only income that is derived from activities conducted within its borders; income generated from property located in Uruguayan territory; or income derived from the economic use of rights within its territory. There also exist preferential tax regimes applicable to free zones, forestry, industrial and qualifying commercial investments.

Uruguay has concluded negotiations of double tax treaties (DTTs) (that follow the Organisation of Economic Co-operation and Development (OECD) model), with Mexico, Spain, Portugal, Switzerland, Finland, Liechtenstein, Malta, Belgium, and Korea, while recently, successfully renegotiating the DTT with Germany. In February 2010, Uruguay signed a memorandum to cooperate in the exchange of information with France, being a first step to conclude an agreement in that regard.

Taxes on corporate income

Net income derived from business activities conducted in Uruguay, obtained by legal entities resident in Uruguay and non-residents operating through a PE in Uruguay, is taxed at a rate of 25%.

In order to determine the net taxable income, all accrued expenses that are necessary for the generation of Uruguayan source income and that are duly documented are allowed as deductions. Additionally, a taxpayer will be able to deduct expenses from its gross income if such expenses are subject to taxation (either foreign or local taxation) in the hands of the other party. A compulsory proportional deduction must be calculated if the tax is at a rate that is lower than 25%.

A 12% withholding tax (with some exceptions) is imposed on Uruguayan sourced income obtained by non-residents except in cases where the income is obtained through the operations of a PE in Uruguay.

Although the Uruguayan tax law follows the source principle, technical services (defined as services rendered in the fields of management, technical administration or advice of any kind), rendered by non-residents but associated with taxable income obtained by the local user in Uruguay is considered to be Uruguayan sourced for tax purposes and, thus, subject to taxation. However, it is also stated that when the taxable income obtained by the local user of the service does not exceed 10% of its total income, then only 5% of the service fee paid or credited abroad will be subject to non-resident income tax ("Impuesto a las Rentas de los No Residentes" or IRNR). Therefore, in these cases the effective withholding rate rises to 0.6% (5% x 12%).

Corporate residence

Legal entities are deemed to be resident in Uruguay when they are incorporated according to the local legislation.

Other taxes

Value-added tax (VAT)
Uruguayan VAT is levied at a general rate of 22% on the provision of services and on the circulation of goods within the limits of the Uruguayan territory. The importation of goods and value-added in regard to the construction of immovable assets are also within the scope of this tax.

The following items are either subject to a 10% VAT rate or exempt from the tax, entirely.

- Items subject to the 10% rate:
  - Food, medicines;
  - Hotel services;
  - Health services; and
  - The first sale of immovable assets.

- Items exempt from the tax:
  - Milk;
  - Books;
  - Magazines;
  - Agriculture machinery; and
  - Accessories.

Net wealth tax (NWT)
All types of legal entities and business enterprise owners are subject to a net wealth tax at a rate of 1.5%. This tax also follows the source principle, whereby only assets located or economically used in Uruguay are taxable. Taxpayers may reduce their capital tax liability in determining the net wealth tax basis, up to their total amount of CIT for the fiscal year. Such reduction may not exceed 50% of the capital tax

U

Uruguay

amount (this regulation is still pending; in practice taxpayers deduct 1%, which was established prior to the tax reform law).

The deduction of liabilities from the amount of taxable assets to determine the net wealth tax basis, is limited to the (i) average of debt with financial institutions, (ii) debt with suppliers of goods and services, (iii) taxes not yet due, (iv) debt with governments, international credit offices of which Uruguay is a member, and with foreign state financial institutions that lend funds for long-term productive projects, or (v) debt documented in debentures and obligations if its emissions are done in a public offering and such papers are quoted in a stock exchange.

Tax of control of corporation
Upon the set up of a corporation, a tax is payable at 1.5% on a notional basis amount which is determined by a variable rate.

This tax is also due annually at the end of each fiscal year, at a rate of 0.75% of the notional amount and may be deducted from the net wealth tax.

Excise tax
In general, this tax applies on the first transaction effected in the domestic market by manufacturers or importers of goods. Exports are not taxable.

Rates vary for each item and are generally fixed by the government within maximum parameters established by law. Goods subject to the highest rates are alcoholic beverages, tobacco, gasoline, fuel, lubricants, and other petroleum products.

Tax on real estate transfer
This tax applies to the transfer of immovable assets. Transfer is defined in an ample sense, as a sale, a cessation of the right to use, a transfer of inheritance rights, etc.

Both parties to the transfer contract are subject to this tax at a rate of 2% on the property's tax valuation (generally lower than market value). When the property is transferred without payment, the beneficiary pays tax at a rate of 4% on the property tax valuation, except in instances where the property is transferred to direct heirs or legatees, who pay tax at a rate of 3%.

Branch income

This annual tax is imposed at a rate of 25% on net income derived from business activities carried out in Uruguay. A 7% withholding tax is imposed on profits remitted or credited to a home office. The dividends and/or profits paid or credited to non-resident shareholders will not be subject to withholding tax when they are paid out of non-taxable income for CIT purposes. This exemption from tax is also applicable in capital redemptions for amounts received by the non-resident over the nominal value of the corresponding shares, as this excess will be considered a dividend/profit distribution.

Uruguay

Income determination

Inventory valuation

Replacement cost is permitted, as well as the first-in, first out (FIFO), last-in, first-out (LIFO) or average cost methods, irrespective of the inventory valuation method elected for accounting purposes. Adjustments for price-level changes may not be made.

Capital gains

Capital gains are treated as ordinary income, except for capital gains on property located in rural areas, which is exempt from tax under certain conditions.

Inter-company dividends

Dividends received from the participation in local subsidiaries are exempt, while dividends received from foreign subsidiaries are beyond the scope of this tax.

Foreign income

Uruguayan legal entities and non-residents operating through a PE in Uruguay are only subject to tax on income from Uruguayan sources under the territorial system of taxation and are not subject to tax on foreign sourced income.

Income derived from activities performed, assets located or rights utilised outside Uruguay, regardless of the nationality, domicile or residence of the parties participating in the transactions and the place where the transaction agreements are subscribed, is not subject to income tax.

As a general rule, duly documented expenses, necessary to obtain and preserve gross taxable income, are tax-deductible. Conversely, those expenses associated with deriving or preserving income not subject to income tax are not deductible from the taxable base.

Other significant items

An income adjustment for inflation has been in force since 1 January 1981, calculated by multiplying the increase in the wholesalers' price index for the financial year by the difference between the following:

1. Total assets at the beginning of the year, excluding fixed assets; and
2. Total liabilities at the beginning of the year

If (1) is greater than (2), then an inflation loss adjustment is deducted from gross income. However, if (2) is greater than (1), then an inflation gain adjustment is added.

Deductions

Depreciation and depletion

Straight-line depreciation over useful life is mandatory. Straight-line rates allowed are 2% per year for urban buildings, 3% per year for rural buildings and no less than 10% per year for new vehicles. Other rates are accepted if economically justified. No conformity between book and tax depreciation is required. The excess of the sales price over the fiscal value of depreciated property, restated for inflation, is considered taxable income.

U

Uruguay

Percentages for depletion computed on the cost of natural resource properties are allowed in accordance with generally accepted criteria.

Depreciation and depletion percentages are computed on the historical cost of the fixed assets revaluated at each year-end on the basis of the increase in the wholesalers' price index. Capital gains derived from the revaluation of fixed assets are not considered taxable income.

Amortization of goodwill is not a deductible expense.

Net operating losses

Losses may be carried forward and deducted from net taxable income for the following five years, once adjusted for inflation. There are no loss carrybacks.

Payments to foreign affiliates

All accrued expenses that are necessary for the generation of Uruguayan source income and that are duly documented are allowed as deductions. Additionally, a taxpayer may deduct expenses from its gross income provided such expenses are subject to taxation (either foreign or local taxation) in the hands of the other party. A compulsory proportional deduction must be calculated if the tax is at a rate that is lower than the corporate income tax rate of 25%.

Taxes

Income and net wealth taxes are not-deductible.

Group taxation

Group taxation is not permitted.

Tax incentives

Capital investment

Please find below the main benefits granted to capital investments:

Income reinvested in fixed assets
- 40% of capital expenditures incurred on the purchase of industrial and agricultural machinery, vehicles and installations, computers, telecommunications equipment and some assets for the tourism industry are exempt.
- 20% of capital expenditures incurred in the construction and expansion of industrial, agricultural and tourism buildings are exempt from income tax (limited to 40% of net taxable income in the year of expenditure).

Fixed assets
- Movable fixed assets directly connected to the industrial cycle and equipment for data processing acquired after 1 January 1998, are exempt from the net wealth tax.

CIT exemption
- Uruguay has modified the investment law (IL), achieving a better framework for local and foreign investments carried out in the country.

- To obtain tax benefits, the IL requires that enterprises obtain a government declaration. The Bureau of Investor Assistance is in charge of monitoring the correct fulfilment of these projects.
- The IL grants two kinds of benefits:
  - Automatic – This kind of benefit is only for manufacturing, extractive or farming/ranching activities, and includes:
    - Exemption from net wealth tax for chattel property directly engaged in the production cycle and data-processing equipment; and
    - Exemption from VAT and from CIT advance on the importation of such goods and reimbursement of VAT in the case of locally purchased items.
- Discretionary – Benefits that may be obtained (not cumulative with automatic benefits):
  - Tax exemptions on importation of fixed assets items;
  - Net wealth tax exemptions, permanent for chattel property items, and for a period of eight years for construction work in Montevideo (capital city) and for a period of 10 years in the rest of the country;
  - VAT reimbursement on local purchase of goods and services for civil construction work;
  - Increased deductions for CIT in respect of fees and remunerations related to technological developments; and
  - Exemption from CIT depending on the nature and size of the project to be carried out. The executive power takes into account the following criteria to grant this benefit:
    - Addition of technology to improve competitiveness;
    - Contribution to export growth and diversification;
    - Contribution to geographic decentralisation;
    - Improvement of technological investigation, innovation and development; and
    - Generation of employment.

Auto-saving canalisation benefit
This benefit allows the company to deduct from the CIT basis, the amount of the capital increase done as a consequence of the reserves capitalisation, or of the in kind distribution of shares, for an amount equivalent to that of the investment carried out with the investor's own funds.

- CIT deduction from taxable income, arbitrarily granted by the government, when the investment is totally or partially funded with the investor's own funds.

Exports
VAT exemption on exports and VAT refund inclusion in the cost of goods and services to be exported.

Other incentives
Other incentives include the following:

Free zones
Commercial, industrial, services or investment activities conducted within or from the free zone to third countries by its users are not subject to tax. Free zone users are also exempt from all national taxes created or to be created, including those taxes for which a specific legal exemption is required, in connection with the activities performed within the free zone territory. Social security taxes as well as certain withholding taxes

U

Uruguay

are excluded from this exemption. Income tax payments of dividends made by these companies to their foreign shareholders are exempted.

Holding companies (SAFIs or "Sociedades Anónimas Financieras de Inversión")
Uruguayan corporations whose principal activity is to invest outside the country in securities, bonds, shares, commercial paper, debentures, commodities, and property or to develop commercial activities abroad are exempt from all taxes under certain conditions. They are subject only to an annual tax of 0.3% on their net worth. These entities will have to comply with the General Tax Regime before 31 December 2010 requiring that from 1 July 2007, the incorporation of new SAFIs is no longer allowed (i.e., they have to reform and adapt to the tax regime and pay taxes like other taxpayers, and will no longer obtain special tax treatment). However, ordinary corporations may be used to hold foreign participations with no effective tax burden, due to the application of the territorial system of taxation.

Trading companies
Uruguayan Corporations that sell and buy foreign goods or services from Uruguay (which are not physically introduced to the country, in the case of goods, or which are not economically used in Uruguay, in the case of services) may determine the net Uruguayan source income on a notional basis of 3% of the gross margin (difference between the selling price and the purchase price). The applicable effective CIT rate is 0.75% (25% x 3%).

Printing industry
Companies that print books and educational material are exempt from the net wealth tax and VAT.

Shipping industry
Imports of material, supplies, and equipment required for the construction, maintenance and repair of shipyards or vessels are exempt from CIT.

Income of water and air transportation companies
This income is tax exempt. In the case of foreign companies, the exemption is subject to reciprocal treatment. The government may exempt from income tax, companies engaged in transportation by land, subject also to the conditions of reciprocal treatment.

Forestry
Income derived from forestry plantations up to July 2007 is tax exempt. Income derived from new forestry plantations is also tax exempt, but under strict conditions, such as wood quality.

Software industry
50% of the income derived from the production, development, implementation, updating and correction of previous versions, amongst others, of software is exempt from CIT for fiscal years ending between 1 January 2010 and 31 December 2010. Some conditions were requirements for exemption, such as those tasks had to be directly developed by the computer support producer. Related services had to be rendered to logical support producers as well.

Industrial parks
Individuals or legal entities that establish industrial parks within Uruguayan territory, as well as companies located within such industrial parks, are entitled to CIT exemption for their industrial equipment; (e.g.,excise tax and VAT exemption on the acquisitions of such goods, amongst other benefits).

Tourism industry
Investments in the tourism industry have tax benefits related to CIT, VAT and NWT, as follows:

* Deduction of up to 40% of CIT in investments made in the fiscal year in hotel equipment and equipment for improving entertainment, moving and information services to tourists;
* Deduction of up to 20% of the CIT in investments made in construction and expansion of hotel buildings;
* VAT refund included in local acquisitions of goods and services for construction, improvement or expansion of Tourist Complexes;
* VAT exemption on import of goods for construction, improvement or expansion of Tourist Complexes;
* The list of operations included in the concept of exports of services for VAT purposes (thus zero-rated) was broadened including, among others, services related to accommodation that hotels, apartments and rural tourism establishments provide to tourists;
* NWT exemption for 10 years on investments in infrastructure and civil work for construction, improvement or expansion of Tourist Complexes;
* NWT exemption for four years on fixed assets investment for Tourist Complexes; and
* 50% exemption of import duties on materials and goods for construction, improvement or expansion as well as fixed assets of Tourist Complexes.

Withholding taxes (WHT)

As a consequence of the introduction of a tax on non-residents, from 1 July 2007, the WHT on certain payments or credit made abroad such as royalties, author rights, technical service fees and dividends/profits remittances is no longer applicable.

All Uruguayan sourced income obtained by non-residents (other than those obtained through a permanent establishment in Uruguay) is taxed at flat rates of up to 12% on gross income, with some exceptions, (i.e., interest on deposits in local currency for terms exceeding one year is taxed at 3%, interest on public bonds is taxed at 0%, dividends paid or credited by CIT taxpayers is taxed at 7%, provided they derived from taxable income), regardless of the tax treatment applicable to such income in the beneficiary country. This tax is basically collected by way of withholding.

Profits originated in the alienation of stock of CIT taxpayer companies obtained by non-residents are exempted only if such alienation is on bearer stocks. The alienation of registered stock is taxed at a rate of 12%.

Tax treaties
Uruguay signed tax treaties with Germany and Hungary several years ago. Recently, Uruguay has concluded negotiations of DTTs that follow the OECD model with Mexico, Spain, Portugal, Switzerland, Finland, Liechtenstein, Malta, Belgium and Korea, while

U

Uruguay

recently successfully renegotiating the DTT with Germany. In February 2010 Uruguay signed a memorandum to cooperate in the exchange of information with France, being a first step to conclude an agreement in that regard.

Tax administration

Returns

Most tax returns are filed on a fiscal-year basis. Some of them require more presentations before the Uruguayan Tax Office (i.e., VAT rules require filing a tax return monthly in addition to the annual return).

VAT, income and net wealth taxes are self-assessed.

Payment of tax

Income and capital taxes are paid monthly by way of advanced payments, which are calculated on the basis of the previous year's tax. The difference between the advanced tax payments and the total annual tax calculated at fiscal year-end, is paid four months after the fiscal year-end.

Corporate taxes in Uzbekistan, Republic of

For more information, contact:

Abdulkhamid Muminov
PricewaterhouseCoopers
5, 1st Proezd Kichik Mirobod Street
Yakkasaray District
Tashkent 100090
Uzbekistan
Tel: +998 71 1206 101
Email: abdulkhamid.muminov@uz.pwc.com

Significant developments

Legislation in the Republic of Uzbekistan has been constantly evolving during the period of economic transition from its pre-independence socialist economy. On 14 April 1997, Uzbekistan introduced its first consolidated tax code, which in certain cases represents a significant change from the previous laws, regulations and decrees. The code became effective on 1 January 1998. Since that time, the tax authorities have issued a number of regulations and procedures on practical implementation of provisions of that tax code.

As of 1 January 2008, a new tax code was introduced. The new tax code unified the underlying principles of taxation and obligatory payments charged in Uzbekistan and provided practical guidance on calculation and payment previously set forth by specific instructions on each tax. With the introduction of the new tax code, all prior instructions have been abolished, and the new tax code is now the primary guidance on tax related matters. The current tax code has been amended as of 1 January 2010.

The information presented in this summary is based on the current tax code with amendments and other laws, regulations and practices as of 1 April 2010.

Taxes on corporate income

The corporate income tax (CIT) rate is set annually by presidential decree. By virtue of the government's annual initiatives for the rate reduction, the CIT rate was reduced as follows:

2010 – 9%	2005 – 15%	2000 – 31%
2009 – 10%	2004 – 18%	1999 – 33%
2008 – 10%	2003 – 20%	1998 – 35%
2007 – 10%	2002 – 24%	
2006 – 12%	2001 – 26%	

In 2010, enterprises (i.e., legal entities) are subject to CIT at the rate of 9%.

Effective 1 January 2009, commercial banks are subject to CIT at the rate of 15%.

There is a local tax on accounting profit (less CIT), an "infrastructure development tax," which is charged at a maximum rate of 8%.

U

Uzbekistan, Republic of

Corporate residence

For Uzbek tax purposes, corporations are classified as resident or non-resident. A resident corporation is an Uzbek legal entity established in accordance with the Uzbek legislation.

Other taxes

Value-added tax (VAT), sales tax
Legal entities are subject to VAT, which is applied to taxable turnover and taxable imports. The rate for taxable turnover is 20%. This rate also applies to taxable imports, for which the tax base is determined as the customs value plus import duties and excise tax (on excise-liable goods). Export of goods for hard currency is generally zero-rated. Insurance and most types of financial services are exempt.

Property tax
The property tax rate in 2010 is 3.5% for legal entities. The tax is computed based on the net book value of the fixed assets adjusted for the effect of revaluation – which should be performed annually on 1 January – residual value of intangibles and value of overdue construction-in-progress. The rate is doubled for equipment not installed in due time.

Newly opened enterprises are exempt from property tax for a period of two years from their date of registration, unless such enterprises have been created on the basis of production facilities or assets of existing enterprises. There is also a rate reduction benefit available to companies engaged in production and export of goods (work, services). Property tax exemption is also available in respect to equipment financed by loan for a period of settlement of the loan not to exceed five years; leased property – for a period of the lease; and new technological equipment – for a period of up to five years.

Turnover taxes
There are three mandatory contributions equaled to taxes that are charged on the enterprise's gross annual turnover (less VAT and excise tax): 2010 road fund, generally imposed at a rate of 1.5%; pension fund imposed at a rate of 1.5%; and school development fund imposed at a rate of 0.5%.

The taxable base (and tax rate in exceptional cases) for these mandatory contributions may differ depending on the type of activity of a company.

Other taxes include a water-use tax, land tax, excise tax on produced and imported excise-liable goods and a subsurface-use tax.

Branch income

There is no "branch" concept in the Uzbek legislation. However, there is a concept of "permanent establishment" (PE) in Uzbekistan, which allows foreign legal entities to perform business activities without establishing an Uzbek company. A PE is generally subject to CIT, property tax, land and water use taxes and net profits tax. Unified social payment on employment remuneration is to be paid in the same manner as applicable for Uzbek legal entities. A PE is also a withholding agent for personal income taxes and individual pension fund contributions.

PEs of foreign legal entities are taxed on their profits from Uzbekistan activities. In 2010, PEs of foreign legal entities are subject to CIT at a standard rate of 9%. The filing deadline for the PE CIT declaration is 25 March following the reporting year. Payment is made annually and due within a month after the assessment note has been issued by the tax authorities. Effective 1 January 2008 PEs of foreign legal entities are subject to net profits tax, which is assessed at 10% on profits retained after the payment of CIT.

Income determination

Inventory valuation
Uzbek legislation permits the application of first-in, first-out (FIFO) and the average cost method for the valuation of inventory for tax purposes.

Capital gains
Capital gains arising from the disposal of tangible and intangible assets are calculated as the difference between the selling price and the net book value of an asset. The capital gain is included in taxable profits, and the capital losses are deductible (only if the disposed asset had been used for business purposes for three or more years). This provision is applicable to Uzbek legal entities and PEs of foreign legal entities duly registered with the Uzbek tax authorities. Capital gains on non-resident companies may be subject to income tax withholding to be assessed on the selling price with no deduction of the net book value.

Inter-company dividends
Dividends paid by a domestic subsidiary will be subject to 10% WHT at the source. The net dividends received by its domestic parent company will then be excluded from its CIT base. Such net dividends received by a foreign parent company would be taxed in accordance with the respective country's internal legislation or double taxation treaty (DTT) provisions (if Uzbekistan has a DTT with this country).

Foreign income
Foreign income/relief is provided for foreign taxes paid in countries with which Uzbekistan has a DTT.

Deductions

The tax base for CIT purposes varies significantly from the computation of taxable profits as in most Western jurisdictions. Expenditures such as entertaining, business trip allowances exceeding the statutory norms, management fees and certain other costs are either non-deductible or restricted to very low levels.

Effective 1 January 2010, the abovementioned expenditures are treated as deductible for calculating CIT by PEs, although there is a different set of add-back rules set out for them (e.g., interest on head office loans, royalty, etc.).

Depreciation and depletion
Fixed assets are pooled into seven groups. Depreciation for tax purposes can be charged at rates not to exceed the maximum rates set by the tax code for each group (ranging from 5% to 20%). If depreciation for accounting purposes is charged at higher rates (compared with the maximum tax code rates), the difference would be treated as a temporary difference for CIT purposes (i.e., deducted in future periods).

U

Uzbekistan, Republic of

Net operating losses
In cases where goods/services are sold below cost (or given for free), the revenue should be adjusted for tax purposes to the cost or purchase price of the goods/services. Production wastes and defects within statutory norms, and losses resulting in force-majeure circumstances are generally deductible. Losses from fixed assets disposal also may be deducted, if the fixed asset has been used for three or more years.

Tax losses
Tax losses may be carried forward for a period of five years, allowing a reduction of taxable income of the respective year by up to 50%. Loss carryback is not permitted.

Payments to foreign affiliates
Transfer pricing rules have been reintroduced in the tax code effective 1 January 2010. The tax authorities may now adjust prices used by interrelated parties in cases where these prices differ from the prices that would have been set forth by independent customers/suppliers.

Taxes
Generally, taxes are deductible for CIT purposes. The exceptions are the infrastructure development tax based on after-tax profits and the net profits tax for PEs.

Interest on short-term loans
Interest is deductible, except for interest on overdue/delayed loans and interest capitalised in the value of fixed assets (i.e., in cases where a loan was obtained to purchase fixed assets).

Group taxation

There is no provision for consolidation of income or losses by related companies for tax purposes.

Tax incentives

The current tax legislation offers certain tax incentives to encourage manufacturers, importers and exporters of strategically important products. There are tax incentives for enterprises in oil and gas exploration/development projects, production enterprises with a substantial foreign investment component, enterprises engaged in the production and export of goods for foreign currency (when export share exceeds 15%), companies rendering certain services, producers of consumer goods, etc.

There are also customs exemptions offered by the legislation for goods imported by individuals within the norms of duty-free import, technological equipment imported by foreign investors as their charter fund contribution, technological equipment imported under projects for creation of new or the modernisation of existing production facilities (with appropriate certificates issued by an authorised bank), property imported for production needs by foreign investors and enterprises with foreign investment with foreign participation in the equity not less than 33%, etc.

Withholding taxes (WHT)

General
The domestic WHT rates are as follows:

	%
Dividends and interest	10
Insurance and reinsurance payments	10
Freight	6
Royalties, services (including management, consulting services), rents, other income	20

Double taxation treaty (DTT) relief
Foreign legal entities that do not carry on activities in Uzbekistan through a PE are subject to WHT on income from sources in Uzbekistan, subject to the terms of a relevant DTT. Uzbekistan has signed DTTs with 49 countries; 44 of them are in force.

DTTs in force establish withholding rates as follows:

Received in	Dividends, %	Interest, %	Royalties, %
Austria	5 (2)/15	10	5
Azerbaijan	10	10	10
Belarus	15	10	15
Belgium	5 (2)/15	10	5
Bulgaria	10	10	10
Canada	5 (1)/15	10	5 (3, 4)/10
China	10	10	10
Czech Republic	10	5	10
Finland	5 (1)/15	5	5 (5)/10 (4)
France	5 (2)/10	0 (7,9,12)/5	0
Georgia	5 (8)/15	10	10
Germany	5 (8)/15	0 (9)/5	3 (3, 10)/5 (4)
Greece	8	0 (7)/10	8
Hungary	10	0 (15)/10	10
India	15	0 (7)/15	10
Indonesia	10	10	10
Iran	8	10	5
Israel	10	10	5 (4)/10
Italy	10	0 (9)/5	5
Japan	15	0 (7,9)/10	0 (4)/10 (3, 5, 6, 10)
Kazakhstan	10	0 (7,9)/10	10
Kuwait	5 (8)/10	0 (7,9)/8	20
Kyrgyzstan	5	5	15
Latvia	10	0 (7,9)/10	10
Lithuania	10	0 (7,9)/10	10
Luxembourg	5 (8)/15	0 (7)/10	5
Malaysia	10	0 (9)/10	10
Moldova	5 (1)/15	0 (7,9)/10	15

Uzbekistan, Republic of

Received in	Dividends, %	Interest, %	Royalties, %
(The) Netherlands	5 (8)/15	10	10
Oman	7	7	10
Pakistan	10	0 (7,14)/10	15
Poland	5 (11)/15	0 (7,9)/10	10
Romania	10	0 (14)/10	10
Russia	10	0 (7,14)/10	0
Singapore	5	5	8
Slovak Republic	10	10	10
South Korea	5 (8)/15	5	2 (10)/5
Switzerland	5 (11)/15	0 (12)/5	5
Thailand	10	0 (9)/10 (13)/15	15
Turkey	10	0 (7,9)/10	10
Turkmenistan	10	0 (7,9)/10	10
Ukraine	10	10	10
United Kingdom	5 (11)/10	5	5
Vietnam	15	0 (9,12)/10	15

Notes

1. Where the beneficial shareholder owns no less than 10% of the voting shares.
2. Where the beneficial owner holds at least 10% of the capital of the paying entity.
3. Where royalties are paid for patents, trademarks, know-how, etc.
4. Where royalties are paid for copyrights on literature, cinema, musical works, etc.
5. Where royalties are paid for secret formulas or processes or know-how.
6. Where royalties are paid for computer software, patents, designs or models or plans.
7. Where one of the following conditions is met: (a) recipient is a local authority or corporate body constituted under public law, including the central bank of the state, or interest paid by local authorities or corporate bodies; (b) interest is paid in respect to debt claims or loans, guaranteed, insured or aided by the state or on behalf of the state; (c) interest is paid in respect to credit sales of industrial, commercial, scientific equipment of goods and merchandise or provision of services by an enterprise to another enterprise; or (d) interest is paid in respect to a loan of any kind granted by a bank.
8. Where the beneficial shareholder owns no less than 25% of the capital of the paying entity.
9. Where the recipients of the interest are governments of contracting states or any governmental body (such interest is exempt from WHT).
10. Where royalties are paid in respect to uses or the rights to use industrial, commercial or scientific equipment.
11. Where the beneficial shareholder owns no less than 20% of the voting shares.
12. Where interest is paid in respect to: (a) a loan made, guaranteed or insured by the government of the other state; (b) the sale on credit of industrial, commercial, or scientific equipment; (c) the sale of merchandise by an enterprise to another enterprise; or (d) a loan of any kind granted by a bank.
13. Where the interest is received by any financial institution (including insurance companies).
14. Where interest is beneficially owned by the other contracting state or local authority or an instrumentality of such other state authority and is not subject to tax by that other state.
15. Where the recipients of the interest are governments of contracting states, National Bank of Hungary, Eximbank Hungary Pte. Ltd., Central Bank of Uzbekistan, or the National Bank of Uzbekistan for foreign economic activity (such interest is exempt from WHT).

There may be other WHT rates offered by protocols to the individual treaties.

Tax administration

Uzbek enterprises, including entities with foreign investment, are required to make advance instalments of CIT in each quarter based on estimated profits in the quarter. The instalments are payable by the fifteenth day of each month. Final quarterly payments based on actual profit figures are payable no later than the filing deadline for the quarterly tax returns (which is the twenty-fifth day of the month following the period of assessment).

U

Corporate taxes in Venezuela

For more information, contact:

Luis Fernando Miranda
Espiñeira, Sheldon y Asociados
Avenida Principal de Chuao
Edificio Del Río
Apartado 1789
Caracas 1010-A, Estado Miranda
Venezuela
Tel: +58 212 7006 124
Email: fernando.miranda@ve.pwc.com

Significant developments

There have not been significant tax or regulatory developments in the past year.

Taxes on corporate income

Corporations domiciled in the country are subject to corporate income tax on their Venezuelan and foreign source income, whereas corporations domiciled abroad with a permanent establishment (PE) in the country are levied on their Venezuelan and foreign-source income attributable to said establishment. They are able to claim any similar taxes paid abroad on foreign source income as a tax credit. Non-domiciled corporations without a PE are subject to the corporate income tax provided that the source of revenue is located in the country.

Corporate income is taxed at the following rates (Tariff 2):

Taxable income			
Over	Not over	% Rate	Subtract
Tax units 0	Tax units 2,000	15	0
Tax units 2,000	Tax units 3,000	22	TU 140
Tax units 3,000	–	34	TU 500

Tax units (TU)

The 1994 Income Tax Law reform established the concept of a taxable unit as an element that reduces the negative effects created by inflation on the determination of the tax rates. The tax code established the initial TU at Bs 1,000, with annual basis adjustments according to the variation on the consumer price index (CPI) from the previous year. During 2009 the TU was Bs 55.00 and for 2010 it is Bs 65.00.

Oil exploitation and certain related income is taxed at a flat rate of 50%. As of 2007, joint venture corporations are also subject to a 50% income tax rate instead of the general corporate income tax rate of 34%. Corporations engaged in the exploration and exploitation of non-associated gas and the processing, refining, transportation, distribution, commercialisation and exportation of the gas and its components or companies exclusively engaged in the refining of hydrocarbons or improvement of extra heavy oil are afforded additional tax considerations.

Municipal business licence tax

Companies and business entities as well as individuals and unincorporated companies are subject to municipal tax on gross income from industrial or trade activities carried on in the municipality during the fiscal year. The rates range from 0.1% to 10.0%, depending on the activity and the municipality.

Corporate residence

According to the Venezuelan tax code, the following companies are regarded as domiciled:

- Companies incorporated in Venezuela and registered with the Mercantile Registry as established by commercial law; and
- Foreign companies registered with the Superintendence of Foreign Investments (SIEX) to be domiciled in Venezuela as branches duly registered with the Mercantile Registry.

The following companies are non-domiciled but subject to Venezuelan taxes:

- Foreign companies registered with SIEX to provide technical assistance, technological services, royalty items and professional services from abroad;
- Foreign banks granting loans to local companies;
- Foreign companies leasing goods to local companies; and
- Foreign companies deriving income from economic activities carried out in Venezuela or from assets in Venezuela.

According to the Venezuela Income Tax Law (VITL), generally, a passive party is deemed to be carrying out operations in Venezuela through a PE when:

1. The passive party, in the Venezuelan territory, owns, directly or through an agent, employee or representative:
   - An office, fixed place of business or an activity centre where its activities are totally or partially carried on;
   - Management head quarters, branches, offices, factories, shops, facilities, warehouses, stores, construction, installations or assembling works, when the duration thereof exceeds six months; or
   - Agencies or representatives authorised (according to the VITL) to contract in the name of or on behalf of the passive party.

2. The passive party, in the Venezuelan territory, performs, directly or through an agent, employee or representative, professional, artistic activities.

3. The passive party, in the Venezuelan territory, possesses, directly or through an agent, employee, representative or other contracted personnel, other work places where the operations are wholly or partially performed.

Any agent acting independently shall be excluded from this definition, except if such representative has the power to conclude contracts in the name of the principal.

V

Venezuela

Other taxes

Value-added tax (VAT)

Federal VAT or (*"Impuesto al Valor Agregado" or* IVA) is a one-time tax payable by the ultimate consumer of all types of products and services. However, each business entity involved in the process, from the sale of raw materials to the production and distribution of finished products to the ultimate consumer, is required to include the tax on its products to customers (output tax) and to pay the tax on its purchases or imports of goods and services (input tax). The amount paid by the business entity is credited against the amount due on its own activities. The net amount payable by each entity represents a tax on the value added.

In general, a VAT does not represent an additional cost to a business enterprise because even though all types of business enterprises, including government departments and agencies (with some exceptions), are required to accept charges of the tax by suppliers on their purchases of goods and services, such amounts are normally deductible from the liability of the business enterprises for the tax on their respective bills to customers.

Exceptions exist, principally when the sales of an enterprise are exempt from VAT, in which case the enterprise is treated as the final consumer and must absorb any VAT charges on its purchases except insofar as its activities are subject to the zero rate. Input tax paid on goods or services used to produce items that are exempt from VAT, may be deducted for CIT purposes.

Taxable transactions

Although a number of significant exceptions are provided by law, in general, VAT is payable on all sales, rental and importation of goods, and rendering of services executed or used in the country.

Sales of goods

The law defines a sale as any transmission of tangible goods, including those made on a conditional basis or through an irrevocable trust. The taxable amount of a sale includes the sales price as well as other amounts charged to the purchaser for other taxes, duties, interest, or surcharges. VAT becomes payable at the earlier of: (1) when the goods are invoiced, (2) shipped to the customers, or (3) when the price is paid in full or in part.

Exempt sales include the following:

- Certain foods and other products for human consumption;
- Fertilisers as well as any natural gas used in the manufacturing thereof;
- Some products for animal consumption;
- Medicine;
- Products derived from hydrocarbons and some raw materials intended to improve the quality of gasoline;
- Wheelchairs;
- Books, magazines, newspapers, and the paper used in producing these products;
- Vehicles, aircraft and trains for passenger transport;
- Machinery and equipment for agribusiness; and
- Scientific equipment purchased by the government.

Services

Taxable services are those rendered within Venezuela by one person to another on an independent basis, transportation of passengers or goods, agency activities, technical assistance and transfer of technology. VAT is payable to service providers at the time the invoice is issued, the service is rendered or the fee becomes demandable, whichever comes first. The taxable amount includes the price of services, as well as charges to the customers for other taxes, interest, etc.

Exempt services include the following:

- Domestic land and maritime transportation of passengers;
- Educational services;
- Accommodations for students and persons with disabilities;
- Healthcare and dental services, surgery and hospitalisation;
- Theatres, sports and cultural events;
- Food services for employees and students;
- Certain utilities (e.g., electricity, water);
- Housecleaning;
- Transport services for hydrocarbon-derived fuels; and
- Services involving livestock, poultry and other minor species including breeding and production.

Exports

Exports are zero-rated. Consequently, VAT is not payable on exports, including exports of in-bond processing companies, technical fees to foreign residents and sales to in-bond processing companies and companies that export their entire production. Sale of natural hydrocarbon by joint ventures regulated by the Hydrocarbon Law to *Petroleos de Venezuela S.A.* (PDVSA) and affiliated companies are also taxable at 0%. Though exporters do not collect VAT on export sales, they may recover VAT charges on their purchases of goods and services by means of a refund certificate. This certificate may be used to pay other tax obligations.

Additionally, a zero rate applies to independent personal services provided by residents in Venezuela that are used solely by and for the benefit of persons abroad without a PE or fixed base in Venezuela.

Tax rates

The rate may change every year, within the range of 8% to 16.5%. Currently the general VAT rate is 12%.

An additional tax rate of 10% is applicable to sales and imports of luxury products: vehicles valued at more than USD 30,000, motorcycles with a cylinder capacity of 500 cc, nickel or token game machines, aircraft used for recreational or sport purposes, fighting bulls, trained horses, caviar, jewellery with precious stones valued at a price exceeding USD 500.

An 8% VAT applies to the following transactions:

- Goats, sheep and minor species for slaughter or breeding;
- Meats in their natural state, or refrigerated, frozen or salted meats, or meats in brine of goats, sheep and poultry;
- Shortening;

V

Venezuela

- Rendering of professional services to any government entity, in any level or branch of government, provided such services do not involve any commercial transactions but rather predominantly intellectual work or efforts; and
- Domestic air passenger transportation.

Payment and collection

Excess VAT charged or chargeable to customers over VAT paid to vendors or customs authorities – *Servicio Nacional Integrado de Administración, Aduanera y Tributaria* (SENIAT) – including the correspondent payment, must be remitted to SENIAT within the first 15 days of the following month.

VAT exoneration

Among the fiscal policy measures applicable pursuant to the conjuncture, sector and regional situation of the country's economy, the National Executive is entitled to exonerate the import and sales of goods and the rendering of services set forth in the respective decree from the payment of VAT.

Refunds/special regime for exporters

The VAT law establishes a special regime for taxpayers engaged in the export of national goods or services (goods produced or services supplied in Venezuela), provided that such operations qualify as exports in the terms set forth in the VAT law. According to this regime, taxpayers are entitled to recover the tax incurred through the purchase of goods and reception of services (input VAT) related to export activities. If such exporters carry out sales in the country, they will be entitled to recover only the input VAT related to foreign sales.

Refunds/special regime for industrial projects

The VAT law stipulates a special regime for taxpayers engaged in the execution of industrial projects, whose duration exceed six taxable periods. Pursuant to this regime, taxpayers will be able to suspend the use of input VAT generated during their operating stage, until the time they begin generating fiscal output VAT.

Taxpayers engaged in the execution of industrial projects aimed at exporting or generating foreign currency may (with prior consent of the tax authorities) choose to recover the tax incurred through the construction operations involving the project, provided that these construction operations are carried out during the pre-operating stage of such project.

Input VAT subject to recovery must be determined after computing output VAT. In other words, input VAT originated from purchasing goods and receiving services is not subject to recovery if the output VAT was not subtracted.

VAT withholding regimes

Taxpayers, qualified by the tax administration as special taxpayers, were designated as liable parties in their capacity as withholding agents in regard to payment of the VAT generated in their purchase of tangible goods or services received by providers that are regular taxpayers for VAT purposes.

Venezuela

The law on the special contribution for hydrocarbon's extraordinary international market prices

This law has been in effect since 15 April, 2008 and establishes a special contribution payable for those who export or transport liquid hydrocarbons, both natural and improved, as well as derivative products outside the country.

This law is applicable when, in regard to any given month, the average price of Brent crude exceeds USD 60 per barrel. The amount of special contribution per barrel is equivalent to 50% of the difference between the aforementioned monthly average and the threshold price (USD 60 per barrel). In addition, when the aforementioned average exceeds USD 100, 60% is to be applied to any difference between the aforementioned monthly average and said threshold price (USD 100).

This contribution is payable monthly in foreign currency to the National Development Fund (FONDEN). The amounts paid in connection to this special contribution are accounted for as costs for income tax purposes.

Gift and inheritance tax

Inter-vivos transfers, inheritances, estates and trusts are taxed individually based on their relationship with the testator/decedent. Both personal and real property located in Venezuela are subject to taxation, as well as property located abroad when transferred to individuals domiciled in Venezuela. The same tax rates and tax treatment apply to both inheritance and gifts.

The following are deemed taxable property:

- Shares, obligations and securities issued in Venezuela and abroad by companies constituted or domiciled in Venezuela;
- Securities issued abroad by foreign companies when they are owned by persons domiciled in Venezuela;
- Rights attached to assets or property in Venezuela; and
- Personal rights or obligations where the legal bases arose in Venezuela.

The tax rates on both inheritance and gifts range from 1% to 55% of the share distributed to the beneficiary or the amount of the inter-vivos gift.

Inherited shares corresponding to ascendants, descendants, spouses, adoptive parents and adopted children under 75 TU are exempt from tax. A tax credit is available for inheritance tax, varying from 5% to 40% of the tax due on each distributed share where the total tax does not exceed 250 TU, depending upon the relationship of the beneficiary or legatee with the decedent.

Donations of assets valued at less than 25 TU are not subject to tax unless the cumulative amount received from the same donor during a five-year period exceeds this amount.

Public registry tax

Commercial companies are registered with the Mercantile Registry Office and are subject to a tax levied upon incorporation of a company and the registration of capital increases. The tax is 1% of the amounts of subscribed or increased capital.

V

Venezuela

The sale of a going concern is also registered in the Mercantile Registry Office and is subject to a tax at a rate of 2%, levied upon the total amount of the sell.

Payroll taxes and other contributions
Contributions applicable to domiciled companies in Venezuela:

Contributions	Basis	Contribution basis (cap)	Employer contributions	Employee contributions	Notes
Mandatory Social Security Regime Contribution	Wages (normal or regular wages)	Up to five (5) minimum salaries for urban workers	9%, 10% or 11%	4%	(1), (2), (5)
Employment Benefit Regime Contribution	Wages (normal or regular wages)	Up to ten (10) minimum salaries for urban workers	2%	0,5%	(1)
Housing Regime Contribution	Total monthly (or integral) salary	No cap (5,6)	2%	1%	(5),
Employee Training Contribution (INCES)	Total salaries paid by the employer for purposes of the employer's contribution.	No cap	2%	0,5% (4)	(3), (4)
Workplace Prevention, Conditions and Environment Contribution (LOPCYMAT)	Total salaries paid to employees	No cap	From 0.75% to 10%	N/A	(6),(7)

Notes

The numbers in parentheses refer to the notes below:

1. As of 1 May, 2010, the minimum monthly metropolitan salary amount was increased to VEB 1,223.39.
2. According to the current system, the employer's contribution to social security will depend on the company's risk qualification (minimum risk, middle risk or maximum risk).
3. Regarding *Instituto Nacional de Capacitación y Educación Socialista* (INCES) contribution, the employer must contribute 2% of the total wages and salaries paid to employees.
4. Employers are also required to withhold 0.5% of the annual profit-sharing bonus paid to employees.
5. According to the *Ley Orgánica del Sistema de Seguridad Social* (LOSSS), generally contribution basis relevant to the new systems, may not exceed 10 minimum salaries. For social security purposes, the transition rules establish a contribution basis of five metropolitan minimum salaries for urban workers. No cap is expressly established in the transition rules for the housing system and the work, security and health regime.
6. Contributions to be made to this regime are exclusively for the employer and vary depending on the risk associated to the company. A company's risk is to be determined by the *Instituto Nacional de Prevención, Salud y Seguridad Laborales* (INPSASEL). To date, INPSASEL has not been created and employers will continue making their contributions to the Venezuela Social Security Institute.

7. *Ley Orgánica de Prevención, Condiciones y Medio Ambiente de Trabajo* (LOPCYMAT) regulations do not establish a cap for the contribution. However, as mentioned, the LOSSS establishes a maximum of the minimum urban salaries. For this reason, there are several contrary interpretations on whether a cap should be applied in this case.

Other contributions	Basis	Contribution basis (cap)	Employer contributions	Employee contributions
Science, Technology and Innovation Contribution (LOCTI) (9)	Total annual income	N/A	0.50%, 1%, 2%	N/A
Contribution against Illicit Traffic and Consumption of Narcotic and Psychotropic Substances (LOCTICSEP) (10)	Total annual income	N/A	1%	N/A

9. *Ley Orgánica de Ciencia, Tecnología e Innovación* (LOCTI).
10. *Ley Orgánica Contra el Tráfico Ilícito y el Consumo de Sustancias Estupefacientes y Psicotrópicas* (LOCTICSEP).

Customs duties

As a general rule, the importation of goods into Venezuela is subject to customs duties. These duties are generally levied on the cost, insurance and freight (CIF) value of the product being imported, excluding VAT. Custom duty rates generally range from 5% to 35%. The duty rates vary depending on the product involved. In general, import tariffs are 5% for capital goods, 10% to 15% for raw materials and intermediate goods, and 15% to 35% for finished products. In addition, all imports are subject to customs handling charges, duty imports and VAT.

Branch income

Branches of foreign corporations are subject to the same tax rules as Venezuelan corporations. Inter-branch income and deductions must be eliminated. The positive difference between a branch's annual book and fiscal income is deemed to be remitted to the branch's head office (branch profits tax). Such remittances are subject to the 34% flat dividend tax regardless of whether there is an actual payment unless the branch can provide proof of reinvestment of its profits for a five-year period. If such proof is established, no deemed remittance is assumed. A Venezuelan taxpayer has to recognise, annually on an accrual basis, income generated in a company or other legal entity it controls which is located in a jurisdiction with low fiscal taxation (JLFT). Further, investments in JLFT must be declared to the SENIAT.

Income determination

Inventory valuation

Inventories may be valued at cost or the lower of cost or market value. Any method generally accepted for accounting purposes can be accepted for tax purposes.

Venezuela

Capital gains

Capital gains are taxable as ordinary income, and capital losses are deductible from ordinary income. Capital losses resulting from the sale of stock, capital reduction or liquidation of a company are deductible under the following conditions:

- The cost of the capital stock was not in excess of the price quoted on a stock exchange or an amount with a reasonable relationship to the book value of the capital stock;
- The holding period of the investment was for at least two years immediately preceding the date of the sale; or
- The stockholder proves that the company selling the shares carried on economic activities for at least two years, preceding the date of sale.

At present, the tax law contains two different rulings relevant to the deductibility of losses incurred through operations on the Venezuelan Stock Market; one of which has been described, above. The second ruling pertains to income obtained from operations on the local market. This income is subject to a final 1% tax that is withheld at the source. Losses in this kind of operation are not deductible against other income (*see above for additional considerations*). Corporate shareholders not domiciled in Venezuela may not deduct such losses from other taxable income other than dividends arising from Venezuelan sources.

Gains upon liquidation or reduction of capital are taxable to the liquidating entity.

A dividend tax is levied at a flat rate of 34% on the positive difference between book income and tax income generated after 2000. Book income is understood to be that approved at a shareholders' meeting and based on the financial statements prepared pursuant to generally accepted accounting principles. To determine the applicable difference, a last-in, first-out (LIFO) method applies. The 34% (domestic) rate can be mitigated under tax treaties to 10%, 5% or even 0%. Withholding is to be made at the moment a dividend is declared or credited to the account a recipient.

Dividends obtained from companies incorporated or domiciled abroad or incorporated abroad and domiciled in Venezuela are taxed at a flat 34% rate.

Foreign income

Beginning 1 January, 2001, extraterritorial income is subject to Venezuelan income tax. The broadening of the territoriality regime is based on the concept of worldwide income taxation, according to which:

- Domiciled companies must pay a tax on total income whether from national or foreign source;
- Companies domiciled abroad with PE in the country will pay tax on their income, whether of national or foreign source, attributable to the Venezuelan PE;
- Non-domiciled companies will pay taxes on their income originated or caused in Venezuela; and
- Domiciled companies as well as companies domiciled abroad with PE in Venezuela may credit the tax paid abroad for earnings of extraterritorial source against the income tax payable in Venezuela, subject to limitations.

Foreign technical assistance and services

Taxable income of foreign taxpayers providing technical assistance or technological services from abroad to individuals or entities that use them in Venezuela or assign them to third parties is presumed to be 30% of gross income for technical assistance fees and 50% of gross income for technological service fees. If the contract does not specify the proportion in which the services are rendered, the law provides that 60% of the technical assistance and technological service fees are deemed to be rendered abroad (i.e., foreign-source) with the other 40% deemed to rendered in Venezuela. The law also provides that 75% of the entire income related to technological services and 25% of that related to technological assistance is rendered abroad if not otherwise specified in the contract. *(See also Withholding taxes).*

International fiscal transparency

A regime of international fiscal transparency is created for the purpose of establishing special standards of fiscal control, governing capital investments in countries classified as JLFT, or tax havens. Under certain conditions a Venezuelan taxpayer may be required to recognise income generated in its JLFT subsidiary on an accrual basis in its tax return.

Stock dividends

Beginning 1 January, 2001, dividends of stock will be subject to payment of the aforementioned tax dividend. Moreover, as of 1 January, 2002, stock dividends will be subject to an advanced payment of dividend tax equivalent to 1% of the dividend distributed. Stock dividends will have no cost for tax purposes.

Transfer pricing

Taxpayers that carry out operations with related parties abroad must calculate their income, costs and deductions by applying a defined methodology of transfer pricing. This regime is applicable to imports, exports and interest paid to recipients abroad as well as technical assistance, technological services and royalty fees. With the amendment of the 2007 income tax law, Venezuela introduced thin capitalisation rules that limit the deduction of interest from debt with related parties in excess of a 1:1 debt-to-equity ratio. Under these rules, if the average of a taxpayer's debt (with related and unrelated parties) exceeds the average amount of its equity for the respective fiscal year, the excess debt is treated as equity for income tax purposes. Consequently, the ability to deduct interest on related-party loans may be affected.

Inflation adjustment

A system for the adjustment of non-monetary assets, non-monetary liabilities and shareholder's equity has been established. "Non-monetary assets" include land, construction, machinery, vehicles, installations, inventories, and investments other than in securities (e.g., bonds and stocks). There are two phases to the adjustments: (1) initial adjustments and (2) annual adjustments. Both phases are mandatory adjustments for taxpayers engaged in commercial, industrial, financial, and insurance operations and in the exploitation of mines and hydrocarbons. The annual adjustment is optional for taxpayers performing non business activities.

Initial adjustment

The initial adjustment on depreciable fixed assets requires a registration tax of 3% on the amount of the adjustment.

V

Venezuela

The initial adjustment must be filed at the closing date of any fiscal year ending after 1 January, 1993. This adjustment is applicable to all non-monetary assets and non-monetary liabilities.

The initial adjustment is calculated by applying the variations between the CPI of the Caracas Metropolitan Area prevailing in the month in which the non-monetary assets were acquired and the month corresponding to the initial adjustment. Assets acquired before 1950 are deemed to have been acquired in January 1950.

A registry tax of 3% is applied exclusively to the initial revaluation adjustment of depreciable fixed assets. For payment, taxpayers must be registered with the Asset Revaluation Registry, maintained by the tax administration. The resulting tax may be paid in three consecutive annual instalments, beginning on the date of registration.

Companies in the pre-operating stage, deemed to end with the first invoice must determine and pay a 3% tax once the pre-operating period has ended.

Depreciation or amortisation (*see below*) on the revaluation adjustment is allowed, based on the original estimated life of the asset.

Annual adjustment
The annual adjustment is applied each year in determining the taxable income. This adjustment, effective as of 1 January 1993, applies to fiscal periods beginning after that date. The adjustment factor must be applied to the following balance sheet items at the closing date of the fiscal year. The resulting adjustment will increase or decrease taxable income.

Balance sheet items	Adjustment factor	Tax effect
Non-monetary assets:		
Inventories (including inventories in transit) (2)	Annual variation of the CPI	Increase taxable income
Fixed assets (3)	Annual variation of the CPI	Increase taxable income
Other assets, trademarks, patents, production licenses, other rights, and investments in stock not registered in the Comision Nacional de Valores (CNV) and deferred charges (except interest).	Annual variation of the CPI	Increase taxable income
Investments in shares registered in the CNV	Adjusted to the share market value at the end of the year	Increase taxable income
Non-monetary liabilities:		
Deferred credits (except interest)	Annual variation of the CPI	Decrease taxable income
Equity:		
Tax initial equity (1)	Annual variation of the CPI	Decrease taxable income

Notes

The numbers in parentheses refer to the notes below:

1. Tax initial equity is defined as the difference between assets and liabilities at the beginning of the tax year, less accounts receivable from administrators, affiliated and related companies. In order to determine the initial tax equity, assets not located in the country as well as goods, debts and liabilities entirely applied to the production of deemed, exempt or exonerated income, are excluded.
2. Inventories are to be valued at historical cost for purposes of applying the CPI. The provisions of the income tax law detail the procedures for applying the CPI. The revaluation of inventories in the tax year is included as part of the initial inventories of the following year.
3. The annual revaluation adjustment of fixed assets is considered part of the cost when the assets are sold.

Net losses arising from the annual adjustment that have not been offset, may be carried forward only to the next tax period (one year).

Gains or losses, originating from the adjustment of accounts receivable or investments, as well as debts and liabilities in foreign currency or with a readjustability clause, are deemed to be carried out during the fiscal year in which they become demandable, collected or paid, whichever comes first.

Deductions

Depreciation and depletion
Depreciation is generally computed on a straight-line basis although any other generally accepted method for accounting purposes is also accepted. Depreciation is not allowed on real estate used as rental property. Depreciation on the stepped-up portion of assets revalued by any method other than the inflation adjustments noted above is not permitted.

Net operating losses
Losses may be carried forward three years. Loss may not be carried back. As previously stated, losses from inflation adjustment may be carried forward only one year.

Foreign losses may be offset only against foreign profits.

Payments to foreign affiliates
A Venezuelan corporation may claim a deduction for royalties and technical assistance and for technical service fees paid to foreign affiliates, subject to the following conditions:

* The contract is registered within 60 days of execution with the Superintendence of Foreign Investments (SIEX);
* Income tax payable by the recipient is withheld at the source;
* Transfer pricing requirements are met; or
* In the case of technical assistance and technological services fees, the expenses maybe deducted if such services cannot be otherwise provided in Venezuela.

Foreign companies domiciled in Venezuela are allowed to deduct royalties paid to parent companies or foreign affiliates. Companies must notify the SIEX of payments

V

Venezuela

made within 60 days *(See also the section on Withholding taxes)*. Branches of foreign companies, however, may not deduct such payments to head offices or related parties.

Taxes

Municipal, state and local taxes are deductible in determining taxable income. Corporate taxes are not deductible.

Other significant items

Deductions for allowable charitable contributions are limited to 10% of taxable income (before deducting contributions) when taxable income does not exceed TU 10,000. When taxable income exceeds TU 10,000, charitable contributions are limited to 8% of taxable income. For oil extraction companies the deduction is limited to 1% of the pre-contribution tax amount.

Payments required by the labour law, such as profit sharing (generally between 15 days' and four months' salary) and severance indemnity accruals are also deductible. In cases of unjustified dismissals, double severance indemnities must be paid. However, accruals for such additional indemnities are generally not deductible until paid.

Group taxation

Group taxation is no longer possible.

Tax incentives

Capital investment

A tax reduction of 10% is available for investments in assets, programmes and activities aimed at the conservation and protection of the environment.

A special 10% investment tax credit is granted on the value of new investments in fixed assets (excluding land) made by those legal entities obtaining income from industrial and agro-industrial activities, construction, electricity, telecommunications, science, technology, and generally any industrial activity that represents an investment in advanced technology. This tax credit may be taken if such new investments are dedicated to effectively improving the productive capacity or creating a new enterprise.

The tourist sector will be entitled to a 75% investment tax credit on the amount of new investments. The agricultural sector will enjoy an 80% investment tax credit.

An additional 10% tax credit is granted on the amount of investments in assets, programmes, and activities aimed at the preservation and protection of the natural environment, the recovery of hydrocarbon and gas exploration and exploitation areas carried out in a production unit's areas of influence.

Investment tax reductions may be carried forward up to three years.

Other incentives

Some customs duty incentives are available, such as drawbacks on the import of materials used for exporting products. This may take the form of a tax refund certificate issued by the Ministry of Finance. The certificate is a negotiable bond and will be accepted by the Treasury Funds Office for payment of national taxes. Determination of the amount of the refund will take into account the import duties effectively paid at the time the materials used in the manufacture of the exported product were received in Venezuela.

Withholding taxes (WHT)

Resident corporations making certain types of payments must withhold taxes. T2 refers to Tariff 2. These include the following:

	Resident (1)		Non-resident	
	Corporation	Individual	Corporation	Individual
	%	%	%	%
Commissions (2)	5	3	5	34
Royalties (3)	5	3	T2 on 90	34 on 90
Interest to foreign financial institutions	N/A	N/A	4.95	N/A
Other interest	5	3	T2 on 95	34 on 95
Professional fees	5	3	T2 on 90	34 on 90
Technical assistance fees (3)	5	3	T2 on 30	34 on 30
Technological service fees (3)	5	3	T2 on 50	34 on 50
Real estate rentals	5	3	5	34
Tangible personal property rentals	5	3	5	34
Contractor and subcontractor services	2	1	T2	34
Film and TV exhibition rights	5	3	T2 on 25	34 on 25
Insurance and reinsurance premiums	N/A	N/A	10 on 30	N/A
Payments to international media organisations	5	3	T2 on 15	N/A
Acquisition of Venezuela commercial funds	5	3	5	34
Payments to non-domiciled international transportation companies (4)	N/A	N/A	T2 on 5	N/A

Notes

1. Withholding taxes constitute prepayments against final tax liabilities as determined by the income tax return when filed.
2. Includes commissions earned in instances other than through a dependent relationship (e.g., employer/employee). Commissions are subject to withholdings in the same manner as salaries and wages.

V

Venezuela

3. The rates for non-residents are similar to those rates applicable for payments to a non-domiciled corporation not resident in a treaty country and rendering services from abroad with no PE in Venezuela.
4. Excludes payments exempted under international shipping agreements.

Tax treaties

There are currently comprehensive treaties for the avoidance of double taxation with the following countries:

Austria	Germany	Portugal
Barbados	Indonesia	Qatar
Belgium	Iran	Russia
Belarus	Italy	Spain
Czech Republic	Korea	Sweden
Canada	Kuwait	Switzerland
China	Malaysia	Trinidad y Tobago
Cuba	Mexico	United Kingdom
Denmark	Netherlands	United States
France	Norway	

Treaties with other countries outside the countries listed above are being negotiated.

The treaties with Brazil, Mexico and Vietnam have been published in the Official Gazette and signed by the contracting parties but have not entered into force since diplomatic notes have not been exchanged.

Tax administration

Returns
Final tax returns must be filed within three months following the end of the tax year. The system is one of self-assessment.

Payment of tax
The total amount of tax due must be paid at the time of filing the annual return. Estimated tax payments must be paid consecutively in six monthly instalments. Companies engaged in mining, hydrocarbon exploitation and related activities must make 12 equal monthly estimated tax payments.

Exchange control
On January 2003 the Venezuelan government and the Venezuelan Central Bank restricted the free foreign currency trade and established an Exchange Control Regime, which is characterised by the following aspects:

The Venezuelan Central Bank (VCB) centralises the purchase and sales of foreign currency.

All foreign currency derived from the export of goods, services, and technology must be sold to the VCB, through the financial system and at the official exchange rate. Exporters are to be registered with the Users Registry and are to consign certain documentation certifying good fiscal status. Likewise, the sale of every foreign currency, introduced in the country for various concepts, including direct foreign investment, to the VCB is mandatory. In such case, said foreign currency is to be registered with the SIEX for re-exportation and remittance purposes. The acquisition of foreign currency for imports is also subject to application for "Foreign Currency Authorisation," which is subject to certain conditions.

The Law on Foreign Exchange Crimes is in effect, thereby establishing the actions that constitute exchange crimes and their respective penalties. Said penalties may be both criminal and pecuniary.

Corporate tax calculation

Taxable income (manufacturing company)	VEB	260,000.00
Divided by the value of the TU (Bs 65,00/1 TU)	VEB	65
Taxable income in TU	TU	4,000.00
Tax thereon:		
Tariff 2-34%	TU	1, 360.60
Subtract (per tax table)	TU	(500)
Total Tax	TU	860.00
Less- Withholding taxes	TU	(100)
Less- Advance payments	TU	(100)
Net income tax payable in TU	TU	660.00
Net Income tax payable in VEF*	VEB	42,900.00

Note

* Multiplied by the TU value, (i.e., VEB 65/1TU).

Corporate taxes in Vietnam

For more information, contact:

David Fitzgerald
PricewaterhouseCoopers Vietnam Co., Ltd.
Saigon Tower, 4th Floor
29 Le Duan Boulevard, District 1
Ho Chi Minh City, Vietnam
Tel: +84 8 3823 0796
Email: david.fitzgerald@vn.pwc.com

Significant developments

There were no significant developments in the corporate income tax (CIT) regulations
from November 2009 to May 2010.

Taxes on corporate income

Standard rates
All taxes are imposed at the national level. There are no local, state or provincial taxes.
The standard CIT rate is 25%. Enterprises operating in the oil and gas industry will be
subject to CIT rates ranging from 32% to 50% depending on each project.

Preferential rates
Preferential CIT rates of 10% and 20% are available where certain criteria are met. *See
Tax incentives for further information.*

Calculation of taxable profits
Taxable profit is the difference between total revenue, whether domestic or foreign
sourced, and deductible expenses, plus other assessable income.

Taxpayers are required to prepare an annual CIT return which includes a section for
making adjustments between accounting profits and taxable profits.

Corporate residence

Enterprises established under the law of Vietnam are subject to corporate taxes. In
addition, Vietnam has a broadly worded permanent establishment (PE) definition.

Other taxes

Value-added tax (VAT)
VAT is applied to goods and services used for production, trading and consumption
in Vietnam (including goods and services purchased from abroad), with certain
exemptions. Depending on the category of goods or services, the VAT rates are 0%,
5%, and 10% (the standard rate). Exported goods and services are subject to 0% rate
(subject to conditions).

Special sales tax (SST)
SST is a form of excise tax that applies to selected goods and services, such as alcohol,
imported automobiles having less than 24 seats, motorcycles, airplanes, boats,
petroleum, air-conditioners up to 90,000 BTU, cigarettes, playing cards, discotheques,

massages, karaoke, casinos, gambling, golf clubs, and entertainment with betting and lotteries. For goods, SST is charged at the production or importation stage. Rates range from 10% to 70%.

Production royalties

Production royalties in the form of a natural resource tax (NRT) are payable in industries exploiting natural resources such as oil and gas, other minerals, forests, fisheries, and importantly, natural water. The tax rates vary depending on the natural resource being exploited, ranging from 1% to 40% and are applied to the production output at a specified taxable value per unit. Various methods are available for the calculation of the taxable value of the resources, including cases where the commercial value of the resources cannot be determined.

Property taxes

The rental of land use rights by foreign investors (if not contributed as capital) is in effect a form of property tax. It is usually known as land rental and the range of rates is wide depending upon the location, infrastructure and the industrial sector in which the business is operating.

Customs duties

Import duty rates are classified into three categories: ordinary rates, preferential rates and special preferential rates. Preferential rates are applicable to imported goods from countries that have most-favoured-nation status with Vietnam (MFN, also known as normal trade relations). The MFN rates are in accordance with Vietnam's World Trade Organization (WTO) commitments and are applicable to goods imported from other member countries of the WTO.

Special preferential rates are applicable to imported goods from countries that have a special preferential trade agreement with Vietnam.

Import duty exemptions are provided for encouraged projects and goods imported in certain circumstances.

Export duties are charged only on a few items, basically certain natural resources. Rates range from 0% to 33%.

Branch income

Branches of foreign entities are subject to the same CIT regime for entities incorporated in Vietnam.

Income determination

Inventory valuation

At present there are no provisions for valuing inventories or determining inventory flows. The tax treatment follows the accounting treatment.

Asset revaluation

Gains from the revaluation of assets (including land use rights with definite term) for the purposes of capital contribution or transfer upon division, demerger, consolidation, merger, conversion of business are subject to CIT at the 25% standard rate.

V

Vietnam

Gains from the revaluation of land use rights with indefinite terms for the purpose of capital contribution or transfer upon division, demerger, consolidation, merger, conversion of business will not be taxed on the basis that the enterprise receiving the land use rights is not allowed to amortise the land use rights. However the enterprise receiving the land use rights shall be taxed if it subsequently revalued the land use rights before contributing the land use rights as capital/transferring to another enterprise.

Gains from the revaluation of land use rights for the purpose of capital contribution to investment projects for construction of houses and infrastructure facilities for sale shall be fully taxed in the year of contribution.

Capital gains

Gains made by a foreign investor on a transfer of an interest in a limited liability company are subject to 25% CIT. The assignee is required to withhold the tax due from the payment to the assignor, and account for this to the tax authorities.

Gains earned by a foreign investor from selling shares in a public joint-stock company irrespective of whether it is listed or non-listed is subject to CIT at a deemed rate of 0.1% of the sales proceeds. However, it is unclear if the same treatment applies to selling shares in a non-public joint-stock company.

Inter-company dividends

Inter-company dividends are generally non-taxable. No withholding tax applies to dividend payments.

Foreign income

Foreign income, under the domestic tax law, is subject to 25% CIT with tax credits available.

Stock dividends

Dividends received from investments in other companies in Vietnam are from after tax profits and are not taxed currently.

Other income

The following other income is subject to 25% CIT and will not be entitled to tax incentives (including preferential tax rate and exemption/reduction):

* Income from transfer of real estate;
* Income from royalty, leasing of assets;
* Income from transfer of assets;
* Interest income;
* Income from trading of foreign currency;
* Reversal of provisions;
* Collected written off debts;
* Unidentified payables;
* Difference between penalties and compensation for breaching economic contracts; and
* Gain from the revaluation of assets .

Deductions

Depreciation and depletion

Tax depreciation may differ from accounting depreciation. Depreciation in excess of the rates specified in the regulations on tax depreciation is not deductible. These regulations specify maximum and minimum permissible effective lives for various classes of assets, including intangibles. Current straight-line tax depreciation rates are as follows:

Depreciation rates	%
Buildings	2 – 16.67
Office equipment	10 – 20
Automobiles	3.33 – 16.66
Machinery and equipment	5 – 33.33

Net operating losses

Losses may be carried forward for five years. Carryback of losses is not permitted.

Payments to foreign affiliates

There are no special restrictions on the deductibility of royalties, loan interest and service fees paid to foreign affiliates (except for those paid by branches). However the payment must be at arm's length as required by transfer pricing regulations. Certain contracts for the transfer of technology and foreign loans must be registered with the competent authorities.

Taxes

Creditable input VAT, CIT, and other fees/charges are not deductible for CIT purposes.

Other significant items

The following are specifically stated to be non-deductible:

- Depreciation of fixed assets which is not in accordance with the prevailing regulations;
- Employee remuneration expenses which are not actually paid or are not stated in a labour contract or collective labour agreement;
- Life insurance premiums for employees;
- Interest on loans corresponding to the portion of charter capital not yet contributed;
- Reserves for research and development not in accordance with the prevailing regulations;
- Interest on loans from non-economic and non-credit organisations exceeding 1.5 times the interest rate set by the State Bank of Vietnam;
- Provisions for stock devaluation, bad debts, financial investment losses, product warranties, or construction work which are not in accordance with the prevailing regulations;
- Advertising, promotion (except certain items), conferences/parties, commissions, prompt payment discounts exceeding 10% of total other deductible expenses (this cap is increased to 15% for newly-established enterprises for the first three operating years);
- Unrealised foreign exchange gain/losses due to the revaluation of foreign currency items other than account payables at the end of a financial year;

V

Vietnam

- Donations except certain donations for education, health care, natural disasters, or building charitable homes for the poor;
- Management expenses allocated to permanent establishments in Vietnam by the foreign company's head office which are not in accordance with the regulations;
- Penalties;
- Creditable input value-added tax, business income tax, personal income tax and other fees/charges.
- For certain businesses such as insurance companies, securities trading, and lotteries, the Ministry of Finance provides specific guidance on deductible expenses for CIT purposes.

Group taxation

There is no provision for any form of consolidated filing or group loss relief.

Tax incentives

Inward investment
Tax incentives are granted based on regulated encouraged sectors and difficult socio-economic locations. The sectors which are encouraged by the Vietnamese Government include education, health care, sport/culture, high technology, environmental protection, scientific research, infrastructural development and computer software manufacture.

The two preferential rates of 10% and 20% are available for 15 years and 10 years respectively, starting from the commencement of operating activities. When the preferential rate expires, the CIT rate reverts to the standard rate.

Investors may be considered for tax holidays and reductions. The holidays take the form of a complete exemption from CIT for a certain period beginning immediately after the enterprise first makes profits, followed by a further period where tax is charged at 50% of the applicable rate. However, where the enterprise has not derived profits within three years of the commencement of operations, the tax holidays/tax reduction will start from the fourth year of operation. Criteria for eligibility to these holidays and reductions are set out in the CIT regulations.

Additional tax reductions may be available for engaging in manufacturing, construction, and transportation activities which employ several female staff, and/or ethnic minorities.

Small- and medium-size enterprises (as regulated) and certain other certain eligible enterprises can enjoy a three month deferral of 2010 CIT payments.

Withholding taxes (WHT)

Interest
An interest WHT of 10% applies to payments to an overseas lender. Offshore loans provided by certain government or semi-governmental institutions may obtain an exemption from the interest withholding tax where a relevant double taxation agreement or Inter-Government Agreement applies.

Royalties, license fees, etc.
A 10% royalty withholding tax applies in the case of payments made to a foreign party for transfers of technology, unless the transfers are contributed as part of legal capital (akin to equity). Transfers of technology are defined very broadly. Certain contracts for the transfer of technology must be registered with the competent authorities.

Management fees, etc.
Withholding tax applies on management fees and head office charges.

Payments to foreign contractors
A withholding tax on payments to foreign contractors applies where a Vietnamese contracting party (including a foreign-invested enterprise incorporated in Vietnam) contracts with a foreign party that does not have a licensed presence in Vietnam irrespective of whether the services are provided in Vietnam or overseas.

Foreign contractors can apply to be deduction-method VAT payers if they adopt the Vietnamese accounting system. If accounting records are adequate, the foreign contractor will pay CIT on actual profits, but otherwise on a deemed-profit basis.

For direct (non-deduction-method) foreign contractors, VAT and CIT will be withheld by the contracting party at a deemed percentage of taxable turnover. Various rates are specified according to the nature of the contract performed. For CIT the withholding tax rate varies from 0.1% to 10%. For VAT, the effective withholding tax rate can also range from 3% to 5%. The VAT withheld by the contracting party is an allowable input credit in its VAT return.

A summary of VAT and CIT rates follow:

Types of income	Effective VAT rate	Deemed CIT rate
	%	%
Trading: distribution, supply of goods, materials, machinery and equipment in Vietnam.	Exempt (*)	1%
Services	5%	5%
Services together with provision of goods	3%	2%
Construction, installation without supply of materials or machinery, equipment.	5%	2%
Construction, installation with supply of materials or machinery, equipment.	3%	2%
Leasing of machinery and equipment	5%	5%
Leasing of aircraft, vessels (including components)	Not specified	2%
Transportation	3%	2%
Interest	Exempt	10%
Royalties	Exempt	10%
Insurance	Exempt	2%
Transfer of securities	Exempt	0.1%
Manufacturing, other business activities	3%	2%

Notes

(*) On the basis import VAT is paid.

Vietnam

Cross-border leases

A Vietnam-based lessee is required to withhold tax from payments to an offshore lessor.

The above deemed CIT rates may be affected by a relevant double tax agreement.

Recipient	Interest	Royalties	Notes
	%	%	
1. Algeria (*)	-	-	-
2. Australia	10	10	-
3. Austria (*)	10	7.5/10	1, 3
4. Bangladesh	15	15	1,2
5. Belarus	10	15	1, 2
6. Belgium	10	5/10/15	1, 2, 3
7. Brunei Darussalam	10	10	1,2
8. Bulgaria	10	15	1, 2
9. Canada	10	7.5/10	3
10. China	10	10	2
11. Cuba	10	10	-
12. Czech Republic	10	10	2
13. Denmark	10	5/15	1, 2, 3
14. Egypt (*)	-	-	-
15. France	Nil	10	-
16. Finland	10	10	-
17. Germany	10	7.5/10	2, 3
18. Hong Kong	10	7/10	2,3
19. Hungary	10	10	-
20. Iceland	10	10	2
21. India	10	10	2
22. Indonesia	15	15	1, 2
23. Israel	10	5/7.5/15	1, 2, 3
24. Italy	10	7.5/10	2, 3
25. Ireland	10	5/10/15	2
26. Japan	10	10	1, 2, 3
27. Korea (South)	10	5/15	-
28. Korea (North)	10	10	1, 2
29. Kuwait (*)	-	-	-
30. Laos	10	10	-
31. Luxembourg	10	10	2
32. Malaysia	10	10	2
33. Mongolia	10	10	2
34. Morocco (*)	-	-	-
35. Myanmar	10	10	1, 2, 3
36. Netherlands	10	5/10/15	2
37. Norway	10	10	1, 2
38. Oman	10	10	1, 2
39. Pakistan	15	15	1

Recipient	Interest	Royalties	Notes
	%	%	
40. Philippines	15	15	1, 3
41. Poland	10	10/15	1, 2
42. Qatar (*)	-	-	-
43. Romania	10	15	1
44. Russia	10	15	-
45. Seychelles	10	10	1, 2, 3
46. Singapore	10	5/15	2
47. Slovakia	-	-	-
48. Spain	10	10	1,2
49. Sri Lanka	10	15	1,2,3
50. Sweden	10	5/15	2
51. Switzerland	10	10	1
52. Taiwan	10	15	1,2
53. Thailand	10/15	15	2
54. UAE (*)	-	-	-
55. Ukraine	10	10	2
56. United Kingdom	10	10	1,2
57. Uzbekistan	10	15	-
58. Venezuela	-	-	-

Notes

(*) Not in force.

1. In some cases the limits set by the treaty are not lower than the present withholding rate under domestic law. Therefore, the domestic rates will apply.
2. Interest derived by certain government bodies is exempt from withholding tax.
3. Royalty withholding tax rates vary for certain types of royalties.

Tax administration

Audit cycle
Tax audits are carried out regularly and often cover a number of tax years. Prior to an audit, the tax authorities send the taxpayer a written notice of time and scope of the audit inspection.

Statute of limitations
The general statute of limitations for imposing tax administration penalties is five years. The tax authorities can collect under declared and unpaid tax at any time.

There are detailed regulations setting out penalties for various tax offences. These range from relatively minor administrative penalties through to tax penalties amounting to various multiples of the additional tax assessed.

In practice, imposition of penalties has been arbitrary and inconsistent. However in recent periods, there has been a much tougher stance adopted by the tax authorities. Hence where tax is paid late, as a result for example of a tax audit investigation, there is a significant likelihood of penalties being imposed. Notably where tax adjustments

V

Vietnam

are made at a tax audit, any resulting additional taxable profits are not eligible for any CIT incentives to which a company may be entitled.

VAT returns and payments

Taxpayers must file monthly VAT returns and remit the VAT payable no later than the twentieth day of the following month.

CIT returns and payments

CIT shall be declared and paid provisionally on a quarterly basis (based on actual revenues and expenses of each quarter). Quarterly CIT returns and payment must be made no later than the thirtieth day of the next quarter. Annual finalisation return and the audited financial statements must be filed within 90 days of the end of the financial year.

The standard tax year is the calendar year. However, different accounting year-ends can be used if approval is obtained from the authorities.

Corporation tax calculation

Fiscal year ending 31 December 2009 (in VND millions)

Net income before taxes	3,360	
Add:		
Fines		50
Expenses without supporting documentation		100
Advertising, promotion and marketing expenditure in excess of limit		200
	350	
	3,710	
Deduct: Loss carried over from previous years	(450)	
Taxable income	3,260	
Tax at 25%	815	

Other issues

Foreign investment restrictions

In several fields, foreign investment will not be licensed or only licensed under special conditions. For sectors in the List of Conditional Investment Sectors, the investment is subject to certain conditions, which include: television, production and publishing cultural products, telecommunication, transportation by all means, cigarette production, exploring and processing natural resources, real-estate business, education, medical services and distribution.

Exchange controls

All buying, selling, lending and transfer of foreign currency need to be made through credit institutions and other financial institutions authorised by the State Bank of Vietnam (SBV).

Outflow of foreign currency by transfer is authorised for certain transactions such as payments for imports and services abroad, refund of loans contracted abroad and payment of interest accrued thereon, transfer of profits and dividends, and revenues from transfer of technology.

All monetary transactions in Vietnam must be undertaken in Vietnamese Dong. Exceptions are applicable to payments for exports made between principals and their agents, and payments for goods and services purchased from institutions authorised to receive foreign currency payments such as for air tickets, shipping and air freight, insurance and international communications.

Forms of doing business

According to the Law on Enterprises, a foreign-invested enterprise may be established as either a single member limited liability or a limited liability with more than one member, a joint-stock company, or a partnership.

Intellectual property

Intellectual property rights are protected by the Civil Code (1995 and 2005), the Law on Intellectual Property (2005) and a host of subordinate legislation.

Vietnam is signatory to the Paris Convention, the Madrid Agreement on International Trademark Registration, and the Patent Cooperation Treaty and is a member of the World Intellectual Property Organisation. Vietnam has entered into an agreement on copy rights with the US. According to the Vietnam- US Bilateral Trade Agreement, Vietnam is further under the obligation to adhere to Berne Convention.

V

For more information, contact:

Manuel Lopes
PricewaterhouseCoopers
Arundel Office Park, Building 4
Norfolk Road
Mount Pleasant
Harare
Zimbabwe
Tel: +263 4 33 8362-8
Email: manuel.lopes@zw.pwc.com

Significant developments

Zimbabwe's annual budget presentation was held on 2 December 2009 by the Minister of Finance, the Honorable Tendai Biti, and the proposed changes have been promulgated into law.

The announcements relating to corporate tax can be summarised as follows:

Value-added-tax (VAT)

It was recommended that all registered operators will have to use electronic tax registers (ETRs) that can be linked to the Zimbabwe Revenue Authority (ZIMRA) beginning 1 April 2010. A notice has since been published by ZIMRA that operators should not undertake the requirement pending further instructions.

Each company or person will have one VAT number only. Presently, the law allows companies or persons to separately register divisions or branches.

The basis for calculating VAT on imports is altered to impose the tax on the value inclusive of customs duty.

Un-beneficiated chrome exports are subject to the standard rate of VAT (15%) beginning 1 January 2010. These were previously zero-rated.

Income tax

The corporate tax rate for companies (other than mining companies with special mining leases, but including branches) was reduced from an effective rate (including a 3% AIDS levy) of 30.9% to 25.75% (which include a base rate of 25% plus a 3% AIDS levy).

Capital allowances are granted on qualifying additions to fixed assets in four equal annual amounts at a rate of 25% (over four years). This was previously allowed over three years (at 50% in the first year and at 25% in the following two years).

It has been proposed to alter the basis of taxation from a 'source basis' to 'residence system'. The legislation to enable this as well as the simplification of the Income Tax Act is being drafted at present.

Taxes on corporate income

Zimbabwe presently operates on a source-based tax system. This means that income from a source within or deemed to be within Zimbabwe will be subject to tax in Zimbabwe unless a specific exemption is available. The government is considering a move to a 'residence'-based tax system.

Income earned by foreign companies from a source within or deemed to be within Zimbabwe will be subject to tax in Zimbabwe. In such a case, one should determine whether the foreign entity is obliged to register a local entity. A company is required to register a branch if it has established a place of business or is otherwise considered to be trading in Zimbabwe. A local subsidiary company may be registered as an alternative to a branch operation.

In the event that Zimbabwe has entered into a double taxation agreement with the foreign company, the entity will only be taxable in Zimbabwe if it operates through a permanent establishment (PE) which, in most cases, includes a fixed place of business. The establishment of a local entity or branch will usually create a PE. The provisions of the related tax treaty should; however, be considered. If a PE exists, only a portion of the income attributable to the PE will be subject to tax in Zimbabwe.

Non-residents who do not have a place of business in Zimbabwe may, however, be subject to withholding tax. *See Withholding tax section for additional details.*

It should be noted that capital gains tax is payable in Zimbabwe on the disposal of immovable property or shares that are held in listed or unlisted companies.

The specific circumstances of a transaction should be considered to determine whether the transaction gives rise to taxation in Zimbabwe.

Anti-avoidance
Please note that Zimbabwe legislation does contain basic anti-avoidance sections that empower the Commissioner General to disregard the implications of a transaction or scheme if it can be proven that:

1. Such transaction or scheme had been entered into to avoid or postpone the payment of any duty or levy imposed by the Act; and
2. It was entered into or carried out by means or in a manner that would not normally be employed in the entering into or carrying out of a transaction, operation, or scheme of the nature of the transaction, operation, or scheme in question; or
3. Has created rights or obligations that would not normally be created between persons dealing at arm's length under a transaction, operation, or scheme of the nature of the transaction, operation, or scheme in question; and
4. Was entered into or carried out solely or mainly for the purposes of the avoidance or the postponement of liability for the payment of any tax duty or levy.

The Commissioner General may at his sole discretion impose this legislation on any transaction or scheme, which will place the onus of proof on the taxpayer to prove that any/all of the requirements noted above will not be applicable to the transaction or scheme.

Z

Zimbabwe

Transfer pricing

No detailed transfer pricing legislation is currently in place in Zimbabwe. The law does, however, allow the Commissioner General to substitute a new sale price to a transaction where he considers the declared sale price to be too high or low.

Thin capitalisation

The law prohibits the deduction of amounts incurred in excess of specified limits in respect of management and general administration expenses as well as interest. This applies to branches or subsidiaries of both local and foreign companies.

The limit on management and general administration expenses is based on such expenses exceeding 1% and 0.75% (respectively for a company already in production and prior to production) of total tax-deductible expenses.

The limit on the deductibility of interest is based on a company incurring interest charged by a subsidiary, a fellow subsidiary, or a holding company when the debt to equity ratio exceeds 3:1.

Treaty relief

Zimbabwe has entered into double tax treaties (DTT) with the following countries:

- Bulgaria;
- Canada;
- France;
- Germany;
- Malaysia;
- Mauritius;
- Netherlands;
- Norway;
- Poland;
- South Africa;
- Sweden; and
- United Kingdom.

Zimbabwe has either negotiated, or is currently negotiating, tax treaties with the following countries:

- Botswana;
- Democratic Republic of Congo;
- Indonesia;
- Iran;
- Jamaica;
- Namibia;
- Serbia and Montenegro;
- Seychelles;
- Tanzania;
- Tunisia; and
- Zambia.

Corporate residence

Currently, the Zimbabwean tax system is based on source and not on residency. Zimbabwe is moving towards a residence-based taxation system, but the details are still to be announced. Income derived or deemed to be derived from sources within Zimbabwe is subject to tax.

Source is the place where income originates or is earned, not the place of payment. If goods are sold pursuant to a contract entered into within Zimbabwe, the source of income is deemed to arise in Zimbabwe, regardless of the place of delivery or transfer of title.

Certain types of income arising outside Zimbabwe may in the hands of a domestic company be deemed to arise in Zimbabwe and be taxed as such. Examples are interest and certain copyright royalties arising outside Zimbabwe. Where the income is deemed to be from Zimbabwe, relief of the foreign tax suffered, up to a maximum of the Zimbabwe tax, may be allowed as a tax credit.

Otherwise, and except for the PE concept embodied in the tax treaties, corporate residence is of little tax significance.

Other taxes

Value-added tax (VAT)
VAT is a transaction tax, and the implications will vary for different transactions. Some transactions are taxed at a rate of 15% or 0% while other transactions are exempt from VAT. Input tax deductions may be claimed, subject to certain provisions. Advice on VAT implications of specific transactions related to corporate operations should be obtained prior to execution of transactions.

VAT shall be levied on every taxable supply by a registered person. A taxable supply means any supply of goods or services in the course or furtherance of a taxable activity.

A taxable activity means any activity that is carried on continuously or regularly in Zimbabwe, which involves the supply of goods or services for consideration.

VAT is payable on all imports for home consumption into Zimbabwe, subject to certain exemptions (e.g., in terms of a technical assistance agreement, donations to the State, goods of which the local supply is zero-rated, etc).

Import VAT is payable on the import value plus the applicable customs duty.

A company/branch is required to register for VAT if it supplies goods or services on a regular basis for consideration and if its taxable supplies (standard-rated and zero-rated supplies) exceed USD 60,000 in any 12-month period.

Registered vendors are required to levy VAT on all taxable supplies at the standard rate of 15%.

A registered VAT vendor is entitled to deduct input tax credits paid in the course of taxable supplies made to such person, provided that a tax invoice is available to support the input tax deduction. It is also important to take note of deemed input tax deductions and prohibited input deductions. Import VAT paid may only be deducted as input tax if the import was in furtherance of a taxable activity and the required documentation (e.g., stamped customs entries) is held by the importer.

Customs and excise
Zimbabwe is a member of Southern African Development Community (SADC) as well as Common Market for Eastern and Southern Africa (COMESA). Customs duties are payable according to the general customs tariffs that are legislated for in Zimbabwe. Preferential duty rates apply on imports from SADC or COMESA countries while goods may be imported free of customs duties from Namibia in terms of the Zimbabwe-Namibia Free Trade Agreement.

Excise duties are levied on local production of excisable products and are included on most excisable products imported from other countries.

Z

Zimbabwe

Excise and fuel levies are levied on petrol, diesel, and illuminating kerosene.

Security is required by Customs on all temporary importations to cover import VAT and customs duties (if applicable). Imports of goods subject to customs duties into registered Customs' bonded warehouses are provided for (i.e., payment of duties may be deferred until the goods are entered for home consumption or acquitted if exported).

Stamp duty

Certain transactions may attract stamp duty. The amount of stamp duty payable will differ and will be based on the nature of every individual transaction.

The basic transactions can be summarised as follows:

Transaction	Stamp duty
Bonds	0.4% (USD 0.40 for every USD 100 or part thereof)
Brokers notes – purchase of securities	0.25% (USD 0.25 per every USD 100 or part thereof)
Brokers notes – purchase/sale of any movable property other than a security	0.10% (USD 0.10 per every USD 100 or part thereof)
Brokers notes – purchase/sale of any immovable property	1% (USD 1.00 per every USD 100 or part thereof)
Off market share transfer instruments	2% or USD 2
Cheques	0.05% (USD 0.05)

Tax advice should be obtained for major transactions in respect of the transactions mentioned above in order to ensure that the correct stamp duty implications are considered.

Transfer duty

Transfer duty is payable on the acquisition value of property acquired.

Transfer duty is payable at the following rates:

Persons	Value of the property (USD)	Rate of transfer duty
All	0–5,000	1%
All	5,001–20,000	2% of the value above 5,000
All	20,001–100,000	3% on the value above 20,000
All	100,001 and above	4% of the value above 100,000

Transfer duty is normally payable by the buyer but the agreement for the sale of the property will determine the person liable to pay these costs. In addition, conveyance costs of up to 3% (plus 15% VAT) must be added on.

Exchange control

Zimbabwe has been operating a multi-currency system since February 2009. The Zimbabwe dollar (ZWD) was demonetarised effective April 2009. This has had a significant impact on the country's exchange control regulations.

The Exchange Control Handbook in Zimbabwe is not available to the public and the banking institutions are the only bodies which have access to these regulations.

Transactions that involve the transfer of funds to countries outside Zimbabwe are generally subject to Bank of Zimbabwe approval.

The issue of shares in a Zimbabwe company to persons residing outside of Zimbabwe requires specific exchange control approvals. In terms of new legislation, a limit of 49% is available for non-residents. A 51% local shareholding by indigenous persons is a requirement. Applications may be made for increased levels; each case will be decided on its own merits.

Branch income

Branch income that is received or has accrued from a source within or deemed to be within Zimbabwe is taxable in Zimbabwe in terms of the normal corporate tax rules.

A branch is regarded as an extension of its foreign head office. A branch may therefore not deduct fees paid to its foreign head office (unless a tax treaty makes provision for such deduction) as it is argued that a branch cannot transact with itself. Reimbursement of actual expenses may, however, be deducted, subject to the normal deduction rules.

A 20% withholding tax is imposed on any payments made in respect of head office charges.

The amount of fees charged by the head office to the Zimbabwe branch is also subject to a limitation, usually based on a maximum of 1% of total expenditure (excluding the charge itself and any capital allowances). Exchange control regulations also limit the remittability of administration and management fees to 2% of turnover.

Income determination

The Zimbabwe Income Tax Act (Act) tax base for corporate taxes is not on profits but rather taxable income. Zimbabwe still uses the 'source' basis of determining income, and as yet has not moved to raising tax on a residence basis. The source and nature of the income determines whether the amount is taxable or not. In addition to amounts received or accrued from actual Zimbabwean sources, there are deeming provisions that bring income from foreign sources into Zimbabwean taxable income.

In general, all receipts from a Zimbabwe source are taxed, excluding amounts that are proven by the taxpayer as being capital receipts. Most expenditure items and some specified exemptions are deductible against income. Capital expenditure is generally not deductible, with amounts on specific items being deductible by way of annual allowances spread over a period.

Deductions

Tax deductions
The Act makes provisions for specific deductions. Some of the deductions, such as the deduction of foreign exchange losses, development and exploration costs, hire purchase allowances, manufacturing allowances, etc, can be more complex.

Z

Zimbabwe

Capital allowances
The cost (including finance charges) of machinery, implements, and other articles used by the taxpayer in the production of income is deductible in four equal annual allowances. No apportionment is required where the asset was held for less than 12 months.

Industrial buildings (including hotels) constructed and used by the taxpayer in the production of income qualify for an initial allowance of 25% of erection cost in the year they are first brought into use. Thereafter, an annual allowance of 25% is deductible for each year following the year of erection. Additions to existing buildings (not alterations or repairs) qualify for the same deductions. It is important to note that the allowance is calculated on the cost of erection and not the cost of acquisition. In these cases the allowances are set at 5% of the cost.

A mining exploration expenditure incurred before commencement of production is deductible in full in the first year of production against income derived from the mine. A subsequent development expenditure is presently written off in the year expended. This aspect of Zimbabwe's mining legislation is currently under review.

Capital allowances may also be deducted in respect of patents, trademarks, leasehold improvements, etc.

A recovery or recoupment of allowances previously claimed should be included in the gross income of a taxpayer in the event that the allowance is recovered or recouped by way of disposal. The recoupment is presently calculated on the capital allowances previously granted.

Trading losses
Assessed tax losses may be carried forward for up to six years provided the company continues to trade. This restriction does not apply to mining companies. Tax laws do not allow for losses to be transferred to other group companies and anti-avoidance provisions may be triggered by transactions designed to transfer or exploit assessed losses.

Assessed losses are reduced in the event of a compromise agreement with creditors.

Group taxation

No taxation of combined operations is allowed in Zimbabwe including where operations are conducted by more than one company.

Tax incentives

It has been announced by the Minister of Finance that Zimbabwe is moving away from taxation incentives; however, the following are still available.

Kindly note that this is a high-level summary, and certain conditions should be met in order to utilise these incentives.

	Tax treatment for normal taxpayers	Tax incentive	Person for whom incentive is available and duration of incentive
1	Capital allowances are calculated as 25% of the cost of erection of industrial building in the year when the building is brought into use and 25% during the three years that follow the year of erection.	The capital allowance is calculated as 25% of the cost of erection of a commercial or industrial building in growth point areas in the year when the building is brought into use and 25% during the three years that follow the year of erection.	Taxpayers operating at designated growth point areas.
2	No investment allowance granted.	Deduction of an investment allowance at 15% on cost of specified assets.	Taxpayers operating at designated growth point areas.
3	Taxed at 25%.	First five years – 0%. Second five years – 15%. Thereafter – normal rate.	For all taxpayers in build, own, operate, and transfer (BOOT) or build, operate, and transfer (BOT) arrangements.
4	Export expenditure incurred is deductible for tax purposes.	An additional allowance of 100% of cost incurred in an export country in order to export Zimbabwean goods to such country may be deducted.	Exporting taxpayers.
5	Taxed at 25%.	Taxed at a reduced rate of 20%.	For all manufacturing taxpayers exporting 50% or more of output (by volume).
6	Taxed at 25%.	Taxed at a reduced rate of 15%.	Mining company holding a special mining lease.
7	Taxed at 25%.	First five years – 0%. Thereafter – normal rate.	Operator of a tourist facility in a tourist development zone.
8	Taxed at 25%.	First five years – 0%. Thereafter – normal rate.	Industrial park developer.

Withholding taxes (WHT)

WHT are applicable where dividends and royalties or similar payments are declared or distributed to non-Zimbabwean residents (and Zimbabwean residents in some instances).

Dividends

Dividends declared by a Zimbabwean company to a non-resident holding company will be subject to non-resident shareholders tax (NRST), a withholding tax. NRST will be payable at a rate of 15% unless treaty relief is available. Dividends from companies listed on the Zimbabwe Stock Exchange have a rate of 10%. NRST is payable within 10 days after declaration of the dividend.

Z

Zimbabwe

Royalties or similar payments
WHT on royalties are payable once a Zimbabwean company pays a royalty to a non-Zimbabwean resident. WHT is levied at a rate of 15% and is payable within 10 days of the date of payment.

A royalty includes payment for the use or right to use any patent or design, trademark, copyright, model, pattern, plan, formula or process, or any other property or right of a similar nature. It also includes the imparting of any scientific, technical, industrial, or commercial knowledge or information for use in Zimbabwe. The nature of the amount payable should therefore be carefully considered in order to determine whether the relevant amount represents a royalty.

Fees
Fees are defined to include amounts that are technical, managerial, administrative, or consultative in nature; costs are paid externally. There are some exceptions, but the definition is broad and brings in most costs that may be charged to a Zimbabwean person.

WHT is levied at a rate of 15% and is payable within 10 days of the date of payment.

Interest
WHT of 15%, calculated on the gross amount of interest, is payable on interest accruing to any person resident in Zimbabwe. This applies to interest arising from a registered banking institution or unit trust scheme. The tax withheld is a final tax, and the financial institution is responsible to withhold the tax.

Non-resident investors, however, are exempt from any withholding tax on interest.

Summary of withholding tax payable
The non-residents withholding tax rates and treaty relief for Zimbabwean double tax agreements can be summarised as follows. It should be noted that the tax treaties contain certain requirements that should be met before the reduced tax rate may be applied.

The definitions of dividends, royalties, and interest in the various treaties should also be considered.

Country	Dividends	Royalties	Fees	Interest
Zimbabwe tax legislation	15%*	15%	Nil	15%**
Bulgaria	10%	10%	10%	N/A
Canada	10%	10%	10%	N/A
France	10%	10%	10%	N/A
Germany	10%	7.5%	7.5%	N/A
Malaysia	10%	10%	10%	N/A
Mauritius	10%	15%	15%	N/A
Netherlands	10%	10%	10%	N/A
Norway	15%	10%	10%	N/A
Poland	10%	10%	15%	N/A
South Africa	15%	15%	15%	N/A
Sweden	15%	10%	10%	N/A

Country	Dividends	Royalties	Fees	Interest
United Kingdom	5%	10%	10%	N/A

* Applies to unlisted companies. The rate for companies listed on the Zimbabwe Stock Exchange is reduced to 10%.

** Resident persons have a 15% WHT on interest arising from financial institutions. Interest from other sources is taxed at the corporate tax rate.

N/A means that the provisions of the tax treaty limited the rate to a rate that is higher than the local Zimbabwean rate. It should be noted that a treaty can only provide tax relief and cannot impose a higher tax rate.

These are payable within 10 days of the date of distribution or accrual.

Tax administration

The due date for filing of returns can be summarised as follows:

Return	Due date
Income tax return	By the end of April in the following year.
Provisional tax return – first payment of 10%	25 March of the respective tax year.
Provisional tax return – second payment of 25%	25 June of the respective tax year.
Provisional tax return – third payment of 30%	25 September of the respective year.
Provisional tax return – fourth payment of 35%	20 December of the respective year.
Employees' tax return (PAYE monthly return)	By the third of the month following the month to which the PAYE relates.
PAYE reconciliation return	Within 30 days from the tax year-end for individuals, i.e., 31 January each year.
VAT return	By the tenth day following the month to which the VAT relates.
Import VAT	At the time that the goods are imported. Can be deferred over a period of 90 days on application to the Commissioner.
VAT on imported services	Within 30 days of receipt of payment or issuance of an invoice (whichever is earlier).
Various amounts subject to withholding taxes	Within 10 days from the date of distribution or accrual.

Global
tax networks

Human Resource Services

Employees are probably your organisation's greatest asset and your biggest challenge. The PwC Human Resource Services (HRS) network helps you create value by helping you actively manage your people.

Working with our network gives you access to specialists in four core disciplines:

- International assignments.
- HR management (including benchmarking services through Saratoga).
- Reward and remuneration.
- People management and change.

We have one of the world's largest human resource (HR) advisory networks to give you all the support you need. Our 6,000 professionals in over 100 countries follow the same multi-disciplinary approach to people management to give you the consistency that is so important when working across borders.

During this decade we expect dramatic change in the global employee competitive landscape. For instance, research[1] shows that 94% of new graduates expect to work across more geographic borders than their parents did – this implies the cost and administrative burden of assigning employees to work internationally will escalate.

Working alongside our specialists in international assignments, we'll help you to stay ahead by:

- Designing and putting in place strategies and policies to align your objectives with your organisation's business strategy;
- Providing cross-border tax advice, so your organisation and your assignees understand the implication of the assignment on their tax bill; and
- Delivering IT solutions so you can remotely control tax and administration details for assigned individuals.

Our specialists have a solid grounding in areas such as tax, compensation, benefits, pensions and HR data metrics so that we can put together the team that is right for you.

To find out more, please contact:

Michael Rendell
Global Leader, Human Resource Services
+44 20 7212 4945
michael.g.rendell@uk.pwc.com

William Owens
Global Leader,
International Assignment Services
+1 704 347 1608
william.f.owens@us.pwc.com

Visit **www.pwc.com/hrs** for more information.

[1]Managing tomorrow's people 2020 – www.pwc.com/managingpeople2020

Indirect Taxes

To give the best advice on indirect taxation, we believe you need to work closely with the people devising it. Over the years we've made a point of building strong relationships with tax authorities, tax policy makers, governments, the Organisation for Economic Co-operation and Development (OECD), the World Customs Organization (WCO) and the World Trade Organization (WTO). We've consciously recruited a large number people from these organisations, who've either created policies or put them in place. Result, we have a thorough understanding of indirect taxes from every perspective.

We appreciate that indirect taxes can be very different depending on which industry sector you work in. So our indirect tax and customs specialists across the world, work closely with PwC industry specialists to really understand the specific issues in your sector, and give you advice with genuine insight.

And because the implications of indirect taxes can be so important to your business, we customise the support we give you, and use the latest technology, to provide you with what you need, wherever you are and whenever you need us.

We inform
- You'll find the latest Value-added tax (VAT)/goods and services tax (GST) news, information, publications, and conference details at globalvatonline.pwc.com

We advise
- Our advice on strategy, structuring and planning will help you mitigate indirect tax costs and risks, to help you get the best from your indirect tax function.
- We can either advise on compliance and reporting, or you can take care of it by outsourcing your compliance to us.
- We can help you improve your processes through automation and digitisation, using tax engines, Enterprise Resource Planning (ERP), e-invoicing, e-archiving and e-filing.

We support
- We can help you with internal controls, Sarbanes-Oxley Section 404 reviews and indirect tax risk management.
- We can help you negotiate with tax authorities, obtain rulings, or manage dispute resolution and litigation.
- We organise conferences, training and regional peer group discussions to keep you abreast of the latest industry sector developments and best practices in indirect taxes.
- We help governments develop VAT/GST systems and provide support with VAT/GST reforms and implementations.

To find out more, please contact:

Ine Lejeune
Global Leader, Indirect Taxes
+32 9 268 8300
ine.lejeune@be.pwc.com

VAT, made simple

Changes to VAT and Goods & Services Tax GST happen all the time. When they do, we can tell you about them, quickly.

Subscribe to our GlobalVATOnline (GVO) service and we'll deliver indirect tax news from over 70 countries to your inbox. From mitigating risk, to making your VAT/GST teams as effective as possible, we'll support you so you understand what these changes mean, and what you need to do about them.

Why subscribe?

Instant updates
As soon as anything changes – anywhere in the world – we'll tell you.

Facts, when you need them
Search online for specific information about VAT and GST topics in one country or several across the world.

Insider reports and knowledge
Read PwC publications and the latest feature articles, from our leading indirect taxes specialists.

A specialist team, on hand
Find details about our indirect tax teams across the world – in more than 130 countries.

Tricks of the trade
Use our tax tools, or learn about the techniques we use, to help you make the most of your indirect taxes teams.

Access to industry events
Get details about our indirect taxes seminars, conferences and courses around the world.

How to subscribe

Subscriptions start from €1,000 a year. To subscribe, go to
https://globalvatonline.pwc.com

International Tax Services

The pressures on business to manage tax across borders – along with growing regulation and the need to stay competitive in a global market – means that a local perspective on international tax is not enough. With specialists experienced in complex international tax matters across the world, our network is well positioned to give you top quality advice. It's this combination of local and global expertise that gives you real insight into managing tax across borders.

Our International Tax Services network helps multinational businesses achieve their goals in the most tax-efficient way, through:

- Identifying locations for tax efficient holding companies;
- Cross-border financing and treasury solutions;
- Tax planning for controlled foreign companies;
- Planning by utilising income tax treaties;
- Profit repatriation;
- Loss utilisation planning;
- Developing tax efficient supply chains and shared services;
- Inbound and outbound structuring;
- Intellectual property and intangible assets planning;
- Addressing regional tax issues e.g., EU tax harmonisation;
- Credit management and planning; and
- Utilising best practice business models.

To find out more, please contact:

Christoph Schreiber
Global Leader, International Tax Services
+49 69 9585 6300
christoph.schreiber@de.pwc.com

Global news, with local knowledge

If your company works around the world, we can help you stay on top of developments in tax, regulation and legislation globally, wherever you are.

Sign up to our International Tax Services (ITS) news alerts and we'll send you breaking news updates. These updates will guide you on the effects on your business operations, the transactions you make and what it means for you.

What you get
Regular news alerts, keeping you up-to-date with changes and developments in international tax.

How to subscribe
To read the latest alerts – and to sign up for future alerts – go to **www.pwc.com**

Legal Services

We support businesses in these areas:

- Asset management;
- Corporate and commercial issues;
- Corporate secretarial;
- Dispute resolution;
- Employment;
- Financial services;
- Immigration;
- Public law; and
- Real estate.

We understand that one size doesn't fit all when it comes to legal services. With over 2,000 corporate lawyers in more than 75 countries, we're able to tackle problems in a way that is genuinely specific to your business. As well as specialist legal advice, we also offer day-to-day general counsel support.

We support businesses with teams drawn from the range of skills within the PwC global network. Depending on your legal issues, we might include tax advisers, human capital consultants, corporate finance specialists, actuaries, management consultants, or accountants. We'll put together whatever it takes to give you the most creative solution in the least possible time.

To find out more, please contact:

Luis Comas
Global Leader, Legal Services
+34 932 532 741
luis.comas@es.landwellglobal.com

Visit **www.pwc.com/legalservices** for more information.

Mergers and Acquisitions

Whether you're buying, selling or merging, it's vital to extract as much value as possible from a deal. With an international network of 700 Mergers and Acquisitions (M&A) specialists, experienced in every type of transaction, we know how to help you structure and finance the deal to your best advantage.

Our M&A specialists support you through every stage of the deal. They work closely with our transactions services, corporate finance and legal teams, so that all aspects of the deal are covered by experienced specialists.

We combine all this experience and insight to:

- Assess and manage acquisition / merger risk;
- Structure acquisitions for the best net cash flows;
- Prepare businesses for disposal;
- Carry out pre-acquisition or pre-sale due diligence;
- Develop tax-efficient deal structuring; and
- Design post deal tax solutions.

To find out more, please contact:

Magnus Johnsson
Global Leader, Mergers and Acquisitions
+46 8 5553 3172
magnus.johnsson@se.pwc.com

See how much you contribute

Do you know what your total tax bill is, beyond corporate income tax? Do you know how it compares with your industry average? More importantly, do your stakeholders understand the total impact of the taxes you pay?

PwC's Total Tax Contribution (TTC) framework helps you grasp all this, and gives you a standardised methodology to measure and communicate your financial contribution to society, either country-by-country or globally. We can help you collect all your data, compare it with the right benchmarks, and communicate the results.

To understand the full value of the taxes you pay, find out more about TTC at **www.pwc.com/ttc**

pwc

Sustainability and Climate Change Tax

Sustainability and climate change continues to evolve as a business issue. Momentum is building. As such, you need more than advice on the current state – you need advice that anticipates what legislative and policy changes are likely to happen. You need that advice to help you to predict how these developments will impact your business. You also need to understand how your organisation is changing to address sustainability and climate change as a business issue and how existing taxes impact on those changes.

Our Sustainability and Climate Change Tax network helps businesses and investors in two ways: it helps them stay on top of global trends and developments in climate change related policy; and it helps businesses address the tax implications of climate change related policy and their own organisation's response to the business issue. Our sustainability and climate change tax services include advice on:

- Tax issues and implications arising from the carbon agenda;
- Monitoring current and potential exposure to taxes;
- Governmental policy consulting;
- Policy and legislative changes;
- Financing sustainability;
- Fund structuring;
- Renewables' investments;
- Green property;
- Environmental taxes;
- Changing behaviours, recruitment and retention; and
- Reward strategies around the adoption of the sustainability and climate change agenda.

To find out more, please contact:

Mark Schofield
Global Leader, Sustainability and Climate Change Tax
+44 20 7212 2527
mark.schofield@uk.pwc.com

For more information, visit
www.pwc.com/sustainability/tax

Tax Controversy and Dispute Resolution

We support businesses across the life-cycle of a controversy (not just resolution or litigation) through:

- Tax dispute prevention techniques;
- Tax audit management practices;
- Tax dispute resolution alternatives;
- Global strategic planning of tax audits and disputes (including policy development); and
- Tax risk management, analysis, and disclosures.

By giving you insight into your company's risks and exposures across different territories and disciplines, we can be the effective option to help you deal with tax disputes, audits, and examinations, from prevention through to management and resolution. Our specialists also use their experience to help businesses put in place consistent and defensible practices and policies, so they know what to expect in the future.

The Tax Controversy and Dispute Resolution network brings together ex-revenue and government officials, accountants, economists, international tax litigators, and industry sector specialists, in all areas of direct and indirect tax, as well as customs duties, employment taxes, and tax fraud. But we think being effective is about more than just knowledge; it's about having an insight into what could happen next. So we build strong relationships with governments and policy makers worldwide. That way, we're close to the people who are setting the dispute agenda, and know how to work with them to get the right result.

To find out more, please contact:

David Swenson
Global Leader, Tax Controversy and Dispute Resolution
+1 202 414 4650
david.swenson@us.pwc.com

Visit **www.pwc.com/taxcontroversy** for more information.

Expert tax insight, around the globe

Keeping up with the increasing pace of change surrounding tax policy and administrative developments worldwide can be a real challenge for multinational companies. We can help you stay up-to-date with the latest developments and explain what these changes mean for you.

What you get
You will receive a monthly Tax Policy Bulletin, with analysis and insights on tax policy changes around the world. By drawing on our experience of tax policy issues and insights from relationships with organisations such as the OECD, we will alert you to new developments and give you guidance on what impact these changes will have on your business.

How to subscribe
To read the latest bulletins – and to sign up for future alerts – visit **www.pwc.com**

Tax Management and Accounting Services

When it comes to managing taxes today, many businesses find that the approaches they've taken in the past no longer work. This could be due to changes in their industry or organisation – whether it's new or changing legislation, structural changes, pressure from shareholders and regulators, or cuts in headcount and budgets.

The specialists in our global Tax Management and Accounting Services (TMAS) network have the experience to help you find an approach that works for your business, so that you retain effective control over your taxes.

We can help you navigate the complex decisions you need to make to update your tax management systems. We can also take you through options to achieve the best delivery model, and how to take advantage of technology that supports you, especially if your business works around the world.

If you'd rather outsource all or part of your tax compliance, we'll take care of it. We can coordinate the outsourcing of your compliance, across borders, for direct and indirect taxes, statutory financial statement production and tax reporting. And our outsourcing arrangements include software that gives you central control, and lets you see the status of compliance around the world, wherever you operate.

Our TMAS network can help you:

Be more efficient
- We help clients develop tax strategies and policies, and review the effectiveness of tax and risk procedures.
- We work with businesses to improve their processes around compliance, tax reporting and statutory financial statements.
- We look for opportunities to introduce technology that supports tax compliance and reporting, improves connectivity and integration with wider finance systems and improves data and process management.

Be more compliant
- We help tax functions work effectively with the wider finance functions to reduce risk, benefit from shared service centres, and other finance transformation projects.
- We produce financial statements both territorially and globally.
- We build cross-border outsourcing models that take care of tax compliance, statutory financial statement production and tax reporting.
- We help businesses to maintain a good relationship with the revenue authorities and support them in carrying out risk assessments.

Be more engaged
- We can help you build a consensus across your organisation, by getting your people behind the business case for change.

To find out more, please contact:

Buddy Tinley
Global Leader, Tax Management and Accounting Services
+1 678 419 8838
buddy.tinley@us.pwc.com

Transfer Pricing

The scrutiny of transfer pricing by tax authorities worldwide has intensified. Our network of transfer pricing specialists has extensive experience in dealing with revenue authorities around the world. Using their expertise in economics, dispute resolution and industry, they can help you prepare for the challenges this scrutiny will present.

As a network of specialists, we help companies develop sustainable, tax-efficient structures, and help make them more compliant with legal requirements. We help them respond quickly to an audit and resolve transfer pricing disputes. We also assist them so they're less exposed to transfer pricing risks in the future.

We've built a network of 1,800 transfer pricing specialists in over 70 countries. Here's how our transfer pricing network can help you manage risks and improve your tax efficiency:

We advise
- We develop coordinated, centralised global documentation and defence processes, building in the requirements of each jurisdiction.
- We draft economic and industry studies.
- We negotiate Advance Pricing Agreements (APAs).
- We benchmark licensing fees for intangible assets and royalties.
- We assess potential benefits and risks of transfer pricing in your existing global operations.

We support
- We assist businesses with experienced testimony and litigation support.
- We help resolve global disputes and Competent Authority negotiations.
- We help multinational organisations centrally control and manage sales to third parties, including managing all accompanying opportunities and risks.
- We perform due diligence.

To find out more, please contact:

Garry Stone
Global Leader, Transfer Pricing
+1 312 298 2464
garry.stone@us.pwc.com

Visit **www.pwc.com/transferpricing** for more information.

Specialist knowledge on transfer pricing. As it happens

If you're looking for the latest news on transfer pricing, sign up to our Pricing Knowledge Network (PKN) updates. We'll keep you up to date with what's happening in transfer pricing. And our specialists will look at the wider effects, and what they mean for your business.

What you get
E-bulletins
We'll send you regular emails, based on what you tell us you want to know – whether it's about specific countries or topics, or both.

Breaking news, to your inbox
As soon as we hear about transfer pricing developments, we'll send it straight to you.

Expert analysis
We'll share analysis of major inter-company pricing issues and related developments from around the world.

Invitations to events
You will receive invitations to our transfer pricing conferences and master classes.

How to subscribe
To subscribe to these free alerts – visit **www.pwc.com/pkn**

Global tax
contacts

Human Resource Services

Global Leader, Human Resource Services
Michael Rendell
+44 20 7212 4945
michael.g.rendell@uk.pwc.com

Global Leader, International Assignment Services
William Owens
+1 704 347 1608
william.f.owens@us.pwc.com

Albania
Laura Qorlaze
+355 4 2245 254
laura.qorlaze@al.pwc.com

Algeria
Stéphane Henrion
+33 1 56 57 4139
stephane.henrion@fr.landwellglobal.com

Angola
Fernando Barros
+244 222 395004
fernando.barros@ao.pwc.com

Argentina
Daniel Santiago
+54 11 4850 6743
daniel.santiago@ar.pwc.com

Australia
Jim Lijeski
+61 2 8266 8298
jim.lijeski@au.pwc.com

Austria
Margit Frank
+43 1 501 88 3200
margit.frank@at.pwc.com

Azerbaijan
Rizvan Gubiyev
+994 12 497 25 ext. 615
rizvan.gubiyev@az.pwc.com

Bahrain
Elham Hassan
+973 175 40554
elham.hassan@bh.pwc.com

Barbados
Christopher Sambrano
+1 246 467 6701
christopher.sambrano@bb.pwc.com

Belgium
Joost De Groote
+32 2 710 7419
joost.de.groote@be.pwc.com

Bermuda
Alistair McNeish
+1 441 298 9708
alistair.s.mcneish@bm.pwc.com

Bolivia
Boris Mercado
+591 2 408 181
boris.mercado@bo.pwc.com

Bosnia and Herzegovina
Mubera Brkovic
+387 33 295 234
mubera.brkovic@ba.pwc.com

Brazil
Edmar Perfetto
+55 11 3674 3722
edmar.perfetto@br.pwc.com

Bulgaria
Maria Toromanova
+359 2 91 003
maria.toromanova@bg.pwc.com

Canada
Dave Peters
+1 403 509 7481
dave.peters@ca.pwc.com

Chad
Elias Pungong
+241 76 24 28
elias.pungong@ga.pwc.com

Chile
Rodrigo Bucarey
+56 2 940 0399
rodrigo.bucarey@cl.pwc.com

China (People's Republic of)
Stacy Kwok
+86 21 2323 2772
stacy.kwok@cn.pwc.com

Colombia
Maria Helena Diaz
+57 1 635 1125
maria_helena.diaz@co.pwc.com

Congo (Republic of)
Emmanuel Le Bras
+242 534 09 07
emmanuel.lebras@cg.pwc.com

Costa Rica
Carlos Barrantes
+506 2224 1555
carlos.barrantes@cr.pwc.com

Croatia
Mirna Kette
+385 1 632 8823
mirna.kette@hr.pwc.com

Cyprus
Philippos Soseilos
+57 22 555 606
philippos.soseilos@cy.pwc.com

Czech Republic
Tomas Hunal
+420 251 152 516
tomas.hunal@cz.pwc.com

Denmark
Mona Lorentsen
+45 3945 3398
mona.lorentsen@dk.pwc.com

Ecuador
Pablo Aguirre
+593 2 256 4142 ext. 361
pablo.aguirre@ec.pwc-ag.com

Egypt
Sherif Mansour
+20 2 2759 7700 ext. 7888
sherif.mansour@eg.pwc.com

El Salvador
Edgar Mendoza
+502 2420 7800
edgar.mendoza@gt.pwc.com

Estonia
Peep Kalamae
+372 614 1976
peep.kalamae@ee.pwc.com

Fiji Islands
Jenny Seeto
+679 331 3955
jenny.seeto@fj.pwc.com

Finland
Risto Lof
+358 9 2280 1811
risto.lof@fi.pwc.com

France
Michael Jaffe
+33 1 5657 4042
michael.jaffe@fr.landwellglobal.com

Georgia
Paul Cooper
+995 32 50 80 50
paul.cooper@ge.pwc.com

Germany
Petra Raspels
+49 21 1981 7680
petra.raspels@de.pwc.com

Greece
Lina Foka
+30 210 6874 546
lina.foka@gr.pwc.com

Hong Kong
Mandy Kwok
+852 2289 3900
mandy.kwok@hk.pwc.com

Hungary
Beata Horvathne Szabo
+36 1 461 9283
beata.horvathne@hu.pwc.com

India
Kaushik Mukerjee
+91 80 4079 6002
kaushik.mukerjee@in.pwc.com

Indonesia
Paul Raman
+62 21 5289 1027
paul.raman@id.pwc.com

Human Resource Services

Ireland
Mark Carter
+353 1 792 6548
mark.p.carter@ie.pwc.com

Israel
Doron Sadan
+972 3 795 4460
doron.sadan@il.pwc.com

Italy
Luca Barbera
+390 2 9160 5300
luca.barbera@it.pwc.com

Jamaica
Tony Lewars
+1 876 932 8383
tony.lewars@jm.pwc.com

Japan
Kojiro Endo
+81 3 5251 2443
kojiro.endo@jp.pwc.com

Jordan
Stephan Stephan
+962 6 5669 629
stephan.stephan@jo.pwc.com

Kazakhstan
Khayrulla Akramkhodjaev
+7 727 298 0448
khayrulla.akramkhodjaev@kz.pwc.com

Korea (Republic of)
Younsung Chung
+82 2 709 0538
younsung.chung@kr.pwc.com

Latvia
Gunita Puzule
+371 6709 4428
gunita.puzule@lv.pwc.com

Lithuania
Monika Zemaityte
+370 5 254 6921
monika.zemaityte@lt.pwc.com

Luxembourg
Michiel Roumieux
+352 49 4848 3055
michiel.roumieux@lu.pwc.com

Macau
Christina Lam
+853 8799 5133
christina.wc.lam@hk.pwc.com

Macedonia
Miroslav Marchev
+389 23 111 012
miroslav.marchev@mk.pwc.com

Malaysia
Sakaya Johns Rani
+60 3 2173 1553
sakaya.johns.rani@my.pwc.com

Malta
Michel Ganado
+356 2124 7000
michel.ganado@mt.pwc.com

Mexico
Claudia Campos
+52 55 5263 5774
claudia.campos@mx.pwc.com

Moldova
Ruxandra Stoian
+40 21 202 8734
ruxandra.stoian@ro.pwc.com

Montenegro
Ivana Velickovic
+381 11 3302 100
ivana.velickovic@rs.pwc.com

Mozambique
Joao Martins
+258 21 307 620
joao.l.martins@mz.pwc.com

Netherlands
Ron Unger
+31 20 568 7012
ron.unger@nl.pwc.com

New Zealand
Neil Haines
+64 9 355 8625
neil.l.haines@nz.pwc.com

Nicaragua
Singrid Miranda
+506 2224 1555 ext. 136
singrid.miranda@cr.pwc.com

Nigeria
Ken Igbokwe
+234 1 270 3119
ken.igbokwe@ng.pwc.com

Norway
Erland Norstebo
+47 95 26 06 69
erland.norstebo@no.pwc.com

Oman
Jeff Todd
+971 2 694 6821
jeff.todd@ae.pwc.com

Pakistan
Naeem Akhtar
+92 21 3241 1628
naeem.akhtar@pk.pwc.com

Panama
Francisco Barrios
+507 206 9217
francisco.barrios@pa.pwc.com

Paraguay
Ruben Taboada
+595 21 445 003
ruben.taboada@py.pwc.com

Peru
Monica Nieva
+51 1 211 6500
monica.nieva@pe.pwc.com

Philippines
Myrna Fernando
+63 2 459 2003
myrna.fernando@ph.pwc.com

Poland
Katarzyna Serwinska
+48 22 523 4794
katarzyna.serwinska@pl.pwc.com

Portugal
John Duggan
+351 213 599 632
john.duggan@pt.pwc.com

Puerto Rico
Jose Osorio
+1 787 772 8057
jose.osorio@us.pwc.com

Romania
Ruxandra Stoian
+40 21 202 8734
ruxandra.stoian@ro.pwc.com

Russian Federation
Karina Khudenko
+7 495 967 5418
karina.khudenko@ru.pwc.com

Saudi Arabia
Dennis Allen
+974 467 5581
dennis.allen@qa.pwc.com

Serbia
Ivana Velickovic
+381 11 3302 100
ivana.velickovic@rs.pwc.com

Singapore
James Clemence
+65 6236 3948
james.clemence@sg.pwc.com

Slovak Republic
Natalia Fialova
+421 2 59 350 612
natalia.fialova@sk.pwc.com

Slovenia
Sonja Omerza
+386 1 5836 023
sonja.omerza@si.pwc.com

South Africa
Gerald Seegers
+27 11 797 4560
gerald.seegers@za.pwc.com

Spain
Joan Daura
+34 932 532 758
joan.daura.cros@es.landwellglobal.com

Swaziland
Paul Lewis
+268 407 2861
lewis.paul@sz.pwc.com

Taiwan
Susan Teng
+886 2 2729 6666
susan.teng@tw.pwc.com

Human Resource Services

Tanzania
Elizabeth Kariuki
+255 22 213 3100
elizabeth.kariuki@tz.pwc.com

Thailand
Prapasiri Kositthanakorn
+66 2 344 1228
prapasiri.kositthanakorn@th.pwc.com

Trinidad and Tobago
Bert Jones
+1 868 623 0281
bert.jones@tt.pwc.com

Turkey
Adnan Nas
+90 212 326 6402
adnan.nas@tr.pwc.com

Ukraine
Marc-Tell Madl
+380 44 490 6777
m.madl@ua.pwc.com

United Arab Emirates
Sharat Seth
+971 4 304 3303
sharat.seth@ae.pwc.com

United Kingdom
Michael Rendell
+44 20 7212 4945
michael.g.rendell@uk.pwc.com

United States
Billy Owens
+1 704 347 1608
william.f.owens@us.pwc.com

Uzbekistan (Republic of)
Akmal Rustamov
+998 71 2536 136
akmal.rustamov@uz.pwc.com

Venezuela
Carmen Cortez
+58 212 7006 679
carmen.cortez@ve.pwc.com

Vietnam
David Fitzgerald
+66 2 344 1500
david.fitzgerald@vn.pwc.com

Indirect Taxes

Global Leader, Indirect Taxes
Ine Lejeune
+32 9 268 8300
ine.lejeune@be.pwc.com

Afghanistan
Syed Shabbar Zaidi
+92 21 24 13 849
s.m.shabbar.zaidi@pk.pwc.com

Albania
Loreta Peci
+355 4 2242 254
loreta.peci@al.pwc.com

Algeria
Stéphane Henrion
+33 1 56 57 4139
stephane.henrion@fr.landwellglobal.com

Angola
Fernando Barros
+244 222 395004
fernando.barros@ao.pwc.com

Antigua and Barbuda
Neil Coates
+268 462 3000 ext. 134
neil.m.coates@ag.pwc.com

Argentina
Ricardo Tavieres
+54 11 4850 6722
ricardo.d.tavieres@ar.pwc.com

Armenia
Paul Cooper
+374 10 59 2150
paul.cooper@am.pwc.com

Australia
Patrick Walker
+61 2 8266 1596
patrick.walker@au.pwc.com

Austria
Christine Weinzierl
+43 1 501 88 3630
christine.weinzierl@at.pwc.com

Azerbaijan
Movlan Pashayev
+994 12 497 7405
movlan.pashayev@az.pwc.com

Bahamas
Kevin D. Seymour
+242 352 8471
kevin.d.seymour@bs.pwc.com

Bahrain
David Stevens
+971 4 304 3304
david.stevens@ae.pwc.com

Barbados
Louisa Lewis-Ward
+246 467 6756
louisa.ward@bb.pwc.com

Belgium
Wouter Villette
+32 2 710 7302
wouter.villette@be.pwc.com

Bolivia
Cesar Lora
+591 721 47 235
cesar.lora@bo.pwc.com

Bosnia and Herzegovina
Mubera Brkovic
+387 33 295 721
mubera.brkovic@ba.pwc.com

Botswana
Seema Ramdas
+26 7 395 2011
seema.ramdas@bw.pwc.com

Brazil
Celso Grazioli
+55 11 3674 3701
celso.grazioli@br.pwc.com

Bulgaria
Nevena Haygarova
+359 895 449 560
nevena.haygarova@bg.pwc.com

Cambodia
Jean Loi
+855 23 218 086
jean.loi@kh.pwc.com

Indirect Taxes

Cameroon (Republic of)
Nadine Tinen
+237 33 43 24 43
nadine.tinen@cm.pwc.com

Canada
Michael P. Firth
+1 416 869 8718
michael.p.firth@ca.pwc.com

Cape Verde
Susana Caetano
+351 213 599 674
susana.caetano@pt.pwc.com

Central and Eastern Europe
Hubert Jadrzyk
+48 225 234 837
hubert.jadrzyk@pl.pwc.com

Chad
Nadine Tinen
+237 33 43 24 43
nadine.tinen@cm.pwc.com

Chile
Sandra Benedetto
+56 2 940 0546
sandra.benedetto@cl.pwc.com

China (People's Republic of)
Alan Wu
+86 10 6533 2889
alan.wu@cn.pwc.com

Colombia
Carlos M. Chaparro
+57 163 405 55 ext. 216
carlos.chaparro@co.pwc.com

Congo (Democratic Republic of)
David Guarnieri
+243 810 336 801
guarnieri.david@cd.pwc.com

Congo (Republic of)
Moïse Kokolo
+242 533 20 57
moise.kokolo@cg.pwc.com

Costa Rica
Ana Elena Carazo
+506 2224 1555 ext. 153
elena.carazo@cr.pwc.com

Croatia
Ivo Bijelic
+385 1 632 8802
ivo.bijelic@hr.pwc.com

Cyprus
Chrysilios Pelekanos
+357 22 555 280
chrysilios.pelekanos@cy.pwc.com

Czech Republic
Peter Skelhorn
+420 251 152 811
peter.skelhorn@cz.pwc.com

Denmark
Jan Huusmann Christensen
+45 3945 9452
jan.huusmann.christensen@dk.pwc.com

Dominican Republic
Andrea Paniagua
+1 809 567 7741
andrea.paniagua@do.pwc.com

Ecuador
Pablo Aguirre
+593 2 256 4142 ext. 361
pablo.aguirre@ec.pwc-ag.com

Egypt
Sherif Mansour
+20 2 2759 7700 ext. 7888
sherif.mansour@eg.pwc.com

El Salvador
Adonay Rosales
+503 2243 5844
adonay.rosales@sv.pwc.com

Equatorial Guinea
Sébastien Lechêne
+240 09 8469
sebastien.lechene@ga.pwc.com

Estonia
Ain Veide
+372 614 1978
ain.veide@ee.pwc.com

Fiji Islands
Jerome S. Kado
+679 331 5199
jerome.kado@fj.pwc.com

Finland
Juha Laitinen
+358 9 2280 1409
juha.laitinen@fi.pwc.com

France
Stephen Dale
+33 1 5657 4161
stephen.dale@fr.landwellglobal.com

Gabon
Laurent Pommera
+241 76 23 71
laurent.pommera@ga.pwc.com

Germany
Götz Neuhahn
+49 30 2636 5445
goetz.neuhahn@de.pwc.com

Georgia
Sergi Kobakhidze
+995 32 508 066
sergi.kobakhidze@ge.pwc.com

Ghana
George Kwatia
+233 21 761500
george.kwatia@gh.pwc.com

Greece
Panagiotis Tsouramanis
+30 210 6874 547
panagiotis.tsouramanis@gr.pwc.com

Guatemala
Edgar Mendoza
+502 2420 7800 ext.844
edgar.mendoza@gt.pwc.com

Guernsey (Channel Islands)
Mark Watson
+44 1481 752 029
m.watson@gg.pwc.com

Honduras
Mauricio Quiñonez
+504 553 3060
mauricio.quinonez@hn.pwc.com

Hungary
Tamas Locsei
+36 1 461 9358
tamas.locsei@hu.pwc.com

Iceland
Elin Arnadottir
+354 550 5322
elin.arnadottir@is.pwc.com

India
Subramaniam Madhavan
+91 11 41150505
s.madhavan@in.pwc.com

Indonesia
Abdullah Azis
+62 21 528 90601
abdullah.azis@id.pwc.com

Iraq
David Stevens
+971 4 304 3304
david.stevens@ae.pwc.com

Ireland
John Fay
+353 1 792 8701
john.fay@ie.pwc.com

Isle of Man
George Sharpe
+44 1624 689689
george.sharpe@iom.pwc.com

Israel
Shay Shalhevet
+972 379 54 811
shay.shalhevet@il.pwc.com

Italy
Nicola Broggi
+390 2 9160 5700
nicola.broggi@it.pwc.com

Ivory Coast (Côte d'Ivoire)
Dominique Taty
+225 20 31 54 67
d.taty@ci.pwc.com

Jamaica
Paul A. Cobourne
+1 876 932 8350
paul.cobourne@jm.pwc.com

Japan
Masanori Kato
+81 3 5251 2536
masanori.kato@jp.pwc.com

Indirect Taxes

Jersey (Channel Islands)
Wendy Dorman
+44 1534 838 233
wendy.dorman@je.pwc.com

Jordan
Jeanine Daou
+961 1 200577 ext. 1691
jeanine.daou@lb.pwc.com

Kazakhstan
Zhanna Klyukanova
+7 727 298 0448
zhanna.klyukanova@kz.pwc.com

Kenya
Nelson Ogara
+254 20 285 5297
nelson.ogara@ke.pwc.com

Korea (Republic of)
Dong-Keon Lee
+82 2 709 0561
dong-keon.lee@kr.pwc.com

Kosovo
Loreta Peci
+355 4 242 254
loreta.peci@al.pwc.com

Kuwait
David Stevens
+971 4 304 3304
david.stevens@ae.pwc.com

Kyrgyzstan
Renat Akhmetov
+7 727 298 0931
renat.akhmetov@kz.pwc.com

Laos
Richard J. Irwin
+856 21 222 718
r.j.irwin@th.pwc.com

Latvia
Ilze Rauza
+371 6709 4512
ilze.rauza@lv.pwc.com

Lebanon
Jeanine Daou
+961 1 200577 ext. 1691
jeanine.daou@lb.pwc.com

Liechtenstein
Niklaus Honauer
+41 61 270 59 42
niklaus.honauer@ch.pwc.com

Lithuania
Kristina Krisciunaite
+370 5 2392 365
kristina.krisciunaite@lt.pwc.com

Luxembourg
Anne Murrath
+352 49 48 48 3120
anne.murrath@lu.pwc.com

Macedonia
Miroslav Marchev
+389 23 111 012
miroslav.marchev@mk.pwc.com

Malawi
Misheck Msiska
+265 1 82 0322
misheck.msiska@mw.pwc.com

Malaysia
Wan Heng Choon
+60 3 2173 1488
heng.choon.wan@my.pwc.com

Malta
Neville Gatt
+356 2564 6791
neville.gatt@mt.pwc.com

Mauritius
Dheerend Puholoo
+230 207 5079
d.puholoo@mu.pwc.com

Mexico
Ivan Jaso
+52 55 5263 8535
ivan.jaso@mx.pwc.com

Moldova
Mihaela Mitroi
+40 21 202 8717
mihaela.mitroi@ro.pwc.com

Monaco
Stephen Dale
+33 1 5657 4161
stephen.dale@fr.landwellglobal.com

Mongolia
Tomas Balco
+7 701 785 7089
tomas.balco@kz.pwc.com

Montenegro
Jovana Stojanovic
+381 11 3302 116
jovana.stojanovic@yu.pwc.com

Morocco
Stéphane Henrion
+33 1 56 57 41 39
stephane.henrion@fr.landwellglobal.com

Mozambique
Joao Martins
+258 21 307 620
joão.l.martins@mz.pwc.com

Namibia (Republic of)
Chantell Husselmann
+264 61 284 1327
chantell.husselmann@na.pwc.com

Netherlands
Bertjan Janzen
+31 20 568 6663
bertjan.janzen@nl.pwc.com

New Zealand
Eugen Trombitas
+64 9 355 8686
eugen.x.trombitas@nz.pwc.com

Nicaragua
Singrid Miranda
+506 2224 1555 ext. 136
singrid.miranda@cr.pwc.com

Nigeria
Yemi Idowu
+234 1 2711700 ext. 3105
yemi.idowu@ng.pwc.com

Norway
Trond Ingebrigtsen
+47 95 26 08 10
trond.ingebrigtsen@no.pwc.com

Oman
David Stevens
+971 4 304 3304
david.stevens@ae.pwc.com

Pakistan
Syed Shabbar Zaidi
+92 21 3241 3849
s.m.shabbar.zaidi@pk.pwc.com

Panama
Francisco Barrios
+507 206 9217
francisco.barrios@pa.pwc.com

Papua New Guinea
David Caradus
+675 321 1500
david.caradus@pg.pwc.com

Paraguay
Karina Lozano
+595 21 445 003
karina.lozano@py.pwc.com

Peru
Rudolf Röder
+51 1 211 6500
rudolf.roeder@pe.pwc.com

Philippines
Mary Bautista-Villareal
+63 2 459 2004
mary.s.bautista-villareal@ph.pwc.com

Poland
Hubert Jadrzyk
+48 22 523 4837
hubert.jadrzyk@pl.pwc.com

Portugal
John Duggan
+351 213 599 632
john.duggan@pt.pwc.com

Qatar
David Stevens
+971 4 304 3304
david.stevens@ae.pwc.com

Romania
Daniel Anghel
+40 21 202 8688
daniel.anghel@ro.pwc.com

Russian Federation
Vladimir Konstantinov
+7 495 967 6236
vladimir.konstantinov@ru.pwc.com

Indirect Taxes

San Marino
Nicola Broggi
+39 02 9160 5100
nicola.broggi@it.pwc.com

Saudi Arabia
David Stevens
+971 4 304 3304
david.stevens@ae.pwc.com

Serbia
Jovana Stojanovic
+381 11 3302 116
jovana.stojanovic@yu.pwc.com

Singapore
Soo How Koh
+65 6236 3600
soo.how.koh@sg.pwc.com

Slovak Republic
Eva Fricova
+421 2 59 350 613
eva.fricova@sk.pwc.com

Slovenia
Marijana Ristevski
+386 1 5836 019
marijana.ristevski@si.pwc.com

South Africa
Charles De Wet
+27 21 529 2377
charles.de.wet@za.pwc.com

Spain
Alberto Monreal
+34 915 685 570 ext. 15570
alberto.monreal@es.landwellglobal.com

Sweden
Lars Henckel
+46 8 555 333 26
lars.henckel@se.pwc.com

Switzerland
Michaela Merz
+41 58 792 44 29
michaela.merz@ch.pwc.com

Syria
Jeanine Daou
+961 1 200577 ext. 1691
jeanine.daou@lb.pwc.com

Taiwan
Lily Hsu
+886 2 2729 6207
lily.hsu@tw.pwc.com

Tajikistan
Elena Kaeva
+7 727 298 06 20
elena.kaeva@kz.pwc.com

Tanzania
Rishit Shah
+255 22 213 3100 ext. 3116
rishit.shah@tz.pwc.com

Thailand
Darika Soponawat
+66 2 344 1015
darika.kriengsuntikul@th.pwc.com

Trinidad and Tobago
Allyson West
+1 868 623 1361
allyson.west@tt.pwc.com

Tunisia
Mabrouk Maalaoui
+216 71 963 900
mabrouk.maalaoui@tn.pwc.com

Turkey
Cenk Ulu
+90 212 355 5852
cenk.ulu@tr.pwc.com

Turkmenistan
Jamshid Juraev
+998 71 120 6101
jamshid.juraev@uz.pwc.com

Uganda
Francis Kamulegeya
+256 414 236 018
francis.kamulegeya@ug.pwc.com

Ukraine
Igor Dankov
+380 44 490 6777 ext. 1173
igor.dankov@ua.pwc.com

United Arab Emirates
David Stevens
+971 4 304 3304
david.stevens@ae.pwc.com

United Kingdom
Michael Bailey
+44 20 7804 3254
michael.bailey@uk.pwc.com

United States
Tom Boniface
+1 646 471 4579
thomas.a.boniface@us.pwc.com

Uruguay
Patricia Marques
+598 2 916 0463 ext. 1348
patricia.marques@uy.pwc.com

Uzbekistan (Republic of)
Abdulkhamid Muminov
+998 71 1204 870
abdulkhamid.muminov@uz.pwc.com

Venezuela
Luis Fernando Miranda
+58 212 7706 124
fernando.miranda@ve.pwc.com

Vietnam
Huong Giang Nguyen
+84 4 9462 246 ext. 3020
n.huong.giang@vn.pwc.com

West Bank and Gaza
Wael H. Saadi
+ 972 2 532 6660 ext. 21
wael.h.saadi@ps.pwc.com

Yemen
Jeanine Daou
+961 1 200577 ext. 1691
jeanine.daou@lb.pwc.com

Zambia
Jyoti Mistry
+260 211 256471
jyoti.mistry@zm.pwc.com

Zimbabwe
Edmore Mandizha
+263 4 338 3628
edmore.mandizha@zw.pwc.com

International Tax Services

Global Leader, International Tax Services
Christoph Schreiber
+49 69 9585 6300
christoph.schreiber@de.pwc.com

Albania
Peter Burnie
+381 11 3302 138
peter.burnie@rs.pwc.com

Angola
Fernando Barros
+244 222 395004
fernando.barros@ao.pwc.com

Argentina
Andres M. Edelstein
+54 11 4850 6722
andres.m.edelstein@ar.pwc.com

Armenia
Paul Cooper
+374 10 59 2150
paul.cooper@am.pwc.com

Australia
Peter Collins
+61 3 8603 6247
peter.collins@au.pwc.com

Austria
Friedrich Roedler
+43 1 501 88 3600
friedrich.roedler@at.pwc.com

Azerbaijan
Movlan Pashayev
+994 12 497 7405
movlan.pashayev@az.pwc.com

Belgium
Axel Smits
+32 2 259 3120
axel.smits@be.pwc.com

Bolivia
Cesar Lora
+591 721 47 235
cesar.lora@bo.pwc.com

Bosnia and Herzogovina
Peter Burnie
+381 11 3302 138
peter.burnie@rs.pwc.com

Botswana
Butler Phirie
+267 395 2011
butler.phirie@bw.pwc.com

Brazil
Nélio Weiss
+ 55 11 3674 3557
nelio.weiss@br.pwc.com

Bulgaria
Orlin Hadjiiski
+359 2 91 003
orlin.hadjiiski@bg.pwc.com

Cameroon (Republic of)
Pierre Roger Ngangwou
+237 33 43 24 43
pierre.roger.ngangwou@cm.pwc.com

Canada
Bill Holms
+1 604 806 7052
william.holms@ca.pwc.com

Chad
Oscar Deffosso
+235 52 38 96
oscar.deffosso@cm.pwc.com

Chile
Francisco Selame
+56 2 940 0462
francisco.selame@cl.pwc.com

China (People's Republic of)
Edwin Wong
+86 10 6533 2100
edwin.wong@cn.pwc.com

Colombia
Carlos Chaparro
+57 163 405 55 ext. 216
carlos.chaparro@co.pwc.com

Congo (Democratic Republic of)
David Guarnieri
+243 810 336 801
guarnieri.david@cd.pwc.com

Congo (Republic of)
Emmanuel Le Bras
+242 534 09 07
emmanuel.lebras@cg.pwc.com

Costa Rica
Carlos Barrantes
+506 224 1555
carlos.barrantes@cr.pwc.com

Croatia
Ivo Bijelic
+385 1 632 8802
ivo.bijelic@hr.pwc.com

Cyprus
Panikos N. Tsiailis
+357 22 555 255
panikos.n.tsiailis@cy.pwc.com

Czech Republic
David Borkovec
+420 251 152 561
david.borkovec@cz.pwc.com

Denmark
Søren Jesper Hansen
+45 3945 3320
soren.jesper.hansen@dk.pwc.com

Dominican Republic
Andrea Paniagua
+1 809 567 7741
andrea.paniagua@do.pwc.com

Ecuador
Pablo Aguirre
+593 2 256 4142 ext. 361
pablo.aguirre@ec.pwc-ag.com

Egypt
Sherif Mansour
+20 2 2759 7700 ext. 7888
sherif.mansour@eg.pwc.com

El Salvador
Carlos Morales Recinos
+503 2243 6344
carlos.morales.recinos@sv.pwc.com

Equatorial Guinea
Sébastien Lechene
+240 09 8469
sebastien.lechene@ga.pwc.com

Estonia
Erki Uustalu
+372 614 1890
erki.uustalu@ee.pwc.com

Finland
Martti Virolainen
+358 9 2280 1396
martti.virolainen@fi.pwc.com

France
Renaud Jouffroy
+33 1 5657 4229
renaud.jouffroy@fr.landwellglobal.com

Gabon
Christophe Relongoue
+241 76 25 08
christophe.relongoue@ga.pwc.com

Georgia
Paul Cooper
+995 32 50 80 50
paul.cooper@am.pwc.com

Germany
Horst Raettig
+49 30 2636 5301
horst.raettig@de.pwc.com

Ghana
Darcy White
+233 21 761576
darcy.white@gh.pwc.com

Gibraltar
Robert G. Guest
+350 200 78777
robert.g.guest@gi.pwc.com

Greece
Vassilios Vizas
+30 210 6874 019
vassilios.vizas@gr.pwc.com

Guatemala
Rolando Díaz
+502 2420 7840
rolando.diaz@gt.pwc.com

Honduras
Ramon Morales
+504 553 3060
ramon.morales@hn.pwc.com

International Tax Services

Hong Kong
Nick Dignan
+852 2289 3702
nick.dignan@hk.pwc.com

Hungary
Gabriella Erdos
+36 1 461 9130
gabriella.erdos@hu.pwc.com

Iceland
Elin Arnadottir
+354 550 5322
elin.arnadottir@is.pwc.com

India
Nitin Karve
+91 22 6689 1477
nitin.karve@in.pwc.com

Indonesia
Ray Headifen
+62 21 528 90800
ray.headifen@id.pwc.com

Ireland
Feargal O'Rourke
+353 1 792 6480
feargal.orourke@ie.pwc.com

Israel
Gerry Seligman
+972 3 795 4476
gerry.seligman@il.pwc.com

Italy
Franco Boga
+390 2 9160 5400
franco.boga@it.pwc.com

Ivory Coast (Côte d'Ivoire)
Dominique Taty
+225 20 31 54 67
d.taty@ci.pwc.com

Jamaica
Eric Crawford
+1 876 932 8323
eric.crawford@jm.pwc.com

Japan
Eiichi Sato
+81 3 5251 2407
sato.eiichi@jp.pwc.com

Jordan
Stephan Stephan
+962 6 569 7431
stephan.stephan@jo.pwc.com

Kazakhstan
Richard Bregonje
+7 727 298 0866
richard.bregonje@kz.pwc.com

Kenya
Simeon Cheruiyot
+254 20 285 5000
simeon.cheruiyot@ke.pwc.com

Korea (Republic of)
Alex Joong-Hyun Lee
+82 2 709 0598
alex.joong-hyun.lee@kr.pwc.com

Kuwait
Fouad Douglas
+965 2299 7894
fouad.douglas@kwt.pwc.com

Latvia
Zlata Elksniņa
+371 6709 4400
zlata.elksnina@lv.pwc.com

Lebanon
Wadih Abou Nasr
+961 1 200577
wadih.abounasr@lb.pwc.com

Lithuania
Kristina Krisciunaite
+370 5 2392 365
kristina.krisciunaite@lt.pwc.com

Luxembourg
Valéry Civilio
+352 49 48 48 3109
valery.civilio@lu.pwc.com

Macedonia
Miroslav Marchev
+389 23 111 012
miroslav.marchev@mk.pwc.com

Madagascar
Andriamisa Ravelomanana
+261 20 22 217 63
andriamisa.ravelomanana@mg.pwc.com

Malaysia
Chuan Keat Khoo
+60 3 2694 6368
chuan.keat.khoo@my.pwc.com

Malta
Neville Gatt
+356 2564 6711
neville.gatt@mt.pwc.com

Mauritius
Anthony Leung Shing
+230 404 5071
anthony.leung.shing@mu.pwc.com

Mexico
Carlos Montemayor
+52 55 5263 6066
carlos.montemayor@mx.pwc.com

Middle East Region
Dean Rolfe
+971 4304 3351
dean.rolfe@ae.pwc.com

Montenegro
Peter Burnie
+381 11 3302 138
peter.burnie@rs.pwc.com

Morocco (Maghreb)
Mahat Chraibi
+212 22 99 98 00
mahat.chraibi@ma.landwellglobal.com

Mozambique
João Martins
+258 21 307 620
joao.l.martins@mz.pwc.com

Namibia (Republic of)
Albé Botha
+264 61 284 1000
albe.botha@na.pwc.com

Netherlands
Jeroen Schmitz
+31 20 568 7018
jeroen.schmitz@nl.pwc.com

New Zealand
Stewart McCulloch
+64 9 355 8751
stewart.j.mcculloch@nz.pwc.com

Nicaragua
Francisco Castro
+505 2270 4346 ext. 102
francisco.castro@ni.pwc.com

Nigeria
Ken Aitken
+234 1 271 1700
ken.aitken@ng.pwc.com

Norway
Steinar Hareide
+47 95 26 04 29
steinar.hareide@no.pwc.com

Oman
Lars Lawall
+49 69 9585 6622
lars.c.lawall@ae.pwc.com

Panama
Francisco Barrios
+507 206 9217
francisco.barrios@pa.pwc.com

Paraguay
Ruben Taboada
+595 21 445 003
ruben.taboada@py.pwc.com

Peru
Rudolf Röder
+51 1 211 6500
rudolf.roeder@pe.pwc.com

Philippines
Alex Cabrera
+63 2 845 2728
alex.cabrera@ph.pwc.com

Poland
Camiel van der Meij
+48 22 523 4959
camiel.van.der.meij@pl.pwc.com

Portugal
Jorge Figueiredo
+351 213 599 636
jorge.figueiredo@pt.pwc.com

Qatar
Ian Clay
+974 467 5581
ian.clay@qa.pwc.com

International Tax Services

Romania
Mihaela Mitroi
+40 21 202 8717
mihaela.mitroi@ro.pwc.com

Russian Federation
Natalia Kuznetsova
+7 495 967 6271
natalia.kuznetsova@ru.pwc.com

Saudi Arabia
Kenny Hawsey
+966 1 465 4240 ext. 1149
kenny.b.hawsey@sa.pwc.com

Senegal
Matthias Hubert
+221 33 849 05 00
matthias.huber@de.pwc.com

Serbia
Peter Burnie
+381 11 3302 138
peter.burnie@rs.pwc.com

Singapore
Elaine Ng
+65 6236 3627
elaine.ng@sg.pwc.com

Slovak Republic
Christiana Serugova
+421 2 59 350 614
christiana.serugova@sk.pwc.com

Slovenia
Janos Kelemen
+386 1 5836 058
janos.kelemen@si.pwc.com

South Africa
David Lermer
+27 21 529 2364
david.lermer@za.pwc.com

Spain
Ramon Mullerat
+34 915 685 534
ramon.mullerat@es.landwellglobal.com

Swaziland
Theo Mason
+268 404 2861
theo.mason@sz.pwc.com

Sweden
Jörgen Haglund
+46 8 555 331 51
jorgen.haglund@se.pwc.com

Switzerland
Armin Marti
+41 58 792 43 43
armin.marti@ch.pwc.com

Taiwan
Steven Go
+886 2 2729 5229
steven.go@tw.pwc.com

Tanzania
David Tarimo
+255 22 219 2201
david.tarimo@tz.pwc.com

Thailand
Paul B.A. Stitt
+66 2 344 1119
paul.stitt@th.pwc.com

Tunisia
Mabrouk Maalaoui
+216 71 963 900
mabrouk.maalaoui@tn.pwc.com

Turkey
Kadir Bas
+90 212 326 6408
Kadir.Bas@tr.pwc.com

Uganda
Francis Kamulegeya
+256 414 236 018
francis.kamulegeya@ug.pwc.com

Ukraine
Ron Barden
+380 44 490 6777
ron.j.barden@ua.pwc.com

United Arab Emirates
Dean Rolfe
+971 4 304 3351
dean.rolfe@ae.pwc.com

United Kingdom
David J. Burn
+44 161 247 4046
david.j.burn@uk.pwc.com

United States
Tim Anson
+1 202 414 1664
tim.anson@us.pwc.com

United States
Tom Moore
+1 646 471 3524
thomas.m.moore@us.pwc.com

Uruguay
Daniel Garcia
+598 2 916 0463
garcia.daniel@uy.pwc.com

Uzbekistan (Republic of)
Abdulkhamid Muminov
+998 71 1204 870
abdulkhamid.muminov@uz.pwc.com

Zambia
Jyoti Mistry
+260 211256471/2
jyoti.mistry@zm.pwc.com

Zimbabwe
Manuel Lopes
+263 4 338 3628
manuel.lopes@zw.pwc.com

Legal Services

Global Leader, Legal Services
Luis Comas
+34 932 532 741
luis.comas@es.landwellglobal.com

Albania
Peter Burnie
+381 11 3302 138
peter.burnie@rs.pwc.com

Algeria
Samir Hamouda
+213 21 48 4183
samir.hamouda@fr.pwc.com

Argentina
Julio Alberto Pueyrredon
+54 11 4850 6912
julio.pueyrredon@ar.pwc.com

Australia
Andrew Wheeler
+61 2 8266 6401
andrew.wheeler@au.pwc.com

Azerbaijan
Farhad Hajizade
+994 12 497 7391
farhad.hajizade@az.pwc.com

Barbados
Ronaele Dathorne
+1 246 467 6652
ronaele.dathorne@bb.pwc.com

Belgium
Karin Winters
+32 2 710 7404
karin.winters@be.pwc.com

Brazil
Fernando Loeser
+55 11 3879 2802
fernando.loeser@lpadv.com.br

Bulgaria
Irina Tsvetkova
+359 2 9355 100
irina.tsvetkova@bg.landwellglobal.com

Cameroon (Republic of)
Nadine Tinen
+237 33 43 24 43
nadine.tinen@cm.pwc.com

Chad
Nadine Tinen
+237 33 43 24 43
nadine.tinen@cm.pwc.com

Chile
Francisco Selame
+56 2 940 0150
francisco.selame@cl.pwc.com

China (People's Republic of)
Anthea Wong
+852 2289 3352
anthea.wong@hk.pwc.com

Colombia
Eliana Bernal
+57 1 634 0527
eliana.bernal@co.pwc.com

Congo (Republic of)
Prosper Bizitou
+242 557 91 98
prosper.bizitou@cg.pwc.com

Costa Rica
Carlos Barrantes
+506 2224 1555
carlos.barrantes@cr.pwc.com

Croatia
Dzenet Garibovic
+385 1 632 8803
dzenet.garibovic@hr.pwc.com

Cyprus
Spyros A. Evangelou
+357 22 559 999
spyros.evangelou@cy.landwellglobal.com

Czech Republic
Vladimir Ambruz
+420 251 152 921
vladimir.ambruz@ambruzdark.com

Dominican Republic
Edgar Orlando Mendoza
+1 502 2420 7800 ext. 844
edgar.mendoza@gt.pwc.com

El Salvador
Edgar Orlando Mendoza
+1 502 2420 7800 ext. 844
edgar.mendoza@gt.pwc.com

Equatorial Guinea
Dominique Taty
+225 20 31 54 67
d.taty@ci.pwc.com

Finland
Jukka-Pekka Joensuu
+358 9 2280 1335
jukka-pekka.joensuu@fi.pwc.com

France
Gilles Semadeni
+33 1 5657 8354
gilles.semadeni@fr.landwellglobal.com

Gabon
Dominique Taty
+225 20 31 54 67
d.taty@ci.pwc.com

Germany
Thomas Fischer
+49 69 9585 5561
t.fischer@de.pwc.com

Gibraltar
Edgar C. Lavarello
+350 200 73520
edgar.c.lavarello@gi.pwc.com

Greece
Mary Psylla
+30 210 6874 543
mary.psylla@gr.pwc.com

Guatemala
Edgar Orlando Mendoza
+502 2420 7800 ext. 844
edgar.mendoza@gt.pwc.com

Honduras
Edgar Orlando Mendoza
+502 2420 7800 ext. 844
edgar.mendoza@gt.pwc.com

Hong Kong
Anthea Wong
+852 2289 3352
anthea.wong@hk.pwc.com

Hungary
László Réti
+36 1 461 9890
laszlo.reti@hu.landwellglobal.com

Iceland
Elín Árnadóttir
+354 550 5300
elin.arnadottir@is.pwc.com

India
Deepak Gupta
+91 11 4115 0307
deepak.gupta@in.pwc.com

Ireland
Edward Evans
+353 1 792 6855
edward.evans@ie.landwellglobal.com

Italy
Gaetano Arnò
+390 2 9160 5210
gaetano.arno@it.pwc.com

Ivory Coast (Côte d'Ivoire)
Dominique Taty
+225 20 31 54 67
d.taty@ci.pwc.com

Jordan
Emad M. Majid
+962 6 567 8707
emad.majid@jo.pwc.com

Kazakhstan
Walter Daniel
+7 727 298 0864
walter.daniel@kz.pwc.com

Laos
Varavudh Meesaiyati
+856 21 222 718
varavudh.meesaiyati@th.pwc.com

Latvia
Vita Sakne
+371 6709 4425
vita.sakne@lv.pwc.com

Liechtenstein
Manuela Lipp
+41 58 792 72 31
manuela.lipp@ch.pwc.com

Legal Services

Luxembourg
Christophe Loly
+352 49 48 48 5114
christophe.loly@lu.pwc.com

Lithuania
Kristina Krisciunaite
+370 5 2392 365
kristina.krisciunaite@lt.pwc.com

Macedonia
Miroslav Marchev
+389 23 111 012
miroslav.marchev@mk.pwc.com

Madagascar
Dominique Taty
+225 20 31 54 67
d.taty@ci.pwc.com

Malta
Neville Gatt
+356 2564 6791
neville.gatt@mt.pwc.com

Mexico
Gabriel I. Aguilar
+52 55 5263 5791
gabriel.aguilar@mx.pwc.com

Moldova
Andrian Candu
+373 2223 8122
andrian.candu@ro.pwc.com

Montenegro
Predrag Milovanovic
+381 11 3302 100
predrag.milovanovic@rs.pwc.com

Morocco
Nicolas Granier
+33 1 5657 8669
nicolas.granier@fr.landwellglobal.com

Mozambique
Joao Martins
+258 21 307 620
joao.l.martins@mz.pwc.com

Netherlands
Frank Erftemeijer
+31 20 568 5930
frank.erftemeijer@nl.pwc.com

Nicaragua
Edgar Orlando Mendoza
+502 2420 7800 ext. 844
edgar.mendoza@gt.pwc.com

Nigeria
Dafe Akpeneye
+234 1 271 3114
dafe.akpeneye@ng.pwc.com

Norway
Kjell Richard Manskow
+47 95 26 11 76
kjell.richard.manskow@no.pwc.com

Panama
Amanda de Wong
+507 206 9219
amanda.de.wong@pa.pwc.com

Paraguay
Sergio Franco
+598 29 160 463
sergio.franco@uy.pwc.com

Peru
Walter Aguirre
+51 1 211 6500 ext 8047
walter.aguirre@pe.pwc.com

Philippines
Alex Cabrera
+63 2 459 2002
alex.cabrera@ph.pwc.com

Poland
Ewa Szurmińska-Jaworska
+48 22 746 7352
ewa.szurminska-jaworska@pl.pwc.com

Romania
Sorin David
+40 21 202 8770
sorin.david@david-baias.ro

Russian Federation
Yana Zoloeva
+7 495 232 5761
yana.zoloeva@ru.pwc.com

Senegal
Pierre Michaux
+221 33 849 05 00
pierre.michaux@ga.pwc.com

Serbia
Predrag Milovanovic
+381 11 3302 100
predrag.milovanovic@rs.pwc.com

Slovak Republic
Andrey Kolchin
+421 2 59 350 604
andrey.kolchin@sk.pwc.com

Spain
Santiago Barrenechea
+34 915 684 406
santiago.barrenechea@es.landwellglobal.com

Switzerland
Gema Olivar Pascual
+41 58 792 43 77
gema.olivar.pascual@ch.pwc.com

Taiwan
Eric Tsai
+886 2 2729 6687
eric.tsai@tw.pwc.com

Thailand
Siripong Supakijjanusorn
+66 2 344 1124
siripong.supakijjanusorn@th.pwc.com

Tunisia
Rachid Tmar
+216 71 862 156
rachid.tmar@tn.pwc.com

Trinidad and Tobago
Allyson West
+1 868 623 1361
allyson.west@tt.pwc.com

Turkey
Nilgun Serdar
+90 212 326 6368
nilgun.serdar@tr.pwc.com

United Arab Emirates
Waseem Khokhar
+971 4 304 3181
waseem.khokhar@pwclegal.co.ae

United Kingdom
Leon Flavell
+44 20 7212 1945
leon.flavell@pwclegal.co.uk

Ukraine
Marc-Tell Madl
+380 44 490 6777
m.madl@ua.pwc.com

Uruguay
Sergio Franco
+598 2 518 2828
sergio.franco@uy.pwc.com

Venezuela
Fernando Miranda
+58 212 7006 123
fernando.miranda@ve.pwc.com

Vietnam
Richard J. Irwin
+66 2286 9999 ext. 4880
r.j.irwin@vn.pwc.com

Mergers and Acquisitions

Global Leader, Mergers and Acquisitions
Magnus Johnsson
+46 8 5553 3172
magnus.johnsson@se.pwc.com

Argentina
Daniel Santiago
+54 11 4850 6707
daniel.santiago@ar.pwc.com

Australia
Mark O'Reilly
+61 2 8266 2979
mark.oreilly@au.pwc.com

Austria
Bernd Hofmann
+43 1 501 88 3332
bernd.hofmann@at.pwc.com

Belgium
Jan Muyldermans
+32 2 710 7423
jan.muyldermans@be.pwc.com

Bolivia
Cesar Lora
+591 721 47 235
cesar.lora@bo.pwc.com

Brazil
Rodrigo Bastos
+55 11 3674 3543
rodrigo.bastos@br.pwc.com

Canada
Doug Frost
+1 416 365 8852
doug.l.frost@ca.pwc.com

Chile
German Campos
+56 2 940 0098
german.campos@cl.pwc.com

Colombia
Eliana Bernal
+57 1 634 0527
eliana.bernal@co.pwc.com

Czech Republic
Viera Kucerova
+420 251 151 255
viera.kucerova@cz.pwc.com

Denmark
Daniel Noe Harboe
+45 3945 9582
daniel.noe.harboe@dk.pwc.com

Finland
Karin Svennas
+358 9 2280 1801
karin.svennas@fi.pwc.com

France
Xavier Etienne
+33 1 5657 8395
xavier.etienne@fr.landwellglobal.com

Germany
Frank Schmidt
+49 69 9585 6711
frank.r.schmidt@de.pwc.com

Greece
Mariza Sakellaridou
+30 210 6874 557
mariza.sakellaridou@gr.pwc.com

Hong Kong
Danny C.W. Po
+852 2289 3097
danny.po@hk.pwc.com

India
Vivek Mehra
+91 11 2321 0542
vivek.mehra@in.pwc.com

Indonesia
Ali Mardi
+62 21 528 90622
ali.mardi@id.pwc.com

Ireland
Ronan MacNioclais
+353 1 792 6000
ronan.mancnioclais@ie.pwc.com

Italy
Nicola Broggi
+390 2 9160 5700
nicola.broggi@it.pwc.com

Japan
Stuart Porter
+81 3 5251 2944
stuart.porter@jp.pwc.com

Japan
Kazuya Miyakawa
+81 3 5251 2462
kazuya.miyakawa@jp.pwc.com

Korea
Alex Lee
+82 2 709 0598
alex.joong-hyun.lee@kr.pwc.com

Luxembourg
Vincent Lebrun
+352 49 48 48 2584
vincent.lebrun@lu.pwc.com

Malaysia
Frances Po
+60 3 2173 1618
frances.po@my.pwc.com

Mexico
Jesus Chan
+52 55 5263 6000
jesus.chan@mx.pwc.com

Middle East Region
Lars Lawall
+49 69 9585 6622
lars.lawall@de.pwc.com

Netherlands
Oscar Kinders
+31 10 407 5348
oscar.kinders@nl.pwc.com

New Zealand
Peter Boyce
+64 9 355 8547
peter.boyce@nz.pwc.com

Norway
Steinar Hareide
+47 95 26 04 29
steinar.hareide@no.pwc.com

Paraguay
Ruben Taboada
+595 21 445 003
ruben.taboada@py.pwc.com

Peru
Orlando Marchesi
+51 1 211 6500
orlando.marchesi@pe.pwc.com

Philippines
Malou Lim
+63 2 845 2728
malou.p.lim@ph.pwc.com

Poland
Mike Ahern
+48 22 523 4985
mike.ahern@pl.pwc.com

Portugal
Maria Torres
+351 225 433 113
maria.torres@pt.pwc.com

Russian Federation
Cherie Ford
+7 495 967 6231
cherie.ford@ru.pwc.com

Singapore
Chris Woo
+65 6236 3688
chris.woo@sg.pwc.com

Spain
David Ramirez
+34 932 532 722
david.ramirez.garcia@es.landwellglobal.com

Sweden
Jörgen Haglund
+46 8 555 331 51
jorgen.haglund@se.pwc.com

Switzerland
Markus Prinzen
+41 58 792 53 10
markus.prinzen@ch.pwc.com

Taiwan
Elaine Hsieh
+886 2 2729 6666
elaine.hsieh@tw.pwc.com

Thailand
Paul Stitt
+66 2 344 1119
paul.stitt@th.pwc.com

Mergers and Acquisitions

Turkey
Kadir Bas
+90 212 326 6408
kadir.bas@tr.pwc.com

United Kingdom
Gaenor A. Bagley
+44 20 7804 5254
gaenor.a.bagley@uk.pwc.com

Uruguay
Sergio Franco
+598 2 916 0463
sergio.franco@uy.pwc.com

United States
Mark Boyer
+1 202 414 1629
mark.boyer@us.pwc.com

Sustainability and Climate Change Tax

Global Leader, Sustainability and Climate Change Tax
Mark Schofield
+44 20 7212 2527
mark.schofield@uk.pwc.com

Australia
Michael Bona
+61 3 8603 3065
michael.bona@au.pwc.com

Belgium
Maarten Tas
+32 2 710 7402
maarten.tas@be.pwc.com

Brazil
Raimundo Christians
+55 11 3674 3642
raimundo.christians@br.pwc.com

Canada
Leanne Sereda
+1 403 509 7586
leanne.a.sereda@ca.pwc.com

Central and Eastern Europe
Peter Burnie
+381 11 3302 138
peter.burnie@rs.pwc.com

China (People's Republic of)
Alan Wu
+ 86 10 6533 2889
alan.wu@cn.pwc.com

France
Jean Sayag
+33 1 5657 8632
jean.sayag@fr.landwellglobal.com

Germany
Frank Schmidt
+49 69 9585 6711
frank.r.schmidt@de.pwc.com

India
Ajay Kumar
+91 12 4330 6509
ajay.kumar@in.pwc.com

Indonesia
Anthony Anderson
+62 21 528 90642
anthony.j.anderson@id.pwc.com

Ireland
Ronan MacNioclais
+353 1 792 6006
ronan.macnioclais@ie.pwc.com

Italy
Valentino Guarini
+390 2 9160 5807
valentino.guarini@it.pwc.com

Japan
Jun Takashima
+81 3 5251 2574
jun.takashima@jp.pwc.com

Korea (Republic of)
Sang-Keun Song
+82 2 709 0559
sang-keun.song@kr.pwc.com

Luxembourg
Wim Piot
+352 49 48 48 5773
wim.piot@lu.pwc.com

Malta
David Ferry
+356 2564 6712
david.ferry@mt.pwc.com

Mexico
Arturo Mendez
+52 33 3648 1013
arturo.mendez@mx.pwc.com

Middle East
Dean Rolfe
+971 4 304 3100
dean.rolfe@ae.pwc.com

Netherlands
Fred Klaassen
+31 10 407 5439
fred.klaassen@nl.pwc.com

Singapore
Sunil Agarwal
+65 6236 3798
sunil.agarwal@sg.pwc.com

Sustainability and Climate Change Tax

South Africa
Kyle Mandy
+27 11 797 4977
kyle.mandy@za.pwc.com

Spain
Araceli Zatarain
+34 963 032 048
araceli.zatarain@es.landwellglobal.com

Sweden
Lars Henckel
+46 8 555 333 26
lars.henckel@se.pwc.com

Switzerland
Markus Hertel
+41 58 792 94 45
markus.hertel@ch.pwc.com

United Kingdom
Mark Schofield
+44 20 7212 2527
mark.schofield@uk.pwc.com

United States
Matthew Haskins
+1 202 414 1570
matthew.haskins@us.pwc.com

Tax Controversy and Dispute Resolution

Global Leader, Tax Controversy and Dispute Resolution
David Swenson
+1 202 414 4650
david.swenson@us.pwc.com

Australia
Michael Bersten
+61 2 8266 6858
michael.bersten@au.pwc.com

Brazil
Durval Portela
+55 11 3879 2800
durval.portela@br.pwc.com

Canada
Charles Theriault
+1 514 205 5144
charles.theriault@ca.pwc.com

China (People's Republic of)
Matthew Mui
+86 10 6533 3028
matthew.mui@cn.pwc.com

France
Michel Combe
+33 1 5657 5657
michel.combe@fr.landwellglobal.com

Germany
Andreas Kempf
+49 21 1981 7304
andreas.kempf@de.pwc.com

India
Pawan Kumar
+91 12 4330 6517
pawan.kumar@in.pwc.com

Japan
Jack Bird
+81 3 5251 2577
jack.bird@jp.pwc.com

Korea (Republic of)
Henry An
+82 2 3781 2594
henry.an@kr.pwc.com

Mexico
Karina Perez Delgadillo
+52 55 5263 6000
karina.perez.delgadillo@mx.pwc.com

Netherlands
Hugo Vollebregt
+31 20 568 6632
hugo.vollebregt@nl.pwc.com

Norway
Morton Beck
+47 95 26 06 50
morten.beck@no.pwc.com

Poland
Hubert Jadrzyk
+48 22 523 4837
hubert.jadrzyk@pl.pwc.com

Romania
Dan Dascalu
+40 21 202 8683
dan.dascalu@david-baias.ro

Russian Federation
Alina Lavrentieva
+7 495 967 6250
alina.lavrentieva@ru.pwc.com

Spain
Javier Gonzalez Carcedo
+34 915 684 542
javier.gonzalez.carcedo@es.landwellglobal.com

Switzerland
Benjamin Koch
+41 58 792 43 34
benjamin.koch@ch.pwc.com

United Kingdom
Simon Wilks
+44 20 7804 1938
simon.wilks@uk.pwc.com

United States
Kevin Brown
+1 202 346 5051
kevin.brown@us.pwc.com

Tax Management and Accounting Services

Global Leader, Tax Management and Accounting Services
Buddy Tinley
+1 678 419 8838
buddy.tinley@us.pwc.com

Africa Central
Rajesh Shah
+254 20 2855326
rajesh.k.shah@ke.pwc.com

Albania
Loreta Peci
+355 4 2242 254
loreta.peci@al.pwc.com

Argentina
Daniel Cravino
+54 11 4850 6000
daniel.h.cravino@ar.pwc.com

Australia
Tim Cox
+61 3 8603 6181
tim.cox@au.pwc.com

Austria
Johannes Mörtl
+43 1 501 88 3400
johannes.moertl@at.pwc.com

Azerbaijan
Jeyhun Huseynzada
+994 12 497 2515
jeyhun.b.huseynzada@az.pwc.com

Belgium
Dirk Vermussche
+32 2 710 7100
dirk.vermussche@be.pwc.com

Bolivia
Cesar Lora
+591 721 47235
cesar.Lora@bo.pwc.com

Brazil
Manuel Marinho
+55 19 3794 5435
manuel.marinho@br.pwc.com

Bulgaria
Zlatka Ignatova
+359 2 9355 106
zlatka.x.ignatova@bg.pwc.com

Cambodia
Richard Irwin
+66 2 286 9999
r.j.irwin@vn.pwc.com

Canada
Betty Jarrett
+1 905 949 7314
betty.ann.jarrett@ca.pwc.com

Chile
Germán Campos Kennett
+56 2 940 0150
german.campos@cl.pwc.com

China (People's Republic of)
Matthew Wong
+86 21 2323 3052
matthew.mf.wong@cn.pwc.com

Colombia
Maria Helena Diaz
+57 1 635 1125
maria_helena.diaz@co.pwc.com

Costa Rica
Carlos Barrantes
+506 224 1555
carlos.barrantes@cr.pwc.com

Croatia
Janos Kelemen
+385 1 632 8880
janos.x.kelemen@hr.pwc.com

Cyprus
Costas Mavrocordatos
+357 22 555 202
costas.mavrocordatos@cy.pwc.com

Czech Republic
Lenka Mrazova
+420 251 15 2553
lenka.mrazova@cz.pwc.com

Denmark
Charlotte Dohm
+45 3945 9428
charlotte.dohm@dk.pwc.com

Dominican Republic
Ramon Ortega
+1 809 567 7741 ext. 2348
ramon.ortega@do.pwc.com

Ecuador
Pablo Aguirre
+593 2 256 4142 ext. 361
pablo.aguirre@ec.pwc-ag.com

Egypt
Abdelkhalek Ahmed
+20 2 2516 8027
abdelkhalek.ahmed@eg.pwc.com

El Salvador
Edgar Mendoza
+502 2420 7800 ext. 844
edgar.mendoza@gt.pwc.com

Estonia
Villi Tontson
+372 614 1816
villi.tontson@ee.pwc.com

Finland
Kaj Wasenius
+358 9 2280 1302
kaj.wasenius@fi.pwc.com

France
Thierry Morgant
+33 15657 4988
thierry.morgant@fr.landwellglobal.com

Georgia
Sergi Kobakhidze
+995 32 508 066
sergi.kobakhidze@ge.pwc.com

Germany
Heiko Schafer
+49 69 9585 6227
heiko.schaefer@de.pwc.com

Greece
Constantine Karydis
+30 210 6874 050
constantine.karydis@gr.pwc.com

Guatemala
Edgar Mendoza
+502 2420 7800 ext. 844
edgar.mendoza@gt.pwc.com

Honduras
Ramon Morales
+504 553 3060
ramon.morales@hn.pwc.com

Hong Kong
Suzanne Wat
+852 2289 3002
suzanne.wat@hk.pwc.com

Hungary
Janos Kelemen
+36 1 461 9310
janos.kelemen@si.pwc.com

India
Vikram Bapat
+91 80 4079 6003
vikram.bapat@in.pwc.com

Indonesia
Ray Headifen
+62 21 528 90800
ray.headifen@id.pwc.com

Ireland
Susan Kilty
+353 1 792 6740
susan.kilty@ie.pwc.com

Italy
Domenico Coldani
+390 2 9160 5800
domenico.coldani@it.pwc.com

Japan
Masanori Kato
+81 3 5251 2536
masanori.kato@jp.pwc.com

Kazakhstan
Elena Kaeva
+7 727 298 0620
elena.kaeva@kz.pwc.com

Korea (Republic of)
Alex Joong-Hyun Lee
+82 2 709 0598
alex.joong-hyun.lee@kr.pwc.com

Latvia
Zlata Elksnina
+371 6709 4400
zlata.elksnina@lv.pwc.com

Tax Management and Accounting Services

Lithuania
Jurate Stulgyte
+370 5 2392 381
jurate.stulgyte@lt.pwc.com

Luxembourg
Wim Piot
+352 49 48 48 5773
wim.piot@lu.pwc.com

Macedonia
Miroslav Marchev
+389 23 111 012
miroslav.marchev@mk.pwc.com

Malaysia
Wee Hong Teh
+60 3 2173 1595
wee.hong.teh@my.pwc.com

Malta
Chris Galea
+356 2564 6911
chris.galea@mt.pwc.com

Meekong
Thavorn Rujivanarom
+66 2 344 1444
thavorn.rujivanarom@th.pwc.com

Mexico
Jesus Chan
+52 55 5263 5766
jesus.chan@mx.pwc.com

Moldova
Andrian Candu
+373 2223 8122
andrian.candu@ro.pwc.com

Montenegro
Aleksandra Cekic
+381 11 3302 143
aleksandra.cekic@yu.pwc.com

Netherlands
Robert van der Laan
+31 40 224 4860
robert.van.der.laan@nl.pwc.com

New Zealand
Ian Rowe
+64 4 462 7274
ian.rowe@nz.pwc.com

Nicaragua
Singrid Miranda
+506 2224 1555 ext. 136
singrid.miranda@cr.pwc.com

Norway
Pål Hasner
+47 95 26 05 50
paal.hasner@no.pwc.com

Panama
Francisco Barrios
+507 206 9217
francisco.barrios@pa.pwc.com

Paraguay
Leonardo Decarlini
+598 29 160 463
leonardo.decarlini@uy.pwc.com

Peru
Rudolf Röder
+51 1 211 6500
rudolf.roeder@pe.pwc.com

Philippines
Fedna Parallag
+63 2 459 3109
fedna.parallag@ph.pwc.com

Poland
Keith Sinclair
+48 22 523 4781
keith.c.sinclair@pl.pwc.com

Portugal
Adriao Silva
+351 213 599 625
adriao.silva@pt.pwc.com

Romania
Ruxandra Stoian
+40 21 202 8734
ruxandra.stoian@ro.pwc.com

Russian Federation
Alexei Ryabov
+7 495 967 6288
alexei.ryabov@ru.pwc.com

Serbia
Aleksandra Cekic
+381 11 3302 143
aleksandra.cekic@yu.pwc.com

Slovak Republic
Sona Krnacova
+421 2 59 350 631
sona.krnacova@sk.pwc.com

Slovenia
Thomas Dane
+386 1 5836 056
thomas.dane@si.pwc.com

South Africa
Gert Meiring
+27 11 797 5506
gert.meiring@za.pwc.com

Spain
Rafael Rebate
+34 915 684 408
rafael.rebate@es.landwellglobal.com

Sweden
Lennart Svantesson
+46 8 555 331 44
lennart.svantesson@se.pwc.com

Switzerland
Donald Compton
+41 58 792 93 28
donald.compton@ch.pwc.com

Taiwan
Lily Hsu
+886 2 2729 6207
lily.hsu@tw.pwc.com

Thailand
Thavorn Rujivanarom
+66 2 344 1444
thavorn.rujivanarom@th.pwc.com

Turkey
Ayse B. Isim
+90 212 355 5812
ayse.b.isim@tr.pwc.com

Ukraine
Marc-Tell Madl
+380 44 490 6777
m.madl@ua.pwc.com

United Kingdom
Angus Johnston
+44 20 7804 2722
angus.i.johnston@uk.pwc.com

United States
Buddy Tinley
+1 678 419 8838
buddy.tinley@us.pwc.com

Uruguay
Leonardo Decarlini
+598 2 916 0463
leonardo.decarlini@uy.pwc.com

Uzbekistan (Republic of)
Tatyana Rososhanskaya
+998 71 1206 101
tatyana.rososhanskaya@uz.pwc.com

Vietnam
Richard J. Irwin
+66 2 286 9999
r.j.irwin@vn.pwc.com

Venezuela
Elys Aray
+58 241 8252 361
elys.aray@ve.pwc.com

Transfer Pricing

Global Leader, Transfer Pricing
Garry Stone
+1 312 298 2464
garry.stone@us.pwc.com

Argentina
Juan Carlos Ferreiro
+54 11 4850 6720
juan.carlos.ferreiro@ar.pwc.com

Australia
Lyndon James
+61 2 8266 3278
lyndon.james@au.pwc.com

Austria
Herbert Greinecker
+43 1 501 88 3301
herbert.greinecker@at.pwc.com

Belgium
Isabel Verlinden
+32 2 710 7295
isabel.verlinden@be.pwc.com

Brazil
Cristina Medeiros
+55 11 3674 2000
cristina.medeiros@br.pwc.com

Bulgaria
Irina Tsvetkova
+359 2 9355 100
irina.tsvetkova@bg.landwellglobal.com

Canada
Charles Theriault
+1 514 205 5001 ext 2254
charles.theriault@ca.pwc.com

Chile
Roberto Carlos Rivas
+56 2 940 0151
roberto.carlos.rivas@cl.pwc.com

China (People's Republic of)
Spencer Chong
+86 21 2323 1135
spencer.chong@cn.pwc.com

Colombia
Carlos Mario Lafaurie
+57 1 634 0492
carlos_mario.lafaurie@co.pwc.com

Croatia
Janos Kelemen
+385 1 632 8880
janos.x.kelemen@hr.pwc.com

Czech Republic
David Borkovec
+420 251 152 549
david.borkovec@cz.pwc.com

Denmark
Erik Todbjerg
+45 3945 9583
erik.todbjerg@dk.pwc.com

Ecuador
Pablo Aguirre
+593 2 256 4142 ext. 361
pablo.aguirre@ec.pwc-ag.com

Finland
Ray A. Grimes
+358 9 2280 1467
ray.a.grimes@fi.pwc.com

France
Pierre Escaut
+33 1 5657 4295
pierre.escaut@fr.landwellglobal.com

Germany
Lorenz Bernhardt
+49 30 2636 5218
lorenz.bernhardt@de.pwc.com

Greece
Antonis Desipris
+30 210 6874 016
antonis.desipris@gr.pwc.com

Hong Kong
Charles Leung
+86 20 3819 2128
charles.leung@hk.pwc.com

Hungary
Zaid Sethi
+36 1 461 9512
zaid.sethi@hu.pwc.com

Iceland
Elin Arnadottir
+354 550 5322
elin.arnadottir@is.pwc.com

India
Rahul K Mitra
+91 33 4400 0484
rahul.k.mitra@in.pwc.com

Indonesia
Ay Tjhing Phan
+62 21 5289 1024
ay.tjhing.phan@id.pwc.com

Ireland
Gavan Ryle
+353 1 792 6425
gavan.ryle@ie.pwc.com

Israel
Vered Kirshner
+972 3 795 4849
vered.kirshner@il.pwc.com

Italy
Gianni Colucci
+390 2 9160 5509
gianni.colucci@it.pwc.com

Japan
Akio Miyamoto
+81 3 5251 2337
akio.miyamoto@jp.pwc.com

Kazakhstan
Bob Jurik
+7 727 298 0448
bob.jurik@kz.pwc.com

Korea (Republic of)
Henry An
+82 2 709 0887
henryan@samil.com

Lithuania
Nerijus Nedzinskas
+370 5 239 2352
nerijus.nedzinskas@lt.pwc.com

Luxembourg
Wim Piot
+352 49 48 48 5773
wim.piot@lu.pwc.com

Malaysia
Thanneermalai Somasundaram
+60 3 2173 1482
thanneermalai.somasundaram@my.pwc.com

Malta
Neville Gatt
+356 2564 6711
neville.gatt@mt.pwc.com

Mexico
Fred Barrett
+52 55 5263 6069
fred.barrett@mx.pwc.com

Netherlands
Arnout van der Rest
+31 10 407 5413
arnout.van.der.rest@nl.pwc.com

New Zealand
Cameron B Smith
+64 9 355 8508
cameron.b.smith@nz.pwc.com

Norway
Dag Saltnes
+47 95 26 06 32
dag.saltnes@no.pwc.com

Philippines
Carlos Carado
+63 2 845 2728
carlos.carado@ph.pwc.com

Poland
Mike Ahern
+48 22 5234 868
mike.ahern@pl.pwc.com

Portugal
Jaime Esteves
+351 225 433 212
jaime.esteves@pt.pwc.com

Romania
Ionut Simion
+40 21 202 8708
ionut.simion@ro.pwc.com

Russian Federation
Evgenia Veter
+7 495 232 5438
evgenia.veter@ru.pwc.com

Transfer Pricing

Singapore
Nicole Fung
+65 6236 3646
nicole.fung@sg.pwc.com

Slovak Republic
Todd Bradshaw
+421 2 59 350 111
todd.bradshaw@sk.pwc.com

Slovenia
Janos Kelemen
+386 1 5836 058
janos.kelemen@si.pwc.com

South Africa
David Lermer
+27 21 529 2364
david.lermer@za.pwc.com

Spain
Javier Gonzalez Carcedo
+34 915 684 822
javier.gonzalez.carcedo@es.landwellglobal.com

Sweden
Mika Myllynen
+46 8 555 344 92
mika.myllynen@se.pwc.com

Switzerland
Norbert Raschle
+41 58 792 42 54
norbert.raschle@ch.pwc.com

Taiwan
Steven Go
+886 2 2729 5229
steven.go@tw.pwc.com

Thailand
Peerapat Poshyanonda
+66 2 344 1220
peerapat.poshyanonda@th.pwc.com

Turkey
Adnan Nas
+90 212 326 6402
adnan.nas@tr.pwc.com

United Kingdom
Ian Dykes
+44 121 265 5968
ian.dykes@uk.pwc.com

United States
Horacio Pena
+1 646 471 1957
horacio.pena@us.pwc.com

Venezuela
Jose G. Garcia
+58 212 7006 802
jose.g.garcia@ve.pwc.com

Vietnam
Van Dinh Thi Quynh
+84 4 3946 2246 ext 4202
dinh.quynh.van@vn.pwc.com

Global Tax Industry Leaders

Consumer, Industrial Products and Services
Jay Oyer
+1 973 236 4177
jay.oyer@us.pwc.com

Automotive Tax
Horst Raettig
+49 30 236 4930
horst.raettig@de.pwc.com

Energy, Utilities and Mining
James Koch
+713 356 4626
james.koch@us.pwc.com

Industrial Products
Michael Burak
+1 973 236 4459
michael.burak@us.pwc.com

Pharma and Life Sciences
Michael Swanick
+1 267 330 6060
michael.f.swanick@us.pwc.com

Retail and Consumer
Clare Bolton
+44 161 247 4032
clare.bolton@uk.pwc.com

Financial Services and Insurance
David Newton
+44 20 7804 2039
david.newton@uk.pwc.com

Banking and Capital Markets
Richard Collier
+44 20 7212 3395
richard.collier@uk.pwc.com

Investment Management Tax
William Taggart
+1 646 471 2780
william.taggart@us.pwc.com

Real Estate
Uwe Stoschek
+49 30 26 36 5286
uwe.stoschek@de.pwc.com

Technology, Information, Communications and Entertainment
Diane Baylor
+1 408 817 5005
diane.baylor@us.pwc.com

Entertainment and Media
Christ Economos
+1 646 471 0612
christ.h.economos@us.pwc.com